# A COMPLETE

ALPHABETICALLY ARRANGED

# BIBLICAL BIOGRAPHY,

CONTAINING A FULL HISTORY OF

## BIBLE MEN AND WOMEN,

WITH AN

## APPENDIX,

EMBRACING A BIOGRAPHY OF UNNAMED PERSONS.

By Rev. T. G. BEHARRELL, A. M.

INDIANAPOLIS:
DOWNEY & BROUSE, PRINTERS AND PUBLISHERS.
1867.

# PREFACE.

In presenting this book to the Christian reader, we have aimed to fill a vacancy in the literature of the Christian Churches, and especially the Sabbath School literature. Sabbath Schools are a blessed auxiliary or help in the great work of training up children in the nurture and admonition of the Lord, and there has been increasing facilities for this great work in Question Books, Reference Books, Library Books, and Books of Song, prepared for use in the schools. With this Biblical Biography we have desired to afford advantages to Superintendents and Teachers in preparing for their work, and the scholars of the Bible classes in the schools in preparing for their recitations; as also, to familiarize all Bible students with the history of Bible characters.

In the history of Bible men and women, we have virtues exemplified that may be admired and imitated—vices that may be detested and shunned. The principles of the religion of the Bible are strikingly exemplified, and the doctrines of religion are beautifully illustrated in the history of holy men and women.

The larger and best prepared Theological Dictionaries are not within the reach of many who are seeking an acquaintance with Bible characters, and those works are so meagre in Bible Biography as to be very unsatisfactory. There are but a few of the men of the Bible referred to.

In this work will be found arranged in alphabetical order a history of nearly all Bible men and women of whom there is a record, and it is adapted to Bible readers of all denominations alike. We have aimed to supply a want existing in the literature of the general church of Christ, and we think the Roman Catholic as well as the Protestant, and Jew as well as the Gentile, may, by perusing these pages, familiarize themselves with incidents in the history of characters in whom they are interested.

The names of the Patriarchs of the Ante-diluvian and Post-diluvian ages are familiar to many, and yet there are many interesting incidents recorded in their lives that Bible readers are not familiar with. And this is also true of the prophets from Moses to the last of the minor prophets, and of their governors and judges from Joshua to Samuel; and of their kings from Saul their first king, to Zedekiah their last one before the captivity. And so from Zerubbabel and Nehemiah to the Herod who was reigning when Jesus was born.

New Testament characters, as their history is recorded, are frought with great interest, and we may well desire an acquaintance with them.

We have aimed to present not only the Biography of Bible men, but of Bible women also—who seem to be almost ignored in the biographical department of our theological dictionaries. There are many important characters among them not referred to at all—and why should not Bible students, many of whom are females, become acquainted with the sacred history of those of their own sex? All Bible students should become familiar with the women as well as with the men of the Bible. Woman was created to be an helpmeet for man, and her formation was the last and crowning work of the great creator. She was made for an associate with man, and has ever been his companion and a full sharer in the woes brought on him by the transgression of the divine law.

The subtile serpent was cursed first, and then the woman, and afterwards the man. And this was the order in sin and of sinners in bringing about the fatal fall; the serpent beguiled Eve, and Eve tempted Adam, and Adam yielded to the temptation.

The curse that was pronounced on the woman was, "I will greatly multiply thy sorrow and thy conception, in sorrow thou shalt bring forth children, and thy desire shall be to thy husband and he shall rule over thee." Though in the creation man and woman was formed with equal rights as to ruling, yet after the fall it was not so—woman was to be subject to the will of her husband.

Though she was thus first in the transgression, and her position to some extent as to equality with her husband changed, yet she was honored beyond man in being the mother of the Redeemer of the fallen race. When the Creator, whose authority had been trampled upon by Satan, by the woman, and by the man, called the two transgressors, Adam and Eve, to an account, before pronouncing the curse upon them, he pronounced a curse upon the serpent. "And the Lord God said unto the serpent, because thou art cursed above all cattle, and above every beast of the field; upon thy belly shalt thou go, and dust shalt thou eat all the days of thy life."

This curse was followed by the promise of a Savior, as the offspring of the woman. And in keeping with this promise that the seed of the woman should bruise the serpent's head, is the declaration of the inspired writer under the New Testament dispensation: "The Son of God was manifested that he might destroy the works of the devil."

In the "Sacred Record" we have the names of many eminent women; and as their history is set forth we behold virtues exemplified and honors conferred that mark them as ornaments to the world, and noble examples for the imitation of their sex.

There were several who were endued with the spirit of prophecy, among whom we might name Miriam, the distinguished sister of Moses and Aaron, who has been styled "The Virgin Prophetess." Deborah, who was the first woman that occupied the position of civil ruler. She left the City of Palm Trees to encourage the heart of her general, Barak, in the battle with Jabin, the king of Canaan. As she occupied a position on the mountain side, where she could see the movements of her victorious general, she composed a song of triumph, full of prophetic declaration.

Huldah was so important as a prophetess, that when the king would have the long-lost copy of the law, that had been found, read, he sent the manuscript to this woman, though the prophet Jeremiah was then living, it is supposed, at Libnah, where he might easily have been consulted. Elizabeth, the mother of John the Baptist, and the Virgin Mary, her cousin, were both favored with the spirit of prophecy. So Anna had the mantle of prophecy on her when she recognized, in the person of the babe of Mary, the Divine Redeemer, and "spake of him to all them that looked for redemption in Jerusalem." And the four daughters of Philip, the Evangelist, were thus favored of God.

Among the women of the Bible are many who were eminent as mothers for their instructions to, and their influence over their children. Of such was Jochebed, who had the early training of the rescued Moses; Sarah, who had the education of the Son of Promise; the wife of Manoah, to whom the angel of the Lord appeared twice, and who followed tenaciously the instructions of the angel in the education of Samson; Hannah, who received the promise of a son while worshiping God at Shiloh, and who, when her son was three years old, placed him in the charge of the venerable Eli; Lois and Eunice, the mother and grandmother of Timothy, who taught him the Scriptures from his early childhood.

And what maternal affection did these and other women exhibit.

Among the women of the Bible we have some of the most touching examples of devotion, in the various relations of life, that are to be found in all the history of the human family. As instances, the two Moabitish women that married the sons of Naomi. How devoted to the interests of their stricken and sorrowing mother-in-law; especially Ruth, who forsook her country and kindred to attend a lone, disconsolate woman to the land of Judea, her former home. Rizpah, the wife of Saul, may be referred to; and her affection, which led her, when her sons were hanged, for many dreary days and nights to watch their dead bodies.

There are many examples among them of pure philanthropy. As such was Esther, the queen of Ahasureus. She risked her station as queen, and even her life, to save her imperiled people. But there are, also, examples of wickedness; as was Jezebel, the wife of Ahab, and Athaliah, the mother of Ahaziah, with many others. For further notice, reference is made to the following pages.

We also present to the reader—in an appendix—a history of Bible men and women not named, running through the Old and New Testaments; and though the persons referred to are, many of them, with their history, referred to in articles in the body of the work, yet a facility for reference to unnamed persons will be found here, that is not given in any other book presented to the Christian public, and we have aimed with it to make our Biblical Biography more complete.

I desire to express my indebtedness, in the preparation of this volume, to the authors of various Dictionaries of the Holy Bible; the biographical departments of which I have consulted, and used in the preparation of the various biographies. Those that have been referred to most are, "Watson's Dictionary," "Wood's Dictionary" of the Holy Bible, "Dymond's Pocket London Edition," and "Barr's Index." I am, also, indebted very much to "Clark's," "Henry's," and "Benson's" Commentaries;" as also, to "Smith's Sacred Annals," and to some extent to other works.

Hoping these pages will be an advantage to Bible readers, especially to Sunday School Teachers and the larger Scholars of Schools, I subscribe myself,

Yours affectionately,

THOS. G. BEHARRELL.

# COMPLETE
# BIBLICAL BIOGRAPHY,
## ALPHABETICALLY ARRANGED.



AARON—[Ay′-ron,] *lofty, mountainous.*

Aaron, the distinguished brother of Moses and Miriam, was a descendant of Levi. He was older than Moses, hence born before Pharaoh, the king of Egypt, decreed that the male infants of the Hebrews should be slain. When he was grown up, he married Elisheba, the daughter of Abinadab, a prince of the tribe of Judah, and he had four sons, viz: Nadab and Abihu, Eleazer and Ithamar, as a result of this marriage. He was associated with Moses in leading Israel out of Egypt, and from Egypt to Canaan. Aaron was with Israel in their bondage, and suffered with them, while his distinguished brother was the adopted son of Pharaoh's daughter, and enjoyed the pleasures of a palace and the honors of royalty.

And so when Moses went to the land of Midian and became a shepherd for Jethro the priest, Aaron was still with his enslaved people suffering oppression. But when Moses, after his call to emancipate his people, left the land of Midian and journeyed towards the capital of Egypt, he met Aaron his brother, who was coming to meet him under the direction of God, who had spoken to him in Egypt, saying: "Go into the wilderness to meet Moses," and so precise was he in following the instructions given him, that he arrived at the sacred mountain just at the time his brother arrived there. They were glad again to look upon each other, and affectionately embraced, when we may suppose they gave each other a relation of the events of their lives for the last forty years. Moses related to Aaron how the God of their fathers had appeared unto him at Horeb, and commissioned him to go to the king of Egypt and demand the freedom of Israel. And Aaron received from Moses the words, signs, and words of explanation that God had given him. Aaron became satisfied that God had appointed his brother to this work, and moreover, that he himself was to be spokesman for Moses, and immediately he certified his willingness to enter upon this mission. It may be that the reason why he was made spokesman was, he spake better Hebrew than Moses, as Moses had been associating in and about the court with Egyptians until forty years of age, and after that with the Midianites; and possibly he had an impediment in his speech, for he says: "I am slow of speech and of a slow tongue;" though St. Stephen says of him: "he was mighty in words as well as in deeds." Ex. 4, 5, 6, &c. After the two brothers arrived in the land of Egypt Aaron called together the Elders of Israel, and spake unto them the words which the Lord had spoken unto Moses. They desired evidence of the truth of what Aaron spake, and of the mission with which he and his brother had been charged. To satisfy them, Aaron cast the rod of Moses upon the ground and it became a serpent, then he put forth his hand and took it up, and it became a rod again in his hand. He then put his hand into his bosom, and when he took it out it was leprous as snow; he put his hand again into his bosom, and when he plucked it out it was turned again as his other flesh. He then took of the water of the Nile and poured it out upon the dry land, and it became blood as it was poured out. As the Elders of Israel and the people beheld these signs and heard the words of Aaron, they believed and rejoiced in the prospect of deliverance from oppression. Moses and Aaron then went in unto Pharaoh to demand the emancipation of their people. Aaron spake boldly for them both, and wrought signs and wonders, but yet Pharaoh would not acknowledge their right to make the demand they made. One plague after another was brought upon Egypt by the divine Ruler, using these brothers as instruments in His hand, until finally He permitted Israel to go out. Moses and Aaron, helped by their sister, conducted Israel to the Red Sea, and through it, (in a road cut by the Almighty power,) to the other side, where they saw the host of their enemies closed in and drowned by the returning waters. When Israel came to Sinai and camped, Aaron was with Moses on the mountain side to hear the first audible words that were spoken by God. In company with his sons and the seventy Elders, he tarried on the slope of the mountain while Moses went up to the summit.

Aaron, in company with Hur, was placed by Moses in charge of the children of Israel during his absence, and to them doubtful matters were to be referred, and by them difficult questions settled; and it was because of the position of Aaron among them that they came to him, and in a tumultuous manner said: "Make us Gods to go before us." Moses had been absent longer than they expected he would be, and probably much longer than he supposed he would be when he left them.

Aaron yielded to their importunities, and bade them bring their wives' and children's ear rings. Having brought them to him, he melted the gold, and then made a calf and dedicated it as an image to the worship of Israel's God; and they engaged in gross idolatry before it, insomuch that the anger of the Lord was kindled against them, and to Moses God threatened to remove from the people the symbols of his presence and destroy them. Aaron himself, in this matter, was not without sin, and he would have been punished had not Moses interceded in his behalf.

After the tabernacle was erected, according to the pattern showed Moses in the mount, Aaron and his sons were set apart to the work and office of the Priesthood. Ex. 28, &c.

Previous to this, public worship was not confined to one place, and the eldest in every family officiated as Priest for the family, but now there was a stated place of worship, viz: the tabernacle, and God had commanded that the Priesthood be retained in the family of Aaron. Accordingly Moses consecrated Aaron to the High Priesthood, anointed him with the holy oil, and invested him with the priestly robes and fixtures—his garments of "glory and beauty."

While the ordinary Priest had on a garment closely fitting the body, a coat, a girdle, and a covering for the head, the High Priest had in addition a robe denoting his superiority, an Ephod, a breast-plate, and a plate of gold on his forehead. The robe was of blue, woven from the top to the bottom without seam, being fastened with a girdle and variously ornamented. The sacred Ephod, or Ephod of the High Priest, was variously colored and ornamented with gold, and had upon each of the shoulders a large button, in which was set a precious stone, and in the stones were engraved the names of the twelve tribes of Israel. It was composed as a garment of "gold, blue, scarlet, and fine twined linen with cunning work." The breast-plate which he wore was four square, "a span shall be the length thereof, and a span the breadth thereof," and fastened with rings to the sacred Ephod. There were twelve precious stones set in the plate, three in a row, and on each stone was engraved the name of a son of Jacob as the head of a tribe of Israel, so that Aaron bore upon his breast, as well as upon his shoulders, the names of the various tribes. Upon the forehead was placed the figured golden plate, on which was engraved the motto: "Holiness to the Lord." This has been called the grand badge of the sacred office, and the motto was certainly appropriate for one engaged as Aaron in a holy calling. It is true that Aaron, after he had been thus consecrated to the office of the High Priesthood, and had served faithfully and efficiently for awhile, sinned against God by indulging in envy, which envy led him with Miriam, his sister, to oppose Moses. But when God led him into the tabernacle, and opened his eyes to see his sin, he acknowledged with a penitent heart his fault, and asked forgiveness of Moses, and of God for himself and for his sister, and their sin was forgiven. Num. xii: 1, &c.

But Aaron himself as a priest, and as the head of the priests, became the object of envy and bitter jealousies. Korah, Dathan and Abiram, with two hundred and fifty Levites—men of influence, "famous in the congregation, and men of renown," turned against Aaron and his brother and spake against them. They were not satisfied with the work they were performing, but desired to set up a priesthood and system of sacrifice of their own, of which system they themselves were to be the ministers. Moses, under the direction of God, required them, with Aaron, to appear before the Lord the next day, which they did with all the opposition they had been manifesting to the priesthood and its operations. God condemned them in the sight and hearing of the people, and the earth opened her mouth and swallowed up these guilty leaders with their families.

After this question that had been vexing Israel was settled, the murmuring against Aaron was stopped by a clear proof that he was the chosen of God. Moses took twelve rods from the princes of the twelve tribes, and wrote upon each rod the name of the tribe to which it belonged, and upon the rod of the tribe of Levi he wrote the name of Aaron. Having prepared the rods he placed them in the tabernacle and near the sanctuary. The next day he entered the tabernacle and took out the rods, and showed them to the whole congregation, and it was discovered that though nothing peculiar marked the eleven rods, yet Aaron's rod "was budded, and brought forth buds, and bloomed blossoms, and yielded almonds." This budded rod was laid up in the ark to perpetuate the memory of the miracle, and continues a standing evidence of Aaron's right to the office. This fact was so unquestionably miraculous that we suppose no doubt could possibly remain in the minds of the people, or even of those who had been envious, who had not been destroyed. Surely their doubts were all silenced and their scruples satisfied, for we hear of no further complaints. Num. xvii: 1, &c. Aaron continued to perform the duties of his office with honor to himself, glory to God, and acceptability to the people, until his mission was ended, and he was called from the priesthood here to the everlasting priesthood on high.

The account given us of Aaron's death is peculiarly affecting. Because of the murmurings of the children of Israel at Meribah for want of water, Moses and Aaron were perplexed. They enquired of the Lord as they had been accustomed to do in time of trial, and they were bidden to gather the children of Israel together, and with the rod to smite the rock before their eyes, and water should come forth in sufficient quantities to meet their wants. They did so, and the waters came forth. But there was something connected with their conduct here with which God was displeased. He determined that as they had not sanctified him in the sight of the people, neither of them should enter the land of Canaan.

Soon afterward they journeyed from Kadesh to Mt. Hor, and then the Lord commanded Moses to make ready for parting with Aaron. "Take Aaron, and Eleazar his son, and bring them up unto Mt. Hor: and strip Aaron of his garments, and put them upon Eleazar his son: and Aaron shall be gathered unto his people and shall die there." How solemn the command! He who had been burdened with Moses for forty years, with the interests of a rebellious people—who had served for many years in the high-priest's office, and who alone had entered the most holy place—who had stood at the door of the tabernacle time after time and observed the divine glory, was now about to die. The summons had come and he himself was made acquainted with it. After giving the Elders and congregation of Israel an affectionate farewell, in company with Moses and Eleazar his successor, he ascended Mt. Hor, all the people gazing in sorrow at the trio, as they slowly made their way up the mountain side. At length they reached the spot upon the mountain summit where Aaron was to die. Moses, who had poured the annointing oil upon his head, and so consecrated him to the work of the priesthood years before—who had clothed him with the sacerdotal robes, and designated him High Priest, now stripped him of his garments, and placed them before his eyes upon Eleazar his son. Aaron witnessed the ceremony, and, it may be, assisted in it until it was closed. He looked a moment upon his successor and rejoiced, then laid him down and died, in the presence of God, his brother and his son.

Thus the spirit of the faithful servant of God, like a bird uncaged, left its house upon the top of Mt. Hor, and hied away to the mountain of God. Whether the form of Aaron was coffined and sepulchred or not, we cannot tell, but the sad intelligence of his death was taken down by Moses and Eleazar, "and when all the congregation saw that Aaron was dead, they mourned for him thirty days, even all the house of Israel." The grave of Aaron, like that of Moses, was left unmarked, lest Israel, in the remembrance of him and his many virtues, and abundant labors, should pay him unwarrantable honors.

ABDAH or ABDA, 1—[Ab′da,] *A servant, servitude.*

Abdah, or Abda, was the father of Adoniram, who was one of the important officers of King Solomon, and by him was placed over his tribute. 1st Kings, iv: 6.

ABDA, 2—*A servant, servitude.*

Abda was the son of Shammua, the grandson of Galal, and the great-grandson of Jeduthun, and is referred to in Neh. xi: 17.

ABDI—[Ab′di,] *My servant.*

Abdi was a Levite, referred to in 2d Chron., xxix: 12, &c. He lived, we suppose, during the reign of Hezekiah, and his son Kish was one of those who were engaged in cleansing the temple.

ABDIEL—[Ab′-de-el,] *The servant of God.*

Abdiel was the son of Guni, a Gadite, and a chief of the house of his fathers. 1st Chron., v: 15. He was, probably, the father of Shelemiah, who, with several others, was commanded to take Jeremiah, the prophet, and Baruch, his scribe; but the Lord hid them. Jer., xxxvi: 26.

ABDON, 1—[Ab′don,] *a servant.*

Abdon was the son of Hillel, the Pirathonite, who judged Israel about eight years after Elon, the Zebulonite. Judges, xii: 13-15. He died in the land of Ephraim and was buried there, in Pirathon of Ephraim, in the mount of the Amalekites. He left behind him forty sons and thirty nephews.

ABDON, 2—*A servant.*

Abdon was the son of Micah. He was one of five messengers of King Josiah, who were sent to consult Huldah, the prophetess. 2d Chronicles, xxxiv: 20.

ABEDNEGO—[Abed′nego,] *a servant of light.*

Abednego was one of the three Hebrews who were companions of Daniel in captivity in Babylon. These young men were selected from among the captives for Chaldean learning, from which fact we may judge that they were approaching manhood—probably eighteen or twenty years of age. And there is another fact which would indicate it, viz: they were promoted to posts of honor in the government. They were appointed to fill civil offices.

These three Hebrews carried their religion with them into Babylon, and maintained their character as servants of the living God amidst the grossest idolatry. They were severely tried because of their convictions of right and their determination to discharge their duty in the fear of God. When they were appointed meat and drink by the king, they refused it, and asked of Melzar, the prince, who had charge of them, the privilege of eating and drinking pulse and water, for their consciences would not allow them to take the apportionment of victuals from the king. They were granted the privilege on the condition that the simple fare they preferred did not have a deleterious effect upon their constitution, vigor and countenance, they being compared with the young men that eat of the portion of the king's meat. At the end of ten days the prince was satisfied, and granted them their desire in taking away the meat and the wine.

These three Hebrews gained the esteem of the king, and, probably through the influence of Daniel, who had been promoted to an important position and office, they, too, became officers of the government. After their promotion, they were envied by some who were in lower offices, and probably by disappointed office seekers, who accused them before the king of disobedience, in that they served not his God, nor worshiped the golden image he had set up in the plains of Dura. The king became angry upon hearing this, and determined at once to have an interview with them. He sent for them, that he might talk with them, and compel them by threats from his own mouth, to obey him. They learned, in a short time, the object had in view—it may have been even before they reached the palace of Nebuchadnezzar they knew his intent—but they faltered not. They come into his presence and stand before him undaunted—though they see in his countenance and learn from the tones of his voice that he is angry.

The voice of the king fell upon their ears in the plain interrogatory: "Is it true, O Shadrach, Meshech, and Abednego, do not ye serve my gods, nor worship the golden image which I have set up?" They are ready with their answer, but the king continues to speak: "Now, if ye be ready," &c. He is willing to admit them to a new trial, hoping they will renounce their religion, and, at the sound of the music, serve his God and worship his image, when they shall be pardoned their former violation of his decree; but if they still persisted in their refusal they should be cast into the fiery furnace.

As soon as the opportunity was afforded them of speaking, they acknowledged the truth of the charge brought against them, and they rejected his overtures. They give him to understand that the case is a clear one. They have no disposition to hide their sentiments or feelings, and unite in saying: "O, Nebuchadnezzar, we are not careful to answer thee in this matter. If it be so, our God whom we serve is able to deliver us from the burning fiery furnace, and he will deliver us out of thine hand, O, King."

What an example do they give, in this language, of faith in God and determination to obey the Divine Will! They are not agitated. They do not tremble. But calmly they look at him, with the threatened fiery furnace before them, and say: "We will not serve thy gods, nor worship the golden image which thou hast set up."

What integrity and decision! They show that their hearts were uncorrupted by the pleasures and government honors they had enjoyed—that they yet maintained determination to do right, cost what it would—yea, though it cost them their lives! The king was full of fury, and in his rage commanded that the furnace be heated seven times hotter than it was wont to be heated. Not that it would increase their punishment, but it would show that he, the king, looks upon their crime as seven times worse than that of others who were cast into the furnace.

He ordered them to be instantly bound; and they were bound, and with their clothes upon them cast into the fire, which was so hot that it consumed the mighty men who were executing the decree. The flames of that furnace that destroyed the executioners did not destroy the Hebrews. "They fell down bound," but the fall did not injure them. The cords that had bound them were snapped asunder or burned, and there, in the midst of the fire, these servants of the living God are walking and praising.

What a strange phenomenon!—three men in the fire of a furnace, praising the God of Abraham, Isaac and Jacob, in the use of some favorite song of Zion, while not a hair of their head is singed, nor had the smell of fire passed upon their garments. Ah, the secret is told in this—that an angel—it might have been the covenant angel—came down and was with them, controling the element. Nebuchadnezzar said: "Lo, I see four men walking, and the fourth is like unto the son of God."

He called them forth, changed his mind toward them and their religion, and again promoted them in the province of Babylon.

Thus we see integrity and decision rewarded. Dan. i: 2, 3.

ABEL—[A′bel,] *vanity, vapor, mourning.*

Abel was the second son of Adam and Eve—born a few years after the creation. Cain, the eldest son of Adam, and the brother of Abel, was raised up by his side and enjoyed the pleasures of childhood and early youth with him.

These two brothers rambled together over the hills and plains of the comparatively new earth. They watched with pleasure the passing seasons, and observed together the changes going on around them, indicating the flight of time. They ate at the same table, slept in the same tent, listened to the same wholesome instructions from their parents, and were governed by the same family rules, and they offered their earliest morning sacrifices together. But as they grew and approached manhood they chose different employments. Abel was a shepherd, while Cain was a tiller of the ground. Abel's employment, through his whole short life, was that of keeping the flock.

He was taught by his parents, as they had been taught by God—that the great Creator and Supreme Ruler—the giver of all mercies, would be worshiped by man—would acknowledge sacrifice.

"In process of time" Cain and Abel brought offerings unto the Lord—the former "brought of the first fruits of the ground"—the latter of the firstlings of his flock and of the fat thereof;" and we are informed that God accepted Abel and his offering, while he rejected Cain and his offering. How the God whom they sacrificed unto, manifested his approval of one and his disapproval of the other we cannot say, but he did; insomuch that Cain complains that "he should now be hid from the face of the Lord." The effect upon Cain of his rejection was to excite anger in him against his brother, and in that anger he meditated revenge upon Abel, and opportunity being afforded him a short time afterwards, "he rose up against Abel his brother and slew him." How strange that he could have been excited to so wicked an act for no other offence than the one set forth in the history.

The sacrifice of Abel is the first one of the kind on record in the sacred scriptures. It was a bloody sacrifice, expiatory and typical of the one great sacrifice for sin, viz: the promised seed of the woman that was to bruise the head of the serpent. The apostle tells us, when speaking of Christ's mission to earth—the object of his coming and the end accomplished—it was to destroy the devil and his works—alluding to this first prophetic promise he says: "for this was the son of God manifested that he might destroy the works of the devil. By faith Abel offered unto God a more excellent sacrifice than Cain, by which he obtained witness that he was righteous, God testifying of his gifts." He, like his brother, brought a thank offering, but that was not all—while Cain, in all probability, stopped there, Abel brings a sin offering, thereby acknowledging his sinfulness and the necessity of atonement for sin. The various sacrifices that he offered are referred to by the gifts that God testifies of. And his faith, in reference to an atonement for sin, may be that referred to by the apostle when he says, "he being dead yet speaketh." This act, thus recorded in the book of God, constantly makes known to mankind the necessity of atonement, and it declares that faith as an internal principle of true worship, must move in the heart when sacrifice is offered to God, or the sacrifice will not be accepted. Gen. iv. and Heb. xi: 4, and xii: 24.

ABI—[A′-be,] *my father.*

ABI was the daughter of Zechariah, and the mother of Hezekiah, a king of Judah. 2d Kings, xviii: 2. She is called Abijah in 2d Chron. xxix: 1. See Abijah.

ABIAH, 1—[Ab-i′-ah,] *the Lord is my father.*

ABIAH, the wife of Hezron, who died in Caleb Ephratah. She was the mother of Ashur, and the grandmother of Tekoa. 1st Chron. ii: 24.

ABIAH, 2—*The Lord is my father.*

ABIAH, with Joel his brother, was a son of the famed prophet Samuel, and was appointed by the father in his old age as a judge over Israel, with Joel his brother. They were not judges in the same sense and to the same extent as Samuel, or to the exclusion of their father. The prophet himself judged Israel until the day of his death, and was their last judge, for Saul, the son of Kish, was chosen and annointed King over Israel by Samuel, at the request of the people and under the direction of God.

They were appointed by Samuel their father as helpers in the affairs of the government, or superintendents of certain things. "They walked not in his ways, but turned aside after lucre, and took bribes and perverted judgment." The people complained to Samuel of the wickedness of his sons, and demanded a king to reign over them. How unfortunate that so great and good a man as Samuel was, should be called to see his own children in a wicked, avaricious and unjust course of life. 1st Sam. viii: 1-5.

ABIALBON— [Ab-e-al′-bon,] *intelligent father.*

ABIALBON, was a native of Arbath, and one of the valiant men of the army of King David. 2d Sam. xxiii: 31.

ABIASAPH — [Abi′-asaph,] *a consuming father.*

ABIASAPH was the son of Korah, and the younger brother of Assir and Elkanah. Ex. vi: 24.

ABIATHAR—[A-bi′-a-thar,] *excellent father.*

ABIATHAR, the son of Ahimelech, was the tenth high priest among the Jews, and the fourth from Eli. When he was divested by Solomon of his office, because he attached himself to the party of Adonijah, the house of Eli failed, as it had been declared it should in 1st Sam. 2d chap. and 31st verse: "Behold the days come that I will cut off thine arm, and the arm of thy father's house, that there shall not be an old man in thine house;" and 35th verse: "And I will raise me up a faithful priest, that shall do according to that which is in mine heart and in my mind; and I will build him a sure house; and he shall walk before mine annointed forever." This was spoken of Zadok, who ministered before Solomon, and kings who reigned after him.

When David fled before the enraged King Saul, he went to Nob and procured from Ahimelech bread to eat from the shew-bread table, and the sword of Goliath of Gath—the Philistine giant that David had slain some time before—for that sword had been placed by King Saul under the charge of Ahimelech.

The priest, knowing that David was the King's son-in-law, and not being aware of the wrath of Saul against him, wondered at his being without attendants; but granted without hesitation his request, when he, with the five loaves of bread and the huge sword, went into the country of Gath and showed himself unto Achish the King. It was not long until Doeg, the Edomite, informed Saul of the help Ahimelech had given David, whereupon Saul sent for him and pronounced the sentence of death upon him and upon all his house.

The sentence was executed by Doeg, the informant, upon all of them save Abiathar, who, to avoid this slaughter and save his own life, fled to David. He carried with him in his flight, probably, his sacerdotal garments, and we are informed that he became high priest for David; while Zadok, the son of Ahitub, of the house of Eleazer, became high priest for Saul instead. He remained in the priesthood through the reign of David, and until Solomon ascended the throne of Israel, when, for the crime already named, he was deposed. 1st Sam. xxii: 20; 2d Sam. xv: 29; 1st Kings, i: 7, and ii: 26.

ABIDAH—[Abi′dah,] *father of knowledge.*

ABIDAH was the son of Midian, and the grandson of Abraham by Keturah. He was the brother of Ephah and Epher, and Hanoch and Eldaah. Gen. xxv: 4.

ABIDAN—[Ab′idan,] *father of judgment.*

ABIDAN was the son of Gideoni, of the tribe of Benjamin. He is referred to as a prince of his tribe, in Num. vii: 60. The chapter contains an account of the offerings of the different tribes at the dedication of the altar and its vessels. His offering, like that of the princes of the other tribes, consisted in "one silver charger, the weight whereof was a hundred and thirty shekels; one silver bowl of seventy shekels, after the shekel of the sanctuary; both of them full of fine flour mingled with oil, for a meat offering; one golden spoon of ten shekels, full of incense; one young bullock, one ram, one lamb of the first year for a burnt offering; one kid of the goats for a sin offering, and for a sacrifice of peace offerings, two oxen, five rams, five he-goats five lambs of the first year.' And his offering was made on the ninth day.

ABIEL—[Ab′-e-el,] *God my father.*

ABIEL was the father of Kish, and the grandfather of Saul, the first king of the Jews. 1st Sam. ix: 1. He was also the father of Ner, and the grandfather of the famous warrior, Abner. 1st Sam. xiv: 51.

ABIEZER—[Ab-e-e′-zer,] *father of help.*

ABIEZER was of the tribe of Benjamin, and from the city of Anathoth. He was one of the thirty men of great valor in David's army. 2d Samuel, xxiii: 27. He was the captain of the ninth month, when David instituted the monthly service of captains over twenty-four thousand men. 1st Chron. xxvii: 12.

ABIGAIL, 1—[Ab′-e-gal,] *the joy of the father.*

ABIGAIL.—There was a woman of this name who was the daughter of Nahash or Jesse. 2d Sam. xvii: 25. Abigail, the daughter of Nahash, sister of Zeruiah, Joab's mother. Joab was the son of Zeruiah, the sister of David. Abigail was also David's sister; and we are informed in 1st Chron. ii: 17, that she was the wife of Jether and the mother of Amasa.

ABIGAIL, 2—*The joy of the father.*

ABIGAIL was the wife of Nabal the Carmelite. She was introduced to our notice in 1st Sam. xxv: 3, as a woman of good sense, and handsome, "A woman of good understanding and of a beautiful countenance." Her husband was what the world would call a great man. He was very rich, and a part of his great wealth consisted in three thousand sheep and a thousand goats, but withal he was churlish, and evil in his doings, and hence was not a fit husband for her. It is likely that she was induced to marry him, as a great many sensible and beautiful women have been induced to marry fools, because of their money and influence in the world.

His character was developed when David sent messengers to him, to greet him in his name, and referred him to the manner in which he had befriended him. Nabal, in a spirit of the most consumate meanness, answered the messengers of David, and they returned to their master with his answer. No wonder that David looked upon this conduct as the grandest insult, and at once determined to revenge the wrong. He ordered his young men to make ready and attend him, and four hundred of them ranged themselves under him and started for Nabal's house.

In the meantime one of the servants informed Abigail of the manner in which Nabal had treated David's messengers, and assured her that evil was determined against the house of Nabal. Abigail made haste and prepared a present, consisting of bread, wine, sheep, raisins, cakes and figs, and went to meet David—if possible to appease his wrath. She showed her good sense and prudence in hastening to bring the present to David, and also in the manner in which she accosted him when they met. She approached him with great deference, and asked the privilege of representing her case in his hearing, and that of the household of Nabal. She confessed to David the true character of her husband, and appealed to him not to shed innocent blood—she begged him to accept a present at her hands—and forgive the trespass that had been offered to him. Her address to David was very beautiful, and very likely won upon his heart—especially the plea she put in, in her own behalf, as she closed her address, "but when the Lord shall have dealt with my lord, then remember thine handmaid." David received her present—accepted her advice, and pronounced his blessings upon her. It was not long after she had returned until she informed Nabal of the narrow escape he had made, by insulting David. The information she gave her husband had a strange effect upon him. He thought of the feast he had held the day before, and of his free indulgence in wine. And of Abigail his wife leaving the family and the enjoyments of the feast, and flying to meet David with a present to appease his wrath, and stay him in his intended work of death. When he thought of the imminent peril to which he was exposed according to this representation of Abigail, he was strangely affected with terror, and became insensible, "his heart died within him, and he became as a stone."

A disease of some kind set in, and in ten days sapped the foundation of life and he died. So Abigail was left a widow. David soon learned that Nabal was dead, and he meditated marriage with the widow. He had been married to Michal, the daughter of Saul, but had been parted from her by the hostility and persecution of Saul, and moreover Saul had given David's wife to another in order to cut off any pretensions he might make to the throne.

When he sent and communed with Abigail on the subject of taking her to wife—she made no serious objections, but made ready and went with the messengers to David, taking with her five damsels. She became his wife, and he in all probability came, through her, in possession of the wealth of Nabal. The property at Carmel and Maon came under his control.

David dwells with his wives, (for he had also married Ahinoam the Jezreelitess,) in Ziklag, a town given him by Achish the king of Gath. The length of time that he lived there was one year and four months, for Ziklag was burnt with fire by the Amalekites who invaded during David's absence. When he returned and saw what was done, and knew that Abigail with his other wife was taken captive, with the wives of his men—he was greatly affected—and mingled his lamentation with those of his men. He hushed the mutinous spirit of his men, however, by telling them that the Lord had commanded him to follow the enemy, and had given him the promise that they should recover all. And they did, and soon Abigail, as the wife of David was happily dwelling in the city of Hebron, awaiting the hour of her husband's promotion as king on the vacated throne of the deceased Saul. While David dwelt in Hebron, Chileab was born unto him of Abigail. We hear but little concerning this woman afterwards—for David took unto himself other wives after he transferred his court to Jerusalem.

ABIHAIL, 1—[Ab′-e-hale,] *father of strength.*

Abihail was the son of Huri and father of Michael and Meshullam, and several others. His name and the names of his children occur in 1st Chron. v: 13, 14.

ABIHAIL, 2—*Father of strength.*

Abihail was the father of Zuriel, who was chief of the house and family of Merari. Num. iii: 35

ABIHAIL, 3—*Father of strength.*

Abihail was the father of the famous Esther who delivered the Jews from their imminent peril, which peril was occasioned by the wickedness of Haman. Esther ii: 15. Esther the daughter of Abihail, the uncle of Mordecai. He died while Esther was a little girl, leaving her an orphan. Esther ii: 7. "She had neither father nor mother." Her cousin adopted her after her father's death as his own daughter.

ABIHAIL, 4—*Father of strength.*

Abihail was the daughter of Eliab, the brother of king David. She became the wife of Rehoboam, the successor of Solomon. She was the mother of Jeush, Shamariah and Zaham, the children of Rehoboam. 2d Chron. xi: 18, 19.

ABIHU—[Abi′hu,] *he is my father.*

Abihu, with Nadab, his brother, ministered in the services of the sanctuary. They were Priests and sons of Aaron, the high-priest. We have an account of their destruction in Lev. x: 1, 2. They offered "strange fire before the Lord, which he commanded them not. And there went out fire from the Lord and devoured them, and they died before the Lord." What their particular sin was we can not certainly determine; but it was sin gross in its character and abominable in the sight of the Lord who had ordained the office and had given the rules and regulations by which the priests were to be governed in the functions of their office. They failed to follow the divine directions, and so, in a few days after their consecration, were visited with a terrible destruction. Though the punishment of Nadab and Abihu may seem to be exceedingly severe, as the crime is not specified, yet we may rest assured that it was of such a character as to justify—nay, more, to demand such punishment.

It is supposed, by many, that these sons of Aaron had indulged, before entering the sanctuary, in the use of wine to such an extent as to unfit them for the duties of their holy office. Some think they were so intoxicated as to forget to take the sacred fire in their censers. And there seems to be some ground for this conjecture in the command God delivered to Aaron immediately after the fallen ones had been removed from the sanctuary where they had been destroyed: "Do not drink wine or strong drink, thou nor thy sons with thee, when ye go into the tabernacle of the congregation, lest ye die; it shall be a statute forever throughout your generations." Thus the priest learned that God would not allow the work of the priesthood to be interfered with by a want of ability to perform its duties because of inebriacy. But this punishment of Abihu and his brother with death may teach us that God will not wink at uncleanliness in his ministers, or, indeed, in any of his servants, when engaged in the performance of religious duties. While the external is being performed the heart must be right. The internal principles of true worship must be exercised.

ABIHUD—[Abi′hud,] *the father of praise.*

Abihud was the son of Zerubbabel or Zorrobabel. The only important item regarding this personage that we give is, he was in the line of the Messiah—one of our Savior's ancestors according to the flesh. Matt. i: 13. He was the son of Zerubbabel and the father of Eliakim.

ABIJAH, 1—[Ab-i′-jah,] *the will of the Lord.*

Abijah was the son of Jeroboam, the first king of the ten tribes of Israel. He died when very young. We have an account of him, his sickness, death, and burial, in the 14th chapter of 1st Kings. When he was taken sick Jeroboam bade his wife disguise herself as the wife of the king and go to Shiloh and inquire of the aged prophet, Ahijah, whether or not the sickness of the child should result in his death. It was natural for Jeroboam, in his anxiety about his son, and desiring to consult a prophet, to apply to this prophet, for it was Ahijah that told him he should be a king over the people.

The wife of the king disguised herself and went, in accordance with the command, to Shiloh, and entered the house of the prophet, who, she found, was very aged and blind, "for his eyes were set by reason of his age." It may be she thought, as she looked upon the blind prophet, the king need not have demanded me to disguise myself that I be not known as his wife, for this prophet has not eyes to look upon the robes of royalty. He can not distinguish a queen mother from the humblest woman in Israel. But in this she was mistaken, for that prophet, though shrouded in constant night, was in communion with God, and by revelation he learned that the wife of Jeroboam was at his house near the door of the apartment, having come to ask of him a question concerning her son who was sick. As she was entering by the door, to her astonishment the prophet said: "Come in, thou wife of Jeroboam, why feignest thou thyself to be another? for I am sent to thee with heavy tidings."

He then informed her of the purpose of God regarding the kingdom and the house of Jeroboam, because of his sin in refusing to honor the God who had promoted him; and then the prophet assured her that the sickness of the child was unto death, and his death would take place upon her entering the city to bear intelligence to Jeroboam from him.

She returned home, we may suppose, with a heavy heart, and when she came to the threshold of the door the child died, and was honored with a prince's burial a few hours afterward. Abijah was the purest and best of the house of Jeroboam.

ABIJAH, 2—*The will of the Lord.*

Abijah, the son of Rehoboam, king of Judah, succeeded his father to the throne. He was the son of Maachah, the daughter of Absalom. She was loved by Rehoboam more than all his wives, and this love that he had for her led him to make Abijah, though he was not his first-born, the chief of his brethren, and his own successor on the throne of Judah. In making this preference the king seems to have violated that law that God gave to govern his people, regarding the first-born. The law to which I refer is in substance as follows: If a man have two wives—one less loved than the other—and the son of the woman less loved be the first-born, then, when he maketh his sons to inherit, he may not make the son of the beloved to inherit before the son of the woman less loved, for the latter is indeed the first-born. Deut. xxi: 15–17. But then Rehoboam had a precedent set by David, in his preference shown to Solomon, the son of Bathsheba, when he made him king.

Abijah, upon ascending the throne of Judah, opened a war upon Jeroboam, the king of Israel, his army consisting of four hundred thousand effective men, while the army of Jeroboam was double that number. Abijah made an appeal to the king of Israel, and to all the people, in which he attempted to show that the govenment of Jeroboam was founded on injustice, and had been carried on in injustice. He rebukes them for their wickedness in rebellion, and for their gross idolatry—asserts the right of the Lord God of his fathers to rule over them, and their obligations to observe the religion that had been instituted for the descendants of Israel, the son of Isaac. Then he declares, while they have the golden calves that they worship as gods, these whom he represented as the kingdom of Judah had the living God with them, and worshiped him. He declared in his appeal, before entering upon the battle, his faith in God, and assured the enemy that God not only dwelt with him and his people, but was their captain, and the priests of the Lord were with them to sound the trumpet and cry the alarm against them.

Jeroboam heeded not the king of Judah, but managed his vast army against Abijah until the peril of Judah seemed to be very great, for with an ambushment their enemy was attacking them behind as well as before. In this their extremity—true to the declaration of Abijah—God's presence among them was manifested, for, as the priests sounded with the trumpets, the men of Judah shouted, *i. e.*, they gave evidence of their trust in the word of the God of their fathers, and Jeroboam and all Israel were smitten before them, and Abijah obtained a great victory, in the destruction of five hundred thousand chosen men of the enemy. Jeroboam never fully recovered the loss he sustained in his position as king. 1st Kings, xv; 2d Chron. xiii.

The Jewish Rabbins have reproached king Abijah because he did not destroy, after his conquest, the profane altar and break up fully the worship of the golden calves. And by many this is supposed to be the only blemish in his character. He was succeeded to the throne of Judah by Asa, his son.

ABIJAH, 3—*The will of the Lord.*

Abijah, the wife of Ahaz, was the mother of King Hezekiah. In 2d Chron. xxix: 1, she was said to be the daughter of Zechariah, but not of the high priest who was slain by King Joash, the account of which murder we have in 2d Chron. xxiv: 21. For had she been the daughter of that Zechariah, she would have been near ninety years of age when Ahaz married her, and had by her a child. 2d Chron. xxix: 1. In 2d Kings, xviii: 2, she is called Abi, the daughter of Zechariah, and the mother of Hezekiah.

ABIMELECH, 1—[Ab-im′-me-lek,] *My father is king.*

Abimelech was a king of the Philistines, who dwelt in the country of Gerer. He is referred to in Gen. xx, from which we learn that he was captivated with the beauty of Sarah, the wife of Abraham; and as Abraham had informed him that she was his sister, he took Sarah into his palace, intending to make her his wife. But the God of Abraham interfered, with a dream or vision, in which he threatened Abimelech with death if he did not restore the woman to her husband. God said to him in a dream, "Behold, thou art but a dead man for the woman which thou hast taken; for she is a man's wife." He immediately restored her, and excused himself before the Almighty on the ground of Abraham's pretense that Sarah was only his sister; and he complained to the patriarch for imposing on him. And he in turn justified himself before Abimelech by saying that Sarah was his sister as well as his wife, "being the daughter of the same father, though not of the same mother."

Abimelech then gave Abraham several presents, and offered him a house in his kingdom if he desired to remain there, and believing him to be a great and good man he asked his prayers to God in his behalf, and in the behalf of his family, and it is quite likely the good man complied heartily with his request. But he made Sarah a present also, it is supposed. Addressing her he said: "Behold I have given thy brother a thousand pieces of silver; behold he is to thee a covering of the eyes, and unto all that are with thee." It is thought by some that this present was to purchase or procure a vail for her that she might cover her face and not subject others to the inconvenience that he had endured, and the peril he had passed through, by being carried away with her beauty. Sarah must have been a very handsome woman, for she was now ninety years old, and yet her countenance was so pleasant and comely that a king of another nation fell in love with her.

Abraham prayed for Abimelech's family and they were converted. We have an account in Gen. xxi: 22, of Abimelech coming to Abraham several years after, in company with Phichol his chief captain, and begging him to enter into a covenant of friendship with him. He probably saw that Abraham's posterity and power were increasing greatly, hence he wanted to form an alliance with him. Abraham readily granted his request.

## ABIMELECH, 2—*My father is king.*

Abimelech was also a king of Gerar the son and successor of the former king. He was about to be imposed upon by Isaac in the same way that Abraham imposed upon his father. But from his window one day he saw evidences of familiarity between Isaac and Rebecca, that led him to conclude she was Isaac's wife and not his sister, as they both pretended. Abimelech at once sent for Isaac and told him what his convictions were, that this woman was his wife; he acknowledged that she was, and the only reason he had to give for deceiving him was that he feared they would kill him if they learned that she sustained the relation of wife to him, and take possession of her themselves.

Abimelech reproved Isaac for taking this course; but he immediately issued orders that none of his subjects should touch or injure either Isaac or Rebecca under pain of death. As Abraham had prospered in that country, so Isaac prospered, until the subjects of the king began to be afraid and envy him. Abimelech then asked Isaac to leave his territory, giving as a reason for the request, he was becoming mightier than they. And soon after this—remembering the course that his father took with Abraham—he took the same course and entered into a league with Isaac. He took with him Ahuzzath his friend, and Phichol his chief captain. Isaac received him at Beersheba and entertained him with a feast, after which they entered into a solemn covenant that each of them ever remembered and continued faithful to. Gen. 26.

## ABIMELECH, 3—*My father is king.*

Abimelech was the name of one of the sons of Gideon, who became a judge of Israel. But he was the son of a concubine of Gideon's that lived in Shechem, *i. e.*, the son of a secondary wife. The children of such wives could not inherit. His name imports: "My father hath reigned." Shortly after Gideon died, he went to Shechem and communed with his mother's brethren, and with all the house of his mother's father. They listened to him, and influenced by his arguments, concluded that he, of all his father's sons should reign over them. And they furnished him money with which he hired wicked persons to assist him in perfecting his plans, and effecting his ends in securing the government. At the head of the hired company of "vain and light persons," he went to his father's house at Ophrah and slew all the seventy sons of Gideon, save Jotham the youngest, who hid himself. Thus by a cunning management of wicked men this revolution was effected, and the government founded in which Abimelech reigned.

When three years had passed away God sent an evil spirit amongst them, or permitted jealousies to take place, which produced among the men of Shechem, factions, contentions, insurrections and civil war. They had no regard for Abimelech as their king longer, but cursed him while they committed their depredations in the land. It may be the very same wicked men that he hired to go with him and slay the seventy sons of his father, and thus in iniquity elevate him to the high position of ruler in the land, now turned against him, and had posted themselves along the road between Shechem, where he lived, and Ophrah, where Gideon had lived, and where his sons had been slain, for they intended to assassinate him. A large part of the people of Shechem set themselves in array against Abimelech, and he fought with them and conquered the city. Afterward he destroyed those who had fled to the "hold of the house of the God Berith," or who had gone to the precincts of the idol temple for safety. He set the hold on fire and so burned a thousand men and women in it. He then went to Thebez, an important city, and took it, and as the men and women of the city had fled to the tower and shut themselves up in it, he opened a siege upon the tower that he might find an entrance and destroy those who had fled thither. He was about to succeed by burning the door down, when a certain woman cast a piece of millstone upon his head, which is supposed to have broken or fractured his skull. Then he called upon his armor-bearer to slay him at once, lest the disgrace of being killed by a woman be affixed to his memory and his death. Then the young man, his armor-bearer, thrust him through with his sword and he died. Thus we behold the sins of the men of Shechem visited upon them in being destroyed by the man they unjustly exalted; and the sins of Abimelech visited upon him by being betrayed in his own government, and finally killed in the manner we have narrated. Jud. ix.

ABIMAEL—[Ab-be-may′-el] *a father sent from God.*

ABIMAEL was the son of Joktan, and the grandson of Eber, and is referred to in the posterity of Shem. Genesis x: 28.

ABINADAB—[Ab-in′-na-dab,] *my father a willing prince.*

ABINADAB was the son of Jesse and the brother of David. 1st Chron. ii: 13. He was the second son of Jesse, and is probably the one who is referred to in 1st Kings, iv: 11, as being the father of one of the officers who were appointed by Solomon to provide victuals for the king's household, and who was married to Taphath, the daughter of Solomon.

ABINOAM—[Ab-in′-no-am,] *father of beauty.*

ABINOAM was the father of Barak, the general of Deborah's army, which army fought against Jabin, king of Canaan. Jud. iv: 6.

ABIRAM, 1—[Ab-i′-ram,] *a high father.*

ABIRAM was the son of Eliab, the Reubenite. He with Korah and his brother Dathan, conspired against Moses and Aaron, and sought to divest them of the powers conferred on them by God. On account of his wickedness he and his whole family were swallowed up with their substance by the earth opening and receiving them, then closing in on them. The account of their sin and destruction is given in Numbers, xvi:

ABIRAM, 2—*A high father.*

ABIRAM was the eldest son of Hiel, the Bethelite. He lost his life while his father was rebuilding the walls of Jericho. His death was in accordance with the prophecy of Joshua, the son of Nun. 1st Kings, xvi: 34—Josh. vi: 26.

ABISHAG—[Ab′-be-shag,] *ignorance of the father.*

ABISHAG was the young woman that was selected as the last wife of David, the king of Israel. It was under the advise of his physician that he married her when he was nearly seventy years of age. Though not as old, probably, as many of his day, yet from constitutional debility and an enfeebled state occasioned by the exposures and hardships through which he had passed, he was almost helpless—premature old age seems to have been upon him.

She was selected that she might minister unto him, and make the latter part of his evening of life as pleasant as it could possibly be made. Abishag had charge of David probably one year, when "he slept with his fathers, and was buried in the city of David."

We may suppose from the account given of her that she was one of the most beautiful women in Israel, for she was selected of all the fair young damsels for this position. But there is another reason why we suppose she was very beautiful, and that is: Adonijah, the brother of Absalom, when he failed to ascend the throne of Israel, desired to take her as his wife, and so anxious was he, enamoured of her beauty, that he asked Bathsheba, the mother of Solomon, to intercede with the king in his behalf, that Abishag might be given him to wife. Solomon, in all probability, mistook the motive of Adonijah, and looked upon his request as treason against his government, and determined that he should die; hence he was slain at the command of his brother Solomon by the hand of Benaiah. 1st Kings, i: 2. She was a native of Shunam, hence called a Shunamite.

ABISHAI—[Ab-bi-sha′-i,] *the father of sacrifice.*

ABISHAI was the son of Zeruiah, David's sister, hence he was the king's nephew, as was also Joab his brother. Abishai was a valiant warrior, and when serving in David's army was one of his principal generals. When David was camped in the wilderness of Ziph, and Saul went out to destroy him with a large company of warriors compared to David's handful of men, Abishai was with him. David asked when night came on, "who will go with me by night into the camp of Saul?" for he had learned where Saul had pitched his tent. Abishai answered that he would go, and the two together went, and as they passed the sleeping guard, and were approaching Saul, who was also sleeping with Abner, the son of Ner, the captain of his host near him, Abishai asked David for the privilege of slaying Saul at once, and so rid him forever of his enemy. But David would not allow it. Abishai thought it very strange that he would allow his enemy this second time to escape, for he had been in his power thus once before. The reason David allowed Saul to escape before was the same reason that allowed him to escape now, viz: he would not injure the Lord's annointed. Abishai served David in his war with Ishbosheth, Saul's son. He also served in the war with the Edomites, and cut off eighteen thousand of them in the Valley of Salt. 1st Chron. xviii: 12. "Moreover Abishai, the son of Zeruiah, slew of the Edomites in the Valley of Salt, eighteen thousand." When David was engaged in a war with the Syrians and Ammonites, Abishai commanded that part of the army which routed the Ammonites, as recorded in 2d Samuel, x: 14: "When the children of Ammon saw the Syrians were fled, then fled they also before Abishai."

In the war with the Philistines, he killed the noted giant Ishbibenob, who was about to destroy the life of David, as recorded in 2d Samuel, xxi: 16. At another time Abishai showed himself a man of great bravery in attacking and killing three hundred men alone. 2d Samuel, xviii: 2. And in the account we have of Absalom's rebellion, we learn that Abishai commanded a third part of the king's army; and he was at the head of the king's household troops that pursued Sheba, the son of Bichri, when he made insurrection against David. 2d Samuel, xx: 6. And when Shimei cursed David, Abishai desired to go to him and take off his head, but the king would not allow him to do it, giving as the reason: "The Lord hath permitted him to curse me, why shall I complain?" David then added, "what is the cursing of Shimei compared with the rebellion of Absalom? My son, which came forth of my bowels, seeketh my life; how much more may this Benjaminite do? let him curse, for the Lord hath bidden him." He served David long and faithfully, and died with the honors of an honorable and successful warrior encircling his brow.

ABISHALOM—[Ab-bi-sha′-lom,] *the father of peace.*

ABISHALOM was the father of Maachah, who was the mother of Abijah king of Judah. 1st Kings, xv: 2.

ABISHUA—[Ab-bi-shu′-ah,] *the father of salvation.*

ABISHUA was the son of Phinehas and the fourth high priest of the Jews. He succeeded his father in that important office. 1st Chron. vi: 50.

ABISHUR—[Ab′-be-shur,] *the father of righteousness.*

ABISHUR was the son of Shammai, and is referred to in the posterity of Judah. 1st Chron. ii: 28.

ABITAL—[Ab′-be-tal,] *father of the dew.*

ABITAL was one of the wives of David. In 1st Chron. iii: 3, she is numbered as the sixth wife of the king, and Shephetiah was her son, born while David was in Hebron.

ABNER—[Ab′ner,] *the father of light.*

ABNER, the son of Ner, was uncle to King Saul, and the commander of his army. He was Saul's first aid, and the prominent person of his body-guard when he was camped at Hachilah, and David was in the wilderness of Ziph.

When David and Abishai entered the camp of Saul by night, Abner was sleeping at Saul's side and did not perceive the intruders, and he was, no doubt, greatly astonished to hear the man whose life they were hunting, calling to him in the morning. He had been wondering from the time they arose from their camp-couch, what had become of Saul's spear and royal cruise. But as David secured his attention he showed him the king's spear and the cruise of water that was at his bolster, that had been taken away the night before. 1st Sam. xxvi: 5–14.

When Saul died Abner made Ishbosheth king, and for several years he headed the troops under the authority of Saul's house. Abner fought frequently with David and his men, but in nearly all the engagements met with loss. He suggested to Joab, the general of David's army, at one time, a very foolish and cruel plan for testing the strength, bravery and tact for fighting hand to hand of twelve men on either side. He proposed that twelve of David's warriors should fight with an equal number of his. Joab agreed thereto, and the twenty-four men engaged. They took each one his fellow by the beard and thrust a sword into each others side, and so the twenty-four men fell down dead together.

A very severe battle followed this foolish slaughter, in which Abner and the troops of Ishbosheth were made to fly. Abner himself fled for his life, and was pursued very closely for death, by Asahel, the brother of Joab, who was very fleet of foot. Abner found that his pursuer was gaining on him and begged him to stop, but he would not; he then struck Asahel with his spear by a back stroke and killed him.

Not long after this, Ishbosheth accused Abner of lewdness toward Rizpah, his father's concubine. On account of this accusation Abner became enraged, and threatened not only to desert him, but betray the whole kingdom of his master into the hands of David; and in order to effect this his threat, he opened a correspondence with David, and afterwards had an interview with him at Hebron.

Joab heard of the interview that Abner had held with David, and the manner in which David had treated him and his men, and remonstrated with David against depending upon Abner accomplishing what he proposed. He gave it as his opinion that Abner had only come as a spy—and then he sent a messenger in the name of the king to invite Abner to come back to Hebron, for he wished to converse with him more fully. Abner returned and went into the presence of Joab to learn, in all probability, more fully for what intent the king had sent for him. Joab, in order to avenge his brother's death, or else moved by jealousy, met Abner in salute and stabbed him mortally. David, when informed of this, complained much of Joab, and declared himself and his kingdom guiltless of Abner's blood—and he showed his regards for the departed by honoring him with a splendid funeral—and he himself was one of the mourners, and composed for the occasion a touching eulogy recorded in 2d Sam. iii: 33–34.

ABRAHAM—[A'bra-ham,] *father of nations.*

ABRAHAM the son of Terah, was born at Ur, a city of Chaldea. He was distinguished more than any other of the Patriarchs. In his eventful life he was noted for his "faith in God," and has sometimes been styled the "father of the faithful." He was an extraordinary man, possessing virtues and excellencies beyond any other person whose history the Bible records. The moral excellence he attained, but few, if any, in all the history of man have attained unto. He presents the portrait of a perfect man, for he walked before God and was perfect.

Of the early life of Abraham we know but little; he grew up and became a man in the country of his birth, and while there the "God of glory" appeared to him and said unto him, "Get thee out of thy country and from thy kindred, and go into the land which I shall show thee." Abraham, though he had not probably been taught the true worship of the true God—yet he believed—he obeyed the voice of God who spake unto him, and he went out not knowing whither he went. His father Terah, and his brother Nahor, and his nephew Lot, went with him. They went to Haran, in Mesopotamia, and lived there for a few years, when Terah died. Abraham, shortly after, with Lot his nephew, left Nahor his brother in Haren, and went into Palestine, having Sarah his wife with him. A remarkable promise, about this time, was made to Abraham, touching the seed of the woman that should bruise the serpent's head. It was in the following language: "In blessing thou shalt be blessed, and in thy seed shall all the nations of the earth be blessed."

When an aged man this promise of God was verified to him. Sarah, his beloved wife, bare him a son. And when God would try the quality of his faith he made him go up to Mount Moriah and offer that son as a sacrifice. This command must have fallen upon the ear and heart of Abraham with ponderous weight, but "staggering not at the promise of God," he made ready to perform this painful duty.

The hours of the night on which he received this command passed away and the morning arrived. He made ready to go to the designated place—his servants that were to attend him made all things ready, and Isaac took an affectionate leave of his mother. Behold the three as they stand within the tent just before the journey is commenced. Abraham alone knew the purpose of God regarding Isaac, and how it must have affected him as he looked upon Sarah, knowing that she was looking upon her son Isaac for the last time, the purpose of God being carried out. Surely paternal love swelled in his heart till he could hardly refrain from whispering in the ear of the mother, "Isaac may never return"—but he did refrain, and with a heavy heart left Sarah in the tent. Abraham listened to the innocent, boyish talk of his son as they rode along, and every sentence of Isaac was like a dagger piercing his heart—yet with solemn looks and melancholy feelings he traveled on, Isaac all the while wondering at the seeming sadness of his father.

At length they arrive at the mountain, and Abraham bids his attendants tarry while he and the lad went up to worship. The two together wended their way up the mountain side and the burden presses the heart of Abraham more and more. His affection for his child is increasing. Isaac walks by his side and receives a glance from his father which seems to say, can I give him up? My son is approaching manhood. I have looked upon him with fond feelings from his earliest infancy. He is the son of my old age and the promised seed in whom all the nations of the earth are to be blessed. But he adds: He who gave me this son of promise has commanded and I must obey. His tempest tossed soul is stilled—his relaxed muscles are strung and his arm nerved to make the preparations for the sacrifice. Soon a rude altar appears upon the mountain, and the fuel is gathered for the fire; when all at once Isaac turns to his father and says, "Father, here is the altar, and here is the wood, but where is the sacrifice?" "My son," said Abraham, "God will provide himself a lamb for the burnt offering."

Abraham then made known to Isaac the command of God. Isaac gave himself up and submitted to be bound and laid upon the altar. Heaven permitted the fond father when he had proceeded thus far, to give his dear son what he supposed was a last fond embrace—then nerving himself for the work, he drew back the knife to plunge it into the bosom of Isaac. Behold the scene! And then think of this mountain as it looms up in moral grandeur among the mountains of the Bible. Here where Isaac was bound and laid on the altar, Solomon's temple was erected, in which was an altar where sacrifices were offered and blood of animals flowed, typifying atonement for sin. Yet, on this mountain God's earthly habitation was fixed. In the Shechinah, in the holiest apartment of the temple, God dwelt between the cherubims. But not far from this spot where Isaac is bound on an altar, Mount Calvary was situated, on which Jesus Christ was bound to a Roman cross and poured out his blood as a libation for man.

But then Abraham was stopped. While the angels of God in heaven were looking upon the scene with the most intense anxiety—their eyes were fixed upon the altar, the sacrifice and the officiating priest, and they wondered as to the result. The solemn stillness around them was broken by the voice of the Almighty saying: It is enough. The command was given a swift winged angel—Fly to the spot and stay the hand of my servant that he slay not Isaac. The angel sped quicker than lightning to Moriah, arrested the attention of Abraham by saying, "Lay not thy hand upon the lad, neither do thou anything unto him, for now I know that thou fearest God, seeing thou hast not withheld thy son, thine only son, from me." Abraham looked up and saw on the mountain a short distance from him a fulfillment of the declaration he had made to Isaac, in a ram caught by the horns in a thicket. He then unbound Isaac, slew the ram, and the two together offered the sacrifice. A short time afterwards Abraham and Isaac with joyful hearts came down from the mountain, and with the servants returned home—when we may suppose Sarah was made acquainted with the trial of her husband's faith.

Abraham has been styled, because of his *trust in God*, and his many virtues, the Friend of God. When he left the land of Egypt and went to Canaan to dwell, he pitched his tent near Bethel, where years before he had lived, and where yet was the altar, it may be on which he had offered sacrifices to his God. His nephew Lot was living near him when he lived in Canaan before, and when he went down into Egypt he went with him, and this time as he enters Canaan the two go together. This gives us to understand that the mutual attachment of these two great men was strong. But as evidence that Abraham possessed and practiced the purest friendship toward Lot, we need but to refer to his conduct there.

Their flocks had multiplied exceedingly, and their substance was great—the land did not give sufficient pasturage for the flocks of each, and moreover, the men that had charge of the flocks of each were quarreling. These things required a separation. Abraham was determined to separate friendly, and addressing himself to Lot he said: "Let there be no strife, I pray thee, between me and thee, and between my herdmen and thy herdmen, for we be brethren." He then directed Lot's attention to the fact that the whole country was before them, and waiving his right of choosing a portion of the country first, and leaving the second choice to Lot, he bade Lot make the selection first. "If thou wilt go to the left hand, then I will go to the right, or if thou depart to the right hand, then I will go to the left."

But we see his affection and good feelings for Lot, his nephew; exemplified still further in the relief he gave him in a time of great need. When Chedorlaomer and the kings associated with him conquered Sodom and Gomorrah, they pillaged the cities and took the goods of Lot, who dwelt in Sodom, and he and his family were taken prisoners. One of the family or servants of Lot escaped, and went and told Abraham. He at once called together the servants born in his own house, numbering three hundred and eighteen—made known to them the captivity and peril of his kinsman, and his determination to pursue the conquerors, then on the way to their own land with the prisoners and spoils. Abraham must have possessed indomitable courage to have meditated an attack upon these four victorious kings and their armies. His true affection led him to risk his life, and the lives of his servants. He followed the army elated with victory, and overtook them, and smote them with great slaughter. These powerful kings fell before him, and their army was cut down by his trained servants, as the grain is cut by the dextrously swung scythe of the mower.

Lot and his family and servants are recaptured, the goods retaken, and all brought back again to the country of Sodom. If Lot was lacking to any extent in good feeling for Abraham before, he surely was not after this bold, daring and effectual effort to release him and his family from the hands and power of his merciless captors.

A beautiful scene presents itself afterwards in the history of this distinguished Patriarch, in connection with the further judgments of God, as they fell upon the cities of the plain. On account of their wickedness they had been conquered, and their country laid waste by the four confederate kings. Lot living among them, though a righteous man, we have seen was taken by the conquerors. But now the Divine Being is about to destroy them with fire from heaven. Abraham is made acquainted with the doom of the cities by one of the three angels in human form, who made him a visit and enjoyed his hospitality in an abundant and healthy repast. He had conducted the men on their way from his tent a short distance, when two of them went toward Sodom, while the other tarried in his presence and made him fully acquainted with the Divine purpose, to destroy the cities of the plain.

Abraham became deeply concerned for the inhabitants, for his feelings were not confined to those of his own relationship—and he prayed earnestly for their deliverance from the coming destruction. So earnest was his prayer and so strong was his faith in God, that the request he made was answered. He asked the Lord if there were fifty righteous persons in the city he would not save the whole city for the sake of the fifty. The Lord answered him he would. But for fear there were not fifty, he asked if forty-five should save it; then forty, afterwards thirty, then twenty, and finally ten. God assured him then, that if there were but ten, for the sake of the ten he would save them all. He supposed, in all probability, that in the family of his nephew there were at least ten persons, but in this he was mistaken. Yet God saved Lot and his daughters, while fire from heaven consumed the cities and their inhabitants.

Abraham had married Keturah, who cherished him in his old age. And when he was called to die, Isaac and Ishmael stood together by his side and listened with interest to his last words. After his death they united as dutiful sons in the last sad office due an honored parent. They bear his cold remains to his family vault—the cave of Machpelah—and lay it beside the mouldering remains of Sarah.

Whilst we admire the almost stainless character, through a long life, of this Patriarch of Patriarchs, let us remember that the God whom he served —who made him so great and good— will make us holy and happy if we submit to him; and when we die we shall sit down with Abraham in the kingdom of our Father. Genesis, xvi to xxvi; Rom. iv: 1–22; Gal. iii: 7; iv: 22; James, ii: 21.

ABSALOM—[Ab′-sa-lom,] *father of peace.*

Absalom, the third son of King David, was greatly beloved by him. His mother's name was Maacah, the daughter of Talmai, king of Geshur. He was distinguished for his fine person—a very comely man. Every year he cut the hair of his head, and it weighed about six pounds.

But he was also distinguished for vice, and an unnatural rebellion, and open war upon his father. He had a fair sister whose name was Tamar, who was disgraced by Amnon, one of the king's sons. As soon as Absalom knew it, he determined to take revenge, and sought that revenge for two years, when an opportunity was offered him and he killed Amnon. He had a sheep-shearing at Baalhazor, to which he invited all the king's sons, and Amnon amongst them. He furnished them wine and Amnon drank until he was drunk, when Absalom ordered his servants to kill him. After Amnon was dead, he fled to Syria, for he knew that David would be grieved and displeased at his course in the matter. Absalom can by no means be justified, however much he loved his beautiful sister Tamar, and the probability is his love for her was great, and that she reciprocated, for she went to Absalom and complained of the insult, injury, and disgrace done her, and became an inmate of his house, and, it may be, fled with him when he went to Geshur, in Syria. His strong attachment for Tamar led him to name his only daughter, we may suppose, after her, notwithstanding this disgrace done her. 2d Sam. xiii: 23–37.

Absalom remained in exile three years, when he was recalled by David, at the instance of Joab, who prompted an artful widow of Tekoah to a speech feigning the danger of her own son, who, she pretended, had killed his own brother in a fit of passion. But after Absalom was recalled, he lived two years in Jerusalem without being privileged to enter the presence of his father. He sent for Joab, with a view of communing with him as to the cause, and to secure him as an advocate for him with David his father. For some cause Joab refused to go to Absalom, and Absalom, being determined to have his attention, set the fields of corn of Joab on fire. When he came to Absalom to get an understanding of this outrage, he learned the cause for which he had done it. Joab then went to King David and procured Absalom's admission to his court, and a reconciliation was effected. "He came to the king and bowed himself on his face to the ground before the king; and the king kissed Absalom."

It was not long after this reconciliation until Absalom prepared to usurp and ascend the throne of his father. He put on the airs of regal state by preparing him "chariots and horses, and fifty men to run before him." He began to make effort to turn the hearts of the people toward him, that they might settle upon him as their king. He knew himself to be of royal blood as the son of David and the grandson of the king of Geshur. Amnon, David's oldest son, was dead, and probably Chiliab, the second son, was dead, for we hear nothing of him; and he was the third, and, therefore, seemed to stand nearest to the throne. But he manifested a shocking degree of vileness in seeking that throne in the way he did, in his father's lifetime.

Absalom "stole the hearts of the people," as he continued, day after day, to stand in or beside the gates and salute them and reason with them, to the effect that his father was not doing them justice, and if he was in power he would meet their wants and wishes.

Absalom made out in mind his conspiracy, and then asked of David his father the privilege of going to Hebron that he might perform a vow unto God that he had made when in Syria, viz: "If the Lord shall bring me again, indeed, to Jerusalem, then I will serve the Lord." The king gave his permission, and he went to Hebron, attended by two hundred persons of note, who were all ignorant of his designs. He soon opened his mind to them, and, through heralds, caused it to be proclaimed all through Israel that Absalom reigned in Hebron. Ahithophel, one of David's principal counsellors, upon an invitation from Absalom, revolted to him, and the body of the Israelites followed his example. David was compelled, when he saw that there was but a handful of men left, to fly from Jerusalem.

Ahithophel became Absalom's counsellor as he had been David's; and one of the first outrages committed by the newly made king was under his counsel, viz: the publicly defiling of ten of his father's concubines. He then advised Absalom to give him the command of twelve thousand men, and he would pursue David, who was flying, with a mere handful of men, for his life. He would overtake him, apprehend and destroy him. This counsel was very proper to answer the end so much desired by Absalom. But Hushai, another of David's counsellors, was with Absalom at the instance of David, that the counsel of the former might be turned to naught. He was consulted by Absalom, and pretended that the counsel that had just been given was not correct, as David and his men were brave and valorous, and, especially now, would be desperate in fight. In order to flatter Absalom's vanity and give David time to put himself in a position for defense, Hushai advised him to assemble every man of Israel capable of bearing arms, and that he should command them in person, and, with such a vast army, he would without fail ruin David and his party, wherever he found them. This advice was approved and followed. Absalom collected and marshalled his troops. He marched over Jordan to attack his father. A battle was fought in the wood of Ephraim. David's general had had time to select a favorable battle ground, and put his troops, well trained, in a proper position. But Absalom headed a raw, undisciplined host; and it was not long after the battle commenced until the probability of a defeat began to dispirit Absalom's men. They broke ranks and fled; and the woods devoured more people that day than the sword devoured.

David had been particularly careful to order Joab and his other generals to spare the life of his rebellious son, for, notwithstanding his cruelty and treason, David loved him. But in the flight that Absalom made when his men had deserted him, as he rode rapidly through the wood, "his head caught in the boughs of an oak, and the mule went away." The Almighty God, in His providence, did for him what David his father probably would not have done, because of his affection for him, viz: executed him by hanging him for his rebellion and treason. When Joab was informed that Absalom was hanging in an oak, he immediately went to the spot and thrust three darts through the heart of Absalom, and so ended his sufferings.

Absalom, in the days of his life, had reared a proud monument to his fame, in the king's dale, but he had not the honor to be buried there. His lifeless corpse was taken down from the tree and cast into a pit, as the carcass of an animal, and a heap of stones thrown over him. We do not know whether his father had it removed to a more honorable sepulchre or not.

David, when satisfied that Absalom was dead, mourned for him with a great mourning. His lamentation was very pathetic. "O, my son Absalom. My son, my son, Absalom. Would God I had died for thee. O, Absalom, my son, my son." 2d Sam. xviii: 33.

ACHAICUS—[A-ka′-i-kus,] *a native of Achaia.*

ACHAICUS was a disciple of Christ, whom Paul recommended to the Corinthians. 1st Epis. xvi: 17. In company with Stephanus and Fortunatus, he is mentioned by the apostle very honorably, and Paul acknowledges their kindness to him.

ACHAN—[A′-kan,] *he that troubles and bruises.*

ACHAN was of the tribe of Judah, of the families of Zerah, Zabdi and Carmi. He was with Israel when they went over Jordan and commenced their conquest of the land of Canaan. He heard, with others, the express charge of Joshua regarding the spoils, but contrary to that charge, actuated by covetousness, he seized a Babylonish garment, a wedge of gold, and two hundred shekels of silver, and hid them in his tent, intending to appropriate to his own private purposes that which God had determined should be destroyed, viz: the garment, and that which should be placed in the Lord's treasury—the silver and gold. The people had not gained the victory, but God had overthrown the city, and they were to have no share of the spoils, for they had no share in the conquest. It all belonged to the Lord. The divine Being was offended with the crime committed by Achan, and declared his indignation by allowing the army of Hebrews, that went to take Ai, to be defeated and suffer a loss of thirty-six men. Joshua inquired of the Lord the cause of their defeat, and was informed that one of the people had sinned in "the accursed thing." Some one had taken of the spoils in the taking of Jericho, and had hid what they had taken among their stuff within the camp. God then informed Joshua that the offender must be found out and punished before he would give them further conquest.

It was customary in those days, and even later, when a doubtful matter was to be settled and the counsel of those concerned was insufficient to settle the matter, to ask direction of God. They did so here in this case, in order to find out the sinner. And God directed that the whole assembly of Israel sanctify themselves and prepare for a solemn search on the morrow. They did, making the search to consist of determining by lot. Joshua caused the tribes of Israel to pass before him, and the tribe of Judah was taken. He then caused the families of that tribe to come before him, and the family of the Zarhites was taken. Then Zabdi of that family was taken, and as the individuals of Zabdi's family passed before him, Achan, the son of Carmi, was taken. He at once confessed his sin and brought forth the stolen goods, so that all Israel could see them. Then Achan, and his children, and cattle, were publicly stoned to death and their dead bodies, with his furniture, they burned to ashes in the valley of Gilgal, called from that event Achor, or the valley of Achor; and a great heap of stones was cast on them.

In the unfortunate Achan we observe a violater of God's law and authority, and in his death a noted instance of the vengeance of God on the transgressor. Joshua, vii: 22, &c.

ACHBOR—[Ak′-bor,] *a rat, bruising.*

ACHBOR was one of the officers of King Josiah, who was sent to consult the prophetess Huldah concerning the long lost copy of the law formed by Hilkiah. 2d Kings, xxii: 14.

ACHIM—[A′-kim,] *preparing, confirming, revenging.*

ACHIM was the son of Sadoc, and the father of Elihud, of the tribe of Judah. His name occurs in the genealogy of Jesus Christ. He was, therefore, in the line of the Messiah. Math. i: 14.

ACHIRAM, OR AHIRAM—[A-hy′-ram,] *brother of craft, protection.*

ACHIRAM, or AHIRAM, was a chief of one of the families of Benjamin, when they came out of the land of Egypt. Num. xxvi: 38.

ACHISH—[A′-kish,] *thus it is, how is this?*

ACHISH was the king of Gath. When David fled from the fury of Saul, he went to this king, who received him kindly, we may judge from the account given in 1st Sam. xxi: 11. But it was not long until the servants of King Achish reminded him that this David was the warrior of Israel, who had slain their giant Goliath and conquered them in a noted battle. That the hearts of the people of Israel were with him, and if not in fact king, he was virtually, for the people had sung one to another of him in dances: "Saul hath slain his thousands, and David his tens of thousands." This led David to be afraid of Achish, and in order to effect his escape he feigned himself mad, which led the king to send him from him, and so he escaped to the cave of Adullam.

About four years after this David came to Achish again. He received him kindly, and gave him with his soldiery, the city of Ziklag to dwell in. After David had lived nearly two years in Ziklag, Achish required David with his men to enter his service and fight with him against the Hebrews, and promised to make him and his men his body-guard, to which David agreed, but the lords of the Philistines complained. They bitterly objected to it. Achish, therefore, dismissed David. The above account is recorded in 1st Sam. 27 and 28.

ACHSAH—[Ak′-sah,] *adorned, bursting of the veil.*

ACHSAH was the daughter of Caleb, the son of Jephunneh, who was one of the two spies that brought back from the promised land a favorable report. Achsah was given to Othniel, her cousin, as a wife, in consideration of his having smitten the city of Kirjath-Sepher.

Caleb had received Hebron as his inheritance from Joshua, who ruled in Israel and appropriated the tribes their inheritance. Joshua, xiv, 13. He had driven out the three sons of Anak, Sheshai, Ahiman, and Talmai, and now he offers his daughter, as a wife, to whoever will smite the city. His nephew Othniel performed the feat and claimed Achsah. She was accordingly given, and, as she entered on the marriage relation with him, she bade him ask of her father a certain field, on which probably she had set her heart. Othniel her husband agreed to the request, and Achsah, having a favorable opportunity, made it herself. Her father saw the desire to say something to him and asked her what it was. She said, in substance, to him: "My father, grant me a particular request." Caleb intimated that he would do it, and asked her what it was. She said: "Thou hast given me a south land; give me also springs of water." And he did, even more than she asked. She probably asked only one district of country that had springs of water; but he gave her two, "the upper springs and the nether springs." He gave her a region of country in the mountains and another in the plains well watered.

Achsah may have lived to see her husband judge Israel; and, for aught we know, she enjoyed, if not all, a part of the forty years of peace consequent upon the deliverance that Othniel wrought, and his wise ruling as judge.

ADAH, 1—[Ay′-dah,] *an assembly.*

ADAH was one of the wives of Lamech, and Zillah the other. Lamech had two wives, and was the first man who broke into what we may suppose was the divine order regarding marriage, viz: that each man should be the husband of one wife. "Thereupon shall a man leave his father and his mother and shall cleave unto his wife, and they twain shall be one flesh." This was the beginning of polygamy. The names of these wives are given in Gen. iv: 19.

The affections of Lamech were divided upon the two women who were sustaining the same relation to him; and this was the first case of the kind in the history of humanity. Yet there does not seem to have been dissatisfaction or jealousy manifested, the one toward the other. They seem alike to have been honored by him, and when the difficulty was upon Lamech, [referred to in Gen. iv: 23,] he addressed his wives together: "And Lamech said unto his wives Adah and Zillah: Hear my voice, ye wives of Lamech; hearken unto my speech, for I have slain a man to my wounding, and a young man to my hurt. If Cain shall be avenged sevenfold, truly Lamech seventy and sevenfold."

It is thought Lamech had slain a man in self defense, and his wives were alarmed lest the friends of the deceased should seek to destroy his life in return; and he quiets their fears by this speech, which probably means, "if God did not allow Cain's willful murder of his brother avenged, surely he will not allow the act that I have committed, which was in self-defense, to be visited with death. If the avenger of Abel's death should suffer a sevenfold punishment, surely the avenger of the young man's death, whom I have slain, shall be a seventy-sevenfold punishment."

Adah was the mother of Jabel, the famous shepherd, "the father of such as dwell in tents, and of such as have cattle." She was also the mother, we suppose, of Jubal, the famous musician, for he is said to be the brother of Jabel. If he had not been the son of the same mother, he would have been only a half brother. Adah may have been the mother, as also Zillah, of several other children, for we have no account of Lamech marrying other wives; and yet it is said "He lived, after he begat Noah, five hundred, ninety and five years, and begat sons and daughters."

ADAH, 2—*An assembly.*

Adah was a wife of Esau, and is referred to in the genealogy of Esau and his sons by his Canaanitish wives. Gen. xxxvi: "Adah, the daughter of Elon the Hittite." Adah was the mother of Eliphaz. She seems to be called by the name of Bashemath in Gen. xxvi: 34. For Bashemath was the daughter of Elon the Hittite, and she was the mother of Reuel. Gen. xxxvi: 10. "Reuel, the son of Bashemath, the wife of Esau."

ADAIAH, 1—[Ad′-a-yah,] *the witness of the Lord.*

Adaiah was the grandfather of King Josiah, and a native of Boscath, in the low lands of Judah. 2d Kings, xxii: 1.

ADAIAH, 2—*The witness of the Lord.*

Adaiah was a Levite of the Gershomite branch, and the ancestor of Asaph. 1st Chron. vi: 41.

ADAIAH, 3—*The witness of the Lord.*

Adaiah was a Benjamite, and the son of Shimhi. 1st Chron. viii: 21.

ADAIAH, 4—*The witness of the Lord.*

Adaiah was a priest, and the son of Jehoram.

ADAIAH, 5—*The witness of the Lord.*

Adaiah was an ancestor of Maaseiah, one of the captains who supported Jehoiada. 2d Chron. xxiii: 1.

ADAIAH, 6—*The witness of the Lord.*

Adaiah was one of the descendants of Bani, who had married a foreign wife after the return from Babylon. Ezra, x: 29.

ADAIAH, 7—*The witness of the Lord.*

Adaiah was the descendant of another Bani, who had also taken a foreign wife. Ezra, x: 39.

ADAIAH, 8—*The witness of the Lord.*

Adaiah was a man of Judah, of the line of Pharez. Neh. xi: 5.

ADAM—[Ad′am,] *earthy, taken out of red earth.*

Adam was the first man, and father of the human race. The account given of his origin is brief, yet clear. After God had made the heavens and the earth, and separated the light from the darkness, he made the firmament, and separated the waters above the firmament from the waters below it—then formed the earth and seas, clothing the earth with herbage. Then followed the creation of the celestial luminaries, sun, moon and stars, to give light by day and by night; also to measure time and make periods and seasons of the rolling years. Then followed the creation of fish, fowls and reptiles in general—aquatic animals, and all cattle and animals that were to subsist on, or derive nourishment from the earth. And then the crowning work was performed—man was made. "And God said, Let us make man in our image, after our likeness, and let him have dominion over the fish of the sea, and over the fowls of the air, and over the cattle, and over all the earth, and over every creeping thing that creepeth upon the earth. So God created man in his own image, in the image of God created he him, male and female created he them."

The manner in which man was created is narrated by the sacred historian, viz: "And the Lord God formed man of the dust of the ground, and breathed into his nostrils the breath of life, and he became a living soul." There is a superiority in the mechanism of the human form over any other creature that God had made. He is made to walk erect, while all other animals move in some other way. He is constructed so that he can use his bodily powers and the different parts of his beautiful form with ease and appropriateness. There is majesty and true greatness marked in the human body when it is compared with the body of any other animal, and it is not to be wondered at that the inspired writer, when contemplating it, exclaimed, "I am fearfully and wonderfully made—marvelous are thy works."

But man was made to govern the world. God gave him dominion over everything else he had made. He was the last, the masterpiece of creation. Everything was prepared for his subsistence, convenience and pleasure. The house was built and furnished, then man was made to tenant the house. He was to be the master of everything else God had made, and hence the dominion and authority was given him by his creator. The sceptre was placed in his hand to rule, and God who made him capacitated him for rule.

Adam possessed, when in his primeval state, a large degree of knowledge. Not only were his bodily powers developed—for he was formed a full grown man—but his powers of mind were also developed, and the feelings of his heart were under sanctifying influence. He was made in the image of God, which consists of righteousness and true holiness. The image of God's own immortality was stamped upon his moral nature. But we may gather some idea of his knowledge in the fact narrated in Gen. ii: that when God caused the animals to pass before Adam, he gave names to them all. How came he to do this? I answer, from an intimate knowledge of the nature and properties of each creature, for he gave to every animal an appropriate name. It is well understood that the names given to different animals in scripture, always express some feature and prominent characteristic of the creature. And so it is with the proper names of the Bible; they denote some peculiarity of the person they designate. Adam's knowledge was complete. And is not this circumstance a strong proof of the perfection and excellence of man while in a state of innocence? Among the numerous beings God had formed, there was no fit companion for Adam, and the great Creator determined to make him an helpmeet, and the following is the statement given of the creation of woman: "And the Lord God caused a deep sleep to fall upon Adam, and he slept; and he took one of his ribs, and closed up the flesh instead thereof. And the rib which the Lord God had taken from man, made he a woman, and brought her unto the man." Adam recognized her at once as a proper helpmeet for him, and by intuition, or by immediate revelation from God, he knew how she had been formed, for he said, "This is now bone of my bone and flesh of my flesh. She shall be called woman, because she was taken out of man."

Adam and his companion thus began life, under the grand law of love. But a precept was given them. I say *them* because Eve, as soon as she took her place beside Adam, became one with him, and was under that precept. The precept was given as a test of obedience and a proof of dependence on the Creator, as well as a proof that the state on which Adam had entered was a trial or probationary state.

Adam took his position in Eden under the precept, "Of the tree of knowledge of good and evil, thou shalt not eat of it; for in the day thou eatest thereof thou shalt surely die." It was not long after Eve was formed until she was tempted to take of the forbidden fruit. The enemy succeeded in planting the spirit of pride in her heart. Desiring to be what Satan had told her they should be, "as gods knowing good and evil," and "seeing that the tree was good for food, and that it was pleasant to the eyes, and a tree to be desired to make one wise, she took of the fruit thereof and did eat, and gave also to her husband with her and he did eat." The deed is done—God's law is violated, and the dark pall of iniquity is drawn over the nature of him who, a few moments before, was pure. The Allseeing eye was upon them when their fidelity was being tested, and when they gave way to the temptation, the recording angel that had written so far the history of their lives, which presented no stain on their character or flaw in their conduct, was compelled to make the register: *Man is fallen!* God's creature has revolted. Oh, what sensations must Adam's fall have produced among angels in heaven! They knew no way of escape from the awful dilemma into which sin had hurled them. They saw that the door of heaven was closed—that God's favor was fully forfeited. And Adam and his fallen companion felt it equally.

In his extremity God had compassion upon man, and in the Infinite and Eternal Mind the plan of salvation, involving the death of Christ, was formed, and God gave to man, in the condemnatory language to the serpent, the promise of a Deliverer.

Adam grasped that promise, and no sooner was he driven from Eden under the blighting, withering curse of sin—a slave of passion and a victim of grief, than he began to offer sacrifice to God, and look, through the type, for the promised atonement for sin; and it is quite likely that the covering or clothing he made from the skins of animals, was the skins of animals offered in sacrifice. That promise of "the seed of the woman that was to bruise the head of the serpent," was the all-important theme for meditation with Adam and Eve, and while the curse that was pronounced upon him, "in the sweat of thy face shalt thou eat bread," was being endured from day to day, he rejoiced in the promised deliverance and anticipated the close of his earthly career and the joys of a purer clime.

Unto Adam and his wife were born sons—Cain the first-born and Abel the second. These sons grew up by each others side and enjoyed the pleasures of life with their parents, but in an evil hour Cain slew Abel, and the anguished parents looked on the lifeless form of the second son, murdered by his own brother. There, in the cold form of their Abel, was the first emblem of their own mortality. What a trial for these first parents. Their elder son a murderer—the second son the murdered—and they called upon to deposit in the earth the mortal remains, while that part of the curse sounded in their ears, "dust thou art and unto dust shalt thou return."

There is no account of the family of Adam further than these two sons and Seth, except that Moses tells us that "Adam begat sons and daughters;" very likely many of them, for the population of earth increased rapidly, and Adam lived nine hundred and thirty years.

Adam has been considered a type of the Lord Jesus Christ; hence St. Paul calls Christ the "second Adam," or calls Adam "the figure of him who was to come." We may mention, as concisely as possible, some points of analogy, or we may look at a few of the striking lineaments of "the first Adam," in which the features of "the second Adam" may be traced. This typical relation may be considered sometimes in similitude, and sometimes in contrast. Adam was formed by God, and Luke, in tracing the genealogy of Christ on the side of his mother, the *virgin Mary*, calls Adam the *son* of God. He was the immediate offspring—the direct workmanship—of the great Creator. So Christ was the son of God—the "only begotten of the father." Adam was created in the image of God, which consisted in righteousness and true holiness; but Christ is the express image God's person as well as "the brightness of His, the Father's glory."

"The first Adam was made a living soul, the second Adam a quickening spirit."

All the generations of the human race have sprung from Adam—and fallen in him, for his currupt fall has tainted every member of his family. Because of his sin, death has passed upon all men, for that all have sinned in him. How eminently did he thus prefigure *that one man*, by whose righteousness the free gift comes upon all unto justification of life. No man, since Christ has become the atonement for sin, will be lost for Adam's transgression. The platform of the atonement is wide as the world is wide—the arms of Jesus' mighty heart encircle the entire family of man. All will be saved in Christ who are not accountable for their conduct, as infants, idiots, and probably a part of the heathen world, and all that are accountable who will be saved, may be saved, upon a compliance with the conditions of salvation—repentance and faith. Adam was the glory of the first creation and former dispensation; Christ was the glory and excellency of the new creation, which we call redemption, and of the latter dispensation. "Redemption 't was creation more sublime."

In Adam human nature shone in beautiful colors in the first state; but by the transgression he tarnished that nature. In Christ the lost beauty is restored, and many lost relationships to God regained. And human nature is presented again in loveliness in the person of the risen and ascended mediatory Savior.

We look on Jesus on the mount of transfiguration and think of the glorification awaiting our humanity. We see him, after his resurrection, appearing at the tomb—at the sea-side—in the country—and in the room in Jerusalem when the disciples met. We hear him saying to unbelieving Thomas, "Handle me, for a spirit hath not flesh and blood as ye see me have." And we see the human nature glorified in heaven as our Advocate, "touched with the feeling of our infirmities," pleads for us. As he is, so shall we be. "We shall be like him, for we shall see him as he is."

Adam and Christ bear a striking resemblance in respect to dominion and authority. "Thou madest him to have dominion over the works of Thy hands." Christ, we are assured, when here among men, exercised unlimited authority over the whole natural world, and in a manner to which Adam could not pretend; for things visible and invisible were under his control. The devils fled at his command—the winds and waves obeyed him—diseases of all kinds were cured at his word—cripples were made sound—and even the dead came back to life at his pleasure, while the grave, when he spake, yielded its victim, and the worms gave up their food. Gen. i, ii, iii, v; Rom. v: 12–19; 1st Cor. xv: 21.

ADBEEL—[Ad′-be-el,] *a vapor, a cloud of God, a vexer of God.*

Adbeel was one of the sons of Ishmael and the head of a powerful tribe or family of the Ishmaelites. Genesis, xxv: 13.

ADDI—[Ad′-di,] *my witness, adorned, passage, prey.*

Addi was the son of Cosam and the father of Melchi. He was one of the ancestors of Christ, according to the flesh. Luke, iii: 28.

ADER.—[A′-der.]

Ader was a Benjamite and the son of Beriah. He was chief of the inhabitants of Aijajon. 1st Chron. viii: 15.

ADIEL, 1—[Ad′-i-el,] *a witness of the Lord.*

Adiel was a prince of the tribe of Simeon and descended from the prosperous family of Shimei. He took part in the murderous raid made by his tribe upon the peaceful shepherds in the valley of Gideon, during the reign of Hezekiah. 1st Chron. iv: 36–43.

ADIEL, 2—*A witness of the Lord.*

Adiel was a priest and ancestor of Maasiai. 1st Chron. ix: 12.

ADIEL, 3—*A witness of the Lord.*

Adiel was an ancestor of Azmaveth, the treasurer of King David. 1st Chron. xxvii: 25.

ADIN—[Ad′-din,] *adorned, dainty.*

Adin was the ancestor of a family who returned with Zerubbabel to the number of six hundred and fifty-five; and there were several others of that family that accompanied Ezra from Babylon, and they joined themselves with Nehemiah, the Tirshatha, in a covenant to separate themselves from the heathen. Ezra, ii: 15; viii: 6; Neh. x: 16.

ADINA—[A-di′-nah.]

Adina was one of David's captains beyond the Jordan and a chief of the Reubenites. 1st Chron. xi: 42. He is represented as having command of thirty men; but it is supposed that the rendering ought to be, that there were thirty officers inferior to him, just as Benaiah was superior to the thirty named in 1st Chron. xxvii.

ADINO—[A-di′-no.]

Adino was an Eznite. He is called in 2d Sam. xxiii: 8, the Tachmonite, but in 1st Chron. xi: 11, Jashobeam the Hachmonite. He was one of David's three mightiest heroes. Next to Adino was Dodo the Ahohite, and after him was Shammah the Hararite. There are thirty-seven valiant men of David mentioned in 2d Sam. xxiii: 8–39. This

Adino "lifted up his spear against eight hundred whom he slew at one time." 2d Sam. xxiii: 8.

ADLAI—[Ad-la′-i,] *my witness, my ornament.*

ADLAI was a herdsman and one of the principal ones in charge of David's herds. 1st Chron. xxvii: 29.

ADMATHA—[Ad′-ma-thah,] *a cloud of death, a mortal vapor.*

ADMATHA was one of the principal officers of King Ahasuerus, referred to with others, in Est. i: 14.

ADNA—[Ad′-na.]

ADNA was a Levite, who married a wife contrary to Jewish law, during the captivity, but after the return of the Jews he forsook her. Ezra, x: 3, &c. He, with several others, had taken a strange wife. But they all entered into a solemn covenant to put them away, with the children that were born unto them.

ADNAH, 1—[Ad′-nah,] *rest, testimony, eternal.*

ADNA was a warrior of the tribe of Manasseh, who joined the party of King David. 1st Chron. xii: 20.

ADNAH, 2—*Rest, testimony, eternal.*

ADNAH was one of King Jehoshaphat's generals He was of the tribe of Judah, and a chief among the warriors. 2d Chron. xvii: 14.

ADONAI—[Ad′-o-na,[ *my Lord.*

ADONAI is one of the plural names of the Deity. The Jews use this name for some cause or other, instead of the name Jehovah. It may be their reverence for God, and awe excited by the manifestation made to Moses at Horeb, or the divine power displayed when Moses went with Aaron his brother to satisfy the elders of Israel that God intended to emancipate them, or when he stood before Pharaoh and demanded their freedom. God said unto Moses, "I am the Lord and I appeared unto Abraham, unto Isaac, and unto Jacob by the name of God Almighty, but by my name Jehovah was I not known." The Jews of modern times read Adonai in the room of Jehovah as often as they meet with the name in the Hebrew text. The ancient Jews were not so scrupulous, and there is no law which forbids them to pronounce it.

ADONIBEZEK—[Ad′-o-ne-bee′-zek] *The lightning of the Lord, the Lord of Bezek.*

ADONIBEZEK, the king of Bezek, was taken as a captive by the associated tribes of Judah and Simon sometime after the death of Joshua. They took his capitol and made him a prisoner, and they punished him by cutting off his thumbs and great toes, that he might never again be able to draw the bow, or handle the sword in war. He seems to have acknowledged, in this punishment, a just vengeance upon him for his cruelty toward conquered princes in Canaan in the days of his prosperity. In Judges i: 7 he says, "Three score and ten kings having their thumbs and their great toes cut off, gathered their meat under my table: as I have done so God hath requited me." He seems to have the knowledge of the true God, and a proper idea of a Divine Providence. He feels that God has brought him to the same state and condition to which he had cruelly reduced the kings whom he had conquered. In this miserable condition he was brought to Jerusalem, and there he died.

The three-score and ten kings that had been taken by him, probably about the time Joshua entered Canaan, were simply chieftains or heads of some tribes inhabiting the land; or it may be they were simply military officers.

ADONIJAH—[Ad-o-ni′-jah] *the Lord is my master.*

ADONIJAH was the fourth son of King David, born at Hebron. Amnon, the oldest, had been killed by Absalom; and Absalom was killed in the rebellion against David; and Chileab was either dead or inactive, for we hear nothing of him; and David himself, though not a very old man, was feeble and infirm.

Adonijah made an attempt to seize the kingdom of Israel and reign in the stead of his father. Like Absalom, his brother, he prepared himself a royal equipage of chariots, horses and horsemen, and fifty men to run before him. David, the king, saw all this, but did not suspect his full designs. He certainly intended Solomon, the son of

Bathsheba, to reign after him; but yet he was not displeased with Adonijah's display, nor did he interfere with him until he was informed by Nathan, the prophet, of the fact that Adonijah had waxed powerful, and that Joab, the general, and Abiathar, the high priest, were with him; that the king's sons, except Solomon, were then attending a feast, or splendid entertainment, at Enrogel, and were making him king; that all the great men of the nation were joining the new king, except the few that were interested for Solomon.

David listened to Nathan, the prophet, and Bathsheba, the mother of Solomon, as they applied to him. The opposers of Adonijah were ordered, at once, to anoint Solomon to the throne. As soon as he was made king, and the shouts of applause went out for him, Adonijah and his party became alarmed and dispersed, wishing no longer to be known as connected with the movement. Adonijah himself flew for protection to the sanctuary and took hold of the horns of the altar, and plead for his life. The newly made king Solomon was informed of his position and terror, and sent him word that his life should be safe, provided he demeaned himself properly in the future. He came and presented himself before Solomon, and was forgiven, and, by the king, ordered to retire to his own house.

After the death of David, Adonijah set his heart upon the beautiful young woman who had charge of his father during the last year of his life, and desired her for a wife; and, so great was his desire, he asked the queen mother to intercede with Solomon in his behalf, that Abishag might be given him to be his wife. Solomon suspected this as a project, on the part of Adonijah, to obtain the kingdom, and ordered Benaiah, his general, to kill him, and he did.

It is very doubtful whether Solomon was justifiable in this act, or whether Adonijah at all deserved death. He knew that Abishag, the Shunammite, was selected for David and married to him without any special affection on the part of either, and that she had faithfully served him as a nurse the last few months of his life, and she was a beautiful woman. There is but very little reason to believe, from what is recorded, that he was at all treacherous in his designs in asking for Abishag for a wife. 1st Kings, i: 5-25.

ADONIKAM—[Ad-o-ni′-kam,] *the Lord is raised, my Lord hath raised me.*

ADONIKAM was one of the captives who returned from the Babylonian captivity. He is mentioned in Ezra, ii: 13, with six hundred and sixty-six of his family or relationship, who went up with Zerubbabel from Babylon to Jerusalem and Judah.

There are two things that have been noticed rather remarkable, respecting Adonikam. The first is his name as a character of Antichrist, and the second is his children numbered six hundred and sixty-six, corresponding with the number of the beast. Rev. xiii: 18.

"Let him that hath understanding count the number of the beast, for it is the number of a man, and his number is six hundred, three score and six."

ADONIRAM—[Ad-o-ni′-ram,] *my Lord is most high, the Lord of might and elevation.*

ADONIRAM was the principal receiver of Solomon's tribute. He was probably the same as is mentioned in 2d Sam. xx: 24, called Adoram, who was the chief receiver of the taxes for David. It is likely that Solomon retained him in that office. When Hiram, king of Tyre, made a league with Solomon to furnish materials for the building of the temple, Solomon raised a levy of thirty thousand men and sent them to the forests of Lebanon to cut and hew timbers with the Sidonians, and he placed Adoniram over the levy as superintendent of the thirty thousand men.

ADONIZEDEK—[Ad′-o-ne-zee′dek,] *justice of the Lord.*

ADONIZEDEK was the king of Jerusalem when Joshua with Israel entered the land of Canaan. When he was informed that Joshua had taken Jericho and Ai, and that the Gibeonites had given themselves up to Israel, he joined himself with the kings of Hebron, Jarmuth, Lachish, and Eglon, to attack and slaughter the Gibeonites. He intended to punish them for giving themselves up, and also deter any other kingdoms from submitting to the invaders.

The Gibeonites informed Joshua, and asked of him protection. He gave it to them by engaging with the allied troops in a hard-fought battle, in which he conquered them; for God helped Israel to fight, for "the Lord cast down great hail-stones from heaven upon them." It was in this contest, on the part of Israel for victory, that the strange phenomenon appeared of the sun standing still and the moon staying. Joshua saw that God had given him a glorious victory—that the enemies of Israel were put to flight; yet he saw that the day was rapidly drawing to a close, and that there was a probability of some of the enemy escaping under the cover of the coming night; and he supposed that those who escaped would rally again, and that he would have to meet them on a field of battle; hence, he desired sufficient time to complete the victory, and make an entire destruction of the confederate armies. Being impressed with strong faith in God, he asked Him to perform the most wonderful miracle that had ever been wrought, viz., to arrest the sun in his course, and so prolong the day that he might accomplish the destruction of his enemies. He said, "Sun, stand thou still upon Gibeon; and thou, moon, in the valley of Ajalon." The miracle was performed. "The sun stood still in the midst of heaven, and hasted not to go down about a whole day." There never had been before, nor has there been since, a period of time when the sun was kept so long above the horizon.

But the five kings hid themselves, for though their soldiery fell, or were captured, they escaped. Their hiding place was a cave near Makkedah. When Joshua learned it he stopped the mouth of the cave with large stones for a few hours, until Israel would have sufficient leisure to execute them. At the close of the lengthened day, when the battle was ended, Joshua had them brought out, and made his principal officers trample on their necks. This was done not only as a token of the present complete victory, but as a token of their approaching triumph over all their enemies now inhabiting this land. This is the interpretation given of the act by Joshua himself. Having thus humbled these five kings, he slew them and hanged them on five trees; and as the sun was setting, he ordered them to be taken down and their bodies to be thrown into the cave where they hid themselves. Josh. x: 3–15.

**ADORAM, 1**—[A-do′-ram,] *their beauty, their power, their praise.*

Adoram is referred to in 1st Chron. xviii: 10. He was the son of Tou, king of Hamath, and sent to congratulate David on his victory over Hadarezer.

**ADORAM, 2**—*Their beauty, their power, their praise.*

Adoram was the general receiver of tribute, and is referred to in 2d Sam. xx: 24, as being "set over the tribute." He may be the same person as Adoniram, who was receiver of Solomon's tribute and the director of the men who cut timber in the forests of Lebanon. 1st Kings, v: 14.

**ADORAM, 3**—*Their beauty, their power, their praise.*

Adoram, or Hadoram, was King Rehoboam's chief treasurer and the overseer of his works. Rehoboam sent him to deal with the ten revolting tribes, and, if possible, reduce them to their allegiance. They became angry at him, and, charging him with encouraging their oppressive taxes, they stoned him to death. 1st Kings, xii: 18; 2d Chron. x: 18.

**ADRAMMELECH**—[Ad-ram′-me-lek,] *the cloak or glory of the king.*

Adrammelech was a son of Sennacherib, king of Assyria, who invaded the kingdom of Judah in the time of Hezekiah. Adrammelech was probably named after one of the gods of the men of Sepharvaim. We know but little about him, save that in company with Sharezer, his brother, he murdered the king, his father. This act was committed by the two sons upon Sennacherib while he was engaged in worshiping in the house of Nisroch, his God. It is supposed that these sons had learned that their father intended to sacrifice them to this god, and that they determined to prevent this by slaying him.

The rabbins say that he consulted his wise men to know why it was that such miracles were performed for the Israelites. They informed him that it was because of the virtue and merit of

Abraham, who offered up Isaac on Mt. Moriah. He then said he would slay his two sons, but they prevented it by slaying him. It may be they were actuated to this by some great prejudice against him and not by fear of being sacrificed by him. After they had murdered him they fled into Armenia, and we hear nothing further of them. 2d Kings, xix: 37.

ADRIEL—[A′-dri-el,] *the flock of God.*

Adriel was the son of Barzillai, to whom Saul gave his daughter Merab to wife, when he should have given her to David. 1st Sam. xviii: 19. "But it came to pass at the time when Merab, Saul's daughter, should have been given to David, that she was given unto Adriel, the Meholathite to wife." In 2d Sam. xxi: 8, he is said to be the son of Barzillai, the Meholathite.

Adriel had five sons as the result of his marriage, and they were all put to death by the Gibeonites, with the sons of Rizpah, Saul's wife—all for the cruelty of Saul to them at some time during his reign.

AGABUS—[Ag′-a-bus,] *a locust, the feast of the father.*

Agabus was a prophet who foretold the famine that happened in the days of Claudius Cesar. It was at Antioch that a number of prophets from Jerusalem had assembled, and among them Agabus "stood up and signified, by the spirit, that there should be great dearth throughout all the world, which came to pass in the days of Claudius Cesar."

We know but little about this prophet, for he is mentioned in only one other place besides the quotation made above. He was probably a Jew, who, whether he was converted to Christianity or not, was under the influence of the spirit of inspiration. This prophecy was fulfilled shortly after it was made.

Agabus visited Paul at Cesarea and foretold his being bound at Jerusalem. He came, it may be, from Judea specially to have an interview with this apostle and tell him what was before him. His actions and language, in prophecy, are very much like those of the Old Testament prophets. He used a very significant emblem in opening his prophecy, viz: the girdle of Paul. The use he made of it was to bind his own hands and feet, emblematical of what was about to be done to him to whom he was speaking. He claimed divine authority for what he was about to utter. The Holy Ghost saith: "So shall the Jews at Jerusalem bind the man that owneth this girdle, and shall deliver him up unto the Gentiles." The meaning of the prophecy was that the Jews would seek his life; but as they had not the power of life and death, they would apply to the Romans and demand that the sentence of death be pronounced upon him.

Now, this prediction of Agabus was literally fulfilled when the chief captain took him and commanded him to be bound with two chains."

It is supposed, by some, that Agabus suffered martyrdom, as a Christian, at Antioch. Acts, xi: 28; xxi: 10.

AGAG—[A′-gag,] *roof, floor.*

Agag was a common name of the kings of Amalek, as Pharaoh was of the kings of Egypt. There are two of these kings that Scripture history speaks of—one in the time of Israel's journeyings in the wilderness and the other in the time of Eli and Samuel. Of the former we learn in the prophecy of Balaam when called to curse Israel. In one single phrase we have the greatness of Agag, as king of Amalek, presented. Of Israel he says: "And his king shall be higher than Agag, and his kingdom shall be exalted."

This Agag was king, probably, when Joshua fought with Amalek and was victorious; for Amalek was discomfited and Israel prevailed; and God determined, at that time, to destroy this people, and made known his determination in the following language: "I will utterly put out the remembrance of Amalek from under heaven." And Moses said: "Because the Lord hath sworn that the Lord will have war with Amalek from generation to generation."

About four hundred years after this, God commanded Saul, by the mouth of Samuel, to destroy the Amalekites, as recorded in 1st Samuel, xv. Saul mustered an army of two hundred thousand footmen and ten thousand men of Judah. The command given by God was, to utterly destroy men, women, and children, with all that they possessed. Saul passed through the country as a conqueror, smiting the Amalekites from Havilah unto Shur, and he took Agag, the king of the people with whom he warred, alive. In this he displeased the Lord; but he also spared the best of the sheep and oxen, and fatlings and lambs; and in this, also, he displeased the Lord.

When Saul met Samuel the next day after he arrived at Gilgal, he declared he had performed the commandment of the Lord. Samuel asked him, if that were the case, what was the meaning of the bleating of the sheep and the lowing of the oxen within hearing. He answered that the people had spared them to sacrifice unto the Lord. Samuel then charged him with disobeying God, and assured him that "to obey was better than sacrifice, and to hearken than the fat of rams;" told him that God was angry with him for his sin—had rent his newly formed kingdom and given it to his neighbor.

Samuel then sent for Agag, the king of the Amalekites, and charged upon him the sins he had committed—especially that of his cruelty in making women childless with the sword—and then assured him that his death had been determined upon, and that his mother should that day be childless among women. And Samuel hewed Agag in pieces before the Lord. 1st Sam. xv: 9-32.

AGEE—[Ag′-ee.]

Agee, the Hararite, was the father of Shammah, one of David's mighty men, who fought bravely against the Philistines. 2d Sam. xxiii: 11

AGRIPPA, 1—[A-grip′-pah,] *one who at his birth causes great pain.*

Agrippa, usually styled Herod Agrippa, was the son of Mariamne and Aristobulus, and grandson of Herod the Great; and he was the brother of Herodias, who was married to Herod the Tetrarch, of Galilee, who beheaded John the Baptist.

Herod the Great sent Agrippa to Rome to procure an education, partly, and partly to make his court to Tiberius. While in Rome he formed strong attachments for the young prince Caligula. Tiberius hearing that Agrippa wished him dead that Caligula might reign in his stead, became enraged at him and cast him into prison. But when the young prince came to the throne he released Herod and gave him a chain of gold and a royal diadem, for the hard treatment of Tiberius did not change the feeling of Caius Caligula toward him. He made him king of Batavia and Trachonitas, and afterward of Abilene.

The newly made emperor, desiring to be worshiped, commanded to have his statue set up in the temple at Jerusalem; but his design in this matter was so much opposed that they who had charge of it were compelled to desist, and in a letter they sent him an account of the resistance which they met. Herod Agrippa was as much opposed to it as were other Jews, and wrote to Caligula, setting forth the impropriety of the scheme, and the wrong that would be done the Jews by thus defiling their temple. He was so influenced by Agrippa's letter that he desisted from his design of setting up his statue in the temple.

Herod Agrippa was still at Rome when Claudius was made emperor, and contributed much to establish his dignity and power, and with his advice and counsel he helped Claudius much in the beginning of his reign. The emperor rewarded him by giving him all Judea and the kingdom of Chalcis, and he entered at once upon the work of governing his dominions, and became very popular among the people. With a desire to please the Jews, who were persecuting the Christians, he put to death James, the son of Zebedee, and cast Peter into prison, intending to bring about his death, too; but in this he did not succeed—Providence defeated his designs.

He went to Cesarea to celebrate games in honor of the Roman emperor. To that place the inhabitants of Tyre and Sidon, who had offended him, sent messengers to him to beg his pardon for the offence. He attended to the message of the deputation, appearing before them dressed in a robe tissued with silver, on which, when the sun shone, a marvelous lustre was created. The conference he had with them was in the theatre. He began his speech, and as he proceeded the audience became enraptured, and began to say "it is the voice of a God and not of man." Instead of rebuking them for their impious flatteries, he received them with an air of satisfaction. The pride of his heart was so great that he looked upon them with complacency. God punished him for his pride. The angel of the Lord smote him directly with a most tormenting disease in his bowels, and he was eaten up by worms and died. It was probably but a few hours from the time that he entered the theatre, dressed in gaudy attire, to have his interview with the deputation until in excruciating agony he departed this life. He left behind him a son of the same name, and three daughters, viz: Bernice, Marianme and Drusilla. Acts, xii.

AGRIPPA, 2—*One who at his birth causes great pain.*

AGRIPPA, the son of Herod Agrippa, was at Rome with the emperor Claudius when his father died. The emperor was much attached to Agrippa, and, though he was very young, was inclined to give him all the dominions possessed by his father at the time of his death; but his courtiers dissuaded him from this.

A short time after this, the governor of Syria thought to compel the Jews to place the ornaments of their high priest in the tower of Antonia, and under the charge of a Roman guard, but, by the influence of Agrippa, the emperor consented that they might keep them themselves.

Herod, king of Chalcis, and uncle to Agrippa, died, whereupon the emperor gave his dominions to him; but four years after the kingdom was taken from him, and, in the stead of it, the provinces of Gaulonites, Trachonites, Batanea, Paneas, and Abilene, were given; and to these provinces Nero added Julius in Perea and a part of Galilee on the west of the sea of Tiberius.

When Festus, the governor of Judea, came to his government, Agrippa and his sister went as far as Cesarea to meet, salute, and congratulate him; and, while they were in conference together, Festus talked with him about Paul, and the pending trial, and his appeal to Cesar. Agrippa was exceedingly curious to see Paul and hear what he had to say for himself, for he had likely heard of him as a prisoner bound for the last two years. On the next day Festus gratified him and his sister Bernice by bringing Paul out into the public hall, where he might represent his cause to King Agrippa. Paul stood up and boldly rehearsed his conversion from a bloody persecutor of Christians into a zealous preacher of the doctrines of Christ's religion. He declared that he had, according to the ancient prophets, preached the resurrection from the dead.

Agrippa was deeply interested in the experience of Paul, and, charmed with the good sense and majesty of his discourse, and with the deference the apostle had shown him, he said: "Almost thou persuadest me to be a Christian."

Here we have a Jew—a king of Jews—listening to the narration of religious experience, and enraptured with the doctrines and eloquent address of a bold and zealous preacher, who was a prisoner; and though Agrippa was surrounded by Jews who hated Paul and had imprisoned him for his faith, yet he said in their hearing he was almost persuaded to be a Christian. The words of the apostle had touched his heart, and he felt that there was something in this new doctrine that Paul preached. It may be that Agrippa never heard the Gospel of Christ afterward, and never became a Christian. But we honor him for his treatment of Paul and his honest expressions of convictions. Acts, xxvi: 1–28.

After the destruction of Jerusalem he and his sister Bernice retired to Rome, where he died.

AGUR—[A′-gur,] *a stranger, gathering.*

AGUR, the son of Jakeh, is the author of the thirtieth chapter of the Book of Proverbs. By some it is supposed that it is an assumed name by Solomon, the king of Israel, and the author of the Proverbs, and that Jakeh, who is the father of him, is intended to represent David, while Ithiel and Ucal, to whom the Proverbs are addressed, are names used to designate Christ. But this is not at all likely, for several of the Proverbs could not consistently have been used by Solomon, such as, "I neither learned wisdom nor have the knowledge of the holy;" and, again, "Give me neither poverty nor riches." This suits no part of Solomon's life or circumstances.

Agur was a person as designated, and addressed these proverbs to two scholars that he taught as a public teacher. In the chapter he professes his great ignorance of the unsearchable greatness and wonderful works of God. He professeth esteem for God's word, and desires a moderate share only of this world's goods. He spoke by inspiration. It would be well for many of the present day, if, from the bottom of their hearts they could pray this same prayer; for many, in their covetousness, are seeking and obtaining wealth to their own destruction. Riches become a snare, and by it they are carried away. "Being full they deny God, and say who is the Lord?" We know nothing more of this teacher than is recorded in this chapter of the Proverbs.

AHAB, 1—[A′-hab,] *the brother of the father.*

AHAB was king of Israel and successor of Omri. He reigned twenty-two years. He was very impious—more so than all the kings of Israel. His marriage may be considered unfortunate, for it was in part the occasion of introducing among Israel the abominations of Baal and Ashtaroth, with which Israel was cursed for several years.

Jezebel, his wife, was the daughter of Ethbaal, king of Zidon, and she brought with her into Ahab's kingdom her prejudices and the idolatry of her country. It was a very great sin on the part of Ahab to take a wife from the heathen, and especially one who was hostile to the true religion as was the daughter of Ethbaal.

Influenced by his wife, Ahab built a temple for Baal, and reared up an altar in that temple. He gave himself up to the influence of this wicked woman. Elijah the Prophet was commissioned to go to Ahab and reprove him for his sin, and declare the divine decree that there should be a grievous dearth in Israel, to last for several years. This came to pass. And during this dearth and famine, Ahab permitted (if he did not, indeed, help) Jezebel to kill the prophets of the Lord wherever she found them throughout the land. She had heard of the prophecy of Elijah, and attributed the public calamity they were enduring to him; and not being able to find Elijah, she wreaked her vengeance on the prophets she found.

It is true that God made Israel, when under Ahab, victorious over the Syrians, who invaded their country; but it was not because of anything good in Ahab, but rather because Benhadad, the king of Syria, boasted and blasphemed God. How wicked Ahab must have been, so far to forget God and his obligations as king of Israel, to go into the grossest idolatry. He made calves and set up the idol Baal, worshipped it himself, and caused Israel to worship it. Then, influenced by his wife, he hunted for the life of the faithful Prophet Elijah, who had reproved him for his sin, and told him of the judgments of heaven coming upon him and his people, as they were now enduring it. And when he could not find Elijah, he put to death, or allowed Jezebel to do it, all the prophets in the land, save those that Obadiah hid, and Elijah, whom God hid.

When God, by the Prophet Elijah, convinced Ahab and all Israel of his power and glory, by sending fire down from heaven to consume the sacrifice that Elijah offered, and then sent rain in abundance upon the parched earth, we might have supposed that the course of the wicked Ahab would have been changed; but no, he still sinned against God and dishonored the throne of Israel.

In 1st Kings, 21st chapter, we have an account of his coveting the vineyard of Naboth. When he made the request of Naboth to give his vineyard and he would give him for it a better vineyard, or if he preferred it he would give him money for it, his request seemed very reasonable. But Naboth called to mind the inheritance law, and showed Ahab that he could not do it. "The Lord forbid that I should give the inheritance of my fathers to thee." Ahab wished him to alienate it finally and fully, and that would be an express violation of God's law; therefore Naboth, consistently with his duty to God, could not indulge him, and it was iniquity in Ahab to tempt him to do it, and his still coveting it shows the deep depravity of his soul, the wickedness of his heart. The Kings of the Jews had no authority to change the old laws or to make new ones. Yet he coveted. He lay upon his bed that night restless, and refused to eat. Jezebel, his wife, asked him the cause of his dejection, and he told her. She upbraided him for it. Thou art King of Israel, and not Naboth; but has he power to refuse thee, then he is greater than the king. She bade him rise up, eat and be merry, for she would procure for him the vineyard. And she did so. She procured false witnesses against Naboth, had him stoned to death, and the probability is that all his innocent family with him were destroyed, so that there should be no heir to his estate. Ahab was informed of the destruction of Naboth, and the next day took possession of the vineyard. But it is said "there was none like unto Ahab, which did sell himself to work wickedness in the sight of the Lord, whom Jezebel, his wife, stirred up."

The end of his wicked life came at last, and the prophecy that had been delivered at his taking possession of the vineyard of another, was fulfilled in his death, "where dogs licked the blood of Naboth, shall dogs lick thy blood, even thine."

Ahab procured the king of Judah to fight with him against the Syrians, and, at the instigation of his helper, he called on Micaiah the Prophet, to say whether he should go up to fight with his enemies or not. He was not pleased with the words of the prophet. But he went to battle, and disguised himself as the king of Israel; and while engaged in the battle, "a certain man drew a bow at a venture and smote him." He died shortly afterwards, and the dogs licked his blood at the pool of Samaria, when his chariot and armor were washed after his decease. 1st Kings, xxii: 34.

AHAB, 2—*The brother of the father.*

AHAB, the son of Kolaiah, and Zedekiah, the son of Maaseiah, were two false prophets, who seduced the Jewish captives at Babylon with hopes of a speedy deliverance, and stirred them up against Jeremiah.

The Lord threatened these two men with a public and ignominious death, as is recorded in Jer. xxix: 21—declared that their names should become a curse; the captivity shall wish for their enemies such a death as Ahab and Zedekiah had, whom the king of Babylon roasted in the fire; and, moreover, that this ignominious death should be before the eyes of those whom they deceived.

AHARAH—[A-har′-ah,] *a sweet brother, an odoriferous meadow.*

AHARAH was the third son of Benjamin, and as such is referred to in 1st Chron. viii: 1.

AHASAI—[A-has′-a-i.]

AHASAI was a priest and ancestor of Maasiai. Neh. xi: 13.

AHASBAI—[A-has′-ba-i,] *trusting in me, brother compassing.*

AHASBAI was the father of Eliphalet, who was one of David's mighty men. 2d Sam. xxiii: 34.

AHASUERUS, 1—[A-has-u-e′-rus,] *prince, chief.*

AHASUERUS, the Mede, is spoken of in the ninth chapter of Daniel and first verse as the father of Darius. He is supposed to have been the son of the Cyaxares who helped Nebuchadnezzar to overthrow the Assyrian empire and destroy the city of Ninevah.

AHASUERUS, 2—*Prince, chief.*

AHASUERUS was Cambyses, king of Persia, and the son of Cyrus. He is supposed to have succeeded his father to the throne of Persia and reigned seven years and five months. The allusion to him in scripture is in Ezra, iii: 6, 7. During the time of his reign the building of the temple was interrupted, which was occasioned by the letter written by the enemies of the Jews to Cambyses. We learn of him that he had scarcely ascended the throne until the Samaritans requested him to stop the work. He did not, however, revoke the decree of his father, for he could not directly. The edict of Cyrus, liberating the Babylonian captives and authorizing them to return to their own land and the city of Jerusalem, and rebuild the house of the Lord, was, like other laws of the Medes and Persians, unalterable. Yet he wrote a letter setting forth his desire, and the groundwork for it, that the work should be stopped. It had the desired effect. "Then ceased the work of the house of God, which is at Jerusalem."

This Ahasuerus was notable for nothing but violence, foolishness, and cruelty. His fits of passion often hurried him into downright madness. In the second year of his reign he entered Egypt, reduced the revolters, wasted their country, killed their sacred ox, and carried off many of their idols. Here he continued five years, and ruined a great part of his army in the dry desert of the country, in his mad attempt to invade Ethiopia; and it is said that he daily sacrificed some principal Persians to his fury—his own brother and sister not excepted. Informed that he whom he had left to govern Persia in his absence had placed a man upon the throne who had no claims to it, and never could have, he hastened back again to his kingdom, and, in his route, he wreaked his vengeance on the Jews as he passed through their territories, destroying great numbers of them. Before he reached home, in mounting his horse, one day, his sword fell from its scabbard and wounded him very severely in the thigh, from which wound, not long after, he died, begging, with his last words, those that were around him not to allow the usurper to translate his government to the Medes. He was the only one that reigned in Persia between Cyrus and Darius.

AHASUERUS, 3—*Prince, chief.*

Ahasuerus, the husband of Esther, was king of Persia, and was, in all probability, the Darius Hystaspes of Persian History. He was the first of the Persian kings who reigned from India to Ethiopia, and he was noted for his imposition of enormous tributes and for his hoarding up of money. The revenues to his kingdom, on account of tributes, were exceedingly great. He appointed governors and ruled over one hundred and twenty provinces.

It was during the third year of his reign that he made a great feast and invited the great men of his nation, including the governors of all his provinces. The feast lasted one hundred and eighty days, during which time he made a great demonstration of his riches as the Persian monarch. But not fully satisfied with this display, he made a further feast of seven days at Shushan, the palace, at which he invited the ambassadors of other nations. Josephus gives us an account of the manner in which this feast was conducted and kept. During the feast the king was desirous to show the multitude the beautiful Queen Vashti, who, it is said, exceeded all other women in beauty; and he sent, commanding her to come to the feast. But Vashti, out of regard for the laws of the Persians, which forbade the wives to be seen by strangers, would not go unto the king. This irritated the king greatly, and, under the advice of Memucan, he punished her by putting her away from being his queen.

Her place was filled by the selection of Hadassah, or Esther, a Jewess, whose nation was not known to those who selected the fair young virgins of the land from whom the king was to make his selection. But the king chose her of them all. Thus God in the order of his province began to open the way for the deliverance of his people.

A thrilling event occurred, not long after this, in the life of Ahasuerus. Bigthan and Teresh, two of his chamberlains, plotted against him to destroy his life, and would have succeeded had not one of the servants made it known to Mordecai, who was the uncle of Esther, the queen, and he made it known to the queen, and she to the king. The king was greatly troubled when he saw the narrow escape he had made with his life; and, by the circumstance of its being made known, probably became more attached to Esther.

After he discovered the truth of the charge against these two chamberlains, he had them executed, and the matter dropped, without rewarding the one who made known the plot.

Not long after this, Haman, the king's privy counsellor, plotted the destruction of all the Jews, and secured a writing, over the signature of Ahasuerus, that on a certain day they should all be slain. Esther was led, in the providence of God, to present, under the most thrilling circumstances, a plea in behalf of this doomed people, to the king, in which plea she made known her own nation and kindred to her husband. The king, in the meantime, had been so dealt with by the divine Being, the God of nations, as to promote Mordecai, the uncle of Esther, to honor for making known the plot of those two chamberlains who aimed to destroy him. Ahasuerus saw the wickedness of Haman, and had him and his family destroyed. Soon after this, Mordecai became his prime minister.

Ahasuerus laid a tax upon his inland territories, and on that part of Lesser Asia and the Islands which belonged to him. He obliged the inhabitants of India to pay him yearly three hundred and sixty-five talents of silver.

He had frequent wars with the Greeks and Athenians, which generally resulted in his loss and disgrace.

He died after a reign of thirty-six years, and was succeeded by Xerxes, his son.

AHAZ—[A′-haz,] *one that takes and possesses.*

AHAZ, the son of Jotham, king of Judah, ascended the throne when about twenty years of age. He married Abijah, the daughter of Zachariah, by whom he had his son Hezekiah. In imitation of the kings of Israel, he gave himself up to the most abominable idolatries. He proved himself most impious towards God and a transgressor of the laws of his country. He reared altars in Jerusalem, and offered sacrifices upon them to idols. He even made his own children pass through the fire; or, as the Jewish historian has it, he offered his own son as a burnt offering, according to the practice of the Canaanites. He shut up the temple, and destroyed its sacred vessels. He ordered Urijah, the Priest, to build an altar, probably like an altar he had seen among the idolatrous Syrians; for it is said, in 2d Chron. xxviii: 23, &c., "He sacrificed to the gods of Damascus; and he said, because the gods of the kings of Syria help them, I will sacrifice to them, that they may help me. And he made high places to burn incense to other gods in every city of Judah." He changed the house of the Lord so as to make it conform to the idolatrous temples which he saw, and he aimed to model the divine worship after the worship of idolaters. In a word, he proposed to honor and worship the gods of Syria, and not the God of Heaven. Thus he offered contempt to the true God and provoked him to anger.

In war with Pekah, king of Israel, assisted by the king of Syria, Ahaz was miserably beaten. Whereupon he procured help of Tilgath Pilneser, king of the Assyrians. With the help of this king, he laid Syria waste, took Damascus, and slew their king, and laid much of the land of Israel waste, and took many captives out of it. At the close of the war he returned to Jerusalem, a worshiper of false gods, and continued to be, we suppose, until he died.

For the impiety which he practiced, he was in dishonor with his people, and they would not, when he was dead, give him a burial with the kings. 2d Chron. xxviii: 27. "And Ahaz slept with his fathers, and they buried him in the city, even in Jerusalem: but they brought him not into the sepulchres of the kings of Israel."

AHAZIAH, 1—[A-ha-zy′-ah,] *possession, vision of the Lord.*

AHAZIAH was the son of Ahab, king of Israel. During the last year of his father's life, he was associated with him, reigning in Israel at the time of the war at Ramoth Gilead, and he reigned about one year after Ahab's death, so that two years was the extent of his reign, and one year of that time he was nothing more than an associate of the king.

Ahaziah imitated his father in the worship of Baal and Ashtaroth, which had been introduced into Israel by Jezebel, his mother, for she was one of another nation than Israel, and Ahab had married her in violation of Israelitish law.

The Moabites, who had been tributary to the kings of Israel from the time that they revolted and separated from Judah during the reign of Ahab, revolted and refused any longer to pay tribute. Ahaziah had not the time, nor had he the power, to subdue them, and make them yield yet longer to tribute. In 2d Kings, i: 1, we have the account of Moab's rebellion. About the time of this revolt, he had the misfortune to fall through a lattice from the top of his house, and by the fall he was considerably injured. Fearing the consequence, he sent messengers to Baal-zebub, the god of Ekron, to know whether he should recover from the injury. The fearless and faithful servant of God, Elijah, met the messengers of Ahaziah, and informed them that he should certainly die. Elijah charged upon Ahaziah his sin of inquiring of a false god, as though there was no God in Israel. Ahaziah, learning where the Prophet Elijah was, with a hostile intent sent a company of fifty men to take him and bring him into his presence. But God, who knew the feelings and intent of the wicked king, sent fire from heaven to consume the company. And, again, another company of fifty men were sent and consumed. A third company was sent, and with them Elijah came down under the direction of *his* master, and stood in the presence of the king, and declared to him the decree, "Thou shalt die;" and he did die in a short time afterwards. 1st Kings, xxii; and 2d Chron. xxii.

AHAZIAH, 2—*Possession, vision of the Lord.*

AHAZIAH was a king of Judah. He was the son of Jehoram and Athaliah. His mother was of the family of Ahab, and probably kept up the idolatry that had been introduced by Jezebel in all its enormity. His reign, like that of Ahaziah, the king of Israel, was short, for he reigned but one year, beginning when he was at the age of twenty-two. When Joram, the king of Israel, went to war with Hazael, king of Syria, at Ramoth Gilead, he was dangerously wounded, and, at his own instance, taken to Jezreel, for the purpose of surgical advice and assistance. Ahaziah was of the same family relation and friendly to Joram, and, indeed, he had probably been engaged in the war with him in which he was wounded. He went to Jezreel to see him, and while there with him, Jehu, the son of Nimshi, an officer in Joram's army, under the appointment of God, rebelled against the king his master, and set himself to destroy utterly the house of Ahab.

When Jorum and Ahaziah, the kings of Judah and Israel, learned that Jehu was coming and nearing Jezreel, they went out to meet him and salute him, knowing nothing of his intention to destroy them. As soon as they met, Joram addressed himself to his officer, saying, "Is it peace, Jehu?" His answer indicated his errand; and, Joram, alarmed, turned to Ahaziah, and said: "There is treachery, Ahaziah."

It was but the work of a few moments. Jehu drew a bow, and an arrow sped swiftly and smote him between the arms. The arrow pierced his heart, and he sunk down dead in his chariot. Ahaziah fled for his life, for he understood the sentence to be against him as one of the house of Ahab, as well as against his kinsman, who had fallen. Jehu's soldiers followed him in his flight, and overtook him at the going up of Gur, and they mortally wounded him. But with failing strength, he continued his flight until he reached Megiddo, where he died. And his servants carried him to Jerusalem in a chariot, and buried him in his sepulcher with his fathers in the city of David." 2d Kings, viii, &c.; 2d Chron. xxii.

AHBAN—[Ah′-ban.]

AHBAN was the son of Abishur, by his wife, Abihail. He was of the tribe of Judah. 1st Chron. ii: 29.

AHI, 1—[A′-hi,] *my brother, my brethren.*

AHI was a Gadite, and chief of a family who lived in Gilead of Bashan in the days of Jotham, king of Judah. 1st Chron. v: 15.

AHI, 2—*My brother. my brethren.*

AHI was a descendant of Shamer, and of the tribe of Asher. 1st Chron. vii: 34.

AHIAH, 1—[A-hi′-ah,] *brother of the Lord.*

AHIAH was the son of Ahitub, the high priest of the family of Eli and his successor in office. 1st Sam. xiv: 3.

AHIAH, 2—*Brother of the Lord.*

AHIAH was the son of Shisha and the brother of Elijah. He was a secretary to King Solomon. 1st Kings, iv: 3.

AHIAM—[A-hi′-am,] *brother of the mother, brother of the nation.*

AHIAM, the son of Sharah, the Hararite, was one of David's mighty men. 2d Sam. xxiii: 33.

AHIEZER, 1—[A-hi-e′-zer,] *brother of assistance.*

AHIEZER was the son of Ammishaddai, of the tribe of Dan. He was chief of his tribe, and was associated with Moses and Aaron in managing the business of their nation at the time of their exodus from the land of Egypt.

Num. i: 12. And when the tabernacle was fully set up, he made an offering for his tribe. Num. vii: 66.

AHIEZER, 2—*Brother of assistance.*

Ahiezer was the chief of the persons who joined themselves to David at Ziklag—the city that Achish, the king of Gath, gave him as a retreat when he fled from the fury of Saul. There were twenty-three Benjamite captains, and with them eleven captains of the tribe of Gad. 1st Chron. xii: 1-12.

AHIHUD—[A-hi'-hud,] *a brother of vanity, a brother of praise.*

Ahihud was the son of Shelomi, of Asher, and was associated with Eleazer and Joshua in dividing the land of Canaan and apportioning to each tribe their inheritance. Num. xxxiv: 27.

AHIJAH, 1—[A-hi'-jah,] *brother of the Lord.*

Ahijah was a prophet of the Lord, who dwelt in Shiloh. He is supposed to be the prophet who spake to Solomon while he was engaged in building the temple. 1st Kings, vi: 11; xi: 12. In this second quotation the announcement is made that God intended to rend the kingdom into parts and give of it to another, because Solomon had not walked in the statutes of the Lord, or observed the divine commandments.

The prophet Ahijah was one of those who wrote the history of the kingdom, or the annals of Solomon's reign. In 2d Chron. ix: 29, it is said: "Now the rest of the acts of Solomon, first and last, are they not written in the book of Nathan, the prophet, and in the prophecy of Ahijah, the Shilonite."

This prophet declared to Jeroboam that he should usurp the kingdom. As Jeroboam was passing out of Jerusalem the prophet Ahijah met him alone in a field. The prophet had on a new mantle, and, securing the attention of Jeroboam, he took the new garment off that he had on, and rent it into twelve pieces, and gave ten of those pieces to Jeroboam. This was a very strange, and yet a very significant act, for, as he gave the ten pieces to him, he explained to him the import in a bold prophecy regarding the future of Israel, "Thus saith the Lord God of Israel, Behold, I will rend the kingdom out of the hand of Solomon, and will give ten tribes unto thee."

This prophet appears again about the end of Jeroboam's reign, predicting the death of Abijah, the son of Jeroboam; and the only pious son of that prince, and the only one of his household that should come to the grave in peace. Abijah, the son of Jeroboam, was taken sick, and he was very desirous to know whether or not his child should recover. In his anxiety he thought of Ahijah, the prophet, at Shiloh—the man of God, who told him he should be king of Israel—and he sent his wife disguised to ask the prophet. Now, Ahijah was nearly blind; but as the wife of Jeroboam approached him, God communicated the fact to Ahijah, and put the words of this last prophecy into his mouth to speak unto her. Under Ahijah's direction she returned to bear to the king the sad intelligence of the certain death of the sick child.

This prophet, as he was quite aged and infirm when he gave this prophecy, died, in all probability, shortly afterward, at Shiloh, and was buried there.

AHIJAH, 2—*Brother of the Lord.*

Ahijah was the treasurer of the House of the Lord, and had the charge of the holy things. 1st Chron. xxvi: 20. Some have thought that this person was the same as Ahijah, the Shilonite.

AHIKAM—[A-hi'-kam,] *a brother that raises up.*

Ahikam, the son of Shaphan and the father of Gedaliah, was a prince of Judah. He was sent by King Josiah, in company with Shaphan, the scribe, who was his father, Hilkiah, the high priest, and Achbor, the son of Michaiah, to Huldah, the prophetess. They went to her to make enquiry of the Lord, through her, as to an old manuscript that had been found by the high priest. This manuscript is supposed to have been the autograph of Moses, containing a part of the book of Deuteronomy where the account is given of the renewal of the covenant on the part of God with Israel in the plains of Moab, which contains the most terrible threats against the corrupters of God's word and worship.

This was a copy of *the law* of Moses, as it is called in 2d Chronicles, xxxiv: 14, "Hilkiah, the priest, found a book of the law of the Lord given by Moses." It is said that Ahaz, Manasseh and Amnon, destroyed all the copies of the law that they found, except this copy found by Hilkiah. The simple fact probably is that this was the original copy of the covenant renewed by Moses with the people, and it was laid up by the ark, and now it is unexpectedly found. Its great age, with the fact that it was not a copy of it, but the original, made it an object of great interest. But then its invectives against the corrupters of God's word were calculated to produce just such an effect in the mind of the young King Josiah (devoted as he was to the service of God) as it did produce. The manuscript was taken by the prince of Judah, Ahikam, and his associates, to Huldah, and they heard her words and prophecy regarding it.

AHILUD—[A-hi′-lud,] *a brother born.*

AHILUD was the father of Jehoshaphat, who was recorder for King David and the writer of the Chronicles. 2d Sam. viii: 16.

AHIMAAZ—[A-him′-a-az,] *brother of the council.*

AHIMAAZ was the son of Zadok, the high priest, and succeeded his father in that important office. They were ministering together in the time of David; and when Absalom rebelled and David found it necessary to leave Jerusalem, Zadok and Abiather would take the ark of the covenant of the Lord along with David; but the king commanded them to return with it to Jerusalem, and they did so, taking Ahimaaz with them.

Ahimaaz performed a very important piece of service for David here. He tarried at Enrogel or the foundation of Rogel without the city, with his companion, Jonathan. To that place a woman, a maid-servant, came to tell them of the resolution which had been made in Absalom's counsel under the advice of Hushai; whereupon they immediately departed to give David the intelligence. They had been discovered, however, by a young man, who had given the information concerning them to Absalom, and that prince had sent orders to pursue them. When they learned that they were being followed, they determined to hide themselves, and, in order to do this, they entered into a man's house at Bahurim and made known their business, probably, when they were hidden in a well in the court, and the woman of the house spread a covering over the well's mouth and spread ground corn thereon so that their hiding place would not be detected when their pursuers came up. Absalom's servant came on and enquired of the woman of the house where Ahimaaz and Jonathan were. She remained true to the servants of David, and the consequence was, they sought ineffectually for them, and returned to Jerusalem, when they came up out of the well and went to David to deliver their message.

After the battle that resulted in the death of Absalom was over, Ahimaaz desired of Joab that he might carry the tidings to David; but, for some cause, Joab preferred to send by Cushi, promising Ahimaaz that he should be the bearer of intelligence on some other occasion; but this did not satisfy him, and, soon after Cushi started, he applied to Joab again, earnestly entreating him to allow him to run after Cushi, when Joab gave him leave, thinking, probably, that Cushi would arrive before him, and so be the first to give the news to King David; but in this he was mistaken, for Ahimaaz, being swift on foot, and probably taking a shorter route, for he ran by the way of the plain, outran Cushi and came to David first with intelligence. It is true he did not know that Absalom was dead, but he knew that David's troops had obtained a victory.

How long he served in the priesthood we do not know precisely, but he was succeeded by his son, Azariah. 2d Sam. xv: to xviii: 1st Chron. vi: 8, 9.

AHIMAN—[A-hi′-man,] *a brother prepared.*

AHIMAN was a giant of the Anak stock, who lived at Hebron, in the land of Canaan, before Israel possessed that land. When Moses sent the spies to look at the land, and bring their brethren word as to the character of the country, Ahiman, as one of the race of giants, lived there. Numb. xiii: 22. This giant, with two of his brethren, Sheshai and Talmai, were expelled by

Joshua, the conqueror of Canaan. Josh. xv: 14.

AHIMELECH, 1—[A-him′-me-lek,] *my brother is a king.*

Ahimelech, the son of Ahitub and brother of Ahiah, whom he succeeded in the office of high priest. He is called, in Mark, ii: 26, Abiathar, probably because Abiathar was the only one of his family that was not put to death by Saul, the king of Israel, and hence the only one that continued in the priesthood. He escaped the destruction of the house of Ahimelech and fled to David, whom he served in the office of high priest.

During the priesthood of Ahimelech, he lived at Nob with other priests, where the tabernacle of God was. When Saul determined to destroy David, and Jonathan, his friend, informed him of it, he determined to fly the country, and in his flight he went to Nob, and asked of the high priest something to eat. As Ahimelech had nothing save the show bread, he gave him that. Then he asked of him a sword, and he gave him the sword of Goliath, the Philistine giant, whom David had killed several years before; for that sword had been kept under the charge of the high priest from the time the giant was killed. Ahimelech, looking upon David as having a right to the use of a sword that he had taken himself, and believing that he was a faithful servant of Saul, and was on important business, probably, without any hesitancy, satisfied him with bread and the sword.

But not long after this, Doeg, the Edomite, reported to King Saul how Ahimelech had received David in his flight and supplied his wants. Saul became very much enraged, and called the priests together, and when they were all convened he made the charge against them of treason, and decided that they should all be slain at once. The guards were unwilling to perform the task—probably they were satisfied that they had done nothing worthy of death, not even Ahimelech. They knew he was innocent of the crime with which the king charged him and his associates. When the guards refused to do it, the king ordered Doeg, who was their accuser, to become their executioner, and he, glad of the opportunity of becoming thus notorious, laid his sacrilegious hand upon eighty-five of them that day, and slew them. Ahimelech was one of the first that was executed.

But Saul did not stop here. He sent a party of cruel men to Nob, who executed his cruel decree to slay men, women and children, and even the cattle, with the edge of the sword. There is supposed to have been no less than three or four hundred of the priests, with their families, that perished in the slaughter. 1st Sam. xxi.

AHIMELECH, 2—*My brother is a king.*

Ahimelech was the son of Abiathar. He and Zadok, whom Saul had made high priests after the murder of the former Ahimelech, were second priests about the latter end of the reign of King David.

Before Ahimelech and other persons of note, Shemaiah, the scribe, wrote down the orders and divisions of the priests, singers, and Levites, and they cast their lots for their turns of service in the temple of God. The Levites were divided into twenty-four orders, and these were appointed to serve by lot under the twenty-four orders of the priests. 1st Chron. xxiv: 3-31.

AHINADAB—[A-hin′-a-dab,] *a willing brother, a brother of a vow, a brother of the prince.*

Ahinadab was son of Iddo, governor of Mahanaim. He lived during the reign of Solomon. 1st Kings, iv: 14.

AHINOAM, 1—[A-hin′-no-am,] *the beauty and comeliness of the brother.*

Ahinoam was the daughter of Ahimaaz, and the wife of Saul. 1st Sam. xiv: 50. We suppose this woman was the only wife of Saul, and the mother of the children whose names are given. Jonathan, Ishui, Malchishua, with Merab and Michal. She was also, it is quite likely, the mother of Ishbosheth, who, it may be, as he is not named in the above passage, was not yet born; or if born, he was an infant, and is not numbered with his brothers, as he could not go with them to war.

AHINOAM, 2—*The beauty and comeliness of the brother.*

Ahinoam, the Jezreelite, was the wife of David. She is referred to in connection with Abigail, the Carmelite, in 1st Sam. xxv: 43: "David also took Ahinoam of Jezreel, and they were also both of them his wives." This passage seems to indicate that David married Abigail first; and yet we judge he did not, for Ahinoam is generally mentioned first among his wives, which we think would not have been the case had he not married her first. And we learn from 2d Sam. iii: 2, that she was the mother of David's oldest son, Amnon.

AHIO—[A-hi′o,] *his brother, his brethren.*

AHIO was with Uzzah, his brother, in charge of the cart into which the Ark was put by David when he removed it from the house of Aminadab to place it in the newly erected tabernacle. 2d Sam. vi: 3.

AHIRA—[A-hy′-rah,] *brother of iniquity or of the shepherd.*

AHIRA was the son of Enan, and chief of the tribe of Naphtali. Num. i: 15.

AHIRAM—[A-hi′ram,] *brother of craft, protection.*

AHIRAM was one of the sons of Benjamin, and an ancestor of the Ahiramites. Num. xxvi: 38. He is thought to be the same as Aher, in the list of Benjamin's children.

AHISAMACH—[A-his′a-mak,] *brother of strength or of support.*

AHISAMACH was the father of Aholiab, a famous artificer, employed by Moses. Ex. xxxv: 34.

AHISHAHAR—[A-hi-sha′-har,] *Brother of the morning or dew, brother of blackness.*

AHISHAHAR was one of the sons of Bilhan, the grandson of Benjamin. 1st Chron. vii: 10.

AHISHAR—[A-hi′shar,] *brother of a prince.*

AHISHAR was an officer in Solomon's household, one of his stewards. 1st Kings, iv: 6.

AHITHOPHEL—[A-hith′o-fel,] *brother of ruin or folly.*

AHITHOPHEL was a native of Giloh, in the tribe of Judah. He was so renowned a counsellor and statesman that his advice was generally received as an order of God. After having been for some time the counsellor of King David, he joined in the rebellion of Absalom, and became his adviser. As soon as David learned that Ahithophel had become Absalom's friend and counsellor, he employed Hushai, another counsellor of his own, to counteract the advice of Ahithophel with Absalom, under the pretense of serving him as the new king. Hushai, true to David's wish, went over to Absalom and became acquainted with Ahithophel's counsel, and he counseled Absalom contrary; which counsel was followed, and Ahithophel's was rejected, at least in part. It is true that Absalom followed the counsel of Ahithophel in defiling his father's wives, and thus laying the ground-work for a degree of feeling on the part of David against Absalom that could not easily be destroyed. Ahithophel intended to make David irreconcilable. But the other thing that he counseled, he was not so successful in. He proposed to Absalom that they should pursue after David at once with an army of men, come upon him while he was weary and weak handed, dispirit him, and frighten his men so that they would desert, when King David should be slain and the way opened for Absalom to ascend the throne. This counsel was received with favor by Absalom, but either to be more certain that this was right, or to show deference to Hushai, who had come over from David to him, or for some other cause, he called Hushai and informed him of the counsel of Ahithophel. Hushai differed from him, and gave his reasons for his contrary counsel. He desired Absalom, instead of pursuing after David at once, to make ready for a campaign, and proceed at the head of his army in person. His counsel pleased Absalom and the men of Israel, and they preferred it to the counsel of Ahithophel. As soon as he learned that his counsel was rejected and Hushai's was taken in its stead he became disgusted and hastened to his house in Giloh, and "put his household in order and hanged himself."

He probably foresaw Absalom's defeat, and dreaded the punishment which would be inflicted upon him as a traitor when David was re-established on his throne and Absalom conquered.

The self-murder of Ahithophel could not be attributed to lunacy, for the steps he took to it were deliberate. He set his house in order, and then deliberately hanged himself. He was a wise man and counsellor, well versed in the affairs of state, but God confounded his wicked devices and brought him thus to a miserable end. Though wise he was very wicked, and died unprepared to meet God. 2d Sam. xvii: 23.

AHITUB, 1—[A-hi′tub,] *brother of goodness.*

Ahitub was the son of Phineas, the son of Eli. Phineas and Hophni were both slain in the unfortunate engagement with the Philistines, in which the Ark of God was taken. This unfortunate affair seemed to be the occasion of the sudden death of Eli, for when he heard that his sons were slain, and that the Ark of God was captured, he fell backward and broke his neck.

Ahitub succeeded his grandfather in the high priesthood, and performed the duties of that office most of the time during the judgeship of Samuel. He was succeded by his sons Ahiah first, and then Ahimelech. His successor is named in 1st Sam. xiv: 3.

AHITUB, 2—*Brother of goodness.*

Ahitub is named in 1st Chron. vi: 7, in the numbering of the sons of Levi, as the son of Amariah and the father of Zadok.

AHITUB, 3—*Brother of goodness.*

Ahitub is mentioned in 1st Chron. vi: 11. He also was the son of Amariah and the father of Zadok.

AHLAI—[Ah′lai,] *beseeching, sorrowing, beginning, brother to me.*

Ahlai was the daughter of Sheshan, and he gave her in marriage to his Egyptian slave Jarha. 1st Chron. ii: 31-35. She became the foundress of an important branch of the family of Jerahmeelites, and from her were descended Zabad, one of David's mighty men, and Azariah, one of the captains of hundreds in the days of Joash. 1st Chron. xi: 41, and 2d Chron. xxiii: 1.

AHOE or AHOAH—[A-ho′ah,] *a thistle, a thorn, a fish-hook, brotherhood.*

Ahoe or Ahoah was the third son of Bela, and a grandson of Benjamin. He is referred to in 1st Chron. viii: 4, where the posterity of Benjamin are given. He was the chief of the family of Ahoites.

AHOLAH—A-ho′lah,] *his tabernacle, his tent.*

Aholah and Aholibah were two feigned names made use of by Ezekiel xxiii: 4. This Prophet represents by them the two kingdoms of Judah and Israel. Aholah signifies a tent, and stands for Samaria and the ten tribes that revolted under Jeroboam. Aholibah signifies my tent is in her, and stands for Jerusalem and the subjects of Judea. Both of these kingdoms went away from God, gave themselves up to their enemies, the Egyptians and Assyrians, and adopted their abominations and idolatries.

Because of this, their wickedness, the Lord abandoned them to those very people for whose idolatry and wicked practices they had shown such a fondness. They were conquered and carried into bondage, and subjected to the severest servitude. There may have been two persons used to represent these two kingdoms.

AHOLIAB—[A-ho′li-ab,] *the tent or tabernacle of the father.*

Aholiab was the son of Ahisamach, of the tribe of Dan, and he was appointed by the Divine Being as a helper unto Bezaleel in the important work assigned him. There may have been many other helpers selected who were wise-hearted. But Aholiab was the principal one. Ex. xxxi: 6.

It seems from Ex. xxxv: 34, that Aholiab was as divinely called and fitted for his work, as was Bezaleel, and we may consider that his position and work was nearly as important. God prepared them alike to teach, "And filled them with wisdom of heart to work all manner of work, of the engraver, and of the cunning workman, and of the embroiderer in blue, and in purple, in scarlet, and in fine linen, and of the weaver, even of them that do any work, and of those that devise cunning work." Moses appointed them to the work, and when it was finished, received it off their hands, and pronounced his blessings upon them. Exodus xxxvi: 2 and xxxix: 43.

AHOLIBAMAH--[A-ho-li′ba-mah] *my tabernacle is exalted.*

AHOLIBAMAH, a wife of Esau. She is called Judith in Gen. xxvi: 34, and in that passage it is told us that Esau was forty years old when he married this woman. She was the mother of three sons, viz: Jeush, Jaalam and Korah, who were born in the land of Canaan. Gen. xxxvi: 5.

AHUMAI—[A-hu′mai.]

AHUMAI was the son of Jahath, a descendant of Judah, and head of one of the families of the Zorathites. 1st Chron. iv: 2.

AHUZAM—[A-hu′zam,] *their taking possession, vision.*

AHUZAM was the son of Ashur by his wife Naarah, and the father or founder of Tekoa. 1st Chronicles iv: 6.

AHUZZATH—[A-huz′zath] *possession, apprehension, vision.*

AHUZZAH was a friend of Abimelech, who, in company with Phichol, came to the patriarch Isaac to establish an alliance with him. The circumstance is recorded in Gen. xxvi: 26.

AIAH—[A-i′ah,] *a raven, a vulture, alas, where is it?*

AIAH was the father of Rizpah, who was secondary wife of king Saul. 2d Sam. iii: 7—2d Sam. xxi: 8.

AJAH—[A′jah.]

AJAH was the son of Zibeon, and the grand-son of Seir, the Horite. Gen. xxxvi: 24.

AKAN.

AKAN was the son of Ezer and the grand-son of Seir, the Horite. Gen. xxxvi: 27.

AKKUB, 1—[Ak′kub,] *the print of the foot where any creature hath been, supplantation.*

AKKUB a descendant of Zerubbabel. 1st Chron. iii: 24.

AKKUB, 2—*the print of the foot where any creature hath been, supplantation.*

AKKUB, one of the sacred porters or door keeper at the east gate of the temple. His descendants succeeded to his office, and are among those who returned from Babylon. Ez. ii: 42; Neh. vii: 45.

AKKUB, 3—*the print of the foot where any creature hath been, supplantation.*

AKKUB, one of the Nathinims whose family returned with Zerubbabel. Ez. ii: 45.

AKKUB 4—*the print of the foot where any creature hath been, supplantation.*

AKKUB was a Levite who assisted Ezra in expounding the law to the people. Neh. viii: 7.

ALEMETH—[Al′e-meth,] *a hiding, youth, worlds, upon the dead.*

ALEMETH was the son of Becher noticed in the 1st Chron. vii: 8. There were nine of them brothers, whose names are given there. In 1st Chron. vi: 60, there is a city mentioned of this name. It was probably named in honor of this man.

ALEXANDER, 1—[Al-ex-an′der,] *one that assists men, one that turns away evil.*

ALEXANDER, in history called Alexander the Great, is supposed to be referred to and described in the prophecy of Dan. vii: 6. He is represented as a leopard with four wings, to signify his great strength and the rapidity with which conquest will succeed conquest under him. So he is understood to be represented in viii; 4, under the figure of a he goat. And the great images which the king of Babylon saw in his dream; with its body of brass is understood to be an emblem of Alexander and the Mace donian empire.

ALEXANDER, 2—*One that assists men, one that turns away evil,*

ALEXANDER was the brother of Rufus, and they were both noted Christians, the sons of Simon the Cyrenian, who was compelled to bear Christ's cross when he fainted under the load. Alexander is referred to in Mark xv: 21.

ALEXANDER, 3—*One that assists men, one that turns away evil.*

ALEXANDER is referred to in Acts iv: 6. He was in company with the chief priests and elders, when they imprisoned the apostles for healing the impotent man.

ALEXANDER, 4—*One that assists men, one that turns away evil.*

ALEXANDER is called the coppersmith. He made pretensions for a while to be a christian, but his conduct was blasphemous and Paul delivered him over to Satan. He may have been sincere at first and may be the one referred to in Acts xix: 33. If so he apostatized. He became enraged at Paul and tried to injure him, as he says in 1st Tim. i: 20 and in 2d Tim. iv: 14–15.

ALMODAD—[Al-mo′dad,] *measure of God.*

ALMODAD was the son of Joktan of the family of Shem. The following are the names of his brothers as given in Gen. x: 26–29. Sheleph and Hazarmaveth and Jerah, Hadoram and Uzal and Diklah and Obal, Abimael and Sheba, Ophir and Havilah and Jobab, in all thirteen, and they had their dwelling from Mesha unto Sephar, a mount of the east.

ALPHEUS, 1—[Al-fe′-us,] *a thousand, chief.*

ALPHEUS was the name of the father of James, the less, who was cousin of our Lord. Alpheus was the husband of Mary, believed to be the sister of the virgin Mary, so that he was the uncle of the son of Mary by marriage, and the father not only of James the less, but of Juda and Joses. They are called the Lord's brothers; but the term brother is too general in its application to fix their relationship. They, with all the children of Alpheus, were cousins. Gal. i: 19; Mark, vi: 3. Many suppose that Cleopas and Alpheus are the same person, the former being the Hebrew name and the latter the Greek, for it was common in those times for persons to have two names—one of them used by their friends and countrymen and the other used by Romans and strangers. [See Cleopas.]

There was another Alpheus, who was the father of Matthew, one of the desciples of our Lord, and one of the evangelists — the first who wrote a history of the Lord.

In the 2d chap. of Mark, 14th verse, where we have the account of Matthew's call, he is denominated Levi, the son of Alpheus. Of this personage we know nothing further.

ALVAN.

ALVAN was the son of Shobal, and the grandson of Seir, the Horite. Gen. xxxvi: 23.

AMAL—[A′mal.]

AMAL was an Asherite, son of Helam. 1st Chron. vii: 35.

AMALEK — [Am′-a-lek,] *a people that licks up or uses ill.*

AMALEK was the son of Eliphaz and the grandson of Esau. There may have been an Amalek long before this one, in the days of Abraham, because there was a people called Amalekites in the days of Chedorlaomer, the king of Elam. That king fought with the Amalekites, and smote all the country, and it is reasonable to suppose that they sprung from an Amalek more ancient than any person bearing that name that we read of.

There is some tradition among the Arabians that there was an Amalek who was the son of Ham; and many suppose that the powerful people who attacked the Israelites in the wilderness, derived their ancestry from Ham rather than from so recent an origin as Amalek, the grandson of Esau; and there is an allusion made by Balaam to Amalekites as "the first of the nations" that will not so well agree with the descendants of Esau as a more ancient stock; and there are other things in which the fitness will not so well appear.

The descendants of the Amalekites that came from Esau were bitter enemies of the Israelites or Jews. They probably were made acquainted with the fact that Jacob, the brother of Esau, had supplanted him and secured his birthright. When Israel had settled in the land of Canaan and were served by judges, the Amalekites associated themselves with the Midianites to invade the land of Israel when they were defeated by Gideon. And when the form of Government of Israel was about to be changed from judges to that of kings, Saul was sent to fight with them, and utterly destroy them. He fought, and conquered them, and destroyed their entire army, but spared Agag, their king.

God did not approve of Saul's course in sparing Agag, and the prophet Samuel took it upon himself to "hew Agag into pieces," thus executing God's decree regarding Amalek.

But Amalek, the grandson of Esau, succeeded Gatem in the government of the Edomites. Gen. xxxvi: 16.

The ducal government prevailed first among the sons of Esau. Amalek was a duke; *i. e.*, a leader or captain of the people. Num. xiv: 25; and 1st Sam. xxvii: 8.

AMARIAH—[Am-a-ri′-ah,] *the strength of the Lord.*

There were two persons of this name who belonged to the tribe of Levi, and in the line of the priests to the captivity. The first was the son of Meraioth, and the second was the son of Azariah. 1st Chronicles, vi: 7; and vi: 11.

AMASA, 1—[Am-ay′-sah,] *a forgiving people, the burden of the people.*

AMASA was the son of Jether or Ithra, and of Abigail the sister of David, was general of Absalom's army in the rebellion. He fought with Joab who was the general of David's army and was conquered. When Absalom was slain and his army scattered, Amasa expected punishment from David but was mercifully spared, and when David became angry at Joab his General he pardoned Amasa and appointed him general in the stead of Joab, and gave him the command of his army. Joab was not pleased at this promotion of him who had fought with the very troops he now commanded in a rebellion, and probably then determined to destroy him, as he afterwards did in a most dastardly and cowardly manner.

When Sheba the son of Bichri revolted against David, he gave orders to Amasa to assemble all Judah and march against him. But while Amasa was delayed in gathering the army together and getting ready for battle Joab and Abishai received orders from the King to go against Sheba the son of Bichri with the six hundred men on hand ready to do battle for the King at any time. And they made ready and went, but they had not proceeded far, when Amasa with the main army overtook them at Gibeon. And when he met Joab in friendship he saluted him according to the custom of that day, heartily. Joab approached near unto him and making as though he intended to kiss him, with one hand he grasped his sword and with the other he caught the beard of Amasa, and he thrust his sword through the body of this General of David's army, so that he expired in a short time. This impious and wicked act of Joab in killing a young man, and his kinsman, and the kinsman of King David, was the effect of jealousy, for Amasa had never wronged him. But he feared that he would become permanently his equal if not his superior, and hence determined to slay him. He was actuated by the same spirit in killing another of the great men of Israel. I mean Abner the son of Ner. 2d Sam. iii: 27.

AMASA, 2—*A forgiving people, the burden of the people.*

In the days of Ahaz King of Judah there was an Amasa the son of Hadlai who occupied a somewhat conspicuous place in the government of Israel or about Samaria the Capitol. For when Israel fought with Judah and conquered them, and brought two hundred thousand captives to Samaria, Amasa with several other heads of the children of Ephraim refused to let the conquerors enter the city with their captives. In 2d Chron. xxviii, we have this account, and from it we may learn that Amasa was a man of some note amongst them. Especially does his address to the conquerors in the 13th verse show that he feared God and desired his blessing upon their nation.

AMASAI, 1—[Am-a-sa′i.]

AMASAI was a Kohathite, and the father of Mahath, and ancestor to Samuel and Heman the singer. 1st Chron. vi: 25.

AMASAI, 2.

AMASAI was chief of the captains of Judah and Benjamin, who deserted to David while at Ziklag. 1st Chron. xii: 18

AMASAI, 3.

AMASAI was one of the Priests who blew trumpets before the Ark when David brought it from the house of Obededom. 1st Chron. xv: 24.

AMASAI, 4.

AMASAI was another Kohathite, and father of another Mahath in the reign of Hezekiah. 2d Chron. xxix: 12.

AMASAI, 5.

AMASAI is referred to in 1st Chron. xii: 16, 19, from which we may judge that he was a chief of Captains of Judah and Benjamin, who went to David in his exile as did many other of his friends to Ziklag and consoled him and joined themselves unto him, while Saul full of wrath was seeking him for death. When David heard they were coming, he went to meet them, asked them if they were for him or against him. "If ye be come peaceably unto me to help me, mine heart shall be knit unto you, but if ye be come to betray me to mine enemies, seeing there is no wrong in mine hands, the God of our fathers look thereon and rebuke it." Amasai stood up and in the name of the whole company said, "Thine are we, David, and on thy side thou son of Jesse. Peace, peace be unto thee, and peace be to thine helpers, for thy God helpeth thee." As David became satisfied that Amasai and his companions would be true to him he received them at once, and made the captains officers in his army.

AMASHAI—[Am-a-sha′i.]

AMASHAI was the son of Azarcel, he was a priest in the time of Nehemiah. Neh. xi: 13.

AMASIAH—[Am-a-si′ah.]

AMASIAH was the son of Zichri and commander of 200,000 warriors of Judah in the reign of King Jehoshaphat. 2d Chron. xvii: 16.

AMAZIAH, 1—[Am-a-zi′-ah,] *the strength of the Lord.*

AMAZIAH was one of the Kings of Judah and the son of Joash. He succeeded his father to the throne. He was twenty-five years of age when he began to reign, and he reigned twenty-nine years at Jerusalem.

There were two important wars prosecuted by Amaziah; the one was against the Edomites and Amalekites, and the other against Israel. He conquered the former, but was conquered by the latter.

Amaziah feared the God of his fathers in the beginning of his reign. "He did good in the sight of the Lord, but not with a perfect heart." As soon as he was settled on the throne he executed just punishment on the murderers of his father, Joash, by putting them to death; but according to the law of Moses, and contrary to the customs of those times and countries, he would not imbrue his hands in the blood of the innocent children. The law of Moses was, "The fathers shall not be put to death for the children, neither shall the children be put to death for the fathers: every man shall be put to death for his own sins." Deut. xxiv: 16.

When about to prepare his expedition against Edom and Amalek, he chose him an army from Judah and Benjamin, of young men in the flower of their age, about twenty years old. His muster resulted in gathering together an army of three hundred thousand men able to bear arms. He sent to the king of Israel and hired one hundred thousand of his men for a hundred talents of silver.

But while he was preparing for the expedition, and about ready to go out to war, a prophet came to him and said, "O, King, let not the army of Israel go with thee, for the Lord is not with Israel." God gave Amaziah to understand through his prophet that he must dismiss the army of the Israelites, for they were bad men. God was angry with them and would not give him success if they went. Now, Amaziah had probably paid the hire, a hundred talents of silver, to the King of Israel, but he is commanded to give up their service and send them back to their master, and he did. But these Israelite soldiers were dissatisfied, and taking their dismission in affront, on their way to Samaria they fell upon the cities of Judah and destroyed them from Bethhoron to Samaria, killing three thousand men and taking much cattle or booty in their conquest.

Amaziah, after dismissing the hired soldiers, made war upon the nations of Edom and Amalekites, and conquered them. In battle he slew ten thousand and took as many prisoners alive, and brought them to a certain place in Arabia where he executed them. He also obtained much spoils and vast riches.

After conquering the Edomites in the Valley of Salt he took their gods and proceeded to worship them. How strange that a king of Judah who had begun his reign as Amaziah had, and had been prospered by the God of his fathers as he had, should be so elated with his victory as to forget his obligations and offer such insults to Jehovah as to engage in the gross idolatry of the heathen nation he had just conquered.

Amaziah it would seem, after his victory over the nations with whom he had fought, thought himself invincible and able to conquer any nation. He meditated in his heart the conquest of Israel. Whether he had any thought of revenging the death of the three thousand men that had been killed from Bethhoron to Samaria by the dismissed soldiery or not, we cannot certainly tell, but it is certain that he contemplated bringing back the revolted tribes, and making his kingdom extensive as it was in the days of his father David. He wrote to the king of Israel to this effect: "Come out with Israel to war with me. Come, let us look one another in the face." It is quite probable that this challenge was made grounded on the matter to which we have referred, viz: the slaughter of the three thousand. He required, probably, of Joash, a repairing of this breach so far as it could be repaired. The king of Israel answered him by the fable of the cedar of Lebanon and the thistle trodden down by a beast. This may be considered a grave rebuke for the challenge and advice to withdraw it. It was not a challenge to a personal combat, to fight a duel, but it was a challenge to bring the forces of Israel and Judah into the field and try the strength of the nations, which would result in the loss of thousands of men. In this fable, recorded in 2d Kings xiv: 9, 11, the King of Israel compares himself to the cedar of Lebanon, and Amaziah to a thistle—a sorry weed. He then tells him that he does not fear him, but rather despised him, and scorned to have anything to do with him, or make any alliance with him, as the cedar would to join its daughter to a thistle. He then foretells the fall of Amaziah—"a wild beast trod down the thistle," and so put an end to the treaty with the cedar. The meaning of this probably was: Israel can crush Judah, or Joash can conquer Amaziah. He then shows him the folly of his challenge: "Thou hast indeed smitten Edom, a weak, unarmed, undisciplined body of men, but thou canst not thus subdue Israel. Thou art proud of the blow given Edom as if that had made thee invincible and unconquerable." He would have Amaziah content with the honor he had won, and not hazard that by grasping for more. But the King of Judah would not hearken, and as he persisted in his resolution Joash met him face to face and defeated him, and took him prisoner and carried him to Jerusalem. The gates of the city were open to receive him, and he took possession of it and plundered it, and carried the gold and silver to Samaria with the rich vessels of the house of God and the treasury of the royal palace, and the sons of his own people that had been hostages in Jerusalem.

Amaziah was thus brought down and humbled by a conqueror. He reigned fifteen years after the death of Joash, but did not return to the God from whom he had wickedly wandered. After this a conspiracy was raised against him and he fled to Lachish, but was assassinated there by the conspirators. Some of his subjects carried his dead body to the city of David and prepared it for burial with his ancestors. 2d Kings xiv: 2d Chron. xxv.

**AMAZIAH, 2**—[Am-a-zi′ah,] *the strength of the Lord.*

AMAZIAH was an idolatrous high priest of the golden calf of Bethel. He is referred to in Amos, vii: 9-17. The prophet Amos predicted the ruin of the high places of Israel, and the utter destruction of the family of Jeroboam the king of Israel. The lying and idolatrous Amaziah then bade Amos flee from Israel into the land of

Judah, and no more prophesy against Israel and her kings. He probably accused Amos to the king as a traitor, and a troubler of the people. But in the stead of heeding his advice, the true prophet assured him that his persecution of him should be resented by the Almighty. He assured Amaziah that his wife should become base and a prostitute, that his children should be cruelly murdered, and his inheritance should be possessed by his enemies. That he himself should die in lonely exile, and Israel should go into captivity.

AMINADAB, 1—[A-min′a-dab,] *prince of the people, a people that vows.*

AMINADAB was the father of Elisheba, Aaron's wife, and is referred to in Ex. vi: 23.

AMINADAB, 2—*Prince of the people, a people that vows.*

AMINADAB is mentioned in Math. i: 4, as of the progenitors of Christ. He was the son of Aram, and father of Naason.

AMINADAB 3, OR ABINADAB—*Prince of the people, a people that vows.*

AMINADAB, or ABINADAB, was a Levite, and an inhabitant of Kirjath-jearim. The ark of God was deposited with him after it was brought from Bethshemesh.

For seven months after it was taken it was with the Philistines, and when they determined to send it back to Shiloh, they took it as far as this place, which was a city of the tribe of Judah, belonging to the priests. Some Levites took possession of it.

Here the order of the divine Being regarding the ark was violated, for some of the people of the city, out of curiosity, looked into the ark. For this the Lord destroyed seventy of the principal men belonging to Bethshemesh, and fifty thousand of the common people. 1st Sam. vi: 19.

The order of Jehovah was that not only the common people should not look into the ark upon pain of death, but even the Levites were solemnly prohibited. Num. iv: 20. "But they shall not go in to see when the holy things are covered lest they die." The people of this city realized that it was a fearful thing to use irreverent boldness with holy things, and so trample upon the authority of God. They besought the men of Kirjath-jearim to come and take possession of the ark, and they did, and deposited it in the house of Abinadab, and his son Eleazer was placed in charge of it. 1st Sam. vii: 1. "And the men of Kirjath-jearim came and fetched up the ark of the Lord and brought it into the house of Abinadab, in the hill, and sanctified Eleazer his son to keep the ark of the Lord."

Abinadab dwelt in Gibeath, that is to say, in the highest part of the city. The chariots of Aminadib are mentioned in the Songs of Solomon, vi: 12. This, of course, is another Aminadib, who, we may suppose, was celebrated as a charioteer. He may have been celebrated for lightness of his chariots and the swiftness of his horses, or he may have been celebrated for his skill in driving, as Jehu the son of Nimshi was.

AMITTAI—[A-mit′tai.]

AMITTAI was the father of Jonah the prophet. Jon. i: 1.

AMMIEL, 1—[Am′mi-el.]

AMMIEL was of the tribe of Dan, and was selected by Moses as one of the twelve spies to search out and examine the state of the land of Canaan. Num. xiii: 12.

AMMIEL, 2.

AMMIEL was the father of Machir, in whose house Mephibosheth, the son of Jonathan, was dwelling when David learned of him, and determined to show him kindness for Jonathan, his father's sake. He is called Ammiel of Lodebar, because he hired them. 2d Sam. ix: 4.

AMMIEL, 3.

AMMIEL was the sixth son of Obed Edom, and one of the sacred porters. 1st Chron. xxvi: 5.

AMMIHUD, 1—[Am′mi-hud,] *people of praise.*

AMMIHUD was of the tribe of Ephraim, and the father of Elishama, the prince of that tribe, who assisted Moses in numbering the tribes of Israel. Num. i: 10.

AMMIHUD, 2—*People of praise.*

AMMIHUD was the father of Pedahel, of the tribe of Naphtali, who was a prince, and assisted in dividing the land of Canaan. Num. xxxiv: 28.

AMMIHUD, 3—*People of praise.*

AMMIHUD was the father of Talmai, king of Geshur. This Talmai was the grandfather of Absalom, and gave him a home the three years he was exiled from his father David for the murder of Amnon. 2d Sam. xiii: 37.

AMMISHADDAI—[Am-mi-shad′-dai,] *the people of the Almighty.*

AMMISHADDAI was of the tribe of Dan, and the father of Ahiezer, the prince, who assisted Moses in numbering the tribes of Israel. Numb. i: 12.

AMMIZABAD—[Am-miz′a-bad.]

AMMIZABAD was the son of Benaiah, is reckoned in the course of his father when the monthly service was instituted. 1st Chron. xxvii: 6.

AMMON—[Am′mon,] *the son of my people.*

AMMON, or the father of the Ammonites, was the son of Lot's youngest daughter, called in Gen. xix: 38, Ben-ammi. He dwelt on the east side of the Dead Sea, in the mountains of Gilead, or his descendants did, and they became very numerous. They were somewhat favored of God, in that the Israelites were forbidden to disturb them. Deut. ii: 19, "And when thou comest nigh over against the children of Ammon, distress them not, nor meddle with them: for I will not give thee of the land of the children of Ammon any possession, because I have given it unto the children of Lot for a possession." Thus we observe that the Lord favored the posterity of the noted kinsman of Abraham. They as well as the children of Moab, Lot's eldest daughter's son, were to be preserved while the Israelites marched through the land as conquerors, though they were not to receive them into the congregation of Israel to the tenth generation, for the reason that they did not render help to Israel when it was in their power, and more than that, they were implicated in hiring Balaam to curse them.

They were idolaters worshiping Molech and Chemosh. In the time of Jepthah, or a little before his time, they engaged in a war with the Israelites. They invaded the land with a view of conquering the tribes of Judah, Benjamin and Ephraim. They were resisted by Israel dwelling in that part of the land, and Jepthah was chosen as their General. Jepthah engaged with and conquered them, with a very great slaughter.

They recovered somewhat from this conquest by Jepthah, and in the days of Saul, they were in battle again with Israel and were conquered. In the days of David they were conquered again. Jehoshaphat routed them during his reign, and Uzziah, King of Judah, entirely overthrew them, and made them tributary to his kingdom. They rebelled in the days of Jotham, but were reduced to the necessity of purchasing peace at very dear rates, viz: "And the children of Ammon gave him the same year a hundred talents of silver, and ten thousand measures of wheat, and ten thousand of barley."

They continued to be enemies of the Jews even after the Babylonian captivity. But at length their animosities ended. The Jews destroyed their city Jasher, and the neighboring towns. They plundered the cities and towns, destroyed the men, and carried the women and children into captivity.

The prophecies regarding Ammon have been fulfilled. "The Ammonites shall not be remembered among the nations"—though they continued a distinct people until the second century of the Christian Era.

AMNON—[Am′-non,] *faithful and true, foster father.*

AMNON was the eldest son of David by Ahinoam, his second wife. He defiled his half-sister, Tamar, who was the daughter of Maachah and the sister of Absalom. This so enraged Absalom that he sought to slay him; and at length an opportunity was offered him. Two years after this wicked act of Amnon, Absalom had a feast to which he invited all the king's sons. He laid his plot, and at the appointed time in the feast, "when Amnon's heart was merry with wine," he gave his order to his servants to kill Amnon, and his order was obeyed.

Thus died one who might have filled the throne of Israel, by the hands of his brother, with a foul stain upon his character of defiling an innocent one. 2d Sam. xiii.

AMON, 1—[Ay′-mon,] *faithful, true.*

AMON, the first one of this name we notice, was a governor of Samaria, whom Ahab, the king of Israel, ordered to imprison the prophet Micaiah because he had not prophesied to please him. He ordered Amon to put Micaiah in prison and "feed him with bread of affliction and with water of affliction" until he returned safe from the war. 1st Kings, xxii: 26, 27.

AMON, 2—*Faithful, true.*

AMON was the son of Manasseh, by Meshullemeth, the daughter of Haruz. He was the fourteenth king of Judah, and began his reign in the 23d year of his age, and reigned two years. He was a very wicked king, for he walked in the way his father had walked. He was, like Manasseh, an idolater; but unlike him in that he did not repent at any time of his wickedness, but went on as a monster in sin, growing worse and worse, until finally his servants murdered him in his own house.

What was the occasion of this act of his servants we do not know. It was not approved by the populace, as is evident from the fact that they rose up and slew the murderers of Amon.

This king, like several other kings that were idolaters and the successors of idolaters, had a short reign, and was brought to an untimely end. It has been said, by Jewish writers, that the sons of Jewish kings, who became idolaters, hardly ever reigned more than two years. This was the fact as to the son of Jeroboam; also Elah, the son of Baasha, and Joram, the son of Ahab.

Amon, after his murder, was buried in the garden of Uzza, supposed to be a family burying ground. 2d Kings, xxi: 2d Chron. xxxiii.

AMON, 3, OR AMI—*Faithful, true.*

AMON, or AMI, was a noted man among the returned captives from Babylon. He is referred to in Ezra, ii: 57, and in Neh. vii: 59. His descendants are referred to there in the transcript of the register of those who had come out of Babylon with Zerubbabel.

AMOS—[A′moz,] *loading, weighty.*

AMOS was one of the twelve lesser prophets. In his youth he was a herdsman of Tekoa which was a small town in the land of Judah, a few leagues south of Jerusalem.

He is supposed to have been born within the territories of the kingdom of Israel, but retired to this little town to dwell in privacy—for his mouth had been closed up by the wicked idolaters of Israel. He was sent to them as a reformer and boldly declared the word of the Lord regarding the kingdoms of Israel and Judah.

He spake against the crying sins of the Israelites—openly charging them with the idolatry of the calves at Bethel—he accuses them of oppression, wantonness and obstinacy. He also accuses Judah of carnal security, sensuality and injustice. He declares the threatenings of Jehovah, and prophesies not only the captivity but the utter ruin of those nations.

His prophecies were given in the time of Uzziah, king of Judah, and Jeroboam the son of Joash, king of Israel.

Amaziah was the high priest at Bethel, and the one that expelled Amos as a prophet. He brought an accusation against him before Jeroboam the king, to this effect. "Amos hath conspired against them in the midst of the house of Israel, the land is not able to bear all his words—for this Amos saith Jeroboam shall die by the sword, and Israel shall be led away captive out of their own land." Amaziah said therefore unto Amos, "O thou seer, go, flee thee away into the land of Judah, and there eat bread and prophesy there, but prophesy not again any more at Bethel for it is the kings chapel and it is the kings court."

Amos gave Amaziah an answer to this address and expulsion from Bethel, in which he declared what the Lord had given him to say.

Some writers have supposed the prophecies of Amos to be wanting in that sublimity and naturalness of expression that other prophets have, but no one can read the book without admiring the imagery he has taken from the scenes around him, and his descriptions of some of them are as eloquent passages as can be found in any of the sacred writings.

The time and manner of his death are not known.—[See Book of Amos.]

AMOZ—[A′moz,] *strong, robust.*

AMOZ, it is supposed, was the son of King Joash and the brother of Amaziah, but of this we cannot be certain, but we know he was the father of Isaiah. Isa. i: 1.

AMRAM — [Am′ram,] *an exalted people, handfuls of corn.*

AMRAM was the husband of Jochebed and the father of the illustrious joint-leaders of Israel, Aaron, Miriam and Moses. He was probably a noted man in the nation, and a devoted servant of the God of his fathers. The Almighty saw fit to select from his family the emancipator of the downtrodden and oppressed race. When Moses was born he was associated with Jochebed the mother in concealing the infant. And in planning for the future of the child. He made and prepared the frail craft in which Moses was placed, committed it to the river Nile, and when Moses was rescued by Pharoah's daughter, and placed in his family to be nursed, he caressed him as his own son, and was satisfied that a glorious future was before him. He died in Egypt at the age of one hundred and thirty-seven years. Ex. vi: 20.

AMRAPHEL—[Am′ra-fel,] *one that speaks of hidden things or of ruin.*

AMRAPHEL was the king of Shinar and was one of the confederates who made war with the Kings of Sodom Gomorrah, Admah, Zeboim and Zoar, Gen. xiv: 1. He with others joined with him conquered the country, and they took Lot and his family prisoners at Sodom. Abraham pursued after them and overtook them and recaptured Lot. [See Chederlaomer.]

AMZI—[Am′zi,[ *strong, mighty.*

There are two persons of this name though there is no history of either recorded. One in 1st Chron. vi: 46. This name occurs in the genealogy of the priests and Levites. He was a descendant of Levi and the sixth from Merari, Levi's son. In Neh. xi: 12. Amzi is numbered with the priests, or at least Adaiah a descendant of Amzi with two hundred and forty-two of his brethren assisted in doing the work of the house of the Lord in Jerusalem.

ANAH—[Ay′-nah,] *one who answers or sings, poor, afflicted.*

ANAH was a Duke of Mt. Seir the son of Zibeon the Horite, and the father of Aholibamah the wife of Esau. In Gen. xxxvi: 24, Anah is said to have found the mules in the wilderness as he fed the asses of Zibeon, his father. This may allude to the statute presented in Leviticus xix: 19. "Thou shalt not let thy cattle gender with a diverse kind," as violated in the existence of these animals.

ANAK—[Ay′-nak,] *a collar, an ornament.*

ANAK was the son of Arbah and the chief of the Anakins who were gigantic. At the time Joshua entered and conquered Canaan, they were considerable as to number, and they dwelt in Hebron, Debir, Anab and other places in that part of the land. Some of them had their dwellings in the mountains of Judah and Israel. But Joshua cut them off until there were none of them left in the land save in Gazar, Gath and Ashdod. Jos. xi: 21, 22. When Moses sent the spies out to view the promised land, ten of them who were unbelieving, when they saw the extraordinary stature, and probably the fierce looks of these children of Anak, were alarmed, and when they made their report to Moses and Israel it was: "The land through which we have gone to search it, is a land that eateth up the inhabitants thereof, and all the people that we saw in it are men of a great stature. And there we saw the giants the sons of Anak, which come of the giants, and we were in our own sight as grasshoppers, and so we were in their sight." Num. xiii: 33.

The sons of Anak were Sheshai, Ahimam and Talmai.

ANAMIM—[Ana-mim.]

ANAMIM was the second son of Mizraim. Gen. x: 13. He was then a descendant of Ham, and his posterity are supposed to have peopled a part of Africa.

ANAN—[A′nan,] *a cloud, a prophecy.*

ANAN was an important personage. He was one of the heads of the people after the return from Babylon, and signed the covenant with Nehemiah. Neh. x: 26.

ANANI—[An-a′ni.]

ANANI was the seventh son of Elioenai, and was descended through Zerubbabel from the royal line of Judah. 1st Chron. iii: 24.

ANANIAH—[An-a-ni′ah.]

ANANIAH was, it is supposed, a priest and the ancestor of Azariah, who assisted Nehemiah in rebuilding the city walls. Neh. iii: 23.

ANANIAS, 1—[An-a-ni′-as,] *the cloud of the Lord.*

There was an Ananias, with his wife Saphira, among the first converts to Christianity in Jerusalem.

The gospel of Christ was to be preached in all nations, beginning at Jerusalem. Among these Christians at Jerusalem there was a temporary regulation that all the converts were to have all things in common. Their estates were to be given in to a common treasury. Ananias sold his estate, but reserved a part of the money to himself. He came to the apostle with a lie in his heart, on his lips, and in his act. The act he performed of handing over to Peter the money, was a lie, for he thereby said: "This is the amount I received for my property." Having the lie in his heart, and having gone so far in developing it, he was prepared to go further. He stood before the apostle, though he knew that he, with his brother apostles, was qualified, by the Holy Ghost, to discern secrets, and affirmed that he had brought the whole price. Peter rebuked him sharply for his wickedness in telling the lie.

He might lawfully have kept the whole, but here he stands before Peter, declaring that he was devoting all to the service of Christ when he was retaining a part to himself. Peter charged him with having "lied unto God;" and hardly had the charge fallen upon his ear until the arrow of the Almighty's vengeance pierced him. He fell down dead at the apostle's feet.

What a solemn scene for Peter and his brethren to witness! and oh, what a terrible lesson to the membership of the infant Jerusalem church. But the terrible scene is not yet all given. The dissimulation on the part of the fallen was by and with the consent of Sapphira, his wife. About three hours after, she came in, not knowing what had been done. Peter asked her the question: "Did ye sell the land for so much?" She answered yes. Then Peter informed her of the fate of her husband, and, probably in the same sentence, that her doom, too, was sealed. "Behold, the feet of them that have buried thy husband are at the door, and shall carry thee out." She died, stricken of God in vengeance, and was buried beside her husband. Together they embraced religion; together they yielded to the temptation to retain a part of the purchase money; and so sinned. They died within three hours of each other, and are buried by each other's side; and together the immortal spirits stand in the presence of the God unto whom they lied. Acts, v.

ANANIAS, 2—*The cloud of the Lord.*

ANANIAS, the disciple of Christ, who lived at Damascus at the time that Saul was persecuting Christians, is supposed to have been one of the seventy sent forth to preach.

He was a preacher at Damascus, and when Saul of Tarsus was a penitant sinner at the house of Judas, on the street which is called strait, he was in the bounds of the pastoral charge of Ananias. That being the case, it is no wonder that God selected him as the instructor of this penitent. He was directed in a vision to go to this house and enquire for Saul of Tarsus. He was also informed in the vision that Saul was praying; but he was also informed that the praying Saul was favored by a vision in which he had seen a man named Ananias coming in and ministering to him.

Ananias begged to be excused, for he had heard of Saul as a great persecutor of Christians, and, moreover, had heard that Saul had recently obtained from Jerusalem authority to imprison all the Christians he could find in Damascus, and that was the errand on which he had come to the city now. The Lord then assured him that he was in no danger at all, for, whatever he was before, he was now a penitent. "Behold, he prayeth," and, more than that, he had also chosen him to be a preacher of the gospel. He had selected him to proclaim the glad tidings of salvation to the Gentile world. He had chosen him to stand before kings and earthly rulers, and be a sufferer for Christ's sake.

Encouraged by these facts, made known to him in vision, he went out from his home in search of Saul, and he found him at the designated place in the condition described—blind and praying. The faith of Ananias increased as he looked on the penitent, and heard his moans, and, approaching him with all the fond feelings of a devoted minister of Christ, he said: "Brother Saul, the Lord, even Jesus that appeared unto thee in the way as thou camest, hath sent me, that thou mightest receive thy sight and be filled with the Holy Ghost."

Saul experienced the desired change and at once took upon himself the name of a Christian by submitting to holy baptism at the hands of Ananias. Acts, ix: 1–8.

ANANIAS, 3—[An-a-ni′as,] *the cloud of the Lord.*

ANANIAS, the highpriest of the Jews, was the son of Nebedeus. He succeeded Joseph to this office about 47 A. D. Quadratus, the Roman governor of Syria, having quelled some disturbances raised by the Jews and Samaritans, sent Ananias to Rome, to answer for his conduct before the Emperor. The high priest cleared himself to the satisfaction of Claudius, and was returned home.

Several years after this, Paul was apprehended and brought before Ananias to be judged. The Apostle, in a very discreet manner, began his defense. He had not proceeded far until the high priest, in a furious manner, ordered those that were near him to smite him on the mouth. Paul not knowing him who had given this order to be the high priest, or else not acknowledging him as such, replied to him in a very cutting manner: "God shall smite thee, thou whited wall," that is to say, thou hypocritical person—God shall judge thee and punish thee, for sittest thou to judge me after the law, and commandest me to be smitten contrary to the law.

Ananias continued to be an inveterate hater of the Apostle Paul. He was ready to accuse him before Felix. With a number of others, he encouraged assassins to murder Paul secretly. But Paul's sister's son became acquainted with their plot, and informed him. Then, under his direction, the young man informed the chief captain, and so thwarted the designs of the murderers, for Paul was sent to Cesarea in the charge of two hundred soldiers. Ananias followed him that he might prosecute him with the assistance of the orator Tertullus. But Paul's appeal to Cesar put off the matter, and changed the place of trial to Rome.

Ananias was smitten of God with severe trials, one of which was his own son Eleazer headed a party of mutineers against the temple and worship, and against him as his own father, pulling down his house and bringing upon them the reproach of rebellious sons. Acts xxiii: 1-5, xxiv: 1.

ANATH—[A′nath.]

ANATH is referred to in Judges iii: 31, as the father of Shamgar, one of the judges of Israel. Whether he was a noted man in Israel or not, his son was, for he slew six hundred men with an ox-goad.

ANATHOTH—[An′-a-thoth,] *answer, affliction.*

We have an account of this personage in 1st Chron. vi: 60, and vii: 8, from which we learn that he belonged to the tribe of Benjamin, and was the son of Becher. It is likely he gave the name to the city of Anathoth. This was a city about three miles north of Jerusalem, which was given by the tribe of Benjamin to the priests.

ANDREW—[An′-drew,] *a stout and strong man.*

ANDREW was one of the apostles of

Jesus Christ. He was a native of Bethsaida, and the brother of the illustrious Peter, for whom, we may judge, he had the fondest feelings, for when, as a disciple of John the Baptist, Christ was pointed out to him as the Messiah, and he was satisfied that Jesus was "the Lamb of God that taketh away the sins of the world," he went at once in search of his "own brother Simon," and gave him the glorious news. He took Simon with him and introduced him, and the two together believed on Jesus. They went with him to the marriage at Cana, in Galilee, and beheld the astounding miracle that was performed there, of turning water into wine. After this they returned home and continued their occupation as fishers, little thinking of the honor and trials before them in life. They were to be called by Christ as witnesses of his miracles, sharers in his privations and sorrows, and after his work was finished they were to be teachers of the living truths he had established—ambassadors for him in extending his kingdom.

Only a few months elapsed after the marriage at Cana until they were called together to leave their ships and nets and become regular attendants of Christ. They left all and followed the Master, under the promise, "I will make you fishers of men."

Andrew was a constant attendant on the Savior, and a witness of his miracles attesting the glory of his character. He received the evidence of Christ's resurrection from the dead, given by Mary Magdalene, his brother Simon, Cleopas, and his fellow-travelers, and he saw him and heard his voice when he said, "Peace be unto you." He was present at Olivet on the ascension morning, and in company with the others received the Savior's blessing.

We are informed by tradition that Andrew preached the Gospel in Scythia and the neighboring countries in the apostolic age. According to an eminent church historian, Eusebius, he came to Patria, in Achia, and made an attempt to convince the Governor of the truth of the christian religion, and lead him to embrace it. That wicked officer became angry and ordered that Andrew be punished by scourging, and then by crucifixion; which order was executed, and his body, it is said, was burned by Maxamilla, a lady of great wealth and quality. John i: 40; xii: 22, and Math. iv: 18.

ANER—[Ay′-ner,] *answer, strong, affliction.*

Aner was a Canaanitish prince, who in company with Eschol and Aner, helped Abraham in his pursuit and conquest of Chedorlaomer and his allies. Gen. xiv: 13–24. From the account given there we learn that he and his associate princes did not follow the example of the generous Abraham, but they took unto themselves a share of the spoils which had been recovered. They took it, however, under the approbation of Abraham, for he said, "let them take their portion."

ANNA—[An′na,] *gracious, merciful.*

Anna was a prophetess, of whom we have an account in Luke ii: 36, 37, and in that account we learn that she was a widow of eighty-four years of age. After her husband died, with whom she had lived seven years, she devoted herself fully to the service of God. She was a constant attendant upon the temple morning and evening service; as the sacrifices were offered up in the service she poured out her soul to God in earnest prayer. She was familiar with the prophecies regarding the coming Savior, and exercised faith in him as the antitype of bloody sacrifices. On the memorable morning that Mary presented the child Jesus in the temple to offer the customary sacrifice of all Jewish women at the end of the days of her purification, Anna was there, and when she saw the venerable Simon with the child in his arms and beheld his countenance lighted up with joy, and heard him in rapturous strains exclaim, "Lord now lettest thou thy servant depart in peace, for mine eyes have seen thy salvation," she caught the holy excitement of the occasion and gave her testimony. "She gave thanks likewise unto the Lord, and spake of him to all them that looked for redemption in Jerusalem." Inspired of God she commended the beautiful babe as the promised Messiah.

Nothing further is known of this woman save that she was the daughter of Phanuel, and of the tribe of Asher.

ANNAS—[An′nas,] *one that answers, that afflicts.*

ANNAS was the father-in-law of Caiphas, a Jewish high priest, who was himself in the office eleven years.

When Christ was apprehended by the mob into whose hands Judas betrayed him, they took him to the house of Annas to be judged, and sent him bound to Caiphas. He is said by Josephus the Jewish historian, to be honored in one particular more than any other man had ever been, viz., in having five sons to succeed him in the office of high priest. It is supposed that he was the high priest at the time Christ was apprehended, and that Caiphas was serving under him as a deputy. But be that as it may he was a hater of Christ and a malicious persecutor of the apostles, on account of their preaching Christ and the doctrines of his Gospel.

We have an account in the 4th chapter of the Acts, of persecution that followed the curing of the lame man at the gate of the temple called Beautiful. Annas the high priest, associated with his son-in-law and with John and Alexander and others of the priesthood line, were the principal movers in the persecution. John xviii: 13.

ANTIPAS—[An′ti-pas,] *against all.*

There is supposed to have been a faithful servant of Christ of this name at Pergamos, a city of Troas. The church of this name was one of the seven churches of Asia which had become very considerably corrupted by the Nicolaitans, for which the church was sharply reproved by St. John, and charged to repent. Rev. ii: 14, 16. Antipas is supposed to have been bishop of this church, and to have suffered martyrdom there. In Rev. ii: 13, he is said to have been slain there as a martyr. The language of the revelation is such as to leave it without doubt that there was such a person as Antipas at Pergamos, and that he sealed his faith with his blood. He was a faithful witness for Jesus, and it is somewhat strange that ecclesiastical history gives no further account of him.

ANTOTHIJAH—[An-to-thi′-jah.]

ANTOTHIJAH was a Benjamite, and one of the sons of Jeroham. 1st Chron. viii: 24.

ANUB—[A′nub.]

ANUB was a son of Coz and a descendant of Judah, through Ashur, the father of Tekoe. 1st Chron. iv: 8.

APELLES—[A-pel′-lees,] *to exclude, to separate.*

APELLES was a christian who is saluted by Paul in Rom. xvi. He is thought by some to have been Bishop of the Church at Smyrna.

APHIAH—[A-fi′-ah.]

APHIAH was one of the forefathers of King Saul. 1st Sam. ix: 1.

APHSES—[Af′-sez,]

APHSES was one of the priests appointed by David, when he divided them into thirty-four orders or courses. Hislot was the eighteenth. 1st Chron. xxiv: 15.

APPAIM—[Ap-pa′-im.]

APPAIM was the son of Nadab, and was descended from Jerahmeel, the founder of an important family of the tribe of Judah. 1st Chron. ii: 30.

APOLLOS—[A-pol′los,] *one that destroys and lays waste.*

APOLLOS was noted for his eloquence. He is brought to our view at Ephesus, as a disciple of John the Baptist. In the 18th chap. of Acts, 24th verse, he is said to have been "a Jew born at Alexandria, an eloquent man and mighty in the Scriptures." He had been baptized with the baptism of John and came to Ephesus at this time to preach the doctrines that John had preached. He was well versed in the Jewish Scriptures, and accustomed to instruct the people in "the way of the Lord," with all the earnestness of his soul and the *fervency* and *fire* of his nature, he preached. He entered into the synaagogue and spake boldly. He acknowledged in the presence of Christ's disciples, himself also as a disciple of Christ. He claimed that he who had been crucified was the Messiah, for whom John, his master, was the forerunner. But Apollos was ignorant of the higher doctrines of the Gospel, and exhibited that ignorance in his teaching—which when Aquila and Priscilla perceived, "they took him unto them" and taught him the way of God more fully. Acts xviii: 26. We may judge that Apollos had some acquaintance with the doctrines of Christ, and his views so far as they went regarding the gospel of Christ were correct. He believed that Jesus was that prophet that should come into the world, and with that important truth, all others that John's ministry taught. These two disciples of Christ named, who were tent makers, living at Ephesus—heard Apollos preach, and no doubt were benefitted by his preaching. They saw that he possessed excellent gifts for public service, and they encouraged his ministry by attendance upon it. But seeing that his knowledge was defective as to the doctrines of Christianity, beyond those taught by John—they took him to their house to lodge, and in the absence of St. Paul and others competent to teach him, they became his instructors. They "expounded to him the way of God more perfectly."

After Apollos had tarried awhile at Ephesus and labored, and received the instructions that these humble and devoted disciples of Christ gave—he desired to go into Achaia, and the brethren at Ephesus wrote letters of recommendation with which he was received in different places, and he was instrumental in doing much good. He was useful in strengthening new converts and proving from the scriptures, to the Jews, that Jesus of Nazareth was the Messiah.

He was admired as a preacher, and it is supposed that his fine address and pleasing manners tended to produce a schism at Corinth, where Paul had planted a church. 1st Cor. iii: 4, etc. "For while one saith I am of Paul; another I am of Apollos, are ye not carnal; who then is Paul and who is Apollos, etc." From this we may learn that there was contention and discord about their ministers, emulations and strife, quarrels and factions. But this contention and strife among the membership did not interfere with the personal friendship of the two ministers. Paul and Apollos were closely united in the bonds of christian affection; and when Apollos heard that he was at Ephesus he went there and was with Paul when the 1st Epistle to the Corinthians was written, and no doubt endorsed the entire letter, and especially the rebukes that Paul gave them for their carnality, as he is pleased to call it—developed in the divisions among them. Paul expresses in this Epistle the great desire that he had for Apollos to return to Corinth; but he could not induce the eloquent preacher to return then, though at a convenient time he intimated he would go, and it is likely he did afterwards go to Corinth and became the Bishop of the church there. But it was not until after the Epistle of Paul had been received and produced a salutary effect upon the church.

AQUILA—[Ak′-quil-ah,] *an eagle.*
AQUILA was a Jew, born in Pontus, in Asia Minor. He, with his wife Priscilla, was early converted to Christianity. By some it is supposed he was converted by Peter's pentecostal sermon. If so, he had been about twenty years a professor of Christ's religion when the young and eloquent preacher Apollos went to Ephesus to preach. With so many years of christian experience we may safely judge that Aquila, with his wife Priscilla, were qualified to instruct him "in the way of God." Acts xviii: 24, 35. By others it is supposed that Paul was the instrument, in God's hands, in their conversion. In either case they had been for years in the service of Christ and were competent to teach.

Aquila, with his wife, lived at Rome, and followed the occupation of making leathern tents for the Roman troops. Acts xviii: 2, 3. But they were banished with all other Jews from Rome, by the edict of Claudius, and on being obliged to leave Rome they returned to Corinth. While they were residing at Corinth Paul lodged with them and worked with them at their business of tent making. Paul afterwards left the house of Aquila and took up his abode with Justus. The reason for this change is not fully known. Some suppose that as Aquila was a converted Jew, and Justus a convert from Paganism, the Gentiles desired he should lodge with Justus, he being the apostle to the Gentiles, and it being preferable for them to go to the residence of a converted Gentile rather than to the house of a Jew to hear the apostle preach.

But this change of the apostle as to the place of lodging, did not change the feelings of Aquila towards Paul. He acquiesced in it, and his attachment to the apostle continued. When Paul left Corinth to go to Jerusalem, Aquila and his wife accompanied him as far as Ephesus, and there they exposed their lives to protect him. The apostle left them at Ephesus, in all probability, with a special work to perform in the church, and when they instructed Apollos they were but performing in part that work.

Aquila returned to Rome, and his house was a place for the meeting and devotion of christians. When Paul wrote his epistle to the Romans, he saluted Priscilla and Aquila as his "helpers in Christ Jesus." He refers in that salutation to the fact that they had endangered their own lives for his sake; that he appreciated their kindness, as did all the churches of the Gentiles. Rom. xvi: 3. And Paul greets the church that is in their house. Aquila afterwards returned to Asia and lived in or near Ephesus, and was there when Paul wrote his 2d epistle to Timothy, for the apostle sends a greeting to them. iv: 19. What became of them after this is not known.

ARAD—[A′rad] *a wild ass, a dragon.*

Arad was a Benjamite, the son of Beriah. He is said to have driven out the inhabitants of Gath. 1st Chron. viii: 15.

ARAH, 2.

Arah was the father of a family that become very extensive. There were seven hundred and seventy-five that returned with Zerubbabel from Babylon. One of his descendants was the father-in-law of Tobiah, the Ammonite. Neh. vii: 10.

ARAM—[A′ram,] *magnificence, one that deceives.*

There was an Aram, the fifth son of Shem, hence the grandson of Noah. He was the father of the Aramites, afterwards called Syrians. Gen. x: 22.

There was also another Aram, or Ram, the great-grandson of Judah, and the father of Aminadab referred to in Ruth iv: 19, and 1st Chron. ii: 10. The same person is referred to in the Genealogy of Christ, as given by St. Luke, while tracing the lineage of Mary, his real mother. Luke iii: 33.

ARAN.

Aran was the son of Dishan, and the grandson of Seir the Horite. Gen. xxxvi: 28.

ARAUNAH—[A-raw′nah,] *ark, song, curse.*

Araunah or Ornan the Jebusite, is thought to have been favored by David at the time that he overthrew the city of the Jebusites, and that their friendship existed for a long time. He is brought to our view in connection with the stopping of the plague which was the consequence of David's sin against God in numbering Israel. David was commanded by the Prophet to go up to the threshing-floor of Araunah, the Jebusite, and build an alter there to God, and offer sacrifice. David hastened to the spot and sought an interview with the owner of the threshing floor, on Mt. Moriah, that he might be permitted to follow out the instructions given him at once, that the destructive plague might be stopped. Araunah and his sons had seen the destroying angel as he hovered about the spot, and in terror and affright, they had left the floor and employment there, and hid themselves in a cave or hole, for fear of the destroying angel. But perceiving David, the king of Israel coming, Araunah came out from his hiding place, and ran to meet him, fell at his feet, and asked him what was his desire. David at once gave him to understand the object of his coming, viz: to make a purchase of his threshing-floor, for the erection of an altar, and the offering of sacrifice unto his God, that the destructive pestilence might be stopped. He may also have informed Araunah that God had selected that spot, hallowed by that most intensely interesting scene—the offering up of Isaac by Abraham, his father—as the spot for the temple site. The place where the God of Abraham, Isaac and Jacob was to record his name.

The good man offered no objection, but proposed the threshing-floor as a free gift, and with it, wood and oxen sufficient for the sacrifice.

David, however, would not accept this, for he did not wish to serve the Lord at the expense of Araunah. He would not take possession of the floor until the price was fixed. David gave Araunah fifty shekels of silver for the threshing-floor and the oxen. 2d Sam. xxiv: 24, and he also bought of Araunah the field in which the threshing-floor was, for six hundred shekels of gold. 1st Chron. xxi: 25.

ARBAH—[Ar′-bah,] *the city of the four.*

ARBAH was the progenitor of the Anakins, or the sons of Anak, and their chief city was named Kirjath Arbah in honor of him. Josh. xiv: 15; xv: 13; and xxi: 11.

ARCHELAUS — [Ar-ke′-lay-us,] *the prince of the people.*

ARCHELAUS who reigned in Judea in the room of his father Herod, according to the last will and testament of Herod, was a very cruel man, a monster with governmental authority. It was this that made Joseph and Mary afraid to reside in Judea with the young child Jesus. Matt. ii: 22, 23. "And when he heard that Archelaus did reign in Judea in the room of his father Herod, he was afraid to go thither. Notwithstanding being warned of God in a dream, he turned aside into the parts of Galilee. And he came and dwelt in a city called Nazareth."

Archelaus was a son of Herod the great by Malthace his fifth wife. Herod had murdered three of his sons Alexander, Anstobulus and Antipater, and had taken by a last will the claim of the kingdom from Herod Antipas, while he constituted Archelaus his successor, on condition that the Roman Emperor was willing to it. As his brother Herod Antipas by a former will of the father was heir to the kingdom, they both repaired to the Emperor and put in their claims. Herod on the former will. He insisted on the ratification of that will because it was made when the judgment of the father was sound while the latter will was made when his understanding was unsound. The two brothers pleaded each his cause through able orators, causing some delay, during which time the Jews petitioned the Emperor to lay aside the Herod family as rulers of the Jews and constitute them into a Roman Province, subject to the governor of Syria. Archelaus then pleaded against the people. The Roman Emperor heard the pleadings of the people and also of this aspirant for office, and in a few days afterwards assigned to Archelaus a part of his fathers dominion, made him ethnarch or governor of a province of the people, with the promise of the crown if his conduct was such in his new office as to deserve it. He had but just received his authority when he exercised it rigourously by deposing Joazas the high priest, professing that this high functionary of the church was to blame greatly in the seditions that had been stirred up against him. Having deposed him he made Eleazer his brother high priest in his stead.

When Archelaus had governed about seven years with a great deal of violence and tyranny, he was accused by the Jews and Samaritans jointly to the Emperor who ordered him brought to Rome for trial. He was taken there and the cause heard, the case went against him and he was banished to Vienna where he continued in exile until his death.

Archelaus was a cruel and bloody man. Almost immediately after he had interred his father's remains in royal pomp and closed up the seven days of mourning, he made a feast and ere the ceremonies of that feast were forgotten he ordered his troops to fall upon a mob who were reproaching his father Herod, and they did, killing three thousand of them on the spot.

This unworthiness and cruelty was punished in the way we have noticed.

ARCHIPPUS — [Ar-kip′-pus,] *governor of horses.*

ARCHIPPUS was, we may judge, a preacher of the gospel at Colosse. In Col. iv: 17, the apostle gives him an important charge, *viz:* "Take heed to the ministry which thou hast received of the Lord Jesus, and so fulfill it," from which we may infer that important interests connected with church had been communicated unto him. The members of that church were required to stir him up to diligence and faithfulness in his ministry. Paul also salutes him in his epistle to Philemon, calling him a fellow-soldier.

ARD.

ARD was one of the sons of Benjamin, and is numbered with the family of Jacob when he went down into Egypt. Genesis, xlvi: 21.

ARDON—[Ar′don.]

ARDON was the son of Caleb, by his wife Azulah. 1st Chronicles, ii: 18.

ARE OR ARAH,—[A′rah.]

ARAH, one of the sons of Jether, the head of the family of the Asherites. 1st Chron. vii: 38.

ARELI—[A-re′li,] *the light or vision of God.*

ARELI was one of the sons of Gad, who went down into Egypt with Jacob, and is numbered with his family. Gen. xlvi: 16.

ARETAS, — [A-re′tas,] *one that is agreeable or virtuous.*

There are said to have been many kings of this name. There is, however, but one mentioned in the scripture, and that one is supposed to be the father-in-law of Herod Antipas. He is said to have been very much offended with Herod for divorcing his daughter to make place for Herodias. He seems to have had authority as a king at Damascus, when Paul was being persecuted there, and he joined in the persecution, and kept the gates shut night and day to apprehend him. 2d Cor. xi: 32: "In Damascus the Governor, under Aretas the King, kept the city of the Damascenes, with a garrison, desirous to apprehend me: And through a window, in a basket, was I let down by the wall."

ARGOB—[Ar′-gob] *a turf of earth, curse of the well.*

ARGOB, it is supposed, was a Gileadite officer, who was governor of the city of Argob. He is thought to have been an accomplice of Pekah in the murder of Pekahiah, and Pekah being afraid of him, slew him also with the King. 2d Kings, xv: 25.

ARIDAI—[A-rid′a-i.]

ARIDAI was the ninth son of Haman. Esther, ix: 9.

ARIDATHA—[A-rid′a-thah.]

ARIDATHA was the sixth son of Haman. Esther, ix: 8.

ARIEL—[A′ri-el] *the altar, light, lion of God.*

ARIEL was one of the chief men who directed a caravan under Ezra, when he led the priests back from Babylon to Jerusalem. Ezra, viii: 16.

ARIOCH—[A-ri′-ok,] *long, your drunkenness, your lion.*

There was a king of this name, who was one of Chedorlaomer's allies. Gen. xiv: 1. "Arioch, king of Ellasar."

ARIOCH, 2.

There was also an Arioch captain of the king of Babylon's guard. He is mentioned in Daniel, ii: 14, as being appointed by Nebuchadnezzer to slay all the wise men of Babylon, because they could not tell the king what the dream was that had gone from him and he could not recall it. Daniel stopped Arioch, and charged the king with being hasty in issuing such a decree, and asked him to delay the execution of it. Arioch did delay, and at the request of Daniel, introduced him to the king, and he engaged with Nebuchadnezzar to tell him the dream and the interpretation thereof. Had not Arioch listened to Daniel, and looked upon him with favor, and introduced him to the king, the wise men of Babylon would all have been slain, and Daniel with his three captive companions, would have fallen under the decree, for, according to verse 13, he, with his three fellows, were sought after to be slain.

ARISAI—[A-ris′-a-i.]

ARISAI was the eighth son of Haman. Esther, ix: 9.

ARISTARCHUS—[A-ris-tar′-kus,] *the best prince.*

ARISTARCHUS was a Macedonian, and a native of Thessalonica. The apostle Paul calls him, in his epistle to the Colossians, his fellow prisoner. He was a zealous Christian, and attended the apostle to Ephesus. He was present in the tumult that was raised there by Demetrius, the silversmith, who made silver shrines for the temple of Diana. He shared with Paul in all the dangers and labors of the ministry there, and dwelt with him the two years he spent at Ephesus. In the mob that was raised by the silversmith, he, with Gaius, was caught and borne into the theatre and exposed to the gaze and insultings of the crowd. Acts, xix : 29.

He attended Paul, we are informed, on his return to Greece ; and when the Jews laid wait for him there, he determined to go into Asia. Aristarchus, with several others, attended him. Acts, xx : 4. He afterwards went with the apostle to Rome. Acts, xxvii : 2 ; and, it is supposed that he died there as a martyr—was beheaded along with the apostle. Col. iv : 10.

ARISTOBULUS–[Ar-is-tob′-u-lus,] *a good counselor.*

ARISTOBULUS is one of the disciples saluted by the apostle in closing his epistle to the Romans.

From the fact that his household is mentioned, we suppose him to have been the head of a family, and that other members of the family were disciples.

It is supposed, by some, that Aristobulus was a brother of Barnabas, and one of the seventy that were sent out to preach ; and it is supposed that he preached with a good degree of success in Britton. But facts, regarding the history of this personage, we are without. He may have been away from home, on a tour of preaching, at the time the apostle wrote the epistle which accounts for the phraseology of the salute.

ARMONI—[Ar-mo′-ni.]

ARMONI was the son of Saul by Rizpah, who was slain to appease the wrath of the Gibeonites. 2d Samuel, xxi : 8.

ARNA—[Ar′-na.]

ARNA was one of the forefathers of Ezra.

ARNAN—[Ar-nan′.]

ARNAN was one of the forefathers of Zerubbabel, and is mentioned in his genealogy. 1st Chron. iii : 21.

AROD—[A′-rod.]

AROD was a son of Gad. Numbers, xxvi : 17 ; but he is called Arodi in Gen. xlvi : 16.

ARPHAXAD—[Ar-fax′ad,] *one that heals or releases.*

ARPHAXAD was a son of Shem, born, we are informed by the sacred historian, two years after the flood. Gen. xi : 10. Why the precise date of his birth, counting from the flood, is given, we cannot tell, unless it be that he was in the line of the promised seed of the woman, from Adam to Mary, the daughter of Heli, the mother of our Lord. His name occurs in the genealogy as given by St. Luke iii : 36.

Arphaxad was the grandson of Noah, and lived four hundred and thirty years.

ARTAXERXES—[Ar-tax-erx′es,] *The silence of light.*

ARTAXERXES is the Smerdis who with Cambyses, hindered the rebuilding of the temple. There were none that ruled in Persia, but these two, from the time that Cyrus gave the edict to the Jews to return and rebuild their city, until Darius renewed it. The account of their opposition is given in Ezra iv.

ARTEMAS—[Ar′te-mas,] *whole, sound.*

ARTEMAS seems to have been a noted preacher of the gospel, and Paul intended to send him or Tychicus to Crete, to supply the place of Titus, while that person come to him to Nicapolis on a visit. Titus iii : 12. "When I shall send Artemas unto thee or Tychicus, be diligent to come unto me to Nicapolis, for I have determined there to winter."

ARZA—[Ar′-za.]

ARZA was steward to Elah, the king of Israel, who was assassinated at a banquet, in his house, by Zimri. 1st Kings, xvi : 9.

ASA—[A′sah,] *physician, cure.*

ASA was a king of Judah, the son and successor on the throne of Abijah. He was educated we learn by Maacah a noted idolater, but yet he himself was a good man, and a worshiper of the true God. As soon as his long reign commenced his opposition to idolatry appears—which opposition continued until in a great measure the kingdom was purged. One of the first things he did was to clear Jerusalem of idols, and the effects of idolatry. He even deprived his own mother Maacah of her office and dignity as queen, because she had made an idol in a grove, and he destroyed her idol and burnt it by the brook Kidron.

The first ten years of his reign he seems to have had no war, but applied himself constantly to reform in his kingdom. There was one thing in which, in his works of reform he probably erred, that was in his not destroying some of the high places. He seemed to think it good policy to tolerate some of them, while he aimed one blow after another at the grosser, and for this sparing he is reproached. It is estimated that his judgment was in error in this; but "his heart was perfect." He took the vessels of gold and silver which his father Abijah had vowed to consecrate to God and deposited them in the house of the Lord for use. He fortified various cities, repaired others and encouraged his people, nay more, he commanded them to cease their idolatry and become true worshippers of the true God. The people acquiesced in the kings judgment and with him entered into a solemn "covenant to seek the Lord God of their fathers, with all their heart, and with all their soul," and they agreed that whosoever did not seek the Lord God of Israel should be put to death, whether man, woman or child, if the child had attained an age of accountability and could understand the two parts of the covenant. The first part of the covenant was, we will seek God with all our heart and soul; and the second part was whoever of us does not worship alone the true God shall be put to death. By this we must certainly understand that king Asa and his subjects determined that idolatry should not be tolerated at all—it should be entirely rooted out of the kingdom. But they did not stop even here, for they confirmed the covenant with an oath of sanctity. 2d Chron. xv: 14. "And they sware unto the Lord with a loud voice, and with shouting, and with trumpets, and with cornets. And all Judah rejoiced at the oath, for they had sworn with all their heart."

But Asa had war for we are informed that Zerah, a king of the Ethiopians came up against him with an army of a million, besides three hundred chariots, but he trusting in God went out to meet in this war this numerous host. He was undaunted by their number or their warlike appearance. He set the battle in array in the valley of Zephathah, and then like a true, sensible and pious warrior he implored with earnestness the divine help. The Lord answered his prayer, and soon the forces of the enemy were struck with terror and began to fly, the victorious army pursued them unto Gerar and destroyed very many of them. Having made the victory complete Asa returned with his army to Jerusalem with very much spoil. 2d Chron. xiv: 9.

After this one of the prophets of the Lord met Asa, and gave him a warm exhortation in which he commended him for his fidelity and trust in God, and encouraged him to go on in his work of reformation in Israel. He gathered new courage from his success, and the favor of God enjoyed by him and his kingdom. After this Asa had war with Baasha the king of Israel, as recorded in Chron. 16th chapter. It seems that Baasha came up against Judah, or set himself against Asa by fortifying a certain town on or near the line of the two kingdoms and then preventing the Israelites who desired, and whose duty it was to go to the temple of the Lord at Jerusalem. This was an imposition upon the kingdom of Judah, and a provocation for war. Asa at once procured the services of Benhadad the king of Syria to assist him in punishing this insult and delivering his people from this enemy at Ramah. It is hardly supposable that Asa could have asked this help, if he had not indulged in a degree of distrust of God. After the Lord had given him such a great victory over an army as we have seen, of more than a million fighting men from Ethiopia, he ought to have trusted in God and gone against Baasha himself. In consequence of this distrust of God on the part of Asa, a prophet named Hanani was sent to him to reprove him. The prophet stood before the king and boldly declared to him his fault in procuring help of the Syrians. Strange as it may seem Asa was wroth with God's messenger. Instead of acknowledging his fault, and humbling himself before God—deprecating the divine displeasure and treating God's messenger with deference due to him, he laid his hands upon the prophet and put him in prison, for "he was in a rage with him because of this thing." He added to the sin of treating the servant of God thus — the sin of oppressing some of the people—probably putting them to death, or loading them with irons in prison. How true it is that the commission of one sin prepares the heart for the commission of another sometimes even worse than the former. God could not lightly look at Asa's conduct in this matter. He stood before him condemned. After this Asa was diseased in his feet, by some it is supposed he had a distressing fit of the gout, that was exceedingly severe and protracted until the day of his death. He is reproached again by the spirit of inspiration, that during his protracted lameness he forgot the Lord, he did not apply to him for help but depended entirely on the skill of the physicians he applied to. The affliction in all probability was sent on him directly for his special good, he should have recognized the hand of the Lord in it.

And Asa died, and probably his body was buried with the great quantity of spices and perfumes that had been provided, after which the bones were taken up and buried in the sepulcher which he had prepared for himself in the city of David. 1st Kings xv: 2d Chron. xv: 16.

ASAHEL—[As'-a-el,] *the work or creature of God.*

Asahel was one of the sons of Zeruiah, and a brother of Joab, King David's chief general. Asahel was one of David's thirty heroes; and he is introduced in 2d Samuel, ii: 18, as being remarkably swift on foot. "He was as light of foot as a wild roe." At the battle of Gibeon, which was a battle between the house of Saul and David, Abner, the son of Ner, commanded the soldiery of Ishbosheth, the son of Saul. Asahel and his two brothers commanded the soldiery of David. Abner was beaten and fled, and Asahel ran after him. His object in all probability was to overtake Abner and kill him, and take possession of his armor, and, as a trophy, show it in the camp of David. Abner besought him to stay in his pursuit of him, but he would not. He bade him lay hold of one of the young men and take his armor; but no, Asahel desired to kill the commander and display his armor to Joab and Abishai. Abner assured him that he would thrust him through with his sword, if he did not stay his pursuit of him. He obstinately pursued until Abner turned him round and thrust him through with his spear. He knew he must kill Asahel or be killed by him.

Joab afterward resented the murder by treacherously killing Abner when he was about to transfer the interests of the house of Saul to David and have him acknowledged the king of all Israel. 2d Sam. iii: 26, 27.

Asahel was taken up and buried in the sepulcher of his father at Bethlehem.

ASAIAH, 1—[As-a-i'-ah,] *the Lord hath wrought.*

Asaiah was one of the servants of King Josiah, who was sent with others to consult the prophetess, Huldah, concerning the book of the law which had been found by Hilkiah in the temple. 2d Chron. xxxiv: 20.

ASAIAH, 2—[As-a-i'ah,] *the Lord hath wrought.*

Asaiah was a servant of King Josiah, and sent by him, together with several others, to seek information of Jehovah respecting the book of the law, found by Hilkiah in the temple. 2d Kings, xxii: 12, &c.

ASAPH—[A'saf,] *one that assembles together.*

Asaph was a celebrated musician in the time of David. He was the son of Berechiah, and of the tribe of Levi. His name is attached to several of the Psalms, but it is probable that he was not the author or composer of the Psalms, but the composer of the music, and the chief singer of the

Psalms bearing his name. We suppose him to have been a master musician, and he was set apart solemnly, with several others, for this special service of the sanctuary. 1st Chron. xv: 19: "So the singers, Heman, Asaph and Ethan, were appointed to sound with cymbals of brass."

The family of Asaph gained more celebrity as choristers of David than any others, and they are mentioned with very peculiar marks of prominence later than the days of David. In the days of Jehoshaphat, Jeiel, a Levite of the sons of Asaph, is mentioned as prominent in worship, and one upon whom the spirit of the Lord came in the midst of the congregation. 2d Chron. xx: 14.

Again, in the days of King Hezekiah, the Levites of that family are engaged in singing praises unto the Lord in the use of the words of David and Asaph the seer. And after the Babylonian captivity there were one hundred and forty-eight of the singers of the family of Asaph returned and were enumerated as singers, while those belonging to other families are hardly spoken of. Neh. vii: 44.

When the nation was reorganized, and especially in numbering the tribe of Levi, where those belonged who were vested with sacred functions, Mattaniah, a descendant of Asaph, was placed over the singers and superintended that interesting part of their devotions. The strong probability is that Asaph's family had cultivated a taste for sacred music, and had entered into the spirit of sacred song more than any other family of the Levites.

ASAREEL—[As-a-re'el.]

Asareel was a son of Jehalaleel, whose name appears in the genealogy of Judah. 1st Chron. iv: 16.

ASARELAH—[As-a-re'lah.]

Asarelah was one of the sons of Asaph, and when the lots were cast, and the singers were divided into twenty-four courses, the seventh lot came to him. He is also called Jesharelah. 1st Chron. xxv: 2 and 14.

ASENATH—[As'-e-nath,] *peril, misfortune.*

We know but little of this woman save that she was the daughter of Potipherah and wife of the illustrious Joseph. She was in all probability an amiable woman, and her father an officer in Pharoah's government. She became the mother of Joseph's two sons Ephraim and Manasseh, who were the heads of the eleventh tribe of Israel. Gen. xl: 45.

ASHBEL—[Ash'bel.]

Ashbel was one of the sons of Benjamin, and is reckoned with the grandchildren of Jacob in Gen. xlvi: 21. He was one of the sixty-six that are said to have come out of the loins of Jacob, that came down into Egypt to sojourn, and he was the head of the family in that tribe called the Ashbelites. Num. xxvi: 38.

ASHER—[Ash'er,] *blessedness.*

Asher, one of the sons of the patriarch Jacob, by Zilpah the handmaid of Leah. He was head of one of the powerful tribes of the Hebrews. A very numerous progeny sprung from his sons Jimna, Jessui, and Beriah. There were fifty-three thousand and four hundred that were twenty years old and upwards, and hence able to go out to war, when the sum of Israel was taken in the plains of Moab. Numb. xxvi: 47.

The second year after they went out of Egypt, commanded by Pagiel, the son of Ocran, they were numbered in the wilderness of Sinai, and they numbered forty-one thousand and five hundred. Numb. i: 1–40.

When Moses sent one from each tribe as spies to see the land of Canaan, Sether, the son of Michael, of the tribe of Asher, was sent. After they entered the land of Canaan and it was divided by lot among them, the lot of this tribe of the Hebrews fell in the north-west of Canaan, where the soil was very fertile, and the country was rich with mines. The cities that were apportioned to them numbered twenty-two, in a wealthy part of the country.

The blessing of Moses, just before he yielded up his life and mission, seemed to be realized in the lot they enjoyed. Deut. xxxiii: 24, "And of Asher he said: Let Asher be blessed with children, let him be acceptable to his brethren; and let him dip his foot in oil."

This tribe was one of the six who were present, and echoed amen to the curses that were pronounced from Mt. Elab, as we find in the song of Deborah and Barak.

They assisted Gideon, the conqueror of the Midianites, and we are informed that when David was to be crowned king of Israel, forty thousand of their expert warriors were present and joined in the coronation ceremonies. 1st Chron. xii: 36. They were loyal to David, and afterward to Solomon, for Baanah, the son of Hushai, was their deputy governor under that king, and in the time of Hezekiah, when he was engaged in a reformation in his kingdom, several of the tribe of Asher with others, are represented as humbling themselves, and rallying round the king. 2d Chron. xxx: 11.

ASHKENAZ—[Ash′ke-naz,] *the fire that distills or spreads.*

ASHKENAZ was one of the sons of Gomer and a grandson of Japheth. We know but little about him. It is supposed his descendants became quite numerous, and peopled the north and north-western portion of Asia Minor, answering in later times to Bethynia, one of the portions of country to which the epistle of St. Peter went, as a letter full of christian sympathy to the scattered disciples of Christ, called "strangers." Gen. x: 3; 1st Chron. i: 6.

ASHPENAZ—[Ash′pe-naz.]

ASHPENAZ was the governor of Nebuchadnezzar's eunuchs. We learn from the book of Daniel i: 7, that he changed the names of Daniel and his companions. "Unto whom the prince of the eunuchs gave names, for he gave unto Daniel the name of Belteshazzar, and to Hananiah of Shadrach, and to Mishael of Meshech, and to Azariah of Abednego. These names imported relations to the Chaldean idols. The office he filled must have been an important one, from the account given of the duties of it, and from the responsibility assumed here, of changing the names of the young captives, to names of such importance.

ASHUR—[Ash′ur,] *one that is happy.*

ASHUR was the son of Shem, and hence the grandson of Noah. He gave his name, it is supposed, to Assyria. Ashur first dwelt in the land of Shinar, as we learn from Gen. x: 11. When Nimrod the mighty hunter entered the land as a usurper, he was probably compelled to leave, and with his posterity, took a position higher up in the country toward the source of the river Tigris. It is supposed from the above text, that he built the cities of Nineveh and Rehoboth, also the cities Calah and Resin. Assyria, it is true, is called the land of Nimrod in Micah v: 6, and it is generally supposed that Ninevah, the capitol of Assyria, was named in honor of Ninus, the son of Nimrod, or of Nimrod himself.

But Nimrod may have driven Ashur and his posterity out of that country, as he had out of the land of Shinar.

ASHURIM—[A-shu′rim.]

ASHURIM was the son of Dedan, and the grandson of Abraham, by Keturah. Gen. xxv: 3.

ASHVATH—[Ash′vath,] *making vestments.*

ASHVATH was one of the sons of Japhlet, of the tribe of Asher. 1st Chron. vii: 33.

ASIEL—[As′iel,] *the work of God.*

ASIEL was a Simeonite, whose descendant, Jehu, lived in the reign of Hezekiah. 1st Chron. iv: 35.

ASNAH—[As′nah.]

The descendants of this person were among the Nethinims who returned with Zerubbabel. Ez. ii: 50.

ASNAPPER—[As-nap′per,] *unhappiness, fruitless.*

ASNAPPER was probably a King of Assyria of whom we are informed in Ezra iv: 10, that he sent them under his command into the country of Israel, the home of the ten tribes. He is supposed by some to be the same as Shalmanezer or Eser Haddon. Of this person we may say there is but little known, he may have been the millitary officer who was appointed to escort this people after the captivity release to Judea.

ASSIR, 1—[As′sir,] *prisoner, fettered.*

ASSIR was the son of Jeconiah a King of Judah, and he is referred to in

1st Chron. iii: 17. It was said of Jeconiah the father of Assir, that he should be childless, by this we understand that his sons should not follow him on the throne. The prophet Jeremiah interprets it thus in xxii: 30. "For no man of his seed shall prosper sitting upon the throne of David and ruling any more in Judah.

ASSIR, 2—*Prisoner, fettered.*

ASSIR with Elkanah and Abiasaph was a son of Korah who was the son of Izhar, of the tribe of Levi. These sons of Korah with their descendants were called Korhites. We have an account of their father being associated with Dathan and Abiram in speaking against Moses and Aaron, and the earth opened her mouth and swallowed them up with the women and children of Dathan and Abiram, but for some cause the children of Korah died not, they were not destroyed with the others. Ex. vi: 24; Num. xxvi: 11.

ATAD—[A′tad,] *a thorn.*

ATAD we suppose was a noted Canaanite, and had a threshing floor at Abel Mizraim. His threshing floor is mentioned in Gen. l: 11. To this floor of Atad, they brought the embalmed body of Jacob, and tarried awhile as they made a great mourning. The Egyptians joined Joseph and his brethren in the mourning seven days, and after the funeral procession passed on they named the threshing floor of Atad Abel Mizraim, "the mourning of the Egyptians."

ATAROTH—[At′a-roth,] *crowns, counsel of making full.*

ATAROTH was the wife of Jerahmeel and the mother of Onam. 1st Chron. ii: 26.

ATHAIAH—[Ath-a-i′ah.]

ATHAIAH was a descendant of Pharez the son of Judah, who dwelt at Jerusalem after the return from Babylon. Neh. xi: 4.

ATHALIAH—[Ath-a-li′-ah,] *the time of the Lord.*

ATHALIAH, the wife of Jehoram, king of Judah, was the daughter of Ahab and grand-daughter of Omri. She was a very wicked woman, and exercised a very baneful influence upon her husband, and also upon Ahaziah, her son. She led them to follow the idolatrous course of Ahab, her father. We learn from 2d Kings viii. that Jehoram the husband, and Ahaziah the son, both walked in the idolatrous way of the house of Ahab; and it is more than intimated that the influence of this wicked woman led both the father and the son. Indeed it is said of Ahaziah, 2d Chron. xxii: 4, "Whereupon he did evil in the sight of the Lord like the house of Ahab, for they were his counsellors after the death of his father, to his destruction."

When Athaliah was informed that Jehu had slain her son and many others of the royal line in Judah, she at once assumed the government; and though we might have supposed she would have wept and bewailed greatly the destruction of her son, the King, and the seventy of the seed royal, many of whom we conclude were her grand children, yet on the contrary, with an ambition for the throne and the authority of the kingdom, she proclaimed herself at the head of the Government, and exercised the cruelty of her wicked heart by hunting up and putting to death all the remainder of the royal family she could find, her object being to secure without fail the government to herself. There was but one of all her grand children that escaped her cruelty, and that was the infant Joash, who was carried off by his aunt and hid for six years in some apartment of the temple. 2d Chron. xxii: 12. During the six years that Joash was hid, Athaliah governed the Jews in that kingdom, in which time she promoted the vilest idolatry.

It was during the seventh year of her reign that Jehoiada, the high priest, brought the young prince from his hiding place and showed him in a public assembly, and at once made known to the people his desire to have Joash made king, and the worship of the true God to take the place of the vile idolatry patronized and supported by Athaliah. He engaged the leading men of the Kingdom in the enterprise, and then caused the people to take a solemn oath of fidelity to the cause of Joash, the young king. He engaged, by a solemn covenant, both Joash and the people to serve the Lord. He armed the Levites and other friends of the enterprise and reform, appointed one part of them faithfully to guard the royal person, another part to secure the gates of the sacred courts. Then he brought forth Joash, put the crown upon his head, annointed him with oil and declared him king. The trumpets were sounded and the vast company of people present proclaimed the child Joash their king.

Athaliah heard the noise and became alarmed, and in her fright she ran to the temple to see the cause of the tumult and shouting. To her horror she saw the young king on his throne. "Then Athaliah rent her clothes and cried treason, treason!"

She discovered then for the first the conspiracy against her. She pressed in among the guards of the temple with her cry of treason. Jehoiada the priest gave orders that she be carried out of the courts of the temple and be slain, and if any one dared to take her part, he ordered that he be instantly slain. Thus died this gross idolater and cruel woman of the house of Ahab.

ATHLAI—[Ath′la.]

ATHLAI was one of the sons of Bebai who put away his foreign wife at the exhortation of Ezra. Ez. x: 28.

ATTAI—[At′ta.]

ATTAI was one of the sons of Rehoboam, born of Maachah the daughter of Absalom. 2d Chron. xi: 20.

AUGUSTUS—[Au-gus′tus,] *increased majestic.*

The Augustus Cæsar spoken of in the New Testament, was the second emperor of Rome, or the successor of Julius Cæsar. History informs us that he was a partner with Mark Antony for awhile, but afterwards fought with him and defeated him in the battle of Actium, and assumed sovereignty, or entire control.

As soon as he had established peace and order in his vast empire, he ordered an enrollment of his subjects and a record of the value of their property, the object of which was to ascertain what was the strength of his empire as to population, or, more particularly, what was his strength as to his subjects that were fit for war. But he also wished to know what tax might be reasonably imposed, and hence, what would be the revenue of his empire.

He made, it is said, three such enrollments, one of which was the occasion of the Virgin Mary and Joseph being at Bethlehem at the time Christ was born. Luke, ii: 1–6, "then went out a decree from Cæsar Augustus that all the world should be taxed, &c."

AZALIAH—[Az-a-li′ah.]

AZALIAH was the father of Shaphan the scribe in the reign of Josiah. 2d Kings xxii: 3. 2d Chron. xxxiv: 8.

AZANIAH—[Az′a-ni-ah.]

AZANIAH was the father of Jeshua the Levite, in the time of Nehemiah. Neh. x: 9.

AZARAEL—[Az′a-ra′el.]

AZARAEL was a Levite musician. Neh. xii: 36.

AZAREEL, 1—[Az-a-re′el.]

AZAREEL was a Korhite, who joined David in his retreat at Ziklag. 1st Chron. xii: 6.

AZAREEL, 2.

AZAREEL was a Levite musician of the family of Heman, in the time of David. 1st Chron. xxv: 18.

AZAREEL, 3.

AZAREEL was the son of Jeroham, and prince of the tribe of Dan when David numbered the people. 1st Ch. xxvii: 22.

AZAREEL, 4.

AZAREEL was one of the sons of Bani, who put away his foreign wife at the request of Ezra. Ez. x: 41.

AZAREEL, 5.

AZAREEL was the father of a priest who dwelt at Jerusalem after the return from Babylon. Neh. xi: 13.

AZARIAH 1,—[Az-a-ri′ah,] *assistance, he that hears the Lord.*

Sometimes Ahaziah or Jehoaz is called Azariah. He who was the grandson of Jehoshaphat and the son of Jehoram and Athaliah. He succeeded his father in the twenty second year of his age, and was destroyed by Jehu, the son of Nimshi, who was commissioned of God to destroy the house of

Ahab so grossly idolatrous. [See Ahaziah.]

### AZARIAH 2, OR UZZIAH.

AZARIAH, or UZZIAH, the son of Amaziah, was a king of Judah. He began his reign when sixteen years of age and reigned until he was sixty-seven.

He was a good king and did that which was right in the sight of the Lord; we are informed that he sought God in the days of Zechariah. This Zechariah, whoever he was, from his character, as given, was a good man, wise and true in the interpretation of prophecies. It is more than intimated that he was quite competent to be the instructor of the young king.

The Lord helped Azariah in his wars with the Philistines and Arabians who dwelt in Gur-baal, and others with whom he fought. The Ammonites paid an annual tribute unto him and his government. He had towers built and fortified in the city of Jerusalem for the protection of the city and its interests. He had towers built in the desert, probably for the defense of the flocks, the shepherds and husbandmen, for it is said of him, 2d Chronicles, xxvi: 10 "for he had much cattle, both in the low country and in the plains, husbandmen also, and vine-dressers in the mountains and in Carmel; for he loved husbandry." How significant that last part of the quotation. Every country depends upon its husbandry, and there must be attention to agricultural interests if there is national prosperity. The ruler and his subjects alike are supplied with the products of the field. To love husbandry is honorable in a king, and, moreover, it is a mark of good sense.

Azariah had a host of warriors and he manufactured implements of warfare, such as shields and spears, and engines to shoot arrows and great stones. This is the first instance on record of any warlike engines for the attack of cities, or for the defense of beseiged cities or places, such engines have been used later but this is the first manufacture and use of them mentioned. The Jews were the inventors of such engines, and the invention dates in the reign of Uzziah. No wonder this king's name spread abroad and struck terror into his enemies.

But Azariah was not without faults. He transgressed against the Lord, "In that the high places were not removed, and the people sacrificed and burnt incense still on the high places." 2d Kings, xv: 4. And we are immediately informed that Uzziah took it upon himself to offer incense in the temple, which work belonged entirely to the priests. God was angry and smote the king so that he was a leper until the day of his death. His disease separated him from the people. He died in "a several house."

The reason why God visited Uzziah with this plague, is well told in 2d Chronicles, xxvi: 16. "But when he was strong his heart was lifted up to his destruction, for he transgressed against the Lord his God, and went into the temple of the Lord to burn incense upon the altar of incense." The priests followed him and besought him to desist, but he would not. He became angry at them because of their warning and reproof, and persisted in holding the censer and burning the incense, and while in the very act of transgression, as he stood beside the altar, God marked him with leprosy in the forehead. When the priests observed the leprosy, they took hold of him and thrust him forcibly from the temple. And he himself felt, as he realized the divine anger in it, anxious to get out of the sacred place.

He was compelled because of this affliction, to shut himself up and have the affairs of his government administered by another. And when he died he was not buried in the royal sepulcher, as was the usual custom when kings died, but was buried in the field at some distance, because he was a leper.

What a striking instance in the history of this king have we of the sanctity of the sacred office, and the wicked presumption of one not called of God to enter the office and perform the work.

### AZARIAH, 3—[Az-a-ri′ah,] *assistance, he that hears the Lord.*

AZARIAH was the son of Oded, the prophet, who prophesied in the time of Asa, and gave one of the most stirring exhortations to that king regarding the low state of religion in his kingdom. He assured Asa that happiness for his people was only to be expected in serving God faithfully; and he encouraged the king to proceed in his work of reforming the kingdom. Asa obeyed his admonition, and completed the reformation which he had begun. His kingdom is very greatly strengthened and blessed, and all the people "entered into a solemn covenant with the Lord." 2d Chron. xv.

Of this prophet we know nothing at all, save what is related of him here. His language to Asa is very striking: "The Lord is with you while you be with him; and if ye seek him he will be found of you; but if ye forsake him he will forsake you." Second verse. And it had a good effect upon him, for, as recorded in the 8th verse, "when Asa heard these words of the prophecy of Oded, the prophet, he took courage and put away the abominable idols out of the land of Judah and Benjamin, and out of the cities which he had taken from Mt. Ephraim, and renewed the altar of the Lord."

There is a striking act in the reform of this king, as a consequence of this prophet's teaching, viz: the removing of the queen mother, Maachah, from her position as queen, because she made an idol in a grove.

Azariah, as a prophet, may have been raised up specially for this time and the accomplishment of this important work.

AZAZIAH, 1—[Az-a-zi′ah.]
AZAZIAH was a Levite, who is referred to in 2d Chron. xxxi: 13, as being exceedingly zealous for the law of the Lord, engaged with others in King Hezekiah's reform.

AZAZIAH, 2.
AZAZIAH is referred to in 1st Chron. xxvii: 20, as the father of Hoshea, of the tribe of Ephraim.

AZBUK—[Az′-buk.]
AZBUK was the father of the Nehemiah who was the prince of part of Bethzur. Neh. iii: 16.

AZEL—[A-zel′.]
AZEL was a descendant of Saul. 1st Chron. viii: 37.

AZGAD, 1—[Az-gad,] *a strong army, a gang of robbers.*
AZGAD was one who returned from Babylon with twelve hundred and twenty-two of his brethren, in company with and under the charge of Zerubbabel. Ez. ii: 12.

AZGAD, 2.
AZGAD is referred to in Ezra viii: 12, as the father of Johanan and Hakkatan.

AZIZAH—A-zi′-zah.]
AZIZAH was a man of the family of of Zattu, who had married a foreign wife after the return from Babylon.

AZMAVETH, 1—[Az′ma-veth.]
AZMAVETH was one of David's valiant men, numbered among the thirty-seven. 2d Sam. xxiii: 31.

AZMAVETH, 2.
AZMAVETH was a son of Jehoadah, of the tribe of Benjamin. 1st Chron. viii: 36.

AZMAVETH, 3.
AZMAVETH was the son of Adiel, and he was over the treasuries of King David. 1st Chron. xxvii: 25.

AZOR—[A′zor.]
AZOR was the son of Eliakim, and the father of Sadoc. His name occurs in the geneology of Christ. Math. i: 13.

AZRIEL, 1—[Az′-ri-el.]
AZRIEL was a man of considerable renown, being the head of a house of the half-tribe of Manasseh, beyond Jordan. 1st Chron. v: 24.

AZRIEL, 2.
AZRIEL was a Naphtalite, and an ancestor of Jerimoth, the head of the tribe in the time of David's census. 1st. Chron. xxvii: 19.

AZRIKAM, 1—[Az-ri′-kam.]
AZRIKAM was a descendant of Zerubbabel, and son of Neariah. 1st Chron. iii: 23.

AZRIKAM, 2.
AZRIKAM was the eldest son of Azel, and a descendant of Saul. 1st Chron. viii: 38.

AZRIKAM, 3.
AZRIKAM was a Levite ancestor of Shemaiah, who lived in the time of Nehemiah. Neh. xi: xv.

AZRIKAM, 4.

He was governor of the house of King Ahaz, who was slain by Zichri. 2d Chron. xxviii: 7.

AZUBAH—[Az-u′bah.]

AZUBAH was the first wife of Caleb, the son of Hezron, and she was the mother of Jesher, and Shobab, and Ardon. 1st Chron. ii:18. When she died Caleb took unto him Ephrath to wife.

AZUR, 1—[A′-zur,] *he that assists, is assisted.*

AZUR was a Benjamite of Gideon, the father of Hananiah, the false prophet. Jer. xxviii: 1.

AZUR, 2—*He that assists, is assisted.*

AZUR was the father of Jaazaniah, one of the people against whom Ezekiel was commanded to prophesy. Ezekiel, xi: 1.

AZZAN—[Az′zan.]

AZZAN was the father of Paltiel, of the tribe of Issacher, who, as a prince assisted in dividing the land of Canaan. Num. xxxiv: 26.

AZZUR—[Az′zur.]

AZZUR was one of the heads of the people, who signed the covenant with Nehemiah. Neh. x: 17.

BAAL, 1—[Ba′-al.]

BAAL was a Reubenite, who is referred to, 1st Chron. v: 5. His son, or descendant, Beerah, was captured by the invading army of Assyria, under Tilgath-Pilneser.

BAAL, 2.

BAAL was the son of Jehiel, by his wife, Maachah. He was the father or founder of Gibeon. He is thought to be a kinsman of Saul. 1st Chron. viii: 30; ix: 36.

BAAL, 3.

BAAL was an idol worshiped by eastern nations, under the emblem of an ox or bull. The Moabites were worshipers of this false god; and when Balak, the king of Moab, hired Balaam to curse Israel for him, he took him to the high places of Baal. Num. xxii: 41.

But even the Israelites, after the death of Joshua, went into idolatry and worshiped this false god. We learn from Judges, ii: 13; iii: 7; vi: 25; and also x: 6, that under their judges, Ehud, Gideon, and Jepthah, they worshiped Baal. And so in the days of Samuel, the prophet, they were thus guilty, for he was engaged in abolishing the worship of this idol in Israel. 1st Sam. vii: 4.

Ahab, by marrying Jezebel, introduced idolatry extensively, and the prophet Elijah, after passing through a severe storm of persecution against true worship and true prophets, put the king, the prophets, and worshipers of Baal to shame, at Mt. Carmel. 1st Kings, xviii.

We have an account in 2d Kings, x, of Jehu's conspiring against Baal's priests and prophets. He pretended, after Ahab and Jezebel and their family were destroyed, to have great reverence and regard for Baal, and convened the priests and prophets in the temple. He proposed to be more ardent and faithful as a worshiper of Baal than Ahab had been. When he had collected them all in their temple he put them all to the sword.

Yet Israel relapsed into Baal worship again, under Ahaz and Manasseh, after Jehoiada had cleared the whole country of Judah of it. The good Josiah, in his reformation, reabolished it; but his son encouraged it again. 2d Kings, xvii; xxi; Jeremiah, xix: 5.

BAAL-BERITH—[Ba′-al-be′-rith,] *idol of the covenant.*

BAAL-BERITH was an idol worshiped by the Israelites after the death of Gideon. "They made Baal-berith their god." And at Sechun there was a temple consecrated to this god. Judges, viii: 33. And in this temple there were seventy pieces of silver deposited, which they who had charge of the temple gave to Abimelech, with which he "hired vain and light persons which followed him." Judges, ix: 4.

BAAL-HANAN, 1—Ba′-al-han′-an.]

BAAL-HANAN was the son of Achbar, who succeeded Saul in the kingdom of Edom. He was the seventh king of the Edomites. He is referred to in Gen. xxxvi: 38; and also in 1st Chron. i: 49.

BAAL-HANAN, 2.

BAAL-HANAN, the Gederite, was placed by King David, over the olive trees and sycamore trees in the low plains. 1st Chron. xxvii.: 28.

BAALIS—[Ba′-al-is,] *a rejoicing, proud lord.*

BAALIS was a king of the Ammonites at the time of the destruction of Jerusalem by Nebuchadnezzar. Jer. xl: 14.

BAAL-PEOR—[Ba-al-pe′-or,] *master of the opening.*

BAAL-PEOR was an idol of the Moabites. Numbers, xxv; v. It is also referred to in Psalms, cvi: 28.

BAASEIAH—[Ba-a-si′-ah.]

BAASEIAH was a Gershonite Levite and one of the forefathers of Asaph, the singer. 1st Chron. vi: 40.

BAAL-ZEBUB—[Ba′-al-ze′-bub,] *the master of flies.*

The idol-god of Ekron. In the scriptures he is called prince of the devils, and chief of devils. Matt. xii: 24; Luke xi: 15.

BAAL-ZEPHON—[Ba′-al-ze′-fon,] *the idol of the north, secret.*

BAAL-ZEPHON is supposed to have been an idol-god, and, as such, is referred to in Ex. xiv: 2; probably set at that place to watch the frontiers of Egypt.

BAANA, 1.

BAANA was the son of Ahilud, and was principal officer in Jezreel and the north of the Jordan valley. 1st Kings, iv: 12.

BAANA, 2.

BAANA was the father of Zadok, who assisted in rebuilding the walls of Jerusalem under Nehemiah. Neh. iii: 4.

BAANAH, 1—[Ba-a′nah.]

BAANAH, with his brother Rechab, was a son of Rimmon, of Besroth, of the tribe of Benjamin. They were both officers of the army of King Ishbosheth, Saul's son. They conceived the idea of putting Ishbosheth, their master, to death, and thereby transferring his kingdom and interests to David, supposing that they would be rewarded by David for it.

To accomplish this purpose they entered the palace of the king at midday, while he was sleeping, and murdered him. They then cut off his head and carried it to David that he might see it and feel satisfied that what they reported was true. The son of Saul was surely dead. David, instead of lauding them for this act, and rewarding them as they desired, charged them with murdering an innocent and a righteous man, in his own house and on his own bed. He at once gave the command that they both be slain. They were accordingly put to death, and to give an expression of the king's judgment as to the horrid nature of their crime, he ordered their hands and feet cut off and their bodies to be hanged over the pool in Hebron. 2d Sam. iv.

BAANAH, 2.

BAANAH was a Netophathite, the son of Heleb, and one of David's thirty-seven valiant men. 2d Sam. xxiii: 29.

BAANAH, 3.

BAANAH was the son of Ahilud. He was a noted governor under King Solomon. From 1st Kings, iv: 12, we learn that he had under his rule and authority the cities of Taanach and Megiddo, and all Bethshean, &c.

BAANAH, 4.

BAANAH was also a governor under King Solomon. He was the son of Hushai. He ruled in Asher and in Aloth. 1st Kings, iv: 16.

BAARA—[Ba-a′rah.]

BAARA was one of the wives of Shaharaim who was sent off, or put away, but afterwards remained. Probably she was the same as Hodesh who was the mother of Jobab, Zibia, Mesha, Malcham, Jeuz, Shachia and Mirma. 1st Chron. viii: 8, 9.

BAASHA—[Ba-a′sha.]

BAASHA was a warrior, the commander-in-chief of the army of Nadab, the son of Jeroboam the King of Israel. He treacherously murdered his master and family, and usurped the crown. After he had smitten Nadab, he destroyed his family until there was not one left of the house of Jeroboam thus the prophecy of Ahijah the Shilonite was fulfilled. When Jeroboam's wife disguised herself and waited on Ahijah to enquire of him whether her son should recover of his sickness, he informed Jeroboam through his wife that his family should be exterminated, not one of them should be left. 1st Kings xiv: 11. "Him that dieth of Jeroboam in the city shall the dogs eat; and him that dieth in the field shall the fouls of the air eat for the Lord hath spoken it." This prophetic declaration involved the refusal of an honorable burial. They should not even come to the sepulcher of their fathers. Baasha though a wicked man was made use of to destroy another wicked man and the entire family to which he belonged, viz: the house of Jeroboam. But Baasha was also very wicked in his reign, and provoked the God of Israel so that he determined to take away his posterity also and make his house as the house of Jeroboam. God declared of Baasha, "Him that dieth of Baasha in the city shall the dogs eat; and him that dieth of his in the field shall the fouls of the air eat." After Baasha's reign ended, Elah his son ascended the throne. He fell by the hand of an assassin. Zimri a servant conspired against him while he was "drinking himself drunk" in the house of Arza, his steward. And after Zimri asscended the throne, he destroyed the whole house of Baasha as Baasha had destroyed the house of Nadab and Jeroboam.

It is not difficult to see why it was that God permitted such judgments to fall on this family. Baasha was a very great offender, as was also Elah his son, for they caused the people to sin, and provoked the God of Israel to anger with their idolatries. 1st Kings xv: 15, 16.

BAKBAKKER—[Bak-bak′ker.]

Bakbakker was a Levite, referred to in 1st Chron. ix: 15, and was, probably, a descendant of Asaph.

BAKBUK—[Bak′buk.]

The children of Bakbuk are referred to among the Nethinims who returned from captivity with Zerubbabel. Ezra. ii: 51, and Neh. vii: 53.

BALAAM—[Ba′lam,] *the old age or ancient of the people, without the people.*

Balaam, the son of Beor, was a noted prophet or divine of the city of Pethor, on the river Euphrates. Some have supposed him to be a false prophet and a hypocrite, but in this they are probably mistaken. He had undoubtedly a knowledge of, and worshiped the true God. He had been a true prophet before he was called on by Balak, the king of the Moabites, to curse the Israelites. This is to be inferred from the extensive account recorded in Numbers, xxii, xxiii, and xxiv. Balak understood Balaam to be a prophet of the God of the people he desired to have cursed, and sent unto him by his servants, making the offer of honor and wealth if he would prophesy against them. But Balaam feared God and evidenced that fear in an honest refusal to meet the wish of Balak, as soon as God let him know that the people should not be cursed; Num. xxii: 12, "for they are blessed." When Balak sent his servants again, and pressed him to come to him at once, renewing the offer of honor and wealth, Balaam still refused and made the honorable reply, "If Balak would give me his house full of silver and gold I cannot go beyond the word of the Lord my God, to do less or more." Balaam certainly appears in this history of him at times in a very favorable attitude. Was he a prophet of God? The scriptures expressly call him one, 2d Peter, ii: 15, 16, "following the way of Balaam, the son of Boser, who loved the wages of unrighteousness; but was rebuked for his iniquity, the dumb ass speaking with man's voice, forbade the madness of the prophet." It is reasonable for us to suppose from this language of the apostle that Balaam had once been a good man, and a true prophet, but that he coveted the wealth and honor that the king of Moab proffered him. The Lord answered him when he inquired the second time: "If the men call thee, rise up and go with them, but yet the word that I shall say unto thee, that shalt thou do." The history would seem to say Balaam was covetous, and this seems to be the language of St. Peter. This permission on the part of the Divine Being was enough. Actuated by covetousness, he did not wait for the call. "And Balaam rose up in the morning, and saddled his ass, and went with the princes of Moab." Here was his sin, and God was angry with him, and his angel withstood him. He confessed his sin at once and proffered to give up the enterprise and return, but the angel bade him go on with the men, and take care only to speak the word of the Lord to Balak. When Balaam stood before the king of Moab he exhibited the same firmness and honesty that marked him when talking with the servants. He stands in the presence of Balak probably for the first time in his life, and the interrogatory was presented to him: "Did I not send unto thee to call thee? Wherefore comest thou not unto me? Am I not able indeed to promote thee to honor?" Balaam was undaunted by such questions coming even from the king, Num. xxii: 38. "Lo I am come unto thee, have I now any power at all to say anything; the word that God putteth in my mouth, that shall I speak." That was a noble resolution, and how well did Balaam keep it. Behold him as he stands upon the high places of Baal, with Balak at his side, and views the mighty host of Israel. Balak is listening for a curse from him as his eyes run over the vast company, but no curse is pronounced because God has not cursed.

Balaam orders seven altars erected, and sacrifices, consisting of seven oxen and seven rams, prepared. These were the animals that the Mosaic law required to be offered in sacrifice, and the number of them—seven—showed that Balaam intended to offer a grand sacrifice. A bullock and a ram were offered on each altar. Balaam having made the offering, left the excited king standing by the burnt offering, while he retired to some point a short distance from the altar to hear what the Lord would say; but he gave Balak to understand that whatever the Lord showed him he would tell him. That was in keeping with what he had stated before: "I cannot go beyond the word of the Lord."

God met Balaam upon the high place to which he had retired, and put words in his mouth. As soon as the revelation was received, he went back to the king and his princes, who were standing all excited to hear his message by the burnt sacrifice. Num. xxiii: 7-10: "And he took up his parable and said, Balak, the king of Moab, hath brought me from Aram out of the mountains of the East, saying, Come curse me Jacob, and come defy Israel. How shall I curse, whom God hath not cursed? or how shall I defy, whom God hath not defied? For from the top of the rocks I see him, and from the hills I behold him. Lo! the people shall dwell alone, and shall not be reckoned among the nations. Who can count the dust of Jacob, and the number of the fourth part of Israel? Let me die the death of the righteous, and let my last end be like his."

Balak being much dissatisfied with this parable, and the sentiment so poetical and sublime,—declaring the future prosperity and greatness of the nation of Israel—complained to Balaam that he had not cursed them as he desired him to, but on the contrary had blessed them altogether. No wonder Balak so understood this language, for it is a beautiful and glowing description of the fact that God had determined to bless and defend Israel, and therefore all efforts to injure or destroy them would be in vain. It declares that they should be preserved as a distinct nation, which has been literally fulfilled through a long series of ages.

But Balaam answered the complainings of Balak with the same honesty that had marked him before: "Must I not take heed to speak that which the Lord hath put into my mouth?" Balak then took Balaam to another point where he could see but a part of the vast company of Israel, thinking, probably, that the sight of such an immense camp had intimidated him; and if he saw but the "utmost part of them" he could curse them—or the part of them that he saw; and then he may have thought, if he could succeed in securing a curse for one part, or portion of the company, he might afterward succeed in getting him to curse another part, and finally the whole host of Israel. So Balak brought him to the field of Zophim, to the top of Pisgah, and built him, as at the former place, "seven altars, and offered a bullock and a ram on every altar." The offerings being thus made, as in the former case, Balak awaited the result. Balaam retired from him a short distance to receive the word of the Lord. The Lord met him and put in his mouth another parable. As soon as he received the message he returned to the altars where Balak and his princes were waiting. The excited king, turning to the prophet, said, "What hath the Lord spoken?"

There seems to be an acknowledgment here on the part of Balak that Balaam was under the influence of Jehovah, and further that he could not be induced to say anything that God had not commanded him. But I suppose he hoped there would be a change in the mind of the God of whom the prophet sought counsel, and that he would yet curse the people he had determined to bless. Balaam answers the question put to him in the following parable: "Rise up Balak and hear; hearken unto me, thou son of Zippor; God is not a man that he should lie, neither the son of man, that he should repent; hath he said and shall he not do it? or hath he spoken and shall he not make it good. Behold I have received commandment to bless, and he hath blessed and I cannot reverse it. He hath not beheld iniquity in Jacob, neither hath he seen perverseness in Israel; the Lord his God is with him and the shout of a king is among them, &c."

Balak listened to this parable with much disatisfaction. He saw that his end was not accomplished, that Israel was not cursed and addressing himself to Balaam, he said: "Neither curse them at all, nor bless them at all." But, said Balaam, did I not tell thee, "All that the Lord speaketh that I must do." Balak then took Balaam to the top of Peor, and at his command built him seven altars and prepared him seven bullocks, and seven rams, and offered them in sacrifice. And again Balaam received a revelation from God, for it is said, "the spirit of God came upon him," and under the influence of that spirit, he spoke another parable, full of beautiful imagery couched in poetry. "How goodly are thy tents, O, Jacob, and thy tabernacles, O, Israel! As the valleys, are they spread forth, as gardens by the river side; as the trees of lign-aloes, which the Lord hath planted, and as cedar trees beside the waters," &c. The parable closes up with, "Blessed is he that blesseth thee and cursed is he that curseth thee." This seemed to be more than Balak could endure, he could hardly contain himself while the prophet was announcing it. In a fit of passion he smote his hand together and with earnestness addressing himself to him, he said: "I called thee to curse mine enemies and behold thou hast altogether blessed them these three times." He ordered Balaam back to his home without the honor he had intended to bestow upon him.

The prophet referred him to the declarations he made when first applied to, *viz:* "If Balak would give me his house full of silver and gold, I cannot go beyond the commandment of the Lord." He then assured Balak that he was ready to return after he had delivered him one more message. He delivered that as recorded in Numbers, xxiv: 15-25.

The message is a succession of parables in which are supposed to be prophecies of the Messiah (who is called "a star out of Jacob" and a "scepter out of Israel,") prophecies of the greatness of Israel, their conquest of mighty nations, &c.

After the message was ended the King of Moab and Balaam the prophet parted, the former sought ease for his troubled soul amid the pleasures of his palace, while the other in possession of a consciousness of having dealt faithfully with him who sought and obtained his service.

But it may be supposed that Balaam after he had returned to his home, thought of the honors and wealth that had been proffered him and as in the first place in transgression he coveted, and under the influence of those covetous feelings, he plotted against Israel, he caused the Moabites and Midianites to send their daughters into the camp of the Israelites and induce them to form matrimonial alliances with them, and so draw them away from God and his protection, by forfeiting his favor in indulgence in idolatry and sins such as were common among them. Num. xiii: 16. "Behold these caused the children of Israel, through the counsel of Balaam to commit trespass against the Lord in the matter of Peor." The prophet says referring to this counsel, it was given to Balak the King of Moab by Balaam the son of Beor. Micah vi: 5. Peter refers to the same counsel. 2d Epistle, ii: 16, as does also the apostle Jude 11, "ran greedily after the error of Balaam for reward." The same thing is referred to and expressed by the Revelator ii: 14, "because thou hast there them that hold the doctrine of Balaam who taught Balak to cast a stumbling block before the children of Israel." Balaam afterwards became fully joined with these enemies of Israel, and in a battle that was fought between them and Israel they were conquered—five of their princes were killed in battle, and a great number of the people, and among them was Balaam.

BALADAN—[Bal-a′dan,] *one without rule or judgment, ancient in judgment.*

BALADAN the king of Babylon. We have an account of him in the Isaiah xxxix. He is called Merodach Baladan the son of one of the same name.

Hezekiah the king had been sick, and had recovered of his sickness, and by the decree of the Almighty fifteen years had been added to his life. Baladan sent messengers to him to congratulate him upon his recovery, at least he was so represented by the messengers.

The true object probably was to secure with his presents and expressions of friendship Hezekiah as an ally and friend. He hoped to be able to secure this king as a helper against his enemies if he needed help. Hezekiah treated Baladan's ambassadors with great kindness, received them gladly and made them a feast, during the feast he took them into his palace and showed them all the treasures of Israel. He showed them his armory, the silver and gold, the spices and precious ointment, and all his wealth and it is said by Josephus the Jewish historian that Hezekiah sent presents to Baladan by the ambassadors when they returned.

Isaiah the prophet approached the king and asked him who these men were and from whence they came, Hezekiah informed the prophet, and also how he had treated them. Then the prophet gave him a prediction regarding the Babylon captivity, which prediction was fulfilled. The successor of Baladan brought Israel into captivity.

BALAK—[Ba′lak,] *who lays waste, who laps.*

BALAK, the son of Zippor, and king of Moab, is presented to our view in the history of Balaam. He and his nation were in friendship and league with the Midianites. He saw the growing greatness of Israel and was alarmed for fear he and his kingdom would be destroyed by them. He did not know that the Israelites were not to meddle with the Moabites or Ammonites, or any other people than those belonging to the land of Canaan, which as a land had been promised to Israel as their future possessions. Sihon, king of the Ammonites, and Og, king of Bashan, were to be conquered, but the Moabites had no reason to fear, and other countries than those named, and that God had promised, were not to be molested. The Hebrews were not to meddle with other countries but to be satisfied with the possessions God had promised them. Indeed they were forbidden to go any further. But Balak in his fright looked upon Israel as his enemies, and without any evidence on the part of Israel of feeling or intention against Moab—he began to move—not for a battle, for he had no desire to fight with a people who had obtained such wonderful success in the recent battle with Arad, king of the Canaanites—and over Sihon and Og, kings of the Ammorites and of the country of Bashan. But he consulted with the elders of Midiam as to what should be done. Num. xxii: 3, 4. "And Moab was sore afraid of the people, because they were many, and Moab was distressed because of the children of Israel. And Moab said unto the elders of Midian: "Now shall this company lick up all that are around about us as the ox licketh up the grass of the field." Balaam who lived by the Euphrates was known as a prophet and Balak sent for him to curse Israel; but he received from the prophet the reply that he could not come—for God was not willing that the people should be cursed. A second time Balak sent for him, urging him to come, giving him the promise of wealth and honor, such as a king only could give, if he would come and meet his wishes. Balaam finally obtained permission of God to go provided the messengers called for him—and after the thrilling circumstance of the angel of the Lord withstanding him in the narrow pass—the dumb animal speaking, reproving the "madness of the prophet;" and his eyes being opened to see the threatening messenger standing before him with a drawn sword in his hand — and his confession of his sin—he is permitted to stand in the presence of Balak. Balak tried in vain to secure a curse on Israel. The Lord had blessed them and they could not be cursed. He was very much dissatisfied and sent Balaam away without any honor. He may have been instructed afterwards by Balaam, and followed the instruction by ensnaring Israel, as they were ensnared by the women of other idolatrous countries. (See Baalam.) Num. xxii.

BANI—[Ba'ni.]

BANI the Gadite, was one of David's mighty men. 2d Sam. xxiii: 36.

BARABBAS—[Bar-ab'bas,] *son of the father*, or *of confusion.*

BARABBAS was a notorious robber, guilty of sedition and murder. He had been imprisoned for his felony. When Christ was taken by his enemies and passed through the mock trial, Pilate, the Roman governor, seemed willing, nay more—anxious to release Jesus. Luke xxiii: 17. "For of necessity, he must release one unto them at the feast." But they refused to have Jesus released, and demanded the release of Barabbas. Thus we see the Jewish rulers demanding the release of a notorious villain. This man was not only charged with, but actually guilty of the very crimes that were falsely charged against Jesus, viz: insurrection. Barabbas, in company with some accomplices, had been in an insurrection, and had committed murder. He had actually violated law, the penalty of which was death. Barabbas deserved to die, and yet they begged for his life, while they demanded the death of the Son of God. And not only did the wicked Jews demand the death of Christ, but they would have him die in the most ignominious manner. The Lord Jesus Christ was sentenced to death, "and a murderer was preferred before him." Peter says, in his Pentecost sermon, Acts iii: 14, "But ye denied the Holy one and the just, and desired a murderer to be granted unto you." With clamor you demanded one of the most infamous men and murderers released; and while you asked for the release of the vile wretch Barabbas, you insolently and wickedly killed the Prince of Life. This seems to be the import of the language of the holy preacher.

It is said of Pilate, Luke xxiii: 24, "He gave sentence that it should be as they required. And he released unto them, him that for sedition and murder, was cast into prison." They took off the irons, and led Barabbas, the hardened criminal, out of the prison a free man, to add other crimes to the list that had already blackened his character, and hardened his wicked heart.

BARACHIAS—[Bar-a-ki'as,] *who blesses God.*

BARACHIAS was the father of Zacharias, who is brought to our view in Matt. xxiii: 35, as having been slain between the temple and the altar as a martyr.

There is a diversity of opinion concerning the person of Zacharias, the son of Barachias, and also concerning Barachias himself. It is generally supposed that Jehoiada had two names, one of which was Barachias, and that the Zacharias spoken of above, was his son who was put to death by the orders of Joash between the temple and the altar, the account of whose death and last words we have in 2d Chron. xxiv: 22. "Thus Joash, the king, remembered not the kindness which Jehoiada his father had done to him, but slew his son, and when he died he said, The Lord look upon it and require it."

BARAK—[Ba'rak,] *thunder*, *in vain.*

BARAK, the son of Ahinoam, was selected by the God of Israel, in company with Deborah, to deliver them from the power of Jabin, a mighty king of the Canaanites. Barak received the message from God through this woman, who was a prophetess as well as judge of Israel. He refused to obey the Divine commands unless she would go with him. Judges, iv: 8: "If thou wilt go with me, then I will go; but if thou wilt not go with me, then I will not go." She agreed to go, and Barak assembled ten thousand men prepared and equipped for war, and went to Mt.

Tabor to show himself to the enemy, and let him know that he would contend for the right in deliverance of Israel. Sisera, the general of the army of Jabin, saw him, and immediately began making preparations for a battle. He gathered together his nine hundred iron chariots and men of war, and marched to a place near the river Kishon and set himself in battle-array. Barak saw him, heard his challenge, and at once made ready for the engagement. He was inspirited for the battle by the declaration of the prophetess. As she looked with him from the heights of Tabor upon the enemy, her declaration was, "For this is the day in which the Lord hath delivered Sisera into thy hand. Is not the Lord gone out before thee?" Barak went down from the mountain, and with his army of ten thousand he soon put Sisera and the host of Jabin to flight. There never was a victory more complete than was this for Barak; for every man of the army of Jabin fell upon the edge of a sword. And though Sisera, the general, to save himself, alighted from his chariot and fled for his life on foot, and took refuge in the tent of Jael, the wife of Heber, the Kenite, yet he, too, fell in death; for when wearied and exhausted, he laid him down to sleep, Jael drove a nail through his temples and fastened it into the ground; so he died. She then hailed the pursuing conqueror, Barak, took him into her tent, and showed him the man he was seeking, as he lay in the sleep of death.

It is supposed that Barak was associated with Deborah in the composition of the beautiful hymn of thanksgiving called the Song of Deborah, and that their voices were united in singing it.

The land had peace for forty years after the conquest of Barak.

BARIAH—[Ba-ri′ah.]

Bariah was one of the sons of Shemaiah, a descendant of the royal line of Judah. 1st Chron. iii: 22.

BARJESUS—[Bar-je′-sus,] *son of Jesus.*

Barjesus is supposed to have been a Jewish magician who lived in the island of Crete. He is also called, by the author of the Acts of the Apostle, Elymus, the sorcerer. He was one who falsely pretended to foretell future events. His name is given him probably because he was the son of one whose name was Jesus or Joshua.

Paul and Barnabas found this man with the deputy of the country, Sergius Paulus, who had called for them to hear from them the word of God. From the character of this deputy, as given, and the efforts of the notorious Barjesus to turn him from the faith, we may judge that he was almost, if not quite, a convert. Acts, xiii: 7, describes him as "a prudent man," and one who "desired to hear the word of God." But the false prophet withstood the apostles. He knew that if the doctrines which these apostles taught were received by the deputy he would lose caste, character, and position. His craft was in danger, and he set himself to work to prevent for himself such a calamity. He tried to hinder the effect of their preaching. To prevent Sergius Paulus from embracing their doctrines, he presented crafty and false insinuations; but, as we shall see, he did not succeed.

Paul seeing the drift of the efforts of Barjesus, in strong, nervous, withering language, rebuked him. Paul was under the influence and direction of the inspiring spirit, and said to Elymus: "O, full of all subtlety, and all mischief, thou child of the devil, thou enemy of all righteousness, wilt thou not cease to pervert the right ways of the Lord?" And then the apostle proceeded to declare the displeasure of the Almighty against him: "And now, behold, the hand of the Lord is upon thee, and thou shalt be blind, not seeing the sun for a season."

What a terrible calamity to come upon a man in the act of fighting against God—so blind that he should not see the sun even at noonday! No sooner had the apostle made the declaration than the fulfillment took place. "There fell on him a mist and a darkness, and he went about seeking some one to lead him by the hand." When Sergius Paulus saw this miracle he doubted no longer, but credited the apostles and believed their doctrine.

Many suppose that Barjesus was converted likewise, and that his blindness continued no longer, if, indeed, as long as the blindness of Saul of

Tarsus; and it is thought that the apostle Paul performed the same office for the converted sorcerer that Ananias did for him, when a weeping, praying penitent in Damascus, viz: restored him to sight.

BARJONAH—[Bar-jo′nah,] *son of Jona, or of a dove.*

BARJONAH is a name used to designate Peter. It was used by Christ when Peter answered the important question presented, "But who say *ye* that I am?" His answer was, "thou art the Christ, the son of the living God." Then said the Savior, Matt. xvi: 17, "Blessed art thou Simon Bar-jona, for flesh and blood hath not revealed it unto thee, but my father which is in heaven." The name simply imports that he was the son of Jona or Jonas.

After Andrew, the brother of Peter was converted, he went in search of him, and finding him, he took him to Jesus. As soon as Jesus saw him, he said: "Thou art Simon, the son of Jona." John i: 42. And after the Savior's resurrection, when he would remind Peter of his fall, in denying him three times when he was in the hands of his enemies, and about to be put to death, he called him by this name. John xxi. Three times the Savior said to him, "Simon, son of Jonas, lovest thou me?"

BARNABAS—[Bar′nabas,] *the son of the prophet, or of consolation.*

BARNABAS was one of the disciples of our lord Jesus Christ, and a companion of the apostle Paul for a long while in his labors. He was in Cyprus whither his parents had retired to shun the ravages of the Syrians or Romans, or other enemies of the Jews in Judea. His name before his conversion to christianity was Joses, but after his conversion he was called Barnabas the son of prophecy or of consolation. He was a gifted and affectionate preacher, and did much towards comforting the early believers to whom he ministered the word of life. We have the following account of him in Acts iv: 36, 37. "And Joses who by the apostles was surnamed Barnabas (which is being interpreted the son of consolation) a Levite and of the country of Cyprus, having land, sold it and brought the money and laid it at the apostles feet." He appears then in this introduction to our notice as one of the primitive converts who so generously contributed of their substance for the relief and living of poor believers. He exchanged his land for money, which he placed in the treasury of the infant church.

It is not to be wondered at, that one who made so noble a start should attain a good degree of excellence, and properly merit the title of "son of consolation."

Barnabas is thought to be one of the seventy disciples chosen by Christ. He was acquainted with Saul the student of Gamaliel, and probably was a fellow student with him under that illustrious teacher.

Three years after Paul's conversion he went to Jerusalem and Barnabas introduced him to the other apostles. They were afraid of him, for they had known him as a persecutor and did not believe him a disciple. But Barnabas extended to him a brother's hand, and a brother's welcome. Acts, ix: 27. "But Barnabas took him and brought him to the apostles and declared unto them how he had seen the Lord in the way, and that he had spoken to him, and how he had preached boldly at Damascus in the name of Jesus." On this introduction and testimony of Barnabas, regarding Paul, they admitted him to their communion.

The church at Jerusalem sent Barnabas to Antioch, having heard of the progress of the gospel there. Acts xi: 22. "Then tidings of these things came unto the ears of the church which was in Jerusalem and they sent forth Barnabas that he should go as far as Antioch." He went joyfully and observed the work of God among them, mingled with them in their devotions, ministered the word of life to them, and exhorted them most earnestly to "cleave unto the Lord."

The testimony is given in connection with the account of his labors at Antioch by the spirit of inspiration that "he was a good man, and full of the Holy Ghost, and of faith, and much people were added unto the Lord." What a concise, clear and satisfactory description of the church and success of this eminent disciple of Christ at Antioch! Sometime afterwards he went to Tarsus in search of Paul, found him and brought him to Antioch, and together they labored there, probably two years. They went together to Jerusalem bearing alms for the poor of that church, from their church at Antioch. When they returned to Antioch they took with them John Mark, a cousin of Barnabas. After they had been at home with their church a short time, they were set apart by the church under the direction of the Holy Ghost to labor among the Gentiles.

They went to Cyprus, where they were instrumental in the conversion of the deputy Sergius Paulus, and probably Elymas the sorcerer. They preached successively in Perga, Derbe, and Lystra. In the latter place, Paul cured a man who had been lame from his birth—Eneas. Acts, xiv: 9, 10. The people of Lystra were greatly astonished at the miracle, and began at once to regard them as gods. It is said they called Paul Jupiter, and Barnabas Mercury. The people were so carried away with them that they would have sacrificed to them had they not hindered them; and yet, strange as it may seem, it was but a short time afterwards they were severely persecuted in this very city. But they returned together again to Antioch. Soon there was a call for them to go to Jerusalem because of disputes that had arisen there. The Church at Antioch sent them as her delegates. They were present in the council, and probably did not fully agree concerning a question that agitated that council; for not long after Peter went to Antioch and there countenanced the observance of the Mosaic distinction. Barnabas was in judgment with Peter, but Paul was opposed to them, and reproved them with considerable sharpness and freedom.

Paul and Barnabas separated shortly after this, and traveled to and labored at different points. A difficulty sprung up between them as to the propriety of taking John and Mark. Barnabas was in favor — Paul was opposed. Paul went towards Asia, and Barnabas towards Cyprus.

This is all that is certainly known of this good man. He probably labored on until death came. With his going to Cyprus and taking Mark along with him, the sacred memoir of him closes.

BARSABAS, 1—[Bar′sa-bas,] *son of return, of rest, of swearing.*

Barsabas was surnamed Justus, and is brought to our view in Acts i: 23. When the apostles would have the place of the traitor Judas filled, they made a selection of Barsabas and Matthias, (they were both of them of the seventy,) and then cast lots to see which of the two should be numbered with the apostles. It had been the custom from time immemorial when a doubtful matter was to be settled, and the counsel of those concerned was insufficient to settle it, to ask direction of God. The apostles did so in this case. They prayed: "Thou Lord which knowest the hearts of all men, show whether of these two thou hast chosen, that he may take part of this ministry and apostleship from which Judas by transgression fell, that he might go to his own place." After this prayer for divine direction they cast lots, and the lot fell upon Matthias, and he was numbered with the apostles. We are not to consider that because Barsabas was not chosen he was not a good man and a faithful preacher. They had both developed the christian character and were in honor in the church, but only one of them could be chosen.

This account of Barsabas is all we have. We know nothing of his life after this.

BARSABAS, 2—*Son of return, of rest, of swearing.*

There is one of this name mentioned in Acts xv: 22, whose surname was Judas. He was sent with some other brethren, by the church at Jerusalem, to the church at Antioch. Paul and Baranbas were in the apostolic council as delegates from that church, and when they returned home Barsabas and Silas attended them, bearing a letter from the apostles signifying to the church at Antioch what the council at Jerusalem had decreed. A copy of the letter they were the bearers of is to be found in verses 23 and 24, inclusive, of the above chapter. They delivered the message to the church when they arrived, and after laboring awhile with the brethren, and enjoying their friendly greetings and christian fellowship, they returned to the apostles at Jerusalem.

This is all that we can learn of Barsabas-Judas.

BARTHOLOMEW—[Bar-thol′-o-mew,] *a son that suspends the waters.*

Bartholomew was one of our Lord's twelve apostles. In Matt. x, his name occurs in the list of the twelve sent out by Christ. He is supposed to be the same person who is called Nathaniel of Cana, in Galilee, who is known to have been one of Christ's disciples in the beginning. John the Evangelist never mentions Bartholomew, but does mention Nathaniel, and the other Evangelists never mention Nathaniel. This indicates very strongly that they were the same person. But the character of Nathaniel as given by John, or rather as given by Christ, seems to indicate it. John i: 47. "Behold an Israelite indeed, in whom is no guile." How much this speaks, coming as it does from Christ, for the purity and holiness of the man.

But Nathaniel is mentioned as having come to Jesus in company with Philip, John i: 45, while the other Evangelist mentions Philip and Bartholomew frequently. And there is another circumstance indicating very strongly that they were one and the same person. After Christ's resurrection, he showed himself to his disciples at the sea of Tiberius, and Nathaniel is particularly mentioned: "Simon Peter, Thomas, Nathaniel, of Cana in Galilee, the two sons of Zebedee, and two other disciples." Would he have been thus favored, and no other one of all the disciples, had he not been an apostle?" Bartholomew and Nathaniel, it is quite probable, mean the same person.

It is thought that this apostle propagated the faith of Christ by preaching his gospel in Judea, and in the northern and western parts of Asia, and that he finally met a martyr's fate. His life and labors are not narrated in the New Testament, and hence it is uncertain what was his field of operation, how long he labored, what trials he passed through, and when and under what circumstances he met his end.

BARTIMEUS—[Bar-ti-me′us,] *the the son of Timeus or of the honorable.*

Bartimeus was the son of Timeus, and was a blind man—one of the blind men that Christ restored to sight in the days of his flesh. We have the account of him in Mark x: 46-52. The account is very interesting, and the miracle a striking example of the sympathy and power of Christ.

Bartimeus sat by the highway side begging, with a blind companion, we may gather from Matthew's naraitive, for he says there were two. Bartimeus was probably the most noted of the two, and when he addressed the Savior, spoke for his companion as well as for himself. He heard that Jesus of Nazareth was passing by, and he began to cry out: "Jesus thou son of David have mercy on me." He seemed to be so deeply impressed with a sense of his own affliction, that he cried out earnestly and vehemently, so much so that the people rebuked him and insisted that he should hold his peace, but instead of staying his cries at their requests and commands he cried the louder. Jesus heard his voice, saw the earnestness of his soul and stopped, and ordered them to bring him near to him. They addressed the blind Bartimeus saying: "Be of good comfort, rise he calleth thee." In the joy of his heart he cast aside his garment and rose and went to Jesus. As soon as he came into the presence of Christ he said, "what wilt thou that I should do unto thee?" In the fullness of his earnest heart he answered, "Lord that I might receive my sight." Jesus perceived his faith and gave him sight—natural and spiritual vision was made clear, and he followed his benefactor.

BARUCH, 1—[Ba′ruk] *who is blessed, who bends the knee.*

Baruch was of the tribe of Judah, the son of Neriah and grandson of Maaseiah. He was a brother of Seraiah one of king Zedekiah's courtiers. This shows him to have been of illustrious birth. He was well skilled, Josephus informs us, in the Hebrew tongue, and was left with Jeremiah, the prophet, in Judea, at the time of the Babylonian captivity. He acted as secretary to the prophet Jeremiah, and was with him in the midst of his persecutions and ill-treatment, and he subjected himself to much persecution and sacrifice by his ardent attachment to the prophet. Where the weeping prophet went Baruch went, and he entered into the spirit and feeling that governed Jeremiah. He shared with him his privations and sorrows, the prison and the dungeon, and was sometimes even charged with prompting the prophet to some of his truthful prophecies that the people treated with contempt. Jeremiah, xliii: 3, "But Baruch, the son of Neriah, setteth thee on against us, for to deliver us into the hands of the Chaldeans that they might put us to death, and carry us away captives to Babylon."

When Jeremiah was thrown into prison in the reign of Jehoiakim, and received an order from God to commit to writing the prophecies that had been delivered unto him up to that time he sent for Baruch, his scribe, and he committed them to writing. And after sometime he took the writing of the prophecies to the temple to read in the hearing of the people there. Michaiah was present and heard them read and immediately gave notice to the king's counsellors.

The king's counsellors at once sent for Baruch and ordered him to repeat what he had read. He did so, and as the prophecies contained some dark tidings concerning the fate of the kingdom they asked him how he came in possession of them. They informed him that they were in duty bound to make the king acquainted with the prophecies, and they did. The king sent for it, and had it read in his hearing, at least in part, for before the reading was finished, he became angry and threw it into the fire. Learning how it came into the possession of his counsellors, *viz:* through Jeremiah and Baruch, he ordered them both seized and punished. But in this Jehoiakim was prevented, for the hand of providence shielded them.

Jeremiah dictated the prophecies a second time, and Baruch wrote them with some additional prophecies. He continued the faithful disciple of Jeremiah until that prophet died.

BARUCH 2—*Who is blessed, who bends the knee.*

Baruch was the son of Zabbai who earnestly repaired a portion of the wall of Jerusalem under Nehemiah. Nehemiah, iii: 20.

The same person is referred to in Nehemiah, x: 6, among those who sealed the covenant, and probably he is the same one who is referred to in Nehemiah xi: 5, as the father of Maaseiah.

BARZILLAI, 1—[Bar-zil′la-i,] *made of iron, son of contempt.*

Barzillai was a Simeonite of Meholah, and the father of Adriel, who married Merab, the daughter of King Saul. His relationship to Adriel is given in 2d Sam. xxi: 8. This daughter of King Saul was to have been given to David, but Saul gave her in the stead unto Adriel. 1st Samuel, xviii: 19.

BARZILLAI, 2—*Made of iron, son of contempt.*

Barzillai, the Gileadite, was one of the chief men of the country near Mahanaim, that supplied David with provisions when he was compelled to flee his throne on the rebellion of the unfeeling Absalom. David had passed over Jordan with a small company as body-guards, and stopped at the beautiful city of Mahanaim, and Barzillai, in company with several others, brought "beds, and basins, and earthen vessels, and wheat, and barley, and flour, and parched corn, and beans, and lentiles, and parched pulse, and honey, and butter, and sheep, and cheese of kine, for David and the people that were with him to eat; for they said the people are hungry and thirsty, and weary in the wilderness." 2d Sam. xvii: 28-29.

BARZILLAI, 3—*Made of iron, son of contempt.*

Barzillai was a priest, and was at the head of a number of priests who returned from the Babylonian captivity. He was probably a descendant of the former Barzillai. Neh. vii: 63.

BASHEMATH—[Bash′e-math,] *perfumed, in desolation.*

Bashemath, a wife of Esau, who is called by another name when married to Esau, viz: Mahaleth. She was the mother of Reuel, a son of Esau, and is called by this name in Genesis, xxxvi: 3, 4

**BASMATH**—[Bas′math.]

BASMATH was the daughter of Solomon, and was given by him to be the wife of Ahimaaz, one of the twelve officers appointed over twelve districts to provide victuals for the king's household. 1st Kings, iv: 15.

**BATHSHEBA**—[Bath-she′bah,] *the seventh daughter, the daughter of an oath.*

BATHSHEBA was the wife of an officer of David's army, *i. e.* Uriah the Hittite, and the daughter of Ammiel. She is represented as a very beautiful woman, and the king was captured with her beauty. After Uriah was murdered by David he took her to be his lawful wife. No wonder that the Lord was so displeased with the conduct of the two, for they probably both sinned in the matter that led to the murder of her first husband—that he struck the child of Bathsheba with death, thus deeply afflicting them both. 2d Sam. xi: 3.

Bathsheba bare unto David four other sons, viz: Shimea, Shobab, Nathan and Solomon. This latter son became the successor of David to the throne of Israel. When David was stricken in years, and was no longer able to manage the affairs of his government, but was ministered unto by Abishag, the Shunamite, as a failing invalid, Adonijah, his eldest son, who supposed himself according to Jewish law, the successor of his father, made ready as Absalom formerly had done to be crowned king. Nathan made the fact known unto Bathsheba, and bade her go unto the king and remind him of his promise and oath, that her son Solomon should sit on the throne. She went to David and did as Nathan had bidden her, and according to a previous arrangement made with her, Nathan the prophet came in and backed her plea, and at the same time gave king David information as to the movements of Adonijah. He listened to this recital of facts by Nathan, and commanded that Bathsheba, who had withdrawn from his presence when the prophet came in, be called in again. She came and stood before the king, not to plead for the crowning of her son, for the pleading was over, and the case was decided in the mind of David, but she came in to hear the decision. She stood before the king with a consciousness from his appearance and the favor to her, marked in his features, that her request was granted and about to be expressed. "And the king swore and said: As the Lord liveth that hath redeemed my soul out of all distress, even as I sware unto thee by the Lord God of Israel, saying, assuredly Solomon thy son shall reign after me, and he shall sit upon my throne in my stead; even so will I certainly do this day." Here we have the spell of a nation broken by the expressed will of the king as to who should succeed him, given to this woman. As she left the presence of the king when Nathan came in, so Nathan left when by the king's order she returned. She is now in possession of a fact that there are no witnesses to, unless Abishag the Shunamite is present, who is now the cherishing nurse of David. But it does not long remain thus, for David determined to consummate the matter at once, and he sends for Zadok the priest and Nathan the prophet, and he made known his will in the matter to them, and gave them commandment to assemble his servants and cause Solomon to ride on the king's mule, and bring him down to the place where he is to be crowned king. He ordered that they set him apart by anointing him, then blow the trumpet and announce that Solomon is king, and they did so that day, so that Bathsheba became before night the queen mother.

Soon after David's death, which occurred not long after Solomon was made king, Adonijah came to Bathsheba with a request to the king. He made known the request to her, thinking she would have more influence with Solomon than any other person. The request was that king Solomon would give him Abishag, the Shunamite, to wife.

This was probably the first time that Bathsheba had seen Adonijah since his rebellion, and she may have been somewhat fearful that he had vengeance in his heart against her as the mother of king Solomon, hence she addressed him as he came into her presence with, "Comest thou peaceably." He answered that he did. He then referred her to the fact that he was the eldest son of the departed David, and of right the kingdom belonged to him; that the people had so understood it, and hence were about to make him king, when

David interfered and put her son on the throne in his stead. And he acknowledged that it was from the Lord. He had no controversy on that subject, and no plea to put in for the kingdom. But he had a petition which he prayed her not to deny him. Bathsheba could see no special objections to it, and she promised Adonijah that she would speak to Solomon for him.

And in conformity with her promise, she went to her son with the petition. Solomon received her very cordially, and seated her beside him as he sat on his throne. She then informed him that she had a petition to ask of him, and true to the promise she had made the petitioner, she put it in a very strong form. She endeavored to commit the king to a favorable answer in presenting it, for she thought it a reasonable request. But Solomon did not thus look at the request. He thought he saw in it a plot for dethroning him, and usurping the kingdom, and hence Solomon passed judgment upon him as a traitor and had him executed at once.

Bathsheba, in being the mother of Solomon, was honored, for he was the wisest of men and of kings.

BAZLITH.

The children of Bazlith were among the Nethinims who returned from Babylon with Zerubbabel. Neh. vii: 54.

BEALIAH—[Be-a-li′ah.]

Bealiah, a Benjamite who went over to David when he was at Ziklag. 1st Chron. xii: 5.

BEBAI, 1—[Beb′a-i.]

His sons, to the number of 628, returned from Babylon with Zerubbabel. Neh. vii: 16. And at a later period, twenty-eight of them, under Zechariah, returned with Ezra. Ezra, viii: 11. And we are further informed that four of his family took foreign wives—Ezra, x: 28; and probably one of them sealed the covenant with Nehemiah, for the name occurs there. Neh. x: 15.

BEBAI, 2—[Beb′a-i.]

Bebai was the father of the Zechariah who is referred to above, and was the leader from Babylon of the twenty-eight men. Ezra, viii: 11.

BECHER—[Be′ker.]

Becher was one of the sons of Benjamin, and is numbered with the family of Jacob who went down into Egypt. Gen. xlvi: 21.

BECHORATH—[Be-ko′rath.]

Bechorath was the son of Aphiah, or Abiah, and grandson of Becher. 1st Sam. ix: 1, and 1st Chron. vii: 8.

BEDAD—[Be′dad,] *alone, in friendship.*

Bedad was the father of Hadad, the King of Edom. Gen. xxxvi: 35, and 1st Chron. i: 46.

BEDAN—[Be′dan,] *only, in the judgment.*

There is a person of this name referred to among the worthy judges of Israel, in 1st Sam. xii: 11, where the prophet is reproving Israel for their ingratitude and disobedience, and gives a summary of their history. It is supposed by some that the Bedan mentioned there refers to Barak, who, associated with Deborah, conquered Jabin, the King of Canaan. Others suppose it refers to Samson; and still others think it refers to Jair, who judged Israel twenty-three years. Judges, x: 3.

BEELIADA—[Be-el-i′a-dah.]

Beeliada was the son of David, born unto him in Jerusalem. 1st Chron. xiv: 7. He is also called Eliada. 2d Sam. v: 16.

BEERA—[Be-e′rah.]

Beera was the son of Zophah, of the tribe of Asher. 1st Chron. vii: 37.

BEERAH.

Beerah was a prince of the Reubenites, carried away by Tilgath Pilneser. 1st Chron. v: 6.

BEERI, 1—[Be-e′ri.]

Beeri was the father of Judith, one of the wives of Esau. Gen. xxvi: 34.

BEERI, 2—[Be-e′ri.]

Beeri was the father of the prophet Hosea. Hosea, i: 1.

BEL—*Ancient, nothing, subject to change.*

Bel, the Chaldean idol, Bel or Baal. Some think it was intended to represent

Nimrod, the mighty hunter and the founder of the empire. Others think it was intended to represent Pul, the king of Assyria. We have our account in Isa. xlvi: 1, and Jer. l: 2, and li: 44, of the existence of this idol at the time that Cyrus and Darius took Babylon. The monstrous image was raised and ruined. "Bel boweth down," &c. "Bel is confounded," &c. The image was brought into utter and absolute contempt.

BELA, 1—[Be′-lah.]

BELA was the son of Beor, and a king in the land of Edom, "before there reigned any king over the children of Israel." The city over which Bela reigned was Dinhabah. At his death he was succeeded by Jobab, the son of Zerah, of Bozrah. Gen. xxxvi: 31–33.

BELA, 2—[Be′-lah.]

BELA was of the tribe of Benjamin, and the head of the family in that tribe called Belaites. Num. xxvi: 38.

BELAH—[Be′-lah.]

BELAH was the name of the elder son of Benjamin, and he with his brothers were reckoned with the family of Jacob, as the reckoning is given in Gen. xlvi: 21. It is likely they were born during the seventeen years that Jacob sojourned in Egypt. The names of his brothers were Becher and Ashbel, Gera and Naaman, Ehi and Rosh, Muppim and Huppim, and Ard.

BELSHAZZAR—[Bel shaz′ar,] *master of the treasure.*

BELSHAZZAR was a king of Babylon. He was probably the grandson of the famous Nebuchadnezzar, for it is said in Daniel, v: 18, "O, thou king, the most high God gave Nebuchadnezzar, thy father, a kingdom and majesty, and glory and honor." And he was the last king of Babylon; for in his fall the kingdom was divided, as it was declared in the handwriting upon the wall it should be, and given to the Medes and Persians.

He had the experience of his father, Nebuchadnezzar, in which were some terribly instructive lessons, but he heeded them not. He knew how his father had been humbled by the God of Heaven, in being compelled for seven long years to eat grass like an ox, until his nails were like birds claws, and the hair of his head like eagles' feathers. He feared not God, but indulged in wickedness. He forgot that the God that had leveled his father with the beasts could tarnish his crown, and blast his hopes.

The account of his reign, as the king of Babylon, is not very extensive. During his first year, Daniel had a vision which represented the revolution of governments in the future. And again during the third year, Daniel had visions which set forth the events that were shortly to come to pass in the monarchies of Persia and Greece. By this vision Daniel was prepared for the overthrow of the kingdom; he was led to see that the destruction of Babylon was not very distant. In Dan. v, we have the destruction of Babylon narrated, and the downfall of her monarch. "Belshazzar made a great feast to a thousand of his lords, and drank wine before the thousand." Cyrus, the Persian conqueror, knew of this feast probably, and as he was engaged with an army then in besieging Babylon, he thought it would be a good time to come upon them for conquest. He managed ingeniously. His stratagem succeeded, and on the night of Belshazzar's feast the city was captured.

This feast of Belshazzar was, probably, a national annual feast in honor of the golden image which Nebuchadnezzar set up in the plains of Dura. Belshazzar not only drank wine before the thousand, indulged in drunkenness and revelry, but he added to that sacrilege by ordering that the golden vessels, which had been taken from Jerusalem's temple and placed in the temple of Belus in Babylon, be brought out, and used on the occasion. These vessels were holy, they had been consecrated to God, and for a long time used in the Jerusalem temple service. But Belshazzar orders them brought into the banqueting room, that he and his princes, his wives, and his concubines, might drink wine therein. The anger of the Almighty waxed hot against him, and he determined to destroy him. The vial of God's wrath was filled and the avenging angel ready to pour it out.

While Belshazzar was engaged in his drunkenness revelry, debauchery and sacrilege, while he was drinking wine from those sacred vessels to his gods of silver and gold, there came forth the fingers of a man's hand and wrote upon the plaster of the wall, over against him, the awful characters that told of his fall and of Babylon's destruction. Belshazzar looked at the fingers as they traced the writing, and his countenance was changed. It was ominous to him of coming ill. The joints of his loins were loosed and his limbs trembled, they smote one against the other. But he longed to know the meaning of the characters, and he called for the astrologers, and the Chaldeans, and the sooth-sayers. They came at his call, looked at the writing, but that was all, for they could not read it, nor tell its meaning. The king was troubled about it, disappointed and dissatified with his wise men. At length Daniel was called in, under the advice of the queen mother. He read the writing and gave the interpretation thereof. The words were few, but they were full of terrible meaning. "Mene, mene, Tekel, Upharsin," Dan. v: 25. Daniel went on to give the interpretation as follows: "*Mene*, God hath numbered thy kingdom and finished it; *Tekel*, thou art weighed in the balances and art found wanting; *Peres*, thy kingdom is divided and given to the Medes and Persians.

This interpretation must have fallen upon the ear of the guilty Belshazzar like a heavy peal of thunder from a midnight storm cloud. But Daniel, the servant of the living God, had read the writing and fearlessly given the meaning and was entitled to the honor the king had promised. Belshazzar gave command, amid the solemn stillness of the occasion, "and they clothed Daniel with scarlet and put a chain of gold about his neck, and made a proclamation concerning him, that he should be the third ruler in the kingdom." This was probably the last public act of Belshazzar, for on that night was he slain. After Daniel had retired from his presence with the royal apparel upon him, and the authority of third ruler, then Belshazzar sat with his courtiers, stupified with wine and horror-stricken by the revelations that had been made unto him. He waited in awful suspense the coming judgments, and he did not have to wait long, for the besiegers had entered the city. Cyrus the conqueror had drawn away the water from the bed of the river that ran under the walls and through the city by means of a canal, and marched a part of his army in the bed of the river under the walls and into the city. Taking possession of Babylon, he opened the gates of brass and broke in sunder the bolts and bars of iron that fastened them. The voice of alarm from a terrified people was soon heard mingled with the clangor of arms, the shrieks and groans of the wounded and dying, all commingled with the shouts and rejoicing of a victorious enemy.

"In that night was Belshazzar slain." It was not long after the victorious foe entered Babylon, until the soldiers had made their way along her streets, leaving devastation and death in their way to the palace of the king. They entered the illuminated mansion in search of him and his great men. He may have tried to hide himself, but he could find no place sufficiently secret for concealment, or sufficiently strong to protect him. He is slain! His pomp and glory have gone. The mantle of death is upon him. His royal robes are rent and stained with his own blood. From his bacchanalian debauchery he is hurried into the presence of the King of Kings. His unprepared spirit is called to stand in the presence of a thrice holy God, with stains of the blackest dye upon it. The prophet Isaiah in chapter xiv represents the kingdom through the reigns of Nebuchadnezzar, Evil Merodach and Belshazzar. He represents Nebuchadnezzar "a serpent," Evil Merodach "a cockatrice," and Belshazzar "a fiery flying serpent." "Rejoice not thou, whole Palestina, because the rod of him that smote thee is broken: for out of the serpent's root shall come forth a cockatrice, and his fruit shall be a fiery flying serpent." Here we have the grand-father, father and the son represented. The delineation would seem to show that Belshazzar was the worst of the three. It is quite certain that his father and his grandfather never made such a use of the captured temple vessels as he made of them on the night he was slain.

BELTESHAZZAR—[Bel-te-shaz′-ar,] *who lays up treasures in secret, secretly endures pain and pleasure.*

BELTESHAZZAR was the name given by the prince of the Eunuchs to Daniel, at the same time he gave the three Hebrew children a Babylon name. Daniel retained the name of Belteshazzar all through his long life and service in the kingdom. Dan. i: 7, and Dan. x: 1.

BEN.

BEN was a Levite of the second degree, and one of the sacred porters appointed by David for the ark. 1st Chron. xv: 18.

BENAIAH, 1—[Ben-a′yah,] *son of the Lord, the Lord's building.*

BENAIAH, the son of Jehoiada, was one of David's valiant men, and captain of his guards. He was of the priesthood by birth, and a man of great valor. 2d Sam. xx: 23: "Now Joab was over all the hosts of Israel; and Benaiah, the son of Jehoiada, was over the Cherethites and over the Pelethites." We have an account of his position in the kingdom of David, and a record of his wonderful deeds in 1st Chron. xi: 22-25. The first wonderful deed he is said to have performed is, "He slew two lion-like men of Moab." By this we may understand he met for fight two princes or nobles of Moab,—men of renown, who were like two strong lions,—and slew them. The next act narrated is, "He went down and slew a lion in a pit in a snowy day." Josephus, in his account of this act of Benaiah, represents him as going—attracted by the noise of the lion which had fallen into a pit—to the mouth of the pit to smite the animal. A struggle commenced between the valorous man and the ferocious beast. Benaiah smote him, as he struggled, with a stake that lay there, and immediately slew him.

The next act narrated is, "He slew an Egyptian, a man of great stature, five cubits high; and in the Egyptian's hand was a spear like a weaver's beam; and he went down to him with a staff and plucked the spear out of the Egyptian's hand, and slew him with his own spear." This Egyptian was, probably, from his height as given—five cubits—seven feet and six inches high. And Benaiah went down to him simply with a staff, and so dextrously used his staff as to render the sword of the Egyptian of no avail. Finally in the contest he got possession of the sword or spear, and with it killed the Egyptian. As a reward for his valor, David made him captain of his body-guard, his own privy counsellor, and confided to him secrets such as no other one was made acquainted with. He was afterward made commander of the troops of Solomon; for he slew, under the direction of that king, Joab, the general of David's army, and Adonijah, who sought to be king, when he had fled to the altar, and was appointed in his stead. He probably continued with Solomon for many years, and executed his commands as he had those of David his father.

BENAIAH, 2—*Son of the Lord, the Lord's building.*

BENAIAH, the Pirathonite, was the captain of the eleventh month, when David instituted the monthly service of captains over twenty-four thousand men. 1st Chron. xxvii: 14.

BENAMMI—[Ben-am′mi,] *the son of my people.*

BENAMMI was one of the two sons of Lot, begotten of his daughters while they dwelt together in the cave in the mountains beyond Zoar. He was the son of the younger daughter, and was the progenitor of the extensive nation of the Ammonites. Gen. xix: 38.

BENHADAD 1—[Ben-ha′dad,] *the son of Hadad, of noise.*

He is mentioned as the son of Tabrimon, and king of Syria, in 1st Kings, xv: 18, who came to the assistance of Asa, the king of Judah, when Asa was contending with Baasha, king of Israel.

Baasha had built and fortified the city of Ramah and had imposed greatly upon king Asa and his subjects by preventing them from coming out or going in. He sent a present to Benhadad and so secured a renewal of the league between their fathers. He secured the attention and services of Benhadad, and Baasha was made to fly from Ramah. It is supposed, by some, that this Benhadad was Hadad, the Edmonite, who rebelled against king Solomon. The rebellion is noticed in 1st Kings, xi: 25, "And he was an adversary to Israel, all the days of Solomon."

BENHADAD 2—*The son of Hadad, of noise.*

BENHADAD, the king of Syria, was a son of the former, and like him, the enemy of the kingdom of Israel. He made war upon Ahab, but was defeated. We have an account of this war in the first part of 1st Kings, xx. At the time he made the proposition for war upon Ahab, there were thirty-two kings or tributary chieftains, associated with him. First verse, "And there were thirty and two kings with him, and horses and chariots: and he went up and besieged Samaria, and warred against it." Camping with his vast army near the capitol of Ahab's kingdom, Benhadad sent messengers to the king with the insulting declaration, "thy silver and thy gold is mine; thy wives, also, and thy children, even the goodliest are mine."

Whether Ahab, by his answer, intended to humble himself before Benhadad, by acknowledging the truth of his declaration, we can hardly tell. He said: "My lord, O, king, according to thy saying, all that I have is thine, and I am thine.

Benhadad evidently was not satisfied with his answer, and sent to him by his messengers a second time. In the second he made the threat that on the morrow he would besiege the city, and after taking the royal treasurers, and the wives and children of the king, he would deliver up the whole to be pillaged by his soldiers. The king made known this message to the elders of Israel and demanded of them advice. They seemed to have no hesitancy in giving their counsel, and all the people joined with them in it. They said, with one voice unto Ahab, "Hearken not unto him, nor consent."

The elders of Israel felt that they had everything at stake, and they preferred to make a desperate effort at defense, rather than tamely yield to such degradation and ruin as would come upon them, if they fell into the hands of Syria.

Benhadad replied sharply to this news brought him by the messengers. "The gods do so to me, and more also, if the dust of the city shall suffice for the handfuls of all the people that follow me." The meaning of this declaration of Benhadad was, "I will bring such an army into Samaria as will fill up the whole city." Ahab answered to that, "Let not him that girdeth on his harness boast himself as he that putteth it off." The meaning of it is "Let not him that goeth out to battle exult as he that has been in battle, and conquered, and returned from his conquest laden with laurels."

When the messengers came this time from the king of Israel to deliver their message, Benhadad was indulging with the kings, that were his helpers, in drinking in the pavillions. He heard the message, and gave orders to his soldiers to prepare for battle. About this time a prophet approached Ahab, and informed him that in the coming battle he should have a victory. And the prophet bade him put himself in charge of the young men, of the princes of the provinces. There were two hundred and thirty-two of them. They were probably the king's own regiment, or the royal guard. After this he numbered the people for war, and there were seven thousand of them. Benhadad heard of their approach and gave orders that they be taken alive, for he was quite confident of victory. But in this he was mistaken, for, under the direction of Ahab, who was himself ordering the battle, the princes and all the soldiers, slew, every one his man, and the Syrians, in alarm, fled before them, and Benhadad saved himself only by escaping on a horse with the horsemen.

It was not long until Benhadad determined to fight with the king of Israel again, and the same prophet that had given instruction before, informed Ahab of his determination and bade him be careful and prepare to meet his enemy. Benhadad gathered together a mighty army at Aphek and determined to conquer the king of Israel. They fought, and Ahab killed a hundred thousand of Benhadad's men. Those that were not killed fled to the city, and the wall fell upon twenty-seven thousand men, thus completely defeating the Syrians. Benhadad fled to hide himself in an inner chamber. He was sought for, probably, but ineffectually. And when it became necessary for him to come from his hiding place, an ingenious stratagem availed. The servants of Benhadad girded themselves with sackcloth and put ropes on their heads, and came to the king of Israel to sound him as to his feelings towards their master. They begged for Benhadad's life. Ahab not only granted their request but gave the conquered king of Syria the greatest liberty, and restored unto him his crown upon certain conditions. He took Benhadad up into his chariot, accepted his proposition to restore to him the cities which his father had taken from Ahab's father. They too made a covenant, and Benhadad returned to his palace and throne.

Twelve years after this Benhadad again declared war against Israel. At this time Jehoram, the son of Ahab was his successor. We have the account in 2d Kings, vi. The prophet Elisha was then in Israel, and when Benhadad plotted for the destruction of Israel, this prophet gave the information and so thwarted his designs.

The Syrian king began to suspect there was a traitor in his own camp. He was informed by one of his servants that it was not a Syrian soldier that was giving this information, but Elisha the prophet. Benhadad soon learned that Elisha was at Dotham, and he sent a company of his soldiers to take him; but the soldiers were stricken with blindness, and were unable to distinguish him from other men. They talked with him and did not know it. He led them into Samaria, into the midst of their enemies, but yet Benhadad was not humbled, and did not cease his opposition to Israel. After this Benhadad went up and besieged Samaria, until the direst want was experienced. The city was reduced to the greatest extremity. A sad representation of its condition was given to King Jehoram by a woman who applied to him for help. The day before she had eaten her own son. The king was greatly humbled, but he charged the calamities they were enduring to the prophet Elisha. Elisha prophesied of plenty, and his prediction was fulfilled the next day, by the Syrian army becoming frightened and deserting Samaria, or their camp near it, leaving a large amount of provisions and arms and garments in the way as they fled. 2d King, vii.

A few months after this Benhadad fell sick and sent his servant to Elisha the prophet with some valuable presents to ask, "shall I recover of this disease?" The servant's name was Hazael. Hazael came to Elisha with his presents and informed him that his master had sent and wished to know of him whether the disease was curable. Elisha's words seem to say it was, yet nevertheless he should die. This appeared paradoxical, but the prophet soon informed Hazael that he would be the murderer of Benhadad. It was not long after this until Hazael returned to the palace and gave to Benhadad what purported to be the language of the prophet regarding his case, and the next day he set himself to accomplish his designs. "He took a thick cloth and dipped it in water and spread it over his face so that he died," and as Elisha had predicted Hazael reigned in his stead. Benhadad died, then, from being smothered or suffocated. 2d Kings, viii.

BENHADAD 3—*The son of Hadad. of noise.*

He was the son of Hazeal, who had murdered the former king of Syria, and he succeeded his father as the king of Syria. 2d Kings, xiii: 24: "So Hazeal, king of Syria, died, and Benhadad, his son, reigned in his stead." During the reign of Benhadad Jehoash recovered from him all that Hazeal had taken from Israel. Jehoash defeated him in three several engagements, and compelled him to surrender all the country beyond Jordan. 2d Kings, xiii: 25: "Three times did Joash beat him and recover the cities of Israel."

BENHAIL—[Ben-ha'il.]

Benhail, w th several others, was sent by King Jehoshaphat to various cities of his dominions in order to instruct the people,—to call them back from their wanderings from God, and to reclaim them from the idolatry into which they had fallen. We have an account in 2d Chron. xvii: 7–10, of the king appointing Benhail, Obadiah, Zechariah, Nethaneel and Michaiah, with a number of Levites and priests, to this important work of reforming the idolatrous people. It was an establishment on the part of Jehoshaphat, of an itinerant ministry, that was to serve in all the cities of Judah; and they did their work faithfully, producing the most beneficial results. This itinerant ministry exerted not only a good effect upon Judah, but upon all the nations around them, inasmuch as they respected the king and made no war upon him; and the Philistines and Arabians brought voluntary tribute, silver, or presents of silver, and flocks of sheep and goats.

BENHANAN—[Ben-ha′nan.]

BENHANAN was a son of Shimon, in the land of Judea, and of the line of Judah. 1st Chron. iv: 20.

BENHUR.

BENHUR is called the son of Hur. 1st Kings, iv: 8. He was one of the twelve officers that provided eatables for King Solomon and his household. (The following are the names of the others: Bendekar, Benhesed, Benabinadab, Baana, Bengeber, Ahinadab, Ahimaaz, Baanah, Jehoshaphat, Shimei, and Geber). These officers served each one month in a year in furnishing the king's table.

BENINU—[Ben-i′nu.]

BENINU, a Levite, who was engaged with Nehemiah in sealing the covenant. Neh. x: 13.

BENJAMIN, 1—[Ben′ja-min,] *the son of the right hand.*

BENJAMIN was the youngest son of Jacob and Rachel, and the full brother of the illustrious Joseph. His mother died at his birth, and dying, she called him Benoni, i. e., the son of my sorrow; but Jacob, from some cause or other, was not willing that this should be his name. It may be that Jacob objected to it because of the import of the name as given above. The name would have been a constant memorial to him of his beloved Rachel's death, for he had loved Rachel with his first love, which was so strong that the years he served for her seemed but days. And though Leah was an amiable woman, yet his attachments were strong for Rachel. He loved Leah "with a less love." It was hard for Jacob to part with Rachel, and as she gave birth to this son while dying, he may have been unwilling that the name Benoni should be settled upon him, lest it would keep constantly before his mind the throes of dissolving nature in the case of her departure.

Jacob called him Benjamin, i. e., "the son of the right hand." When Joseph was torn by his cruel brethren from the father's side, and the society of his smaller brother, Benjamin, as the only son of Rachel, was doubly dear to Jacob.

When the famine prevailed in Canaan, and when he sent his sons down to Egypt to buy corn, Joseph, the brother of Benjamin, was lord of the land. One of the first things that he thought of on seeing his brothers, was the boy Benjamin that he used to play with, and he asked them of their other brother. He then required of them that they bring that other brother with them the next time they came down into Egypt, and they did. Joseph looked upon Benjamin, and knew him. But Benjamin did not know his brother. He was but a small boy when the cruelty of his brothers parted them, and he had learned to think of Joseph as dead—torn by wild beasts. By a stratagem, Joseph detains Benjamin, allowing the others to go their way if they would, but they would not.

There had been to them a strange management on the part of the governor of Egypt, in supplying them all at his table, himself serving them, and giving to Benjamin a mess five times as large as to any of them, and his language to Benjamin when they first introduced him was peculiar. "God be gracious to thee my son." But now Benjamin is accused and convicted, and he proposes to detain him. Judah plead for him in the most eloquent strains, and with his speech so touched the tender chords of Joseph's heart, that he could hide his relationship no longer. He affectionately embraced his brother Benjamin, and disabused his mind as to the fate of his brother Joseph.

Soon Jacob and his whole family were living in Egypt, in Goshen, the fat of the land. And day after day the two brothers, Joseph and Benjamin, were permitted to see each other, and enjoy each other's society.

Benjamin married when quite young, for he was a young man when he was the father of ten sons. Their names are given in Gen. xlvi: 21, five of whom we will find by tracing out their history, died childless. And yet Benjamin became the head of a powerful tribe called the Benjamites.

BENJAMIN, 2—*The son of the right hand.*

Was a man of the tribe of Benjamin, and the head of a family of warriors. 1st Chron. vii: 10.

BENJAMIN, 3—*The son of the right hand.*

Was one of the sons of Harim, an Israelite, who lived at the time of Ezra, and with several others, had married a foreign wife. Ezra x: 32.

BENO—[Be'no.]

BENO was one of the ministers in the temple, under the order of service instituted by David. 1st Chron. xxiv: 27.

BERA—[Be'-rah.]

BERA was the king of Sodom, upon whom Chedorlaomer and his allies made war. Gen. xiv: 2. "These made war with Bera, king of Sodom, and with Birsha, king of Gomorrah, Shinab, king of Admah, and Shemeber, king of Zeboim, and the king of Bela which is Zoar." It seems that these five Canaanitish kings had been for twelve years so far subdued as to be compelled to pay tribute to their conqueror, but being desirous to obtain their liberty they revolted in the thirteenth year. In consequence of which Chedorlaomer summoned to his assistance three of his subdued kingdoms, and invaded Canaan, and discomfited these five kings, and pillaged their cities and took many prisoners. Lot, Abram's nephew lived in Sodom, and he and his family and their goods were taken. As soon as Abram learned it, "he armed his trained servants, born in his own house, three hundred and eighteen, and pursued them unto Dan." Though the army of these kings was large, and they elated with victory, yet Abram attacked them and conquered them, and recovered all the baggage with the prisoners. He recovered from the enemy Lot and his family, and the people. On his return, Bera the king of Sodom went out to meet him, and he proposed to the patriarch to take to himself as a reward for his valor the whole booty. "Give me the persons and take the goods to thyself." But Abram refused any part of it. He said to Bera, "I will not take from a thread even to a shoe latchet; and that I will not take anything that is thine, lest thou shouldst say, I have made Abram rich." He would have all his wealth then possessed, as well as his future wealth attributed to Jehovah.

BERACHAH—[Ber-a'-kah,] *blessing.*

BERACHAH was a Benjamite, who attached himself to David at Ziklag. 1st Chron. xii: 3.

BERAIAH—[Ber-a-i'ah.]

BERAIAH was the son of Shimhi, a chief man of Benjamin. 1st Chron. viii: 21.

BERECHIAH, 1—[Ber-e-ki'ah.]

BERECHIAH was one of the sons of Zerubbabel, and a descendant of the royal line of Judah. 1st Chronicles, iii: 20.

BERECHIAH, 2.

Is mentioned as the father of Meshullam, who assisted in rebuilding the walls of Jerusalem. Neh. iii: 4.

BERECHIAH, 3.

Was a Levite, of the line of Elkanah. 1st Chron. ix: 16.

BERECHIAH, 4.

Was a door-keeper of the ark. 1st Chron. xv: 23.

BERECHIAH, 5.

Was one of the chief men in the tribe of Ephraim, in the time of King Ahaz. 2d Chron. xxviii: 12.

BERECHIAH, 6.

Was the father of Asaph, a singer. 1st Chron. xv: 17.

BERECHIAH, 7.

Was the father of the prophet Zechariah. Zech. i: 1.

BERED—[Be'red.]

This was a son or descendant of Ephraim. 1st Chron. vii: 20. He is thought to be the same person as Becher, in Num. xxvi: 35.

BERI—[Be'ri.]

Was the son of Zophah, of the tribe of Asher. 1st Chron. vii: 36.

BERIAH—[Be-ri'ah.]

Was one of the sons of Asher, and a grandson of Jacob. He is reckoned with the souls belonging to Jacob's family in Egypt during the seventeen years he sojourned there, Gen. xlvi: 17; is referred to in the genealogy of Asher in 1st Chronicles, vii: 30, and was the father of Heber and Malchiel. He was the head of the family in the tribe of Asher called Beriites. Numbers, xxvi: 44. There was also a Beriah of the children of Joseph, of the tribe of Ephraim, referred to in 1st Chron. vii: 23. When he was born his father called his name Beriah, "because it went evil with his house," and still another in the posterity of Benjamin. 1st Chron. viii: 13.

BERNICE—[Ber'nice,] *one that brings victory.*

BERNICE was the daughter of Agrippa the Great, and the sister of Agrippa his son, of whom we have an account in Acts, xxv. Paul delivered his noble defense before Festus and King Agrippa, and Bernice. She sat beside her brother when in the presence of an assembled multitude he permitted the persecuted apostle to speak for himself. She listened attentively to the address of Paul, in which he related his wonderful conversion, and his experience as a minister of Christ. She heard the noble Festus cry out with a loud voice, interrupting the apostle in his defense, "Paul, thou art beside thyself! Much learning hath made thee mad." And a little while after she heard her brother Agrippa say, "Almost thou persuadest me to be a Christian." And no doubt she had some of the same feelings that moved them to the language given above. Bernice was associated with the king and the governor in passing opinion upon the case. And when he (Paul) had then spoken, the king rose up, and the governor and Bernice, and they that sat with them; and when they had gone aside they talked between themselves, saying, "This man doeth nothing worthy of death or of bonds."

History informs us that Bernice was first married to Mark, the son of Alexander, governor of the Jews at Alexandria. Afterward she married her uncle Herod, king of Chalcis; and after his death she married Polemon, king of Pontus, but did not continue long with him. She was very strongly attached to her brother Agrippa, with whom she probably staid.

BESAI—[Be'sa.]

The children of this person were among the Nethenims who returned to Judea with Zerubbabel. Ezra, ii: 49, Neh. vii: 52.

BESODEIAH—[Bes-o-di'ah,]

The father of Meshullam, one of the builders of the walls of Jerusalem, under Nehemiah. Neh. iii: 6.

BETHUEL, 1—[Beth-u'el,] *filiation of God.*

BETHUEL was the father of Nahor and Milcah, and the cousin of Abraham. He was also the father of Laban and Rebekah. Gen. xxii: 23. It is probable that Bethuel was dead before Eleazar went to the city of Nahor in search of a wife for Isaac; for we hear nothing about him in the conference that resulted in Abraham's servant securing Rebekah as a wife for his master's son. Laban and his brother Bethuel consulted with Eleazar, and granted him his desire, when Eleazar gave presents to Rebekah, her brother, and her mother. Gen. xxiv.

Padan-aram was called the country of Bethuel long after he was dead; for when Isaac blessed Jacob, he sent him there to secure from the family of Bethuel his mother's father a wife. And Jacob married the two daughters of Laban. Gen. xxix.

BETHUEL, 2—*Filiation of God.*

BETHUEL was the son of the former, as we have already supposed; and in company with Laban, the elder brother, he heard the account of Eleazar's errand, and the circumstances that had attended him and the two brothers said, "The thing proceedeth from the Lord: we cannot speak unto thee bad or good." Gen. xxiv: 50.

BEZAI—[Be'-zai.]

The children of Bezai, to the number of three hundred and twenty-three, returned from captivity with Zerubbabel. Ezra, ii: 17.

BEZALEEL—[Be-za-le′-el,] *in the shadow of God.*

BEZALEEL, son of Uri, was of the tribe of Judah, and Aholiab the son of Ahisamach, who was his helper, was of the tribe of Dan. They are brought to our view in connection with the account we have of the erection of the ancient tabernacle. In Ex. xxxviii: 23, 24, we have the following language: "And Bezaleel, the son of Hur of the tribe of Judah, made all that the Lord commanded Moses. And with him was Aholiab, the son of Ahisamach of the tribe of Dan, an engraver, and a cunning workman and an embroiderer in blue, and in purple, and in scarlet, and in fine linen."

These two men were noted artificers, and were called of God, hence eminently qualified with wisdom to plan and skill to perform in the erection of the movable temple. It was made according to the pattern showed Moses in the mount. From Exodus, xxxi: 1-11, and from Exodus, xxxv: 30-35, and from the 36th chapter, we learn that Bezaleel was placed with Aholiab as a helper. He is said to be "filled with the spirit of God in wisdom and in understanding, and in knowledge, and in all manner of workmanship." By which we may understand that he was acquainted with the arts and sciences. He was skilled in ornamental work. The tabernacle itself shows that. But the wisdom Bezaleel possessed came from God. The genius which he possessed was the special gift of God, as in the case of all wise men. Solomon exhibited that genius, even before he offered up his earnest prayer to God for wisdom; and even the prayer itself shows that God had blessed him naturally. And the answer to his prayer proves the fact that God is the author of wisdom, and imparts it in an eminent degree to those called to fill important posts, and to perform a special work.

Under the direction of Bezaleel the wise-hearted men, appointed of God through Moses, made the garments for the priests—the breastplate and ephod and broidered coat; the mitre and the girdle. The breastplate of judgment, with its Urim and Thummin. He was the overseer in the erection of the tabernacle of the congregation, and the ark of testimony, and the mercy seat that covered it, and the cherubims at each end of the mercy seat. And he made the rings and placed them at each side of the ark; and he made the staves and put them into the rings that the priests might bear the ark. He made the table of shew bread with its vessels. He made the holy candlestick with its six branches and ornaments. He made the golden altar of incense, with the anointing oil and its perfume. Bezaleel also made the altar of burnt offering—the laver and its foot. He made the court and its pillars and hangings, the sockets for the pillars, and the hooks and their fillets; and even the pins that were used to fasten it together. The work, unto which God called him, with the assistance of Aholiab and the wise men, was all performed according to appointment, and it was pleasing to God.

In Ex. xxxix: 43, we have Moses, the leader of Israel, presented to our view inspecting the work of Bezaleel, when finished. He looked upon it all and compared it with the God-given pattern. After examining it closely at every point, he declared it to be according to the commandment of the Lord—exactly agreeing with the pattern laid before them in the beginning of the work. "And Moses blessed them." He gave them praise for their skill and faithfulness. He assured them, in all probability, that the God of Israel, for whom they had wrought with such fidelity, approbated them and their labor, and would assuredly reward them.

BEZER.

Was one of the sons of Zophah, and one of the heads of the houses of Asher. 1st Chron. vii: 37.

BIDKAR—*In compunction, in sharp pain.*

Was a fellow-officer of Jehu, and after Jehu's accession to the throne, his captain. He completed the sentence on Jehoram, son of Ahab. 2d Kings, ix: 25.

BIGTHA.

Was one of the seven chamberlains or eunuchs of Ahasuerus. Est. i: 10.

BIGTHAN—*Giving meat.*

Was also a chamberlain in the court of Ahasuerus, and he in company with Teresh conspired against the king's life. Est. ii: 21. This conspiracy was detected by Mordecai, and he with Teresh was hung. It has been thought that they were degraded when Vashti was deposed, and were seeking revenge by the murder of the king.

BIGVAI—[Big-va′-i.]

The children of Bigvai to the number of 2,067 returned from the captivity with Zerubbabel. Neh. vii: 19.

BILDAD—[Bil′dad,] *old friendship.*

BILDAD, the Shuhite, one of Job's three friends, named first in Job ii: 11, in connection with Eliphaz and Zophar. He was a descendant of Abraham by Keturah, probably the son of Shurah. He visited Job, as did the others, when the hand of the Lord was so heavily laid upon him. He looked at Job in his sufferings and distress, and said to himself, surely he is a noted transgressor, for God does not punish in such a way, except great sinners. He intimates that Job was a deceiver in religion, and that it was hypocrisy, the worst of all crimes, that God had visited him with the sore calamities that were upon him. The eighth chapter contains this address. Job answers him in the next chapter. In which answer he acknowledges to the general truth of the maxims presented by Bildad, and he confutes the error that had been presented—that God only afflicts the wicked. He maintains that God afflicts the innocent, as well as the wicked, and then he maintains boldly, his own innocence.

Bildad presents another address to Job, 18th chapter, in which he accuses Job with impatience and impiety. He shows the fearful end of the wicked and their posterity, and applies the whole of his remarks to Job whom he threatens with a ruinous end. Job answers this as he had answered the former speech of Bildad. He complains severely of the cruelty of his friends, and in a very pathetic manner, laments his sufferings, complains of his being forsaken by his relatives and friends, and even by his own wife. After detailing his sufferings in a touching manner, he calls upon his friends for pity and compassion. He expresses his hope in the glorious doctrine of the resurrection, and closes with a warning to his persecutors to desist, lest the judgments of God fall upon them.

In the twenty-fifth chapter, Bildad closes his address to Job. This speech, though very short, is more creditable to him than either of the others. In it he celebrates the greatness and goodness of the Divine Being, and his infinite purity.

The Almighty called Bildad, with his companions, to an account for the manner in which they had treated Job, and in which they had spoken of him. Job xlii: 7. "My wrath is kindled against thee, and against thy two friends, for ye have not spoken of me the thing that is right, as my servant Job hath." They were then commanded to go together to Job, and recognize him in his true character as a servant of the *Most High God*, and through him as a patriarchal priest, make a burnt offering, and accompany it with prayers and intercession.

Job was to make their offering and pray for them. He did this for his sons before they died. 1st chapter, 5th verse, "Job sent and sanctified them, and rose up early in the morning and offered burnt offerings according to the number of them all."

Bildad and his two friends made preparations, offered their seven bullocks and seven rams. God accepted the sacrifice, and heard the intercession of Job in their behalf, and forgave them.

BILGAH—[Bil-gah.]

Was one of the priests appointed by David when he divided them into twenty-four orders. His lot was the fifteenth. 1st Chron. xxiv: 14.

BILHAH—[Bil′hah.]

BILHAH was the handmaid of Rachel. Upon Rachel's marriage it is said, Gen. xxix: 29, "Laban gave to Rachel his daughter, Bilhah his handmaid to be her maid." When Rachel saw that she was not blessed with children as was her sister Leah, she gave him Bilhah her maid to be his wife, and when Bilhah bare children Rachel claimed them as her children. This woman was the mother of two of Jacob's sons that became heads of powerful tribes. It is thought by some that after Rachel died Jacob loved Bilhah more than he loved Leah or Leah's maid, who was also given him to wife, and that Reuben, the eldest of Jacob's sons, became enraged at this. Being in sympathy and feeling with his mother Leah, he committed an offense against Bilhah, viz: that of overturning her bed—not of incest, as is generally understood by Genesis, xxxv: 22.

BILHAN—[Bil′han.]
Was the son of Ezer and the grandson of Seir the Horite. Genesis, xxxvi: 27.

BILSHAN.
Was one of Zerubbabel's companions on his expedition from Babylon. Ezra ii: 2.

BIMHAL.
Was one of the sons of Japhlet in the time of Asher. Ist Chron. vii: 33.

BINEA—[Bin′-e-a.]
Was one of the sons of Moza, and a descendant of Saul. 1st Chron. viii: 37.

BINNUI, 1—[Bin′-nu-i.]
Was a Levite, and the father of Noadiah in Ezra's time. Ezra viii: 33.

BINNUI, 2.
Was one of the sons of Pahath-moab, who had taken a foreign wife. Ezra x: 30.

BINNUI, 3.
Was a Levite, son of Henadad, who assisted in repairing the walls of Jerusalem under Nehemiah. Neh. iii: 24, and x: 9, and xii: 8.

BIRSHA—*In evil, son that beholds.*
Was the king of Gomorrah at the time the confederate kings made war upon the cities of the plain. He, in company with the kings of Sodom, Admah, Zeboiim, and Zoar made a stand for battle against the confederates in the vale of Siddim, and they were routed, destroyed, and taken by the enemy, and their cities pillaged. Gen. xiv.

BISHLAM.
Seems to have been an officer of Artaxerxes in Palestine at the time of the return of Zerubbabel from captivity. Ezra iv: 7.

BITHIAH—[Bith-i′ah,] *daughter of the Lord.*
This person is represented as the daughter of Pharoah. Some think that this was the name of the princess who rescued Moses when an infant, and who, it is thought, afterwards became a convert to the Israelite faith, and married him whose name is recorded as Mered. 1st Chron. iv: 18.

BLASTUS—[Blas′tus,] *one that sprouts and brings forth.*
BLASTUS was the chamberlain of King Herod Agrippa. Acts, xii: 20. The inhabitants of Tyre and Sidon had offended Herod until he was very greatly displeased with them. They were quite anxious to have the difference between them and the king made up. In order to effect a reconciliation, they made Blastus their friend, and so secured his influence with Herod in their favor; and the king granted the deputation an interview with him, that they might make their concessions and express their desire for peace.

BOANERGES—[Bo-a-ner′gez,] *the sons of thunder; James and John, the sons of Zebedee.*
BOANERGES was a name given by Jesus to James and John. Mark, iii: 17: "And he surnamed them Boanerges, which is, the sons of thunder." Why Jesus gave these two disciples this name is not known; some have thought it was because of their manner of teaching or preaching,—others think it was because they wanted the Savior to bring fire down from heaven to burn up and destroy some Samaritan cities that refused to let them remain in them to preach. The account is given in Luke, ix: 53, 54: "Lord, wilt thou that we command fire to come down from heaven and consume them, even as Elias did?"

BOAZ—[Bo′-az,] *in strength, in the goat.*
BOAZ was the son of Salmon. Ruth iv: 21. And from Matt. i: 5, we learn that Rachab or Rahab was Salmon's

wife, and the mother of Boaz. This Rahab was probably the harlot, a Canaanite of the city of Jericho. She entertained the spies that Joshua sent, and with whom they entered into a covenant which Joshua recognized and faithfully observed when he conquered the city. Salmon was of the tribe of Judah, hence Boaz was in the line of Judah to Christ. The book of Ruth closes up with the genealogy of David, from Pharez the son of Judah. That genealogy shows David to have been the great grand-son of Boaz. Boaz was a kinsman of Elimelech. The widowed and childless Naomi, who returned from the country of Moab with her daughter-in-law Ruth, thought of him and spoke of him to Ruth. What the relationship was we are not informed, but probably he was a nephew. Boaz was an extensive cultivator of the soil, quite likely a very wealthy man. Ruth proposed to go and glean ears of corn, and with the advice and consent of Naomi she went. She fortunately, or we might say providentially was led to the part of the field belonging to Boaz. He came into the field and observed her gleaning, and addressing himself to the reapers, he asked, "Whose damsel is this?" The servant told him who it was, and that she had made the request to glean among the sheaves, and that he had allowed her. Boaz approved of this and very likely commended his servant. He addressed himself in kind words to her, "Hearest thou not my daughter, go not to glean in another field, neither go from hence, but abide here fast by my maidens," &c. Ruth felt herself greatly honored by this kindness, and would probably have felt more so at that time, had she known that her appearance and conduct had already very considerably won upon the feelings of Boaz. That she had done so is evident in that he extended his favors still further. He said to her, "At meal time come thou hither and eat of the bread and dip thy morsel in the vinegar. And she sat beside the reapers, and he reached her parched corn and she did eat and was sufficed and left."

But his expression of feeling did not stop even there. He commanded the young man to give her the privilege of gleaning among the sheaves without check or reproach. This was not allowed to other gleaners; they could not glean until the sheaves were all bound, and the shocks set up. But he bade the reapers to let some handfuls fall on purpose for her, and they did so, and she threshed out what she had gleaned during the day, and took it to Naomi. It was an Ephah, or a little more than seven gallons and a half. She narrated the kindness of Boaz, and Naomi thought it a very favorable omen. It was not long until Boaz obligated himself to take Ruth to be his wife, unless a nearer kinsman that he knew of would meet the requirements of the Jewish law and wed her. He went through the form of ascertaining whether or not this kinsman would take her, all the time hoping he would not, for Boaz had learned to love the amiable, accomplished and industrious Ruth, and really desired her as his own wife. The matter ended as he desired, and Boaz became the husband of Ruth. Their marriage was honorable, and their union was happy. Though Ruth was a Moabite, and the Moabite men were not allowed, even to the tenth generation to come into the congregation of the Lord, she had been received and incorporated into an Israelite family as the wife of Mahlon. She had left her own country, and people, and gods, and had become a proselyte to the Jewish faith, and a worshipper of the God of Abraham, Isaac and Jacob.

BOHAN—[Bo′-han.]

BOHAN was a noted Reubenite, who did, it is supposed, some wonderful exploits during the time of the war for the conquest of Canaan; but what those exploits were we are not informed. There was a stone reared to perpetuate his name somewhere near the line dividing Benjamin and Judah's possessions. In Joshua xv: 6, it is said, "the border went up to the stone of Bohan the son of Reuben." The stone marked the event or events it was intended to commemorate, as the stone of Jacob set up at Bethel marked that particular point in Jacob's history.

BUKKI—[Buk′ki.]

Was the son of Jogli, of the tribe of Dan, and was one of the princes that assisted Joshua and Eleazer in dividing the land of Canaan among the tribes of Israel. Num. xxxiv: 22.

BUKKIAH—[Bukki′-ah.]

Was one of the sons of Heman, and when the lots were cast and the singers were divided into twenty-four courses, the sixth lot came to him. 1st Chron. xxv: 13.

BUZ—*Despised, plundered.*

He was one of the sons of Nahor, by Milcah. Gen. xxii: 21. Elihu, who reasoned very sensibly with Job, was probably a descendant of Buz, the son of Nahor. He is called Elihu the Buzite. His posterity, it is likely, dwelt in Arabia, and were among those who were sorely distressed and carried into captivity by Nebuchadnezzar, the king of Babylon. Jeremiah prophesies of the utter overthrow of the Arabian kings, and of the kings of the "mingled people that dwelt in the desert." Jer. xxv: 24.

BUZI—[Bu′zi,] *my contempt.*

He was the father of the prophet Ezekiel. Ezekiel, i: 3.

CAIN—[Kain,] *possession.*

CAIN was the eldest son of Adam, the first one born into our world. He was first an infant, then a child of days, then a youth, and afterwards a man full grown,—the first one that passed through the earlier stages of life up to manhood; for Adam and Eve, the father and mother of the human family, were created of full stature. When Cain was born his mother looked with joy upon him, and exclaimed, "I have gotten a man from the Lord." She had often thought of the curse pronounced upon the Serpent, and of the promised seed that should bruise the head of the Serpent, and probably thought, as she looked upon her infant, Cain, and pressed him to her bosom with the fond feelings of a mother, This is the promised seed. She saw in her little babe the beginning of the increase of the family of man.

It is supposed by many that Cain and Abel were twin brothers, but Cain was the oldest. The two brothers grew up together and chose different employments. Cain was a tiller of the ground, while his brother was a keeper of sheep. At a particular season of the year Cain brought an offering of the first fruits of the ground to the Lord, and Abel brought also an offering. His was the firstling of his flock. There was something wrong in the spirit and feeling, or in the character of the offering Cain made—probably he had an unbelieving and wicked heart—and God was not pleased with it. He gave Cain no mark or token of approbation, but on the contrary was displeased. "Unto Cain and to his offering he had not respect." Abel's offering was accepted, and Cain was enraged. He could not bear the idea of his brother being preferred to him. His wicked heart recoiled at the idea of his brother Abel being designated thus the favorite of God, the darling of heaven. He indulged in a surly, wicked temper, and very likely in a sullen and disagreeable countenance and demeanor. God saw it and reproved him, and expostulated with him in tender and affectionate language. Oh! what an exhibition does the language give of the goodness and mercy of God to a transgressor! Gen. iv: 6, 7: "And the Lord said unto Cain, Why art thou wroth? and why is thy countenance fallen? If thou doest well shalt thou not be accepted? and if thou doest not well, sin lieth at the door: and unto thee shall be his desire, and thou shalt rule over him." In this last sentence, the Lord would have Cain remember that he was the eldest, and should ever have the right of primogeniture if his conduct was proper and right, such as he could approve. But the anger of Cain was not allayed; on the contrary, it waxed worse and worse, until in his heart he meditated the murder of Abel. Soon an opportunity was afforded, and his murderous feelings, that had ripened into settled purpose, led him to the cruel act. "He rose up against Abel his brother, and slew him." Soon the Almighty clearly convinced him that his sin was discovered. He charged the death of Abel upon him, and assured him that he would hold him accountable for the horrid deed. "Thy brother's blood crieth unto me from the ground." And then the Divine Being adds, in order to strike conviction to the guilty soul of the murderer still more keenly, and give him to realize his condition and peril, "And now art thou cursed from the earth, which hath opened her mouth to receive thy brother's blood from thy hand. When thou tillest the ground, it shall not henceforth yield unto thee her strength; a fugitive and a vagabond shalt thou be in the earth." The divine threatening seems to come upon him stronger and stronger—the lashings of his guilty conscience are more and more severe—and in agony he cries out, "My punishment is greater than I can bear." He contemplated the import of the curse as it had just fallen upon his ear and heart from the mouth of the God against whom he had sinned, and he exclaimed, under the most intense feeling, "Behold, thou hast driven me out this day from the face of the earth; and from thy face shall I be hid; and I shall be a fugitive and a vagabond in the earth; and it shall come to pass that every one that findeth me shall slay me."

We may suppose from this language that Cain repented of his sin—was truly sorry that he had been so vile and heartless—and was willing openly to acknowledge to his distressed parents and the entire family how wicked he had been; and it would seem that the Almighty, in "setting a mark upon him, lest any finding him should kill him," or giving him a sign or token that his life should not be taken, recognized his repentance. We may reasonably suppose that Cain abhorred the deed, and himself for its commission. Though he could not restore the life he had taken, he freely confessed his guilt, and never afterwards committed so barbarous an act.

He went and dwelt in the land of Nod. This was a region of country lying east of Eden. While he dwelt in Nod his son Enoch was born. He seems to have dedicated that son to God, which is certainly some proof of his repentance. He built a city there and called it after the name of his son; and it is supposed that Enoch ministered in the sacred office of Patriarchal Priest for the family of Cain, it being understood that Cain was forever excluded from that office because of his crime in the murder of Abel. His family increased and was blessed of God, for a host of very honorable men in the early patriarchal times trace their genealogy to him, and amongst them were the first artists and musicians. Gen. iv.

CAINAN—[Ka'-nan,] *possessor, one that laments.*

CAINAN was the son of Enoch and the father of Mahalaleel. Gen. v: 9, 11. He was seventy years old when Mahalaleel was born unto him, and lived after that eight hundred and forty years, so that his whole life was nine hundred and ten years. He is referred to in Adam's line to Noah, in 1st Chron. i: 2; as, also, in the genealogy of Christ as given by St. Luke, iii: 37.

CAIPHAS—[Ka'-a-fas,] *a searcher.*

CAIPHAS, the son-in-law of Annas, was high priest of the Jews when Jesus was put to death. He succeeded Simon, the son of Camith, about the year of our Savior, 25, and continued until after the crucifixion of Christ. He did not, however, enjoy the dignity long after this, for he was deposed, according to Jewish history, by Vitellus, governor of Syria, two years afterward.

He uttered a strange prediction when he was first brought to our view. The priests had been deliberating on the subject of seizing and delivering Christ to death. They, with the Pharisees, were sorely vexed because Jesus had raised Lazarus from the dead. In the prediction to which I refer he seems to upbraid them for their stupidity, and declares that there is no room for contention or debate. John xi: 49, 50: "And one of them, named Caiphas, being the high priest that same year, said unto them, Ye know nothing at all; nor consider that it is expedient for us that one man should die for the people, and that the whole nation perish not."

We might judge from this language that some of the council of priests apprehended some danger in attempting to take, condemn, and deliver to death, a man who was innocent so far as they knew, and who performed such wonderful miracles—whose whole conduct being closely scanned by their jealous, Jewish brethren, presented no grounds for accusation against him. He seems to reprove them for their ignorance—"Ye know nothing at all." The plea he then presents in favor of putting Christ to death may be looked upon as a plea of political expediency—that it was better for their nation that an innocent man be judged without law and put to death than that their whole nation be destroyed. This language of Caiphas is declared to be a prophecy that Jesus should die for their nation. Though the high priest said it from a principle of human policy, yet the Almighty overruled it. These words were given as an important prediction of Christ's meritorious death and his "gathering together into one (church) the children of God that were scattered abroad."

When Jesus was betrayed by Judas Iscariot into the hands of his enemies in the garden, they took him before Annas, a former high priest; but Annas, who probably lived in the same house with Caiphas, the acting high priest, refused to judge him, and sent him into the apartment of Caiphas. John, xviii: 24: "Now, Annas had sent him bound unto Caiphas, the high priest."

Christ is brought into the presence of this high functionary, and the trial commenced. Those that were to pass judgment in the case were all enemies of the accused. They were the priests and doctors of the law. They brought the charge, and supported it, or endeavored to do so, with the depositions and oral evidence of false witnesses. Matthew tells us, xxvi: 59, 60: "The council sought false witness against Jesus to put him to death; but found none. Yea, though many false witnesses came, yet found they none. At last came two false witnesses." These two witnesses went on to testify against Christ—that he had spoken against the temple. But there was nothing in this evidence sufficient to condemn him, and he remained all the while silent. Caiphas, the high priest, was dissatisfied with his silence, and, rising in a passion, he demanded of the innocent Jesus, under oath, an answer to the question: "Art thou the Christ, the son of God?" The language of Caiphas was: "I adjure thee, by the living God, that thou tell us whether thou be the Christ, the son of God." Jesus, without hesitancy, said: "Thou hast said"—that is to say, I am. As soon as this answer was given, Caiphas "rent his clothes," to signify his horror at the blasphemy, as he considered it, of Jesus in claiming to be the son of God. Caiphas, turning to the priests and doctors of the law, said: "What need have we of further witness? Behold, now, ye have heard his blasphemy." And, waxing still hotter in his opposition and hatred to the innocent Jesus, he said: "What think ye?" They answered and said: "He is guilty of death." And then, in the presence of Caiphas, they began the most disgraceful conduct toward Jesus. They spit into his face, and buffet him, or strike with the clenched fist; and they smote him with the palm of the hand, and they derided, and scoffed, and mocked him, because of his pretensions as Messiah. They said: "Prophesy unto us, thou Christ. Who is he that smote thee?"

Caiphas saw all this and did not rebuke it. Had they possessed the power of life and death, they would at once have put Christ to the most cruel torture and death; but they had not. Hence, under the direction of Caiphas, Christ was taken to Pontius Pilate, the Roman governor, that he might confirm their sentence, and order the condemned Jesus to be executed.

No wonder that the God of Heaven did not allow this wicked high priest to enjoy much longer the honors of that honorable office. Matt. xxvi: 57–66; Luke, xxii: 54–69; Mark, xiv: 53–64; John, xviii: 13–28; Acts, v: 27–32.

CALEB 1—[Ka′leb,] *a dog, a crow, a basket.*

CALEB was the son of Jephunneh, and the one that was selected by Moses from the tribe of Judah to go to the land of Canaan, and view it and bring Israel back word as to the country that had been promised unto them by the God of their fathers, as the land of their possession.

There were twelve selected and deputed by Moses to examine the country and the deputation consisted of one from each tribe. Num. xiii: 2. "Send thou men that they may search the land of Canaan which I give unto the children of Israel, of every tribe of their fathers shall ye send a man, every one a ruler among them." By this we understand that Caleb was an important man in the tribe of Judah. They were all men of consideration and importance in their respective tribes. These went into Canaan and traversed the country in every direction. They did not satisfy themselves with viewing a locality or two, but they traveled through the country and observed its inhabitants. They visited different parts of the country, and saw that it was a land "flowing with milk and honey."

At Eschol they cut down a large cluster of grapes and carried it between two of them on a staff, and they said to their brethren when they returned "this is the fruit of the land."

The Israelites looked with wonder and astonishment at it, and began to long for their promised inheritance in Canaan. But their ardor and anxiety was cooled by ten of the company uniting in saying. Num. xiii: 28. "Nevertheless the people be strong that dwell in the land, and the cities are walled, and very great and moreover we saw the children of Anak there." They then went on to tell them of the strong nations that inhabited the south part of the land, and then of those that dwelt in the mountains, and by the sea and by the coast of Jordan. When the people were dispirited by this presentation of the case Caleb stood up and if he did not openly contradict the report he joined issue with the ten spies. Their report was as though they had said, we can not take the land. If we do not give up the idea, but prosecute our purpose we shall all be slain. "Caleb stilled the people before Moses and said: Let us go up at once and posses it, for we are well able to overcome it." Then the ten spies openly contradicted Caleb, for they said, "we be not able to go up against the people for they be stronger than we." And then they reiterated what they had said before. And as they represented the sons of Anak "which come of the giants," they declared "we were as grasshoppers in our own sight, and so we were in their sight. The impression made upon their minds by this evil report not withstanding the efforts of Caleb and Joshua led all the congregation of Israel to rebel. "They lifted up their voices and cried and wept all night."

They proposed to elect for themselves a captain to take them back into the land of Egypt. At this Moses and Aaron were greatly wounded. They felt that the people they were leading, were committing a great sin against God, and they feared the result. "They fell on their faces before all the assembly of the children of Israel." They were horror-stricken at the rebellion. Joshua and Caleb came in at this point with their defense before all the murmering people. They said, "the land which we passed through to search it, is an exceedingly good land. If the Lord delight in us, then he will bring us into this land and give it us; a land which floweth with milk and honey. Only rebel ye not against the Lord, neither fear ye the people of the land; for they are bread for us; their defense is parted from them, and the Lord is with us; fear them not."

In the stead of this address in defense stilling the tumult and rebellion, it only incensed them more and more, insomuch that they were about to stone them with stones. It would seem from history, that had not the glory of the Lord shone, and so arrested the attention of the rebels, they would have put Caleb and Joshua to death. But God had determined it otherwise, and soon his determination was made known. God declared that their carcasses should fall in the wilderness, and not one of those murmurers should enter Canaan, while Caleb, the son of Jephunneh, and Joshua, the son of Nun, should enter it, and enjoy possession. This promise may be looked upon as a reward for their faithfulness to God, and their fidelity to the nation, especially when it is considered that their ten companions in the beginning of the plague that broke out in Israel, were struck dead on the spot. There is a passage regarding Caleb, worthy of remark. God said, Num. xiv: 24, "But my servant Caleb, because he had another spirit with him, and hath followed me fully, him will I bring into the land whereinto he went, and his seed shall possess it." By this we may understand that Caleb had natural and moral courage—a noble and heroic spirit; but more than that, the spirit and influence of God was upon him, and with him. This faith was so strong in God's ability and willingness to give them the land, that there was no room for doubt or distrust.

When Joshua had entered the promised land, and conquered a good part of it, and was about to divide it by lot among the tribes of Israel, Caleb made a petition to him to have a certain part of the country allotted to him.

In the 14th chapter of the book of Joshua, we have the petition of Caleb. In it he refers to the circumstances of his being selected as one of the spies, of his following the commandment of the Lord in his report, while his brethren intimidated and frightened the people. He referred to his age at the time he was sent out as a spy, *viz:* forty, the years that rolled away since that time, *viz:* forty-five; but though he was eighty-five years old, yet he was strong as when forty—that he was as able now for war, as he was then. He precedes his petition for a particular locality with the above, and being desirous of that particular locality for an inheritance. He says, Josh. xiv: 12, "Now, therefore, give me the mountain whereof the Lord spake in that day; for thou heardst in that day, how the Anakins were there, and that the cities were great, and fenced, if so, the Lord will be with me, then I shall be able to drive them out, as the Lord said." As though he had said, though I am eighty and five years old, I have no desire to sit down and do nothing in the further conquest of the country. On the contrary I am willing to fight, and so drive out the Anakins, these giants who frightened the people. I am as able and as willing to do it as I was when I urged the children of Israel, in the rebellion, to go up and possess the land. So Joshua gave Caleb Hebron for his inheritance. The very place where Arba, the father of the Anakins, dwelt, or the country that was inhabited by the giants.

Caleb entered at once upon the conquest of his inheritance. He warred with the three sons of Anak, and drove them out. He gave his daughter Achsah, to Othniel, his nephew, to wife, as a reward for taking in war Kirjath Seper, with a considerable amount of property. He gave him the south land and springs of water, "the upper springs and the nether springs," this we may consider to have been a large portion of the territory included in his own possession.

We cannot learn from the scripture account of Caleb, the time of his death, or the manner of it. As long as he lived, we doubt not, he continued a faithful servant of the most high God, and when he died, he left behind him sons who were an honor to him as their father, and the posterity became very numerous, maintaining for ages an honorable rank among the people of Israel. The names of Caleb's descendants are given in 1st Chronicles, iv: 15-20.

CALEB 2—*A dog, a crow, a basket.*

CALEB was the son of Hezron, and the brother of Jerahmeel. In 1st Chronicles, ii: 9, he is called Chelubai, but in the 18th verse, he is called Caleb, the son of Hezron; as, also, in the 42d verse, from which references we learn that he had several wives. Azulah, Jerioth, Ephrath, Ephah and Maachah, and by these wives he had several sons, whose names are given as follows: Jesher, Shobab, Ardon, Hur, Mesha, Haran, Moza, Gazez, Sheber, Tirhanah, Shaaph and Sheva, in all twelve, and he had a daughter, whose name was Achsah. The posterity of this Caleb was very numerous.

CALEB 3—*A dog, a crow, a basket.*

CALEB was the son of Hur, and the grandson of the former Caleb. In 1st Chronicles, ii: 50-55. The names of his sons are given. They were: Shobal, Salma and Haroeh, and we are left to infer that the posterity of this Caleb was quite extensive. One of his sons settled and named the cities and countries of Bethlehem, Kirjath-jearim, &c.

CANAAN—[Ka'nan,] *a merchant, a trader.*

CANAAN was the youngest son of Ham, and hence the grandson of Noah. When Noah stained his character with a fit of drunkenness, the fact of his drunkenness and exposure was known first to Ham, and it is supposed Canaan was with his father when Noah was discovered. They treated Noah with contempt, and probably indulged in unfeeling remarks or reprehensible levity. But Ham told Shem and Japheth the condition in which they had found their father, and probably the manner in which he with his son

Canaan had treated him. They could not find it in their hearts to treat him thus, but on the contrary, they kindly threw a garment over their shoulders, and ran backwards and covered the nakedness of their father. "When Noah awoke and knew what his younger son had done," (this alludes, probably, to Canaan) he said, "cursed be Canaan—a servant of servants shall he be unto his brethren." This is a curse against Canaan, involving the basest servitude. He was destined to be a servant of servants; and how has this been fulfilled in the history of his descendants. It did not fall on him individually at once, nor upon his ungrateful father, but upon the Canaanites. And no one can read the history of this people but they will freely acknowledge that this curse was fully deserved. Their profligacy was very great, and their conduct very wicked. This profligacy and wicked conduct was foreseen by the Lord, and was the cause of the curse.

When the Israelites were about to pass over Jordan to expel the inhabitants of the land of Canaan, the Almighty cautioned them not to suppose that they were to conquer the Canaanites and take possession of their land because of their own righteousness. Deut. ix: 4: "Speak not thou in thine heart after that the Lord thy God hath cast them out from before thee, saying, For my righteousness the Lord hath brought me in to possess this land, but for the wickedness of these nations the Lord doth drive them out before thee." They had transgressed the laws of God, had resisted his spirit, and he would no longer tolerate them as possessors of so goodly a land as was the land of Canaan. God determined that the Israelites should possess it, not because they were very righteous and deserved it, but they were less wicked than the descendants of Canaan, and God had chosen them as a nation amongst the nations of earth, where he might manifest his greatness and glory, and begin the great work of his salvation among men. The wickedness of this people, the descendants of Canaan, is presented in Deut. xii: 31: "For every abomination to the Lord which he hateth, they have done unto their gods, for even their sons and their daughters they have burnt in the fire to their gods." What a dark picture is this of the corruption and iniquity of the children of Canaan.

It is quite probable that Canaan lived and died in the land that bears his name, and that he gave it the name. His posterity were very numerous, of this we may form an idea from the generations of Canaan as given in Gen. x: 6–15. There we learn that the Sidonians, Tyrians, Hittites, Jebusites, Amorites, Gergashites, Hivites, Arkites, Sinites, Arvadites, Zemarites, Hamathites, Perrizites and the tribe called the Canaanites descended from him. According to the customs of the times they were divided into a great number of kingdoms, and in each kingdom was a king or a ruler. Almost every city of note had a king residing within it. We have an account of the conquest of two of these kings by Moses. Joshua in the conquest of the land subdued thirty-one of the kings of the Canaanites, and Adonibezek, the king of Bezek slew seventy of them and cut off their thumbs and great toes. Judges i: 7. "And Adonibezek said, threescore and ten kings having their thumbs and great toes cut off gathered their meat under my table; as I have done so God hath requited me." From those conquests of Canaanitish kings we may learn they were formed at one time in their history into not less than one hundred kingdoms.

Melchizedek the king of Salem, and his kingdom we may suppose adhered to the worship of the living God—but nearly all of them were gross idolaters and indulged in the most daring wickedness. The cities of the plain with their kings were desperately wicked, and God visited them with the most terrible destruction that ever fell upon any portion of the country. He rained fire and brimstone from heaven upon the cities of Sodom and Gomorrah, Admah and Zeboim. Because of their vileness they became marks for the arrows of God's indignation. They were made public examples of the vengeance of the Almighty, and the very site of those cities is now the bed of a heaving lake or sea.

After Israel was established in Canaan and Joshua their leader was dead, they went on conquering and exterminating the different tribes of Canaanites. Judah and Simeon reduced them to subjection throughout their possessions. The same is true of Ephraim and Manasseh. For when they allowed them to remain in possession of cities in many cases they subjected them to tribute in their possessions.

It is true the Canaanites reduced the children of Israel to a servitude twenty years under Jabin their king who was a powerful king, and had a vast army led by Sisera his general, who had in his command nine hundred iron chariots. But God raised Israel up a deliverer in the person of the prophetess Deborah, the wife of Lapidoth. She with her general, Barak, fought with Jabin and gained one of the most complete victories recorded in the world's history. For the entire soldiery of Sisera fell by the hand of the conquerors, while Sisera the general who alighted from his chariot and fled for his life, fell by the hand of a woman in the tent of Heber.

When David ascended the throne of Israel, the descendants of Canaan made war upon him, and he made war upon them and conquered them. He took Jebus or Jerusalem one of their strongest places. Their fort upon Mt. Zion came into David's possession, and he transferred his court from Hebron to it, and afterwards it was included within the limits of the city of Jerusalem, as was Mt. Moriah in another direction from the old city, the place where the celebrated Jewish temple was erected. In the days of Solomon the Canaanites were reduced still more, especially by the conquests of Pharoah, the king of Egypt, whose daughter Solomon married. Gezar with its inhabitants was given to Solomon. And when Solomon was engaged in building the temple, that noble structure which he dedicated to God, and God accepted and honored with his special presence in the Shechinah, it is said he had one hundred and fifty-three thousand and three hundred Canaanites employed in servile work. They were required to perform the hard labor of the enterprise. Indeed since that time the Canaanites as a people seem to have enjoyed but little freedom—and down even to the present time the curse of Noah and of God is upon them. "A servant of servants shall he be." Gen. x: 15, 18, 19. Num. xiv: 20, 21. Jud. i: 1, 3, 4. Ez. ii: 55. Neh. xi: 3. 2d Sam. v: 6-9. 1st Kings v: 9.

CANDACE—[Kan-da′ce,] *who possesses contrition.*

CANDACE was a queen of the Ethiopians, and the royal mistress of the Eunuch who was converted fully to christianity under the preaching of Philip. This servant of Queen Candace had renounced idolatry, and attended the worship of God at Jerusalem. He needed some instruction, and Philip received a commission to teach him. He joined himself to the Eunuch's chariot and entered into conversation with him regarding the prophecies of Esaias that he was reading. He explained them to him so much to his satisfaction, that he wished at once to take upon himself the christian name and character, which he did by submitting to the ordinance of baptism at the hands of Philip.

The passage of scripture presenting this royal personage to our minds is Acts viii: 27. "And behold man a of Ethiopia a Eunuch of great authority under Candace, Queen of the Ethiopians, who had the charge of all her treasure, and had come to Jerusalem for to worship." Now as this servant of Queen Candace had come to Jerusalem for the special purpose of worshiping the God of Israel, we may reasonably suppose that he had fully renounced idolatry though not well informed regarding the religion of God's people. And we may also suppose that he was at Jerusalem by the permission and favor of Candace. And it is also quite reasonable to suppose that she favored the religion and worship of the Jews. The idea received and advanced by some, that she was converted to the christian faith is not improbable. From the position he occupied in her government and influence he had over her, this is quite likely, though there is no direct evidence of it recorded on history.

CARCAS — [Kar-′kas,] *the covering of a lamb.*

CARCAS was one of the seven chamberlains or Eunuchs of King Ahasuerus. Est. i: 10.

CARMI—[Kar′mi,] *my vineyard the knowledge of the lamb of the waters.*

CARMI was of the tribe of Reuben and from him came the family of the Carmites. Num. xxvi: 6.

CARPUS—*Fruit, fruitful.*

Was a christian at Troas with whom St. Paul states that he left a cloak. 2d Tim. iv: 13.

CARSHENA—[Kar-she′-na.]

Was one of the wise men or princes of Persia, whom Ahasuerus consulted as to what should be done with Vashti, the queen, who had refused to come unto the king when sent for to display her beauty. He joined with Memucan, another of them, in suggesting to the king that he issue a decree that Vashti be deposed and her royal estate be given unto another. Est. i: 14–21.

CASLUHIM—[Kas-lu′-him.]

Was the son of Mizraim, and the grand-son of Ham, and is referred to in the posterity of Ham. Gen. x: 14.

CEPHAS—[Ce′-fas,] *a rock or stone.*

Was a name given by our Savior to Peter. John i: 42. "Thou art Simon the son of Jona; thou shalt be called Cephas, which is by interpretation a stone." See Peter.

CESAR—[Ce′-zar,] *one cut out.*

CESAR was a name given the emperors of Rome—as Augustus Cesar—Tiberius Cesar—Claudius Cesar, &c. Luke ii: 1. "Then went out a decree from Cesar Augustus, that all the world should be taxed." Luke iii: 1; Acts xi: 28; Phil. iv: 22.

CHAIMIS.

CHAIMIS was a son of Melchiel, one of the rulers of a district of country.

CHEDORLAOMER—[Ked-or-la-o′mer,] *as a generation of servitude.*

CHEDORLAOMER was the king of Elam who subdued the five kingdoms and the kings of Sodom and Gomorah, Admah, Zeboim and Zoar. He kept them in subjection after he had conquered them, for twelve years, when they rebelled. In a few months after the rebellion he determined on an attempt at least, to subdue them again. He associated with him the three following kings: Amraphel, Arioch and Tidal. As his allies, they marched with him against the kings of these five cities, situated in the plain of Siddim. Chedorlaomer conquered them, ravaged the whole country, gathered much spoil, and took many captives. Among those that were taken as captives, and were being borne away to a strange country as trophies of a conqueror, was Lot, Abraham's nephew, and the family of Lot. As soon as Abraham heard of it, "he armed his trained servants, born in his own house," and pursued after them, and overtook the conqueror with his captives and spoils. Abraham fought with them and conquered them. Gen. xiv: 16. "And he brought back all the goods, and also brought again his brother Lot, and his goods, and the women also, and the people." Abraham seems to have had a complete victory over Chedorlaomer and his allies. And when he returned with the recaptured people, and women, and Lot with his family, the king of Sodom and other kings met him and greeted him. As also did Melchizedek, the king of Salem, and blessed him. Chedorlaomer himself, was not killed in the battle, but in all probability escaped to his own country and kingdom.

CHELUB.

CHELUB, the father of Ezri, was the overseer of those who did the work of the field for the tillage of the ground. He was one of David's officers. 1st Chron. xxvii: 26.

CHELUBAI—[Ke-lu′-ba.]

CHELUBAI was the son of Hezron, of one of the chief families of Judah. 1st Chron. ii: 9.

CHENAANAH—[Ke-na′-a-nah.]

Was the father of Zedekiah, who smote the prophet Micaiah on the cheek and reproached him. 1st Kings xxii: 24.

CHENANIAH—[Ken-a-ni′-ah,] *preparation, rectitude of the Lord.*

Was one of the Levites who were engaged in the solemn service of removing the ark to Jerusalem, and placing it in the tent which David prepared for it. 1st Chron. xv: 27.

CHERAN—[Ke′-ran.]
Was one of the sons of Dishon, the Horite, a duke. Gen. xxxvi: 26.

CHESED—[Ke′-sed,] *as a devil, a destroyer.*
Was the fourth son of Nahor. Gen. xxii: 22.

CHILEAB—[Kil′-e-ab,] *totality or perfection of the father.*
Was the son of David by Abigail, the Carmelite. 2d Sam. iii: 3. But he is called Daniel in 1st Chron. iii: 1. [See Daniel.]

CHILION—[Kil′-i-on,] *finished, complete.*
Was one of the sons of Elimelech and Naomi. He was the husband of Orpah, and is described as an Ephrathite of Bethlehem-judah. Ruth i: 2–5, and iv: 9.

CHIMHAM—[Kim′-ham,] *as they like, like to them.*

CHIMHAM was the son of Barzillai, the Gileadite. He received the demonstrations of kindness from David that had been intended for his father. After the rebellion of Absalom had been quelled, as David was returning to Jerusalem, Barzillai met him and conducted him over Jordan. David proposed to take him with him to Jerusalem to live, and to be fed from the king's treasury. But as he was an old man, he declined this honor, and proposed that Chimham should go on with the king. He had probably acted an important part in the matter of furnishing David with sustenance while he lay at Mahanaim. David was pleased with the proffer and took Chimham with him, and it seems gave him a portion of land near Bethlehem, where he and his posterity dwelt. In Jer. xli: 17, we learn that Chimham, a city built by Barzillai's son, was near to Bethlehem. 2d Sam. xix: 31–40.

CHISLON—[Kis′-lon.]
Was the father of Elidad, of the tribe of Benjamin, who as a prince of his tribe assisted in dividing the land of Canaan. Num. xxxiv: 21.

CHLOE—[Klo′-e,] *green herb.*
Is supposed to have been a religious matron in the church at Corinth, whose family were converted and also members of the same church. There were dissensions in the church, and some member of the household of Chloe informed the apostle of them. It is thought by some that Stephanas, Fortunatus, and Achaicus were sons of this woman. They are referred to in 1st Cor. xvi: 17, as the persons who were the bearers of letters to the apostle, and they may have brought his answer back with them. The Epistle was designed to be an answer to the letter from the church.

CHOZEBA—[Ko-ze′-bah.]
The men of Chozeba are named among the descendants of Shelah, the son of Judah. 1st Chron. iv: 22.

CHRIST—*The anointed of God.*
CHRIST is the name given our Lord and Savior. He is so frequently called Christ, that some have denominated this a surname. Hence he is often called Jesus Christ. He was sent and anointed by God to execute the work of deliverance for a lost, ruined and guilty race, and to perform the office of mediator. Christ the anointed was divine. He was the Son of God, equal with the Almighty Father in his divine and infinite perfections. "God so loved the world that he gave his only begotten Son, that whosoever believeth in him should not perish, but have everlasting life." He was promised and prophesied of through the patriarchal and prophetic ages. His character was set forth in those promises and prophecies as Messiah, which in New Testament language is Christ. Those promises and prophecies were all fulfilled in the birth, life, character and work of Christ, in the suffering of body and soul until his death-warrant was signed and sealed, and his enemies executed that warrant in putting him to death upon a Roman cross. His work of conquering sin, death and the grave, was accomplished when he rose from the dead. After his ascension into heaven, and as a consequence of his mediation before the eternal throne for man, he imparted the gift of the Holy Ghost to the apostles. The whole work of redemption was consummated,

for the accomplishment of which he was the anointed—the Christ.

The first promise of a Messiah was made to Adam and Eve, shortly after the fatal fall. Gen. iii: 15: "And I will put enmity between thee and the woman, and between thy seed and her seed; it shall bruise thy head, and thou shalt bruise his heel." This was the first promise of a Redeemer ever made to man, and in the work of Christ we behold the promise gloriously fulfilled. Though four thousand years rolled away after the prophecy was made, we behold "the seed of the woman" in the person of Jesus Christ, the son of Mary and the son of God. And as he wrought his mighty miracles attesting the truth of his Messiahship and the glory of his character, he was performing the work prophesied of him. 1st John, iii: 8: "The Son of God was manifested that he might destroy the works of the devil."

There is a prophecy of the time when the Messiah should come, Gen. xlix: 10: "The sceptre shall not depart from Judah, nor a lawgiver from between his feet, until Shiloh come." That important prediction was fulfilled by Christ's coming at the time he did. Gal. iv: 4. "When the fullness of the time was come God sent forth his Son," &c. The sceptre was trembling in the hand, partially wrested from Judah. The Jews had not the power of life and death over criminals. As a nation they were subject to the taxing of Cesar Augustus, and were paying him tribute.

There were prophecies regarding the persons of whom he should be born. He should come in the line of Abraham, Isaac, Jacob, Judah, Jesse, and David; and a virgin was to be his mother. Woman, that was first in the transgression, is to be honored in giving birth to the Redeemer of man. He was to be "the seed of the woman."

The apostle tells us he was "made of a woman; made under the law," &c. Genesis, xii: 3: "In thee shall all the families of the earth be blessed." That promise was confirmed unto Isaac; and also unto Jacob, and is set forth in the genealogy of Christ as given by Matthew and Luke. The former traces his lineage by the side of Joseph to Abraham, through Isaac and Jacob, and the latter by the side of his real mother, calling Joseph the son of Heli, because he was the son-in-law of Heli, having married Mary, the daughter. According to Luke's genealogy, Mary was the forty-first from David, and the seventy-fourth from Adam. The lineage shows Isaac and Jacob, Judah, Jesse and David, as in the line of Christ from Adam to Abraham.

In Isaiah, vii: 14, we have the following: "Behold, a virgin shall conceive and bear a son, and shall call his name Immanuel." In the history of Christ's advent, we are informed that the angel Gabriel appeared unto the virgin Mary and declared unto her the will of God—that she would be the mother of the world's Redeemer. Luke, i: 30, 32: "Fear not, Mary; for thou hast found favor with God. And, behold, thou shalt conceive in thy womb and bring forth a son, and shalt call his name Jesus. He shall be great, and shall be called the son of the Highest," &c. And Matthew says: "Now, all this was done that it might be fulfilled which was spoken of the Lord by the prophet, saying, Behold, a virgin shall be with child, and shall bring forth a son, and they shall call his name Immanuel." The place where he should be born was mentioned in the prophecies of Micah, v: 2: "Thou Bethlehem Ephratah, though thou be little among the thousands of Judah, yet out of thee shall he come forth unto me that is to be ruler in Israel." Christ was born in Bethlehem. Matt. ii: 1. The facts and circumstances of his birth agree with the prophecy.

The declaration is made in prophecy that he should attest his Messiahship and establish his doctrines with miracles. Isaiah, xxxv: 5, 6: "Then the eyes of the blind shall be opened, and the ears of the deaf shall be unstopped; then shall the lame man leap as an hart, and the tongue of the dumb sing." When John the Baptist sent his disciples to Christ to ask him: "Art thou he that should come, or do we look for another?" Jesus said, Matt. xi: 4, 5: "Go and show John again those things which ye do hear and see. The blind receive their sight, and the lame walk, the lepers are cleansed, and the deaf hear; the dead are raised up, and the poor have the gospel preached unto them."

There are many other prophecies, clear and plain, regarding Messiah, and their fulfillment is recorded in the New Testament. There are many types presented in the Old Testament dispensation that are met in the person, character, sufferings, and works of Christ.

As the high priests of the order of Aaron were set apart by washing with water and annointing with holy oil—the "precious ointment upon the head that ran down upon the beard, even Aaron's beard," so Christ by his baptism by John, just before entering upon his public ministry, was set apart to his work and office. And though oil was not used as in the case of the Aaronic priesthood, yet the Holy Spirit, in the shape of a dove, came down, and amid the solemn and interesting initiatory ceremony, sat upon the head of Christ, while the voice of the father was heard saying, "This is my beloved son in whom I am well pleased."

The word Christ is usually given to denote office or dignity, for example: Mat. i: 16, 'Jesus who is called Christ;' Mark viii: 29, "Thou art the Christ, the son of the living God;" Luke ii: 11, "Savior, which is Christ the Lord;" John i: 41, "We have found the Mesias, which is being interpreted, the Christ;" John vii 26, "This is the very Christ;" Acts viii: 5, "preached Christ unto them;" Acts ix: 22, "Proving that this is the very Christ;" Acts xvii: 3, "Whom I preach unto you is Christ;" Acts xviii: 5-28, "And testified to the Jews that Jesus was Christ," showing by the scriptures that Jesus was Christ. Romans v: 6-8, "Christ died for the ungodly;" Romans viii; 34, "It is Christ that died;" Romans x: 4, "Christ is the end of the law for righteousness to every one that believeth;" Romans xiv: 9, "To this end Christ both died and rose again;" 1st Cor. i: 23, "We preach Christ crucified;" 24: "Christ the power of God and the wisdom of God;" 1st Cor. iii: 23, ye are Christ's and Christ is God's;" v: 7, "Even Christ our passover is slain for us;" Gal. iii: 13, "Christ has redeemed us from the curse of the law, being made a curse for us."

The evangelists Matthew and Mark, begin their gospels with the use of this term as a surname for the purpose of distinction we may suppose, for there were many among the Jews that have the name Jesus, hence it was necessary to distinguish between the Jesus who was the son of Mary, and those of other families that bore that name.

The gospel was written by Matthew after Christ had finished his work, and ascended into Heaven. Mark i: 1, "The beginning of the gospel of Jesus Christ, the son of God. [For further history, see Jesus.]

CHUZA—[Kew′-zah,] *the prophet, Ethiopian.*

She was the wife of the steward of Herod Antipas, she had charge of the house probably, and with Susanna and Mary Magdalene ministered unto Jesus of their earthly substance. Luke viii: 3.

CLAUDIA—[Klaw′di-a,] *lame.*

CLAUDIA was a Roman woman, who is supposed to have been converted to christianity through the instrumentality of the apostle Paul. She is brought to our view in 2d Tim. iv: 21, in the salutations to disciples from the Church of Rome. "Eubulus greeteth thee and Pudens and Linus and Claudia and all the brethren." She is thought to be the wife of Pudens mentioned in the salutation just before her. Whether that be the case or not she was an eminent christian woman or her name would not likely appear in the closing sentences of this letter to Timothy.

CLAUDIUS 1—[Klaw′di-us.]

CLAUDIUS was a Roman Emperor and hence is called Claudius Cesar. He was the fifth Emperor and succeeded Caligula. And he reigned nearly fourteen years. King Agrippa assisted him very much in gaining the throne, and after he was crowned he acknowledged his obligations, and rewarded Agrippa by giving him the the sovereignty of the kingdom of Judea, and conferring other favors upon him. We learn in Acts xi: 28, that a famine came on the people in the time of this Emperor, "And then stood up one of them named Agabus, and signified by the spirit, that there should be great dearth throughout all the world, which came to pass in the days of Claudius Cesar." Roman and Jewish historians agree in regard to this famine, that it was very severe.

We have an account in Acts xviii: 2, of a cruel and unjust edict of this Emperor against the Jews. It was an edict for expelling all the Jews from Rome, "because that Claudius had commanded all Jews to depart from Rome." This edict is spoken of in history and the reason given for it is, "The Jews are a turbulent people upon the account of Christ, some being for him, and some against him, which accasioned great heats, such as gave umbrage to the government, and provoked Claudius to order them all to be gone, for he was a timorous, jealous man." It is likely that the christians as well as the opposers of christianity were banished by this decree.

## CLAUDIUS, 2.

CLAUDIUS is denominated Claudius Felix. He ruled in the government of Judea. He managed to induce Drusilla, the sister of Agrippa, to leave her husband and marry him. Paul appeared before him at Cesarea—for Felix lived there—and made a defense before him. He did not condemn him, nor did he set him at liberty. He treated Paul with great kindness, and permitted his friends to minister unto him; and it is said he hoped the Apostle or his friends would procure his redemption with a sum of money. Acts, xxiv: 26. He was sent to Claudius Felix by Lysias, the commander of the soldiers at Jerusalem, for he had taken him by force from his enemies, and he sent the following communication to Felix: Acts, xxiii: 26–30: "Claudius Lysias unto the most excellent governor Felix sendeth greeting. This man was taken of the Jews, and should have been killed of them: then came I with an army and rescued him, having understood that he was a Roman. And when I would have known the cause wherefore they accused him, I brought him forth into their council: whom I perceived to be accused of questions of their law, but to have nothing laid to his charge worthy of death or of bonds. And when it was told me how that the Jews laid wait for the man, I sent straightway to thee, and gave commandment to his accusers also to say before thee what they had against him. Farewell." The officer presented this letter with the prisoner; and Felix waited five days, when Paul's accusers came down, bringing with them the orator Tertullus to plead against him. They presented their charge and the evidence, and the orator plead against him to the satisfaction and admiration, we suppose, of his employers, the high priest and elders; after which, Paul made his defense in answer to the charge and pleadings, and it was a noble defense. Felix could not pronounce him guilty; on the contrary, he adjourned the cause for the present, intending to hear him again. He left Paul in custody, but allowed his friends to minister unto him. The high-priest and elders were disappointed and dissatisfied that he did not convict Paul, or else place him back in their charge and power. He did not do that, and yet he did not release him as he should have done. But after a few days, true to his promise, he called Paul before him again, and in company with his wife Drusilla, he heard him reason of "righteousness, temperance, and judgment to come." Paul's discourse seemed to have an effect upon Felix to convict him, for he trembled and said, "Go thy way for this time; when I have a convenient season I will call for thee." But he still retained Paul as a prisoner, being desirous to show the Jews a pleasure.

About this time Felix was recalled to Rome, and Paul as a prisoner passed into the hands of his successor, Porcius Festus. Felix was called to answer to charges brought against him by the Jews; and would, it is thought, have been put to death by the emperor Nero, had it not been for the earnest solicitations of his brother Pallas, who was at that time in the highest reputation with the emperor.

## CLAUDIUS 3, OR CLAUDIUS LYSIAS.

CLAUDIUS was the chief captain that relieved Paul at Jerusalem, by coming upon his persecutors and rescuing him from their hands. Tidings were brought to Lysias of the mob then persecuting Paul and seeking to put him to death. He came down upon them with his soldiers and quelled the tumult and took charge of their prisoner. Paul addressed himself to the chief captain who was greatly astonished to find that he was a Jew, born in Tarsus, a city in Cilicia, and he further informed him that he was a Roman citizen, free born.

The chief captain allowed him to speak, which he did boldly, and in his address he claimed his rights and privileges as a Roman citizen. The chief captain himself had done him a wrong in allowing him to be scourged, and Paul asks the centurion, "Is it lawful for you to scourge a man that is a Roman and uncondemned." The centurion went at once and told the chief captain Lysias, that Paul was a Roman.

Claudius Lysias went to the persecuted apostle and asked him, "art thou a Roman?" Paul answered him "Yes." He ought to have known it from what Paul had said before. Paul had probably attained his citizenship by the place of his birth, the city of Tarsus, a city privileged by the emperor, because of services given him. Some suppose that his father or grandfather had served so faithfully in war, that this great favor was bestowed upon them and their family. "I was free-born." Lysias said, "with a great sum obtained I this freedom." On account of Roman citizenship Lysias showed him favor.

When the Jews bound themselves by an oath to slay Paul before they ate again, Paul heard of it through his sister's son, and sent him to Claudius Lysias to give him the information. He received it secretly, and at the third hour of the night, under the charge of two hundred soldiers, sent Paul to Felix, and sent an explanation of his course in a letter. Acts, xxiii.

CLEOPAS—*The whole glory.*

Cleopas was an early devoted disciple of our Lord. He is thought to have been brother of Joseph, the husband of the virgin Mary. He was the father of four of the distinguished disciples of our Lord, *viz:* Simon, James the less, Jude and Joses. The Mary who was his wife and the mother of his sons, was the sister of the blessed virgin. He was, therefore, according to the flesh, the uncle of Jesus, and his sons were first cousins.

Cleopas, with all his family, were followers of Christ, and in all probability were near him when suffering death upon the Roman cross. Like many others of the disciples, Cleopas was somewhat dispirited when he found the Master had yielded up his life. Up to that time, he, with others, had expected to see a kingdom established and temporal deliverance wrought for Israel. When he was conversing with a supposed stranger on the road between Jerusalem and Emmaus, he said, Luke, xxiv: 21, "But we trusted that it had been he which should have redeemed Israel."

It was on the morning of the first day of the week, the third day after the savior's crucifixion, that Cleopas, in company with a disciple, that we suppose to have been Saint Luke, went to Emmaus. That it was Luke, is inferred from the fact that he narrates so minutely the circumstances. He professes to write nothing in his gospel but what he can vouch for, to have been an eye witness to things which he records. Luke, i: 2, "Unto us which were from the beginning eye witnesses, and ministers of the word." He does not give his own name in the narration, but gives the name Cleopas. If he had not been the person, he would have given, it is quite likely, the name of the other.

Cleopas, and his companion, as they left Jerusalem and journeyed towards Emmaus, were conversing together earnestly about their master, his death and burial, and the intelligence that had that morning reached them by the women that went early to the sepulcher to embalm the body, that he had risen. That Peter and John had also gone to the sepulcher and had found that the body was gone as the women had said. They were discussing these things together, and probably trying to reconcile them with the prophecies regarding Messiah, and the teachings of Christ himself when among them. While they were thus talking, Jesus, the risen Savior, appeared unto them, but they did not know him. The first they knew of the presence of a stranger, his voice fell upon their ear, and his form stood before them. The voice was changed so that they did not recognize it, and their eyes were supernaturally affected, so they did not know him.

But he said, "what manner of communications are these that ye have one to another and are sad?" Cleopas looked up and said, "Art thou only a stranger in Jerusalem, and hast not known the things which are come to pass there in these days?" Cleopas seems astonished that the stranger who seemed like themselves to be traveling from Jerusalem, should ask such a question, having just come from the city. He then, in a very condensed form, presented the character of Christ, attested by his wonderful miracles. He then referred to his having been prosecuted by the chief priests and rulers of the nation—condemned and put to death. He then rather ingeniously acknowledged that he and his traveling companions once believed this personage to be the deliverer of their nation, and that they were his disciples; but that their faith was somewhat shaken, for he had been dead three days. He then went on to say that some women of their acquaintance astonished them very much that morning with news from the sepulcher of his resurrection. They declared that they had seen a vision of angels, which told them that he was alive, and that two of their companions had gone to the sepulcher before they left Jerusalem and found the report of the women correct as to the sepulcher being empty and the body gone.

Then the seeming stranger began to talk with them in a way that greatly astonished them. He reproved them, and assumed the position and office of teacher. He referred them to the prophecies and types of the former ages, and showed them that he of whom they had been speaking was the Messiah, "and beginning at Moses and the prophets he expounded unto them in all the scriptures the things concerning himself." The discourse with which these two disciples were favored was so interesting and instructive that they "took no note of time" or of distance. Ere they were aware they were at the place of their destination, and they asked the distinguished stranger to tarry with them. He did, and as soon as the repast was provided, he, at the wish of the disciples, took a position at the head of the table, where he could distribute to them as the Jewish heads of families distributed to their guests. He took the bread and blessed it and gave thanks, just in the same way as he had often done with these and other of his disciples previous to his crucifixion. "Their eyes were opened." The supernatural effect upon their sight was taken off. The sound of a familiar voice fell upon their ears, and the language and sentiment of an often-heard blessing was recognized. "He vanished out of their sight." He suddenly became invisible, having accomplished the end he designed when he joined them as travelers on the road.

As soon as they recovered from their great surprise and interchanged a few words as to their feelings, they rose up and went to Jerusalem. Though it was quite late in the day, for it was toward evening when they stopped, yet they felt that they could not long withhold or defer giving the disciples at Jerusalem the testimony they had received of Christ's resurrection. "They rose up the same hour." When they arrived at Jerusalem and at the room where the disciples were accustomed to meet, they found them also in possession of important testimony to the same truth, viz. "The Lord hath risen indeed, and hath appeared unto Simon." Cleopas related as soon as an opportunity was afforded, and the disciples gave attention to him, "What things were done in the way, and how he was known of them in breaking of bread." And their testimony comforted the hearts of the disciples. Luke xxiv: 13—35.

This is all the sacred account gives of this disciple. There is no other record made.

COLHOZEH—[Kol-ho′zeh,]

A man of the tribe of Judah, in the time of Nehemiah. Neh. iii: 15.

CONANIAH—[Ko-na-ni′ah,]

One of the chiefs of the Levites in the time of Josiah. 2d Chron. xxxv: 9.

CONIAH—[Ko-ni′ah,] *the strength or stability of the Lord.*

Was the son of Jehoiakim. He is also called Jehoiachin. He succeeded his father by the appointment of Nebuchadnezzar. Coniah reigned but three months and ten days and was succeeded by Zedekiah. Jer. xxxvii: 1, and 2d Chron. xxxvi: 9.

**CONONIAH,**

A Levite director of the offerings and tithes in the time of Hezekiah. 2d Chron. xxxi: 12.

**CORNELIUS**—[Kor-ne′li-us,] *a horn*

Cornelius was the first Gentile convert to Christianity. He was a Roman officer who had his quarters in Cesarea. He was "a centurion of the band called the Italian band." This was an important band of Roman soldiers. It is supposed that all of them were native Italians, who had distinguished themselves for their true loyalty and fidelity to the government. They may have been the acting governor's life-guard.

Cornelius was a devout man, and one that feared God; and he taught and impressed his family with the necessity and importance of fearing God. He and his house served God according to the light they had. He was a charitable man—"gave much alms to the people." And he was a man of much prayer—"he prayed to God always." God favored him with a vision, and the ministry of an angel. The angel that appeared unto him in the vision spoke unto him in the midst of his fears, and assured him that God accepted his devotions, and looked with favor upon his sacrifices. "Thy prayers and thine alms are come up for a memorial before God." He was then directed to send for Peter, who would instruct him in the word of life, and tell him what he ought to do. In accordance with the instructions thus received, he dispatched two messengers to Joppa from his household servants, and with them a devout soldier—a soldier who, like himself, feared God. Peter was prepared by a vision for these messengers and their message. He had seen a great sheet, knit at the four corners, let down from heaven, "wherein was all manner of four-footed beasts of the earth, and wild beasts and creeping things, and fowls of the air." He had been commanded to eat, and had made objections on account of the laws that governed him as a Jew,—he must not eat anything that is unclean. But the voice that fell upon his ear in the command is heard again; and this second voice is a proclamation of the repeal, for the time being and for the present case, of the law to which Peter refers. "What God hath cleansed, that call not thou common." Three times did God show him in the vision this collection of animals, and three times did he say unto him, "Rise, slay and eat." This was to show him that the thing was certain. He awoke from his vision and was wondering what could be the meaning of it, when the messengers from Cornelius arrived before the house and were making enquiry for him. Peter was immediately instructed by the spirit to go with them; and in order to make the matter sure and satisfactory to Peter, the spirit told him there were three men, and he was to go with them without any doubting because God had sent them. Peter went out and invited them in. He received their message, hospitably entertained them for a night, and on the morrow, procuring six of the Joppa Christians to go with them, he went to Cesarea. Cornelius and his family were together awaiting the arrival of Peter, and he had called together his kinsmen and acquaintances.

An important event was about to transpire, and an important era about to be ushered in on the church, *viz.*: the breaking down of the middle wall of partition that had existed between the Jewish and Gentile world. Soon these two important personages are brought together, Cornelius and Peter meet, the one to be taught and the other teacher. Cornelius "met Peter as he was coming in and fell down at his feet and worshipped him." He did not intend to be sinful, but he felt his obligations to Peter for coming. Peter affectionately checked him, he took him up saying, "stand up, I myself also am a man." He then entered into a familiar conversation with Cornelius, in which he learned from Cornelius' mouth what the servant had told him. Peter then compared the revelations that had been made to him, with statements made by Cornelius, and at once earnestly entered upon his work as an ambassador from God to the Gentiles. In the opening sentence of his sermon to Cornelius he expresses his confidence in the honesty and candor of Cornelius, and the purity of his intentions. "I perceive that God is no respecter of persons, but in every nation he that feareth God and worketh righteousness is accepted of him. He unfolded to him in a sermon the truths of the

Gospel of Christ. Cornelius and his friends heard and received that word, the Holy Ghost was imparted, and the gifts of that spirit as enjoyed by the believing Jews in the beginning were manifested by these Gentile converts. They were baptized at once in the presence and by the order of Peter.

The name of Cornelius will go down to the latest generation of man—immortalized as it is by the circumstance of Peter's preaching to him—his faith and acceptance with God as the beginning of that glorious work which shall not end until the world shall be brought to Christ.

COZBI—[Koz′bi,] *a liar, as sliding away.*

COZBI was a Midianitish woman, but a princess. Zimri, a prince of the tribe of Simeon, married her, thereby committing a great crime against God. She may not have been guilty of sin by forming this alliance with Zimri as he was. Yet when Phineas the son of Eleazer went to the tent of Zimri and put him to death, he also put to death Cozbi his wife. Num. xxv: 6–8.

CRESCENS—[Kres′-cens,] *growing, increasing.*

CRESCENS was one of the fellow preachers of Paul, to whom he refers in 2d Timothy iv: 10. Crescens seems to have left the apostle Paul while a prisoner at Rome, and went unto Galatia to preach, while Titus went to Dalmatia, and possibly he was the bearer of the apostle's epistle to the Galatians.

CRISPUS—[Kris′-pus,] *curled.*

CRISPUS was one of the very few that were baptized by the apostle Paul. He was chief of the synagogue at Corinth, and converted to christianity under the apostolic ministry, and received baptism at his hands. Acts xviii: 8, and 1st Corinthians i: 14.

CUSH—[Kush.]

CUSH was the eldest son of Ham, and the grandson of Noah, as we learn from Gen. x: 6-8. "And the sons of Ham, Cush &c." He was the father of Seba, the founder of the Sebeans, Havilah, Sabta, Raamah and Sabtechah. Each one of these sons became the head of a large family, and settled in different parts of the country.

Cush was also the father of the famous Nimrod, who was a mighty one in the earth. He is called "the mighty hunter before the Lord." Cush was the father of this distinguished person who founded by tyranny, oppression and violence, a mighty kingdom.

CUSHAN RISHATHAIM—[Kush′-an Rish-a-tha′im,] *ethiopian, blackness of iniquities.*

CUSHAM RISHATHAIM was a King of Messopotamia, into whose hands Israel was sold because they did evil in the sight of the Lord. For eight years Israel was compelled to serve him. At length the Lord raised them up a deliverer in Othniel the son of Kenaz. On Othniel the spirit of the Lord rested, and in the beginning of his judgeship he warred with Cushan Rishathaim, and prevailed against him and delivered them out of his hands, after which Israel had peace and prosperity for forty years. Jud. iii: 8–10.

CUSHI 1—[Kush′-i,[ *ethiopia, blackness, heat.*

CUSHI was one of servants of King David. He was intrusted by Joab with private information of the death of Absalom and sent by that officer to tell the king that the rebel Absalom was dead. No sooner had he received the order, than he started on the embassy. "Cushi bowed himself unto Joab and ran." When he arrived he delivered his official report of the battle and in a prudent manner made known to David that Absalom his son was dead. David asked, "Is the young man Absalom safe." And Cushi answered. The enemies of my Lord the king and all that rise against thee to do thee hurt, be as that young man is. By this language of Cushi David learned that Absalom was dead. 2d Sam. xviii.

CUSHI 2—*Ethiopian, blackness, heat.*

He was the father of the prophet Zephaniah. Zep. i: 1.

CYRENIUS—[Cy-re′-ni-us,] *who governs.*

CYRENIUS is brought to our view as the Governor of Syria, in Luke ii: 2.

"And this taxing was first made when Cyrenius was governor of Syria." The tax referred to, ordered by Cesar Augustus was levied and collected while this person was President of Syria. Jewish history informs us that he was not governor at the time the decree went forth, nor for ten years afterwards. But when he entered on the duties of his office he discharged them promptly and with fidelity to the government that had placed him in the position.

He demanded that it be done faithfully. It is thought by some that he was in office in the Roman Government at the time of the ordering of the enrollment and was sent with several others by the Emperor to Syria to enforce it. He succeeded Herod and Archelaus as Governor of Syria.

It was this enrollment that led Joseph and Mary to Bethlehem their own city at the time Jesus was born.

CYRUS—[Cy′-rus,] *as miserable, as heir, the belly.*

Cyrus is often denominated the Persian conqueror. He was at the head of a large number of the Persian soldiery, assisting his uncle Cyaxares when he was contending with the mighty empire of Babylon. In company with his uncle, he gave the Babylonians battle, and put them to flight. He gained many laurels as a warrior, and finally besieged the city of Babylon. He effected his ends in the taking of the city during the ceremonies of an annual feast—a feast that Belshazzar, the king, made in honor of the image that Nebuchadnezzar, his grandfather, set up in the plains of Dura. It was during the third year of Belshazzer's reign that Babylon was conquered and taken by Cyrus by stratagem. He diverted the course of the river that ran under the walls and through the city, by means of a canal dug by his soldiers. Having drained the river, he marched his soldiers into the bed, under the walls. and into the city.

Cyrus was an important personage —the subject of prophecy as the conqueror of Babylon and the deliverer of Israel. His name was declared by Isaiah in prophecy more than a hundred years before he was born. Isa. xliv: 27, 28: "That saith to the deep, Be dry; and I will dry up thy rivers. That saith of Cyrus, He is my shepherd, and shall perform all my pleasure, even saying to Jerusalem, Thou shalt be built, and to the temple, Thy foundation shall be laid."

Here is not only his name given, but a clear allusion to the mode of entering and conquering Babylon, viz: by the drained river. There is also an allusion to the benefit that shall flow to Israel by his conquest—their deliverance from Babylonian captivity—their return to their own land—and their rebuilding Jerusalem, the holy city, and the temple or house of the Lord. He was spoken of frequently by this prophet, and all his prophecies have been fulfilled. He is referred to in some of the visions of Daniel. In Dan. viii: 20, he is represented by Daniel's ram with two horns. "The two horns are the kings (or kingdoms) of Media and Persia." These two kingdoms were united in the person of Cyrus. In Dan. vii: 5, Cyrus is represented by a bear: "A second like to a bear, and it raised up itself on one side, and it had three ribs in the mouth of it, between the teeth of it, and they said thus unto it, Arise, devour much flesh,"

After Cyrus had conquered Babylon, Darius, the Mede, was king; but his reign was short. In two years he died, and Cyrus, having married his only daughter, fell heir to the crown, and reigned king on the throne of Babylon. We learn, from the book of Ezra, that in the first year of his reign, he made a written proclamation throughout his kingdom in favor of the Jews.

It may be that he was not specially acquainted with the prophecies regarding him as the deliverer of Israel from captivity; but yet the Lord, who had inspired the prophet, "stirred up the spirit of Cyrus" to issue the decree. Ezra, i: 2: "Thus saith Cyrus, king of Persia, The Lord God of Heaven hath given me all the kingdoms of the earth, and he hath charged me to build him an house at Jerusalem, which is in Judah."

This was in accordance with the prophecy of Jeremiah. He called upon the Jews throughout his kingdom, as many as would, to go up to Jerusalem and rebuild the house of the Lord; and he ordered that those who were comfortably settled, and did not wish to go, should assist those that did go. As none of them were compelled to go, but whoever went, went of their own free will and accord, and, as the journey was a long one, and the work a hard one, they who staid in Babylon should give silver and gold, and goods, and beasts; and under his instructions they thus acted. They gave vessels of silver and gold, or articles of value to those who designated themselves as volunteers in this great and good work, and so "strengthened their hands."

Cyrus brought forth the vessels of the house of the Lord from the temple of Belus. They had been deposited there by Nebuchadnezzar when he conquered Jerusalem, and ransacked and pillaged the temple, and probably had never been moved or used, save when Belshazzar was indulging in the ceremonies and sacrilegious revelry of his last feast. Cyrus gave these vessels into the hands of Zerubbabel, the prince of Judah, who had been a *stranger in Babylon*, but now enters with joy upon the work of returning to his native country and the land of his people. Cyrus gave over to him the vessels of gold and silver to the number of five thousand and four hundred; and in possession of these important treasures, he went to Judea and began his work, and, about twenty years after Cyrus gave him commandment to rebuild the house, it was finished.

Cyrus is supposed to have died at the age of seventy years, but the manner of his death is not known. He was a very remarkable person, who, in the labor of life accomplished the divine purpose regarding Israel.

DAGON—[Da′-gon,] *corn, a fish.*

DAGON was the principal idol-god of the Philistines—half man and half fish. The upper part represented a man and the lower part a fish. When the ark of God was captured by the Philistines, and placed in the temple of Dagon, at Ashod, the image or idol Dagon fell before it, and the head and hands were broken off on the threshold. 1st Sam. v. It seems that the first morning after the ark was placed in the temple beside the image, the image fell, but was not seriously damaged. The men of Ashdod raised it up and set in its place again. 1st Sam. v.

But the next morning when they went into their temple, Dagon was fallen upon the threshold and broken. On account of this affair, the priests and men of Ashdod never afterwards trod upon the threshold, but when they came to the temple jumped or bounded through the door.

DALAIAH—[Dal-a-i′ah.]

DALAIAH was the sixth son of Elioenai, and a descendant of the royal family of Judah. 1st Chron. iii: 24.

DALPHON—[Dal′-fon.]

DALPHON was one of the ten sons of Haman who were hanged in Shushan, the palace, on the day of the slaughter of the enemies of the Jews. The names of his brothers were Parshandatha, Aspatha, Poratha, Adalia, Aridatha, Parmashta, Arisai, Aridai, and Vajezatha. Esther ix: 7-9.

DAMARIS—[Dam′a-ris,] *a little woman.*

DAMARIS was an Athenian woman converted to christianity through the instrumentality of Paul's preaching. Acts xvii: 34. She is thought by some to have been the wife of Dionysius, the Areopagite.

DAN—*Judgment, he that judges.*

DAN was the fifth son of Jacob, and the oldest son of Bilhah, who was given to Jacob to wife by his beloved Rachel. Gen. xxx: 4. "And she gave him Bilhah, her handmaid to wife." When she brought forth unto Jacob a son, Rachel claimed him as her son and gave him the name Dan. This son of Jacob had but one son, and he was named Hushim, or Shuham. Gen. xlvi: 23. "And the sons of Dan, Hushim." But though Dan had but one son his family greatly increased afterwards. It was a little over two hundred years when the Exodus from Egypt took place, and they then numbered sixty-two thousand seven hundred, under the command of Ahiezer, the son of Ammishaddai, "all that were able to go forth to war." The name and work of Ahiezer their commander, and of the number of warriors in their tribe is given in Num. i: 12–38. "They greatly increased as a tribe of Israel while they were in the wilderness." Num. xxvi: 42, 43. "These are the sons of Dan after their families: of Shuham, the family of the Shuhamites. These are the families of Dan, all the families of the Shuhamites according to those that were numbered of them were three score and four thousand and four hundred." When Moses selected spies to search the promised land and bring him and all Israel word as to the country, he selected Ammiel, the son of Gemalli. Num. xiii: 12. And when the Lord gave Moses instruction as to how the land should be divided, he ordered that their prince Bukki, the son of Jogli should act for Dan in the division of it. Num. xxxiv: 22. He did so, and they took their inheritance according to Joshua xix: 40–49. In that possession they were plagued with the Amorites, who drove them into the mountains for a while, as we learn from Judges i: 34. "And the Amorites forced the children of Dan into the mountains, for they would not suffer them to come down into the valley." The house of Joseph, or the tribe of Ephraim, came to their relief, conquered the Amorites, and obliged them to be tributaries.

DANIEL 1—[Dan'iel,] *judgment of God.*

DANIEL was a son of David by Abigail formerly the wife of Nabal the Carmelite. 1st Chron. iii: 1. "Now these were the sons of David which were born unto him in Hebron; the first-born Amnon the son of Ahinoam the Jezreelitess; the second Daniel of Abigail the Carmelitess." It is quite likely that this was the same person called in 2d Sam. iii: 3, by another name. "And his second (son) Chileab of Abigail the wife of Nabal the Carmelite." It is certain that the mother of him who is called Daniel, was the mother of Chileab, and they are said to be the "second," hence they must be the same person.

DANIEL, 2—*Judgment of God.*

DANIEL, there was a Daniel who was a priest, and who attended Ezra to the land of Judea. When Ezra went up from Babylon in the reign of Artaxerxes, the king, "of the sons of Ithamer, Daniel went up with him." Ezra viii: 2. Several years after this when Nehemiah remembered and confessed the sins of Israel, for which they had been punished, the mercy of of God as it had been manifested to them in sparing them amidst their wickedness, was acknowledged, and he entered into a solemn covenant with God. He then set his seal as the governor, to the covenant, after him the priests sealed, and then the chiefs of the people. Daniel was among the priests that sealed. Neh. x: 6.

DANIEL, 3—*Judgment of God.*

DANIEL the prophet was of the tribe of Judah. He was a descendant of the kings. Yet he was taken along with many others as a captive into Babylon. Being of royal line and that fact being known, may have had something to do with his selection by Nebuchadnezzer, the king of Babylon, for a place in his court. He with his three companions Shadrach, Meshach and Abednego, was educated in the Chaldean language and learning, and he was raised to great rank and position in the mighty empire of Babylon, and afterwards in the empire of Persia. His Assyrian name was Belteshazzar. The name was given to him by the prince of the Eunuchs. Dan. i: 7. This name given him was in accordance with the wishes of Nebuchadnezzar. The king recognized it as his proper name, for in Dan. iv: 8, he says: "But at the last Daniel came before me, whose name was Belteshazzar, according to the name of my God." He was probably about eighteen or twenty years of age when he was carried away captive to Babylon, but he was a devoted servant of the living God, and took his religion with him and maintained his character as a pious Jew, surrounded by the idolatry and wickedness of the corrupted Babylonian court. When the course of education of Daniel and his companions commenced, under what many would have considered very favorable circumstances, for they were appointed a daily provision of the king's meat, and of the wine which the king drank. Daniel became aroused to a sense of duty. Dan. i: 8. "But Daniel purposed in his heart that he would not defile himself with the portion of the king's meat, nor with the wine which he drank, therefore he requested of Ashpenaz that he might not defile himself." Daniel made known this purpose of his heart unto Melzar first. This servant of the prince of the Eunuchs had charge of Daniel and his companions, as to giving them food and clothing, proper apartments, healthy exercise, etc. And Melzar may have made it known unto Ashpenas; at any rate Daniel's request was granted.

The reason why he demanded a change of diet for himself and his companions from that appointed was, in all probability, that it would be a violation of the Jewish law regarding the eating of meat. The Babylonians ate those beasts which were unclean according to the Jewish law. They ate beasts which had not been properly bled, but had been strangled to death. The Babylonians also ate animals that were offered in sacrifice to their gods. No wonder that Daniel objected.

He asked of Melzar that they might have a vegetable diet. "Give us pulse to eat and water to drink." At first Melzar was unwilling; for he thought that the effect of living on such diet under him would be that they would not prosper—that such hard living would reduce them, and that soon a complaint would be lodged against him and his course in changing their diet from the king's appointment. It would be known, and his life would be in danger. Daniel then entered into an agreement with Melzar, that they should be tried for ten days on the diet he proposed, and if their countenances had changed for the worse, or if they did not compare favorably in appearance with the young men that continued to eat the portion of the king's meat, then he would give it up. He would no longer insist upon a change. Melzar agreed to this, and at the end of ten days was satisfied that they were not injured at all, but that they looked better, healthier than before, and he acquiesced in the wishes of Daniel for himself and his companions.

For three years this was their diet, and they had prospered physically, and they had rapidly improved under their educators. They became learned in the Chaldean language and literature, so that when they were brought unto the king, and he examined them as to the progress they had made, the king's decision was, "that in all matters of wisdom and understanding they were ten times better than all the magicians and astrologers that were in all his realm."

Thus we behold the self-sacrifice and industry of Daniel rewarded. The king acknowledged his wisdom and promoted him in a short time to high positions. By this the envy of aspirants for office among the Babylonians was excited, and they became his enemies, and sought to ruin him by bringing accusations against him before the king.

It was during the second year of the reign of this king, for he reigned two years in connection with his father before he reigned alone, that he had a succession of dreams which greatly troubled him. He called to him the wise men of Babylon and demanded of them what a particular dream was which had troubled his mind. They thought it a very hard requisition on the part of the king, and promised him if he would only give them the dream, they would give him the interpretation thereof. This, however, he could not do, for he could not call it up. It is true, that this demand, and the threat if they did not, "they should be cut in pieces," was exceedingly tyrannical. It seemed to be cruel in the extreme. They plead against the injustice, but their pleading was all in vain, the king became furious and in his anger commanded to destroy them all. Hence the decree went forth and would have been executed in a short time, had not Daniel heard of it and interfered. It is quite probable that he, with his three companions, were numbered among the wise men, and would have fallen in the slaughter. Daniel and his fellows were sought for. When the king's captain, Arioch, was about to execute this decree, or see that it was executed, Daniel checked him by saying, "why is the decree so hasty from the king?" It is not likely that he had been applied to and yet his life was sought after in executing the decree. Arioch thus stopped in his work of death, went to inform the king that Daniel had spoken and had indicated that after all the dream might be recalled and the interpretation given.

The king was glad to hear it, especially from one who had developed so much wisdom as Daniel, during his examination. Daniel appeared in person before the king, and expressed a desire that he would stay the execution of the decree for awhile. "Give me," said Daniel, "a little time and I will show the king the interpretation." Daniel then went to his three companions and informed them of the interview he had had with the king and of the promise he had made. They heard, as he represented the case, and in all probability engaged with him in earnest prayer to God for a revelation, that Daniel might make known unto the king, both the dream and the interpretation thereof. They realized that in the execution of the decree, they would perish with the wise men of Babylon. In the visions of that night God revealed to Daniel, the lost dream of king Nebuchadnezzar. He acknowledged the divine goodness and praised the Lord; and in possession of the secret, he hastened to Arioch, who was waiting to enter upon the slaughter, and bade him not destroy the wise men, for he was now in possession of the dream and the interpretation thereof.

Arioch then brought Daniel in before the king in haste, and informed him that he was ready to give the king the desired information. The king then bade Daniel proceed, which he did, attributing the revelation to the God of Heaven. The first thing he developed was, that the dream was concerning things that should take place in the latter days. He then gave Nebuchadnezzar the dream of the image composed of gold, silver, brass, iron and clay, and the stone cut out of the mountains without hands, that smote the image and broke it to pieces, and crushed it to dust, and that became a great mountain, and filled the whole earth. He then went on to give the interpretation of the dream. Nebuchadnezzar acknowledged this to be the dream, and he witnessed such wisdom in Daniel while he gave the meaning of it, as he had never seen in any other man, insomuch that he fell upon his face before Daniel, and worshiped him, supposing him to be a god or divine being. Daniel, we may suppose, forbade him, and endeavored to impress his mind with the greatness of God who had made it known unto him, for he had told the king when he was brought into his presence to reveal the secret, that it was not because of any wisdom he had more than any living man that he could do it, but because there was a God in heaven that revealeth secrets. The king then declared that Daniel's God was "the God of Gods, and the Lord of Lords," greater than all others, and the ruler in heaven and earth. Because of the interpretation of this dream, Daniel was greatly promoted. It is said the king made him a great man. "He gave him many great gifts, and made him ruler over the whole province of Babylon, and chief of the governors over all the wise men of Babylon." After Daniel was thus favored and promoted, he spake to the king in behalf of his three companions. As they had shared his peril and his anxieties, and prayed with him to their God for light and help, he wished them to share in the promotion. Accordingly through his influence, they were set over the affairs of the province of Babylon. While Daniel was the chief officer, and the confidant and counsellor of the king, his three companions were officers under him in the province of Babylon.

We find Daniel again engaged in interpreting a dream for King Nebuchadnezzar, recorded in the 4th chapter of Daniel. The wise men of Babylon who had been applied to had failed, and the king came to Daniel and rehearsed his dream. It was the vision of the tree hewn down and the stump left. He heard it and was not a little perplexed, for he saw its import: that himself the king for seven years should be humbled by the God of Heaven for his wickedness, by being driven out from men and made to dwell with the beasts of the field. It is not strange that Daniel was astonished for a time, and that he felt that the task imposed upon him was a difficult and a delicate one. He saw that the king would wander as a maniac for seven years, but after that he should return to his kingdom.

Having given in an unvarnished way the interpretation of the dream, he ventured to give the king a bold and earnest exhortation to repentance and reformation. "Wherefore, O King, let my counsel be acceptable unto thee, and break off thy sins by righteousness, and thine iniquities by shewing mercy to the poor, if it may be a lengthening of thy tranquility." Here he charges the king with having been an oppressive man—one that oppressed the poor. He pleads with him to cease from his sins —to stop his course of wickedness and bring forth fruits meet for repentance. But it seems he did not heed or profit by the exhortation; for not long afterwards, with a heart inflated with pride, as he walked in the palace of Babylon and contemplated the greatness and glory of his dominions, he said, "Is not this great Babylon, that I have built for the house of the kingdom by the might of my power and for the honor of my majesty?" He attributed everything to himself, and acknowledged God in nothing. God was angry with him for this pride and wickedness; and while the words were yet on his lips, the voice of God fell upon his ear, saying, "The kingdom is departed from thee." He had time, it may be, to call to mind Daniel's interpretation of his dream, and the earnest exhortation he gave him, when behold! the blast of the breath of an angry God came on him,—reason was hurled from her seat, and the king from his throne. A dreadful fit of madness came upon him, and he deserted the city and palace and sought a home with the beasts in the woods and deserts. Here was the commencement of the fulfillment of Daniel's declaration.

During the time of Nebuchadnezzar's insanity, Evil Merodach, his son, exercised authority as his regent, and Daniel remained in office. And when Belshazzar, the grandson of Nebuchadnezzar, ascended the throne of Babylon, Daniel was still in office, though for a while not so prominent as he had been in an earlier day. But at length, in the third year of this king, a circumstance occurred that for a short time placed Daniel in possession of great honor, for he was clothed in scarlet and a chain of gold was put about his neck, and a proclamation made that he should be the third ruler in the kingdom.

Belshazzar, on the night of his bacchanalian feast, was terrified by the handwriting on the wall, and he called his wise men to read it and interpret it, but they could not. Belshazzar, prompted by the queen mother, sent for Daniel, and he came and looked upon it and understood it at once. It may be the characters belonged to the language in which Daniel was born, and that he had learned before his captivity in Jerusalem, or in the land of Judea. And though the writing imported the speedy dissolution of the king and of the kingdom, because the decree of God was that Media and Persia should divide Babylon as a prey, yet Daniel boldly declared the import of the writing, preceding it with a solemn charge of the sins of which he was guilty.

When Darius became the king of Babylon, Daniel was made the first of the presidents that were set over the one hundred and twenty princes that Darius gave provinces to in his kingdom. When the two presidents and the princes saw that Daniel was preferred above them all, they set themselves to work to find something against him by which they might accuse him to the king. But they were unsuccessful; for Daniel's whole course was marked with the strictest fidelity to the king and his vast kingdom. They therefore determined to seek an occasion against him concerning the law of his God. They determined to assail his religion. Their plan for accusing him was deeply laid. They knew he was as faithful to the God of his fathers, as he was to Darius and the interests of his government, and that it would be very difficult to make him abjure his religion. They called a convocation of the princes, and the two presidents under Daniel, and after consulting together they concluded on their course.

They matured a plan and went to the king with it. The plan was to destroy Daniel, and it was involved in a proposition to the king to do him homage for thirty days; to make him alone the object of worship. The king's ambition was flattered by this proposition, and he agreed that there should be such a law passed. He issued the decree and stamped it with the seal of the empire, so that it became unalterable for thirty days. The king himself had not the power to change it until the time was out. Daniel saw this deep laid scheme of his enemies to destroy him, but he was not alarmed. Undaunted, he continued his devotion to his God: "He went into his house, and his windows being opened in his chamber towards Jerusalem, he kneeled upon his knees three times a day, and prayed and gave thanks before his God, as he did aforetime." He might, it may be, have secluded himself from the gaze of the world or his enemies. He might have closed his windows, and yet turned his face towards Jerusalem and the temple, as probably was the custom of all the Jews when in captivity or in a foreign land, as Solomon indicated it should be when he dedicated the temple. He prayed to God that he would hear the prayers of those who might be in strange lands, or in captivity, when they should turn their faces toward their own land, the city which God had chosen, and the house dedicated to his name. Daniel was not afraid to be seen. The same decision of character that had marked him before, marked him now.

His enemies went to the king with the charge against him of violating the royal statutes. There was no trial to prove him guilty, for he did not deny the charge. When the king saw that his first president was about to be destroyed, he was much displeased with himself for his great folly in signing such a decree, and he tried ineffectually to have it annulled, so that Daniel might be saved. The princes and presidents met together, and insisted that the law should be executed at once. Darius had no power to resist, and hence commanded that they cast Daniel into the den of lions. But as he signed Daniel's death warrant with a heavy heart, he thought of his many excellencies—his fidelity to the government ever since he was made an officer, and his wisdom manifested in his counsel, in framing of laws, and interpretation of dreams, and he said to him: "Thy God whom thou servest continually will deliver thee."

Daniel was cast into the den, but when he reached the floor where the wild beasts were, he found them mild and gentle and playful as so many lambs. Their ferocity had been allayed by the power of Daniel's God. They were all in the charge of a new master. They had an angel-keeper, and Daniel an angel companion. The king was so troubled over the execution of the decree in Daniel's case, that he could not sleep. He would have no music, neither would he eat. Darius went to the den of lions early in the morning, and laid his royal hand upon the signet with which the stone had been sealed, and in full confidence that the God of Daniel had taken care of him, "He cried with a lamentable voice," and his heart was so full of sorrow and grief that he exclaimed, "O Daniel, servant of the living God, is thy God whom thou servest continually able to deliver thee from the lions?" By this time his heart was greatly eased of its burden, for his eye rested on him probably as he stood surrounded by the lions, but if not, his voice fell upon the ear of the king in the oft repeated salutation: "O king, live forever." Then Daniel related to the king how he had been preserved, and why that innocency was found in him, both toward God and the king, and the innocency had been proved by his preservation. King Darius was exceedingly glad, and took Daniel up out of the den, and then ordered that the conspirators and accusers of Daniel, with their wives and children, be cast into the den, and ere they reached the bottom, the lions destroyed them.

Daniel took his position again in the government, and continued to retain it through the reigns of Darius the Mede and Cyrus the Persian.

It is worthy of remark that Daniel served under five kings, Nebuchadnezzar, Evil Merodach, Belshazzar, Darius and Cyrus, and unlike the courtiers of kings, he never flattered, but always faithfully discharged his duty. When it became necessary for him to reprove, he reproved. And when the judgments of God were decreed against any of them, he fearlessly declared the decree, and specified the judgments coming upon them.

Daniel had renown for wisdom and piety when a youth, for the prophet Ezekiel ranges him with Noah and Job. Eze. xiv: 14: "Though these three men, Noah, Daniel and Job, were in it," &c. And again, Ezekiel xxviii: 3: "Behold, thou art wiser than Daniel—there is no secret that they can hide from thee." These passages represent Daniel when a young man, and he increased in wisdom and piety all through his life.

It is quite likely that he did not return to his native land, but continued in Babylon in office until he died. We do not know when he did close up, in the providence of his God, his eventful earthly career; but the impression is that he died soon after his last vision, which is dated in the third year of the reign of Cyrus.

The book of Daniel is a genuine and authentic book. The Jewish church and nation have so taken it, and Josephus puts Daniel down as the greatest of the prophets. Our Savior cites his words and styles him "Daniel the prophet," and the apostles have, several of them, referred to his prophecies. Many of his prophecies have been literally fulfilled, and others of them are now in course of fulfillment.

DARDA — [Dar′-dah,] *house of the shepherd.*

Darda, a son of Mahol, one of four men of great fame for their wisdom, but surpassed by Solomon. They are referred to in 1st Kings iv: 31. He is the same person it is thought who is called in 1st Chron. ii: 6, Dara.

DARIUS, 1—[Da-ri′-us,] *he that inquires and informs himself.*

Darius the Mede succeeded Belshazzar to the throne of Babylon. He was the son of Astyages a king of the Medes, and a brother of the mother of Cyrus the conqueror of Babylon. He was also the brother of the mother of Evil Merodech. He was therefore the uncle of Cyrus and the great uncle of Belshazzar whom he succeeded. There seems to have been considerable war between Babylon and Media and Persia, before Cyrus the Persian conquered it in the reign of Belshazzar, and it was taken as a prey and divided between the Medes and Persians according to Daniel's interpretation of the last character of the hand-writing on the wall. Though Daniel in his book of history and prophecy has not given us an account of wars during the reigns of the three kings under which he served previous to Darius becoming the king in Babylon; yet the prophets Isaiah and Jeremiah have given in prophecies, an account of wars upon Babylon, and finally its capture and conquest by Cyrus and the release of the Jews.

As soon as he was crowned king in Babylon he appointed one hundred and twenty princes as governors of provinces in his kingdom, and over these governors three presidents or principal governors, of whom Daniel was one and the first of them. He was very much vexed by the conspiracy of these princes for the destruction of Daniel. But after the latter was delivered from the den of lions, the king published an edict that all his subjects should fear the God of Daniel and of the Jews. He demanded that they reverence the God of heaven. The language of his decree was as follows: "I make a decree in every dominion of my kingdom that men tremble and fear before the God of Daniel, for he is the living God and steadfast forever, and his kingdom that which shall not be destroyed, and his dominion shall be even unto the end, etc." A strange decree this for a heathen king, but the proof of Daniel's innocency and the power of his God in his preservation among the hungry lions was such that he was fully convinced.

Darius was sixty-two years old when he became king in Babylon—he reigned only two years when he died and Cyrus succeeded him.

DARIUS, 2—*He that inquires and informs himself.*

Darius Hystaspes or the son of Hystaspas is supposed to have been the Ahasuerus of scripture, the husband of the devoted and sacrificing Esther. See Ahasuerus.

DARIUS, 3—*He that inquires and informs himself.*

Darius Codamannus was the last of the Persian Kings of that age. He is mentioned in Neh. xii: 22. "The Levites in the days of Eliashib, Joiada, Johanan and Jaddua were recorded chief of the fathers; also the priests to the reign of Darius the Persian." It is supposed that this Darius was raised up from a low condition and position in the government to be the king. He is said to have been a courier to Darius Ochees who promoted him to the governorship of Armenia. The feat he performed which brought him notoriety and honor was that of fighting a duel and coming off a conqueror. Any man the Persian army could produce for a single combat was challenged, and Darius took up the challenge of the enemy and came off the victor. He was of royal blood, but not very near the throne. Yet one of the servants of the King of Persia determined to make him king, and to accomplish his work murdered the reigning king and placed him on the throne, so that he became the king of Persia. Alexander the great, the Macedonian conqueror, warred with his kingdom and took it, Darius was slain, and so ended, accord- to the prophecies of Daniel the Persian dynasty.

DARKON—[Dar′-kon.]

The children of Darkon were among the servants of Solomon who returned from Babylon with Zerubbabel. Ez. ii: 56 and Neh. vii: 58.

DATHAN—[Da′-than,] *laws, rites.*

DATHAN was associated with Korah and Abiram in the rebellion against Moses. He was the brother of Abiram and the son of Eliab, as we learn from Num. xvi: 1. In the 13th and 14th verses we have a very seditious speech of these two sons of Eliab. Moses had sent for them to come to him, for he desired a conversation with them, and, if possible, to quell their mutinous spirit and feeling; but they sent him word that they would not. The following is their speech:

"Is it a small thing that thou hast brought us up out of a land that floweth with milk and honey, to kill us in the wilderness, except thou make thyself altogether a prince over us? Moreover, thou hast not brought us into a land that floweth with milk and honey, or given us inheritance of fields and vineyards. Wilt thou put out the eyes of these men? We will not come up?"

What insolent language this to the meek and God-fearing Moses. He was destroyed, with all that he had, as was Korah and Abiram.

DAVID—[Da′-vid,] *beloved, dear.*

DAVID was the youngest son of Jesse. He was of the line of Judah, from whom the Savior of mankind was to descend.

He is first introduced to our notice as a shepherd boy. When Saul, the first king of Israel, proved unfaithful to the command of God, who had erected a throne in Israel, and selected him as king to sit on that throne, it was determined that the kingdom should not remain in his family. And the prophet Samuel, who had been the last judge of Israel, was sent to the house of Jesse to select a successor for Saul from among his sons. It was Samuel that had anointed Saul king. Saul had been disobedient, and now the prophet is commissioned to anoint another. He prepared a horn of oil, and went to Bethlehem. He called Jesse and his sons to the sacrifice, and without letting the principal object of his visit from Ramah at this time be known unto the people, he sought an interview with the family of Jesse, and Jesse caused his sons to pass before the prophet that he might look upon them. When he looked upon Eliab, the eldest, he said, "Surely the Lord's anointed is before him." But in this he was mistaken. The Lord let him know that he was not to judge of stature or outward appearance, for "the Lord seeth not as man seeth, for man looketh on the outward appearance but God looketh at the heart." All the sons of Jesse passed before Samuel except David, who was in the field with the sheep.

When Samuel saw that God had not selected either of the seven, he asked, "are here all thy children?" Jesse answered that they were all here except the youngest. He bade Jesse send for him, and he did. As soon as Samuel saw the lad, he was satisfied that this was the one that was to be anointed. And in the company of Jesse and his other sons, Samuel poured the oil upon the head of David, and so designated him as the Lord's anointed for the throne of Israel. 1st Samuel, xvi: 12.

From the time that Samuel anointed David he was blest with the spirit and favor of God. He increased under the influence of that spirit, in wisdom, prudence, courage and true magnanimity. He had natural gifts that were probably not developed so as to attract particularly the attention of his father, and of his brothers, previous to the visit of Samuel. But it was not long after that until he made himself known as a prodigy in slaying with a sling and stone the Philistine giant.

His brothers, at least the three eldest, were warriors in the army of king Saul, who was engaged in a contest with the Philistines. 1st Samuel, xvii: 13. Jesse sent David to the army to see his brothers, with some parched corn, loaves of bread and cheese. At the time he reached the army, they were about entering into an engagement with the enemy. He heard the shouting to the battle, he saw the armies were arranged for the contest, and he ran into the army with the message from his father and the presents he had brought. While he talked with his brethren, Goliath, the Philistine giant, came out to show himself and defy the army of the living God. Now David heard his defiant words, and his courageous soul was fired with ambition to rid Israel of this dreaded enemy. He intimated that he was ready to meet Goliath in single conflict. He talked with a considerable degree of animation, and attracted the attention of the soldiers. David said What did ye say shall be done to the man that killeth the Philistine, and taketh away the reproach from Israel? And they told him that king Saul would give him great riches, and his daughter for a wife, and make his father's family free in Israel.

Eliab, the oldest brother of David, complained of him when he heard him talk thus, and reproved him, but David defended himself by asserting "that there was a cause" why he should talk thus, and the complaint and reproof of Eliab did not stop him. Soon it was told Saul that David was willing to meet Goliath. Saul sent for him and communed with him. He looked upon David's slender form and youthful appearance, and made an objection, "thou art but a youth, and he a man of war from his youth." David then presented an argument in favor of his being permitted to go against the giant in battle. His reasoning was: "I kept my father's sheep, and a lion came and took a lamb out of the flock, and I followed the lion and smote him and recovered the lamb. And at another time I was attacked by a bear, and I slew him. Now as I slew a lion and a bear I will slay this uncircumcised Philistine. The Lord gave me deliverance in the first case, and he will give me deliverance in this latter case." Saul saw that there was a force in David's reasoning, and he bade him go with his blessing. He admired the courage of David, and his trust in the God of Israel. In order to place David in as good a condition for defense as possible, he put on him his own armor. The first time probably the king of Israel had ever offered the loan of his armor to a warrior, or placed it upon any person, not even upon Jonathan, his son. And he must have had a degree of confidence in David's success, or he would not have risked his armor, when it would certainly fall into the hands of his enemies, the Philistines, if David was killed. 1st Samuel xvii. But the armor was rejected. David was but a youth, slender and not very tall, while Saul was a head and shoulders taller than any other man in Israel. It probably did not fit, and beside that it would be an incumbrance to David who was unaccustomed to the use of armor.

He left the presence of the king with no weapon of war about him, except, indeed, his staff might be considered such. As he passed on toward the Philistine army, he crossed a brook, and, from the bed of it, chose him five smooth stones. With one of these stones in his sling, he approached the defiant giant. He heard the bitter words and cursing of his enemy as he neared him, and, trusting in God for deliverance, he threw a stone from his sling with such violence that, as it smote the giant in the forehead, it broke through and sank in, producing almost instant death. David, upon seeing that his enemy had fallen, ran up, and, with the massive sword of the fallen champion, cut off his head, and took it to Jerusalem to show it unto Saul and all Israel. And he took possession of Goliath's sword and armour, and probably deposited them with the king as testimonials of his conquest. Saul placed them in the charge of the high priest, for afterward, when David was in imminent peril, Abimelech gave him the sword. 1st Sam. xxi.

David cultivated, while a shepherd, his talent for music, and an evil spirit from the Lord troubled Saul. It was thought, by some of the king's servants, that music would have a salutary effect upon him. They suggested this to Saul, and he agreed that they should provide him a man that could play well. Some of them had heard the sweet tones of David's harp borne on the morning and evening breezes in and near Bethlehem, where Jesse lived, and they reported the son of Jesse to Saul as a skillful player, and, moreover, "a mighty valiant man, and a man of war, and prudent in matters, and a comely person"—one that would be an honor to the king's court. King Saul accordingly sent for David, and Jesse, his father, sent him to the king with a present. Thus was David introduced to Saul as a musician.

Early after David was admitted to the court, he formed strong attachments for Jonathan, the king's son. They became true friends, and, as years rolled on and David suffered from the jealousy of Saul, he and the young, magnanimous prince, were bound together in the strongest of mutual covenants. The jealousy of Saul led him twice to cast a javelin at David to kill him; but the Lord preserved him. Saul was determined to rid himself of David, who had already secured to himself a great name in Israel as a valorous man; for he had not only slain Goliath, but he had other and very great victories over the Philistines. Saul gave orders to his officers to kill David.

When David returned from the slaughter of the Philistines, the women sang as they came out of the cities of Israel to congratulate them: "Saul hath slain his thousands, and David his tens of thousands." This was exceedingly unpleasant to the jealous king. He had murder in his heart, and would indeed have spilled the life-blood of David with his own hand had not God prevented. He sent his servants to David's house to watch for him as he left it in the morning, and kill him. And when David escaped with the aid of Michal, who deceived her father by saying that he was at home sick, Saul sent his servants to the house and bade them enter and bring him in his bed, that he might slay him. He wished to effect his end in murdering David without shocking Michal by committing the deed before her eyes, and hence bade them lie in wait for him and kill him; but upon hearing that David was sick, he bade them bring him to him in the bed and he would slay him at once. David having thus escaped fled to Ramah and had an interview with Samuel. Soon Saul heard of it, and he went in person to seize David, but was prevented. David afterward sought and obtained an interview with Jonathan, which resulted in the young prince making another effort to reconcile his father to David, but it proved a failure; and David fled to Nob, where Ahimelech the priest was, and from him he procured bread and the sword of Goliath, the Philistine giant. Having provided himself thus with bread and a sword, he went to Achish, the king of Gath. He had not been there long until he was recognized as the man who had killed their giant. It may be they saw the sword of Goliath in his possession and knew it. Their suspicions were aroused against him, and he began to realize that he was in great danger—that his life was in imminent peril. He became, it is supposed by some, greatly alarmed, and his alarm threw him into a kind of madness accompanied with epilepsy; but 1st Sam. xxi: 13, favors the idea that his madness was not real but feigned: "And he changed his behavior before them, and feigned himself mad in their hands, and scrabbled on the doors of the gate, and let his spittle fall down upon his beard." The king of Gath was under the impression that he was deranged or very sorely diseased, and sent him away.

David then went to the cave of Adullam, where he was joined by four hundred men, who placed themselves under him as his soldiers. David left the cave of Adullam and went to Mizpeh of Moab. Having an interview with the king of Moab, he made arrangements for the safety of his parents, supposing they were not safe in the reach of Saul. After this he went to the forests of Hareth. Here he was joined by Abiathar, the son of Ahimelech, the high-priest; for he, with all his sons except this one, had perished.

Not long after this he helped the fortified town of Keilah, when the Philistines rose up against them, and God gave him a victory over the Philistines. It was not long until Saul heard of the victory, and supposing David was in the town he had thus delivered, he determined to go in search of him; but

David had fled from the place and had encamped in the wilderness of Ziph. Saul was quite anxious to take David; but having heard of his escape, he determined not to go until he learned where he was. After hearing that he was in the wilderness he sought him, but in vain. While David was wandering one day in the wood skirting the wilderness, he had an interview—and it was the last he ever had on earth—with Jonathan. Soon after this the inhabitants of the city of Ziph tried to betray David into the hands and power of Saul. Having heard of, or understanding this plot, David changed his position to Maon. His enemy sought him there; but he was called from his pursuit of David by the Philistines invading his kingdom, and its interests demanded his attention. David takes advantage of Saul's stay in pursuing him, and encamped in the wilderness of Engedi. Saul having heard that he was there goes in search of him with three thousand men, and being wearied he went into a cave to rest and sleep. It was the place where David and his men were concealed, and an opportunity was thus afforded David of killing Saul, but he would not, nor would he allow his men to do it; but he cut off the skirt of Saul's robe, and afterwards showed it to him. Saul was confounded at the generosity and kindness of David toward him, and determined to give up the pursuit of him. He acknowledged his convictions that David was to be the King of Israel, and asked a promise of him of kindness to his father's house. David readily made the promise, for he had made it before to Jonathan in their covenant. 1st Sam. xix, xx, and xxi.

Not long after this David was severely tried by the churlishness and meanness of Nabal, the Carmelite, and he would have destroyed the family of Nabal, but for the kindness to him, and the influence over him, of Abigail, Nabal's wife. This Carmelite was informed afterwards of the danger he had escaped by her interference, which had such an effect upon him that in ten days afterwards he died, when David took Abigail to be his wife. 1st Sam. xxv.

Again Saul was induced to go in search of David, the Ziphites having informed him where David was. He went as in the former case with three thousand chosen soldiers. He encamped with his men in the hill of Hachilah which is before Jeshimon. David sent out some spies to ascertain where Saul had pitched his royal tent, and in company with Abishai, David went under the cover of night and softly approached the tent where Saul lay sleeping, as also the captain of the host. Again Saul was in David's power, but he would not harm him. He took his spear that was sticking in the ground near him, and a cruise of water and went away. David then goes off a distance and awakes Abner and chides him for being so careless of his master's life; shows the spear and cruise of water. He enters into a conversation then with Saul in which he complains bitterly of his hostility and continued seeking after him to destroy him.

David seemed to have so far lost confidence as to conclude that he will certainly perish by the hand of Saul. He had no confidence in the seeming humiliation of Saul or his promises to cease hostility, and he flies to Achish the king of Gath, or joins the enemies of God and of his country. He was kindly received and Achish gave him Ziklag, and he lived there for more than a year. And when Achish made war with the Israelites he proposed to David to go out to battle with him, and he seemingly consented. But a question of propriety rose among the officers of the Philistine army as to David's going with them, they objected, and their king finding that they were all against him, advised David to return and he did so reluctantly. But when he arrived in the land of the Philistines he found his city Ziklag burnt with fire, and his wives and the wives of his men carried away captives by the Amelekites who had taken advantage of his absence. Added to the loss of his wives and of the city, and the cries of his men for their losses, they turned against him in mutiny and talked of stoning him. But David went in pursuit of the enemy and finding them he attacked them and destroyed the whole company except four hundred, who made their escape by the fleetness of their camels. They recovered their wives and families and all their goods, and he took much spoils for we are informed that he sent of the spoils that were taken to various cities of Judah, and to those persons and places where favor had been shown him.

The battle between the Philistines and Israelites that David would have been in, had not Achish sent him back, was a severe one, and Israel was made to flee before the enemy. And Saul and three of his sons fell in battle, among them was Jonathan. The information reached David that the Gilboe battle had gone against Israel, and that Saul and Jonathan were slain. David and his men engaged in a lamentation, and the composition of David is a most touching elegy. After this David by the direction of the Almighty, goes to Hebron with his family, and his men and their families, and they dwell in Hebron cities, and David was taken up by the men of Judah and anointed king.

One of the first acts on reaching the throne was to congratulate the inhabitants of Jabesh Gilead, over their kindness to the kingdom in rescuing the bodies of Saul and his sons from the Philistines. At first when David began to reign Ishbosheth, the son of Saul was also reigning in Hebron, and he probably continued to reign as long as David remained there, which was seven years and six months. 2d Sam. ii: 11. But two years after Ishbosheth began to reign, the house of Judah attached themselves to the interests of David, leaving him whom they had served two years. The first war in which David's kingdom was engaged was with the house of Saul, not because he desired to be at war with them, or had forgotten the covenant entered into and confirmed with Jonathan under the most solemn circumstances, and afterward with Saul when he parted with him the last time, having delivered him up his spear and cruise of water.

If David had been determined to extirpate the house of Saul, Ishbosheth would not have reigned for two years even in peace as he did. The wars seemed to be brought on and prosecuted by Abner and Joab, the former the chief servant of Ishbosheth, and the latter the captain of David's host. But we are informed that the house of David waxed stronger and stronger, and the house of Saul waxed weaker and weaker, until finally Abner proposed to David to transfer to him the interests of his master. But it was not long until, (even before this matter was consummated,) Abner fell by the murderous hand of Joab. David was much afflicted over this treachery of his servant in the death of Abner, and broke out in the most touching and pathetic lamentations: "Died Abner as a fool dieth? Thy hands were not bound, nor thy feet put into fetters. As a man falleth before wicked men. so fallest thou." Soon after this Ishbosheth was murdered by two of his captains, who came and informed David what they had done, and they brought as evidence of their deed, the head of Saul's son to him. David instead of looking upon them with favor, charged them with a most wicked act. They had murdered an innocent man in his own house, and upon his own bed, and one that they ought to have defended, which was the meanest treachery, and for this act declared that they should die. David thereby proving to all Israel that he was not the enemy of Saul's house.

All the people of Israel that up to this time had adhered to Saul's son, now turned their attention to David, and submitted to his authority as king. They gave three reasons why they rallied around him as king. One was, he was their countryman. "We are thy bone and thy flesh." Another reason was, in the days of king Saul, David was the general of Israel's armies, and led them to victory against their enemies. "Thou wast he that leddest out and broughtest in Israel." But a third reason was, God had selected him evidently as king and successor of Saul. "The Lord said to thee, thou shalt feed my people, and be a captain over Israel." With these convictions regarding David, it is not to be wondered at that they accepted him as King. For their satisfaction, David was anointed the third time to be king of Israel. First by Samuel, when he fed his father's sheep. Second at Hebron, seven years and six months before this third anointing done at Hebron, and he was now acknowledged by all Israel as king.

One of the first acts of David as king of all Israel was to retake the city of Jerusalem; for by some means it had come into the hands and was under the authority of the Jebusites. They had a strong fort upon the hill called Zion, which David took and transferred his court to it from Hebron. He then enters into friendly relations with Hiram, king of Tyre, who furnished him workmen and materials to build a house. Soon after this he is called upon to fight with the Philistines, who had so long been the bitter enemies of Israel, in the valley of Rephaim. He conquered them, and captured their images or false gods that they were accustomed to take with them when they went to war, and he burned them. The Philistines not being satisfied, met Israel again upon the same battlefield. David did not wish to fight with them, though flushed with victory, unless the Lord was willing. He enquired of the Lord as to whether he should go or not, and the Lord told him to go. He received direction as to the route he should take. God marked out the way for his army, and the precise time when he should make the attack. 2d Sam. v: 23–24: "Fetch a compass behind them and come upon them over against the mulberry trees. And let it be when thou hearest the sound of a going in the tops of the mulberry trees that then thou shalt bestir thyself," &c. He followed the divine direction, and soon the army was smitten.

He brought the ark of the Lord from Kirjath-jearim to Jerusalem, but a circumstance occurred that led him to leave it for awhile in the house of Obed-Edom. It was detained there three months, when he brought it up to his own city with gladness and joy. This made Jerusalem the centre of worship.

When David realized peace in his kingdom, (for his enemies were subdued) and prosperity among his subjects, he began to contemplate building a temple for the Lord, and made the prophet Nathan acquainted with his thoughts on the subject. The prophet encouraged him in it. But there was a barrier in the way, and that was the divine will. God let David know that he should not build a temple, but that Solomon, his son, should. The reason given was, (1st Chronicles, xxii: 8,) "Thou hast shed blood abundantly and hast made great wars."

David, in carrying on his kingdom, continued in war with his enemies. He fought and conquered the Philistines again, and the Moabites, and the king of Zobah, and the Syrians in general. He continued to increase in power as a king and in popularity with his subjects.

He is afforded an opportunity of showing friendship to the house of Saul in the person of Mephibosheth, Jonathan's son, and he improves it. David was injured by having his motives impugned by a king of the Ammonites, to whom he sent messengers and a message of condolence. They treated the messengers shamefully, by cutting off one-half of their beards and their garment. He resented the injury, and though they hired the Syrians to help them in war against him, yet he defeated them. The Syrians, chagrined over their defeat, determined to replenish their army and try it again, and they did, but were defeated, with a loss of seven hundred chariots and forty thousand horsemen, and the death of their commander, Shobach.

The Ammonites still war with David and there is a long contest, as Joab besieges the city of Rabbah, and finally a loss to Israel. It was about this time that David committed the darkest deed of his life, viz. the murder of Uriah the Hittite, and the crime which led to that murder. He was reproved in the most searching manner by Nathan the prophet, and was deeply humbled before the Lord. His sin in this matter seems to have been visited upon him when Ammon defiled Tamar. And again when Absalom killed Ammon. And again when Absalom rebelled and tried to lead the kingdon away from him, and finally was hung in an oak and fell in death by the darts of Joab. If he wept when the child of Bath-shebah was dying he wept still more when Absalom was dead.

When Absalom rebelled he was compelled to leave Jerusalem and fly for his life, but after he was dead David returned to Jerusalem.

An insurrection was raised by a wicked man named Sheba, but it was finally quelled and the leader of the insurrection was thrown over the wall of the city to which he had fled. Joab saw it, was satisfied, and retired from the city.

When the Gibeonites demanded at the hand of David seven sons of Saul, that they might hang them as an atonement for Saul's cruelty to them, David gave them up and no doubt thought he did right in doing so.

It was not because David had anything against the house of Saul, or desired to destroy them, but the requisition was made and he complied with it, saving the son of Jonathan because of the oath between them.

David took up the bones of Saul and Jonathan that were buried by the men of Jabesh Gilead under a tree, and interred them in the sepulcher of Saul's father in the country of Benjamin.

The Philistines yet made war upon Israel and David went in person to battle, and while fighting with his enemy "waxed faint;" this circumstance seems to have led Abishai to suggest to him that he go out to battle no more, *lest the light of Israel be quenched.*

We have an account of a wrong committed by David in numbering Israel, for which the Lord was angry with him, and in his anger determined to punish him. David realized that he had done wrong and confessed his sin. But confession was not enough then, and the Lord sent the prophet Gad to him with a proposition regarding the punishment. "Thus saith the Lord, I offer thee three things; choose thee one of them that I may do it unto thee," &c. David acted very sensibly and nobly in this matter. He showed his power of mind and wisdom in the choice. "Let us now fall into the hands of God, for his mercies are great; and let me not fall into the hands of man." *i. e.* I choose the pestilence. This choice brought him and his household on a level with all his subjects. The pestilence came and seventy thousand died, when the plague was stayed, and an altar was erected on the threshing floor of Ornan the Jebusite.

When David had reigned forty years, or nearly so, it was quite evident from his feebleness that his end was nigh, they procured a fair damsel whose name was Abishag, to cherish and minister unto the king.

Adonijah the eldest son of king David, seeing the feebleness of his father and knowing that he would soon die, followed the example of his brother Absalom in procuring chariots and horsemen, and arranging to have himself proclaimed king.

Nathan the prophet knew that Solomon was to be the successor of David, and he bade Bathsheba go in unto the king and remind him of the oath he had given, that Solomon, her son should reign after him. She did so, and while she was talking to the king Nathan came in to talk on the same subject, and inform him of the movement of Adonijah. David then commanded that Solomon be crowned king at once. Soon after this the dying David gave his last charge to Solomon—a charge relative to his personal conduct as a king in the affairs of his government and the manner in which he should treat Barzillai the Gileadite, who befriended him in a time of great peril, and also of the manner in which he should treat Joab who had been captain of his host—who had murdered two great men who were innocent, *viz.*, Abner the son of Ner, and Amasa. He also gave direction as to the treatment of Shimei, who cursed him as he went to Mahanaim, after which his work being all done and the affairs of his reign closed up, he died.

The life of David had been a remarkable one. A chain of Providence is clearly discoverable, formed of unbroken links from his boyhood until threescore and ten years were numbered. He lived well in the main, and he died well. He distinguished himself as a man of war; as a poet and musician; as a father full of kindness and love to his children, even where, as in the case of Absalom, they were guilty of the grossest wrongs toward him. And he was a faithful friend to those who were in league with him. He was buried with royal honors by Solomon in the city of David, and Josephus tells us that immense treasures were deposited in his sepulcher and remained there unmolested for thirteen hundred years.

The immortal spirit of the illustrious David went home to heaven.

DEBIR—[De′ber.]

DEBIR was a king of Eglon, who is referred to in Joshua x: 3. He was one of the four kings that Adonizedek, king of Jerusalem, called to his help when he heard that Ai was captured, and that the Gibeonites had made peace with Israel. The king of Jerusalem, and his four helpers, encamped before Gibeon, to fight with them. The Gibeonites at once sent to Joshua to help them, and he answers to the call, and quickly falling on the confederate forces, defeats them. In the 38th and 39th verses, we have an account of Joshua fighting against Debir, and taking it and the king thereof.

DEBORAH, 1—[Deb′o-rah,] *a word, a bee.*

DEBORAH was the nurse of Rebekah. We have no account of her, save her death and burial, which is narrated very briefly in Gen. xxxv: 8. "But Deborah, Rebekah's nurse, died, and she was buried beneath Bethel, under an oak, and the name of it was called Allonbachuth," the oak of weeping. This is the woman that was sent from Nahor with Rebekah by the faithful servant of Abraham, Eleazar.

But she is represented here as being in the family of Jacob. If she was we may suppose that as Jacob was the beloved of Rebekah, for she evidently loved him more than Esau, at the death of her mistress, she may have taken up her abode with Jacob, to live with him or his family, until her mortal career ended.

But she may have died and been buried here several years before, and the arrival of Jacob and his family at this place, may have led to a rememberance of her, and the facts recorded that here she died and was buried.

DEBORAH, 2—*A word, a bee.*

DEBORAH was a prophetess, and the wife of Lapidoth. The sins of Israel were numerous and aggravating in their nature, after their entrance into the land of Canaan, as well as while they were in the wilderness. God says: "Forty years long was I grieved with this generation, and said it is a people that do err in their hearts, and they have not known my ways."

Their sins were especially great in Canaan after the death of Joshua, their leader. He had conducted them safely into the country, commanded them in conquests, and ratified the apportionment of the conquered land to the different tribes. The people revolted from the true God, and went into gross idolatry. On account of it the Lord was angry with them, and delivered them into the hands of the "spoilers." When they repented a judge was raised up among them, who delivered them out of the hands of their enemies. But after the judge died they returned to their idolatry and corruption; and again the Lord was angry with them, and determined to punish them. He would leave the nations that were in the conquered country where Joshua died, that through them Israel might be proved. They corrupted themselves by doing evil in the sight of the Lord, and went into the service of "Baalim and the groves." Again God's anger was toward them, and he sold them into the hand of an enemy. They repented and cried to God for deliverance. He had mercy upon them, and raised them up a judge and deliverer in the person of Othniel. For forty years they had peace and prosperity; but when their judge died they relapsed into their former habits of wickedness and corruption; and again God gave them up. Their enemies over-powered them; took them captives, and took possession of the beautiful plain of Jericho, with the "city of palm trees."

Israel again repented, and entreated God to deliver them; and God raised Ehud, who first slew the king of Moab, to whom Israel had been in service for eighteen years. Ehud then led them against the Moabites, and they slew them by thousands, and soon Israel was again in peace and prosperity.

After him was Shamgar, who delivered Israel and triumphed against their enemies. But after eighty years they again went into grievous sins, and Jabin, king of Canaan, the captain of whose host was Sisera, greatly afflicted them. This was the most powerful king which had come against them, and Sisera was the most expert commander. Israel looked upon the nine hundred iron chariots of Jabin, and the large and well-trained army led on by Sisera, and they were afraid. They cried mightily unto God, and in the remembrance of their sins they were penitent. Their prayers for help were earnest and continued.

At length the Lord heard them, and a star arose upon them amid the darkness of their night, in the person of Deborah. Her influence in her country in this time of trouble is told in the following language: "At her word the stars in their courses fought against Sisera." Deborah was raised up to judge Israel. And this is the first instance of female government on record, save that of Miriam governing among the women of Israel during their sojourn in the wilderness. The husband of Deborah seems to have had no hand in the affairs of the government. She occupied the high position of head of affairs, civil and religious. She called to her aid Barak, the son of Abinoam, and appointed him general of the army. She was favored with revelations from God, which told her that the enemy should be conquered. She thus declared to Barak, her general, the revelations God had made to her, viz: that the enemy should be delivered into his hands. He credited what she said, but yet he refused to go out to battle unless she would accompany him. His refusal to go without her was probably because he saw that she was guided by divine influence—the spirit of inspiration was upon her, and he wished to have her along with him that he might know from her, when and how to make the attack. She agreed to go with him without any hesitancy, and with an army of ten thousand men, Barak made ready for battle.

As Sisera gathered the hosts of Jabin together for battle, Deborah was there and gave to her general, Barak, the word of command with the promise that Sisera should be delivered into his hands, for she knew full well that the Lord was gone out before him and would fight for Israel.

Having thus performed the part she was desired to perform by Barak, he at the head of his army went down from the top of Tabor where he had been encamped, and Deborah tarried on the mount to see how the battle went. She looked with intense anxiety upon her general and soldiers as they marched against the enemy. She saw them as they came near each other and commenced their attack. She witnessed the confusion and disorder in the ranks of the enemy. She saw the destruction of the iron chariots. It may be that she saw the chariot in which Sisera rode, and saw him as he alighted from it and fled on foot from the scene of action, and she might have seen the remaining soldiers as they wheeled and made an effort to escape, while Barak and his men pursued them in their flight, and cut them off until there was not a man of that vast army left. Even Sisera himself fell in death by the hand of Jael, the wife of Heber, though he escaped the slaughter on the battlefield. Deborah had prophesied that he should thus fall. "For the Lord shall sell Sisera into the hands of a woman."

Under the inspiration with which Deborah was blessed while she was yet on Mount Tabor, or after her return to the city of "palm trees," she composed the song of triumph usually styled the song of Deborah and Barak. The song itself is a sublime composition. Piety and true devotion to God shine forth in bold relief from its beginning to its end.

It is difficult to see where the conduct of this celebrated woman is most to be admired. Whether, when she was a judge of Israel, residing in the city of the plain, deciding difficult cases referred to her, and so winning the hearts of the people; or when she settles the generalship upon Barak, and commands him to enlist ten thousand men in the service of his country, or when she accompanies him to the scene of action and gives direction as to when he shall make the attack, and encourages him to hope for victory; or when she stands upon the mountain, and with intense anxiety watches the armies as they come in conflict; or when associated with Barak after the battle is over, her voice of song falls upon the ears of her soldiers and the delighted people, made free by the recent wonderful victory, in this song of glorious triumph. From every standpoint that we thus behold her she appears beautiful, but especially as a poetess and singer of this, her song, so full of sublime prophecy.

DEDAN 1—[De′-dan,] *their breasts, friendship, uncle.*

DEDAN was the son of Raamah, and the grandson of Cush, referred to in Genesis, x: 7, with Sheba, his brother. It is supposed that the posterity of Dedan settled a part of Arabia. They probably gave the name to the city of Dedan in Arabia Felix.

DEDAN 2.—*Their breasts, friendship, uncle.*

DEDAN was the son of Jokshan, and the grandson of Abraham. He is referred to in Genesis, xxv: 3, with his three sons Asshurim, Letushim, and Leummim. These three names are supposed to represent three tribes, and the Dedanites who traded with the Tyrians in ivory, ebony and fine clothes, for chariots, were the descendants of this Dedan. They are referred to in Ezekiel, xxvii: 15–20, as also, in Jeremiah, xxv: 23 and Isaah, xxi: 13.

DEKAR—[De′-kar,]

DEKAR was the father of one of the officers who were appointed by Solomon to provide victuals for his household. 1st Kings, iv: 9.

DELAIAH 1—[De-la-i′-ah,]

DELAIAH was one of the seven sons of Elioenai, and is referred to in the account given of the regal line of David and Solomon. 1st Chronicles, iii: 24.

DELAIAH 2.

DELAIAH, was one of the family of the priests, and is mentioned in the division that David made of the priests into twenty-four courses. Delaiah was the three and twentieth lot. 1st Chronicles, xxiv: 18.

DELAIAH 3.

DELAIAH was the father of Shemaiah, into whose house Nehemiah went when Tobiah and Sanballat were seeking to destroy him, having hired a false prophet to deceive him. Neh. vi: 10.

DELAIAH 4.

DELAIAH was a prince of Judah, and a counsellor of king Jehoiakim. He is referred to in Jeremiah, xxxvi: 12, with others who were in the king's house when Micaiah the son of Gemariah went there to report what he had heard from the roll of threatening prohecies that were written by Baruch from the mouth of Jeremiah. Delaiah and the other princes, sent after Baruch to read the roll to them. They reported it to the king, and on its being read to him he ordered it to be burnt. Delaiah with two others plead with the king not to burn it, but he would not hear them.

DELILAH—[Del′i-lah,] *poor, head of hair, bucket.*

DELILAH was a woman of the Philistines who resided in the valley of Sorek, to whom Samson became strongly attached. Judges, xvi: 4: "And it came to pass afterward that he loved a woman in the valley of Sorek, whose name was Delilah." He probably married her; if so, this, like his former marriage, was unfortunate. However much Samson loved this woman, there was a defect in her love—if, indeed, there was any love for him.

When the lords of the Philistines came to her and bade her entice Samson and see where his strength lay, they plainly told her the object they had in view: to prevail against him. She urged no objection to making the effort; but in the meanness of her heart she fixed her eyes upon the eleven hundred pieces of silver they promised to give her, and preferred that to the affection of a true man. She made effort as soon as opportunity was afforded to find out the occasion of Samson's great strength, that she might betray him into the hands of his enemies. Samson told her, "If they bind me with seven green withes that were never dried, then shall I be weak as another man." She gave the information to his enemies, and they provided her with the withes, then she bound him with them. Having bound the man that loved her so ardently, with a traitor's heart and lip she said, "The Philistines be upon thee, Samson," and he brake the withes as tow is broken when it toucheth the fire. She thought she was about to possess the eleven hundred pieces of silver, but she was mistaken. She then charges Samson with mocking her and telling her lies, and urges him to tell her the truth. He gave her another plan which she followed out, but it, too, failed; and yet the money was not hers. He gave her another plan, and she followed it up, but failed again. She then used a mode of persuading that took the strong man captive; she laid a snare that caught him. She said: "Samson, how canst thou say, I love thee, when thine heart is not with me. Thou hast mocked me these three times, and hast not told me wherein thy great strength lieth." She had touched the chord by this speech which vibrated through the heart of the strong man. He knew he loved her, and probably this was the first time she had ever given an expression indicating that she suspected his love. It was more than he could bear, and he told her all his heart. She saw the reasonableness of this last plan, and rejoiced in the prospect of her gain. She said to the Philistine lords, "Come up this once." Oh! what consumate meanness in Delilah! She made him sleep upon her lap, and while he was asleep she caused his locks to be shaved off, and then she began in person to insult him; and being satisfied that his strength was gone, she gave him over to the Philistines, and they put out his eyes.

Delilah proved herself unworthy of the love of Samson; and her conduct toward him and her treatment of him, was mean and detestable.

DEMAS—[De′mas,] *popular.*

Demas was a professor of christianity in the apostolic age, and it is thought by some, he was a preacher. But whether he was or not, he was for a while a companion of the apostle Paul, and useful to him during his imprisonment, and when that apostle writes his epistle to the Colossians, Demas, with St. Luke, sends his greetings to the church. Col. iv: 14.

But Demas did not remain faithful. He forsook Christ and the church, and turned his attention to some worldly business, for Paul in writing his 2d epistle to Timothy, says: "For Demas hath forsaken me, having loved this present world." 2d Tim. iv: 10. From which we may reasonably suppose he went into some more lucrative business. He followed, after this, some occupation in which there was more money than in that of preaching.

DEMETRIUS—[De-me′tri-us,] *belonging to Ceres, to corn.*

Demetrius was a silversmith of Ephesus, who made shrines for the temple of Diana.

Paul preached with wonderful success at this place, and the opposers of christianity were sorely vexed, and especially the tradesmen who were patronized by the priests of the goddess Diana, among whom was Demetrius. He headed a mob of workmen, and he secured them to act with him by telling them the craft was in danger.

Influenced by Demetrius, the mob became very furious, and for the space of two hours cried out, "Great is Diana of the Ephesians." The excitement was intense, and in the midst of it, they caught Aristarchus and Gaius, and dragged them into the theatre, with a view of having them condemned at once. They also seized Alexander, who was probably manifesting some disposition to allay the excitement. But as they saw he was a Jew, and hence not of their religion, they would not hear what he had to say, but dragged him into the crowd, and continued on in their shouts of, "Great is Diana of the Ephesians."

At length a man of some note and influence in the city, secured the attention of the mob, and allayed the excitement by telling them that these men they had seized were not blasphemers of their goddess, nor robbers of their temple—that they had nothing to fear as to the honor of Diana, or the fidelity of her Ephesian worshipers. He then informed them that they were altogether unjustifiable for the uproar they had made, and that they had laid themselves liable to be called to an account and punished for their conduct. He further told them that if Demetrius, who was heading this mob, or any one else had a charge against any one, they should bring it up, and prosecute according to law, and not fill the city with confusion thus. The city officer succeeded in quelling the excitement, and in dispersing the mob.

It is thought that Demetrius afterwards became a christian, and is the person referred to in the 3d epistle of John 12, in the following language. "Demetrius hath good report of all men, and of the truth itself."

DEUEL—[De-u′-el,] *the knowledge of God.*

DEUEL was of the tribe of Gad, and the father of the prince Eliasaph, who assisted Moses in numbering the tribes of Israel. Num. i: 14.

DIANA—[Di-a′-nah,] *luminous, perfect.*

DIANA was a goddess of the heathens, called one of the superior deities. This goddess was especially popular in Ephesus, as we see from Acts xix.

DIBLAIM—[Dib-la′-im.]

DIBLAIM was the father of Gomer, whom the prophet Hosea is represented as marrying, and she was the mother for him of two sons, viz: Jezreel and Lo Ammi, and one daughter, viz: Lo Ruhamah. Hosea i.

DIDYMUS—[Did′-i-mus,] *a twin.*

DIDYMUS was the surname of the Apostle Thomas. The phrase occurs, "Thomas, who is called Didymus," in John xi: 16. [See Thomas.]

DIKLAH—[Dik′-lah.]

DIKLAH was the son of Joktan and the grandson of Eber, and is referred to in the posterity of Shem. Genesis x: 27.

DINAH—[Di′-nah,] *judgment, who judges.*

DINAH was the daughter of Jacob and Leah and was probably quite young when Jacob enters the country of the children of Hamor and buys a parcel of ground for a home, and erects an altar to God, the God of Israel.

Dinah becomes acquainted with Shechem the son of Hamor the lord of the land. She is chargeable with folly in forming so intimate associations with the "daughters of the land." But her acquaintance with Shechem ended in crime and after the crime he endeavored to gain her affections that a marriage union might be consumated and she in some sort, be reconciled to the disgrace now come upon her. It does not appear that she acquiesced in the judgment of the prince as to marriage, but she seems by violence to have been detained in the house of Shechem, for when Simeon and Levi revenged the wrong done to their sister, and the folly that had been wrought in Israel, they found her in the dwelling of Hamor and Shechem and took her home. Gen. xxxiv: 1, &c.

DIONYSIUS—[Dy-o-nish′-e-us,] *divinely touched.*

DYONYSIUS is called the Areopagite. He was the judge in the Court of Areopagus referred to in Acts xvii: 34. He seems to have been a subject of converting grace through the instrumentality of Paul at Athens, for he and a woman named Demetrius with others are said to have believed.

It is said of him that he was a very learned man, but after his conversion became an humble evangelist, and finally suffered martyrdom for the cause of Christ.

DIOTREPHES—[Di-ot′-re-fez,] *nourished by Jupiter.*

This person is referred to in 3d John, 9. He was probably in membership in the church, but was not a true christian. He was exceedingly ambitious to be preferred to all others, and hence when John sent messengers with an epistle, Diotrephes opposed the reception and indulged in malicious and wicked language. "I wrote to the church, but Diotrephes, who loveth to have pre-eminence among them, receiveth us not, wherefore if I come, I will remember his deeds, which he doeth, prating against us with malicious words and not content therewith, neither doth he himself receive the brethren."

DISHAN—[Di′-shan.]

DISHAN was the son of Seir the Horite, and is referred to as a duke. Genesis, xxxvi: 21.

DISHON 1—[Di′-shon.]

DISHON was the son of Seir the Horite, whose posterity is referred to in Genesis, xxxvi: 21.

DISHON 2.

DISHON was the son of Arah, and grandson of Zibeon. He and his posterity are referred to in Gen. xxxvi: 25.

DODAI—[Do-da′-i.]

DODAI was one of David's mighty men, and the captain of the second month, when David instituted the monthly service of captains over twenty-four thousand men. 1st Chronicles, xxvii: 4.

DODANIM—[Do′-da-nim.]

DODANIM was the youngest son of Javan, and the grandson of Japheth. Genesis, x: 4, and 1st Chronicles, i: 7. Where his family settled is not known.

DODO 1—[Do′-do.]

DODO was of the tribe of Issacher, and the grandfather of Tola, one of the judges of Israel. Judges, x: 1.

DODO 2.

DODO is called the Ahohite, and was one of David's mightiest men. He is said to have smote the Philistines until his hand was weary and clave unto the sword. 2d Samuel, xxiii: 9.

DOEG—[Do′-eg,] *who acts with uneasiness, a fisherman.*

DOEG was called the Edomite. He was a servant of king Saul, and a great enemy of David. 1st Samuel, xxi: 7. His employment was that of a herdman, and he was the chief of them. He was at the city of the priests the day David procured the sword of Goliath, and the loaves of the shew bread, and reported the fact to Saul, which brought about the death of all the priests. 1st Sam. xxii: 17. It seems when Saul determined to slay the family of Ahimelech, he at once ordered his footmen, who were probably his body guard, to do it, but they would not. He then ordered Doeg to do it, and in obedience to the king's command he slew them, to the number of eighty-five. And when Abiathar, the only one that escaped, fled, and went to David, and told him what had been done, he moaned over it, and seemed disposed to reproach himself. And David wrote Pslams lii: cxx: cxl: upon this circumstance.

DORCAS—[Dor′-cas,] *the female of a roe-buck.*

DORCAS is brought to our view in Acts ix: 36, as a disciple. She was a good woman, had a reputation in the church for faith, and as proving her faith by good works. She was well known by the christians at Joppa, and many of them who were poor had fond remembrance of her kindness and ministrations to them in times of necessity. We learn from Acts ix: 36, "this woman was full of good works and almsdeeds which she did." But her reputation among the christians of Joppa, and her faith so nobly developed were not proof against sickness and death. God in his Providence saw fit to bring upon Dorcas sickness—disease took hold of her, and she died. In all the membership of that church, there probably was not one that, (in the estimation of its members,) could not have been better spared. A true friend in the church to her poor is a christian philanthropist indeed. As soon as she died, her friends with sorrowing hearts prepared her grave clothes and dressed her for the tomb.

Having heard that the apostle Peter was at Lydda, a place about six miles from Joppa, they sent for him to come at once to Joppa. They communicated to him through the messengers the sad intelligence that Dorcas was dead. The real object of this sending for him probably was that he might comfort them in their great sorrow with words of truth, and that he might be with them in performing the last sad duty due to the dead from the living, viz: the burial. When the messengers arrived and informed Peter for what intent they had come, and that the church at Joppa desired that he would not delay to come to them, without any hesitancy he arose and went with them. It does not appear that Peter went expecting to be used as an instrument in so great a work as the raising of Dorcas from the dead. But God intended to work this miracle, and inclined Peter to arise and go to this scene of sorrow.

As soon as the apostle arrived, they conducted him into the upper chamber where the christian woman lay in the embrace of death and shrouded for the tomb. He was not alone in that chamber of death. As he stood and looked upon the clay-cold form, motionless and speechless, he heard the cries of the anguish-stricken hearts around him. The widows who had been relieved by Dorcas in her life time were then pronouncing blessings upon her memory as their benefactress, and they wept in the remembrance that they could no more enjoy her counsels and share in her charities, and to satisfy the apostle that their sorrow was called for, and that their tears were the over-flowings of hearts over charged, they showed him the coats and the garments which she made while living. This that they were exhibiting was clothing with which this woman, when alive, "clothed the naked." She was the friend of all, and her death was a common loss.

Peter then under the direction of the inspiring spirit began to prepare for the forthcoming display of Almighty power. He "put them all forth" invited them to leave the upper chamber—that he might with more freedom and less disturbance pour out his soul to God in prayer. He then knelt down and earnestly prayed for her restoration to life. Behold the scene; an honored apostle kneeling beside the corpse of a departed Christian woman, and praying for a display of resurrection power. The virtues of this good woman as they had been represented were fresh in his mind, but he desired a new attestation to the truth of his own mission as an apostle—and to the truth of the gospel he preached. After praying, he turned to the still lifeless form before him and said, "Tabitha arise." Oh what faith he must have had; how firm must have been the hold he took on God while praying, to close his prayer and speak to the yet unconscious matter "arise." Divine power was displayed as he thus spake, and Dorcas opened her eyes and looked upon the apostle. The first object her eyes lighted upon in coming back to life was Peter. He saw her gaze fixed upon him, and reaching forth his hand as she sat up, he assisted her. Peter then called the saints and widows and presented Dorcas alive to them.

There was we may reasonably suppose a large amount of surprise on the part of her who was raised as well as on the part of those who had lamented her death. And whether it was a matter of rejoicing on her part or not it was undoubtedly on the part of those who were so deeply wounded in her death. But the miracle was a glorious confirmation of the gospel, and as such was a matter of rejoicing to all the Christians and especially to the devoted Dorcas.

How long she lived after this we do not know. It may be that for several years she continued her work of *ministry to the necessity of saints*, and doing good especially to the poor—until again she crossed the mystic river, no more to return to a life in a state of probation.

DRUSILLA— [Dru-sil′-lah,] *watered by the dew.*

DRUSILLA was the youngest sister of Agrippa, Bernice and Mariamme. The fathers name was Agrippa and her mothers name was Cyprus. Drusilla was married to Azezus, but this marriage was dissolved by Felix who had fallen in love with her and persuaded her to forsake her husband and marry him. She did so and we have an account of her in the New Testament as the wife of Felix. When Paul defends himself before Felix, and preaches Christ unto him, and when he "reasoned of righteousness, temperance and judgment to come," Drusilla the wife of Felix was present. Acts xxiv: 24. And after certain days when Felix came with his wife Drusilla who was a Jewess, he sent for Paul and heard him concerning the faith in Christ. It is said by Josephus that she had a son by Felix who was buried in melted lava by an eruption of the volcanic Mount Vesuvius.

DUMAH—[Du′-mah,] *silence, resemblance.*

Was a son of Ishmael hence the grandson of Abraham. Gen. xxv: 14. It is generally supposed that the posterity of this man gave his name to a place called Dumah in Arabia, and in Isa xxi: 11. This place is the subject of prophecy. The prophecy is called "the burden of Dumah."

EBAL—[E′-bal,] *a heap, collection of old age.*

EBAL was the son of Shobal, and the grandson of Seir the Horite. Gen. xxxvi: 23.

EBED-MELECH—[E′bed-me-lek,] *the king's servant.*

EBED-MELECH was an Ethiopian slave of King Zedekiah. We have an interesting account of him in Jer. xxxviii. When he heard of the imprisonment of the prophet Jeremiah in a gloomy dungeon, he went to the king and represented it to him as cruel treatment of so good a man. He told

Zedekiah that the prophet was in the mire and filth, and moreover was in danger of being starved. He wrought upon the king's sympathies so that he ordered him to take thirty men with him and draw the prophet up.

Ebed-melech, glad of an opportunity to assist the persecuted servant of God, went to him, and let down ropes, by which to draw him up; and that the ropes might not hurt the prophet's arms, he let down old rags, and instructed Jeremiah to put them under his arm-holes and under the ropes. Then they drew him up and took him out of the dungeon, and Jeremiah remained, after this kindness of Ebed-melech, in the court of the prison. In Jer. xxxix: 15, 18, we have an account of the reward for this kindness shown to Jeremiah. The Lord ordered the prophet to go and tell Ebed-melech, the Ethiopian, that evil was purposed upon the city and its inhabitants, but that evil should not come upon him. He was assured that he should not be given into the hands of the men of whom he was afraid, neither should he fall by the sword; but his life should be precious in the sight of God. And the reason given for this, his deliverance, was "because thou hast put thy trust in me, saith the Lord." He had manifested that trust by caring for the prophet Jeremiah, and pleading affectionately for him before King Zedekiah.

EBER—[E′-ber,] *one that passes, anger, wrath.*

EBER is the same as Heber, the son of Shebah, and grandson of Shem. 1st Chron. i: 25.

EBIASAPH—[E′-bi-a′-saf,] *a father that gathers together.*

EBIASAPH was a Kohathite Levite, of the family of Korah, one of the forefathers of the prophet Samuel and of Heman the singer. 1st Chron. vi: 23-27.

EDEN—[E′-den,] *pleasure, delight.*

EDEN was a Gershonite Levite, and son of Joah. 2d Chron. xxix: 12. He lived in the days of King Hezekiah, and is probably the same person that is referred to in 2d Chronicles, xxxi: 15.

EGLAH—[Eg′-lah,] *heifer, chariot, round.*

EGLAH was a wife of David and the mother of the sixth son, whose name was Ithream. It is thought that Eglah was the same as Michal, Saul's daughter; but as it does not apppear that Michal had a child "to the day of her death," it is likely that this woman was one which he had while in Hebron. 1st Chron. iii: 3.

EGLON — [Eg′-lon,] *heifer, chariot, round.*

EGLON was the King of Moab, and is thought to have been the immediate successor of Balak. He fought against Israel and had success as we may judge by the especial appointment of God. This King of Moab, together with the Amalekites had greatly oppressed Israel. He had prevailed against them, they were subdued by him and his allies and served him eighteen years. Judges iii: 12, 13. "And the children of Israel did evil again in the sight of the Lord, and the Lord strengthened Eglon the King of Moab against Israel, because they had done evil in the sight of the Lord. And he gathered unto him Ammon and the children of Amalek and went and smote Israel, and possessed the City of Palm Trees." Thus we observe the power of God was with Eglon, for he strengthened him to conquer Israel.

The children of Israel recognized the judgment of God upon them in the oppression they endured, "they cried unto the Lord." By this we may understand that they repented of their sins, and implored God against whom they had sinned, to grant them pardon, and deliver them from Eglon the King of Moab. God heard them, and raised them up a deliverer in the person of Ehud a Benjamite. The children of Israel sent a present to Eglon by the hand of this man. In which they pretended submission to him. Eglon received their messenger and present. But before Ehud returned to his people he approached the king under pretence of a secret errand. He pretended to have a communication which was to be made to him alone. Accordingly Eglon sent all his servants from the apartment where he was, and awaited the message of Ehud, who approached the unsuspecting king and drew a dagger with which he had provided himself and thrust it into the body of Eglon, so that he died almost instantly. Ehud escaped leaving the mangled body of the king in his parlor. His servants waited for awhile and wondered that their services were not demanded. At length they procured a key and opened the door, when, to their horror and astonishment, they saw the dead body of their King lying on the floor, and at once they understood that the messenger from Israel had murdered him.

EHI—[E′-hi.]
Was one of the sons of Benjamin and was numbered with the family of Jacob who went down into Egypt. Gen. xlvi: 21.

EHUD—[E′-hud,] *he that praises.*
Ehud was raised up as a deliverer for Israel after they had been subdued by Eglon, the king of Moab, who was assisted by Ammon and Amalek. Their eighteen years submission and servitude was ended by Ehud, the son of Gera, a Benjamite, killing the king of Moab, while pretending to give him alone, a message from God. He is said to have been left-handed, and we learn that as his sword or dagger was hanging by his right side, he grasped it with his left hand, and thrust it into the body of Eglon, which resulted in almost instant death.

After Ehud had killed the king, he fled to Mt. Ephraim, and collected a body of Hebrews, with which he took at once from the Moabites, the fords of Jordan, to prevent the return of any of them, who were panic stricken, when they heard that their king was dead. He slew with his Hebrew soldiery, ten thousand of them in their attempt to cross the Jordan at the fords. Judges iii: 29. "And they slew of Moab at that time, about ten thousand men, all lusty, and all men of valor, and there escaped not a man." These men that Ehud killed at the fords were in all probability, Moabite soldiers, and the most valorous troops—such as Eglon had stationed among the Israelites to keep them in submission. Through the influence and conquest of Ehud, Moab was conquered and Israel had rest for eighty years.

It is quite likely that Ehud had a divine call, and hence the killing of the king was not murder, or the act of a base and deceiving assassin, but a compliance with the divine will, made known to him "when he was raised up as a deliverer." It may be his commission involved the duty of the killing of Eglon, of putting the tyrant and oppressor of Israel to death. His call is not fully specified, nor his motives expressed. The sacred historian simply recorded the fact. He judged Israel we suppose, till he died, with honor to himself, and profit to the people. It is thought by some, that Shamgar, the son of Anath, who is generally reckoned as the third judge of Israel, judged Israel in the western part of the country, and Ehud in the eastern at the same time. For while Judges iii: 31 intimates that Shamgar was his successor, Judges iv: 1, seems to intimate that Ehud was succeeded by Deborah, who delivered Israel from Jabin, king of the Canaanites, to whom they became subject after Ehud was dead. We might infer from the history contained in Judges iv, that Shamgar was not numbered with the judges of Israel.

EKER.
A descendant of Judah, through the families of Hezron and Jerahmeel. 1st Chron. ii: 27.

ELADAH.
A descendant of Ephraim, through Shuthelah. 1st Chron. vii: 20.

ELAH—[E′lah,] *an oak, oath, an imprecation.*
Elah was the son of Baasha, and king of Israel. His reign was very short, lasting only two years. 1st Kings, xvi: 8: "In the twenty and sixth year of Asa, king of Judah, began Elah, the son of Baasha, to reign over Israel in Tirzah two years." He was murdered by his servant, Zimri, while drinking himself drunk in the house of Arzah, his steward. The precise manner in which Zimri accomplished this murder of the king of Israel is not recorded; but if Elah was drunk, as the history states he was, it was not very difficult for him to accomplish the murder. The reason why God permitted the family of Baasha to be cut off and

Elah to be murdered, was, they were grievous offenders against God—caused Israel to sin and provoke divine anger. 1st Kings, xvi: 13.

ELAM—[E'lam,] *a young man, a virgin, secret, an age.*

ELAM was the eldest son of Shem, whose posterity were called Elamites. His name occurs in Gen. x: 22, where the names of the children of Shem are given. The celebrated Chedorlaomer was king of a country that was named probably from Elam, the son of Shem. Gen. xiv: 1. There is also an Elam mentioned in Ezra, ii: 7, and twelve hundred and fifty-four of his children came up from Babylon with Zerubbabel; and still another Elam mentioned in the 31st verse, whose children numbered the same as the former. There was also an Elam one of the sacred porters. 1st Chron. xxvi: 3.

ELASAH, 1—[El'a-sah,]

A priest in the time of Ezra, who had married a Gentile wife. Ezra, x:22.

ELASAH, 2,

The son of Shaphan, one of the two men who were sent on a mission by King Zedekiah to Nebuchadnezzar, at Babylon. Jer. xxix: 3.

ELDAAH—[El-da'ah,]

One of the sons of Midian, and the last one named. Gen. xxv: 4; 1st Chron. i: 33.

ELDAD—[El'-dad,] *loved or favored of God.*

ELDAD was the associate of Medad, which two were among the seventy appointed by Moses as his assistants. Whether they modestly declined the office, or were detained from going to the tabernacle at the time the others went, by some unavoidable hindrance, we are not certain. These two men remained in the camp, but while the other elders were engaged in the active work at the tabernacle, the spirit of prophecy came upon them, and they prophesied in the camp. They used the functions of their office among the people in the camp. Supposing it was a breach of the order that should prevail among those who were in the sacred office, a young man ran and told Joshua, and Joshua being of the same opinion, asked Moses to forbid them. Moses reproved him for the request. "Art thou jealous on my account, afraid I shall be eclipsed. I am not afraid. On the contrary, I would be glad if all the Lord's people were prophets. If the same spirit that rests upon me, rested upon all the people. Numbers, xi: 26–28.

ELEAZAR 1—[El-e-a'-zar,] *the help, or court of God.*

ELEAZAR was the third son of Aaron. Long after the death of Nadab and Abihu, he was with his father, and assisted in the high and holy work of the priesthood. He succeeded Aaron as high-priest, and was inducted into that office as we learn from Num. xx: 25–28, by Moses on Mount Hor. The circumstances under which he entered the high-priesthood, are thrilling, intensely so. God had declared that Aaron's pilgrimage was ended: his work was done, and he should now be gathered unto his people. Moses was commanded to take Aaron and his successor, Eleazar, and bring them up into Mount Hor, and strip Aaron of his sacred vestments and put them upon his son, this was to denote the transfer of the office from the father to the son. Aaron went in company with his brother and son, after ministering for the last time in the tabernacle, after looking the last time at the Urim and Thummim, the divine presence in the pillar of cloud and fire, up to the top of Mount Hor, resigned his charge, saw his son inducted into the office, pronounced upon him a father's blessing, then laid him down upon the mountain and died, and Moses and Eleazar closed his eyes. After his death, they buried him, and then came down from the Mount, and announced the sad intelligence to all Israel. Eleazar, his son, was recognized as his successor.

Eleazar assisted Joshua to divide the land of Canaan. Numbers, xxxiv: 17. "These are the names of the men which shall divide the land unto you, Eleazar, the priest, and Joshua, the son of Nun." They were associated with one of every tribe.

Eleazar executed the office of high-priest about twenty-three years at Shiloh, and died, and was buried in a hill that belonged to Phineas, his son and successor. Joshua, xxiv: 33. It is likely he died a very few years after Joshua. He was among the last, we may suppose, that witnessed the miracles with which God favored them in the wilderness.

ELEAZAR 2—*The help, or court of God.*

Eleazar was the son of Dodo, the Ahohite. He was one of David's mighty men. 2d Sam. xxiii: 9. He seems to have been the second of the three mighty men. Adina being the first, and Shammah the third. He was with David at Ephas-damim, and contended with the Philistines, when he was deserted by his fellows, he stood his ground in or near a barley field, and fought with the enemy and smote them. It is said he smote "until his hand was weary and his hand clave unto the sword." Along with Shammah, he defended a field of barley so valorously, that the Philistines fled before them. 1st Chronicles, xi: 12–14.

ELEAZAR, 3—*The help or court of God.*

A Merarite Levite, son of Mahli and grandson of Merari. 1st Chron. xxiii: 21, 24–28.

ELEAZAR, 4—*The help or court of God.*

A priest who took part in the feast of dedication, under Nehemiah. Neh. xii: 42.

ELEAZAR, 5—*The help or court of God.*

One of the sons of Parosh, an Israelite, who had married a foreign wife and put her away. Ezra, x: 25.

ELHANAN, 1—[El-ha′-nan,] *grace, gift, or mercy of God.*

The son of Dodo, a Bethlehemite. He was one of David's mighty men. 1st Chron. xi: 26.

ELHANAN, 2—*Grace, gift, or mercy of God.*

The son of Jair, who slew a brother of Goliath of Gath, the Philistine giant. The name of the giant he slew was Lahmi, and the place where he slew him was Gob. 1st Chron. xx: 5, gives an account of the slaying, and 2d Sam. xxi: 19, gives an account of the place and the act.

ELI—[E′-li,] *the offering or lifting up.*

Eli was a Jewish high priest, who was descended from Ithamer the son of Aaron. His history is recorded in 1st Samuel i: ii: iii: how it came that the high priesthood passed from the family of Eleazer to that of Ithamer, from whom Eli was descended we cannot certainly tell. We gather from the history of Eli that he was a good man and a faithful judge in Israel. He was judge as well as high priest. It is said in i: 9, "Eli sat upon a seat by a post of the temple of the Lord." This imports that he sat upon a seat of judgment. He heard the case of Hannah and changed his mind as it regarded her condition, and sent her away with his blessing. Though he was a good man his sons Hophni and Phineas were very wicked. They committed very great crimes which were reported to their father. He was pained at their wickedness and reproved them, but his reproof seems to be very mild. It was in the following language "why do ye such things? for I hear of your evil doings by all this people. Nay my sons for it is no good report that I hear; Ye make the Lord's people to transgress. If one man sin against another the judge shall judge him; but if a man sin against the Lord who shall entreat for him?" This reproof shows the kindness of his heart toward his sons, but it exhibits the secret of his failure in their education. He had been an affectionate, yet an over-indulgent father. He had probably failed to bring them under proper restraints and discipline, and now though their conduct was so unbecoming he continued them in their offices. He had the anthority to disrobe them but did not use it.

Samuel the son of Hannah was placed under his charge when but three years of age, and was made at that early age the medium of communication on the part of the divine Being with Eli. The child came to him three times supposing he called him—when Eli told him it was the Lord who was talking to him and bade him answer the next call, which he did, and faithfully reported to the venerable high priest. Eli had been warned by a prophet of God whose name is not given, 1st Sam. ii: 27. But now his little pupil receives from God for the aged man a reiteration of the calamities that are to come upon him, and reports them. Through Samuel Eli learned that these trials were just at the door—they were about then to fall upon him. He should soon see his beloved country invaded by a foe; his sons slain both of them in one day, and some other family take the honors of the priesthood that had belonged to his. He received the denunciations without murmuring, for he knew full well that it was just, hence he bowed to the divine will.

It was not long after Samuel had thus communicated the divine will, until the Philistines invaded the country, fought with the Hebrews and conquered them, killing thirty thousand of them, and Hophni and Phineas, the sons of Eli, were slain according to the prediction. But this was not all. They had taken the ark of God, which ought to have remained at Shiloh, with them to battle. They thought it would be an advantage to them and had sent for it to the camp, but the battle went against them and it was taken possession of by the enemy. It was not long after the defeat until a messenger went and told Eli. He could bear to hear that Israel was defeated, and even to hear that his sons were slain, though that intelligence was sad and filled his soul with grief, but when he heard that the ark of God was taken, he could not endure it, "he fell backward from off the seat by the side of the gate, and his neck brake and he died."

Eli was an old man, ninety years of age when these calamities came upon him, and he had judged Israel for forty years. The prediction regarding his family was fulfilled. His two sons and his daughter-in-law died the same day he did. Ahitub, the brother of Ichabod succeeded Eli, and Ahiah succeeded him. Ahimelech succeeded him, and his family were all murdered by Saul except Abiathar, who fled for his life and went to David, when the high priesthood was again settled in the family of Eleazar in the person of Zadok. Solomon deposed Abiathar, the only remaining descendant of Eli, who had served in the priesthood during the reign of David.

ELIAB, 1—[E-li′-ab,] *god my father.*

Eliab was the son of Helon, of the tribe of Zebulun. He was the chief of that tribe, and was associated with Moses and Aaron in managing the business of their nation, at the time of their exodus from the land of Egypt. Num. i: 9. And when the tabernacle was fully set up, he made an offering for his tribe. Numbers vii: 24.

ELIAB, 2—*God my father.*

Was a Reubenite, the son of Pallu, the father of Dathan and Abiram, or progenitor. Numbers xxvi: 8; xvi: 1-12. Deut. xi: 6.

ELIAB, 3—*God my father.*

Was one of David's brothers, and the eldest of Jesse's family. His daughter is represented as marrying her cousin Rehoboam. 1st Sam. xvi: 6. 2d Chron. xi: 18.

ELIAB, 4—*God my father.*

Was a sacred porter in the time of David. 1st Chron. xv: 18.

ELIAB, 5—*God my father.*

Was one of the Gadites who came over to, and joined David in the wilderness. 1st Chron. xii: 9.

ELIAB, 6—*God my father.*

Was one of the forefathers of Samuel, the prophet. 1st Chron. vi: 27.

ELIADA, 1—[E-li′a-dah,] *the knowledge of God.*

Eliada was one of David's sons, born unto him after Jebus was taken, and Jerusalem established. 2d Sam. v: 16.

ELIADA, 2—*The knowledge of God.*

Was a mighty man of war, who led two hundred thousand of his tribe, Benjamites, to the army of Jehoshaphat. 2d Chron. xvii: 17.

ELIAHBA—[E-li′ah-bah,]

The Shaalbonite, was one of David's mighty men. 2d Sam. xxiii: 32.

ELIAKIM 1,—[E-li′a-kim,] *the resurrection of God, God the avenger.*

Eliakim was the son of Hilkiah, and was associated with Shebna the scribe, and Joah the recorder, in an embassy to Sennacherib, king of Assyria, from King Hezekiah. The office that Eliakim filled under King Hezekiah was that of chief treasurer and master of the household. He was probably chief of the embassy. He stood before Sennacherib's servant, Rab-shakeh, and delivered the message. 2d Kings, xviii: 26. They received nothing from Rab-shakeh but abusive language, and protested against it. They especially complained that he used such words in the hearing of the Jews, and asked him not to speak longer in the Jews' language, but to speak in the Syrian tongue. But Rab-shakeh would not cease; on the contrary, spoke yet in the Jews' language and louder than before. When they found they could obtain nothing but abuse from him, they returned to King Hezekiah weeping, with their clothes rent, and told him the words of Rab-shakeh. 2d Kings, xviii: 37.

Not long after this King Hezekiah sent Eliakim and one other of the former embassadors, with a company of the elders of the priests, to Isaiah, the prophet, the son of Amoz; and in the ears of that prophet they poured out their complaints. They set the case of their imminent peril before him, and earnestly desired his prayers and intercessions in their behalf. Isaiah received Eliakim and his associates, and prophesied evil concerning their enemies. Eliakim went back to Hezekiah from the interview with Isaiah with very different feelings to those which he had when he returned from Rab-shakeh. He came not now weeping over the city —doomed, as he thought, to destruction—and over the blasphemy of the enemies of God and his people, but expecting divine deliverance, as promised by the prophet Isaiah.

Eliakim is spoken of in very high terms in Isa. xxii: 20, &c. The Lord called him to the high and important position of chief treasurer and master of the household. He was to wear the king's robe, be girded with his girdle, govern in his kingdom, and be a father in Jerusalem and to the inhabitants of Judah.

Because of his position and his many excellencies, he has sometimes been styled an important type of Christ. Like Christ, he was over the household of God. He was the messenger of peace; and he wept over Jerusalem and the inhabitants of Judah.

ELIAKIM 2 — *The resurrection of God, God the avenger.*

Was the same as Jehoiakim King of Judah. 2d Kings xxiii: 34.

ELIAKIM 3 — *The resurrection of God, God the avenger.*

Was one of the priests in the days of Nehemiah, who helped to build and dedicate the walls of Jerusalem. Neh. xii: 41.

ELIAKIM 4 — *The resurrection of God, God the avenger.*

Was in the line of Joseph the husband of Mary, and appears as the eldest son of Judah or Abiud. Matt. i: 13.

ELIAKIM 5 — *The resurrection of God, God the avenger.*

He appears in the line of Christ as the son of Melea and the father of Jonan. Luke iii: 30, 31.

ELIAM 1—[E-li′-am,] *the people of God.*

Was the father of Bathsheba, the wife of David. 2d Sam. xi: 3.

ELIAM 2—*The people of God.*

Was the son of Ahithophel the counsellor. 2d Sam. xxiii: 34.

ELIASAPH—[E-li′-a-saf.]

Eliasaph was the son of Deuel, of the tribe of Gad. He was chief of his tribe, and was associated with Moses and Aaron in managing the business of their nation at the time of their exodus from the land of Egypt. Num. i: 14. And when the tabernacle was fully set up he made an offering for his tribe. Num. vii: 42.

ELIASHIB, 1—[E-li′-a-shib,] *the God of conversion.*

Eliashib was one of the priests appointed by David when he divided them into twenty-four orders. His lot was the eleventh. 1st Chronicles, xxiv: 12.

ELIASHIB, 2—*The God of conversion.*

Eliashib is brought to our view in Neh. iii: 1, as also xiii: 4–7. He is represented as a leader in the important work of rebuilding the walls of the sacred city. As he was a high priest, it was right that he should superintend. He is represented as building the sheep-gate, that may have been the gate by which the offerings were brought into the temple.

But in the latter quotation he is represented as committing a great wrong by preparing a chamber in the temple for a heathen—Tobiah, the Ammonite. He was allied to this heathen in some way, how, we do not know, but probably he had married his daughter. His conduct in this respect was very wicked, and not approved by the church or nation. It was an abuse of power on his part as high priest, having the oversight of the temple. The error was afterwards corrected. Neh. xiii: 8. "And it grieved me sore; therefore I cast out all the household stuff of Tobiah out of the chamber." Nehemiah cleansed the temple of this impurity. Whether Eliashib was punished for his unfaithfulness to the high charge he had received, and the reproach he had brought on the priesthood, we know not.

ELIATHAH—[E-li′-a-thah,] *thou art my God, my God comes.*

ELIATHAH was one of the sons of Heman, and when the lots were cast, and the singers were divided into twenty-four courses, the twentieth lot came to him. 1st Chron. xxv: 27.

ELIDAD—[E-li′-dad.]

ELIDAD was the son of Chislon, of the tribe of Benjamin, and was one of the princes that assisted Joshua and Eleazar in dividing the land of Canaan among the tribes of Israel. Numbers xxxiv: 21.

ELIEL, 1—[E′li-el,]

One of the heads of the tribe of Manasseh, settled on the east of the Jordan. 1st Chron. v: 24.

ELIEL, 2.

A son of Toah, and a forefather of Samuel the prophet. 1st Chron. vi: 34.

ELIEL, 3.

A chief man of the tribe of Benjamin, referred to in 1st Chron. viii: 20.

ELIEL, 4.

Is called the Maharite, and was one of the heroes of David. He is referred to in the list of the king's guard. 1st Chron. xi: 46.

ELIEL, 5.

One of the Gadites who came to David when he was in the wilderness, and being hunted by Saul. 1st Chron. xii: 11.

ELIEL, 6.

Was a Kohathite Levite at the time of removing the ark from the house of Obed-edom to Jerusalem. 1st Chron. xv: 9.

ELIEL, 7.

Was a Levite in the time of Hezekiah, and one of the overseers of the offerings made in the temple. 2d Chron. xxxi: 13.

ELIEZER, 1—[E-li-e′-zer,] *help or court of my God.*

ELIEZER was the servant of Abram, "born in his house." He was of Damascus. Abram had no son, and realized that his servant, Eliezer was for the present, and was likely to be, instead of a son unto him. Gen. xv: 2. "And Abram said, Lord God what wilt thou give me, seeing I go childless, and the steward of my house is this Eliezer of Damascus." He had committed unto this servant the care of his estate, who might be faithful as a servant until his master died, when Eliezer would have control and bear rule over all that he had. Abram seemed as yet to be in doubt as to whether it would be his seed begotten or his seed adopted of whom God would make a great nation, and who should be as the dust of the earth in number. Genesis xii: 2, and xiii: 16. But the promise of a son was made to Abram, and in due time Isaac was born. When Isaac was grown up, and Abram sought for him a wife, he called Eliezer his faithful servant unto him, and bound him by a solemn oath not to take a wife for Isaac of the daughters of the Canaanites, but to go to Messopotamia, and procure one from amongst the kindred. Eliezer was also charged not to enter into arrangements that would make it necessary for Isaac to go there either for a temporary or permanent residence. Gen. xxiv: 1–6.

Eliezer went to Nahor and tarried at a well until Rebekah, the daughter of Bethuel came out with a pitcher to draw water. He had prayed earnestly to the Lord to give him "good speed." He had indicated the manner in which the damsel that was to return with him should speak and act. Rebekah filled the request of Eliezer, then invited him to her father's house to tarry for the night, and he agreed to do so, thankful in his heart to God for the indications he had of success in his undertaking. Finding that the maiden was a neice of his master Abram, he presented her with a set of golden ear-rings and a pair of bracelets. She soon introduced the stranger to her father's family, and he made known at once to them his embassy and the dealings of the Lord with him. He designated Rebekah as a wife for his master, and asked that they send her without delay with him. He demanded a positive answer at once. The father and brother expressed their convictions that it was of the Lord, and hence they dare not oppose it. They threw the responsibility of settling the matter upon her, and she decided to go. Eliezer then presented her with fine jewels and rich apparel, he also gave valuable presents to her mother and her brother, and the next morning he took his departure for Beersheba, and in a few days arrived there. When Eliezer neared his master's tent, he saw Isaac in the field, informed Rebekah who it was, and the two met and in a short time afterwards were married, according to the Patriarchal customs. Genesis xxiv.

ELIEZER, 2—*Help or court of my God.*

ELIEZER was the son of Moses and Zipporah, his Midianitish wife. He was the younger son, Gershom being the older. His name is not mentioned where he is first referred to, viz: when Moses makes ready to go with his wife and sons into Egypt, on the mission to which Jehovah had appointed him. Ex. iv: 20. The name of Eliezer occurs in Ex. xviii, when Jethro, the father-in-law of Moses brings Zipporah and her two sons to him. The family of Eliezer, like that of Gershom, was incorporated with the Levites, and they had together with the family of his brother, care of the tabernacle and tent. Num. iii: 21–26. They served at the tabernacle and were appointed to carry burdens. Num. iv: 24–28.

ELIEZER, 3—*Help or court of my God.*

The son of Zichri, was the ruler of the tribe of Reuben. 1st Chronicles, xxvii: 16.

ELIEZER, 4—*Help or court of my God.*

ELIEZER, the son of Dodavah was a prophet who foretold king Jehoshaphat that the fleet which he had built in conjunction with the wrecked king Ahaziah, should be so far disabled as to be unable to go on the contemplated voyage to Tarshish. 2d Chron. xx: 37. "Because thou hast joined thyself with Ahaziah, the Lord hath broken thy works. And the ships were broken, that they were not able to go to Tarshish."

ELIHU, 1—[E-li'hu,] *he is my God himself.*

ELIHU was the son of Barachel. He visited the afflicted patriarch Job, in the midst of his distress. When he attended the conference between Job and his three friends, Eliphaz the Temanite, Bildad the Shuite, and Zophar the Naamanite. He listened to the remarks on both sides, and was displeased alike with Job and his friends. He thought their accusations and insinuations against Job, were unjust—that they had no good grounds for calling the afflicted man a hypocrite, and making such severe censures, and using such hard speeches against him. Yet he thought that Job, in defending himself, had used improper language, and had used expressions which savored very strongly of self-righteousness. He also thought that Job had charged the Divine Being wrongfully. Had questioned God's goodness and love, mercy and justice, in the mysterious providences through which he had passed.

Elihu being a young man, did not intrude his views and feelings until the conference was about to close. He waited until they had said all they wished to say, then he unburdened his heart fully to them. His address is lengthy, including the 32d, 33d,

34th, 35th, 36th and 37th chapters of Job. He first expresses his disapprobation of Job and his three friends. He then proposes to reason with Job in meekness and sincerity, and after showing him how his expressions are irreverent, he vindicates the Divine providence. Then follows an earnest exhortation to the three friends. It may be said of the entire address of Elihu, that it is a masterly defense of God, his attributes and providence, and a reproof for irreverence on the part of Job, with severe reprimand and condemnation of Eliphaz, Bildad and Zophar, for their very uncharitable views and expressions against Job.

Elihu is supposed to have been a descendant of Nahor, the brother of Abraham, by Buz, his second son.

ELIHU, 2—*He is my God himself.*

Was the great-grandfather of Samuel. The name occurs with his relation to Elkanah in 1st Sam. i: 1.

ELIHU, 3—*He is my God himself.*

Elihu or Eliab was the eldest son of Jesse. He is called Elihu in 1st Chron. xxvii: 18, When Samuel was sent to anoint David to be king, as soon as he saw Elihu or Eliab, he said: "Surely the Lord's anointed is before him," but in that he was mistaken. 1st Sam. xvi: 6. This brother of David was in the army of king Saul, and complained of the shepherd boy when he proposed to meet the Philistine giant in battle. 1st Sam. xvii: 28.

ELIHU, 4—*He is my God himself.*

Elihu was a descendant of Obed Edom, and one of the sacred porters. 1st Chron. xxvi: 7.

ELIJAH—[E-li′-jah,] *God the Lord, the strong Lord.*

Elijah, the Tishbite, was a noted prophet in Israel. He is referred to in the New Testament by the name of Elias. He was a native of Gilead, and prophesied in the time of King Ahab. Ahab sinned greatly against God, especially by turning to idolatry, and in marrying Jezebel, a heathen woman and a gross idolater. He countenanced the worship of Baal and the Groves, and God determined to punish him, and the nation over which he reigned. Elijah, under a commission from God, assured Ahab that there should be neither dew nor rain for a length of time, only as he, the prophet, prayed for it. Consequently the drought began, and Elijah went to the brook Cherith that he might drink of its waters until it failed. He concealed himself near this brook, and was fed miraculously by ravens who "brought him bread and flesh in the morning and bread and flesh in the evening." What a beautiful sight is presented here, in the history of this prophet. Somewhere in the country of Israel, it may be in some secluded spot, angels, or possibly men, were employed by the Divine being to prepare Elijah two meals every day, and after preparing it, await the coming of the ravens, who were also employed by God, to take charge of the meal and bear it away to the solitary home of Elijah. About the same time each morning and each evening, as the prophet became hungry, he looked up in the direction they were accustomed to come, and saw them on wing approaching him with his meal. They left it with Elijah, and he partook of it with a thankful heart.

But at length the brook dried up, and under the direction of God Elijah sought another home. He went to the city of Zerephath, and as he was entering it he saw a poor widow engaged in gathering a few sticks with a view to preparing the last meal; for she had only a handful of meal and a little oil left, with which to make one small cake for herself and her only son. Elijah saw the woman and called her attention to his wants. He bade her bring him a little water. He had probably traveled all the way from the brook Cherith without a drink of water. The woman saw him a wearied traveler, and sympathizing with him, she started in the direction of her humble cottage to procure him drink, but he called her attention again to him, and bade her bring him also a piece of bread. She ventured then to unfold her wretched condition to him. "I have not a cake, but a handful of meal in a barrel, and a little oil in a cruise, and behold I am gathering two sticks that I may go in and dress it for me and my son, that we may eat it and die." This was a sad tale indeed; the poor widow was at the point of starvation—she saw no hope for the future. Elijah bade her not fear, but go bake a cake for him first, and then for herself and her son; and then he assured her that the meal should not waste nor the cruise of oil fail until the famine was ended. The parched earth should again be blessed with rain, and the labor of the husbandman be rewarded. There were many other families in the city that were suffering from the famine, and so all through the land there were those that were like this woman in extremity, but unto none of them was Elijah sent save unto this woman." The poor woman believed the prophet and followed his instructions. And Elijah entered her house and tarried there during the remainder of the dearth, living with the woman and her son upon the multiplied meal and oil. So that Elijah was not only fed miraculously at Cherith for a few months, but he was sustained miraculously through the whole dearth.

A very interesting circumstance occurred about two years after he came to the house of this widow and her son. It illustrates the doctrine of the soul's immortality and immateriality, and the power of Elijah's God. The son died, and with a sorrowing heart the widow bent over his fallen form and mourned as none but a mother can sorrow for the loss of an only son. She came to Elijah and complained that he had come to call her sins to remembrance and to slay her son. The prophet deeply sympathized with the sorrow-stricken woman, and took the child up into his own room and laid him on his own bed. He became deeply interested in the case, and in the fullness of his heart laid it before the Lord. "And he stretched himself upon the child three times, and cried unto the Lord and said, O Lord my God, I pray thee let this child's soul come into him again." His prayer was earnest and importunate. The Lord heard it, and the request was granted—"the soul of the child came unto him again and he revived," and he gave him to his mother alive; and while she in the joy of her heart embraced her son, she declared her strong convictions that Elijah was a man of God—that the word of the Lord in his mouth was truth. 1st Kings, xvii.

After the drought and famine had continued for three years and six months, the prophet Elijah was commissioned to go to Ahab the king, and inform him that the land should be blessed with rain. This scene in the history of Elijah is exceedingly thrilling. He met Obadiah one of the servants of Ahab, and bade him go and inform his master that he desired to see him; Obadiah made objections to reporting to the king, the chief of which were that the king with murderous intent had searched the whole kingdom and the adjacent country and kingdoms for Elijah, and would surely kill him if he came within his power; and furthermore, he feared that if he informed Ahab of the presence of the prophet that the spirit of the Lord would carry him away, and then his king enraged at him, would murder him in the stead of Elijah. He earnestly desired to be released from the painful duty of periling the life of the prophet and his own life, partly on the ground that he had been the friend and protector of the Lord's prophets—a hundred of whom he had fed in two caves with bread and water. The prophet then assured Obadiah that he need not fear, for he had determined to show himself that day to Ahab. Being thus assured, Obadiah hastened to Ahab and informed him of the whereabouts of Elijah, and of his desire to see him. The king went without delay to where Elijah was, and accosted him rather roughly by charging him with being the troubler of Israel. Elijah repelled the charge and in his reply told the king that he himself and his family, by their wickedness and idolatry, were the troublers of Israel. They had brought this dearth and famine upon the land by erecting heathen temples and countenancing and worshiping false Gods. Elijah then asked the king that the people of Israel be assembled at Mt. Carmel with four hundred and fifty prophets of Baal, and four hundred prophets of the groves to test the matter as to whether Jehovah or Baal was the true God. Ahab accordingly gave orders to that effect, and soon the people with these false prophets were convened. And Elijah stood before the people and boldly rebuked them for their sins, in "halting between two opinions," hesitating as to whether they would serve God or Baal. He then made a proposition to test the power of God and Baal by offering sacrifices that should be consumed by fire from heaven. They agreed to the proposition. Baal's prophets erected their altars and offered their sacrifices first. In the midst of the ceremonies of their sacrifice, in their earnestness and intensity of feeling they cut themselves with knives, leaped upon the altar and cried "O Baal hear us." But it was a signal failure. Elijah then stepped forward in the presence of the multitude and erected his altar, slew his bullock and laid it thereon. He then drenched his sacrifice and altar with water until a large trench was filled to the brim around the altar. And Elijah prayed to his God for a display of divine power in consuming the sacrifice in the sight of all the people. Scarcely had he commenced praying until fire was seen flashing from heaven, and that sacrifice and altar was its center of attraction. It was not long until the fire consumed the flesh, and wood and stones and water, and even the earth where the altar stood. The people were astonished and cried out, "The Lord he is God." Elijah then ordered the prophets of Baal to be slain, and his order was obeyed, none escaping. He then informed Ahab that the drought was at an end, soon there should be rain.

As the people were dispersing from the place of execution of the prophets of Baal, Elijah returned to the summit of the mount and prostrated himself before the Lord in prayer for rain, having Gehazi his servant with him to observe. After praying seven times Gehazi reported a cloud arising out of the sea. Elijah then bade him tell Ahab "there is the sound of abundance of rain," to make ready and go to Jezreel at once lest the rain stop him, while Elijah himself girded up his loins and ran before the king to the entrance of the city. 1st Kings xviii.

The success that crowned Elijah in the recent demonstrations, and the slaughter of the prophets of Baal enraged Jezebel the Queen, and she determined that his life should pay for his conduct, and she sent Elijah the word. He received the intelligence and determined at once to flee to Beersheba. As this was probably not more than one hundred miles from Jezreel, he determined to pursue his course further. But he dismissed his servant at this place, and went on alone toward the Arabian desert. The first night after he commenced his lonely travel, wearied and fatigued he laid down under a juniper tree, and as he thought of the persecutions through which he had passed, the destruction of the Lords prophets throughout the kingdom of Israel, he wished to die.

In his solitude and sadness his attention was arrested by an angel, who touched him and bade him rise up and eat provisions he had brought him. He did so, and then slept. After a few hours he awoke from his sleep, an angel appeared again and bade him eat and drink of that which he had brought him, and he did so, after which he resumed his journey and traveled for forty days without refreshments, and came to the mount of God called Horeb. Here he took up his home for a time in a cave, and at this cave the Almighty communed with him. Elijah's God bade him stand in the mouth of the cave and as he did so a strong wind passed over it. He heard its roaring and probably felt its influence. That wind was followed by an earthquake, and the earthquake was followed by a flaming fire, and that flaming fire was followed by a still small voice, and in that voice the Lord addressed himself to Elijah, and assured him that there were seven thousand in Israel that had not bowed the knee to Baal. The Lord then bade the prophet go back again to his own country, and anoint Hazael to be King of Syria, and Jehu the son of Nimshi to be king over Israel, and Elisha the son of Shephat to be prophet in his stead. This was a very important mission. Not long after this Elijah called Elisha whom he found plowing in a field with oxen, and he referred the anointing of the two kings to him. 1st Kings xix.

Elijah again threw himself in the way of Ahab and told him of the judgments that God would visit upon him and his wicked family. 1st Kings xxi. He denounced Ahaziah and told him of his approaching end.

Two companies of soldiers composed of fifty men each, went to him, to apprehend him and place him in the power of his enemies, and they were consumed. The captain of the third company begged for his life and the life of his men, and they were spared, for Elijah went with them under the protection of his God.

When Elijah was about to be translated he made efforts to get out of the company of Elisha that his translation might be secret, but in this he failed, for his successor followed him closely. When they came to Jordan Elijah struck the waters with his mantle and they divided and the two went over. Elijah then asked Elisha what should be done for him, and he answered "let a double portion of thy spirit fall on me." Elijah told him his request was a great one, and yet it should be granted on condition that he saw him when his translation occurred. The two together passed on a little further, when a company of angels, and the form of a chariot and horses of fire appeared, and Elijah understanding that they had come for him, quick as thought left the side of Elisha and entering the chariot was borne by a whirlwind into heaven. Elisha in the excitement looked at the ascending chariot and cried after Elijah, "My father, my father, the chariot and horsemen of Israel." The mantle of Elijah had fallen from him as he ascended, and Elisha took it up and returned to the Jordan that they two had crossed a little while before, and with the mantle he smote the waters and they divided again. Elijah thus went up to heaven and there he has ever since with Enoch of an earlier age, represented man in glorified humanity.

After his translation, fifty of the youthful prophets sought his body by the permission of Elisha for three days. 2d Kings, 1 and 2.

In the time of Jehoram, king of Judah, a writing of the prophet Elijah was presented, in which the sins that had been committed were brought to remembrance, and the judgments of God declared as they should fall upon the king and his family. 2d Chron. xxi: 12–15.

The New Testament refers to this important person frequently, and John the Baptist because of his temper, apparel, method of living, and faithful manner of reproving vice, with his zeal for the right, and his gifts, is called Elijah or Elias. Matt. xvii: 10–13. The above reference is made in the above passage to the notion existing among the Jews that Elijah would come before the Messiah should make his appearance, and John the baptist declared to be that Elias.

At the transfiguration of Christ, Elias with Moses, descended from Heaven, and in shining raiment, stood near Jesus and conversed with him. Matt. xvii: 5.

ELIKA—[E-li′ka,] *pelican of God.*

Was one of David's guard. He is called an Harodite. 2d Sam. xxiii: 25.

ELIMELECH—[E-lim′e-lek,] *my God is king.*

Was a man of the tribe of Judah, who dwelt in Bethlehem in the days of the Judges. Because of a famine in the land, he, with his wife Naomi, and their two sons, went to sojourn in Moab, where he and his sons both died. Ruth.

ELIOENAI, 1—[E-le-e′-na-i,] *toward him are my eyes, my fountains, toward him is my poverty or misery.*

Was the eldest son of Neariah. 1st Chron. iii: 23.

ELIOENAI, 2—*Toward him are my eyes, toward him is my poverty or misery.*

Was the head of the family of the Simeonites. 1st Chron. iv: 36.

ELIOENAI, 3—*Toward him are my eyes, toward him is my poverty or misery.*

Was a Benjamite, and head of one the families of the sons of Becher. 1st Chron. vii: 8.

ELIOENAI, 4—*Toward him are my eyes, toward him is my poverty or misery.*

Was the seventh son of Meshelemiah, of a Korhite Levite family, and one of the doorkeepers of the house of the Lord. 1st Chron. xxvi: 3.

ELIOENAI, 5—*Toward him are my eyes, toward him is my poverty or misery.*

Was a priest of the line of Pashur. He was one of those who had married a foreign wife. Ezra x: 22. He was one of the priests who assisted Nehemiah at the dedication of the wall of Jerusalem. Neh. xii: 41.

ELIOENAI, 6—*Toward him are my eyes, toward him is my poverty or misery.*

Was an Israelite of the sons of Zathe, who had also married a foreign wife.

ELIOSEPH—

ELIOSEPH and his brother Ahia, were the sons of Shesha, scribes for king Solomon.

ELIPHAL—[El′i-fal.]

Was a son of Ur, and one of David's body-guard. 1st Chron. xi: 35.

ELIPHALET, 1—[E-lif′a-let,] *the God of deliverance.*

Was the thirteenth son born to David after his establishment in Jerusalem. 2d Sam. v: 16.

ELIPHALET, 2—*The God of deliverance.*

Was a son of Abashai, one of the thirty warriors of David, who served as his body-guard. 2d Sam. xxiii: 34.

ELIPHALET, 3—*The God of deliverance.*

Was one of the leaders who returned from Babylon with Ezra. Ez. viii: 13. He may be the same one who had married a foreign wife. Ez. x: 33.

ELIPHAZ, 1—[El′-i-phaz,] *the endeavor of God.*

ELIPHAZ was the son of Esau and Adah. It may be supposed he was Esau's eldest son, as he is named first in the genealogy given in Gen. xxxvi: 10, &c.; also in 1st Chron. i: 35, &c. This Eliphaz was the father of six sons. The following are their names as given: Teman, Omar, Zepho, Gatam, Kenaz, and Amalek. The last-named was the son of Timna, the concubine of Eliphaz.

ELIPHAZ, 2—*the endeavor of God.*

ELIPHAZ, who was one of the visitors and pretended friends of Job in his affliction, was probably the son of Teman and the grandson of the former Eliphaz. He is called Eliphaz the Temanite. He was, we may judge from Job, xv. 10, an old man. "With us are both the gray-headed and very aged men, much elder than thy father." And as he is the first to speak to Job of the three who are visiting him, it is likely he was the eldest of the company. The object he had in view with his companions was to mourn with the afflicted, and to comfort him. Job, ii: 10. He commences his address in the fourth chapter, in which he refers to Job's character as an instructor—the work he had performed of ministering to the afflicted —"strengthening the weak hands," and reproves him for his faintness, as he calls it, in the midst of his afflictions. He insinuates that Job had been wicked and hypocritical. He endeavors to convince him that none are punished in such extraordinary manner as he was being punished, but gross sinners; and he pleads with Job to repent of his sins —to renounce his wickedness, and plead with God for deliverance. See chapters xv and xxii.

As evidence that Eliphaz was mistaken regarding Job, in chapter xlii, we learn that the wrath of God was kindled against him and his friends who had joined him in his false charges; and under the direction of God Job prayed for them, and their sin was forgiven.

ELIPHELEH—[E-lif′e-leh,]

Was one of the Levites who was engaged in the solemn service of removing the ark to Jerusalem, and placing it in the tent which David had prepared for it. 1st Chron. xv: 21.

ELISHA—[E-li′-shah,] *salvation of God.*

ELISHA the son of Shaphat and the successor of Elijah was a prophet in Israel. He was called to the work and office as he drove one of his father's twelve plows. 1st Kings xix: 19. While Elijah was in the cave at Horeb, God prepared him for an important revelation he was about to make to him, by displaying his presence and majesty in a strong wind that rent the mountains and brake the rocks around him, which wind was followed by an earthquake, and the earthquake by fire, and the fire by a still small voice, in which voice the revelation was made and a part of that revelation was "Elisha the son of Shaphat of Abel-meholah shalt thou anoint to be prophet in thy room." 1st Kings xix: 16. Elijah found Elisha in the field plowing, and as he approached him he cast his mantle over him, thereby intimating his desire that he should follow him, and succeed him in the office of prophet. Elisha understanding the import of the act, and probably already feeling the divine influence upon him that afterwards made him so distinguished as a prophet, signified his willingness to leave his native city—his father's house and his employment as an agriculturist. Feeling himself to be under the charge of Elijah he asked the privilege of going home to bid his father and mother farewell. "Let me, I pray thee, kiss my father and my mother and then I will follow thee." Elisha went back and slew a yoke of oxen, and made a great feast for the people—probably the laborers over whom he had charge, as servants of his father. After they had ate together of the boiled flesh of the oxen he left home, taking an affectionate leave of the household, especially of his father and mother. From this time until Elijah was translated they were companions. Elisha was made acquainted with the revelations that had been made to Elijah at the cave, and he referred the anointing the two kings to Elisha; Hazael to be king of Syria, and Jehu the son of Nimshi to be king of Israel. In 2d Kings viii: 12, we learn that Hazael meets Elisha and soon the prophet assures him that he shall be king of Syria, and in 2d Kings ix: 1, 3, we have the account of Elisha anointing Jehu.

Elisha witnessed the wonderful display of divine power and glory in the translation of Elijah, and the same mantle that was cast upon him while plowing, signifying his call to the work and office of a prophet, now falls by his side as he looks wonderingly at the chariot of fire bearing Elijah away. When Elijah had passed away—the strange scene of his ascension was over, Elisha was reconciled to the separation, took up the mantle and went back to the Jordan where they two, a little while before had crossed it. And as Elijah smote the waters with that mantle, and they divided "hither and thither," so Elisha with the mantle smote the waters and they divided, and the second time he passed through on dry ground. The sons of the prophets were standing upon the bank of Jordan as Elisha approached and they saw the waters divided before him as they had seen the waters divide a short while before when Elijah smote them, and they said, "the spirit of Elijah doth rest on Elisha." This was the very thing that Elisha had asked for, 2d Kings ii: 9, and it had been promised him on condition that he saw him when he was taken from him. He did see him as long as human vision could follow him.

The young prophets met him as he came up from the Jordan, and satisfied that he was the honored successor of Elijah, they bowed to him as their superior. They asked the privilege of him to go in search of Elijah, supposing that the "spirit of the Lord had taken him up and cast him upon some mountain, or into some valley. He tried to dissuade them, but they importuned and insisted, until he gave them permission, at the same time assuring them that their search would be in vain. They went and searched three days but found him not.

While the search was being made, Elisha tarried at Jericho. A complaint was made to him by the inhabitants of Jericho, to the effect that though they were pleasantly situated in many respects, yet there was one very serious difficulty under which they labored "the water is naught, and the ground is barren."

Pleasant as the city of Jericho was and its surrounding country, the curse of God seemed to rest upon it, in bad water, and in a barren land. Elisha called for a new cruise and filling it with salt, he cast the salt into the springs, and told the people of Jericho, that the waters were healed and that the land should no longer be barren. He then left Jericho and turned his face toward Bethel, and, as he was going he was wickedly mocked by a company of children. They were probably the school of some celebrated teacher, who was an idolater, and probably the parents of the children were idolaters.

They had heard of Elijah's ascent, and had learned the relation Elisha sustained to him, and they mocked him by saying, "Go up thou bald head; Go up thou bald head." The prophet cursed them in the name of the Lord. The offense was against the Lord, and his servant but executed his purpose when he cursed them in his name. Scarcely had the sound of Elisha's voice died upon the ears of the company of children thus mocking him, until two she bears came out of the wood. It may be these bears were tracing the footsteps of the murderers of their young, when they came upon the children insulting the prophet, "and they tare forty and two children of them." 2d Kings, ii.

The allied army of Israel, Judah and Edom, while contending with Mesha, king of Moab, applied to Elisha to enquire of the Lord for them. It was through the influence of Jehoshaphat, the king of Judah, that the application was made to him. As soon as the interview was had, Elisha addressed himself to Jehoram, the king of Israel, in a very just and cutting reproof, for he was an idolater. "What have I to do with thee? get thee to the prophets of thy father, and to the prophets of thy mother." For the sake of the king of Judah, who worshiped the true God, Elisha attended unto their request, and enquired for them of the Lord. He received the revelation and made it known unto them that there should be an abundance of water for their refreshment, though they should see no wind or rain, and it was according to his word. 2d Kings, iii.

A few days after this a widow of one of the prophets came to Elisha and complained that her husband's creditor had certified his intention to sell her two sons to pay the debt. The prophet intent on relieving her, asked if she had anything in the house. She answered nothing save a pot of oil. He then bade her borrow vessels, which she did, "not a few," and the prophet told her to shut the door of her house upon herself and her two sons, and pour out from her vessel of oil into the empty vessels, which she did, until they were all filled with oil. When they were all full the oil stayed, and the woman reported to the man of God who bade her sell the oil and pay the debt, and live, she and her two sons off the rest. 2d Kings, iv: 1–7.

Elisha became acquainted with the woman of Shunem and ate with her and her husband. And after that, on an invitation from them, as often as he passed that way "he turned in thither to eat bread." His acquaintance with them extended, and their mutual esteem and regard increased. The Shunemite prepared a little chamber specially for the prophet, and furnished it with a bed, and a table, and a stool, and a candlestick, and in that chamber the prophet often rested. As a reward for the kindness shown the prophet Elisha, this Shunemite was blessed with a son; and when the child was about five years of age, he died suddenly. Elisha restored him to life, to the joy of his parents. 2d Kings, iv: 8–37.

Elisha visited Gilgal, and while there the sons of the prophets gathered about him and welcomed him among them. There was a dearth in the land, and consequently food was scarce. One of the young prophets had gathered herbs for a mess of pottage—wild gourds, a bitter and poisonous herb. His fellow-prophets had no sooner tasted it, than they cried out, "There is death in the pot!" Elisha took a little meal and cast it into the pot, which removed the bitter taste and poisonous quality. 2d Kings, iv: 38–41. Then Elisha multiplies twenty barley loaves, so that more than a hundred persons ate plentifully, and yet left some remaining.

This prophet was applied to by Naaman, the Syrian general, who was a leper, to be healed of his leprousy. He bade him go wash seven times in Jordan and he should be healed. He did so and was cured; then returned to Elisha and offered him large presents, but he would not receive them. And afterwards, when Gehazi, his servant, covetously followed the Syrian and received from him a present, Elisha rebuked him, and assured him that the leprousy of Naaman should cleave to him. 2d Kings, v.

Not long after this the young prophets went to the banks of the Jordan to cut wood, and procure beams of timber with which to enlarge their dwelling; and while one of them was cutting the axe-head fell into the water, and he could not find it. He came to Elisha and informed him. The axe was a borrowed one, which made the young prophet the more anxious to procure it. Elisha went to the place where it had fallen in, and taking a stick he threw or thrust it into the water, "and the iron did swim," and so was recovered.

About this time Benhadad, the king of Syria, waged war against Israel; and Elisha informed Jehoram of the plans and machinations of the Syrians, and so they were defeated. At this Benhadad became troubled and perplexed, and learned that Elisha disclosed his thoughts and plans to his enemy. Having heard that Elisha was at Dothan, he sent soldiers to take him, but Elisha was environed with horses and chariots of fire. His servant saw them coming and was frightened, and turning around to Elisha he said, "Alas! my master, what shall we do?" The prophet prayed first that the young man's eyes might be opened, and his prayer was answered and his fears relieved. He then prayed that the Lord would smite the soldiers with blindness, and his prayer was answered. Then he led the blind soldiers into Samaria, where they were in the power of the king of Israel, who would have destroyed them had not Elisha stopped him, and indicated a more humane and sensible mode of treatment: to give them bread and water to eat and drink, and send them home to their master unharmed. 2d Kings, vi: 1–24.

When Benhadad had besieged Samaria and cut off their supplies, until provisions were exceedingly scarce, even the unclean head of an unclean animal was sold for about twenty dollars, and other things used for food in proportion; and thousands were starving. One poor woman cried to the king against another woman who had agreed, the day before, while with her, eating her son, that on that day they two should eat her son also, but now she refused. The king heard her cries and lamentations, and was deeply grieved. He attributed, in his grief, these calamities to Elisha, and determined that he should die. He sent a messenger to execute his purpose at once; but in this Jehoram was foiled.

Elisha foretold abundant relief to the inhabitants of Samaria in the next twenty-four hours, which came to pass; for the Syrians became alarmed at a noise they were made to hear, and, supposing it to be forces coming to help the inhabitants of Samaria, they fled hurriedly from their camp, leaving their tents, horses and equipage. Soon the fact was made known by four lepers, and plenty was enjoyed in the city. 2d Kings, vii.

Elisha went to Damascus to appoint Hazael king of Syria, as Elijah had directed him. He finds Benhadad sick, and that king probably hearing him, sends Hazael to enquire of him as to whether he will recover from his sickness. He tells Hazael that Benhadad will die, and that he is to be king in his stead. He then indicated to Hazael the policy he would pursue —atrocities and wickedness of which he would be guilty as the king of Syria; and, although he seemed to be struck with horror at the prediction, yet he went home, and, with a wet cloth, smothered or suffocated King Benhadad; then ascended the throne.

About this time, Elisha sent a young prophet to anoint Jehu to be king over Israel, that he might cut off the idolatrous house of Ahab.

The work of Elisha being nearly done, he was taken sick of the disease of which he died. 2d Kings, xiii: 14. During his sickness, Joash, the king of Israel, came down to see him, and wept in his presence, using language precisely like the language that Elisha used when Elijah was translated: "My father, my father, the chariots of Israel and the horsemen thereof." He looked upon the pale form of the dying prophet and felt that the kingdom of Israel was about to lose a prophetic protector. Elisha directed the king to take bow and arrows and shoot out of the window eastward; and he did so. The prophet told him the shot presaged deliverance from the Syrian yoke: "Thou shalt smite the Syrians in Aphek till thou hast consumed them." The prophet then bade the king take the the arrows and smite them on the ground; and he did, smiting the ground thrice. The dying prophet blamed the king that he did not smite five or six times, that he might as often have defeated the Syrian troops instead of three times.

Elisha died, and they buried him;

and, a short time afterward, a marauding party of the Moabites were invading the land, and a funeral procession passing along saw the band and were alarmed; and as the grave in which Elisha was buried was open, they who were carrying the dead man to burial let him down into Elisha's sepulcher, and as soon as the corpse touched the bones of the prophet the dead man was restored to life. "He revived and stood up on his feet." 2d Kings, xiii.

ELISHAH—[E-li′-shah,] *son of Javan; it is God, God that gives help.*

ELISHAH was a descendant of Japheth, and the son of Javan. He is referred to in Gen. x: 4. As he is numbered first of the sons of Javan, he was probably the eldest. Elishah probably settled at Elis, in Peloponesus, and his descendants are referred to as trading with the Tyrians in Ezekiel, xxvii: 7. "Fine linen with bordered work from Egypt, was that which thou spreadest forth to be thy sail; blue and purple from the isles of Elishah was that which covered thee."

ELISHAMA, 1—[E-lish′a-mah,] *God hearing.*

ELISHAMA was of the family of Ephraim, of the children of Joseph. He was the son of Ammihud, and chief of the family of Ephraim. He was associated with Moses and Aaron in managing the business of their nation at the time of their exodus from the land of Egypt. Num. i: 10. And when the Tabernacle was fully set up he made an offering for his tribe. Num. vii: 48.

ELISHAMA, 2—*God hearing.*

A son of king David born unto him after his establishment in Jerusalem. 2d Sam. v: 16.

ELISHAMA, 3—*God hearing.*

A descendant of Judah, the son of Jekamiah. 1st Chron. ii: 41.

ELISHAMA, 4—*God hearing.*

The father of Nethaniah, and grandfather of Ishmael. 2d Kings xxv: 25.

ELISHAMA, 5—*God hearing.*

The scribe to king Jehoiakim. He is referred to in Jer. xxxvi: 12, 20.

ELISHAMA, 6—*God hearing.*

He was a priest in the time of Jehoshaphat. 2d Chron. xvii: 8.

ELISHAPHAT—[E-lish′-a-fat.]

A son of Zichri, and one of the captains of hundreds in the time of Jehoiada. 2d Chron. xxiii: 1.

ELISHEBA—[E-lish′-e-bah,] *God hath sworn, the fulness of God.*

ELISHEBA was the wife of Aaron, the daughter of Aminadab, and sister to Naashon, who was one of the princes of Judah. The name is the same as Elisabeth, a name of the Christian age. The mother of John the Baptist, whose name was Elisabeth, was a daughter of Aaron, and she bare, as we see, the name of Aaron's wife. Elisheba was the mother of Nadab and Abihu, who offered strange fire unto the Lord, and were destroyed. Lev. x: 1, 2. "And offered strange fire before the Lord, which he commanded them not. And there went out a fire from the Lord and devoured them, and they died before the Lord." She was also the mother of Eleazar and Ithamer. Eleazar succeeded his father to the office of the high priesthood.

ELISHUA—[El-i-shu-ah,] *God is my salvation.*

ELISHUA was one of the sons of David, born unto him in Jerusalem. 1st Chron. xiv: 5.

ELIZABETH—[E-liz′-a-beth,] *God hath sworn, the fulness of God.*

ELIZABETH was the wife of Zacherias a descendant of Aaron and the mother of the forerunner of our Lord, John the Baptist. She was also related to the Virgin Mary. When the angel talked with the mother of our Lord, he refers her for confirmation of her faith to facts regarding her "cousin Elizabeth."

According to the description given of Elizabeth and her husband in Luke i: 6, we learn that she was a good woman, "righteous before God," and with her husband she obeyed all the divine commandments. She held the moral code that God had given, to be sacred, and was blameless in all the ordinances. The ceremonial as well as the moral law was observed. She attended faithfully to the duties of religion.

Elizabeth lived many years with her honored husband and had no children, but when "stricken in years," God gave her a son. An angel appeared to Zacharias while he was engaged in ministering in the order of his course in the temple, and spake to him of the son that should be born to Elizabeth, and of his character and work. The husband of Elizabeth did not believe fully the divine message that had been delivered, and ventured to express his doubts. This was evidently an offense, and his being deaf and dumb until John was born was a chastisement for his doubts. But the prediction of the angel was fulfilled and John was born. On the eighth day after his birth the Levitical law was complied with. Elizabeth with her husband being present to witness the sacred ceremony, and enter into a covenant with God and name their child. Those that were present, and engaged in the solemn service, supposed that the child was to be named after his father hence they called him Zacharias. But Elizabeth corrected them in their mistake, for in all probability her husband had told her in writing what the angel had said to him. "And his mother answered and said not so; but he shall be called John. They seemed to be astonished at the name and ventured some objections to it. "There is none of thy kindred called by this name." But in order to satisfy themselves as to the name they made signs to Zacharias what he would have him called. And he asked for a writing table and wrote saying, "his name is John." Thus they discovered that Elizabeth was not mistaken.

If the Virgin Mary was honored more than any other woman in being the mother of our Lord. Elizabeth was next to her in being the mother of our Lord's forerunner, one of the greatest of men, and the "prophet of the highest." John was not only a prophet but "he was more than a prophet" according to our own Lord's declaration.

How long Elizabeth lived after the birth of John, we do not know, but it is likely she died before John commenced his ministry, so that she witnessed not the sorrows that fell to the lot of her cousin Mary when Christ was crucified. No, nor the fulfillment of the expressed wish of Herodias, and the cruel edict of Herod, that her son should be beheaded.

ELIZAPHAN, 1—[E-liz′-a-fan.]

Elizaphan was the son of Uzziel, and a cousin of Moses and Aaron. He is spoken of in Num. iii: 30, as the chief of the family of the Kohathites. This family had charge of the ark, and the table and the candlesticks, and the altars, and the vessels of the sanctuary. Hence we observe that the position of Elizaphan was a very important one, which he and the family of the Kohathites retained in the wilderness. In Lev. x: 1, 2, we have an account of the sin of Nadab and Abihu, the sons of Aaron, in offering strange fire unto the Lord, and their punishment, viz: sudden death in the sanctuary. As soon as the vengeance of the Lord had thus struck them dead Moses called Elizaphan, and Mishael his brother, and bade them carry the dead bodies of the two fallen priests out from the sanctuary and without the camp.

In 1st Chron. xv: 1–10, we have an account of David preparing to bring the ark of God from the house of Obed-Edom to the tent that had been provided for it. He musters the Levites, and they sanctify themselves and prepare to bear the ark upon their shoulders in accordance with the commandment of Moses. Num. iv: 5–15. Of the sons of Elizaphan there were about two hundred engaged in this important undertaking.

ELIZAPHAN, 2.

Was the son of Parnach, of the tribe of Zebulun, and was one of the princes that assisted Joshua and Eleazar in dividing the land of Canaan among the tribes of Israel. Numbers xxxiv: 25.

ELIZUR—[E-li′-zur.]

The son of Shedeur, was a man renowned in the tribe of Reuben, and a prince of that tribe. He was appointed to assist Moses in numbering the tribes of Israel. Num. i: 5, and vii: 30.

ELKANAH—[Elka′nah,] *God the jealous, the reed of God.*

Elkanah seems to have been a common name among the Levites, hence the name occurs several times in the genealogy of Levi and Aaron, as given in 1st Chron. vi. In the 25th and 26th verses the name occurs, also in the presentation of the offices of the priests and Levites. But the most important personage in Bible history of this name was the son of Jeroham, the husband of Hannah, and Peninnah, and the father of the prophet Samuel. From 1st Sam. 1, we learn that Elkanah was an Ephrathite, who devoutly worshiped the God of his fathers. He was accustomed to go early to Shiloh, where the ark of God was, to sacrifice, and his wives attended him, to whom he gave a portion also to sacrifice unto the Lord, and the children of Peninnah were also supplied by Elkanah, their father. He sympathized greatly with Hannah in the sorrows that pressed her soul, as she earnestly petitioned the Lord for a son, and vowed that the son, if given her, should be given unto the Lord all the days of his life. The Lord heard her prayer, and granted the petition.

The next year when Elkanah went up to sacrifice at Shiloh, Hannah remained at home with the child Samuel. He acquiesced fully in the expressed wish of the mother that she might remain at home until her child was weaned, when he could be given unto the Lord. It is likely he provided Hannah with the consecration offering, which consisted of a bullock or heifer, of three years old, an ephah of flour, and a bottle of wine, and attended her when she presented Samuel to Eli the priest. He heard the sentiment of his wife's prophetic song, and joined with her in adoring the God of his fathers. After the ceremony of presenting the child unto the Lord was all over, and the devotions of the feast ended, Elkanah, with his wife Hannah, returned to Ramah.

Elkanah, as well as Hannah, received the blessings of Eli, the priest, for the *loan* which they together *lent* unto the Lord. After Samuel was thus left with the venerable Eli, three sons and two daughters were born unto Elkanah by Hannah.

ELNATHAN—[El-na′than,] *God has given.*

ELNATHAN was the son of Achbor, and the father of Nehushta, the wife of Jehoiakim, and his residence was in Jerusalem. 2d Kings xxiv: 8. He was probably an officer under the king, his son-in-law. When Jehoiakim sent to Egypt to bring back Urijah, the prophet, that he might put him to death, he placed Elnathan in charge of the men that went on the errand. They found the prophet, and brought him back, and took him into the presence of the king, who slew him with the sword, and had him buried without honor in the graves of the common people. Jeremiah xxvi: 22.

Elnathan is counted with the princes of Jehoiakim, and it is quite likely he had considerable influence with the king. He used that influence at one time unsuccessfully. The king had determined to burn the roll that had been prepared by Baruch, who was the scribe for the prophet Jeremiah. The prophecies had been publicly read, which declared that the king of Babylon should come and destroy the land. Elnathan, with two of the other princes, plead with the king of Judah not to burn the roll containing the prophecies of Jeremiah, "but he would not hear them." The above account is recorded in Jeremiah xxxvi.

ELON, 1—[E′-lon,] *oak, grove, strong.*

ELON was a son of Zebulon, hence a grandson of Jacob. He is referred to in the summing up of Israel which occurred in the plains of Moab. Num. xxvi: 26. Here Elon is called the father of the Elonites. This was one of the three families composing the tribe of Zebulon. The Sardites and the Jahleelites were the other two families.

ELON, 2—*Oak, grove, strong.*

Was a judge of Israel, and a descendant of Zebulon. He succeeded Ibzan in the office of judge, and filled it for ten years. During the time that he was judge as well as his two predecessors, Jepthah and Ibzan, and Abdon his successor, Israel had rest, a period of thirty-one years, but afterwards they corrupted themselves and were delivered into the hands and power of the Philistines.

Elon having served his ten years, died and was buried in Aijalon in the country of Zebulon. Judges xii: 11, 12.

ELPALET.

ELPALET was one of the sons of David born unto him in Jerusalem. 1st Chron. xiv: 5.

ELZAPHAN—[El′-za-fan.]

ELZAPHAN with his brother Mishael was a son of Uzziel, the brother of Amram, the father of Moses and Aaron. Ex. vi: 18. Hence Uzziel is called in Leviticus x: 4, the uncle of Aaron. When Nadab and Abihu the sons of Aaron offered strange fire unto the Lord and were suddenly destroyed, Moses called Elzaphan and Mishael and bade them go and carry the dead bodies of the fallen priests with their clothing upon them, out of the sanctuary, and without their camp. "So they went and carried them in their coats out of the camp as Moses had said."

ELZABAD—[El′-za-bad.]

ELZABAD was a descendant of Obed-Edom, and one of the sacred porters. 1st Chron. xxvi: 7.

EMMOR—[Em′-mor,] *an ass.*

EMMOR, or Hamor, the father of Shecham who defiled the daughter of Jacob. Gen. xxxiv: 2. He in company with his son was murdered by Simeon and Levi, who revenged their sisters injury.

ENAN.

ENAN was of the tribe of Naphtali, and the father of the prince Ahira, who assisted Moses in numbering the tribes of Israel. Num. i: 15.

ENOCH, 1—[E′-nok,] *dedicated, disciplined, well regulated.*

ENOCH was a son of Cain, after whose name his father called the city which he built in the land of Nod. Gen. iv: 17. As the import of the name is "instructed, dedicated, initiated," it is supposed that we have here in the naming of this child and in the building of this city, an evidence of Cain's repentance, for he appears to have dedicated his son to God that he might minister in his stead in the sacred office, he being excluded forever for the high crime he had committed in the murder of his brother. This Enoch was the father of Irad, the grand-father of Mehujael, and the great grand-father of Methusael.

ENOCH, 2—*Dedicated, disciplined, well regulated.*

ENOCH was the son of Jared, and the father of Methuselah. Genesis v: 18, &c. He was a great and good man, for it is said of him, "he walked with God after he begat Methuselah three hundred years, and begat sons and daughters. His entire age was three hundred and sixty five years, and it is furthermore said of him, he "walked with God and he was not, for God took him." He evidently formed a character for serving God in early life, and he developed that character till the day of probation closed, and then went to heaven without dying. He lived a holy life, walking with God in constant close communion. His faithfulness was rewarded while he lived, "for he had this testimony, that he pleased God."

In Heb. xi: 5, it is said: "By faith Enoch was translated that he should not see death, and was not found because God had translated him, for before his translation he had this testimony, that he pleased God."

He prophesied regarding the judgment of the great day. We have his prophecy referred to and recorded in Jude 14 and 15. "And Enoch also, the seventh from Adam, prophesied of these, saying: Behold the Lord cometh with ten thousand of his saints, to execute judgment upon all, and to convince all that are ungodly among them of all their ungodly deeds which they have ungodly committed, and of all their hard speeches which ungodly sinners have spoken against him." Enoch has sometimes been looked upon as a type of Christ. He was dedicated, as his name imports, to God and to His service, as was Christ. He walked with God, was in constant fellowship and communion, as was Christ. But the most remarkable resemblance is this: he entered heaven without corruption of his body, and is the only person save Elijah, that has thus entered the heavenly world. There is the glorified humanity of Enoch who represents the Patriarchal age, of Elijah who represents the Prophetic age, and of Christ the Christian age.

ENOSH, or ENOS—[E′-nosh,] *fallen man, subject to all kinds of evil.*

ENOSH, or ENOS, was the son of Seth, and the father of Cainan. In connection with the announcement of his birth, in Genesis, iv: 26, we have the significant expression, "then began men to call upon the name of the Lord." The marginal reading for the phrase, is: "Then began men to call themselves by the name of the Lord." The true servants of God began to distinguish themselves from those who were not the servants of God by the title, "sons of God," while the others were titled, "children of men."

It is supposed that idolatry had its origin in the history of man just here. Enosh is supposed to be one of those that erred in laying the ground-work for the system of idolatry that has dishonored God and disgraced humanity. The import of the name is, "a fallen man," which would seem to indicate that he was one of those that erred; and, before he ended his days, the descendants of Seth, his father, profaned the name of the Lord by intermarrying with the offspring of Cain who was cast off for the cruel murder of his brother. The offspring of Cain were the children of men, and those of Seth sons of God. Gen. vi: 1, 2.

Enosh lived nine hundred and five years, and he died. Gen. v: 11.

EPAPHRAS—[Ep′-a-fras,] *covered with foam.*

EPAPHRAS was a native of the city of Colosse. From the reference made to him in Col. i: 7, we learn that Paul was strongly attached to him. He calls him "Our dear fellow-servant and a faithful minister of Christ." He had boldly declared the gospel in Colosse, and had been instrumental in the conversion of many souls to Christ. When Paul was at Rome, Epaphras went to see him, and in his love for him identified himself with him. He became Paul's fellow-prisoner.

It is thought while he was with Paul he heard that false teachers had corrupted and troubled the Colossian church, and he reported the same to the apostle, which led him to write this epistle from Rome to the Colossians. From Col. iv: 12, we learn that he was with Paul when the epistle was written and sent by Tychicus and Onesimus, and the apostle certifies to the interest Epaphras took in the church of the Colossians, "laboring fervently with you in prayers, that ye may stand perfect and complete in all the will of God."

EPAPHRODITUS—[E-paf-ro-di′-tus,] *agreeable, handsome.*

EPAPHRODITUS, a noted preacher of the Christian faith, who lived and labored at Philippi. From Phil. ii: 25, and iv: 18, we learn that he was sent by the church at Philippi with a supply of money and such other things as they thought Paul needed to make him comfortable during his imprisonment at Rome. He is supposed to have brought on himself an indisposition which threatened his life, by his executing with care and zeal the mission to which he was appointed. The account of his sickness reached the church at Philippi, and they were greatly concerned about him, as was Paul, who was with him in his sickness. Paul wrote to the church as follows: "For indeed he was sick nigh unto death: but God had mercy on him, and not on him only, but on me also, lest I should have sorrow upon sorrow." Thus the apostle acknowledges the mercy of God, both to the Philippian church and to himself, in raising up Epaphroditus from the bed of death. Having written the epistle to that church he sent him back to them as the bearer of the same.

EPHAH, 1—[E′fah,] *weary, to fly as a bird.*

EPHAH was the eldest son of Midian, and is referred to in Gen. xxv: 4. The descendants of Midian and Ephah probably settled in a country south-east of the Dead Sea; and they gave their name to the country where they settled. Their country abounded with camels and dromedaries; and when the prophet Isaiah represents the ingathering of the Gentiles to Christ, he refers to this people. Isa. lx: 6: "The multitude of camels shall cover thee; the dromedaries of Midian and Ephah, all they from Sheba shall come; they shall bring gold and incense," &c.

EPHAH, 2—*weary, to fly as a bird.*

EPHAH was a secondary wife of Caleb, the son of Hezron; and she was the mother of Haran, and Moza, and Gazez. 1st Chron. ii: 46. She was probably the same as Ephrath, referred to in 1st Chron. ii: 19, as the mother of Hur.

EPHER.

Was also a son of Midian, and is referred to in Gen. xxv: 4, as the second son. He is also referred to in the genealogy as given in 1st Chron. i: 33. It is not certainly known what country his posterity peopled. One historian says he conquered Lybia and called it Affrica, and that he was accompanied in the expedition by Hercules.

EPHOD—[E′fod,]

Was the father of Hanniel, the prince of the tribe of Manasseh, who assisted in dividing the land. Num. xxxiv: 23.

EPHRAIM—[Ef′-ra-im,] *that brings forth fruit or grows.*

EPHRAIM was the younger son of Joseph, and the brother of Manasseh. These two sons were born unto Joseph in Egypt, before his father Jacob came down to see him. Genesis, xlviii: 5. And when Jacob called his sons together to receive their father's blessing, he claimed the two branches that sprung from Joseph, *viz:* Ephraim and Manasseh, as his own children. They were to be numbered in Israel as Reuben and Simeon were numbered, though any children that Joseph might be blessed with afterwards, were to be called by his own name, or counted his own children. These two sons of Joseph were adopted into Jacob's family, and were ever after to have a place among his twelve sons, being entitled to an equal interest in the spiritual and temporal blessings of the covenant.

A very interesting and significant circumstance occurs in the apartment of the dying Jacob. As Joseph approaches near to him with his two sons, Jacob's eyes were dim with age, and indeed the film of death was gathering over his eye balls. He asked Joseph, who are these? He answers they are my sons whom God hath given me in this place. Then Jacob bade him bring them near him that he might bless them, and he did so.

The dying patriarch kissed them and embraced them, and then addressing himself to Joseph he said: "I had not thought to see thy face: and lo, God hath showed me thy children." Ephraim was then presented with Manasseh to the dying Jacob for his blessing, by Joseph, the father. As Ephraim was the youngest, Joseph presented him to Jacob in such a manner as that he could place his left hand on his head, and his right hand on the head of Manasseh, the eldest. Laying the hand on the head was a significant act in ancient times. It was used as in the present case, in giving blessings, also in designating men to particular offices, and in the consecration of solemn sacrifices. Jacob instead of placing his right hand upon the head of Manasseh as Joseph thought he would, crossed his hands and placed them on the heads of the lads.

This crossing of his hands "wittingly," brought his right hand on the head of Ephraim. Joseph supposing it to be a mistake, was about to correct it. He took hold of his father's right hand to remove it from Ephraim's head unto Manasseh's head. But Jacob gave Joseph to understand that he had not made a mistake. The mantle of prophecy was upon him, and he saw that Ephraim's tribe was to be the most numerous and powerful. Gen., xlviii: 19, "he also, shall become a people, and he also shall be great; but truly his younger brother shall be greater than he, and his seed shall become a multitude of nations," which declaration of Jacob is fulfilled in the history of Ephraim's descendants.

In Numbers, xxvi: 35, we learn that Shuthelah, Becher and Tahan, were each heads of numerous families of Ephraim. He had several other sons who are named in 1st Chronicles, vii: 21. Four of his sons were killed by the Philistines of Gath, while they were trying to defend their herds of cattle from the robbers. How many of the families of these sons of Ephraim were thus slain we do not know, but it is quite probable many of their children were slain with them. "Ephraim, their father, mourned many days, and his brethren came to comfort him.

No wonder he mourned this slaughter, for he was left by it almost childless. But another son was given to him about this time whose name was Beriah. He had also a daughter whose posterity was very numerous. They built the upper and nether Bethhorens, and Uzzen Sherah.

When the children of Ephraim, or the tribe of the Ephraimites, went out of Egypt in the exodus, they numbered forty thousand five hundred, and Elishama, the son of Ammihud, was their chief prince and captain. Num. ii: 18, 19. When the sum of Israel was taken in the plains of Moab the Ephraimites numbered thirty-two thousand five hundred, so that we discover a decrease of eight thousand of this tribe in the wilderness. Num. xxvi: 37. And it is further remarkable that there was but one single man of the tribe, and but two of all the tribes of Israel, that Moses and Aaron numbered in the census taken at Sinai—Joshua, the son of Nun of the tribe of Ephraim, and Caleb, the son of Jephunneh. These two men were of the spies, and the only ones that brought back a favorable report to Moses. Numbers, xiii: 8; xiv: 38.

The Ephraimites occupied an important position in the encampment of the Israelites. Their position was behind the tabernacle. In a march they followed after the ark, with its sacred deposits, borne, as it was, on the shoulders of the priests; and in this circumstance we may discover the ground-work for the expressions of inspiration. Psalms, lxxx: 1, 2: "Give ear, O Shepherd of Israel, thou that leadest Joseph like a flock; thou that dwellest between the cherubim, shine forth." For their position as a tribe, see Num. ii: 18–24; x: 21–24.

This tribe furnished a head, or a leader, of the Israelites after Moses died, in the person of Joshua, who greatly distinguished himself in the conquest, under God, of Canaan, and settling the tribes, by lot, in their inheritance. He assigned the tribe of Ephraim their lot in the very heart of the land. In their inheritance was the parcel of ground that Jacob bought of Hamor, which was afterward taken from him by the Amorites, but which he wrested from them with his sword and with his bow. Genesis, xlviii: 22. Jacob, when dying, indicated that that piece of ground should be in the inheritance of Joseph's family; and probably Joshua had reference to Jacob's dying language when he included it in Ephraim's inheritance.

We have an account in Judges, i: 22–29, of the Ephraimites and Manassites enlarging their possessions by going up against Bethel and conquering it, and so adding to their inheritance.

Deborah, a prophetess and a judge of Israel, was of the tribe of Ephraim when she went into war with Jabin, king of Canaan. It was thought that a body of Ephraimites were detached from the army to attack the Amalekites who were on their way to join Sisera, the general of Jabin's army; and this may be what Deborah refers to in her song. Judges, v: 14: "Out of Ephraim was there a root of them against Amalek."

When Gideon defeated the vast army of the east, on the plains of Moab, the Ephraimites complained and censured him because he did not call them to his assistance; but Gideon pacified them by referring them to what they had done in slaying Oreb and Zeeb, princes of the Midianites.

When Jepthah arose as a deliverer in Israel he invited the Ephraimites to join him and war with Ammon, but they would not, and when Jepthah had conquered and was returning, the Ephraimites crossed the Jordan and taunted and abused his troops, and threatened to do him personal injury. Provoked by their abuse he fell upon them and put them to flight, then took possession of the passage of Jordan before them and killed them as they attempted to cross. They were detected as Ephraimites by pronouncing the word Shibboleth, Sibboleth. There were forty-two thousand of them that fell. Judges xii: 6. After this Abdon an Ephrathite judged Israel. xii: 13.

Shiloh was in the tribe of Ephraim and the ark and tabernacle was there about three hundred and twenty years. This tribe seemed to occupy an important position in the tribes of Israel. When David was crowned, twenty thousand eight hundred attended and joined in the ceremonies. 1st Chron. xii: 30.

Jeroboam who revolted from Rehoboam and Judah and led off the tribes of Israel was of the tribe of Ephraim, and it is worthy of remark that nearly all the Kings of Israel, which kingdom lasted two hundred and fifty-four years, were of the tribe of Ephraim, and Samaria the capitol of Israel, as also the royal city of Shechem, was in the inheritance of Ephraim. Indeed so important was the tribe of Ephraim that sometimes the whole ten tribes received its name. As in Hosea ii: iv: v: vi. In 2d Chron. xxv: 7. It is said "let not the army of Israel go with thee, for the Lord is not with Israel, to-wit, with all the children of Ephraim."

EPHRATH—[Ef′-rath,] *abundance, bearing fruit.*

EPHRATH was the second wife of Caleb the son of Hezron, and she is brought to our view in 1st Chron. ii: 19, as the mother of Hur. Bethlehem th city of Rachel—the birthplace of David and of Christ—is supposed to be called Ephratah in honor of this woman.

EPHRON—[E′fron,] *dust.*

EPHRON was a Hittite who generously offered Abraham the field of Machpelah with its cave for a burying place, that he might bury his beloved Sarah out of his sight and have a family burying ground there. Abraham wished to buy it, but Ephron wished to give it to him, and could hardly be persuaded to take money in lieu of it. Ephron received for the field and the cave which was in it, "four hundred shekels of silver, current money with the merchant." And the property thus bought by Abraham was secured unto him by Ephron. This is the earliest account we have on record of the purchase of land. Gen. xxiii.

ER.

ER, with his brother Onan, sons of Judah and grandsons of Jacob, died in the land of Canaan. Gen. xlvi: 12. The account of their death and the sin that occasioned it is given in Gen. xxxviii. The sin of Er is not given, but it is said he "was wicked in the sight of the Lord;" and the Lord slew him. We are justified in considering that it was some great sin by the phrase above.

ERAN—[E′-ran.]

ERAN was of the sons of Joseph in the tribe of Ephraim, and the head of the family of that tribe called Eranites. Num. xxvi: 36.

ERASTUS—[E-ras′tus,] *lovely, amiable.*

ERASTUS was a chamberlain or treasurer of the city of Corinth. He was a convert to christianity, and early became an attendant and confident of St. Paul. He resigned the office of city treasurer at Corinth, and went with the apostle to Ephesus. He was sent in company with Timothy to Macedonia, by Paul, probably to prepare contributions for the poor christians of Judea. Acts xix: 22.

When Paul wrote his epistle to the Romans, Erastus was residing at Corinth, and sends his salutation to the Roman christians. Romans xvi: 23. And so afterwards, when Paul wrote his epistle to Timothy, Erastus still abode at Corinth. 2d Timothy, iv: 20.

It is thought by some, that he was afterwards bishop of Macedonia, for several years, and that he finally suffered martyrdom, for the cause of Christ at Philippi.

ERI.

ERI was one of the sons of Gad, and is numbered with the family of Jacob, who went down into Egypt. Gen. xlvi: 16.

ESAR HADDON—[E′sar Had′don,] *that binds, joy, or closes the point.*

ESAR HADDON was the son and successor of Sennacherib, King of Assyria. He is referred to, and his ascension to the throne, in Isa. xxxvii: 38. It is declared that Adrammelech and Sharezer, the sons of Sennacherib, smote him with the sword while he was worshiping in the house of his god, Nisroch; after which they escaped into the land of Armenia, and Esar Haddon reigned in his stead. During his reign he carried Manasseh a prisoner to Babylon, the account of which is given in 2d Chron. xxxiii: 11: "Wherefore the Lord brought upon them the captains of the host of the king of Assyria, which took Manasseh among the thorns, and bound him with fetters, and carried him to Babylon." Esar Haddon is referred to by name in Ezra, iv: 2.

It seems that the adversaries of Israel, having heard that the returned Jews were building the temple, proposed to Zerubbabel to assist in the work, declaring that since the days of Esar Haddon they were serving the God of Israel; but Zerubbabel and his associate chiefs refused them.

ESAU—[E′-saw,] *he that does or finishes.*

ESAU, or EDOM, was the elder son of Isaac and the twin brother of Jacob. He was called Esau because he was hairy. He was probably called Edom because his hair and his color were red. The account of his birth is given in Gen. xxv: 25. When he grew up to be a young man, he engaged mostly in hunting, and it was a common thing for him to come in from his hunting excursions and supply his father with venison. One day Isaac bade him go and procure him some venison, then dress it and prepare it for use, bring it to him, that he might eat it of his hands, and bless him before he died. He went out as he had often gone before, and while he was gone, Jacob under the instructions of his mother, killed a kid. She dressed it, making savory meat, such as Isaac loved. Jacob took it to Isaac, and pretending himself to be Esau, received his father's blessing. Jacob had but gone from the presence of Isaac, when Esau came in with savory meat and presented it, asking him to arise and eat of it that his soul might bless him. Isaac was astonished, for he thought that Esau had just gone from him with the blessing. The old Patriarch became agitated, and trembling exceedingly, he said: "Who is he that hath taken venison and brought it to me, and I have eaten of all before thou camest, and have blessed him? Yea, and he shall be blessed!" Esau heard the words of his father with sorrow, and he cried out in the bitterness of his soul: "Bless me, even me also, O, my father." It was a sad hour for Esau, and he called to mind in all probability the circumstances that occurred not long before that, when he sold his birth-right for a mess of red pottage. He came home one day from a hunting excursion, wearied, hungry and faint, and he asked Jacob to give him a little of his pottage. He agreed to do it, if Esau would yield the birth-right in his favor, and he did so, as is recorded in Gen. xxv: 24-34. Isaac then said to Esau: "Thy brother came with subtlety and hath taken away thy blessing." But still he plead with his father for a blessing, and Isaac blessed him, using the following language: "Behold thy dwelling shall be the fatness of the earth, and of the dew of heaven from above, and by thy sword shalt thou live and shalt serve thy brother; and it shalt come to pass when thou shalt have the dominion, that thou shalt break his yoke from off thy neck."

Esau was led by this act of Jacob supplanting him to hate him, and in his heart he determined to slay him. Rebekah, the mother, was informed of Esau's intention to take vengeance on Jacob, she therefore advised her beloved son to go to Haran and tarry awhile until Esau's wrath was pacified. Under the direction of Isaac he accordingly went, thus leaving Esau alone with the aged father. Gen. xxvii.

Esau married two women of Canaan, Judith the daughter of Beri, the Hittite, and Adah, or as she is sometimes called, Bashemeth, the daughter of Elan, the Hittite. These marriages did not please his parents, for they were wicked women of another nation. When Jacob was sent away, his father charged him not to take a wife of the daughters of Canaan, but rather go to his kindred in Padan-aram. When Esau found his marriages were disagreeable to his aged parents, he went and took wives of the descendants of Abraham, through Ishmael, Mahalath, the sister of Nebajoth. He also married Aholibamah, the daughter of Anah. Gen. xxviii: 6-9 and xxxvi: 2.

After Jacob had been in Padan-aram about twenty years, he returned to his own country with his wives and children, and flocks and herds. He remembered the fury of Esau when he left, and his threat to kill him, and was afraid. In order to appease the wrath of Esau, he sent him a present. It may be when Esau left Mt. Seir with his four hundred armed men to meet Jacob, he intended to injure him. If so, he lost the disposition before they met, for all his feelings developed were kind feelings. Jacob made him the present, but he was disposed to decline it, because he had enough; but he was finally induced to accept it. He then invited Jacob to Mt. Seir, and proposed to conduct him, but as Jacob expressed a wish that he should go on, and let his party take their time, he returned to his house. Whatever difference there was between them, was made up, and the two together attended their father in his last hours, and united in affectionately placing his remains in the cave of Machpelah. Genesis, xxxii: xxxiii: xxxv: and xxxvi: 6–7.

Esau had five sons, Eliphaz, Reuel, Jeush, Jaalam and Korah, and some of them had a very numerous posterity. They were altogether called Edomites. We may suppose from the account given of them in Gen. xxxvi: when Esau's family in Canaan is represented, that they were a strong and powerful nation, while the Israelites were in bondage in Egypt.

We have various accounts of the kings and dukes of the Edomites, in Deuteronomy ii; 1st Chronicles i: 35–34. And in the days of the reign of the kings of Judah and Israel, there were eighteen thousand of them slain by David's generals in the valley of Salt. We read of them in the days of Solomon being governed by deputies under the king of Judah. They helped Jehoshaphat and Jehoram against the Moabites, and again they joined the Moabites and Ammonites against Jehoshaphat, but they were afterwards destroyed in great numbers by their allies. 2d Sam. viii: 14; 1st Kings xi: 14–25, and xxii: 47; 2d Kings iii.

The Edomites became and continued inveterate enemies of the Jews and hence enemies to the church of God. Christ is represented in Isaiah lxiii: 1–3, in the following language: "Who is this that cometh from Edom, with dyed garments from Bozrah, &c."

ESHBAAL—[Esh-ba′al,] *the fire of the idol.*

ESHBAAL is the same as Ish-bosheth, the son and successor of Saul, made a king by Abner, the son of Ner, and murdered by two of his servants. See 2d Sam. ii and iv. In the account of the posterity of Benjamin, given in 1st Chron. viii: 33, we have this name given to Ish-bosheth. [See Ish-bosheth.]

ESHBAN.

Was the son of Dishon and the grandson of Anah. Gen. xxxvi: 26.

ESROM—[Es′rom,] *the dart of joy, division of the song.*

See Ezrom or Hezrom.

ESTHER—[Es′-ter,] *secret, hidden.*

ESTHER was the cousin of Mordecai, being the daughter of his uncle, but she was an orphan and he adopted her as his own daughter. She was young, but very beautiful. And when Vashti, the queen of Ahasuerus dared to disobey the king, the crown was taken from her, and preparations were made to give her royal estate to another. The fair young virgins were collected together at Shushan—and as Esther's kindred was not known, or her relation to Mordecai the Jew—she was numbered among the fair virgins and placed in the charge of the keeper of women, that the king might see the company, and choose from among them one to take the place of the queen Vashti who had been expelled the royal palace. Esther found favor with the king, and she of all the fair young virgins was selected by him.

Though she was a Jewess the fact was not known, "for she had not shown her people and her kindred." Mordecai had charged her that she should not show it. The king was so charmed with her beauty that he made no enquiry as to her family. She gained upon his feelings more and more, until he loved her above all the women, and advanced her to the highest honor, that of wearing the royal crown and being mistress of all the rest.

Shortly after Esther's promotion, through the influence of Haman, the Jews were brought into imminent peril—Haman had plotted their destruction, and had so far succeeded that he had procured the royal decree for their extermination. Mordecai the relative of queen Esther, knew of the decree and to whom it was attributable. He therefore besought the queen to use her influence to deliver her people. The feelings of Mordecai were intense, and he developed them by lamentations and cries, fasting[a] and sackcloth. He made the whole matter known unto Esther and besought her to make a request before the king for her people. She was deeply affected at the perilous condition of the Jews, but knew not what to do. She sent her cousin word that she had not had an interview with the king for thirty days—and that according to the law she would risk her life if she went unto the king uncalled. He received her answer, and no doubt appreciated the difficulty; but feeling that his case and that of his countrymen was desperate, he sent her back a solemn, searching charge, Est. iv: 14: "If thou altogether holdest thy peace at this time, then shall there enlargement and deliverance arise to the Jews from another place, but thou and thy father's house shall be destroyed: and who knoweth whether thou art come to the kingdom for such a time as this?"

We are now to look upon Esther as she perils her life for the safety of the Jews. She resolved on attempting their deliverance, even though in that attempt she might fail, and sacrifice her own life. Esther sent word to Mordecai to gather the Jews together at Shusham for a fast of three days, and she promised him, that she and her maids would fast. She thus entered into an agreement with them to humble themselves in supplication to God, for his mercy and for prosperity in her perilous undertaking. She agreed to go in unto the king and make her request, and said she, "If I perish, I perish." If I lose my life in the attempt to save my people, I shall lose it cheerfully. What magnanimity and true nobleness. Here is a woman risking station, honor, a crown and even life itself, to save a periled people. Feeling that it was her duty, she humbled herself before God, implored his help, and entered upon the task of bringing Haman down, and lifting her oppressed and periled people up.

On the third day of the fast she felt herself fully ready for the undertaking, and attiring herself in royal apparel she approached the court where the king was, and as she stood in the attitude of one desiring an interview with the king, he saw her. There she stood unveiled. The king, it may be, called to mind the law she was violating, and for a moment was angry at her approach. He was jealous for his honor as the Persian Monarch, and for this law that came so near deifying an earthly king, and was about to expel her from the court and declare her place vacant as queen, when he saw her terror and alarm, (for it is said she was so frightened that she fainted.) His sympathies were aroused, the fire of his affection for her was kindled afresh, and touched with tenderness he descended from his throne and in the most endearing manner took her up in his arms, allayed her fears, then held out to her the golden sceptre and she touched it. May we not suppose that the king in his tenderness laid the golden sceptre upon her neck, that upon her recovery from the swoon into which she had fallen, her eyes as they were opened might rest upon it, and her heart be at once comforted in the knowledge of the fact that she had secured favor and the way was open for her request in behalf of her people. As soon as she had returned to consciousness she saw the sceptre and touched it. Then the voice of the king fell upon her ear expressing his forgiveness and an acknowledgment of her station as queen. "What wilt thou, Queen Esther? What is thy request?" She must have felt that the king was condescending to address her with such expressions as these. She could hardly have supposed that she had so won upon him that he would make the magnanimous offer to her of meeting her wishes, whatever the request might be, even though it should equally divide his glory as a king. "It shall be given thee, even to the half of my kingdom."

Now we observe a movement on the part of Esther in making her request known to the king, that at first sight we can hardly understand. Why did she not at once declare to the king her errand? Why not unburden her heart without delay to him whose heart had been so wonderfully opened? It may be she thought that by her gracefulness and winning smiles at a banquet of wine, she could win still more upon him, and so increase the probabilities of success. She asked the king that he and Haman might come to a banquet of wine she had prepared. The king agreed to it, and left his throne, and in company with Haman attended. Knowing that she had a request to make, he asked her at the banquet, "What is thy request? Tell it me and it shall be granted." Esther saw that she was gaining on the king's affections more and more; but yet she was not fully satisfied that the time had come for her openly to declare her kindred, and put in her plea for her people. She stood before the king and requested that he and Haman should come to a banquet that she would prepare on the morrow, when she would fully make known her request. The king agreed to it, and Haman was lifted up with pride at the high honor conferred upon him; and that night in his own home he spake of his glory and his wealth—of his position in the government, and the honor of being invited to Queen Esther's banquet on the morrow. Ah! little did he think that Queen Esther's plea on the morrow would condemn him, and that in less than twenty-four hours he would be publicly executed by the order of the king.

While Queen Esther was preparing for the banquet, and nerving herself for the task of the coming day, God in his providence was preparing to favor her by promoting her kinsman Mordecai to honor.

The time had come when the banquet was prepared, and the king and Haman were being expected. There sat the queen in her apartment awaiting the arrival of her distinguished guests, and wondering that they did not come. She had made up her plea in an ingenious manner, and was ready, as soon as the opportunity afforded, to make it known; but the guests came not. How strange it is, thought Esther. What can be the occasion of this lack of promptness? Why do they tarry? Ah! there was a reason for it. Haman was the cause of the delay. He was at home with his family, with dreadful forebodings of coming ill. He was filled with mortification at the humbling process through which he had passed in honoring Mordecai. The king sent for Haman, and when he arrived they started for the queen's apartment. Their arrival was announced to her, and she received them with all the gracefulness due to their positions, and the banquet commenced. The king was anxious to know her request, and asked her, "What is thy request, and it shall be performed, even to the half of my kingdom."

The time had now come for her to declare her wishes, and, in answer to his question, with a true woman's heart, and in such language as none but a true woman could use, she said: "If I have found favor in thy sight, O King, and if it please the King, let my life be given me at my petition, and my people at my request; for we are sold, I and my people, to be destroyed, to be slain, and to perish. But if we had been sold for bondmen and bondwomen, I had held my tongue, although the enemy could not countervail the King's damage."

This address astonished the king, and, in a high state of feeling, he asked: Who is he? and where is he that durst presume in his heart to do so? Is it possible, he continues, that the queen, whom I most tenderly love, is thus in peril—that her life, so dear to me, is in danger?

Esther, having thus presented her cause, and seeing that the king was deeply enlisted for her and those for whom she plead, said: "The adversary and enemy is this wicked Haman," pointing with her delicate finger to Haman, who sat near them. The king arose and looked upon Haman with anger; then walked out into the garden. And while the king was absent from the apartment, Haman arose and stood before Queen Esther, in great agitation, to plead for his life, for he saw that the king was angry, and that his life was in danger. But Esther dared not exercise mercy to one so wicked and cruel as he was—whose fall God, in his providence, was bringing about. She heard the words of the king pronounced in sentence of death upon Haman, and rejoiced that this enemy of her nation was condemned.

When Esther saw that Haman was dead, and that her life and the life of her cousin was no longer in danger, she again besought the king in behalf of the Jews, against whom a decree had gone forth. She plead that the decision might be reversed—virtually at least. Though the law could not be revoked by a succeeding edict, or repealed, yet she asked that one of a similar character for the Jews, against the Persians, might be enacted and sealed with the royal signet.

The king granted her request, and the decree went forth, giving the Jews authority to slay their enemies; as their enemies had authority to slay them. Thus Esther succeeded in her noble work, and comforted the hearts of all the Jews.

Upon this deliverance through the influence of Esther, the Jews formed one of their annual feasts, called *Purim, or the feast of lots.*

In view of the interesting and thrilling scenes narrated—the sacrifice and devotion of Esther to the interests of her people—the Jews to the present day consider her one of their greatest benefactors.

ETHAN, 1—[E′-than] *strong, the gift of the Island.*

Was a son of Zerah, and the grandson of Judah. He is referred to in 1st Chron. ii: 6.

ETHAN, 2—*Strong, the gift of the Island.*

Was the son of Kishi, and a descendant of Merari. He is supposed to be the author of the eighty-ninth Psalm, and it is thought penned the Psalm on the occasion of the revolt of the ten tribes under Jeroboam. This Ethan was a wise man, and as such is referred to in 1st Kings iv: 31. The wisdom of Solomon is compared to the wisdom of Ethan, and Solomon is said to be the wisest of the two. Ethan is thought to be the same as Jeduthun who is referred to in 1st Chron. xxv: 3–17, and was the father of several sons who were temple singers. This Jeduthun was the author of several Psalms, xxxix and xlii, &c.

ETHBAAL—[Eth-ba′-al,] *toward the idol, he that rules.*

Was King of the Zidonians and he was the father of Jezebel, the wife of Ahab, King of Israel. 1st Kings, xvi: 31.

ETHNAN—[Eth′-nan.]

He was one of the sons of Helah the wife of Ashan. 1st Chron. iv: 7.

ETHNI—[Eth′-ni.]

A Gershonite Levite, referred to in 1st Chron. vi: 41.

EUBULUS—[U-bu′-lus,] *a prudent counselor.*

A Christian at Rome, referred to by Paul in 2d Tim. iv: 21.

EUNICE—[U-ni′-se,] *good victory.*

Eunice was the mother of Timothy, whom St. Paul calls his son in the gospel. She was a Jewess by birth, but married to a Greek. Acts, xvi: 1: "Then came he to Derbe and Lystra; and behold a certain disciple was there, named Timotheus, the son of a certain woman, which was a Jewess, and believed; but his father was a Greek."

Eunice and her son Timothy had been converted to Christianity through the instrumentality of some of the early ministers; for when Paul became acquainted with them they were considerably experienced in grace and Christian virtues. They were "well reported of by the brethren which were at Lystra and Iconium." From this we may learn that their reputation as Christians was unblemished; and as devoted members of the church the apostle was made acquainted with them. As a Christian mother, she taught her son the ways of religion, and gave him a practical insight into the principles of Christianity in her own life. She said to her son, Follow me, as I follow Christ; and her instructions and example were not lost upon him, as is evident from the position he attained in the church of God, and from the testimony of the great apostle Paul, who wrote epistles to him.

Eunice taught her son to read the Holy Scriptures; and Paul, when referring to Timothy's education, says: "From a child thou hast known the Holy Scriptures, which are able to make thee wise unto salvation through faith, which is in Christ Jesus."

But Paul gives his testimony to the piety and devotion of Eunice in the following language, writing to Timothy: "When I call to remembrance the unfeigned faith that is in thee, which dwelt first in thy grandmother Lois, and thy mother Eunice."

The teachings and example of this Christian woman had a salutary effect upon the mind and heart of her son, and helped to prepare him for his high and holy work.

EUODIAS—[U-o′-di-as,] *sweet scent.*

EUODIAS was a pious woman, who was probably a deaconess of the church at Philippi. She is mentioned by the apostle in his epistle to the church at that place. The reference is Phil. iv: 2. Euodias had some doctrinal difference with Syntyche, which accounts for the exhortation, "be of the same mind in the Lord." She may have been the wife of him, who in the next verse is called a "true yoke fellow," and who is entreated to "help these women."

EUTYCHUS—[U′-ti-kus,] *happy, fortunate.*

We have an account of this person in Acts, xx: 9-12. He lived at Troas, where Paul with his travelling companions tarried seven days. On the Sabbath day he celebrated the Lord's Supper with the disciples there, and preached to them a lengthy sermon. It is said he "continued his speech until midnight." The room they occupied was probably crowded, and Eutychus sat in the window. During the sermon he fell asleep, and losing his balance as a sleeping man is likely to do, he fell from the window outside. It was the third story of the house they were occupying, and the young man was killed. "He was taken up dead." The circumstance created alarm and deep interest throughout the congregation. Paul went down and took the young man up in his arms; told the alarmed friends not to be troubled, for his life was in him. Paul continued on in worship with them all night until the break of day, but he left the young man Eutychus alive, and his friends comforted, by his being thus raised from the dead.

EVE—*Living, enlivening.*

EVE was the helpmate of Adam, and the mother of the human family.

The man was formed first, and then the woman. How much time elapsed from the creation of Adam, to the formation of Eve, we are not informed, but we suppose only a short time. God looked upon man as he stood erect in Eden bearing his image, and pronounced him good, as he had declared the other work of the creation. Adam may have been alone for a few hours, enjoying the refreshing and invigorating air of Eden, and beholding the beauties and excellencies of the new formed world, and moving about among the newly created animals, when the Great Creator said, "It is not good for man that he be alone—I will make him an helpmeet for him," and this seems to imply, that the woman was to be an equal of the man. She was not to be his inferior, nor his superior.

It was while Adam was sleeping, probably the first time he ever slept after his creation, that God formed Eve, his partner, and we are to observe a difference between the creation of the man and the woman; and between the formation of her body, and that of every other being God had made. In Gen. i: 24, it is said, "And God said let the earth bring forth the living creature after his kind, cattle, and creeping thing, and beast of earth after his kind." And in Genesis, ii: 19, it is said, "And out of the ground the Lord God formed every beast of the field, and every fowl of the air, and brought them unto Adam." And when the body of Adam was formed, it was made of the dust of the ground, "And the Lord God formed man of the dust of the ground, and breathed into his nostrils the breath of life, and he became a living soul." But when *woman* was to be formed, "The Lord God caused a deep sleep to fall upon Adam and he slept; and he took one of his ribs, and closed up the flesh instead thereof: and the rib which the Lord God had taken from man made He a woman, and brought her unto the man."

As Adam awoke from the deep sleep that had fallen upon him, he fixed his eyes upon this resemblance of himself, and readily perceived in the new formed creature, a companion provided for him. But he seemed to understand how nearly that personage was allied to him. He felt the ties of new formed nature, and the endearment of relationship, and he said,

"This is now bone of my bone, and flesh of my flesh. She shall be called woman, because she was taken out of man." Adam claimed her as his companion, and He who had created them both, joined them together as hushand and wife, and the strength of that endearing relation was felt under the announcement for the first time to the ear and heart of man. "Therefore shall a man leave his father and his mother, and shall cleave unto his wife and they twain shall be one flesh."

God our Creator thus instituted the rite of marriage by joining Adam and Eve as husband and wife in the garden of Eden. Thus united, they traveled the pathway of life, sharing each others woes and bearing each others burdens, as well as partaking of each others joys. Their lives, as the lives of all their progeny, was a mixed cup. They sinned, and as a consequence were brought into sorrow. How long Eve remained innocent and happy, we do not know, only that her time in the innocent state was a little shorter than was that of her companion. She was not created until after Adam commenced the enjoyments of life, and she was first in the transgression—hence first to feel and endure the effects of the transgression.

They were equally happy in their first state, and equally under obligations to keep the law that had been given them. And when the tempter approached Eve and referred her to the delicious fruit on the tree in the midst of the garden, she said: "We may eat of the fruit of the trees of the garden; but of the fruit of the tree which is in the midst of the garden, God hath said ye shall not eat of it, neither shall ye touch it lest ye die." Here we observe that Eve couples herself with Adam, acknowledges the obligation upon them both alike. She knows herself to be under the great law of love with Adam, and bound to obey the law regarding the forbidden fruit.

But under the temptation presented by the enemy, she yielded. The serpent said unto her, "ye shall not surely die. For God doth know that in the day ye eatthereof, then your eyes shall be opened, and ye shall be as gods, knowing good and evil." The principle that the enemy succeeded in planting in her heart was pride—the sin that led to the fall of the angels. She credited the tempter, desired to gratify the appetite that had been created in her by eating the fruit. It appeared to be good, for "it was pleasant to the eyes;" but another incentive was, "and a tree desired to make one wise." Here was a development of what the apostle calls "the desires of the flesh, the lusts of the eye, and the pride of life." Eve took of the fruit thereof. Adam made himself a party in the transgression by failing to administer reproof, and by following her in eating. "She took of the fruit thereof and did eat, and gave also unto her husband with her and he did eat." Some are disposed to blame Eve much more than Adam for listening to the voice of the tempter, taking of the fruit and exercising her influence over her husband to lead him also to transgression. But if he favored her violation, and without any hesitation took the fruit from her hand and did eat, who can surely say that he would not have yielded to the tempter earlier, even, than did Eve; for she did venture objections when talking with the serpent, but so far as we know he made none, but readily took the fruit and did eat.

They both realized immediately after the act, that they had fallen; they felt the dark pall of iniquity shrouding their moral nature. But their sin is to be brought home to them, and God calls them to an account. Adam, at the trial, attached blame to Eve—and Eve charged the serpent with the cause of her action. "The serpent beguiled me and I did eat." The Lord God pronounced a curse upon the serpent, but as he looked upon the guilty pair, and the numerous progeny that would spring from them, he had compassion upon them, and he coupled with the curse of the serpent the promise of a Redeemer for man, "And I will put enmity between thee and the woman, and between thy seed and her seed, it shall bruise thy head, and thou shalt bruise his heel."

How much compassion is to be seen in the divine procedure here. The woman was to be cursed, but before the announcement of that curse, the promise is made her of a Savior. It is not made directly to Adam—God is talking with the woman, and for the woman, while declaring the curse upon the serpent. We may suppose she was thus strengthened to endure the curse that fell upon her. "I will greatly multiply thy sorrow and thy conception, in sorrow thou shalt bring forth children, and thy desire shall be to thy husband, and he shall rule over thee." Here we may observe a change in the position of the woman, she was no longer to be the equal in all the respects she had been before of Adam. We suppose she had as much right to rule as Adam, but now she is to be ruled—subjection to the will of her husband, is a part of the curse pronounced upon her, "and he shall rule over thee." Adam heard the words of the curse pronounced upon Eve, and from it he learned that she was to be the mother of a numerous progeny—and that from her was to come a Redeemer, "the bruiser of the serpent's head." With this knowledge that had been imparted unto him he "called his wife's name Eve, because she was the mother of all living." After the two were driven from the garden of Eden as the victims of grief, and the slaves of passion—they lived together as happily as possible in their fallen state. It was not long until Eve was blessed with children; Cain and Abel were born. When she looked upon her first-born she thought of the promised seed, and probably said in her heart, this is he who is to bruise the serpent's head. We may imagine the interest with which, as the first mother, she ministered to her two children—watched them as they passed from infancy to later childhood and to youth, and then to early manhood. She felt the satisfaction and maternal pride that mothers have felt in all ages, when looking at their sons—succeeding in life and promising good for the future. She acquiesced in the choice they had each made of employment. But one day the sad intelligence reached her that Cain had killed his brother Abel. Though she had never seen a human form wrapped in death's cold embrace, yet she had an idea of its meaning, and the intelligence was like a dagger to her heart. Her devoted, affectionate Abel is dead, and, worse than all, her eldest son has killed him. Oh, what a trial must this have been upon the first mother of our race!

After this Eve bare another son, and by a direct divine communication she learned that it was a son that was to take the place of her murdered Abel, in the line of Messiah or the promised Redeemer. The progeny of Seth continued in the person of Noah and his family. How long Eve lived we do not know, but it is quite likely she died long before Adam closed his mortal career, and went to join the spirit of her much loved Abel in the purer climes of bliss.

EVIL MERODACH — [E′-vil Me-ro′-dak,] *the fool of Merodach, despising the bitterness of the fool.*

Was the son of Nebuchadnezzar, and his successor on the throne of Babylon. He was the father of Belshazzar, who was the reigning monarch when the Babylonian dynasty closed, and the city was taken by Cyrus. He is referred to in Jeremiah lii: 31, as ascending the throne of Babylon and showing kindness to the captive King of Judah, Jehoiakim.

It is thought that Evil Merodach governed the Empire as proxy for his father, during his mental imbecility or madness. His reign as the king of Babylon, was short and rather unimportant. The generally received impression regarding this king is, that he was a very weak man.

EZBAI—[Ez′-ba-i.]

Was the father of Naarai, who was one of David's mighty warriors. 1st Chron. xi: 37.

EZBON, 1—[Ez′-bon.]

Was of the tribe of Gad, and founder of one of the Gadite families. Gen. xlvi: 16.

EZBON, 2.

Was a son of Bela, the son of Benjamin, and is referred to in 1st Chron. vii: 7.

EZEKIEL—[E-ze′-ki-el,] *the strength of God.*

Ezekiel was the son of Buzi, a prophet and priest. He was carried captive to Babylon with Jehoiakim, king of Judah, and in the fifth year of his captivity, was engaged in prophesying. Ezekiel, i: 2. He prophesied among the captives by the river Chebar, in the land of the Chaldeans.

Ezekiel was favored with some of the most sublime visions that are recorded in the sacred book. As such, is his vision of the "chariot of God," 1st chapter; "vision of the valley of dry bones," xxxvii; "vision of holy waters," xlvii. Under the inspiration of the Holy Ghost, he gives graphic descriptions, and uses the strongest and most nervous language. His descriptions are often wrought up to a holy energy and possess a daring grandeur. There never have been revelations made to mortal man, exceeding in sublimity, those made to Ezekiel. And among all the prophets, none were more bold and rapturous.

He predicted the overthrow of Jerusalem by Nebuchadnezzar. Though he was six hundred miles from the place, yet he said to his fellow captives, "the king of Babylon set himself against Jerusalem this same day." Ezekiel, xxiv.

He predicted the overthrow of the kingdoms of Ammon, Moab, Edom, Philistines, Tyrians and Egyptians, by the hand of the Chaldeans, and his prophecies were fulfilled.

He is supposed to have prophesied about twenty-two years—about six years before the destruction of Jerusalem by Nebuchadnezzar, and sixteen after it. There is a prophecy made in the twenty-fifth year of the captivity of Jehoiakim, king of Judah. Ezk. xl: 1.

It may be said of this prophet, in reproving sin, he was exceedingly plain and pointed, though many of his visions are hard to understand; and it is said that the Jews do not read the first or the last nine chapters, until they are thirty years of age. They suppose that the mind should be considerably developed before this part of Ezekiel's prophecies are read. When and where he died is not certain.

EZER—[E′-zer.]

Ezer was the son of Seir, the Horite, and, with his brothers, is referred to as a duke of the Horites. Genesis, xxxvi: 21.

EZRA—*A helper.*

Ezra was the son of Seraiah, who was of the sacerdotal line. He was a direct descendant from Aaron, and, as we learn in the book that bears his name, vii: 1, "a ready scribe in the law of his God." Ezra was sent from Babylon into Judea by King Artaxerxes during the seventh year of his reign, and he was the bearer of letters from that king, and a commission to correct errors in the church and state of the Jews. We have an interesting account of his embassy, and of his filling it, and of the effect it had upon the Jews in the last four chapters of Ezra. The first six chapters give an account of the edict of Cyrus, also of the return of the Jews under Zerubbabel, and their re-establishment in their land with the rebuilding of the temple at Jerusalem, and its solemn dedication to the service of God.

It is thought, with some degree of probability, that Ezra attended the Jews after the seventy years' captivity, to their own land, and was with Zerubbabel in building the second temple, and after it was finished he returned to Babylon to represent the condition of his people. This, however, is not certain. He was commissioned by Artaxerxes Longemanus to go to Judea and correct the error that had crept into the church and State. When he started for Judea with his commission, a large number of Jews attended him. He made a stop with his companions at the river Ahava, and thought of sending back to the king of Babylon for a band of soldiers, to attend and guard them on their way to Jerusalem. But remembering he had declared unto the king, saying: "The hand of our God is upon all them, for good that seek him; but his power and his wrath is against all them that forsake him," he was ashamed to require of the king such protection. Ezra, viii: 22. Feeling that he could not consistently ask for an escort of soldiers, he procured priests and Levites to the number of two hundred and fifty-eight, and after a solemn fast, during which they implored earnestly the protection and guidance of the God of their fathers, they made ready for the journey. They remained at the river Ahava three days, when Ezra delivered into the hands of Sherebiah, Hashabiah and ten of their brethren, the gold and silver which the king had granted for the service of the temple.

Ezra weighed the silver to the amount of six hundred and fifty talents; and silver vessels to the amount of one hundred talents; and gold to the amount of one hundred talents; also twenty basins of gold and two basins of fine copper, the whole amounting in value to more than five million dollars. And these twelve men that were separated to take charge of these things, received a solemn charge from Ezra to retain them in their possession, to take care of them until they reached Jerusalem, and then place them in the possession of the chief of the priests, then at the temple.

Having made all their arrangements, they started, and in four months their journey was completed. There were one thousand, seven hundred and seventy-five of them with Ezra when he arrived at Jerusalem, and on the fourth day after their arrival, the twelve men who had been set apart to guard the valuables, delivered them up in the house of their God. Ezra, vii: viii.

Ezra entered at once upon the important work to which he had been assigned. He found that a great many of the Jews had married heathen women; and among those who had thus offended, were princes and rulers in the land. He becomes greatly affected on account of their sin, and gives the strongest signs of grief. He rent his garment and his mantle, plucked out his hair and his beard, and secreted himself to meditate and mourn until the evening sacrifice. Then he ventured to make supplication and prayer unto God in their behalf. His prayer for them evinces the most intense feeling. Ezra, ix: 6–15.

The people saw him in his agony of soul, and heard the expressed anguish of his heart on account of their sins and the divine anger. They saw their errors and regretted their folly; "they wept very sore." One of the chiefs (who was not probably himself guilty) Shechaniah, the son of Jehiel, stood up before Ezra and confessed for the people their sin, and proposed that they who had transgressed should put away their strange wives and the children born unto them. He asked Ezra to issue a proclamation to that effect, promising that he would stand by him, and as an officer assist him. The commission of Artaxerxes authorized Ezra to do anything that the law of God required. He accordingly arose and brought the priests and Levites and all Israel into a solemn engagement to stand by him in correcting this gross error. He then issued a proclamation calling all together at Jerusalem, within three days, upon pain of excommunication from the church and the nation. Accordingly they came together, and Ezra stood before them, and charged the sin they had committed upon them. He bade them make confession, and resolve to forsake it at once. They agreed to do so. Commissioners were appointed to see that the matter was executed.

In the space of three months they made a thorough investigation, and one hundred and thirteen priests and other Jews put away their strange wives, notwithstanding some of them had children by those wives. It is not certain that they put away the children or disowned them entirely. They probably educated them in the religion of the Jews.

Ezra had the principal authority in Jerusalem, and was the director of the church and state for thirteen years He entered upon his work in the seventh year of Artaxerxes, and Nehemiah was appointed to succeed him, by the same king, in the twentieth year of his reign.

Nehemiah was commissioned to rebuild the walls and gates of Jerusalem, and Ezra, assisted by twenty-six Levites, read the law to the people, and expounded it in their hearing. Neh. viii. We have an account of the Feast of Tabernacles in Neh. ix; and, on the second day, Ezra read the law; and so every day till the feast ended—seven days. The people confessed their sins and renewed their covenants with God.

It is probable that Ezra wrote the book that bears his name, and he is generally looked upon as the restorer and publisher of the Sacred Scriptures after the Jews returned from the Babylonian captivity. It is thought he corrected some errors which had crept into the copies then extant through the negligence or mistakes of transcribers. He is thought to have collected the books of Scripture then received and disposed them in the order in which they appear in his time. And he is supposed to have added something in connecting the chain of Bible History. As for instance he is thought to be the author of the account of the death and burial of Moses, in the last chapter of Deuteronomy. Ezra is thought to be the author of the books of Nehemiah and Esther.

There has been an opinion extant that Malachi and Ezra were the same person, but of this we cannot be certain. The generally received opinion is that they were not the same, that the prophet Malachi was a native of Sapha, and of the tribe of Zebulon.

EZRI—[Ez′-ri.]

We have an account of this person in 1st Chron. xxvii: 26, as the son of Chelub, and an officer of David, who had charge of those who were in the king's employ as agriculturists or tillers of the ground.

EZROM or HEZRON—[Hez′-ron,] *the dart of joy, division of the song.*

He was the son of Pharez, and is brought to our view in the genealogy of David, as given in Ruth, iv: 18. In the genealogy of Christ, as given by Matt. i: 3, tracing the lineage of Joseph the husband of Mary, this person is referred to, and also in the genealogy of Mary, the mother of Christ, as is given in Luke, iii: 33. He was honored then in being in the regular line from Adam to Christ.

FELIX—[Fe′-lix,] *happy, prosperous.*

FELIX was a deputy for the Romans in the government of Judea. He enticed Drusilla to leave her lawful husband, and marry him. For his history and operations as given in the "Acts of the Apostles," see Claudius Felix.

FESTUS—[Fes′-tus,] *festival, joyful.*

FESTUS, whose name is Porcius Festus, was the successor of Felix in the government of Judea. Acts, xxiv: 27. And an account is given of the part he took in the affairs of St. Paul. This apostle had been two years a prisoner, and Felix, contrary to the expressed wish of the Jews, who were persecuting the apostle, would not condemn him, though "willing to show the Jews a pleasure, he left Paul bound." When Festus first arrived at Jerusalem, some of the principal Jews applied to him to condemn Paul, but he would not without a hearing. He told them that the Romans did not condemn a man until they heard his defense. They desired Paul to be brought from Cesarea to Jerusalem, under the pretense of trying him, but their intention was to murder him on the way. Festus rejected their request, and told them that he would return to Cesarea in a few days, and he invited them to go down with him, and lay in their charges against Paul and prove them, if they had it in their power to do so; and if he was guilty of wickedness, he should be punished. Accordingly in ten days after his arrival at Jerusalem, he returned to Cesarea, and Paul's accusers attended him. The day after his arrival, he sat upon the judgment-seat, and commanded Paul to be brought, and his enemies brought against him their charges. "They laid many and grevious complaints," which they were unable to prove. From the defense that the prisoner made, we judge that they accused him of breaking the law, of defiling the temple, and of treason against Cesar, and his government; for Paul says, Acts, xxv: 8: "Neither against the law of the Jews, neither against the the temple, nor yet against Cesar have I offended anything at all." Festus, with a desire to please the Jews, made a proposition to Paul to go to Jerusalem, and be judged before him there. He may have been bribed by the Jews to change the place of the trial, but he knew he could not do it without Paul's consent, as he was a Roman citizen; therefore he asked him, "Wilt thou go to Jerusalem?" The apostle answered that he was already at Cesar's judgment-seat, where he ought to be judged, being a freeman of Rome. He plead against the change, and his plea was successful. Paul demanded that he either be tried there at Cesarea, or be taken to Rome, and tried before Cesar. Festus probably explained to the council, that Paul had a right, as a Roman prisoner, to demand his trial there, or at Rome, and after his consultation with them as to which they would prefer, and they choosing to have him tried at Rome, he said to Paul, "Hast thou appealed unto Cesar? Unto Cesar shalt thou go."

Not long after this, King Agrippa and Bernice, his sister, came to Cesarea to salute Festus; and as Festus was declaring the case of Paul the prisoner unto him, and how it met him at Jerusalem upon his entering upon the duties of his office, Agrippa expressed a wish to hear him himself. He reported to Agrippa the manner in which he had disposed of the case, giving him at some length an account of the trial before him; and he informed Agrippa that as the prisoner had appealed to Cesar, he had entertained the appeal, and was waiting a favorable opportunity to send him to Rome. In accordance with the wish of the young king, the next day Festus had Paul brought out for a hearing, and he answers for himself before Agrippa. Acts, xxvi. Festus seems to have had it in view to gather from the defense the apostle was to make before Agrippa, some facts from which he could make out more clearly and distinctly a case to the emperor. He seems to have listened very attentively to the prisoner as he stands before Agrippa and makes his noble defense. He notices the compliment paid to the king, followed with an account of his education from his youth up. He listens to the defendant as he refers to his persecutions, and the reason he gives why the Jews had thus persecuted him, viz.: for maintaining the hope of the resurrection. Paul gives an account of his persecution of Christians previous to his conversion. He speaks of his miraculous conversion and his call to the ministry; of his obedience to that call, and of his success in preaching Christ crucified.

Festus becomes so intensely interested as the prisoner proceeded in his defense, and excited by the manner and matter of it, that he interrupted him; and, as we may judge from the account, became greatly moved, for he cried out with "a loud voice, Paul, thou art beside thyself; much learning hath made thee mad." Paul modestly, yet with sound sense and discretion, answered him, "I am not mad, most noble Festus, but speak forth the words of truth and soberness." Festus may be excused for supposing the prisoner was deranged; for he being a heathen, was ignorant of those things of which he had spoken; but he certainly must have considered Paul's answer well-timed and sensible. It did not increase his convictions of the prisoner laboring under mental derangement.

Not long after this Festus sent him to Rome under the charge of Julius, a centurion of Augustus' band; and although the vessel in which he sailed was completely wrecked in the Adriatic sea, yet from the island of Melita, after tarrying there three months, he was taken by Julius, in a ship of Alexandria, to Rome. Acts, xxvii and xxviii.

Festus, as a governor, was very active in suppressing and breaking up bands of robbers and assassins in Judea, and we are told that he also suppressed a magician, that drew a great many people after him, and was doing great harm. Jewish historians tell us that Festus died after filling the office two years and performing its duties, and that he was succeeded by Albinus.

FORTUNATUS—[For-tu-na'-tus,] *happy, prosperous.*

FORTUNATUS is mentioned in connection with Stephanus, in 1st Cor. xvi: 17, as a messenger from the church of Corinth to the apostle Paul, who was at Ephesus. Fortunatus was one of the first converts to christianity in Achaia, and hence a proper person to be the bearer of a letter from the church to the apostle. The occasion of his being sent was to acquaint Paul with the condition of the churches at Corinth. The apostle honors Fortunatus and his companion for the faithful discharge of their duty in the delivering of the message, and declares himself to be greatly refreshed in spirit. He bids the church respect them, "For they have refreshed my spirit and yours; therefore acknowledge ye them that are such."

GAAL—[Ga'-al,] *contempt, or an abomination.*

GAAL was the son of Ebed, and is brought to our view with his conspiracy against Abimelech, in Judges, ix. He was probably a Canaanite, and possibly a descendant of Hamor, the ancient king of Shechem. Abimelech had murdered all his father's sons, save Jotham, and was made king by the men of Shechem.

But it was not long until they became dissatisfied with Abimelech, for in about three years they began to deal treacherously with him, and they laid plans to destroy his life. Gaal observed the dislike, and in order, if possible, to increase it, he went over and dwelt awhile with them. He succeeded. The dissension increased, and he caused the men of Shechem to commit depredations in the adjacent fields and vineyards. And in the midst of their ravaging and carousing, they cursed Abimelech. Gaal endeavored to excite them against him by asking who is Abimelech? and intimating that he was a silly fellow and unworthy of rule and authority among them. He urged them to go in with him to make some descendant of Hamor, the father and founder of the city, their king. Gaal expressed a wish that he were captain, or leader of the people, and he would soon dethrone Abimelech and "as he expressed this wish" he challenged Abimelech to come out and meet him.

Zebul, the deputy, heard the words of Gaal, and reported them to Abimelech, so that the next morning he came out with an army and appeared on the top of an adjacent hill. Gaal saw them and talked with Zebul, Abimelech's deputy, regarding them. Zebul dissembled by saying, "thou seest the shadow of the mountains as if they were men." And he upbraided Gaal who had so recently boasted of his superior ability, and urged him to go out and fight with Abimelech. And he did so, and was defeated. "Abimelech chased him and he fled before him, and many were overthrown and wounded."

It seems that he rushed with his remaining men into the city thereby acknowledging himself conquered. But Zebul would not allow them to remain there, but thrust them out of the city of Shechem. What became of Gaal after this, we are unable to tell.

GABRIEL—[Ga'-bri-el,] *a man of God, God's strength.*

Gabriel was a noted angel of the living God. We have an account of his appearing unto Daniel the prophet, and giving him information of the seventy prophetic weeks or four hundred and ninety natural years which should elapse from the date of the edict to go forth and rebuild Jerusalem and the temple, to the death of Messiah the Prince, in Dan. ix: 20-27.

Gabriel was the angel who appeared in the form of a man at different times to Daniel and gave him important information. In the seventh chapter this angel deciphers the hieroglyphics that represent in Daniel's vision the four great empires that should succeed each other. He is, in all probability, the messenger that God sent to confront and confound the Persian prince for three weeks, and who then comes to the prophet to give him an understanding of what shall befall the Jews in the latter days. Dan. x: 13–20. And we may suppose that it was Gabriel that gave Daniel the important instructions that are recorded in the 12th chapter, supposed to be in reference to the general resurrection.

It was Gabriel that appeared unto Zacharias and informed him of the birth of John the Baptist, and of his character and work. The good man saw the angel and was afraid. Gabriel allayed his fears, and assured him that his announcement might be relied upon. Notwithstanding his age and the age of his wife, Elizabeth, they should surely be blessed with a son, and his name should be called John. They, as his parents, should have joy and gladness, and many of the people of Israel should rejoice at his birth. He assured him that their son should be great in the sight of the Lord, and should drink neither wine nor strong drink, and should be filled with the Holy Ghost, even from his mother's womb. And as though that was not enough fully to satisfy the priest Zacharias, he announced his name as Gabriel, and his position among the angels "that stand in the presence of God." And he further declared his special embassy from the King Eternal, to be to make known these glad tidings. He then informed Zacharias that he should be dumb until these things were accomplished, which came to pass.

Six months after Zacharias was informed of the birth of John, the angel

Gabriel appeared unto Mary, and informed her of the honor that God had conferred upon her, in selecting her as the mother of the world's Redeemer. She was informed by the angel of her conception, and of the coming birth of Messiah, and then the angel told her Elizabeth, her cousin, had conceived in her old age. Mary seemed to credit the information thus given her by Gabriel regarding herself and her cousin. The same angel appeared unto Joseph, the husband of Mary, and bade him retain his wife. Afterwards he appeared unto Joseph, and bade him flee into Egypt, and remain there until Herod was dead. And when Herod was dead the angel informed Joseph that he was dead, and bade him go back into the land of Israel with the young child and his mother. Luke, i., and Matt. ii.

GAD, 1—*A troop.*

GAD was the son of Zilpah the handmaid of Leah, and as the son of Jacob he was the head of one of the twelve tribes. Gad had seven sons, who were all fathers or heads of numerous families. Their names and the number of their families are given in Gen. xlvi: 16, and in Num. xxvi: 15, 18. When the tribe of Gad came out of the land of Egypt under their prince Eliasaph, the son of Deual, it numbered forty-five thousand six hundred and fifty, but in the wilderness it was reduced five thousand one hundred and fifty. This tribe was represented among the spies Moses sent over to view the promised land, by Geuel the son of Machi. Num. xiii: 15. We have an account in Num. xxxii, of their petitioning for an inheritance on the east side of the Jordan, and they obtained it, as did also the Reubenites who petitioned at the same time. This tribe have its part in the wars by which the country west of the Jordan was conquered. They were engaged in the war about seven years when they retired to their inheritance and houses, as we learn from Josh. xxii. There is an interesting account given in 1st Chron. xii: 8, 17, of eleven of the captains of this tribe who visited David when in the hold in the wilderness of Ziklag for the purpose of joining themselves to him and assisting him in his defense against Saul, who sought his life. They came to him from their own inheritance east of the river, and performed the feat of swimming the Jordan when swollen to its upper banks, and they put to flight several persons of the enemy of Israel in their rout. And when David was made king in the stead of Saul, who was killed at Mt. Gilboe, many of the tribe of Gad resorted to him and joined in the coronation ceremonies.

GAD, 2—*A troop.*

GAD was a prophet who was with David when he was being persecuted by Saul. He had fled to the cave of Adullam, and was joined by four hundred men who placed themselves under him. The prophet Gad came to David, and advised that he leave his hold and go to the forests of Hareth, which he did. As this prophet was with David before he was established on the throne, so he was afterwards, and we find him standing before the king of Israel late in his reign, when he had sinned against God in numbering Israel, and he charges the sin upon him and declares that punishment awaits him. Under the divine direction the prophet Gad bade David make choice between three plagues —famine, pestilence or war. David, with deep feeling for his sin, made the choice, and the plague fell upon him and his people.

And as the destroying angel stood by the threshing floor of Ornan the Jebusite, Gad was commissioned to say to David, "set up an altar in the floor of Ornan the Jebusite." David obeyed — purchasing the floor of its owner, he made the altar, and offered sacrifice and the plague was stayed. It would seem from 1st Chron. xxix: 29, that the prophet Gad wrote a history of David's life, and certainly he was well qualified to do it. As he was with David in Moab before he was king, and had probably been with him all through his reign as the king of Israel, contemporary with Samuel who annointed him, and with Nathan who ministered to him in his last hours.

GADDI—[Gad′-dy,] *my happiness, a troop, a kid.*

GADDI was the son of Susi, of the tribe of Manasseh, and was selected by

Moses as one of the twelve spies to search out and examine the nature and state of the land of Canaan. Numbers, xiii: 11.

GADDIEL—[Gad′-di-el,] *goat of God, the Lord is my army.*

Was the son of Lodi, of the tribe Zebulun, and was selected by Moses as one of the spies to search out and examine the nature and state of the land Canaan. Num. xiii: 10.

GAIUS—[Ga′-yus,] *Lord, or an earthly man.*

GAIUS was a noted Christian of the apostolic age, who abode, we are informed, at Corinth. He was one of the two converts of St. Paul whom Paul baptized himself. 1st Cor. i: 14. "I thank God that I baptized none of you but Crispus and Gaius." The apostle St. Paul wrote his epistle to the Romans from Corinth, and was dwelling at the time he wrote it with Gaius, and the apostle sends the salutations of Gaius his host to the Church at Rome. Rom. xvi: 23. From Acts, xix: 29, we learn that Gaius with Aristarchus had accompanied Paul to Ephesus, and he was severely persecuted by the mob that was raised there; they were dragged to the theatre and threatened, but were not severely injured. He is called in the next chapter, Gaius of Derbe, for we suppose it to be the same person, but why he is thus designated we cannot tell. The apostle St. John directs his third Epistle to Gaius, a devoted member of the church and dearly loved by the apostle. It may be the same person referred to above, for certainly the same virtues are referred to that were developed in the "host" of St. Paul.

GALLIO—]Gal′-lio,] *he that sucks or lives upon milk.*

GALLIO was the brother of Seneca, the famed moralist and philosopher. He is said to have changed his name in honor of his adopted father, from Novatus to Gallio, which was the father's name.

He was deputy or governor of Achaia under the Emperors Claudius and Nero. It was the latter Emperor who put him and his brother to death.

The Jews were greatly enraged at the apostle Paul for converting many Gentiles. The Corinthians heard him preach and were brought to Christ; they became Christians, and the Jews became so embittered and mad that they dragged the apostle before Gallio, and arraigned him at his tribunal, under the charge of teaching men to worship God contrary to the Roman law. Paul was about to speak for himself, when Gallio dismissed the case. He told the Jews that if their charges had been of a criminal nature, he would have given them a hearing; but since they pertained to matters of their law, he would have nothing to do with it. He ordered them out of his presence. Some heathen Jews probably taking license from the temper and action of Gallio in this case, took Sosthenes, the ruler of the synagogue, and beat him before the tribunal, but he did not concern himself at all about it. His carelessness in this matter has placed his name in a reproachful proverb. A man regardless of all piety, is called "a Gallio," and is said, "Gallio-like to care for none of these things." The above account is recorded in Acts, xviii: 12–17.

GAMALIEL, 1—[Ga-ma′-le-el,] *recompense of God.*

GAMALIEL was a prince of the tribe of Manasseh, numbered among the princes as they prepared under Moses for their exit from the land of Egypt. His name and position, is given in Numbers, i: 10.

GAMALIEL, 2—*Recompense of God.*

GAMALIEL was a celebrated Rabbi and doctor of the Jewish law. He was a Pharisee, at whose feet the young Pharisee, Saul of Tarsus, was brought up, and by whom "he was taught according to the perfect manner of the fathers." It is thought that Barnabas and Stephen were also pupils of Gamaliel. It is very likely that the first named was an intimate friend and associate of Saul, but converted before him. When Saul went from Damascus to Jerusalem, Barnabas received him and introduced him to his brother apostles.

It was not long after the day of Pentecost, and the astonishing display of divine power, that the Jewish Sanhedrim began to be alarmed at the progress of the gospel, and they desired to put the preachers of this new doctrine to death, in the hope thereby to stop the progress of the cause. They accordingly apprehended the apostles, and brought them before the National Council, of which this man was a member. Gamaliel checked the council in their heat and earnestness to put the apostles to death, by prudent advice. He had the arraigned apostles to withdraw for awhile from the presence of the Sanhedrim, that he might give his counsel without their hearing. He then told the council that if these men were impostors, the fact would soon be discovered, and they could be brought to justice, while their cause would die. But if, on the other hand, they were true men, and their cause was the cause of God, it was in vain for them to attempt to stop it, for they would be contending against the Almighty which was the height of folly. The council saw the wisdom of Gamaliel's advice, and changed their purpose from putting the apostles to death to mere corporeal punishment. Acts, v: 34, &c. If the Jewish Sanhedrim really believed the forged account of Christ's body being stolen by his disciples, Gamaliel, as one of them, would not have talked thus, and they would not have listened to such advice from him, much less have been influenced by it. From the report of the soldiers who had guarded the tomb, they knew full well that a very extraordinary circumstance had occurred. It is thought by some that Gamaliel was the son of the famous Rabbi Hillel, and the uncle of Nicodemus, who was instructed by Christ regarding the great doctrine of regeneration or the new birth. He is thought to have been the president of the Jewish Sanhedrim for about thirty-two years. Whether he was president or not, he certainly had a very considerable influence in that council. Acts, v: 34–40.

GAMUL—[Ga′-mul.]

Gamul was one of the priests appointed by David when he divided them into twenty-four courses. His lot was the twenty-second. 1st Chron. xxiv: 17.

GAREB—[Ga′-reb.]

Gareb, an Ithrite, was one of David's mighty men. 2d Sam. xxiii: 38.

GASHMU, or GESHEM—[Ge′-shem.]

There is a person of this name brought to our view frequently in the book of Nehemiah. He was associated with Sanballat and Tobiah against Nehemiah while engaged in building the walls of Jerusalem. He is called Geshem, the Arabian. They despised the workers, and taunted them while at their labor. Nehemiah, ii: 19.

Geshem and Sanballat tried to secure the attention of Nehemiah and divert him from his purpose and labor; but they could not, even by craft. He sent a messenger to them, stating that he could not come. The work in which he was engaged was a great work, and he could not think of letting it stop. "Why should the work cease, while I leave it and come down to you?"

When Sanballat and Geshem found they could not succeed in getting Nehemiah to a conference with them in the plain of Ono, Geshem charged him with intention to rebel and make himself a king. Neh. vi: 1–6.

GATAM—[Ga′-tam,] *their lowing, their touch.*

He was the son of Eliphaz, and the grandson of Esau. Gen. xxxvi: 11.

GEBER—[Ge′-ber.]

He was the father of one of the officers who were appointed by Solomon to provide victuals for his household. 1st Kings, iv: 13.

GEDALIAH, 1—*The greatness of the Lord.*

Gedaliah was one of the sons of Jeduthun, and when the lots were cast and the singers were divided into twenty-four courses, the second lot came forth to him. 1st Chronicles, xxv: 9.

GEDALIAH, 2—[Ged-a-li′-ah,] *the greatness of the Lord.*

Gedaliah was the son of Ahikam, a Jewish prince. He was made a governor over the poor people that were left in the land of Judah by Nebuchadnezzar, the king of Babylon. We suppose he was simply made an overseer, or appointed to regulate the husbandmen. As the overseer, his residence was at Mizpah, not very far from Babylon, and where he could easily receive the instructions that were to govern him. He pledged himself in the most solemn manner to the poor Jews, to encourage, protect and defend them—assured them if they would serve the king of Babylon it should be well with them. Jeremiah the prophet and Baruch went to Mizpah and placed themselves under the charge of Gedaliah, and claimed the protection he offered, and a great many Jews who fled into the land of Moab and Ammon came back. Baalis, the king of the Ammonites, instigated Ishmael the son of Nethaniah to murder Gedaliah, and he set himself about the work. He came to Mizpah with ten men, accomplices in the work of death. Gedaliah was informed by Johanan of the intention of Ishmael, but he would not believe it; hence took no precaution to save his life. He invited the party to an entertainment, and in the midst of the feast they murdered him. The Jews that were under him at Mizpah were alarmed lest the king of Babylon should charge the murder of Gedaliah upon them, and they fled into Egypt, notwithstanding the prophet Jeremiah tried to pacify them. For the account of the prince Gedaliah and his position as a ruler, and his murder by Ishmael, etc., see 2d Kings xxv.; Jer. xl: xli: xlii.

GEHAZI—[Ge-ha′-zi,] *the valley of vision.*

Gehazi was the servant of the prophet Elisha for several years; and it is thought by some that he was Elijah's servant before Elisha was called to be a prophet. Of this there is no certainty, for the first time we hear of Gehazi is at the house of the Shunamite, when Elisha bids him call her for a conference as to how she desired to be compensated for her kindness and hospitality to him.

When the Shunamite woman's son died she made ready and went to Carmel, where Elisha was to inform him of her bereavement and sorrow and urge him to come to her house. Elisha saw her coming in the distance, and, recognizing her, he bade Gehazi run and meet her, and inquire of her: "Is it well with thee? Is it well with thy husband? Is it well with the child?" He obeyed the prophet and received her answer: "It is well."

When she came to Elisha, and, in her sorrow, caught him by the feet, Gehazi approached to thrust her away and would have done so, had not Elisha stopped him. As soon as she told her trouble, Elisha sent Gehazi, with his staff, to her house, and bade him lay it upon the face of the child, and he did so, but with no visible effect. When his master arrived he told him "the child is not awaked." Elisha restored the child to life, and Gehazi called the Shunamite to take him.

When Naaman, the Assyrian, was healed of his leprosy and returned from the Jordan, he offered the prophet money, but he refused it. Gehazi had a love of money, and yielded to a temptation to run after Naaman and demand it, notwithstanding his master had refused it. He demanded it and secured a large amount—two talents of silver. He only asked for one talent, but Naaman gave him two. As soon as the servants of Naaman that carried it were dismissed, Gehazi hid the money and went into the presence of Elisha, who asked him: "Whence comest thou?" With a lie he answered: "Thy servant went no wither." Elisha then informed him that he was acquainted with his recent movements; that the prophetic spirit in him had made him acquainted with the whole affair, and with his intentions when he procured the money, viz: to set up a splendid establishment; to have men and maid-servants, olive yards and vineyards, and sheep and oxen. He rebuked him for his covetousness, and assured him that the leprosy of Naaman should cleave unto him and unto his seed forever. And the leprosy did cleave unto him at once, for he retired from the presence of Elisha a "leper as white as snow." 2d Kings, v.

Gehazi was punished very severely, but the sin that he committed was very heinous, actuated by the principle of covetousness, and indulging in pride and vanity. He would become a great man. He lied in order to impose upon Naaman, and in effect committed theft. He had asked for the silver and two changes of garments from Naaman, for Elisha, but intended to appropriate them to himself; and he closed the infamous acts by lying to his master, saying: "Thy servant went no wither."

About six years after, this same Gehazi confers with Jehoram, a king of Israel, concerning Elisha's miracle. The Shunamite woman had sojourned in the land of the Philistines during the famine. She solicits the king to give her land back. Gehazi certified that she was the woman whose son was restored to life, and the king answered her petition. 2d Kings, viii: 1–6.

GEMALLI—[Ge-mal′-li.]

GEMALLI was the father of Ammiel, who represented the tribe of Dan among the spies sent out by Moses. Numbers, xiii: 12.

GEMARIAH, 1—[Gem-a-ri′-ah.]

GEMARIAH was the son of Shaphan, the scribe, and father of Micaiah. He was one of the princes of Judah, and had an apartment in the house of the Lord, and Baruch was in this room when he read the alarming prophecies in the ears of the people referred to in Jer. xxxvi.

GEMARIAH, 2.

GEMARIAH, the son of Hilkiah, was a messenger from Jeremiah to the captive Jews, and the bearer of a letter from that prophet. Jer. xxix.

GENUBATH—[Gen′-u-bath,] *theft, garden or protection of the daughter.*

GENUBATH was the son of Hadad by an Egyptian princess, the sister of Tahpenes, the wife of Pharoah, who was governing in Egypt during the reign of Solomon. 1st Kings, xi: 20.

GERA—[Ge′-rah,] *pilgrimage, dispute.*

GERA was one of the sons of Benjamin, and is numbered with the family of Jacob who went down into Egypt. Gen. xlvi: 21.

GERSHOM—[Ger′shom,] *a stranger there.*

GERSHOM was the son of Moses and Zipporah, his Midianitish wife. The account of his birth is given in Ex. ii: 22, where it is said the reason Moses gave him that name was, "I have been an alien in a strange land." Gershom was the elder of the two sons of Moses, we judge from the fact that the birth of Eleazer is not yet announced, and where the two sons are mentioned his name occurs first. It is supposed that he and his family with his brother Eleazer and his family were united with the Gershonites and had the employment of taking care of the tabernacle and the tent. Num. iii: 21–26. They served at the tabernacle and were appointed to carry burdens. Num. iv: 24–28.

GERSHON—[Ger′-shon,] *his banishment.*

GERSHON was the eldest son of Levi, and prince of one of the extensive families of the Levites. At the time the children of Israel left the land of Egypt the Gershonites numbered seven thousand five hundred males, of which number there were two thousand six hundred and thirty that were fit for service. Eliasaph, the son of Lael, was chief of the family. They had their position as Levites at the west end of the tabernacle and their appointed work was to carry the vails and curtains as ordered by Ithamar the son of Aaron. Num. iii: 21–25, and iv: 24–28.

When the Israelites entered Canaan and the land was divided among these, the family of the Gershonites had thirteen cities assigned them. They are referred to in Joshua xxi: 27–33, as also in 1st Chron. vi: 71–76. This family continued to be an important family for many ages. It was divided into two parts or branches, Laadan was at the head of one, and Shinei at the head of the other. We have an account of them and their importance in the days of David; and some of them are reported as overseers of the treasuries in the house of the Lord. See 1st Chron. xxiii: 7, 11; and xxvi: 21, 22.

GETHER—[Ge′-ther,] *the vale of trial.*

GETHER was the son of Aram and the grandson of Shem, and is referred to in the posterity of Shem. Gen. x: 23.

GEUEL—[Ge-u′-el.]

GEUEL, the son of Machi, of the tribe of Gad. He was selected by Moses as one of the twelve spies to search out and examine the nature and state of the land of Canaan. Num. xiii: 15.

GIDDALTI—[Gid-dal′-ti.]

GIDDALTI was one of the sons of Heman, and when the lots were cast, and the singers were divided into twenty-four courses, the two-and-twentieth lot came to him. 1st Chron. xxv: 29.

GIDEON—[Gid′-e-on,] *he that breaks or bruises.*

GIDEON was the son of Joash, who belonged to the tribe of Manasseh, and was of the city of Ophrah. Gideon is the same with Jerubbabel, the seventh judge of Israel. He was called, under very extraordinary circumstances, to deliver Israel from the Midianites, who had sorely oppressed them for seven years. The enemy had devoured the crops of the Israelites, and seized and taken away their cattle, and impoverished them greatly. They became deeply affected and cried unto the Lord for deliverance. The Lord sent a prophet unto them to tell them why this evil had come upon them, viz: "ye have not obeyed my voice." But the Lord had mercy upon them, and sent an angel unto Ophrah to confer with Gideon who was engaged in threshing wheat, and the heavenly visitant let him know that he was selected to deliver his people. Thus we observe a call made upon one in agricultural life to become the general of an army, and the deliverer of his people. We may suppose from what the angel said to him, he had performed some feats that exhibited his courage and personal powers. What those feats were, we are not informed, but the angel says, "the Lord is with thee, thou mighty man of valor." Probably the thrilling circumstances that had occurred in the life of Gideon, that made him a mighty man of valor, were known to his countrymen, and would tend to excite confidence in him as their deliverer. Gideon heard the charge given him by the angel, but he ventured what seems to be an objection, "My family is poor in Manasseh," &c. The angel answered him that the Lord would be with him, and that the Midianites should be smitten by him. The confidence of Gideon seemed to increase, but he ventured to ask the angel to work a miracle, that he might feel more fully satisfied that this mission he was authorizing was of God: "Show me a sign that thou talkest with me." Gideon secured the attention of the angel and received a promise from him to tarry until he prepared for him a repast. He made ready to entertain him by slaying a kid and preparing unleavened cakes, and he brought the prepared victuals out to the angel who remained in the shade of a tree. The angel, however, did not eat, but bade Gideon place the prepared flesh and cakes upon a rock near by, and he proceeded before the eyes of Gideon to work a miracle. The angel touched the food with the end of his staff, and as he did so there came up fire out of the rock and consumed the flesh and the bread and the broth, thus making it an offering unto God. The proof of a supernatural agency was satisfactory to Gideon. He knew that he had seen an angel of the Lord, and became alarmed lest he should be struck dead. He had evidently adopted the opinion which prevailed under the legal dispensation, that if a man saw God or his representative angel he must surely die; hence he says: "Alas, O Lord God! for I have seen an angel of the Lord face to face." But his fears are allayed by a secret inspiration in his own heart, or it may be by an audible voice, for it is God himself that speaks: "Peace be unto thee; fear not; thou shalt not die."

His fears were allayed, and as he was left alone; the angel having departed from him, he engaged in adoration and praise to God. He built an altar and called it Jehovah Shalom: "The Lord send peace:" a very appropriate name for an altar at that time. The same night Gideon received a message from the God who had commissioned him to the important work of delivering Israel. That message required him to cut down the grove at once, and demolish the altar of Baal which his neighbors had erected, and at which they had been worshiping, and offer his father's bullocks upon the altar on the rock where the fire had miraculously devoured his provisions. He accordingly did so, having ten of his father's servants to assist him. Early the next morning the city was thrown into confusion, as the idolatrous men beheld the altar of Baal demolished, and the grove cut down, and another altar erected, on which already two bullocks had been sacrificed to another god than Baal.

These idolators were greatly enraged, and learning that Gideon had done it, they demanded of Joash, his father, his life. It may be that the father of Gideon was a worshiper of Baal, and that was the reason why "he feared his father's household." But now that the altar was torn down and the grove destroyed, and his son had done it, and the enraged idolaters were clamoring for Gideon's blood, Joash remonstrated with them, and urged that if Baal was a god, he ought to exert his power and punish the person who had broken down his altar. He insisted that Baal, if a true god, should avenge his injured honor, should stand up in his own defense. He probably renounced his idolatry, and from that hour looked with anxiety upon Gideon and his movements.

It is probable that the Midianites heard what Gideon had done in destroying the altar and grove of Baal, and thinking that his bold act was a forerunner of an attempt to come out from under their power, they associated with them the Amalekites and the children of the east, and encamped a mighty army in the valley of Jezreel. It was an army of nearly two hundred thousand.

Gideon, under divine influence, commenced to gather together an army. His friends the Abiezrites and warriors from the tribes of Manasseh, Asher, Zebulun and Naphtali, to the number of thirty-two thousand, were gathered under him. Gideon desired of the Lord additional evidence that he would save Israel by his hand. This request seems to be very bold, and yet we doubt not it was suggested to him by the divine spirit. "Behold I will put a fleece of wool in the floor; and if the dew be on the fleece only, and it be dry on all the earth beside, then shall I know that thou wilt save Israel by mine hand as thou hast said."

He made the test. Early the next morning he went to the floor, and while the ground was dry all around, the fleece contained a bowl full of water. Gideon then asked of the Lord one more test, viz: "Let me leave the fleece another night on the floor, and let it now be dry only upon the fleece, and upon all the ground let there be dew." God condescended to give him this request, and so settle his mind. It had the desired effect, and Gideon at once marched his forces towards the encampment of the enemy. After the march, he pitched by the well of Harod. Here his faith was severely tried, as he learned that some of his men were timorous and faint-hearted. His army only numbered thirty-two thousand, while the army of the enemy numbered two hundred thousand;—and yet the Lord told him the people were too many. All the fearful of his men were to be discharged. Twenty-two thousand took the benefit of this order and left him, which only left him ten thousand. The Lord spake to Gideon again, and told him that yet the people were too many—his army must yet be reduced. And the singular plan was proposed and followed of bringing the army down to a watering place to be tried by the manner in which they drank; and every one that lapped of the water with his tongue as a dog lappeth, was to be placed together, and every one that bowed on his knees to drink was to be placed together. And it was so that but three hundred of the ten thousand lapped; all the others bowed down upon their knees to drink water. The Lord then informed Gideon that the three hundred was to compose his army, to conquer the Midianites; the other nine thousand seven hundred were to be discharged. Whether there was anything in the manner of drinking indicative of the character of the men, we know not. It has been thought that the army had been on a very fatiguing march, during which they became very much heated and very thirsty, and that the mode of drinking adopted by the three hundred was less dangerous than that of drinking quickly and abundantly, as it is thought the others did. The fact is, the Lord had determined to use Gideon as an instrument to conquer the enemies of Israel, and he had determined to do it in such a way as to convince the people that his hand had saved them, and not their own hands.

Gideon sent the army all home save the three hundred, while he ordered them to prepare food for several days, and provide themselves with a trumpet, an empty pitcher and a lamp, for each soldier. They did so. The night before Gideon made his attack, he went, in company with his servant Phurah, into the Midianitish camp, or near enough to the camp to see them, and hear conversation passing between them. It may be that it was not the regular army, but Midianites who were camped very close to them, and were in feeling with them, and on friendly relations, who were expecting a battle, and in hopes of securing plunder after the battle was over. They approached near enough to hear the conversation of two men, which consisted of relating a dream on the part of one, and the interpretation of the dream by the other. He was afresh inspirited for the conflict, as he listened to the talk, and returned to his men confident of success. So confident was he that he said, "Arise, for the Lord hath delivered into your hand the hosts of Midian."

He divided his men into three companies, and attacked the camp of the enemy on different sides. Before making the charge and rushing into the enemy's camp, he had ordered his men to follow his example—all of them do as he did. When he reached a certain point, he blew his trumpet, broke his pitcher, and held his lamp in his hand, and cried, "the sword of the Lord and of Gideon." His men all followed his example, and together broke their pitchers, blew their trumpets, and held their lamps, while as with the voice of one man they united in the war cry, and their enemies alarmed, fled, supposing the army charging upon them was mixed up with them, they smote friend for foe, and killed one another. The three hundred men of Gideon kept their position, and continued to blow their trumpets until all the vast army of their enemy that was not killed had escaped from the plain. As the news of Gideon's victory went abroad, the men of Naphtali, Asher and Manasseh pursued after them. The Ephraimites were invited by Gideon, and they came up and took the fords of Jordan, and slew the two kings of Midian, Oreb and Zeeb. In the battle not less than one hundred and twenty thousand Midianites were slain, and the fifteen thousand that escaped with their kings, Zebah and Zalmunna, were overtaken and destroyed. There were two cities through which Gideon passed with his men, that denied his men food when they were hungry and faint. He punished the inhabitants on his return.

The Ephraimites were angry because Gideon did not invite them earlier to his assistance, but he was able to pacify them. The people, immediately after this great victory, desired Gideon to be their governor, but he told them the Lord was their rightful sovereign. He declared that he would not rule over them, neither should his son, but the Lord should rule. He requested the people to give him the earrings of their prey, which they did, and it amounted to one thousand seven hundred shekels of gold, (eleven thousand nine hundred dollars,) and out of this gold he made an ephod, and placed it in his native city. Probably he intended it simply to be a memorial of his victory, but it proved a snare to Gideon, and a ruin to his family, for it led to idolatry. Gideon judged Israel forty years, and died leaving seventy sons, all of whom were murdered, except Jotham, by Abimelech, a son of a secondary wife. See Judges, 6th, 7th and 8th chapters. We may say of Gideon, as the angel said, he was "a mighty man of valor." We may also say he was a true patriot, and an instrument in the hands of God in delivering Israel, from Midian. His private character, after he became a judge of Israel, was not exemplary in all respects. He had many wives, and seventy children, besides one by a concubine who succeeded him and murdered all his other sons. It has been thought Gideon was a type of Christ, but the spirit of inspiration has not designated him as such.

GIDEONI—[Gid-e-o′-ni,]

Was of the tribe of Benjamin, and the father of Abidan, the Prince who assisted Moses in numbering the tribes of Israel. Num. i: 11.

GILEAD, 1—[Gil′-e-ad,] *the mass of testimony.*

Was the son of Machir, and the grandson of Manasseh, as we learn from Num. xxvi: 29, and Jos. xvii: 1. He was the head of the tribe called the

Gileadites and the father of the following six sons: Jezer, Helek, Azriel, Shechem, Shemida and Hepher, who had a numerous posterity. They were settled beyond Jordan on the noted ridge of mountains of the same name. Num. xxxii. 40.

GILEAD, 2—*The mass of testimony.*

Was the father of the famous Jephthah, who was a mighty man of valor. Judg. xi: 1, and who delivered the Israelites from the hand and power of the Ammonites. This Gilead had a numerous family, and was probably a descendant of the former Gilead.

GINATH—[Gi′nath.]

GINATH was the father of Tibni, and is referred to in 1st Kings, xvi: 21.

GINNETHO—[Gin′ne-tho.]

GINNETHO, one of the chief priests and Levites who returned to Judea with Zerubbabel. Neh. xii: 4; and he is the same person who is referred to in Neh. x: 6. who sealed the covenant.

GISPA—

GISPA, one of the overseers of the workmen in rebuilding the walls of Jerusalem after the return from the captivity. Neh. xi: 21.

GOG—*Roof, covering.*

GOG was a Reubenite, the son of Shemaiah. 1st Chron. v: 4.

GOLIATH—[Go-li′ath,] *A captivity, a passing over.*

GOLIATH was a Philistine giant. He was the champion of the enemy of Israel who defied the armies of the living God. His size was enormous as it is given in 1st Sam. xvii. He was ten feet six and a half inches high, and had an armor of great weight. His brazen helmet weighed fifteen pounds; his target or collar weighed thirty pounds; his spear was twenty-six feet long, and the head of it weighed thirty-eight pounds. His sword weighed four pounds, his greaves or the covering for his legs thirty, and his coat of mail one hundred and thirty-six, so that all the weight of his armor was two hundred and seventy-three pounds.

He went out from the Philistine camp for forty days in succession, and defied the Hebrews to produce a man that would meet him in single combat, and he offered to let the fate of the two armies be decided by a single combat with him. If the Israelites could produce a man that could conquer him he agreed that the Philistines should be subject, and if the man that met him was conquered then the Israelites should be subject. This, however, Saul would not agree to for they were dismayed and terror-stricken at the sight of the giant and at his bold words of defiance.

But David came to the camp of the Hebrews one day during the forty days that the giant defied Israel. He heard his defiant words and with pure love of his nation and a jealousy for her honor, he meditated an individual contest with Goliath and made known his thoughts to some of Saul's warriors. Soon David appeared in the presence of Saul and agreed to meet the giant. He attacked Goliath with a staff—his sling and a few small stones which he took from the brook. The giant looked with disdain upon David as he approached him, and cursed him by the gods of the Philistines. He bade the youthful warrior come on and he would tear his flesh in pieces, and give it to the fowls of the air and to the beasts of the field. David, undaunted by the words of Goliath, said unto him, "I come to thee in the name of the Lord of hosts, the God of the armies of Israel." He assured his enemy that he was sanguine of victory, he expected and would surely have success. In a little while the Philistines would see their champion fallen. The preliminaries for the battle having been all gone through with, Goliath arose and began to approach David, who put a stone into his sling and threw it at his enemy's head, and it struck him a deadly blow. He suddenly fell dead, when David ran up and severed his head from his body, and took his head and his armor to the city as a trophy of victory.

Goliath had four brethren who were afterward slain by the warriors of David; the names of two of them are given, *viz:* Ishbi-benob and Saph; another is distinguished as the brother of Goliath the Gittite, and the other as one having six fingers on each hand, and six toes on each foot. 2d Sam. xxi: 16, 21.

GOMER, 1—[Go′mer,] *to finish, complete.*

GOMER was the eldest son of Japheth, and hence a grandson of Noah. He is referred to in the generations of Noah and his sons, Gen. x: 2; and this person, or his descendant, is referred to in Eze. xxxviii: 6. Gomer is suppose to have been the head of a numerous progeny.

GOMER, 2—*To finish, complete.*

GOMER was the wife of the prophet Hosea, and the daughter of Diblaim. Hos. i: 3. The prophet seems to have married this woman because he was commanded to do so. She is brought to our notice as a woman of ill fame. She had never been married, but had lived a life of scandal. She was the mother for the prophet of a son whose name was Jezreel, and a daughter whose name was Loruhamah. Hos. i: iv: vi. And afterwards she bare another son, and called his name Loammi.

GUNI—[Gu′-ni.]

GUNI was the son of Naphtali, and is numbered with the family of Jacob, when he went down into Egypt. Gen. xlvi: 24.

HAAHASHTARI—[Ha-a-hash′-ta-ri,]

A man or a family immediately descended from Ashur, the father of Tekoe, by his second wife Naarah. 1st Chronicles, iv: 6.

HABAIAH—[Ha-ba′-yah.]

Was among the sons of the priests who returned from Babylon with Zerubbabel. Ezra, ii: 61; and Neh. vii: 63.

HABAKKUK—[Hab′-ak-uk,] *a wrestler.*

HABAKKUK was a prophet supposed to be of the tribe of Simeon. There is nothing certainly known as regards his birthplace or parentage. He is thought to have prophesied during the reign of Manasseh, and was cotemporary with the prophet Jeremiah. It is supposed he was alive at the time of the destruction of Jerusalem by Nebuchadnazzar. In his prophecies he foretells the destruction of Judea by the Chaldeans, with the captivity of the people of the Jews. He also declares their deliverance from the oppressor at the appointed time, with the ruin of the empire that subdued them. He refers, in his prophecies, to the promise of the Messiah, and confirms it, and concludes the subject of his teachings with a prayer or hymn, in which he sets forth, in the most grand and glowing language, the wonders which God had wrought for his people. The poetry of the third chapter is almost unrivalled for sublimity in the sacred records.

If Habakkuk was alive when Judea was conquered by Nebuchadnezzer, and the Jews were carried into captivity, it is likely he remained in Judea and died there. [See Book of Habakkuk.]

HABAZINIAH—[Hab-a-zi-ni′-ah.]

Was one of the Rechabites, whose fidelity to the temperance principles of the family was tried, by placing pots full of wine, and cups before him to drink. He joined the others in refusing to drink, and thereby secured the divine favor. Jer. xxxv: 3.

HADAD, 1—[Ha′-dad,] *joy, noise.*

HADAD was a king of Edom. He was the son of Bedad, who smote Midian in the field of Moab. Gen. xxxvi: 35. Why the record of this circumstance is made here we can not tell. It may be because it was a circumstance talked about in the land of Midian during the time that Moses was there with Jethro, and pointed to as a calamity. The capital of his kingdom was Avith, and his successor was Samlah of Masrekah. 1st Chronicles, i: 46.

HADAD, 2—*Joy, noise.*

HADAD was the son of a king whom David conquered in the land of Edom. 1st Kings, xi: 14, &c. While Joab, the general of David's army, was ravaging the conquered country, Hadad fled for his life, and was placed by his father's servants under the protection of Pharaoh, king of Egypt. He was but a child when thus exiled from his native land. The king of Egypt cared for him, treated him kindly, and when he grew up to be a man, he gave him the sister of Tahpanes, his own wife, to be his wife, and she bare him a son, whose name was Genubath.

When David was dead, and Joab his general, Hadad desired to go back to his native land and recover his kingdom. In order to recover it he became the adversary of Solomon. Through the influence of Pharaoh, who parted very reluctantly with Hadad, he was permitted by Solomon to govern Edom as his deputy. He was, however, an enemy to Israel, and did much mischief. 1st Kings, xi: 25.

HADADEZER or HADAREZER—[Had-ad-e′zer,] *the beauty of assistance.*

He was the son of Rehob, and a very powerful king of Syria. He is called king of Zobah, which was a kingdom in Syria. 1st Chron. xviii: 3. It has been thought he was king of all Syria, except the province of Phonœcia. From the account given of him in 2d Sam. viii, we learn, extensive as were his dominions, he desired still to extend them; and in order to do so, he invaded the dominions of King David. He brought into action a large army, which the king of Israel met and conquered. David defeated Hadadezer's hosts and took twenty thousand of them prisoners, seven hundred horsemen with their horses, and one thousand chariots.

He had engaged in a war with Toi, the king of Hameth, who made himself an ally of David; for when that king had conquered Hadadezer, Toi sent his son to salute him and bless him, and intimated his joy and sincerity by sending David, as presents, vessels of silver, and gold, and brass.

About seven years after this, Hadadezer associated with him three other Syrian princes, and with the Ammonites fought against David again, but they were defeated. The Syrians fled and the Ammonites followed them; but Hadadezer, being unwilling yet to give it up, sent and brought the Syrians out in great numbers from beyond the river Euphrates, and they gathered together for a battle at Helam. The army of Israel met them and fought with them, and again defeated them. They fled before Israel, and seven hundred chariots were captured, and the men of the chariots slain, and beside them forty thousand of their horsemen were slain with Shobach, their general.

The consequence of this defeat was, the Syrian princes that were under Hadadezer deserted him and made peace with Israel, and became servants of King David. They abandoned the Ammonites whom they had helped, and for whom they had fought, and soon the children of Ammon were completely conquered. 2d Sam. x, and 1st Chron. xix.

HADAR—[Ha′-dar.]

Hadar was a king of Edom who succeeded Baal-hanan, the son of Achbor. The capital of his kingdom was the city of Pau. The name of the wife and mother-in-law of Hadar is given, viz: Mehetabel, the daughter of Matred the daughter of Mezahab. Gen. xxxvi: 39.

HADORAM—[Ha-do′-ram,] *their beauty, power, praise.*

Hadoram, called also Joram, was the son of Toi, king of Hamath, who had been engaged in battle with Hadadezer, the king of Syria. He had carried on wars with him, but probably not with the amount of success that David had. When David conquered that powerful Syrian king, Hadoram was sent by his father to the king of Israel to congratulate him upon his success; and he was the bearer of presents of silver and gold, and brass vessels, which David received and dedicated to God. 2d Sam. viii: 10; 1st Chron. xviii.

HAGAR—[Ha′-gar,] *a stranger, that fears.*

Hagar was the hand-maiden of Sarah, and was greatly honored in being given unto Abraham to wife; and still more was she honored in being made the mother of a child for the honored patriarch. Though Hagar may have had faults, she surely had excellencies. When she was treated hardly by her mistress, she fled from her presence into the wilderness, and there, in solitude and sadness, she wandered until she was wearied, and, coming to a fountain of water, she sat down to rest and refresh herself. While sitting by that fountain and meditating upon the sadness and sorrow of her lot, all at once her attention was arrested by the angel of the Lord, who, addressing her, asked whence she came, and whither she was going. She answered, without any equivocation: "I flee from the face of my mistress." The angel then bade her return and submit herself to her mistress; at the same time he gave her the promise that she should be the mother of a numberless multitude. Without any hesitancy she obeyed the instructions given; and it is quite probable she believed the promise of the angel as to her offspring. She returned to the tent of Abraham and submitted herself to Sarah.

The exercises of Hagar's mind, when she sat down to rest by that fountain, and one grand expression that she gave, are worthy of record in her history. Though she was a fugitive from her mistress and all alone in the wilderness, she said: "Have I here also looked after Him that seeth me? And she called the name of the Lord that spake unto her, thou God seest me."

After Hagar returned home she remained seventeen years with Sarah. In the meantime she bare a son to Abraham. Ishmael was his name, and afterward Isaac was born, the son of her mistress. Not long after this a thrilling scene presents itself in the history of Hagar. Her mistress became dissatisfied and determined to send her away. She made known her wishes to Abraham and he had objection to it. But Sarah was determined. She said to her husband: "Cast out this bondwoman and her son, for the son of the bondwoman shall not be heir with my son, even with Isaac." Abraham had his mind satisfied on this subject by the divine purpose being made known unto him, and he concluded to send her away. Early the next morning he provided her with bread and a bottle of water, and sent her with her son into the wilderness. She had not traveled far, oppressed in spirit as she was, until she lost her way.

We can not wonder that she was sad and sorrowful as she looked upon herself without a home, and upon Ishmael, her son, having been disinherited by his father—virtually an orphan. Neither do we wonder that she missed her way, and failed to find the fountain of water—(for she was probably seeking it)—that she had named Beer-lahai-roi, where the angel of God met her seventeen years before, and spake to her of Ishmael as the beginning of a mighty nation.

As she wandered about in the wilderness sorrowing, the bread she had been provided with failed, and the water gave out. Hunger began to press her and her son, and their thirst became extreme. She saw nothing but starvation and death for herself and her child, and in their extremity, she bade Ishmael lie down in the shade of a shrub to die. She desired him to screen himself from the rays of the burning sun, and then she went off from him a distance, for she said: "I will not see the child die." And she sat and wept until the fountain of tears was almost dried up, and her heart could no longer gather ease, overcharged as it was with sorrow, by crying.

In this, her greatest extremity, relief came. It may be that the same angel that appeared to her many years before when alone, was the angel that appeared to her now. The angel that came to her, assured her that the voice of the lad was heard, and bade her go and lift him up, and while she was in the act of raising the head of her dying child, the promise that had been made to her before he was born, was reiterated, viz: That he should be the beginning of a great nation. Just at this time the angel showed her a fountain of water. And softly laying the head of Ishmael down, she went to the fountain, and filling the empty bottle, she gave him a drink, and he revived. Hagar instructed her son as he grew up in the religion of Abraham, and taught him to practice the virtues of the patriarchal system, and we behold this son of Hagar, many years after, though driven from his father's house when a boy, standing beside the dying Abraham, ministering to him in union with Isaac, the child of promise. He harbored no ill feeling in his heart toward his father or his brother. Hagar, his mother, had no doubt taught him to forgive.

HAGGAI—[Hag-ga′-i,] *feast, solemnity.*

HAGGAI was one of the lesser prophets who flourished after the

Babylonian captivity. He is supposed to have been born in Chaldea, and he was of the sacerdotal race. Under the edict of Cyrus he returned with Zerubbabel to Jerusalem to assist, and encourage in the important work of rebuilding the temple of the Lord. He was associated with Zechariah in prophesying while the builders of the temple were engaged. The entire prophecy of Haggai has reference to the temple. He first reproves the people for their delay in building it and remonstrates with them upon the impropriety of permitting the temple to lie in ruins, while their own habitations were in excellent condition. He charges them boldly with wrong in living in ceiled houses while the house of their God was desolate. He represents the Divine Being as punishing them for this neglect by sending them the unfruitful seasons they had experienced. Haggai earnestly entreats them at once to enter upon the important labor and not stop until it was completed, and he encourages them by an important prediction regarding the glory of the latter house: "The glory of this latter house shall exceed that of the former." The meaning of this prediction was that though the second temple might be inferior as to its outward appearance—its external magnificence and grandeur, and though it might lack the ark with its sacred deposits, and the holy Shechinah or visible presence of Almighty God—yet it should be honored with the presence, authority and teaching of the Savior of mankind. He told them of terrible convulsions that should follow; of a mighty revolution that should precede the second coming of the Lord Jesus Christ. [See book of Haggai.]

HAGGI—[Hag′-gi.]

Haggi was one of the sons of Gad and is numbered with the family of Jacob who went down into Egypt. Gen. xlvi: 16. And he was the head of the family called Haggites. Num. xxvi: 15.

HAGGITH—[Hag′-gith,] *rejoicing.*

Was a wife of king David, and the mother of his fourth son, Adonijah, who was born in Hebron. 1st Chron. iii: 2.

HAKKOZ—[Hak′-koz.]

Was one of the priests appointed by David, when he divided them into twenty-four orders. His lot was the seventh. 1st Chron. xxiv: 10.

HAM—*Hot, brown.*

Ham was the youngest son of Noah. There is a circumstance recorded in his history when a young man, that is given as the cause of the curse that was pronounced upon him and his posterity. Noah, his father, was drunk, and in his state of drunkenness lay uncovered within his tent. Ham saw him, and treated him in his disgrace with levity and contempt. He went and told his brothers, Shem and Japheth, of the condition in which their father was, and they immediately performed the part that dutiful children were under obligation to perform to a father thus in disgrace. They threw a garment over their shoulders, and hurriedly ran backward and covered the nakedness of their father. When Noah awoke from his wine and learned how he had been treated by Ham, and the part that his other two sons had acted, he cursed the former and pronounced blessings upon the latter. This curse, pronounced by Noah upon Ham, was under the spirit of prophecy, and it was literally fulfilled, if not upon the person of Ham, or Canaan his son, yet upon their descendants, called Canaanites. Gen. ix: 20–25.

Ham had four sons, viz: Cush, Mizraim, Phut and Canaan, and they seem to have peopled Africa and a part of Asia. The name of Ham, which signifies *burnt*, or *black*, was peculiarly significant of the regions allotted to his family. We learn from 1st Chron. iv: 40, that part of the race of Ham dwelt on the south borders of the tribe of Simeon.

The powerful empires of Assyria and Egypt were founded by the descendants of Ham, and the cities or republics of Tyre, Sidon and Carthage were noted for their commerce; but they were destroyed, and Egypt, as a mighty kingdom, was subdued, as we learn from Eze. xxix: 14; "and they shall be there, a base kingdom."

**HAMAN**—[Ha′-man,] *noise, tumult, he that prepares.*

Haman was the son of Hammedatha, the Agagite, i. e., a descendant of Agag, the Amalekite. He was the prime minister of Ahasuerus, the Persian monarch, promoted by his king above all the princes of the court. The princes themselves, with the common people, bowed the knee at his approach, because the king had so ordered it. There was one man, who was a Jew, that would not obey the command, viz: Mordecai, the kinsman of Esther, the queen. Haman became enraged at this refusal to do him homage, and he determined to revenge himself on the whole nation of the Jews, by securing the passage of an edict, that on a certain day they should all be slain throughout the empire. In order to effect his purpose, he represented, on a favorable occasion for him to do so to king Ahasuerus, the people of the Jews as a burden and a nuisance in his empire, because of their peculiar laws and customs for which they were exceedingly tenacious; and he begged of the king that they might be destroyed, while he proposed, being immensely wealthy, to balance the loss of their tribute by giving the great sum of ten thousand talents of silver into the treasury. His king accepted his proposition, and an order went forth under the signet of the empire, to extirpate the Jews. Haman dispatched letters in the king's name to all the provinces of the empire, bidding the people to put all the Jews to death on the thirteenth day of the twelfth month, and in order to encourage the people to execute this decree, he placed before them as a temptation, the effects of the Jews, including in many cases great wealth, as prey.

In the midst of Haman's seeming success, Queen Esther invited him to a banquet alone with the king. He was lifted up with pride at this honor conferred upon him, but his pride was severely wounded at the refusal of Mordecai, who sat at the king's gate, to do him reverence, and he told Zeresh, his wife, that he could not enjoy himself, notwithstanding his honors, while this Jew remained there. She with other of his friends advised him to erect a gallows, and procure permission of the king to have the man hanged before the day of general slaughter of the Jews. Haman accordingly erected a gallows, fifty cubits high, and the next morning went unto the king to ask the privilege of hanging Mordecai at once. During the night that Haman was erecting the gallows, God was working with the feelings of the Persian king, and he had determined to honor the Jew Mordecai, who had some time before this saved his life when two of his chamberlains plotted against him.

The king was glad to hear in the morning that Haman had arrived for an audience with him; and as he entered his apartment without detailing to him the troubles of the night, he asked Haman, "What shall be done to the man whom the king delighteth to honor?" Haman was glad to hear such a question proposed to him, for it was calculated to impress his mind with the favor of the king towards him, and the probabilities of the petition, he had prepared and was about to make, being granted him. He answered the king, supposing he was to be the favored one: "Let a royal robe be brought, the apparel of a king, and the horse that the king rideth upon, and let one of the king's noble princes place the favored one appointed, in a king's robe upon the horse, and lead the horse through the streets of the city of Shushan, and proclaim in the hearing of the people, 'Thus shall it be done to the man whom the king delighteth to honor.'" Haman was then bidden to do thus unto Mordecai.

This order, so unexpected, must have fallen upon his ear like a loud clap of thunder from a clear sky. It must have filled his mind suddenly with forebodings of coming ill. What! the very man who had been in his way to enjoyment for months, and whose refusal to honor him had led him not only to meditate his death but the death of all the Jews,—this man is to be taken by him through the streets of the city and proclaimed the favorite of the king! But the task was given him, and he must do it. As soon as he had performed the office, stung with grief and mortification, he went to his house and told his wife and friends the strange and humbling circumstances of that morning. They were astonished, and feared it was an ill omen. They feared that Haman's favorite project would fail—that the Jews that he had plotted against, after all, would not be destroyed. But Haman had been invited that day to a banquet with the queen. The time arrived, and messengers were sent after him. He had been to the banquet the day before with a light heart and a merry countenance, but this day he goes with a heavy heart, and, no doubt, a sad and dejected countenance. During the banquet, at the earnest request of the king, Esther made known her petition. She made her bold and magnanimous plea, and in the presence of the quailing and trembling Haman, charged his sin upon him. The king was angry. Haman was frightened, and plead for his life, but he plead in vain, for the king ordered him to be hanged, and he was, upon the very gallows he had erected on which to execute Mordecai; and a little while after his ten sons were also hanged. [See book of Esther.]

HAMATH—[Ha′-math,] *anger, heat, a wall.*

There was a son of Canaan of this name whose family is referred to under the title Hamathite, in Gen. x : 18; also in 1st Chron. i: 16, where the genealogy of Noah's family is given.

HAMMEDATHA — [Ham-med′-a-thah,] *he that troubles the law.*

He was the father of the infamous Haman who sought the destruction of the Jews. Esther, iii : 1–10.

HAMMELECH—[Ham′-me-lek.]

He was the father of Jerahmeel one of the men sent to take Jeremiah and Baruch when the Lord hid them. Jeremiah, xxxvi : 26.

HAMMOLEKETH— [Ham-mo′-le-keth.]

She was the daughter of Machir, and the sister of Gilead. 1st Chron. vii : 17.

HAMOR, or EMMOR—[Ha′-mor,] *an ass, clay, wine.*

Hamor, or Emmor, was the father of Shechem, the man who defiled Dinah, Jacob's daughter. Hamor was a Hivite and prince of the country. At the earnest request of his son, he communed with Jacob to procure his daughter in marriage for Shechem. Jacob permitted his sons to join in the conference; and they laid a plot together, keeping it from their father, to destroy Shechem and Hamor for the offense that had been committed against their sister. Simeon and Levi executed the plot and slew Hamor and his son with the men of the city. Gen. xxxiv. [See Shechem.]

HAMUEL—[Ha-mu′-el.]

A man of Simeon of the family of Shaul. 1st Chron. iv : 26.

HAMUL—[Ha′mul] *godly, merciful.*

He was the son of Pharez, and the grandson of Judah, and he is numbered with the family of Jacob who went down into Egypt to dwell. Gen. xlvi : 12.

HAMUTAL — [Ha-mu′-tal,] *shadow of his heat, the heat of the dew.*

She was the daughter of Jeremiah of Libnah, and the mother of Jehoahaz, who was the son and successor of the good King Josiah. 2d Kings, xxiii : 31.

HANAMEEL — [Ha-nam′-e-el,] *grace or pity from God.*

Hanameel was the son of Shallum and the cousin of Jeremiah the prophet. He came to the prophet by divine appointment, and offered him a parcel of ground, as his kinsman. He wished to sell, and the law did not allow the estate of any family to be alienated; and, moreover, the nearest relative had the right of purchase given him. When Hanameel approached Jeremiah, he said: "Buy my field, I pray thee, that is in Anathoth, for the right of inheritance is thine, and the redemption is thine; buy it for thyself."

The price was settled on, which was seventeen shekels of silver, and weighed out to him; and he, in turn, gave Jeremiah a deed to the property in the presence of witnesses. The deed was duplicated, after which it was closed up in an earthen vessel to preserve it from accident, while the duplicate was left open for the inspection of all concerned. Jeremiah, xxxii: 7–14.

HANANI, 1—[Ha-na′ni,] *my grace or mercy.*

Hanani was a prophet who went to Asa, king of Judah, and reproved him because he hired the Syrians to help him, when engaged in a war with Baasha, king of Israel. Baasha had built or fortified Ramah, with a view of cutting off communication between Israel and Judah. Asa and the kingdom of Judah could have succeeded, but he was fearful, and hence hired help of another country to subdue Israel. The Lord was not pleased with him, and sent this prophet to inform him, and moreover to let him know that for his sin and foolishness, henceforth in his reign, he should have wars. Asa, instead of acknowledging his sin as he should have done, and humbling himself before God, and deprecating divine displeasure, became angry at Hanani, the prophet, and persecuted him by imprisonment. 2d Chron. xvi.

HANANI, 2—*My grace or mercy.*

HANANI was one of the sons of Heman, and when the lots were cast, and the singers were divided into twenty-four courses, the eighteenth lot came to him. 1st Chron. xxv: 25.

HANANIAH, 1—[Han-a-ni′ah,] *grace or mercy of the Lord.*

HANANIAH was the son of Heman, and when the lots were cast, and the singers were divided into twenty-four courses, the sixteenth lot came to him. 1st Chron. xxv: 23.

HANANIAH, 2—*Grace or mercy of the Lord.*

HANANIAH was a false prophet—one who prophesied lies in the name of the Lord. We have an account of him and his protested prophecy, in Jeremiah, xxviii. There we learn that Hananiah was the son of Azur, the prophet. The father and son were probably priests, as they were of a sacerdotal city, "Gibeon." He pretended to be commissioned of God to say that within the next two years, the vessels of Jerusalem's temple, that had been carried away by Nebuchadnezzar, should be brought back, and that the captives in Babylon should return to the land of Judea. The prophet Jeremiah arrays himself in teaching against the false prophet, and the people heard his words. Hananiah then approached the prophet Jeremiah, and took the yoke from off his neck, and brake it in pieces. He intended to palm off upon the people, this significant act as symbolic of his prediction. The prophet Jeremiah then received the word of the Lord regarding Hananiah, which was, that he was a false prophet, a transgressor of God's law, and for his wickedness, should die—he should be cut off in death during that year. It was during the fifth month of the year that he prophesied, and two months after, he died. Jeremiah, xxviii: 17. "So Hananiah, the prophet, died the same year, in the seventh month."

HANNAH—[Han-′nah,] *gracious, merciful, taking rest.*

HANNAH was the wife of Elkanah, a devoted servant of God and of the Jewish church, and the mother of Samuel, the last judge of Israel. The husband of Hannah went every year to Shiloh where the ark of God was, for the purpose of celebrating the great national festivals of the Jews. The temple, or place of public worship, was there. And Hannah, the wife of Elkanah, accompanied him yearly with a portion to sacrifice unto the Lord.

She had been sorely tried by the insinuations of Penninah, another wife of Elkanah. The actions and expressions of this other wife were provoking to Hannah. The other wife had sons and daughters, and she had none. She was not bound to her husband by the endearing ties of children, and her heart was grieved because of it. She could not hide her grief, even when she went up to the house of the Lord. Her husband saw it and was troubled, for he greatly loved her, and had evinced that love by giving her a "worthy portion" year after year. He endeavored to comfort and console her in her sorrow by declaring his especial affection for her.

She listened to his declarations and for a time dried up her tears, rose up, and ate, and drank. But soon her sorrow returned, and tears were again coursing down her cheeks. She was weeping in her devotions. And she began to tell the Lord the bitterness of her soul in prayer and supplications.

Eli, the priest, was sitting near where Hannah was praying and he was watching her closely; he saw her lips moving, and concluded she was intoxicated and made the charge of drunkenness upon her. She denied the charge and vindicated herself in a delicate yet pointed manner. "No, my lord, I am a woman of a sorrowful spirit; I have drank neither wine nor strong drink, but have poured out my soul before the Lord. Count not thy handmaid for a daughter of Belial, for out of the abundance of my complaint and grief have I spoken hitherto." God had heard her prayer, and the solemn vow she made in her deep engagedness was recorded in heaven. Eli was satisfied with her vindication, and sent her away with his benediction.

A year after this the husband of Hannah went up to Shiloh again, but she tarried at home for she had charge of a babe who had been named Samuel.

The vow that she had taken a year before, was upon her, "I will give him unto the Lord, all the days of his life, and there shall no razor come upon his head." She determined to remain at home with her child untill he was weaned, when she would take him to the temple, that he might appear before the Lord and abide there as long as he lived. When the child was three years of age, Hannah accompanied her husband, bearing little Samuel in her arms in the journey from Mt. Ephraim to Shiloh. And making an appropriate sacrifice, in company with her husband, she presented her child at the house of the Lord to Eli the priest. And addressing herself to him she said: "O, my Lord, as thy soul liveth, O Lord, I am the woman that stood by thee here praying for this child. I prayed, and the Lord hath given me my petition." Four years before she was compelled to vindicate her own cause, under a charge alleged against her; now she is prepared to explain (and does so) the subject of her deep devotion at that time.

Faithful to her vow she gave Samuel into the charge of Eli, and engaged in heartily praising the Lord, while the aged priest received his precious charge, and acknowledged the hand and mercy of God in his dealings with his handmaiden, and he united his voice with hers in praising God.

Hannah having dedicated her child unto God, appears before us as a poetess and a prophetess of the first class. The poetry of the prophetic hymn excels much Bible poetry even in the simplicity of its composition, the beauty of its style and the piety of its sentiment. It is recorded in 1st Samuel, ii. It seems that the inspiring spirit was given to her when she made the vow and gave up the child, and under the influence of that inspiration she composed and probably sang, as she composed it, this hymn of praise. Her song contains important prophecies that were afterwards fulfilled. Her son became a great prophet, as the hymn represents him. The judgments of God are prophesied as they were afterwards poured out upon Israel's enemies. In it John the Baptist, and Christ are foretold; and it is remarkable that in her prophecy of the Savior, she is the first one to give him the title "annointed."

Hannah continued, after she had "lent her son unto the Lord," year after year, to come to Shiloh, as she had done before, and she gave, in her annual visits, evidence of her attachment to Samuel by presenting him yearly with a new coat. The son of Hannah grew up and became a famed prophet in Israel. He lived to a good old age, then died, honored and lamented by all.

HANNIEL—[Han'-ni-el.]

HANNIEL was the son of Ephod of the tribe of Manasseh, and was one of the princes that assisted Joshua and Eleazer in dividing the land of Canaan among the tribes of Israel. Numbers xxxiv: 23.

HANOCH, 1—[Ha'-nok,] *dedicated.*

HANOCH was one of the sons of Midian, and a grandson of Abraham by Keturah. He is referred to, with the other sons of Midian, in Gen. xxv: 4. His brothers' names are Ephah, Epher, Abidah and Eldaah.

HANOCH, 2—*Dedicated.*

HANOCH was the eldest son of Reuben, and his name is given in connection with the names of his three brothers, Phallu, Hezron and Carmi, in Gen. xlvi: 9. Here the names of all the grand-children of Jacob are given, who went with Jacob and his sons into Egypt.

**HANUN**—[Ha′-nun,] *gracious, merciful, he that rests.*

HANUN was the son and successor of Nahash, king of the Ammonites. When the father of Hanun died, David for some cause showed kindness unto him, by sending messengers to him to comfort him. He probably would have received these expressions kindly but for the counsel and influence of some of the princes of Ammon, who assured Hanun, their king, that David was not sincere. That he had no respect, indeed, for Nahash his father; but on the contrary these his servants were spies, and their object was to come in possession of knowledge whereby they might successfully plot the overthrow of the their city and kingdom. Hanan believed his princes and treated the servants of David shamefully. He cut off half of the beard of each one and mutilated their garments, then sent them back to their king. The beard was never cut off save in mourning, or as a sign of slavery, and the object of Hanun was to make them have the appearance of slaves. It was a gross insult to David, and he so regardrd it. He sent his men word to tarry at Jericho until their beards were grown; but he looked upon the conduct of the Ammonites as abominable. The phrase used to represent David's abhorrence of Hanun's conduct is "*they stank before David.*" Hanun supposed this treatment would be resented and he prepared at once for a war with the Hebrews. He procured help from the Syrians, but David defeated them in sundry battles and the kingdom of the Ammonites was taken and Rabbah, the capital, was destroyed, after besieging it several months. It is supposed that Hanun was killed, and that his brother Shobi became a deputy governor of the subdued kingdoms under David, who had subdued it. This person is referred to in 2d Sam. xvii: 27, 29, as associating himself with Machir and Barzillai in furnishing David with provisions at Mahanaim.

**HARAN**—*Mountainous country, which is enclosed.*

HARAN was the eldest son of Terah, and the brother of Abraham and Nahor. The account of him is given in Gen. xi: 27-29, from which we learn that he died in the land of his birth before Terah, his father, died; and he left behind him two daughters, viz: Iscah and Milcah. The latter was married to Nahor, her father's brother. And Haran also left a son, viz: Lot, who was provided for by his grand-father, and became the intimate of Abraham, and spent several years pleasantly in his society in the land of Canaan, to which they went when they left the land of their nativity.

**HARIM**—[Ha′-rim.]

HARIM was the third in the division of the families of Eleazer and Ithamar, made by David when he formed the twenty-four courses of priests, and arranged for the rest of the sons of Aaron to serve under them. 1st Chron. xxiv: 8, &c.

**HARSHA**—[Har′-shah.]

Was among the families of the workmen who came back with Zerubbabel from Babylon. Ez. ii: 52, and Neh. vii: 54.

**HARUM**—[Ha′-rum.]

Was the father of Aharhel, in the genealogy of Judah. 1st Chronicles, iv: 8.

**HARUMAPH**—[Ha-ru′-maf.]

Was an ancestor of Jedaiah. Neh. iii: 10.

**HARUZ**—[Ha′ruz.]

Was a man of Jotbah, who was the father of the queen of Manasseh. 2d Kings, xxi: 19.

**HASADIAH**—[Haz-a-di′-ah.]

Was one of five persons of the royal line of Judah, referred to in 1st Chron. iii: 20. They were probably sons of Zerubbabel.

**HASENUAH**—[Haz-e-nu′-ah.]

Was a Benjaminite, one of the chief families of the tribe. 1st Chronicles, ix: 7.

**HASHABIAH, 1**—[Hash-a-bi′-ah.]

Was one of the sons of Jeduthun, and when the lots were cast, and the singers were divided into twenty-four courses, the twelfth lot came to him. 1st Chron. xxv: 19.

HASHABIAH, 2.
Was the son of Kemuel, and was the ruler of the tribe of Levi. 1st Chron. xxvii: 17.

HASHABNAH—[Hash-ab′-nah.]
HASHABNAH was one of the chiefs of the people, who sealed the covenant with Nehemiah. Nehemiah, x: 25.

HASHABNIAH — [Hash-ab-ni′-ah,]
HASHABNIAH was a Levite, and was among those who officiated at the great fast under Ezra and Nehemiah, when the covenant was sealed. Neh. ix: 5.

HASHBADANA—[Hash-bad′-a-nah]
HASHBADANA was one of the men who is represented as standing on Ezra's left hand when he read the law to the people of Jerusalem. Nehemiah, viii: 4.

HASHUB, 1—[Hash′-ub.]
HASHUB was a son of Pahath-moab, who assisted in the work of repairing the wall of Jerusalem. Neh. iii: 11.

HASHUB, 2.
HASHUB was one of the heads of the people who sealed the covenant. Nehemiah, x: 23.

HASHUBAH—[Hash-u′-bah.]
HASHUBAH was one of the five men referred to in 1st Chronicles, iii: 20, probably a part of the family of Zerubbabel.

HASHUM—[Hash′-um.]
HASHUM was one of the priests, or Levites, who stood on Ezra's left hand, while he read the law to the congregation. Nehemiah, viii: 4.

HATACH—[Ha-′tak,] *he that strikes.*

HATACH was one of the eunuchs in the court of Ahasuerus. Esther, iv: 5.

HATTUSH, 1—[Hat′-tush.]

HATTUSH was a descendant of the kings of Judah. He is thought to be one of the sons of Shechaniah. 1st Chronicles, iii: 22. He was probably the same person that accompanied Ezra from Babylon, or that accompanied Zerubbabel. Ezra, viii: 2; and Nehemiah, xii: 2.

HATTUSH, 2.
HATTUSH was a son of Hashabmiah, one of those who assisted Nehemiah in building the walls of Jerusalem. Nehemiah, iii: 10.

HAVILAH, 1—[Hav′-i-lah,] *that suffers pain, brings forth, declares to her.*
HAVILAH was the second son of Cush, and the grandson of Ham. His name occurs in the numbering of the sons of Cush in Genesis, x: 7. The land of Havilah was probably peopled and named by the descendants of Havilah.

HAVILAH, 2.—*That suffers pain, brings forth, declares to her.*
HAVILAH was the son of Joktan, referred to in the account of the posterity of Shem, in Genesis, x: 29. He was the twelfth son.

HAZAIAH—[Ha-za′-yah.]
HAZAIAH was a man of Judah, of the family of the Shilonites. Nehemiah, xi: 5.

HAZAEL—[Ha′za-el,] *that sees God.*
HAZAEL was a principal officer of Benhadad, the king of Syria, and was spoken of by the prophet Elijah, under the instructions which God gave him, to his successor Elisha, as the future king of Syria. We have the account of the revelation to Elijah regarding Hazael, in 1st Kings, xix.

It was several years after Elijah's translation, that Elisha went to the wilderness of Damascus, and Benhadad, who had heard of his coming, and being sick, he sent his servant Hazael to the prophet to enquire of him whether he would recover of his sickness. Hazael made his errand known to Elisha, who told him, that so far as the danger of the disease was concerned, he might recover—the sickness was not mortal, but yet he was well assured that he would not recover. And looking steadily at Hazael for a time, Elisha burst into tears. This was strange conduct to him, and he asked the prophet the cause of it. Elisha answered, "Because I know the evil that thou wilt do to the children of Israel, their strong holds wilt thou set on fire, and their young men wilt thou slay with the sword, and dash their infants against the stones, and rip up their women with child."

Hazael seemed to be struck with horror, and indignation at this declaration. "Is thy servant a dog, that he should do this?" Hazael, it may be, answered the prophet, that he had no power to do this, nor inclination, if, indeed, he had the power. Elisha then informed him that he was to be king of Syria, and then he would do these things. He returned to Benhadad, and told him a lie. He assured him that he should recover. But the next day Hazael murdered his master by taking a wet cloth, and spreading it on his face, and thereby smothering or stifling him. Hazael occupied a very prominent position in the kingdom and army of Syria, and immediately on the death of his master, who had no son to reign after him, ascended the throne, and was declared king of Syria..

He soon set himself to work to inflict upon Israel the very cruelties which Elisha had foretold. He ravaged the country of Israel beyond Jordan, inhabited by Reuben, Gad, and Manasseh. He burnt the cities with fire—dashed their little children to pieces. 2d Kings, x: 32.

He warred with Israel all the days of Jehoahaz, and God delivered them up into his hand, so that there was left to king Jehoahaz but "fifty horsemen, ten chariots and ten thousand footmen; for the king of Syria destroyed them." 2d Kings, xiii: 3-7 and 22.

Hazael laid siege to Jerusalem, but Joash, the king, diverted him by large presents, from his purpose. He however, did besiege it afterwards, and prevailed against it, and destroyed all the princes of the people, and sent the spoils that he took, unto the king of Damascus. 2d Chron. xxiv: 23. Upon the death of Hazael, Benhadad, his son, reigned in his stead. 2d Kings, xiii: 24.

HAZARMAVETH—[Hay′-zar-may′-veth,] *court or dwelling of death.*

HAZARMAVETH was a son of Joktan, hence a descendant of Shem. He is ranked as the third son of thirteen, and was probably the head of a numerous family. Gen. x: 26.

HAZELELPONI—[Ha′zel-el-po′ni,] *shade, sorrow of the face.*

This name occurs in the second genealogy of Judah, 1st Chronicles iv: 3. She was the sister of Jezreel, Ishma and Idbash.

HAZO.

HAZO was the son of Nahor and the grandson of Terah. Gen. xxii: 22.

HEBER, 1—[He′-ber,] *one that passes, anger.*

HEBER was the son of Salah, who was the grandson of Shem, and he was the father of Peleg and Joktan, who had a numerous posterity and peopled the country of Mesopotamia. Some have thought that Abraham and his descendants were called Hebrews in honor of Heber. His name occurs in Gen. x: 24, as the son of Salah. In Gen. xi: 16 and 17, we learn that he was but thirty-four years old when Peleg was born, and that he lived after that four hundred and thirty years, and begat sons and daughters.

HEBER, 2—*One that passes, anger.*

HEBER was a Kenite, of the family of Jethro, and who lived amongst the children of Israel, or near them at the time that Jabin, the king of Canaan, oppressed them. It seems from Judges, iv: 17, that there was peace between the king of Canaan and this family, and that they professed more friendship for him than for Israel. Hence, Sisera looked upon her invitation as the result of friendship, and went into the tent feeling secure from Barak, who was following after him. Jael, who killed Sisera, was the wife of Heber, the Kenite.

HEBER, 3—*One that passes, anger.*

HEBER was of the family of Beriah, of the tribe of Asher, and the head of the family called the Heberites. Num. xxvi: 45.

HEBRON—[He′-bron,] *society, friendship, enchantment.*

HEBRON was one of the four sons of Kohath, the son of Levi. The names of the other three are Amran, Izhar and Uzziel. As Moses, Aaron and Miriam were the children of Amram, the brother of Hebron, he was their uncle. Ex. vi: 18.

HELAH—[He′-lah.]
HELAH was one of the wives of Ashur, and she was the mother of his three sons, Zereth and Jezoar and Ethnan. 1st Chron. iv: 7.

HELDAI—[Hel′-da-i,] *the world.*
HELDAI, the Netophathite, was the captain of the twelfth month, when David instituted the monthly service of captains over twenty-four thousand men. 1st Chron. xxvii: 15.

HELEB—[He′-leb.]
HELEB, the son of Baanah, the Netophathite, was one of David's mighty men. 2d Sam. xxiii: 29.

HELEK—
HELEK was of the family of Manasseh through Gilead. He was the head of the Helekites, an extensive family referred to in the posterity of Joseph. Num. xxvi: 30.

HELEZ—
HELEZ, the Pelonite, was the captain of the seventh month, when David instituted the monthly service of captains over twenty-four thousand men. 1st Chron. xxvii: 10. Helez, the Paltite, may be the same person. 2d Sam. xxiii: 26.

HELI—*Ascending, climbing up.*
HELI was the father of Mary, the mother of our Lord, and his name occurs in the genealogy of Christ, as given by St. Luke. Luke iii: 23. Joseph is there called the son of Heli because he was his son-in-law, having married his daughter.

HELON—[He′-lon.]
HELON was of the tribe of Zebulun, and the father of Eliab, the prince who assisted Moses in numbering the tribes of Israel. Num. i: 9.

HEMAN, 1—[He-man,] *their trouble, their tumult, much.*
HEMAN was one of the sons of Zerah, the son of Judah. There are five of them named in 1st Chron. ii: 6. It is likely that the Heman who is mentioned in 1st Kings, iv: 31, is the son of Zerah, who, in the latter quotation, is called Mahol. If so, this Heman ranked with three of his brothers among the wisest of men. The wisdom that God gave Solomon is compared to the wisdom of these men and declared to be superior.

HEMAN, 2—*Their trouble, their tumult, much.*
HEMAN was a son of Joel and a grandson of Shemuel, and he was a principal singer in the time of King David. 1st Chron. vi: 33; xv: 19. He was associated with Ethan and Asaph. In 1st Chron. xv, he had fourteen sons, who were the heads of fourteen families, which constituted fourteen classes of the sacred musicians. It is not known certainly whether Heman composed poetry or not—but he is thought by some to be the author of the eighty-eighth psalm.

HEMDAN—
HEMDAN was the son of Dishon, and the grandson of Anah. Genesis, xxxvi: 26.

HEPHZIBAH—[Hef′-zi-bah,] *my pleasure.*
Was the wife of Hezekiah and the mother of Manasseh. 2d Kings, xxi: 1. "And his mother's name was Hephzibah." The church is called by this name in Isa. lxii: 4. "Thou shalt be called Hephzibah, and thy land Beulah, for the Lord delighteth in thee, and thy land shall be married."

HERMAS—[Her′-mas.]
Was the name of a christian resident at Rome, to whom St. Paul sends greetings in closing up his Epistle to the Romans. Rom. xvi: 14.

HERMES—[Her′-mes,] *mercury, gain, refuge.*
Was another christian to whom Paul sends his salutations. Rom. xvi: 14

HERMOGENES—[Her-mog′-e-nes,] *begotten of Mercury, of lucre.*

This person is mentioned by St. Paul in his epistle to Timothy. Many had turned away from him, and from the faith, and he mentions "Phygellus and Hermogenes," as two of them. 2d Tim. i: 15.

**HEROD, 1**—[Her´-rod,] *the glory of the skin.*

HEROD is usually styled Herod the Great. He was the king of the Jews. His father, Antipater, is thought by some to have been a Jew, by others an Idumean, who embraced Judaism. Others think him to have been a heathen guardian of an idol temple—the temple of Apollo, at Askelon, and who was captured by a scouting party of Idumeans, and while in Idumea was induced to embrace the religion of the Jews. History informs us that at the early age of twenty-five years, if not indeed earlier, he was appointed by his father, with the consent of the high priest, governor of Galilee, and while in that office he distinguished himself for valor by the suppression and utter riddance of the country of a band of robbers. He apprehended and executed Hezekiah, their leader. He had received no order from his superiors in the government for this purpose, and hence was considered an offender against law, and by some of his enemies among the Jews he was accused and brought before the Sanhedrim to answer for his conduct. He succeeded, however, through the influence of his friends, in escaping censure, but he went in the night to Syria, and was intrusted by Sextus, the governor, with authority in the government of Hollow Syria.

Herod felt himself aggrieved by the Jews, and determined, as soon as an opportunity offered, to avenge himself. He accordingly marched an army, and would have laid siege to the city of Jerusalem, but for the influence of his father and brother, who succeeded in dissuading him from his purpose.

After this a hundred principal men of the Jews brought accusations against Herod and his brother Phasael before Mark Antony. Hyrcanus, the high priest, befriended him, and represented Herod and his brother as being much better qualified to govern the Jews than those men who had brought accusations against them; whereupon Antony destroyed the lives of several of Herod's adversaries, and would have put them all to death, had not Herod interfered and plead for their lives. The two brothers were then appointed Tetrarchs, and the kingdom of Judea was conferred upon Herod.

Immediately after his appointment he assumed the government, and in about three years he secured possession of the whole country. Jerusalem held out against the siege of Herod nearly six months, but he finally conquered and took Antigonus a prisoner of war. He put him to death, and obtained peaceable possession of the kingdom. He put Aristobulus, the brother of his wife Mariamne, in the office of the high priesthood. Aristobulus being the grandson of Hyrcanus, was entitled to the office, probably, and he became exceedingly popular and much loved by the Jews. Herod, it is thought, was jealous of him, because the people loved him, and he ordered him, about a year after, to be thrown into a bath and drowned.

Some time after this, an accusation was lodged against Herod by Cleopatra to Mark Antony. He was accordingly summoned to answer to the charge; but, before leaving home, he gave a charge to Joseph, whom he left to govern in his absence, regarding Mariamne, his wife, to whom he was devotedly attached. That charge required Joseph to put her to death in case he was convicted of the charge on which he was to be tried, for he was unwilling, in any event, for Mariamne to be the wife of any other man. He was, however, cleared, and returned in credit to his government in due time.

He found, on his return, that Joseph had communicated to Mariamne the secret he had committed to him, and he put him to death. Afterward he put Mariamne to death, who was incensed against him from the time that Joseph made known the secret to her.

After the ruin of Antony, Herod sought and obtained the clemency and favor of Augustus, who continued to heap honors upon him, which he was illy prepared to enjoy because of remorse for the murders he had committed, especially that of his wife.

In order to acquire popularity among the Jews, he set himself to work at the vast enterprise of rebuilding or repairing the temple of Jerusalem. He thought they would honor his attachment to their religion, developed by so noble an enterprise. He prosecuted the work with vigor, and finished it in a magnificent style in about a year and a half.

He placed his two sons, Aristobulus and Alexander, at Rome, to be educated, and, after their return, he married them to Bernice and Glaphyra. These two sons afterward offended him, and were put to death. And not long after this, Antipater, another son who had instigated him to the murder of the other two, laid a plot to put Herod to death; but his plot was detected, and he was imprisoned, and afterward, by order of his father, put to death.

This cruel king was reigning when Jesus was born in Bethlehem of Judea. Matt. ii: 1. He was in a languishing and troubled state when the wise men announced the birth of the Messiah. He was exceedingly disturbed, and the principal Jews with him. No sooner had Herod found out the place of the birth of the Messiah than he resolved to murder him while he was yet an infant. He, therefore, pretended to the wise men to be desirous of worshiping the Messiah, and charged them, when they found the young child, to bring him word where he was, and how he might know him, so as to do him homage.

The wise men passed on from Jerusalem toward Bethlehem, with an intention, in all probability, of returning the same way and giving to the king the information he asked for. They found the young child, and worshiped him; but, being warned by an angel, they returned to their own country another way. Herod was greatly disappointed and provoked by the fact of the wise men not returning to give him word. He at once, in his rage, issued an edict to his soldiers, requiring them to go to Bethelehem and put all the male children to death, from two years old and under, that he might make sure of putting the Messiah to death.

It was this cruel work of Herod that led to the touching language: "In Rama was there a voice heard, lamentation and weeping and great mourning, Rachel weeping for her children and would not be comforted because they are not." But the cruel king was disappointed again, or at least his end was not accomplished, for Mary and Joseph with the young child fled into Egypt.

Herod died a most wretched death. The disease under which he was dying, was exceedingly painful and loathsome. He tried to commit suicide by plunging a dagger into his own body, but was prevented by those that were near him. His last acts were acts of cruelty. In the agonies of his last sickness he had forty young men burned alive for committing an offense. He shut the principal men of the kingdom up in the circus and gave orders to have them executed the moment he should expire. And from his death-bed he ordered his son, who was in prison, executed. He died about seventy years of age, having reigned thirty seven years. He is said to have had eight or ten wives and fifteen children. Archelaus, his son, reigned in Judea in his stead, while Philip and Herod Antipas ruled in other parts of his kingdom. Matt. ii: Luke iii: 1.

HEROD 2.—*The glory of the skin.*

He was Herod Antipas, the son of Herod the Great. His father left him the tetrarchy of Perea and Galilee. In this appointment he was confirmed by Augustus, the Roman emperor. He set himself to work, at once, in fortifying the principal places of his dominions, and adorning his government. He married the daughter of Aretas, king of Arabia, from whom he was afterwards divorced, that he might marry his sister-in-law, Herodias, the wife of Philip; and it is said his divorcing the daughter of Aretas, threw him into a war with the Arabs. For the unlawful marriage of Herod to Herodias, John the Baptist reproved him, on which account Herod imprisoned him, and would have killed him, had he not feared an insurrection of the people.

While John the Baptist was a prisoner, Herod's birthday was celebrated. Sometime during the festivities Salome, the daughter of Herodias, danced before Herod, and pleased him so well, that he promised, with an oath, to give her whatever she would ask. Salome, being instructed by her mother, who was exceedingly bitter in her feelings against John, and desired revenge, asked of Herod the head of John the Baptist, in a charger. Herod, in order to show regard for his word and oath, and the persons in whose hearing he had rashly made her the promise of whatever she would ask, sent one of his guards, who beheaded John in the prison. Soon the head was delivered to her in a charger. Matthew, xiv: Luke, iii: and Mark, vi.

Pontius Pilate sent our Savior to Herod, the king of the Jews. But Herod mocked him, dressed him as a king and then returned him to Pilate. "Herod, with his men of war, set him at nought." Luke, xxiii: 7–11. Herodias grew jealous of Agrippa, deputy king of Judea. and influenced her husband to solicit that dignity of the Roman emperor. When Agrippa heard of his efforts to displace him, he accused him before the emperor of a plot against Tiberius. Agrippa gave, as one evidence of the correctness of his charge, the fact that Herod Antipas had seventy thousand stand of arms. Herod did not attempt to deny it, for he knew it was true, and could be easily proven. He was convicted of having these arms in his arsenal. Caius was banished by him at once, to Lyons, in Gaul. The emperor offered to pardon Herodias, and recall her for the sake of her brother; but she preferred banishment with her husband. Herod Antipas and his accomplice, Herodias, died in exile. Matthew, xiv: and Mark, vi.

HEROD 3.—*The glory of the skin.*

Herod, who was usually styled, Herod Agrippa. [See Agrippa.]

HERODIAS—[He-ro-di′as.] *the wife of Herod.*

Herodias was the wife of Herod, the Tetrarch of Galilee, who procured, through the request of her daughter, the death of John the Baptist. Matt. xiv: 3. "For Herod had laid hold on John, and put him in prison, for Herodias' sake, his brother Philip's wife." John the Baptist reproved Herod for marrying her, for in doing so he had violated law, she having another husband. Herodias was angry at John, and had induced her husband to imprison him, and tried to have him carry his persecution still further. It is likely he would at once, had he not feared the people. But he seemed to have a degree of reverence for John, for when Salome, the daughter of Herodias, danced before Herod, and pleased him so well that he promised, with an oath, to give her whatsoever she would ask, he was troubled. The daughter had been instructed before by her mother, to demand the head of John the Baptist. Herodias was thus the murderer of him, of whom the Savior said, "there was not a greater man born of woman."

We may imagine the feeling of the cruel woman, when her daughter presented the head to her in a charger. She, and Herod too, were visited by judgments for this cruel crime. It is said they were both banished from the land in which they had enjoyed honors, and died at Lyons, in Gaul, in banishment.

HESED—[He′-sed.]

Was the father of one of the officers who were appointed by Solomon to provide victuals for his household. 1st Kings, iv: 10.

HETH—*Trembling, fear.*

Heth was the father of the men with whom Abraham transacted the business of purchasing the field of Machpelah with its cave, or at least he was the father of those from whom the company called "children of Heth," and "sons of Heth," were descended.

Ephron the Hittite was the owner of the field and cave, but as he dwelt among the children of Heth and Abraham, had no special acquaintance with him. He asked the children of Heth to agree with him for a price, and he would pay it. They accordingly did so, and made the field and cave sure unto Abraham for a possession of a burying place, for four hundred shekels of silver, and there Abraham buried Sarah. Gen. xxiii.

HEZEKIAH—[Hez-e-ki′-ah,] *strong in the Lord.*

Hezekiah was the son of Ahaz, a king of Judah, he was twenty-five years old when he succeeded his father in the kingdom and the length of his reign was twenty-nine years. Ahaz left the kingdom in a very bad condition for he had plunged it into idolatry. The circumstances under which Hezekiah began his reign were very unpropitious. He set himself at at once to the work of reforming the kingdom. In the first month, in the first year of his reign, he caused the principal doors of the house of the Lord to be opened and repaired. He ordered the priests and Levites to purify the temple, to sanctify the honor of the Lord God of their fathers, and carry forth the filthiness out of the holy place—repair the the altars and offer sacrifice. 2d Chron. xxix. After this was done he and his princes dedicated the cleansed temple to God, and offered sacrifices. He then ordered the Feast of the Passover to be observed—not at the usual time, for the temple was not clean until the second month. It was observed probably a month after the usual or proper time. He did not confine these exercises in and about the temple to his own people, but he invited those of the kingdom of Israel who were in his kingdom to join them in the celebration. Some of them did, and others ridiculed his devotion and would not join in it. The Feast of the Passover was observed with more solemnity than it had been for many ages, and Hezekiah took a more active part in the ceremonies and devotions than was the custom of the kings. 2d Kings, xviii: xix.

Hezekiah broke down the idolatrous altars and idols throughout his dominions, and also the dominions of Hoshea, who took no offense at the efforts this reformer made to bring even Israel back again to the true worship of the living God. Hezekiah appropriated means for the maintenance of the priests and Levites.

He refused to bear the yoke that the Assyrians had placed upon the neck of his people in the days of his father Ahaz. He would not pay tribute; which brought on him an invasion by Sennacherib, of which invasion a particular account is given in Isa. xxxvi. Sennacherib took most of Hezekiah's fenced cities and environed the city of Jerusalem. After besieging it for awhile, the king begged of Sennacherib terms of peace. The Assyrians demanded three hundred talents of silver and thirty talents of gold—amounting probably to one million seven hundred and fifty-five thousand dollars, and on condition that this amount was paid he proposed to leave the country with his army. Hezekiah set himself about raising this sum, but in order to do it he was compelled to exhaust his own treasuries, and pull off the golden plates with which he had adorned the doors of the temple.

When the Assyrian found that Hezekiah was disqualified for war he violated his obligation to leave the country, and sent three of his principal officers to Hezekiah to demand his surrender of the city. Hezekiah sent three of his men to answer the demand. The conversation was very unsatisfactory and indeed the words of Sennacherib's officers were blasphemous. They were shocked, and returned and reported to their master. Hezekiah realized that he was in great extremity. He sent to the prophet Isaiah, and besought him to intercede with God in their behalf. By the prophet he was assured that the Assyrian army should be quickly ruined. The words of the prophet were fulfilled. Sennacherib was not allowed to come against the city, or so much as shoot an arrow in the direction of it; and we are informed, in 2d Kings, xix: 35, that the angel of the Lord went forth that night and in the camp of Sennacherib slew one hundred and eighty-five thousand of his warriors, and he fled to his own country to report the sad disaster.

About this time Hezekiah fell dangerously ill of an ulcer, it is thought. The sacred historian strongly intimates that the heart of Hezekiah was improperly elevated on account of the deliverance God had wrought out for him and his people, and this was the cause of his sickness "unto death." Isaiah was sent to the king with the solemn message: "Set thy house in order, for thou shalt die and not live." It was a solemn communication, and Hezekiah had recourse to God in earnest prayer and supplication for his recovery. God heard his prayer, and determined to prolong his life. The prophet had scarcely left the threshold of the king's house after delivering his message, until the Lord commanded him to return to Hezekiah and tell him, "Thus saith the Lord, I have heard thy prayer, and I have seen thy tears. I will heal thee."

Hezekiah was informed that he should go up to the house of the Lord in three days from that time, and that he should live fifteen years more. He was ordered to apply a lump of dry figs to the ulcer in order to his recovery, and was informed that the Assyrians should not capture the city. In addition to all this, the Lord gave him a sign of the certainty of the events. "The sun went back ten degrees upon the sun-dial of Ahaz." In accordance with the prediction of the prophet, Hezekiah was able, in three days, to walk to the temple.

After his recovery he composed a hymn of thanksgiving, and an account of his temper of mind in his trouble. He was very much elated by the miracles which had been wrought in his favor, but did not properly thank and praise God, who had so wonderfully blessed him. Isa. xxxviii: 10-11.

When Merodach-baladan, the son of Baladan, the king of Babylon, sent messengers to Hezekiah to congratulate him upon his recovery, elated with the honor thus conferred upon him by the king of a powerful empire, he made a pompous display of his treasures, spices, and rich vessels, to the messengers. He took them all through the palace buildings, and showed them all the treasures of Israel.

In this the pride of Hezekiah was gratified, but the Lord was displeased with him. He sent Isaiah to the king to inform him of his displeasure, and also to tell him that the time was coming when all the treasures of Israel, of which he had vainly boasted as he showed them to the messengers, should belong to the King of Babylon, and that his own offspring should be carried captives and serve as eunuchs in that foreign palace. Isa. xxxix. Hezekiah saw his wrong and confessed it, and acknowledged the divine mercy to him, in promising truth and peace throughout the remainder of his reign. He accordingly passed in tranquility his last years, and was in a good degree prosperous in his kingdom. Manasseh, his son, succeeded him. 2d Chron. xxxii: 32.

HEZIR—[He′-zer.]

Was one of the priests appointed by David when he divided them into twenty-four orders. His lot was the seventeenth. 1st Chron. xxiv: 15.

HEZRAI—[Hez′-ra-i.]

The Carmelite, was one of David's mighty men. 2d Sam. xxiii: 35.

HEZRON—[Hez′ron,] *the dart of joy, division of the song.*

Hezron, and his brother Hamul, were the sons of Pharez, the son of Judah, and are numbered with the grandchildren of Jacob, when his family went down into Egypt to sojourn. It has been thought that Pharez was not more than ten years of age when he went with his father, and grandfather into Egypt. If this be so, we must consider that Hezron and Hamul were born unto Pharez, during the time that Jacob sojourned in Egypt, which was about seventeen years, and it may be that they are mentioned because of the importance of Judah's family in the families of the patriarchs. Pharez was in the line of the Messiah.

HIDDAI—[Hid′da-i,] *praise, cry.*

Hiddai was one of David's mighty men, and is said to have dwelt by the brooks, or in the valley of Gaash. 2d Sam. xxiii: 30.

HIEL—[Hi′-el,] *the life of God.*

Hiel, the Bethelite. He assisted in rebuilding Jericho in the days of Ahab, King of Israel. It is said of him in building the city and its walls: "he laid the foundation thereof in Abiram, his first-born, and set up the gates thereof in his youngest son Segub, according to the word of the Lord, which he spake by Joshua the Son of Nun." 1st Kings xvi: 34. The meaning of which probably is, his first-born son died when he began the work, and his youngest son died before or about the time he finished it.

HILKIAH, 1—[Hil-ki′-ah,] *God is my portion, the Lord's gentleness.*

Was of the tribe of Levi, and in the line of the priests from Aaron to the captivity. 1st Chron. vi: 13.

HELKIAH, 2—*God is my portion, the Lord's gentleness.*

Was the son of Hosah, and one of the sacred porters. 1st Chronicles, xxvi: 11.

HILLEL—[Hil′-le′,] *praising*, *folly*, *Lucifer*.

Is called a Pirathonite. He was the father of Abdon, one of the judges of Israel. Judges, xii: 13.

HIRAH—[Hi′-rah.]

HIRAH was a Canaanite, of the city of Adullam, who became intimate with Judah, the son of Jacob. He probably had some influence over Judah in the matter of his marriage to Shuah, the Caananitish woman. When a death occurred in the family of Judah, in the daughter of Shuah, his wife, he mourned as was the custom of the times; and at the end of his mourning was comforted, and in company with Hirah, the Adullamite, he went up unto his sheep-shearers. This person is called Judah's friend, and he was sent by Judah to Tamar, his daughter-in-law, to redeem the pledge he had left with her—"his signet, and bracelets, and staff." Gen. xxxviii.

HIRAM, 1—[Hi′-ram,] *exaltation of life*, *their whiteness*, *he that destroys*.

HIRAM was a king of Tyre, became a friend of David immediately after his accession to the throne of Israel. He sent messengers to congratulate him, and also sent him cedar trees, and carpenters and masons—experienced workmen—to build David a house. 2d Sam. v: 11. He probably continued the friend of David all through his reign, and is the same person who congratulated Solomon as the successor of David, and became more intimate with him than he had been with his father. Hiram furnished Solomon with timber, stone and workmen, for the temple and Solomon's house, the house of the forests at Lebanon, and the house for Pharoah's daughter, his wife. He lent Solomon one hundred and twenty talents of gold, and he assisted him in establishing a trade with the people of Ophir.

We judge from the account given in 1st Kings, v and ix, that Hiram engaged with Solomon to render him all the assistance needed, if in his power, and he was glad of an opportunity of associating himself in so good a work with so good and great a man as king Solomon. Hiram was made acquainted with the draft prepared by the Almighty architect for the temple, and entered joyfully upon the work of preparing the materials for the magnificent structure. He received from Solomon every year, twenty thousand measures of wheat for food for his household, and twenty measures of pure oil. They were engaged seven and-a-half years in building the temple, and twelve and-a-half in erecting Solomon's own house. And Solomon gave Hiram in return for his cedar trees, and fir trees, and gold, and for the attention and assistance he had given in person, and the labor and skill of his servants, twenty cities in the land of Galilee. Whether these were heathen cities which Solomon had conquered and had a right to give away, or whether they were cities of Israel that were given to Hiram until such time as the revenue from them would repay the king of Tyre, we know not. But we learn that Hiram was not pleased, for some cause, to take them and restore them to Solomon, and he satisfied Hiram in some other way, probably by a direct tax, which was burdensome for years to the people. And this tax may be the thing that the elders of Israel complained of to Rehoboam, Solomon's successor. 1st Kings, xii: 3-4. "Thy father made our yoke grievious; now, therefore, make thou the grievious service of thy father, and his heavy yoke which he put upon us lighter, and we will serve thee." It is quite certain that an intimacy existed between these two kings, and was kept up for many years, if not as long as both lived.

HIRAM, 2.—*Exaltation of life*, *their whiteness*, *he that destroys*.

HIRAM was an artificer who lived in Tyre. His father before him had lived there, and was a worker in brass, gold, silver, iron, stones and timber. He was a worker in blue, purple, and fine linen, and an engraver. 2d Chronicles, ii: 14. Hiram's father was dead, but he was engaged in the same occupation, and with his skill and labor, was supporting a widowed mother. This Hiram was an Israelite. It is thought his father was of the tribe of Naphtali, and his mother a descendant of the tribe of Dan. In 1st Kings, vii: 14, he is said to be of the tribe of Naphtali, and in 2d Chronicles, ii: 14, his mother is said to be of the tribe of Dan.

Solomon sent and brought this artificer out of Tyre and associated him with himself, in the building and adorning of their temple. He was exceedingly skillful in designing and executing the most curious and magnificent workmanship, especially in the metals that were used to construct the pillars with their ornaments, the sea-lavers, shovels, basins, and other utensils of the temple. From the description given of the two pillars which Hiram made and set up in the porch, one of which he named Jachin, and the other Boaz, we must conclude they were an exhibit of wonderful skill in workmanship. See 1st Kings, vii: 15–22.

Nor less skillful was the work presented in the molten sea, which he made to contain two thousand baths and placed upon twelve oxen—verses, 23–26. And he made ten bases, four cubits long, four cubits wide and three cubits high, and ornamented them beautifully. He also made ten lavers to contain forty baths, that were set upon the ten bases he had made and adorned. These, with other things, he cast in his foundry, established in the plains of Jordan between Succoth and Zarthan, and brought to the temple and placed in their order and position, and used in accordance with the design of the Great Architect.

HOBAB—[Ho′-bab.] *favored and beloved.*

Hobab was the son of Ruel, the brother of Zipporah, and hence, the brother-in-law of Moses. It is supposed that Reuel or Raguel was dead at the time that the Lord appeared to Moses in the burning bush, and commissioned him to emancipate his downtrodden countrymen; and that Jethro, the son of Reuel, had succeeded his father in the office of prince and priest of Midian. As Moses had served Reuel in his lifetime, so now he was serving Jethro the son, as a shepherd. It is said, "Now Moses kept the flock of Jethro, his father-in-law, the priest of Midian." It is thought the translation should have been "brother-in-law." If this be true, then Jethro is the same person as Hobab mentioned in Num. x: 29. He visited Moses as he, with the children of Israel, was about to leave Mt. Sinai, after having been encamped there over eleven months. Moses addresses himself to Hobab, saying, "Come thou with us, and we will do thee good, for the Lord hath spoken good concerning Israel." It seems that Hobab had brought Zipporah and the two sons of Moses with him to visit her husband and father and the camp of Israel. This visit is narrated at length in Ex. xviii. How long Hobab stayed with Moses we know not, but his visit was continued for some time. He witnessed the working of the administration and government of Israel, and gave Moses advice so that his labors might be made lighter. Moses followed this advice, and chose heads of the people, rulers of thousands, rulers of hundreds, rulers of fifties and rulers of tens. This influence that the Midianite prince and priest had over Moses, was complained of by Aaron and Miriam, who were afterwards reproved, and Miriam was severely punished, by being made leprous for seven days.

Hobab did not accept the invitation of Moses to go with him and with Israel, but "he went his way into his own land." Ex. xviii: 27. It is said, in Num. x: 30, Hobab "said unto him, I will not go, but I will depart unto mine own land, and to my kindred." And yet it is thought he did afterwards return from Midian, and identified himself with the children of Israel; for it is said in Judges, i: 16, that the Kenites, the descendants of Moses' father-in-law, dwelt in the City of Palm Trees and united themselves with the tribe of Judah in an attack upon Arad. And in Judges, iv: 11, Heber, the Kenite, whose wife slew Sisera, the general of Jabin's army, was of the children of Hobab. And the remarkable people called Rechabites, of whom we have such an interesting account in Jer. xxxv, are said to be children of Hemath the Kenite or the head of the Kenites. 1st Chron. ii: 55.

HODESH.

Hodesh was the wife of Shaharaim, who with Hushim, another of his wives, was the mother of a numerous progeny. 1st Chron. viii: 9.

HODIAH—[Hod-i′-ah.]

HODIAH is represented as the sister of Naham and the daughter of Mered and Bithiah. This name occurs with the account of the relationship in the genealogy of Judah. 1st Chron. iv: 19.

HOGLAH—[Hog′-lah,] *his festival, his dance.*

HOGLAH, was one of the daughters of Zelophehad, who was a man of Manassah, and "died for his own sins, and had no sons." Num. xxvii: 3. There were five daughters who came to Moses and Eleazar, the priest, with a plea that demanded an additional law in their civil code: "Give unto us therefore, a possession among the brethren of our father." Their reason for making the demand is given thus: "Our father died in the wilderness and he was not in the company of them that gathered themselves together against the Lord, in the company of Korah; but died in his own sins, and had no sons. Why should the name of our father be done away from among his family, because he hath no son?" The case was a new one to Moses, and he brought it before the Lord. The Lord gave him to understand that their request was a reasonable one, and that their demand must be met. "Thou shalt surely give them a possession of an inheritance among their father's brethren, and thou shalt cause the inheritance of their fathers to pass unto them."

Moses accordingly determined that their request should be granted. And then he determines that heiresses shall marry in their own tribe, that no part of the ancient inheritance be alienated from the family. The daughters of Zelophehad are commanded to marry, making choice of companions in their own tribe. Num. xxxvi: 6.

This law was simply to affect the heiress. "Every daughter that possesseth an inheritance in any tribe of the children of Israel, shall be wife unto one of the family of the tribe of her father, that the children of Israel may enjoy, every man, the inheritance of his fathers." Num. xxxvi: 8. We are further informed regarding these daughters of Zelophehad, that they were married unto their father's brother's sons, into the families of the sons of Manasseh, where their inheritance was given them, and where it remained, that being the tribe of the family of their father.

HOHAM—[Ho′-ham.]

HOHAM was the king of Hebron. When Adonizedek, king of Jerusalem, found that the inhabitants of Gideon had made peace with the Hebrews, he sent unto Hoham, and unto Piram, king of Jarmuth, and unto Japhia, king of Lachish, and unto Debir, king of Eglon, asking them to come up and help him to smite Gibeon. They accordingly did so; but the men of Gibeon procured Joshua's help, and the Amorite kings were smitten, and their armies, with great slaughter. Josh. x: 1-10.

HOPHNI—[Hof′-ni,] *he that covers, my fist.*

HOPHNI was one of the sons of Eli, the priest, of whom we have an account in 1st Samuel, i: 2, 3. He and his brother Phineas were priests of the Lord, with Eli, their father, at Shiloh. Hophni and his brother were perverse and wicked men. They are said to be sons of Belial; that is, they were profligate men—children of the devil. They were ungodly themselves and because of the influence they exerted as priests, were the cause of much ungodliness among the people. We are almost shocked at their conduct as set forth in 1st Sam. ii: 13, 17, and 22. It appears that the people were satisfied that they were destitute of piety, nay more, that they were constantly committing sacrilege, showing that they had no regard for God, or his service. They even committed, under the most aggravating circumstances, the sin of adultery with the women who were employed about the tabernacle, or who came there with their sacrifices.

Eli, their father, complained of their conduct, and charged their sin upon them; but he reproved them so mildly, that we can hardly suppose such hard-hearted and villainous men were troubled in their consciences by that reproof. It was not long after Eli talked thus to Hophni and Phineas, until a prophet of the Lord, whose name is not given, came to the aged priest, and told him of the end of the priesthood in the family to which he belonged, and that because of the wickedness of his sons, it should go back again into the family of Eleazar, the eldest son of Aaron. The prophet told him that an enemy should invade the country, and that his two sons should be slain in one day.

Shortly after this, the Lord directed the child Samuel to reiterate these things in the ears of Eli. Soon the Philistines invaded the country, and Israel made war with them, and the ark of God was taken along with the army, probably in charge of Hophni and Phineas. The battle grew hot, and of Israel were smitten by their enemies, thirty thousand footmen, and while these two corrupt priests were guarding or defending the ark, it was taken, and they were slain. Thus was the prophecy fulfilled, "thy two sons, Hophni and Phineas, shall be slain both in one day."

HORI, 1—[Ho′-ri.]

Hori was the son of Lotan, and the grandson of Seir, the Horite. Gen. xxxvi: 22.

HORI, 2.

Was of the tribe of Simeon, and the father of Shaphat, who was the spy selected by Moses from that tribe. Num. xiii: 5.

HOSAH—[Ho′sah.]

Was one of the sacred porters, and was associated with Shuppim, another sacred porter, in keeping the westward gate. 1st Chron. xxvi: 16.

HOSEA—[Ho-ze′-ah,] *savior*.

Hosea was the son of Beeri. He was the first of the lesser prophets, and he prophesied in the days of Uzziah, Jotham, Ahaz, and Hezekiah, kings of Judah, and in the days of Jeroboam, the son of Joash, king of Israel. His father is said to have been of the town of Belemoth, in the tribe of Issachar; but he was probably of the tribe of Reuben, and is the person called, in 1st Chron. v: 6, Beerah, who was a prince of that tribe, and was carried by Tilgath-Pilneser, with others of Israel, into captivity.

The prophet lived in the kingdom of Samaria, and prophesied there; but he delivered some prophecies regarding the kingdom of Judah. He prophesied about sixty years, and was one of the oldest prophets whose writings are left for our perusal. From the first chapter in the book we learn that the Lord commissioned him to show Israel their exceeding sinfulness, and the hatefulness of their sins in His sight; and his marriage, under the divine direction, to a woman of ill fame, was intended to set forth their wickedness and folly. He married Gomer, the daughter of Diblaim, and she bare two sons, Jezreel and Loammi, and one daughter, Loruhamah.

It is thought that Hosea witnessed the captivity, already referred to, brought about by Tilgath Pilneser, and endured with his father some inconveniences from it; and that he also witnessed the destruction that was brought upon Samaria, by Shalmaneser.

The principal prophecies in the book of Hosea, are the captivity of Israel, and their return at the end of their captivity. [See viii and x.] He also declares, regarding the people of Judah, that though they should remain for some time after the captivity of Israel in their country, yet they also should be carried captives beyond the river Euphrates, but should be brought back after a certain number of years. [See i: 10 and 11.]

The prophecies of Hosea are more obscure than the writings of succeeding prophets, yet it must be said there is much to admire in the force and energy of the prophet, and the boldness with which he denounces sin. The figures and similitudes he uses are very striking.

HOSHEA, 1—[Ho-she′a,] *savior*.

Hoshea, the son of Azaziah, was the ruler in the tribe of Ephraim, in the time of David. 1st Chronicles xxvii: 20.

HOSHEA, 2—*Savior*.

Hoshea, the son of Elah, murdered Pekah, the son of Remaliah, a king of Israel, and after a struggle of several years civil war, he succeeded in settling himself on the throne of Israel, which was his intention when he committed the murder. 2d Kings, xv: 30; and xvii: 1.

Hoshea was less wicked than many of his predecessors, though he himself did evil in the sight of the Lord. It could hardly be expected that one coming to the throne as he did, and meeting with the opposition from the elders of Israel, that he met with, would be virtuous and good.

He allowed such of his subjects as desired it, to go to Jerusalem and worship the Lord. His predecessors had forbidden that, and had the road leading to Jerusalem guarded to prevent it.

He entered into a conspiracy with So, the king of Egypt, to throw off the yoke of Assyria, to which his kingdom had been subject for many years. Shalmenezer being informed of Hoshea's intention to revolt, and of the plans and measures he had concerted with the king of Egypt, marched against him with an Assyrian army and besieged Samaria, the capital of his kingdom. The war continued three or four years, and he took the fenced cities and reduced the city to ruins, captured Hoshea, the king, and killed him. In the most barbarous and cruel manner, Shalmanezer killed the women and children, and removed the Israelites to countries beyond the Euphrates, and thus ended the kingdom of the ten tribes.

HOTHIR—[Ho′-thir.]

HOTHIR was one of the sons of Heman, and when the lots were cast, and the singers were divided into twenty-four courses, the one-and-twentieth lot came to him. 1st Chronicles, xxv: 28.

HUL, OR CHUL—*infirmity, bringing forth children.*

HUL, or CHUL, was the son of Aram, and the grandson of Shem. He is referred to in Genesis, x: 23, and it is supposed that his descendants peopled a part of Armenia. Some of his descendants, it is thought, resided in the desert of Syria, near to Tadmor, where once stood a city called Cholle, named, possibly, after Hul, or Chul.

HULDAH—[Hul′-dah,] *the world, a prophetess.*

HULDAH was a prophetess and the wife of Shallum. She was applied to under the direction of God, who had given her the spirit of prophecy, to give instruction upon the copy of the law and the testimony that had been found by Hilkiah, the high priest. The book had been handed by Hilkiah to Shaphan the scribe, and he presented it to the king. Josiah was astonished at the contents of the book, as it was read to him by the scribe. He commanded Hilkiah the high priest with others to enquire of the Lord concerning the words "of this book that is found," and they did so. 2d Kings, xxii: 14. "So Hilkiah the priest, and Ahikam and Shaphan and Asahiah went unto Huldah the prophetess." She received them, and under the spirit of inspiration she gave the meaning of the contents of the book in the following language: "Thus saith the Lord God of Israel, tell the men that sent you to me: Thus saith the Lord God: Behold I will bring evil upon this place, and upon the inhabitants thereof, even all the words of the book which the king of Judah hath read." She then goes on to give the reason why God will do this: They had gone into idolatry, and their God was angry with them. She then instructed them to say unto the king, that though desolation and a curse was before the people, yet that desolation and curse should not come on them in his day, because he had humbled himself before the Lord, had rent his clothes and wept. He should therefore close his days in peace and not see the evil that should be brought upon the people and Jerusalem.

What this book was that gave the king so much trouble, and that Huldah was inspired to interpret, we cannot certainly tell, but it is quite likely it was a manuscript copy of the words by Moses, which had been deposited in the tabernacle. The reason why we may conclude it was prepared by Moses, is found in the parallel passage. 2d Chron. xxxiv: 14. "Hilkiah, the priest, found a book of the law of the Lord given by Moses." Some supposed it was the renewing of the covenant in the plains of Moab, recorded in the the book of Deuteronomy, which contains the most terrible invectives against the corrupting of the words and worship of God.

It seems quite strange that Huldah, a prophetess, should be applied to for light in this matter when the prophet Jeremiah was then living in

Israel, and was dwelling in all probability at that time at Anathoth and could have been consulted readily. Zephaniah was also prophesying during the reign of this king, but he was not applied to in this case. A woman was the honored instrument in the hands of God, of giving the needed information. And further, it is a woman of whom we know nothing, save what we learn in this circumstance.

An eminent author, Dr. Priestly says: "It pleased God to distinguish several women with the spirit of prophecy as well as other great attainments, to show that in his sight, and especially in things of a spiritual nature, there is no essential pre-eminence in the male sex."

HUPHAM—[Hu′-fam.]

HUPHAM was of the tribe of Benjamin and the head of the family in that tribe, called the Huphamites. Numbers, xxvi: 39. He is probably the same as Huppim one of the sons of Benjamin, who is numbered with Jacob's family in Egypt. Gen. xlvi: 21.

HUPPAH.

HUPPAH was one of the priests appointed by David when he divided them into twenty-four orders. His lot was the thirteenth. 1st Chron. xxiv: 13.

HUR, 1—*Liberty, whiteness, cavern.*

HUR was the son of Caleb and the grandson of Hezron. He was the son of Caleb by his wife Ephrath. 1st Chron. ii: 19. He is thought by some to have been the husband of Miriam, and if she was ever married, possibly he was. He was the father of Uri, and the grandfather of the famous workman, Bezaleel. Hur was intimately associated with Aaron, and when Israel entered into an engagement at Rephadim with the Amalekites, Hur was engaged with Aaron on the mountain side, holding up the hands of Moses. So important was their work here that faithfulness on their part seemed under God to be the pivot on which the interest of the nation turned. If they held up Moses' hands Israel prevailed, but if they let his hand fall Amalek prevailed. Ex. xvii. And when Moses went up to Mt. Sinai to talk with God, and receive the decalogue, not knowing how long he would be gone, he appointed Aaron and Hur to act in his place in governing the people and settling disputed questions among them until his return. Ex. xxiv: 14.

HUR, 2—*Liberty, whiteness, cavern.*

HUR was the father of one of the officers who were appointed by King Solomon to provide victuals for his household. 1st Kings, iv: 8.

HURAI—[Hu′-ra.]

One of David's body guard. 1st Chron. xi: 32.

HURAM, 1.

HURAM was a Benjamite, the first-born son of Bela. 1st Chron. viii: 5.

HURAM, 2.

Is the same as Hiram, King of Tyre, and so Hiram the artificer is called Huram. See 1st Chron. xiv: 1; 2d Chron. ii: 11, 13.

HURI.

HURI was a Gadite, and the father of Abihail. 1st Chron. v: 14.

HUSHAI—[Hu′-sha,] *their haste, sensuality or silence.*

HUSHAI, the Archite, was a trusty friend and counsellor of king David, who rendered him important service during the rebellion of Absalom. When Absalom conspired against his father, he gained Ahithophel over to his cause, and when David learned fully of the conspiracy, and of Ahithophel, his counsellor, deserting him and joining in the rebellion, he, with his life-guard and friends, fled from the city to go to the wilderness. As he was going up the mountain, probably Mount Olivet, engaged in earnest prayer that the counsel of Ahithophel might be turned into foolishness, Hushai, the Archite, met him, and was deeply affected by the calamity which had befallen David, "he rent his coat and put earth upon his head," and he expressed a desire to identify himself with David and his interests—probably he expressed a wish to become a warrior. As he was not skilled in war, David made an objection to his going with him, but appointed him, as he was a wise and discreet man, to the important work of detecting the enemy's plans so that they might be thwarted. He accordingly entered into a strict confederacy with Zadok and Abiathar, the priests, and engaged their sons to act as couriers between Jerusalem and David's camp.

Hushai went into Jerusalem, and meeting Absalom who had just entered the city, he proposed to serve him as he had served David, his father. Absalom seemed to be somewhat suspicious at first, but his fears were all relieved, we judge, by the words of Hushai to him, and he secured the full confidence of Absalom. For after Ahithophel had counseled Absalom, with twelve thousand men, to follow his father, Absalom would not, until he had counseled Hushai, and his counsel was against the counsel of the former. It was so plausible, and there seemed to be so much wisdom in it, that Absalom forsook the counsel of Ahithophel, and followed that of Hushai. As soon as he found that Absalom would follow his counsel, probably, he informed the priests who were confederated with him, how he had counseled, and also how Ahithophel had counseled. He bade them send David word at once by Jonathan and Ahimaaz, who had secreted themselves at Enrogel. They accordingly did so, and these two sons of the priests succeeded in bearing the intelligence to David, who followed their instruction, and that night crossed the Jordan, and encamped at Mahanaim. The counsel of Hushai thus given and followed by Absalom, gave David more time for flight, and preparations for defense, and so was the means of saving his life. 2d Sam. xv and xvi.

It is thought that Baanah, who was a deputy governor of king Solomon, was the son of this Hushai, as Hushai was the name of Baanah's father. 1st Kings, iv: 16.

HUSHAM—[Hush′-am.]

Reigned as a King of Edom, and the successor of Jobab. Gen. xxxvi: 34. He is said to be of the land of Temani. At his death he was succeeded in the kingdom by Hadad, the son of Bedad, who smote Midian in the field of Moab.

HUSHIM, 1—[Hu′-shim.]

Was the son of Dan, and the grandson of Jacob, and is reckoned with the children and grandchildren of Jacob in Gen. xlvi: 23. He was the only son of Dan. All the other sons, of the patriarch had more children in Egypt than he had.

HUSHIM, 2.

Was one of the wives of Shaharaim, who was sent off, or put away, but afterwards re-married. She was the mother of Ahitub and Elpaal. 1st Chron. viii: 8.

HUZ.

Was the son of Nahor and Milcah. He was the eldest and is mentioned in connection with Buz, Kemuel, Chesed, Hazo, Pildash, Jidlaph and Bethuel, who were all sons of Nahor by Milcah. Gen. xxii: 21, 22.

HUZZAB—[Huz′-zab,] *molten.*

Who is referred to in Nah. ii: 7, is supposed to have been the queen to the king of Nineveh. The city was to be destroyed and her king taken, and Huzzab, with her maidens, was to be led away captive.

HYMENEUS—[Hy-men-e′-us,] *nuptial, marriage.*

HYMENEUS was once a christian. He was probably a native of Ephesus, and converted to christianity through the labors of Paul. He had faith and a good conscience for a while, but made shipwreck thereof, and indulged, we may judge, in grievous sins and gross errors. Paul refers to him in his epistles to Timothy, and to his backsliding and to his being excommunicated from the church. 1st Timothy, i: 20. We have an account of this same person in connection with Philetus. 2d Tim. ii: 17, where he is represented as teaching new and dangerous doctrine. Their words are said, "to eat as doth a canker," they were denying the doctrine of the resurrection from the dead, and overthrowing the faith of some.

IBHAR—[Ib′-har,] *election, he that is chosen.*

IBHAR is mentioned in 2d Samuel, v: 15, as also 1st Chronicles, iii: 6, as one of David's sons, born unto him in Jerusalem.

IBRI.

IBRI was one of the ministers in the temple under the order of service instituted in the time of David. 1st Chron. xxiv: 27.

IBZAN.

IBZAN was of the tribe of Judah, and of the city of Bethlehem, a judge of Israel. He was the successor of Jeptha, and served his people in the capacity of judge seven years. He had sixty children, thirty of them were sons, and thirty daughters, all of whom he lived to see married. We have nothing further regarding him recorded, save that he died, and was buried in his own city, Bethlehem. Judges xii: 8–10.

ICHABOD—[Ik′-a-bod,] *where is the glory?*

ICHABOD was the son of Phineas, the son of Eli. He and his brother were very wicked and desecrated the priest's office in the most abominable manner, on account of which, the priestly office in the family of Ithamar, ended, and was transferred back again to the family of Aaron's eldest son, Eleazar.

Ichabod was not born until after his father fell in battle, and as his mother gave birth to him under the distressing intelligence that her husband and father-in-law were dead, and that the ark of God was taken, she named him Ichabod, which signifies, "where is the glory? or there is no glory; or the glory is departed from Israel." 1st Samuel, iv: 19–22.

IDDO, 1—[Id′-do,] *his hand, power, praise, witness.*

IDDO, the son of Zechariah, was the ruler in the half tribe of Mannasseh, in the time of David. 1st Chronicles, xxvii: 21.

IDDO, 2—*His hand, power, praise, witness.*

IDDO was a prophet of the kingdom of Judah, who prophesied in the times of Rehoboam and Abijah. He is said to have written the acts of Rehoboam in 2d Chron. xii: 15; the acts and ways and sayings of Abijah, in 2d Chron, xiii: 22. We have nothing particular marked out in the life of this prophet, and the supposition that he prophesied against Jeroboam may be correct. Josephus with other historians are of opinion that he was the prophet that was sent to Jeroboam while he was at Bethel dedicating an altar to the golden calves he had made, and who spoke in warning against the altar in Bethel, and against all the high places and houses of the high places in the city of Samaria. If this be the same person, then he was killed by a lion and buried under the direction of the old prophet of Bethel, and a place reserved in the sepulcher for his own form after death, beside him. See 1st Kings, xiii.

IGAL—[I′-gal.]

IGAL belonged to the tribe of Issachar, and was selected by Moses as one of the twelve spies to search out and examine the nature and state of the land of Canaan. Num. xiii: 7.

IGDALIAH—[Ig-da-li′-ah,] *the greatness of the Lord.*

IGDALIAH was a prophet or holy man, called "the man of God." Jer. xxxv: 4. He is only named the once, and is said to be the father of Hanan.

IGEAL—[Ig-e′-al.]

IGEAL was a son of Shemaiah, and a descendant of the royal line of Judah. 1st Chron. iii: 22.

IKKESH.

IKKESH was the father of Ira the Tekoite. 2d Sam. xxiii: 26.

ILAI—[I′-la.]

ILAI was a warrior of David, and one of his body guard. 1st Chron. xi: 29.

IMLAH—[Im′-lah,] *plentitude, repletion, circumcision.*

IMLAH was the father or progenitor of Micaiah the prophet. 1st Kings, xxii: 8.

IMMANUEL—[Im-man′-u-el,] *a name given to our Lord Jesus Christ, signifying God is with us.*

IMMANUEL a name given by the prophet Isaiah to him who shall be born of a virgin. Isa. vii: 14. And it is applied by Matthew to the Messiah. Matt. i: 23.

IMMER.

IMMER was one of the priests appointed by David when he divided them into twenty-four orders. His lot was the sixteenth. 1st Chronicles, xxiv: 14.

IMNA.

He was a descendant of Asher, and was the son of Helam, of that tribe. 1st Chron. vii: 35.

IMNAH, 1.

He was the first-born son of Asher. 1st Chron. vii: 30.

IMNAH, 2.

He was a Levite, who assisted in the reform of king Hezekiah. 2d Chron. xxxi: 14.

IMRAH—*A rebel, changing.*

He was a descendant of Asher, of the family of Zophah. 1st Chron. vii: 36.

IMRI, 1.

He was a man of Judah, belonging to the extensive family of Pharez. 1st Chron. ix: 4.

IMRI, 2.

He was the father or progenitor of Zaccur. Neh. iii: 2.

IPHEDEIAH—[If-e-di′-ah,] *the redemption of the Lord.*

A descendant of Benjamin, and a man of great importance among them. See 1st Chron. viii: 25.

IRA, 1—[I′-rah,] *city, watch, spoil, heap of vision.*

He was an Ithrite, one of David's mighty men. 2d Sam. xxiii: 38.

IRA, 2—*City, watch, spoil, heap of vision.*

The son of Ikkesh, the Tekoite, was the captain for the sixth month, when David instituted the monthly service of captains over twenty-four thousand men. 1st Chron. xxvii: 9.

IRAD—*Wild ass, heap of descents, of empire.*

He was the son of Enoch, and the grandson of Cain, and the father of Mehujael. Gen. iv: 18.

IRAM—[I′-ram.]

IRAM was of the family of Esau, and one of the dukes of Edom. He is mentioned in connection with ten others in Gen. xxxvi: 40-43. They were persons, it is supposed, that were chiefs in their respective families, and were governors over the districts of country settled by their families.

ISAAC—[I′zak,] *laughter.*

ISAAC was the child of promise, born unto Abraham and Sarah in their old age. His birth was promised by an angel of the Lord. Gen. xviii: 10-12.

He was educated in the religion of his father—his training was of the purest kind. God said of Abraham, "I know him that he will command his children and his household after him." Sarah, the wife of the patriarch, and the mother of Isaac, was strongly bound to him—she loved him with true maternal affection; and no wonder, for he was her only son, and given to her when she was very far advanced in life. At an early period of life, Isaac was the object of the contempt of Ishmael, the son of Hagar, the bondwoman. When Sarah saw Ishmael mocking or making himself merry by ridiculing Isaac, she said to her husband, "cast out this bondwoman and her son, for the son of this bondwoman shall not be heir with my son, even with Isaac. Gen. xxi: 10; Gal. iv: 30. The desire on the part of Sarah thus expressed, was that Hagar might be divorced—that some legal act might be performed by which Ishmael might be excluded from all claim on the inheritance, and Isaac be the sole heir. This requisition was painful to Abraham, for Ishmael, for seventeen years, had been the object of his paternal love, and he had trained him up to the service of that God who had promised that his seed should be innumerable. God allayed the fears and anxieties of Abraham in this matter by answering him that, "in Isaac, his seed should be called."

When Isaac grew up, and had arrived at a state of maturity or manhood, he was called upon to give a striking proof of his entire devotion to God. Abraham was commanded to offer up his beloved son in sacrifice. Gen. xxii: 1. Abraham's faith was tested, and proved genuine, for he drew back the knife and would have slain Isaac, had he not been stopped.

But turning from the father and his act to the son, we see something to admire. There is an expression of faith and dutiful obedience, hardly equalled, not to say surpassed, by any act on record, save the actual sacrifice of the Lord Jesus Christ, "who was led as a lamb to the slaughter, and as a sheep before her shearers, is dumb, so he opened not his mouth." He submitted without any resistance, to be bound by his honored parent, and laid upon the altar with his body exposed to the glistening knife raised to destroy him.

He was about forty years of age when Sarah, his mother, died, and he sorrowed greatly on the occasion of her death. He no doubt attended with his father, the burial of Sarah in the cave of Machpelah.

Shortly after the death of Sarah, Abraham sent Eliezer to the land of Mesopotamia to procure from among his kindred, a wife for Isaac. Guided by the hand of Providence, the servant of Abraham went to Nahor, and in the family of Bethuel, who was Abraham's nephew, procured his son a wife in the person of the beautiful Rebekah.

Eliezer immediately returned home with the maiden of Nahor under his charge, and as he came near his masters tent Isaac was walking in the fields engaged as was his custom, in meditation. And as he lifted up his eyes, he saw the camels coming. Eliezer and his company were returning from Abraham's former country. About the time that Isaac saw the train, and his eyes lighted upon Rebekah, she also saw Isaac and asked who he was; she was informed that it was her future husband, when she at once lighted off the camel on which she rode, and quickly veiled herself as a sign of chastity, modesty and subjection. Isaac at once took charge of her and brought her into the tent that had formerly been occupied by Sarah his mother. And Isaac took Rebekah to be his wife and loved her.

It was not long after this until Abraham died and Isaac is seen performing the last tribute of respect due the honored dead from the living. Abraham died and "was gathered to his people," and Isaac and Ishmael united in carrying his mortal remains to the cave and placed it beside those of Sarah, so that whatever jealousies and contentions existed before between those two sons of Abraham, they had now ceased. Gen. xxv: 21. God renewed the promise unto Isaac that had before been made unto Abraham, to make his seed very numerous. Soon two sons were born unto Isaac concerning whom the divine purpose regarding the posterity was made known unto the parents, "the elder shall serve the younger." Jacob and Esau became the heads of mighty nations the Israelites and Edomites.

A second famine visited the land of Canaan and Isaac went with his family to dwell in Gerar, and while he dwelt there as his father had done before him, he denied his wife saying, "She is my sister." In the case of Abraham it was literally true, but it was not true in the case of Isaac, for the relation that Rebekah sustained to him previous to their marriage, was that of cousin, while Sarah was the daughter of the same father with Abraham, though not of the same mother. It is quite likely that Isaac considered himself in some sort justifiable for these words spoken with an intention to deceive, since he supposed his life would be periled by his claiming the relation he really sustained to the beautiful Rebekah.

When Isaac became old, and his sight failed, so that he could not distinguish one of his sons from the other, for he was then one hundred and thirty-seven years of age, he desired to receive savory meat at the hands of his eldest son, and pronounce the blessings of primogeniture. But Jacob deceived him and craftily obtained Esau's blessing, and although this supplanting on the part of Jacob proved the occasion of a break between the brothers, and brought about a separation which continued for many years, yet the brothers were afterwards reconciled, and they united in comforting their father in his last days, and when he died, they joined in filial affection to peform the last sad office for their amiable, and truly pious father. Gen. xxvii and xxv. Though Isaac may not have been in many respects as remarkable a man as was Abraham his father, or Jacob his son, yet he was as virtuous and pious-minded as either of them, and as free from faults.

ISAIAH, OR ESAIAS—[I-za′-yah.] *the salvation of the Lord.*

ISAIAH was the son of Amoz. He prophesied in the days of Uzziah, Jotham, Ahaz, and Hezekiah, kings of Judah. Isaiah, i: 1. It has been supposed that he was of royal blood, being nearly related to Uzziah, in whose reign he began the prophetic work.

The first five chapters of Isaiah, are supposed to have been written in Uzziah's life-time, and the sixth shortly after his death. That chapter contains an important vision of the Redeemer and his kingdom, given to the prophet in the year of Uzziah's death. The Redeemer is represented as attended and praised by seraphs, angels and ministers. Isaiah is humbled by the glorious vision and bewails his own unworthiness and loathsomeness. In the midst of his self-abasement, a seraph flew towards him, having a live coal, which he had taken with the tongs, from off the altar, and laid it on his mouth, thereby symbolizing the preparation to preach and to teach. Realizing the qualification he had received, he at once offered himself for the work. "Here am I, send me." In his labors as a prophet, he faithfully declared the divine will unto those to whom he ministered.

He had two sons, the name of the first was Shear-Jashub, and the name of the second was Maher-shalal-hashbaz. When God sent him to meet Ahaz, he bade him take the first named son with him, and tell him, among other things, that Syria, and the ten tribes should be without a king, and assured him that the circumstances that should produce the event, should take place in a short time, even before the child should come to years of discretion. He also assured the Jews that before his second son, Maher-shalal-hashbaz, should learn to talk, or be able to cry, "my father, or my mother," the kingdoms of Syria and Samaria should be utterly ruined by the Assyrians, and that the kingdom of Judah itself, should also be brought to the very brink of ruin. See Isaiah, vii and viii.

When king Hezekiah was sick, Isaiah was moved by his request to pray for him, to petition the God of the Jews in his behalf. He afterward comforted the king. But when the messengers of Baladen were received by the king, and honored by being shown the treasures of Israel, and the magnificence of Hezkiah's palaces, Isaiah went to the king and reproved him; he also prophesied regarding the future kingdom and family of Hezekiah. See chapters, xxxviii: xxxix.

The prophet is represented as going barefoot and almost naked, for nearly three years, to prefigure the distressed condition of two countries under the Assyrian yoke, *viz:* Egypt and Ethiopia. Isaiah, xx. He is supposed to have prophesied forty-five, and some think sixty years, and probably was put to death.

Isaiah was uniformly spoken of in the scriptures as a prophet of great honor and dignity. He is called by some writers, the prince of all the prophets. He has also been denominated the evangelical prophet, because of the number and variety of his prophecies regarding the person, character, ministry, teaching and miracles, with the sufferings and death of Messiah; and also, because of his prophecies regarding the kingdom of Christ. He has been said to be the most eloquent of all the prophets. There is fire and energy, and purity in his language and expressions, and his writings are sublime poetry, almost without any exception.

His wife is styled a prophetess, though her name is not given. Isaiah, viii: 3.

There is a tradition extant regarding Isaiah, that he wrote other books; one regarding the reign and actions of Uzziah, referred to in 2d Chronicles, xxvi: 22; and also, that he wrote a book called the "ascension of Isaiah." It is also, reported that he was buried near Jerusalem, under the Fuller's oak, not far from the pool of Siloam, and that his body was afterwards removed to a point near the source of the Jordan; and later, was removed to Constantinople. But of these things we have no evidence, nor are they of any great importance.

ISCAH—[Is′-cah,] *he that anoints, or covers.*

ISCAH is referred to in Gen. xi: 29, as the daughter of Haran. Some have supposed that she was the same person as Sarah, the wife of Abraham, but this cannot be so, since Iscah is expressly said to be the daughter of Haran, while Sarah was the daughter of Terah, and the half-sister of Abraham, before she became his wife.

ISCARIOT—[Is-kar′-ri-ot,] *is thought to signify a native of the town of Iscarioth.*

Judas, one of the twelve. He betrayed Christ for thirty pieces of silver. This is his surname. [See Judas Iscariot.]

ISHBAK—*Empty, forsaken, abandoned.*

He was one of the sons of Abraham, by Keturah, and is referred to in Gen. xxv: 2.

ISHBIBENOB—[Ish′-bi-be′-nob,] *he that sits in the prophecy, conversion.*

ISHBIBENOB was a Philistine of the race of the giants. 2d Sam. xxi: 16, 17. We learn that his spear weighed three hundred shekels. He had a new sword girded upon his thigh, which in size and weight answered to the spear. Equipped with these weapons, he went forth to slay David, and was on the point of effecting this purpose and end, when Abishai, the son of Zeruiah came to David, helped him and smote the Philistine giant, and so succored and saved the king.

ISHBOSHETH—[Ish′-bo-sheth,] *a man of shame.*

ISHBOSHETH was the son of King Saul, and his successor on the throne of Israel. Abner the chief general of Saul made Ishbosheth king over the tribes of Israel, except the tribe of Judah, which clave to David. And Ishbosheth reigned in peace for two years, when Abner drew on a war with the kingdom of David. It was not a general conflict, but was made up of skirmishes between parties of the soldiers of Ishbosheth and David.

Ishbosheth gave offence to Abner by accusing him of improper conduct with Rizpah his father's second wife. Abner became enraged at the charge, and deserted him. He began to set on foot a plan for transferring the kingdom of Ishbosheth with all its interests to David. He conferred with David by messengers, and also in person. But David would not allow Abner to see him until he brought Michal, Saul's daughter, and his own legitimate wife to him. He accordingly made the demand of Ishbosheth, who sent and took her from Phaltiel, the son of Laish, and had her conveyed to David at Hebron. Abner then engaged to bring all Israel over to David, but he was murdered by Joab the general of his army.

Ishbosheth was not aware of the designs of Abner as to his government, and was deeply affected by his death. He lost his courage, "his hands were feeble and all the Israelites were troubled." Ishbosheth was a very feeble prince, and had but few of the qualities requisite for a successful sovereign. In the sorrow that pressed him he went into his chamber about noon, to rest and to sleep; there were two of his captains who were brothers, that had plotted his death—and they entered his bed chamber stealthily and murdered him, then made their escape, with the head of the murdered king to David, who was at Hebron. Baanah and Rechab who had performed this cruel act, supposed that David would laud them for their conduct, and honor them with a higher position in his army than they had occupied in the army of Ishbosheth; but in this they were mistaken, for no sooner had they reported their deed to David, than he accused them of being guilty of a great crime. They had murdered an innocent man, in his own house, and on his own bed, while to his face they had pretended to be his friends. David ordered his young men to put them to death, and they did at once, cutting off their hands and their feet—and he ordered their bodies to be hung up over the pool of Hebron, and the head of Ishbosheth to be honorably buried in the tomb of the fallen Abner. See 2d Sam. iii:

With the death of Ishbosheth the authority and rule in Israel, of the house of Saul failed.

ISHI, 1—[I′-shi.]

A man of the descendants of Judah, and belonging to the extensive family of Hezron. 1st Chron. ii: 31.

ISHI, 2.

He was a head of a family in the tribe of Simeon. 1st Chron. iv: 42.

ISHI, 3.

He was the head of a family in the tribe of Manasseh, on the east of the Jordan. 1st Chron. v: 24.

ISHIAH—[I-shi-′ah.]

ISHIAH was the fifth son of Izrahiah, and one of the heads of the tribe of Issachar in the time of David. 1st Chron. vii: 3.

ISHIJAH—[I-shi′-jah.]

ISHIJAH was an Israelite returned from the captivity, who had married a foreign wife. Ez. x: 31.

ISHMA.

A man named in the genealogy of Judah's tribe. 1st Chron. iv: 3.

ISHMAEL, 1—[Ish′ma-el,] *God who hears.*

ISHMAEL was the son of Abraham, by Hagar, the handmaid of Sarah, who was given to the patriarch to wife.

He was about thirteen years of age, when Isaac was born; but when Isaac was four or five years of age, his mother saw Ishmael, the son of Hagar, mocking him or indulging in some kind of ridicule of her son, and she determined to send Hagar, with her son, away. At first, Abraham was unwilling to meet Sarah's wishes in this respect, but by a revelation from God, he was required to grant her request.

Abraham disinherited Ishmael, and dismissed him, with his mother, from the family, though he provided them with bread and water for their journey into the wilderness. It was not long until the bread gave out, and the water was spent in the bottle. She felt that she was in extremity, and with her son, was about to resign herself to death from starvation and thirst, when God miraculously supplied her with water, and with it she refreshed herself and her dying boy.

Ishmael and his mother took up their residence in the wilderness of Paran, and he procured for himself and mother a living by shooting—"he became an archer."

At length Ishmael married an Egyptian woman, under the direction of his mother, and became the head of a numerous family. He had twelve sons who were all heads of extensive Arabian tribes, and thus the prediction was fulfilled, made by the angel to Hagar at the well, and also to Abraham, regarding Ishmael's descendants.

He had also a daughter called Mahalath or Bashemath, who became the wife of Esau. Gen. xxi and xxviii: 9.

Although Ishmael was disinherited, yet he seems afterwards to be associated with Isaac, if, in nothing else, in burying their father; for when Abraham was "gathered to his people," Isaac and Ishmael, his sons buried him in the cave of Machpelah. Gen. xxv: 9. This shows that the son of Hagar had a regard for Abraham, notwithstanding the seeming hardness of being disinherited by Abraham. The posterity of Ishmael are called Ishmaelites, and took up their abode between Havilah and Shur. Havilah was situated near the confluence of the Tigris and Euphrates, and Shur was on the Isthmus which separates Arabia from Egypt, and hence we may suppose that they possessed nearly all of Arabia. Josephus styles Ishmael the founder of the Arabian nation. Gen. xxv: 17-18. Ishmael died at the age of one hundred and thirty-seven years, surrounded by his friends, and in the presence of his brethren.

ISHMAEL, 2—[Ish-ma′-el,] *God who hears.*

ISHMAEL was one of the royal families of Judah. He was the son of Nethaniah, and was sent by Baalis, the king of the Ammonites, to murder Gedaliah, the deputy governor of the Jews, who were left in Canaan after the captivity. Gedaliah was filling that office under the direction of Nebuchadnezzar. He was unwilling to believe the report made to him of the intention of Ishmael to kill him. He was admitted, with several others, by the unsuspecting governor, into his presence, and to the enjoyment of a repast with him. No sooner was an opportunity afforded, than Ishmael rose up with the men that were with him in the plot, and smote Gedaliah; and he added to the murder of this man, the murder of other Jews, and also the Chaldeans, who were associated with Gedaliah. A great number were slain thus, and cast by Ishmael into a pit; and he took a great many captives, and started with them on a march to the country of Ammon, as captives taken in war. But Johanan, the son of Kareah, hearing what he had done, gathered a company of warriors and pursued after Ishmael, and overtaking him, he retook the captives and recovered the spoils, and would have taken Ishmael and his accomplices had he not fled with them to the country of the Ammonites. Jer. xl. and xli.

ISHMAIAH—[Ish-ma-i′-ah.]

Was a son of Obadiah, the ruler of the tribe of Zebulon, in the time of David. 1st Chron. xxvii: 19.

ISHMERAI—[Ish′-me-ra.]

Was a Benjamite, and one of the family of Elpaal. 1st Chron. viii: 18.

ISHOD—[I′-shod.]

Was one of the tribe of Manasseh, on the east of the Jordan. 1st Chron. vii: 18.

ISHPAN—[Ish′-pan.]

Was a Benjamite, and one of the family of Shashak. 1st Chronicles, viii. 22.

ISHUAH—[Ish′-u-ah.]

Was one of the sons of Asher, and is numbered with the family of Jacob, who went down into Egypt. Genesis, xlvi: 17.

ISHUAI—[Ish′-u-a.]

Was the third son of Asher, and the founder of a family bearing his name. Numb. xxvi: 44; 1st Chron. vii: 30.

ISHUI.

Ishui was one of the sons of Saul, the first king of Israel. 1st Samuel, xiv: 49. He is called Abinadab in 1st Sam. xxxi: 2, where the account of his death, with the death of his father and two brothers Jonathan and Melchishua is given.

ISMACHIAH—[Is-ma-ki′-ah.]

Ishmachiah was one of those who were engaged in Hezekiah's reform, and is referred to with several others in 2d Chron. xxxi. He was an overseer.

ISRAEL—[Is′-ra-el,] *a prince with God, prevailing with God, that wrestleth with God.*

This was a name given to Jacob by the angel of the covenant when he wrestled with him all night, even until the break of day at Peniel. Gen. xxxii: 28. "Thy name shall be called no more Jacob, but Israel; for as a prince hast thou power with God and with man, and hast prevailed." See Jacob.

While the descendants of Abraham are called Hebrews, because they came from the other side of the Euphrates into Canaan; they were afterwards called Israelites from their progenitor Israel, as afterwards they were called Jews, from Judah a son of Jacob from whose loins the Messiah was to come, and whose tribe was the most important of all the tribes.

ISSACHAR—[Is′sa-char,] *price, reward.*

Issachar was the son of Leah, the wife of the patriarch Jacob. He was the fifth son of Leah, and the circumstances narrated regarding his birth, are remarkable. The name is supposed to have reference to the mandrakes which Leah gave to Rachel. Gen. xxx: 14.

Issachar had four sons whose names are given in Gen. xlvi: 13, and his descendants, through these sons, became numerous. When they left the land of Egypt, they numbered fifty-four thousand and four hundred, and were under the charge of Nathaneel, the son of Zuar, and their spy, to view the promised land, was Igal, the son of Joseph, while their agent, to assist in dividing, was Palteel, the son of Azzan. Num. i: 3-29. Also Num. x: 15 and xiii: 7. The position of this tribe in the wilderness was before the tabernacle, and they increased in the wilderness nine thousand and nine hundred. Num. xxvi: 23.

The tribe of Issachar enjoyed a rich lot in the land of Canaan. They are said to have been very industrious and wealthy, and continued to worship the God of their fathers, as predicted by Moses when he blessed the tribes of Israel.

We know nothing particular regarding the life of Issachar, and but little regarding individuals of his tribe. Tola, who was a judge of Israel, was of this tribe, and Baasha, a king of Israel, belonged to the tribe of Issachar. The princes of Issachar were associated with Deborah and Barak, in overthrowing the army of Jabin, the king of Canaan. Judges v: 15. When David was crowned, two hundred of the principal men attended, and with Zebulun and Naphtali, brought much provisions with them to use during the coronation feast. 1st Chron. xii. The tribe was very numerous in the time of David, containing one hundred and forty-three thousand and six hundred warriors—men that were able to draw the sword. And even as late as the day of Hezekiah, this tribe is spoken of as a tribe of very considerable number, and importance. Multitudes of them attended Hezekiah's passover. 1st Chron. vii: 1-6, and xii: 32, and xxvii: 18, and 2d Chron. xxx.

ISSACHAR, 2—[Is′-sa-kar,] *price, reward.*

He was one of the sons of Obed-Edom, and one of the sacred porters. 1st Chron. xxvi: 5.

ISSHIAH.

He was one of the ministers in the temple, under the order of service instituted in the time of David. 1st Chron. xxiv: 21.

ISUI—[Is′-u-i.]

He was one of the sons of Asher, and is numbered with the family of Jacob, who went down into Egypt. Genesis xlvi: 17.

ITHAMAR—[Ith′-a-mar,] *island of the palm tree, woe to the palm or change.*

ITHAMAR was the fourth and youngest son of Aaron. In the time of Eli and his children, for some cause or other, the high priesthood rested in the family of Ithamar. It had been transferred from the family of Eleazar. It, however, returned to the family of Aaron, because of the wickedness of Eli's sons, Hophni and Phineas. Though the high priesthood went back to Eleazar, yet Ithamar's descendants continued in the office of priests, for David divided them into twenty-four orders, and gave to Eleazar sixteen parts, and to the family of Ithamar eight, or in other words David constituted eight of the orders of the priests of the descendants of Ithamar. 1st Chron. xxiv.

ITHMAH—[Ith′-mah.]

He was a Moabite, one of the warriors of David, and of his body guard. 1st Chron. xi: 46.

ITHRA—[Ith′-ra.]

Was an Israelite, or Ishmaelite, the father of Amasa, by Abigail, David's sister. 2d Sam. xvii: 25; 1st Chron. ii: 17.

ITHRAN—[Ith′-ran.]

Was a son of Dishon, a Horite, referred to in Gen. xxxvi: 26; 1st Chron. i: 41.

ITHREAM—[Ith′-re-am,] *excellence of the people.*

Was a son of David, born unto him in Hebron, and said to be the sixth. His mother's name was Eglah. 2d Sam. iii: 5; 1st Chron. iii: 3.

ITTAI—[It′-ta-i.]

ITTAI was a native of Gath, a Philistine in the army of David. He was in the army, as an officer, during the rebellion of Absalom. He commanded six hundred warriors, who were about David's person when he made his flight. 2d Sam. xv: 18. And afterward, when the army was numbered and organized by David, at Mahanaim, it was divided into three parts, and Ittai was placed in command of one third of the entire army. 2d Sam. xviii: 12.

IZEHAR—[Iz′-e-har.]

IZEHAR was of the family of Kohath, of the tribe of Levi. The family to which he belonged were privileged beyond other families in the tribe of Levi, in that they had charge of the holy things, such as the ark, table, candle-stick, altars, and the holy vessels. Numb. iii: 27-31.

IZHAR—[Iz′-har.]

There were two of this name in the tribe of Levi, and in the line of the priests, being the sons of Kohath. 1st Chron. vi: 2 and 18.

JAALAM—[Ja-a′-lam,] *hidden, young man, kids.*

JAALAM was one of the sons of Esau by his Canaanitish wife, Aholibamah. He had two full brothers, they were Jeush and Korah. Genesis xxxvi: 5.

JAAREOREGIM—[Ja-a r-e or′-a-gim.]

JAAREOREGIM was the father of Elhanan, who slew the brother of Goliath the Gittite. 2d Sam. xxi: 19. He is also called Jair. 1st Chron. xx: 5.

JAASIEL—[Ja-a′-si-el.]

JAASIEL the son of Abner, was the ruler in the tribe of Benjamin in the times of David. 1st Chronicles, xxvii: 21.

JAAZANIAH OR JEZENIAH—[Ja-az-za-ni′ah.]

JAAZANIAH the Maachathite is referred to in 2d Kings, xxv, and in Jer. xl. He was associated with Ishmael in the murder of Gedaliah the governor of the Jews, appointed by Nebuchadnezzar.

JABAL—[Ja′-bal,] *which glides away, produces.*

JABAL was the son of Lamech and Adah. He was remarkable as the inventor of tent-making, and the first person mentioned as raising cattle. Gen. iv: 20. "And Adah bare Jabal: he was the father of such as dwell in tents, and of such as have cattle." He was not the first shepherd, for Abel was a "keeper of sheep," but Jabal engaged extensively in the business, which became so common among the Patriarchs. Abraham and Lot had extensive flocks and herds. Laban and Jacob's wealth consisted in such, and so all the sons of Israel from Reuben the eldest, to Benjamin, the youngest.

JABEZ—[Ja′-bez,] *sorrow, trouble.*

JABEZ was a descendant of Judah by Ashur. 1st Chron. iv: 9. The pain and sorrow of his mother, at his birth, is expressed by the name that was given him. She "called his name Jabez, saying: because I bare him with sorrow." Though we know nothing of him but what is mentioned here, for his name does not occur anywhere else in the sacred scriptures, we are satisfied that he was an honorable man. His religious character, with his authority growing out of his position in the family, made him "more honorable than his brethren."

He worshipped God most devoutly, and his prayer recorded is full of earnestness and fervor. He prays that God would enlarge his family and his inheritance, and would help and direct him in all his undertakings; keep him from everything dangerous and sinful, that he might not be grieved. The following is his prayer which was granted to him; "Oh that thou wouldest bless me indeed, and enlarge my coast, and that thine hand might be with me, and that thou wouldest keep me from all evil that it might not grieve me." The name of Jabez occurs in 1st Chron. ii: 55, but it is the name of a place and not of a person.

JABIN, 1—[Ja′-bin,] *he that understands, he that builds.*

JABIN was a Canaanitish king, and one of the most powerful of that country. He was the king of the city of Hazor, who associated with himself the King of Madon, and the King of Shimron, and the King of Achshaph with several others, to oppose Joshua in his conquest of the land. He determined if possible to stop his march, and cool his ardor as a conquering general. Josh. xi. He consequently gathered their whole forces together at the waters of Merom to fight with Israel. The confederate kings laid their plans, but the Lord delivered them into the hands of Joshua. They fled from the battlefield, and were pursued in their flight and many of them cut off. When Joshua gave up the pursuit, he returned to Hazor, which was not far from Merom, and burnt the city with fire, and killed Jabin the King.

JABIN, 2—*He that understands, he that builds.*

JABIN was also a King of Hazor, and probably a descendant of the former king. Hazor where he reigned, was the same as the former, for after Joshua conquered it, and gave it to the tribe of Naphtali, it was afterwards possessed by the Canaanites. In Judges iv: 2, it is said "the Lord sold them into the hand of Jabin, King of Canaan, that reigned in Hazor." This Jabin was also a powerful King, and for twenty years he mightily oppressed the children of Israel. At the time that Deborah arose "a mother," and a deliverer of Israel, this Jabin had nine hundred iron chariots and a very large army under the management of Sisera. They fought a battle which resulted in the defeat of Jabin, and the utter distruction of his vast army, armor and weapons of war, and the death of his general Sisera. Jud. iv.

JACHIN, 1—[Ja'-kin,] *that strengthens.*

JACHIN was one of the sons of Simeon. He was numbered with the family of Jacob, who went with him down into Egypt. Genesis, xlvi: 10.

JACHIN, 2.—*That strengthens.*

JACHIN was one of the priests appointed by David, when he divided them into twenty-four orders. His lot was the twenty-first. 1st Chronicles, xxiv: 17.

JACOB—[Ja'-kob,] *he that supplants, the heel.*

JACOB was the youngest son of Isaac and Rebekah, and the grandson of the patriarch Abraham. He was a very remarkable personage, whose fortunes were varied, but he proved himself, in his trust in God, equal to every emergency, and though dark portentious clouds at times hung over him so as to make his life shady, through the mercy of the God of his fathers, he passed the storms and trials of his eventful life, and his last days were his brightest and best.

He possessed a strong mind and a heart influenced by divine grace. The strength of his mind is exhibited in his whole life, and the goodness of his heart is attested by the wonderful manifestation of God's favor made to him at Peniel. Jacob continued to be a man of strong mind until his work was all done. His intellect did not fail until the last sentence had fallen from his lips, and his weeping children had beheld him breathe his last in death.

Jacob was the twin brother of Esau, and before they were born, the mother was advised by the Lord that they should become heads of mighty nations, very different in their temper, circumstances and government; but the "elder should serve the younger." Gen. xxv: 26. Esau being born first, was the eldest, and justly claimed the birthright, which gave him superiority to Jacob. That superiority consisted in part of a double portion of the father's inheritance, and his peculiar blessing. The birthright, important as it was, was transferable, as the sequel in the history of these two brothers proves. One day, as Esau came in from a hunting excursion very hungry, his eye rested upon some vegetables that Jacob had cooked, and he asked him that he might eat of them. Jacob accordingly proposed him the cooked vegetables in lieu of the birthright. Esau accepted his proposition, and under oath transferred it to Jacob.

Some years after this, when Isaac was old and his eyes were dim, he bade Esau, who was a hunter, take his weapons and go out and procure him venison, and prepare him meat that he could relish, that his soul might bless him before he died.

Now Rebekah, who was partial to Jacob, was near by when Isaac gave the order to Esau, and heard it; and being anxious that Jacob should have the first blessing, she bade him go to the flocks and procure two kids of the goats, and she would prepare savory meat such as she knew that Isaac loved, and he should go in with the meat to his father, and procure the blessing that Isaac was intending for Esau. The conscience of Jacob was rather tender, and he ventured an objection; but his mother so far removed it as to induce him to carry out her plan. Jacob killed the kids and his mother dressed them. She then put the raiment of Esau upon Jacob, and the skin of the kids that had been slain upon his hands and his neck. Thus prepared he went into the presence of his father, and deceiving him, Isaac pronounced upon him the peculiar blessing.

Esau became greatly enraged at his brother who had supplanted him, and resolved to murder him. This led to Jacob's leaving home some time after; but before he left he received the confirmation of the blessing he had obtained through subtlety.

Jacob went, under the instruction of his father, to Padan-aram, to take a wife of the daughters of his mother's brother. He left home privately, and on the second day of his journey neared, in the shade of the evening, the city of Luz; "and he lighted upon a certain place and tarried there all night because the sun was set." And taking a stone of that place for a pillow he laid him down and slept; and in the vision of that night the sublime scene passed before him of a ladder reaching up into heaven, and the angels of God ascending and descending upon it. At the top of the ladder stood the Lord God, and assured him that he was the God of his fathers, Abraham and Isaac, and that he would give him and his seed the land of Canaan for their inheritance, and make his posterity numerous as the stars of heaven and as the sands of the sea-shore, and all nations should be blessed in him.

Under the pleasant sensations produced by the ladder-dream, early in the morning Jacob consecrated, with solemn ceremony, the spot where he had been thus favored. He took the stone which he had for a pillow and erected it as a monument, then poured oil on the top of it and called the name of the place Bethel, or the house of God. He also entered into a solemn covenant with God, that if he would protect him, provide for him, and prosper him, he would give him one-tenth of his entire income; and further, that he would make Bethel a place of solemn worship. Genesis xxviii: 20, 21, 22.

Jacob, encouraged by the vision and the divine promise made to him, proceeded on his journey to Haran, where Laban, his uncle, dwelt. The first member of the family he was permitted to see was Rachel, who afterwards became his wife. When he first made himself known unto her at the well, as she was watering the flock, he testified his friendship as a cousin in the simple and pure method, in primitive times, of kissing. He offered thanksgiving unto God, and wept tears of gratitude for the success with which he had been favored so far. She ran from the well and informed her father that the son of Rebekah, her aunt, had come. Laban went out and conducted Jacob to his house, which became his home. After he had been with his uncle one month, and nothing had been said about wages, Laban, desirous of retaining his services, asked him what wages he should give him. Jacob had already formed strong attachment for the beautiful Rachel, and had meditated marriage with her. He therefore said, "I will serve thee seven years for Rachel, thy younger daughter." Laban accepted the proposal, and Jacob served according to agreement,—years seemed but as a few days, because of the love he had for Rachel. He then said to Laban, "Give me my wife." The father consequently made a marriage feast, but in the place of giving Rachel, his younger daughter, he deceived Jacob and gave him Leah.

As is reasonable to suppose, Jacob expressed dissatisfaction, and earnestly upbraided Laban for the deception. He gave the reason for thus acting, that Leah was the eldest and should be married first, as that was the custom in Mesopotamia. Jacob was not acquainted with this custom of the country, and probably was reconciled to it, when his father-in-law promised, after the lapse of a week, to give him Rachel also, provided he would give him seven years of service for her in addition to the other seven years. Jacob agreed to this, and Rachel on whom his affections were set was given to him, when he commenced and completed the service; after which, for other wages, he continued in charge of the flock of Laban, which was greatly increased, and he himself was prospered and became very wealthy.

Of the two wives, Jacob much preferred Rachel, but God favored Leah with children, while Rachel was barren. She then gave Bilhah, her maid unto Jacob as a secondary wife, who bare two sons that Rachel looked upon as her own children, and gave them names. In imitation of Rachel, Leah gave her maid also to Jacob, and she bare him two sons. In all Jacob had eleven sons born unto him in Mesopotamia, and one daughter.

When he desired to return to his own country, and to the land of his kindred, having been instructed in a vision by the angel of the Lord, he made known his desire to his wives, Rachel and Leah, and they heartily acquiesced in the will of the Lord. Hence, while Laban was away from home, Jacob gathered all together and started with his wives and children to go to Isaac, his father, in the land of Canaan. When Laban returned home, and it was told him that Jacob was gone, he determined to pursue after him. He overtook him in a few days, and would have dealt harshly with him, but for the caution he received from God. Laban made the charge upon Jacob of having dealt unfairly with him, and he especially complained that he had carried away his gods. Jacob defended himself, and especially denied the charge of theft. He bade his father-in-law examine all his goods, and feeling very certain that no one of his family was guilty, he agreed that whoever of his family should be convicted, might be put to death, for he had no thought that Rachel was guilty. Laban searched for his idols, but found them not, because of the iniquity of Rachel, who sat upon them and complained of indisposition that prevented her rising up. The difficulty between Laban and Jacob was finally settled, and they made a solemn covenant of perpetual friendship, and reared a heap of stones in testimony of their covenant, when Laban "kissed his sons and daughters, and blessed them," then turned his face towards his home, and Jacob with his family went on his way. Before they parted, however, each one gave a name to the place. Jacob called it Galeed, and Laban called it Jegar-Sahadutha, both of which signify the heap of witness.

Shortly after this Jacob was favored with another vision of angels in the wilderness of Mahanaim. Here a host of angels met him. The Almighty showed him that he was guarded on every side. He had just passed the severe trial and inspection of Laban, and now he was dreading the vengeance of Esau, whom, years before, he had supplanted, and who had threatened to destroy his life. As in other times of trial he had recourse to God, in prayer, having sent his family on, and being left alone, he earnestly plead with God for help, for he felt himself to be in extremity. And while he prayed, the angel of the covenant, in the form of a man, came down, and he became deeply exercised. He wrestled with the man until the break of day. So earnest was he that he took hold of the garments of the heavenly visitant. He said to the angel: "I will not let thee go, except thou bless me."

He prevailed in his supplication; and his name was changed from Jacob, a supplanter, to Israel, because, as a prince, he had wrestled and prevailed with God. From this name the children of Abraham, or the descendants of the Patriarchs, have received the appellation of Israelites. Jacob honored the place where he had thus prayed and prevailed, by calling it Peniel; *i. e.*, the face of God.

Joining his wives and children in the morning, he pursued his journey, to meet his brother. He had prepared large presents for Esau: two hundred and twenty goats, two hundred and twenty sheep, thirty milch camels with their colts, forty kine, ten bulls, twenty she asses, and ten foals. These he divided into five droves, and gave orders to the drivers to tell Esau, as they met him, that they were a present to him; and by this means he hoped to appease the wrath of his brother. He divided his family into three divisions, that, if Esau murdered, with his four hundred men, the first company, the others might escape. He put the two handmaids and their children first; Leah and her children next, and Rachel and her son last. He probably thought that was the safest place for her, and, in case of necessity for flight, would give her an advantage over all the rest. But the fears of Jacob were soon allayed, for, as he lifted up his eyes and saw Esau coming to meet him, he saw nothing but the purest friendship indicated in the appearance or conduct of his brother. "Esau ran to meet him, and embraced him, and fell on his neck and kissed him, and they wept." The present that had been arranged was offered Esau, but he generously refused it, because he had much wealth already. Esau then offered to attend Jacob to Mt.

Seir, but he begged him not to trouble himself, as the flocks and little ones could but move slowly.

Jacob soon came to the spot where Succoth was afterwards built, and reared for himself a house, and booths for his cattle. Soon we hear of him crossing the Jordan, and coming to Shalem, where he bought a piece of ground from Hamor, the father of Shechem, for one hundred pieces of silver. Here he erected an altar, and called it El-elohe—Israel. He had not dwelt long here, when Dinah, his daughter, went out to see the young women of the country, and was seduced, and disgraced, by Shechem, a prince of the country. After this, Shechem and Hamor, his father, begged her in marriage, offering Jacob any price he would name. He waited till his sons came home, and they made a proposition, which was, that the men of Shechem should all be circumcised as the terms, and the only terms, of obtaining Dinah for a wife, for Shechem.

They accordingly submitted to it, and on the third day after the rite was performed, Simeon and Levi fell upon the Shechemites, and murdered all the male inhabitants. This they did to revenge the disgrace of their sister. This act of the sons of Jacob, was not approved by him, and he feared the resentiment of the Canaanites. He was directed by the Lord to go to Bethel to dwell.

Jacob, remembering his vow, which he had made, as he went to Padanaram, ordered his family to put away all strange gods and purify themselves. They accordingly delivered up their idols to him. It is likely that Rachel gave up the gods she had stolen from her father, and Jacob hid them all under an oak. At Bethel he offered sacrifice to God, who appeared unto him and renewed his former covenant and blessing. He did not remain at Bethel long, but went to Hebron to visit Isaac, his father, and during the time he was at Hebron, Deborah, his mother's nurse, who, possibly, was now a member of his family, died and was buried. Rachel, the beloved wife of Jacob, died also in a short time after she gave birth to Benjamin, and he buried her near Bethlehem, which was called, in honor of her, "the city of Rachel." Not long after this he was sorely tried, no doubt, by the conduct of Reuben, his eldest son, who committed a disgraceful act towards Bilhah, one of his secondary wives, that of overthrowing her bed. He continued with his family, near Isaac, his father, a few years, when Isaac died, and in company with Esau, his brother, he buried him in the honored cave of Machpelah, beside Rebekah. . Genesis, xxvi, and xxix, inclusive.

Jacob was very sorely tried in the loss of Joseph, the elder son of his beloved Rachel. His brothers had dealt cruelly with him, by selling him to Midianitish merchants, and quite as cruelly with their father, in deceiving him with a report that Joseph was devoured by wild beasts in the woods.

Several years after Joseph was sold, the country where Jacob dwelt, was visited by a distressing famine, and he sent his ten eldest sons down to Egypt to buy corn. The long lost Joseph was lord of that land, and after a succession of thrilling circumstances was announced to his father. Jacob being satisfied that he was alive, went down to Egypt to see him; they met and embraced each other; and Jacob spent the last part of his life in peace and plenty, and day after day looked with pleasure upon the growing greatness of the dreamer.

Jacob was undoubtedly a great and good man. He was celebrated for his practice of virtue, and his devotion to the God of his fathers. He was an aged and venerable man when he went into Egypt, as we see from his introduction to Pharaoh. The king was so impressed with his appearance, that he asked him the question, "Jacob how old art thou." His answer was beautiful. "The days of the years of my life are a hundred and thirty years: few and evil have the days of the years of my life been, and have not attained unto the days of the years of my fathers, in the days of their pilgrimage."

When Jacob was about to die, he blessed both the sons of Joseph, claimed them as his own children, and required that they bear his name. He then gathered all his sons together, and with the mantle of prophecy around him, his nature's failing fire rekindled, and he told them what should be in the latter days. And beginning with Reuben, the eldest, he passed through the entire family, closing with Benjamin, and in the most sublime language; and in the use of the most apt and beautiful figures, he indicated the future of each one, and his posterity. Having finished his blessings and closed his admonitions to them, he gave directions calmly as to his burial, then "gathered up his feet into the bed" and died.

Joseph had his body embalmed, according to the custom of the Egyptians, then attended by all the adult relationship, and a large number of Egyptians, he took it to the land of Canaan, and buried it beside the remains of Leah his wife in the cave of Machpelah. In all the grave yards of this world there is to be found no family vaults containing six persons, who were honored of God in their lifetime, as the six that were buried there. Abraham and Sarah, Isaac and Rebekah, Jacob and Leah.

## JACKAMEAM.

JACKAMEAM was one of the ministers in the temple under the order of service, instituted in the time of David. 1st Chron. xxiv: 23.

## JAKIM.

JAKIM was one of the priests appointed by David when he divided them into twenty-four orders—his lot was the twelfth. 1st Chron. xxiv: 12.

## JADDUA OR JADDUS—[Jad-du′-ah.]

JADDUA was the son of Jonathan, and the high priest of the Jews. He is referred to in Neh. xii: 11, and officiated, we may judge, some time after the captivity—Josephus gives an interesting account of him. He went in company with other priests to meet Alexander the Great as he was coming toward Jerusalem for the purpose of destroying the city. He was dressed in his priestly garments, and Alexander was so favorably impressed with his appearance that he immediately gave up his hostile intentions against the city, and it is said worshiped the Lord in the temple, and granted special privileges to the Jews—though some think this a Jewish fable.

## JAEL—[Ja′el,] *he that ascends, a kid.*

JAEL was the wife of Heber, the Kenite, and the Kenites were the descendants of Jethro, the father-in-law of Moses. This people became attached to the Israelites, and were probably with them during their wanderings in the wilderness. Moses cordially invited Hobab, and it is likely that he accepted the invitation and accompanied them to the promised land, and received a lot with one of the tribes.

They were dwelling in "the city of Palm Trees" during the life of Joshua, and probably not far from it when God raised up the prophetess Deborah to be judge of Israel, and their deliverer out of the hand of Jabin, king of Canaan.

Heber, the husband of Jael, had for some cause severed himself from the Kenites, and was on friendly terms with the king of Canaan, and with Sisera, the captain of Jabin's army. Jael, the wife of Heber, is introduced to our view in connection with the flight of Sisera from the field of battle—his securing from her what seemed to him to be, an hospitable and safe shelter from the pursuing enemy.

The plain of Zanaim, where Heber's tent was pitched, was probably in the country of the king of Canaan, for Sisera, as soon as he lighted off his chariot fled on foot directly to the tent of Jael. She saw him coming and went to meet him, and gave him a cordial invitation to hide himself within her tent. He seemed to have fixed upon her apartment of the tent, because of secrecy. According to the custom of those times, when any one approached a tent, they never intruded into the apartments of the women, which were always separate from the apartments of the men. Sisera felt that he would be safe there, for no one would dare to enter the apartment in search of him. He had broken over the custom for he was in extremity, but he knew his pursuers would not be likely to do it. But seemingly, to avoid his being found, she covered him with a mantle, and then under his advise took her position in the door of the tent, to tell any one who might enquire of her that there was no man within the tent.

Sisera was greatly fatigued with labors he had performed as commander during the battle, and the loss he had sustained and the flight he had made on foot.

He asked her for water; she recognized his wants in being greatly fatigued as well as thirsty, hence she gave him milk or cream, that would answer the double purpose of quenching thirst and nourish and restore his exhausted nature. After thus ministering to him, she covered him again with the mantle and took her station at the door of the tent. And now the scene in her history changes. She has appeared in the character of a friend to the conquered general. Who could suspect her kindness, when she met him and so cordially invited him to hide in her apartment of the tent, and then to make him feel safe, with her own hands covered him with a mantle? Who could suspect her friendship? "When he asked for water and she gave him milk; she brought forth butter (cream) in a lordly dish;" not in an ordinary dish, but a vessel suitable to the rank and dignity of him to whom she ministered.

She stands in the door of her tent while the fatigued general resigns himself to sleep, feeling certain, in his own mind, that she who had ministered to his wants would defend his life; and when confident that he was fast asleep, she carried out her purpose. "She took a nail of the tent"—which was probably a spike to which they fastened the tent cord—and she "took a hammer in her hand and went softly in to him." There he lay unconscious of his danger, insensible to her presence, dreaming, it may be, of the battle that had just been fought, which had gone against him, and of the enemy following hard after him and overtaking him. Just as he, in his dreams, felt the weapon of an enemy pierce his vitals, Jael smote the nail or spike into his temple with the hammer, and fastened it into the ground on which he was lying. He struggled, it may be, for a few moments, and then stretched himself in death. Having performed this seemingly cruel deed, she took her position again at the door of the tent, and watched for the pursuers of Sisera. Soon Barak appears in sight, and Jael left the door of her tent and went to meet him, and invited him to come into her tent, promising to show him the man he was seeking. He attended to her invitation, intending, probably, to take Sisera alive as a captive in war; but, to his astonishment, there Sisera lay in death, and the spike was yet in his temples, fastening him to the ground.

We are not authorized to suppose that Barak applauded Jael for the deed she had committed, though Deborah, in her song, does. Judges, v: 24: "Blessed, above woman, shall Jael, the wife of Heber the Kenite, be; blessed shall she be above women in the tent."

She was thought of, in ages afterward, as a heroic woman. It may be that she was under divine direction when she performed this heroic and bloody deed, and perfectly justifiable before God, who has a right to dispose of human life as it pleases him. It may be that Sisera had been a very wicked man and his cup of iniquity was full, and God, in his infinite wisdom, appointed and directed her in this whole matter. Deborah was under divine influence when composing her song, and she declares Jael to be "blessed above women." This would seem to indicate that her conduct was pleasing to God. We are not called upon to justify all her conduct in this matter; nor are we fully authorized to condemn. This deed, whether justifiable or not, will give her name, as a heroine, to the latest generation of man.

## JAHATH, 1.

Jahath was the son of Libni, the son of Gershom, of the tribe of Levi. 1st Chron. vi: 20.

## JAHATH, 2.

Belonged to the tribe of Judah. 1st Chron. iv: 2.

## JAHATH, 3.

Was the son of Shelomoth a Levite. 1st Chron. xxiv: 22.

## JAHATH, 4.

Was the son of Shimei. 1st Chron. xxiii: 10. He was the elder of four sons, who were chiefs in the family. Their families were larger, hence they were considered more important than their two brothers of whom it is said "they had not many sons."

## JAHAZIEL—[Ja-haz′-i-el.]

Jahaziel was one of the ministers in the temple under the order of service instituted in the time of David. 1st Chron. xxiv: 23.

JAHDAI—[Jah-da′-i.]
He appears in the genealogy of Caleb as the father of six sons. 1st Chron. ii: 47.

JAHDIEL—[Jah′-di-el.]
A chief man of Manasseh on the east of the Jordan. 1st Chron. v: 24.

JAHLEEL—[Jah′-li-el.]
The third of the three sons of Zebulun, and he was the founder of an extensive family in that tribe. Gen. xlvi: 14; Num. xxvi: 26.

JAHMAI—[Jah-ma′-i.]
A man of the tribe of Issachar, and one of the heads of an important house. 1st Chron. vii: 2.

JAHZEEL, 1—[Jah′-ze-el.]
The oldest of the four sons of Naphtali, and the founder of an extensive family of that tribe. Num. xxvi: 48.

JAHZEEL, 2.
Was the son of Naphtali and is reckoned with the children and grand children of Jacob in Gen. xlvi: 24. He had three brothers, Guni, Jezer and Shillem.

JAHZERAH—[Jah-ze-rah.]
A priest of the house of Immer. 1st Chron. ix: 12.

JAIR, 1—[Ja′er,] *my light, who diffuses light,*
Was the son of Segub, and the grandson of Hezron, of the tribe of Judah. He seems to have fallen heir to an immense estate. It is thought he inherited it from his grandmother, the daughter of Machir. He had twenty-three cities in the land of Gilead. 1st Chron. ii: 22.

JAIR, 2—*My light, who diffuses light,*
Was a judge of Israel who succeeded Tola, and he governed in Israel about twenty-two years. He was a Gileadite, probably of the tribe of Manasseh. We may judge, from the account given of him in Judges, x: 3–5, that he had peace and prosperity during the time that he governed, for there is nothing said to the contrary; and his thirty sons are said each one to have rode upon an ass colt, and were each provided by their father with a city or village of his own. The inference to be gathered is, that Jair was prosperous, and that his sons were all of them men of dignity and importance. Jair died and was buried in Camon, which was a city in the tribe of Manasseh, east of the Jordan.

JAIRUS—[Ja′-i-rus,] *is enlightened.*
JAIRUS was a ruler of the synagogue at Capernaum. We have an account of Christ raising his daughter to life in Matt. ix: 18–26. His daughter had been sick for several days, and he had watched with anxiety over her, while all the means that had been used had proved ineffectual. He thought of Christ and went in search of him, and when he found him, he entreated him earnestly to go to his house and restore her to health. Jesus perceiving that he had strong faith in his healing power, went with him. They had not arrived however at the ruler's house, when a messenger came to tell him his daughter was dead. Jesus looked with sympathy upon the anguish stricken father, and said to him, "be not afraid, only believe." When they entered the house of the ruler, they found the child dead, and the family and relations in great distress. Jesus in the presence of the father and mother, and three of his disciples, raised the damsel to life.

JAMES, 1—*He that supplants, the heel.*
JAMES is sometimes called James the Great, to distinguish him from the less. He was the brother of John the Evangelist, and one of our Lord's apostles. He was the son of Zebedee and Salome, and was called from his occupation as a fisherman to follow Christ and become an apostle. Matt. iv: 21. In company with his brother John he was permitted to behold some exhibitions of Christ's divinity that all the apostles were not favored with. He witnessed the Savior's transfiguration. Matt. xvii: 2. In company with his brother, he asked the Savior's permission to call fire down from heaven to consume the Samaritans, who would not receive him. He rebuked them by

telling them that they were ignorant of themselves—they knew not the spirit they were of. Luke, ix: 54. They seemed to have had an idea that their Master would certainly establish a temporal kingdom, and they possessed an ambition to occupy an important position in that kingdom; and hence, made a request through their mother to the effect that he would favor them. It is likely she was quite willing to make the request for them, as she saw that he had a particular regard for them. He told them they knew not what they were asking, and then addressed the question to them, "Are ye able to drink of the cup that I shall drink of, and be baptized with the baptism that I am baptized with?" They answered that they were willing to undergo sufferings with him. Christ then told them that his Father had the disposal of the eminent places in his kingdom. Matt. xx: 20–24; Mark, x: 35–45.

It would seem, from John, xxi: 2, that James, with his brother, returned to their business of fishing after Christ's resurrection, for awhile; but he was present on the day of Pentecost, and received, in the gift of the Holy Ghost, qualification for his important mission as an apostle.

James was put to death as a martyr early in the apostolic age. We have an account of his murder by Herod, who "killed James, the brother of John, with a sword," in Acts, xii: 2.

JAMES, 2—*He that supplants, the heel.*

JAMES, who is called James the Less, was the son of Cleophas or Alpheus, and Mary, the sister of the Virgin Mary. He was, therefore, the kinsman of our Lord. He was surnamed the Just on account of the holiness and purity of his heart and life. He is called by Paul the "Lord's brother." Gal. i: 19. He was honored with a personal interview with the Savior after his resurrection, and Paul refers to it as occurring early in the first week after he rose. 1st Cor. xv: 7. And he was with the apostles when their Master appeared to them together.

After the conversion of Paul, James was at Jerusalem, during the fifteen days that the newly initiated apostle was at Jerusalem forming an acquaintance with Peter and others who were members of the church there, he also formed an acquaintance with James, who was the only apostle save Peter that Paul was then privileged to see. Gal. i: 19.

Several years after this there was a council of the apostles at Jerusalem. Acts, xv. James the less was present, and took a part in the discussions of the council. He listened attentively to Peter in his address, and then to Paul and Barnabas, as they declared the miracles and wonders that God had wrought by them among the Gentiles; then he himself, secured the attention of those present as he declared his sentiments regarding the main question before the council, the question of circumcision. He stated clearly, that as God had accepted the Gentiles—called them to himself—and through the instrumentality of the apostles who had spoken, established a church among them, that Gentile churches ought not to be burdened with Jewish ceremonies which were hard to be borne. He favored their forbearing to eat things strangled, and blood; and to abstain from fornication and meats offered to idols. And this advice of James was received, and was the substance of the agreement of the council, and in the form of letters from the council, was sent by messengers to all the gentile churches.

Sometime after this James wrote an epistle to the Jewish believers, wherein he refers them to the importance of an exercise of faith in Christ, developed by good works, and he sharply reproves those who pretended to faith, and did not show their faith by their works. He encourages them to bear any sufferings they might be exposed to, with fortitude and patience, and enforce by precept and practice, the genuine doctrines of Christ's gospel. He declares the divine will in threats against those who use the world and its riches improperly, or indulge in sensual, or sinful passions.

It is said that this apostle was severely persecuted, and finally stoned to death. Annanias ordered James to ascend one of the galleries and renounce his religion, and declare that Jesus of Nazareth was not the Messiah. He did ascend the gallery, and speak to the multitude but not as they desired him to speak. He declared, with a loud voice, that Jesus was the son of God, and that he would appear in the clouds of Heaven and judge the world. It is said the Pharisees were so enraged at him that they threw him over the battlement. By the fall he was sorely bruised but raising up on his knees began to pray for his murderers, as Stephen had done before him, amid a shower of stones, under which he died. There have been converted Jews, who attributed the destruction of Jerusalem, and of their nationality, to the cruel murder of this just man.

JAMIN—[Ja'-min.]

Jamin was one of the sons of Simeon, and is numbered with the family of Jacob, who went with him down into Egypt. Genesis, xlvi: 10.

JANNES and JAMBRES — [Jan'-nez.] *who speaks, who answers, affliction.*

Jannes and Jambres are referred to in 2d Tim. iii: 8, 9, in the following language. "Now as Jannes and Jambres withstood Moses, so do these also resist the truth; men of corrupt minds, reprobate concerning the faith. But they shall proceed no farther, for their folly shall be manifest unto all men, as theirs also was." From this it seems they were two principal magicians of Egypt, or the names rather of the magicians who imitated Moses when performing miracles in the land of Egypt. Exodus vii: 11.

When Moses and Aaron went into the presence of Pharoah and his courtiers and cast down the rod and it became a serpent, the King of Egypt called Jannes and Jambres with other magicians, and they cast down their rods, and each rod became a serpent, when Aarons rod swallowed up theirs. And so when Moses and Aaron smote the waters, and they were turned to blood, Jannes and Jambres with their associates did so also. And afterwards they imitated Moses and Aaron in bringing frogs out of the waters of the rivers. These two persons probably excelled in magic among the magicians of Egypt, at the time the Israelites made their Exodus under the direction of Moses and Aaron.

JAPHETH — [Ja'-feth,] *persuades, handsome.*

Japheth was the son of Noah. Though we are accustomed to name the sons of Noah in the following order—"Shem, Ham, and Japheth"—it does not follow that he was the younger. It is likely he was the oldest son of Noah, as he is said to be the elder brother of Shem. Gen. x: 21. Shem is probably put before him for the same reason that Abraham is named as first of Terah's sons; so Isaac is often named before Ishmael, in the Scripture history, and Jacob before Esau.

His modest behavior, and the service he rendered in company with Shem, of covering his father's nakedness when reported to him by Ham as drunken and uncovered within his tent, were rewarded, while Ham, for his unfeeling neglect, was punished. The promise was made him that his posterity should be greatly enlarged, and that he should dwell in the tents of Shem, and Canaan should be his servant.

The posterity of Japheth was very numerous. He had seven sons, whose names were Gomer, Magog, Madai, Javan, Tubal, Meshech, and Tiras, who were each the heads of large families. The descendants of Japheth are understood to have peopled the Northern part of Asia, the islands of the Mediterranean sea, the continent of Europe; and probably from Northern Asia they went into and settled North America. Indeed, the prophecy contained in Gen. ix: 27, seems to have been clearly fulfilled.

JAPHIA—[Ja-fi'ah,] *which enlightens, groans.*

He was one of the sons born unto David, in Jerusalem. 2d Sam. v: 15; 1st Chron. xiv: 6.

JAREB—[Ja'-reb,] *a revenger.*

He is referred to in the prophecies of Hosea as a king of Assyria. We know nothing further of him than is recorded there. Hosea, v: 13; x: 6.

JARED—*He that descends or commands.*

Jared was the son of Mahalaleel, and the father of Enoch. We know but little about him, save that he was one hundred and sixty-two years old when Enoch was born, and that he lived after that eight hundred years—so that he attained the great age of nine hundred and sixty-two years. Gen. v: 18, 20. We also learn from Luke, iii: 37, that he was in the line of the Messiah. Mary the daughter of Heli, and the mother of Christ was descended from him.

JARESIAH—[Jar-e-si′-ah.]

JARESIAH was a Benjamite, and is referred to in 1st Chron. viii: 27.

JARHA.

JARHA was the Egyptain servant of Sheshan, to whom he gave his daughter to wife, and constituted him heir to an estate. 1st Chron. ii: 34. Of this Sheshan we learn that he had no sons, but daughters, and it is supposed that the children of this Egyptian servant were called his children, being the children of his daughter.

JARIB, 1.

Was the son of Simeon. 1st Chron. iv: 24.

JARIB, 2.

One of the chiefs who accompanied Ezra from Babylon to Jerusalem. Ezra viii: 16.

JARIB, 3.

Was a priest of the house of Joshua, the son of Jozadak, who had married a foreign wife, and like others put her away. Ez. x: 18.

JAROAH—[Ja-ro′-ah.]

Was a chief man of the tribe of Gad. 1st Chron. v: 14.

JASHEN—[Ja′shen,] *righteous.*

JASHEN was the father of the Jonathan who was numbered with David's mighty men. 2d Sam. xxiii: 32.

JASHOBEAM—[Ja-sho′be-am.]

JASHOBEAM, the Tachmonite or Hachmonite, was one, perhaps the chief, of David's mighty men. 1st Chron. xi: 11. It is said he was chief of the captains, and slew three hundred men at one time. In 2d Sam. xxiii: 8, it is said he attacked eight hundred men at one time, and slew them. If it be the same circumstance that is referred to in both passages, we may suppose that he routed eight hundred and slew three hundred of them himself, and probably his associates slew the other five hundred, making the slaughter to be really eight hundred men as reported in the latter place.

In company with Eleazar and Shammah, two other mighty men, he broke through the army of the Philistines, and brought David water from the well of Bethlehem. Being not far from the well David had expressed a desire for some of the water of it, as he was very thirsty. They overheard his expression, and determined to procure it, and they did so at the hazzard of their lives. When David looked at their boldness and daring that had been crowned with success, he determined, thirsty as he was, to deny himself, hence would not drink of it, but "poured it out unto the Lord."

It is likely that Jashobeam was the commander of the royal guard of twenty-four thousand for the first month referred to in 1st Chron. xxvii: 2. He was appointed over the first course for the first month. There is a descendant of Benjamin by Korah referred to by this name in 1st Chron. xii: 6, and he was one of David's men—possibly the same person as above.

JASHUB.

JASHUAB was of the tribe of Issachar, and the head of the family in that tribe called Jashubites. Numb. xxvi: 24.

JASON — [Ja′-son,] *he that cures, gives medicines.*

JASON was a kinsman of the apostle Paul, and is spoken of in Acts xvii: 5 as the host of the apostle when at Thessalonica. By the labors that were performed there, and the success that attended them, a persecution was raised against Paul and his companions. They raised an uproar in the city, and went with a mob to the house of Jason and assaulted it. They demanded that Paul be brought out, but he escaped out of their hands. They then determined to take vengeance on Jason, and they caught him and took with him several others unto the ruler of the city, with a charge against them of "turning the world upside down," by which they meant producing commotion and disorder among the people. They knew that Jason was a resident among them, but they charged him with being equally guilty in receiving the apostles into his house, and taking care of them while desseminating their strange doctrine. But Jason was finally liberated.

If he is the same person referred to by Paul, in Rom. xvi 21, of which we have no doubt, he with the others named was related to Paul and had changed his residence from Thessalonica to Rome.

JATHNIEL—[Jath′-ni-el.]

Was one of the sons of Shelamiah, and one of the sacred porters. 1st Chron. xxvi: 2.

JAVAN—[Ja′-van,] *that deceives, clay.*

JAVAN was the son of Japheth, and the grandson of Noah. Gen. x: 2. The posterity of Javan are referred to in Isa. lxvi: 19, as also in Ez. xxvii: 13, 19, from which we may learn that they were a people of very considerable importance, and engaged as merchantmen. It is generally understood in history that he was the father of the Ionians or Greeks.

JAZIZ.

The Hagerite was placed by King David over his flocks. 1st Chronicles, xxvii: 31.

JEATERAI—[Je-at′-e-ra.]

Was of the tribe of Levi, and in the line of the priests from Aaron to the captivity. 1st Chron. vi: 21.

JEBUS—[Je′bus,] *treads under foot, contemns.*

JEBUS was the son of Canaan, and the head of the family of the Jebusites. Gen. x: 16. In the time of David, they inhabited the ancient city of Jerusalem, and round about in the mountains, and had occupied it for many years. They had a strong fort on one of the mountains that David took when he conquered them, and transferred his court from Hebron to that place, or to Mt. Zion, which was their strong hold; and afterwards David brought the ark from Kirjath-jearim, to that place. 2d Samuel v, and vi.

JECOLIAH—[Jek-o-li′ah.]

This woman was the mother of Azariah, king of Judah, and is called a woman of Jerusalem. She was probably born in that city. 2d Kings xv: 2.

JECONIAH OR JEHOIACHIN—[Jek-o-ni′-ah,] *preparation or the steadfastness of the Lord.*

JECONIAH, or JEHOIACHIN, was the grandson of Josiah. 1st Chron. iii: 16. It seems that his father designated him as his successor when he was but eight years of age. Indeed, he seems to have placed the honor of a king upon him at that early age. He was eighteen years old when his father died and he entered upon the sole government of the kingdom as his successor. He reigned only three months and ten days, when Nebuchadnezzar, king of Babylon, took Jerusalem and captured Jeconiah.

It was a complete conquest for the king of Babylon, for he took the city with all its treasures—the king, and his mother and wives, and all his princes and men of might, and the craftsmen and warriors. 2d Kings, xxiv; 2d Chron. xxxvi; Jer. xxii.

After he had been imprisoned many years in Chaldea he was released by Evil Merodach, the son and successor of Nebuchadnezzar. 2d Kings, xxv: 27-30; Jer. lii: 31-34. It appears that the king of Babylon promoted him to great dignity and honor. After he had been imprisoned thirty-seven years he lifted him up from his low condition, spoke kindly to him, changed his prison garments for the robes of royalty, and fed him from the kings table; and this kindness continued until his death.

The prophet Jeremiah was commissioned by God to write Jeconiah childless—to declare that he should have no children to sit on the throne of Judah; and he had none. There are seven sons of Jeconiah mentioned in 1st Chron. iii: 17, 18—Salathiel, Malchiram, Pedaiah, Shenazer, Jecamiah, Hoshama, and Nedabiah. We find him in the genealogy of Christ as given by Matt. i: 11, though the name is changed to Jechonias. He is also called Coniah.

JEDAIAH—[Je-da′-yah.]
JEDAIAH was a priest who returned with nine hundred and seventy-three of his brethren from the Babylonian captivity. Ezra, ii: 36.

JEDIAEL, 1—[Jed-i-a′-el.]
JEDIAEL is referred to in 1st Chron. xi: 45, and xii: 20, from which we learn that he was an officer in the kingdom of Israel, and a brave man. He was one of Saul's warriors, but he abandoned him, and with several others joined David at Ziklag, and rendered him very important service.

JEDIAEL, 2.
JEDIAEL one of the sons of Shelemiah, was one of the sacred porters. 1st Chronicles, xxvi: 2.

JEDIDAH.
JEDIDAH was the mother of Josiah, who ascended the throne of Judah, when only eight years of age. She was the daughter of Adaiah, of Boscath. 2d Kings, xxii: 1.

JEDIDIAH — [Jed-i-di′-ah,] *beloved of the Lord.*
JEDIDIAH was a name given by Nathan, the prophet, to Solomon, to designate him "the beloved of the Lord." 2d Samuel, xii: 25. It does not seem that he was to be called by that name. [See Solomon.]

JEDUTHUN—[Jed-u′-thun,] *his law, who gives praise.*
JEDUTHUN was probably the same as Ethan, one of the four great masters of the temple music. He is referred to in 1st Chron. xvi: 41–42, as one of the chosen men to give thanks unto the name of the Lord, He is appointed with Heman to sound cymbals and trumpets in the worship of God. His six sons were heads of so many bands of the temple singers. 1st Chronicles, xxv: 3–17. A good many of the Psalms bear his name, which may simply import that they were placed in his hands, or in the hands of his sons, to be put to music, and sung by them. As such, are the following Psalms, xxxix, lxii, lxvii, &c. [See Ethan.]

JEEZER—[Je-e′-zer.]
Was of the sons of Gilead in the tribe of Manasseh, and the head of the family in that tribe called Jeezerites. Numb. xxvi: 30.

JEHDEIAH, 1—[Jeh-di′ah.]
Was one of the ministers in the temple, under the order of service instituted at the time of David. 1st Chron. xxiv: 20.

JEHDEIAH, 2.
The Meronothite, was placed by king David over the asses. 1st Chron. xxvii: 30.

JEHEZEKEL—[Je-hez′e-kel.]
Was one of the priests appointed by David when he divided them into twenty-four orders. His lot was the twentieth. 1st Chron. xxiv: 16.

JEHIEL, 1—[Je-hi′el.]
Was the son of Laadan, and a chief of the family. He, with his two brothers, Zetham and Joel, was over the treasures of the Lord's house. 1st Chron. xxiii: 8.

JEHIEL, 2.
Was the son of Hachmoni. He was an important man in David's kingdom, for he is said to have been with the king's sons. 1st Chronicles, xxvii: 32.

JEHOADDAN—[Je-ho-ad′den.]
Was the mother of Amaziah, a king of Judah, and the wife of Joash, the former king. We know nothing further of this woman, than that she was a daughter "of Jerusalem." 2d Kings xiv: 2, and 2d Chronicles xxv: 1.

JEHOAHAZ, 1—[Je-ho′-a-haz,] *the prize or possession of the Lord.*
He was the same as Ahaziah, the grand-son of Jehoshaphat. [See Ahaziah.]

JEHOAHAZ, 2—*The prize or possession of the Lord.*
JEHOAHAZ was the son of Jehu, king of Israel, and succeeded him on the throne. 2d Kings x: 35. He was very wicked, following the example of Jeroboam, the son of Nebat. The wickedness of this king was punished by the Lord, who gave him and his kingdom up to the fury of Hazael, the king of Syria, who conquered him and

greatly reduced the ten tribes. It is said that Jehoahaz, after he was conquered, had but ten chariots left him, and fifty horsemen, and ten thousand footmen, for the king of Syria had destroyed them, and had made them like the dust by threshing. 2d Kings xiii: 7. This king reigned seventeen years, when he died, and Joash reigned in his stead. It seems that Joash had been installed into the office of king two years before, but now that Jehoahaz was dead, he entered upon the sole government.

JEHOAHAZ, 3—*The prize or possession of the Lord.*

JEHOAHAZ, sometimes called Shallum, was the son of Josiah, a king of Judah. Jer. xxii: 11. He was not the eldest son of Josiah, but he was supposed by the people to be the fittest to govern in that critical time. Josiah had been wounded by Pharaoh-nechoh, king of Egypt, and died at Megiddo. 2d Kings xxiii: 30. But his reign as a king was short; only three months. Nechoh returning from Carchemish a conqueror, ordered Jehoahaz, whose promotion he did not approve of, to come to him at Riblah. Then he stripped him of his royal robes, loaded him with chains, and took him as a prisoner into Egypt, where he died. Jer. xxii: 11. And the king of Egypt placed Jehoiakim, or Eliakim, the oldest brother of Jehoahaz, on the throne in his stead. 2d Chron. xxxvi: 1–4.

JEHOASH—[See Joash.]

JEHOHANAN, 1—[Je-ho-ha′-nan.]

Was a Korhite Levite, one of the door-keepers of the house of the Lord, according to the appointment of David. 1st Chron. xxvi: 3.

JEHOHANAN, 2.

Was one of the princes of Judah, at the reign of Jehoshaphat. 2d Chron. xvii: 15.

JEHOHANAN, 3.

Was the father of Ishmael, one of the "captains of hundreds," whom the priest Jehoiada took into his confidence. 2d Chron. xxiii: 1.

JEHOHANAN, 4.

Was one of the Israelites who had taken a foreign wife during the captivity, and was forced by Ezra to put her away. Ezra x: 28.

JEHOHANAN, 5.

Was a priest who represented the house of Amariah in the time of Nehemiah. Neh. xii: 13.

JEHOHANAN, 6.

Was another priest of that name, who took part in the dedication of the walls of Jerusalem. Neh. xii: 42.

JEHOHANAN, 7.

Was the sixth son of Meshelemiah and one of the sacred porters. 1st Chron. xxvi: 3.

JEHOIADA—[Je-hoy′-a-dah] *knowledge of the Lord.*

JEHOIADA was the high-priest whose wife, Jehoshabeath, preserved the young prince Joash, from the murderous designs of Athaliah, who aimed to destroy all the seed royal. 2d Chron. xxii: 11. Jehoiada the high-priest, under the direction of God, gave commandment that Joash should be made king. They acted in concert with him notwithstanding Athaliah was then reigning. He succeeded in gathering together a large number of the nobles and captains, and in their presence he put the crown upon the head of young Joash, and anointed him, and they clapped their hands and said, "God save the king!" He then ordered the cruel Athaliah slain, and restored the worship of the true God. 2d Kings, xi: and 2d Chronicles, xxiii: 16.

We have an account of the death of Jehoiada, at the advanced age of one hundred and thirty years, after assisting Joash many years in his reign. He was a great and good man and was honored and lamented in his death. They honored him with a burial among the kings, in the city of David, and the reason given for this honor is, "he had done good in Israel toward God and toward his house." 2d Chronicles, xxiv. [See Joash.]

JEHOIAKIM or ELIAKIM—[Jehoy′-a-kim,] *the resurrection of the Lord.*

JEHOIAKIM or ELIAKIM was the elder son of Josiah. He was entitled in preference to other sons, to be his successor. He may have been taken prisoner by the King of Egypt when he conquered his father, while his younger brother was not a prisoner, which accounts for the people making him king. Jehoahaz was reigning, when Pharoah-nechoh returned to go to Egypt. He dethroned the younger brother, loaded him with irons and took him a prisoner to Egypt, but made Jehoiakim king and exacted of him a large tribute. 2d Kings, xxiii: 34. He raised the tribute required and paid it to the King of Egypt who had placed him on the throne, and had exacted it. He began to reign at the age of twenty-five years, and reigned eleven years. From the prophecy of Jeremiah that was made against Jehoiakim, it is inferred that he was very wicked. He oppressed his subjects in order to procure money to build himself a splendid palace, and he kept back a part of the hire of his workmen, and abandoned himself to cruelty and avarice. Jer. xxii: 13–23. He was a hater of the prophets of the Lord, especially of the prophet Jeremiah, and others who prophesied to him, and of him and his kingdom; who warned him to repent of his wickedness, and announced to him the judgments of the Almighty. Urijah was one of the prophets who was hated by Jehoiakim, and who fled into Egypt to save his life from the fury of the king. But he sent a troop of soldiers under Elnathan, the son of Achbor, to bring the fugitive prophet back, and they found him and brought him to the king, who slew him with the sword, and then cast his dead body into the graves of the common people. Jeremiah xxvi: 20–23.

In the beginning of the reign of this king, Jeremiah was commanded to make bonds and yokes and put them upon his neck—symbolic of the yoke that the king of Babylon would put upon the king and nations around him—including Israel and Judah. Jer. xxvii. And in the fourth year of the reign of Jehoiakim, a copy of Jeremiah's predictions were brought before him. He became enraged as they were being read by Jehudi the scribe—the king took the roll from his hand, and cut it with a penknife, and cast it into the fire, and then sent several of his servants to apprehend Jeremiah and Baruch his scribe. His intention was to put him to death as he had already put Urijah to death, but the Lord knowing his murderous designs, kept the prophet out of his hands. Jer. xxxvi: 26. Nebuchadnezzar, the king of Babylon, made himself master of Canaan—took Jehoiakim prisoner and carried him in chains to Babylon. The first time he took him he submitted to the terms of the king of Babylon, and was released and settled on his throne as a tributary, but three years afterwards when he was designing to break the yoke of the king of Babylon, he was detected and conquered, when Nebuchadnezzar took him and put him to death, and then cast his dead body into a common sewer, in the manner of the unburied carcass of an ass; as Jeremiah had prophesied, xxii: 19, "He shall be buried with the burial of an ass, drawn and cast forth beyond the gates of Jerusalem." This cruelty in the murder of Urijah the prophet, and burying him in a common grave, seems to be thus visited upon himself, as the king of Babylon puts him to death and buries his body in a common sewer. His death is recorded in 2d Chron. xxxvi; 2d Kings, xxiv. Thus the words of the prophetess Huldah are fulfilled, 2d Kings, xxii: 16. "I will bring evil upon this place and upon the inhabitants thereof, even all the words of the book." And the other prophecy was fulfilled, for Johoiakim had no son to reign as king after him. His kingdom was tributary, and the son who is said to have reigned after him three months, was not a king but a mere vassal to the Babylonians, "he shall have none to sit upon the throne of David, or rule any more in Judah." Jer. xxii: 30.

JEHOIARIB—[Je-hoy′-a-rib.]

Jehoiarib was the head of the first family of priests established by David. 1st Chronicles, xxiv: 7, and it has been considered that the illustrious family of the Maccabees, descended from Jehoiarib.

JEHONADAB—[Je-hon′-a-dab,] *who acts as a prince.*

Jehonadab was the son of Rechab. 2d Kings, x: 15; Jer. xxxvi. In the former passage we have an account of Jehu, the son of Nimshi meeting this important personage. Jehu was engaged in destroying the house of Ahab, and the progeny of the wicked and idolatrous Jezebel—and meeting Jehonadab he saluted him, and ascertained most certainly that he was with him in heart, in the prosecution of a reform in Israel, by the restoration of the worship of the true God and the destruction of the idolatry that had been encouraged and settled by the house of Ahab. He gave the reformer his hand, stepped up into his chariot and rode with him, thereby approving his course, and encouraging him in his work. The other reference is to the descendants of Jehonadab, when obedience to the command of their father was tried and proven. It was probably two hundred and fifty years before they were tested as set forth in the record of Jeremiah, xxxv, that Jehonadab lived and gave them the commandment that they should drink neither wine nor strong drink. He lived in the time of Jehu the reformer, and Jeremiah, in the time of Jehoiakim. He required his children to abide by the customs of their fathers, as to living in tents, cultivating the ground, and the vine. They scrupulously observed his commands—and would not swerve even under the trial that Jeremiah used; and because of their faithfulness God promised that "Jehonadab the son of Rechab should not want a man to stand before him forever."

JEHORAM—[See Joram.]

JEHONATHAN—[Je-hon′-a-than.]

JEHONATHAN the son of Uzziah, was placed by King David over his storehouses in the fields, cities, villages and castles. 1st Chron. xxvii: 25.

JEHOSHAPHAT—[Je-hosh′a-fat,] *God judges.*

JEHOSHAPHAT was a king of Judah, the son and successor of Asa. His mother's name was Azubah, the daughter of Shilhi. 1st Kings, xv: 24; 2d Chron. xvii: 1. He was thirty-five years of age when he ascended the throne, and he reigned twenty-five years. To strengthen himself against the kingdom of Israel, he placed strong forces in all the cities that Asa, his father, had taken from the children of Ephraim. His riches and his honor increased as a king of Judah, until he became very great. 2d Chron. xvii: 12. "And Jehoshaphat waxed great exceedingly, and he built in Judah castles and cities of stone."

In the third year of his reign he ordered the priests and Levites to go through his kingdom and teach the people the law of the Lord. The zeal he manifested in the ways of the Lord was rewarded, for God made the nations around him to respect and revere him and his kingdom; and some of them brought him presents and tribute—silver and flocks.

He had a very large army—his enrolled militia numbered one million, one hundred and sixty thousand, and he had five generals in command under him. Their names are given in 2d Chron. xvii: 14–18, viz.: Adnah, Jehohanan, Amasiah, Eliada, and Jehozabad. These generals are all represented as men of great valor, with large numbers of soldiers under them.

Jehoshaphat, in his prosperity and greatness, formed an alliance with Ahab, the king of Israel, for which the Scriptures reproach him. He married his son, Jehoram, to Athaliah, the daughter of Ahab. As Ahab and his house were idolatrous, this affinity led him and his family to too great intimacy with that which was evil.

He helped Ahab to retake Ramoth-gilead from the Syrians, and came very near losing his life on account of the treachery and meanness of Ahab, who arranged it to place him in imminent danger. He went into the battle in his robe, and the Syrians took him to be Ahab, and was about to kill him. When he found that he was sorely pressed, he cried out, and they, discovering their mistake, permitted him to escape, while the king of Israel was followed up and slain. 2d Chron. xviii: 33. Jehoshaphat then returned to Jerusalem in peace, when he was accosted by Jehu, the son of Hanani, a prophet, and sharply rebuked for entering into the alliance and helping so wicked a king as Ahab. He was assured by the prophet that the anger of the Lord was against him, and his family and kingdom. He seems to have been properly exercised under the reproof given him, and set himself to work with the greatest care and earnestness to repair the injury he had done, by good regulations and the good order which he established in his dominions, both with regard to civil and religious matters. He appointed honest and able judges, regulated the discipline of the priests and Levites, and required them to be punctual and faithful in the observance of their duties. The Sodomites were removed.

About the time he had completed this reformation, he was informed that there was an alliance of several nations against him, the Edomites, Ishmaelites, Haggerites, Giblites, Moabites, Ammonites, Amalakites, Philistines, Tyrians and Ashurites, and he was informed that a part of them were already advanced to Hazazon-tamar, which was only about thirty-eight miles from Jerusalem. He went immediately to the temple, and put up prayers to God in company with his people. He proclaimed a fast throughout all Judah. The Lord looked with favor upon his humility, and expressions of need of divine help, and answered his prayer. By the mouth of Jahaziel he said to the king, "Be not afraid nor dismayed by reason of this multitude, for the battle is not yours, but God's." The king was assured that on the morrow, they should have a victory, and that the victory should be secured on their part without hard fighting, for the Lord should make them to "rejoice over their enemies." And so they did, for the king and people of Judah beheld the dead bodies of their fallen foes, and for three days they were engaged in taking the spoil, consisting of much riches and precious jewels, and the fourth day they assembled in Berachah, and prepared to return in triumph to Jerusalem. [See 2d Chron. xx.]

A few months after this, Jehoshaphat sinned against God again by forming an alliance with the wicked Ahaziah, the elder son of Ahab. He joined his fleet with that of the king of Israel to go to Tarshish. With this the Lord was displeased, and Eleazar was commissioned to prophesy against him saying, "Because thou hast joined thyself with Ahaziah, the Lord hath broken the works." The consequence was, the whole fleet was wrecked or dashed to pieces by a storm, at or before Ezion-geber. 2d Chron. xx: 35.

We have an account in 2d Kings, iii, of Jehoshaphat being associated with the second son of Ahab, in warring with the Moabites. The two kings traveled in the wilderness of Edom for seven days, and they suffered greatly for water. Jehoshaphat became alarmed, and enquired if there was not a prophet of the Lord there, by whom they might enquire of the Lord in their extremity. He was answered that Elisha, the son of Shaphat was there. Jehoram and Jehoshaphat went down to see him, and enquire of the Lord by him. Elisha seemed to have strong regards for the King of Judah, and moved by these regards, gave attention to Jehoram. He prophesied that there should be a miraculous supply of water in that valley. And in the morning after, the ditches in the valley had been filled with water. The appearance of the water to the Moabites, which was as though it had been mixed with blood, induced them to go up at once against Israel. They thought, from the appearance of the water, that there had been a great slaughter, and rushed along into the valley to take the spoils. But the Israelites rose up against them, and smote them.

Jehoshaphat died after a reign of twenty-five years, and was buried with his fathers, in the city of David, and Jehoram, his son, reigned in his stead. He had several other sons, whose names are given in 2d Chron. xxi: 2, to all of whom he gave large portions. He gave them silver and gold, and precious things, and fenced cities. It was but a little while until Jehoram, his eldest son, slew all his brothers.

The Lord thus visited with vengeance the house of Jehoshaphat for his sin in forming alliance with the idolatrous family of Ahab.

### JEHOSHEBA—[Je-hosh′-e-bah.]

Jehosheba was the daughter of king Joram, and the sister of Ahaziah. She took Joash, the son of Ahaziah, and secreted him from the infamous and wicked Athaliah, who attempted to slay the last of the royal family. She kept him hid for six years from that cruel queen, who reigned that length of time over the land. 2d Kings, xi: 1-3. She is called Jehoshabeath in 2d Chron. xxii: 11.

JEHOVAH—[Je-ho′-vah,] *the incommunicable name of God, self-existing.*

JEHOVAH is the proper and incommunicable name of the *divine essence.* God revealed himself to Moses by this name when he called him to the work of emancipating his down-trodden and enslaved people. "He spake unto Moses, saying, I am the Lord; and I appeared unto Abraham, unto Isaac, and Jacob, by the name of God Almighty; but by my name Jehovah was I not known to them." The Jews had so great a veneration for this name that they called it the ineffable name. They had such superstitious regards for it, after their captivity in Babylon, that they left off pronouncing it and lost its proper pronunciation. Whenever the name Jehovah is given to an angel, it is to the covenant angel—he who appeared in the office, though not in the nature of an angel. For the Lord Jesus Christ of the New Testament was the Jehovah of the Old; and, as saith the prophet Isaiah: "In all their afflictions He was afflicted, and the angel of His presence saved them. In His love and in His pity He bare them, and He carried them all the days of old." He was with Moses, and spoke to him from out the flame of fire; in the pillar of cloud and fire from Egypt to Canaan, &c.

JEHOZABAD, 1—[Je-hoz′a-bad,]

Was the second son of Obed-edom, and one of the sacred porters. 1st Chron. xxvi: 4.

JEHOZABAD, 2.

Was the son of Shomer. He was one of the murderers of King Joash in the house of Millo. 2d Kings, xii: 21.

JEHOZADAK—[Je-hoz′a-dak,]

Was of the tribe of Levi, and in the line of the priests from Aaron to the captivity. 1st Chron. vi: 15.

JEHU, 1—*He that is, or exists.*

JEHU was said to be the son of Nimshi; yet he was the son of Jehoshaphat and the grandson of Nimshi, and he was captain of the army of Jehoram or Joram, king of Israel. When Elijah received the commission to anoint Jehu king, he is called the son of Nimshi. 1st Kings, xix: 16; but when Elisha was sent to execute this commission several years after, he is called the son of Jehoshaphat, the son of Nimshi. 2d Kings, ix: 2. The prophet came to Jehu to anoint him king while he was commanding the army of Jehoram at Ramoth-gilead, the king himself being absent. Elisha did not go in person to Ramoth-gilead on this important errand, but he sent a young prophet, who, when he reached the camp, called Jehu aside and poured oil upon his head, and said unto him, "Thus saith the Lord God of Israel, I have anointed thee to be king over the people of the Lord, even over Israel." He then told Jehu what the Lord had determined concerning the house of Ahab, and the descendants of Jezebel. After the young prophet had thus commissioned him, he retired from the camp and fled to his home that he might not be known. When Jehu returned to the officers from whom he had been called away, they asked him who the man was, and what was his errand. He informed them that it was a prophet, and that the prophet had declared him king and anointed him. They at once acknowledged that it was from the Lord, and blew the trumpet, saying, "Jehu is king." He entered at once on the conspiracy against the king Joram; and he gave orders to all the officers and soldiers to stay in camp and carry no tidings to Jezreel, and he himself made ready and went there to surprise Joram, who had been for some time in a state of indisposition, owing to wounds that he had received in the seige of Ramoth-gilead.

When Joram heard that Jehu was coming, not suspecting any intentions against him, he sent a messenger to meet him and ask him if all was well with the army. Jehu ordered the messenger to join his company without giving him a satisfactory answer. Soon another messenger came up, and he ordered him as he had ordered the former, to join his company. Joram may not have known certainly, when he dispatched his messengers, who it was that was coming to him from the army; but as he observed the furious driving of the chariot, he supposed it was his general; and in company with Ahaziah, the king of Judah, who was visiting him at the time, he set out in his chariot to meet Jehu. As they came within speaking distance he asked him if all things were well and peaceful in the army. His answer astounded the king Joram: "How can there be peace so long as the whoredoms of thy mother, Jezebel, and her witchcrafts, are so many!" Joram had only time to turn to Ahaziah and say, "We are betrayed!" when an arrow from the bow of Jehu smote him between his shoulders and pierced his vitals, so that he died in his chariot instantly. Jehu then gave orders to Bidkar, his captain, to take up his lifeless form and cast it into the field of Naboth, the Jezreelite, thus fulfilling the prediction of the prophet Elijah. He then ordered the company that was with him to follow the king of Judah, who was fleeing for his life, and slay him also; and they did, wounding him mortally, and a little while after he died at Megiddo.

Jehu having smitten the kings of Israel and Judah, went on to Jezreel to carry out the purpose of God expressed in his commission—the entire destruction of the house of Ahab. As he rode to Jezreel, Jezebel, who had painted her face and attired herself in gorgeous apparel, looked out at a window and saw him, and then addressed him, in substance as follows: "Had Zimri much prosperity, who slew his master? or can he who has slain his master hope for peace?" Jehu, looking up to the window, asked if there was any one in the apartment where she was that favored him and his cause. Two or three eunuchs looked out and answered affirmatively. He then bade them throw her out of the window, which they did, and she was trampled upon by the horses of Jehu's company. And then, to complete the matter as to her destruction and fulfill the threats of the prophet, the dogs came and devoured her body, so that when Jehu gave orders to bury her, nothing could be found but some of the principal bones. 2d Kings, ix.

Jehu then sent to Samaria, the capital of the kingdom of Israel, and asked the inhabitants which one of Ahab's seventy children they would place upon the throne of Israel. They informed him that they were his servants, and would in all things obey him. He then told them to put all the children of their former king to death, and bring him, as evidence that they had done this, the head of each one of the sons of Ahab. They accordingly put them all to death, and the next day the heads were sent into his presence. He then put to death all the relatives and special friends of Ahab, with the officers of court and the priests at Jezreel. Having done this, Jehu proceeded to Samaria in person, and, on his way, he met the friends of Ahaziah, king of Judah, going to Jezreel to salute the sons of the fallen king of Israel, who were unacquainted with the scenes that had transpired. Jehu asked them who they were, and whither they were going. They told him, when he apprehended them and put them all to death. There were forty-two of them. And meeting Jehonadab, the son of Rechab, he took him up into his chariot and told him what he had already done, and what he would yet do; and, wishing him to be an eyewitness of his zeal for the Lord of Hosts, he took him with him to Samaria, when he slew all that remained of Ahab's family, not sparing a single individual.

He then called together the people of Samaria, and proposed to them to honor Baal with a very solemn festival. He ordered all the priests, ministers and prophets of Baal, to come together from all parts of the kingdom, and worship in the temple of Baal, and there was to be no worshipers of the Hebrew God among them. When they were all thus together, he ordered his guards to fall upon them in their temple, and slay them, not allowing a single man to escape. He then broke down the image of Baal, demolished the temple, and reduced the site of the temple to a dunghill.

To reward Jehu for his faithfulness in cutting off the idolatrous house of Ahab, and destroying Baal, and his worship in the kingdom of Israel, God promised him that his seed should inherit the throne and crown of the ten tribes to the fourth generation. [See 2d Kings, x.]

Though Jehu had been the instrument in the hands of God in taking vengeance on the wicked house of Ahab, yet he is accused of not entirely forsaking the sins of Jeroboam, the son of Nebat, who made Israel to sin in worshiping the golden calves. It also appears that in executing the divine purpose and indignation, he was actuated by improper feelings, and motives at times. 2d Kings x: 31.

He reigned twenty-eight years over Israel, and when he died, was succeeded by his son Jehoahaz. But the reign of this son was made unpleasant because of the war that was carried on by Hazael, king of Syria. This was commenced in the time of Jehu, but it was continued for many years and Israel was "cut short" by it. His four descendants who followed him on the throne of Israel, were Jehoahaz, Joash 2d, and Zechariah.

JEHU, 2.—*He that is, or exists.*

There was a prophet of this name, called the son of Hanani, who rebuked Baasha, the king of Israel, for his wickedness in walking in the way of Jeroboam, and leading Israel into gross sins. 1st Kings, xvi: 1. And the same prophet rebuked Jehoshaphat, the king of Judah, because he had helped them that hate the Lord and were ungodly, though he had done many good things. 2d Chron. xix: 2–3. [See also Baasha and Jehoshaphat.]

JEHUDI—[Je-hu′-di.]

Jehudi was the son of Nethaniah, and the grandson of Shelemiah. He was sent by the princes of Jehoiakim to Baruch, after the roll of Jeremiah. that contained declarations against the king. When the contents of the roll were reported to the king, Jehudi was required to produce it, and read it in his ears. He did so, and the king being enraged, took it from him in the midst of the reading, and cut it with a penknife, then threw it into fire and it was consumed. And Jehudi was not allowed to read it all. Jer. xxxvi.

JEHUDIJAH—[Je-hu-di′-jah,] *praise of the Lord.*

This name occurs in the second genealogy of Judah, and is thought to be a name (recorded) of Moses's mother, while Jered, whom she bare, is thought to be a name of Moses. She is represented as the wife of Eshtemoa. 1st Chronicles, iv: 18.

JEIEL, 1—[Je-i′-el.]

Jeiel was a Reubenite, of the house of Joel, referred to in 1st Chron. v: 7.

JEIEL, 2.

Jeiel was a Merarite Levite, one of the guards, or gate-keepers to the sacred tent. 1st Chron. xv: 18. A part of his duty was to play on the harp, or the psaltry, in the service of the tabernacle. 1st Chronicles, xv: 18, and xvi: 5.

JEIEL, 3.

Jeiel was a principal Gershonite Levite, in the time of Jehoshaphat. 1st Chron. xv: 20.

JEIEL, 4.

Jeiel was the scribe who kept the account of the numbers and names of king Uzziah's irregular warriors. 2d Chron. xxvi: 11.

JEIEL, 5.

Jeiel was one of the chiefs of the Levites in the time of king Josiah. 2d Chron. xxxv: 9.

JEIEL, 6.

Jeiel was one of those who formed a part of Ezra's company from Babylon, Ezra, viii: 13, and is probably the same person referred to in Ezra, x: 43, who had taken a foreign wife.

JEKAMEAM—[Jek-a-me′-am.]

Jekameam was a Levite, in the time of king David the fourth, of the sons of Hebron, the son of Kohath. 1st Chron. xxiii: 19, and xxiv: 23.

JEKAMIAH—[Jek-a-mi′-ah.]

Jekamiah was the son of Shallum, in the line of Ahlai. 1st Chron. ii: 41.

JEKUTHIEL—[Je-ku′-thi-el.]

Jekuthiel was one of the tribe of Judah, referred to in the genealogy, as the son of Ezra, or Mesed, by his Jewish wife. 1st Chron. iv: 18.

JEMIMA—[Je-mi′-mah,] *handsome as the day.*

JEMIMA was the eldest daughter of the man of Uz. Job had been severely afflicted in the loss of his property, servants and children, as recorded in the first chapter of the book of Job. He had also been sorely afflicted in the body, and his wife had turned against him; while pretended friends had brought the gravest charges against his moral and religious character. But God justified him, and made the evening of his life prosperous and happy. In his old age, sons and daughters were born unto him. Jemima, with her two sisters, Kezia and Keren-happuch, were exceedingly fair—more handsome than all the women of the land. Job, xlii: 15.

JEMUEL—[Jem′-u-el.]

JEMUEL was the son of Simeon, and is referred to in Genesis, xlvi: 10. As he is ranked first, he was probably the eldest son. The same person is called, in 1st Chron. iv: 24, Nemuel.

JEPHTHAH—[Jef′-thah,] *he that opens.*

JEPHTHAH was one of the judges of Israel. He was the successor of Jair, and the son of Gilead by a concubine. Judges, xi: 1, 2. His father had several other children by his lawful wife, and those children expelled him from the family, because he was the son of a strange woman, for they insisted that such a child was not to inherit with lawful children. Like Ishmael the son of Abraham, who was disinherited, Jephthah withdrew from the family. He retired into the land of Tob, where he became the chief of a band of robbers, or a marauding party who subsisted mainly by plunder. They were persons without property and employment, and profligate in their manners. It seems that the Hebrews on the east of the Jordan had been for a long time oppressed by the Ammonites, and knowing that he was a valorous man they insisted that he would espouse their cause, and as a captain lead them against their enemy. He at first reproached them for the manner in which he had been treated—the injustice that had been done him in expelling him from his father's house. They repeated their entreaties and he yielded to them, and became their leader, on the condition that if he was successful in an expedition against the Ammonites and delivered them, they would acknowledge him as their chief. They agreed to the proposal, and in the most solemn manner pledged themselves at the end of the war to make him their judge. "The Lord be witness between us, if we do not so according to thy words." Judges, xi: 10.

As soon as Jephthah had thus obtained the command of the Israelites, he sent a deputation to the enemy to know why they had taken up arms against them. They answered that it was to retake the territory which the Israelites took from them when they first came out of the land of Egypt, and through the deputation they made the demand of Jephthah: "Now therefore restore those lands again peaceably." Jephthah told them that the Israelites were not in possession of any land except that which the Lord their God had given them, and he used the following mode of reasoning with them: "Wilt thou possess that which Chemosh thy God giveth thee to possess? So will *we* possess that which the Lord our God gives us." As though he had said, you will not relinquish what you may consider as a nation you hold by divine right, or by commandment of your God, so we will not relinquish our right that our God has given us; therefore, if you will not let us alone we will decide the matter by the sword.

The Ammonites despised Jephthah and his reasonings and expostulations, and he at once proceeded to raise an army for the purpose of conquering them. While collecting his troops together, and preparing them for the contest, the spirit of the Lord came upon him and animated him with courage, and inspired him with a spirit of reliance and implicit confidence in the God of the armies of Israel. Judges, xi: 17; Heb. xi: 32. And in the midst of his preparations he made a vow to the Lord. "If thou wilt without fail, deliver the children of Ammon into mine hands, then it shall be that whatsoever cometh forth of the doors of my house to meet me, when I return in peace from the children of Ammon, shall surely be the Lord's, and I will offer it up for a burnt offering." The contending armies met upon the battlefield, and Jephthah conquered, and his army ravaged the whole country. He returned home and his only daughter met him with her maidens, with timbrels and dances to celebrate his victory. At the sight of her, he was greatly troubled, and at once told her the reason of this trouble. She consented to be made a sacrifice, after bewailing her virginity for two months. At the expiration of that time, the vow was consummated, which in all probability, simply involved a celibacy to which she was devoted. And it is said, "That the daughters of Israel went yearly to lament the daughter of Jepthah, the Gileadite, four days in the year." As long as she lived, they went from year to year to talk with and comfort her.

The men of Ephraim became enraged at him because he did not call on them to help when he fought with the children of Ammon, and in their jealousy, they determined to arm themselves, and destroy him with the Gileadites. He vindicates himself, but they were still dissatisfied, and in order to defend himself, he armed the Gileadites against the Ephraimites, and fought against them and conquered them. It is supposed they had two battles, and the latter was occasioned by the taunting language of the Ephraimites to the Gileadites after the first victory. "Ye Gileadites are fugitives of Ephraim." Jephthah and his army took the passages of the Jordan, and as the Ephraimites attempted to cross, they were detected by their dialect. They pronounced Shibboleth, Sibboleth, and as they were detected, they were slain in great numbers. Jud. xii: 6. "There fell at that time, of the Ephraimites, forty-two thousand."

After Jephthah had judged Israel six years, during which time they had peace, which for thirty years after his death continued under his successors, he died and was buried in Gilead.

JEPHUNNEH—[Je-fun′-neh,] *he that beholds.*

Jephunneh was of the tribe of Judah, and the father of Caleb, who with Joshua, brought back a good report of the promised land. Numb. xiii: 6.

JERAH—[Je‵-rah,] *the moon, to scent or smell.*

He was the son of Joktan, and the grandson of Eber, and is referred to in the posterity of Shem. Gen. x: 26.

JERAHMEEL—[Je-rah-me′-el] *the mercy or love of God.*

He was one of the ministers in the temple under the order of service instituted in the time of David. 1st Chron. xxiv: 29.

JEREMIAH—[Jer-e-mi′-ah,] *the grandeur of the Lord.*

Jeremiah was a prophet of the Lord of the sacerdotal race. He was the son of Hilkiah, who was a priest, probably of the line of Ithamar. He was a native of Anathoth, and resided in that city, which was about three miles north of Jerusalem. From his commission to prophesy, as set forth in Jer. i, we may gather that he was very young when called. He calls himself a child and begs to be excused, on account of his age, from entering upon the office. But young as he was, the Lord promised to be with him and give him boldness in the presence of the wicked against whom he should prophesy. His boldness in opposing the wickedness of the kings, princes, and people of Judah, is represented by a brazen wall.

Jeremiah began to prophesy in the thirteenth year of Josiah. We have an account, in 2d Chron. xxxv; 25, of his lamenting over king Josiah when he died, and all the chiefs and matrons joined him in the lamentation, and the day was set apart and annually commemorated in Israel.

Jeremiah was directed to prophesy in the gates of Jerusalem in the presence of the king and the people, and urge them to an observance of the Sabbath day. They had probably violated that command and the Lord was angry with them, and now the prophet is commissioned to say to them: "Take heed to yourselves, and bear no burden on the Sabbath day; nor bring it in by the gates of Jerusalem; neither carry forth a burden out of your houses on the Sabbath day; neither do ye any work, but hallow ye the Sabbath as I commanded your fathers." Jer. xvii: 21, 22.

He prophesied faithfully as God commanded him; but he complains that he was not received, and that his messages were rejected. Jer. xx: 7: "I am in derision daily; every one mocketh me."

He was applied to by the king, to enquire of the Lord for him as to the result of Nebuchadnezzar's war against him. He did enquire, and gave the word of the Lord to the king of Judah, in which he advised him to yield to the king of Babylon; and the prophet foretold a dreadful siege through which the kingdom was to pass on account of the sins of the people. Jer. xxi. He reproves the Jews for their disobedience to God, and foretells the Babylonish captivity that was to last seventy years. Jer. xxv.

Because of the faithful manner in which Jeremiah declared the word of the Lord and uttered reproofs against them, they apprehended him, and some of them were determined to put him to death. But in this they did not succeed, for he was acquitted. Jer. xxvi: 16.

It was about the beginning of the reign of Jehoiakim that Jeremiah foretold that the kingdom of Judah and the city of Jerusalem should be rendered a desolation. Pashur, the son of Immer, the priest, who was the chief governor of the temple, was enraged at the prophet, and smote him, and put him in the stocks that were in the high-gate of Benjamin, which was by the house of the Lord. Jer. xx: 1. The prophet assured his persecutor that he would be punished in his person, and that he and his family, with other Jews, should be carried into captivity: and, further, that he should die a captive and be buried in the land of Babylon.

Jeremiah seems to feel very sorely his persecutions and trials, and he indulges in bitter complaints. He even curses the day of his birth. "Cursed be the day wherein I was born, let not the day wherein my mother bare me be blessed. Cursed be the man who brought tidings to my father, saying: A man child is born unto thee, making him very glad."

He prophesied calamities that should come upon the various nations called Egyptians, Philistines, Phœnicians, Edomites, Arabians, Moabites, Ammonites, Syrians and Persians, as well as upon the Jews. And that Nebuchadnezzar should be the instrument under God to punish them. Jeremiah xxv: 8–38.

It was in the beginning of the reign of Jehoiakim, the son of Josiah, that the prophet Jeremiah made yokes of wood to be sent to several nations by embassadors, as a token of their servitude to Nebuchadnezzar, the King of Babylon, and his successors Evil Merodach and Belshazzar. Jer. xxvii: 6, 7. In the fourth year of the reign of Jehoiakim, the prophet Jeremiah predicted terrible calamities that should come upon the nations of whom he had prophesied that they should be servants to Nebuchadnezzar, and he reproved the Jews, his own nation, for their disobedience and wickedness in abusing the servants of the Lord, and refusing to incline their ears to their words, and foretold clearly the seventy years captivity. Jer. xxv. It was during this same year that Jeremiah caused his scribe to write out a copy of all his prophecies, and present them unto the people on the day of a fast appointed by Jehoiakim. The object of Jeremiah was to lead the people to repentance. Baruch accordingly wrote the prophesies, and the fast being in the ninth month of the fifth year of the reign of the king, as the people gathered together from all the cities of Judah to Jerusalem and to the house of the Lord, Baruch read it unto them in the chamber of Gemariah the son of Shaphan the scribe, and as Michaiah heard it, he went at once and reported it to the princes and great men of the nation in the king's house. They sent Jehudi, a servant of King Jehoiakim to Baruch to come unto them with the roll and read it in their ear, and they were afraid for their king and nation, because of the prophecies against them, and said one to another, "we will surely tell the king all these words." And they asked Baruch how he wrote all these words, he told them that Jeremiah pronounced them, and he wrote them down with ink as the prophet pronounced them. They then went into the king and reported the words of this prophecy, and the king sent Jehudi to fetch the roll and read it in his ears in the presence of his courtiers, and Jehudi brought it and began to read it in the ears of the king. He had but read three or four leaves, when Jehoiakim stopped him, and taking it from him, mutilated the roll by cutting it with a pen-knife, after which he threw it into the fire that was burning on the hearth, and it was consumed. He then issued orders that Jeremiah and his scribe should be taken and put to death, but the Lord hid them, and Jehoiakim could not find them. His servants sought them in vain. Jeremiah then received commandment from the Lord to prepare another roll, and write in it, all the prophecies that were in the former, and then to add other predictions regarding the unhappy death of Jehoiakim, and that he should have no son to sit upon the throne of David, and that his dead body should be cast out in dishonor. Jer. xxxvi:

Jeremiah, during the reign of this king, was appointed of God to try the fidelity of the Rechabites to the command of Jonadab, their father, which was, "Ye shall drink no wine, ye nor your sons, forever," &c. He accordingly set pots of wine before them, and cups, and invited them to drink, but they would not. The prophet approved of their obedience, and declared that it should be rewarded, by Jonadab, the son of Rechab, having representatives to stand before God in all future time.

In the beginning of the reign of Zedekiah, the successor of Jehoiakim, the prophet Jeremiah placed a yoke upon his own neck and wore it with a chain, to signify the slavery of the Jews; and he advised the king to submit to the authority and bondage of the king of Babylon as a means of preventing ruin. His teaching at this time was interfered with by a false prophet named Hannaniah, who approached him and broke the yoke that was upon his neck; and as he did this, he told the people present that the Lord would in two years break the bondage of the nations subject to the Babylonians. Jeremiah charged Hananiah with false teaching, and assured him that he should be punished with death that very year. Jer. xxvii and xxviii.

Jeremiah about this time had his vision of two baskets of figs—the one good and the other bad,—by which he represented the piety and devotion to God of many captive Jews in Babylon, and the wickedness of many who remained in Jerusalem. Jer. xxiv. He sympathized with the pious captives, and sent them a letter containing advice as to their conduct. He urged them to cultivate lands and build houses, and marry wives and enjoy the endearments of the home-circle, so far as it was possible for them as captives, and to pray for the peace of the country in which they were captives; for that the bondage was to continue seventy years, when it should end, and they should be delivered. He declared a terrible death to be awaiting the two false prophets, Ahab and Zedekiah.

This letter of the prophet to the captives produced a sensation, especially with Shemaiah, a dreamer, who informed Zephaniah, the priest, by letter at Jerusalem, and he begged that Jeremiah might be put in the stocks as a madman. The letter was read in the hearing of the prophet, when he declared the coming ruin of Shemaiah and his family. Jer. xxix. This same priest who was applied to, was twice sent, by king Zedekiah, to Jeremiah to beg his prayers in behalf of the kingdom. See Jer. xxi and xxxvii. He boldly warned King Zedekiah of the destruction awaiting the kingdom for the wickedness of the people.

At length the Chaldeans fought with the Egyptians, and in making ready for it they raised the seige of Jerusalem. Many of the inhabitants thought they would gain advantage thereby, but the prophet told them in this they were mistaken; for the Chaldeans would certainly take their city and burn it with fire.

About this time Jeremiah was apprehended by Irijah the son of Shelemiah, who had been imprisoned in a dungeon. King Zedekiah sent for him, to ask him *secretly* for the word of the Lord regarding himself as the king of Judah. He assured him that he should fall into the hands of the king of Babylon. And he begged Zedekiah not to return him to his dungeon, as he had given no offence—either against him, or his princes, or his people. The king attended to his petition, and did not return him to the dungeon, but bade his keepers to remand him to the court of the prison and feed him every day with bread.

from the baker's street. Jer. xxxvii: But there were some of the princes that were very greatly offended at Jeremiah's faithful predictions, and they begged the king to put him to death. Zedekiah accordingly gave him into their hands to do with him as they pleased, and they threw him into a filthy dungeon, or rather let him down with cords and he sunk in the mire that was in the bottom of the dungeon.

It was not long until Ebed-melech, a servant of the king interested himself in the behalf of Jeremiah, and prayed Zedekiah to release him. He accordingly gave him orders to take thirty men and go to the prophet and draw him up from the dungeon; he did so and placed Jeremiah again in the court of the prison and had food allowed him every day. The king then sought a private interview with the prophet, and pledged himself to Jeremiah that he should not die for speaking the truth to him. He then told him if he would go forth and surrender himself fully to the king of Babylon, he should live and the city should not be burned with fire, but if he did not, then the city should be taken and burned, and he himself should fall into their hands. Jeremiah xxxviii.

It was probably about this time that Jeremiah foretold the return of the Jews from their mournful captivity, and he bought a piece of ground from Hanameel his cousin, and had the writings drawn and his claim clearly certified unto. He subscribed the evidence and sealed it, and in the presence of witnesses weighed the money and gave it unto the former owner of the field. Jer. xxxii: 6, 12. This is the first instance in which we find written instruments used in such transactions. There seems to have been a deed and a duplicate, and the one that was signed and sealed in the presence of witnesses was carefully preserved in an earthen vessel, as a token that his seed should return from Babylon and possess it.

When Jerusalem was taken, Jeremiah was released from his prison, and under the direction of Nebuchadnezzar the captain of the guard gave him the choice of going to Chaldea, and being well provided for there, or remaining in Jerusalem with him who was the governor, viz, Gedaliah. He preferred to stay, and no doubt was the fast friend of Gedaliah, until he was murdered by Ishmael and his associates. Jer. xli: 2.

One of the friends of Gedaliah, Johanan, the son of Kareah, who had advised the governor of his danger, and of the intentions of Ishmael, asked the prophet to consult the Lord as to what they should do; and he did so, and gave them the result. Jeremiah xlii. They charged the prophet with prophesying falsely, and would not follow his instructions, but went and took Jeremiah and Baruch, his scribe, with them into the land of Egypt, and in that country he prophesied.

It is not known when Jeremiah closed his days, or in what manner he died, but it is evident that he prophesied a little over forty years, during the latter part of the reign of Josiah, and through the reign of Jeconiah, Jehoiakim and Zedekiah, and while Gedaliah was governor under an appointment of the king of Babylon, and still later in the land of Egypt whither he was taken by Johanan.

Jeremiah was the author of the book of the Lamentations, as also of the prophecies of the book of Jeremiah. The Lamentations were composed on the destruction of Jerusalem. He sets forth the miseries of the seige, his own personal and particular afflictions, with the ruins of the beautiful temple and city, and the miseries and hardships of all the people, and his language is exceedingly pathetic. It seems to be the language of a heart overcharged with sorrow, and yet seeking for ease in mourning and tears. He has been called the weeping prophet, and no wonder, when he expresses himself in such language as the following: Jeremiah ix: 1, 2, "Oh that my head were waters, and mine eyes a fountain of tears, that I might weep day and night for the slain of the daughter of my people, &c." And again, Lamentations, i: 12, "Is it nothing to you, all ye that pass by; behold and see if there be any sorrow like unto my sorrow which is done unto me, &c." He breathes in sighs, and speaks in groans.

We may say of Jeremiah, in the course of his ministry, he met with many difficulties, and had much opposition and hard treatment from his own people; but he retained his own integrity. He was, in truth, a man of unblemished piety, a true patriot and philanthropist.

JERIAH—[Je-ri'-ah.]

JERIAH was one of the ministers in the temple, under the order of service instituted in the time of David. 1st Chron. xxiv: 23.

JERIMOTH, 1—[Je-ri'-moth.]

JERIMOTH was one of the sons of David, and the father of Mahalath, the wife of Rehoboam. 2d Chronicles, xi: 18.

JERIMOTH, 2.

JERIMOTH was one of the sons of Heman, and when the lots were cast, and the singers were divided into twenty-four courses, the fifteenth lot came to him. 1st Chronicles, xxv: 22.

JERIMOTH, 3.

JERIMOTH, the son of Azriel, was a ruler in the tribe of Naphtali, in the time of David. 1st Chronicles xxvii: 19. He may be the same person (of that name) referred to in 1st Chronicles, xxiv: 30, who was a minister in the temple, under the order of service instituted in the time of David.

JEROBOAM, 1—[Jer-o-bo'-am,] *fighting against, increasing the people.*

JEROBOAM was the son of Nebat and Zeruah. When King Solomon saw that he was a daring, bold, enterprising youth of the tribe of Ephraim he made him ruler over the house of Joseph, the tribes of Ephraim and Manasseh. We understand that he was appointed to levy the tax for those tribes. See 1st Kings xi: 26, 28. As he left the city of Jerusalem for the purpose of filling his appointment, he was met by Ahijah the prophet, who set forth the future of Jeroboam, and of the kingdom of Israel, by rending a new garment into twelve pieces, and giving ten of the pieces to him. The prophet told him that he should be made king over ten of the Hebrew tribes. Jeroboam accordingly began to set himself about preparing for a revolt. He was detected in his preparations and Solomon issued orders to apprehend him. He saved himself by a flight into Egypt where he formed an alliance with Shishak, the king of Egypt, who was an enemy to Solomon, and he remained there until the king's death. 1st Kings, 11. Rehoboam was the successor of Solomon on the throne of Israel. No sooner had Jeroboam heard of the death of Solomon than he left Egypt and returned to the land of Israel. Being recognized by his former friends, at their request he went into the presence of the king to represent them and their cause. They had suffered oppression from very heavy taxes under King Solomon, and desired to have them lightened. Jeroboam said to Rehoboam: "Thy father made our yoke grievous, now therefore, make thou the grievous service of thy father, and his heavy yoke which he put upon us lighter, and we will serve thee." The king counseled with the old men who advised him to do so, but he afterwards counseled the young men and they advised contrary, and he forsook the counsel of the old men, and followed that of the young men. The people of Israel were enraged at the foolish answer that Rehoboam gave to their petition, *viz.*, "My little finger shall be thicker than my father's loins—my father chastized you with whips, I will chastize you with scorpions," and they revolted and made Jeroboam their king. After he was made king he fortified Shechem the place where he was crowned and rebuilt Penuel. The God who had selected Jeroboam to be king had promised him that the kingdom of Israel should be established in him and his offspring, if he walked in the ways of David. But he did not; scarcely was he settled on the throne until he disregarded the terms on which he was to keep it. He saw some of his subjects in their devotion to God going up to Jerusalem, and the temple to worship, and fearing this would result in their going back again to the king of Judah, he made two golden calves and set them up, one at Bethel and the other at Dan, and ordered his people to worship at those two points, and not endure the fatigue and inconvenience of travel to Jerusalem to worship. He succeeded in thus leading the people away from God, and into gross idolatry. He built houses where these idols were, and set apart priests that were not of the family of Levi, but from among the common people. And he appointed a great feast about a month after the feast of tabernacles, when he offered sacrifices on these altars to the calves which he had made, and burned incense before them. 1st Kings, xii.

About the time Jeroboam was engaged in the ceremonies of the feast at Bethel and the worship of these idols, a prophet of Judah appeared among them and cried out against the altar, and declared that at some future time a descendant of David, Josiah by name, should pollute that altar, and should burn the bones of the idolatrous priests who should serve at it; and then, in token that his prophecy should be fulfilled, he gave a sign at once in the rending of the altar and the pouring out of the ashes, with the withering of Jeroboam's hand and arm in a moment. No wonder that Jeroboam was alarmed at these declarations, and especially at the signs that were given of the truth of the prophet's mission; and he besought the prophet to pray that his hand and arm might be restored. Accordingly the prophet besought the Lord, and the king's hand was restored to him again as it was before. Jeroboam then asked the prophet to go with him and take some refreshment and receive of him a reward, but he refused because the Lord had forbidden him; yet he did afterward, and was punished with death, for a lion met him and slew him. 1st Kings, xiii.

These events transpiring in the history of Jeroboam, did by no means lead him to reformation. He continued to encourage his subjects to idolatry; nay more, he obliged them to it, and established the accursed system by law, which finally brought on the ruin of the nation.

Jeroboam was punished in different ways. Many of his best subjects forsook him and joined the kingdom of Judah. Jeroboam had battles with Rehoboam and Abijah, his son, in one of which he lost five hundred thousand chosen men. 2d Chron. xiii: 17. He had but one pious son, or, rather, but one that came to the grave in peace, and that was Abijah, who died in early life. While he was sick Jeroboam was intensely interested in the case, and sent his wife to Ahijah, an aged prophet, to ask him if his son should recover. The prophet assured her that he should not; and, further, he declared the ruin that was coming on the family of Jeroboam. 1st Kings, xiv.

He died after a reign of twenty-two years, and Nadab, his son, succeeded him. In about two years he was murdered by Baasha at the siege of Gibbethon, and the entire family of Jeroboam was put to death and their bodies were left to be eaten by the dogs and wild beasts. 1st Kings, xv: 29.

JEROBOAM, 2—*Fighting against, increasing the people.*

Jeroboam was the son of Joash, and the great grandson of Jehu.

This Jeroboam was also a king of Israel, and followed in the way of the former, as an idolater. He reigned about forty-one years, during which time the kingdom of Israel attained great splendor. But like the former Jeroboam, a short time after his death, the Lord cut off his idolatrous house. The prophet Jonah is understood to be prophesying of this king and the kingdom of Israel in his day, when he represents the ten tribes in their greatest glory, as he does in 2d Kings, xiv: 25.

About twenty-three years after the death of Jeroboam, his son, Zechariah, succeeded upon the throne, but in six months he and the entire family were murdered. 2d Kings, xv: 8. His reign was thus short. He was wicked like the former Jeroboam, and Shallum conspired against him, and slew him, and reigned in his stead.

JEROHAM—[Jer-o´ham.]

Was the son of Elihu and the grandson of Tohu, and he was the father of Elkanah, and hence, the grandfather of the prophet Samuel. In the genealogy given of Elkanah, 1st Sam. i: 1, we learn they were inhabitants of the country of Ephrath, and they are called Ephrathites. So Elimelech and his family are called Ephrathites of Beth-lem-judah, because they lived there. Ruth, i: 2.

JERUBBAAL—[Je-rub'ba-al,] *he that revenges the idol, let Baal defend his cause.*

The same as Gideon. [See Gideon.]

JERUSHAH—[Je-ru'shah,] *he that possesses the inheritance, exiled.*

JERUSHAH was the daughter of Zadok and the wife of Uzziah, who began his reign piously and prosperously, but at last became wicked, and invaded the priest's office; and as a punishment for this sin was struck with leprosy. Jotham, the son of Jerushah and Uzziah, reigned in the stead of the leprous father. We know nothing further of this woman than is stated above. She was the daughter of Zadok, and the wife and mother of a king. 2d Chron. xxvii: 1.

JESHAIAH—[Jesh-a-i'ah,]

One of the sons of Jeduthun. When the lots were cast, and the singers were divided into twenty-four courses, his lot was the eighth. 1st Chron. xxv: 15.

JESHEBEAB—[Jesh-eb'e-ab,]

Was one of the priests appointed by David. His lot was the fourteenth. 1st Chron. xxiv: 13.

JESHUAH—[Jesh'u-ah,] *a savior.*

Was one of the priests appointed by David when he divided them into twenty-four orders. His lot was the ninth. 1st Chron. xxiv: 11.

JESSE—[Jes'-se,] *to be my present.*

JESSE was the son of Obed and the grandson of Boaz, and he was the father of David. In Ruth iv: 18–22, his genealogy is traced back as far as Pharez. He had seven sons and two daughters, whose names are given in 1st Chron. ii: 13–16. The prophet Samuel was sent to the house of Jesse, to select from among his sons a successor on the throne of Israel, when Saul was rejected from being king. Samuel seemed somewhat reluctant to go to the house of Jesse and anoint one of his sons to be king, lest Saul should hear of it, and kill him. The Lord commanded the prophet to go to Bethlehem with a sacrifice, and as he called the elders of Israel he called Jesse also with his sons to the sacrifice. After the public services were over, or else before they began, Samuel had a private interview with Jesse and his family, during which interview the sons of Jesse passed before him, and he selected the shepherd youth, and anointed him as the future King of Israel. The following are the names of the sons of Jesse: Eliab, Abinadab, Shimma, Nethaneel, Raddai, Ozem and David, and the following are the names of his daughters: Zeruiah (who was the mother of Joab, Abishai and Asahel) and Abigail (who was the mother of Amasa.) Jesse was certainly greatly honored of God in that the sacred King of Israel was selected from his family in the person of David. And moreover, most of the kings of the Hebrews, both of the kingdoms of Judah and Israel, were descendants of Jesse, and in the genealogy of Christ Jesse appears in the regular line of the promised Messiah. Christ is called the son of David according to the flesh, and the Lord of David as a divine personage, and he is called a branch from the root of Jesse. Isa. xi: 1. "And there shall come forth a rod out of the stem of Jesse, and a branch shall grow out of his roots, &c."

Jesse it is likely was growing old when David his younger son was selected as the successor of Saul, and keenly felt the separation when David was received into the kings court, and became the constant attendant of the diseased king, as a musician, but he still more keenly felt the exile of David when Saul was seeking to kill him. He fled to David fearing for his own life and that of his family. But on account of the feebleness and infirmities of age, he with his wife could not attend David so as to be supported and protected by him. Accordingly David went to Mizpah of Moab, and made an arrange- with the King of Moab for the protection of his father and mother. He was unwilling to risk his parents any longer within the reach of Saul, and he knew that they could not endure the hardships and fatigues of military life. Jesse went to the King of Moab and dwelt while David "was in the hold." How long he remained in Moab we do not know. It is supposed by some that when David fled under the direction of the prophet Gad to the forests of

Hareth, the Moabites murdered Jesse and his family, and that was the reason why David afterwards considered and treated the Moabites as enemies. 1st Sam. xxii. He smote the Moabites. 2d Sam. viii: 2.

JESUI—[Jes′-u-i,] *who is equal, flat country.*

JESUI was of the tribe of Asher, and the head of the extensive family called Jesuites. Numbers xxvi: 44. This person is referred to in Genesis xlvi: 17, under the name Ishauh.

JESUS—[Je′sus,] *the holy name Jesus, Savior, who saveth his people from their sins.*

JESUS is the name by which our blessed redeemer is called, and the reason given why this should be his name is, "for he shall save his people from their sins." Matthew i: 21. This name was given by the angel of the Lord, who appeared unto Joseph in a dream, informing him that the coming son of his espoused wife was the Messiah—the long-looked for Savior of mankind. Consequently as soon as the son of Mary was born, Joseph called his name Jesus. For the divine character of the Savior, see Christ.

The history of Jesus is full of interest. It abounds with striking incidents that will be read with deep emotion by our redeemed race, down to the latest generation. Every line of the recorded history of Jesus, is fraught with infinite and intense interest to man, from his birth in the manger in the stable at Bethlehem, to his vicarious death upon the cross.

The first thing appearing in the recorded history of Jesus is, his genealogy as given by Matthew i: 1–16. This is the genealogy by the side of Joseph, his reputed father, because he married his mother, and here is the line from Joseph the son of Jacob, to Abraham.

St. Luke gives his genealogy by the side of Mary, his real mother, from Joseph, the son-in-law of Heli, to Adam, the federal head of the human family.

It would seem to be more important to trace his lineage through Mary, his real mother, on up to Adam, than to have traced it to our federal head in Joseph; and hence the Evangelists under inspiration, have thus given his genealogy. The conception and birth of Jesus, is narrated specially and particularly in Matthew i: 18–25, and Luke i. He was conceived by the Holy Ghost, born of the Virgin Mary. Infidels have dared to cavil, and indeed to indulge in obscenity, and wicked expressions regarding the conception and birth of Jesus. But we will always admire the love of God in providing such a Savior for man, and his wisdom in providing him in such a way. He was made of a woman, made under the law, to redeem such as were under the law. He identified himself with humanity, by taking upon him our nature. Woman, who was first in the transgression, is honored in being the mother of the Savior of the transgressor.

On the eighth day after his birth, he was circumcised, and the name which was given him by the angel, was settled upon him, and recorded according to custom. Luke ii: 21. "And when eight days were accomplished for the circumcising of the child, his name was called Jesus, which was so named of the angel, before he was conceived in the womb."

We have an interesting account of the Magi passing through Jerusalem in search of the new-born king of the Jews. Matthew, ii. They had an interview with Herod, the king, who was troubled on account of their embassy, and the earnestness they manifested, and the confidence they expressed, that the king of the Jews was born. Herod succeeded in hiding his fear and trouble from the Magi, as he gathered together the readers and expounders of the law and prophecy, and demanded of them "where Christ should be born," and they told him in Bethlehem, of Judea. He then charged them when they found him to bring him word, that he might come and render him homage. His intention was to put him to death, but his plan was thwarted, for after the Magi found him and presented him with their gifts of gold, frankincense and myrrh, they were instructed by the Lord to return to their own country another way than through Jerusalem. Joseph and Mary probably used the presents of the Magi, to bear their expenses in their flight into Egypt, whither they went under the direction of an angel, to elude the grasp and power of the wicked Herod. The king of the Jews, became greatly enraged when he found the Magi did not bring him word as to this new-born king, and he vented his fierce rage upon the families of the city of Bethlehem, by issuing a decree that the male children under two years of age, should all be put to death. The decree was executed, and thereby the prophecy of Jeremiah fulfilled. "A voice was heard in Ramah, lamentation and bitter weeping; Rachel weeping for her children, refused to be comforted for her children, because they were not." Jer. xxxi: 15. Though these words were originally spoken relative to the captivity of the ten tribes, they are here applied to the murder of the innocent children by Herod, in his determination to kill Jesus.

Not long after this, Herod put his son Antipater to death, and five days aftewards he died a most horrible death. When he was dead, an angel of the Lord appeared to Joseph in his exile in Egypt, with Mary and the young child, and told him that Herod and Antipater were dead, and that Archelaus had the kingdom of Judea apportioned to him, and was reigning there. The angel bade Joseph go with the young child and his mother, into Israel. And he went to Nazareth and dwelt there, and this dwelling of the family at Nazareth, as they did for many years, gave Jesus the title of the Nazarene. Matthew, ii: 23.

Forty days after the birth of Jesus, according to the Jewish law, his parents brought him to Jerusalem, to present him in the temple, and offer the customary sacrifice. The law is recorded in Lev. xii: 2-6. It seems that his mother took the benefit of the provision made in that law for the poor, while the rich brought their lambs of the first year, the poor brought a pair of turtle doves, or two young pigeons. Mary being poor, brought the sacrifice of a pair of turtle doves, or two young pigeons, and so prepared herself according to law to appear in, and take part in public worship.

It was while she presented Jesus thus in the temple, that Simeon, a devout and holy man, who had long waited for the consolation of Israel, was inspired to see in the person of that child, the Lord's Christ. He had been divinely informed that he should not die before he had seen the Savior of mankind; and as he entered the temple that morning, and looked upon the parents and upon the child Jesus, he saw the Messiah; and taking the child from the arms of the mother to his own arms, he said, "Lord, now lettest thou thy servant depart in peace, for mine eyes have seen thy salvation which thou hast prepared before the face of all people—a light to lighten the Gentiles, and the glory of thy people, Israel."

It was probably while Simeon was engaged in praising God in rapturous strains, that Anna, a prophetess, came in and spake of him to all them that looked for redemption in Jerusalem. Luke, ii: 22-38.

The only circumstance recorded further of the childhood of Jesus up to twelve years of age, is, that "he grew, and waxed strong in spirit, [was] filled with wisdom; and the grace of God was upon him:" that is, his body was in perfect health and fully developed—the mental powers also expanded. His excellency as to moral nature was made manifest more and more, for he grew in the favor of God. He manifested the graces of the Holy Spirit, and the glory of his divine nature.

When he was twelve years of age he went up with his parents to celebrate the Passover, an annual feast of the Jews. He may have attended them before in their annual visits, for they went every year; and the law required, anciently, that all the men children appear before the Lord thrice in the year. Ex. xxiii: 17, and xxxiv: 23. Though Jesus may have been at Jerusalem at the feasts before, yet nothing peculiar and striking had transpired so far as the records show. It is likely that the age of twelve years was that at which the parents were required to bring their children to the great feasts without fail, that they might witness the ceremonies of the feast, and probably take a part in some of the exercises of worship of which they were capable.

After the eight days of the feast were accomplished,—the Passover day and the seven days of unleavened bread,—Mary and Joseph started for Nazareth, their home, and they traveled a day's journey before they found that Jesus was not with them. It is probable that the men and women traveled in separate companies, and that the children sometimes traveled with the men and sometimes with the women, and that Mary supposed Jesus was with the company of the men, and Joseph supposed he was with his mother; hence, they traveled until evening before they found that he was left behind. They immediately turned back to Jerusalem, and the third day they found him in the temple sitting in the midst of the Rabbi, or teachers. He was listening to them as they taught their disciples regarding the law, the doctrines, and ceremonies of the Jewish religion. But he had not contented himself with hearing them, for he asked them questions, and confounded them with his wisdom and knowledge. Though they were teachers of the law, he was not among them as a scholar to learn, but he assumed the position of a teacher of these teachers. He proposed questions as a teacher proposes questions to his pupils, and then gave the answers and explanations in order to instruct; for it is said "they heard him and were astonished at his understanding and answers."

His mother approached him with a degree of amazement, to see him in the temple thus, and making himself familiar with the Rabbi. She said affectionately, "Son, why hast thou dealt thus with us? Behold thy father and I have sought thee sorrowing." The answer that he gave her, may have been intended as a gentle reproof, but it certainly does not express a want of feeling for her on his part, or a disposition to insubordination. He said, "How is it that ye sought me? Wist ye not that I must be about my father's business." He may have meant that they need not to have been concerned about him, knowing him as they did. As they left him in his father's house, or at the temple, they might have been sure that he was there yet. Though this saying was not fully understood, yet Mary kept it with many other sayings in her heart, as the few following years rolled on. Luke ii: 41–51.

The four Evangelists have given us an account of the baptism of Jesus by John the baptist in Jordan. Mat. iii: 13; Mark i: 9; Luke iii: 21; John i: 32. Jesus went from Galilee to Jordan to be baptized, and he demanded baptism of John, who it seems was well satisfied of the exalted character of Jesus, and earnestly opposed it. How strange, that he who had baptized the inhabitants of Jerusalem, the country of Judea, and all the region round about Jordan, now, as Jesus approaches him as a candidate for baptism, urges objection on the ground that he was not worthy to baptize him. "I have need to be baptized of thee, and comest thou to me." But Jesus urged it on the ground that it was an ordinance of God, the author of that dispensation—"suffer it to be so now; for thus it becomes us to fulfill all righteousness." Jesus probably intended, that as baptism was the initiatory ordinance into the dispensation of John, which was the preparation for his own, to give the dispensation and baptism of John his sanction. And again, as Jesus was himself to be the high priest over the house of God, it was important that he should be properly inducted into the office. John was the only proper person then living to initiate him, for he was the forerunner or messenger of the Messiah. The Jewish high priest was inducted into the office with washing with pure water, anointing with holy oil, and the offering of sacrifice. Hence Jesus was baptized or washed with water, and anointed by the Holy Ghost, while the devotions of the subject of the ordinance, and of the administrator, and of the already discipled multitude, was the sacrifice, which sacrifice was acceptable to God, for the Holy Spirit descended in the form of a dove, and lighting upon the head of Jesus, a voice was heard speaking from heaven saying, "this is my beloved son, in whom I am well pleased." Matthew, iii: 13–17.

The next important circumstance in the history of Jesus, was his temptation in the wilderness. Matt. iv: 1–11 and Mark i: 12, &c. It seems that he went into the wilderness very shortly after his baptism, and that he was still under the especial influence of that spirit that sat upon him in the bodily shape of a dove; he was "led up of the spirit into the wilderness to be tempted of the devil." Here we have the first act of our Savior's ministry narrated; the official account of the first battle he fought as the captain of our salvation. It was a combat with Satan, and Jesus was the victor. He went into the wilderness for this special purpose. And like Moses the great law giver of Israel, when on the mount of God within the foldings of the cloud that capped that mountain, fasting forty days and forty nights; and like Elijah, who went in the strength of one meal forty days, Jesus fasted in the wilderness. Thus we have a representative of the patriarchal age in the person of Moses, a representative of the prophetical age in the person of Elijah, and Jesus of the Christian age, fasting forty days and forty nights, and though nothing is said of the inconvenience endured by the two former from fasting, yet of Jesus it is said "he hungered."

The temptation of Jesus was of three kinds, there were three special and particular onsets, and how judiciously, speaking after the manner of men, were they made. First the tempter said: "If thou be the son of God, command these stones, that they be made bread." As though he had said, why art thou here suffering the cravings of hunger, when if thou art what thou claimest to be, thou canst make bread, and so meet the pressing wants of nature. Jesus answered him: "It is written man shall not live by bread alone, but by every word that proceedeth out of the mouth of God." Thus with the sword of the spirit as a heaven invented weapon, he struck at his foe, and as Satan beheld the blade gleaming in the light, wielded so dexterously by the hand of Jesus, he fled before him.

Shortly after this temptation he went to Jerusalem and entered the temple, and he occupied a position for a time on what is called a "pinnacle of the temple," which was probably the king's gallery, or as it is termed *Solomon's porch*. This was a magnificent piazza which was founded on a vast terrace that was raised from the valley beneath, four hundred cubits high, for the purpose of giving foundation for the temple, according to the plan presented in the draft of the Almighty architect, or rather it was the summit of the royal gallery built by Herod upon the masonry wall that King Solomon built from the valley to increase the area of the temple site. Josephus tells us that its height was seven hundred feet, and the eyes were almost unable to reach so vast a depth. The temptation of Jesus is expressed in the following language by Satan: "If thou be the son of God cast thyself down, for it is written he shall give his angels charge concerning thee; and in their hands they shall bear thee up, lest at any time thou dash thy foot against a stone." Jesus had already maintained the position that he was the Son of God, by resisting the former temptation, and now he is called upon to give an exhibit of his heroism. He is requested to prove the divinity of his mission by leaping from the summit of that porch down into the depth of the valley of the Kidron, and thus astonish the world by a leap of seven hundred feet without realizing injury. But Jesus unsheathed the sword of the Spirit and struck at Satan by saying: "It is written thou shalt not tempt the Lord thy God." While the former appealed to the animal appetite, this latter appealed to the *mental tastes*—the love of show and the gratification of universal admiration. Again he put his enemy to flight. But a third time Satan approached Jesus to tempt him. It is said he "taketh him up into an exceedingly high mountain and showeth him all the kingdoms of the world and the glory of them, and saith unto him: All these things will I give thee if thou wilt fall down and worship me." We may suppose that Satan pointed in the direction of the different kingdoms of the world, and painted their glory with his deceptive tongue—represented his position as "the God of this world," and promised Jesus unlimited lordship if he would fall down and worship him. Here was an appeal to ambition. The rock on which many have split. But Jesus unsheathed the sword of the spirit again and drove the tempter from his presence as he said "Get thee behind me Satan, for it is written thou shalt worship the Lord thy God, and him only shalt thou serve." After Satan had departed from him angels came and ministered unto him. The darkness of a night of temptation receded, and the bright, clear light of a beautiful day dawned upon him. The faintness of hunger, and the fatigue of the terrible combat through which Jesus had passed, was soon counteracted as angels spread a table before him, and waited on him and supported him as he ate. Matt. iv: 11.

Jesus then left the place of his trial and triumph, and went into Galilee, but he did not tarry there long, and for some cause changed his residence from Nazareth to Capernaum, a town situate on the western shore of sea of Galilee. He was born at Bethlehem, spent his childhood and youth at Nazareth, but Capernaum was his home during his ministry. Matt. iv: 13. The first place at which Jesus preached in commencing his ministry was in the synagogue in Galilee. At Nazareth, he preached probably the first sabbath after he arrived at home. And this is the first account we have of his preaching, and the foundation of his discourse was a remarkable prophecy of himself, recorded in Isa. lxi; 1. "The spirit of the Lord God is upon me; because the Lord hath annointed me to preach good tidings unto the meek; he hath sent me to bind up the broken-hearted, to proclaim liberty to the captives, and the opening of the prison to them that are bound," etc.

He informed the worshipers in the synagogue at Nazareth that the scripture he had just read was fulfilled. They heard with astonishment, but would not receive his word, for they said: "Is not this Joseph's son?" Jesus knew their thoughts and unbelief, and said unto them: "A prophet is not without honor, save in his own country and among his own kindred."

They seemed to draw conclusions, from what Jesus said unto them, that he had intended to tell them that the Gentiles were more precious in the sight of God than the Jews, for he had referred them to the goodness of God to the widow, Serepta, in providing for her during the dearth and famine in Israel; and he had referred them to Naaman, the Syrian, who was cleansed of his leprosy while Jewish lepers remained unclean; and in their wrath they drove him from the city, making an attempt to destroy his life by casting him down the hill on which the city stood; but they were not allowed to do this. He quelled their murderous feeling toward him, or placed some obstacle in their way so that they could not harm him, and passed from their midst away from the city. Luke, iv: 16-30.

This treatment of Jesus was probably the cause of his changing his residence to Capernaum. And shortly after commencing his residence there, he called his first disciples from their employment as fishers on the sea of Galilee. They were Simon Peter and Andrew, his brother, and James and John, the sons of Zebedee.

We have an account earlier than this of Andrew's faith in Christ as the Messiah, and his laudable zeal, and successful effort to lead his brother Peter to embrace the faith that he had. John i: 40. Hence we may suppose that Jesus was acquainted with these two fishermen, and they with him, when he called them to be "fishers of men." Matthew iv; 18: Mark i: 16. And soon after this he increased the number of his disciples to twelve.

Jesus attended a marriage in Cana, of Galilee, where he performed the miracle of changing water into wine in the presence of his mother, his disciples, and some of the servants, and other guests. John ii: 1. And after the marriage feast was over, he went with his mother to Capernaum, and was there a few days, when the Feast of the Passover came on, and Jesus went up to Jerusalem to join in the solemn ceremonies.

This was the first Passover Feast after the baptism of Jesus, and he may have exercised some authority about the temple, as indicated in John ii: 13-17, though many suppose that the circumstance recorded there of the cleansing of the temple by driving out the money changers, and those that sold doves, with a scourge of small cords, &c., refers more particularly to the act of Jesus recorded in Matthew xxi: 12; Mark xi: 15; and Luke xix: 45. If so, then John anticipates three years, for these latter quotations refer to the fourth Passover Feast during his ministry, which was just before he was condemned, and crucified. During this feast, he taught the people, and many of those who heard him believed on him. His teachings were pure, and his miracles strong attestations of his divinity.

Shortly after this, he had the important conversation with Nicodemus on the doctrine of the new birth,—John, iii: 1–13,—in which he taught its necessity, and the importance of faith in his testimony.

He left the country of Judea again to go to Galilee, and in making the journey passed through Samaria; and when he came to Sychar, which was the ancient Shechem—then a somewhat important city, near which was Jacob's well—he did not go himself into the city, but stopped at the well and sent his disciples in to buy provisions; and while alone at the well he had the conversation with the woman of Samaria, during which he satisfied her that he was the Messiah. And she so far declared her convictions as to induce many of the Samaritans to believe on him, who went to him and besought him to tarry with them, and he did two days, during which time many others heard for themselves, and believed not on the evidence of the woman merely, but on what they themselves heard; for they said, "We have heard him ourselves, and know that this is indeed the Christ, the Savior of the world."

Having spent two days at Sychar in Samaria, in company with his disciples, he went into Galilee, and in Cana of Galilee he cured the son of a nobleman. The nobleman was of Capernaum, and had applied unto him, and expressed strong faith in his healing power; with great earnestness he begged him to heal his son. Jesus said unto him, "Go thy way, thy son liveth." He remained at Cana, but cured the nobleman's son at Capernaum. John, iv.

After he had been at Cana a short time he returned to his home at Capernaum, and on the Sabbath day taught in their synagogue, and astonished the people with the matter of his teaching and the manner of his delivery, for he taught with authority; but his teaching was attended with miracle-working power, for there was a demoniac in the synagogue whom he cured. Mark, i: 23. After the synagogue service was over, he entered into the house of Peter. It is likely Peter's house was his Capernaum home. Jesus belonged to Peter's family; hence, we find in Matt. xvii: 24, that the tribute-receivers came to Peter and demanded tribute for him and his master, and Jesus provided Peter with money in the mouth of a fish with which to pay tribute for them both. But as Jesus entered into Simon's house, he saw his wife's mother under the influence of a malignant fever, and he cured her with a word, so that she rose up at once and ministered unto them. Mark, i: 30; Matt. viii: 14; Luke, iv: 38.

It was probably about this time that Jesus preached his memorable sermon on the Mount, recorded in Matt. v, vi and vii, and a similar sermon not on the mountains, but in the plain recorded in Luke vi: 17–49.

About this time, he cured a leper, who came to him and besought him to make him clean; and he charged the cleansed leper to go and show himself to the priest, and offer the gift for cleansing required by the Mosaic law. Mark i: 39; Matthew viii: 1; Luke viii: 22. Immediately after this, he went into Capernaum, and on being applied to by a centurion to heal his servant, who had been suddenly struck with paralysis, he signified his intention to go, but upon the centurion asking him to cure him with a word, Jesus did. Luke vii: 2; Matthew viii: 5.

The day after he had cured the servant of the centurion, he left Capernaum, and went to Nain, and as he came near the city, he met a funeral train. The deceased was the only son of a poor widow, with whom the inhabitants of Nain greatly sympathized, for they attended the stricken mother to the burial of her son. "Much people of the city were with her." Jesus had compassion and comforted the woman. He bade the bier-bearers stop, and then called the young man back to life, and gave him to his mother. Luke vii: 11. About this time, or not long after, he was waited on by two of John's disciples with the question, "Art thou the Messiah, or do we look for another?" His answer to them was, "Go your way and tell John what things ye have seen and heard, how that the blind see, the lame walk, the lepers are cleansed, the deaf hear, the dead are raised, to the poor the gospel is preached." Luke vii: 22. These disciples reported to John, and he gave his testimony to the truth of Christ's Messiahship, and gave them to understand that they were no longer to complain that his glory was being eclipsed in the rising popularity of Jesus. His language is, "he must increase, but I must decrease. John iii: 30.

About this time Jesus and his disciples were crossing the sea of Galilee, and a great storm of wind arose and the waves of the tempestuous sea were threatening to destroy them, so that the disciples were afraid and awoke their master who was asleep. Jesus saw their fears and charged them with a want of faith in him. He then spoke to the winds and waves, and there was a sudden calm. Mark iv: 37; Matthew viii: 24; Luke viii: 22. The storm having ceased, they made a safe landing, and proceeded to the country of the Gergesenes, where he met the demoniac of Gadara, and cast the devils out of him, who, when they were cast out, were permitted by Jesus to enter the herd of swine that were feeding on the plain, and the whole herd ran into the sea and perished, while the demoniac, clothed in his right mind, returned to his home, and to his family. Matthew viii: 28; Mark v: 1; Luke viii: 27. Jesus then recrossed the sea of Galilee, and came to Capernaum, when they brought unto him a man sick of the palsy to be cured. Jesus saw their faith, and the faith of the palsied man, and said, "Son, be of good cheer, thy sins be forgiven thee." He healed the soul, while he cured the body.

There was an objection raised by some of the scribes to the form of expression used by Jesus—they called it blasphemy. But he claimed the right as God to forgive sins, yet he changed the form of address to the cured man by saying, "Arise, take up thy bed and walk," and the man arose, and went unto his house. Matthew ix: 1; Mark ii: 1; Luke v: 18. He then enters into a conversation with the Pharisees, and delivered a discourse on the subject of fasting, in which he reproved them, and showed them that their system was inconsistent with christianity—that Phariseeism and christianity could never harmonize. And while Christ was engaged in addressing these Pharisees, a certain ruler of the synagogue of Capernaum came to him, and with great earnestness, besought him to come to his house and cure his little daughter, who was lying at the point of death. The ruler had faith in Jesus and his healing power, for he said, "come and lay thy hand on her, and she shall live." He immediately started with him to his house, but on the way a crowd gathered about him and among the crowd were diseased persons, one of whom was a woman whose disease was of twelve years standing, and a distressing one, for it excluded her from the congregation of Israel. She pressed her way through the crowd and touched the hem of Jesus' garment, and was cured. As soon as opportunity afforded, Jesus and the ruler passed on, but before they reached the house, intelligence was brought the anxious father, "thy daughter is dead." Jesus comforted his sorrowing heart, and hastened on to the dwelling, and putting all that were present out of the appartment save the father and the mother of the damsel, he took her by the hand and commanded her to arise, "and she arose and walked, for she was of the age of twelve years. Mark v: 22–42 and Matt. ix: 18–25. When Jesus departed thence he was followed by two blind men who expressed their faith in him as the Messiah and begged him to restore them to sight. He asked them if they believed he was able to do it? They answered him, Yea Lord. He then touched their eyes and gave them sight. Matt. ix: 27. These men that were cured of their blindness, spread abroad the fame of Jesus in all that country, and it may be that they brought the dumb man possessed with a devil, who was relieved, for Jesus cast the devil out of him, in the presence of the multitude, who were greatly astonished at his power and said: "It was never so seen in Israel." Matt. ix: 32. On the performance of the last miracle the Pharisees made a charge against Jesus of being in league with the devil. In their malice and wickedness, they attributed the power of God to the devil. Jesus asserted his Godhead and declared his equality with the father, declares himself the quickener of the dead, and the judge of the world. He refers to the testimony of John the Baptist, concerning him, and adds to that the testimony appearing in the works that he had already performed, with the declarations of scripture regarding him and their fulfillment. Matt. ix: 32 and John v: 17-39.

On a Sabbath morning Jesus and his disciples passed through a cornfield, and as the disciples were hungry, they plucked ears of corn and did eat. There was a complaint among the Pharisees that they had done that which was unlawful to do on the Sabbath day. Jesus defended his disciples by referring the Pharisees to the act of David, recorded in 1st Sam, xxi: 6, of entering the house of God when he was hungry, and taking the shew bread to eat, which was not lawful for any except the priests, and yet they did not blame him. And, again he referred them to the priests work on the Sabbath, how they slay and offer sacrifices on the Sabbath as a common day and are blameless, and he declares himself as Lord even of the Sabbath day. Matt. xii: 1, Mark ii: 23 and Luke vi: 1.

They were probably on their way to the synagogue when they passed through the cornfield, for as the conversation with the Pharisees closed, he entered into the synagogue, and there was a man there which had a withered hand. Jesus after setting forth clearly the fact that it is proper to heal on the Sabbath day, cured the man with the withered hand. With a word he restored it whole like the other. Matt. xii: 10, Mark iii: 1 and Luke vi: 6.

About this time he designated his disciples apostles. He gave the twelve their names and authority against unclean spirits, and power to heal sickness and all manner of disease. He gave them particular instructions relative to the objects of their ministry, their mode of preaching, &c. He foretold the afflictions and persecutions they would have to endure, and cautions them against unfaithfulness in any respect. Matt. x: 1, &c., Mark, iii: 12, Luke, vi: 13, &c. Jesus cured a man who was possessed with a devil, blind and dumb. This was a remarkable cure and amazed the people, and the Pharasees renewed the charge they had brought against him before, viz: "He casteth out devils by Beelzebub, the prince of the devils." In connection with his defense at this time, he charges upon his enemies the sin against the Holy Ghost which is unpardonable, which sin seems to be, as Jesus sets it forth, attributing to satanic agency the power by which he wrought miracles. Matthew. xii: 24, Mark, iii: 22, Luke, xi: 15.

Before the above conversation fully closed, the mother of Jesus and the children of Mary, the wife of Cleopas, who was the sister of the virgin Mary, were reported as without, desiring an interview with him. Jesus asked the significant question, "Who is my mother? and who are my brethren." His object in asking this question evidently was to declare the nearness of spiritual relationship, for he says, "whosoever shall do the will of my father in heaven, the same is my brother and sister, and mother." Matt. xii: 46; Mark, iii: 31; Luke, viii: 19.

Not long after this he dines with Simon, the Pharisee; and while in Simon's house a woman, probably a converted heathen, whose love for Jesus was great, entered the house with an alabaster box of ointment. She stood at Jesus' feet, and wept tears of gratitude for what he had done for her. Her tears fell upon his feet as he reclined, and she washed them, wiping them with the hairs of her head. She kissed his feet and anointed them with the precious ointment. Jesus commended her, but mildly reproved Simon for his lack of proper courtesy. Luke, vii: 36-46.

We next hear of Jesus in a desert place apart, and the people in multitudes following him, to be benefitted by his teachings and the curing of their sick. And when the evening was come his disciples proposed that he should send them away to their homes, or to the villages to buy themselves something to eat. But Jesus told them no, he would not send them away, but would himself provide them a meal, and he did, multiplying five loaves and two fishes, with which he fed five thousand men, beside women and children, taking up twelve baskets full of fragments after the meal was over. Matt. xiv: 15; Mark, vi: 30; Luke, ix: 10, and John vi: 1.

Immediately after this he bade his disciples get into a ship to go over the sea, and in the fourth watch of the night h e overtook them in their voyage. He had been up the mountain side praying for a season, while they, at his command, had started out to cross the sea. When they saw him coming they were afraid, but Jesus stilled their fears, and entered the ship with them, and crossed over. Matt. xiv: 22; Mark, vi: 45, and John, vi: 15.

The day after this, some of those who were present and did eat of the loaves and fishes, followed Jesus to Capernaum, and when they found him they asked how he came there, for they knew that he did not enter the ship with his disciples the night before. Jesus then charges them with seeking him, not so much to see his miracles or hear his words, to be benefited, but rather to be fed again. He then presents himself as the bread of life, and urges them to seek after spiritual food. John, vi: 26.

About this time one of the important annual feasts occurred, and Jesus went up to Jerusalem where he cured a lame man at the pool of Bethesda, and discourses concerning his important mission, and the tradition of the elders which the Pharisees held was transgressed by the disciples of Jesus in eating with unwashed hands. John, v: 2, 17; Matt. xv: 1; Mark, vii: 1. When Jesus left Jerusalem this time he departed into the coasts of Tyre and Sidon, and cured the Syro-phenician woman's daughter. Matt. xv: 21; Mark, vii: 24, and he also cured in the coasts of Decapolis, after he left Tyre and Sidon, a person who was deaf, and had an impediment in his speech. He opened the ears of the deaf man and loosened his tongue so that he spake plainly. Mark, vii: 32. And Matthew tells us that multitudes that were blind, dumb and maimed were healed, xv: 30. There seems to have been a great multitude about the Savior while performing these miracles, and they continued with him three days, so deeply interested that they did not leave to seek for something to eat. Having compassion upon them Jesus multiplied seven loaves, and a few fishes, with which he fed four thousand men, beside women and children. Mark, viii: 1. Having sent the multitude away Jesus took ship and came into the coast of Magdala.

The Pharisees and Sadduces joined together to demand from him a sign from heaven—they feigned a desire to have his doctrine fully proved to them that they might credit it and become his disciples. He severely rebuked them for their hypocrisy and wickedness, and then cautions his disciples to beware of their doctrines. Mark, viii: 11; Matt. xvi: 1; Luke, xii: 54. He then cames to Bethsaida and as a blind man was brought to him, he restores him to sight. Mark, viii: 22. Soon after this he began to teach his disciples regarding his coming sufferings. He tells them he will be rejected of the elders and chief priests and scribes, and be put to death, and after three days rise again. Peter was astonished and objected to this teaching but Jesus rebuked him. Matt. xvi: 21; Mark, viii: 31; and Luke, ix: 18. And six days after he thus taught his disciples, he took Peter and James and John up into a mountain to be witnesses of his transfiguration. He gave these three disciples a more glorious view of his divinity than they had ever had before. He caused the divine nature to shine forth through the human as they had never before seen it. They reached the spot on the mountain selected by Jesus, and immediately his face shone as the sun and his raiment was white as the light, and Moses and Elias appeared and talked with him. The disciples saw them and knew them—and proposed to their master to build tabernacles and detain the two heavenly visitants: "let us make three tabernacles, one for thee, and one for Moses, and one for Elias." A bright cloud overshadowed Jesus and his attendants, and the voice of the father was heard by all the company, saying: "This is my beloved son in whom I am well pleased." The disciples were afraid and fell on their faces. They were dismayed by the voice, and dazzled by the glory of the cloud, Jesus dispelled their fears and they lifted up their eyes and saw him standing before them alone. Matt. xvii: 1, 8; Mark, ix: 2; Luke, ix: 28, and the apostle Peter in his 2d Epistle i: 16, refers to this glorious manifestation as he says, he "was an eye-witness of his majesty." When Jesus and his disciples came down from the mountain a man came to him and besought him to cure his son who was a lunatic, and affected most with his disorder at the full and changes of the moon. It was a very severe case, and the paroxysms sometimes threw him into the fire and sometimes into the water. While Jesus and the three disciples were on the mount of transfiguration, he had probably applied to the other disciples for a cure and they could not affect it. He says "I brought him to thy disciples and they could not cure him." Jesus at once rebuked the devil and healed the child. Matt. xvii: 14; Mark, ix: 17; Luke, ix: 37. He again spake to his disciples regarding his sufferings, and declared that he would be betrayed into the hands of men. Matt. xvii: 22. He then went to Capernaum, and while there the demand was made of Peter for tribute, which seems to indicate that Jesus was a member of his family. The money was miraculously supplied and the tribute paid by Peter for them both.

While he, with his disciples, were at Capernaum, they came to him with a question, which seemed to indicate a desire for position and rank in his kingdom. He takes occasion to give them a very important discourse on the virtue of humility, and the proper mode of treatment of an offending brother. Matthew xviii; Mark ix: 33; Luke ix: 46. At the close of this discourse, John informed him that they, the disciples, had seen one casting out devils in his name, and they forbade him, because he was not of their number. Jesus reproved them for rebuking that man, and informed them that no man can do a miracle in his name, who does not possess a proper spirit. Mark ix: 38; Luke ix; 49. He then left Galilee, and went into Judea, and to the Jews he foretold the destruction of Jerusalem. He gave the declaration contained in the following passage: Luke xiii: 34—"O Jerusalem, Jerusalem, thou that killest the prophets, and stonest them that are sent unto thee; how often would I have gathered thy children together as a hen doth gather her brood under her wings, and ye would not."

The declaration was made just after certain Pharisees told him of Herod's intention to kill him. In Matthew xxiv, and Mark xiii, the same subject is spoken of, and Jesus follows the expostulation above with other predictions of the destruction of the temple, and the taking of Jerusalem, and the uprooting of the Jewish polity. He illustrates the whole by the parable of the fig tree. Matthew xxiv: 32–33.

As Jesus was on his way to Jerusalem, he passed through Galilee and Samaria, or from his own city, passed several other towns until he came to Samaria, and then passed through it, teaching and preaching, and curing diseases, and in one of the villages, he cured ten men who were lepers—whether they were all Samaritans or not we cannot tell—but one of them was, for, being healed, he glorified God with a loud voice, and fell down at Jesus' feet giving him thanks—"and he was a Samaritan," and he was the only one of the ten men that were cleansed, that returned to glorify God. Luke xvii: 12–18.

It is probable, that about this time, Jesus sent forth the seventy, two and two, into the various towns and cities, whither he himself would come. He sent them forth to preach and to heal. They went in the name of Jesus and were very successful. In a tour, of a few days, they performed many wonderful works, and returned to Jerusalem and reported, saying: "Lord even the devils are subject to us, through thy name." Luke x: 1–17. Jesus was, it is likely, at Jerusalem at this time, attending the feast of Tabernacles. There was a variety of opinions among the Jews regarding his character. Some declared him to be a good man, and others said he was a deceiver. John vii: 11. But about the middle of the feast, Jesus entered the temple, and declared his divine mission. He confounds the Jews, as he unfolds openly their secret designs against him. They were greatly enraged, and desired to kill him, but notwithstanding their hatred toward him, he keeps on teaching, until the last day of the feast, when he made an earnest appeal.

He saw the priests as they brought water from the pool of Siloam to use in the temple, and improved the circumstance by crying in their ears, "If any man thirst, let him come unto me and drink." The consequence of his searching appeals and earnest invitation was, many believed on him. John, vii: 37.

He continued in Jerusalem after the feast was ended, and still taught in the temple, and we have an account of a woman brought unto him by the Scribes and Pharisees, taken in the act of adultery. They referred him to the law of Moses, and its penalty for such an offense, which was death. They probably desired him to say that she should be stoned to death; that they might accuse him before the Roman governor, for arrogating to himself the power of life and death, which the Romans had taken away from the Jews. Yet he did not answer them, so that they could thus accuse him. Though he did not countenance the crime of which she was guilty, yet he did not condemn, for the witnesses against her had all fled. He bade her go and sin no more. John, viii: 1–11.

Jesus discoursed with the Jews regarding himself as the light of the world. He confutes the Pharisees in their cavils, and shows his authority, convicts them of sin and foretells their dying in it, because of their unbelief. When the Jews cavil again and declare the nobility of their birth, being Abraham's children, he shows their vanity, and the wickedness of their habits, and declared them to be children of the devil, doing his lusts, and murderers in their hearts, for they were constantly seeking to kill him. John, viii. They even attempted to stone him in the temple.

As Jesus was leaving the temple where the Jews had intended to stone him—to go it may be to the Mount of Olives, he saw a man who had been blind from his birth. The disciples were deeply interested in the case and asked him the question, "Master who did sin, this man or his parents, that he was born blind?" They referred to an idea that existed in many Jewish minds, that bodily afflictions or disabilities were marks of sin in the soul; and from this idea arose the proverb: "Mark him whom God marks." Jesus satisfied their enquiring minds as it regarded this matter, but restored the blind man to sight. John, ix: 1, &c.

It is likely that Jesus went to Bethany after he left Jerusalem, and was entertained at the house of Martha, and Mary, and Lazarus; and this was probably the time when Jesus mildly reproved Martha for her anxiety to provide a splendid repast, while he commended Mary who was complained of by her sister. Luke, x: 38-42.

Jesus was invited to the house of a Pharisee to dine. He accepted the invitation; and the Pharisee was very much astonished that he did not wash before dinner. He may not openly have made an objection, but Jesus knew his thoughts, and exposed the hypocrisy of this sect, and he denounced the wickedness of the lawyers, and condemned them. Luke, xi: 37–54.

He discourses about the Galileans, whose blood Pilate had mingled with their sacrifices, and the eighteen upon whom the tower of Siloam fell; and preaches in a powerful manner the necessity of repentance. Luke, xiii: 1. And while teaching in the synagogue on the Sabbath day, he cured a woman who had been seriously afflicted for eighteen years. Luke, xiii: 11. This cure was performed on the Sabbath, or shortly after the former cure. He entered into the house of a chief Pharisee to enjoy his hospitality, and while there he cured a man that had the dropsy. Luke, xiv: 1–6; and followed the cure with the discourse on humility which he gives in a parable. He also gave the parable of the great supper, and taught how men were to become his disciples. Luke, xiv.

He probably returned to Jerusalem about the time the feast of dedication came on, which was in the winter. John, vii: 14; and during that feast, to the Jews who came to him, he asserted his divinity, and declared himself to be equal and one with the Father. Because of this, the Jews sought to stone him. He vindicated his conduct and character, and appealed to his works. They strove to apprehend him, but he escaped out of their hands, left Jerusalem again, and went away beyond Jordan, where John at first baptized. John, x.

It was here that the question concerning divorce was presented by the Pharisees; and he answered it. Matt. xix: 1, &c.; Mark, x: 1, &c. And it was here that the little children were brought to him that he should put his hands on them and bless them; and he uttered that glorious declaration that comforts the hearts of Christian parents—especially when bereft of their children in death: "Suffer little children, and forbid them not, to come unto me; for of such is the kingdom of Heaven." Matt. xix: 13; Mark, x: 13; Luke, xviii: 15.

As he was leaving the coasts of Judea, when he had thus addressed the multitude, probably to go to Jericho, where we learn from Matt. xx: 29 he went, a young man came to him with the question, "good master, what good thing shall I do, that I may inherit eternal life." Jesus gave him a plain, pointed answer, laying down for him a course of conduct which would have resulted in his salvation, had he attended to it. Matt. xix: 16, Mark x: 17 and Luke xviii: 18. From the conduct of this young man Jesus was led to address his disciples on the subject of the dificulties of a rich man's being saved. About this time Lazarus the brother of Martha and Mary died, and Jesus with his disciples went to Bethany and there he raised Lazarus from the dead. John xi. After the miracle of raising Lazarus to life, Jesus retired to the City of Ephraim where he tarried awhile with his disciples, probably until the feast of the passover, which was the last passover he attended, and the one at which he suffered. John xi: 55. Here he foretold his sufferings the third time clearly. He said to his disciples, "Behold we go up to Jerusalem; and the son of man shall be betrayed into the hands of the chief priests and scribes, and they shall condemn him to death, &c." Matt. xx: 18, Mark x: 33 and Luke xviii: 31. On the way to Jerusalem he was entertained by Zaccheus. Luke xix: 2, and having made a stop at Jericho, as he was leaving it, Bartimeus a blind man implored him to restore him to sight. One of the evangelists says, "two blind men sitting by the wayside," and he informs us Jesus had compassion on them, and restored them to sight, and they followed him. Matt. xx: 29, Mark x: 46 and Luke xviii: 35.

Before he came to Jerusalem, Jesus lamented its condition and wept, because of its coming destruction. Luke xix: 41. He stopped at Bethany, which was but a short distance from Jerusalem, and took supper, for "they made him a supper and Martha served; but Lazarus was one of them that sat with him at the table." This was a few days before the Passover.

While Jesus was at Bethany in the house of Simon the leper, who may have been a person whom Jesus had healed of leprosy, a woman came to him and anointed his head with precious ointment. The person who performed this anointing was evidently Mary, the sister of Martha, if there was but one anointing; but possibly there may have been two, one in the house of Simon and the other in the house of Martha. Jesus commended the act, and took occasion again to speak of his coming death. Matt. xxvi: 6; Mark xiv: 1, and John xii: 1. Having made his triumphant march into Jerusalem, Mark xi: 1; Luke xix: 28, and John xii: 12, it is probable that the last six days before Jesus was apprehended and crucified, he spent the time in Jerusalem and about the temple, teaching the people, and each night lodged at Bethany, and it was during this time that he cleansed and purified the temple as set forth by the Evangelists. Matt. xxi: 12; Mark xi: 11; Luke xix: 45, and John ii: 14. After lodging at Bethany on one of those nights, in the morning as he returned to Jerusalem, he cursed the barren fig-tree, which miracle wonderfully astonished his disciples. While Jesus ministered in the temple, after he had used his authority in cleansing it, while engaged in prayer, the singular phenomenon of a voice from heaven was heard by those about the temple. It was the voice of God, the Father, declaring that his name had been glorified in Jesus, and should be glorified again. John xii: 28. Jesus called their attention to that voice as they had heard it, and he took occasion to discourse to them concerning his blessed mission and the ministration of John. John xii, and Luke xx. In that discourse he refers them to the question of obligation to pay tribute to Cesar. Matt. xxii: 16–22. In the same discourse he brings up the subject of his resurrection; teaches a lawyer the greatest commandment: Love to God; the next to it in importance: Love to our neighbor. He speaks about himself as the Messiah—as the son of David. Matt. xxii; Mark xii, and Luke xx. Jesus sat in the temple over against the treasury, and saw the worshipers casting their money in, and amongst them he saw a widow casting a farthing or two mites. He called the attention of his disciples to it, and greatly commended the widow for her gift. Mark xii: 41, and Luke xxi: 1. He delivered a discourse on the necessity and importance of watchfulness, during which he gave the parable of the evil and oppressive servant. Matt. xxiv; Mark xiii, and Luke xxi, and he refers to the destruction of Jerusalem, and the coming general judgment.

Judas, one of the twelve, engages, with the chief priests to betray Jesus for thirty pieces of silver, and having settled the arrangement with them, he sought a fit opportunity to accomplish it. Matthew xxvi: 14; Mark xiv: 10; Luke xxii: 3. Jesus then began to make the arrangements for celebrating the last Passover with his disciples. He sent Peter and John into the city, to a man whom he designated, who had a large upper room, and who offered them the use of the room, and they made ready the Passover, and Jesus, with his disciples, resorted thither. While there, a contest arose among the disciples as to who of them should be the greatest. Jesus taught them the importance of humble views of self in the simple yet significant manner of washing the feet of each one of them. In Matt. xxvi: 17; Mark xiv: 12; Luke xxii: 7; John xiii: 1, we find he instituted the sacred supper, and bade Judas, after he had designated him as the one that would betray him, "do what thou doest quickly." In the above quotations, with 1st Cor. xi: 23, we have the institution of the Lord's supper clearly set forth with all its solemnity and interest. He then delivered his farewell discourse to his disciples, contained in John xiv, offers up an earnest prayer for them, John xvii, and retires with some of them to the garden of Gethsemane, where he entered into the unspeakable agony that preceeded his crucifixion. Matthew xxvi: 36; Mark xiv: 32; Luke xxii: 39. The mob came by night to Gethsemane, headed by the traitor Judas, who betrayed him with an hypocritical kiss. They secured him and took him to the house of Annas, the father-in-law of Caiaphas, to be judged. John xviii: 13. Annas refusing to judge him, sent him to Caiaphas, and Caiaphas delivered him over to Pontius Pilate, who tried him, and condemned him to be crucified, after he had allowed him to pass a trial before Herod, and be mocked of his men of war. Jesus was not only subject to the abuses of these wicked men, but he was forsaken by all his disciples save Peter, and he did even worse than forsake him, for he denied him with bitter oaths and curses.

After Jesus was condemned he was led from Pilate's judgment hall to Calvary; they put a crown of thorns upon his head—clothed him in a scarlet robe; placed a reed in his hand, and then placed the cross on which he was to die, upon his shoulder, and compelled him to carry it toward the place of execution. He did carry it until he fainted beneath his load. They compelled him to rise up and bear it on; he fell a second time, but they compelled him to rise and feel its weight again; but a third time he faints beneath his load, and lest he should expire before they reached the top of the hill, and they not have the pleasure of crucifying him, they compelled a Cyrenian to bear it for him. When the designated place is reached they fastened him to the wood, and he is raised up to die. There were two malefactors crucified with him. The agony of Jesus on the cross cannot be told, but it may well be imagined as indiscribable by the language that escaped his lips while enduring it; "My God! My God! Why hast thou forsaken me," as well as the various attestations that were given of his divinity, in the darkened sun, and trembling of the earth, and rending of the vail of the temple in twain. He exercised his sin-pardoning power by preparing the moral nature of the dying penitent for heaven; but he himself gave up the ghost. He said "it is finished." For the account of the vicarious sufferings and death of Jesus see Matt. xxvi: 27; Mark, xiv: 15; Luke, xxii: 23; John xviii: 19.

After his death his body was given to Joseph of Arimathea, and he took it down from the cross, and preparing it for burial placed it in his own tomb. The Jews remembered how, in his life time he taught that he would rise from the dead, and they asked of Pilate a band of Roman soldiers with which to guard the sepulcher. He granted them their request, and they sealed the sepulcher and placed a Roman guard to watch; but on the third morning, or the first day of the week he rose from the grave. Matt. xxvii: 27, 28; Mark, xv: 43; Luke, xxiii: 24; John, xix: 20.

The fact of his resurrection was sufficiently attested. He was seen of Mary Magdalene, Simon, Cleopas and St. Luke, then of all the apostles, and at one time by five hundred brethren at once. Mark, xvi: 9; Luke, xxiv: 13, 24, 34; 1st Cor. xv: 6. He appeared to his disciples at different times for forty days; but having given them his final instructions, he led them to Olivet and ascended up into heaven. Mark, xvi: 19; Luke, xxiv: 51: Acts, i: 9. And the last they heard of him on the morning of the ascension was, "Ye men of Galilee why stand ye gazing up into heaven? this same Jesus whom ye now see," &c. He has become for man a mediator, having borne humanity with him to the skies—he has all the feelings of a man with all the compassion of a God; he is touched with the feelings of our infirmities.

JETHER—[Je′ther,] *he that excels, remains, searches.*

Jether was the husband of Abigail, the sister of David, and the father of Amasa, who commanded the army of Absalom in his rebellion. 1st Chron. ii: 17, "And Abigail bare Amasa, and the father of Amasa was Jether, the Ishmaelite."

JETHRO—[Jeth′ro,] *his excellence, or posterity.*

Jethro was a priest of Midian, and the father-in-law of Moses. When Moses fled from the land of Egypt, having been concerned in killing an Egyptian, he went to the land of Midian; he first formed an acquaintance with Jethro's daughters, at the well where they watered the cattle. He kindly rendered the young women assistance in watering their father's cattle, and driving away some shepherds who were disposed to impose upon them. They informed their father of the service he had rendered them, and Jethro invited him to his house, and he came, and there entered into an engagement to tarry with him, and be a shepherd, and Jethro gave him his daughter, Zipporah in marriage. Ex. ii: 15, 22.

Moses remained with Jethro forty years, when he was favored with revelations from God, and a commission to emancipate his enslaved countrymen in Egypt. He made known the revelations to Jethro, and asked his permission to go with his wife and sons to his own country. Consent was given, and he pronounced upon Moses and his mission, his blessing—"Go in peace." Ex. iv: 18. Moses started, but for some cause, his wife and children returned to Jethro, where they remained until after the Israelites had left the land of Egypt, and were encamped at the foot of Mt. Sinai, where Jethro, Moses' father-in-law, paid him a visit, taking Zipporah, and her two sons with him. Exodus, xviii: 1-3. He probably sent Moses word that he was coming before he reached the camp, and he went and met him, and fell prostrate before him, took him into his tent, and related the wonderful dealings of God with him and his people. Jethro acknowledged the hand of God, and engaged in offering burnt offerings and peace offerings, and he ate with Moses and Aaron, and the elders of Israel. And, as the next day Moses took his seat in order to judge Israel, from morning till evening, Jethro observed it and thought it too much for him, and ventured to suggest a change in the administration of justice among the people. Moses listened to it and accepted it, and soon had helpers to judge in all the trivial cases, while he himself, reserved the important cases for judgment.

When the Israelites were about moving from the wilderness of Sinai, Moses invited his father-in-law to remain with his people, and go on to the promised land. Jethro refused to do so, for he had interests in Midian that demanded his attention, but it is thought he left Hobab, his son, with the Israelites, and he became one with them in their travels, and in his posterity had an inheritance in Canaan. We hear nothing more of Jethro after he left Moses, as Israel moved from the wilderness of Sinai. Many think he was a true priest of the living God, and maintained the true religion as a descendant of Midian, one of Abraham's sons, by Keturah. Moses offered sacrifice to God with him for forty years in Midian, and as we have seen, they sacrificed together in the camp of Israel. He evidently worshiped the same God that the Israelites did.

JETUR—[Je′tur,] *he that keeps, succession, mountainous.*

Was the son of Ishmael, and the grandson of Abraham. Genesis xxv: 15.

JEUSH, 1—[Je′ush,] *devoured, gnawed by the moth.*

Was one of the four sons of Shimei. They were Jeush, Jahath, Zizah and Beriah, and it was said of Jeush and Beriah, that they had not many sons, and for that cause, they were reckoned as one family in their father's house. 1st Chron. xxiii: 11.

JEUSH, 2—*Devoured, gnawed by the moth.*

Was one of the sons of Rehoboam, and born unto him of one of the wives he took in the family of David. 2d Chron. xi: 19.

JEZEBEL—[Jez′-e-bel,] *island of the habitation, wo to the habitation, isle of the dunghill.*

Jezebel was the daughter of Ethbaal, the king of Zidon, and was the wife of Ahab, the king of Israel. She was from an idolatrous country, and was herself an idolater. Though she became the wife of Ahab, she did not become a worshiper of the God of Israel; but, on the contrary, she used witchcraft, and was given to idolatry. She maintained among the people of God the religion of her own country. At her own expense she supported four hundred priests of the groves, sacred to Ashtaroth of the Zidonians. Ahab committed a sin against God in taking her to wife, she being a heathen and hostile to the true religion. She was the idolatrous daughter of an idolatrous king. Ahab knew this fact well, for she practiced idolatry openly, nay more, she persecuted the true religion. Under her influence Ahab was lead to countenance idolatry and himself to serve Baal. 1st Kings, xvi: 32, 33: "And he reared up an altar for Baal in the house of Baal, which he had built in Samaria. And Ahab made a grove."

What a spectacle is presented to our minds here! A heathen woman selected for a wife of the king of Israel, and in Israel patronizing the religion of her native country, and influencing her husband to the grossest idolatry. While she fed four hundred prophets of the goddess Astarte at her table, Ahab supported four hundred of Baal's prophets as ministers of his false gods.

Soon God visited Israel for their sin with a dearth that prevailed for three years and six months. During the time of this dearth, Jezebel had wreaked her vengeance in persecution by murdering the prophets of Israel. When Obadiah met Elijah and was commanded to go tell Ahab, "Behold, Elijah is here," Obadiah made objection, and referred to the cruelty of Jezebel. 1st Kings, xviii: 13: "Was it not told my Lord what I did when Jezebel slew the prophets of the Lord, how I hid a hundred men of the Lord's prophets in a cave and fed them with bread and water?"

It is quite likely that Jezebel, as she was a bad woman, attributed the public calamity, in the dearth that was prevailing, to Elijah, who could not be found. And as she could not find him, she determined to kill all the prophets of the Lord that could be found, or that were within her reach. But Elijah had determined to show himself to Ahab, the king, that day. Obadiah informed the king, and soon afterward the two distinguished personages met. Elijah, after giving the king, in a coversation, the true ground of the present dearth, bade him bring all Israel to Mt. Carmel, with the prophets of Baal, four hundred and fifty, and the prophets of the groves, four hundred. These latter named prophets were those who were supported by Queen Jezebel. They were all residents of Samaria, and ate at her table. These prophets of Baal, with the multitude of Israel, assembled on the mount, and Elijah made a proposition, which they accepted, to try the power of Israel's God, and their god Baal. The trial was made, and Elijah's God answered by fire. The multitude of spectators declared in favor of Elijah.

Though Elijah demanded of Ahab the presence of Jezebel's prophets, it seems they were not present to witness the stirring and convincing scene on Mount Carmel. After the fire came down from Heaven and consumed the sacrifice, Ahab consented to the death of the prophets of Baal, and Elijah slew all by the brook Kishon. This demonstration was followed by an abundant rain, in answer to the continued earnest prayer of Elijah. It was not long after Ahab arrived at the palace that he told Jezebel what Elijah had done—that he had slain all the prophets with the sword. As soon as she heard it she determined to take vengeance on him, and she sent a messenger to the prophet, 1st Kings, xix: 2, saying, "So let the gods do to me, and more also, if I make not thy life as the life of one of them, by to-morrow about this time." She meant, by this form of expression, to say, If I do not slay thee, Elijah, let the gods put me to the most painful death. When the prophet received this message from Jezebel, he fled for his life, and escaped out of her hand.

King Ahab desired the vineyard of Naboth the Jezreelite, yet Naboth was unwilling to give it up or sell it, for in doing so he would violate one of the Levitical laws, which forbids alienating parental inheritance. As the King was troubled about it, Jezebel counseled him, as such a wicked woman was capable of counseling, and she undertook the infamous work of murdering this man and placing his vineyard in the possession of Ahab. She proclaimed in the name of the King a fast, set Naboth on high—brought him to a public trial—procured two witnesses to swear falsely against him, and had him stoned to death for the alleged offence. She then informed Ahab that Naboth was dead, and bade him arise and take possession of the vineyard, and he did so. Elijah appeared unto Ahab while in the vineyard, and declared unto him the word of the Lord, in which it was given that Ahab's blood should be licked up by the dogs in the place where Naboth's blood was spilled. And further, the prophet declared that Jezebel's body should be eaten, by the walls of Jezreel, by the dogs, and we are informed in 2d Kings ix: 34, &c., that this declaration of the prophet was literally fulfilled.

Jezebel's influence over Ahab was very great. She was the means of leading him into idolatry and many other gross sins that mark his course. She was a curse to all Israel, and though the judgments of God were turned aside from Ahab because he humbled himself before the Lord, yet her wickedness brought those judgments upon Ahab's sons. When Ahab was killed in battle and died in his chariot, as that chariot was afterwards washed at the pool of Samaria, cleansing it from the blood of the slain King, the prediction of Elijah was fulfilled, "Dogs shall lick thy blood, even thine." Ahaziah, his son, reigned in his stead; but his reign was short. Jehoram also reigned. These sons, in all probability, were under her influence, and when Jehoram fell by the hand of Jehu, the son of Nimshi, the witchcraft and abominations of Jezebel, his mother, was the last thing he heard of.

Jehu went to Jezreel in seach of Jezebel. "She painted herself and tired her head, and looked out at a window." The object she had in view, probably, was to improve her appearance so that Jehu would be charmed and captured by her beauty, and be induced to take her for a wife. Had she succeeded in her designs in this respect, she might still have corrupted the court and reign of Israel's king. But she did not succeed. As Jehu entered the city she attracted his attention, and ventured to address him with words of conciliation. "Had Zimri peace who slew his master?" It is supposed by some that the meaning of this address to him was, "If thou hast slain thy master, it is no more than Zimri did, who slew Elah."

But Jehu was not to be pacified with any words or acts of this wicked woman. He had come to find her and slay her, and looking up to the window where she was, he asked two men, who had designated themselves as being on his side, to throw her down, and they did. "And some of her blood was sprinkled upon the wall, and upon the horses; and he trod her under foot. How terrible was the death of Jezebel. Thrown down from a window, in sight of the people, almost killed by the fall, and then her mangled body trod upon by the horses Jehu and his aids rode upon. Thus mangled, her lifeless form was left, while he and his companions went into some house and ate and drank. After he had feasted awhile he gave orders concerning the burial of Jezebel's body. "Go see now, this cursed woman, and bury her, for she is a king's daughter."

Jehu knew her lineage and position as to royalty. He knew she was the daughter of the king of Tyre; wife of Ahab, king of Israel; mother of Joram, another king; the grand-mother of Ahaziah, king of Judah; also the mother-in-law of another king of Judah.

They went in search of the body of Jezebel, but to their astonishment they found "no more of her than the skull, and the feet, and the palms of her hands." How terribly had the vengeance of God been displayed in the punishment and death of this wicked woman, and devouring of her body by dogs. And how literally had the prediction of the prophet Elijah been fulfilled. "The dogs shall eat Jezebel by the wall of Jezreel."

Though she was a woman of rank, because of her birth, relationship, and alliances, yet she was not honored with a burial, but dogs ate her flesh. No funeral followed this calamity and no monument was erected to mark the spot where one of royal blood lies. "And the carcass of Jezebel shall be as dung upon the face of the field in the portion of Jezreel; so that they shall not say, this is Jezebel."

JEZER—[Je'zer.]

Jezer was the son of Naphtali, and the third of his sons as they are named in order in Genesis, xlvi: 24. This person was the head of the family of the Jezerites. Num. xxvi: 49.

JEZRAHIAH—[Jez-ra-hi'-ah,] *the Lord is the east, the Lord arises.*

There was a person of this name who was a chief of the singers in the ceremonies of dedicating the walls of Jerusalem, rebuilt by Nehemiah. He is called the overseer of the singers. Neh. xii: 42.

JEZREEL, 1—[Jez'-re-el,] *seed of God, dropping of the friendship of God.*

Jezreel was the son of Etam, of the tribe of Judah, referred to in 1st Chron. iv: 3.

JEZREEL, 2.

Was the son of the prophet Hosea, by his wife Gomer. Hosea, i: 4.

JIDLAPH—[Jid'-laf,] *he that distils.*

Was the son of Nahor, and the grandson of Terah. Gen. xxii: 22.

JIMNAH.

Jimnah was one of the sons of Asher, the son of Jacob, and he is reckoned with the children and grandchildren of the old Patriarch in Gen. xlvi: 17. The names of his brothers as given were Ishuah, Isui and Beriah. The name of his sister is also given, Serah, and also the names of two nephews, the sons of his brother Beriah, viz., Heber and Malchiel. Jimnah was head of the family in the tribe of Asher, called the Jimnites. Num. xxvi: 44.

JOAB—[Jo'-ab,] *paternity, having a father, voluntary.*

Joab was the son of Zeruiah, David's sister, and the brother of Abishai and Asahel, hence he was the nephew of King David—he was also David's general. He was faithful and valiant as a warrior, true as a commander, yet he was cruel and revengeful. We have an exhibition of his character in this particular, in his compliance with the proposal of Abner to have a duel fought between twelve of the men of Ishbosheth, and twelve of the men of David. 2d Sam. ii: 15. This trial of twelve men on each side was at Gibeon. That very day he fought with the troops of Ish-bosheth and conquered them, though his brother Asahel was killed by Abner. 2d Sam. ii: 27. This greatly enraged Joab, and he determined to revenge his brother's death, and an opportunity being afforded he treacherously slew Abner. 2d Sam. iii: 27. David did by no means approve this cruel act. He declared himself guiltless before the Lord, as was also his kingdom, of the blood of Abner, the son of Ner, and charged guiltiness upon Joab, and more than indicated that Joab would be punished in his posterity; that the members of his household, or his descendants, would be diseased; some of them would fall by the sword and others of them would lack bread.

It is probable that David would have punished him for his cruel act in murdering Abner, had it not been for his wonderful influence with the troops; for Joab and his brother Abishai were in the confidence and esteem of the army, for they had just been led by them to a victory. Joab led the troops at Jerusalem, entered the city and drove back the guards, and by his heroic conduct he secured the position of chief commander of all the forces of Israel. He directed the army in their battles with and conquests of the Moabites, Philistines, Edomites, Syrians and Ammonites, who all became tributary to Israel.

When David desired the murder of Uriah, the Hittite, Joab became accessory, and put Uriah in the forefront of the battle. 2d Sam. xi: 15. It was through the influence, and management and cunning of Joab, that David was induced to send and fetch Absalom from his exile; and he afterwards obtained Absalom's admission to court. This return of the king's son from Geshur was through the stratagem of Joab, though the woman of Tekoa made the plea in Absalom's behalf; yet, after the return of Absalom, Joab was evidently his enemy and opposer. And when he rebelled against his father David, and raised an army with an intention of usurping authority and making himself king, Joab led the army of David to battle, and refused to regard the instructions of the father as to the manner of treatment of the rebellious son. He was ordered to deal gently with the young man, Absalom, and spare his life; yet, contrary to orders, after the tide of battle turned in his favor, hearing that Absalom's head was caught in an oak, he went with his armor-bearers to the place and thrust three darts through the body of Absalom. 2d Sam. xviii: 14.

When David mourned because Absalom was dead, Joab reproved him and showed him that his sorrow was excessive and ill-timed. He more than intimated that the king should be engaged in commending his brave warriors, rather than in excessively mourning the death of his rebel son. We may judge that David did not take the reproof of Joab kindly, and especially the violation of his orders, for he displaced him from the generalship and appointed Amasa in his stead. 2d Sam. xx: 4.

Joab volunteered and attended his brother Abishai's troops in the pursuit of Sheba, the son of Bichri, who had raised a rebellion, and at the great stone in Gibeon he murdered Amasa. In pretended friendship he approached him to kiss him; and taking hold of Amasa's beard with his right hand, with his left hand he plunged his sword into his body, and thereby occasioned his death suddenly. Having committed this murder he took command of the troops again, and pursued Sheba unto the city of Abel of Bethmaachah. He besieged the city and would have destroyed it had not the wise woman of the city agreed to throw him the head of Sheba over the wall. This was done, and Joab returned unto Jerusalem to the king, with the head of the rebel, it may be, in his possession, to show to David as evidence that the rebellion was ended. 2d Sam. xx.

When David determined to number Israel, and issued orders to that effect, Joab wisely remonstrated with him; but his opposition did not avail, and he was obliged to enter upon and execute that task; and at the end of nine months and twenty days he had performed the task, save the numbering of Jerusalem. When the whole task was completed he reported the number. 2d Sam. xxiv.

After serving David for a long time in company with his brother Abishai, he was engaged in a rebellion which contemplated the placing of Adonijah on the throne, as David's successor, contrary to the wishes and designs of that king. Joab knew full well that Solomon was to be the successor of David, but he took advantage of David's premature age and infirmity, and his little concern in the government of the kingdom. His attempt to make Adonijah king, failed, and as his efforts became known to David, they served to increase his displeasure at Joab. When the king gave his deathbed charge to his successor, he bade him punish the son of Zeruiah, for the murder of the two captains of the hosts of Israel, Abner and Amasa. Adonijah was put to death by Solomon, for laying a plan as the king supposed, to usurp authority, and increase his claims to the throne of Israel, by securing as a wife, the last wife of his father David. When Joab learned that Adonijah was slain by Solomon's orders, he became alarmed, supposing that he too, would be put to death, and he fled to the brazen altar at Gibeon for refuge, and caught hold of the horns of the altar. When Solomon heard that he was there, he sent Benaiah to fetch him, who, when he had come to the tabernacle said to Joab, "thus saith the king, come forth." He refused to come forth, preferring rather to die there. He had fled there for protection and would not quit the place. Solomon then ordered Benaiah to execute him there, and he did so. He seems to have served David faithfully throughout his entire reign, except failing to carry out his orders regarding Absalom, and so wickedly putting to death the two captains of the hosts of Israel. After his death, he was buried in his own house in the wilderness. 1st Kings ii: 34.

JOAH, 1—[Jo′-ah,] *who has a brother, brother of the Lord.*

JOAH was a servant of King Hezekiah, and the son of Asaph the recorder. He was sent by Hezekiah in company with Eliakim and Shebna, to receive the propositions of Rabshakeh the agent of the King of Assyria. 2d Kings xviii: 18. They were improperly treated by Rabshakeh, who blasphemed before them, and the Jews. They were deeply affected, and with clothes rent they reported the result of their conference to Hezekiah.

JOAH, 2—*Who has a brother, brother of the Lord.*

JOAH was the secretary to King Josiah. He was the son of Joahaz the recorder, and we learn from 2d Chron. xxxiv: 8, that he was associated with Shaphan and Maaseiah under an order of Josiah, in repairing the house of the Lord.

JOAH, 3—*Who has a brother, brother of the Lord.*

JOAH was the third son of Obed-Edom, and one of the sacred porters. 1st Chron. xxvi: 4.

JOANNA—[Jo-an-′na,] *the grace or mercy of the Lord.*

This woman was the wife of Chuza, the steward of Herod. Luke viii: 3. She is represented as associating herself with Mary Magdalene and Susanna, and others in ministering unto Christ. She was a woman of position, for the office her husband filled was one of honor and profit, overseer of the kings domestic affairs. She had probably heard Jesus preach, witnessed some of his miracles, and believed him to be the Messiah. If she had not believed him to be Christ she would not have "ministered unto him of her substance," as it is said she did.

JOASH, 1—[Jo′-ash,] *who despairs, burns, is on fire.*

JOASH was the son of Ahaziah, king of Judah. When he was a child one year old his grandmother, Athaliah, made an attempt to murder him, with the other members of Ahaziah's family, but Jehoshebah, the wife of Jehoiada, the high priest, and the aunt of the young child Joash, kept him from her. She hid him six years in a chamber of the temple. And when he was seven years old the high priest entered into a solemn covenant, with several important personages in the kingdom, to make Joash, young as he was, the king of Judah, and thereby dethrone the wicked Athaliah. 2d Kings, xi.

After Jehoiada, with his associates, had prepared matters in the kingdom by bringing the Levites, and others that they could trust, to Jerusalem, they made Joash king, crowning him in the court of the temple with great ceremony and solemnity. Athaliah heard their acclamations, and alarmed, ran to the court of the temple, where she was secured and quickly carried forth and slain. Jehoiada then entered into a solemn covenant to serve the Lord and him only. At once an important revolution took place. Baal's temples and statues were torn down, and the priest Mattan was slain, and Jehoiada, who became the tutor to Joash, began repairing the house of the Lord. 2d Chron. xxiii.

Joash was zealous in the reformation as long as Jehoiada lived, but when he died the king was influenced by wicked courtiers. He neglected the worship of God, and soon idolatry again prevailed. When Joash had thus lapsed into idolatry, Zechariah, the son of Jehoiada, who was his successor in the priesthood, uttered faithful warnings; and because of those faithful warnings he was stoned to death in the court of the house of the Lord, by order of King Joash. 2d Chron. xxiv: 21. While Zechariah was dying under the shower of stones he assured his murderers that his death should be revenged; and it was. Hazael invaded the kingdom of Judah, and Joash was compelled to redeem his capital from plunder with a large sum of money and the valuable treasures in the house of the Lord, which he gave to Hazael, the king of Syria, and so, for the time being, saved Jerusalem. 2d Kings, xii: 18.

About a year after this a company of Syrians ravaged the country, defeated the army of Joash, pillaged the capital, and murdered the princes. They heaped disgrace upon the king; and not long after his own servants murdered him in his bed; and so the blood of Zechariah, who was murdered between the porch and the altar, was revenged. 2d Chron. xxiv: 25. He was buried in Jerusalem, but not in the sepulcher of the kings.

JOASH, 2—*Who despairs, burns, is on fire.*

Joash was the son of Jehoahaz, and the grandson of Jehu. He was a king of Israel. He reigned two years in conjunction with his father and fourteen years alone. 2d Kings, xiii: 9.

Joash copied after the wickedness of Jeroboam, the son of Nebat. He departed not from the course of his father in that he too walked in the ways of Jeroboam.

When Elisha, the prophet, was sick, Joash sent to him and was encouraged by the declaration of the prophet that he should deliver his people from their Syrian oppressors. Elisha, in his instructions, indicated a triple victory for Joash by ordering him to shoot arrows out of the window of the apartment where they were, eastward. 2d Kings, xiii: 15. He accordingly did defeat Benhadad. He routed the Syrians and recovered the cities they had taken from Israel.

Amaziah, the king of Judah, provoked Joash to war with him, and he defeated him. 2d Kings, xiv: 15. After he had conquered him he pillaged the capital of Judah, and returned to Samaria, his own capital, in triumph, where he died soon afterward, and was succeeded by Jeroboam, his son.

JOB—[Jobe,] *he that weeps, cries, or speaks out of a hollow place.*

Job was a noted servant of the living God; and he is introduced to our view, in the beginning of the book which bears his name, as an inhabitant of Uz—(a region of country eastward of Gilead)—a perfect man and upright, one that feared God and eschewed evil. He is thought by some to have been the same as Jobah, one of the ancient kings of Edom, hence a descendant of Esau; but it is quite probable that he was before Esau, and cotemporary with the patriarch Abraham. It has been thought that he was a descendant of Nahor by Huz, his eldest son, as Elihu, one of Job's counsellors, was by Buz, Nahor's second son. It is impossible to tell certainly from whom he was descended, and at what particular time he lived. There are some important circumstances that he mentions or refers to, which lead us to suppose that he was cotemporary with the great Patriarch.

There can be no doubt but there was such a person as Job, and that the afflictions spoken of in the book of Job were real. The Spirit of Inspiration refers to him as a righteous man. Ezek. xiv: 14: "Though these three men,

Noah, Daniel and Job, were in it, they should deliver but their own souls by their righteousness." And the apostle James, v : 11, says: "Behold, we count them happy which endure. Ye have heard of the patience of Job, and have seen the end of the Lord; that the Lord is very pitiful and of tender mercy." And in addition to this, the book itself expressly specifies the names of persons, places, facts, &c., usually related in other histories, which are considered reliable. Job's name is given; his wealth is described, and his piety; and the number of his children, with the names of some of them, at least. His wife is referred to, and her conduct is a recorded fact. It is quite likely he was comparatively a young man when he passed through the severe trials recorded of him; for Eliphaz, one of his counsellors, addresses him as a young man compared with himself. Job, xv: 10: "With us are the gray-headed and very aged men, much elder than thy father." Job speaks of the sins of his youth, and also of the prosperity of his youth. Job, xiii: 26. He survived his trial one hundred and forty years. xlii: 16. His afflictions were in all probability some time before the departure of the children of Israel from Egypt; and the book was written before that, or there would have been, we think, some allusion to that circumstance.

The history of Job begins with his character as a devoted servant of the living God. His family consisted of seven sons and three daughters, who all lived in affluence, and for aught we know, in harmony. His wealth was abundant, consisting of oxen and asses, sheep, camels, &c. He was probably the wealthiest and greatest man in all that country—noted for his piety and integrity. He not only attended to his own spiritual interests, but, like Abraham, to the spiritual interests of his family. When his sons held their annual feasts, which they probably did regularly on their birth-days, Job always rose early next morning, and with deep devotion offered up sacrifices for them, fearing lest in their mirth they had forsaken God and committed sin against him. Job, i: 5, informs us that this was his constant custom.

Job was marked by Satan and his destruction aimed at. God permitted seven calamities to come upon him for the trial of his faith. On a certain day, when the worshipers of God were assembled together for devotion, Satan presented himself among them. And the Almighty questioned him as to whence he came, where he was going, and what his object was. And God asked Satan if he had set his heart upon the destruction of his servant Job. He indicated that he had, and told the Almighty that Job was devoted to him from mercenary motives. He insinuated that Job was a hypocrite, that he was serving God for the purpose of preserving his uncommon wealth and to add to it, and that if he was afflicted a little he would soon give up his religion and curse his Maker. God then permitted Satan to try Job, by destroying his property, but he was not allowed to touch his person.

Satan incited the thievish Sabeans to fall on his cattle, and they drove them all away and murdered his servants. He next caused fire to fall upon Job's flocks and burn them up and the servants that kept them. He next incited the savage and unprincipled Chaldeans, to fall upon the camels and take them and murder the servants who were attending them, and about the same time, while the seven sons and three daughters of Job were attending a feast at their elder brother's house, probably a birth-day feast, Satan raised a terrible storm that blew down the house and buried the ten children in the ruins.

It seems that in every one of these calamities that fell upon Job, some one who witnessed them was preserved and bore the sad news to him, and they came in succession as messengers of sad tidings. When the last one told the heart-rending tale of the death of his sons and daughters, severe as was the stroke, he resigned himself to the will and providence of God, and having exhibited his grief by rending his clothes and shaving off the hair of his head, he broke out in the following language: "The Lord gave, and the Lord hath taken away; blessed be the name of the Lord." It was not long after this until Satan presented himself again as the enemy of Job. The Lord referred him to the conduct of Job, under the heavy afflictions through which he had passed. Satan then suggested that Job had maintained his integrity because his person was untouched, and he alleged that if he was afflicted in person, he would then curse God and give up his service.

Satan was then permitted to do all that he could in afflicting Job in body, but was limited in that he could not destroy his life. He immediately afflicted him with sore boils from the crown of his head to the soles of his feet. He became, because of these, a loathsome object to look upon. He clothed himself with sackcloth and sat in ashes, and scraped himself with a potsherd, thus removing the putrid matter that ran from his sores.

In addition to all his other afflictions, his wife upbraided him because he did not complain. "Dost thou still maintain thine integrity? curse God and die." But as he had behaved in the former trials, so did he in this. He said to his wife "thou speakest as one of the foolish women. Shall we receive good at the hands of the Lord, and not also evil." He felt that it became him to receive affliction from God's hand, that had so often bestowed favors. Job, ii: 10.

His three friends, Eliphaz, Bildad and Zophar, hearing of the calamities that had befallen him, the sad disasters through which he had passed and was passing, came to visit him, and counsel him, and with them came a young man named Elihu. The counsel, advice and admonitions of the four friends are given in the the book of Job.

It seems that the patience of the good man was almost overcome, and he was led to curse the day of his birth. He seems to wish that he had never been born, or that he had died in early infancy. When his three friends charged him with hypocrisy, and gave it as their opinion that his severe afflictions were punishment for his sins. He plead his own cause before them and declared that he was not a deceiver. He protested against their charge, and certified his integrity in such a manner that he put them to silence.

The youthful Elihu then spoke, and in his address he admitted that Job was a saint, a true servant of the living God, yet he reproved him for some of his unguarded speeches. And this address of Elihu was probably approved of God, for he follows it with a solemn address that seemed to strike conviction to Job's heart. He was convinced of error and repented before God. He sought, and obtained divine favor, and the Almighty appointed him as a priest and a minister of religion to his three friends who had falsely charged him.

After Job had prayed for their forgiveness the scenes in his life begin to change. The burden that was upon him was taken off, and his friends came to him from every direction with compliments and presents of money. He soon became wealthy again, much more so than before the destruction of his property. And again the Lord blessed him with children, in number the same as he had before, seven sons and three daughters, and we are informed that he gave to his daughters the following names: Jemima, Kezia and Keren-happuch. It is said they were very fair, not excelled in beauty by any women of the land.

Job lived, after he was thus restored to prosperity, one hundred and forty years, and saw his children to the fourth generation. Job is to be pointed to in all time to come as an example of patience in affliction, of triumph in the darkest hours, of strong faith in God, and bright hopes of a future glorious inheritance. [See the Book of Job.]

JOB, 2—*He that weeps, cries, or speaks out of a hollow place.*

Job was one of the sons of Issachar, and is mentioned with his three brothers among the grand children of Jacob, who went down into Egypt to sojourn there. Gen. xlvi: 13.

JOBAB, 1—[Jo'bab.]

Jobab was the son of Joktan, and the grandson of Eber, and is referred to in the posterity of Shem. Genesis x: 29.

JOBAB, 2.

Jobab, a king of Edom, was the son of Zerah, of Bozrah, and the successor as a king, of Bela, the son of Beor. He was succeeded by Hushan of the land of Temani. Some have thought that this person was the same as Job, the man of Uz; but the history of him in Gen. xxxvi: 34, does not present him as a man remarkable for his trials, patience and faith.

**JOCHEBED**—[Jok′e-bed,] *glorious, honorable, a person of merit, the glory of the Lord.*

JOCHEBED was the wife of Amram. "There went a man of the house of Levi and took to wife a daughter of Levi." And this woman of Levi was the mother of the illustrious Moses. The names of Amram and Jochebed are not given where the thrilling narrative of their son commences, Exodus ii. But their names occur in Exodus vi, where the family of Levi is spoken of by name. And the marriage of Amram with Jochebed, with the relation they sustained to each other before their marriage, and the two sons, Aaron and Moses, that she bare. Ex. vi: 20. "And Amram took him Jochebed, his father's sister, to wife, and she bare him Aaron and Moses." She sustained then the relation of aunt to him on his father's side.

Aaron, the eldest son of Jochebed, was born before the cruel edict of the king of Egypt, but Moses was born during the existence of the cruel law. His mother determined, if possible, to save him. "When she saw him that he was a goodly child, she hid him three months." This would seem to intimate that the babe was more beautiful than her other children had been, when in early infancy, and possibly this may be so, and is a part of the reason which led the daughter of Pharoah to adopt him as her son, and make him an Egyptian Prince. Jochebed succeeded for three months in concealing her child and so preserving its life. And fearing to attempt hiding him any longer, she collected together from the marshy grounds near the river Nile, reeds or rushes, and with them constructed an ark, and having made it water-proof, and prepared it to be a comfortable habitation for a short time for the infant, she lulled him to sleep, imprinted the kiss of fond affection upon his little cheek, then committed him to his home. She placed the ark in the flags of the river's brink. Though she did not doubt but the ark was water-proof, yet she was not willing because of the precious treasure within it, to put it out on the water, where it would be bourne down by the current. She placed it among the flags by the brink not very far from the place where Pharoah's daughter was accustomed to come, it may be, every day, to perform a religious ablution. The princess saw the ark, had it brought to her, looked at the beautiful babe, and determined almost at once to adopt it as her own son.

Soon, in the order of Divine Providence, Jochebed had her darling babe placed in her arms again, to nurse it for Pharoah's daughter for wages. How must her heart have swelled with gratitude to God, when she pressed that infant to her bosom, and thought of the future greatness destined for him.

When he had come to sufficient age, she took him to the princess, and he became her son. How often she saw him after this, we do not know, but it is reasonable to suppose that Moses occasionally visited her, and that when she died she had a firm conviction that her son would be a great man, and a friend to his oppressed people.

**JOEL, 1** — [Jo′-el,] *that wills, commands, or swears.*

JOEL was the son of Pethuel, one of the minor prophets. He is thought to have prophesied in the time of Hezekiah or Manasseh. He is the author of some very important prophecies. He told of a fearful famine, that would come upon his people on account of a want of rain, and an abundance of destructive vermin. He calls upon the people to engage in humbling themselves before God, by fasting and prayer, and tells them that they shall be delivered from the famine and destruction, by being thus properly exercised. He also prophesies of the pouring out of the Holy Spirit in the last days, and under the glorious effusion on the day of Pentecost. Peter in his memorable sermon refers to Joel's prophesy, in the following language: "These men are not drunken as you suppose, seeing it is but the third hour of the day, but this is that which was spoken by the prophet Joel: Behold, I will pour out of my spirit in the last days, saith the Lord, &c."

Joel predicts the ruin of the Philistines and other nations, and then refers to the deliverance of the Jews in the last days. [See book of Joel.]

JOEL, 2—*That wills, commands, or swears.*

JOEL was the name of the eldest son of Samuel. He with Abiah assisted Samuel as a Judge of Israel. 1st Sam. viii: 2, &c. [See Abiah.]

JOEL, 3—*That wills, commands, or swears.*

JOEL was the son of Josibiah. 1st Chron. iv: 35.

JOEL, 4—*That wills, commands, or swears.*

JOEL was the son of Zichri. He is referred to in Neh. xi: 9, as a person of considerable importance. He was an overseer among the dwellers at Jerusalem.

JOEL, 5—*That wills, commands, or swears.*

JOEL was the son of Pedaiah, the ruler in the half tribe of Manasseh in the time of David. 1st Chronicles xxvii: 20.

JOGLI—[Jog′-li.]

JOGLI was the father of Bukki, the prince of the tribe of Dan, who assisted in dividing the land of Canaan. Num. xxxiv: 22.

JOHANAN—[Jo-ha′-nan.]

JOHANAN was the son of Kareah, the brother of Jonathan, and an associate of Seraiah and Jezaniah, captains of the forces that were under Gedaliah at Mizpah. He informed Gedaliah of Ishmael's conspiracy against him. He refused to credit Johanan or to allow him to go as he proposed, secretly to Ishmael and slay him, and so break up the conspiracy. Gedaliah even charged Johanan with speaking falsely of Ishmael. Jer. xl: 13. Johanan with his associate captains, after the murder of Gedaliah by Ishmael, pursued the murderer and overtook him, yet Ishmael escaped out of his hands and went to the Ammonites. Johanan recovered the captains that Ishmael had carried away and brought them to Chimham which is by Bethlehem, and there they dwelt. Johanan and his associates, with the people that were with them brought the prophet Jeremiah to pray to God for them, that they might enjoy the divine benediction, and be divinely directed in their walk and conduct in the future. Jeremiah promised to pray for them and faithfully to report the word of the Lord to them. And he did.

It seems that Johanan and those that were with him desired to go to Egypt and reside, and the prophet enquired of the Lord for them, whether they should go, and the prophet reported to them, that they should remain in their own land and should be saved from the hand of the king of Babylon. But if they determined to go to Egypt for the purpose of escaping war and hunger, these things should surely overtake them and they should die in that land. They would not obey the Lord and suffered for their disobedience. Jer. xlii.

When Johanan went into Egypt he carried the people, left in the land, down with him, and the prophet Jeremiah among them, and in the course of fourteen years they suffered from various invasions of the Chaldeans—war, the sound of the trumpet, pestilence and famine were visited upon them, and they died. Jer. xliii.

JOHN, 1—[Jon,] *the gift or mercy of the Lord.*

JOHN THE BAPTIST was prophesied of as the forerunner of Messiah—the messenger of the coming Savior. He was spoken of by Isa. xl: 3, and Mal. iii: 1. Because of the important position he was called to occupy he is called the Elias.

He was the son of Zacharias and Elisabeth. This Zacharias was an aged priest of the course of Abia. This aged couple were holy and devout—they "walked in all the ordinances and commandments of the Lord, blameless." The birth of this distinguished person, and the important work he should perform were predicted by the angel Gabriel. His father was ministering at the altar in the order of his course, when the angel appeared unto him, and spake of his coming son. On account of his unwillingness to credit the prediction of the divine messenger, he was struck dumb, and he was unable to speak until after John was born. At the time that Zacharias gave him his name, his tongue was loosed and he praised God, and as the spirit of prophecy came upon him he predicted the appearance and work of Christ shortly, as also the character and work of this his infant son. Luke, i: 67.

It had been declared by the angel regarding John that he should be a Nazarite from his mother's womb, "and he shall drink neither wine nor strong drink, and he shall be filled with the holy Ghost." Luke, i: 15. Of the early part of the life of John the Baptist, we know but little. It is said of him that he grew, and waxed strong in the Spirit, and was in the deserts until the day of his showing unto Israel." Though John was consecrated to God from his mother's womb, yet he did not enter upon the ministerial office until he had attained the age of thirty years. He spent much of his time in solitude, alone in meditation and prayer. He retired to the deserts where he lived for some time, and we are informed that "his raiment was camels hair, and a leathern girdle about his loins—and his meat was locust and wild honey." According to the prediction of the prophet Isaiah, John's ministry was commenced in the wilderness. "The voice of one crying in the wilderness, prepare ye the way of the Lord—make straight in the desert a highway for our God." The evangelists tell us that he went forth "preaching in the wilderness and saying, repent for the kingdom of heaven is at hand." He declared the coming of the Messiah, and called on the people to repent because the kingdom of God, (or the New Testament dispensation) was about being revealed. It "is at hand." The people heard his words and many of them heeded his admonitions and faithful warnings, they repented and were baptized. We judge from the account given that all who repented or professed to repent, and confessed their sins, were baptized with water by John. And they credited John's words, that the Messiah was about to make his appearance, and that he would baptize them with the holy Ghost.

He was so mighty as a teacher that many of the people thought surely he was the Messiah; but he told them he was not. He was far inferior to him who should come—his language is, "He that cometh after me is mightier than I, the latchet of whose shoes I am not worthy to unloose." He further told them that the Messiah should shortly be designated by the holy Spirit descending, and to their sight, resting upon him.

While John was baptizing in Jordan the multitudes that heard him preach, Christ approached him and demanded of him baptism; but John, understanding to some extent, if not fully, the glory of Jesus, the superiority of his person and character, said, "I have need to be baptized of thee, and comest thou to me?" He seemed to feel that he was not worthy to perform baptism upon such a subject, but Jesus said unto him, "Suffer it to be so now, for thus it becometh us to fulfill all righteousness." John then baptized Jesus in the presence of the multitude; and the Holy Spirit descended, and in the form of a dove sat upon the head of Jesus, while a voice was heard, saying, "This is my beloved Son, in whom I am well pleased." John pointed Jesus out to two of his disciples the next day as the "Lamb of God that taketh away the sin of the world." See Matt. iii; Luke, iii; John, i.

It was not long after this that John was baptizing at Enon, near to Salim, when his disciples came to him and informed him that Jesus was baptizing, and that great multitudes were following him. They seemed to be afraid that the glory of their master would be eclipsed in the rapidly-growing popularity of Jesus. The information they gave John was rather in a complaining mood: "Master, he to whom thou barest witness beyond Jordan, behold he baptizeth, and all men come unto him." John hushed their complaining by saying, "He that hath the bride is the bridegroom, but the friend of the bridegroom which standeth and heareth him rejoiceth greatly because of the bridegroom's voice. This my joy, therefore, is fulfilled. He must increase, but I must decrease." He thus gave his testimony to the truth of Christ's Messiahship. John, iii: 29, 30.

John the Baptist was revered and respected by Herod, the Tetrarch, of Galilee; but having occasion to reprove Herod, he did so fearlessly. The offense he had committed was an offense against the Jewish law. He had married his brother Philip's wife. He told Herod it was not lawful for him to have her. The consequence of his thus reproving sin in high places was, he was cast into prison, where he remained for some time. During the time of his imprisonment he sent two of his disciples to Christ to ask him if he was the Messiah, or if they should look for another. It is quite probable that John was satisfied, but he wished to have his disciples satisfied and their faith confirmed. Hence, Jesus said to John's disciples, "Go and show John the things which ye do hear and see: the blind receive their sight, the lame walk, the lepers are cleansed, and the deaf hear; the dead are raised up, and the poor have the gospel preached unto them." John received this report from Jesus, and it is quite likely he referred his disciples to the prophecy that Jesus thus copied as his answer. Matt. xi.

Soon after this the daughter of Herodias danced before Herod and greatly pleased him, so that he promised to give her whatever she would ask of him. She consulted her mother as to what she should ask. This gave the wicked woman an opportunity to gratify her malice and hatred of John. It may be she had sought revenge from the time John was cast into prison. Now an opportunity is afforded, and she bids her daughter ask Herod for the murder of the good man, and she asked that the evidence of his having been put to death might be given her, by his head being brought to her in a charger. It was accordingly done, though on the part of Herod with reluctance. Matt. xiv.

After John was thus beheaded, Herod permitted his disciples to take the body and give it a decent and respectable burial. It is thought that John the Baptist was thus put to death about a year and a half before our Savior's crucifixion. As it regards him, the Savior testifies that he was a great and good man. He was a firm and constant believer, and a noted teacher in the things of God. The Savior says he was a prophet and more than a prophet. He was one of the greatest men that ever appeared in any age of the world. "Of them that are born of woman, there hath not risen a greater than John the Baptist." His age and dispensation connects the old and new Testaments—the prophetical age and the age of Christ. Because of his austere life and self-sacrifice, the wicked Pharisees said, "He hath a devil," though he was so thoroughly respected that they were afraid to disseminate their sentiments. "John the Baptist came neither eating nor drinking, and they say he hath a devil. The son of man came eating and drinking, and they say, behold a glutton and a wine-biber, a friend of publicans and sinners."

JOHN, 2.—*The gift or mercy of the Lord.*

JOHN THE EVANGELIST was the son of Zebedee and Salome, and the brother of James the greater. He was a fisherman on the sea of Galilee, and the account of his call from his employment to be a disciple and attendant of Jesus, is given in Matt. iv: 21. It has been thought that he, with his brother James, was a disciple of John the Baptist, and if so, they might have been present at the baptism of Jesus and joined in the devotions that were so signally honored. John is thought to have been the youngest of all the apostles, being not more than twenty-five or twenty-six years of age when he entered upon the work of a follower of Jesus. He seems to have been loved by Jesus with a particular love, and he is called "that disciple whom Jesus loved." And he was favored by our Savior with several scenes that all the the disciples were not favored with. He accompanied Jesus when he restored the daughter of Jairus to life, with James his brother, and Peter. So he was present at the transfiguration. He was with Jesus in the garden of Gethsemane, when he endured the dreadful agony there. He leaned on Jesus' breast at the eucharistic feast, and when Peter wished to know who it was that would betray Jesus, he asked John, because he was on such terms of intimacy, to ask the master who would betray him, John xiii: 24, and his question was directly answered by giving the sop to Judas when he had dipped it.

John was present at the crucifixion of Jesus, for just as the Savior was expiring on the cross, he addressed his mother in the most affectionate manner, "woman behold thy son," and he said to the disciple whom he loved, "behold thy mother." This was understood to be on the part of the dying Jesus, as placing his mother under the care, and committing her to the attentions of John, for "from that hour that disciple took her unto his own home." John xix: 26.

John was one of the first witnesses of the resurrection. He in company with Simon Peter, received the intelligence from one of the women that the sepulcher was empty, and the body gone. They hurried to the sepulcher and found it as the women had reported. It is said of John that he outran Peter and came first to the sepulcher. John xx: 4. When John made the examination of the tomb, notwithstanding he did not understand the doctrine of the resurrection, yet he believed that Jesus had risen. John xx: 9. He was with the disciples at different times when Jesus showed himself to them after his resurrection, and he was present at the Mount of Olives on the ascension morning, and heard the last audible words of Jesus just as the cloud of glory settled upon him and the Angel escort surrounded him. Mark xvi: 19 and Luke xxiv: 51.

From the acts of the apostles we may judge that he preached the gospel for some time in Jerusalem, and we learn in Acts iv, that in company with Peter he was tried by the Jewish Sanhedrim, and cast into prison.

He and Peter had performed a noted miracle of healing in the name of their master, of the lame man at the beautiful gate of the temple, and the hypocrisy of Annanias and Sapphira had been detected, and they had both died with a lie in their mouth.

After they were released from prison, John and Peter were sent by the other apostles to some Samaritans, to whom Philip, the Deacon, had preached with a good degree of success. The object of the apostles and church in sending them there, was to instruct them more fully regarding the completed gospel, and impart to them the Holy Ghost. Acts viii: 14, &c.

John was one of the evangelists to whom our Lord delivered his predictions regarding the destruction of Jerusalem, and the calamities that should come upon their nation and polity, and it is thought by some that he wrote his gospel containing those predictions in the year ninety-seven, which was long after the destruction of Jerusalem. Whether he wrote it so late as that or not, it is quite likely that the other gospels were written first. His gospel is more spiritual and doctrinal than either of the others, and the first chapter especially, is a clear presentation of the doctrine of Christ's humanity and divinity conjoined. The historical narrative is not so extensive as the other gospels, but it accords with them in that particular, while it is a standard of doctrine or faith for all ages.

St. John was banished to the Isle of Patmos. This was an island in the Ægean sea. He tells us in Revelation i: 9, he was "in the isle that is called Patmos, for the word of God, and for the testimony of Jesus Christ." Which one of the Roman emperors banished him, is not certainly known, but it was probably Nero, if not Domitian, in the latter part of his reign. He wrote three epistles, probably during his exile. The first was written to the Ephesian church. The second was written to a worthy female called "the elect lady." And the third was written to Gaius.

John received the revelations commonly styled the apocalypse while on the island of Patmos, and what a glorious series of revelations does the book contain. He is supposed to have been recalled from his exile, and in his old age, to have met with the church in Ephesus, to which he ministered in the days of his strength. And after counselling, advising and strengthening them, he died, it is supposed, a natural death among them, and he is the only one of the apostles that did not suffer martyrdom. It is likely that our Savior was referring to the fact that John should die a natural death, when he said to Peter, John xxi: 22, "If I will that he tarry till I come, what is that to thee; follow thou me."

JOKSHAN—[Jok′-shan,] *hard difficult, scandalous.*

JOKSHAN was one of the sons of Abraham, by Keturah, and is referred to in Gen. xxv: 2, and he was the father of Sheba and Dedan. 1st Chron. i: 32.

JOKTAN—[Jok′-tan,] *small, disgust, weariness, dispute.*

JOKTAN was the son of Eber, and the grandson of Salah, and is referred to in the posterity of Shem. Genesis x: 25.

JONADAB—[Jon′-a-dab,] *who acts in good earnest.*

JONADAB was the son of Shimeah, David's brother; hence he was the nephew of David and the cousin of Absalom. He is presented to our view as a very subtle and wicked man, in 2d Sam. xiii: 5. When Amnon was sick in love with Tamar, his half-sister, or feigned sickness, Jonadab was guilty of giving him the most diabolical advice. Amnon followed it, and it resulted in his disgrace and the disgrace of Tamar, and finally in the murder of Amnon by her brother Absalom.

JONAH—[Jo′-nah,] *a dove, he that oppresses.*

JONAH was a prophet of Gath-Hepher, in Galilee. He ranked as the fifth of the minor prophets, and was the son of Amittai. He is thought to be the most ancient of the prophets who wrote, or whose writings are preserved. Some of the Jewish Rabbi have thought him to be the son of Serepta, and that he was raised to life when a child by the prophet Elijah. But of this we have no certain proof.

There is an important prophecy in 2d Kings, xiv: 25, referred to as the prediction of Jonah, the son of Amittai. It was a prediction that God would restore the cities which the Syrians had taken from the Hebrews during the reigns of Ahab, Jehoram, Jehu, and Jehoahaz.

We have a narrative of this prophet in the book that bears his name. In that narrative we learn that he was commanded to go to Nineveh and warn them of the anger of God and their approaching destruction. He was either afraid of the Ninevites or he feared that the Lord would be merciful unto them and forbear to punish them, if they repented, and so prove him to be the author of a prediction that was false. He seems to have been afraid that his honor as a prophet would be tarnished. And at Joppa he found a vessel ready to sail to Tarshish, and he went on board, paid his fare, and set sail, thus fleeing from the path of duty and refusing the work to which God had appointed him. The vessel had not proceeded far until a storm overtook them, and the frightened crew began to call upon their gods for deliverance; but no deliverance came. The storm did not abate, and their peril was all the while increasing. They remembered this Hebrew that had taken passage on board their ship and sought for him. He was in the side of the ship asleep, and they quickly awoke him, saying: "What meanest thou, O sleeper; arise, call upon thy God, if so be that God will think upon us that we perish not."

There was a custom prevailing among the Hebrews as well as other nations, when a doubtful matter was to be settled and the counsel of those concerned was insufficient to settle it, to ask direction of their God; and they usually did this by casting lots. They therefore cast lots to ascertain who was the cause of the storm, and the lot fell upon Jonah. He acknowledged, like an honest man, his nation, occupation, and sin in fleeing from the presence of the Lord; and he bade them take him up and cast him into the sea, and assured them that the storm should cease and the sea should be calm. They seemed to regard Jonah as an honorable man, and they wished if possible to save his life; hence they rowed hard to bring the boat to land, but could not. They threw him overboard, calling upon God to witness their reluctance to proceed to this extremity of destroying the life of this disobedient prophet. Immediately, upon Jonah's being cast into the sea, the storm was stilled and the waves ceased their raging, which led these heathens to acknowledge the God of Jonah to be the Lord.

The Lord prepared a fish to swallow up the prophet as soon as he was committed to the waves, and in the belly of the fish he earnestly prayed to God, and after three days and nights the fish vomited him up on dry land. This was a wonderful miracle performed by the Lord. The fish was prepared miraculously for that purpose; God made Jonah to live and breathe in the fish miraculously, and by miracle caused the fish to vomit him up on the dry land. He was then recommissioned to go to Ninevah and declare the message that had been given him before. He went, and for three days proclaimed as he walked around the walls, or upon the wall, "Yet forty days, and Nineveh shall be overthrown." The people heard him and credited his message, and repented. Their king ordered them to apply themselves to fasting and prayer. God recognized their humiliation and repentance and forbore to execute His vengeance upon them. Jonah seemed to be greatly displeased. In a hasty and inconsiderate manner he looked upon the mercy that had been shown them, and was very angry; and in his anger he wished to die rather than live, seeing the prediction he had made was to be unfulfilled. His language was, "Take my life from me, for it is better for me to die than to live." Jonah then went out of the city, and sat on the east side of it to wait and see what would become of the city. While he was there waiting, the Lord caused a gourd to spring up quickly and overshadow him from the scorching rays of the sun. It may be that it was a plant that had grown up in that place, and he took his seat under it to enjoy the shelter that it gave. But a worm began eating at the root, and the consequence was the plant soon withered, and so failed to shade him. The growth of this plant may have been supernatural as also its withering. The next day, as the sun arose and a vehement east wind accompanied it, beating upon the head of Jonah, he fainted, and still angry, he wished to die. He even averred to God that he was right in wishing to die, "It is better for me to die than to live." The Almighty bade him take time to think—to consider what he was saying. As though God had said, If thou hast pity on the inanimate plant, on the short-lived gourd, how much more reason is there for me to have pity upon the inhabitants of Ninevah, who are all immortal, and who are penitent before me. How strange it seems that Jonah should desire the destruction of the thousands of the inhabitants of Ninevah just because he had prophesied—for among them were one hundred and twenty thousand innocent infants, or persons that did not know their right hand from their left, beside much cattle. Jonah typified our Savior lying part of three days in the grave, Matt. xii: 40, "For as Jonah was three days and three nights in the whale's belly, so shall the son of man be three days and three nights in the heart of the earth." Christ thus speaks of his burial and resurrection. And as Jonah, after his deliverance, preached to the Ninevites, so after the gospel was consumated, its glorious doctrines were promulged to men. See Book of Jonah.

**JONATHAN**, 1—[Jon′-a-than,] *given to God.*

JONATHAN was a young Levite. He was the son of Gershom and perhaps the grandson of Moses. Judg. xviii: 30. He was selected by Micah to serve as his priest, and for the sum of ten shekels of silver a year, with a suit of apparel and his victuals he agreed to serve. Micah seemed to feel confident that the Lord would bless him, seeing this Jonathan, a Levite, was his priest. There were five Danites who were passing through this country as spies, and coming to Mt. Ephraim they tarried for a night at the house of Micah, and during the evening they overheard some conversation of the young Levite, and they knew his voice. They had probably been acquainted with him before, and addressing him they said: "Who brought thee hither? And what makest thou in this place, and what hast thou here?" He told them he was hired as a priest for Micah. They then asked him to ask counsel of God for them, whether or not they should prosper in their way. He pretended to consult his idol, and assured them that their undertaking at Laish should prosper. And when they did accomplish their end—six hundred of the Danites took Jonathan away from Micah, and with him they took the graven image, and all the equipments of the priest. They had not proceeded far from Mt. Ephraim until Micah overtook them, and demanded of them his images and his priest; but they would not hear him or satisfy his demands. Being stronger than he, they compelled him to give it up, and so he lost his gods and his priest.

Jonathan kept charge of the gods of Micah, and the vestments of his priest—and as a priest he served the children of Dan in a city that they named Dan. He and his posterity were priests until the captivity of the land. Judges, xviii: 30.

JONATHAN, 2—*Given to God.*

JONATHAN was the son of Saul, king of Israel. He was a very excellent prince and greatly distinguished himself by his valor, excellent qualities, and especially by his sincere friendship for David, the son of Jesse.

When the Philistines had invaded the country of Israel, and wrought up the whole nation of the Hebrews to a state of alarm and terror, Jonathan delivered them. Actuated by true courage, he went over to a garrison of the Philistines against Michmash. In approaching the garrison he went up between the two sharp rocks called Bozez and Senah. Having made the difficult passage between the rocks, he proposed to his armour bearer that they should approach the garrison in the name of the Lord. The young man agreed to follow him wherever he should go, assuring him that he was with him in heart, and would be in person, even to death. Jonathan must have been on terms of intimacy with the Divine Being, and his faith in God was strong, for he said to the young man: We will show ourselves to the Philistines, and their conduct towards us shall indicate our course. If they say to us tarry, then we will not go, but if they bid us come up unto them, then we will go, for the Lord hath delivered them into our hands. They did show themselves, and the Philistines said, "Come up unto us," Jonathan turned to his armor-bearer and bade him come on, for the Lord had delivered their enemies into their hands and power, though they were but two, and their enemies were numerous. They climbed up on their hands and feet until they came to the top of the rock, when Jonathan and the young man slew twenty men within about half an acre of ground.

When the Philistines saw how the soldiers of the garrison fell, and supposed that the Hebrews had the advantage of them, and would destroy them, they fled in great confusion. When Saul saw that they fled he made ready to pursue them; and calling the roll of his officers and soldiery, it was discovered that Jonathan and his armor-bearer were absent. The noise among the Philistines increased, and Saul hurried to the pursuit. While making his preparations he made a rash vow: "Cursed be the man that eateth any food until evening, that I may be avenged on mine enemies." Jonathan knew nothing of this vow of his father, and as he passed through the woods, seeing some honey, he put forth the end of his staff and touched it, and then putting it to his mouth tasted the honey, and so brought himself into danger. As soon as he had done so, one of the soldiers informed him of his father's charge or vow; and soon Saul was made acquainted with the fact that his order had been violated, and that Jonathan had tasted honey. He determined that he should die; but the people interfered, and boldly told Saul that Jonathan should not die, for he was innocent, as he knew nothing of his father's charge; and moreover, he had wrought a great deliverence in Israel, for the conquest they had made was the result of his valor. "So the people rescued Jonathan that he died not." 1st Sam. xiv.

He formed a friendship for David immediately after Goliath was slain, and manifested that friendship by presenting him with his robe, girdle and bow. When David was Saul's musician, and afterwards a warrior, Jonathan tenderly loved him, and more than once he risked his life for the safety and deliverance of David. When Saul was determined to kill him, so strong was the attachment of Jonathan under their mutual covenant, that he stood before his angered father and plead that David was innocent, and thereby narrowly escaped death at the hands of his father. He went to the field and shot an arrow, thereby indicating to David, who was hid at the stone Ezel, the anger of his father whom he had just sounded. 1st Sam. xviii, xix, xx.

Jonathan did not forget David or their mutual covenant, though they were separated the one from the other.

When he heard that David was at Ziph he sought him out and had a confidential conversation with him in the woods, during which he renewed his covenant, and encouraged David to hope (though now an exile) for the throne of Israel.

How strange that the heir-apparent to the throne, after the decease of the reigning king, should encourage another, not of the royal family even, save that he was the husband of Michal, the king's daughter. Jonathan knew that David was appointed of God, and was to be king. After an intimate and affectionate interview they parted. 1st Sam. xxiii.

At length an important battle was fought between Israel and the Philistines at Mt. Gilboa, and Saul, the king, and Jonathan were both slain in battle, with the other two brothers of Jonathan; and the day after the battle the Philistines stripped them of their armor and fastened their bodies to the walls of Beth-shan. And the men of Jabesh-gilead hearing of it went by night and recovered their bodies and brought them to Jabesh and burnt them, then buried the bones under a tree at Jabesh, and fasted seven days. 1st Sam. xxxi.

Soon after this battle David heard of it, and lamented in the most tender and affectionate manner, especially the death of Jonathan. 2d Sam. i: 26: "I am distressed for thee, my brother Jonathan: very pleasant hast thou been unto me: thy love to me was wonderful, passing the love of women." And true to his promise and covenant with Jonathan, David showed kindness to Mephi-bosheth, his son. [See David; also Mephi-bosheth.]

JONATHAN 3.—*Given to God.*

Jonathan, the uncle of David, was one of his great men. He was one of his chief counsellors and a secretary, and is numbered among the wise men. 1st Chronicles, xxvii: 32.

JORAH—[Jo′-rah.]

Jorah was the head of a family of one hundred and twelve, who returned from Babylon with Ezra. Ezra, ii: 18. He is presented by Nehemiah under another name, viz. Hariph. Nehemiah, vii; 24.

JORAI—[Jo′-ra-i.]

Jorai was one of the Gadites who dwelt in Gilead, in Bashan, in the reign of Jotham, king of Judah. 1st Chronicles, v: 13.

JORAM, 1—[Jo′-ram,] *to cast, elevated.*

Joram was the son of Jehoshaphat, and the son-in-law of king Ahab. Upon the death of his father, he ascended the throne of Judah. He was one of several sons of Jehoshaphat, unto whom the father gave gifts of silver and of gold, and of precious things, with fenced cities in Judah. The father gave the kingdom to Joram, because he was the elder son, or the first-born. As soon as Joram had settled himself upon the throne, for some cause or other, he slew his brothers, and with them many of the princes of Israel. Probably he feared that one of them would dethrone him, and to prevent this, he cruelly murdered them all. 2d Chronicles, xxi: 1-4.

Joram was instigated to much of the wickedness that marked him in his reign, by Athaliah his wife. He was a wicked idolater, following in the way of Ahab, whom he made his pattern. His reign was by no means peaceful and happy. He had wars, distresses, and reproofs. In 2d Chronicles, xxi: 8, we learn that his impiety was punished by the revolt of the Edomites, who not only went away from him, but made themselves a king and became his enemies. He warred with them, but could not subdue them. At the same time Libnah revolted from him. This was a city of the priests unwilling any longer to be governed by a king who was utterly forsaken of the Lord, their God. The prophet Elijah, under direction of God, wrote letters to Joram, reproaching him for his wickedness, and the prophet announced the severest judgments awaiting him. "Behold with a great plague will the Lord smite thy people, and thy children and thy wives, and all thy goods, and thou shalt have sickness by disease of thy bowels, until they fall out, by reason of the sickness, day by day." 2d Chronicles, xxi: 14-15.

These threatenings were fulfilled for the Philistines and Arabians ravaged his kingdom, plundered his palace and carried captive his wives and children.

all of them, save Ahaziah, the youngest, who afterwards succeed him on the throne of Judah. It was not long until he and nearly all his family, came to a miserable end. Joram, himself, was seized with a terrible distemper, from which he suffered excruciating torment for two years, when his bowels fell out, as the prophet had predicted, and he died. He was not honored as the kings of Judah usually were; "for they made no burnings for him like the burnings of his fathers," and though they gave him a burial in the city of David, it was not in the sepulcher of the kings. 2d Chron. xxi: 19–20.

JORAM, 2.—*To cast, elevated.*

JORAM, or JEHORAM, the son of Ahab, was a king of Israel. He succeeded his elder brother, Ahaziah, on the throne of Israel. He removed the statues of Baal, which his father had introduced into the kingdom. "He put away the image of Baal, which his father had made." 2d Kings, iii: 2.

Joram, king of Israel, had Jehoshaphat, the king of Judah, as an ally, with the Edomites, who were then tributary to Judah. He marched against the king of the Moabites with these, his allies; and after a very fatiguing march they came near perishing for want of water. Joram was in a great strait and knew not what to do. It seemed certain to him that he, with his allies, would be delivered into the hands of the king of Moab. Jehoshaphat asked him if there was no prophet of Israel near that they might enquire of as to the will of the Lord. One of the servants of Joram overheard the question and answered it by saying: "Here is Elisha, the son of Shaphat, which poured water on the hands of Elijah." 2d Kings, iii: 11. The three kings went down to see the prophet; and when Joram applied to him, he answered him roughly and charged upon him his sins against God. And the prophet told him that if it were not for the presence of Jehoshaphat the king of Judah, whom he regarded, he would have nothing to do with him. He would neither entertain his application nor look toward him. Elisha prophesied an abundance of water speedily; and it came; and these allied kings met the Moabites on the battle field and conquered them. Those of them that were not slain in battle fled to their own country. 2d Kings, iii.

Some time after this Benhadad, the king of Syria, sent Naaman to Joram to be healed of his leprosy, for Naaman had learned, through a captive maid, that there was a prophet in Israel who could cure him, and he had reported it to his lord. The application was made to Joram by Benhadad by letter; and when he read the letter he looked upon it as evidence that the king of Israel desired to go to war with him; and soon Benhadad and Joram were engaged in war.

The prophet Elisha rendered Joram important assistance by thwarting the plans and machinations of Benhadad, who became so enraged that he sent a host of Syrian soldiers to take him at Dothan. The Lord smote the Syrian soldiery with blindness, and Elisha led them into the city of Samaria, and into the hands and power of Joram. The king would have smitten them at once, but the prophet bade him treat them kindly by giving them bread to eat and water to drink. He accordingly did so; then sent them away to their master.

When the Syrians besieged Samaria, the capital of Israel, so that famine and want pressed the inhabitants until women did eat their own children, Joram blamed Elisha for the distress of the city, and intended to murder him, but he was prevented from it. 2d Kings, vi. He sometimes honored the prophet, and at other times aimed to injure and destroy him. When the woman whose son Elisha had restored to life asked Joram to restore her her house and her land that she had left before the famine became so sore, he seemed to take delight in having Gehazi, who had been the prophet's servant, relate the miracles that Elisha had performed, and he readily restored her the inheritance that belonged to her.

When the famine was ended, Samaria, and the Syrians no longer beseiged the city, but fled to their own country, all leaving the land of Israel, Joram laid siege to Ramoth-Gilead; but during the seige, being wounded, he repaired to Jezreel to be healed.

He had not been there long until Elisha sent one of the young prophets to the army with a box of holy oil to anoint Jehu, the son of Nimshi, to be king in the stead of Joram. The young prophet immediately prepared to execute the divinely appointed mission. The appearance of the young prophet in the camp, awakened suspicion among the soldiers, and they asked Jehu the cause of his coming. He told them what he had said and done. They immediately proclaimed Jehu king. After giving directions to the army, he started for Jezreel, where Joram yet was, not having fully recovered from his wounds. As one of the watchmen on the tower of Jezreel saw Jehu coming, he reported to Joram, who immediately ordered a horseman to go and meet him, and salute him. Jehu ordered the horseman to fall into the ranks behind him, and he did so. Joram then sent another, and he did as the former. The king then ordered his chariot made ready, and he and Ahaziah, his kinsman, the king of Judah, who had come to Jezreel to see him, went up into the chariot, and went to meet Jehu. As soon as they came within speaking distance, Joram saluted him with, "Is it peace Jehu?" His answer struck terror to the heart of Joram, and he turned to Ahaziah, and said, "There is treachery, O Ahaziah." Scarcely had he given this note of alarm, until an arrow from the bow of Jehu smote him, and pierced his heart, so that he sunk down in his chariot. His dead body was thrown, by the order of Jehu, into the field or vineyard of Naboth. And this murder of Joram was followed by the destruction of the house of Ahab. 2d Kings ix; 2d Chron. xxii.

JOSEPH, 1—[Jo′-sef,] *increase, addition.*

JOSEPH was the eldest son of Rachel, the first choice for a wife of the Patriarch Jacob. He was born in Messopotamia. For some cause Jacob manifested strong partiality for Joseph, when he was yet a child. It may be, it was because he was the eldest son of Rachel, or by a divine influence, he may have been impressed with the fact that Joseph's life was to be very eventful. He had a coat of many colors, which as the gift of his father, manifested very strikingly his partiality for him. This love of Jacob for Joseph, led his brothers to hate him, "and they could not speak pleasantly to him."

Joseph was afterwards distinguished as a dreamer. He told his dreams in such a way that his brothers and his father divined the interpretation, and they were displeased. His brethren hated him more and more. Not long after Joseph had his dreams, and made them known, his brothers were feeding their father's flock in Shechem, and Jacob sent Joseph to see how they were getting along, and bring him word. When he reached Shechem, and made inquiry for them, he learned that they had gone to Dothan, and he followed after them. And when he came in sight of them, moved with envy they conspired against him to slay him, and they probably would have done it, had not Reuben the elder brother interfered by proposing to cast him into a pit in the woods to perish. Reuben's intention was, as soon as an opportunity offered, to take him up from the pit, and restore him to his father. But while Reuben was absent, his brothers sold him to Midianitish merchants for twenty pieces of silver, or about two pounds six shillings, less than two dollars apiece, and these merchantmen took him to Egypt and sold him to Potiphar an officer of Pharoah, and captain of the guard. Gen. xxxvii.

Joseph's good behavior gained him the esteem of his master, and he soon made him his steward. It was not long however until his sky was clouded, and an attempt was made to blast his character by an infamous lie. The wife of Potiphar indulged a criminal passion for him, but he closed his heart to her entreaties, and urging that it would be on his part the basest ingratitude to his master, as well as wickedness in the sight of God, and he would not yield. Unmoved by what he said, she caught hold of his garment, but he fled away leaving it in her hand. She brought her false charge against Joseph to Potiphar when he came home, and he, believing his wife, cast him into prison. Here his good behavior gained upon the keeper of the prison, and soon the other prisoners were entrusted to his care. There were two of the king's servants, his chief butler and his chief baker, and they both dreamed, Joseph interpreted their dreams, and the chief butler pledged himself to Joseph that he would remember him to Pharaoh after he was restored to his office. But two years passed away, and the chief butler in the enjoyment and pleasures of his office, forgot Joseph. In the course of events Joseph was remembered. Pharaoh dreamed a dream, and his wise men could not explain it. The chief butler spoke of Joseph to the king, and he sent and brought him from the prison.

Joseph gave a satisfactory interpretation of the dream, and the king honored him by releasing him from the prison, clothing him in royal costume, and he took the ring from his finger in which was set his signet—the national seal. He then put a golden chain upon his neck. It may be that that chain was intended to represent the union which the king desired should exist in all parts of his government, or possibly he intended it as a badge of office, and to show forth the authority with which Joseph was invested. For he rode in the second chariot in the nation, and rulled over all the land. During the seven years of plenty, he collected the surplus corn of the land, and stored it in granaries for the coming famine. He was married to Asenath, the daughter of Poti-pherah, priest of On, and in the course of time, there were born unto him two sons, Manasseh and Ephraim. Genesis, xxxix, xl, xli.

As the famine came on, Canaan, where Jacob dwelt, was suffering, and the old patriarch, in extremity, hearing that there was corn in Egypt, sent his ten sons down to buy bread. As soon as they came to Egypt, Joseph saw them and knew them, but they did not know him. He was governor of the land, and was approached by his brethren just as the interpretation of his dream, when a boy indicated that they would, "for they bowed themselves before him with their faces to the earth. Joseph, in all probability, remembered his dream, and in their conduct its fulfillment. He spake roughly to them, and charged them as being spies. But after enquiring into their family circumstances, he dismissed them on the condition that Benjamin, their younger brother should come with them the next time, and Simeon should be retained until their second visit to insure the bringing of him.

In the manner in which Joseph made himself known to his brethren, we can see a degree of wisdom, and high-toned feeling, truly touching and sublime. On the arrival with Benjamin, he made a great feast for them. The preparations were all made and they were invited the first day after their arrival to dine with him at noon. According to his direction they all sat before him, ranged according to their respective ages, and he, himself, served them, "for he sent messes unto them;" but what must have been exceedingly remarkable to them, and especially to Benjamin, the mess sent to Benjamin was five times as large as that to either of the others. They may all have remarked a peculiarity in the appearance of Joseph, when he first met them and looked upon the son of his own mother, and asked "Is this your younger brother, of whom ye spoke unto me?" and he said, "God be gracious unto thee, my son." He had no sooner said this, than he hurried from their presence, sought his chamber where he might weep.

The next day they were furnished with corn, and started for home. They had not proceeded far when the steward of Joseph followed after them and overtook them, and charged them with stealing. Conscious of innocence, they all agreed that with whomsoever the cup should be found he should die, and the rest of them should be servants in Egypt. Search was made and the silver cup of Joseph was found in the sack of Benjamin. They were all greatly troubled and returned, and standing before Joseph, they plead for Benjamin. They looked at the dilemma into which they were thrown as a punishment for their sin in so cruelly treating their brother Joseph several years before. Their language was, "We are verily guilty concerning our brother, in that we saw the anguish of his soul when he besought us and we would not hear him; therefore is this evil come upon us." Judah addressed Joseph in the most affecting manner, and asked to be retained as a bondman instead of the lad. Joseph was exceedingly affected by the address, and at its close found himself unable to refrain any longer from giving vent to the feelings of his heart. He then ordered the Egyptians all to leave him, and being left alone with his brethren he said, "I am Joseph; doth my father yet live?" The announcement fell upon their ears like the sudden pealing thunder of a midnight storm, and they could not answer. He entreated them to come near him, and pale and trembling they approached him. He said, "I am Joseph your brother, whom ye sold into Egypt;" here they wept, if possible, still more, for their unfeelingness and inhumanity was brought before him. Joseph knew full well that their hearts were wrung with bitter anguish, and to alleviate, if possible, their sorrows, he referred them to the doctrine of divine providence, as it had been exemplified in his eventful life. "Now, therefore, be not grieved nor angry with yourselves that ye sold me hither, for God did send me before you to preserve your life." If true nobleness was ever exemplified by man, it was exemplified here by Joseph. He not only freely forgave them, but wished them to forget the injury they had done him. As though he had said: It was not you that sold me, but God that sent me, and had I not been sent, Egypt and Canaan would have perished.

He then told his brethren that the famine would continue five years longer, and he desired them to hasten back to Canaan and inform Jacob their father that Joseph his son was yet alive and Governor of Egypt, and tell him to come without delay, and he should dwell with his family and herds in the best of the land. In order to satisfy Jacob, his father, that he was yet alive, Joseph sent wagons to facilitate his journey to Egypt, and asses burdened with good things, and corn, and bread, and meat, for their sustenance during the journey. He sent his brothers away with the affectionate injunction, "See that ye fall not out by the way."

As soon as they arrived at home they communicated to their father the fact that Joseph was alive and governor of the land of Egypt. Jacob listened to them, and was so overpowered with the intelligence that he fainted, and when he recovered he could not fully credit them until he saw the wagons and presents and provisions. He said, "It is enough; Joseph my son is yet alive. I will go and see him before I die." Jacob accordingly made ready and went to Joseph his son in Egypt. As he neared the land of Goshen, he sent Judah to inform Joseph of his coming, and he went out in his chariot to meet his father. When Jacob could so far control his feelings as to speak, after they met, he exclaimed, "Now let me die, since I have seen thy face and because thou art yet alive." Shortly after Jacob arrived in Egypt, Joseph introduced him to Pharaoh, and procured for him and his family and herds the land of Goshen.

A few years after this Jacob called his children around him to give them his parting admonition, and declare the will of God regarding them. He blessed both the sons of Joseph, "leaning upon the top of his staff." He then died and Joseph according to a promise made, embalmed his body and took it into the land of Canaan and buried it in the cave of Machpelah.

Joseph as a true man continued his friendship and forgiveness to his brethren, but at length the end of his eventful life came. He called his brethren around him and told them he was about to die, but that God would visit them and bring them out of Egypt and give them the land of Canaan as their inheritance. He then exacted of them a solemn and binding obligation to carry his remains with them: "By faith Joseph when dying made mention of the departure of the children of Israel, and gave commandment concerning his bones."

As to the character of this great and good man we may safely say, his piety cannot be questioned, for it was fully and fairly tested. And whether we look at him as the chattel of the Midianitish merchant, as the slave of Potiphar, as a prisoner in an Egyptian jail, or as the governor of Egypt, fidelity and faithfulness mark him in his course and conduct. He proved himself an honorable politician, one who had the interests of the ruler and subjects at heart. For ages the government of Egypt enjoyed advantages which were the results of his prudence and wisdom. His body was embalmed and coffined in Egypt, and when Moses, long after, prepared for the Exodus of Israel, he took care to carry up Joseph's body with them. After Moses died Joshua took charge of the bones of Joseph, and when Canaan was conquered the remains of Joseph were buried in Shechem in a parcel of ground that Jacob bought of Hamor, which ground with its grave yard came in possession of Joseph's descendants. Gen. xliii and l, inclusive. Ex. xiii: 19; Joshua, xxiv: 32.

JOSEPH, 2—*Increase, addition.*

JOSEPH was the first born son of Asaph, the great singer of Israel, in the time of David. When the lots were cast, and the singers were divided into twenty-four courses, the first lot came forth to Joseph. 1st Chronicles, xxv: 9.

JOSEPH, 3—*Increase, addition.*

JOSEPH was the husband of the virgin Mary. He was espoused to Mary at the time that the angel designated her as the mother of the coming Messiah. The angel of the Lord appeared unto Joseph in a dream and informed him that his espoused wife would shortly be the mother of a son, and that son should be the world's redeemer; the angel encouraged him to consumate at once the marriage contract. He was informed that the name of Mary's son should be Jesus, "for he shall save his people from their sins." Joseph as a reader of the Jewish scriptures was familiar with the prophecy in Isaiah, vii: 14. "Behold a virgin shall conceive and bear a son and they shall call his name Immanuel," which, being interpreted is God with us. And from what the angel had just announced to him, he knew that this prediction was to be fulfilled in the coming son of Mary. Matt. i: 21, 23.

He was the son of Jacob and the grandson of Mathan, a descendant of David and Abraham. Matt. i: 15, 16. His occupation was that of a carpenter, Matt. xiii: 55. And it is likely that our Lord wrought at the same trade previous to his entering upon the work of the ministry; and this may be what is referred to in Luke, ii: 51: "He went down with them to Nazareth, and was subject unto them."

The place of Joseph's residence was Nazareth. There he lived, and in all probability died. It is likely he died before Jesus commenced his public ministry, for he is not mentioned in the history given by the Evangelists of the work of Jesus, though Mary is often mentioned. And when Jesus was dying on the cross, he committed his mother to the care of the Evangelist John; and we can hardly suppose he would have done so if Joseph, her husband, had still been living. John, xix: 25. We are informed by the Evangelist, Matt. i: 19, that Joseph was a just man, by which we may understand he was a pious Jew that had been looking for the coming Messiah for a long time, and rejoiced in his appearance.

JOSEPH, 4—*Increase, addition.*

JOSEPH of Arimathea was a Jewish senator, who, while the other members of the Sanhedrim gave their consent to the death of Christ, he did not. He believed in the divine mission of our Lord Jesus Christ, and was a good and just man. John, xix: 38; Luke, xxiii: 50. He did not consent to Christ's condemnation or crucifixion, but sympathized with him and his scattered disciples. After the death of Jesus he went to Pilate, the Roman governor, and begged the body. His request was granted, and he took the body down from the cross, and with the help of Nicodemus and others prepared it for burial. John, xix: 39, 40. They wrapped the body in clean linen and laid it in Joseph's tomb — "a new tomb hewn out of the solid rock." In this circumstance we observe the prophecy fulfilled: "He made his grave with the wicked and with the rich in his death." He probably openly avowed his faith in Jesus, and after the crucifixion identified himself with the disciples, and no more attended the Sanhedrim, or Jewish high council.

JOSEPH, 5—*increase. addition.*

JOSEPH or JOSES, was the brother of James the Less, and the son of Cleopas. He was the kinsman of our Lord, In Matt. xiii: 55, he, with James, and Simon, and Judas, is called the brother of our Lord. The term is probably used to denote near relative. He is supposed to be the same with Barsabas, one of the seventy disciples, and the defeated candidate for the apostleship when Matthias was selected. Acts, i: 21–26. [See Barsabas.]

JOSHBEKASHAH—[Josh-bek′-a-shah.]

He was one of the sons of Heman, and when the lots were cast and the singers were divided into twenty-four courses, the seventeenth lot came to him. 1st Chron. xxv: 24.

JOSHUA, 1—[Josh-u-a,] *the Lord, the Savior.*

Joshua, the son of Nun, was probably one of the elders called together by Moses and Aaron when they came into the land of Egypt to demand of Pharaoh the freedom of their people. It is quite probable he heard the words of Aaron declaring the divine determination that their bondage should end. He saw the miracles wrought attesting the truth of the mission of Moses and Aaron, and was fully satisfied that they were appointed of God.

After the visitation of God's wrath upon Egypt, in the plagues, and the preparation of Israel for their exodus, Joshua was appointed as the captain of the army of Israel, which was a high and important position, and tells us plainly that he was a favorite with God and greatly esteemed by Moses and Aaron.

The first time the name is mentioned is after the Red Sea had been crossed and some travel had been performed in the desert. The Israelites had come to Rephidim, and after being encamped there awhile, the Amalekites made war upon them. The manner in which they made the attack was mean and dastardly. They came in unawares upon the rear of Israel. Instead of inviting them to a battle, or challenging them to a contest, they treacherously attacked them when faint and weary with the fatigues of travel, and cut off the feeble ones that they might procure the baggage under their charge as spoils. Moses commanded Joshua to fight with Amalek, and he did, "discomfiting Amalek with the edge of the sword." Ex. xvii: 13.

After this victory God directed that a record should be made of it, and that in the ears of Joshua, who had gained the victory, it should be rehearsed, that the very remembrance of Amalek should be utterly put out from under Heaven. Probably the reason why this rehearsal was to be made to Joshua, was this: God had determined that he should be the successor of Moses.

Joshua had close acquaintance with the leader of Israel, and was on terms of the greatest intimacy with him. When Moses ascended Mt. Sinai to receive the revelations that were made there, Joshua ascended with him; and though he did not go up into the midst of the cloud that capped the mountain, yet he went up to the highest station under it. And there, just under the foldings of the cloud, amid the majestic thunder and the terrific lightnings, he waited for forty days for the return of Moses.

Joshua appears to rank next to Moses himself in the manifestations made of divine power and glory at Sinai, for the seventy elders, with Aaron, Nadab, and Abihu, tarried at a station on the mountain lower down than Joshua.

He was filled with the spirit of wisdom and so qualified for the arduous and responsible station of governor of Israel.

After Moses died, Joshua was divinely appointed to this important work, and exhibited a piety, and courage and integrity, throughout his whole life, that was truly commendable. There are incidents in his history worthy of record. He was one of the spies selected by Moses to explore the promised land. Num. xiii: 16. All the spies, save Joshua and Caleb, brought back an unfavorable report, and as a punishment they were not permitted to go over Jordan, but died in the wilderness. Indeed Joshua and Caleb were the only men that left Egypt, that secured an inheritance in person, in the promised land.

In accordance with the appointment of God, Joshua succeeded Moses as the leader of Israel. Numbers xxvii: 18. "And the Lord said unto Moses, take thou Joshua, the son of Nun, a man in whom is the spirit, and lay thy hand upon him; and give him a charge in their sight." And Moses did as the Lord commanded him.

Joshua led the children of Israel across the Jordan and began the conquest of the land by taking Jericho. As one of the spies he had entered into an engagement with Rahab, the harlot, and being satisfied as he took the city, that she had kept her vows to keep the approach of Israel secret from the people, he fulfilled his part of the engagement, and he did it faithfully. "He saved Rahab, the harlot, alive." He acknowledged the obligations the Israelites were under to her, and tendered her, in the name of Israel, sincere thanks, and moreover, he rewarded her by giving her and her kindred, citizenship and a portion among them. Josh. ii.

Joshua continued to lead Israel against the nations inhabiting the land of Canaan, until they were all conquered and the land divided among them, as the lot of their inheritance. He did not retire from active labor and peril, until the work was all done, and the dangers all passed. He did not resign his office until the last battle for the conquest of the country was fought. And when he did retire, he retired laden with well-earned laurels. He was the general when they fought their first battle with Amalek, and was the first on the battle-field. He continued in command until the last battle was over in the campaign, and he was the last to leave the field.

He was greatly honored of God, in that an angel, styling himself the captain of the Lord's host, came to him, and conversed with him, encouraging him in his work, as he was before Jericho, and preparing to take the city. Joshua, v: 14. It may have been the same angel that appeared to Moses at the base of Horeb, for the language he uses, is very much the same as that used when Moses was commissioned. Josh. v: 15. "Loose thy shoe from off thy foot, for the place whereon thou standest is holy."

Joshua received from the children of Israel, as their leader, an inheritance, after he had made a division of the conquered land. Josh. xix: 49. This inheritance consisted of Timnath-serah, in Mount Ephraim, where he built a city and dwelt. It was comparatively little earthly reward for the services, which, as a successful general, he had given to his country.

His work being done, he delivered his valedictory, in which he refers them to the gracious dealings of God with them, from the days of their father, Abraham. He earnestly exhorted them to abolish idolatry in all its forms, and tells them of his own and his family's resolution. Josh. xxiv: 14–25.

He died, being one hundred and ten years old, and his body was buried in his own inheritance, while the immortal man ascended to the association again of Moses, Israel's former leader and law-giver.

JOSHUA, 2—[Josh′ua,] *the Lord, the Savior.*

Joshua was the son of Josedech, He was the high priest of the Jews, when they returned from Babylon, the land of their captivity. Haggai i: 1–2, and Ezra, iii: 8. In the former passage, he is associated with Zerubbabel in hearing the word of the Lord by the mouth of the prophet Haggai, which was a command to rebuild the sacred temple, and encouragement in the work; and in the latter passage, he is represented as engaged in the work with his associates, and in encouraging the people.

In Zechariah iii, and vi, Joshua is represented as standing before the Lord in filthy garments, and Satan standing at his right hand to resist him and accuse him. The Lord is represented as rebuking Satan, and arraying Joshua in pure raiment, and not long after that, the prophet was directed to make a golden crown and set it upon the head of Joshua, the high priest, and thereby make him a type of the glorious Messiah.

JOSIAH—[Jo-si′-ah,] *the fire of the Lord.*

Josiah was the son of Amon, and a king of Judah. He was very young when he succeeded his father to the throne, but eight years of age. 2d Kings, xxii: 1, and 2d Chron. xxxiv: 1. While he was yet a child he began to be noted for his piety, and his zeal for the Lord God of Israel. At eight years of age he began to seek after the God of David his father, and in his twelfth year he began to purge Judah and Jerusalem. Idolatry was practiced among them, and Josiah set himself to work destroying the idols. He cut down the groves, and broke down the altars after he had burned the bones of the deceased priests on them, and so he cleansed Judah and Jerusalem. 2d Chron. xxxiv: 5, 6. He also extended his reformation over the ten tribes, and destroyed all their idols and idol-temples, and broke up their system of idol worship. He demolished the altar of Bethel after he had burned dead men's bones on it. He repaired the temple of the Lord, employing many workmen, and using much material, and expending much money.

While Hilkiah the high priest was engaged in repairing the temple, he found a copy of the laws of Moses, which is supposed to have been the original one put by Moses in the sides of the ark. Shaphan the scribe informed Josiah of this manuscript. He had it brought to him, and a part of it read in his hearing. The contents of it affected him greatly, for he feared, as the laws it contained had been wickedly broken, that fearful judgments would fall upon the people. Being deeply affected with what he considered was the peril of his people, he sent a deputation, headed by Hilkiah the high priest, to the prophetess Huldah, who was the wife of Shallum, the keeper of the royal wardrobe. Huldah received the deputation, and read the book, then assured them that what was threatened in that book should come to pass, but yet not in the days of King Josiah. The stroke should be delayed on account of the piety of the king, and his great grief at the wickedness of the people.

Josiah was born and attained the Kingdom of Judah, as we have seen in an age of idolatry, and we may reasonably suppose he was unacquainted with many important things written in the laws of Moses. From the reading of the newly found copy of the laws, he discovered that the three great solemn feasts of the Jews had been neglected, and he ordered his subjects at once to make preparations for celebrating the feast of the passover. 2d Chron. xxxv: 1. They killed the passover on the fourteenth day of the first month, and he caused his subjects to renew their solemn covenant with God. In the account given of this feast we find Josiah completed his work of reformation. He destroyed the soothsayers and Sodomites out of the land, and pulled down all of the remaining idols. He filled the valley of Hinnom with dead men's bones, and broke down the last statue of idolatry there, and nearly all his subjects turned or professed to turn unto the Lord.

After Josiah had reigned thirty-one years, his kingdom was invaded by the King of Egypt, and he levied a large army and led them in person to battle to stop the invaders, and while engaged in the battle in the valley of Megiddo, the archers shot at him and wounded him mortally. As soon as he received the wound, he reported it to his servants and they placed him in another chariot and took him to Jerusalem, where he died, and they buried him with great mourning in a royal sepulcher, and the people made Jehoahaz, his son, king in his stead. 2d Chron. xxxv, and 2d Kings xxiii.

Josiah was much loved by the people and the lamentation of Jeremiah over his death was joined in by the army, and especially the singing men and the singing women, and the prophet established an annual lamentation for Josiah.

JOTHAM, 1—[Jo′-tham,] *perfection of the Lord.*

Jotham was the youngest son of Gideon. When Gideon died, Abimelech who was an illegitimate son, being the son of the concubine in Shechem—usurped authority, and rising up slew all the sons of Gideon except Jotham, who fled for his life after hiding himself during the slaughter of his brethren. Sometime after Abimelech had been made king by the men of Shechem, Jotham showed himself to them and charged upon them their cruelty and injustice, in countenancing the murder of his brethren, and placing Abimelech over them as their king. He addresses them by a parable which, it may be remarked, is the oldest parable on record. By this he intimated to the people that while his father and worthy brethren refused to reign over Israel, they had made the worst and basest of his father's children their king, and that they might expect to suffer for it. After he had finished his parable he left the top of the hill where he delivered it, and fled to Beer, lest Abimelech should kill him as he did his brothers. Judges, ix: 1, 21. The imprecations he uttered against the men of Shechem, and against Abimelech were fulfilled.

JOTHAM, 2—*Perfection of the Lord.*

JOTHAM was a king of Judah, the son and successor of Uzziah or Azariah. We learn from 2d Kings, xv: 5, and 2d Chron. xxvi: 19, etc., that when Uzziah became a leper, Jotham or Joatham, became the acting ruler for his father, he being confined as a leper in a separate house. It is said Jotham "was over the house judging the people of the land." When the leper king died, Jotham was crowned, and so became the sole governor, after ruling several years as his father's viceroy.

He was twenty-five years of age when he began to reign. As a king he was much better than many that had reigned before him, but yet he permitted the people to sacrifice in high places. Jotham did many things that were pleasing to the Lord. He built the great gate of the temple, or house of the Lord. He fortified the walls of Jerusalem, and built cities and castles, and towers on the mountains of Judah, and in the forests. He fought with the king of the Ammorites and prevailed against them, so that they were tributary to him, and paid him large sums for at least three years. During the latter part of his reign his kingdom was invaded by Rezin, the king of Syria, and Pekah, the king of Israel. He seems to have died a natural death after a reign of sixteen years, and was succeeded by Ahaz his son. 2d Chron. xxvii: 1, 9.

JOZABAD, 1—[Joz′a-bad.]

Was a captain of a large number of the Manassites who deserted Saul's army before the Mt. Gilboa battle, and went over to David. 1st Chronicles xii: 20.

JOZABAD, 2.

Was a Levite in the reign of Hezekiah. 2d Chronicles xxxi: 13.

JOZABAD, 3.

Was a Levite in the reign of Josiah. 2d Chronicles xxxv: 9.

JOZABAD, 4.

Was a Levite who returned with Ezra from Babylon, and like others, had married a foreign wife, and was compelled to put her away. Ez. x: 22. He is probably the same that is referred to in Neh. viii: 7, who presided over the outer work of the temple.

JOZACHAR—[Joz′a-kar.

Was the son of Shimeath, and was one of the murderers of king Joash, in the house of Millo. 2d Kings xii; 21.

JUBAL—[Ju′bal,] *he that runs, he that produces, a trumpet.*

JUBAL was the son of Lamech, and Adah, his wife, and he was the brother of Jabal. He is referred to in Gen. iv: 21, as "the father of all such as handle the harp and organ." By this we understand that he was the inventor of musical instruments—of all string and wind instruments—and in all probability he was a teacher in the use of instruments in that early age when the science was in its infancy.

JUDAH—[Ju′dah,] *the praise of the Lord.*

JUDAH was the fourth son of Jacob by Leah; and in the record of his birth we have the reason given for his name Judah. His mother said, "Now will I praise the Lord." Gen. xxix: 35.

When Joseph was sent by his father in search of his brethren, and he found them, at first they conspired against him to slay him, but Reuben interfered, and they cast Joseph into a pit to die. Judah proposed that they should take him up out of the pit and sell him to Midianitish merchantmen, in preference to being guilty of his blood; and they did so, all joining in the sale except Reuben, the elder. Gen. xxxvii: 26, 27

When Judah was a young man he contracted a familiarity with Hirah, the Adullamite, and this friendship led him to form an intimacy with Shuah, a Canaanite, which resulted in marriage. Shuah bare him three sons, Er,

Onan, and Shelah. When the eldest of these three sons was yet quite young Judah married him to Tamar, a woman of Canaan; but the young man committed sin, and the Lord destroyed his life. Judah then gave the widow the next eldest son for a husband, but he sinned as did his brother, and the Lord slew him also. Judah then gave her the promise of Shelah for a husband when he should have attained a proper age; but his daughter-in-law was filled with disgust because that Judah did not fulfill his promise, and she laid a snare successfully to entrap him. Hearing that Judah was to pass along a certain way to his sheep-shearing, she laid off the garments of her widowhood and attired herself as a harlot by the wayside. He was caught in the snare, and left with her his staff and bracelet as a pledge that he would furnish her a kid. But when he sent the kid to redeem his staff and bracelet, the harlot was gone and could not be found.

It was not long after this until Tamar was reported to Judah as having played the harlot, and as being with child. He immediately gave orders that she be put to death. She then exhibited the bracelets and the staff that had been left by Judah, and thereby brought his own sin to his remembrance as well as the wrong done her in failing to give her Shelah as a husband. Tamar bare him two sons, Pharez and Zarah. Gen. xxxviii.

When Jacob sent his sons down to Egypt the second time to buy corn, and reluctantly sent Benjamin with them, Judah entered into the most solemn engagement with his father to return Benjamin to him safe. And when it appeared that Benjamin would be detained in Egypt, he plead with the lord of the land in behalf of his younger brother, and he offered himself as a slave instead of Benjamin, who was charged with stealing the silver cup. His pleadings were so affecting that they melted the heart of Joseph, and he could no longer refrain from making himself known unto his brethren. Gen. xliv.

Just before Jacob died, he predicted the superiority of Judah over his brethren, and declared that from him should come the Messiah, and that the kings should descend from him, and that the apportionment of the land of promise that should fall to him should abound with vines. Gen. xlix: 8–12.

The three sons of Judah, viz: Shelah, by his Canaanite wife, and Zarah and Pharez, by his daughter-in-law, became the heads of numerous families forming the tribe of Judah. When they went out of Egypt, their fighting men amounted to seventy-four thousand six hundred, with Nashon, the son of Aminadab, as their head. They increased nearly two thousand in the wilderness, and Caleb the son of Jephunneh, was their spy sent to search out the land, who with Joshua brought back a favorable report. And they marched in the first division of the grand army in the wilderness. Num. i, xiii, xxvi.

The tribe of Judah were very active and energetic, and successful, in expelling the Canaanites from their land, and especially from that part of the territory apportioned to their tribe. When a judge was selected by them to rule among them, and deliver them from their enemies, Othniel, of the tribe of Judah, was the one. He was their first judge and deliverer. Judg. iii. Of this tribe, in the time of king Saul, the first king of Israel, we learn it was extensive, for when king Saul warred with Nahash, the king of the Ammonites, there were thirty thousand of the tribe of Judah with him. 1st Sam. xi: 8. And so when Saul went to war with Amalek, there were ten thousand men of Judah with him.

After Saul, David was king, and he was of this tribe as were many of his successors. The revolt of the ten tribes from Rehoboam, under Jeroboam, led to the establishment of the kingdom of Judah, of which Jerusalem was the capital, and David's posterity the kings. The government of Judah remained until the Messiah appeared in accordance with the prediction, "The sceptre shall not depart from Judah, nor a lawgiver from between his feet, until Shiloh come."

JUDAS, 1.—[Ju′-das,] *the praise of the Lord.*

JUDAS, or JUDE, was the same as Thaddeus or Lebbeus. He was the son of Mary, the wife of Cleopas, hence the brother of James the less, and the cousin of our Lord. Acts i: 13. He was one of our Lord's apostles. Matt. x: 3; Mark iii: 18; Luke vi: 16. When Jesus instituted the last supper, this apostle asked him the significant question, John xiv: 22, "Lord, how is it that thou wilt manifest thyself unto us, and not unto the world?" Jesus answered and said unto him, "If a man love me he will keep my words, and my father will love him, and we will come unto him and make our abode with him." This apostle wrote the Epistle of Jude, and it was probably the last of the epistles written by the inspired apostles.

JUDAS, 2,

Or JUDAS ISCARIOT. He was one of our Savior's disciples, numbered with the apostles. He was placed by the Savior in charge of the money and provisions that the company carried about with them. He was in good repute with his brethren until Jesus was closing up his ministry, when he turned traitor and sold his Lord for thirty pieces of silver. He heard the Savior's preaching and witnessed his miracles, and, for aught we know, himself preached and wrought miracles, as did the other apostles. We do not know that he was inferior, as a teacher, to any of them; but the fact seems to be exhibited, in the history given of Christ and his apostles, that there was some defect in his character. We may judge he was covetous. He loved the world too much. When Mary anointed the Savior's head with precious ointment, in the house of Simon the leper, there were several present that objected to it, and Judas Iscariot was among them and urged objection. Christ rebuked him and commended the woman. It is likely that Judas became angry at the master for justifying what he pretended was a great waste, and determined on revenge by betraying Jesus into the hands of his enemies. It was not long after this, when Judas found the chief priests and elders, and agreed to deliver him into their hands for thirty pieces of silver, which is supposed to be less than seventeen dollars. It was probably after he had made the agreement to deliver Jesus into the hands of his enemies, that he was present with the disciples as the supper was celebrated. For though his brethren did not know what he had done, yet Jesus did, and he plainly told them that one of them would betray him. John, who was on terms of very great intimacy with Jesus, asked him who it was that should betray him, and Jesus told him, so that all the apostles at once learned that Judas was a traitor. He became, it is likely, enraged at being thus designated, and went directly to those with whom he had made the contract, and they made arrangements at once to go on the expedition of apprehending Jesus of Nazareth. He led them to the place where Jesus was —the garden of Gethsemane—and there, with a hypocritical kiss and salutation, he gave the mob the signal whom to apprehend.

No sooner had Judas Iscariot seen his master condemned by the Jewish council, than his conscience began to trouble him, and the heinous wickedness of his conduct in betraying innocent blood loomed up before him, he knew not what to do. The money he had secured by this wicked act was detested by him, and he took it back to those from whom he had received it—confessed to them that he had betrayed innocent blood, and would no longer keep the money. They would not receive it and place it in the treasury because it was the price of blood. They, therefore, acting as agents for Judas to whom the money belonged, bought the Potter's field to bury strangers in, and while they were engaged in making this disposition of the money Judas himself filled with remorse went out and hanged himself. Matt. xxvii: 5. The author of the Acts of the Apostles says in i: 18. "Now this man purchased a field with the reward of iniquity, and falling headlong he burst asunder in the midst, and all his bowels gushed out. Some think that the rope with which he hanged himself broke, or that the branch of the tree, to which the rope was tied, gave way, and he fell and his body burst asunder, and others think that the word hanged might be rendered "choked with grief," and that in the extreme of his anger and agony he threw himself with such violence on the earth that he burst asunder and his bowels gushed out.

After Judas had thus hanged himself, his place was filled by the selection of Matthias to be numbered with the apostles. Acts, i: 26.

JUDAS, 3—*The praise of the Lord.*
JUDAS of Galilee. He is represented as having been engaged in an insurrection, by Gamaliel the famous Jewish teacher, at whose feet Saul of Tarsus was brought up. Acts, xxii: 3. When the apostles were apprehended and examined before the council, this learned man gave very prudent advice to the council, in which he refers to Theudas and Judas of Galilee. They both raised insurrection. Judas perished and those who were associated with him were destroyed or dispersed. The Jewish historian Josephus mentions this Judas of Galilee and his insurrection, and says that it was when Cyrenius was governor of Syria. It is thought he based his insurrection on the sentiment that it was sinful for Jews to obey a heathen ruler. Acts, v: 37.

JULIA—[Ju′lia,] *downy.*
Was a friend of the apostle Paul, to whom he wrote a salutation in closing up his epistle to the Romans. Romans xvi: 15.

JULIUS—[Ju′li-us,] *downy.*
JULIUS was the centurion of Augustus' band, and he had the apostle Paul committed to his care by Festus, when sent as a prisoner to Rome. The account is given in Acts xxvii: 1. Julius treated the apostle kindly. At Sidon as the ship in which they were sailing touched, or tarried for a little while, Julius permitted Paul to go ashore, giving him liberty to go among the christians and refresh himself. And when afterwards in the voyage, the vessel was wrecked at the island of Melita, and the soldiers counseled together to kill the prisoner lest he should escape, Julius kept them from it, and loosening Paul and the other prisoners, he commanded those of them that could, to swim to the shore, and those that could not to secure broken pieces of the wrecked ship, and they did, so that all of them escaped to the land.

JUNIA—[Ju′nia,] *youth.*
JUNIA was a christian saluted by the apostle as a kinsman and fellow prisoner. It has been thought by some that Junia was a woman and the wife of Andronicus. These two persons may be looked upon as having been active and zealous in propagating the christian faith, and probably they were at one time, fellow prisoners with Paul. Romans xvi: 7. He remembers their virtues and holds them in high esteem. They were converted to christianity before Paul was. They may have been joined to Christ under his ministry, if not converted on the day of Pentecost.

JUSTUS, 1—[Jus′tus,] *upright.*
Was the surname of Barsabas. Acts i: 23. See Barsabas.

JUSTUS, 2—*Upright.*
Was a pious man in whose house Paul preached at Corinth. Acts xviii: 7.

JUSTUS, 3—*Upright.*
Was also called Jesus, and was a fellow laborer with Paul. He was associated with Aristarchus and Marcus, the nephew of Barnabas. They were all of the circumcision, or formerly Jews. The apostle says of them "they had been a comfort unto him." Col. iv: 10-11.

KADMIEL—[Kad′-miel,] *God of rising.*
Was one of the Levites who with his family returned from Babylon with Zerubbabel. He is also called Hodariah or Hodaviah. The house or family of this man was prominent. Ezra iii: 9, Neh. ix: 4 and x: 9.

KALLAI—[Kal′-la-i.]
Was a priest in the days of Joiakim. He represented an extensive family. Neh. xii: 20.

KAREAH—[Ka-re′-ah.]
Was the father of Johanan and Jonathan who acknowledged the authority of Gedaliah, and supported it and avenged his murder. Jer. xl: 8-16, xli: 16 and xlii: 1-8.

KEDAR—[Ke′-dar,] *blackness, sorrow.*
KEDAR was a son of Ishmael and the head of a numerous family, called the Kedarenes, who resided in Arabia. He was the second son of Ishmael. Gen. xxv: 13. Like nearly all the Ishmaelites, the Kedarenes dwelt in tents,

though sometimes they were collected together in villages, and David refers to one of these collections of them, when he says in Psalms, cxx: 5, "I dwell in the tents of Kedar." He sought refuge among them when his life was hunted by Saul. Their greatness and wealth consisted chiefly in flocks and herds, and Isa. refers to it in xxi: 16, and lx: 7. The children of Kedar traded with the ancient Tyrians, in sheep and goats, as we learn from Ezek. xxvii: 21. The prophet Jeremiah predicted their conquest by the Chaldeans. It is declared that Nebuchadnezzar shall smite Kedar, their tents and their flocks shall be taken away. Jer. xlix: 28. And when the prophet Isaiah is prophesying regarding the kingdom of Christ, and the ingathering of the Gentile nations to him, he says in Isa. lx: 7, "All the flocks of Kedar shall be gathered together unto thee, the rams of Nebaioth shall minister unto thee; they shall come up with acceptance on mine altar, and I will glorify the house of my glory."

KEDEMAH—[Ked′e-mah,] *oriental.*

KEDEMAH was the youngest son of Ishmael. Gen. xxv: 15. Like others of the the posterity of Ishmael, the children of Kedemah roved about. It is supposed that their territory was mainly eastward of Gilead, and that they gave the name of Kedemoth to a city near the river Amon, referred to in Josh. xiii: 18, and xxi: 37.

KEMUEL, 1—[Kem′-u-el,] *God is risen.*

KEMUEL was the third son of Nahor. He is supposed by some to have been the father of the Kamelites, who, it is thought, dwelt on the east of Syria, and a little westward of the river Euphrates.

KEMUEL, 2.—*God is risen.*

KEMUEL was the name of a prince belonging to the tribe of Ephraim. He is referred to in Num. xxxiv: 24, from which passage we discover, that he was the representative of his tribe in dividing the land of Canaan.

KENAZ, 1—[Ke′-naz,] *this nest, lamentation, possession.*

KENAZ was the fourth son of Eliphaz, the son of Esau, and one of the dukes of Edom referred to in Genesis, xxxvi: 15.

KENAZ, 2.—*This nest, lamentation, possession.*

KENAZ was the father of Othniel, and the younger brother of Caleb. Joshua, xv: 17, and Judges. i: 13,

KEREN-HAPPUCH—[Ker′-en-Hap′-puch,] *the horn or child of beauty.*

She was one of the three daughters of Job, born unto him in his old age, and, with her sisters, more handsome than all the other women of the land. Job, xlii: 14, 15.

KETURAH—[Ke-tu′-rah,] *he that burns, or makes the incense to fume, odoriferous.*

KETURAH was the name of a wife of Abraham. Gen. xxv: 1: "Then again Abraham took a wife, and her name was Keturah." When the patriarch married this woman, we are not informed. It was, in all probability, in the life-time of Sarah, the mother of the child of promise. Some have thought Keturah the same person as Hagar, who was given to Abraham as a wife; but this is not at all likely, since the two second wives of the patriarch are so distinguished in their history and in their descendants, Hagar's son being the head of the powerful nation of Ishmaelites, while the sons of Keturah were the heads of powerful tribes. The first of Abraham's second wives is mentioned as the mother of the one son, Ishmael, who, though disinherited by his father and sent away from home when a boy, was present when Abraham died, and assisted Isaac, his half-brother, in burying him—while Keturah's sons were six in number.

These sons were sent away before Abraham died, with their father's blessing. Gen. xxv: 6: "But unto the sons of the concubines, which Abraham had, Abraham gave gifts and sent them away from Isaac, his son, (while he yet lived,) eastward into the east country." The object Abraham had in view was to avoid any disputes among them as to inheritance after he, their father, was dead. He intended, because he knew it was the divine purpose, that the descendants of Isaac should settle in the land of promise. He therefore sent them "eastward into the east country" to procure them habitations and inheritance, so that they would have no occasion to dispute with Isaac the settlement of the land of Canaan.

Keturah may have become the wife of Abraham shortly after Isaac was born, or about the time that Hagar, with her son Ishmael, was sent away, and these sons of hers were born unto him when he was a very aged man.

KEZIA — [ke-zy′-ah,] *superfices, angle, cassia.*

Was a daughter of Job, born unto him after his afflictions were passed. She joined with her sisters in making the evening of her father's life pleasant. Job xlii: 14, 15.

KISH, 1—*Hard, difficult, straw.*

Was the son of Abiel. He was of the tribe of Benjamin and a man of great wealth or substance. He was the father of Saul the first King of Israel. 1st Sam. ix. Some of the asses of Kish were lost and he sent Saul his son, with one of the servants to search for them, and it was while Saul was searching for them, that the prophet Samuel, of whom he went to enquire anointed him king.

KISH, 2—*Hard, difficult, straw.*

Was the third son of Gibeon, and is referred to in 1st Chron. viii: 30.

KISH, 3—*Hard, difficult, straw.*

Was the second son of Mahli, and he was a Levite. Eleazar his brother died having no sons, and the sons of Kish took the sons of Mushi, their father's uncle, and placed them in offices that would have been filled by sons of Eleazar, had sons been born unto him. 1st Chron. xxiii: 21, &c.

KISH, 4—*Hard, difficult, straw.*

Was the son of Abdi and is referred to in 2d Chron. xxix: 12. He was a descendant of Merari the brother of Mahli and Mushi. 1st Chron. xxiii: 21.

KITTIM—[Kit′-tim,] *they that bruise, gold, coloring.*

Was one of the sons of Javan, and the grandson of Japheth, and is referred to in Gen. x: 4.

KOHATH—[Ko′-hath,] *congregation, obedience, to make blunt.*

KOHATH was the second son of Levi, hence the grandson of the patriarch Jacob, Gen. xlvi: 11, and from him were descended the extensive family of the Kohathites. He was the father of Amram and the grandfather of Moses, Aaron and Miriam The Hebrew priests, who were the children of Aaron, sprung from Kohath. Ex. vi. It seems that the family of the Kohathites numbered eight thousand six hundred males at their departure from the land of Egypt. Num. iii: 28. There were two thousand seven hundred and fifty of them that were fit for service, and they were under the charge of Elizaphan, the son of Uzziel. Num. iv: 36. They pitched their tents on the south side of the tabernacle, and in the marches they were immediately behind the tribe of Reuben. They were the bearers of the ark and other of the sacred things connected with the tabernacle. Num. x: 21.

They had their apportionment of cities made them, in the land of Canaan. The number and names of the cities are given in Joshua xxi: 20–26.

The names of the chief men of the Kohathites, in the time of David and Solomon, are given in 1st Chron. xxiii: 12–20. There were four of them—Shebuel, Rehabiah, Jesiah and Micah. The first two men were descendants of Moses, and had the charge of the sacred treasures. 1st Chron. xxvi: 24–25.

KOLAIAH—[Kol-a-i′-ah.]

Was the father of Ahab, the false prophet who, in company with Zedekiah, the son of Maaseiah, prophesied a lie; and were slain by Nebuchadnezzar, the king of Babylon. Jeremiah, xxix: 21.

KORAH, 1—[Ko′rah,] *bald, frozen.*

Was the son of Esau, by his wife Aholibamah. He seems to have been the third son. Gen. xxxvi: 14, and he has the rank of a duke of Esau or a prince and governor.

KORAH, 2—*Bald, frozen.*

KORAH was the son of Izhar, and the great-grandson of Levi, hence he sustained the relation of a cousin to Moses and Aaron. He was the father of Assir, Elkanah and Abiasaph. Ex. vi: 21. He was associated with Dathan and Abiram, in envying Moses and Aaron, and speaking against them. We have an account of their rebellion in Num. xvi, in which two hundred and fifty princes were gathered with them against the leaders of Israel. Korah seems to be leader, as his name occurs first in the trio, and Moses speaks unto Korah and the company with him. He is recognized at the head of the mutiny. He haughtily upbraided Moses and Aaron for taking too much authority and making themselves too prominent in the camp.

Moses meekly replied that it was very wicked in them thus to find fault with the arrangement of the Almighty, and he assured them that the Lord would show them the next day who were proper persons to officiate in the priesthood. He bade Korah and his company come up with their censers prepared with incense, and have the matter about which they complained tested. They accordingly did so, and Korah, Dathan and Abiram brought up together a large number of them, and induced them to rail on Moses and Aaron. They probably suggested to the people that God was about to accept their incense, and they wished to have a large number present to witness the acceptance. God appeared among the people and the cloud of his glory overshadowed the tabernacle. The anger of God towards the mutineers was exhibited as he ordered Moses and Aaron to separate themselves from them that he might destroy them. They begged that he would not destroy the whole congregation for the sin of a few, and their prayer was heard, and their request granted. They then under the divine direction, ordered the congregation to get away quickly from the tents of these wicked men. They all left them except the two hundred and fifty men that offered incense with Korah. The earth opened its mouth and swallowed up the three guilty leaders with their tents and families, unless it be that some of the sons of Korah who were not with their father in the rebellion were saved. Num. xvi: 32. After they were thus destroyed, fire from God consumed the two hundred and fifty men also. Num. xvi and xxvi: 9-11. It is supposed that several of the Psalms were delivered to the sons or descendants of the sons of Korah for the purpose of being set to music. In the account of the Levites and their families in 1st Chron. vi, several or the sons of Korah are referred to as musicians, and in 1st Chron. xxvi, some of them are represented as porters to the temple.

KUSHAIAH—[Kush-a′-iah.]

KUSHAIAH was the father of Ethan, who was of the family of Merari, and who was one of the singers engaged in the solemn service of removing the ark to Jerusalem and placing it in the tent which David had prepared for it. 1st Chron. xv: 17.

LAADAN—[La-a′-dan.]

Was a Gershonite, who was connected with the sacred offices in the time of David. He was among those who were gathered together of the princes of Israel, with the priests and Levites. He was affected by the appointment of David of the priests and Levites to serve in the sacred offices. 1st Chron. xxiii: 8.

LABAN—[La′ban,] *white, shining, gentle.*

LABAN was the son of Bethuel and the brother of Rebekah; hence he was the uncle of Jacob. He is brought to our notice in connection with the reception of Eliezer at Nahor. Abraham had sent this faithful servant in search of a wife for his son Isaac; and, as he tarried at a well near the city, Rebekah, who had come to the well to draw water, entered into converse with him. She kindly drew water and gave him to drink; then watered his thirsty camels, received presents at his hand, and ran home to give report of the stranger to her father's family. Laban immediately ran out to the man at the well and cordially invited him to the family circle. Laban took care of, and gave food to the camels, and brought water to wash the feet of Eliezer and the men that were with him. Gen. xxiv: 29, &c. And when the stranger made known his errand, and gave the family of Bethuel the reasons that he had for believing that the Lord had prospered him, and that it was the divine purpose that Rebekah should become the wife of his master's son, Laban acceded without hesitancy to the proposal.

When Jacob left home with the blessing of his father and his mother upon him, in search of a wife, he went to Padan-aram, to the house of Bethuel, and took a wife from the family of Laban his mother's brother. He met Rachel his first choice at the well near the city, and made himself known to her. She ran and told her father, and he came out and gave him a friendly reception, and afterwards he agreed to give Jacob his daughter to wife in lieu of seven years labor. The labor was performed on the part of Jacob and he claimed at Laban's hand the reward. The marriage was arranged for, but Laban deceived Jacob by substituting Leah for Rachel, and then defended himself by the custom of that land which was to marry the elder before the younger. He however in order to pacify Jacob who had been deceived, agreed at the end of the marriage feast to give him Rachel also as a wife, if he would serve seven other years, which he did. Laban then fixed upon other wages, and Jacob with his wives still tarried in his employ. Gen. xxix. Several times Laban changed the wages of Jacob, but still kept him as the overseer of his flocks, until finally Jacob determined to leave him, and go back to his father's land. He made known his determination to his wives, and they both acquiesced in his wishes, and agreed to go with their husband. Getting all things in readiness they left while Laban was absent from home. As soon as he returned, and learned that they had gone, he pursued after them and overtook them after seven days travel in Mt. Gilead. He charged Jacob with committing a great wrong in stealing away as he had done, but Jacob gave him the reason why he had done so, viz: "I was afraid thou wouldst take thy daughters by force from me." Laban had been favored with a vision from the God of Jacob advising him to deal justly with Jacob, and he did so. The difficulty between them was settled and they entered into a covenant to do each other no harm and continue so far as they had opportunity in friendly relations. They gathered together a heap of stones to be a standing memorial of their covenant; Laban called the memorial Jegar-sahadutha, and Jacob called it Galeed which signifies "the heap of witnesses."

They stayed together in the mount all day, offered sacrifice unto God, and did eat bread together. Early the next morning they parted in friendship. Laban kissed his sons and his daughters, blessed them and returned to his home. Gen. xxxi.

LAEL—[La'el,] *to God, to the Almighty.*

Was the father of Eliasaph, and was the chief of the Gershonites, who had a very important work assigned them, viz.: the charge of the tabernacle and its sacred fixtures. Num. iii: 23-27.

LAHMI—[Lah'mi,] *my bread, my war,*

Was the brother of Goliath, the Gittite. He was slain by Elhanan, the son of Jair.

LAISH—[La'ish,] *a lion,*

Was the father of Phalti, the man to whom King Saul gave Michal, David's wife. This Laish was a resident of Gallim. 1st Sam. xxv: 44.

LAMECH, 1.—[La'-mech,] *poor, made low, who is struck.*

Lamech was a descendant of Cain by Mathusael, and is referred to in Gen. iv: 18. He is the first man who is reported to have married more than one wife. He was the first who practiced poligamy. The names of his two wives were Adah and Zillah. By the former he had two sons, viz: Jabel and Jubal. Jabel, who was the elder, was the inventor of tents, and roved about with herds of cattle. He is called the father of such as dwell in tents, and of such as have cattle, while Jubal, the younger, was the inventor of musical instruments, such as harps and organs. By the other wife, Lamech had a son whom he called Tubal-Cain, who was the first worker in metals. He had also a daughter whom he named Naamah. Gen. iv: 22.

There seemed to be no jealousy existing between the two wives of Lamech, the one toward the other. They had the regards of each other, and alike the affection and esteem of their husband. One day Lamech approached his wives, and with a solemn air told them he had slain a young man. It is supposed that they became alarmed lest the death should be avenged with his destruction, and so they would be left widows. He quieted their fears by telling them that if Cain should be avenged seven fold, surely Lamech seventy and seven fold. If Cain, who was a cruel murderer of his own brother, was not to be destroyed, surely he who had slain a man unintentionally, or possibly in self-defense, would not be destroyed.

LAMECH, 2—[La′-mech,] *poor, made law, who is struck.*

Was the son of Methuselah, and is referred to in Gen. v: 25. He was the father of Noah. Though he did not live to be as old as Methuselah his father, yet he lived to a good old age, for he was seven hundred and seventy-seven years old when he died, which was probably not more than five years before the flood destroyed the inhabitants of the old world. He was living when Noah was engaged in preparing the ark for the safety of his family. From the genealogy of Christ, as given by Luke, we find Lamech was in the line from Adam. Luke, iii: 36.

LAPIDOTH—[Lap′-i-doth,] *enlightened, lamps.*

LAPIDOTH was the husband of the prophetess Deborah, who delivered her people from the hand and power of Jabin, king of Canaan. Jud. iv: 4. He seems to have had no hand in the affairs of the nation, as to administering the laws or leading in the army, or even consulting regarding the movements of the army with Deborah or Barak, her general.

LAZARUS, 1—[Laz′a-rus,] *the help of God.*

LAZARUS was the brother of Martha and Mary, who lived at Bethany. He was a disciple of our Savior, and, with his sisters, was strongly attached to their Master. Their house was always open for the reception of Jesus when at Bethany; and we may judge from the account given of the Savior's visit, as recorded in Luke, x: 38–42, that he was often with them and enjoyed their hospitality. At this visit Martha was extremely anxious to give him a handsome entertainment, and complained to Jesus that Mary, her sister, had left her to serve alone; for while she was engaged in the domestic affairs her sister was listening to his instructions and receiving his admonitions and counsels. Jesus did not, as Martha hoped he would, send her away from him to assist her, but on the contrary, commended Mary and reproved her.

A few months before the Savior closed his ministry, Lazarus fell dangerously sick and died. As soon as the sisters began to despair of their brother's recovery, they sent to Jesus, who was then preaching and teaching beyond Jordan, and informed him of the sickness of Lazarus, and besought him to come and cure him. It would seem from the manner in which the case was presented to Jesus, that he was especially attached to Lazarus: "Lord, behold he whom thou lovest is sick." Jesus at once informed his disciples that the sickness of Lazarus would not shut him up in the tomb, or in the state of the dead, but would result in a manifestation of God's power and glory. He thereby intimated, though the disciples did not understand it, that Lazarus would be raised from the dead. In order to make the miracle more noted, he tarried, when he was beyond Jordan, two days. He then intimated to his disciples his determination to go into Judea again. They tried to dissuade him because of the persecutions he had met with when last there, but he would not be turned from his purpose. He then told his disciples that Lazarus was asleep in death, but he was going to Bethany to awake him out of sleep, or to raise him from the dead.

It was the fourth day after Lazarus died that Jesus with his disciples came to Bethany; and being in the outskirts of the town Martha went out and met him, and poured the sorrows of her soul out in his hearing, saying, "Lord, if thou hadst been here my brother had not died." He sympathized with her and indicated his intention to raise him up from the dead. Mary afterwards came out and addressed him in the same language used by her sister, and the Jews that were friends of these bereaved sisters also gathered about Jesus and expressed their feeling and sympathy. The Master himself was greatly moved. "He groaned in the spirit and was troubled," and asked where the sepulcher of Lazarus was; and as they went to the grave he wept."

When they reached the grave he bade them remove the stone from the mouth of it. Martha at first ventured an objection, but Jesus answered her objection by referring her to the conversation they had had when she met him, regarding the resurrection, and he admonished her to believe and she should soon see a display of the glorious power of God in the resurrection of her brother.

They then took away the stone from the mouth of the sepulcher and Jesus lifted up his voice in prayer to God the father, after which "he cried with a loud voice Lazarus come forth." The dead body immediately started up into life. He who was dead came up from the grave freed from the power of the monarch of the tomb. Jesus ordered them to take off the clothes with which his body was bound for burial; and they did so, and Lazarus was again living—restored to the home and hearts that four days before had been made desolate. John, xi.

The Jewish priests and rulers became very much enraged at this miracle and determined to kill Jesus, and Lazarus also, whom he had raised from the dead—for they desired the report of it to die away. John, xii: 10.

A few days before Jesus was crucified he was at Bethany, and lodged at the house of Lazarus. This Bethany family for the last time entertained him. Martha served as she had been accustomed to at other times. Lazarus sat at the table, and Mary anointed the head of Jesus with costly ointment. Jesus commended this act of hers and declared that it should be spoken of to her honor in all the world. John, xii: 1, 8.

How long Lazarus lived after he was raised from the dead we know not, nor in what manner he met death the second time.

LAZARUS, 2—[Laz′-a-rus,] *the help of God.*

LAZARUS was the name of the poor man in the history or parable, as it is denominated of the "Rich man and Lazarus." It was designed by the Savior to illustrate the doctrine of a future state, and of rewards and punishments. He is represented as being a very poor man, and with his poverty sorely afflicted. He had no home or shelter of his own; no money or provision and very poor clothing. He had his position at the rich man's gate, and begged the crumbs that fell from his table. His clothes were not sufficient to shelter him from the weather, for the dogs had access to his sores. He was a feeble, emaciated, suffering man. Nature gave way under the hardness of his lot and he died; but when dying, angels bent over his failing form, and took possession of the immortal spirit as soon as it was let loose from the clay tabernacle, and they carried it into the heavenly state. We hear of Lazarus after he left earth, "in Abraham's bosom."

In a little while after the death of Lazarus the rich man also died, and was buried, no doubt in great pomp and splendor, and a costly monument was raised over him, while the form of Lazarus was rudely coffined and laid in the Potter's field or stranger's burying ground. While Lazarus was in heaven enjoying the companionship of Abraham, the rich man was in hell, and in torment calls ineffectually for water to cool his parched tongue. The rich man saw Lazarus now in paradise, and remembered him as a beggar at his gate, and he begged that Abraham would send him to his five brethren and warn them, lest they also should come to that place of torment; but this request was also denied him. Luke, xvi: 19, 31.

It makes but little difference to us whether this account is real history or parable, the great truth it is intended to teach is the same. If history it is a relation of facts as they have been, if parable merely, it is a relation of facts as they may be.

LEAH—[Le′-ah,] *weary, tired.*

LEAH was the oldest daughter of Laban, who became the wife of Jacob. From the history we learn, she did not become the wife of the patriarch by choice on his part, but by the custom of the country, and the management of Laban, the father.

Jacob had agreed to serve Laban seven years for Rachel, his younger daughter. But when his service was ended, and he demanded the hand of Rachel in marriage, Laban made a great feast, and made as though he was about to meet his promise to Jacob, but instead of giving him Rachel to wife, he gave him Leah, thereby deceiving him. Jacob was dissatisfied, and ventured to express that dissatisfaction to Laban. The father-in-law then gave as his reason for practising the fraud upon him, that the custom of that country was to give daughters in marriage by seniority. The eldest must be married first. This was not only custom but in all probability it was law in the country of Mesopotamia; but Jacob had not learned that fact, and hence his dissatisfaction. The matter was finally settled between Jacob and Laban, by the latter agreeing to give him Rachel also to wife at the end of the present marriage feast.

Jacob had no feelings against Leah, he loved her as a sister, but had never meditated marriage with her, for his affections had centered upon the younger daughter. He had served the proposed time for her, seven years, and the seven years seemed to him as days for the love he had for her. Leah was an amiable woman, and worthy the affections of the shepherd who was destined to be a mighty man and the head of a mighty nation.

In Gen. xxix: 17, it is said "Leah was tender-eyed." By this it need not be understood that her eyes were weak or diseased, for it may mean that she had a soft, delicate, beautiful eye, as to its color and expression—that her beautiful eye was an adornment that her sister had not—while Rachel excelled her in shape, person and carriage.

It was quite natural for Jacob to love Rachel more than Leah, as she was the object of his first love, but yet we are not to suppose that Jacob did not love Leah at all; because it is said "Leah was hated," Jacob loved her with a less love than the love he bare to her sister. She was the honored mother of Reuben, Simeon, Levi and Judah. She was also the mother of Issachar and Zebulun and of Jacob's daughter, Dinah. Thus we behold her as the honored mother of one half of the heads of the tribes of Israel. But in addition to these Gad and Asher, two other of the sons of Jacob were considered Leah's children because they were born unto Zilpah, her handmaid. There is one other circumstance worthy of record regarding Leah—when she died she was buried in the cave of Machpelah beside Abraham and Sarah, Isaac and Rebekah—and Jacob of choice was taken when he died, from Egypt by his son Joseph, and buried by her side.

LEBBEUS—[Leb-be′us,] *a man of heart.*

LEBBEUS or THADDEUS, was one of the twelve disciples, and the same as Judas, the son of Cleopas, and the brother of James the less, hence a kinsman of our Lord. Matthew, x: 3; Mark, iii: 18; Luke, vi: 16; Acts, i: 13. See also Judas or Jude.

LEMUEL—[Lem′u-el,] *God with them.*

This real or supposed person is referred to in Proverbs, xxxi: 1, and important lessons of instruction are given him by his mother. It has been supposed that Lemuel is another name for Solomon. If so, his mother is the author of those excellent lessons.

LETUSHIM—[Le-tu′-shim.]

Was the son of Dedan, and great grandson of Abraham by Keturah. Genesis, xxv: 3.

LEUMMIM—[Le-um′-mim.]

Was the son of Dedan, and great grandson of Abraham by Keturah. Genesis, xxv: 3.

LEVI—[Le′-vi,] *who is held and associated.*

LEVI was the third son of Jacob and Leah. His birth and position in the family of Jacob is given in Gen. xxix: 34. He was engaged with his brother Simeon in revenging the disgrace of their sister Dinah. Together, these two brothers deceived the Shechemites and murdered them. Jacob by no means approved their act. He remembered it against them, and, when dying, denounced Levi and declared that his seed should be scattered about among the tribes of the land of Canaan. Jacob, in his dying words, referred to this act of Simeon and Levi, Gen. xlix: 6, "O my soul, come not thou into their secret," &c. He associates them together as having instruments of cruelty in their habitations. Gen. xxxiv.

Levi had three sons, viz: Gershon, Kohath and Merari, and one daughter whose name was Jochebed, who afterwards became the wife of Amram and the mother of the leaders of the children of Israel. Ex. vi: 16–20. The sons of Levi were each the head of extensive families, called the Gershonites, Kohathites and Merarites. Levi himself died at the age of one hundred and thirty-seven years. His tribe, consisting of the above named families, was not as extensive as some other tribes, at the time of the Exodus from Egypt, for they numbered but twenty-two thousand two hundred and seventy-three males that were over one month old.

We have an account of the wickedness and idolatry of Israel at Sinai, in making and worshiping a golden calf. The tribe of Levi, to which Moses and Aaron belonged, sinned greatly, and God was angry with them, and many were slain. We are informed in Ex. xxxii: 28, that three thousand men of them fell in the slaughter of idolaters. They were faithful in cutting them off for their wickedness, until there were no idolaters left in the tribe of Levi. God rewarded them for their zeal and faithfulness in this matter.

Aaron and his immediate descendants were set apart to be priests; but the entire tribe of Levi were not to be numbered and apportioned as the other tribes, but exist among the other tribes as agents or actors in holy things. The whole tribe was to be taken for tabernacle or sanctuary service and to minister unto the Lord, under Aaron and his sons. Moses, under divine direction, numbered them by the three families, gave them their position in the grand army, and appointed their chief. The family of Gershon had Eliasaph as their chief; the family of Kohath Elizaphan, and the family of Merari had Zuriel as their chief.

The Levites were consecrated to their work with solemn ceremony. They were to be sprinkled with pure water, to shave off their hair and wash their clothes. They were then to bring two young bullocks to the door of the tabernacle. The hands of Israelites were to be laid upon the heads of the Levites, thereby resigning them to their station in the sacred worship. The Levites then laid their hands on the two young bullocks and offered them, one for a burnt offering and the other for a sin offering. Thus consecrated, they were required to walk to and fro before the tabernacle door for awhile, thereby signifying that they were dedicated to God and had entered upon their important work. The age at which they began this service was twenty-five, and they closed the active service at fifty. The first five years was a kind of probation, so that really they were thirty when the active service commenced. Num. iv: 47, and Num. viii.

The Levites had no special sacred apparel, and yet they performed much sacred work, such as bearing things pertaining to the tabernacle during their tented state; afterwards in the land of Canaan they took care of it and its sacred things, as also the temple and its furniture. They were often engaged in teaching the people and assisting the priests.

In the land of Canaan they had forty-eight cities with their suburbs assigned them, six of which were appointed as cities of refuge. Some of the judges of Israel were Levites, as Eli and Samuel. 1st Samuel; and the tribe was quite numerous in the days of the kings. More than eight thousand were engaged in the coronation ceremonies of David, and there were thirty-eight thousand of them fit for service during David's time. We are informed that twenty-four thousand of them officiated in the service of the tabernacle or temple; six thousand of them were judges; four thousand were porters, and four thousand were musicians. They were divided into twenty-four classes or courses, and had their service appointed them by lot. 1st Chron. xii, xxiii, and xxvi.

The Levites refused to remain with the idolatrous Jeroboam. Very many of them left his kingdom and returned to the kingdom of Judah, where Jerusalem and the temple were and the worship of the true God continued. They were teachers of religion, and we learn that Jehoshaphat sent them all through his kingdom with the princes to teach the people. They were very active in the reform of the young king Josiah; they directed in the repairs of the temple, and assisted at the solemn passover. 2d Chron. xi and xii; also xix to xxxv.

Many of them were carried into Babylon and were in captivity there, but some of them returned with Zerubbabel, others with Ezra, and ten of them are mentioned in Ezra x: 23, 24, as putting away strange wives they had married in Babylon. Some of them assisted Nehemiah in reading the law at his solemn fast, Neh. viii, and ix, and seventeen of them subscribed to Nehemiah's covenant for reformation. Neh. x. Nehemiah required the people to attend to the tithes due the Levites, as their neglect had made it necessary for them to go into other employments instead of being faithful to the temple service. Nehemiah x.

The Levites became demoralized greatly after our Savior's death, for they tell us the high priesthood was disposed of to the highest bidders, while the common Levites wore the robes of the priests which had not been allowed from the time the tribe was consecrated.

LIBNI—[Lib′ni,] *white, whiteness.*

Libni was the son of Gershon, of the tribe of Levi. His family, with the family of his brother Shimi, had the charge of the tabernacle of the congregation, that is, so much as pertained to the curtains, and coverings, and cords. Exodus vi: 17. Numbers, iii: 25.

LOIS—[Lo′is,] *better.*

Lois was the mother of Eunice, and the grandmother of Timothy. We may gather from the testimony of Paul regarding the piety of these women, that while Timothy owed much to the instructions of his mother; he also owed much to his grandmother. She taught Eunice, and associated herself with her daughter in raising up the son "in the nurture and admonition of the Lord." Paul said, 2d Timothy, i: 5, "When I call to rememberance the unfeigned faith that is in thee, which dwelt first in thy grandmother Lois, and thy mother, Eunice." And referring to Timothy's early education, he says, "from a child, thou hast known the holy scriptures, which are able to make thee wise unto salvation through faith which is in Jesus Christ." 2d Timothy, iii: 15.

LOAMMI—[Lo-am′mi,] *not my people.*

Was one of the sons of the prophet Hosea, by Gomer, the daughter of Dibliam. The name is significant of a future event. Hosea, i: 9.

LO-RUHAMAH—[Lo-ru-hay′mah] *not having obtained mercy, not pitied.*

Was the daughter of the prophet Hosea, by Gomer, the daughter of Dibliam, and her name was significant of a future event. Hosea, i: 6.

LOT—*wrapt up, myrrh, rosin.*

Lot was the son of Haran, and a nephew of Abraham, and some suppose the brother of Sarah the wife of the great Patriarch. If Sarah was the daughter of Haran and the granddaughter of Terah, and the same as Iscah referred to in Gen. xi: 29, then she was the sister of Lot. But of this we cannot be certain. After the death of Haran, Lot traveled with Abraham and lived with him. They went down together into Egypt, and tarried during a famine there. Together they left Egypt and went into the south country and pitched their tents between Bethel and Hai. Lot and Abraham were both quite wealthy, and their wealth consisted in extensive flocks and herds. So extensive that the land would not afford pasturage for them both. There was a difficulty between the herdsmen of Lot and Abraham, probably regarding the pasturage, and when Abraham learned it he made a peaceful offer to Lot to separate, which offer was accepted on the part of Lot, and he chose the country about Sodom for his residence and pasturage. So the two separated.

It was not long until the Sodomites began to develop great wickedness of heart. Lot saw it, mourned over it, and his very life became a burden unto him. God punished the wicked people of that country by permitting the confederate kings to conquer and ravage their country, and carry them captive.

Lot himself and his family were taken captive, but Abraham, his uncle, hearing of it, armed his trained servants born in his own house, and pursued after Chedorlaomer and recovered Lot and his family and goods.

A few years after that God determined to destroy the cities of the plain of which Sodom was one, by fire and brimstone from heaven. Lot was visited by two angels, and with his family hastened out of the city before it was destroyed. These angels had feasted with Abraham, and made known the divine will and purpose to destroy Sodom. They went on to the city wearied and fatigued with travel. Lot saw them, and begged of them, that they would come in and lodge that night in his house. At first they manifested a disposition—probably to try his hospitality—to stay all night in the street, but he pressed them to come in, and they did, and ate with him.

Scarcely was the repast over when a rabble crowd of Sodomites beset the house of Lot, and demanded that he bring out the strangers, that they might insult them, but he would not. They became furious and rushed at the door to break it down, but the angels drew Lot in and shut the door, fastening it securely, then smote the wicked crowd with blindness. They became confused and astonished, and at last left the habitation of Lot and went to their homes. The angels then informed Lot of the divine determination to destroy the City of Sodom, and the other cities of the plains, for the wickedness of the people, and they bade him with his relations leave the place. He sent to his intended sons-in-law and begged them to go with him and his wife and daughters; but they would not. Early the next morning Lot, his wife, and two unmarried daughters left Sodom, urged by the angels, and started for the mountains.

They were warned to flee and not tarry, or look back. Lot felt an anxiety to have a home in some town or village, and not in the mountains that were inhabited but by wild beasts, and he asked for the privilege of fleeing to Zoar, which was the smallest of the five cities marked for destruction. The Lord granted this request, and permitted him to go there. When he arrived at Zoar, there was one less of his family than when he started from Sodom. For some cause or other, his wife had disobeyed the divine command, and was overtaken by the vengeance of the Almighty. She became a pillar of salt, while the cities, with their inhabitants, were destroyed. Lot was afraid to dwell in Zoar. It may be, he could view from that place, the desolated and ruined country, and possibly he could see the saline monument into which his wife was turned, and so shocking was the sight of the country, and the destruction that had befallen his wife, that he retired to the mountains, where he was first bidden to go. It was while he dwelt in the mountains beyond Zoar with his daughters, that he committed sin against God in indulging in drunkeness, and evil concupiscence. The snare was set by his daughters, and he was entrapped. The sin Lot committed here was almost the only blemish in his moral conduct.

Both the daughters bare a son, and the elder called the name of her son Moab, and he was the father of the Moabites; and the younger called the name of her son Ben-ammi, and he was the father of the Ammonites. Both of these two powerful tribes seemed to be under the malediction of Heaven. The Moabites became gross idolaters, and the Ammonites who dwelt near them, engaged with them in their idolatries, and they were alike enemies to Israel. Judges, xi: 24; Deut. xxiii: 3–4.

It can hardly be supposed, from what is recorded regarding Lot in Genesis, xiii: 5–13, that he became a vicious and wicked man, as there is but a single wicked act recorded. Nor does Peter, in his epistle, 2d Epistle, ii: 6–8, even condemn him, as we are accustomed to condemn this act, though he had a knowledge of it.

LOTAN—[Lo′tan.]

Was the son of Seir, the Horite, whose posterity is referred to in Genesis, xxxvi: 20.

LUCIFER—[Lu′ci-fer,] *bringing light.*

LUCIFER is a title by which the prophet Isaiah describes the proud tyrant and wicked king of Babylon, Nebuchadnezzar. His glory and power is represented as far surpassing that of other kings. Isaiah, xiv: 12, "How art thou fallen, O Lucifer," &c. The title is used to represent the head of the fallen angels, and the king of Babylon is compared to him.

LUCIUS—[Lu′shi-us,] *luminous.*

Of Cyrene, was probably the same as Luke, the author of the Acts of the Apostles, and the gospel. He is referred to in Acts, xiii: 1.

LUD OR LUDIN, 1—*Maturity, generation.*

LUD or LUDIN was the son of Shem, and is referred to in Genesis, x: 22. He is supposed to be the progeniture of those Lydians who dwelt in lesser Asia, who became a very wicked people, and one of the prophets refers to Lud, or the descendants of Lud, who were ignorant of God, and had not seen his glory, among whom he would exile some of the Jews for their wickedness. Isaiah, lxvi: 19.

LUD OR LUDIM, 2—*Maturity generation.*

LUD or LUDIM was the son of Mizraim, probably the elder son, as he is named first of the sons in Genesis, x: 13. His descendants are supposed to be the same as the Nubians, who settled on the south or west of Egypt. They were famous as archers, and are referred to in Jeremiah, xlvi: 9, as helping Pharaoh-necho against the Chaldeans; but Ezekiel, xxx: 5, tells us that these Lydians, with those whom they were in league, shall be exterminated.

LUKE—*Luminous.*

LUKE was an Evangelist, the author of the gospel bearing that name, and also the author of the "Acts of the apostles." He was a native of Antioch, and by profession a physician. He became we suppose during Christ's ministry a disciple, and constant attendant on the master. His gospel or history of Jesus Christ, is very complete, there are several important circumstances related, that are not mentioned by Matthew and Mark. He records incidents in Jesus' public life, and relates parables and instructions that the other Evangelists omit. He gives especially a full and clear account of the two disciples that journeyed to Emmaus, and received evidence satisfactory to them, that their lord had risen from the dead. The strong probability is that he was one of the two, for he gives the name of Cleopas, but not of his traveling companion. As he relates the circumstance so clearly in the twenty-fourth chapter of his gospel, it is quite likely that he was "that other disciple," and modestly refrained from giving his own name, as sometimes others of the sacred writers do. In Luke i: 2 he professes to be an eye-witness of the scenes and circumstances he is about to relate. He seems to have written or directed his gospel as also the Acts of the Apostles, to a noted Christian, and special friend of his, whose name was Theophilus. Luke i; 3. Acts i: 1. In his gospel he has given a clear and satisfactory account of the birth of Jesus, and his genealogy by the side of Mary, his real mother, calling Joseph the son of Heli, who was the son-in-law, having married Mary, Heli's daughter. His account of the messenger, or forerunner of Messiah is very clear and satisfactory. He gives the names, character and position of John the Baptist's parents, John's birth and life, and work and death. He gives the important testimony of the aged Simeon regarding Christ's Messiahship, and the testimony of the aged widow Anna. He gives the conversation of Jesus with the doctors in the temple when but twelve years of age. He gives several striking parables which are omitted in the other gospels. The parable of the good Samaritan; prodigal son; rich man and Lazarus; also, the unjust judge, and the Publican and Pharisee, who went up to the temple to pray. He relates the cure of the woman who had been bowed down by affliction for eighteen years; the cleansing of the ten lepers; the restoring to life of the widow's son at Nain. He gives the account of Zaccheus and his conversion.

It is not very certain whether Luke was a Jew or a Gentile but the probability is that he was a Jew. Some have supposed he was a kinsman of Paul; they think that Lucius named in Rom. xvi: 21 was the same as Luke. He was a companion of that apostle, traveled extensively with him, and frequently in giving the travels of Paul he associates himself with him, or in writing his account he uses the first person plural. In Acts xvi: 11, "Wherefore loosing from Troas we came with a straight course to Samothracia." This gives us to understand that Luke was with Paul on his first voyage, and visit to Macedonia, and when Paul reached Philippi he and Luke probably separated for a time, for as Luke continues the account of the apostle's travels and labors, in his writing he uses the third person plural. Acts xvii: 1. "Now when they had passed through Amphipolis, &c," but after that he uses the first person again. Acts xx: 5, 6. "These going before tarried for us at Troas," &c. "We sailed from Philippi." We may learn from 2d Tim. iv: 11, Philemon twenty-fourth verse. Col. iv: 14, that Luke "the beloved physician," was with Paul during the years of his confinement as a prisoner at Rome.

It is supposed that he was more learned than either of the other evangelists. His language is considered more varied, copious and pure and his style of writing generally superior to the style of the others. It is not known when he died or where; historians have not mentioned him among those who suffered martyrdom, hence we may suppose he died a natural death.

## LYDIA—[Lyd′-i-a.]

Lydia was a woman who had been born in Thyatira, but was a seller of purple, or purple silks in Philippi. It is not certain whether she was a Jewess or a Gentile. From the account given of her in Acts, xvi: 14, 15, we suppose she was a worshiper of God, but became a convert to the Christian religion through the preaching of Paul at the river side, not far from the city of Philippi, where she was engaged in her calling. Her employment was honorable and demanded attention and application, but she found time to worship God according to the knowledge she had, and was probably very devout in her worship; but she heard the apostle preach on that memorable Sabbath after he arrived in the country of Macedonia. And she did not hear the word preached in vain; it was made instrumental in her conversion. "The Lord opened her heart and she attended to those things which were spoken of Paul." She at once acknowledged the truth, declared her faith in Christ, and openly took upon herself his name and the obligations of his religion. She was baptized with her household, and immediately showed her strong attachment to the cause, and her gratitude to the ministers who had been instrumental in her conversion, by pressing them to come into her house and abide there. There were several reasons why she besought them, if they judged her faithful, and her conversion to be genuine, to come into her house and abide there. One of the principal reasons in all probability was she desired to receive further instruction from them. She would have them in her family, that she and her household might have their counsel and instruction daily—that she might ask them questions and have their teaching and prayers in her family. She had learned something of Christ and desired to learn much more. Thus beginning, it is not strange if she became a noted and Christian woman.

Paul and his companion were soon cast into prison at Philippi and during their imprisonment were instrumental in the conversion of the jailor. As soon as they were delivered from the prison and the stocks, they went into the house of Lydia where they found the Christians engaged in prayer for them. Lydia was not afraid to show her friendship and feeling for these despised and persecuted ambassadors of Christ—she did not shun them or their company lest the patronage she had as a seller of purple should be cut off.

After encouraging Lydia and the other converts, Paul and his companion departed from Philippi to preach in other cities of Macedonia. Lydia probably remained faithful until the pilgrimage of life ended, when she entered upon the glorious reward of the righteous.

## LYSIAS.

Lysias was the chief captain of a Roman band at Jerusalem, and in Acts, xxi, he is presented to our view as rescuing Paul from the hands and power of a mob. The apostle had been received gladly by the brethren at Jerusalem, and he declared the things that God had wrought by his ministry among the Gentiles. At the request of James and the elders of the church there, Paul showed his respect for the law of Moses, by purifying himself and certain others who were with him that were under a vow. After the days of purifying were ended, certain Jews finding him there, raised an insurrection against him and would have killed him had not Lysias taken charge of him. He came with an armed force and bound him with two chains to two soldiers, and ordered him to be placed in the castle. As Paul was ascending the stairs, he asked of Lysias the privilege of speaking, who permitted him, and standing on the stairs, out of the reach of the mob, he delivered a powerful address, Acts, xxii, during which he plead his privileges as a Roman citizen, and by that plan escaped the torture that he was about to endure by scourging. The next day he brought Paul before the chief priests and their council. The apostle defends himself there also. A great dissension arose during the examination of the case, and Lysias closed up the examination and placed Paul again in the castle. When Lysias heard that forty persons had conspired to kill Paul, he sent him by night under a strong military escort to Cesarea, to Felix the Governor. Acts, xxiii: 26–30, is a copy of the letter that the chief captain wrote to Felix, setting forth the case. (See Claudius.)

MAACAH—[Ma-a'cah,] *to squeeze.*

MAACAH was one of the wives of David. She was the daughter of Talmai, the king of Geshur. David probably formed some acquaintance with this woman while he dwelt in Ziklag, the town that Achish, the king of Gath, gave him. During the time that David lived there, he warred with the Geshurites, and some neighboring nations, and conquered them.

Absalom was the son of Maacah, and when he killed Amnon, his brother, he fled to the country of Geshur, and put himself under the charge of Talmai, the king, who was his grandfather on his mother's side, where he remained for three years. Tamar, who was disgraced by Amnon, was the daughter of Maacah, and hence sustained a near relation to Absalom, who revenged her disgrace by an act that exiled him for three years from David, and from Maacah, his mother. 2d Samuel, iii: 3.

MAACHAH, 1—[Ma-a'kah,] *to squeeze.*

MAACHAH was the son of Nahor, by his concubine Reumah. She was the mother of four children, of whom Maachah was the youngest, we judge, from Genesis, xxii: 24. It is thought he was the father of the Maachahthites, who inhabited a tract of land on the east of what was called the springs of Jordan. We have an account in Deut. iii: 14, of the conquests of Jair, the son of Manasseh, who took all the country of Argob unto the coasts of Geshuri and Maachathi. In Joshua, xii: 5, we learn further of the country of the Maachathites. But Maachah was probably the same country, and as it was not far from Padan-Aram, the country where Nahor, the father of Maachah, lived, and not far from the place where the rest of Nahor's posterity dwelt. The Hebrews when conquering the land seemed disposed to spare the Maachahthites, and we can see no special reason for it, except that they had a regard for them because of their origin and relationship.

We have an account afterwards of the Maachahthites helping the Ammonites against David. 2d Sam. x: 8–9. They took a position on the battle field, and fought with the Syrians, who were also helping Ammon against David, but Joab, the general of king David's army, conquered the Ammonites and their helpers, and subdued their country.

MAACHAH, 2—*To squeeze.*

MAACHAH, or MICAIAH, was the daughter of Absalom and Uriel. 2d Chron. xiii: 2. She was the wife of Rehoboam and the grand-mother of King Asa. She was the mother of Abijah, one of the kings of Judah, who succeeded his father, Rehoboam, to the throne. Maachah was an idolater, and probably debased herself very much in her worship of the obscene idols of the land. When King Asa executed the covenant that he had entered into with God, he stripped Maachah of what authority she had. He removed her from being queen for her idolatry, cut down her idol and stamped it and burnt it by the brook Kidron. 1st Kings, xv: 13. From 2d Chron. xi: 21, we learn that she was loved by Rehoboam above all his wives and concubines, numbering in all seventy-eight.

MAACHAH, 3—*To squeeze.*

There was a man of this name who is referred to in 1st Kings, ii: 39, as king of Gath, and father of Achish. Some of the servants of Shimei had fled from their master to him.

MAACHAH, 4—*To squeeze.*
Was the father of Shephatiah, who, in the time of David, ruled over the house of Simeon. 1st. Chron. xxvii: 16.

MAADAI—[Ma-ad′-a.]
MAADAI was one of the sons of Bani who had married a foreign wife. Ez. x: 34.

MAADIAH—[Ma-a-di′-ah.]
MAADIAH was one of the priests at the head of a family who returned from Babylon with Zerubbabel. Neh. xii: 5.

MAAI—[Ma-a′-i.]
MAAI was one of those who took part in the musical service when the walls of Jerusalem were dedicated by Nehemiah. xii: 36.

MAASEIAH, 1—[Ma-a-si′-ah,] *the work of the Lord.*
There were four persons of this name who returned with Ezra from Babylon, and had each married a strange wife. Ez. x: 18, 30.

MAASEIAH, 2—*The work of the Lord.*
Was the father of Azariah, one of the priests who helped Nehemiah to build Jerusalem. Neh. iii: 23.

MAASEIAH, 3—*The work of the Lord.*
Was one of those who stood on the right hand of Ezra when he read the law to the people. Neh. viii: 4.

MAASEIAH, 4—*The work of the Lord.*
Was a Levite who assisted Ezra in the same way. Neh. viii: 7.

MAASEIAH, 5—*The work of the Lord.*
Was one of the heads of the people whose descendants signed the covenant. Neh. x: 25.

MAASEIAH, 6—*The work of the Lord.*
Was the son of Baruch and descendant of Pharez, the son of Judah. Neh. xi: 5.

MAASEIAH, 7—*The work of the Lord.*
A Benjamite and the ancestor of Sallu. Neh. xi: 7.

MAASEIAH, 8—*The work of the Lord.*
There were two priests of this name who took part in the musical service of dedicating the wall. Neh. xii: 41, 42.

MAASEIAH, 9—*The work of the Lord.*
Was the father of Zephaniah, a priest in the reign of Zedekiah. There were some other persons of this name referred to in Jer. xxi: 1; Jer. xxix: 21; 2d Chron. xxiii: 1, xxvi: 11; xxxiv: 8; Jer. xxxv: 4; xxxii: 12; 1st Chron. ix: 12.

MAASEIAH, 10—*The work of the Lord.*
Was the son of Ahaz, a king of Judah. He was assassinated by Zichri, a mighty man of Ephraim. 2d Chron. xxviii: 7.

MAAZIAH—[Ma-a-zi′ah.]
Was one of the priests appointed by David, when he divided them into the twenty-four orders. His lot was the twenty-fourth. 1st Chronicles, xxiv: 18.

MACHI—[Ma′chi.]

Was the father of Geuel, who was one of the twelve men that were sent to examine the nature and condition of the land of Canaan. He was of the tribe of Gad. Num. xiii: 15.

MACHIR—[May′-kir,] *he that-sells or knows.*

MACHIR was the son of Manasseh and grand-son of Joseph. Gen. l: 23. Of his children, it is said they were brought up upon Joseph's knees, by which we may understand they were educated by Joseph or under his direction, and they looked upon him as the Patriarchal head of their father's family. He had three sons, and also a daughter who was married to Hezron, of the tribe of Judah. 1st Chron. vii: 16.

To the family of Machir Moses gave the land of Gilead, and they dwelt in it. Num. xxxii: 40.

In Numb. xxvi: 29, we learn that Machir was chief of the family of the Machirites.

MADAI—[Mad′-a-i.]

MADAI is reckoned as the third son of Japheth. Gen. x: 2. It is thought by some that he was the father of the Macedonians. In support of this it is said the ancient name of Macedonia was Madai; and again, it is asserted in the ancient history of that kingdom that there was a king of that name in early times. Others think he was the father of the Medes, as Media answers so well to the name Madai.

MAGOG—[Ma′-gog,] *roof, that dissolves.*

MAGOG, as we learn from Gen. x: 2, was the son of Japheth and brother of Madai and others.

MAHALATH, 1.—[Ma-hay′lath,] *melodious song, infirmity.*

MAHALATH was the wife of Esau, the daughter of Ishmael and sister of Nebajoth. Gen. xxviii: 9. "Then went Esau unto Ishmael, and took unto the wives which he had, Mahalath, the daughter of Ishmael, Abraham's son, the sister of Nebajoth, to be his wife." Thus Esau married a woman who sustained the same relation to Isaac his father, that Rachel, whom Jacob married, sustained to Rebekah the mother. Esau married his father's niece, and Jacob married his mother's niece. It is quite probable that Esau made this selection to please his father, actuated by a sincere desire to do what he gathered from the instructions Isaac had given him, would be a gratification to him.

MAHALATH, 2—*Melodious song, infirmity.*

MAHALATH was the daughter of Jeremoth the son of David, and a wife of Rehoboam. 2d Chron. xi: 18.

MAHALALEEL.—[Ma-ha-la-lee′-el] *he that praises God.*

MAHALALEEL is referred to in the genealogy of the ten antediluvian patriarchs, as they succeeded each other, from Seth, who was appointed to take the place in the family of Adam of the murdered Abel. Gen. iv: 26. He was the son of Cainan and the grandson of Enos. Mahalaleel was the father of Jared, the sixth from Adam, and was sixty-five years old when Jared was born, and as he lived, after the birth of this son, eight hundred and thirty years, at the time of his death he was eight hundred and ninety-five years old. Gen. v: 15, &c.

MAHARAI.—[Ma-ha′-rai.]

MAHARAI, the Netophathite, was the captain of the tenth month, when David instituted the monthly service of captains, over twenty-four thousand men. 1st Chron. xxvii: 13.

MAHAZIOTH.—[Ma-ha-zi′-oth.]

MAHAZIOTH was one of the sons of Heman, and when the lots were cast and the singers were divided into twenty-four courses, the three-and-twentieth lot came to him. 1st Chron. xxv: 30.

MAHER-SHALAL-HASHBAZ—[Ma′-her-shal′-al-hash′-baz,] *in making speed to the spoil he hasteneth, &c.*

MAHER-SHALAL-HASHBAZ was a child whose name is given in Isa. viii: 1, and an account of him in the verses following. The name is significant of a future event. Its meaning is Haste to the spoil—fall upon the prey. It was intended to set forth the destruction of Damascus and Samaria by the Assyrians. Maher-shalal-hashbaz was the son of a prophet, born unto him by the prophetess, and before he was three years old the prophecy was fulfilled which was set forth by his name.

MAHLAH—[Mah′-lah,] *melodious song, infirmity.*

MAHLAH was one of the daughters of Zelophehad, who obtained with her sisters an inheritance in the tribe of Manasseh by a special law added to the Jewish civil code. Numbers, xxvii: 7.

MAHLON—[Mah′-lon,] *song, infirmity.*

MAHLON was the elder son of Elimelech and Naomi. When his father and mother left the land of Judah and went to sojourn in the country of Moab, he and his brother Chilion went with them. It was not long until the father died, when Mahlon married Ruth a Moabitish damsel, while his brother married Orpah a Moabite woman also. Soon, however he died, leaving his wife a widow and childless. Ruth, i: ii: iii.

MAHOL—[Ma′-hol.]

MAHOL was the father of Ethan, the Ezrahite, and his three brothers, Heman, Chalcol and Darda. These four men were all famous for their wisdom, next to Solomon himself. 1st Kings, iv: 31.

MALACHI—[Mal′-aki.]

MALACHI was one of the lesser prophets, and the last in order as to time of prophesying and position in the book of prophecies. He wrote his predictions about four hundred years before the coming of Christ, and they close up the great and important prophetical age. John, the Baptist, whose appearance Malachi so clearly foretold, was the next prophet to him, and the age and ministry of John links the prophetical age to the Christian era.

It has been pretended that Malachi was the same as Zerubbabel, others say he was the same as Ezra, and still others say he was the same as Mordecai, the Jew, who was promoted to honorable position in the service of the Persian king, Ahasuerus, and still others say he was the same as Nehemiah; but we know as it regards these distinguished men, neither of them is ever called a prophet, or presented to our view as performing the particular work and office of a prophet. Again, it has been asserted that Malachi was of the tribe of Zebulun, and a native of the city of Sephoris, and that he died a young man.

He lived and prophesied about the time that Nehemiah was governor of Judea, or probably a few years after the death of Nehemiah. He prophesied after the building of the second temple, and contributed his influence, as a prophet of God, to the full restoration of the Jewish polity, and the reform begun and established by the good governor, Nehemiah.

His prophecies have been divided into two discourses, in the first of which he refers the Jews to the goodness of God, their benefactor. He shows them how irreverent and wicked they had been, and denounces the divine judgments against them. In the second discourse, he sets forth the coming of Christ, and of his messenger, John, the Baptist. He speaks of the work of John, and of Christ, viz: to purify the sons of Levi, the priests, and to visit the land with a curse unless they repented. (See book of Malachi.)

MALCHIAH, 1—[Mal-ki′-ah.]

MALCHIAH was the keeper of the prison in Jerusalem at the time Jeremiah was prophesying, and in Jer. xxxviii: 6, the miry dungeon into which the persecuted prophet was let down with cords, is called the dungeon of Malchiah, the son of Hammelech. By this we understand that he had the charge of the prisoners that were incarcerated there.

MALCHIAH, 2.

He was appointed by David to the office of the priest, with other Levites. 1st Chron. vi: 40.

MALCHIAH, 3.

He is referred to in Ezra x: 25, amongst those who had trespassed against God by marrying strange wives.

MALCHIJAH, 1—[Mal-ki′-jah.]

MALCHIJAH was one of those who was engaged by Nehemiah in rebuilding the walls of Jerusalem. In company with Hashub, he is represented as working on the wall, and also repairing "the tower of the furnaces." Neh. iii: 11. And still there is another Malchijah represented as the son of Rechab, who repaired the dung-gate, and was the ruler of the village or town of Beth-haccerem. Nehemiah iii: 14.

MALCHIJAH, 2.

He was one of the priests appointed by David, when he divided them into twenty-four courses. His lot was the fifth. 1st Chron. xxiv: 9.

MALCHI-SHUA—[Mal-ki-shu′ah,] *my king is a savior.*

MALCHI-SHUA was the third son of Saul, the first king of Israel. He was engaged with his father and with his brothers, Jonathan and Abinadab, in the battle at Gilboa, and with them he was slain by the Philistines. His body was rescued from the enemy with the bodies of the others of the king's household, by the inhabitants of Jabesh-Gilead, who brought them to Jabesh, and buried them in a grave under a tree. 1st Sam. xxxi.

MALCHIEL—[Mal-ki′-el.]

He was one of the two sons of Beriah, and the grand-son of Asher, and is numbered with the family of Jacob, who went down into Egypt. Gen. xlvi: 17.

MALCHUS.—[Mal′-kus,] *king or kingdom.*

MALCHUS was a servant of Caiphas the high priest. He is brought to our notice in John, xviii; 10. Though his name is not given by the other three Evangelists, yet the transaction recorded by St. John is given by them all. He was one of the company that went to the garden to take Jesus, when Judas had agreed to betray him into the hands of his enemies. Peter, who a little while before had declared to Jesus that his enemies should not take him, stood near his master when the mob approached, and, true to his purpose of defending him, he took out his sword and cut off the right ear of Malchus. It may be that this man was at the head of the mob, or in the front of the rabble crowd, and this may account for his being wounded by Peter. The bold, ardent, courageous apostle probaby aimed to kill him, with his sword to cleave his skull in twain; but Jesus turned it aside and only permitted Peter to cut of the ear, and probably would not have permitted that, but that he might be afforded an opportunity of attesting the truth of his divinity by a very convincing miracle, wrought in the presence and before the eyes of some of his worst enemies. Luke tells us that Jesus touched the ear of Malchus and healed him. Luke, xxii: 51. Why the other three Evangelists, Matthew, Mark and Luke, do not give the name of Malchus, whose ear was cut off, or of Peter who cut it off, we do not certainly know. It may be because they were both living at the time they wrote these gospels, and St. John, who wrote his later, may have given the names in relating the circumstance, because they were both dead. Whether Malchus ceased his opposition to Jesus after this miracle was performed, or continued to lead the crowd and join in the rabble shout while the innocent Redeemer was led to his mock trial, we know not.

MALLOTHI.

MALLOTHI was one of the sons of Heman, and when the lots were cast and the singers were divided into twenty-four courses, the nineteenth lot came to him. 1st Chron. xxv: 26.

MALLUCH, 1—[Mal′luk.]

Was a Levite of the family of Merari, and an ancestor of Ethan, the singer. 1st Chron. vi: 44.

MALLUCH, 2,

Was one of the sons of Bani. Ezra, x: 29.

MALLUCH, 3,

Was one of the descendants of Harim, who had married foreign wives. Ezra, x: 32.

MALLUCH, 4,

Was a priest or family of the people who signed the covenant with Nehemiah. Neh. x: 4.

MALLUCH, 5,

Another priest or head of the people, who signed the covenant with Nehemiah. Neh. x: 27. He may be the same person who is said to have returned with Zerubbabel. Neh. xii: 2.

**MAMRE**—[Mam′re,] *rebellious, bitter, that changes.*

MAMRE, in company with Aner and Eschol, his brothers, was friendly to Abraham, insomuch that he dwelt in the plain of Mamre. These three brothers were Amorites, and they seem to have held a conference with Abraham about the time of the conquest on the part of the confederate kings of the cities of the plain, and the conference resulted in their joining themselves unto him.

When the news was brought to Abraham that Lot, his nephew, was taken captive, he prepared at once to pursue the conquerors. He armed his trained servants, born in his own house, to the number of three hundred and eighteen. Then Aner, Mamre and Eschol, with the force they could command, joined themselves to Abraham, and they together followed the confederates, flushed as they were with victory. They overtook them by night and fell upon them, in all probability, unawares. This produced confusion and flight in the army, and they left their prisoners of war, among whom were Lot and his family, and the goods that had been taken, as well as a large amount of their own army stores and provisions, and they returned with their prisoners and spoils. Abraham would take nothing as his own that his army brought back or recovered, save what his young men had eaten; but he did not claim to prescribe as to the compensation that Mamre, Aner and Eschol should have. By right of conquest the recaptured booty belonged, in part, to them. They probably claimed it. They certainly had not the same reason for refusing it, or generously giving it all up, that Abraham had. Gen. xiv: 23. See whole chapter.

**MANAEN**—[Ma-na′-en,] *a comforter, he that conducts them.*

MANAEN was a prophet at Antioch, who in company with Simon called Niger, and Lucius of Cyrene, appointed Paul and Barnabas to preach in other places. The holy Ghost bade them set these two apostles apart to the work whereunto they were called. "And when they had fasted and prayed and laid their hands on them they sent them away." Acts, xiii: 1, 3.

**MANAHATH**—[Man′-a-hath.]

MANAHATH was the son of Shobal, and the grandson of Seir the Horite. Gen. xxxvi: 23.

**MANASSEH, 1**—[Ma-nas′-seh,] *forgetfulness, he that is forgotten.*

MANASSEH was the eldest son of Joseph, born unto him of Asenath in Egypt. We have an interesting account of the children of Joseph being brought to the dying Jacob to receive his blessing. Gen. xli: 50; Gen. xlviii: 8, 14. The reason given by Joseph for naming his elder son Manasseh was "for God hath made me forget all my toil and all my father's house." Manasseh and Ephraim are brought into the presence of the dying Jacob, and he asked his son Joseph, "Who are these?" Joseph told him they were his sons that God had given him. Jacob then bade him bring them near him and he would bless them. He did so, and the dying Patriarch kissed them, and embraced them. But the eyes of Jacob were dim and moreover the film of death was beginning to gather on his eye-balls, so that he seemed not to know the elder from the younger—so thought Joseph, as he placed Manasseh near his father's right hand, and Ephraim near his father's left hand. When Jacob crossed his arms and placed his right hand upon the head of Ephraim and his left hand upon the head of Manasseh, Joseph took hold of his father's right hand as it was placed upon the head of the younger, to put it upon the head of the elder—when he was checked by his father who told him, "I know it my son, I know it, Manasseh shall become a people and shall be great, but truly Ephraim shall be greater than he, and his seed shall become a multitude of nations."

What a beautiful picture is here presented to our minds. The venerable patriarch in a dying condition, and his much loved, and long lost Joseph with his two sons receiving the father and grandfather's blessing, and the trembling voice of the departing Patriarch is heard by them, saying, "The God which fed me all my lifelong unto this day, the angel which redeemed me from all evil, bless the lads."

In accordance with the prophecy of Jacob, the tribe of Manasseh was less numerous and honored than the tribe of Ephraim. Manasseh seems to have had but two sons, they were Ashriel and Machir. 1st Chron. vii: 15. The latter was the son of a concubine, she is called the Aramitess.

When the Israelites departed from the land of Egypt, the warriors or fighting men of Manasseh amounted to thirty-two thousand two hundred, and their chief or commander was Gamaliel, the son of Pedahzur. Num. i: 10, We learn from Num. ii: 20, that they had their position in the camp with Ephraim, and that they marched next to that tribe. Their spy who was to search the land of Canaan was Gaddi, the son of Susi, Num. xiii: 11, and their prince to divide the land after it was taken, was Hanniel, the son of Ephod. Num. xxxiv: 23. The tribe of Manasseh was divided and one half of them received their inheritance in one place and the other half in another — they are sometimes called eastern and western Manassites. Joshua advised those of them who received their inheritance west of the river Jordan to increase their territory and advantages by expelling those Canaanites who were near them; but they did not expel from at least five of the principal cities that they inhabited. Judges, i: 27. Bethshean, Taanach, Dor, Ibleam and Megiddo were still inhabited by Canaanites.

The tribe of Manasseh was noted in many respects. There were several persons of eminence among the Hebrews that sprung from it. Gideon and Abimelech, Jair and Jepthah who were judges of Israel were Manassites. Barzillai the Gileadite, and Elijah the prophet were of the tribe of Manasseh.

About eighteen thousand of the Western Manassites, called the half tribe of Manasseh, assisted in the coronation ceremonies. They did however as a tribe afterwards revolt from the family of David with the other nine tribes under Jeroboam, who became the king of Israel while Rehoboam ruled in Judah. But in after ages when Asa was King of Judah, many of the people of Manasseh who are called strangers, returned to the kingdom of Judah, and dwelt there. Abhoring the idolatry of the kingdom of Israel they turned to the kingdom of Judah that they might enjoy the pure worship of God. 2d Chronicles xiii: 19, xv: 9, &c.

We have an account in Isaiah, of a civil war that the Manassites were engaged in with Ephraim. In which the one did not spare the other, and yet they two together were against Judah.

Many of the Manassites went into captivity, and a part of them returned again from Babylon, and inhabited the land of Canaan and dwelt in Jerusalem the capital of Judah, in the days of its glory. 1st Chron. ix: 3.

MANASSEH, 2—*forgetfulness, he that is forgotten.*

Manasseh was a King of Judah, and the son and successor of King Hezekiah. He was the son of Hephzibah, Hezekiah's wife. Manasseh was very young when he ascended the throne of Judah, being but twelve years of age when he began to reign, and he reigned fifty-five years in the city of Jerusalem. 2d Kings xxi: 1.

He was a very wicked king, he dishonored the throne of Judah, by rebuilding the high places which his father had broken down and destroyed. Manasseh went into the grossest idolatry, for he established Baal's worship and planted groves in honor of his idols. He went so far in idolatry as to to worship the sun, moon and stars, and rear up altars in the court of the temple to these objects of his adoration. He even set up one of his idols in the temple, thus polluting it, and trampling upon the commands of God, as they were given to David and Solomon, regarding the sanctity of the temple. He caused his children to pass through the fire in the "valley of the sons of Hinnom." He had intercourse with devils and practised witchcraft and sorcery, and it is not to be wondered at that his subjects became impious and unholy. They were even more wicked than the Canaanites had ever been, who because of their wickedness and idolatry were driven out of their land. He not only practiced thus wickedly, but he compelled his subjects to follow his idolatrous ways, by murdering those who refused. He even made the streets of Jerusalem run down with innocent blood.

When the king of Assyria and Babylon, (Esarhaddon) invaded the kingdom of Judah and conquered it, he found Manasseh hid among the thorns and carried him a prisoner to Babylon, having bound him with fetters. While Mannasseh was a captive in Babylon, he repented of his sins, besought the Lord, his God in his afflictions and humbled himself greatly. He prayed earnestly to God for deliverance. The Lord heard his supplication, and in his mercy and providence restored him again to Jerusalem, his kingdom and his throne. Then he knew and acknowledged the Lord as God.

As soon as he was re-established on the throne he partially forsook idolatry. "And he took away the strange gods, and the idols out of the house of the Lord, and all the altars he had built in the court of the temple, and around the temple, on the sacred mount, and within the walls of Jerusalem, and cast them all out of the city. And he repaired the altar of the Lord and sacrificed thereon peace offerings;" and issued a royal order that Judah should worship the Lord God of Israel. Yet it seems he permitted the high places to continue, and the people sacrificed thereon. Mannasseh, after this, fortified Jerusalem, and added a new city on the west side. For a history of his life and acts, see 2d Kings, xxi, and 2d Chronicles, xxxiii. Then he died and was buried in royal pomp, in his own garden, and was succeeded in the kingdom, by Amon his son.

It should not be forgotten, that though Manasseh was so very wicked, yet when he repented, and implored forgiveness, God had mercy on him, and though he had filled Jerusalem with wailing and misery, by shedding innocent blood very much, and making Judah to sin in doing that which was evil in the sight of the Lord, yet he was returned to his kingdom, and God dealt out mercy to his soul. Yet temporal punishment of the Jewish nation was still visited upon them, for their sin in complying with Manasseh's injunctions, when trampling upon the divine authority, and it may be that the fate of Amon, his successor, whose servants conspired against him, and slew him in his own house, was in part punishment for the sin of Mannasseh, the father.

MANOAH.—[Ma-no′-ah,] *rest, a present.*

MANOAH was the father of Samson, that great prodigy of human strength. He was, as we learn from Jud. xiii: 2, of the tribe of Dan and of the city of Zorah, in the inheritance of that tribe. The wife of Manoah for a long time was childless. The angel of the Lord appeared unto her and told her that she should conceive and bear a son, and that that son should be a Nazarite from his birth. She was instructed by the angel to keep herself from that time from the slightest touch of wine or strong drink, and to be careful not to eat any unclean thing. She was also informed that her son should deliver Israel out of the hand and power of the Philistines. Filled with joy at the promise of a son, she went quickly to her husband Manoah and informed him of the revelation that had been made to her. He at once credited the revelation, and earnestly entreated the Lord that the man of God that had appeared to his wife should appear again, that he might hear his declarations and the instructions regarding the manner of raising the child.

The prayer of Manoah was answered, for the angel appeared again unto his wife as she sat in the field. Without waiting to hear any revelations to be made further, she ran and told Manoah, and in company with her he went out into the field to hold an interview with the angel. As he came near the visitant, he said, "Art thou the man that spakest unto the woman? and he said, I am." He then asked the angel to repeat in his hearing the instructions regarding his coming son, and the angel rehearsed them. Manoah, without hesitancy, believed the angel and asked him to remain awhile and partake of his hospitality. He manifested a willingness to be detained awhile, but refused to eat bread with him. As Manoah had proposed to kill a kid and dress it, the angel bade him kill the kid, but offer it as a burnt offering to the Lord, and he would tarry and take part in his devotions. Manoah was filled with wonder, and ventured to ask the angel, "What is thy name?" The angel, however did not tell him his name, but as he prepared his kid with a meat offering, and offered it upon a rock there in the field, and as the flame enveloped the sacrifice upon that rude altar, the angel did wondrously, thereby declaring his name "wonderful," for he ascended in the flame that consumed Manoah's sacrifice up to heaven. The good man then realized that the visitant was a divine personage, and immediately expressed his fears to his wife that they would both die because they had seen God. But his wife reasoned thus with him: "If the Lord were pleased to kill us, he would not have received a burnt offering and a meat offering at our hands, neither would he have shown us all these things, nor would, at this time, have told us such things as these."

Samson was born, and Manoah observed the divine injunctions regarding him; and he often thought of the interview he had with the angel as the child grew, and the Lord blessed him; and especially did he recur in his thoughts and feelings to that scene as the spirit of the Lord rested upon the young man and began to move him to deliver Israel.

At length Samson determined to marry the woman of Timnath, and told his father and his mother, and bade them get her for him as a wife. Manoah ventured an objection to Samson to marrying that woman, as she did not belong to the tribe of Dan, or indeed to the Israelitish stock, which would be a violation of law regarding marriage; but Samson insisted upon it that she should be his wife. He therefore said unto his father, "Get her for me, for she pleaseth me well." It seems to have been the divine will that Samson should marry this woman, but Manoah knew it not. Manoah and his wife went down with their son to Timnath to consummate the marriage that he had determined upon, so far as forming the espousals. After this was done they returned again to their home, and about a year after that, we suppose,—since one year was the time usually that elapsed between espousing and wedding—Manoah went down with Samson again, and the marriage contract was consummated. See Judges, xiii and xiv.

MAOCH—[Ma′-ok.]

He was the father of Achish, the king of Gath, with whom David found refuge when Saul sought after him. 1st Sam. xxvii: 2.

MAON—[Ma′-on,] *house, crime.*

Maon was the son of Shammai and the father of Bethzur, or of the inhabitants of Bethzur. We may suppose this son of Maon gave the place its name. 1st Chron. ii: 45. We have an account in 1st Sam. xxiii: 24–25, of a wilderness called Maon, in which David and his men were concealed when Saul was hunting his life. In or near this wilderness Nabal, the Carmelite, dwelt. 1st Sam. xxv: 2. It is possible that the wilderness takes its name from Maon.

There was also a tribe of Arabians called Maonites, referred to in Judges x: 12, who may have received their designation from this person, though he was of the family of Caleb.

MARK—*polite, shining.*

Mark, the Evangelist, was the son of one Mary, in whose house Peter found the Christians praying for his deliverance from prison, at the time he escaped under the guidance and with the assistance of an angel. Acts, xii.

He wrote the gospel which bears his name, and in it he begins with the preaching of John the Baptist. He relates several of the scenes and circumstances recorded in Matthew's gospel somewhat abridged; and to some of the parables, &c., he adds several particulars which further illustrate the subject. It will be seen, by comparing his gospel with that of Matthew, that he has added several important miracles, as, the cure of the demoniac, the cure of a deaf man at Decapolis, and a blind one at Bethsaida.

Mark was the cousin of Barnabas, and, as we learn in Acts, xii: 25, accompanied those apostles as they traveled together preaching the gospel. He went with them as far as Perga in lesser Asia, but when he found that they were intending to go to Pamphylia and other places, he deserted them and returned to Jerusalem. After some time Paul and Barnabas went to Jerusalem to attend a council of the apostles, at the close of which they were about starting out on another tour together, when Barnabas certified his intention of taking his cousin Mark with him. Paul was opposed to it, and openly objected, giving as a reason that Mark had once deserted them when laboring in that field before. Barnabas would not give up to Paul, but insisted that Mark should go with them. The contention was so sharp that they parted, Paul choosing another companion, and Barnabus taking Mark with him to Cyprus.

Mark was afterwards reconciled to Paul, and was with him at Rome, where he was very useful to him, as may be seen by the salutations to the Collossians. Col. iv : 10. He is also referred to in the salutations of the Epistle to Philemon, 24th verse. And from 2d Tim. iv : 11, we learn that the apostle Paul desired Mark to return from Asia, whither he had sent him, to Rome, where he might be with him, because he was profitable to him for the ministry.

Mark seems to have been with the apostle Peter at the time he wrote his first Epistle, for in the salutation from Chaldea, beside the church that was at Babylon, he says "Marcus my son saluteth you." 1st Peter, v : 13. It is thought that Mark afterwards preached in Egypt and Cyrene, and that he was put to death by a cruel mob.

MARTHA—[Mar′tha,] *who becomes bitter.*

MARTHA was the sister of Lazarus who was raised from the dead, and of the Mary of Bethany. Martha was in all probability the elder of the two sisters, and the mistress of the house, and she may have been as some suppose, a widow with whom Lazarus her brother, and Mary her sister lived.

When Jesus went to Bethany he enjoyed the hospitality of this family, and we have an account in the 10th chapter of the gospel of St. Luke, of one of these visits. Martha was exceedingly anxious to entertain her distinguished guest hospitably, and she made arrangements to this effect. But in the labor of providing a splendid repast, she desired the assistance of her sister Mary, and it seems did not get it, on account thereof she complained to the Savior that Mary had left her to serve alone. While she was performing the labor her sister was enjoying the company and teachings of Christ. Her address to the Savior is a complaint, "Carest thou not that my sister hath left me to serve alone? bid her therefore that she come and help me." Jesus in his answer commended Mary, and in a mild yet forcible manner reproved Martha: "Thou art careful and troubled about many things, but one thing is needful, and Mary hath chosen that good part which shall not be taken away from her." He probably intended to reprove her for so much care and anxiety and trouble in providing to entertain him with a great variety of the good things of this life, when he was constantly engaged in pressing the interests of the soul upon the attention of the children of men. And in this striking manner, he taught her that the salvation of the soul was more important than all things else. Though the Savior saw fit to reprove Martha, yet we can see some things in this account to admire in her. She loved the Savior, and was evidencing that love in providing for him. She puts many of the present day to the blush, in that she performed the labor of providing for guests—she worked with her own hands.

A short time before the ministry of Jesus closed—Lazarus the brother of Martha and Mary, was taken sick, his sisters felt that his case was a critical one, and they sent for Jesus saying, John, xi : 3. "Lord, behold, he whom thou lovest is sick." In the message they sent they urged him in all probability to come without delay to Bethany and cure him. Jesus did not go at once but remained where he was two days longer. In the meantime he had intimated to his disciples the course he had determined to take with regard to his friend. And when he started for Bethany he said, "Our friend Lazarus sleepeth, but I go that I may awake him out of sleep." He meant by this, Lazarus is dead, but that I am going to raise him from the dead. In accordance with this determination he went, and when he had reached the outskirts of the town, Martha who had heard that he was coming, went out to meet him, and poured out the bitterness of the sorrow of her soul in the touching sentence, "Lord, if thou hadst been here my brother had not died." Jesus knew full well the anguish of her aching heart, as he said, "Thy brother shall rise again." She knew that, and expressed her faith in the doctrine of the resurrection by saying, "I know that he shall rise again in the resurrection at the last day." Jesus said to her, "I am the resurrection and the life; he that believeth in me, though he were dead, yet shall he live. And he asked Martha the significant question, "believest thou this?" she replied that she believed he was the Christ, the son of the living God.

She then went and informed her sister that the master had come, and desired an interview with her. Afterwards, the Savior went with the two sisters to the grave of their brother. And when he ordered them to remove the stone, Martha ventured an objection. She thought the corpse would be offensive, as he had been dead four days already. But Jesus, as was his intention when he went to the grave with them, restored him to life, and to the society of the sisters. Lazarus came forth with his grave clothes about him, and in the presence of the company of sympathizing Jews, he embraced his sisters from whom he had been parted four days.

Six days before the Savior's crucifixion, he lodged again with his Bethany friends. John, xii: 1–8. And Lazarus, whom he had raised from the dead, was one of those that sat with him at the table, while Martha performed the same part she had been accustomed to when they had entertained him at their house before—"Martha served." She first engaged in preparing the repast, and then presided at the table, or served those distinguished guests with that which had been provided.

MARY, 1—[Ma′-ry,] *exalted*, *bitterness of the sea*, *mistress of the sea*.

MARY, THE VIRGIN, was of the family of Heli, who was descended from David, Judah and Abraham. Luke gives her genealogy in the third chapter of his gospel, calling Joseph, her husband, the son of Heli, because he was the son-in-law of Heli, having married his daughter Mary. Joseph, the husband of Mary, was the son of Jacob. Matthew, i: 16. She was espoused to Joseph, when selected to be the mother of the world's redeemer.

She had been the subject of prophecy, but did not know it until the angel of the Lord announced it unto her. When informed that the important prophecy should be fulfilled in her, "Behold a virgin shall conceive and bear a son, and shall call his name Immanuel." she was filled with joy. When she learned that from her should come the Messiah, in her faith and piety, and devotion to God, she exclaimed, "Behold the handmaid of the Lord, be it unto me according to thy word," and when a few days after, she was in company with her cousin Elisabeth, and received an expression marking her as this honored personage, she broke out in rapturous strains of praises to God, saying, "My soul doth magnify the Lord, and my spirit hath rejoiced in God, my Savior, &c."

In this sublime song, which is the first piece of poetry in the New Testament, there is an offering, on the part of Mary, to God, for what had been done for herself, for what he had done against his enemies, and for what he had done, and was about to do for his church. How different was the conduct of Mary, and her expressions, when advised by the angel of the birth of Christ, and the conduct of Zacharias, when informed of the birth of John. While Zacharias hesitated to believe the announcement, she believed it with all her soul.

It was during an edict of Cesar Augustus, taxing the subjects of his empire, and requiring each one to go to their own city to register their names, that Mary and Joseph were at Bethlehem, the city of David. And while they were there, the world was blessed with the promised Savior. The glorious event transpired that has dispelled the darkness of earth, and lit up the moral world—Jesus Christ was born.

During the stillness of that memorable night, which the christian world designates the twenty-fourth of December, the Son of Man was born in an humble place, the manger of a stable.

While the inhabitants of Heaven were looking on with intense anxiety, a command was given from the eternal throne, to a swift winged angel, to go to the fields of Bethlehem, and tell the shepherds the glorious news. Quick as thought, the angel sped to the spot and arrested the attention of the watchers, who at first were alarmed, but hearing the voice of the angel, saying, "Fear not, for behold we bring you glad tidings of great joy, which shall be to all people, for unto you is born this day, in the city of David, a Savior, which is Christ, the Lord," the fears of the shepherds were allayed. And they left the field and their flocks, and went to Bethlehem. There they found it as the angel had said.

As they looked upon the tender babe lying beside its mother in the manger, they were led to adore him as the Savior of mankind.

After eight days were accomplished, true to the requirements of the Jewish law, Mary named her child, and consecrated him to God. And at the end of forty days, she presented herself with her child at the temple, having brought the sacrifice to offer, that the Jewish women presented at the end of the days of their purification. And it is worthy of remark, that the mother of Jesus Christ was poor, and her sacrifice on this occasion indicates it. "She offered a pair of turtle doves, or two young pigeons, in the stead of a lamb. Thus we behold her taking the benefit of a law under the Levitical economy enacted especially for the poor. The law referred to is recorded in Lev. xii: 8. "And if she be not able to bring a lamb, then she shall bring two turtles, or two young pigeons, the one for a burnt-offering, and the other for a sin-offering." Well may it be said of Christ, "He who was rich, for our sakes became poor."

But whilst Mary entered the temple with the child Jesus, the attention of an aged and devout man, one very remarkable for his piety, was arrested by her approach. This aged man had long been waiting for the "consolation of Israel," and in his services in the temple, had often spoken rapturously of the coming Redeemer. He saw her as she approached, bearing her tender infant in her arms, and as he looked his nature was strangely touched; his vision dimmed with age, was suddenly cleared. The hand of the Lord was upon him, and the divine spirit was within him, and favoring him with a revelation regarding the child fraught with infinite interest. He saw in the pious woman before him, one greatly honored of God, and in the lovely babe, he beheld the Lord's anointed. And taking the child in his arms, his nature's flickering fire flashed high, as under the spirit's inspiration he gave his testimony to Christ's Messiahship: "Lord now lettest thou thy servant depart in peace, for mine eyes have seen thy salvation." Simeon thus resigned himself to a dismissal from earthly labor and enjoyment, at the will of God, having lived long enough to see the long expected Messiah, and hence have the grand aim and desire of his life accomplished.

In addition to the testimony of Simeon to Christ's Messiahship, Mary was cheered by the testimony of an aged holy widow, who entered the temple while Simeon was exulting. For Anna "spake of him to all them that looked for redemption in Jerusalem."

Because of the spirit of persecution in Herod the King of the Jews, Mary was instructed by an angel to flee with her child into Egypt, and she did, remaining there until the death of the wicked tyrant. After this the angel of the Lord directed her to the land of Israel, and in company with Joseph her husband, and the child Jesus, she went to Nazareth, which after that became her place of residence.

Mary faithfully performed the part of a mother for her son, and Jesus in turn entertained the kindest regards, and the most tender and endearing affection for her.

She took him with her to the temple to worship God in the celebration of the annual feasts, after he was twelve years of age. She looked upon him with joy, "as he grew and waxed strong in spirit; was filled with wisdom and the grace of God."

The evangelist gives us an interesting account of the attendance of the son of Mary at the annual feast. His parents returned toward home a day's journey, before they found he was not with them. As the men and women traveled in companies by themselves, and sometimes the children were with the men, and sometimes they were with the women, Mary supposed he was in the company of the men, but night came and Jesus was not with them. She returned to the temple in search of him, and she found him there sitting among the teachers of religion, asking them questions and requesting answers to his enquiries. The anxieties of Mary for him in the search were all gone, for the lost one was found. Approaching the child Jesus, she said with fond affection, "thy father and I have sought thee sorrowing." Mary received his answer, "Wist ye not that I must be about my father's business," and laid it up in her heart as she had laid up other sayings.

Mary was probably present at the baptism of Christ by John in Jordan, and so saw him as he entered upon his work of teaching. She engaged, it may be, in the devotions of that sacred hour, when to "fulfill all righteousness," Jesus was baptized, and she was one of those that looked wonderingly and adoringly at the Holy Ghost in the bodily shape of a dove, sitting upon his head. It may be she was of those who heard the voice that come down from heaven—"This is my beloved son in whom I am well pleased."

She was present at the marriage in Cana, of Galilee, where he performed the first miracle attesting the glory of his character, and she performed an interesting part on that occasion. She approached him when the necessity existed for more wine in the feast, and said to him, "My son, the wine is out," and though his answer seemed to be somewhat indirect and strange, yet she said to them, "whatsoever he saith unto you, do it." She seemed to understand that he was about to work a miracle.

Mary was in the synagogue at Nazareth on the memorable Sabbath that Jesus entered it, and unrolled the manuscript to read from the prophet Isaiah, and comment upon a noted prophecy of himself describing the character and effect of his works. "The spirit of the Lord God is upon me, because he hath anointed me to preach the gospel to the poor; he hath sent me to heal the broken-hearted, to preach deliverance to the captives; and recovering of sight to the blind, to set at liberty them that are bruised, to preach the acceptable year of the Lord."

She often listened with admiration and devoutness to the teachings of Jesus, and it may be, witnessed his miracles. She was present at Jerusalem at the last Feast of the Passover Jesus celebrated before his passion. She saw all that was transacted there in all probability, and she stood near Christ's cross while he was suffering the agonies of crucifixion. Ah, and she realized the truth of the aged Simeon's declaration, "Yea, a sword shall pierce through thine own soul also." Who can suppose, even, the anguish of Mary's heart, when she stood beside her suffering son, expiring on the Roman cross. Jesus, amid the pains of death, looked down and saw his widowed and weeping mother, and moved with feelings of true affection, he said, "woman, behold thy son." Turning his eyes from Mary, his mother, he fixed them upon John, the beloved disciple, who a few hours before, had leaned on his breast at the Eucharistic feast, deeply moved in sympathy and sorrow, he said: "Behold thy mother." By this expression, he gave his mother in charge of John, and "from that hour, that disciple took her unto his own house."

MARY, 2—*Exalted, bitterness of the sea, mistress of the sea.*

MARY, the wife of Cleopas, was a disciple of Christ, and was the mother of James the less, of Joses, Simon, and of Judas. She is also supposed to have been the sister of the Virgin Mary; hence her children are represented as the kinsmen of our Lord. They were his kindred according to the flesh. That she was the sister of the Virgin Mary is evident from John, xix: 25: "Now, there stood by the cross of Jesus, his mother and his mother's sister, Mary, the wife of Cleopas," &c. And the fact that she was the mother of James, Joses, &c., is evident from Matthew's presentation of the crucifixion scene. He says, Matt. xxvii: 56: "And many women were there, among which were Mary Magdelene, and Mary the mother of James and Joses."

This Mary was an early believer in Christ, and attended him in many of his journeys; and with others she ministered unto him; and she shared, in common with other disciples that attended him, his trials. She was present at the last passover, when the holy supper was instituted; and she mingled in the sorrowing company that followed Jesus to calvary. She stood beside the anguish-stricken mother (her sister) during the tragic passion of her son. When Joseph, of Arimethea, took the lifeless form from the cross to inter it in his own tomb, she was present and assisted in preparing the body for burial. She engaged, with mournful pleasure, with the little company that attended Joseph to the garden, and wept at his burial.

Having performed the office of burial, in company with other women she returned to the city, and prepared spices and ointments for embalming the body after the Sabbath. Luke, xxiii: 56: "And they returned and prepared spices and ointments, and rested the Sabbath day," &c. Very early on the morning of the first day of the week she went, with others, to the sepulcher to perform this work. Having arrived, to the astonishment of all the company they found the sepulcher empty and the body gone. Two angels appeared in shining raiment and declared that Christ was risen. In company with all the women that attended her, except Mary Magdalene, she went back to the city to tell the disciples the language of the angels.

Mary, the wife of Cleopas, appears thus as a disciple of the despised Nazarene. One of the last at the cross, and one of the first at the sepulcher, and one of the first to declare his resurrection.

MARY, 3—[Ma'ry,] *exalted, bitterness of the sea, mistress of the sea.*

MARY, the sister of Lazarus, lived with her sister Martha and their brother at Bethany, a small town not far from Jerusalem. When the Savior visited this town he was entertained at their house Luke, x: 38–42. "Martha received him into her house;" but while Martha cordially received him, and made preparations to entertain him hospitably, Mary took her position as a disciple of Jesus, an enquiring scholar. She listened attentively to his instructions, and thought it an honor to sit at his feet. Martha complained to the Savior that Mary had left her to provide the repast alone, and she said, "Bid her, therefore, that she come and help me." The Savior reproved her for her dissatisfaction, and commended Mary for her course. As often as Jesus visited this family he found Mary constant and devoted to him, as well as to her own spiritual interest.

As acquaintance increased, the affection of Jesus for these two sisters increased, until, when Lazarus died, and the sisters poured out the feeling of their sorrowing and bereaved hearts into his ear, it so deeply affected him that he wept with them. See him as he approaches the little town, knowing as he did that Lazarus was dead—Martha and Mary meet him and express the sorrow of their hearts by saying, "Lord, if thou hadst been here my brother had not died." He sympathizes with them in their anguish, and intimates his determination to bring their brother back to earth. He attends them to the sepulcher and mingles true tears with theirs; but he calls their brother back to earth and restores him to their arms and hearts.

A few days before the Passover, after Jesus raised Lazarus from the dead, he came to Bethany, and being invited to sup with Simon, he accepted the invitation, and Mary, her sister, and Lazarus, who had been raised from the dead, were invited guests. It was whilst this company were together that Mary took a pound of costly ointment of very pleasant perfume, and poured it upon the head of the Savior, and the whole house was filled with the odor of the perfume. There was one present who objected to this anointing, and possibly there were others besides that one; but Jesus commended her for it. "She hath wrought a good work on me; she is come aforehand to annoint my body to the burying." Thus Mary is presented as having done the very work that the illustrious women spoken of went to the sepulcher on the morning of the resurrection to do.

MARY, 4.—*Exalted, bitterness of the sea, mistress of the sea.*

MARY, THE MOTHER OF MARK. She was a disciple of Christ, won by the apostles, who lived at Jerusalem, and by many it is supposed that her house was the place where the persecuted followers of Christ met, and where they prayed and encouraged one another with words of exhortation, even after their master was taken from them and put to death. Her house furnished the room where Christ showed himself to his disciples after his resurrection in all probability, and where they assembled after the ascension and received the Holy Ghost, qualifying them for their high and holy work.

During the severe persecutions of christians by Herod, when James, the brother of John, was killed by the sword, her house was probably the place where the faithful disciples assembled and prayed.

Peter was cast into prison during this persecution, and was guarded by sixteen soldiers, four of them serving on each watch. But while Peter was there bound and guarded, "prayer was made without ceasing of the church unto God for him." And on the night before he was to be brought forth by Herod from the prison, he was delivered by an angel of the Lord. The angel awoke him from his prison sleep and bade him bind on his sandals and follow him out; and he did. He followed the angel through the different apartments to the outer gate, which opened of its own accord. Soon, with the angel, he was threading his way along the streets of the city toward the house of Mary. Before they reached her house, the angel left Peter, and being satisfied that he was at liberty—was really delivered out of the hand of his enemies—he went to the house of this good woman and found many gathered together praying. He went into their midst and declared how the Lord had delivered him out of the hand of his enemies.

Mary, the mother of Mark, was then a disciple of Christ in the apostolic age, and furnished them with a place of worship in perilous times.

MARY, 5—*Exalted, bitterness of the sea, mistress of the sea.*

MARY was probably called Magdalene as a disciple of Christ to distinguish her from the other Marys, Magdala in Galilee being the place of her residence, and it may be her birth place. She was a devoted disciple of Christ, and probably a woman of very great respectability previous to her following Christ. If she had not been a woman of respectability, it is not at all likely that she would have been allowed to follow Christ and his apostles, as she did from city to city. She appears beautiful to us, as her character is developed as a disciple. Constant and kind in her ministrations to the Savior in life, she was true to him at his crucifixion, and to the body when in the grave. The circumstance of her remaining at the sepulcher when the other woman returned to the city would seem to indicate that her love for the Savior excelled the love of the other women. It may be possible that the Savior had done more for her than for either of the others, yet we can by no means conceive that she was prostitute and vicious, as some think, before she became Christ's disciple.

She was one of the women who followed Jesus in his last journey to Jerusalem, and was near the cross beside the Virgin Mary when he was crucified. After the crucifixion and the body was interred, she went with other women to Jerusalem to buy and prepare the necessary articles for embalming the body after the Sabbath. Early on the morning of the first day of the week in company with Mary, the mother of James, and with Salome and other women, she started for the sepulcher. They had not proceeded far, when a difficulty presented itself to the minds of some of the women. And one of them said, "we are going to embalm the body, but who shall roll us away the stone from the door of the sepulcher." As they were so near, notwithstanding the difficulty, they proceeded, and coming to the garden, and approaching the tomb, to their astonishment they saw "that the stone was rolled away," and as they examined still further, they saw "that the body was gone." Soon two angels appeared, and they were affrighted but their fears were allayed as the angels said to them: "He is not here but is risen;" and further they charged the women to go and tell Peter and the other apostles, that Jesus was risen, and that he would appear unto them in Galilee. The women ran to tell the news. It may be Mary Magdalene herself went, but if she did, she soon returned to the sepulcher; and there all alone she stood weeping. She mourned the absence of the body of her Lord. The thought that pressed itself upon her mind as she stood weeping, she could not endure, (that she would see that lovely form no more,) and the anguish of her heart was told in sighs and crying and tears.

She was not unobserved in her sorrow, for, as she stooped down and looked into the sepulcher, she saw two angels—probably the same angels that had been seen before, but they had changed their position. Now they were sitting "the one at the head and the other at the feet where the body of Jesus had lain." John, xx: 12. They saw the anguish of her heart, and, addressing her, said: "Woman, why weepest thou?" She answered that she was weeping because of the absence of the body of her Lord. Just then another voice fell upon her ear, saying: "Woman, why weepest thou? Whom seekest thou?" She, supposing the one now addressing her to be the gardener, saith unto him: "Sir, if thou hast borne him hence, tell me where thou hast laid him, and I will take him away." Scarcely had this sentence died upon her lips until a well known voice fell upon her ear, and that voice proceeded from the person who was speaking to her in the question above. He said to her: "Mary." She stopped not a moment to reflect, for he who now called her name had done it frequently before, and she recognized the voice as the voice of her Lord. Turning herself, she said unto him: "'Rabboni,' which is to say Master." Overpowered with joy she fell at his feet and embraced him. He said unto her: "Touch me not, for I am not yet ascended to my Father; but go to my brethren and say unto them, I ascend unto my Father and your Father; to my God and your God." After this, Mary Magdalene went to the disciples and told them that she had seen the Lord, and that he had spoken these things unto her.

Thus she appears as the first witness of the truth of the crowning doctrine of Christianity—the resurrection of Jesus Christ from the dead. Thus, while the Virgin Mary was honored in being the mother of the world's Redeemer, and in beholding him first when he entered this sindefiled world, Mary Magdalene's love was rewarded as she looked with adoring rapture, first of all the disciples, upon the risen and glorified form of him who conquered death and cleared the way for man to the joys of immortality.

## MASH.

Mash was probably the same as Meshech, the fourth son of Aram, and the grandson of Shem. Gen. x: 23. In 1st Chron. i: 17, he is called Meshech. He was probably the father of Morcheni, or as they are called, Masians, who are said to have resided in the south part of Armenia. There is a mountain near there called Mt. Masius, and now called Mazeka, to which probably the descendants of Mash or Meshech, gave these names.

## MASSA—[Mas′-sah,] *temptation.*

Massa was the son of Ishmael, and the grandson of Abraham. Gen. xxv: 14.

## MATRI—[Ma′-tri,] *rain, prison.*

We have no special account of this personage except where Saul, the son of Kish was selected and proclaimed king of Israel. Samuel caused the tribes of Israel to pass before him and the tribe of Benjamin was taken He then caused the tribe of Benjamin to pass before him, and the family of Matri was taken. He then caused the family of Matri to pass before him, and Saul the son of Kish of that family was taken. He is thus presented as one of Saul's progenitors. 1st Sam. x.

## MATTAN—*The reins, the death of them.*

Mattan was a priest of Baal that was slain before the altar of his false God, during the reformation from idolatry under Jehoiada the priest, at the time he crowned Jehoash in the place of the wicked Athaliah. 2d Kings, xi: 18; 2d Chron. xxiii: 17.

## MATTANIAH—[Mat-ta-ni′ah.]

Mattaniah was one of the officers among the singers and players on musical instruments. 1st Chron. xxv: 21. David formed the several orders of priests, dividing by lot into twenty-four courses.

Mattaniah was the second son of Heman, one of fourteen sons whose names are given in 1st Chron. xxv: 4, and he had three sisters. These officers were blessed with the spirit of prophecy. "All these were the sons of Heman the king's seer, in the words of God to lift up the horn," *i. e.*, the horn of prophecy, to sound with the trumpet in the words of prophecy before the Lord. The ninth lot was appointed to Mattaniah.

MATTHAN.

MATTHAN was the son of Eleazar, who is referred to in the genealogy of Christ, as given by Matt. i: 15–16. There we learn that Matthan was the father of Joseph the husband of Mary, the mother of Christ.

MATTHEW—[Mat′thew,] *given a reward.*

MATTHEW is sometimes called Levi, the son of Alpheus. He was born in Galilee—was a devout Jew in his religion—but was a tax gatherer. His residence, it seems, was at Capernaum, the place that Jesus adopted as a place of residence when he left Nazareth, and called it his "own city." His office as a publican, was near the sea of Galilee, and it was while Jesus was by the sea side that he saw Matthew sitting at the receipt of customs, and bade him follow him. Matthew, ix: 9; Mark, ii: 14; Luke, v: 27. He seems to have had but little hesitancy, for without stopping to arrange his affairs or settle up his business, he followed the Savior and identified himself at once with Christ's followers.

It was not long after Matthew was called to be a disciple, that he gave an entertainment at his house to Jesus, and invited other publicans with himself to be present, and enjoy the company of this distinguished personage. It would seem from Mark, ii: 15, that the company was quite large. "Many publicans and sinners sat with Jesus and his disciples," and as Matthew had been before them, they became prejudiced in his favor and followed him.

This occasioned a complaint among the Pharisees against Jesus and his course. They said to his disciples, "How is it that he eateth with publicans and sinners?" Jesus heard their censure, and justified his conduct before them by saying, "They that be whole need not a physician, but they that are sick." It was the sin-sick that needed a Divine Physician, and he was come into the world not to call the righteous, but sinners to repentance.

We have an account in Matthew, x: 3; Mark, iii: 18: Luke, vi: 15, of his being numbered with the apostles.

Matthew was one of the evangelists who wrote a history of Christ, which is the gospel bearing his name; and it was probably the first of the gospels written, and, for that reason mainly, was placed first in order. His gospel begins by showing the royal descent and genealogy of Jesus Christ. He gives us an account of the birth, life, and labors of Christ. Many of his conversations and discourses are recorded, and the miracles he performed attesting his divinity, and the glory of his character. The sermon of our Lord upon the mount is beautiful, and inimitable; also the life and various conversations of Christ as given by this evangelist. He seems to enter into the particulars more than either of the others, and gives, more abundantly, rules for the conduct of life, with lessons of pure morality. It may be said of Matthew, he has all the characteristics of a good historian—sufficiently plain, and yet dignified.

After Matthew was called to the work and office of an apostle, he seems to have been a constant witness of Christ's works, and a hearer of his words. He attended on his Master's person, when before the public, as also when in private. He saw very many of the miracles that were performed, and was, with his brethren, the apostles, a witness of Christ's resurrection; and he was also at the Mount of Olives when Jesus ascended. After the ascension he remained in Jerusalem, and was with them, in the upper room, on the day of Pentecost, when they received the Holy Ghost to qualify them for their high and holy work.

It is not known how long he remained in Judea after the descent of the Holy Ghost on the day of Pentecost, nor how long he lived and labored, nor when and where he died. His labors were confined mostly to Judea, probably, and he wrote his gospel there for the Jewish nation, the object evidently being to confirm those who had believed in Christ, and to convert to the Christian faith those who were unconverted. From his gospel we gather that he wished the Jews to compare the circumstances, as he had narrated them, of the birth, life, labors, death and resurrection of Jesus, with their ancient prophecies relative to the Messiah. He wrote early in the apostolic age—perhaps in the year of our Lord, 38.

Matthew probably preached the gospel in other countries, as did the other apostles, and, like them all, except John, died a martyr.

MATTHIAS—[Mat-thi′-as,] *the gift of the Lord.*

MATTHIAS was a disciple of Jesus Christ; it is probable one of his earliest disciples. From Acts i: 21, 22, we may judge that Matthias was one of the disciples of John, the Baptist, and was present at the baptism of Christ by John in Jordan. He may have been one of those who saw the Holy Spirit descending, and in the form of a dove lighting upon the head of Jesus, and he may have heard the voice of the Father saying: "This is my beloved Son in whom I am well pleased." He heard the testimony of John concerning Christ, and became a firm believer in Christ and his Messiahship; and according to the account given above we judge that the course of Matthias was marked with fidelity to Jesus through his whole mission. It is declared of him that he companied with the disciples all the time that the Lord Jesus went in and out among them, beginning from John's baptism until Christ ascended up into heaven.

It is thought that Matthias was one of the seventy commissioned by our Lord to preach and teach.

Judas, one of the twelve apostles, had fallen, having wickedly betrayed his Lord for thirty pieces of silver, and his bishopric was thereby vacated. Peter proposed to fill the vacancy; and the apostles all agreed that one who had been a constant witness of Christ's miracles, who had heard his teachings and had seen his sufferings, should be the successor of the fallen Judas. They therefore selected from among the disciples two, viz: Barnabas and Matthias, one of whom they would choose. But the apostles, it may be, were divided in their opinion, some of them being in favor of the one, and some in favor of the other. They all wished to do right, but differed in opinion as to which of them was the proper person. They were both good men, eminently qualified for the position, as they had both been with Christ all through his ministry. But the apostles feared to make the selection, lest they might err. They accordingly resorted to a long established custom among the people of God, that of casting lots. This was a custom with ancient Israel. When a doubtful matter was to be settled, and the counsel of those concerned was insufficient to settle it, they asked of God divine guidance. The ancient priests consulted the Urim and Thummim, or Breastplate of Judgment. Moses was directed to settle the vexed question as to the priesthood in the family of Aaron, and it was determined by the rod of Aaron budding and blooming, and bearing almonds in a night. Joshua was directed by the Divine Being how to determine the transgressor in the accursed thing before the victory could be had at Ai. Jonah, when awaked from his sleep in the sides of the ship, storm-driven on the voyage to Tarshish, agreed to cast lots to determine who as a transgressor was the cause of the storm, and when the lot fell upon Jonah, he confessed his sin, and they cast him overboard. The wise man had reference to this custom, and makes a statement of it in the following language, Prov. xvi: 33: "The lot is cast into the lap, but the whole disposing thereof is of the Lord."

When the apostles were all ready to fill the vacancy, they prayed thus: "Thou Lord, which knowest the hearts of all men, show whether of these two thou hast chosen, that he may take part of this ministry and apostleship, from which Judas by transgression fell, that he might go to his own place." They then cast lots, and the lot fell upon Matthias, and he was numbered with the eleven. Acts i: 15-26. After he had thus entered the apostleship, he began preaching as an apostle. Where he labored, and how long is not certain. The Greeks believe he preached at Colchis, and died there. And it is quite likely that his death, like others of the apostles, was the death of a martyr, though we have no certain account of it.

MATTITHIAH—[Mat-tith-i′-ah.]

MATTITHIAH was one of the Levites who were engaged in the solemn service of removing the ark to Jerusalem, and placing it in the tent which David had prepared for it. 1st Chron. xv: 21. He was probably the same person who, when the lots were cast, and the singers were divided into twenty-four courses, the fourteenth lot came to him. 1st Chronicles, xxv: 21.

MEBUNNAI—[Me-bun′-na.]

MEBUNNAI, the Hushtathite, was one of David's mighty men. 2d Samuel, xxiii: 27.

MEDAD—[Me′-dad,] *he that measures, the water of love.*

MEDAD, and Eldad, are referred to in Numbers, xi: 26. When Moses gathered together the seventy elders to meet God at the tabernacle. These two, and they were of the seventy, for some cause did not go. It is likely they were lawfully hindered, and as they continued in the camp, they were engaged in prophesying there. And a young man went and told Moses. Joshua was standing near enough to hear the intelligence, and addressing himself to Moses, he said, "My Lord, Moses, forbid them." But Moses, instead of forbidding them, reproved Joshua by saying, "Enviest thou for my sake? Would to God that all the Lord's people were prophets, and that the Lord would put his spirit upon them." As they were probably prevented from going with the other elders to the tabernacle, they preformed the functions of their office in the camp.

MEDAN—[Me′dan,] *judgment, process, measure, covering.*

MEDAN was the third son of Abraham by his wife, Keturah. Though the account of the patriarch's marriage to this woman, and of the children he had by her, is not given until after the death of Sarah is recorded, yet it may be possible that Moses has given us the account out of its chronological order. Facts are sometimes thus related in the sacred writings. He was one of the six sons of Keturah, whose names are given in Gen. xxv: 2. Where the descendants of Medan settled is not certainly known; but it is thought they dwelt in that part of Arabia Petrea contiguous to the land of Moab, eastward of the Dead Sea, for the people of this country are called Madianeans or Madianites.

MEHETABEL—[Me-het′a-bel,] *how good is God.*

Was the wife of Hadar, a king of Edom, who succeeded Baal-hanan. She was the daughter of Matred and the grand-daughter of Mezahab. Gen. xxxvi: 39.

MEHUJAEL.—[Ma-hu-jay′-el,] *who proclaims God, God that blots out.*

Mehujael was the son of Irad and the father of Methusael, and he is referred to among the descendants of Cain. Gen. iv: 18.

MEHUMAN—[Me-hu′-man.]

MEHUMAN was one of the seven chamberlains that served in the presence of Ahasuerus, who were commanded to bring Vashti the queen before him, that he might show her beauty to the people, but she refused to come and was deposed.

MELCHISHUA—[Mel-ki-shu′-a.]

MELCHISHUA was one of the sons of Saul who was engaged with him in war with the Philistines, and his death is recorded in 1st Sam. xxxi: 2.

MELATIAH—[Mel′-a-ti-ah,] *affording honey.*

MELATIAH was a Gibeonite who assisted in rebuilding the walls of Jerusalem. Neh. iii: 7.

MELCHI, 1—[Mel′-ki,] *my king, my counsel.*

Was son of Janna, and ancestor of Joseph in the genealogy of Jesus Christ. Luke, iii: 24.

MELCHI, 2—*My king, my counsel.*

Was the son of Addi, and his name occurs in the same genealogy. Luke, iii: 28.

MELCHIAH—[Mel-ki′-ah.]

Was a priest, and the father of Pashur. Jer. xxi: 1.

MELCHIEL—[Mel-ki′-el.]

Was the father of Channis, who was one of the three governors of Bethulia.

MELCHIZEDEK— [Mel-kiz′-ze-dek] *king of righteousness.*

There has been much conjecture as to who this person was. Disputes have arisen, and much discussion has been elicited regarding him. Some have thought he was a divine person and not a man. Some believe him to have been Christ, or the Son of God, the second person in the Trinity, and others he was the Holy Ghost, the Divine Spirit. But when we come to consider the representation given of him by Moses in the Old Testament, and by Paul in the New Testament, we are forced to the conclusion that he was a mere man.

Melchizedek was the king of Salem, Gen. xiv: 18, and priest of the most high God, Heb. vii: 1. The account given of him in Gen. xiv is as follows: When Abram was returning from the pursuit of the confederate kings, and the conquest of them, with the recovery of his nephew Lot and his family, with the spoils he had taken in war, Melchizedek met him with a blessing on his lips, for he blessed Abram in the name of the most high God, and he brought forth to him bread and wine. The object he had in view evidently was to refresh the conquerer, with his weary and exhausted men. They had made a rapid march after Chedorlaomer and his allies, had engaged them in battle and had conquered them at Hobah, and now had returned with the prisoners and spoils. He knew they were wearied and fatigued, and hence had prepared them this repast, and now offered it to them. Abram acknowledged the favor, and heard the praises that Melchizedek gave to the most high God, and he gave the good king of Salem tithes of all, intending those tithes as a tribute to his God, whose priest Melchizedek was.

Upon the circumstance thus narrated we have the representation given of Melchizedek by the apostle Paul, Heb. vii. From the characteristics given by the apostle, we learn that he was a great and good man, being "King of Righteousness, and after that also King of Salem, which is King of Peace—without father, without mother, without descent, having neither beginning of days nor end of life, but made like unto the Son of God abideth a priest continually." That is, he was not reckoned in Jewish genealogies as a priest, not descended from the Jewish Sacerdotal tribe, or the stock that God had appointed for the office of priest in the family of patriarchs, or from the tribe that was afterwards consecrated, that of Levi, to officiate in the sacred office. Melchizedek was probably of the seed of Canaan, a descendant of Ham, which seed was under the malediction of heaven, accursed of God, and therefore without the honor of genealogy. It is possible that the father and mother of Melchizedek were unknown, which accounts for the phraseology, "without father, without mother," &c. His parentage, the time and place of his birth, not being recorded, were not known. As a mortal man, he had assuredly beginning of days and end of life. He was born, lived and died; but his birth and death are not recorded. Melchizedek was a great man, the most important character in all that country, a sort of universal priest, having none superior to him. He was confessedly superior to Abraham himself. "Now consider how great this man was, unto whom even the patriarch Abraham gave the tenth of the spoils." And the apostle tells us, "without all contradiction, the less is blessed of the better," and he tells us further, that even "Levi, who was appointed to receive tithes, paid tithes in Abraham, for he was yet in the loins of his father when Melchizedek met him."

Melchizedek is made a type of Christ, and his priesthood typical of the priesthood of Christ. Ps. cx: 4; "Thou art a priest forever, after the order of Melchizedek." The priesthood of Christ is to abide. There is something typical in the person, name, office, and residence. His person we have referred to already as being typical of Christ. Melchizedek was not of the line of Priests; so Christ was not of the tribe of Levi, but of Judah.

The name Melchizedek signifies the righteous king, or king of righteousness, and this is one of the titles of our blessed Lord. He is the ruler of a kingdom established in righteousness, and carried on under the principle of righteousness. He is a king of righteousness,—essential righteousness belongs to him and to no other king; hence, Melchizedek could only bear the name as a type or representative of Christ. But as to his office, he was a priest of the Most High God, and a prince as well as a priest. He sustained the double office of king and priest, and in this typified the Lord Jesus Christ. And his residence, and the centre of his kingdom and authority as a teacher as well as a ruler, was Salem, which signifies peace. So Christ is called the "Prince of Peace." He came to earth on the glorious embassy of establishing peace between God and his revolted creatures—man. His gospel on earth is, peace and good will to man. Through him alone are we reconciled as offenders, to God the offended.

## MELZAR.

MELZAR was the first steward of Babylon, and placed in charge of the captives Daniel, Hananiah, Mishael, and Azariah. These four young men desired not to eat of the portion that had been appointed them by the king, and they proposed to Melzar that he should feed them with pulse and water. Daniel requested he would permit them to try the diet, that he proposed, ten days, and if, at the end of the ten days, he and his companions did not look fairer and fatter in flesh than any of those who eat the portion of the king's meat, they would submit. Melzar accordingly tried them, and, at the end of the ten days, was satisfied that their diet agreed with them. He therefore met their wishes by taking away the portion of the king's meat, and continued to give them pulse to eat and water to drink. Daniel, i: 11-16.

## MENAHEM—[Men′-a-hem,] *comforter, who conducts them.*

MENAHEM was the son of Gadi, and probably a general under Zachariah, the son of the second Jeroboam. They were both of them kings of Israel. Zachariah's reign was very short, only six months, when he was slain by Shallum, the son of Jabesh, who usurped authority and ascended Zachariah's throne. 2d Kings, xv.

Shallum had scarcely ascended the throne until Menahem, hearing that his master was murdered, went against him with an armed force and cut him off, then seized the crown for himself. He was not readily acknowledged by the inhabitants of the country between Tirzah and Tiphsah, at which he became enraged and vented his cruel spite upon them, by murdering them, ripping up the women with child, and dashing the little infants to pieces, in Tiphsah, and the surrounding country.

It was not long after he commenced his reign, thus in blood, that the Assyrians invaded his kingdom, and he proposed friendship with them by giving them a thousand talents of silver.

Menahem procured this money of the people of Israel. He exacted of all the mighty men of wealth, fifty shekels of silver, to give to Pul, the king of Assyria, that his hand might be with him to confirm the kingdom and establish it. He succeeded in this matter so that Pul gave up the conquest of Israel.

Menahem reigned ten years over Israel, in Samaria, and followed in the way of Jeroboam, the son of Nebat, who made Israel to sin. He was succeeded on the throne by Pekaiah, his son, who reigned two years, and was murdered in his own house by Pekah, the son of Remaliah, one of his captains. Thus was the sin of Menahem visited upon his posterity.

## MEPHIBOSHETH, 1—[Me-fib′-o-sheth,] *out of my mouth proceeds reproach.*

MEPHIBOSHETH was a son of King Saul by his concubine Rizpah. He was the brother of Armoni, and one of the seven sons of Saul who were delivered by David into the hands of the Gibeonites to be hung in Gibeah, as an atonement for an injury inflicted upon them by Saul in his lifetime. Rizpah watched the dead bodies of her sons from the beginning of harvest until the autumnal rains, which was probably about five months. 2d. Sam. xxi: 8, 9.

MEPHIBOSHETH, 2—*Out of my mouth proceeds reproach.*

MEPHIBOSHETH was the son of Jonathan, and a grandson of King Saul. He was a little child in the arms of a nurse at the time his father Jonathan was killed in battle. On the day of the Gilboa battle the intelligence reached the household of the king, and the nurse who had charge of Mephibosheth was so alarmed at the tidings, and so terrified, that she let the child fall—and the fall inflicted an injury that made him lame in both his feet his whole lifetime. 2d Sam. iv: 4. He was five years old when he received this injury. He spent his childhood and youth in the family of Machir, the son of Ammiel of Lodebar, and was probably kept in this family secretly, lest the enemies of the house of Saul should slay him, as the last member of his family, and so put royal honors for descendants of the fallen king beyond all hope.

When David the successor of Saul was established on the throne of Israel, and had conquered a peace with the Philistines, and also with the Moabites—he heard of Ziba a servant of King Saul, and he sent for him and examined him to see if he was the one who had saved the first king of Israel. He then asked him if there were any left of the house of Saul "that he might show the kindness of God unto him." He wished to show the highest degree of kindness, because of the covenant of God, or the covenant that God was a witness to—made between him and Jonathan. Ziba then informed the king that there was one left of the house of Saul, and he was a son of Jonathan, Mephibosheth, and that he was lame in his feet.

David was glad that there was one left, and especially that that one was a son of Jonathan. He asked where Mephibosheth was, and was informed that he was in Lodebar. He bade Ziba bring him to him; Mephibosheth was accordingly brought and entered into the presence of King David. Fearing lest some harm was to befall him, "he fell on his face and did reverence." David addressed him kindly and affectionately and so quieted his fears, "Fear not for I will surely show thee kindness for Jonthan, thy father's sake, and will restore thee all the land of Saul thy father," all the landed estate of Kish, the father of Saul. David as king might have retained this, but in doing so he would have violated the law of the Israelites regarding estates going to the family or descendants of the deceased.

David proposed not only to restore him the land of Saul, but to bestow upon him the honor of eating bread at his table. The former was but justice; but this latter was voluntary kindness, and it was kindness that could hardly be excelled. He was lame on both his feet, and so unfit for public employment. Mephibosheth accepted the favor with humility and complaisance, and entered at once upon the enjoyment of the honor· but he was not alone in the enjoyment of this honor, for he had a young son whose name was Micah who shared with him in the inheritance. David ordered Ziba and his family of fifteen sons and twenty servants to cultivate for Mephibosheth and his son the entire inheritance 2d Sam. ix.

Some years after this Absalom rebelled against David, his father, and forced him to quit his capital and flee for his life from the violence of a rebel son. Mephibosheth desired very much to accompany David in his flight, for he felt gratitude to him as a benefactor; hence, he ordered Ziba, his servant, to saddle him an ass that he might accompany him. Since he could not go on foot on account of his lameness, he wished to ride. Ziba instead of obeying him turned a traitor to Mephibosheth and his interest, and set himself to work to turn David against him, and secure the estate for himself and his family. He left his helpless master in Jerusalem and followed after David himself with a present of two hundred loaves of bread, and a hundred bunches of raisins, and a hundred summer fruits, and a bottle of wine. Ziba then told David that Mephibosheth was waiting in Jerusalem in the hopes that his enemies would prevail against him; and in the event they did succeed he hoped in some way to be restored to the throne of his grandfather Saul. "And Ziba said unto the king, Behold, he abideth at Jerusalem; for he said, To-day shall the house of Israel restore me the kingdom of my father." What a base wretch was Ziba! and how unfounded was the accusation brought against the peaceable, loyal and innocent son of Jonathan! David acted very rashly in this matter, for he credited the foul slander, and transferred the estate, or the proceeds of the estate, at once to Ziba and his family. He ought to have examined the circumstance, and not inconsiderately have spoiled an innocent man to reward a villain. But so it was.

After the defeat of Absalom, David returned to Jerusalem, and one of the first persons he met was Mephibosheth in deep mourning, for he had not dressed his feet nor trimmed his beard, nor washed his clothes from the day that David fled in haste from Jerusalem, until the day that he returned again in peace. He asked Mephibosheth why he had not gone along with him. He then told the king that he had intended to go, and had ordered his servant Ziba to saddle him an ass. David then probably told him the report that had come to him. Mephibosheth refuted the slander, and told how Ziba had deceived him; but he added in this conversation, "My lord, the king is as an angel of God; do therefore what is good in thine eyes." He did not complain that the king had so rashly decided against him and given the lands to Ziba. He did not ask to have it restored to him; but he said, "Let Ziba take it; I am content, since the king has safely returned to his throne." But David did annul the gift he had made to Ziba, and placed the estate just where it was before. He did not punish Ziba for his treachery and villainous conduct; but since he had been so long a servant in the house of Saul, and there were so few of Saul's family to whom he could show kindness, he left him in his position. 2d Sam. xix: 24-30.

In 1st Chron. viii: 35, we learn that Micah, the son of Mephibosheth, had four sons, and these four sons in all probability had a numerous posterity.

MERAIOTH, 1—[Me-ra'-yoth.]

Meraioth was the son of Ahitub, the high-priest. 1st Chronicles, ix: 11. The high-priest here is called "the ruler of the house of God." As Joshua, the son of Jozedek, appears to have been the high-priest at this time, and Seraiah, the second priest. It is thought by some that Meraioth is the same person.

MERAIOTH, 2.

Meraioth was the son of Seraiah, and the father of Amariah, who is named among the high-priests, in 1st Chron. vi: 6. Here the genealogy of Levi and Aaron is given, and the offices of the priests and Levites, are set forth, with the cities that were assigned to them.

MERARI—[Me-ra'ri,] *bitter, to provoke.*

Merari was the third son of Levi, and the father of Mahli and Mushi, Num. iii: 20. The families of these two sons of Merari were very numerous, for when the Hebrews came out of the land of Egypt, it is said of the Merarites that their males from a month old and upwards were six thousand two hundred, and they had amongst them fit for service about three thousand two hundred, who were between the ages of thirty and fifty years.

The chief of the family was Zurial, the son of Abihail, and their position in marching was on the north side of the tabernacle. They went first of all the Levites, were in the front, and having in their custody and charge the boards of the tabernacle, and the bars, and the pillars, and the sockets, and all the vessels thereof, and all that serveth thereto; and the pillars of the court round about, and their sockets, and their pins, and their cords; and these Merarites were placed under the charge of Ithamar, the son of Aaron. See Numbers, iii and iv chapters.

Some of the posterity of Merari were sacred porters in the time of David, and are referred to in 1st Chron. xxvi: 19.

When the Levites applied to Eleazar, the successor of Aaron, and to Joshua with the elders of Israel, for cities to dwell in according to the promise that had been given them by Moses, their request was granted, and the children of Merari had twelve cities appointed them out of the tribes of Reuben, Gad and Zebulun. The names of their cities as given in Jos. xxi: 34–40, are Jokneam, Kartah, Dimnah, Nahalal, Bezer, Kedemoth, Jahazah, Mephaath, Ramoth-Gilead, Mahanaim, Heshbon and Jazer, and these same cities are referred to as given to Merari in 1st Chronicles vi: 77–81.

MERCURIAS—[Mer-cu′-ri-as,] *a false god; from the Latin word mercari, "to buy or sell," because he presided over merchandise; in Greek, hermes, "orator" or "interpreter."*

MERCURIUS or MERCURY was one of the fabulous heathen gods. He was worshiped by the heathens, as the god of learning, eloquence and trade, and it is said was famous for lying and deceit. There is a reference made to this false god in Acts xiv: 12, where we have an account of Paul and Barnabas performing the miracle of healing an impotent man, who was a cripple in his feet from his birth. Paul is the actor and speaker in the scene described. The people of Lystra looked on with wonder and astonishment and exclaimed, "The Gods are come down to us in the likeness of men, and they called Barnabas, Jupiter; and Paul, Mercurias, because he was the chief speaker.

MERAB—[Me′-rab,] *he that fights, he that multiplies.*

MERAB was the eldest daughter of Saul, the first King of Israel. When the Philistines were fighting against Israel, and Goliath, the giant of Gath, was defying the armies of the living God, King Saul promised to enrich with great riches the man who should kill Goliath; and in addition to rewarding him with riches, he promised to give the conqueror of his enemy, his daughter to wife. So the men of war informed David, when he visited the army. 1st Sam. xvii: 25. And Saul himself said to David, (after having failed to give him his daughter to wife upon his killing Goliath,) when he removed him from his presence and made him captain over a thousand; "be thou valiant, and I will give thee my elder daughter Merab to wife." But the intention of Saul was to rid himself of David, of whom he was very jealous. David was valiant in "fighting the Lord's battles," but Saul gave his daughter Merab to another, and not to him. Merab became the wife of Adriel the Meholathite, and was the mother of the five sons of Saul or grandsons, who were given with the two sons of Rizpah, to the Gibeonites to be hung. We have an account of the circumstance of the death of the five sons of Adriel, the Meholathite, which sons were brought up by Michal, the daughter of Saul, for Adriel. 2d Sam. xxi: 8. It may be that Merab died while these sons were small, and that her sister Michal took charge of them and brought them up, or trained them as the sons of a king. It is certain that Adriel was not married to Michal, for she was first the wife of David, and afterwards Saul gave her to Phaltiel. And when David was made king in Hebron, and Abner was about to transfer the house of Saul to David and his kingdom. David demanded of Ishbosheth, his wife Michal, and she was taken from her husband Phaltiel, and delivered up to David.

MEREMOTH, 1—[Mer′-re-moth.]

MEREMOTH was a son of Urijah the priest, the head of the seventh course of priests instituted by David. We have an account in Ezra, viii: 33, of his being appointed to weigh and register the gold and silver vessels of the temple. In the rebuilding of the wall he took an active part, and his position as a workman is given us in Neh. iii: 4.

MEREMOTH, 2.

Was one of the people of the sons of Rani who had married a foreign wife. Ez. x: 36.

MEREMOTH, 3.

Was at the head of a family of priests who sealed the covenant with Nehemiah, the name also occurs in the list of those who went up with Zerubbabel. Neh. x: 5; Neh. xii: 3.

MERES—[Me′-rez.]

Was one of the seven counselors of king Ahasuerus—they are said to be wise men who knew the times. Est. i: 14.

MERODACH, 1—[Me-ro′-dak,] *bitter, contrition; in Syriac, the little lord.*

MERODACH who is called Merodach Baladan, was the son of Baladan, king of Babylon. After Hezekiah had been sick and had recovered, he sent messengers to him to congratulate him upon his recovery. In 2d Kings, xx, and also in Isa. xxxix, we have the account of the king's sickness and the prophet's message to him, urging him to prepare for death in the following language: "Set thine house in order for thou shalt die and not live." Hezekiah prayed that his life might be extended. His prayer was heard and fifteen years were added to his life—so the prophet Isaiah informed him. As the means were being used to restore him to health, the king asked for a sign that he should be restored. A sign was given him in the shadow going back ten degrees in the sun dial of Ahaz.

Merodach Baladan in all probability had heard of the miracles connected with Hezekiah's recovery, and especially the backward motion of the sun, and he wished to congratulate him upon these miracles, and especially upon his recovery to health. The messengers were treated with great courtesy and respect.

Merodach was a great king, and much honored after his death. A massive image was erected to his memory and worshiped, and when Cyrus the Persian conqueror took the city and country, the image of Merodach was broken in pieces.

MERODACH, 2—*Bitter, contrition; in Syriac, the little lord.*

MERODACH is called Evil Merodach, and was the son of Nebuchadnezzar, the great king of Babylon. It is thought Nebuchadnezzar supposed this son would be like the former Merodach, and hence gave him his name, but he turned out to be a very weak man, and incompetent for governing a kingdom. [See Evil Merodach.]

MESHA—[Me′-shah.]

Mesha was a king of Moab. 2d Kings, iii and iv. He was tributary to Ahab, the king of Israel, paying yearly one hundred thousand lambs and a hundred thousand rams, with the wool; but after Ahab died, he revolted and denied to the kingdom of Israel the yearly tributes. Joram, or Jehoram, the son of Ahab, was king of Israel, and at once set himself, with the assistance of the Jews and the Edomites, to subdue Mesha and the Moabites. He invaded the kingdom of Moab and routed Mesha's army, without giving him time to put himself and his army in battle array against him, with his allies.

Mesha shut himself up in Ar, the capitol of his kingdom. The king of Israel, the king of Judah and the king of Edom, then made a march upon the capitol and besieged it. In a march of seven days, the army suffered much for lack of water, and the king of Israel and the king of Judah felt themselves to be in extremity. They inquired of Elisha the prophet as to what they should do in their want for water, and whether they should persist in following up Mesha, the king of Moab. Elisha told them that the valley where they were camped should be full of water, so that their want and the want of their cattle and beasts should be supplied, and furthermore, that the Moabites should be delivered into their hands—that they should certainly succeed in the conquest of Mesha and his country. In the morning, according to the words of Elisha, the valley was full of water, and the water had the appearance to Mesha and the Moabites of blood, as the rising sun shone upon it. Mesha thought that the confederate hosts had fallen into confusion in the darkness of the night and destroyed each other, as the Midianites did when Gideon marched against them in the plain of Moab, and he accordingly gave orders for the Moabite soldiers to hasten to the spoil. Not being properly drilled for war, they rushed out in a disorderly manner and easily fell a prey to their enemies.

When Mesha saw that the battle was against him, and that his capitol was about to be taken, he took with him seven hundred warriors and made an attempt to escape by breaking through the troops of the king of Edom, as he thought that was the weakest part of the army; but his attempt was ineffectual and he fell back into the city. He then took his oldest son, who was heir to the crown, and offered him for a burnt sacrifice on the wall. He offered him as a sacrifice to his god, and on the wall that his enemies might see it. This was evidence that Mesha was in great extremity. The enemy saw it and they immediately raised the siege and went back again to their own country.

We have an allusion in Amos, ii: 1, to the king of Moab burning the bones of the king of Edom into lime, but whether it was Mesha, or some other king of Moab, we do not know.

MESHACH—[Me′-shak,] *that draws with force, that surrounds the waters.*

MESHACH, otherwise called Mishael, was one of the three Hebrew children, taken with Daniel, captives to Babylon. The prince of the eunuchs of the king of Babylon, changed his name from Mishael to Meshach. Daniel, i: 7. For the history of Meshach, see Abednego.

MESHECH—[Me′-shek,] *who is drawn by force, shut up, surrounded.*

MESHECH was the sixth son of Japheth, and is referred to in Gen. x: 2. The posterity of Meshech, no doubt, became very numerous, though it is not certain who they were. It is thought, by some, that the descendants of Meshech are referred to in Ezek. xxxii: 26, under the title Meshech-Tubal, "and all her multitude: her graves are round about him; all of them uncircumcised, slain by the sword, though they caused their terror in the land of the living."

Gog is called the chief prince of Meshech and Tubal. Ezekiel, xxxviii: 2, and some think the descendants of Meshech will assist the Turks against the Jews, about the time of the beginning of the Millenium, but will perish in the attempt, as Gog is represented as perishing in Ezekiel, xxxix.

MESHELEMIAH — [Mesh-el-e-mi′-ah,] *peace, perfection, retribution of the Lord,*

Was a Korhite, and one of the sacred porters. 1st Chron. xxvi: 1 He is referred to under the name of Shelemiah, as the keeper of the eastern gate. 1st Chron. xxvi: 14. He is also supposed to have been captain of a thousand men.

MESHULLEMETH — [Me-shul′-le-meth,]

Was the mother of Amon, a king of Judah, and she was the daughter of Haruz of Jotbah. She was the wife of Manasseh, Amon's father. 2d Kings, xxi: 19.

METHUSAEL—[Me-thu′-sa-el,] *who demands his death,*

Was the son of Mehujael, a descendant of Cain; and he was the father of Lamech, who was the first one to introduce polygamy among the family of man. Gen. iv: 18, 19.

METHUSELAH — [Me-thu′-se-lah,] *he has sent his death.*

METHUSELAH was the son of Enoch, that great and good man, whose character as a servant of the Most High has been admired in all ages of the world since he lived and passed away to heaven without dying. Gen. v: 21.

Methuselah had a religious training. He had constantly before him the pious example of a father who walked with God, and we may reasonably suppose that example exerted a good influence upon him—that he, too, was virtuous and good. We know of him that God blessed him with the longest life of any man whose age the Scriptures present; and it is quite likely that his life was the longest one ever lived. It was within thirty-one years of a thousand—nine hundred and sixty-nine years.

Methuselah lived one hundred and eighty-seven years and begat Lamech; and as Lamech was the father of Noah, Methuselah was his grandfather. He lived not only to see his grandchild, but his great-grandchildren—the three sons of Noah who were preserved in the ark, and whose posterity peopled the new world. It is said of him, he lived after he begat Lamech seven hundred and eighty-two years; and it is further said that Lamech begat Noah when at the age of one hundred and eighty-two years.

The import of the name Methuselah is, "his death produces, or at his death shall break out—the flood." Agreeably to this the flood commenced the very year in which Methuselah died. Gen. v: 27.

MEZAHAB—[Mez′-a-hab,]
Was the father of Matred and grandfather of Mehetabel, the wife of Hadar, a king of Edom. Gen. xxxvi: 39; 1st Chron. i: 50.

MIAMIN, 1—[Mi-a′-min,]
A layman of Israel, of the sons of Parosh, who had married a strange wife and put her away at the suggestion of Ezra. Ezra, x: 25.

MIAMIN. 2,
A priest who went up from Babylon with Zerubbabel. Neh. xii: 5.

MIBHAR—[Mib′-har,]
Was one of David's warriors. 1st Chron, xi.

MIBSAM, 1—[Mib′-sam,]
A son of Ishmael. Gen. xxv: 13.

MIBSAM, 2,
A son of Simeon, referred to in 1st Chron. iv: 25.

MIBZAR—[Mib′-zar,]
Was one of the dukes of Edom after the death of Hadad. Gen. xxxvi: 42; 1st Chron. i: 53.

MICAH, 1—[Mi′-cah,] *poor, humble, who strikes, is there,*
MICAH was a native of Mt. Ephraim, near Shiloh, the son of a very wealthy widow who was a superstitious idolater. He is brought to our view in Jud. xvii, from which we learn that he stole from his mother eleven hundred shekels of silver. As soon as the widow missed the silver she pronounced the bitterest curses on the thief who had stolen her money, and Micah heard her curses; he heard the imprecations and was alarmed lest the curses should fall on his head. He therefore came to his mother and confessed to having taken the money. She was very glad to find that the money was yet in the family, and when he offered to return it to her, she was so overjoyed that she blessed him, and bade him keep it to himself. He however would not keep it. She then told Micah that she had dedicated it to the Lord to make a graven image and a molten image for their family worship. Micah's mother then gave two hundred shekels of the silver to the founder who made the images. One was graven, the other molten. Whether they were made to resemble something belonging to the tabernacle, we do not know. But they were placed in a house or room of the dwelling house, and Micah made an ephod and teraphim, and consecrated one of his sons as a priest.

Sometime after this a young man out of Bethlehem-Judah, a Levite who had probably married into the family or tribe of Judah, or his mother may have been of the tribe of Judah, and his father of the tribe of Levi—this young man was in search of a home, and he came to Mt. Ephraim to the house of Micah. No sooner had Micah learned that he was a Levite, than he invited him to stay with him, and be a priest in his family. The young Levite agreed to tarry and serve Micah and his family, for the sum of ten shekels of silver a year, and a suit of apparel and his food. This young Levite after tarrying awhile with Micah concluded to leave him without letting him know; and he went away secretly, and carried with him the idols of Micah. He went in company with six hundred Danites to Laish. No sooner had Micah missed his gods than almost frantic with grief he called his neighbors together and with them he pursued after the Danites and over took them. As soon as they saw him they mocked him by saying: "what aileth thee that thou comest with such a company?" Micah answered "Ye have taken away my gods, which I made, and the priest, and ye are gone away; and what have I more? and what is this ye say unto me, What aileth thee?"

They mocked him still more, and threatened him with the loss of life of himself and his household, if he did not cease to complain thus of them. Though he told them that they had rendered him wretched and miserable by taking away his gods, yet would they not pity.

When Micah saw that they were too strong for him, he turned in his wretchedness and went back to his house, and his neighbors, who attended him, went with him. Judges, xi: 8-26.

MICAH, 2—*Poor, humble, who strikes, is there.*
MICAH was one of the lesser prophets. He was an inhabitant of Morashath near Gath; he was cotempo-

rary as a prophet with Isaiah, and prophesied during the reigns of Jotham, Ahaz and Hezekiah. That he prophesied as late as the last named king is evident from Jer. xxvi: 18. "Micah the Morasthite prophecied in the days of Hezekiah."

Micah prophesied during a period of about fifty years, and from his prophecies we learn that he had a fair share of trial, affliction and persecution. The first part of his prophecies were delivered during the reign of Jotham, a king of Judah, contained in the first chapter in which he pronounces fearlessly God's judgment against Israel and Judah for their sins.

The second part are prophecies made during the reign of Ahaz, king of Judah, and Tekah, king of Israel, ii and iv chapters inclusive.

The third part contains prophecies delivered during Hezekiah's reign, and a part of the reign of Hoshea, the last king of Israel, 5th and 7th chapters inclusive. In the 5th chapter there is a very clear prophecy of Messiah, and the spread of his gospel among men—and he clearly sets forth the spiritual peace and prosperity of the church of God under the coming New Testament dispensation.

Micah v: 2, is a prophecy relative to the very place where Christ should be born. "But thou Bethlehem Ephratah, though thou be little among the thousands of Judah, yet out of thee shall he come forth unto me, that is to be ruler in Israel; whose going forth have been of old, from everlasting."

MICAIAH—[Mi-ka'-yah,] *Who is like to God? the lowliness of God.*

MICAIAH was a prophet of the Lord, who prophesied in the days of Ahab, a king of Israel. He was the son of Imlah, an Ephraimite. The character of Micaiah was that of a faithful prophet, who reproved the wicked Ahab for his wickedness, which led that king to hate him.

Jehoshaphat, the king of Judah, had associated himself with Ahab against the Syrians. 1st Kings, xxii. Ahab enquired of four hundred false prophets whether he should go against Ramoth-Gilead to battle, and they told him to go, for he should surely succeed. Jehoshaphat was not altogether satisfied with these false prophets, and he asked: "Is there not here a prophet of the Lord, besides, that we might enquire of him?" Ahab answered him that there was yet one man, Micaiah by name, but that he disliked him very much for the reason that he never prophesied good concerning him, but evil; and the king of Judah said: "Let not the king of Israel say so."

We have an account of a prophet who approached King Ahab, or waited by the road side, disguised, and, after a conversation with him, reproved him for dismissing Benhadad, the king of Syria, when he had it in his power to slay him. 1st Kings, xx: 35-43. The prophet declared that his life should go for the life of his enemy. This displeased the king very much, and he went to Samaria sad and dejected; and now that he was about to go against Ramoth-Gilead, he probably thought of this interview with the prophet; and it may be that Micaiah was the prophet who had thus spoken. Ahab seems more than to intimate that he had held interviews with this prophet, and that he had always prophesied evil concerning him.

Ahab being willing to gratify Jehoshaphat, his ally, sent for Micaiah that he might be consulted as to the matter of besieging Ramoth-Gilead. As soon as he was introduced into the presence of the two kings, some of the attendants told him that the prophets of Baal had been consulted, and that they had, without a dissenting voice, advised the king to proceed and assured him of success in the war; and they begged him that he would give the same assurances and advice. He told them he was there to tell them what the Lord directed, and that he would speak nothing else. Ahab then asked him if he should go up to Ramoth-Gilead to battle or forbear? And Micaiah answered: "Go, and prosper, for the Lord shall deliver it into the hand of the king." Micaiah gave this answer with an air and a manner that satisfied Ahab that it was irony. The manner in which he said it was as though he had said: You applied to your prophets, and they have predicted your success.

Now you wish me to speak as they speak. Trust in your prophets, and in their advice, and go against your enemies.

Ahab then adjured Micaiah to speak nothing but the truth. When thus appealed to, the prophet seriously told him of a vision given to him, which was prophetic, and pointed out the disasters which were to ensue. "I saw all Israel scattered upon the hills, as sheep that have not a shepherd; and the Lord said: These have no master; let them return every man to his house in peace." He then went on to tell him that a lying spirit had entered the prophets of Baal, that they might entice him to go up and fall at Ramoth-Gilead. The king of Israel complained to the king of Judah of these declarations and teachings of Micaiah, and said: "Did I not tell thee he would prophesy no good, but evil concerning me!" With this Zedekiah, the son of Chenaanah, approached Micaiah and smote him on the cheek, and then insolently said to him: "Which way went the spirit of the Lord from me to speak unto thee?" Micaiah turned to this insolent man and said: "Behold, thou shalt see in that day when thou shalt go into an inner chamber to hide thyself," alluding in all probability to some severe judgment of God that should fall upon this deceiver.

Ahab ordered Micaiah carried back unto Amon, the governor of the city, and placed in his charge, and in the charge of Joash, the king's son. He ordered that they put Micaiah in prison, and feed him with bread of affliction, and with water of affliction, until he comes in peace. Micaiah heard these instructions to the king, and said: "If thou return at all in peace, the Lord hath not spoken by me." That was as much as to say, If thou dost return safe I am willing to be counted as a false prophet.

MICHAEL—[Mi′-ka-el,] *Who is like to God? the lowliness of God.*

MICHAEL is referred to as an arch-angel, and sometimes signifies the Lord Jesus Christ. He is represented as being at the head of the angelic host, and an opposer of Satan and his allies. Rev. xii: 7. "And there was war in heaven; Michael and his angels fought against the dragon, and the dragon fought and his angels, and prevailed not, neither was there place found any more in heaven."

In Dan. xii, when the general resurrection is foretold, and the glorious millenial era prophesied of, Michael, the arch-angel, is represented as an important actor in bringing about the events; and again, as one of the chief powers or principal angels, he is said by Jude, 9th verse, to have disputed with the devil about the body of Moses, and it is said of him that he durst not, that is, thought it unbecoming his dignity to bring a railing accusation against the devil, but rebuked him in the name of the Lord.

Michael then was a created angel, though the name may sometimes be used to represent Jesus Christ and his work, as the conqueror of sin, death, and the grave.

MICHAH.

MICHAH was one of the ministers in the temple, under the order of service instituted in the time of David. 1st Chron. xxiv: 24.

MICHAIAH—[Mi-ka′-yah,] *Who is like to God? the lowliness of God.*

The daughter of Uriel, of Gibeah, and the mother of Abijah, a king of Judah. 2d Chron. xiii: 2.

MICHAL—[Mi′-chal.]

MICHAL was the daughter of King Saul, and was given David to wife—probably at her own request. It may be that she knew that David, having slain Goliath of Gath, was entitled to the hand in marriage of her sister Merab—but she saw that her father did not give her to David but to Adriel the Meholathite. And as David had performed a feat that entitled him to be the king's son-in-law, she desired to be his wife, and it is quite likely made known that desire to Saul. She would certainly have been justifiable in making the request of Saul from the fact stated in 1st Sam. xviii: 20. "And Michal, Saul's daughter, loved David." As soon as the fact was communicated to the king he said, "I will give him her that she may be a snare to him."

He desired the death of David, and supposing that Michal's love for

David, and his love in return for her would induce him to place his life in imminent peril. He agreed with David to give him his daughter to wife, if he would kill a hundred Philistines, and bring proof to him that he had done so. It was not long until the feat was performed and David and Michal were married. It is a significant fact that Michal loved David. Soon an opportunity was afforded of testing that love. Saul determined to slay David, and sent messengers specially charged to waylay and murder him. Michal became aware of it, and informed David, and successfully planned his escape. She let him down through a window, probably at the back part of the house, where there were no liers-in-wait, and so he escaped.

Then to detain pursuit after him for awhile, she put an image in the bed to represent David, and reported to her father, who was intent on killing him, that he was sick. Saul then sent messengers to take him from the bed where he was lying as was supposed; but the astonished messengers looked upon an image in the stead of a man. The reason why Saul did not send the messengers in the night to his house to kill him probably was, he was unwilling that Michal should be shocked by a scene of murder in her own chamber.

Saul gave his daughter Michal, the lawful wife of David, to Phalti, the son of Laish, who had lived in Gallim a town belonging to the tribe of Benjamin, which was the tribe to which he himself belonged. 1st Sam. xxv: 44.

When David was settled as king in Hebron, he demanded of Saul's son, who was also reigning, his wife Michal. 2d Sam. iii: 14. "David sent messengers to Ishbosheth, Saul's son, saying, Deliver me my wife Michal which I espoused to me for a hundred foreskins of the Philistines." It was very hard for her husband Phalti to give her up, but David had a right to demand her, for she was his own lawful wife. Moreover she was a king's daughter, and as he was the reigning king, prudence and policy might have demanded that a princess be not the wife of a man, who possibly might build a claim to the throne upon his relation to the daughter of the late king. But he had been divorced from Michal, and when she was taken from him it was by violence, and moreover her last act was the shielding him from the fury of her father.

When the ark of God had remained three months in the house of Obed-Edom, David made ready to bring it, with sacrifices and solemn rejoicings, to Jerusalem. We have this account in 2d Sam. vi. Michal saw David as he entered Jerusalem dancing before the ark. There was something in his appearance and actions during the sacred ceremony that she did not approve of, and although she did not speak out against it to her attendants, yet "she despised him in her heart." As soon as an opportunity was afforded her of speaking to King David about the matter, she did so. Her language, which was in accordance with her judgment, was very unbecoming. If she was the first wife King David ever had, and the daughter of a king, she had no right to talk as she did in irony to the king, 2d Sam. vi: 20. "How glorious was the King of Israel to-day," &c. David was not at all pleased with her severe criticism, and his language may be considered a strong reproof. But God was not pleased with it. It is said, "Therefore, Michal, the daughter of Saul, had no child until the day of her death."

It may be after this that she took the charge of the children of Merab her sister. Five of them were hanged by the Gibeonites, when the two sons of Rizpah, the wife of Saul, were put to death, for it is said in 2d Sam. xxi: 8, that the five sons of Michal, the daughter of Saul, whom she brought up for Adriel, were delivered to the Gibeonites and hanged. Michal was never the wife of Adriel, but Merab was: and it is not said that she was the mother of these five sons of Adriel, but simply that she brought them up.

MIDIAN—]Mid′-i-an,] *judgment*, *measure*, *covering*.

MIDIAN was the fourth son of Abraham, by Keturah, Gen. xxv: 2, and he was the father of the extensive tribe called Midianites. This tribe, or family, inhabited the land called the land of Midian. To this land Moses fled when he left the land of Egypt, and here Jethro, the priest, dwelt, who was the father-in-law of Moses. Exod. iii:1. The descendants of Midian were divided into five different parts, or tribes, the heads of those tribes were, Ephah, Epher, Hanoch, Abidah, and Eldaah, and each one had their own kings, or rulers. Gen. xxv: 4.

The Midianites trafficked with the Egyptians in spices, balm, and other things. And it was a company of these trafficking Midianites that the sons of Jacob sold their brother Joseph to, who took him down to Egypt and sold him to an officer of Pharoah.

It seems, from Num. xxii: 6. that the Midianites were associated with the Moabites in trying to induce Balaam to curse Israel. The elders of Midian attended the elders of Moab where they waited on the prophet, and by his advice, a number of the Midianitish women went into the Hebrews' camp and decoyed, enticed and carried away the Hebrews from the fear and worship of their God, to whoredom and idolatry, the consequence of which was, a plague from the Lord destroyed twenty-four thousand of the Hebrews.

In order to revenge this on the Midianites, the Lord directed Moses to send twelve thousand of the Hebrews into the country of Midian and cut off all the people except the virgins, and they did so, and five kings of Midian were killed, viz: Eri, Rekem, Zur, Hur and Reba, and Balaam the false prophet, who had identified himself with them, was also slain. These Hebrews burnt the cities of Midian and carried off as booty, thirty-two thousand virgins, six hundred and seventy-five thousand sheep, seventy-two thousand beeves, sixty-one thousand asses, which were equally divided among the soldiers, except what was assigned to the Lord. Num. xxxi.

There were Midianites that escaped this destruction, who afterwards greatly increased, and for several years grievously oppressed the Hebrews; but they were conquered by Gideon with his handful of men, the Lord working miraculously for their destruction. Their kings, Oreb and Zeeb, with Zebah and Zalmunnah, were slain, and with them about thirty-five thousand fell by the sword. Jud. vii: 15–22. Thus the descendants of Midian were almost annihilated or destroyed. They became, after this, incorporated with other nations—the Moabites and Arabians.

MIJAMIN—[Mi′-ja-min,]

Was one of the priests appointed by David when he divided them into twenty-four orders. His lot was the sixth. 1st Chron. xxiv: 9.

MIKLOTH—[Mik′-loth,]

Was the ruler in the course of Dodai the Ahohite, when the monthly service was instituted. 1st Chron. xxvii: 4.

MIKNEIAH—[Mik-ni′-ah,]

Was one of the Levites who were engaged in the solemn services of removing the ark to Jerusalem and placing it in the tent which David had prepared for it. 1st Chron. xv: 21.

MILCAH, 1—[Mil′-kah,] *queen.*

MILKAH was the daughter of Haran and the wife of Nahor, the brother of Abraham. Gen. xi: 29: "And the name of Nahor's wife, Milcah, the daughter of Haran." After Abraham had offered up Isaac, and God had accepted the offering, but spared the sacrifice—providing Abraham a lamb for a burnt offering instead of his son—we are informed that he heard from Nahor, his brother, that Milcah had borne children unto him. Gen. xxii: 20. This fact seems to be introduced to begin the thrilling history of the family of Nahor furnishing a wife in the beautiful Rebecca for Isaac, the son of promise.

Milcah was the mother of Bethuel and the grandmother of Rebecca.

MILCAH, 2—*queen,*

Was one of the daughters of Zelophehad, who obtained an inheritance and a husband in the tribe of Manasseh. [See Hoglah.]

MILLO—[Mil′-lo,] *fullness, repletion.*

MILLO was a person of some note, whose family assisted the Shechemites in making Abimelech king. It is said in Judges, ix: 6: "all the house of Millo assisted the men of Shechem." In the curious and instructive parable of Jotham, the Shechemites and the house of Millo are reproved, and it is declared that Abimelech, whom they have made king, shall be the cause of kindling a fire of civil discord that shall consume and destroy them.

Thus Millo and his house were destroyed by Abimelech. Judges, ix: 6–20.

MIRIAM—[Mir′i-am,] *exalted, bitterness of the sea, mistress of the sea.*

MIRIAM was the sister of Moses and Aaron. She was a celebrated woman among the Hebrews, and several years older than her brother. Aaron was but three years older than Moses, while she was of sufficient age to be entrusted by her mother with the ark in which the innocent babe had been placed. Ex. ii: 4. "And his sister stood afar off, to wit what should be done to him." And she was sufficiently ingenious to manage the stratagem. Miriam watched the ark faithfully as it rested among the flags by the river's brink until Pharaoh's daughter came with her maidens to wash. She saw them passing along near the shore, and close to the spot under her eye, her heart fluttered and her whole soul was full of anxiety. She thought to herself, they may pass that spot, and their attention not be arrested by the ark and its inmate. But her fears were suddenly relieved by the company halting, and one of the maidens approaching the spot to divine. She saw that the ark was being brought to the Princess, and without fearing to be considered an intruder, she approached the royal lady and looked, with them, with seeming wonder and astonishment at the babe. It was a babe on which she had often looked before, but that fact she artfully concealed. Addressing herself to the Princess, she said: "Shall I go and call a nurse for the child?" The lady said yes. She went accordingly, and called the child's mother and her own mother, so that under the management of Miriam, Moses' own mother became his nurse.

Miriam had been trained up, as were Aaron and Moses, in the religion of patriarchs, which accounts for her occupying the high position she held among the women of Israel. She was constituted joint leader with her two brothers. The prophet Micah says: "For I have brought thee up out of the land of Egypt, and I sent before thee, Moses, Aaron and Miriam." Because of her devotion to God, and the part she took in their religious exercises, she is called the Virgin Prophetess. She was the leader of the Jewish women, and the first woman, so far as we know, thus honored in all the history of the family of man. It is quite likely that she was appointed of God to instruct the women, as Moses and Aaron instructed the men. She regulated the time and places of their devotional acts, and led in those of them that were public. When they crossed the Red Sea, she led that vast host of women through in the bed of the sea, between the wall of waters, encouraging the timid, at every step.

She stood beside her brothers on the other side of the sea, and listened with admiration, "As God opened the mouths of the dumb, and made the tongues of infants eloquent."

She heard the song of victory sung by Moses and the children of Israel, as they drowned the roar of the recently closed sea, with melody such as human voices had never made before. And she headed a company of Israel's maidens, whose souls were fired with song, and who were all ready to respond to the eloquence and enrapturing music of the men. Scarce had the last sound of the sacred anthem been given, when the excited prophetess, followed by the women attending her, led off in the chorus. She sounded—

"The loud timbrel o'er Egypt's dark sea:
Jehovah has triumphed, his people are free."

Miriam was a tender and affectionate sister, and never but once in all their trials did she wound the heart of Moses. She was associated with Aaron in speaking against him in relation to Zipporah, his wife. It is possible that they thought his wife's relations had too much influence over him, since his father-in-law induced him to appoint officers over thousands, hundreds, and tens, and Moses gave evidence that he thought much of Hobab. He had said to them, "Come thou with us and we will do thee good, for the Lord hath spoken good concerning Israel." Aaron and Miriam were alike guilty. Their brother did not attempt to reproach them for their unkindness to him. But God directs the three to enter the tabernacle, and then he charges the sin upon Aaron and Miriam. The punishment inflicted upon Miriam seemed to be severe—she became "leprous, as white as snow." The affectionate Moses forgave her and earnestly prayed for her restoration. His prayer was heard, the disease destroyed, and at the end of seven days she resumed her labors in the camp.

Miriam bore her share of toil, suffering and reproach. With her gifted mind and warm heart, her noble and generous nature, and her devotion to the God of Israel, she acted in union with her brothers in promoting and maintaining order, and elevating her people.

For nearly forty years she had thus acted her part, when the pillar of cloud and fire led them again to the borders of Canaan, and they encamped at Kadesh, in the desert of Sin. Here Miriam died and was buried; and we may well suppose, from the part she had acted so long, the Jewish women greatly mourned her departure. But her work was done; the infirmities of age were upon her, for she was one hundred and thirty years old. Her brothers both followed her to the spirit-land in less than one year; hence, neither of them attained her age.

MISHAEL, 1—[Mi-sha′-el,] *asked for, lent, God takes away.*

He is referred to in Ex. vi: 22, as the eldest son of Uzziel and a descendant of Kohath, the son of Levi.

MISHAEL, 2—*Asked for, lent, God takes away.*

Was also a Levite, and was one of those who were associated with Ezra and Nehemiah in reading and interpreting the law to the people. Neh. viii: 4.

MISHAEL, 3—*Asked for, lent, God takes away.*

Was one of the captives taken to Babylon with Daniel, and whom the prince of the eunuchs called Meshech. Dan. i: 6. [See Meshech.]

MISHMA—[Mish′-mah.]

Was the son of Ishmael and the grandson of Abraham. Gen. xxv: 14.

MITHREDATH, 1—[Mith′-re-dath.]

Was the treasurer of Cyrus, king of Persia, to whom the vessels of Jerusalem's temple were committed, to be transferred to Sheshbazzar. Ezra, i: 8.

MITHREDATH, 2.

Was a Persian officer stationed at Samaria by Artaxerxes. Ezra, iv: 7.

MIZRAIM—[Miz-ra′-im,] *tribulation in straits.*

MIZRAIM was the son of Ham, and the father of Ludim, Anamim, Lehabim, Naphtuhim, Pathrusim, and Casluhim. Gensis, x: 6; 13: 14. The descendants of Mizraim were certainly very numerous, for, from Casluhim, the last named, sprang the nation of the Philistines, "out of whom came Philistim."

MIZZAH—[Miz′-zah.]

MIZZAH was the son of Reuel, and the grandson of Esau. Gen. xxxvi: 13.

MNASON—[Na′-son,] *a dilligent seeker, betrothing, an exhorter.*

MNASON was a disciple of Christ in the apostolic age, converted by Christ himself, and was put into the rank of the seventy disciples. Mention is made of him in Acts xxi: 16. He lived at Jerusalem, and while Paul was there, some of the disciples of Cesarea, who probably were acquainted with Mnason and knew him as an old disciple, brought him into the presence of Paul, and he invited the apostle to lodge with him, and he did so until he was apprehended by a mob and imprisoned.

MOAB—*Of the father.*

MOAB was the son of Lot, by his eldest daughter. From Gen. xix, we learn of Lot's departure from Sodom, where he dwelt with his wife and his two daughters. His wife was punished with death for her disobedience, and his daughters went on with him to the city of Zoar, where Lot was unwilling to tarry long, and with the daughters he went and dwelt in a cave in the mountains. And while dwelling there he committed sin against God by drunkenness and what too often accompanies drunkenness.

Moab and his posterity dwelt in the land of Moab, and were associated with the Ammonites and Midianites. The former conquered them, taking all their territory north of the river Arnon. Num. xxi: 26. After this Balak, the son of Ziphor, became king of Moab, and hired Balaam to curse the Hebrews, and as a punishment God decreed that the Moabites, with the Ammonites, who would not let Israel pass through their land, should not enter the congregation of Israel to the tenth generation. Deut. xxiii: 3-6.

The posterity of Moab were enemies to the Hebrews, and under Eglon, their king, subjected the Hebrews to oppression for eighteen years; but at length they were delivered; for Ehud, a judge of Israel, killed Eglon, and the Hebrew troops killed ten thousand of the Moabites, and thereby recovered their liberty. Jud. iii.

It was among this people that Elimelech, with his family, sought a home during a famine in Canaan, and the sons, Mahlon and Chilion married Moabitish women, Ruth and Orpah. Ruth i. We have an account in 1st Sam. xiv: 47, of Saul, the first king of Israel warring with the Moabites, for they were still the enemies of Israel. And yet when David fled from the violence of Saul, being persecuted by him at one time, he went to the land of Moab and secured the protection of that king for his aged parents. It may be, since David's great grandmother was a Moabite, Ruth, his father's grand-mother, he claimed protection on that ground for them, and he secured it. 1st Sam. xxii: 4. It is thought by some that the Moabites killed the aged parents of David, and that was the reason why David afterwards so terribly ravaged their country, and reduced the soldiery that he took as prisoners of war to such base servitude. 2d Samuel viii: 1, 2. "He smote Moab, and measured them with a line, casting them down to the ground; even with two lines measured he to put to death, and with one full line to keep alive," from which we may suppose that he put two-thirds of them to death.

MOLOCH—[Mo′-lok,] *king.*

Moloch, or Molech was the principal idol of the Ammonites. It is said to have had the face of an ox. It was a brazen image, and hollow within; and the fire was placed within it to heat it, that it might burn the offerings that were made to it, and it is clearly intimated that various nations sacrificed their children unto it. 2d Chron. xxviii: 3; Jer. vii: 31.

The Divine Being prohibited, among the Hebrews, the worship of Moloch. Lev. xviii: 21. They were sometimes guilty of breaking over God's charge in this matter, and Stephen refers to it in his defense. Acts vii: 43. "Yea, ye took up the tabernacle of Moloch, and the star of your god Remphan," &c.

MORDECAI—[Mor′-de-ka,] *contrition, bitter, bruising; in Syriac, pure myrrh.*

Mordecai was the son of Jair, of the family of Saul and Kish, and one of the chief of the tribe of Benjamin. He was carried to Babylon with Jehoiachim, king of Judah, when he was quite young. For his history we depend mainly upon the book of Esther for he was a kinsman of her, and had charge of her in her orphanage. It has been thought that he was one of the chiefs who conducted the Jews from Babylon to Judea, as the name occurs in Neh. vii: 7, among the princes who attended Zerubbabel. But if he did he must have returned again to Shushan in Persia.

Mordecai agreed that Esther his cousin should be counted among the fair young virgins, and should be placed in the charge of Hegai, the king's chamberlain, and stand her chance in the company to be selected as queen in the stead of Vashti, who had been deposed. And Mordecai charged her not to show her kindred, as that might be prejudicial to her interests with the king, and he himself walked every day before the court of the women's house, that he might know how she did and what became of her.

It may be possible that Mordecai occupied some honorable position as an officer of the king, if not before, immediately after the marriage of Esther. For he "sat in the king's gate." About this time two of the king's chamberlains conspired against him to kill him; they were Bigthan and Teresh; what it was, or how they intended to effect, their purpose is not known, but Mordecai learned of it, and he informed the queen—she gave the information to the king and the traitors were convicted and hanged, and the circumstance recorded in the chronicles of the nation, and Mordecai's name was entered there as the king's deliverer in this his imminent peril.

The prime minister of king Ahasuerus, Haman by name, was greatly honored in that the king commanded all his servants to bow before and reverence him. Mordecai, however, for some reason would not do it. Haman became very angry, and on learning that he was a Jew—scorning to lay hands simply on Mordecai he meditated revenge on all the Jews. He laid a plot to destroy them all throughout the entire kingdom and succeeded in it so far that he procured a royal edict for a general massacre of the nation. Mordecai heard of this decree and immediately informed Esther, and earnestly begged that she would intercede with the king for the life of her people. She sent him back word that she had no opportunity, for she had not been called into the presence of the king for thirty days, and there was a law punishing with death any one who went into the king's presence uncalled. Mordecai feeling that it was a desperate case, sent back to Esther a solemn charge in the following language, Esther, iv: 14. "For if thou altogether holdest thy peace at this time, then shall there enlargement and deliverance arise to the Jews from another place; but thou and thy father's house shalt be destroyed; and who knoweth, but thou art come to the kingdom for such a time as this?"

At the request of Esther, Mordecai caused all the the Jews in Shushan to fast three days for her, or rather for success in the attempts she would make to rescue her people. While Esther and her maidens were fasting in the palace, Mordecai and the Jews were fasting without, and God in his providence was working upon the heart and mind of the king. Ahasuerus had a sleepless night, and he called for the annals of the nation and had that part of them read which mentioned Mordecai as the discoverer of the two traitors who had planned to destroy his life, and when he found that no reward had been given Mordecai, he determined to make up this lack and nobly reward this man. Haman came early in the morning to the court, to procure the signature of the king to a death warrant he had drawn up for Mordecai, or to procure permission to hang him on the gallows he had erected for that purpose. But what was the consternation of Haman, when the king bade him do honor to Mordecai by setting him on the king's own horse, and himself leading the horse through the streets of the city, and proclaiming, "Thus shall it be done to the man whom the king delighteth to honor." After this honor had been done Mordecai, he returned to the king's gate. He went back again to his position, and to the performance of his work and office, whatever it was.

Before the night of that day Haman was condemned and hanged on the gallows he had erected on which to hang Mordecai, and Mordecai was promoted to his office. As soon as he took his position as prime minister, in company with Esther he sent letters to the different provinces of the empire reversing, so far as it could be reversed, the former decree, and so stopped the massacre of their nation.

Mordecai was clothed in royal apparel, and not only enjoyed the esteem of the king, but the respect of the people of Shushan and the whole realm. "The city of Shushan rejoiced and was glad." But he became great in the king's house, and his fame was noised through all the provinces, "for this man Mordecai waxed greater and greater." He, in company with Esther, instituted the feast of Purim, or Lots, and enjoined it upon the Jews to be observed as an annual feast, to commemorate their deliverance.

He continued for several years to fill the important post to which, in the providence of God, he had been called in that nation.

MOSES—[Mo′-zez,] *taken out of the water*.

MOSES was the brother of Aaron and Miriam and the son of Amram, and

Jochebed. His birth is announced in Exodus, ii: 2.

After Joseph died another king arose in Egypt, who did not approve of the system of government brought about and sustained by Joseph; and that king began to deal hard with, and afflict the children of Israel, who had become very numerous. Task masters were appointed over them, and burdens were imposed upon them beyond endurance, yet still they prospered. Their lives were made better as the chains of bondage were riveted tighter, and the yoke of their service made more and more galling. At length the king made known his pleasure throughout the entire country regarding the Hebrews, which was that their male children should be put to death as soon as they were born. Not succeeding in his first attempt, he sent forth an edict to all his people, that Israelitish male children should be cast into the river as soon as they were born, and thus the increase of the nation be stopped.

Moses was born during this cruel edict, but his birth was kept secret for three months, for his parents hid him. When they found they could no longer hide him, his mother made a small boat, or basket, of the reeds that grew on the bank of the Nile, and making it water-proof, she placed her babe tenderly in it, then committed it to the river. She placed it upon the water among the flags by the brink, or near the shore.

Not long afterwards the king's daughter was passing along, and having her attention attracted by the boat, she bade one of her maidens bring it to the shore, take it out of the water, and place it beside her on the bank. She took off the covering and discovered the beautiful babe. Though the little child may have learned to recognize its mother, before its commitment to the ark, and after being awaked from its infant sleep, it may have met the eye of the woman with an innocent smile. Yet this was not the mother bending over it, with a heart filled with love and anxious care, but the daughter of Pharoah and her maidens. The countenances of all being strange, it may have been afraid, for it wept. This fear and seeming distress, awakened the compassion of the woman, and she gave orders that a nurse be procured for the child. A Hebrew nurse.

The anxious mother herself was called, and entrusted, for wages, with the care of the child. How must that mother's heart have bounded with joy, when all alone that night she clasped to her bosom her precious charge and thought of the adventures of the day! How her heart swelled with gratitude to God that his hand had provided her child a shelter and a home under her own roof, and a cradle in her own arms.

Moses became the adopted son of Pharaoh's daughter, and received his name from her. The reason she gave for naming him Moses, was, "because I drew him out of the water." He was learned in all the wisdom of the Egyptians; and it is said, by a Jewish writer, that he was appointed, and served, as general of the Egyptian forces.

When he was about forty years of age—remembering, it may be, some of the facts that had been given him by his mother, regarding his oppressed people, and, guided by the principles of the religion of the patriarchs that had been instilled into his mind in his earliest education—"It came into his heart to visit his brethren." And while he looked upon them in their sorrows, and beheld the burdens that were laid upon them by their taskmasters, his soul was stirred within him. He saw an Egyptian taskmaster smiting one of his brethren, a Hebrew. It is probable that Moses, considering himself justifiable according to the law God gave to Noah—"whoso sheddeth man's blood, by man shall his blood be shed"—made himself the avenger of blood by killing the Egyptian, and then buried him in the sand of the river. It was but a few hours afterward, still anxious about his oppressed people, that he was walking out again, and he saw two Hebrews striving together. He approached them and would have made up the difference between them, when one of them addressed him roughly and charged him with the murder of the Egyptian yesterday. He had hoped that the transaction referred to was not known; but in this he was mistaken. And it was not long until it came to the ears of Pharaoh, and he sought Moses to slay him. He felt that the time had now come for him to leave that land; and, as the apostle informs us, Hebrews, xi: 24, &c., "By faith Moses, when he was come to years, refused to be called the son of Pharaoh's daughter; choosing rather to suffer affliction with the people of God, than to enjoy the pleasures of sin for a season; esteeming the reproach of Christ greater riches than the treasures of Egypt: for he had respect unto the recompense of the reward." He fled from the land of Egypt to the land of Midian.

He sat down, one day, wearied, near a well in Midian, and while there the daughters of Jethro came to the well to water their father's flocks. Just after they had filled the troughs with water, some barbarous fellows, who had also flocks in their charge which they wished to water, made an attempt to drive the daughters of Jethro away. Moses came to their assistance and drove these men away, and then helped them to water their flocks. They reported his kindness to their father, and he bade them call him in to take some refreshments; and soon we see Moses with a shepherd's crook in his hand, in the employ of Jethro, the priest of Midian, feeding his flock in the desert near Horeb.

While Moses was engaged in faithfully watching his fleecy charge, his attention was arrested one day by the angel of the Lord, who "appeared unto him in a flame of fire out of the midst of a bush." He saw the bush in flames. It was a wonderful phenomenon, and especially so as the bush was not consumed. He said, "I will approach and see this great sight, why the bush is not burnt." Well might Moses call it a great sight, for it was the presence and glory of the uncreated spirit—the Eternal God. As he approached the Lord saw him, and from out the blazing fire spake thus: "Moses, Moses, draw not nigh hither; pull off thy shoes, for the place whereon thou standest is holy ground." He obeyed the divine injunction, and with sacred ceremony was set apart by Jehovah for the important work of emancipating his down-trodden and deeply injured countrymen. At first Moses made objection to entering upon this work, feeling his insufficiency. He seemed surprised that God should appoint him to so great a work. He distrusted himself; but God assured him that he should prosper, and that his people should be brought out of Egypt and serve him in this mountain. God condescended to give him an answer to the question he asked—"What shall I say to my people when they ask, What is the name of him that sent you?" God said unto him, "Say unto them, I Am hath sent me unto you." And as though this was not enough to satisfy Moses, God said unto him, "What is that in thine hand? And he said, A rod. And he said, Cast it on the ground. And he cast it on the ground, and it became a serpent." Moses was afraid and fled before the serpent; but the Lord commanded him to take it by the tail, and as he did so it became a rod in his hand again.

That rod of Moses in all probability was taken down into Egypt, and with it mighty signs and wonders were wrought to convince Pharaoh that his message was a heavenly one. Afterward held in the hand of Moses, it was stretched over the waters of the Red Sea, and they divided so that a road was made for Israel to pass over. And again it was stretched out, and the waters came back to their place, and Pharaoh and his hosts were drowned. When the Israelites were in the wilderness it was used for smiting the flinty rock, and the waters gushed forth to quench the thirst of the famishing thousands. And it may be that was the same rod that afterwards was called Aaron's rod, that budded and blossomed and bore almonds in a single night, and so was the means of settling the vexed question as to who should serve in the important office of the priesthood. From the time that Moses produced the budded rod the priesthood was decided to be in the family of Aaron, and the rod was laid up as a standing memorial of God's decision.

And yet still further to satisfy Moses of his mission, the Lord said unto him, "Put now thy hand into thy bosom; and he put his hand into his bosom, and when he took it out, behold his hand was leprous as snow. And he said put thy hand into thy bosom again, and he put his hand into his bosom again, and plucked it out of his bosom, and behold it was turned as his other flesh."

The Lord also informed him that he should give other signs to the Egyptians, if these were not sufficient. But Moses ventured still another objection to taking upon himself the work and office of emancipator of Israel. "O my Lord, I am not eloquent, neither heretofore nor since thou hast spoken unto thy servant, but I am slow of speech and of a slow tongue."

It may be that the meaning of Moses was, he was not sufficiently accustomed to the use of the Hebrew language spoken by the Israelites at that time, to speak it distinctly and fluently, for he had been brought up from childhood as the adopted son of Pharaoh's daughter, in the Egyptian court until forty years of age; and beside that, he had been forty years in the land of Midian. And though the Egyptian language, as that of the Midianites, might have been very similar to the Hebrew, yet it is hardly likely that it was his own language. But it may be that Moses had an impediment in his speech, though it is said, Acts, vii: 22, "he was mighty in word and in deed." But the Lord removed this objection also, and gave him Aaron, the Levite, his brother, to be the spokesman for him unto the people. See Exodus ii, iii and iv.

Moses took an affectionate leave of his father-in-law, and with his wife and the two sons that were born unto him, Gershom and Eleazar, and he started for the land of Egypt, but as they stopped at an inn by the way, an angel threatened to slay Moses on account, it is thought, of his neglect to circumcise his children. To prevent his death, Zipporah performed the rite, and then with a strange degree of warmth of temper said to Moses, "surely a bloody husband art thou to me." It may be that this was the reason why Zipporah and her children returned to their father. It was not long after this until Moses, as he was pursuing his journey alone, met Aaron, his brother. The meeting was tender and affectionate—for forty years they had been absent from each other—but now that they meet and embrace each other, they find that the fire of true brotherly affection had not expired. In company they go down into Egypt, and begin the work of their great and important mission.

After making their mission known to the elders of Israel, they went into the presence of the king and delivered their message, simple, yet fraught with intense interest to them and their oppressed people. Pharaoh replied harshly to their request, "Who is Jehovah, that I should obey his voice to let Israel go?" Moses proceeded to expostulate with him, but Pharaoh became angry and ordered that the burdens of the unoffending Hebrews be increased. Under the direction of God, plagues of blood, frogs, lice, flies, murrain, boils, and blains, hail, locusts, darkness, and finally death in every family were brought upon the Egyptians. By the hand of Moses and Aaron, the Hebrews were led out from under the hand of their oppressors and began their journey towards Canaan.

By the way of Succoth and Etham, Moses led the children of Israel being guided by the pillar of cloud and fire, to a point on the Red Sea. Here his meek spirit was greatly grieved by reproaches heaped upon him by the murmuring Israelites. They charged him with bringing them there to die. He did not reproach them in turn, but bade them "stand still and see the salvation of God." He then engaged in earnest prayer, committed himself and his people, with their interests, into the hands of God. The answer to his petition came, "Speak to Israel, that they go forward." And so he led them through the way opened up in the sea, and Pharaoh and his hosts essaying to follow were drowned. And Moses and all Israel joined in a song of triumph to God, their deliverer. Exodus, xv.

Ere three days were passed the Israelites were again reproaching Moses, because that the waters of the spring of Marah were bitter. He sought direction of God, and was shown a tree which, when he had cast into the waters, they were made sweet. In the desert of Sin they murmured again, and charged Moses with the design of killing them all with hunger in bringing them into that wilderness, for their supply of provisions was exhausted. Soon their complainings were stopped by a supply of quails for flesh, and manna for bread, and the manna continued to be supplied them for forty years.

Soon they were murmuring again because of a lack of water to drink, and Moses, standing on the rock of Horeb, with the rod in his hand, smote the rock and a fountain was opened there, and the murmuring thousands of Israel quenched their thirst, not only for the time being, but the waters flowed along the way of their future travels and supplied them for years.

When Israel were encamped at Sinai, Moses went up under the direction of God to the top of the mountain, and amid the folds of that majestic cloud, that terrified and struck with awe, the hosts of Israel by its blackness and thunder, he received the ten commandments, and bearing the tables on which they were written in his arms, he came down after an absence of forty days from his people. He had been all that time in glorious converse with God—fasting he had devoted himself to the interests of his people. But as he came down he beheld the cause of the divine anger, which had been intimated to him when he left the mountain summit. Israel was engaged in idolatry. Moses beheld their wickedness in sorrow—his soul was grieved, especially that God was threatening to remove from them the symbols of his presence. Throwing down the tables of the law he brake them in pieces and began earnestly to plead with God for the offenders. His prayer of faith prevailed. After Moses had destroyed the golden calf, the object of the worship of the multitude, and called Aaron his brother to an account for his conduct—he set the sin of the people before them, and earnestly prayed for them again. O how must his soul have been pressed when he said in prayer, "Forgive the sin of this people; if not blot me I pray thee, out of thy book which thou hast written."

The Lord commanded Moses to hew out two tables of stone like unto the first, and take them up on to the mountain. He did so and after receiving a variety of instructions with the re-written decalogue—forty days being ended he went down from the mount; but so glorious was his appearance that Aaron and the children of Israel could not look upon him for the halo of glory that surrounded him; veiling himself he came into their midst and declared to them all the words of the Lord.

Aaron and Miriam for some cause became dissatisfied with Moses, and complained of him. They had been associated with him in bringing the children out of Egyptian bondage, and his sister was the leading female in the camp. They thought that in the administration of the affairs of the government they did not share as largely as they should. Moses heard their complaints, but practiced the same meekness which had marked him in his course up to that time. Though deeply injured and depressed in spirits, he was silent under their reproaches.

Shortly afterward while they were in the tabernacle, God declared the faithfulness and innocence of Moses, and charged upon them their sin in speaking against his servant. As the cloud of divine presence began to withdraw, they understood that God was angry with them, and Aaron fearing, looked upon Miriam "and beheld she was leprous, white as snow." The fear of Aaron increased to dread alarm—for before him in his leprous sister was a terrible token of God's displeasure. He prayed for forgiveness for his sin, and turning to Moses he entreated him to pray for Miriam, Moses always ready to forgive injuries, earnestly supplicated God in behalf of his sister. His prayer was heard and her sin was forgiven, and the disease removed and after seven days she entered the camp and resumed her labors.

Moses led the children of Israel to the borders of Canaan, and, selecting twelve of their chief men, he sent them to spy out the land and bring back a report. They were to report concerning the inhabitants, whether they were "strong or weak, many or few;" whether they dwelt in tents or strongholds; and whether the land was fat or lean, wooded or not; and whether it was productive or not; and to bring of the fruits of the land. The spies made their search and returned, and, with the exception of two of them, they brought back an evil report. This evil report of the ten created fear in nearly all the congregation; and soon they were murmuring against Moses and Aaron, and a spirit of mutiny was clearly visible, for they proposed selecting a captain and returning into Egypt. Moses beheld their sin with sorrow, and he heard the threatening of the divine being to cast them off utterly. Again he resorted to prayer. His prayer was answered, but a sentence was pronounced against the whole murmuring congregation—that their carcasses should fall in the wilderness, and that for forty years they should wander from place to place, and die, and that Caleb and Joshua, of the old stock, alone should enter the promised land.

An extensive mutiny broke out after this, in which there were two hundred and fifty princes of the congregation, headed by Korah, Dathan, and Abiram. It was a very extensive and formidable rebellion. Moses again resorted to prayer. After which he asked those heading the rebellion to hold an interview with him. This they would not do, but continued in their opposition to Moses and the Lord; and the next day the earth opened and swallowed up these guilty leaders, with those who adhered to them. Before the mutinous spirit was fully quelled and the priesthood was miraculously decided to be in the family of Aaron, fourteen thousand seven hundred guilty ones perished.

When the forty years Israel was destined to wander in the wilderness were coming to a close, and nearly all of the generation that came out of Egypt were dead, and a new generation was risen up under the laws and regulations that governed them in their tented state, with the noble example of their great leader before them, they drew near again to the promised land. And while they were camped at Kadesh, Moses was called to part with his beloved sister Miriam. She had done a noble part toward elevating her people, and had borne her share of toil and suffering with her brothers. Miriam died in Kadesh and was buried there. The sensitive heart of the meek Moses was pained as he paid the last tribute of respect to the memory of her "who had acted the double part of sister and mother" for him, and who probably never acted unkindly toward him but once.

About four months after this, Aaron was called up to Mt. Hor, and by Moses divested of the vestments of his office, when he yielded up his spirit to God and joined the pure spirit of his sister, who had preceeded him. And Moses put the robes of Aaron upon Eleazar, his son, and constituted him his successor.

A few months after this, Moses received warning of his approaching end. The Lord let him know that because of his fault in the desert of Sin, he should not pass over Jordan, and enter the promised land; but yet he should be favored with a view of that country from the summit of a neighboring mountain. After appointing Joshua his successor, and settling the portion for Reuben, Gad and the half-tribe of Manasseh, on the east side of Jordan, in the already conquered country, he made arrangements for his departure. He then gives his instructions and charges to the people and Joshua, and at the age of one hundred and twenty years, he ascends Nebo at the command of the Lord, and takes a view of the promised land.

Behold him as he closes his address and pronounces his last benedictions upon the people he had so long served. He takes an affectionate leave of all, but especially of the elders of Israel, of Eleazar, the successor of his brother, and Joshua, his own successor. He climbs the mountain side all alone, and finally reaches Pisgah, its summit, and with his vision strengthened, he stands and looks upon the land flowing with milk and honey. Its hills and plains, mountains and valleys, rose up before him, and his soul was filled with rapture as he saw its coming greatness. Having his desires fully satisfied, he laid him down upon the mountain top, and slept the the sleep of death. He closed his eyes after looking upon the earthly Canaan, and waked up amid the joys of the heavenly Canaan, and joined at once in the enrapturing anthems of glory, with Abraham, Isaac and Jacob, Aaron and Miriam. Having died, his mortal remains were intered by God himself, (an honor which no other human being has ever received) in a valley, in the land of Moab, and no man knoweth his grave until this day. See Exodus, xxxiii; Numbers, xi: 7; Deuteronomy, i: xxxiv: &c.

Moses appeared with Elias in a glorified body on the mount of transfiguration. Matthew, xvii: 1-6.

He wrote the first five books of the Bible, and the ninetieth Psalm. Other writings are ascribed to him by the Jews, but these alone the spirit of inspiration has ascribed to him.

He was an illustrious type of Christ and his name and character is destined to go down to the latest generation of man, and the redeemed in Heaven are to sing the song of "Moses and the Lamb."

MOZA, 1—Mo'za.

Was the son of Caleb, the son of Hezron. 1st Chron. ii: 46.

MOZA, 2.

Was a son of Zimri, and a descendant of Saul. 1st Chron. viii: 36.

MUPPIM—[Mup'pim,]

Was one of the sons of Benjamin, and was numbered with the family of Jacob, who went down into Egypt. Gen. xlvi: 21.

MUSHI—[Mu'shi,] *he that touches, withdraws himself.*

Was the son of Merari, the son of Kohath. Exodus, vi: 19; 1st Chronicles, vi: 19; xxiii: 21; xxiv: 26.

NAAMAH—[Na'-a-mah,]

Was an Ammonitess, and the mother of Rehoboam, the successor of Solomon, from whom the tribes of Israel revolted and formed the kingdom of Israel. 1st Kings, xiv: 21.

NAAMAN, 1—[Na'-a-man,] *beautiful, agreeable, that prepares himself to motion,*

Was one of the sons of Benjamin, and is numbered with the family of Jacob who went down into Egypt. Gen. xlvi: 21.

NAAMAN, 2—*Beautiful, agreeable, that prepares himself to motion.*

NAAMAN was a general of Benhadad, the king of Syria. It is said of him, "he was a great man with his master, and honorable, because by him the Lord had given deliverance to Syria." He has been supposed to be the warrior who drew the bow at a venture and smote Ahab. The death of that king is referred to in 1st Kings, xxii: 34; and the deliverance he had given to Syria is supposed to allude to his slaying Ahab, the king of Israel, in consequence of which the Syrians obtained the victory. It is further said, "he was a mighty man of valor," by which we may understand that he was an able and experienced general.

But of Naaman it is said, he was a leper. This was a very heavy affliction indeed for one occupying the position he did. He not only felt it keenly but his king also felt it. It was very humbling to him, and a great tax upon his grandeur. So anxious was the king about Naaman, his general, that when he heard, through a little captive maid in the house of Naaman, that there was a prophet in Israel who could cure Naaman, he sent a letter unto the king of Israel, setting forth the case of his servant, and asking that he would have him cured; and he sent with it a present of ten talents of silver and six thousand pieces of gold, and ten changes of raiment. When the king of Israel read the letter, he rent his clothes and said, "Am I God, to kill and make alive, that this man doth send to me to cure a man of his leprosy?" He then concluded that the Syrian king sought a quarrel with him, in desiring him thus to do a work that none but God could do. Elisha, the prophet, heard of the circumstance, and he sent the king word to send Naaman to him, and the power of the God of Israel should be made manifest in his cure. Jehoram, the king, accordingly sent him, and Naaman with his chariots and train appeared at the door of the prophet's house. Elisha did not come out to speak with him, but gave him orders through Gehazi, his servant. The reason Elisha did not go out may be, he desired to observe a proper distance from a leper; or it may be he wished to mortify Naaman's pride, and manifest clearly that the cure was wholly of God. He sent orders to Naaman to go wash seven times in Jordan and he should be cleansed of his leprosy. It was not because there was any special virtue in the waters of the Jordan that he bade him do this; but God chose to make this the means by which he would convey healing power to Namaan. The leper was angry that Elisha showed so little regard for him. He expected the prophet would come out and stand by him, and implore the help of his God, and lay his hand upon the part affected and cure him; but instead of that, he bids him go wash in Jordan. Naaman then ventured to reason against this mode of proceeding. "Are not Abana and Pharpar, rivers of Damascus, better than all the waters of Israel? So he turned and went away in a rage." His servant ventured to talk with him as to the propriety of following the directions of the prophet. He asked him to remember how cheerfully he would have undergone the most painful operation to get rid of his disease. "My father, if the prophet had bid thee do some great thing wouldst thou not have done it? How much rather, then, when he says, wash and be clean." Naaman was persuaded, and in conformity to the instructions given him went to Jordan and washed seven times, and he was restored; "his flesh came again like unto the flesh of a little child, and he was clean."

Naaman, when cured of his leprosy, hurried back to the residence of the prophet and offered him a present. He made a bold acknowledgment of the fact that the God of Israel was the true God, and he declared his faith in him. Elisha would not accept his present, but received his profession of faith in God, and granted him two mules' burden of Israelitish earth, that he might build him an altar for sacrificing to Israel's God. He acknowledged his wrong in engaging in idolatry, by worshiping the idol of Syria in the house of Rimmon, when he attended the king of Syria there. He confessed his sin, and asked that he might be pardoned, and pledged himself that he would ever after worship the God of Israel.

Naaman went from the prophet very joyful, for he was returning to his family, and kindred, and nation, clean. But the servant of the prophet was not pleased that his master had refused a present from Naaman, hence he followed after him with a view of securing one, and appropriating it to his own private purposes. Naaman saw him coming, and recognized him as the servant of Elisha. He humbly alighted from his chariot, and asked him what was his desire. He told a falsehood to accomplish his end. "My master desires a talent of silver and two changes of garments, to meet the wants of two young prophets who have just come to him, and are in necessitous circumstances." He was so gratified for what had been done for him that he complied with the request, only that he gave him two talents instead of one; and, having bound them in the two suits of clothes, he sent two of his servants to carry them for Gehazi. These servants carried them as far as the lying servant would permit, when they returned to their master. Gehazi laid the present up as secretly as he could, when he presented himself before Elisha, and the prophet asked him where he had been. He denied having been anywhere. Elisha then gave him to understand that he was acquainted with the terrible sin he had committed. He boldly charged him with the commission of the crime, and added: This is not the time for buying fields, olive-yards and vineyards, which he had intended to do with that money. He then told him as he had wickedly obtained that money, his falsehood, and covetousness, and treachery should be remembered against him, for the leprosy of Naaman should cleave to him and his posterity forever. "And he went out of the presence of Elisha a leper as white as snow."

As Hazael became the Syrian general shortly after this, we suppose that Naaman died, or gave up his position in the army. We may safely suppose that he remembered ever after the favor done him in curing him of his leprosy, and that he would not lead the Syrians against the Hebrews.

NAARAH—[Na′-a-rah.]

One of the wives of Ashur. She was the mother of three sons whose names are given in 1st Chron. iv: 5.

NABAL—[Na′-bal,] *a fool, senseless.*

NABAL was a rich man of the tribe of Judah and a descendant of Caleb, but he was a very churlish man. He had large flocks and extensive wealth. While David, with his warriors, was staying in the wilderness of Paran, the flocks of Nabal were pasturing near

Maon or about Carmel. David and his men, being near there, protected the flocks from the wild beasts and also from the Arabs, and, it is supposed, often rendered valuable assistance to Nabal's herdmen.

David hearing that Nabal had a sheep-shearing at Carmel, sent ten of his young men to greet him in his name, and to desire of him a present, and left it optional with Nabal as to what the present should be. "Give, I pray thee, whatever cometh to thy hand, unto thy servants and to thy son David." He had a right to demand a present of Nabal for the kindness he had shown him, and the essential service he and his men had given. David's kindness had been of more advantage than the service of any of those who were being honored by Nabal at his feast. Nabal, in a harsh and surly manner, told David's ten messengers that he would not give their master presents; that he knew better than to give his provisions to a contemptible fugitive from his master such as David was. "Who is David? and who is the son of Jesse? There be many servants, now-a-days, that break away every man from his master." Now, the request that had been made of him was a very just and reasonable one, and the manner in which it was refused was a very gross insult. No wonder, indeed, that his own servants said of him, "He is such a son of Belial, that one cannot speak to him." The messengers went back and informed David of the treatment they had received, and David at once rashly resolved that he would put Nabal and all his family, and all that he had, to the sword, that others might be deterred from acting toward him as Nabal had. He would have executed his purpose in this matter, but for the prudence, caution and kindness of Abigail, Nabal's wife. One of Nabal's young men reported to Abigail the manner in which David's messengers had been treated. He referred her to the fact that David had rendered very valuable assistance to their master Nabal, in that he was a "wall unto them by day and by night, while they were with him keeping the sheep." The young man then urged her to take some course, if possible, to appease the wrath of David, occasioned by the insult offered him by Nabal.

Abigail made haste and prepared a present, consisting of two hundred loaves, and two bottles of wine, five sheep ready dressed, and five measures of parched corn, and a hundred clusters of raisins, and two hundred cakes of figs; and she then bade her servants go on quickly and meet David, and tell him of her approach. All this she did without the knowledge of her churlish husband. She met David and disarmed his rage, and won his feelings and affections, and thereby saved David spilling the blood of Nabal, and killing his innocent household. Abigail then went home. Nabal was still engaged in the feast, and having indulged in wine to drunkenness, she could not tell him that day how narrowly he had escaped death, but the next morning when he was sober, she told him these things. She portrayed the danger into which his conduct had brought himself and family. Nabal had not thought by refusing David to provoke him to anger, and that he had it in his power to injure him; and when his wife reported to him the manner in which she had appeased his wrath, and stayed David from slaying him, "Nabal's heart died within him, and became as a stone." He was thunderstruck; terrified in a very great degree at what he had done, and how he and his family had escaped destruction. Fear overcame Nabal, and he became insensible. He was thrown into severe sickness, of which in ten days he died. See 1st Sam. xxv.

NABOTH—[Na'-both,] *words, propheccies, fruits.*

NABOTH was a Jezreelite, or rather an Israelite of the city of Jezreel. He was probably a man of considerable wealth, for he had a very fine garden not far from the palace of Ahab, the king. This garden or vineyard had often attracted the attention of Ahab and he desired to own it—he wished to possess it for a kitchen garden, or as he calls it, a garden of herbs. He did not wish to take it from Naboth without compensating him for it; he proposed to give him the value of it in money. This request seems at first view to be fair and honorable, and moreover reasonable, that Naboth should accommodate the king by selling it or exchanging it for another vineyard. Naboth objected to it, because there was a prohibition in the divine law to alienating an inheritance. Hence he answered Ahab's proposal in the following language, "God forbid that I should give the inheritance of my father's to thee." Indeed it was out of the power of an Israelite finally and forever to alienate the inheritance that came to him from his parents. He might sell or mortgage it till the jubilee year, but then it must revert to the original owners if not redeemed before. Lev. xxv: 14, 17, 25, 28.

Ahab was displeased at Naboth that he refused him the garden, and went to his house with a heavy heart, dispirited and sorrowful; he even refused to eat bread. Jezebel his wife became greatly concerned about him, and asked him what it was that ailed him, "why is thy spirit so sad that thou eatest no bread?" and he told her how he desired the vineyard of Naboth, and had offered him money for it, or another vineyard; but that the man had utterly refused. She reproached him as the king of Israel for giving such demonstrations of feeling over such a matter. She told him as he was the king of Israel he should not be troubled thus—she bade him make himself easy and she would see to it, that the vineyard of Naboth should be given him. She accordingly wrote letters in Ahab's name and placed on them the signet of the kingdom of Israel, and then sent the letters to the elders and nobles of the city of Jezreel. She bade them proclaim a fast and set Naboth on high among the people, and then set two wicked men to bear witness against Naboth, accusing him of blaspheming God and the king—condemn him by those witnesses and then carry him out of the city and stone him to death. These wicked and abandoned rulers executed her orders. Having set him on high, they brought the charge of treason and blasphemy against him, then condemned him and carrying him without the city, they stoned him with stones that he died.

Having done this, it is likely they destroyed the whole of his family, so that the inheritance had no longer an heir. When Jezebel found that Naboth was stoned and dead, she bade the king arise and take possession of the vineyard, and he did so. But God remembered this wicked conduct of Ahab and Jezebel against them, and His vengeance as the Almighty God pursued them, and dogs licked the blood of Ahab at the place where Naboth was slain, and as for Jezebel, she was thrown down from a window and the horses trod upon her, and the dogs ate her flesh by the wall of Jezreel. See 1st Kings, xxi; 2d Kings, ix: 10 37.

**NADAB**, 1—[Na′-dab,] *free and voluntary gift, prince.*

NADAB was a son of Aaron and the brother of Abihu. Being the sons of Aaron they acted in the sacred office of the priesthood. The fact of their offering up strange fire unto the Lord, and of their sudden and strange death, is narrated in Lev. x. They violated the divine injunctions in some way in the performance of their work. It is said "they took either of them his censer and put fire therein, and put incense thereon, and offered strange fire before the Lord, which he commanded them not. And there went out a fire from the Lord and devoured them, and they died before the Lord." Why they used strange or common fire instead of sacred, we cannot tell; but from the instructions that immediately followed, we are disposed to think that they had been indulging in the use of strong drink, the consequence of which was their understanding was not clear—their judgment was not correct—they were not capable of discerning between clean and unclean—pure and impure.

It was soon known to Aaron that Nadab and Abihu had sinned, and that God had punished their sin with death; and though they were his own children he dare not murmur or complain. He acknowledged by his silence the justness of the divine power thus made known so terribly. Moses gave orders to two of the priests, Mishael and Elzaphan, the sons of Uzziel, to go and take charge of the dead bodies, and carry them without the camp that they might be buried.

After Nadab and Abihu had been taken out and buried, the Lord gave Moses and Aaron further instructions regarding the sanctity of the priest's office. He charged Aaron not to drink wine or strong drink, he nor his sons, when they went out into the tabernacle of the congregation, lest they die as those two had died. They were to put a difference between clean and unclean, holy and unholy.

NADAB, 2—*free and voluntary gift, prince.*

NADAB was a king of Israel. He was the son and successor of Jeroboam. 1st Kings, xiv : 20 ; xv : 25, &c. He began to reign over Israel in the second year of Asa, king of Judah, and reigned but two years. Nadab walked all through his reign in the sins of Jeroboam, his father. He was slain by Baasha at Gibbethon, a city in the tribe of Dan. Baasha not only smote Nadab, but he smote all the house of Jeroboam. According to the saying of Ahijah, the Shibonite, God made one wicked man to slay another. 1st Kings, xiv : 10–14.

NAHARAI—[Na-har′-i,] *my nostrils, hoarse, hot,*

The Beerothite, was one of David's mighty men. 2d Sam. xxiii : 37.

NAHASH, 1—[Na′-hash,] *snake, one that foretells, brass.*

NAHASH was a king of the Ammonites. 1st Sam. xi. It is said he came up and encamped against Jabesh-Gilead. When the inhabitants of the city saw them they were affrighted, for they saw they were in no condition to enter on a war with Nahash, and hence they made a proposition to enter on a course of servitude to him. They said : "Make a covenant with us and we will serve thee." Nahash agreed to it, on the condition that they would submit each one to have his right eye thrust out, to be a standing badge of their slavery, and a means of incapacitating them from serving as soldiers. "He who opposes his shield with his left hand, thereby hides his left eye, and looks at the enemy with his right eye. They, therefore, who pluck out that right eye, make men useless in war." This was a very cruel condition, and no wonder they were slow to agree to it. They asked a respite of seven days, when they agreed to give him an answer as to the course they would take. They sent their messengers all through the kingdom and inquired if there was no help for them. The messengers went to Gibeah of Saul, the place where Saul lived, and told their sorrowful tale in the hearing of the people, and, deeply sympathizing with the people of Jabesh-Gilead, those of Gibeah wept. Saul was coming out of the field after the herd, and he asked what ailed the people that they wept; and they told him the tidings that had come from Jabesh-Gilead—that Nahash had besieged the city and and offered them the humbling conditions of a covenant, that of putting out the right eye of each one. It is said that the Spirit of God came upon Saul. He felt himself strongly excited to attempt their relief. He felt that he ought to espouse their cause, and that if he did he would have success. He hewed a yoke of oxen in pieces, and sent them in pieces thoughout all the coasts of Israel, thereby calling the warriors together, to defend their brethren. The people heard the call and came out with one consent. They rendezvoused in Bezek to the number of three hundred and fifty thousand men, marshalled under Saul for battle, and putting the army in three companies or divisions, he marched all night, and came to the camp of the Ammonites about daybreak and slew them, and so delivered the inhabitants of Jabesh-Gilead, as the Ammonites "were scattered so that two of them were not left together." It is quite likely that Nahash escaped, and it may be he was the same person who afterwards showed kindness to David. He is referred to as the king of Ammon and the father of Hanun, to whom David showed kindness for his father's sake. 2d Sam. x : 2.

NAHASH, 2.—Same as Jesse.

NAHATH, 1—[Na′-hath.]

Was the eldest son of Reuel, who was Esau's son by Bashemath. There are three others, named who were brothers of Nahath, viz: Zerah, Shammah and Mizzah, they are called the sons of Bashemath, Esau's wife, because they were the sons of Reuel her son. Gen. xxxvi: 13.

NAHATH, 2.

Was of the tribe of Levi, and in the line of priests from Aaron to the captivity. 1st Chron. vi: 26.

NAHBI—[Nah'-bi.]

Was of the tribe of Naphtali, and was selected by Moses as one of the twelve spies to search and examine the nature and state of the land of Canaan. Num. xiii: 14.

NAHOR—[Na'hor,] *hoarse, hot, angry.*

NAHOR was the son of Terah, and the brother of Abraham. He lived at Haran, in Messopotamia. Sometimes the place where he lived is called after him, or by his name. Eleazar is reported to have stopped at the city of Nahor, when seeking a wife for Isaac, from among his master's kindred.

He married Milcah, the daughter of his brother Haran. Gen. xi: 29. This was not as near a relation as his brother Abraham married, for he married Sarai, the daughter of his father Terah. Nahor had a numerous progeny. Having eight sons by his wife Milcah, and he had four sons by his concubine Reumah. Huz was his firstborn, and is supposed to have been the father of Huzites. Buz the second son, is thought to have been the father of the Buzites, from whom Elihu was descended. Kemuel, who is called the father of Aram, is thought to have been the father of the Arameans or Syrians, and Chesed was the father of at least one tribe of the Chaldeans. So others of his children were supposed to have been the heads of large families. Gen. xxii: 20.

NAHSHON—[Na'shon,] *that foretells, serpent.*

NAHSHON was the son of Amminadab, of the tribe of Judah. He was the chief of that tribe, and was associated with Moses and Aaron in arranging the business of the nation at the time of their exodus from the land of Egypt. Numbers, i: 7. And when the tabernacle was fully set up, he made an offering for his tribe. Numbers, vii: 12.

NAHUM, [Na'-hum,] *comforter, penitent, their guide.*

NAHUM was one of the lesser prophets of the city of Elkoshai, and the author of the book of prophecies that bears his name. He flourished about seven hundred and thirteen years before Christ.

In his prophecies he speaks of the Assyrian ravages of Egypt and the destruction of the populous city of No. Nahum, iii: 8. He represents the Assyrian king as imagining an evil thing against the Lord. It is thought from the prophecies contained in Nahum, i: 9–11, and iii: 9–10, that he uttered those prophecies just at the time that Sennacherib was returing from the conquest of Egypt. But there is no certainty as regards this. He gives a very grand description of God in his first chapter, and of the armies against Nineveh, and the fall of that city, in the second and last chapters. And many of those predictions have been fulfilled to the very letter.

NAOMI—[Na-o'-mi,] *beautiful, agreeable.*

NAOMI was the wife of Elimelech who lived in Bethlehem Judah, in the land of Judah, and she was the mother of two sons Mahlon and Chilion. Ruth i: 2. Because of a famine in the land, Elimelech with his wife and sons went to sojourn in the country of Moab. They had not been in Moab long until the husband and father died; thus Naomi was left a widow. She was called to bury her companion among strangers, and with her two sons in loneliness to weep over his grave. After the days of mourning for her husband were over, she married her two sons to Moabitish women, the names of which were Orpah and Ruth. In about ten years both of these sons of the widow died. and with a crushed heart she buried them beside her husband, and resolved desolate, and alone as she was, to go back again to her own land, for she had heard that the Lord "had visited his people in giving them bread." As the famine was ended, and there was plenty in the land of Judea, she thought it better, being a widow and childless, to return to her own people, let them know of her affliction, and demand of them sympathy and help. She made known her determination to her daughters-in-law; and after an affectionate parting with Orpah, accompanied by Ruth she returned, and arrived safely in Bethlehem, the town of her former residence.

Naomi was extensively known, and highly respected when a resident there, and her arrival was soon noised abroad. Her former friends came to see her and learn from her own lips the tale of her sufferings—the bitter dealings of the Almighty with her. They looked with astonishment upon her thin and pale visage, her feeble and emaciated form. They looked upon her poverty and distress, and said one to another in low whispers, for they did not wish to open the wound in her womanly heart afresh: "Is this Naomi." She overheard them, and with deep emotion said: "Call me not Naomi, (i. e., pleasant,) call me Mara, (i. e., bitter,) for the Almighty hath dealt very bitterly with me. When I left you I had an affectionate companion and husband, and two noble sons, but the three are dead. I went out full, but the Lord hath brought me home again empty."

Naomi began her residence in Bethlehem with Ruth, as her companion in poverty. Soon, however, fortune favored her. The God who had afflicted her smiled upon her. The kindred of Elimelech noticed, and pitied and helped. Soon Boaz married Ruth, and so provided Naomi with a comfortable and pleasant home. The clouds in her sky were scattered, and the evening of her life was made calm and pleasant. She lived to see her daughter-in-law the mother of a son, and she took that son as her own kinsman, and "laid it in her own bosom, and became nurse unto it." Ruth iv: 16.

NAPHISH—[Na′-fish,] *the soul, he that refreshes himself, that respires; in Syriac, that multiplies.*

He was the son of Ishmael, and the grand-son of Abraham. Genesis xxv: 15.

NAPHTALI,—[Naf′-ta-ly,] *comparison, likeness, that fights.*

NAPHTALI was one of the sons of Jacob by Bilhah, the handmaid of Rachel, and he was the head of one of the twelve tribes of Israel. The names of his sons are given in Genesis, xlvi: 24. They were Jahzeel, Guni, Jezer and Shillem, all of whom were the heads of a numerous progeny.

The prophetic blessing of his father upon him is given in Gen. xlix: 21. "Naphtali is a hind let loose, he giveth goodly words." It may be intended to set forth the activity and courtesy of that tribe. There is another translation which renders the passage thus, "Naphtali is a tree shot out, bringing forth goodly branches." This would be calculated to set forth the fertility and increase of that tribe.

When the tribe of Naphtali went out of Egypt they had fifty-three thousand four hundred fighting men, who were under the command of Ahira, the son of Enan. Num. i: 15–43. The tribe decreased while they were in the wilderness, several thousand, for they only numbered forty-five thousand four hundred, when the sum of the children of Israel was taken in the plains of Moab. Numbers, xxvi: 50.

Their spy to search the land was Nahbi, the son of Vophsi. Numbers, xiii: 14. And their agent to divide the land and secure them their inheritance, was Pedahel, the son of Ammihud. Numbers, xxxiv: 28. Their inheritance was a rich one, for their land was very fertile.

But in their inheritance they permitted the Canaanites to retain Bethanath and Bethshemesh, two of their cities, on the condition that they would pay tribute to them. The Canaanites continued in possession of these two cities, but were tributaries to the tribe of Naphtali. Judges, i: 33.

They seemed to be associated as a tribe, intimately with the tribe of Zebulun, and when Deborah arose "a mother" and a deliverer of Israel, from the hand and power of Jabin, king of Canaan, she called Barak, the Naphtali general, and he came up to her help, and undertook the work with her, and he brought with him ten thousand warriors of Naphtali and Zebulun. They fought with distinguished bravery and conquered Jabin. Judges, iv.

When Gideon fought with the Midianites and the children of the east, and conquered them, the descendants of Naphtali associated with other tribes at the request of Gideon, pursued the

Midianites, and so helped to make the victory complete. Judges, vii: 23.

At the coronation of David, thirty-seven thousand of the tribe of Naphtali assisted, under the command of a thousand captains, and it is said that when they came they did not intend to be chargeable to David or the nation for subsistance, for they brought great quantities of provisions with them.

There are but two persons of very distinguished note that we know of in this tribe. One we have mentioned, Deborah's general. The other was Hiram, the artificer, and assistant of king Solomon in the building of the temple. It is said of this Hiram, 1st Kings. vii: 14, "He was a widow's son, of the tribe of Naphtali, and his father was a man of Tyre." We have an account of their country being terribly ravaged by Benhadad, the king of Syria, in 1st Kings, xv: 20. In 2d Kings, xv: we have an account of many of them being carried captives by Tilgath-Pileser, king of Assyria. Their country became idolatrous, but Josiah in his reformation cleansed it.

While the Savior was here on earth, and preaching his own gospel, he, with his disciples, resided a part of the time and preached in the land of Naphtali. Matthew, iv: 13. "He dwelt in Capernaum, which is upon the sea coast, in the borders of Zebulun and Naphtali."

NAPHTUHIM—[Naf'-tu-him.]

NAPHTUHIM was the fourth son of Mizraim. Genesis, x: 13. It is supposed that the family of Naphtuhim was extensive, though it is not certainly known where they settled, who they were, or by what name they were called.

NARCISSUS—[Nar-sis'sus,] *astonishment.*

NARCISSUS was probably a disciple, whose household were also converts to christianity. The household is referred to by the apostle Paul in his epistle to the Romans, xvi: 11, "Greet them which be of the household of Narcissus, which are in the Lord." He has been thought to be of the number of the seventy disciples, and to have become a noted preacher of the gospel, and a martyr for the cause of Christ. Indeed the Greeks suppose him to have been a bishop of the church at Athens.

NATHAN, 1—[Na'than,] *who gives, or is given.*

NATHAN was a prophet of considerable fame, who flourished in the time of David, and had a place in the confidence and esteem of that king. He was a prophet in Israel at the time David ascended the throne, and in 2d Samuel, vii: 3, we have an account of his commending David for his intention of building a temple to the Lord. David addressing himself to Nathan, said: "See now I dwell in a house of cedar, but the ark of God dwelleth within curtains." The prophet was pleased with the suggestion of the king, and gave him encouragement, not as a prophet, but as a pious man. He was not under the divine afflatus, or actuated by the divine spirit. He said to David, "Do all that is in thy heart, for the Lord is with thee." He thereby encouraged David to the important undertaking without waiting for divine instruction. It was not long after this until he was divinely instructed to forbid this work he had encouraged. He received a message from God, to the effect that David should not build the house, but that his son, who should come after him, should build it, and he told these words of the Lord unto David, and in 1st Chronicles, xxii: 8, there is the additional reason given: David had shed blood abundantly, and had been a man of wars.

Some time after this, when David had sinned against God, by defiling Bathsheba, and murdering her husband, who was one of the officers in the army, this prophet reproved David for the great sin he had committed, and his reproof was administered by a parable of a man who had a great many flocks of his own. But when his friend came to visit him, and he desired a lamb for a repast, he went and took from a poor neighbor, an only lamb, and dressed and prepared it to entertain his friend.

David little thinking he was about to condemn himself, was very angry against the man who had thus treated his poor neighbor, and quickly said to Nathan, "As the Lord liveth, the man that hath done this thing shall surely die; and he shall restore the lamb fourfold, because he did this thing and had no pity." Nathan then as a prophet of God emboldened, by the spirit of inspiration, said to David, "Thou art the man." He thereby declared the king a guilty criminal, and the one intended to be represented by the parable he had just delivered. For he, though the ruler of all Israel, who had several wives of his own—had defiled the only wife of Uriah the Hittite and in addition to that crime had virtually murdered the man, by sending word to Joab his general to put him in the forefront of the battle and retire from him that he might be smitten. The consequence of this sin on the part of David was that God determined severely to punish him, and so Nathan the prophet assured him. David made an humble acknowledgement of his sin, and Nathan was commanded to say to him, "The Lord also hath put away thy sin; thou shalt not die." The king of Israel dare not to object to the rebuke Nathan had given him, but while he humbled himself before the Lord he honored the prophet, and it seems that he named one of his own children after him, one born unto him by Bathsheba after she became his wife. 1st Chron. iii: 5.

When he was very aged and infirm, Adonijah made an attempt to settle himself upon the throne of Israel. In his attempt to usurp authority he took with him Joab, David's general, and Abiathar, who had been his priest. Nathan brought the intelligence to Bathsheba that Adonijah had been crowned king, and was already reigning. Nathan at once adopted a plan of informing David and reminding him of his oath and promise that Solomon should reign after him. He bade Bathsheba go in unto the king and inform him and remind him of his promise to her, and he agreed while she was yet talking to the king, he would come in and confirm her words. She accordingly went in and began to unfold these things to David, and about the time she had concluded Nathan came in and set the matter before him. David determined at once to set Soldmon on the throne, and he gave orders to have arrangements made at once for his coronation, and entrusted the authority to crown Solomon king, to Zadok the priest and Nathan the prophet, and Benaiah the general. He gave orders to blow the trumpet and say "God save King Solomon." Nathan in company with Zadok anointed Solomon king in Gibeon. See 1st Kings, i.

Nathan, in company with the prophet Gad, wrote the history of David; and who can we suppose was better prepared to write it than he was, having been with him through his reign, and having been his especial confidant.

As the last part of the first book of Samuel and the second book contain the history of David, it is probable Nathan wrote them. And he and Abijah wrote the history of Solomon. 1st Chron. xxix: 29: "The acts of King David, first and last, behold, they are written in the book of Samuel, the seer, and in the book of Nathan, the prophet, and in the book of Gad, the seer." 2d Chron. ix: 29: "The acts of Solomon, first and last, are they not written in the book of Nathan, the prophet," &c.

It is possible that he was the Nathan who was the father of Azariah and Zabud, who were officers in the kingdom of Solomon. 1st Kings, iv: 5.

NATHAN, 2—*Who gives, or is given.*

He was one of the sons of David, born unto him in Jerusalem of Bathsheba. Hence he was the full brother of King Solomon. 1st Chronicles, iii: 5.

NATHANAEL—[Na-than′-a-el,] *The gift of God.*

NATHANAEL was a disciple of Christ, who is referred to in John, i: 45, &c. He seems to have been brought to Christ through the influence of Philip.

When he was coming for the first time into the presence of Jesus, and he saw him he saith unto those about him, as he pointed to Nathanael: "Behold an Israeliie indeed, in whom is no guile." Nathanael seemed somewhat astonished that Jesus knew him, and asked him: "Whence knowest thou me?" Jesus let him know that he saw him when engaged at his devotions in his bower of prayer; "Before Philip called thee when thou wast under the fig tree, I saw thee." The good man at once aknowledged him as the son of God, the king of Israel. He was truly converted to the Christian religion, and listened with intense interest to Jesus as he assured him that he was blind because of his faith, and that he should see in the future greater things than he had seen. "Ye shall see Heaven open and the angels of God ascending and descending upon the Son of Man." We can not well suppress the conviction that Jesus had reference, in his conversation with Nathaniel, to the dream of Jacob.

Many have supposed Nathanael to be the same as Bartholomew, since the evangelists who mention the one do not mention the other. John informs us that Nathanael was a witness of Christ's resurrection from the dead, in company with Peter, Thomas, James and John, at the seaside. John, xxi: 1, 2.

NEARIAH, 1—[Ne-a-ri′-ah.]

One of the six sons of Shemaiah, in the line of the royal family of Judah, after the Babylonian captivity. 1st Chron. iii: 22.

NEARIAH, 2.

A son of Ishi, and one of the captains of the five hundred Simeonites, who in the days of Hezekiah drove the Amalekites away from Mt. Seir. 1st Chron. iv: 42.

NEBAI—[Ne-ba-i.]

He was the head of an important family who signed the covenant with Nehemiah. Neh. x: 19.

NEBAIOTH — [Ne-ba′-yoth,] *prophecies, fruits.*

NEBAIOTH was the oldest son of Ishmael. He was one of the twelve sons, whose names are given in Gen. xxv: 13, &c. He was a prince and a chief of a large tribe. The Nebatheans sprung from him, and they are said to have been the most civilized tribe of the Arabians, and the most friendly to the Jews. In Isa. lx, we have prophecies setting forth the conversion of the Gentiles, and the descendants of Nebaioth are referred to in the following language: "All the flocks of Kedar shall be gathered together unto thee; the rams of Nebaioth shall minister unto thee; they shall come up with acceptance on thine altar, and I will glorify the house of my glory." The descendants of this person were no doubt converted to Christ.

NEBAJOTH—[Ne-ba′-joth.]

Was the eldest son Ishmael, and he is referred to with his brothers, whose names are as follows: Kedar, Adbeel, Mibsam, Mishma, Dumah, Massá, Hadar, Tema, Jetur, Naphish and Kedemah. Gen. xxv: 13—15.

NEBAT—[Ne′-bat,] *that beholds.*

NEBAT was the father of Jeroboam, the first king of Israel, and he under whom the ten tribes revolted from Rehoboam and the house of David. Nebat was of the tribe of Ephraim, and the descendant of Joshua. 1st Kings xi: 26; and we suppose that he died while Jeroboam was a child, for it is said of Jeroboam that he was the servant of Solomon, and his mother Zeruah was a widow woman.

NEBO—[Ne′-bo,] *that speaks, prophesies, or fructifies.*

NEBO is referred to in Isa. xlvi: 1, as an idol of the Chaldeans, "stooping" or bowing before God, and the worship of the idol failing before the worship of the true God. The name is compounded with the names of princes, kings, and great men of Chaldea.

NEBUCHADNEZZAR—[Neb-u-kad-nez′zar,] *tears and groans of judgment.*

NEBUCHADNEZZAR was the great king of Babylon. He is first referred to in 2d Chronicles, xxxvi: 6, as coming up against Jehoiakim, king of Judah. He bound the king with fetters, and carried him to Babylon. He took the sacred vessels of the house of the Lord in Jerusalem, and carried them also to Babylon, and put them into the idolatrous temple, where they remained for many years; for when Belshazzar had his feast, he brought those vessels out, and his wives and concubines drank wine in them. Dan.

v: 2. Jehoiakim ascended the throne when his father was deposed by Nebuchadnezzar, but he was only allowed to reign three months and ten days, when he too was carried captive to Babylon, and Nebuchadnezzar appointed Zedekiah, the brother of Jehoiakim, and set him on the throne of Judah and Jerusalem. 2d Chronicles, xxxvi: 10.

He carried many captives to Babylon, among whom were Daniel, Hananiah, Mishael and Azariah, who were princes of Judah, and there were many others of rank taken captives at the same time.

But the four young men had names given unto them in exchange for their Jewish names. They were called Belteshazzar, Shadrach, Meshech and Abednego, which names import connection with their idol gods.

Nebuchadnezzar caused those, with other captive princes, to be trained in all the learning of the Chaldeans, that they might serve in the court. He bade Ashpenaz, the master of his servants, take such of the princes of Judah as had no blemish, and were well favored and skillful in all wisdom, and cunning in knowledge, and understanding science, and such as had ability to stand in the king's palace, whom they might teach the learning and the tongue of Chaldea. He appointed them a daily provision of the king's meat and wine for the space of three years. Dan. i: 3.

During the second year of Nebuchadnezzar's reign, he had a singular dream which occasioned him much trouble. He was so greatly troubled that he could not sleep. But what troubled him so greatly was, the dream had gone from him and he could not call it up. He assembled his wise men, the magicians, and the astrologers, and the sorcerers, and the Chaldeans, and demanded of them to show him his dream. They told him it was impossible for them to tell him the dream; but if he would tell it to them, they would show him the interpretation thereof. But the king told them it was gone from him and he could not tell them, and that they must call it up and tell it to him, else they "should be cut in pieces and their houses should be made a dung-hill," and he promised them, if they did succeed, they should receive of him gifts, rewards and great honor. They ventured to expostulate with him, "Let the king tell his servants the dream and we will tell the interpretation thereof." He reiterated his threat, and told them he would not swerve from the decree he had uttered. But they ventured to urge the matter once more before the king, and, feeling that their lives were in imminent peril, they said, "There is not a man upon the earth that can show the king's matter; therefore there is no king's lord nor ruler that asks such things of any magician, astrologer or Chaldean; none other can show it unto the king except the gods, whose dwelling is not with flesh." The king became angry at their words and commanded them to be slain at once, and the decree of Nebuchadnezzar would have been executed had not Daniel interfered. He asked and obtained leave to tell the king the dream and the interpretation thereof. He went unto the three captives, Hananiah, Mishael and Azariah, and made the fact known unto them that he had undertaken this matter, and he asked them to pray to the God of Heaven to reveal unto him the secret, that he and they and the wise men of Babylon might have their lives spared, for Nebuchadnezzar had determined to destroy them all. They attended to his request, and that night in a vision the lost dream was recovered, and Daniel was prepared to tell the king the dream and the interpretation. Daniel at once reported himself to Arioch and asked him to spare the wise men, for he was now prepared to meet the king's wishes.

Arioch took Daniel into the presence of Nebuchednezzar, and he asked him art "thou able to make known unto me the dream and the interpretation thereof?" He modestly answered: There is a God in heaven, that revealeth secrets, and maketh known unto the king the interpretation of his dream, or, "telleth what shall be in the latter days." He fully satisfied Nebuchednezzar as to the dream, insomuch that the king fell on his face before Daniel and worshiped. And he ordered an offering or oblation of sweet odors unto Daniel as though he were a God. He acknowledged the God of Daniel to be the God of Gods, and the Lord of Lords. Nebuchednezzar then gave orders that Daniel should be ruler over the whole province of Babylon. He made him a great man, and gave him many gifts, and in addition to promoting Daniel, he promoted his three friends, making them subordinate governors. Daniel ii: 49.

Nebuchadnezzar in about the twentieth year of his reign, having amassed a large amount of gold, in his various expeditions and conquests, and from those who were tributary to him, 2d Kings xxiv: 10–17, 2d Chronicles xxxvi, Daniel iii: and Ezek xxi: made a massive image to his God Belus and he erected it in the plains of Dura in his province, It is said to have been ninety feet high and nine feet broad, composed of gold. After he erected it he called together his princes, governors, judges, captains and other officers and dedicated the idol, and in connection with the dedication ceremonies he issued a decree that every one in his kingdom should fall down on his knees and face and worship this image. He proclaimed that there should be a concert of music by cornet, flute, sackbut, psaltery, dulcimer, &c. It should sound in the ears of all, and at its sound, the image should be worshiped, and whoever refused should be cast into the burning fiery furnace.

The Hebrew children were reported as not obeying the proclamation, but refusing to worship the idol; Nebuchadnezzar called them to him and interrogated them as to it, and they freely acknowledged that they had not obeyed his decree, and more than that they boldly declared that they would not worship the image, and though they knew what the penalty was, they expressed to the king the confidence that they had in their God, that he would deliver them even from the burning fiery furnace. Nebuchadnezzar became very much enraged at their language and ordered his servants to heat the furnace to a sevenfold degree, and then bind them and cast them bound into it. The furnace was so hot that the flames consumed those who cast them in. They were burnt to death in their attempt to execute the king's decree of casting the Hebrews into the furnace; but though the flames were so hot, and the Hebrews were cast into it, yet were they delivered. The son of God appeared in human form and walked with them through the fire. The fire was allowed to consume their bonds; but a hair of their head was not singed, neither did the smell of fire pass upon their garments.

It was not long until the king saw them walking through the fire unharmed, and was astonished and addressing his counselors said, "Lo! I see four men walking, and the fourth is like the son of God." He then called Shadrach, Meshech and Abednego to come forth from the midst of the furnace, and they came forth and stood in the presence of the king. Nebuchadnezzar then blessed their God and sent forth a decree that every people, nation and language should no longer speak against the God of Shadrach, Meshach and Abednego; if they did they should be cut in pieces, and their house should be made a dunghill, and the reason he gave for this decree was, there is no God that can deliver after this sort. These three Hebrews were again promoted in the province of Babylon to important offices. Dan. iii: Soon after this Nebuchadnezzar engaged in wars which are referred to in Jer. xxv; Isa. xxiii; Ezek. xxv.

In the thirty-fifth year of his reign his kingdom had reached its hight, and the astonishing structures of the capital were completed, and Nebuchadnezzar, in the pride of his heart, said: "Is this not great Babylon that I have built?"

He had a dream that troubled him, and he desired to have it interpreted. He saw a tall and flourishing tree laden with delicious fruit, and the tree was a place of refuge for birds and beasts out of number; and yet, all at once, orders were given by an angel to hew the tree down, shake off its fruits and leaves, but leave the stump, and fasten the roots in the ground as if with a band of iron and brass, for seven years, that it might be wet with the dew of heaven and have its portion with the beasts of the field in the grass of the earth. After the king had laid the dream before Daniel he asked him to declare the interpretation, since the spirit of the holy gods was in him; and he could interpret dreams when all the other wise men failed. And, furthermore, Nebuchadnezzar bade him tell it, whatever the interpretation was, for he probably saw that there was something in it that troubled him. He then told him that it meant that for seven long years he, the king of Babylon, should be reduced to the condition of a beast, and be driven from human society, until his nails should become as birds' claws and the hair of his head as eagles' feathers, and that, after the acknowledgement on his part of the divine supremacy, he should be restored to his kingdom and his throne. And Daniel besought Nebuchadnezzar to break off from his sins and wickedness—to quit his unjust course of life, and show mercy to the poor Jewish captives that he had taken, who were now scattered about and doing service in his kingdom. But the king was regardless of the admonition, and continued as proud as ever. Again he looked upon the grandeur of the city, and, as he looked from the palace, or, possibly, from the hanging garden, and surveyed its greatness and glory, he said, (we suppose, in the hearing of his courtiers and attendants:) "Is not this great Babylon that I have built by the might of my power and for the honor of my majesty?" Just as these words escaped his lips, God condemned him. A voice from Heaven answered him, that he should be immediately driven from among men—that he should be lost to human society and should be as a beast. In accordance with the declaration, he was struck with a kind of madness in which it is thought he fancied himself a beast and imitated one in action. His friends stood around him astonished, and, finding it necessary in order to prevent his doing injury, bound him; but he broke the bonds and escaped out of their hands, and, on escaping, fled to the fields and there, according to the prediction of Daniel in interpreting the dream, he lived for seven years on the grass of the field, without clothing.

At the end of the seven years he was restored to reason, when he humbled himself before God, and ordered the account of his dream and the striking fulfillment of it to be made a matter of clear record. He glorified God by an acknowledgment of his pride that had been so signally punished, and wished all his subjects to know about it and profit by it.

During the time he was thus incapacitated for governing, his son, Evil Merodach, ruled in the kingdom. But as soon as Nebuchadnezzar was restored it is said he cast his son into prison to punish him for his follies and weakness, or else he found it necessary to do so in order to restore his kingdom to peace and quiet. It is said he cast him into the same prison that Jehoiakim had laid in for thirty-six years. Dan. iv.

About a year after this Nebuchadnezzar died, it is thought in the forty-third or forty-fourth year of his reign. After his death it is probable Evil Merodach was taken from prison and ascended the throne; but after occupying it two years died or was murdered. Belshazzar, his son, succeeded him, and reigned until the Chaldean empire closed.

NEBUZARADAN — [Neb-u-zar′-a-dan,] *fruits or prophecies of judgment, winnowed, spread.*

NEBUZARADAN was the general of the armies of Nebuchadnezzar. We have an account in 2d Kings, xxv: 8, &c., of his leading the army successfully against Jerusalem, burning the house of the Lord and the king's house, and breaking down the walls of the city and carrying away into Babylon such of the Jews as had been marked for captivity, while he left the poor of the land to be vine-dressers and husbandmen. He broke the pillars of the temple in pieces and carried the gold and silver, and brass, and vessels of the house of the Lord, to Babylon; and he took Seraiah, the chief priest, and Zephaniah, the second priest, and the three keepers of the door. He also took the officer that was set over the men of war, and five of the king's body-guard, and the king's principal scribe, and sixty other men, and carried them to Babylon, and Nebuchadnezzar put them to death. But as we learn from Jer. xl: 1–6, he liberated Jeremiah the prophet. He took his chains from off him and gave him the privilege of going on with him to Babylon, or going back to Gedaliah, the son of Ahikam, the son of Shaphan, who had been appointed by Nebuchadnezzar governor over the cities of Judah, and he kindly apportioned to Jeremiah victuals, and let him go.

NECHO—[Ne′-ko,] *lame, who was beaten.*

[See Pharaoh-Necho.]

NEHEMIAH, 1—[Ne-he-mi′-ah,] *consolation, repentance, or rest of the Lord.*

NEHEMIAH was the son of Hachaliah, Neh. i: 1, and the author of the book that bears his name. It is supposed he was of the royal family of David. This thought may have arisen from the fact that he was the royal cupbearer in the Prussian court, and succeeded Zerubbabel in the government of the Jews. Like all the Jews who were in Babylon, he was deeply concerned about his native land, and especially about Jerusalem, the holy city, and when he was informed by Hanani, that Jerusalem was still in ruins, that the walls were broken down, and the gates were burned with fire, he was deeply affected. He sat down and wept, and mourned for several days. He fasted and prayed most devoutly. Neh. i: 4-11, He ask God that he might meet with favor in the eyes of the king of Persia, for whom he was cup-bearer. He had formed the intention of asking the king's permission to go and rebuild Jerusalem. He was careworn and sorrowful, but he still kept on in the discharge of his duty, and one day, while giving wine unto the king, his sad and sorrowful countenance attracted the attention of the king, and he asked him, "why is thy countenance sad, seeing thou art not sick?" (or excused from service.) The king wished to know why it was that he looked so sad, for his countenance indicated sorrow of heart. There was something about the king's language, or the manner in which he said it, that alarmed Nehemiah, but he answered the question by saying, "let the king live forever."

He then set forth before the king and his queen, who was sitting beside him, the cause of his sadness. The city and place of his fathers' sepulchers was lying waste, and the gates of the city were consumed with fire. The king then asked what he desired. He answered that he desired to be sent to Judah and Jerusalem to build up the city.

His request was attended to and he was granted a respite from service in the court for the length of time he asked to accomplish the work, and the king empowered him with authority to go and rebuild the walls of Jerusalem. Having procured his letters of recommendation to the governors through whose territory he would pass, with orders that they should convey him on to Judah. The king also gave him a letter to Asaph, the keeper of the forests of Lebanon, with instructions that he should give Nehemiah timber to make beams for the gates of the palace which appertained to the house, and for the wall of the city, and for his own house.

When Nehemiah arrived at Jerusalem with the commission of the king, he and his servants went round the wall of the city in the night. He surveyed the ruins and saw clearly what a wonderful work was before him, but nothing daunted or discouraged, he assembled the chief of the Jews, and informed them of his intention, and of the powers with which he had been invested by the Persian king, and encouraged them to take hold vigorously with him, and to begin at once the work.

They saw that he was properly empowered, and readily agreed to his proposal. They said, "let us rise up and build; so they strengthened their hands for this good work." The different portions of the wall were assigned to the principal men as set forth in Nehemiah, iii. As soon as they had entered vigorously upon the work, Sanballat, the Horonite, and Tobiah, the Ammonite, opposed them. They were extremely vexed to think that the Jews would undertake to repair the walls of Jerusalem, and that they carried the work on with so much ardor. To discourage the Jews, they scoffed at them saying, "What do these feeble Jews? Will they fortify themselves? will they sacrifice? will they make an end in a day? will they revive the stones out of the heaps of the rubbish which are burned?" And Tobiah said that which they did build would be so weak and insecure, that even a fox passing over would break it down. When they found that they could not thus stop them or discourage them, the Arabians, Ammonites and Ashdodites, conspired against them, and came up against them to fight. They made several attempts to surprise and murder them whilst engaged in the work. Nehemiah placed a guard on the outside of the workmen, and required every builder to keep his sword by him, that he might quit the work of building, and be prepared to fight at the shortest notice. And the workmen kept on and ceased not until the work was finished. They never put off their clothes day or night, except for washing them, and Nehemiah was always with them, watching and ready to give the alarm, or the word of command, and he kept his trumpeter always with him, to sound the alarm at his command in time of danger. When Sanballat and Tobiah found they could not otherwise retard their progress in the work, they had recourse to a mean stratagem. Tobiah, some time before, had married the daughter of Shechariah, a prince of Judah, and had thereby secured the feelings of many of the Jews; and these Jews associated themselves with him to dispirit Nehemiah and his friends, but they could not succeed. At length they sent four letters to Nehemiah inviting him to a friendly conference with them in the plain of Ono. He sent them word back, that he was engaged in a great work, so that he could not come down—that if he did, the work would cease. Sanballat then wrote to him the fifth letter charging him with the design of rebelling, and causing himself to be made king. He denied the charge, and returned an answer, in which he expressed his convictions that they had been feigning desire for a friendly conference, when really they were aiming at his destruction. Which was true, for they had caused a party to lie in wait to murder him by the way.

They urged him to come and answer to the charge brought against him by Gashmu, and clear himself, if indeed he was clear; else the Persian king would hear of it and enquire of them, and they were unable to confute it. Nehemiah would not go, he was conscious of his innocence, therefore he resolved to trust in God, and hope that the king would not be turned against him by this report, if it should come to his ears.

When Sanballat and Tobiah found that they could not succeed thus against Nehemiah, they bribed the prophet Shemaiah, and the prophetess Noadiah, to murder Nehemiah, and thus prevent the work, and Shemaiah did impose on Nehemiah a little. He tried to get him to shut himself up with him in the temple or house of God at midnight, under the pretext that his enemies would come to kill him, and that would be the safest place; but Nehemiah utterly refused, and it was not long until he was satisfied that Shemaiah was not a true prophet, but was hired by his enemies against, him. Thus notwithstanding all that his enemies did against him he prospered, and went on with his work until it was finished. In fifty two days from the time the repairs were begun, it was ended. Neh. vi: 15.

About a year after the work was finished it was dedicated with solemn ceremonies; sacrifices and offerings were made unto God, and their thanksgivings were rendered. Neh. xii: 27-43.

After the wall was completed he took proper precaution in guarding the city gates. He reckons the people according to their genealogies and finds a complete register of those who came out of Babylon with Zerubbabel. He commenced at once rectifying disorders. He curbed the inhumanity of the nobles and princes and rich men, who held the lands of the poor men with mortgages, and held their children in slavery. He enters into a covenant with the priests and Levites and chiefs of the people, by which, with him they all solemnly promised not to have affinity with the people of the land. They promised to observe the Sabbath, to provide for the support of the sanctuary and its service according to law, and to pay the regular tithes for the support of the priests and Levites and other officers of the temple. Nehemiah then required one tenth of the people to come from their country residences and dwell within the city to guard it. The people of the country were all divided into companies of ten, and lots were cast to see which one of the ten should reside in the city. There were some of the people that willingly offered themselves to dwell in Jerusalem or volunteered rather, in the service of the city. It was an expression of patriotism on their part, that was highly lauded by the people, for "they blessed all the men that offered themselves to dwell at Jerusalem."

The feasts of trumpets and of tabernacles were observed with great care and exactness, and Ezra the scribe, with a sufficient number of helpers, read and explained the book of the law to the people. Immediately after this, Nehemiah cleansed the house of God and rectified various evils, among which was that of various Jews who had married heathen women, and one of the priests had married the daughter of Sanballat the Horonite. This man was expelled from office, and he required all of them to put away their strange wives. They acceded to his request, confessed their sins, renewed their covenants with God, and solemnly promised obedience to his law. They especially promised not to espouse or marry heathen women. They promised to hallow the Sabbath and buy no goods on that day; to observe the year of release, give their first fruits and firstlings to the Levites. They promised to allow this every year for the service of the temple. There were twenty-two priests, seventeen Levites and forty-four chief men of the people that subscribed to this covenant, while all the people about them declared their adherence. Neh. vii to xii.

In order to show himself a distinguished pattern of generosity, Nehemiah never required of the kingdom the salary prescribed him by the Persian king, but maintained himself and family on the products of his own fields, with the salary he had received as the king's cup-bearer.

After he had governed the Jews several years, he returned to King Artaxerxes and remained with him for a time, but was returned by him from Persia to Judea. It was during his absence that Tobiah had been allowed by the priest to fix his residence in Jerusalem and in a chamber of the house of the Lord. He drove him at once out of the house and threw his furniture out, and deposed the priest who had allowed the house to be thus desecrated.

After Nehemiah had governed in Jerusalem or with the Jews in all about thirty-six years, he died, having written the chief part of his own history as we have it in the book of Nehemiah.

NEHEMIAH, 2.—*Consolation, repentance, or rest of the Lord.*

NEHEMIAH, who is referred to in Ezra, ii: 2, is not the same as the one above, but was one of those who returned many years before with Zerubbabel from Babylon, under the decree of Cyrus, king of Persia, the object of which was particularly to build the house of the Lord God of Israel. Ezra, i: 3.

NEHUSHTA—[Ne-hush′-tah,] *snake, soothsayer.*

Was the daughter of Elnathan, of Jerusalem, and the mother of Jehoiakim. 2d Kings xxiv: 8.

NEMUEL, 1—[Nem-u′-el.]

Was the son of Eliab, and the brother of Dathan and Abiram. Num. xxvi: 9. And he belonged to the tribe of Reuben.

NEMUEL, 2.

Was of the tribe of Simeon, and the head of the family of that tribe called Nemuelites.

NEPHEG, 1—[Ne′-feg.]

NEPHEG, with Korah and Zichri, were the sons of Izhar, the son of Kohath, of the tribe of Levi. He, with his brothers, sustained the relation of cousin to Moses, Aaron and Miriam, as Amram was their uncle. Ex. vi: 21.

NEPHEG, 2.

Was one of the sons of David, born unto him in Jerusalem. 1st Chron. xiv: 6.

NER—*Lamp, brightness, land new tilled.*

Was the father of Abner, who was the general of Ishbosheth, the son of Saul. 2d Sam. ii: 12.

NERGAL—[Ner′-gal.]

Was the name of an idol of a tribe of the Chaldeans or Persians, viz: the Cuthites. 2d Kings xvii: 30. And we learn from Jer. xxxix: 3, that two of the generals of Nebuchadnezzar were named after this idol, Nergal-Sharezer.

NERIAH—[Ne-ri′-ah,] *light and lamp of the Lord.*

Was the father of Baruch, who was the scribe of Jeremiah, and attended him through much of his affliction. Jer. xxxvi: 4.

NERO—[Ne′-ro.]

Nero was a Roman emperor who ruled in the Apostolic age, from A.D. 54 to 68. He was an infamous, cruel man, one of the most wicked of all the Roman emperors. In the first part of his reign we are informed he was mild, and behaved with decency and justice, for he pretended a desire to copy after an illustrious predecessor, Augustus. But near the end of his reign he became very tyrannical and cruel—and he was guilty of some of the darkest deeds that ever disgraced the conduct and character of any man. Among those foul deeds was the cruel murder of his own mother, he also put to cruel torture and death many of his friends and important personages in his empire.

We have an account in Acts, xxv, of the apostle Paul appealing to Cesar, which was the appellation of Roman emperors. Nero was the emperor to whom he appealed, and before him he went to be tried; Nero does not condemn him; for the apostle is permitted to preach, and for two full years he continued at Rome proclaiming with great freedom the doctrines of the cross, and we may safely judge that he was instrumental in converting to the Christian religion some of the members of Nero's family or household—for in writing his epistle to the Philipians, which was written from Rome, and sent by Epaphroditus, he says, iv: 22. "All the saints salute you, chiefly they that are of Cesar's household." But Paul was brought before Nero the second time and was condemned to be beheaded, and about this time he wrote his second epistle to Timothy. In that epistle he gives a most solemn charge to his son in the gospel, in which charge he declares to Timothy "I am now ready to be offered up, and the time of my departure is at hand. I have fought a good fight," &c. It may be supposed that Nero was greatly enraged at Paul because that some of his own family had become Christians, and probably that was the reason why he was so severe in his persecutions of the apostles and christians. It is said he caused the city of Rome to be set on fire and like a fiend, sung while the flames were progressing, and the cries of the sufferers were rending the air. The Roman senate was outraged by him, and in order to appease their wrath he put the blame upon the innocent Christians—and he kept on persecuting them, putting them to all kinds of torture and cruel death. But he rendered himself intolerable to the senate and they declared him an enemy of Rome, when he feared their action regarding him and fled from the palace. They sought him to put him to death, and he to prevent this, committed self-murder.

NETHANEEL, 1 — [Ne-than′-e-el,] *the gift of God.*

Was the son of Zuar, of the tribe of Issachar. He was the chief of that tribe, and was associated with Moses and Aaron in managing the business of the nation at the time of their exodus from the land of Egypt. Num. i: 8.

NETHANEEL, 2—*The gift of God.*

Was the fifth son of Obed-edom, and one of the sacred porters. 1st Chron. xxvi: 4.

NETHANIAH, 1 — [Neth-a-ni′-ah,] *the gift of the Lord.*

Was the father of the Ishmael who, in company with ten men—or rather as the captain of a company of ten men—slew Gedaliah at Mizpah. Nethaniah was the son of Elishama, of the seed royal. 2d Kings, xxv: 25.

NETHANIAH, 2—*The gift of the Lord.*

Was one of the sons of Asaph; and when the lots were cast and the singers were divided into twenty-four courses, the fifth lot fell to him. 1st Chron. xxv: 12.

NIBHAZ—[Nib′-haz,] *that fructifies, to prophesy, to speak.*

Was an idol god of the Avites, which, it is said, was made like unto a dog. 2d Kings, xvii: 31, refers to this idol and the worship of it: "And the Avites made Nibhaz and Tartak."

**NICANOR**—[Ni-ca′nor,] *a conqueror, victorious.*

NICANOR is referred to in Acts vi: 5, as one of the seven deacons of the church at Jerusalem. He was selected with his colleagues to attend to some of the interests of the church there, that the twelve apostles wished not to be burdened with. They wished to devote themselves "wholly to prayer and to the ministry of the word." We learn of Nicanor and his companions, that they were "men of honest report, full of the Holy Ghost and of wisdom." They were ordained or set apart by the apostles, by the imposition of hands, to the work and office for which they had been selected.

**NICODEMUS**—[Nik-o-de′mus,] *innocent blood; in Greek, the victory of the people.*

NICODEMUS was a Pharisee and ruler of the Jews, and as such is introduced to our notice in John iii: 1. "There was a man of the Pharisees named Nicodemus, a ruler of the Jews." He seems to have been prejudiced in favor of Jesus, and by some means to have been led to highly esteem him, and yet he was ashamed openly to profess it. He desired to make a confession to the Savior of his regards, and to be instructed by him in the way of life. He therefore came to Jesus by night, and said unto him: "Rabbi, we know that thou art a teacher sent from God, for no man can do these miracles which thou doest, except God be with him." He thereby acknowledged Christ as a worthy teacher, but in addition, he intimated a desire to learn of him. Jesus was always willing to impart instruction to those who approached him, but he clearly intimated to Nicodemus that he ought not to be ashamed to acknowledge his convictions. He told him that though he was a member and ruler in the Jewish Church, and faithfully observed the forms and ceremonies of religion, there was something more required. The heart must be renewed, and the internal principles of true worship must be exercised—that he must be born again in order to see the kingdom of God. The spirit must change his heart and renew his nature. There was something very strange to Nicodemus in this doctrine of the new birth, and being grossly ignorant of it, he asked the Savior how it was possible for a man to be born again. "Can he enter the second time into his mother's womb and be born?" Jesus asked if it were possible that he, being a Jew and a teacher in Israel, one who had read the divine oracles, was ignorant of these things. Jesus then discoursed to him more fully regarding the doctrine of regeneration, and demanded of him faith in it as a vital doctrine. "If I have told you earthly things and ye believed not, how shall I tell you of heavenly things." But the Savior informed him that, "As Moses lifted up the serpent in the wilderness, even so the Son of Man must be lifted up; that whosoever believeth in him should not perish, but have everlasting life." The Savior thereby gave Nicodemus to understand that as the brazen serpent was raised up by Moses in the camp of Israel, for the cure of bitten Israelites, so he himself should be lifted up on the cross, that the dying children of men might look by faith to him, and have the poison of the serpent, sin, extracted, and a spiritual cure performed for them. John iii: 1-21.

It is quite reasonable to suppose that Nicodemus after this conversation became a true Christian, and it is likely that he openly attended the ministrations of Christ as he had opportunity. We have an account in John 7: 45, of a session of the Sanhedrim where the case of Jesus was brought up. The members were angry and raged at their officers for not apprehending him and bringing him before them—they derided and scoffed at the people who believed in him, but the officers said "Never man spake like this man." They railed still more and declared that they who believed on Jesus were ignorant and accursed. Nicodemus sat there and heard all this—and he asked them if it were according to the law that they pretended to understand and be governed by to condemn a man before they heard him. They had probably suspected him for being a believer in Jesus. The question had been asked have any of the rulers, or of the Pharisees believed in him. They asked him if he too was a Galilean, and they bade him search the Jewish scriptures and he would find that there came no prophets out of Galilee.

But as evidence that Nicodemus became a disciple of Jesus, he showed his sympathy and feeling for Jesus and his cause at the crucifixion. Whether he was near Jesus when apprehended, or when passing through his mock trial, we know not, or whether he was really a witness of the agonies of Jesus. Yet he came out and showed himself a disciple by assisting Joseph of Arimathea to prepare the body for burial, and placing it in the tomb, while Joseph provided a sepulcher, and begged of Pilate the body. Nicodemus provided a hundred pounds of myrrh and aloes, and probably the linen clothes with which the body was wrapped. After the two had prepared the body for burial they bare it to the garden and placed it in the new tomb.

It has been said that when the other members of the Jewish Sanhedrim heard of Nicodemus becoming a Christian, and being baptized, they deposed him from his office and excommunicated him from the Jewish church, and that he retired to the country residence of Gamaliel where he lived in peace, until he died a natural death, but of this we cannot be certain.

NICHOLAS—[Nik′o-las,] *victor of the people.*

NICHOLAS was one of the seven deacons of the Jerusalem church. He was selected, as were his companions, because he was a man of "honest report, and full of the Holy Ghost, and of wisdom." Acts, vi: 5. (See Nicanor.) It is not known certainly whether the sect of the Nicolaitans received their name in honor of him, or took to themselves the name, because of his fame for sanctity. They were a very detestable and corrupt sect, revelling in abomination and wickedness. They were addicted to the use of meats offered unto idols; but one of the worst features of their system was, they imputed their wickedness to God. Their deeds are declared in Revelations, ii: 6, to be hateful to God, and the church of Ephesus, though partially backslidden, also hated the deeds of the Nicolaitans.

NIMROD—[Nim′rod,] *rebellious, sleep of descent.*

NIMROD was the son of Cush, and a celebrated hunter. He is referred to in Genesis, x: 8–11. This passage with 1st Chronicles, i: 10, is the only place in the scriptures where he is mentioned. He is supposed to have been a tyrant, and oppressor of the poor. We learn that he founded a kingdom at Babylon, and set himself up as a king. He extended his dominions to Erech, Accad and Calneh, in the land of Shinar. In this land the tower of Babel was built, and it is thought that Nimrod promoted the building of it.

NISROCH—[Nis′roch,] *flight, standard, proof.*

Was an idol of the Assyrians, referred to in 2d Kings, xix: 37.

NOAH, 1—[No′-ah,] *repose, rest, consolation.*

NOAH was the son of Lamech. He was born when his father was one hundred and eighty-two years old. Gen. 5: 28. As the name given him imports rest, repose, consolation, and as the language of Lamech, when Noah was born, was: "This same shall comfort us concerning our work and toil of our hands," there was probably an allusion to the preservation that he and his family should have in the ark while the inhabitants of the world should be drowned. The language of Lamech seems to be prophetical. We are informed in Gen. viii: 21, after the waters were assuaged from off the face of the earth and Noah came forth from the ark to offer sacrifice to God, he used the following language: "God smelled a savour of rest and said he would not curse the ground any more for man's sake." By this language we can hardly fail to be reminded of Lamech's language when he named him.

But the character of Noah is set forth in Gen. vi: 9: "Noah was a just man and perfect in his generation, and Noah walked with God." When it is said he was a just man, we understand that he gave to all their due. And when it is said he was a perfect man in his generations we understand he was in all things consistent in his character, and never departed from the truth in principle or practice. And again; when it is said he walked with God we understand that he was truly pious—devoted to God and to the great interests of his soul. Like Enoch, he enjoyed union and communion with God. But while Noah was thus just, perfect, and walked with God, the inhabitants of earth around him were wicked, insomuch that it is said the earth was corrupt before God and filled with violence; nay more, it is said all flesh had corrupted his way upon the earth. The wickedness of man was so great in the earth that it is said "every imagination of the thoughts of his heart was only evil continually; and it repented the Lord that he had made man on the earth, and it grieved him at heart." God determined to destroy man from the face of the earth. He determined to destroy all the earth with water. But while the wicked inhabitants were swept off with the besom of destruction, God rewarded the piety in life and fidelity in teaching of his servant Noah. He bade him make an ark of gopher wood. God gave him all the necessary directions concerning it, and at once he began its erection, for the safety of his family and the animals with which the world was to be peopled after the flood. It is supposed that he spent a hundred and twenty years in building the ark, and all that time continued faithfully to preach to the wicked antediluvians. Had they repented the judgment of God might have been turned aside; but they did not. They continued in their sins "until the flood came and swept them all away." He warned them of the coming flood, but they heeded not his warnings.

At length the ark was completed, and in company with his wife and his three sons, Shem, Ham and Japheth, and their wives, under the divine direction he entered the ark, taking with him seven of all clean animals that could not live in water, and two of all unclean. Having provided in the ark food for his family and the animals, he shut himself up, and the flood came and destroyed all living things.

After he had been about a year in the ark, as the waters were to him evidently much decreased, he opened a window and sent out a raven to see if the earth was dry. The ark rested on Mt. Ararat, and the tops of the surrounding mountains in a few weeks were visible from the windows of the ark. He, it may be, thought that the waters were assuaged, and said, "I will send forth the raven," and it went forth to and fro until the waters were dried up from off the earth. As the raven was a kind of bird that could pick up food floating on the surface of the water, or food that had been left by the receding waters on the mountain side, until it was fully satisfied, it may have had no disposition to go again within the ark. Noah next sent forth a dove. It found no dry place and speedily returned to the ark, when Noah put forth his hand and took it in. He waited seven days and sent out the dove again. Again she returned, bearing in her mouth an olive leaf. This olive leaf was an emblem of peace restored betwixt God and the earth. Still Noah seemed not to be fully satisfied that the waters had dried up, and he waited seven other days and sent out the dove again, and she returned to him no more, from which circumstance he understood the waters were sufficiently dried up to justify his removing the covering from the ark. Soon after, he and his family, and the animals that had been preserved with them, went forth. From the sacred historian we learn that their stay in the ark had been one year and ten days.

One of the first things that Noah did after leaving the ark was to build an altar and offer unto God clean beasts and clean fowls as a burnt offering on his newly erected altar. He thus offered thanksgiving and praise to God for his preservation, and God accepted his sacrifice, and promised him that he would not again curse the ground for man's sake, and that he would not again smite every living thing as he had done. He furthermore promised unto Noah that as long as the earth remained there should be seedtime and harvest, and cold and heat, and summer and winter, and day and night. God also charged Noah and his sons to multiply and replenish the earth. He allowed them to eat the flesh of clean animals, provided they did not eat them with the blood; and he gave them a law, which, so far as we know, has never been repealed: "Whoso sheddeth man's blood, by man shall his blood be shed; for in the image of God made he man." Thus we are taught that punishment is to be in proportion to crime. Whoever kills a man, unless it is unwittingly, as the Scripture expresses, shall for doing so forfeit his own life.

The Almighty also marked the establishment of his covenant with Noah for the future preservation of the world, by "setting his bow in the clouds." The rainbow is a natural effect of a natural cause. It has always been seen when the sun shines on a watery cloud directly opposite to it, and never in any part of the heavens except opposite to the sun. It existed then before the flood; but God took it as a thing existing in nature and made it a sign to Noah and his posterity that the world should not again be drowned —a token that the waters should no more cover the earth. See Gen. vi: 7–8.

Not long after the flood, Noah became a husbandman and planted a vineyard and cultivated the vine. Shortly after the vine had been cultivated and the juice of the grape had been expressed, Noah learned from its effects upon him as he drank it, its intoxicating power, "for he drank of the wine and was drunken, and lay uncovered within his tent." He may have been innocent, not knowing the intoxicating power of the wine; but it has the appearance of a stain upon the character of this great and good man. Ham, the younger son, was probably informed of the condition of Noah, who lay drunken and uncovered within his tent, by his son Canaan. The two were evidently associated in reprehensible conduct toward him. Ham, in a sportive manner, informed his two brothers of their father's drunkenness. They wondered that Ham should treat him thus, and throwing a garment or mantle hurriedly over their shoulders, they ran backward and covered their father's nakedness, that they might not behold their father's shame. When Noah awoke from his wine and became duly sober, and learned what Ham, his younger son, had done, and what part Canaan performed in the scene that had transpired, and also how Shem and Japheth had acted, he pronounced a curse of servitude upon the descendants of Ham, but pronounced blessings upon Shem and Japheth and their posterity. Of Ham's children, he declared they should be slaves to the descendants of his brothers, and should be sorely oppressed by them. Of the posterity of Shem he predicted the Messiah should come, and of the posterity of Japheth, which "should be enlarged," he should at last seize upon the territory of Shem, or should literally compass the whole earth. We learn of Noah that he died at the age of nine hundred and fifty years, only a little while before Abraham was born.

The generations of the sons of Noah as given in Genesis x: show that his immediate posterity was very large. Very favorable mention is made of him in connection with Job, the patriarch, and Daniel the prophet, by Ezek. xiv: 14. "Though these three men, Noah, Daniel and Job, were in it, they should deliver but their own souls by their righteousness, saith the Lord." By this we are to understand that these three men were singularly righteous.

The faith of Noah is celebrated by the apostle in his epistle to the Hebrews, xi: 7. "By faith Noah being warned of God, of things not seen as yet, moved with fear, prepared an ark to the saving of his house; by the which he condemned the world, and became the heir of the righteousness which is by faith." And Peter, in 2d Epistle, ii: 5, calls him "a preacher of righteousness." Christ refers to Noah and his history, with the flood and the destruction of the inhabitants of the old world. Matthew, xxiv: 37–38. "But as the days of Noe were, so shall also the coming of the son of man be. For as in the days that were before the flood, they were eating and drinking, marrying and giving in marriage, until the day that Noe entered the ark, and knew not until the flood came and took them all away."

Noah has been looked upon as prefiguring Jesus, his name signifying rest. His upright and holy life in the midst of a wicked and perverse world; his faithful preaching to the people, warning them, and boldly denouncing sin, is much like the work and character of the Savior. The ark which he built for the saving of his house, prefiguring the salvation that has been provided for lost guilty man. It was the only deliverance for Noah and his family, so Christ is the only Savior for our race, and his salvation the only salvation provided.

NOAH, 2—*Repose, rest, consolation.*
NOAH was one of the five daughters of Zelophihad, that demanded of Moses an inheritance. Num. xxvi: 33.

NOBAH—[No′bah,] *that barks or yelps.*
Was an Israelite warrior probably of the tribe of Manasseh, who conquered the city of Kenath, with the villages dependent upon it, gave the conquered territory his own name, and dwelt there. Numb. xxxii: 42.

NOGAH—[No′gah.]
Was one of the thirteen sons of David, born to him in Jerusalem. 1st Chronicles, iii; 7, and xiv: 6.

NYMPHAS—[Nim′fas,] *spouse, bridegroom.*
NYMPHAS was a christian in the city of Laodicea, devoted to the cause of Christ in the apostolic age. The apostles had enjoyed his hospitality, and worshiped God in his house. The reference to Nymphas is in Col. iv: 15. "Salute the brethren which are in Laodicea, and Nymphas and the church which is in his house." From which we may certainly gather that he was a pious man, and that his household was religious.

OBADIAH, 1—[O-ba-di′-ah,] *servant of the Lord.*
OBADIAH was a good man who occupied a high position in the government of Ahab, King of Israel. Though the king his master and all the family of of the king were wicked, yet Obadiah feared God and practiced righteousness. When Jezebel, the wife of Ahab, sought out the Lord's prophets to have them murdered, he took their part, so far as he could without being deposed. He hid a hundred of them in two caves, thereby running a risk of being found out as a devout worshiper of Israel's God, and a lover of her prophets, and he supplied the hundred men with the necessaries of life. He must have had some difficulty in supplying them secretly as he did, for he was required to go out through the land and see if he could find provender for the starving beasts. The land had been without rain for three years, and dire famine prevailed, and yet Obadiah secretly fed one hundred of the Lord's prophets. This persecution of the prophets by Jezebel was, it is supposed, during the dearth, and she charged the public calamity upon Elijah, and not being able to find him, she wreaked her vengeance upon such of the prophets as she could find. Elijah having spent six months at the brook Cherith, and three years with the widow of Serepta, was commanded by his God to go and show himself unto Ahab, and as he was going he met Obadiah, who was on an excursion of hunting water and provender. As soon as he saw the prophet he knew him, and fell on his face before him. Elijah told him to go and tell the king, "Behold Elijah is here." Obadiah objected to doing this, for his impression was, that the Lord who had taken care of Elijah during the persecution of the prophets, would by his spirit take him away, and his life would be placed in jeopardy from the anger of Ahab, exasperated by such disappointment. But Elijah told Obadiah that he was determined that day to show himself unto Ahab. When Obadiah was fully satisfied, he went to meet Ahab, and inform him that Elijah was coming after him to see the King. It was but a little while until the prophet and the King of Israel met.

OBADIAH, 2—*Servant of the Lord.*
OBADIAH was one of the lesser prophets, and he wrote the book which bears his name. It is supposed by some that he was the same as the governor or steward of Ahab's house, but this is not very likely. There is a striking similarity between his prophecies, and some of those which were uttered about the time of, or indeed after the destruction of Jerusalem by the Chaldeans. The prophecies that are referred to as being similar are Jer. xlix, Ezek. xxv. Usher insists that he prophesied within a year or two after the taking of Jerusalem.

The prophecy of Obadiah consists of one chapter, wherein he severely reprimands the Edomites for the part they acted in conquering the Jews, and rejoicing in their destruction.

OBADIAH, 3.—*Servant of the Lord.*
OBADIAH was one of the valiant men who came to join David's army at Ziklag, or in the wilderness. 1st Chronicles, xii: 9.

OBADIAH, 4.—*Servant of the Lord.*
OBADIAH was one of the ministers sent out throughout the land by Jehoshaphat, the king of Judah. 2d Chron. xvii: 7. The king established a system of instruction, or as some have called it, an itinerant ministry, and sent them through all the cities of Judah to teach the people. Obadiah was one of those ministers. They went about taking the law of the Lord with them, and from it they taught, and the instructions they gave, and the labor they performed were very beneficial.

We may suppose that the effect was to improve the moral tone and make the kingdom of Judah prosperous, for the "fear of the Lord, fell upon all the kingdoms of the land that were round about them, so that they made no war against Jehoshaphat."

But that was not all the effect of this ministry, for the "Philistines brought Jehoshaphat presents, and tribute of silver, and the Arabians brought him flocks to the amount of seven thousand seven hundred rams, and seven thousand and seven hundred he goats.

OBADIAH, 5.—*Servant of the Lord.*

OBADIAH was a principal man of the Jews in the days of Nehemiah. One of those who subscribed to, or sealed the covenant made with the Lord. Neh. x: 5. There were four classes of persons who sealed: viz: 1st, the governor, Nehemiah; 2d, the priests; 3d, the Levites; 4th, the chief of the people. Obadiah belonged to the priests.

OBAL—]O′-bal,] *inconvenience of old age, of the flux.*

OBAL was the son Joktan, and the grandson of Eber, and is referred to in the posterity of Shem. Gen. x: 28.

OBED, 1.—[O′-bed,] *a servant.*
OBED was the son of Boaz and Ruth and the father of Jesse, hence the grandfather of David. Ruth, iv: 17. When an infant he was placed in the hands of Naomi, for "she became nurse unto it." This good woman had been disconsolate for several years, having lost her husband and her two sons; but Ruth had attended her to her native land and married Boaz. As soon as Obed was born the women of Bethlehem said, "Blessed be the Lord which hath not left thee this day without a kinsman, that his name may be famous in Israel. And he shall be to thee a restorer of thy life and a nourisher of thine old age; for thy daughter-in-law which loveth thee, which is better to thee than seven sons, hath borne him." And it is further said that the women, Naomi's neighbors, gave him the name Obed.

OBED, 2.—*A servant.*
OBED was one of King David's valiant men. 1st Chron. xi: 47. In this chapter there is a list of thirty-seven valiant men, divided into four parts: 1. A captain general; 2. The first three; 3. The second three; and 4. Thirty who occupied the same position. Obed belonged to that thirty.

OBED, 3.—*A servant.*
OBED was the son of Shemaiah and the grandson of Obed-Edom, and one of the sacred porters. 1st Chron. xxvi: 7.

OBED-EDOM—[O′-bed-E′-dom.]
OBED-EDOM was the son of Jedutham, a Levite, and the father of Shemaiah, Jehozabad, Joah, Sacar, Nathaneel, Ammiel, Issachar and Peulthai. 1st Chron. xxvi: 4, 5. We have an interesting incident of Obed-Edom recorded in 2d Sam. vi: 10, also 1st Chron. xiii 14. King David was bringing the ark from Kirjath-jearim to Jerusalem. He placed it on a new cart drawn by oxen. As Uzzah and Ahio were conveying the ark thus, or driving the oxen toward Jerusalem, they came to a threshing floor and Uzzah put forth his hand to steady the ark — in doing which he violated a law that God had given to the Levites, Num. iv: 15, 20, and for that violation the Lord slew him and

he died there by the ark. David was struck with terror at the sudden death of Uzzah, for touching the ark —and he was afraid at that time to take it on to Jerusalem; so he removed it to the house of Obed-Edom the Gittite, that was near by the threshing floor where Uzzah had died and he left it there.

Obed-Edom received the ark and gave it a place in his house, and it remained there three months, during which time the Lord blessed the house of Obed-Edom, and blessed all that pertained unto him because of the ark being there. The family did not suffer inconvenience from the ark being with them, but were prospered in various ways. It is likely it increased in numbers as well as being otherwise blessed, for we learn from 1st Chron. xxvi: 8, there were sixty-two able bodied men of the house of Obed-Edom that were appointed porters of the temple. This was several years after the ark was in his house, and the Lord blessed his house because of it.

We do not know why he is called a Gittite, except it be that he was born in Gathrimmon, or had lived awhile in some place, that had given him the title. It may be in Gath of the Philistines.

OBIL—[O′-bil,] *that weeps, deserves to be bewailed, ancient.*

Obil an Ishmaelite, was placed by King David over his camels. 1st Chron. xxvii: 30.

OCRAN—[Ok′-ran,] *disturber.*

Was of the tribe of Asher, and the father of Pagiel the prince who assisted Moses in numbering the tribes of Israel. Num. i: 13.

ODED—[O′ded,] *to sustain, to lift up.*

Oded was a prophet of the Lord, who is referred to in 2d Chronicles, xxviii: 9. We have the history of Ahaz, a king of Judah, given, from which we learn that he reigned wickedly for sixteen years. He restored idolatry in its worst forms into his kingdom, and as a punishment for his wickedness, the Lord delivered him into the hands and power of the king of Syria, and of the king of Israel. Pekah slew in Judah, one hundred and twenty thousand of the Jews, and carried captive two hundred thousand of the people. Just at this point, Oded, the prophet, is introduced to our view, and he makes an appeal to the conquerors for humane treatment toward the captives. His address is exceedingly beautiful and touching. "Behold because the Lord God of your fathers was wroth with Judah, he hath delivered them into your hand, and ye have slain them in a rage that reacheth up unto heaven. And now ye purpose to keep under the children of Judah and Jerusalem for bondmen and bondwomen unto you; but are there not with you, even with you, sins against the Lord your God? Now hear me therefore, and deliver the captives again, which ye have taken captive of your brethren, for the fierce wrath of the Lord is upon you." They were well affected by this speech, and moved by the remonstrance it contained. They not only dismissed or released the captives, but they took the spoils which they had taken from them, and with those spoils they clothed and fed and shod them. And those of them who were too feeble to walk or endure the march to Judea, they set upon asses and escorted them safely to Jericho. And after they had done this, they returned to Samaria, and to their own kingdom. It is almost, if not quite impossible, to find a parallel to this case in all the history of the world, and its wars. And the prophet Oded had much to do with this action of Israel towards their brethren of Judah.

OG—*A cake, bread baked in the ashes.*

Og was the king of Bashan. He belonged to the race of men who were of extraordinary stature, called giants. These persons were doubtless not as large as they are commonly believed to have been. The spies who went under the direction of Moses to search the promised land and see what it was, and what was the strength of its inhabitants, brought a very disheartening report back, except Caleb and Joshua. See Num. xiii: 33. They said: "We saw giants, the sons of Anak, which come of the giants; and we were in our own sight as grasshoppers, and so we were in their sight;" from which we may understand that they were a robust, sturdy, warlike race of men. But Og is judged to have been a man of very great stature. His bedstead was of iron, and it was nine cubits long and four cubits broad. This is reckoned by some to be sixteen feet in length, and seven feet three inches in breadth. Og is supposed to be considerable shorter than his bedstead, but supposing him to be but three-fourths as long, he was of great stature. This wonderful piece of furniture for the king's sleeping apartment is thought to have been taken by the Ammonites in battle, and as a trophy of victory carried to their royal city, Rabbah, for it is called the royal city of the children of Ammon, in 2d Sam. xii: 26. The Ammonites probably kept this bedstead there as a curiosity for a long time.

The children of Israel warred with Og, king of Bashan, at Edrei, and the battle went against Og, and in favor of Israel. They defeated him, and took three score fortified cities, with many unwalled towns. The Israelites made an utter destruction of the people of his kingdom, and they took all his cattle and spoils as a prey. And they took possession of his land, with the land of Sihon, king of the Amorites, and it was given unto the Reubenites, Gadites, and to the half tribe of Manasseh. Deut. iii: 1-14. And Og was slain by the Israelites afterwards, if not at the time his country was taken. Psalms cxxxv: 10, 11. "Who smote great nations, and slew mighty kings; Sihon, king of the Amorites, and Og, king of Bashan."

OHAD.

Was one of the six sons of Simeon, who went down with the family of Jacob into Egypt. The children and grandchildren of the aged patriarch are enumerated, and their names are given in Gen. xlvi.

OLYMPAS, 1—[O-lim′-pas,] *heavenly.*

Was a believer in Christ of the apostolic age, who is referred to in Rom. xvi: 15, with several other persons of distinguished virtue and merit. The Christian salutations of Paul are given to him.

OLYMPAS, 2—*Heavenly.*

OLYMPAS-JUPITER was a heathen god whose statue was set up in the temple of Jerusalem by the order of Antiochus-Epiphanes, and it remained there for three years. It is supposed that this idol is referred to in Dan. xii: 11, when it is said "And from the time that the daily sacrifices shall be taken away, and the abomination that maketh desolate set up, shall be one thousand, two hundred and ninety days."

OMAR—[O′-mar,] *he that speaks, bitter.*

Was one of the sons of Eliphaz, the son of Esau. There were six of them, Teman, Omar, Zepho and Gatam, and Kenaz and Amalek. These six are reckoned as the sons of Adah, Esau's wife, because she was the mother of Eliphaz. Gen. xxxvi: 11, 12.

OMRI, 1—[Om′-ri,] *a sheaf of corn, rebellion, bitter.*

OMRI was the general to the forces of Elah, king of Israel, and was engaged in besieging Gibbethon with the army at the time the intelligence reached him that Zimri, who was "captain of half of Elah's chariots," had conspired against the king and slain him while in the house of Arza, his steward. He also learned that Zimri had slain all the house of Baasha that there might be none to sit on the throne, and himself had usurped authority and ascended the throne at Tirzah. He left Gibbethon at once and hurried to Tirzah, and laid siege to it, and took it. When Zimri saw that the city was taken he hurried into the king's palace and set it on fire, and himself perished in the flames. He thus chose rather to die by his own hands than to fall into the hands of his enemy.

The kingdom of Israel was then hurried into a civil war that lasted about four years. It was headed on the one side by Omri and on the other by Tibni, the son of Ginath. It is said half the people followed the one and half followed the other. The army, however, we suppose, was for Omri, and he prevailed. They were both aspiring for the honorable position of king, vacated by the murder of Elah by his dastardly servant.

As Omri prevailed, and the other aspirant was dead, he ascended the throne, and reigned twelve years. His reign was by no means a good reign, for "he wrought evil in the eyes of the Lord, and did worse than all before him."

He purchased the hill Samaria from one Shemir, for two talents of silver, and built on it; then called it after the name of its former owner. He made the city he built on that hill the capital of his kingdom, and it became the capital of the ten tribes.

What all the acts of his wicked reign were we can not tell; nor, indeed, what the principal of them were; but the sacred history informs us that he was more wicked than Jeroboam or any of his predecessors. He was, we doubt not, an idolater in principle and practice. He gave them royal precept and royal example, and, in all probability, he enacted laws and circulated edicts making idolatry the religion of the land. Micah, vi: 16, is a clear reference to them: "For the statutes of Omri are kept, and all the works of the house of Ahab."

Omri died and was buried in Samaria, and Ahab, his son, reigned in his stead. 1st Kings, xvi: 8-28.

OMRI, 2—*A sheaf of corn, rebellion, bitter.*

OMRI, the son of Michael, was the ruler in the tribe of Issachar, in the time of David. 1st Chron. xxvii: 18.

ON—*Pain, force, iniquity.*

ON, the son of Peleth, of the tribe of Reuben, was engaged with Korah, Dathan and Abiram in the rebellion, which resulted in the earth opening her mouth and swallowing up the guilty leaders, and those who adhered to them. Num. xvi.

ONAM.

ONAM was the son of Shobal, and the grandson of Seir the Horite. Gen. xxxvi: 23.

ONAN—[O′-nan,] *pain, strength, iniquity.*

ONAN was the son of Judah, he was the second son of the Canaanite woman, Shuah. His father bade him marry his elder brother's widow—he did so, but sinned against God, and for his sin was punished with death. His crime was evidently that of refusing to raise up seed unto his brother, children who should inherit the possessions of the former husband of their mother, the first husband having died childless. Gen. xxxviii: 4, 10.

ONESIMUS—[O-nes′si-mus,] *profitable, useful.*

ONESIMUS was a Phrygian by birth, and the slave of Philemon. He deserted his master and made his way to Rome, where he heard the apostle Paul preach and teach, and through the apostles instrumentality he was converted to Christianity. It is likely that he told the apostle at once, that he had left his master's service, and Paul advised him to return and sent with him the epistle to Philemon. The epistle is strongly persuasive; he urges Philemon to receive Onesimus for his sake, and to forgive him any wrong he had committed, declaring that he had been soundly converted, "Whom I have begotten in my bonds." He also declares that he had been so far faithful, and had greatly won upon his feelings, "a brother beloved" he is unto me. As he returned him to Philemon he commends him to his esteem and Christian regards.

Onesimus became an eminent Christian and a faithful worker in the church. It is said that Paul made him a bishop of the church in Berea, in Macedonia. [See Epistle to Philemon.]

ONESIPHORUS — [On-e-sif′-o-rus,] *who brings profit.*

ONESIPHORUS was probably a native of Ephesus, and one of the most ardent and devoted Christians of that place. We have an account in 2d Tim. i: 16, &c., of his great kindness to the apostle Paul. When Onesiphorus went to Rome, and Paul was there in prison, he sought him out, had a conference with him, and to the utmost of his power comforted and assisted the apostle. "When he was in Rome, he sought me out very diligently, and found me." But he was a devoted friend of Paul at Ephesus, giving him, no doubt, the hospitalities of his house, and in many ways ministering unto him. Paul greatly loved him, and in closing up his epistles he saluted him and his household in the Lord. 2d Tim. iv: 19.

OPHIR—[O'-fir,] *ashes.*

Was a son of Joktan and descendant of Shem. He is referred to in Gen. x: 29, as one of thirteen sons who had their dwellings from Mesha unto Sephar. The country which is called Ophir was probably settled by the descendants of Ophir, who, it may be, gave the country the name. It abounded in gold and precious stones. For the building of Solomon much gold was brought therefrom. 1st Kings, ix: 28: "And they came to Ophir and fetched from thence gold four hundred and twenty talents, and brought it to King Solomon." See, also, x: 11, and xxii: 48.

OREB—[O'reb,] *a raven, caution, evening.*

OREB was a prince of the Midianites, who with Zeeb, another prince, was pursued by the men of Ephraim under the direction of Gideon, after he had had the miraculous victory over the mighty army that were encamped on the plains of Moab.

The Ephraimites followed them in their flight from their own country to Beth-barah and Jordan, and overtaking them they totally overthrew them, and taking the princes they slew them. Oreb they slew on the rock Oreb, and Zeeb at the wine press of Zeeb. It is thought that Oreb took refuge among the rocks or in a cave of the rocks, and they named the rock Oreb, while the other took refuge in the vat of a wine press. Having slain them, the Ephraimites brought their heads to Gideon, as evidence of their victory. Jud. vii: 25.

ORNAN—[Or'nan,] *that rejoices, their bow on ark.*

See Araunah, the Jebusite.

ORPAH—[Or'pah,] *the neck, skull, nakedness of the mouth.*

ORPAH was a Moabitish woman, who was married to one of the sons of the widowed and disconsolate Naomi. She, with her sister-in-law, Ruth, was left a widow, her husband dying. When Naomi determined to return to her own land, and seek a home among her kindred, Orpah, like Ruth, being strongly attached to her, concluded to go to Judah with her. She endeavored to dissuade them, but at first failed, and afterwards, with Orpah, she succeeded.

The three widows had passed out of the city or village where they lived towards Naomi's country, and Naomi gave them her mind as to the propriety of their remaining where they were, while she returned alone. She gave them to understand that she appreciated their kindness, but thought it was best for them not to go with her. She gave them a solemn and touching charge: "Go return each to her mother's house; the Lord deal kindly with you, as you have dealt with me, and with the dead. The Lord grant that you may find rest each of you in the house of your husband. Then she kissed them, and they lifted up their voices and wept." What a touching scene. But they were not changed from their purpose. They were both determined to accompany her, and see her safely lodged among her own people. Naomi again plead with them, setting forth her position and circumstances, to tarry in the land of Moab, while she went on to Beth-leham-Judah. Her reasoning with them had force in it, and the picture she drew was so dark that Orpah concluded to remain in her own country, and she was commended by Naomi for her good sense, and propriety in doing so. The parting scene must have been very affecting. They spent a few moments, it may be, calling up reminiscences of the past—wept together at the remembrance of their losses, when Orpah kissed her mother-in-law," and they parted, the one to Judea, and the other to take up her life residence with her own people.

OTHNI—[Oth'-ni,] *my time, my hour.*

OTHNI was the son of Shemaiah and the grandson of Obed-Edom, and one of the sacred porters. 1st Chronicles, xxvi: 7.

OTHNIEL.—[Oth'-ni-el,] *the hour of God.*

OTHNIEL was the son of Kenaz. He belonged to the tribe of Judah, and was the first Judge of Israel. He was the nephew of Caleb and married Achsah his daughter. The Canaanites inhabited a part of the inheritance that had been apportioned Caleb, and he was exceedingly anxious to free Dibir, or Kirjath-Sepher, from the hands and power of those who inhabited it. He promised to give Achsah his daughter to wife to him who should smite the city. Othniel, the son of Kenaz, undertook it and succeeded; he thereby purchased Achsah. Josh. xv: 16, &c.

While Achsah was preparing to depart from the house of her father to that of Othniel her husband, she moved Othniel to ask for her of her father a marriage present. It would seem from the account that he was not willing; hence she undertook it herself. She met her father and indicated a desire to make a request of him. He told her to ask what she would, and she asked an additional blessing: "Thou hast given me a south land, give me also springs of water; and he gave her the upper springs and the nether springs."

In Jud. iii: 8–11, we have an account of Othniel delivering his people from the power of the king of Mesopotamia, who had enslaved them for eight years. Chushan-rishathaim was their oppressor. God stirred up Othniel to levy an army sufficient to war with him. He routed the king of Mesopotamia and his troops, and fully delivered Israel, after which the land had rest for forty years, or till the fortieth year of their settlement in it. After living and acting to profit through his life, he died in honor.

OZEM — [O′-zem,] *that fasts, their eagerness.*

Ozem was the sixth son of Jesse, and the brother of David. 1st Chron. ii: 15. We have an account in 1st Sam. xvi: of the sons of Jesse being called to pass before Samuel, that he might select and anoint, from amongst them, one to take the place of Saul. Ozem we suppose was the last one that passed before him, before David was sent for.

OZIAS—[O-zi′-as,] *strength from the Lord.*

Was the son of Joram, and the father of Joatham. He was one in the line of the Messiah, as the genealogy is given. Matt. i: 8, 9.

OZNI—[Oz′-ni.]

Was of the tribe of Gad, and at the head of the family in that tribe called Oznites. Num. xxvi: 16.

PAARAI—[Pa′-a-ra,] *opening.*

Was one of the mighty men of David, referred to in 2d Sam. xxiii: 35. He is called Paarai, the Arbite.

PAGIEL—[Pa′-gi-el,] *prevention or prayer of God.*

Pagiel was the son of Ocran, of the tribe of Asher. He was chief of his tribe, and was associated with Moses and Aaron in managing the business of their nation, at the time of their Exodus from the land of Egypt. Num. i: 13. And when the tabernacle was fully set up he made an offering for his tribe. Numbers vii: 72.

PALLU—[Pal′-lu.]

Was of the tribe of Reuben, and from him came the family of the Palluites. Num. xxvi: 5. He was the grand-father of Dathan and Abiram, who were so famous in the congregation of Israel for striving against Moses and Aaron, and who were destroyed in the company of Korah. Numbers xxvi: 9.

PALTI—[Pal′-ti,] *deliverance, flight.*

Belonged to the tribe of Benjamin, and was selected by Moses as one of the twelve spies, to search out and examine the nature and state of the land of Canaan. Num. xiii: 9.

PALTIEL—[Pal-ti′-el.]

The son of Azzan, of the tribe of Issachar, was one of the princes that assisted Joshua and Eleazar in dividing the land of Canaan among the tribes of Israel. Num. xxxiv: 26.

PARMASHTA—[Par-mash′-tah.]

Was one of the ten sons of Haman, who were hanged, as Haman, their father, had been hung. Esther, ix: 9.

PARMENAS—[Par-me′-nas,] *that is permanent.*

Was one of the seven deacons of the church in Jerusalem, referred to in

Acts, vi: 5, 6. Like Stephen and his other companions, he was a good man, one "of honest report, full of the Holy Ghost and wisdom." With the others he was ordained to the work and offices for which he had been selected by the imposition of the apostles' hands.

PARNACH—[Par′-nak.]

Was the father of Elizaphan, the prince of the tribe of Zebulun, who assisted in dividing the land of Canaan. Num. xxxiv: 25.

PARSHANDATHA—[Par-shan-da′-thah,] *revelation of corporeal impurities, of his trouble.*

Was another one of Haman's sons who was killed in the slaughter by the Jews of their enemies in Shushan. Esther, ix: 7.

PASHUR—[Pash′-ur,] *that extends the hole, whiteness.*

PASHUR was the son of Immer. Jer. xx. It was about the beginning of the reign of Jehoiakim, that Jeremiah predicted the desolation and destruction of Judah and Jerusalem. Pashur occupied a high position in the temple, and pretended to be very jealous of the temple's honor. He smote Jeremiah, and put him in the stocks that were in the high gate of Benjamin, on account of his prophecy. The next day Pashur brought Jeremiah out of the stocks, when the prophet told him that his name was to be changed from Pashur to Magor-missabi, and he gave him the reason for the changing of the name.

He was to be sorely punished for his abuse of the prophets. Jeremiah told him that the word of the Lord concerning him was, "Behold I will make thee a terror to thyself and to all thy friends: and they shall fall by the sword of their enemies." And further that he, himself, should see the cruelties that should be practised towards them. He furthermore declared to him that Judah should be given into the hand of the king of Babylon, and he should carry her inhabitants away and slay them with the sword. The strength of the city, and its wealth and beauty, should be destroyed, its precious things should be taken for spoil, and carried into Babylon. But that he, and all his family, should go into captivity, and should die in Babylon, and be buried there. He, and all his friends, to whom he had prophesied lies, should come to the same sad end.

Pashur occupied a high place and his sins were sorely punished. We have his sin and punishment thus set forth as a warning to those who are in authority, and wearing sacred vestments. His name, Pashur, signified "whiteness, or freedom," but the new name which the Lord gave him, Magor-missabib, signifies "fear round about."

PATHRUSIM—[Path-ru′-sim.]

PARTHRUSIM was the son of Mizraim, and the grandson of Ham. Gen. x: 14.

PAUL—*A worker. His former name was Saul, a sepulcher, a destroyer.*

PAUL was the great apostle to the Gentiles. He was of the tribe of Benjamin and both his parents were Hebrews. He was born in Tarsus, a city of Cilicia, was by birth a citizen of Rome. He asserted his Roman citizenship at different times in his addresses and defences before his persecutors. And he demanded the privileges that belonged to him as a Roman citizen at different times, when being persecuted and punished without law. It was on the ground of his citizenship that he appealed unto Cesar, and was sent to Rome for trial.

His name previous to his conversion, and for sometime after, was Saul, which signifies "a destroyer," very significant of his conduct towards christians previous to his conversion, for he persecuted them to death.

During his early life he enjoyed the advantages of a thorough education, under the direction of Gamaliel, one of the most noted doctors or teachers of the law of that age. "Brought up at the feet of Gamaliel, and taught according to the most perfect manner of the law of the fathers." He made great progress in his studies, and was zealous in the observance of the law as he learned it. He was of the sect of the Pharisees. He calls himself "a Pharisee of the Pharisees," by which we may understand that his father and mother were of that sect. He was a faithful observer of the law of Moses. And as a Pharisee he thought it was his duty with all his might to oppose the religion of

Christ Jesus, and persecute his followers. In the account we have in Acts vii, of the stoning to death of that good man Stephen, we learn that Saul was present, and though he did not take an active part, such as throwing the missiles of death at the dying martyr, yet he held the clothes of the young men who stoned him. He heartily consented to Stephen's death, and the persecution of christians, that followed immediately after the death of Stephen, was carried on mainly by him we may judge. He seems to be the principle actor in the scene, the most noted of all the persecutors. He entered the houses of christians, arresting men and women, and committing them to prison. He even went into the sacred sanctuaries or synagogues where christians met, and took them and caused them to be beaten and abused. He procured letters from the high priest authorizing him to go to Damascus and enter the synagogue and either compel christians to blaspheme the Savior, or go to Jerusalem bound, to be punished. He was on his way to Damascus, bearing these letters, when the Lord stopped him by his power, and convinced him of the error of his way. Acts ix.

As he and his attendants were drawing nigh unto Damascus, all at once a great light shone among them, and they were all terrified, for it was an unaccountable phenomenon, and they threw themselves on their faces on the ground in their fright. But there was one in that company who was especially agitated, and that one was Saul; for in addition to the light he heard the voice of the Savior, saying unto him, "Saul, Saul, why persecutest thou me?" He trembled at the sound of the voice of the majestic Jesus, and in his trembling asked, "Who art thou, Lord?" The reply came back in the same tone, "I am Jesus whom thou persecutest." Saul still trembling and astonished, asked in humility, "Lord, what wilt thou have me to do?" Jesus told him, "Arise and go into the city, and it shall be told thee what thou must do." He arose at the command of Jesus and went into Damascus. He did not walk alone, for he had been struck blind—they who were with him led him into the city, and into the street called Straight, and to the house of Judas, where he remained until he was instructed in the word of life, and informed more fully of the divine will. His condition now was that of an awakened and deeply-convicted sinner. The divine spirit attending the law had opened the eyes of his understanding, aroused his moral fears, and made tender his conscience. He saw himself a condemned sinner, and was deeply penitent before God. He gives his experience at this point in the following language: "Before the law came I was alive, but when the law came sin revived and I died." He had accounted himself before this one of the best of men; but now he was convinced of sin, deeply convicted for sin, and his soul was filled with anguish and sorrow. He felt himself condemned to endless ruin. For three days he was without sight, and did neither eat nor drink.

God appointed Ananias, a Christian minister, to go to him and administer spiritual comfort in his sorrow of heart. At first Ananias objected, for he had heard of this man as a noted persecutor and blasphemer. The preacher was afraid of him, but God told him to go; for whatever he had been before he was now an earnest enquirer after truth—"behold he prayeth." Ananias was further informed that this man had seen a vision, and in the vision had seen a man of his name coming unto him and putting his hands on him that he might receive his sight. And yet still Ananias objected; but his objection was removed by his being told that this man was a chosen vessel to bear the glad tidings of salvation to the Gentile world, and that he who had been so noted as a persecutor should be a great sufferer for the cause of Christ. Ananias then went to the place where he was, and entering into the apartment, said, "Brother Saul, the Lord, even Jesus, that appeared unto thee in the way as thou camest, hath sent me that thou mightest receive thy sight." It was but a few moments until Paul was a converted man, and rejoiced in God his Savior. He at once took upon himself the Christian name by submitting to holy baptism.

After fasting during his conviction and penitence, now that the chains that had bound him were broken, and the scales had fallen from his eyes, and the burden had rolled from his heart, he ate with the disciples and was strengthened; and he at once entered upon his high and holy calling. He tarried awhile with the brethren at Damascus; and to them, in their synagogues, he first preached the word of life. He preached from the beginning of his ministerial course with power and with the demonstration of the Holy Spirit. The people of Damascus were astonished at the power with which he preached, and at the unction and success that attended him. He confounded the Jews, proving that Jesus is the very Christ. Acts, ix; Gal. i: 11–24; Acts, xxii: 1–16; xxvi: 9–11; Romans, vii: 8–13.

Many of the Jews about Damascus were converted and others of them, in their madness, resolved to murder him. They determined, if possible, to stop the circulation of his astonishing conversion, and his influence and work as a votary of this new religion. They therefore watched the gates of the city night and day, to prevent his escape, or to waylay and murder him. But his friends among the disciples learned this, and they let him down from a window of a house built on the wall of the city, and he thereby made his escape in the night and directed his steps toward Jerusalem. "He assayed to join himself to the disciples; but they were all afraid of him, and believed not that he was a disciple." It is supposed this was more than two years after his conversion, and he desired to see Peter, who had begun the great work of converting the Gentiles. This was the great work to which he had been called. But Peter, with the other disciples, hesitated to receive him, and would not, until Barnabas had introduced him and declared his wonderful conversion. They then admitted him into their society and confidence; and, as he had preached with power in Damascus, soon he was proclaiming the doctrines of the cross of Christ in Jerusalem. He went in and out before the disciples, developing the Christian character. He disputed with the opposers of Christianity, and confounded them, till in Jerusalem they went about to kill him. When his brethren, the disciples of the church at Jerusalem, saw it, they consented to his leaving them and going to Cesarea, or, rather, to Tarsus. They went with him as far as Cesarea, and sent him by ship to Tarsus in Cilicia, his native city. Acts, ix: 26–29; xxii: 17–21; 2d Cor. xi: 31–33; Gal. i: 15–21.

It is worthy of remark that Paul preached first at Damascus, the place where he had gone with letters of persecution. Then in Jerusalem, the place where he had received his letters, and now in the providence of God, he is in Tarsus, his native city, and in different parts of Cilicia, for five years, he boldly preached the doctrines of the cross of Christ.

Barnabas was appointed by the church at Jerusalem to go to Antioch. Under his ministry, there was a glorious work of grace, and with earnest exhortation, and wholesome teaching he established the christians in the faith. Barnabas then went to Tarsus to seek Saul, and found him and brought him to Antioch, to labor as his colleague for that church, and for a year, together they went in and out before the people with great acceptability and usefulness. Acts x: 11–26.

This Antioch church raised a collection for the poor saints at Jerusalem, and in Judea. Their want was occasioned by a dearth. Acts xi: 28. Paul and Barnabas were appointed to bear the contribution, and place it in the hands of the elders of the church there. After they had accomplished their mission at Jerusalem, they returned to Antioch, and took with them John, whose surname was Mark. They had not been long at Antioch, until certain prophets, directed by the Holy Ghost, sent them out to preach the gospel in other places. It is said, "As they ministered to the Lord and fasted, the Holy Ghost said, separate me Barnabas and Paul, (or Saul) for the work whereunto I have called them. And when they had fasted and prayed, they laid their hands on them and sent them away." The names of those prophets as given, are Simeon, Lucius and Manaen.

Paul and Barnabas went to Seleucia, and from that point sailed to Cyprus, having John Mark with them. At Salamis, they entered into the Jewish synagogue and preached Christ. While they were preaching in the island of Cyprus, a certain magician, whose name was Barjesus, withstood them; and while the deputy of the island, Sergius Paulus, desired to hear the word of God from them, this bad man tried to turn him away from the faith, and as a punishment for this, his wickedness, he was struck blind. Paul rebuked him for his wickedness in a very cutting and severe manner: "O full of subtilty, and all mischief, thou child of the devil, thou enemy of all righteousness, wilt thou not cease to pervert the right ways of the Lord. And now behold the hand of the Lord is upon thee, and thou shalt be blind, not seeing the sun for a season," and immediately upon the apostle making this declaration, a mist gathered about the eyes of the sorcerer, and he submitted himself, as a blind man, to the hand and will of a guide. This demonstration of power fully convinced the governor, and he became a convert to christianity.

From Cyprus they went to Pamphilia, where John left them and went back probably to his home and to his mother in Jerusalem. Paul and Barnabas went on in their work, and the next place we hear of them is in Pisidia. There they entered the Jewish synagogue on the Sabbath day. The ruler of the synagogue invited them to give words of exhortation, whereupon Paul after reading the law delivered a long address in which he preached the doctrines of the cross of Christ. And the next Sabbath day they went into the synagogue again and the whole city came together to hear them. The Jews became jealous and envious at the vast concourse of Gentiles that came together, and broke out in opposition to the apostles and their teachings—they contradicted the apostles and refused any longer to hear them. They then turned to the Gentiles and preached, and multitudes of them believed. The Jews then stirred up devout and honorable women, and chief men of the city to persecute the apostles; and they expelled them out of the coasts. Acts, xiii.

They went to Iconium and in the synagogue there they preached Jesus, and multitudes of Jews and Greeks believed. Many miracles were wrought by the apostles here, among them was a lame man who was cured at Lystra; he had been lame from his birth and had never walked. This was a very remarkable miracle and astonished the multitude insomuch that the people of Lystra took them for gods—they said in the speech of Lycaonia, "the gods have come down to us in the likeness of men." And they called Barnabas, Jupiter; and Paul, Mercurius, because he was the chief speaker.

The idolatrous people carried this matter so far, that the priests of Jupiter brought oxen and garlands, and would have done sacrifice unto them but the apostles prevented it—they rushed out into the mob and told them they were but men like themselves, and they begged them to refrain from these demonstrations towards them. They tarried here we suppose for some time, and taught and preached; but at length there came some Jews from Antioch and Iconium and stirred up this people against the apostle, the consequence was, Paul was stoned, and they dragged him out of the city and left him for dead. But his Christian friends gathered about him and ministered unto him and he revived, and the next day went in company with Barnabas to Derbe. He preached there awhile and returned again to Lystra, and to Iconium and Antioch. In all these places where the apostles had been before they labored, we are informed "confirming the souls of the disciples and exhorting them to continue in the faith, and that we must through much tribulation enter heaven." They also preached in Perga and Attalia, and then returned to Antioch, Syria, in the place where they labored so successfully together at first, and there among their brethren who sent them out, they rehearsed how great things the Lord had wrought by them in the places where they had been, and they remained a long time with the church at Antioch. Acts, xiv.

While they were here, and serving the churches of Cilicia, there were certain persons who came from Judea, pretending to be sent by the apostles, who taught that circumcision, according to the law of Moses was necessary to salvation. Paul and Barnabas disputed with them, and at length they agreed to refer the matter to a council of the apostles at Jerusalem. They were sent as delegates from the church at Antioch. The apostles and elders met together, and Paul and Barnabas rehearsed in their presence their labors and successes, and the matter that was referred to the council was discussed, and finally it was decided that the Gentile converts were under no special obligation to observe the ceremonial law. They declared that those teachers who had harrassed the churches of Cilicia were false teachers, and that they gave them no such commandment as they pretended, that Gentile converts were to be circumcised. The council prepared a pastoral address, or wrote a letter and decree to the churches of Antioch, Syria and Cilicia, and sent it by the hands of Paul and Barnabas; and they sent with them Barsabas and Silas. Paul had been cordially greeted, and his actions fully endorsed by the apostles who were at Jerusalem. They continued at Antioch awhile, and at length Paul proposed to Barnabas that they should go and visit the churches they had formed in different places. He readily agreed to it, but he insisted on having John Mark with him. Paul was opposed to Mark going with them, for the reason that he had left them when they were on the tour of establishing the churches. The contention became so sharp that they parted assunder, and Barnabas took Mark with him and sailed into Cyprus; and Paul chose Silas, and went through Syria and Cilicia confirming the churches. Acts xv.

Paul, and Silas, his companion, went to Derbe and Lystra. Here was a young disciple, whose name was Timothy. His mother was a Jewess, but his father was a Greek. He selected him also as a companion, but before taking him he caused him to be circumcised, that he might not be objectionable to the Jews. They then went on through the cities, delivering the decrees of the council at Jerusalem, and their labors were greatly blessed. The churches were established, and increased in numbers daily. They went through Phrygia and the region of Galatia, and they came to Troas. Here Paul had the vision in which he heard the Macedonian cry: "Come over and help us." He immediately determined to go and preach the gospel in Macedonia. From Troas he went to Philippi, a chief city of that country by the way of Samothracia and Neapolis, and near Philippi, on the Sabbath day, he went to a place of resort by the river side. He sat down amongst those who had resorted there and taught them, and Lydia was converted with her family; and many of her neighbors and friends also. Lydia opened her house, and offered its hospitalities to the apostle while he stayed there. "And when she was baptized and her household, she besought us saying: "If ye have judged me to be faithful to the Lord, come and abide in my house."

There was a damsel possessed with a spirit of divination, that followed the apostles about in their labors day after day, and annoyed them and those who attended them. Paul had compassion upon her, and healed her. This occasioned much disatisfaction with her masters, and they proceeded at once against the apostles. They dragged them into the market place, and before their rulers, and brought their accusations against them. The magistrates gave judgment against them, and after beating them they cast them into prison, and made their feet fast in the stocks. But undaunted by persecution and stripes and imprisonment, at midnight they prayed and sang praises to God. The prisoners heard them, and their shout of praise astonished them.

There was an earthquake that shook the prison so furiously, that the bolts flew back, and the doors opened, and the bonds of every prisoner were loosed. The terrible shock awakened the jailor, and springing from his bed, he was alarmed to see that every door was open and every prisoner was loose, and supposing that all would make their esacpe, and he would be suspected of unfaithfulness, he was about to kill himself with his own sword, but the voice of Paul fell upon his ear, saying, "Do thyself no harm, we are all here." The jailor then tremblingly besought the apostles to show him the way of life: "What must I do to be saved?" Paul said to him, "Believe on the

Lord Jesus Christ, and thou shalt be saved."

The jailor did believe, and that night he and his whole family, were converted to God, and took on themselves the christian name and character in holy baptism.

The next day the magistrates who had condemned them ordered the jailor to give them their liberty. But Paul asserted his Roman citizenship, and demanded that the magistrates who had beaten them uncondemned should come in person and dismiss them. When they heard that they were Roman citizens, they were affrighted. They then came and besought them to go free and depart out of their city. They accordingly departed from the prison, but not at once from the city, for they went to the house of Lydia, and comforted the disciples that resorted there. Acts, xvi.

From Philippi they went to Thessalonica. Here, for three Sabbath days, the apostle preached the doctrines of the gospel, "reasoned with them out of the scriptures," in the Jewish synagogues. The consequence was, many believed, and the jealous and wicked Jews raised a mob and assaulted the house of Jason, where Paul lodged. As the mob did not find Paul and his companions there, they arrested Jason, and took him before the magistrates, under the charge of harboring rebels against the emperor and empire. But he proved his loyalty, furnished security, and was dismissed.

The persecution being so severe, the christians conducted Paul and Silas out of the city that night, and the next day they went to Berea and began there to preach Jesus in the synagogues of the Jews. The people of Berea were more noble than those of Thessalonica. They heard the apostles preach and received their words readily, and searched the scriptures daily to compare them with the teachings they received. The consequence was, very many believed, and among them were many women and men of note. The Jews who were so cruel and malicious at Thessalonica, heard of their success in Berea, and they came there and stirred up the people insomuch that a mob was raised there, and the brethren of Berea sent Paul away. Silas and Timothy tarried awhile to instruct the new converts. Paul went to Athens, from which point he sent for Silas and Timothy, and they immediately made ready and went. But while Paul waited for them, his soul was stirred within him at the idolatry of the city, and he could not forbear to lift up his voice against their sin. He went into the Jewish synagogues and disputed with them. He met the philosophers of the Stoics and Epicureans and disputed with them. They brought accusations against him and arraigned him before the court of Areopagus. A great many persons attended his trial, and before them all he preached against their idolatry, and proclaimed the doctrine of the gospel, and especially the doctrines of the resurrection and the judgment. His defense was masterly, and resulted in the conversion of some. Dionysius the Areopagite and a woman of some note named Damaris clave unto him and believed. Acts, xvii.

Silas and Timothy came to Paul at Athens, and, as it is thought, reported to him the suffering of the christians, especially at Thessalonica, which led the apostle to write the Epistles to the Thessalonians, and he probably sent them by the hands of Silas and Timothy, and caused them to return to comfort, and encourage them. Paul then left Athens and went to Corinth, where he preached with much success. He lodged in Corinth at the house of Aquila and Priscilla. Every Sabbath day he preached in the Jewish synagogues, and among those who were converted here were Stephanus and his family, Crispus and Gaius. Paul continued here one year and six months. He had glorious success amid much opposition. Silas and Timothy came to him, and were with him in labor at Corinth part of the time. For some reason Paul removed his lodgings from the house of Aquila to the house of Justus. But the Jews were determined to rid themselves of Paul if possible. They therefore accused him before Gallio, the deputy of Achia. They charged Paul with being an enemy of the Roman Governor, but Gallio gave the mob no encouragement, and he told them he would not be a judge for them in such matters as they brought before him, "and he drave them from the judgment seat."

They then took Sosthenes, the ruler of the synagogue, and beat him, probably for letting Paul preach in the synagogue, but of this Gallio took no notice. After some time Paul determined to go to Jerusalem, and be there at the coming Pentecost season. He went through Ephesus, Cesarea, Antioch, and the churches of Galatia, and Phrygia, and in the churches he strengthened the brethren. Aquila and Priscilla attended him as far as Ephesus, and he left them there. Acts, xviii.

The account of his travels and labors—his successes and persecutions. is recorded in Acts, xix and xx. He performed several miracles at Ephesus, and by the laying on of his hands conferred the miraculous influence of the Holy Ghost—such as the gift of prophecy and the speaking of languages. Demetrius, a silver smith that made shrines for the temple of Diana, raised an uproar against Paul, and brought on him a severe trial, and it is supposed that he wrote his epistle to the Galatians from this place.

Paul left Ephesus after the uproar was over, and went to Macedonia, probably to Philippi, and then into Greece, where he stayed three months. He left Philippi and went to Troas, being five days on the route, and he spent seven days at Troas. The last day he spent there was the Sabbath, or first day of the week. He held a sacramental meeting with them, and prepared the next day to leave them. He continued the services that night until after midnight. A young man who was in the congregation had fallen asleep, and being seated in the window of the upper room where they were assembled, he fell down and was taken up for dead. Paul by a miracle restored him to life. Paul then pursued his journey. He stopped at Miletus, and had a conference with the elders of the church. He spake to them of his trials and abundant labors, and of the trials that yet awaited him, and he exhorted them to fidelity, then commended them to God and the word of his grace. They then kneeled down together and after an earnest prayer from the apostle, during which they were deeply affected and wept sorely, Paul and these elders parted to meet no more in time. There is, probably, an allusion to these circumstances and trials, in Paul's life, in 1st Cor. xv: 32; 2d Cor. 1-8; and vii: 5-6; xi: 23-28.

Paul then went to Rhodes, Patara and Tyre, making at each place a short stay, when he went to Ptolemais, and thence to Cesarea. At Cesarea, he lodged at the house of Philip, the deacon, and while there, he was visited by Agabus, the prophet from Judea, who prophesied regarding the bonds that awaited Paul at Jerusalem. The friends of the apostle tried to prevent him from going, or rather to disuade him, but he would not be stopped, for he was ready to suffer imprisonment and even death, for the cause of his adorable master.

At length he reached Jerusalem, and was received with cordiality by the church. James, the apostle, was there, and Paul called on him, and the elders of the church assembled together at the house of James, when Paul gave them an account of his labors and travels. He acceded to the wishes of the brethren at Jerusalem to prepare himself, by purifying, to enter the temple. Seven days were accomplished, and he came into the court of the temple with his offerings; but scarcely had he entered before he was arrested for polluting the temple, and they drew him out of it and shut the doors, and they were about to kill him, but he was rescued by Lysias, the chief captain of the Roman Guards. He had observed the uproar in time to save Paul from being killed. Taking charge of Paul, Lysias hurried toward the castle with him. Paul asked very courteously of the captain the privilege of speaking a word. He granted it, when the apostle told him he was a Jew, and born in the famous city of Tarsus. Lysias, hearing this, gave him the privilege of speaking. He then rehearsed his conversion and his manner of life since.

The Jews became very clamorous for his blood, especially when he declared his mission to preach among the Gentiles. Lysias, in order partly to appease the wrath of the Jews, ordered Paul to be scourged. Just at this point he asserted his Roman citizenship, which alarmed the centurion and led Lysias to have him loosed, and the next day he called a council of priests and elders to have Paul deliberately tried. Acts, xxi.

As the council were gathered together the apostle appeared before them and began his defence. Acts, xxiii. Scarcely had he begun his speech when Ananias, the high priest, gave an order to smite him on the mouth. He looked at him and said: "God shall smite thee, thou whited wall, for sittest thou to judge me after the law, and commandest me to be smitten contrary to law." This was a severe but merited rebuke. Paul then proceeded with his defence, when the Pharisees and Sadducees fell to disputing, and Lysias dismissed the council and ordered Paul back to the castle. That night the persecuted apostle was favored with a vision in which the Lord told him that he should bear testimony in Rome.

There was a plot, laid by the Jews, to kill him. About forty of them vowed they would neither eat nor drink until they had accomplished their purpose. Paul's sister's son revealed the plot, and the design of these murderers was thwarted. The chief captain sent him bound and guarded to Cesarea, to the governor, Felix.

Some time after this Ananias and others of the Jewish rulers came down to Cesarea to prosecute Paul, and they brought with them Tertullus, an orator, who accused the apostle as a disturber of the peace and a wicked profaner of the temple. Paul was permitted to answer to the accusations, which he did in a defence before Felix.

The governor dismissed the trial for that day, and promised to bring it up again when he could have Lysias, the chief captain, present, who had sent him. Felix commanded the centurion who had charge of Paul to let him have liberty, and let his friends and acquaintances come to see him and minister unto him. Felix, and Drusilla his wife, sent for Paul and heard him reason of righteousness, temperance, and judgment to come, and it is said, Felix trembled. He kept Paul yet as a prisoner.

When Festus entered on his government the apostle had been a prisoner two years. The Jewish rulers accused Paul to him, and requested that he would send him up to Jerusalem for trial. Festus was unwilling to do that, and bade them come to Cesarea. They did so, but failed. Festus then asked Paul if he was willing to go up to Jerusalem and be tried. He certified his unwillingness by appealing to Nero. His appeal was entertained, and he was notified that he should be sent to Rome.

A little while after this Agrippa and his sister Bernice came to pay Festus a visit. When Paul's case was reported to King Agrippa he desired to see him and hear for himself. Paul was therefore brought before Agrippa and set forth his conversion, his call to the ministry, and his labor. Both Festus and Agrippa were touched by the apostle's presentation of his cause, and especially the king, for he said, "Almost thou persuadest me to be a Christian." He gave it as his opinion that he might have been set at liberty if he had not appealed to Cesar, and his appeal been granted. Acts, xxv and xxvi.

Not long after this, in company with other prisoners he was put on board a vessel bound to Rome, under a guard. Julius, a centurion of Augustus' band, had all the prisoners in his charge. Julius was very kind during the voyage to Paul. They were affected by contrary winds, but gained Lycia, when they were put on board of an Alexandrian vessel bound for Rome. Contrary winds, storms and disagreeable weather came on them so that they traveled slowly; but at length a terrible storm came up, and they were driven into a small island called Clauda. They took down the sails, and cast out the tackling. For several days they saw neither sun nor stars, the storm continuing; and all on board except Paul were discouraged, and thought all was lost. He was advised by an angel of God that the lives of all should be saved, though the vessel might be an utter wreck. On the fourteenth night they drew nigh to an island, cast out their anchors and anxiously waited for daylight. There were two hundred and seventy-six souls, and so far none had been lost. They weighed anchor and tried to make the land, but the vessel struck a rock and broke in two. The centurion ordered those who could swim to throw themselves into the sea and swim to shore, and those who could not, clung to broken pieces of plank and made their way to the shore, so that every one of them escaped—not one life was lost. The inhabitants of the island showed them great kindness, for they kindled a fire and warmed them after their exposure to the cold and storm, and rain and sea. A venomous serpent came out of a bundle of sticks that had been cast on the fire and fastened on Paul's hand. The superstitious inhabitants of Melita thought that circumstance was an evidence of Paul's guilt, and they looked every moment for him to die; but instead of that he shook the viper off and realized no harm. Then they changed their minds and said he was a god. He cured many diseases of the people of the island, and among them the father of Publius of a dangerous disease.

They tarried at the Island three months, when in a ship of Alexandria, which had wintered in that Island, they departed for Rome, and landing at Puteoli they tarried seven days, during which time Paul associated with the brethren whom he found there when he set out for Rome. The brethren had learned that he was coming, and many of them came to meet him as far as the "Three Taverns." He was greatly encouraged by their demonstrations of christian fellowship and feeling, "he thanked God and took courage." Julius who had had him in charge, handed him over, or delivered him to the captain of the guard, where for two full years he was permitted to live in his own hired house with the soldiers that kept him, and all that time he preached the gospel to those who came to hear him.

Those who had brought the accusation against him in Jerusalem did not follow him up and persecute him at Rome. He then sent for the principal Jews of Rome and laid his case before them. They told him that it had not been represented to them by their brethren of Judea. He had occasion as he thus represented the case, to preach to them the doctrines of the cross, and he did it with a good degree of success. Acts xxvi. xxvii.

Whether he was released after two years imprisonment and went back into the countries where he had formerly preached, and then returned to Rome we cannot certainly tell. But during these two years, he made many converts, and among them some of Cesar's own household. He had many friends, who, when they came to Rome ministered unto him, such was Onesiphorus, who sought him out. Onesimus, Philemon's runaway slave, was converted, and was very useful to the apostle. He wrote his epistle to Philemon, and sent it by Onesimus. Epaphroditus came from the Philippian church to him, and brought with him to Paul money and presents from the brethren at Philippi. About this time Demas forsook him, and he wrote his Epistle to the Philippians. He alludes to the fall of Demas overcome with the world in Col. iv: 14, 2d Tim. iv: 10. He sent the epistle by Epaphroditus on his return. The epistle to the Galatians, he sent by Crescens, and that to the Ephesians, by Tychicus. He also wrote his second Epistle to Timothy about this time, and in it desires him to come to Rome. He did go and was imprisoned there, it is thought, and was afterwards liberated. When Paul wrote his Epistle to the Hebrews, Timothy was the one in whose charge Paul placed it.

Paul knew full well that his end was approaching, for which he wrote his second epistle to Timothy, he was aware that Nero was greatly enraged at him, and he expected a violent death by his hands. He wrote "I am now ready to be offered up, and the time of my departure is at hand. I have fought a good fight, I have finished my course, I have kept the faith, henceforth there is laid up for me a crown of life," etc. It seems when he was first tried before Nero his friends all forsook him, for he says "all men forsook me." At his second trial he was condemned and put to some violent death, but exactly how he suffered death we do not know.

The epistles of Paul are highly commended by Peter, "even as our beloved brother Paul also according to the wisdom given unto him hath written unto you, as also in all his epistles," etc. 2d Peter, iii: 15.

He has been called the great apostle to the Gentiles, because God selected him as a chosen vessel to bear the glad tidings of salvation to the Gentile world, and he confined his ministry mainly to them. The treasure of a measure of the gospel was committed unto him and he used it, giving God the glory due unto him. He did not preach himself but Christ Jesus the Lord, and of his qualifications he says, "For God who commanded the light to shine out of darkness, hath shined into our hearts to give the light of the knowledge of the glory of God in the face of Jesus Christ."

Paul had a large degree of spirituality—occupied a high state in grace. He says, "I am crucified with Christ. I live, yet not I but Christ liveth in me; and the life which I now live in the flesh, I live by the faith of the son of God. And again he says, "God forbid that I should glory save in the cross of our Lord Jesus Christ, by whom the world is crucified to me and I unto the world." He was bold and ardent in his temperament before his conversion, and so he was after. He was as noted as a preacher as he had been as a persecutor. The principles of firmness, stability, decision of character were very marked in his whole ministerial life. He stood firm at his post until his work was done — when he exchanged earth for heaven; the sorrow and trials of life for the rest and enjoyments of that pure clime where the wicked cease from troubling, and the wearied soul is forever at rest.

PEDAHEL—[Ped′-a-hel.]

The son of Ammihud, of the tribe of Naphtali, was one of the princes that assisted Joshua and Eleazar in dividing the land of Canaan among the tribes of Israel. Num. xxxiv: 28.

PEDAHZUR—[Ped-ah′zur,] *savior, strong and powerful, stone of redemption.*

Was of the tribe of Manasseh, and the father of Gamaliel, the prince, who assisted Moses in numbering the tribes of Israel. Num. i: 10.

PEDAIAH, 1—[Ped-a′-yah,] *redemption of the Lord.*

The father of Zebudah, and grandfather of Jehoiakim. 2d Kings xxiii: 36.

PEDAIAH, 2—*Redemption of the Lord.*

The brother of Shealtiel and uncle of Zerubbabel. 1st Chron. iii: 18.

PEDAIAH, 3—*Redemption of the Lord.*

Was the son of Parosh, who assisted Nehemiah in building the walls of the city. Neh. iii: 25.

PEDAIAH, 4—*Redemption of the Lord.*

One of those who stood at Ezra's left hand when he read the law to the people.

PEDAIAH, 5—*Redemption of the Lord.*

The father of Joel, a prince of the half tribe of Manasseh in the time of David. 1st Chron. xxvii: 20.

PEKAH—[Pe′-kah,] *he that opens, or is at liberty.*

PEKAH was the son of Remaliah. He was a general of the king of Israel's army. 2d Kings, xv: 25. He conspired against Pekaiah, the king and slew him in the palace, in Samaria, having as his helpers, Argob and Arieh, with fifty Gileadites. He then usurped authority and reigned as king in the stead of Pekaiah, and the length of his reign was twenty years. He was a wicked king, and his history and reign, were disgraced with many sins.

Pekah entered into a league with Rezin, the king of Syria, to vex and destroy Judah and the house of David. They intended to conquer Judah, and make it tributary to them, setting up a king of their own selection. Isa. vii: 1-7.

We have an account in 2d Chronicles, xxviii: 6-10, of Pekah's war with Judah, in which he slew one hundred and twenty thousand, and took two hundred thousand captives, or prisoners. But he was induced by Oded, the prophet, to return the prisoners to their own land, clothing and feeding them out of the spoils he had taken, and with great humanity he conveyed the feeble ones, on asses, to Judea.

At length Tiglath-Pileser, the king of Assyria, warred with Pekah, the king of Israel, and he took several cities and carried the inhabitants captive to Assyria, and finally Hoshea murdered Pekah, and reigned in his stead. 2d Kings,. xv: 26-30.

PEKAHIAH—[Pek-a-hi′-ah,] *it is the Lord that opens.*

PEKAHIAH became the king of Israel in the fiftieth year of Azariah the king of Judah. He was the son of Menahem, and reigned but two years in Samaria. "And he did that which was evil in the sight of the Lord: he departed not from the sins of Jeroboam, the son of Nebat, who made Israel to sin." 2d Kings, xv: 24. He was slain by Pekah, the son of Remaliah, who had fifty-two others associated with him in the murder, when he ascended the throne and reigned in the stead of Pekahiah.

PELATIAH — [Pel-a-ti′-ah,] *let the Lord deliver.*

PELATIAH was the son of Benaiah. The prophet Jeremiah urged Zedekiah to go out and submit himself to the mercy of Nebuchadnezzar, who was besieging the city of Jerusalem. Palatiah, it is supposed, dissuaded the king from doing so, and as a punishment died. We have also a clear account of his sin and death in Ezek. xi: 1-13, from which it appears that when Ezekiel came to the east gate of the Lord's house to prophesy, he saw Jaazaniah and Pelatiah, with twenty-three other men, and the Lord told him that these men had given wicked counsel in the city and that they should be punished for it; and while he was prophesying, Pelatiah fell suddenly dead. Whether his companion, the other prince, died thus suddenly or not, we cannot tell.

PELEG—[Pe′-leg,] *division.*

PELEG was the son of Eber and the brother of Joktan. In connection with the announcement of his birth, it is said, "for in his days was the earth divided." Gen. x: 25. His birth is supposed to have been about one hundred years after the flood, which was probably the time when the earth was divided among the sons of Noah. In the 5th verse of the chapter there is a reference to this division, when it is said: "By these were the isles of the Gentiles divided in their lands; every one after his tongue, after their families in their nations." There is an allusion to the confounding of languages, and the dispersion which took place on account of it in the days of Peleg. The building of Babel may have occurred some time after his birth, and his father may have given him the name which signifies division, under the spirit of prophecy. And, indeed, it is understood that the event did not transpire until just before Peleg's death, which was probably more than two hundred years later, for he was thirty years old when Reu, his son was born, and lived after that two hundred and nine years. Genesis xi: 18, 19.

He was the same as Phalec, whom Luke places in the genealogy of Christ. Luke iii: 35.

PENINNAH—[Pe-nin′-nah,] *precious stone, his face.*

PENINNAH was one of the wives of Elkanah, who was a Levite of Mt. Ephraim, at the time that Eli was high priest and the center of worship was at Shiloh, because the ark of God was there. Hannah was also a wife of this Levite, and was greatly loved by him—loved beyond what Peninnah was loved—and yet the latter had children, while the former had none.

They were accustomed, as the wives of this devoted Levite, to go with him every year to worship in Shiloh, and he gave them a portion to offer unto the Lord. 1st Sam. i: 4. "And when the time was that Elkanah offered, he gave to Peninnah his wife, and to all her sons and daughters, portions." Peninnah seems to have been jealous of the other wife of Elkanah. She saw that her husband made Hannah his favorite, notwithstanding she had no children. And her jealousy led her to become an adversary to Hannah, and to provoke her sore because she had no children. Peninnah certainly did wrong in constantly trying to irritate and vex Hannah, and so make her unhappy. But she did wrong especially to take the opportunity of vexing her when they were going to the annual feast to sacrifice unto the Lord. If she would provoke her, ought she not to have selected some other time than when making their yearly visits to Shiloh, thereby disturbing the solemn services of the religious feast. But there was a circumstance connected with Elkanah's treatment of the two wives that was groundwork for the temptation. That was, when he gave Peninnah and her sons and daughters each a portion to sacrifice, "unto Hannah he gave a worthy portion, for he loved Hannah." In whatever Hannah's portion differed from the others, it was intended as a special exhibit and proof of especial love to her.

Possibly, had Elkanah been more careful in his expressions of stronger love for Hannah than for Peninnah, the latter would not have had the jealousy she had, and hence would not have become the open adversary of the other wife.

PERSIS—[Per′-sis.]

PERSIS is supposed to have been a very laborious and efficient female in the church, saluted by Paul in closing up his epistle to the Romans. Rom. xvi: 12. "Salute the beloved Persis, which labored much in the Lord." We would suppose that she was the most noted for efficient labor of the three women saluted in that verse. Of the other two it is said they labored in the Lord, but of Persis, she labored *much* in the Lord. Thus we may suppose she excelled as a holy woman.

PETER—[Pe′-ter,] *a rock, a stone.*

PETER was a native of Bethsaida, the son of Jonas and the brother of Andrew. His first name was Simon, which continued to be used as his name even by Christ and his apostles, after his name was changed to Cephas, or Peter. John, i: 40-42. He was a married man and lived at Capernaum, being engaged in the occupation of a fisherman. One of the first miracles that Christ performed at Capernaum, which became his place of residence, or is called "his own city," was that of curing Peter's wife's mother of a fever. Mark, i: 29.

After Andrew formed acquaintance with Jesus, and was convinced that he was the promised Messiah, he went in search of Simon and found him, and invited him to go and see Jesus. He said, "We have found the Messiah, which is, being interpreted, the Christ." Andrew brought him to Jesus; and when Jesus saw him he changed his name to Cephas, and they spent the night together.

About a year after that Peter and Andrew, with the two sons of Zebedee, were engaged in fishing on the sea of Galilee. They had spent a whole night in fruitless toil and given it up; preparatory to putting away their nets they were washing them. Jesus came to them and asked for the use of their fishing boats to sit in while he taught the people on the shore. They granted his request, and after Jesus had finished his teaching he bade them push out from the shore and cast their net into the sea for a draught. They had been fishing without success, but yet they made no objection. They followed his instructions and cast the net, and it was soon filled with great fishes—such a draw as they had never made before, and yet the net was not broken. Peter was greatly astonished at the number of fish taken, and, turning to Jesus, he entreated him to depart from him, for he was too holy to stay in the company of one so sinful and polluted as he was. Jesus did not depart from him as requested, but on the contrary, called Peter, with his brother Andrew, and James and John, the sons of Zebedee, to be his disciples. Luke, v: 1-11.

In the account given of his call to follow Christ, in Matt. iv: 19, Jesus said unto them, "Follow me and I will make you fishers of men." Peter and his brother were the two first called, and so they were the two first of the apostles sent forth, and it is quite likely that they were the two oldest of the apostles. They are the first ones named in the account and number of the apostles. Luke, vi: 14; Matt. x: 2.

Peter was bold and ardent in his temperament—more forward than any of the apostles, and he often appears as spokesman for them, because of his natural ardor, he was exceedingly liable to rashness. There are several circumstances related in the history of Christ as given by the Evangelists, setting this forth. We have an account in Matt. xvi: 22 of Peter daring to rebuke Jesus. He had told his disciples that he must go to Jerusalem and suffer much from his enemies, and be killed, and the third day rise again from the dead, "Then Peter took him and began to rebuke him saying, Be it far from thee Lord, this shall not be unto thee." This was probably the first time that Jesus had spoken plainly of his coming suffering and death. Peter in his ardent love said, "It shall never be as thou hast said." This led Jesus very sharply to rebuke Peter, "Get thee behind me Satan; thou art an offence unto me, for thou savorest not the things that be of God, but those that be of men." When Jesus came to the disciples on the sea of Galilee and Peter saw him coming, on the water, as soon as he was satisfied that it was Jesus, he asked him if he might come to meet him. He saw his master walking on the water and conceived the idea that he too could walk on it. Jesus bade him come, but scarcely had his feet touched the water until he felt that he was sinking. His faith failed him, he felt that he was sinking and cried, saying, "Lord, save me." Christ put forth his hand and saved him, but rebuked him for his lack of faith. Matt. xiv: 28, etc.

Jesus asked his disciples at one time if they would leave him, as many others had done, "for many of his disciples went back and walked no more with him." Peter answered for them all, "Lord, to whom shall we go? thou hast the words of eternal life." John, vi: 67.

At one time Christ was with his disciples at Cesarea Philippi, and asked them, "Whom do men say that I, the Son of Man, am?" They told him that some said he was John the Babtist, some said he was Elias, and others Jeremias, or some one of the prophets; but turning to Peter, Jesus said, "Whom say ye that I am?" He promptly answered, "Thou art the Christ, the son of the living God." Jesus pronounced a blessing upon him, and assured him that through his instrumentality the church should be built upon the truth he had thus confessed, and that "the gates of hell should not prevail against it." He told Peter that he and his brother apostles, and their successors in the ministry, should have the power vested in them of founding and governing the church. "Whatsoever ye shall bind on earth, shall be bound in Heaven, and whatsoever ye shall loose on earth shall be loosed in heaven." Matt. xvi: 13, &c.

A short time after this, Peter, in company with James and John, went up with Jesus on the mount of Transfiguration, and they beheld together the divine glory as it gathered about the person of Jesus; and they saw the two shining ones that represented the patriarchal and prophetical dispensations—Moses and Elias. Peter knew the heavenly visitants, and said unto Jesus, "Lord, it is good for us to be here. Let us make three tabernacles, one for thee, and one for Moses, and one for Elias." Matt. xvii: 1-4.

As Peter's home was at Capernaum, and that was the home of Jesus, too, they were both enrolled as residents, and hence were liable for tribute. The tax-collectors asked Peter if his master paid tribute. Jesus knowing that the question had been asked him, bade him go and cast a line into the sea and open the mouth of the first fish he caught, and he should find a piece of money with which (it being of sufficient value) he should pay tribute for them both. Matt. xxvii: 24, &c.

At one time Jesus was discoursing, probably to his disciples, on the duty of forgiving injuries when forgiveness was sought. Peter desired some further instruction, and asked, "If my brother sin seven times shall I forgive him?" Jesus told him he should, and even more than that—seventy times seven, or four hundred and ninety times. The true meaning of the Savior was, he should forgive just as often as necessary—as often as forgiveness was properly sought. Matt. xviii: 21.

When the Savior was imparting instruction regarding the deceitfulness of riches and the danger to which rich men were exposed,—having the case of the young man who refused to sell what he had and distribute to the poor before him,—he said, "A rich man shall hardly enter into the kingdom of heaven." And in order more fully to impress their minds with the danger of riches, he said, "It is easier for a camel to go through the eye of a needle than for a rich man to enter into the kingdom of God." The disciples were all amazed, and Peter returned to ask what would be their (the disciples') reward, having left all to follow him. He told Peter that if they were faithful they should gain much—they should receive a hundred fold in this world, and in the end everlasting life. Matt. xix: 23, &c.

A little while before our Savior's passion he cursed a barren fig-tree, and in a short time it withered away. Peter pointed it out to his master, and referred to the curse he had pronounced upon it because there was no fruit thereon. Mark, xi: 11, &c. And still a little later, Jesus gave his disciples a striking lesson on the virtue of humility, in washing the disciples' feet. Jesus took a towel and girded himself, poured water into a basin, and began the service. When he came to Simon Peter he refused to allow Jesus to wash his feet, nor would he yield until Jesus told him he could have no part in him unless he submitted. Peter then said, "Lord, not my feet only, but my hands and my head." John, xiii: 1, &c.

Either at this time, or very shortly after, Jesus indicated clearly that one of them would betray him. They were very anxious to know which one it was, for they each enquired, "Lord, is it I?" Peter was especially anxious to know, and he beckoned to John, the beloved disciple, who was then leaning on Jesus's breast, to ask him. John did ask him, and the traitor was pointed out. John, xiii: 25.

On Thursday before Christ's crucifixion, Peter and John, under the direction of Jesus, went into the city to prepare the Passover, that he might eat with them once more, and institute the sacred supper. He gave all the necessary directions, and they following them, soon had an upper chamber provided and prepared; and soon after Jesus and his disciples met there, and he gave them the emblems of his broken body, and shed blood. Luke, xxii: 8-20.

Soon after the sacred supper was ended, Jesus referred to the fact again that one of them would betray him. Peter, with his accustomed ardor and rashness, declared that though all others prove recreant to the master, yet he would not. Jesus told him in an affectionate manner, that Satan desired to have him that he might sift him as wheat, but that he had prayed for him that his faith might not utterly fail. Peter felt very confident that he could stand—that his love for Jesus would lead him to prison and to death. "Though I die with thee, yet I will not deny thee." Jesus answered him that the cock should not crow until he should deny him thrice. John, xiii: 36; Matthew, xxvi: 31; Luke, xxii: 31-34. Shortly after this, Jesus retired to the garden of Gethsemane, and he took with him there Peter and James and John. Just as he had entered the garden he said to the three disciples, "Stay ye here, and I will go yonder and pray." It was but a little while till they all fell asleep. Jesus waked them up after each of the three prayers he had offered up to the father in his agony, with the affectionate question, "What! could ye not watch with me one hour?" He knew full well that they were willing, but were overcome with sleep. He kindly said to them, "the spirit indeed is willing, but the flesh is weak." It was not long after he awoke them the last time, until Judas, heading a mob, entered Gethsemane, and approached the company—with the kiss of a hypocrite he designated Jesus, and the band seized him. Peter, true to the purpose he had formed, and a little while before expressed, determined to defend his master. He took out his sword and cut off the ear of Malchus, the servant of the high priest. Jesus rebuked him for the rash act, and bade him put up his sword. He gave Peter to understand that he needed no defense of that kind, nor was his religion to be propogated by the sword. "They that take the sword shall perish by the sword." As the band led Jesus away, Peter followed at a distance. He went on to Caiphas, the high priest, and by some means, gained an entrance into the hall, and mixed up with the servants till he should learn the result of the investigation. A damsel approached him, and asked him if he was not with Jesus, of Galilee. He said he was not. He passed out into the porch, and another maid saw him, and accused him of being one of the disciples of Jesus. He again denied it, and confirmed his denial with an oath, declaring he knew not the man. After awhile, one of the company approached him, and affirmed that he was positively a disciple of Jesus.

Several others of the company said that they were confident he was. His speech betrayed him, and finally a kinsman of Malchus, whose ear he had cut off, one who probably saw his act and heard the rebuke of Jesus when he bade him put up his sword, said to Peter, "Did I not see thee in the garden?"

At this Peter became furious and cursed, and swore that he knew not the man. Just then the cock crew, and he remembered the words of Jesus, "before the cock crow, thou shalt deny me thrice." His conscience smote him for his wickedness, and to add to the bitterness of his soul Jesus looked on him. That gaze seemed to penetrate his inner heart, and show him his treachery and wickedness. He withdrew from the crowd, and sought a place to weep. His heart was over-balanced with sorrow, and he wept bitterly. Matt. xxvi; John xviii. Though Peter thus denied his Lord, yet he repented. His sin was sudden; his contrition was deep and genuine. He still thought well of his master, and his anxieties and feelings clustered about the tomb where he lay. On the morning of the Resurrection, Peter and John heard by the women who went early to the sepulcher that the body was gone, and they ran to the sepulcher to see. They found it as the women had said. The body was gone, but the grave-clothes were there. Peter made an examination, and full of sorrow and perplexity the two went back to the city and reported to the rest what they had seen. The women had been charged especially to tell Peter that Christ was risen from the dead. But not long after this Jesus appeared to Peter himself, for when the two disciples returned from Emmaus, they found the disciples gathered together and saying: "The Lord hath risen indeed, and hath appeared unto Simon." Soon after this Christ appeared unto all the disciples together in Jerusalem. Luke xxiv: 34; and 1st Cor. xv: 5. When Peter and some other of the apostles were fishing on the Sea of Galilee, Jesus appeared to them on the shore. They had fished all night and caught nothing. He asked them: "Have ye any meat?" They answered, no. He then directed them to cast the net on the right side of the ship; they did so, and they were not able to draw it for the multitude of fishes. The circumstance, it is likely, strongly reminded John and Peter of their call to the ministry, for it was just after a miraculous draught of fish. John suggested to Peter that it was the Lord. Peter at once girt his fisher's coat about him and swam to the shore; all anxiety to be near him in haste. Soon the disciples all gathered about Jesus, and they ate together of the fish which they had caught. After they had dined, Jesus asked Peter, who by this time was fully satisfied it was the Savior: "Simon, son of Jonas, lovest thou me." This question was asked him three times, probably to remind him of his having denied him three times. He answered promptly, but the third time very significantly, "Lord, thou knowest all things; thou knowest that I love thee." Jesus then informed Peter that severe trials awaited him in the future. He told him that he would be called to endure bonds, imprisonments, and even death for his sake. He did not shrink from the task before him, but manifested a willingness to have his faith thus tested. But fixing his eyes on John, he asked: "Lord, and what shall this man do." He wished to know something as to the future course and fate of the beloved disciple. John xxi; and Mark xvi: 7, &c. He was present at Olivet on the ascension morning, and was one of the gazing Galileans addressed by the angels.

It was but a little while after the ascension that Peter proposed to the disciples to have the place of Judas filled. Accordingly Matthias was chosen, after earnest prayer to God to direct, and settle for them the question, as they cast lots. A few days after this, the Pentecost came on, and Peter and his fellow apostles were endowed with "power from on high." They received the Holy Ghost, the promise of the father, to qualify them for their mission. There was a vast concourse of Jews gathered in, from the different parts of the empire, and Peter spoke to them as did his brethren in their own language.

The other apostles may have preached as did Peter, but the Pentecost sermon, as recorded, is awarded to him. He defended his brethren and the excited and happy multitude, and preached with power, the doctrines of the cross of Christ. A great many received the word, believed in Christ, and were added to the Lord. Three hundred thousand that day took upon them the name and character, in baptism. Acts, i, and ii.

A remarkable case of healing is next recorded in the history of Peter. He and John were going up together to the temple, at the hour of prayer, a poor man was sitting there, who had been a cripple from his birth, and he asked alms of them. Peter said unto him, "Silver and gold have I none, but such as I have give I unto thee. In the name of Jesus Christ, of Nazareth, rise up and walk." The man was at once cured, and went with them into the temple.

Peter and John improved this circumstance, and it is thought that there was a large addition that day to the church. But in the evening the priests and Saducees apprehended Peter and John, and put them in prison, and kept them there until the next morning, when they brought them before the council and questioned them, as to the manner in which they had cured this lame man. This afforded Peter an opportunity of preaching another sermon, and he improved it. The council was astonished at their answers, and at the boldness and power, with which they spoke, seeing they were unlearned men. They, however, charged them to preach no more in the name of Jesus. But Peter and his companion gave them to understand that they would follow the leadings of the divine spirit, and the openings of divine providence. They then threatened them further, and let them go.

They went at once to their own company and reported all that the chief priests and elders had said, and done unto them. They all at once joined the two liberated apostles in praising God, and they engaged in a prayer meeting, during which the power of God was manifested. The very place where they were assembled was shaken, and they were all filled with the Holy Ghost. Believers were multiplied greatly, and the poor christians about Jerusalem, were provided for by voluntary contributions, constituting a church treasury, "distribution was made unto every man according as he had need." Acts, iii, and iv.

Among those who sold their possession and placed the proceeds in this treasury, was Ananias and his wife Sapphira. At least they pretended to have so done, but secretly agreed together, to keep back a part of the price. Peter discerned their deception and wickedness, charged it upon them, and they both fell dead at his feet. Peter no doubt improved this solemn circumstance by preaching Jesus to the people, and many of them believed on him. Then the high priests and Sadducees laid hands on Peter and his brother apostles, and cast them into prison. "But the angel of the Lord by night opened the prison doors and brought them forth and said, go stand and speak in the temple to the people all the words of this life." They went at once and preached in the courts of the temple. Morning came and the council sent for them to have them tried, but to the astonishment of the officers, though the prison doors were all shut, the prisoners were out. They were wondering about this strange affair when a report came to them that these men were teaching in the temple. The convened council sent for them, and when they were brought before them, the high priest asked them why they had kept on preaching, after they had been charged to stop. Peter answered charging them with the murder of the prince and Savior. He declared the resurrection of Jesus. At this they were very much enraged, and took council together to slay them. Gamaliel stepped forth and asked the council to hear him a little while. He then delivered an address that induced them to let the apostles go. Acts v.

Some time after this a severe persecution broke out, during which Stephen, one of the seven deacons suffered martyrdom. The persecution scattered the apostles, and Peter and John went to Samaria, where Philip, one of the deacons had introduced the gospel. There Peter detected Simon the sorcerer as an imposter, and confounded him with the most scathing rebukes. Simon saw that by the laying on of the apostle's hands, the Holy Ghost was communicated. He offered Peter money to invest him with the same power, but Peter said to him. "Thy money perish with thee, because thou hast thought that the gift of God may be purchased with money. Thou hast neither part nor lot in this matter, for thy heart is not right in the sight of God," &c. Acts viii: 9–24. After preaching in different parts of Samaria Peter and John ventured back again to Jerusalem. And the persecution having somewhat abated, probably because their leader, Saul of Tarsus, was converted, Peter went into different parts of Judea, Galilee and Samaria. It is said Peter "passed throughout all quarters, and came down to Lydda." In this place he cured Eneas of the palsy. He preached effectually there and at Saron. The death of Dorcas led him to go to Joppa, for the disciples there hearing he was at Lydda sent for him. He went and entered the apartment where Dorcas lay in the stillness of death. There were present a large number of her beneficiaries in the chamber, and they showed Peter the coats and garments she had made in her life time.

Peter put them all out, and offered up an earnest prayer to God to give this good woman back to the Joppa church. He then bade her arise from dead, and she arose, and the weeping church was soon rejoicing. Peter then took up his abode for a while in Joppa, lodging with Simon, a tanner, by the sea side. Acts, ix.

While he was residing here, Cornelius, the centurion, sent for him to hear from him words whereby he should be saved.

To prepare Peter for his mission to Cornelius, the Lord favored him with a vision, in which he saw a great sheet knit at the four corners, in which were clean and unclean animals, and a voice was heard by him saying: "Rise Peter, kill and eat." He made objections, but his objections were removed by the voice saying: "What God hath clensed, that call not thou common." This was repeated twice, when the sheet was taken up, and Peter awoke. Just at the time of his awaking, the messengers from Cornelius arrived, and enquired after him. He received their message, and at once knew the import of his vision, and agreed to go with them. He went and preached to Cornelius, thus introducing the gospel into the Gentile world. He was fully satisfied that it was his duty to preach the gospel to the Gentiles, for while administering the word of life, the Holy Ghost fell on all those that heard the word. Cornelius and his family and friends were baptized. Acts, x.

It was soon noised about at Jerusalem, that Peter had preached to the Gentiles, and they were offended. When he came to Jerusalem, they complained of his course, but he rehearsed the circumstances which led him to go there; and he told them the effect of his preaching: "The Holy Ghost fell on them as on us at the beginning." They were satisfied, "and glorified God saying, then hath God also unto the Gentiles granted repentance unto life." Acts, xi: 1–18.

Not long after this, Paul was in Jerusalem and tarried with Peter fifteen days, during which time they no doubt conversed freely regarding Paul's life-work—preaching the gospel to the Gentiles.

About this time Herod killed James and he imprisoned Peter, intending at a certain time to bring him forth to the people. While he was in prison, the christians were engaged in earnest prayer to God for him. And the very night before he was to be executed, they were praying in the house of Mary, the mother of John Mark. And the angel of the Lord went into the prison and waked Peter, and bade him bind on his sandals and follow him out. He did so, for the prison doors opened before them, and soon Peter, with his angel guide, was in the street. He went to the house of Mary and knocked at the gate. Rhoda came to the gate, and seeing him for joy opened not the gate, but ran in, and told the company that Peter was there. They did not at first believe her, but as he kept on knocking, they went and opened the gate, and he went in among them, and told them how that the Lord had delivered him. Acts, xii.

It is likely after this Peter went to Pontius, Galatia, Cappadocia, Asia and Bithynia. Into these countries many persecuted christians had fled, and to these disciples called strangers, he wrote his epistle. 1 Peter, i: 1. Several years after this Peter was in Jerusalem at the council that received Paul and Barnabas, and heard the report of their labors; and then set them apart, with others of their company, to preach the Gospel to the Gentiles of Antioch, and Syria, and Cilicia. Peter related in the council how that God had first granted the Gospel by him to the Gentiles, and he insisted that they ought not to impose any such ceremonial rites upon the Gentiles as circumcision, &c. Peter, and James the less, and John gave Paul the right hand of fellowship, and agreed that he should confine his labors chiefly to the Gentiles. Gal. ii: 9. Peter met Paul at Antioch, some time after this, and there was a sharp disputation between them, regarding the Gentile converts, and some ceremonies that Paul did not approve. Gal. ii: 14. Where Peter traveled and labored the latter part of his life is not certain. He wrote his Epistles to the Jews scattered about in the different portions of country named in 1 Peter, i: 1. He finally died, it is supposed, by crucifixion. It is reported of him that he asked the privilege of being crucified with his head downwards, not being worthy to suffer death as his master did. His Epistles are full of comfort to those for whom they were designed, and peculiarly appropriate to them in their exile and persecutions.

Peter occupied a high position among the apostles, and performed a great work; but it is not true that he possessed superiority over the others as the apostatized church imagined, and that he conveyed this supremacy to successors. He had weaknesses and imperfections, and failings equal to any of them, yet he enjoyed a large degree of religious experience. He often called up the reminiscences of his eventful life, and it has been said that he never heard a cock crow without having grief revived in his heart at his wicked denial of his Master. When writing his 2d Epistle, he calls up the transfiguration scene, and gives his testimony to it again. "And this voice which came from heaven, we heard, when we were with him in the holy mount."—i: 18.

PETHAHIAH—[Peth-a-hi′-ah.]

Was one of the priests appointed by David when he divided them into twenty-four orders. His lot was the nineteenth. 1st Chron. xxiv: 16.

PETHUEL—[Peth-u′-el,] *mouth or persuasion of God.*

Was the father of the prophet Joel. Joel i: 1.

PEULTHAI—[Pe-ul′-tha.]

Was one of the sons of Obed-Edom, and one of the sacred porters. 1st Chron. xxvi: 5.

PHALLU—[Fal′-lu,] *admirable, hidden.*

Was the second son of Reuben, and is referred to in Genesis xlvi: 9. He is one of four sons named there: "Hanoch, Phallu, Hezron and Carmi." And we learn from Num. xxvi: 5, that he was the head of the family of the Phalluites.

PHALTI—[Fal′-ti,] *deliverance, flight.*

PHALTI, sometimes called PHALTIEL, was the son of Laish. We have an account of him in 1st Sam. xxv: 44. He was of the city or tower of Gallim of the tribe of Benjamin. For some cause Saul, gave Michal, David's wife, to him, after he took her away from David. We know not that he was an officer in the kingdom, or a man of any special note. Saul may have selected him, and given Michal to him, mainly because he was of his own tribe.

After David was anointed king in Hebron, over the house of Judah, a war was carried on between his house and the house of Saul, in Ishbosheth, who had been made king by Abner, the son of Ner, over Israel. David waxed stronger and stronger, and the house of Saul waxed weaker and weaker. David at length demanded of Ishbosheth, Michal, his wife, who had been given to Phalti. Ishbosheth sent and took her from her husband. The separation from Michal greatly distressed Phalti, and he followed her crying. It was certainly very hard for him to be parted from her, for he loved her greatly. But David was her legitimate husband, and his interest in the government demanded that he should not leave a princess in the possession of another man who was his own legitimate wife as well as the daughter of a king. Had David left her as the wife of Phalti, she might sometime have presented a double plea to the throne.

When they reached Bahurim, on the way to Hebron, Abner, who had Michal in his charge, bade Phalti go back again to his home. He accordingly did so, and Michal was received by David and numbered with his other six wives. 2d Sam. iii: 13-16.

PHANUEL—[Fan-u´-el,] *face or vision of God.*

Phanuel was the father of the prophetess Anna, who entered the temple just after Simeon had given his testimony to the Messiahship of Jesus. It is said "she spake of him to all them that looked for redemption in Jerusalem."

This man was of the tribe of Asher. Luke, ii: 36.

PHARAOH, 1—[Fa´-ro,] *that disperses, that discovers.*

The first Pharaoh mentioned in the Bible, was that king of Egypt that was reigning at the time that Abraham went down into Egypt because of a famine.

Abraham was afraid lest the beauty of his wife, Sarah, would lead the Egyptians to kill him, that they might possess her. He said to Sarah, when the Egyptians see thee they will say, "This is his wife, and they will kill me, but they will save thee alive; say I pray thee, thou art my sister." Abraham had fears, and they were not groundless, for as soon as he reached Egypt, her beauty was observed, and and commended. The princes of Pharoah saw her and commended her before the king, and he took her to the palace, that she might be prepared to be brought into his presence, and supposing that she occupied only the relation of sister, Pharaoh treated Abraham well for her sake. But the Lord interfered on behalf of Sarah's husband, by plagueing the king and his house with great plagues. Whatever these plagues were, they were understood by Pharaoh as proofs of disapprobation, and he called for Abraham and interrogated him as to the relation Sarah sustained; he frankly confessed that she was his wife, but that she was also his sister. He very likely explained to Pharoah as he did afterwards to Abimelech. Gen. xx: 12. Then he said, "she is indeed my sister. She is the daughter of my father, but not the daughter of my mother, and she became my wife."

Pharaoh more than intimated that if he had told him she was his wife, he would not have taken her. He then commanded his men concerning him, and sent Abraham away, and his wife, and all that he had. Genesis, xii.

PHARAOH, 2—*That disperses, that discovers.*

Pharaoh was the king of Egypt who reigned at the time that Joseph was taken down, enslaved, and cast into prison. This Pharaoh had become wroth with two of his servants, the chief butler, and the chief baker, and had put them in ward in the captain of the guard's house. Both of these servants of the king dreamed a dream and were sad over it, the next morning. Joseph saw them, and asked them why they were sad. They told him, and he interpreted the dreams, and each dream was fulfilled according to the interpretation.

At length Pharaoh dreamed a dream. The magicians and wise men of Egypt were applied to, but could not interpret it for the king. The chief butler, whose dream had been interpreted, and who had promised faithfully to remember Joseph, made an acknowledgment to the king of his fault in forgetting that promise, and he suggested that the dream be referred to Joseph. Pharaoh accordingly sent for Joseph, told him his dream, and he gave him the interpretation thereof. And, as a reward, Pharaoh set him over all the land of Egypt, to gather corn during the seven years of plenty, for the coming seven years of famine, and he put his ring upon Joseph's hand, arrayed him in royal robes, and put a gold chain about his neck, and made him to ride in the second chariot. He made Joseph next to himself in Egypt, gave him the name of Zaph-nath-Paa-neah, and gave him to wife, Asenath, the daughter of Potipherah, the priest of On.

When Joseph's brethren went down to Egypt to buy corn, and he made himself known unto them, and Pharaoh heard of it, he bade Joseph invite his brethren and his father to come down into Egypt, under the promise that they should dwell in the best of the land. He told Joseph to send wagons out of the land of Egypt to bring their little ones, and their wives, and their fathers, and not to be careful about their stuff, because the best of the land of Egypt was theirs. As soon as Joseph's father and brethren arrived, he took five of his brethren and went into the presence of Pharaoh, the king, and told him they had arrived with their flocks and herds, and all that they had. Pharaoh asked the five brethren what their occupation was, and they told him they were shepherds. Pharaoh then repeated to Joseph what he had said before:—that the land of Egypt was before them, and to have them make choice of a place to dwell. In a short time after their arrival, Joseph introduced his aged father to Pharaoh, who was struck with Jacob's venerable appearance, and asked him, "How old art thou?"

After Jacob died Joseph embalmed his body in Egypt, and certified his desire to Pharaoh to take the remains to the land of Canaan and bury them in the family vault of his grandfather. So Pharaoh granted his request. How long Pharaoh lived after this we cannot tell; but we learn that after he died another king arose who knew not Joseph. Gen. xlii: 1.

PHARAOH, 3—*That disperses, that discovers.*

Pharaoh was that king of Egypt who began sorely to oppress the children of Israel. He proposed to the Egyptians that they should deal wisely with the Hebrews and stop their increase, lest if they as a nation were led into war with any other nation, they would raise an insurrection and help their enemies to fight against them and liberate themselves. He set taskmasters over them to afflict them with burdens and make them public servants; for under their taskmasters they built for Pharaoh towns and cities. But the oppression of Pharaoh did not have the desired effect, for the more they afflicted them the more they multiplied and grew. At length Pharaoh ordered the midwives to kill every male child of the Hebrews as soon as born; but these women feared God and disobeyed the king's orders. He then ordered all his people to mark every son that was born unto the Hebrews and cast him into the river, but save the daughters alive. His daughter had some of the milk of human kindness about her, and when she found a Hebrew babe floating in an ark on the river Nile, she adopted it as her own son. That child was Moses. Pharaoh's daughter educated him, and he remained with her in Egypt until forty years of age.

When Moses slew the Egyptian who was fighting with a Hebrew, and Pharaoh learned it, he sought to slay him, and Moses fled from the face of Pharaoh. Ex. i and ii.

PHARAOH, 4—*That disperses, that discovers.*

Pharaoh was the king who was reigning in Egypt at the time that Moses went from Midian and demanded the emancipation of all the Hebrews. He may have been the son or grandson of the former king. Moses and his brother went fearlessly into his presence, and demanded of him the freedom of Israel, "Thus saith the Lord, let my people go that they may hold a feast unto me in the wilderness." But Pharaoh refused. They then told him that God had met with them and required them to go three days journey into the wilderness to sacrifice unto him—and they represented the danger they would be in if they did not obey, viz, their God might fall upon them with pestilence and with sword. Pharaoh talked roughly to them and bade them in the stead of trying to make the slaves discontent, to let them alone, and themselves go to their burdens. In the stead of granting them their request, he bade the task-masters of the Hebrews deal more hardly with them and thereby quell any disposition among them to insurrection. He bade them require the Hebrews to make the number of bricks they were accustomed to make without furnishing them straw, which was used in the manufacture of Egyptian bricks. They were obliged to go all over the cornfields and gather the straw and make the same number of bricks as when there was plenty of straw furnished them. And they were punished by their cruel task-masters when they failed, as some of them did. This led them to complain of Moses, and he in turn prayed to God for direction. God gave Moses directions, and again he went into the presence of Pharaoh and wrought signs and wonders before him to convince him of the truth and divinity of his mission. The next day Moses met Pharaoh as he was going out to the water, probably to bathe or to perform some religious ablution, and he addressed him again on the subject of letting Israel go, and he gave him the divine threatening of serious and dreadful plagues if he did not. The first plague was visited upon Pharaoh and Egypt, which was turning the waters into blood and slaying all the fish, and for seven days this plague afflicted him and Egypt. The fish died and the river stank so that the people could not drink of the water. The whole land of Egypt was filled with blood.

At the end of seven days Moses was directed to threaten Pharaoh with the plague of frogs, and that plague was visited upon him, and after it the plague of lice, then flies, then murrain, after that boils and blains, then hail and locusts—in all eight plagues; but these did not prove sufficient to humble the haughty heart of Pharaoh, so as to induce him to let the people go. God then brought upon Pharaoh the ninth plague, which was a plague of darkness that continued for three days. And still another, it was the destroying angel, who passed through the land slaying one of every family of the Egyptians, from the royal family to the lowest family in his realm. Under the sorrows that pressed the nation, with every family in mourning for the sudden death of its first-born, the king called for Moses and Aaron, and bade them go with the people and serve the Lord as he had said. Moses led the people out. It was not long until Pharaoh repented letting them go, and pursued after them to bring them back. He followed them with the Egyptian army into the bed of the sea, the waters of which had been parted to make Israel a road, and while the whole Egyptian army, with the enraged Pharaoh at their head, were marching through, suddenly the parted waters closed and they were all devoured. Ex. iv to xv inclusive.

PHARAOH, 5—*That disperses, that discovers.*

PHARAOH was the father-in-law of Solomon. He, too, was a king of Egypt. The king of Israel made affinity with him, and married his daughter, and brought her after the marriage into the city of David. 1st Kings, iii: 1. We have an account in 1st Kings ix: 16, of this Pharaoh taking Gezer from the Canaanites, and slaying them, and then giving it as a present unto his daughter, Solomon's wife. And it is likely this Pharaoh was the one that gave his wife's sister to Hadad, the Edomite, as a wife, whose children were raised up in Pharaoh's palace, and who in company with Rezon and Jeroboam were enemies to king Solomon. 1st Kings, xi: 19, &c.

PHARAOH, 6—*That disperses, that discovers.*

PHARAOH is called Pharaoh-necho. He is referred to in 2d Kings, xxiii and xxiv. Like the other Pharaohs he was a king of Egypt. He went in battle against Josiah, because he refused to let him pass through his territories. They fought at Megiddo, and Josiah was mortally wounded. His servants put him into another chariot and took him to Jerusalem, where he died. See 2d Chron. xxxv: 24. "The archers shot at king Josiah, and the king said to his servants, have me away, for I am sore wounded." Jehoahaz was made king in the stead of Josiah, but Pharaoh dethroned him, and made Eliakim, his brother, king, and changed his name to Jehoiakim; and putting the land under tribute he returned to his own country.

In about four years the army of Pharaoh, was routed by the Chaldeans, the city of Jerusalem taken and Jehoiakim was made tributary to Nebuchadnezzar, while Pharaoh-necho and his army were driven into Egypt and confined there. Jer. xlvi, gives an account of the defeat of Pharaoh and his army.

PHARAOH, 7—*That disperses, that discovers.*

PHARAOH is called Pharaoh-hophra. He is supposed to have been the grandson of Pharaoh-necho, and to have reigned twenty-five years as the King of Egypt. Many of the Jews were scattered about in his dominions, and Jeremiah himself was at Tahpanhes the royal city or the city where was the palace of Pharaoh. Jeremiah was commissioned to prophesy the downfall of this kingdom. Zedekiah depending upon Pharaoh to assist him, rebelled against the King of Babylon, and refused to follow the instructions of Jeremiah the prophet. But when the action commenced the Egyptian army retreated, and left Zedekiah, and he was taken. The prophet was commanded of the Lord to say: "Behold I will give Pharaoh-hophra, King of Egypt, into the hands of his enemies, and into the hands of them that seek his life; as I gave Zedekiah, King of Judah, into the hands of Nebuchadnezzar, King of Babylon, his enemy and that sought his life." Jer. xliii and xliv. He became exceedingly unpopular with his people, and it is said that they turned against, and hated him. When he was taken prisoner, his captor and conqueror would have dealt kindly with him, but the people would not allow him. They forced Pharaoh out of his hands, and strangled him to death it is said after they had made his conqueror, Amasis king in his stead. Isaiah xix, Ezekiel xxix, xxx, xxxi and xxxii.

Pharaoh was a common name of the Kings of Egypt and was aften added to other names. It is said there were not less than sixty of Egypt's kings of this name, through the various dynasties of the empire. There is one mentioned in the days of Hezekiah with whom he made a league. 2d Kings xviii: 19–21, that was probably a different person from any whom we have referred to.

PHAREZ—[Fa′rez,] *division, rupture.*

PHAREZ was the twin brother of Zarah, the son of Judah, by his daughter-in-law, Tamar. Genesis, xxxviii: 27. He was not the elder of two, but the younger, hence the privileges and honors of birthright belonged to Zarah, and yet as they were twins, we may suppose that the privileges to some extent were conjoined. Pharez was the one that was in the line of Christ's genealogy. Matt. i: 3.

Like the other two living sons of Judah, he became the head of a powerful family, for when Israel came out of Egypt, the tribe of Judah numbered seventy-four thousand fighting men. Numbers, i: 27.

PHEBE—[Fee′be,] *shining, pure.*

PHEBE was an early christian, and is very strongly commended by Paul, as he closes up his epistle to the Romans. Romans, xvi: 1–2. Phebe may have been the bearer of this epistle, and this language is a strong recommendation for her on the part of Paul. It may be she was, as some think, a person of quality and estate, of whom there were few among the early christians. And she may have had business at this time at Rome, where she was a stranger, and hence Paul recommended her to their acquaintance and assistance, so far as they had it in their power to assist her in her business. He desired them to extend christian courtesy to her, and give her the hand of fellowship. "I commend unto you our sister Phebe, who is a servant of the church, which is at Cenchrea. That ye receive her in the Lord as becometh Saints, and that ye assist her in whatsover business she hath need of you, for she hath been a succorer of many, and of myself also." Here we learn that Paul considered her a sister in the Lord, and a faithful member of the church—one that ministered to the wants of those who were in necessity and who entertained the ministers of Christ in her house.

PHICOL—[Fi′-col,] *the mouth of all, perfection.*

PHICOL was the captain of the host of Abimelech, the king of Gerar. He was the chief of Abimelech's officers, and was associated with his master, the king, in exacting a solemn promise, or covenant, of Abraham that he would deal kindly with him and his sons, and his sons' sons, in return for the kindness he had done him in permitting him to dwell in his land, and in returning his wife Sarah unto him. Gen. xx: xxi. Abraham acceded to their wishes and entered heartily into the covenant.

It is probable that the Phicol mentioned in Gen. xxvi: 26, is the same person that is mentioned above. He was the chief captain of Abimelech's army, and is mentioned in connection with Ahuzzath, one of the king's friends.

PHILEMON—[Fi-le′-mon,] *that is affectionate.*

PHILEMON was a disciple of Christ in the apostolic age. He lived at Colosse and is supposed to have been very wealthy, and the Christians held meetings in his house. His wife was probably with him early converted to the Christian faith.

Philemon had a servant whose name was Onesimus, who ran away from him and went to Rome. While at Rome, Onesimus was converted under Paul's ministry, and made himself quite useful to Paul in his imprisonment. After he had been with Paul awhile he sent him back to Philemon, his master, and wrote an epistle in which he relates the fact of the servant's conversion and recommends Philemon to receive him kindly and forgive his errors; and he wrote Philemon to charge what his servant might have wronged him in running away, to his account. See the epistle, which is a very affectionate letter, full of natural and touching eloquence.

It is thought, by some, that Philemon, suffered martyrdom with Appia, his wife, in the persecution under the emperor, Nero.

PHILETUS — [Fi-le′-tus,] *amiable, beloved.*

PHILETUS is mentioned by the apostle Paul in his Epistle to Timothy, (ii: 17, &c.,) in connection with Hymeneus. Philetus erred concerning the truth. They had embraced, we suppose, the error of the Gnostics, referred to in 1 Tim. i: 4; as also Titus iii: 9, and Jude iv. In that system there were "fables and endless genealogies,—foolish questions and contentions and strivings about law." "For there are certain men crept in unawares, turning the grace of God into lasciviousness and denying the only Lord God and our Savior Jesus Christ." It is said "they say that the resurrection is passed already, and overthrow the faith of some." Paul exhorts Timothy to shun profane and vain babblings—to be sure not to split upon the fatal rock on which these two men had been wrecked.

PHILIP, 1—[Fil′-lip,] *warlike, a lover of horses.*

PHILIP was one of the apostles called by Jesus, and a witness with the others of his miracles. He was of Bethsaida, the city of Andrew and Peter. Jesus called him to be his disciple and follow him, he obeyed the call. He had an interview with Nathaniel in which he invited him to an acquaintance with Jesus of Nazareth. Nathaniel did not believe his report that this person was the Messiah, and he asked Philip, "Can any good thing come out of Nazareth?" Philip invited him to come and see for himself and he did.

When Jesus was about to feed the multitude miraculously he turned to Philip and asked him, "where shall we buy bread that these may eat?" He said this to Philip with a view of proving him, for he was intending to multiply the few loaves and fishes that were there. Philip answered Jesus, "Two hundred penny-worth of bread is not sufficient for them, that every one of them may take a little." John, vi: 5.

We have an account in John, xii: 20, of certain Greeks coming to Jesus to see and converse with him. They did not at once go into his presence but approached Philip, and asked him to introduce them. He reported their presence and desire to Andrew, and the two together introduce them to Jesus.

At the last supper he expressed a desire to see the father's glory, "Show us the father and it sufficeth us." Jesus told him that as he and his father were one and inseparable, he that by faith had seen him, had seen the father. He gave Philip to understand that he had been showing forth the father and his glory in all his works and acts. John. xv: 8.

His labors as an apostle are not narrated as are the labors of some others, but it is thought he preached the gospel in upper Asia, and at last died a martyr at Hierapolis, a city in the neighborhood of Colosse, where Christianity was early planted.

**PHILIP, 2**—*Warlike, a lover of horses.*

PHILIP was one of the seven deacons who were all declared to be men of "honest report—full of faith and of the holy Ghost," appointed to that work and office by the apostle in the Jerusalem church. Acts, vi: 5. We have an account in Acts, viii: 5, of his going to Samaria and preaching Christ unto the people there. He not only preached but also wrought miracles there—he healed the sick and cast out devils. Under his ministry there was a glorious revival and the whole city was excited. "There was great joy in that city." Among those who professed conversion in the city of Samaria was Simon the sorcerer. He was afterwards confounded by the apostle Peter, and as we may suppose excluded the church. Not long after this Philip was bidden by an angel to go toward the south, to the road that went from Jerusalem to Gaza. He accordingly went and met a man of Ethiopia, an eunuch of great authority under Candace, the queen of Ethiopia. The man was engaged in reading the prophecy of Esaias. He went near the chariot and overheard the reading of the 53d chapter of Isaiah. Philip asked the nobleman if he understood what he was reading—he readily acknowledged he did not, and supposing the stranger did understand it, from his having asked the question he invited him to a seat in the chariot with him. He re-read the passage possibly, then asked Philip "of whom speaketh the prophet this, of himself or some other man?" Philip then preached Jesus to the eunuch, from the prophecies read.

The instructions were received humbly and believingly, and as they came to water, he said to Philip, "See here is water, what doth hinder me to be baptized." Philip told him he might be, if he believed. He said he did believe that Jesus Christ was the son of God. They went down to the water, both Philip and the eunuch, and he baptized him. The nobleman then re-entered his chariot, and the spirit of the Lord carried Philip to Azotus, where he engaged in preaching the gospel, passing through all the cities till he came to Cesarea. He lived at Cesarea when Paul stopped there on his way to Jerusalem, and that apostle entered his house, and tarried there many days; and Paul tells us he had four daughters who prophesied. Where the future labors of this good man were performed, we do not know. Acts, viii, and xxi: 8-9.

**PHILIP, 3**—*Warlike, lover of horses.*

PHILIP or Herod Philip was the son of Herod the great, and of Mariamne, who was the daughter of Simon, the high priest. We learn from Matt. xiv: 3, that the Herod who laid hold on John the Baptist, and cast him into prison, had married Philip's wife Herodias. This Herod was the brother of Philip, and John had said to him, "It is not lawful for thee to have her." She was so enraged at this that she induced Herod to imprison him. See also Mark, vi: 17. See Herod Philip.

**PHINEHAS, 1**—[Fin′-ne-as,] *a bold countenance.*

PHINEHAS was the son of Eleazar and the grandson of Aaron, and he was the third high priest of the Jews. We have an account in Num. xxv: 6, &c., of his remarkable zeal for God and the religion of his fathers. There is an account given of the Midianitish women coming into the camp of the Hebrews and leading the Israelites away to uncleanness and idolatry. Zimri, a prince of the Simeonites, led Cozbi, who was a daughter of Zur, a prince of the Midianites, into the camp and into his own tent. Phinehas saw him and followed after him with a javelin in his hand; and approaching the guilty Zimri and the heathen princess he thrust the javelin through them both, and so they died. It may look like a rash act on his part, but Israel was being scourged at that time with a dreadful plague—twenty-four thousand had died. He saw this demonstration of the wickedness that had occasioned the plague, and he rushed upon these destroyers of the peace and happiness of Israel and put them to death. God approved and rewarded him for it. The plague was immediately stopped, and God assigned the high priesthood to Phinehas and his family for many generations, because he had manifested this zeal and stayed his anger. Num. xxv.

There is an allusion made in Ps. cvi: 30, 31, to this act of Phinehas, and he is justified and lauded for it. "Then stood up Phinehas and executed judgment, and the plague was stayed; and that was counted unto him for righteousness unto all generations for evermore."

In Josh. xxii, we have an account of several princes who were sent to expostulate with the Reubenites, the Gadites, and the half tribe of Manasseh regarding an altar they had erected by the side of Jordan, for they were suspected as having reared an altar for idolatrous purposes. Phinehas headed the deputation of princes, and when they were satisfied that the altar Ed was not for purposes of idolatry, they went back and reported to their brethren, and they united in praising God.

When the tribe of the Benjamites were cut off on account of their conduct in the affair of Gilead, Phinehas was with the army, and enquired of the Lord and received directions. Judg. xx: 28. When Phinehas died he was succeeded in the office of high priest by his son.

PHINEHAS, 2—*A bold countenance.*

PHINEHAS was the son of Eli. He also was a priest, but like his brother was wicked before God. 1 Sam. i: 2, 3. The sons of Eli ministered before the Lord, but though in the same office and having the example of a good father, they desecrated the sacred office, and profaned the sanctuary at Shiloh.

Phinehas and his brother abused the women that assembled at the door of the tabernacle of the congregation. It is supposed by some that these women assembled there for devotional purposes. Others suppose they were employed as nightwatchers. Women were employed about the house of the high priest in our Lord's time. A woman kept the door of the palace of the high priest when Jesus was hurried from the Garden to Caiphas. John xviii: 17. "Then saith the damsel that kept the door, unto Peter," &c. But in Ex. xxxviii: 8, the ancient custom is referred to.

Eli heard of this conduct of his sons, and said unto them, "Why do ye such things, for I hear of your evil doings by all this people. Nay, my sons; for it is no good report that I hear ye make the Lord's people to transgress," &c. How affectionate is the admonition and reproof from the aged Eli to his erring sons. Eli was the Judge in Israel, and might at once have deposed his sons, but he did not. A prophet of God reproved him because he honored his sons by retaining them in the office after their flagrant crimes complained of by all the people. Some time after this, while Samuel was yet a child, the Lord revealed his will to Eli through Samuel, in which he declared his coming judgments against his house, because of the wickedness of his sons; and God gave Eli to understand that the terrible trial should soon come upon him of his two sons, Hophni and Phinehas, both dying in one day. 1 Sam. iii: 11.

Soon after this there was a battle between Israel and the Philistines, and Israel was defeated. Phinehas and his brother were in the camp of Israel with the ark of God. They were both slain, and the ark was taken. The news of the defeat of Israel was taken to Eli by a Benjamite, and as soon as the aged priest heard it, filled with sorrow, he fell suddenly from his seat backward and died. Soon the intelligence reached the wife of Phinehas, and she too sank under the sorrows that were produced by the news that the Israelites were defeated—the ark of God taken—and her father-in-law and her husband were both dead.

The wife of Phinehas named her son Ichabod, just as she was dying—that name was expressive of her own sad feeling, and the facts as it regarded her nation, viz., "The glory is departed."

PHLEGON—[Fleg′-on,] *zealous, burning.*

Was a christian who is merely mentioned by Paul in his salutations to the Roman christians. Rom. xvi: 14. He is thought by some to have been a bishop of the church of Marathon.

PHURAH—[Fu′-rah,] *that bears fruit, that grows.*

PHURAH was a servant of Gideon, and is mentioned in Jud. vii: 11. The Lord bade Gideon arise in the night and go down to the camp of the Midianites, and take Phurah, his servant with him, and he should hear things by which he should be strengthened. He did so accordingly and the two together overheard a man telling a dream to a fellow soldier, which was interpreted by the soldier to whom the dreamer talked. Gideon was inspirited for his work and he and Phurah went back again, to the camp, and that night the Midianites were conquered.

PHUT—[Fut.]

PHUT was one of the sons of Ham, hence the grandson of Noah, and is referred to in Noah's posterity. Gen. x: 6. His posterity are supposed to have settled first in Egypt, and that they were in league with, if not indeed subject to the Egyptians in the time of Hezekiah. Nahum, iii: 9: "Ethiopia and Egypt were her strength, and it was infinite. Phut and Lubim were thy helpers."

PHUVAH—[Fu′-vah,] *that bears fruit, that grows.*

PHUVAH was the son of Issachar, and is numbered with the family of Jacob, who went down to Egypt to dwell. Gen. xlvi: 13.

PHYGELLUS—[Fi-gel′-lus,] *fugitive.*

PHYGELLUS is noticed in 2d Tim. i: 15, in connection with Hermogenes. They were professed Christians, and, for a time, the seeming friends of Paul. Whatever is true as regards their real character, it is certain that they forsook Paul in the time of his distress and imprisonment, as did "all they which were in Asia."

PILATE—[Pi′-lat,] *who is armed with a dart.*

PILATE, commonly called Pontius Pilate. He was the successor of Gratus in the government of Judea. Pilate is represented in history as a very cruel and wicked man; putting innocent people to death and to torture, without even the form of trial; and the Bible history of him is in keeping with this. We have an account in Luke xiii: 1, 2 of his cruelty to certain Galileans. He had probably taken offense at something they had said or done, and while they were in the court of the temple, he murdered them, and mingled their blood with Jewish sacrifices, as they were offered in the temple.

When Christ was taken from Gethsemane to Annas the father-in-law of Caiaphas, for judgment. Annas refused to judge him, and sent him bound to the acting high priest, and the high priest sent him to Pontius Pilate, after having bound him. John xviii: 14, Luke xxiii: 1.

The Jews brought their accusations against Jesus, the principal one was for sedition and heresy against the Roman Empire, and declaring himself to be King. At first Pilate was disposed to refuse to sit in judgment on the case. He told the Jews to take Jesus whom they accused and judge him according to their own law, but they said no, "It is not lawful for us to put any man to death," we Jews have not the power of life and death. He was induced to enter into his judgment hall and permit the case to be opened before him. He then asked Jesus, "Art thou the King of the Jews." He answered the question by asking Pilate if he asked this question of his own accord, or for his own satisfaction. "Sayest thou this of thyself, or did others tell it thee of me." Pilate told Jesus that the chief priests of the Jews had delivered him to him for judgment, and he desired to know what he had done. Jesus answered him "my kingdom is not of this world; if my kingdom were of this world, then would my servants fight that I should not be delivered to the Jews, &c." Pilate asked him the question again. "Art thou a king." He told him plainly he was. Pilate then asked him the significant question, "what is truth," but without waiting for an answer, prejudiced in favor of Jesus he went out to the Jews and referred them to a custom of the Roman government releasing a prisoner to them on the occasion of their Passover, and he asked them if he should release unto them Jesus, who styled himself the king of the Jews. They all cried out no, preferring Barabbas a noted robber. Pilate then to gratify the Jews, scourged Jesus and permitted the soldiers to put a crown of thorns upon his head, and a purple robe upon him in mockery of royalty, and they said "Hail king of the Jews." Pilate then stood before the Jews, and freely declared that he found no fault in him. But the chief priests were full of rage. and cried out crucify him! crucify him!!

Pilate had made friends that day with Herod, and referred the case of Jesus to him, and he had found no fault in him, or if he had found fault, he had not judged him worthy of death; and he referred them to that fact, but they would not be pacified.

Pilate tried several methods to preserve the life of Jesus, whom he looked upon as an innocent man. The wife of Pilate had sent him word to have nothing to do in condemning him; and, her judgment thus expressed, had its influence on him.

In the course of the trial he had heard the Jews say: "We have a law, and by our law he ought to die, because he made himself the son of God." This declaration had made Pilate afraid, and now he appears before the Jews and again insists on releasing him; but the Jews cried out: "If thou let this man go, thou art not Cesar's friend. Whosoever maketh himself a king speaketh against Cesar." This alarmed Pilate, and, lest he should be reported on and superceded as the governor, he went into the judgment hall again, and, sitting in his seat, prepared to give judgment against him. But, in connection with this act, he determined to give one more evidence of his convictions that Jesus was innocent. He called for a basin of water and washed his hands, saying: "I hereby declare my innocence of this man's blood." Exulting that their hopes were so near being consummated, they said: "His blood be on us, and our children." He then pronounced the sentence of death upon Jesus, and the Jews took him away to crucify him. Pilate wrote a title and put it on the cross; and, in order that all who witnessed the crucifixion might read it and understand it, the inscription was written in Hebrew, and Greek, and Latin. The chief priests were mortified at this inscription and asked Pilate to change it from "This is the king of the Jews" to "He said, 'I am the king of the Jews;'" but Pilate would not change it. When Joseph begged the body of Jesus, for a decent burial and honorable interment, Pilate readily granted it. And so, when the Jews applied to him to make the tomb secure, he granted them the use of the seal and a guard of Roman soldiers; and those soldiers performed faithfully their work of watching till the divine power was displayed, breaking the seal of Pilate and striking terror and consternation into the soldiers, who fell back like dead men. Matt. xxvii; Luke, xxiii; John, xix.

It is supposed that Pilate was finally deposed, for his cruelty, by the governor of Syria, and sent to Rome to give an account of his conduct before the emperor. The emperor banished him to Vienna, in Gaul, where he was subject to extreme inconveniences, which occasioned such a state of mind that he was driven to commit suicide.

Pilate was a consummate hypocrite and coward or he would never have put Jesus to death, with the impressions he had of his innocence.

PILDASH—[Pil′-dash.]

Was the son of Nahor, and the grandson of Terah. Gen. xxii: 22.

PORATHA—[Por′-a-tha,] *fruitful.*

Was one of the ten sons of Haman who were slain by the Jews in the slaughter in Shusham. They were ordered by King Ahasuerus to be hanged. Est. ix: 8, 13.

POTIPHAR—[Pot′-i-far,] *bull of Africa, fat bull.*

POTIPHAR was an officer of importance, for Pharaoh the king of Egypt at the time that Joseph was taken down into Egypt by the Midianitish merchants. He is supposed to have been captain of the royal guards. He bought Joseph of the Midianites, and after he had tried him found him to be worthy of his confidence and esteem—for every thing seemed to prosper in Joseph's hands. Potiphar had such confidence in Joseph that he put the entire management of his affairs and household arrangements in his hands. But the wife of Potiphar blasted Joseph's character with a lie. He credited the charge brought against Joseph and cast him into prison. Gen. xxxvii: 36; Gen. 39.

POTIPHERAH—[Pot-i-fe′-rah,] *that scatters or demolishes the fat.*

POTIPHERAH was a priest of On. He was the father-in-law of Joseph.

Gen. xli: 45. Pharaoh after promoting him gave him Asenath, the daughter of Potipherah as a wife. He was priest of On, a city about forty-five miles from Zoan, the royal city. He was a man of great prominence and importance in Egypt. The fact that the king selected his daughter for a wife for the man who rode in the second chariot of the nation, and was the governor of all the land, indicates it. It can hardly be supposed that this person was the same as Potiphar, for Joseph could hardly have been satisfied to marry the daughter of a woman who had so wickedly traduced him.

PRISCILLA—[Pris-sil′-lah,] *ancient.*

PRISCILLA with her husband Aquila was originally of Rome, but banished by the edict of Claudius. Acts, xviii: 2. They were tent makers, and when Paul became acquainted with them at Corinth and as he had learned in his younger days the same trade, he lived at their house and wrought with them at tent making. Paul greets this woman with her husband as an "helper in Christ Jesus." Rom. xvi: 3. And they were his helpers; for when the eloquent Apollos began to preach, Priscilla with her husband took him unto them and expounded unto him the way of God more perfectly." They taught him what they had learned from Paul while he resided with them—and then gave him the benefit of their own experience. Acts, xviii: 26. So strong was their attachment for Paul that they even laid "down their own necks." The apostle appreciated their kindness and presses upon the church of Rome the duty of kindness to these noted persons, for the benefit they had conferred upon the church in saving his life.

PUA.

Was of the tribe of Issachar, and the head of the family in that tribe called the Puaites. Num. xxvi: 23.

PUAH, 1.

Was of the tribe of Issachar and the father of Tola, one of the Judges of Israel. Jud. x: 1.

PUAH, 2.

Was one of the Egyptian midwives who was commanded by the king of Egypt to put the male children of the Israelites to death, as soon as they were born. Ex. i: 16. [See Shipsah.]

PUBLIUS—[Pub′-li-us,] *common.*

Was the governor of Melita or Malta, the Island on which Paul and his companions were cast when shipwrecked on the way to Rome. Paul cured his father of a dangerous disease. Acts xxviii: 8.

PUL—*Bean, destruction.*

He was the first King of Assyria that invaded the kingdom of Israel. We have an account of that invasion in 2d Kings xv: 19.

Manahem prevailed on Pul to withdraw his troops, by giving him one thousand talents of silver. He waged war with the Reubenites, Gadites and the half tribe of Manassah, conquered them and carried them away captive. 1st. Chron. v: 26.

RAAMAH—[Ra′-a-mah,] *greatness, thunder, evil, bruising.*

RAAMAH was the fourth son of Cush. Gen. x: 7. His sons that are mentioned are Sheba and Dedan, both of which became heads of powerful tribes. The former it is thought settled beyond the Euphrates, and the latter in Arabia, on the confines of Idumcea. It is likely that the posterity of Raamah carried on a trade with the Syrians in spices, precious stones and gold, &c.

In Ezek. xxvii: 20, &c. it is said "Dedan was thy merchant in precious clothes for chariots. The merchants of Sheba and Raamah, they were thy merchants: they occupied in thy fairs with chief of all spices, and with all precious stones, and gold."

RABSARIS—[Rab′-sa-ris,] *grand master of the eunuchs.*

RABSARIS was one of the servants of the king of Assyria, associated with Tartan and Rabshakeh in sending an insulting and blasphemous message to King Hezekiah. 2d Kings, xviii: 17.

RABSHAKEH—[Rab′-sha-keh,] *Cup-bearer of the prince, chamberlain.*

RABSHAKEH was one of the principal generals of Sennacherib, the king of Assyria. We have an account, in 2d Kings, xviii, of Hezekiah, the king of Judah, making an effort to shake off the yoke of the king of Assyria. Sennacherib invaded his kingdom and took the fenced cities of Judah, and then besieged Jerusalem, the capital. Hezekiah had sent a message to him, asking him to desist, with the promise that he would pay him any tribute he would impose. He accordingly imposed a tribute of three hundred talents of silver and thirty talents of gold; but he violated his agreement and still warred with Hezekiah. Sennacherib sent Rabshakeh with an insulting and blasphemous message to the king of Judah. It was in effect: "Speak ye now to Hezekiah. Thus saith the great king, the king of Assyria: What confidence is this wherein thou trusted? Thou sayest, I have counsel and strength for the war. Now, on whom dost thou trust that thou rebellest against me? Now, behold thou trustest upon the staff of this bruised reed—even upon Egypt, on which, if a man trust, it will go into his hand and pierce it. So is Pharaoh, king of Egypt, unto all that trust in him."

Rabshakeh insinuates to Hezekiah that he had offended Jehovah in removing the high places and breaking down the altars, cutting down the groves and breaking in pieces the brazen serpent, thereby depriving the people of their religious rights. He added to this another insult: "Were I to give thee two thousand Assyrian horses, couldst thou find riders for them? How, then, canst thou think of being able to stand against my master in war?" He added yet to this insult and injury by trying to make the people believe that God had departed from Israel and had become allied with the Assyrians. And in order that this speech might have the effect upon the people to stir them up to sedition, Rabshakeh made it in the Jews' language. Eliakim, and Shebnah, and Joah, who represented Hezekiah in this conference, asked him to speak in the Syrian language, as they understood it. But Rabshakeh spoke the louder in the Jews' language. The people were instructed by their king not to answer Rabshakeh, and they did not. "They held their peace and answered him not a word." Thus the conference ended, and Hezekiah's representatives returned to him. God understood their cause, and Judah was delivered, for the destroying angel slew, in the camp of the Assyrians, one hundred and eighty-five thousand men.

RACHEL—[Ra′-chel,] *a sheep.*

RACHEL was the younger daughter of Laban and the beloved wife of the patriarch Jacob. When Isaac called Jacob unto him and confirmed the blessing that had been pronounced upon him, when he supplanted Esau his brother, he charged him to go to Padan-aram, and to the family of his uncle Laban, and take a wife of his daughters—and he did so.

After a long and fatiguing journey, during which he had his ladder dream — and entered into a special covenant with the God of his fathers, in which he pledged himself to give to God the tenth part of all he should have if prospered—he arrived safely in the suburbs of the city where Laban dwelt. He saw three extensive flocks of sheep in a field—where was a well that afforded water for watering the sheep. He saw some men near the well, and he approached them, and entered into conversation with them. He asked who they were and where they lived. They answered him—when he asked them if they knew Laban the grandson of Nahor, they told him they did. He then asked them of Laban's health; they answered, "He is well;" and then they proceeded to say, "Behold Rachel his daughter cometh with the sheep." She was probably then in sight, and Jacob the wearied traveller looks for the first time upon his beautiful kinswoman. The lovely maiden approaches the well, being in charge of her father's sheep, and seeing the stranger standing there she probably wondered who it was. Before he made himself known unto Rachel his cousin, he assisted the shepherds to roll off the stone from the well's mouth, and watered the flock for her. He then told her who he was, and in the simple and pure method of primitive times "he kissed Rachel and lifted up his voice and wept." She had no doubt often heard her father Laban speak of Rebekah his sister, and the extraordinary circumstances under which she left Nahor in the charge of Eleazar, to become a wife for Isaac. As soon as Rachel learned who he was "she ran and told her father." Soon Laban was at Jacob's side, giving him strong evidences of his feeling for him as his nephew. And Jacob became an inmate of Laban's house, and a member of his family.

It was not long after Jacob arrived in the family of Laban until his affection was kindled toward Rachel—and that affection ripened into thoughts of marriage. As he had come to Mesopotamia to procure a wife, it is likely he thought of Rachel from the time he first met her by the well and assisted in watering the flocks, until Laban asked him what wages he should pay him, he said, "I will serve thee seven years for Rachel thy younger daughter." The agreement was made and the service was performed, and though Jacob was sadly disappointed by a fraud practiced upon him in giving him the older sister, Leah, yet in a few days he was made the happy husband of Rachel also.

After the marriage Rachel was greatly troubled that she was not blessed with children, as her sister Leah was. And she gave Bilhah, her handmaid to Jacob to wife and claimed her two children as her sons, naming them Dan and Naphtali. But afterwards Rachel bare a son, the illustrious Joseph who became governor of Egypt, and the deliverer of his fathers family.

When Jacob had been greatly blessed, and his flocks and herds had increased, he determined to go back to the land of his father and to the home of his youth, with his wives and children and all his substance.

Rachel in the preparation for departure, which preparation was unknown to Laban committed an offence in stealing her father's images, and she managed to hide her theft, when Laban following, overtook them and examined all their stuff. It may be as some suppose, that her object in taking them was to break up a system of idolatry that he had established in the use he made of these images. Or it may be that she thought their flight would be detected, and the direction they had taken would be indicated in some way, by these gods that he was in the habit of consulting, and she wished her husband to succeed, in his endeavor to get away from their father.

When Jacob was about to meet Esau, his brother, and was in dread lest he was yet angry with him and would destroy him, he showed his partiality for Rachel and her son by placing them as the last in the train. Gen. xxxiii: 2. "And he put the handmaids and their children foremost, and Leah and her children after, and Rachel and Joseph hindermost."

Shortly after Jacob arrived in his own land, Rachel died at Ephrath. She had given birth to a son, and named him Benoni, the same was Benjamin the youngest of the twelve patriarchs. Because of her death and burial at Ephrath, which is Bethlehem, the city has been called the city of Rachel. When Christ was born, or shortly after it, as by the edict of Herod the young children were slain. It is said, "In Rama was there a voice heard, lamentation and weeping and great mourning, Rachel weeping for her children, and would not be comforted, because they are not."

RAGUEL—[Rag'-u-el,] *shepherd or friend of God.*

RAGUEL, or REUEL, was the father-in-law of Moses. Ex. ii: 18. After Moses had helped the daughters of the priest of Midian to water their flock, "they came to Reuel, their father." He asked them how they came so soon, and they answered that an Egyptian had helped them.

The name Raguel occurs in Num. x: 29. Moses' father-in-law is called Jethro in Ex. iii: 1, and Hobab in Judges, i: 16. [See Hobab, Jethro, and Reuel.]

RAHAB—[Ra'-hab,] *proud, strong, quarrelsome.*

RAHAB was a Canaanitish innkeeper in the city of Jericho, who received the spies that Joshua sent and concealed them from the gaze and knowledge of the citizens of Jericho. "And they went and came into a harlots house, named Rahab, and lodged there." Josh. ii: 1.

There is no evidence that this woman was a bad woman, or a prostitute. We have frequent allusions in the scripture to women where the term harlot is not used to designate them as wicked and lost to virtue. As, for example, in Judges, xvi: 1: "Then went Sampson to Gaza, and saw there an harlot, and went in unto her." This woman was probably an inn-keeper at Gaza, and Sampson, while there, stayed at her house. Again; the two women who came to Solomon for judgment relative to a dead and living child are called harlots. 1st Kings, iii: 16. They were probably inn-keepers.

But had Rahab been a woman lost to virtue it is not at all probable that the spies, who were men of high standing in Israel, would have lodged with her. They were men who were in favor with God, and had the confidence and regards of Joshua, the leader of Israel. They felt the importance of their commission, and realized that their errand to Jericho at that time was fraught with intense interest to them and to their nation. They would not have periled their own interests and the interests of Israel by going where the curse of God was, or endeavoring to secure the co-operation and help of a wicked violator of sacred laws. But there is another strong reason for supposing Rahab to be an honorable woman, and engaged in an honorable employment. The spies agreed to show kindness to her and her father's house; and afterward, when Jericho was taken and razed to the ground, she and her father's house were preserved alive. She was honored with a place among Israel; nay more, she was married to a prince in Israel, Salma, and became the mother of Boaz, which Boaz was the great grandfather of the illustrious king of Israel, David.

Thus we observe this woman of Canaan adopted by the nation of Israel, and appearing in the genealogy of our Lord Jesus Christ. Her husband was one of his ancestors. The apostle Paul reckons her among the ancient worthies who had faith in God, and was moved by that faith to receive, and entertain, and deliver the spies. Heb. xi: 31: "By faith the harlot Rahab perished not with them that believed not when she had received the spies with peace."

Rahab, then, was an inn-keeper in the city of Jericho. The spies, when they entered it, took particular notice of the mode of approach to it—its fortifications and strength, and the best plan of besieging it. Having made all the examination that they could without being suspected as spies, they went to the house of Rahab to tarry for the night. They had been observed as they entered the city, and though not suspected while engaged in making their discoveries, yet they were afterwards suspected, and some men of Jericho gave information to their king, and expressed their suspicions to him; whereupon he sent to Rahab and commanded her to bring forth the two men; probably for examination as to their business in the city, what point they hailed from, &c.

As soon as the command reached her, she secreted them temporarily, and prevaricated by telling those who were in search of the spies, that they were gone, and urged them to pursue after them at once, make no delay, for they should overtake them. This falsity on her part is by no means justifiable. God could have accomplished the work of their deliverance without it. "Evil is not to be done that good may come of it." This was a stratagem of her own, and it succeeded. For the men hurried in pursuit as they thought, of the spies, to the fords of Jordan. When they were gone, Rahab removed the spies to the house top, and covered them with stalks of flax, lest others should come and insist on searching her house, and so find them.

Rahab then expressed her belief to them plainly, that Israel would conquer that city and the land of Canaan. She then asked them to swear unto her by the Lord that they would show kindness unto her and her father's house, and, said she, "give me a true token." Rahab believed in their God, and in his power to deliver the country of Canaan into their hands. She desired her own safety, and the safety of her father and mother, and her brothers and sisters. The spies then entered into a solemn covenant with her. They pledged their lives for her deliverance, and the deliverance of her father's house, if she remained faithful to her part of the agreement, "not to make known their business." She then let them down by a cord from the window, outside the city, her house being upon the town wall, and they obligated her to fasten a line of scarlet thread in her window, and so designate her house from all others when they came to destroy the city. She was also obligated to have her father and mother, and all the members of her father's household at her house. As soon as they were gone from the walls of the city to the mountains, where they were to hide themselves for three days, Rahab bound the scarlet line in the window, where it remained until Jericho was besieged and taken. And the same two men who were the spies, and were hid in Rahab's house, and were delivered by her stratagem, at the command of Joshua, went into her house, and finding that she had faithfully observed the agreement between them, brought her and all her father's house out, and placed them in the charge of Israel. Joshua gave her and her father's family a dwelling in Israel, as soon as they could be purified and prepared for citizenship.

If, when Rahab was a woman of Jericho—a Canaanite, she believed that the true God was on the side of the Hebrews, and her faith led her, as the apostle tells us, to receive the spies with peace, we may suppose from the position to which she attained, that her faith in the God of the Hebrews increased until she became a noted woman among them.

RAM—*Elevated, who rejects.*

Was the son of Hezron, and the father of Amminadab. He is referred to in the genealogy of David, from Pharez, the son of Judah. Ruth, iv: 19.

RAPHU—[Ra′fu,] *cured, comforted.*

Was of the tribe of Benjamin, and the father of Palti, who was selected by Moses as a spy of the land of Canaan, for that tribe. Numb. xiii: 9.

REBEKAH—[Re-bek′-ah,] *fat, quarrel, appeased.*

Rebekah was the daughter of Bethenel, of Nahor, a city in the country of Mesopotamia. She became the wife of the illustrious Patriarch Isaac, the son of Abraham.

When Abraham was one hundred and forty years of age he called unto him his faithful servant Eleazar, for the purpose of sending him on the mission of procuring a wife for Isaac, who was then about forty years of age. Gen. xxiv: 4. He bade the ruler of his house go to his former country, and take a wife of his kindred for Isaac. Eleazar accordingly made ready and went to the city of Nahor. He saw a fountain or well outside the limits of the city, and tarried there a short time to rest. Being very anxious for prosperity in his errand he prayed earnestly for "good speed," and while he was praying Rebekah, the daughter of Bethuel, came out from the city with her pitcher upon her shoulder to draw water from the well. As she approached Eleazar left his camels and ran to meet her and said, "Let me, I pray thee, drink a little water of thy pitcher." He desired the use of the pitcher to draw water from the well for himself and also for his camels. Rebekah was very kind and said—for she knew the traveler was fatigued with his journey—"Drink, my lord, and I also will draw water for thy camels." Having said this she hastened and let down her pitcher upon her hand, and gave the stranger to drink, then watered his weary and thirsty camels. This was an exhibition on her part of pure friendship. Eleazar, confident in his own mind of success, because the Lord was thus prospering him, asked Rebekah of her kindred, and she told him. She then invited him to tarry that night at her father's house, assuring him there was room, and moreover plenty of straw aud provender for the camels. If Eleazar was confident that the Lord was blessing him with success when he met her, and she proposed to give him drink, and water his ten thirsty camels, how much more confident must he have felt when she told him whose daughter she was, and invited him so cordially to stay that night at her father's house.

Ah, little did the artless and beautiful maiden of Nahor think, as she waited upon the stranger, and received at his hands the presents of an earring and bracelets of gold, that the camels she had watered, and the man from whom she had received these gifts, would the next day bear her away from her father's house and kindred, and her native country, to be the wife of one she knew not. But so it was.

Eleazar was introduced by Rebekah and soon made known the object of his journey, and he procured the consent of the family, and the promise of Rebekah to go with him the next day. Gen. xxiv: 58. "And they called Rebekah and said unto her, wilt thou go with this man?" and she said, "I will go;" and on the following morning, attending the stranger she began her journey toward her new home, with the blessings of her kindred upon her.

Isaac, it may be, was expecting the return of his father's servant from Mesopotamia with a wife for him; and on the evening of the day of his return, he was walking in the fields meditating. What the subject of his meditation was we are not informed—it may have been the being and attributes of God, which nature at eventide so beautifully develops. But he chanced to lift up his eyes and saw the camels coming. Just about this time, Rebekah, raising her eyes and looking ahead saw Isaac, and asked Eleazar who it was: "What man is that walking in the field to meet us?" He answered that it was Isaac. She quickly vailed herself, and alighting from the camel was introduced to Isaac by Eleazar.

Thus these two remarkable personages for the first time look upon each other. They are at once united in marriage according to the ceremonies in use in patriarchal families. "And Isaac brought her unto his mother's tent, and she became his wife, and he loved her." Rebekah was honored in being mother of two noble sons, Jacob and Esau, who each became the head of a great and mighty nation.

As it was with Abraham, so it was with Isaac. He went to Egypt to sojourn because of a famine in his own land, and he dwelt awhile in Gerar. Here we learn of Rebekah what we have learned of Sarah—that she "was fair to look upon—a beautiful woman;" and Isaac was afraid that the Gerarites would be so charmed with her beauty that they would desire his death; hence, he charged her to claim the relation of sister to him, though previous to their marriage they were only cousins.

Rebekah exhibited many excellencies during her life with Isaac, but we cannot say she was without faults. Her attachment to Jacob beyond her attachment to Esau, may have been a fault, as also her management to procure the birthright may have been a fault; though undoubtedly the divine purpose regarding the descendants of the two was thus brought about—"the elder shall serve the younger." Isaac, her honored husband, buried her imperfections with her body, in the cave of Machpelah; and Jacob learned with deep sorrow of her death, and no doubt, on his return to his own country, visited the family vault where her remains were mouldering. Gen. xlix: 31.

RECHAB, 1—[Re′-kab,] *square, chariot, rider.*

RECHAB, and his brother Baanah, were the sons of Rimmon the Beerothite. They were captains in the army of Ishbosheth. It may be that Ishbosheth kept marauding parties, and that these two men of Benjamin were in charge of two such bands. But when they heard that Abner was dead, they conspired together to slay their master; and they came to the palace about noon, or in the heat of the day, with an intention of slaying the king. They entered his bed chamber feigning business for their master, that their designs might not be suspected. He was probably asleep when they approached him. They smote him and cut off his head, and then bore it away to Hebron to show it unto David. They came into the presence of David with the head and showed it unto him, under the full conviction that he would approve their conduct. In this they were mistaken, for no sooner had they made their report than David condemned them, and ordered his young men to slay them and cut off their hands and their feet, and hang them up over the pool in Hebron, because they had slain a righteous man in his own house. David compared their conduct to the man who brought him intelligence of Saul's death, thinking he would be rewarded, and charged them with a greater crime in killing Ishbosheth.

RECHAB, 2—*Square, chariot, rider.*

RECHAB was the father of Jonadab, whose descendants attended faithfully to a solemn charge of their father never to drink wine or strong drink, nor to build any houses, but to dwell in tents and feed cattle. They kept this charge so faithfully that when they were tried by pots full of wine being placed before them three hundred years after, and they were urged to drink of the wine, they utterly refused. The Lord approbated them for their refusal, and promised to reward them by ever preserving their family. See Jonadab, or Jehonadab, Jer. xxxv.

REHOB—[Re'-hob,] *breadth, extent.*

REHOB was the father of Hadadezer, the king of Zobah, who was smitten by David after he had conquered the Philistines and the Moabites. 2 Samuel, viii: 3.

REHOBOAM—[Re-ho-bo'am,] *who sets the people at liberty, space of the people.*

REHOBOAM was the son and successor of Solomon. 1st Kings, xii: 1, and 2d Chron. x: 1. His mother's name was Naamah, an Ammonitess. 1st Kings, xiv: 21. He was by no means a wise man, as was his father, and we may well suppose that the wise instructions of Solomon to him were lost. The Proverbs contain wholesome lessons from a father to his son, but Rehoboam, as his life and reign proves, broke over those restraints and refused to be governed in his life by them. He was crowned king in Shechem, and commenced his reign there. Jeroboam, the son of Nebat, had been unfriendly to Solomon, but when Rehoboam was made king, returned from Egypt where he was. He approached the king with a request from the people, that he would relieve them from the heavy burdens that had been laid upon them by Solomon, his father. Their language to him was: "Thy father made our yoke grievous; now, therefore, make thou the grievous service of thy father, and his heavy yoke which he put upon us lighter, and we will serve thee." Rehoboam asked for three days to consider it, when he would give them an answer. He consulted with the aged men who had been his father's counsellors. They advised him to agree to make their service lighter, and their taxes less; by so doing he would soon get the affections of the people, and they would love him as their king. He then called together the younger men of his counsellors, and consulted with them. They advised him differently. They told him to tell the people that he intended to load them with far more grievous burdens, and punish them much more severely than even his father had done. They counseled him to say: "My little finger shall be thicker than my father's loins. My father did put upon you a heavy yoke, but I will put upon you a heavier one. He chastised you with whips, but I will chastise you with scorpions." Forsaking the sensible advice of the old men, he took that of the younger, and the consequence was the ten tribes rebelled under Jeroboam. There was Reuben, Simeon, Ephraim, Manasseh, Dan, Zebulon and Issachar, Naphtali, Gad and Asher. The cry was raised throughout the whole kingdom: "We have no portion in David, and no inheritance in the son of Jesse; to your tents, O Israel!" That part of the children of Israel that dwelt in the cities of Judah alone continued with Rehoboam. When they went off thus in a body, Rehoboam sent Adoram after them to induce them to return. As Adoram was the superintendent of the tribute, he probably went after them demanding of them their usual tax; but in the stead of answering to his call and returning to Rehoboam, they killed Adoram, and the king himself fled hastily to Jerusalem for the sake of his own life; and the ten tribes took Jeroboam and made him king, while the two tribes of Judah and Benjamin clave unto Rehoboam and acknowledged him their king.

King Rehoboam then gathered together an army of one hundred and eighty thousand chosen warriors to fight against the revolted tribes, and subdue them. The prophet Shemaiah spoke the word of the Lord unto the king, dissuading him from the attempt, He gave up the enterprise, and discharged his army, and the soldiery returned to their homes. He then set himself to work to strengthen his kingdom in the way of fortifying the cities that were in it. The principal cities that he fortified were Bethlehem, Etam, Tekoab, Bethzur, Shoeba, Adullam, Gath, Manshah, Ziph, Adoram, Lachish, Azekah, Zorah, Aijalon and Hebron. He furnished each of these cities with a sufficient number of men to protect them, and placed provisions, arms and ammunition in them. We are informed that the priests and Levites that were in all Israel, resorted unto Rehoboam, and for three years after the revolt of the ten tribes, the kingdom of Judah was prosperous, for the king and his subjects followed the Lord. But after that Rehoboam became wicked and his people became idolatrous. They abandoned the worship of the true God, and gave themselves up to all kinds of enormity and wickedness. They made statues and idols, erected idolatrous altars, they made groves, and built high places, and even appointed women as public prostitutes. 1st Kings, xiv: 21–24.

The God of their fathers was angry with them and he permitted the king of Egypt to invade their land. Shishak, the king of Egypt, entered Jerusalem and ravaged the city. He took possession of the treasures of the house of the Lord, and the treasures of the king's house, and all the shields of gold, which Solomon had made.

From 2d Chron. xii: 5, we learn that Shemaiah, the prophet, approached the king and his princes, and told them why the Lord had delivered them into the hands of their enemies; because they had forsaken him. Accordingly they humbled themselves before the Lord. Because they did humble themselves, God had mercy upon them and said, "I will not destroy them, but I will grant them some deliverance, and my wrath shall not be poured out upon Jerusalem by the hand of Shishak.

Sometime after this the Egyptian conqueror left the country, and Rehoboam and his people restored the kingdom of God, but the reformation was not thorough and complete, for they broke not down the high places.

Rehoboam made brazen shields in the stead of the golden ones that Solomon had left in the king's house, which had been taken by Shishak, and carried into Egypt. These brazen shields were used by the king's guard, when they attended with him in the temple, and such times as these shields were not used, they lay in the king's arsenal.

We are informed that there "was war between Rehoboam and Jeroboam all the days of his life." By this we may understand there was a continual spirit of hostility kept up between the two kingdoms. There were skirmishes between bordering parties, but no open war, for that was forbidden by the divine being. When king Rehoboam gathered together one hundred and eighty thousand of Judah and Benjamin, he thought a war would be justifiable, but God would not allow it, hence he disbanded them.

Rehoboam reigned seventeen years, and died, and was buried in the city of David, and Abijah, his son, became his successor. 1st Kings, xii: 14, and 2d Chronicles, x: 11–12.

REMPHAN—[Rem′-fan,] *the name of an idol, which some think to be Saturn.*

It is thought there was a king of Egypt by this name, who, after his death, was worshiped; for Remphan was an idol god. Remphan is referred to in connection with Moloch, by Stephen, in his address before his persecutors and murderers. Acts vii: 43. "Yea, ye took up the tabernacle of Moloch and the star of your god Remphan, figures which ye made to worship them." Chiun is supposed to be the same, and is mentioned in connection with Moloch, in Amos, v: 26. "But ye have borne the tabernacle of your Moloch and Chiun your images, the star of your god, which ye made to yourselves." A deity was worshiped in the form of a bull in Egypt, and the Hebrews, it may be supposed, had some reference to the Remphan of Egypt when the golden calf was made and worshiped at Sinai, while Moses was upon the mount.

REPHAEL—[Re′-fa-el.]

Was the son of Shemaiah and grandson of Obed Edom, and one of the sacred porters. 1 Chron. xxvi: 7.

REU—*His friend, his shepherd.*

Reu was the son of Peleg, born unto him when he was thirty years of age, and at the age of thirty-two had Serug born unto him. Gen. xi: 20. He was a descendant of Shem, who was the lineal ancestor of the Messiah. Luke, iii: 35.

REUBEN — [Ru'-ben,] *who sees the son, vision of the son.*

Reuben was the eldest son of Jacob by Leah. Gen. xxix: 32. It is said Leah "called his name Reuben; for she said, Surely the Lord hath looked upon my affliction; now, therefore, my husband will love me."

When Reuben was a small boy he found mandrakes in the field in the time of wheat harvest, and brought them to his mother. These his mother sold to Rachel. Gen. xxx: 15.

Reuben grew up to be a man, and when about forty years of age he grieved his father greatly by offering the grossest insult to one of his secondary wives, Bilhah, the handmaid of Rachel. Gen. xxxv: 22.

Reuben, being the eldest son of Jacob, was entitled to privileges and blessings that did not belong to the others; and it is probably safe to say he had more right to complain of Jacob's partiality to Joseph than either of the others. He saw Joseph's coat of many colors, and beheld his father's demonstrations of affection for Joseph day after day. He heard Joseph relate his dreams which indicated that he should be first of them all—that his father and all his brethren should bow down unto him. He does not seem to have harbored as strong feeling against Joseph as the other brothers. When the others were disposed to murder Joseph, he did all in his power to keep them from it. He proposed that they should cast him into a pit and leave him there to die, and not stain their hands with his blood. He really intended as early as he possibly could, to rescue Joseph and send him home to his father. While Reuben was away his brothers sold Joseph to Midianitish merchants. When he came back and found that the lad was gone he was deeply affected, and "rent his clothes; and he returned to his brethren and said, The child is not; and I, whither shall I go?"

When Joseph became ruler of the land of Egypt, and Reuben with his brothers went there to buy corn, the lord of the land treated them roughly, and demanded that they should bring their youngest brother Benjamin down into Egypt. They had all been kept under guard three days, during which time they had thought of their cruelty to their brother Joseph in selling him, and they said, one to another, "We are, verily, guilty concerning our brother, in that we saw the anguish of his soul when he besought us and we would not hear him; therefore is this evil come upon us." Reuben then remembered the efforts he had made to save his brother, and to prevent this reproach they now felt. He said unto them, "Spake I not unto you, saying, Do not sin against the child, and ye would not hear? Therefore behold, also his blood is required." Gen. xlii: 21, &c.

When they returned unto their father and told him that the Lord of the land of Egypt demanded to see their younger brother, Jacob was unwilling to let Benjamin go. Reuben, as the elder son, then addressed his father, urging him to let Benjamin go and he said, "Slay my two sons, if I bring him not to thee; deliver him into my hand and I will bring him to thee again;" but Jacob utterly refused. At length necessity demanded that they have more corn, and Jacob sent him down, we may suppose, under the charge of Reuben and Judah.

In Gen. xlix, we have an account of Jacob's death, and his blessing upon his sons, in which he gives prophetic declarations concerning their posterity. As Reuben was the eldest, he is the first one to whom Jacob addressed his dying language; it is contained in the 4th and 5th verses: "Reuben, thou art my first-born, my might and the beginning of my strength, the excellence of dignity, and the excellency of power; unstable as water, thou shalt not excel, because thou wentest up to thy father's bed, then defilest thou it; he went up to my couch." In this language he refers to Reuben's birthright and the dignity and blessing that belonged to it; to his forfeiture of it in the sin referred to—or the transfer of it to the sons of Joseph. That the birthright was given to the sons of Joseph we have evidence in 1st Chron. v: 1, "for he was the first-born; but forasmuch as he defiled his father's bed, his birthright was given unto the sons of Joseph, the son of Israel."

The sons of Reuben were Hanoch, Pallu, Hezron and Carmi, who were each of them heads of extensive families. Numbers, xxvi: 5, 6. The families of Hanochites, Palluites, Hezronites and Carmites, their number as given is forty-three thousand seven hundred and thirty; and this was a much smaller number than when they left the land of Egypt, for then their number of fighting men amounted to forty-six thousand five hundred, and they were under the command of Eleazar, the son of Shedeur. The great army of Israel was divided into divisions, and in their marching the tribe of Reuben with Simeon and Gad formed the second great division, and they marched just before the ark. The spy that Moses appointed for Reuben was Shammua, the son of Zaccur. Dathan and Abiram who, along with Korah, rebelled against Moses and Aaron, were of the tribe of Reuben, as was also On. Num. xvi: 1. We have an account in Numbers, xxxii, of the Reubenites and Gadites coming to Moses and asking him to give them their inheritance on this side of Jordan. Moses expostulated with them and reproved them for making the request because it was calculated to discourage Israel from going over to possess the land on the other side of Jordan. They explained themselves—they wanted an inheritance in which they could build houses, etc., and make their wives and children comfortable, then they would go over Jordan with the other tribes as warriors, and after the conquest was made and the land subdued they would return to their families.

Moses agreed to this, and gave them their inheritance, or commanded Joshua and Eleazar, on the condition named, to give it to them. Whether they and the half tribe of Manasseh were fully true to this promise and covenant or not, we cannot tell certainly. The last census that had been taken of the tribes, would make the warriors of the two full tribes and the half tribe, one hundred and ten thousand five hundred and eighty. Numbers, xxvi. And yet when these tribes made up their army to go over Jordan, there were but forty thousand armed men. If they were not reduced in number, there would have been seventy thousand five hundred and eighty men left behind, which we may suppose was more than was necessary to guard the women and children, and their stuff, especially when we consider that the people of the land were panic stricken by the successes that the Israelites had over them. Josh. iv: 13. Though Joshua does not charge them with failing to furnish their quota of warriors, but on the contrary, at the close of the war, he blesses them and dismisses them when they return to their inheritance, and to their families. Joshua, xxii. After they returned, they builded an altar by the side of Jordan. When the other tribes heard of their altar, they suspected that they had built the altar for idolatrous worship, hence they prepared to go to war with them. But they first sent a deputation to ascertain the facts in the case. The Reubenites, Gadites, and the half tribe of Manasseh, received the deputation, and explained to them the reason of their building the altar. Instead of designing to become idolatrous, this was to prevent it. They made a noble defense, and the deputation returned to report that they were satisfied that their brethren had not done wrong, and all Israel praised the Lord. In Deut. xxxiii: 6, there is a prophetic declaration regarding the tribe of Reuben. "Let him live and not die, and let his men not be few."

The Reubenites were not able to send warriors in the time of Deborah, to assist Barak against Jabin, king of Canaan. From the song of Deborah, we may suppose that they had divisions among them, and hence could not heartily join with the other tribes and possibly they were suffering from foreign invasion, and could not leave their interests, "for the divisions of Reuben there were great searchings of heart." The other tribes seemed to feel uneasy when they found that Reuben did not join with them. Judges, v: 15.

During the reign of King Saul, as we learn from 1st Chron. xii, they, with the Gadites and Manasites, numbered very largely. Of those that rallied to David and assisted in his coronation, there were of them one hundred and twenty thousand. There are several important persons of the tribe of Reuben noticed, among whom Eliezer, the son of Zichri, who was their governor, and Adina the son of Shiza, who was one of David's great men. 1st Chron. xxvii: 16; 1st Chron. xi: 42.

During the reign of Jeroboam the country of the Reubenites was ravaged by Hazael, the king of Syria. It is said, in 2d Kings, x: 33: "Hazael smote them in all the coasts of Israel, from Jordan eastward all the land of Gilead, the Gadites, the Reubenites and the Manasites; from Aroer, which is by the river Arnon, even Gilead and Bashan." In 1st Chron. v, we have the genealogy of Reuben given, as also of Gad, with various exploits of these two tribes, and the half tribe of Manasseh. We have an account of their running into idolatry, and of their captivity by the Assyrians. Pul and Tilgath-pilneser conquered them, and carried them to Halah, and Habor, and Hara, supposed to be in the north-east part of the Assyrian Empire.

REUMAH—[Ru′mah] *lofty, sublime.*

REUMAH was the concubine or second wife of Nahor, Abraham's brother. Her name occurs in Gen. xxii: 24, and her relation to Nahor is given for the first time with the fact that she was the mother of the following named sons of Nahor: Tebah, and Gaham, and Thahash, and Maacah.

REZIN—[Re′zin,] *voluntary, runner.*

REZIN was a king of the Syrians, cotemporary with, and a confederate of Pekah, the king of Israel, in a war with Ahaz, the king of Judah. He was probably a descendant of Hazael, and the last of the kings of ancient Syria. 2 Kings, xvi: 5. The king of Israel and Rezin were unable to take Jerusalem, but they ravaged the country; when Rezin with his army returned to his own country. But sometime after this, Rezin's army again plundered the country, and Ahaz, the king of Judah, hired Tilgath-Pileser, king of Assyria, to help him, and he invaded Syria, and conquering Rezin's army slew him, taking Damascus and carrying the people captives to Kir. Isa. vii: 8, gives us an account of his joining Pekah against Ahaz, and he was commissioned to comfort Ahaz as the representative of David's family, and declare that Rezin should be destroyed.

REZON—[Re′-zon,] *lean, secret, prince.*

REZON was the son of Eliadah who revolted from Hadadezer, his master. He was a captain of the Syrians whom David defeated. At the time of the defeat of Hadadezer, Rezon escaped with the company he commanded, and lived for some time, it is supposed, by plunder. At length he seized Damascus, and made himself king, and remained king there until David took possession of it. As David conquered Syria, Rezon was driven from it. But after Solomon's departure from God, Rezon learned that God was not with Israel and her king, as in the days of David, and he came up against Solomon and recovered Damascus. In 1st Kings, xi: 25: "And he was an adversary to Israel all the days of Solomon." Here we have the fulfillment of God's threatening, by Nathan the prophet. "If he commit iniquity, I will chastise him with the rod of men, and with the the stripes of the children of men." 2d Sam. vii: 14.

RHODA—[Ro′-dah,] *a rose.*

RHODA was one of those who were at the house of Mary on the memorable night that Peter was released from prison by an angel. There were engaged in prayer to God many of the disciples at this house. As soon as the apostle was led out of prison, he made his way to the residence of Mary, and knocked at the door of the gate. "And a damsel named Rhoda came to hearken." Acts, xii: 13. It seems that Peter spoke, and that Rhoda recognized his voice. No wonder that she knew it, for she had often heard it. She had heard him pray and preach, and with the other disciples she had intense anxiety as to his welfare. When she heard Peter's voice, she did not stop to open the gate, but ran into the house and told the company that he was at the gate. They did not believe it, for they knew he was in prison; but she insisted upon it that it was Peter, for she knew his voice. They began to feel that they must credit Rhoda, for she was so confident. But they said: "It is his angel." Peter continued knocking, and at last they let him in, when he informed them how he had escaped the prison.

RIPHATH—[Ri′-fath,] *remedy, release.*

Was the second son of Gomer, and the grand-son of Japheth. His brothers were Ashkenaz and Togarmah. Genesis, x: 3.

RIZPAH—[Riz′-pah,] *bed, extension, coal.*

RIZPAH was a second wife of Saul, the first king of Israel. She was the mother of Armoni and Mephibosheth, the sons of Saul, and was the daughter of Aiah. 2d Sam. xxi: 8. Soon after David was made king in Hebron, Ishbosheth, the son of Saul, charged Abner, the captain of his host, with improper familiarities with Rizpah, who had survived Saul. Abner, whether guilty or not, became angry at the son of Saul, and made arrangements to transfer the interest of his master's kingdom to David, and would have done it had he not fallen by the murderous hand of Joab.

Late in the reign of King David there was a famine that lasted for three years in succession. 2d Sam. xxi: 1: "Then there was a famine in the days of David, three years, year after year." David became anxious to know the cause of it, and enquired of the Lord. He was informed that "it was for Saul and for his bloody house, because he slew the Gibeonites." David then enquired of the Gibeonites what would make atonement to them for the injury done them by Saul. They replied to him that they wanted not silver or gold of Saul or of his house, but they wanted seven men of his sons to be delivered unto them that they might hang them in Gibeah. David agreed to give them seven of Saul's sons, and he did. Two of them were the sons of Rizpah, and the other five were the grandsons of Saul, as the sons of Michal, his daughter.

Rizpah was greatly grieved at the loss she sustained in the death of her two sons. It is hardly possible to read the account of their being thus sacrificed, and of her maternal affection, without dropping the tear of sympathy with her in her sorrows. She "took sackcloth and spread it for her upon the rock from the beginning of harvest until water dropped upon them out of heaven, and suffered neither the birds of the air to rest on them by day, nor the beasts of the field by night." The probability is that this poor broken-hearted mother watched these bodies for several months before the periodical rains came on. What a sad and mournful employment for a lone woman—a widow and childless—from the beginning of early harvest until the autumn rains!

ROMAMTI-EZER—[Ro-mam′-ti-e′zer,] *exultation of help.*

ROMAMTI-EZER was one of the sons of Heman, and when the lots were cast and the singers were divided into twenty-four courses, the four-and-twentieth lot came to him. 1 Chron. xxv: 31.

ROSH—*The head, the beginning.*

ROSH was one of the sons of Benjamin, and was numbered with the family of Jacob who went down into Egypt. Gen. xlvi: 21.

RUFUS, 1—[Ru′-fus,] *red.*

RUFUS was the brother of an Alexander, and they were both the sons of Simon the Cyrenian, whom the soldiers that were taking Jesus to Calvary, met, and compelled to bear the cross for the fainting Savior. Mark, xv: 21.

RUFUS, 2—*Red.*

RUFUS was a disciple of Christ in the apostolic age, and endeared to the apostle Paul, who salutes him, Rom. xvi: 13, in the following language: "Salute Rufus chosen in the Lord and his mother and mine," from which some have supposed that Rufus was related to Paul; but probably he intended to say that the natural mother of Rufus had been as a mother to him, or in her kindness to him, had filled the place of a mother.

RUTH—*Filled, satisfied.*

It is thought by some that this woman was of royal blood as the daughter of Eglon, the King of Moab; but this is mere conjecture. For her history we refer to the book of Ruth. She was a Moabitish damsel, who was married to Mahlon, the son of Elimelech and Naomi. She appears endowed with all the virtues and charms of true womanhood. It may be that her tender affection and sympathy to Naomi and her sons, when bereft of the husband and father, her watching by the couch of pain, and ministering to the suffering and dying Elimelech, was what led to the undying affection that afterward existed between her and Naomi. And it may be that the womanly virtues she developed was the reason why Naomi selected her as a wife for her son.

She was married to Mahlon, but he soon died, and she was left a widow, and not long afterwards the husband of Orphah died also, so that the family consisted of three widows. Naomi, in her bereavement and sorrow, determined to return from the country of Moab, to the land of Judah, and accordingly informed her daughters; they said "we will also go with thee." She dissuaded them from that, or attempted to; with Orphah she succeeded, but with Ruth she could not. While Orphah kissed her mother-in-law and parted with her, Ruth "clave unto her," and utterly refused to be parted from her. She said "Entreat me not to leave thee, or to return from following after thee; for whither thou goest, I will go; and where thou lodgest, I will lodge; thy people shall be my people, and thy God my God; when thou diest, I will die, and there will I be buried." She then confirmed her purpose by an oath of the greatest sanctity and importance amongst the daughters of Israel, viz: "The Lord do so to me, and more also, if aught but death part thee and me."

The mind of Ruth was fully made up to leave her own land, and friends, and wealth, (if she was heir to wealth,) and the false gods that were worshiped by the Moabites. She wished to share in all the storms and trials that might break, and spend their fury upon Naomi, to whose interests she was so unflinchingly devoted.

How disconsolate Naomi would have been, had she been traveling alone, for she was leaving three graves of loved ones behind her in the land of Moab. Though she left Judah vigorous and happy, she was returning with a care worn brow, furrowed cheeks and sad visage. She was alone. No not alone either, for the affectionate Ruth was with her, pleasing in person, winning in manners, kind in actions and words. Day after day, as they traveled on, their affection for each other increased until finally they reached the city and entered its gates. It may be they rented an humble cottage and poorly as it was furnished called it their home, while Ruth labored daily for their support.

They had come to Bethlehem in the beginning of barley harvest. Ruth, addressing her mother-in-law, said: "Let me now go to the field, and glean ears of corn after him, in whose sight I shall find favor." She desired to go out as a gleaner, and Naomi said unto her: "Go, my daughter." Accordingly she went. Now it was her fortune in her ramblings to be found gleaning in that part of the field belonging to Boaz. And as he was passing along from the city to the fields where his men were reaping, he saw her engaged in her work, and looked with a degree of interest upon her, wondering in his own mind who it was. Her modest bearing, flushed cheeks, flowing locks, and her womanly address, won his admiration, and when he reached the reapers, he asked them: "Whose damsel is this?" They told him it was the Moabitish damsel that came back from the country of Moab with Naomi. Boaz thought of Elimelech, who was his kinsman; of Naomi, who had passed through dark providences, and of the two sons who had died, leaving widows, of which this woman was one; and he thought of this woman's tenderness and care for Naomi, and addressing her, he said: "Hearest thou not, my daughter; go not to glean in another field, neither go from hence, but remain here fast by my maidens. I have given commandment to the young men that they shall not touch thee, and when thou art athirst go and drink of that which the young men have drawn." Ruth was astonished at this kindness, and asked why it was. He told her he had heard of her kindness to Naomi. But the affection of Boaz increased for her. "He reached her parched corn and she did eat." He commanded the reapers to let some handfuls fall on purpose for her, and bade her remain in his fields through the harvest. She did, when she claimed of him the protection and obligation of a kinsman. He acknowledged the correctness of her claim, and gladly set himself about consummating what in all probability he had been meditating—marriage to her, for he had learned to love the modest, industrious and accomplished Ruth.

Soon she became his wife, and found in him a gentle and loving companion. She rested on the arm and bosom of a generous and noble man, and felt herself more than compensated for her sacrifices in leaving her native land and kindred, and in a strange country stooping to the service of a menial, and performing hard labor for weeks as a gleaner, to support herself and her mother-in-law. Boaz claimed her as his wife. She became the mother of a son, and that son was the grand-father of David, the king of Israel. Ruth, iv: 22.

SABTA.

Sabta was the third son of Cush, and the grandson of Ham. He is supposed to have settled in Arabia. Gen. x: 7.

SABTECHA—[Sab-te′-kah,] *that surrounds.*

Sabtecha was the fifth son of Cush, and is supposed to have settled with his family in the east of the Persian Gulf—for there are said to be some vestiges of the name in various things found by travellers. Genesis, x: 7

SACER.

Sacer was the fourth son of Obed Edom, and one of the sacred porters. 1st. Chron. xxvi: 4.

SALAH—[Sa′-lah,] *mission, dart; according to the Syriac, that spoils.*

Salah was the son of Arphaxed, and the grandson of Shem, and he is referred to in the posterity of Shem. Gen. x: 24.

SALMON—[Sal′-mon,] *peaceable, perfect, that rewards.*

Salmon was of the descendants of Judah by Pharez his son. He is recorded in the genealogy of David as given in Ruth, as the son of Nahshon and the father of Boaz. Ruth, iv: 18, 22. And in the genealogy of Christ as given by Matthew, i: 5, he is said to have begat Booz of Rahab or Rachab, from which we learn that Salmon married the Canaanitish innkeeper—and thus connected her who had hid the spies with the honorable tribe of Judah.

SALOME—[Sa-lo′-me.]

Salome was the wife of Zebedee, and the mother of James and John. She was one of the holy women that followed our Savior, and ministered unto him during his travels and labor. She made a strange and foolish request of Christ, indicating her ignorance of the nature of the kingdom he was about to establish on earth. That request is recorded in Matt. xx: 21. "She saith unto him, grant that these, my two sons, may sit, the one on thy right hand and the other on thy left hand, in thy kingdom."

Just before Salome made this request Christ had taken the twelve disciples apart, and told them, in a feeling manner, of his approaching sufferings and death. He had told them that he was about to be betrayed into the hands of the chief priests and scribes, and would be condemned to death. That in the execution of his sentence, the Jews would deliver him to the Gentiles, "to mock and scourge and to crucify him." And yet Salome made this request of him. But it is quite likely that she was not altogether to blame in making it.

From the presentation of this circumstance, Mark, x: 35, it would seem that the sons themselves led her to make the request, or rather, that they made it through their mother. Christ recognized it as their request, as is evident from his answer. "Ye know not what ye ask. Are ye able to drink of the cup that I shall drink of, and to be baptized with the baptism that I am baptized with?" And when they answered him "we are able," he said

"Ye shall, indeed, drink of my cup, and be baptized with the baptism that I am baptized with."

But while Salome was expressing their wishes, she was also expressing her own. It was her desire that her two sons, James and John, might occupy important positions in Christ's temporal kingdom.

Salome was present when Christ was crucified, though with other women, standing some distance from the summit of Calvary. They were sufficiently near to witness the terrible scene. Matt. xxvii: 55: "And many women were there, (beholding afar off,) among which were Mary Magdalene, and Mary the mother of James and Joses, and the mother of Zebedee's children." It is impossible for us to imagine the feelings of these pious women, and the strong sympathy for Mary, the mother of Jesus, whose soul a sword was now piercing, as Simon predicted.

Salome was one of the women who went to the sepulcher, early on the morning of the first day of the week, with spices and perfumes to embalm the body. Mark, xvi: 1. "And when the Sabbath was past, Mary Magdalene, and Mary the mother of James, and Salome, had bought sweet spices, that they might come and anoint him." This good woman was true to the master while he lived and labored among men. She was true to him when he was put to death; visited his grave as early as an opportunity afforded after his burial, and was one of the first to receive the first evidence of his resurrection, viz: an empty sepulcher.

SAMLAH—[Sam'lah,] *raiment, his left hand, his name.*

Was a king of Edom, who succeeded Hadad. His place of residence was Masrekah, where he entered upon the duties and honors of the office. Gen. xxxvi: 36. And he was succeeded by Saul, of Rehobeth.

SAMSON—]Sam'son,] *his sun, according to the Syriac, his service, here the second time.*

SAMSON was the son of Manoah, a Danite. His birth is announced in Judges, xiii; 24: but there are some things remarkable regarding this person recorded, before we have his birth announced. The angel of God appeared to Manoah's wife, who had not been blessed with children, and informed her that she should be the mother of a son, who should be a deliverer for Israel out of the hand and power of the Philistines, who had began to oppress them, and she was further instructed to keep herself from everything unclean. She was also informed that the child should be a Nazarite from his mother's womb. She went to her husband and informed him that an angel had appeared unto her, and had told her these things. He became very anxious that the angel should appear again, insomuch that he prayed for it. The angel did appear again to the woman, and she ran and told her husband. Manoah went at once to the place where the angel appeared to the woman this second time, and he repeated unto him the declaration he had made to her. Judges, xiii. [See Manoah.]

Samson was born, and the scripture account of him is, that "he grew and the Lord blessed him, and the spirit of the Lord began to move him at times, in the camp of Dan." By this we may understand that when Samson was quite young, his mind was being developed, and at times he showed an uncommon bravery; while his body was endowed with supernatural strength. His parents dwelt between Zorah of Esthaol. We have an account of his going to Timnath, and becoming acquainted with a woman that he desired to marry. He requested his parents to procure her for him for a wife. They at first objected because she was a woman of another nation, and enemies to their nation. But he was so intent on it, that his father and mother thinking it might be from the Lord procured her for him.

Manoah and his wife accompanied Samson to Timnath, to consummate the espousal. On the road Samson turned aside and a lion roared against him, threatening to destroy him. He had not even a staff in his hand to defend himself with. But the spirit of the Lord came upon him, and he took hold of the lion and rent it as he would a kid, then passed on his way following his father and mother, but he told them not what he had done.

The parents having accomplished what they wanted to, went to Timnath, and afterwards returned home, and Samson with them.

Some time after this, Samson went there again, to consumate the marriage, and his parents went with him. On the way, he turned aside to see the carcass of the lion, and, to his astonishment, there was a swarm of bees, and honey, in the carcass; and he took some of the honey in his hands, and went on eating it, and gave to his father and mother, but yet did not tell them of his having killed the lion. The marriage feast was prepared according to the custom of that age, and they began to enter into its enjoyments when Samson put forth a riddle to the thirty companions that had been brought him, with the agreement, on his part, if they found it out during the feast, he would give them thirty sheets and thirty changes of garments, and if they failed, were to give him the same.

They then bade him put forth the riddle and he did as follows: "Out of the eater came forth meat, and out of the strong came forth sweetness." They studied over it three days and could not expound it—they then came to Samson's wife and urged her to tell them, threatening to burn her and her father's family with fire, if she did not procure information for them. She accordingly entreated Sampson to tell her, but he would not, notwithstanding her entreaties and tears. He told her he had not told his father and mother. On the seventh day, "as she lay sore upon him," he told her—she then told them, and they, in turn expounded the riddle. He knew full well that they had informed themselves through his wife, and he charged it upon them, "If ye had not ploughed with my heifer, ye had not found out my riddle." The spirit of the Lord then came upon Samson and he went to Askelon and killed thirty Philistines, and took their spoil, and gave thirty sheets, and gave change of garments to each of the thirty companions one. He thought his wife had dealt treacherously with him, and he left her and went to his father's house, not intending to abandon his wife altogether; but her father did not understand it, and married her to one of his thirty companions. Samson not knowing that her father had given her to be the wife of another, went some time after to visit his wife, when her father told him that he had supposed he had forsaken her, and hated her, and hence he gave her to his companion. But the father proposed to give him a younger daughter to be his wife in the stead of the other. Samson was displeased and determined on revenge. He, therefore, went forth and caught three hundred foxes—which animals, we may suppose were very numerous in that country; and fastening them together in twos he put a firebrand between them and sent them into the standing corn of the Philistines and among the shocks into which in their fright they would run to hide. The corn being ripe caught fire, and soon the standing corn and the shocks were consumed. But this was not all the injury done, for their vineyards and oliveyards were also destroyed. As soon as the Philistines ascertained who had done this, and that he had done it because of the injury and insult he had received in connection with his marriage, the Philistines then went up and burnt Samson's wife and her father with fire. He told them, after they had thus cruelly murdered his wife and father-in-law, that he would be further avenged on them for it. "And he smote them hip and thigh with great slaughter."

After thus avenging himself he went down to a rock called Etam—probably a fortified place—and dwelt there. When the Philistines found he was there, they invaded the country and demanded of Judah that he should be given up to them that they might punish him as their destroyer. They thought it would be better to deliver him up than to enter upon a war with this people. Accordingly three thousand of them went up to the top of the rock, and they told Samson that they had come to bind him and deliver him to the Philistines. He asked them if they would enter upon an oath that they would not kill him themselves if he delivered himself up to them. They vowed that they would not harm him, but simply bind him and give him to them. They then bound him with two new cords and brought him from the top of the rock and delivered him up. The Philistines were very joyful when they found Samson was in their hands and power, and they began to shout and exult against him. Just at this time the spirit of God came upon Samson, and the cords with which the men of Judah had bound him were snapped asunder as though they were burnt with fire, and the bands were loosed from his hands; and seeing the jawbone of an ass lying near him, he took it up and began to kill the Philistines with it. He went on slaying one after another until he had slain a thousand men with it. He then broke out in triumphant song, saying, "With the jawbone of an ass heaps upon heaps; with the jaw of an ass have I slain a thousand men!"

Having performed this wonderful feat he threw down his weapon; and as the excitement of the engagement died away he became thirsty, and began in his thirst and faintness to think, after all, he would perish. He prayed humbly to the Lord to help him in his extremity, and he did, by miraculously filling the hollow place in the jawbone with water. Samson drank of the water and was revived, and commemorated the event by calling the fountain En-hakkore, *i. e.* the well of him that cried, while the place was called Lehi, or Ramoth-Lehi, *i. e.* the lifting up of the jawbone. Judges, xiv and xv.

The next account we have of Samson is, he is at Gaza, boarding at a house of public entertainment. When the Philistines heard that he was there, they thought surely he was in their power. They accordingly guarded the house and set watches at the gates of Gaza, with instructions to kill him as he went out in the morning. But about midnight he rose up and started out. The closed gate was no barrier to him, for he tore it down and carried the posts and doors with him to the top of the hill Hebron, or a hill on the road to Hebron.

Not long after this he became strongly attached to a woman in the valley of Sorek, whose name was Delilah, and it is likely he married her. Whether she was a woman of the Philistines, or a daughter of Israel, is not known. It is said "he loved her."

As soon as the Philistines knew of Samson's relation to Delilah, their lords came to her and demanded that she entice him and ascertain where his great strength lay, and how they might prevail over him. They promised each of them to give eleven hundred pieces of silver. This she undertook to do—loving the money more than she loved Samson. Delilah pressed him to tell wherein his strength lay, and how he might be bound to afflict him. He told her if they bound him with seven green withes, that were never dried, then he should be weak as another man. She called the lords of the Philistines and told them. They brought her the withes, and she bound him with them and told him the Philistines were upon him. "He brake them as a thread of tow is broken, when it toucheth the fire." She urged him again to tell her, and tell her the truth. He told her to bind him fast with new ropes that were never used, and he would be weak as another man. She did so, and upon trying him, as in the former case, the ropes proved of no avail. She then reproached Samson with telling her lies, not only in the matter of the great secret of his strength, but in mocking her. He then told her to weave the seven divisions of his hair or the locks of his head, with a web. She did so, and fastened it with a pin, then said: "The Philistines be upon thee." He awoke from his sleep, and went away with the pin of the beam, and the web. She then charged him with lying unto her as it regarded his love. She said, "thine heart is not with me, thou hast mocked me these three times, and hast not told me wherein thy strength lieth." Samson with all his strength of body, shows himself to possess a very weak mind in being influenced by her as he was, for his soul became vexed, and without seeing that it was Delilah's intention to ruin him, he made known to her the great secret, viz: That his strength lay in the preservation of his hair, as a Nazarite; there was his strength and security. When she found that he had told her the secret, she called the lords of the Philistines to come up once more, and they come. She then caused Samson to sleep upon her lap, and she cut off his hair as he lay sleeping. She then began to afflict him, and his strength went from him. Soon the Philistines rushed upon him, and apprehending him, they put out both his eyes, and taking him to Gaza, they put fetters of brass upon him, and made him their slave, and compelled him to grind at their corn mill.

Thus he continued for a year, when his hair was again of considerable growth, and his strength began to return; and on a festival during which they offered sacrifice unto their God Dagon, who they said had delivered Samson, their enemy, into their hands. And in the midst of their feast, they called for Samson to be brought from his prison-house, that they might deride him, and compel him to make sport for them. They accordingly brought him to their temple, and they set him between the pillars of the temple. The various apartments of the building were thronged with delighted spectators. Samson could not see them, but he could hear the bustle of the multitude, and the insults they were heaping upon him. He asked the Philistine that had him in charge, to let him feel the pillars whereon the house stood, that he might rest himself upon them. He was granted his request, and he lifted his heart in prayer to his God, saying, "Remember me, I pray thee, and strengthen me, I pray thee; only this once, O God, that I may be at once avenged of the Philistines for my two eyes." He then took hold of the pillars, the one with his right hand and the other with his left, and asked of his God that he might die with the Philistines. He then put out his strength in lifting these central pillars, and tore them from their place; and the whole temple fell with a crash upon the multitude, the consequence of which was, several thousand of them died with Samson. There were three thousand men and women in and about the temple; and the account tells us that in this slaughter, Samson killed more than he had killed in his lifetime.

Samson was a judge of Israel for twenty years. We are not certain as to the precise time that his magistracy commenced, or when it closed, or over how great an extent of country he exercised it. Many have thought he was cotemporary with Eli, if so he probably judged in the tribe of Dan, on the border of the Philistine country, only.

After he was buried in the ruins of the Dagon temple, his relatives of the tribe of Dan took his body from the ruins and carried them to the former residence of his father, and where he was born and raised, and they buried him between Zorah and Eshtaol in the family burying place of Manoah. Jud. xvi.

With all his faults and failings Samson had excellencies, and the spirit of inspiration under the New Testament dispensation refers to him among the ancient worthies who had faith in God. Heb. xi; 32, 33. There he is mentioned with Gideon, Barak, Jephthah, David and Solomon.

SAMUEL—[Sam′-u-el,] *heard or asked of God.*

Samuel, the prophet and judge of Israel, was the son of Elkanah and Hannah. For an account of the remarkable circumstances connected with his birth, see Elkanah and Hannah. His parents devoted him to the service of God. As soon as Hannah, his mother, weaned him, she took him to Shiloh and placed him under the charge of Eli. This priest was very old when Samuel was placed under his charge, and the child, while very young, ministered unto the Lord before Eli. There was no prophet in those days—no accredited prophet—to whom, as in after years, the people might go to have difficult matters settled, and to receive open visions of revelations from God.

One night, while Eli was sleeping in his apartment, near to the place where the ark of God was, and the child Samuel near him, if not in the same apartment, under the same roof, while the lamp of God was still burning, the Lord called to Samuel. He, thinking it was Eli, ran to him and asked him what he had called him for. The aged priest said, "I called not, my son; lie down again." Samuel was called by the Lord a second time, and he ran to Eli, confident that he had called him; but he told him he had not called him,—to lie down again. A third time the Lord called him, and he reported himself to Eli. The aged priest suspected that the Lord had spoken unto him, and bade him lie down, and if he heard the voice again, to say, "Speak, Lord, for thy servant heareth." The voice called him again, and he followed the directions of Eli. The Lord then informed Samuel that calamities were about to fall on Israel, and that the family of Eli should sadly suffer. When the child Samuel came into the presence of Eli, he requested him to make known unto him the saying of the Lord, which he did, but not without some reluctance. It is said he told Eli every whit, and hid nothing from him.

Samuel continued with Eli, and probably had many revelations made to him, which he made known; for it is said "Samuel grew, and the Lord was with him, and did let none of his words fall to the ground." And it was not long until all Israel, from Dan to Beer-sheba, understood that Samuel was a prophet of the Lord. 1st Sam. iii.

When Eli died Samuel succeeded him as judge of Israel. The ark was taken by the Philistines in the battle in which Hophni and Phinehas, Eli's sons, were slain; and it was this sad calamity that brought about Eli's death. After the ark had been seven months in the land of the Philistines, they consulted their priests about sending it back to Shiloh. They advised them to send it back on a new cart drawn by two milch kine. The calves of these cows were to be confined, and if the cows in drawing the cart were to take the way of Beth-shemesh in going to the Israelite border, then the Lord had afflicted them; but if not, their afflictions, that had led them to think of sending the ark back, were accidental. The kine went the way of Beth-shemesh, and the men of that place committed error in curiously looking into the ark, and were smitten by the Lord. They became alarmed, and sent to the inhabitants of Kirjath-jearim to come and fetch the ark away. Samuel assembled the people on the occasion, and warned them to put away their idols and return to the Lord, and they should be delivered. He bade them meet him at Mizpah; then he appointed a solemn fast, during which they confessed their sins and mourned before the Lord.

The Philistines came against them in battle, and they were afraid, and entreated Samuel to pray for them. He did so, and offered sacrifices to God, and he helped them, for God confounded the Philistines with thunder, and they fled before the Israelites. Samuel acknowledged the deliverance God had wrought out for them, and built a monument to perpetuate the memory of it, calling it Ebenezer, i. e., hitherto the Lord hath helped us. Samuel then became a judge in Israel. 1st Sam. vi and vii.

Samuel had two sons, Joel and Abiah, and he appointed them as his helpers in his old age. Like the sons of Eli, they were wicked and unworthy of their father. It is said: "His sons walked not in his way, but turned aside after lucre, and took bribes and perverted judgments," insomuch, that the elders of Israel complained to Samuel of them, and they came to him, asking that their form of government be changed. They said: "Make us a king to judge us like all the nations." Samuel was displeased at this, their request, but he consulted the Lord in prayer as to what he should do, and the Lord bade him hearken unto the voice of the people, charging it upon them that they had forsaken him, and were weary of the divine government; but at the same time, Samuel was directed to warn them what manner of tyrants they would have to rule over them. They would be obliged to serve their king in wars—to serve him in his household, and to bear heavy taxes for the support of his government. They persisted however in having a king. 1st Sam. viii. Samuel was then directed to anoint Saul, the son of Kish, to be their king. He found Saul on a search for the asses of his father, for they had strayed away, and he invited him to dine with him, and he intimated to Saul that he was to be king in Israel. They communed together on the top of the house, and when Saul was about ready to start home to his father's house, Samuel attended him to the outskirts of the city. He told Saul to bid his servants pass on before him, that they might have a secret counsel together, and he did so. Samuel then took a vial of oil and poured it on his head, and kissed him as the Lord's anointed. He then told Saul that when he reached Rachel's sepulcher in the border of Benjamin, he would see two men who would tell him that the asses of his father were found, and that now he was the object of his father's search; and further, when he came to the plains of Tabor, he should meet three men going up to Bethel, one of them carrying three kids, and another three loaves of bread, and the other carrying a bottle of wine. He told him how they would salute him, and give him the bread. He told him further that when he came to the hill of God, he should meet a company of prophets coming down with instruments of music, such as were used in worship, and they should prophesy, and the spirit of prophecy should also come upon him. All these were to be signs confirmatory of the declaration he had made to him, as to his being selected of God to rule over Israel. But this was not all, for just as he turned from Samuel to pursue his way, "God gave him another heart."

Samuel calls the people together at Mizpah and confirms the kingdom to Saul. He solemnly challenges the people to accuse him, if they could, of any injustice since he had been their judge. They acknowledged that they could not accuse him.

He then referred them to the mercy of God, as it had been displayed to them, and warned them faithfully to take heed and serve the Lord under the new form of government, that his blessings might be continued unto them. He told them again that they had done wrong in asking a king, and as evidence that they had done wrong, they should now have a sign from heaven. Though it was wheat-harvest, and thunder and rain seldom happened at that time, yet there should be a storm that day, to testify to God's displeasure. Accordingly "Samuel called on the Lord, and the Lord sent thunder and rain that day." Samuel then delivered a faithful warning to the people, against apostacy from God's service, and dismissing the people, he went to his house and never afterwards acted as a judge of Israel. 1st Samuel, ix to xii.

After Saul had been acting as king twenty years, he sinned against God, in his conduct towards the Amalekites, and the aged prophet, Samuel, reproved him sharply for it. Saul took Agag, their king, a prisoner, and saved the best of the spoil. When Samuel reproved him, he tried to justify his conduct, but the prophet convinced him that he had done wrong. Samuel then calls for Agag, and as he came delicately into his presence, he said unto him, "As thy sword hath made women childless, so shall thy mother be childless among women. And Samuel hewed Agag in pieces before the Lord, in Gilgal." After this Samuel went to Ramaah, and no more visited Saul to council or advise him. It is true that Saul visited Samuel at Ramah, when David was there, but there was no friendly counsel between him and the prophet.

Samuel was grieved because that Saul was disobedient, and the Lord comforted him by sending him to the house of Jesse, the Bethlehemite, to anoint his son king, as successor of Saul. When he went to Bethlehem on this errand, he went there under divine direction with sacrifices, that his true errand might not be known. Having a private interview with Jesse, he asked that all his sons might pass before him. His object was to select the one that was to be king, and before he returned home anoint him. When he saw Eliab, the eldest, he thought surely this was the one, but the Lord told him he was not the selection. The outward appearance was not to be the criterion, "for God looketh at the heart." Six others passed before him, but neither of them were selected. Samuel learned that David the younger was in the field with the sheep, and he sent for him. He saw at once, as David came, that he was the one, and he sought an opportunity, probably in company with Jesse only, to anoint the lad as Saul's successor. After which Samuel returned again to Ramah. 1st Sam. xvi: 13.

Samuel seems to have presided for several years over a school of young men, who were devoting themselves exclusively to the service of God. When David fled from the persecuting Saul, he went to Ramah to Samuel probably to ask his advice as to what he should do; and Samuel thought it best to retain him with him awhile, and he did so, and they dwelt together at Naioth. 1st Sam. xix: 18-24. We have an account of the death of Samuel.

Sam. xxv: 1. He was greatly lamented by all Israel, and they buried him in the tomb he had provided for himself at Ramah.

Samuel was the first of that line of prophets that ended with Malachi. He is seemingly the first who established schools for the prophets, a custom that continued at least until the Babylonish captivity. In his day he reformed many abuses. He was a zealous and ardent advocate for true religion. He was the last judge of Israel, and the prime minister of the first king. He anointed the first and second kings to their offices, and his public and private character was without a blemish, and in this respect his equal is not to be found in modern or ancient history.

The first two books of the kings are called the first and second books of Samuel. As it is certain that he wrote in a book rules for the government of the kingdom, in which rules he pointed out the duties and privileges of king and subjects. It is likely he wrote nearly all of the first book of Samuel. All that part of it that gives the history, up to his death, of himself, of Eli, and of Saul and his kingdom. He is also thought to have written the books of Judges and Ruth. 1st Chron. xxix: 29; xxvi: 28; ix: 10. The style of these two books with the first twenty-four chapters of 1st Samuel is easy and exceedingly plain. It has been thought that Samuel typified Christ; and to prove this, his supernatural birth has been referred to, his growth in wisdom and favor with God, the revelations made to him, and the prophecies uttered by him when a child. He occupied the position of prophet for Israel, also priest, and judge, the prime minister of the king, &c.

SANBALLAT—[San-bal′-lat,] *bush or enemy in secret.*

SANBALLAT was the governor of Samaria at the time that Nehemiah came with his helpers from Persia to rebuild the walls of Jerusalem, and in company with Tobiah and Gesham, he was sorely vexed that this work was going on, and the welfare of the children of Israel was sought after. In a contemptible manner he tries to dissuade Nehemiah from the work. They accused him of rebelling against the king. Sanballat arrayed himself against Nehemiah as an open enemy, having tried several methods of fraud to prevent the work without success. He tried to secure a conference with Nehemiah in which he intended to kill him. He then accused him of rebellion, and afterwards hired a false prophet against him; but in all he failed—for the walls of Jerusalem were built in spite of him and his allies. Neh. ii: 10; Neh. vi. Sanballat was of Horanaim, hence called the Horanite.

SAPH—[Saf,] *rushes, end, threshold.*

SAPH was of the sons of the giants. He was slain in a battle that the Israelites had with the Philistines. Sibbechai the Hushathite slew him, 2d Sam. xxi: 18. We do not know that he was related to Goliath the Gittite, but he was of the race of Philistine giants.

SAPPHIRA—[Saf-fi′-rah,] *that tells, that writes books.*

SAPPHIRA was the wife of Ananias, an insincere professor of faith in Christ. He was not a true believer, neither was Sapphira; if she had been she would not have concurred in the lie that her husband told the apostle. They were false professors so far as they went in their profession. They had not as yet, probably, been baptized, but they were candidates for baptism. Ananias sold his possessions,—whatever they consisted in,—and, with the consent of his wife, kept back part of the price, "his wife also being privy to it." Their sin was that of attempting to deceive—holding back a part of the money, and yet professing to give all up, and so professing to stand on a level with those who had given all, when in reality they reserved money.

Peter made the charge upon Ananias of lying to the Holy Ghost, and the deceiver fell dead at the apostle's feet. About three hours afterward, this woman, not knowing that the deception was detected and her husband was dead, came into the place where Peter was, expecting, in all probability, that the apostle and all present would laud the act of their selling their property and putting the proceeds into a common treasury, and thereby becoming benefactors to this fund. But she was greatly mistaken. As she approached the apostle he demanded of her an answer to the following question: "Tell me whether ye sold the land for so much?" and she, without any hesitancy, answered with a lie. She thought Ananias was near by and would hear her testimony, according to their agreement; but how was she mistaken—Ananias was dead! And as she answered Peter, "Yea, for so much," the startling intelligence was given her, Thy husband is dead! God in his anger struck him down with a lie upon his lip. Sapphira, thou hast committed the same sin, and the same punishment is awaiting thee! And just as she awoke to the fact that she was a widow, the announcement was made by the apostle, "Behold, the feet of them which have buried thy husband are at the door, and shall carry thee out." How solemn and startling this declaration! She had hardly time to think, when the arrow of the Almighty pierced her vitals, and she fell dead at Peter's feet. Her immortal spirit joined her husband's—both alike with the stains of sin upon them. Without time for repentance, they were hurried into the presence of the Great God to render their account.

Her dead body was prepared for burial, and by the young men that had buried her husband it was carried out from the presence of the apostle and those that were with him, and buried beside his form. Acts, v: 1-11.

SARAH, 1—[Sa′-rah,] *lady princess of the multitude.*

SARAH was the wife of Abraham, the illustrious Patriarch and friend of God. Her name was Sarai when married to the son of the same father with her. Gen. xi: 29, and xii: 13. But her name was changed to Sarah. Gen. xvii: 15. "And God said unto Abraham: As for Sarai, thy wife, thou shalt not call her name Sarai, but Sarah shall her name be."

She was a remarkable woman, and has been styled "chief among the women of the Bible." Sarah was the mother of Patriarchs. Though she was childless until she was aged, yet in her old age the son of promise was born, "he in whom all the nations of the earth were to be blessed."

The promise was made her of a son at the advanced age of eighty-nine years, and in a few months Isaac was born, when she in company with her husband, dedicated him devotionally to God, and afterwards true to her obligation as a mother, she directed Isaac's feet in moral instructions in the pathway of virtue and peace. As a consequence in part, when he grew up to manhood he was a noble specimen of humanity—a loving and dutiful son—an honor and joy to his mother in her old age. Gen. xvii: 18.

Sarah was a beautiful woman, not only in the estimation of her husband, but she possessed a very pleasing person and was really handsome in the judgment of others.

When Abraham left Ur of the Chaldees, to go to Canaan because of a famine in his land, he was led down into Egypt to sojourn awhile, and on arriving there he charged Sarah to claim the relation of sister to him, as she could do it with some degree of consistency, being the daughter of the same father though not of the same mother. "I know," said Abraham, "thou art fair to look upon, and when they shall see thee, they will say, this is his wife; and they will kill me, but they will save thee alive." And so it was that when the princes of Pharaoh saw Sarah, they commended her for her beauty, and Pharaoh entreated Abraham well for her sake. She must have been very handsome in early life, if at the age of sixty-five the great men of Egypt spake of her beauty, and the king himself desired her for his wife. It was not long until all the truth was made known to Pharaoh, viz: that she was Abraham's wife, as well as his sister. About twenty-five years after this, Abimelech, king of Gerar, sent and took her while her husband was sojourning for a short time there. As she was now ninety years of age, her beauty must have faded to some extent, and yet either on account of it, or the greatness of the man she called her brother, with whom he wished to form an alliance, he sent and took Sarah to be his wife. God interposed and she was soon restored to Abraham.

When Abraham dwelt in the plains of Mamre, as he sat one day at noon in the door of his tent, three weary pilgrims attracted his attention. They were coming toward him to enjoy for awhile the shade of his tent, and realize his genuine hospitality. Going beyond the common courtesy of that age, Abraham went to meet the strangers and bowed himself toward the ground and entreated them to tarry with him for awhile. As soon as they manifested their willingness, Sarah united with her husband to make their guests feel that they were in the tent of a friend. She quickly made ready three measures of meal and baked it upon the hearth, prepared the calf brought by her husband, butter and milk, and set them before the strangers and they did eat.

When she determined to send Hagar her handmaid away with Ishmael, and told Abraham, he was grieved for he loved Ishmael, and remembered the promise of God to make his posterity innumerable. There was something harsh to Abraham in Sarah's expression, "Cast out the bondwoman and her son, for the son of the bondwoman shall not be heir with my son, even with Isaac." But Sarah was right as Abraham afterward learned. She acted and spake regarding that matter under inspiration.

At the age of one hundred and twenty-seven years she died at Hebron in the land of Canaan. Behold the patriarch of patriarchs as he bends in sorrow over her failing form, or see him when she is dead, weeping over her cold remains, and asking of the children of Heth a burial place, that he may bury his beloved out of his sight. He makes the purchase of the cave of Machpelah, with the field in which it is situated, and there he placed the coffined remains, reserving for himself a place in that sepulcher, for he wished to be placed beside her in the sleep that is not to be broken until the trump of God shall sound. Gen. xxiii.

SARAH, 2—*Lady princess of the multitude.*

Was the daughter of Asher, and is referred to in Num. xxvi: 46.

SARAPH—[Sa-'raf.]

SARAPH and Joash are referred to in 1st Chronicles, iv: 22. It is supposed by some, they are characters used to represent Mahlon and Chilion, the two sons of Elimelech and Naomi, but this is hardly likely, for they are represented as rulers, while the sons of Naomi, were poor. Their father emigrated to Moab, because of famine and poverty in his own land, staring him in the face. These two men, Saraph and Joash were rulers in Moab. It may be they were the deputies of David.

SAUL, 1—[Sawl,] *demanded, sepulcher, destroyer.*

SAUL of Rehoboth was one of the kings of Edom. He succeeded Samlah, and was succeeded by Baal-hanan, the son of Achbor. Gen. xxxvi: 37

SAUL, 2—*Demanded, sepulcher, destroyer.*

SAUL was the son of Kish, of the tribe of Benjamin, and the first king of Israel. He is brought to our notice in 1st Samuel, ix, just at the time that Israel's elders came to Samuel, their judge, and demanded a king, that they might be governed as other nations were governed. The young man went in search of his father's asses, which had wandered away. He and the servant that attended him, hunted several days ineffectually for them. At length the servant proposed that they should consult the prophet Samuel, who lived not far from where they were, who he suggested might, for a small consideration, give them information regarding them. They made enquiry of some maidens, as to where the seer lived, and they directed him to his house. Samuel had called a convention that day, of the chief persons of that place, to a sacrifice. As soon as he saw Saul he welcomed him, and told him that the lost asses were found. The prophet treated him very kindly, and in the conversation, hinted to him very clearly, that he would be the king of Israel. He took the hint and observed that it was not at all likely, because he belonged to the tribe of Benjamin, the smallest of all the tribes of Israel, and his family was one of the smallest families of the small tribe. He, however, accepted Samuel's invitation to tarry at the feast, and Samuel placed him at the head of the table, and served his dish very bountifully, thus marking him as a distinguished guest.

Saul lodged with Samuel that night and they had a secret conference on the top of the house. The next morning the prophet went with him a short distance, and before they parted Samuel took a vial of oil, and anointed Saul to be king over Israel, thereby giving him clearly to understand that he was to be Israel's first king. He then gave Saul a threefold token of this purpose of the God of Israel. First, near Rachel's grave, he should meet two men, who would inform him that the asses of his father were found. Second, at Tabor he should meet three men, who were going to Bethel to worship the Lord, and that they would make him a present of bread. Third, in or near the hill of God, he should meet a company of prophets, and the spirit of God should come upon him, and he would join them in their devotions. All these things as they occurred, were calculated to strengthen the faith of Saul in the declarations of Samuel. But when he joined those prophets in their exercises, it was said, "Is Saul also among the prophets?" Not long after this, Samuel assembled the people, at Mizpah, and they cast lots as to who should be the king.

The lot fell upon the tribe of Benjamin, and the family of Matri, the household of Kish, and upon Saul of that family. Saul had hid himself among the stuff, but they found him and presented him before the people as the Lord's selection. And here it is said of Saul that he was a very tall man—a head and shoulders taller than any other man of the vast and delighted crowd. The people called him at once their king, and shouted: "God save the king." The main body of the people then went home; and Saul went to his home in Gibeah, and a band of men followed him, divinely influenced to be his body-guard, it may be. But there were some wicked men who insulted him, and declared him incapable of governing as a king. Though they despised him, and brought him no presents, yet he held his peace. It seems that, though he was a king, he returned to his usual labor. 1st Samuel, x.

It was not long after he was thus made king until the inhabitants of Jabesh-Gilead were in great distress, because that the Ammonites had besieged their city and offered them the most humbling conditions of peace. They were in great distress, and asked a seven days' truce of their enemies. They granted it. And the men of Jabesh-Gilead sent messengers to Gibeah to inform them of their peril. All the people sympathized with them and wept, but Saul was in the field plowing, and when he enquired the cause of their distress and they told him, he hewed a yoke of oxen to pieces and sent pieces into all parts of Israel, thereby calling the people to arms. He threatened them with destruction of their property if they did not come at the call and meet him and Samuel at Bezek. He soon had an army of thirty thousand men of Judah and three hundred thousand of the other tribes. It was not more than five days from the call until this vast army was marshalled for fight, and they began their march at once, crossing Jordan, toward Jabesh, to attack the Ammonites. They came upon their enemy unawares and conquered them, cutting them to pieces. This victory gave Saul at once a strong hold upon the feelings of all the people; and they were now in favor of killing those sons of Belial who had formerly contemned him. Saul, however, was not willing to this. He said: "There shall not a man be put to death this day; for to-day the Lord hath wrought salvation in Israel." They then went up to Gilgal, and the kingdom was confirmed by Samuel unto Saul, and all the men of Israel rejoiced greatly. 1st Samuel, xi.

After Saul had reigned a short time, probably two years, he levied a standing army of three thousand men, two thousand were under his own command, and one thousand were under the command of Jonathan, his son, and with this army they warred with the Philistines. They endeavored to take some posts from the Philistines, that they had occupied for several years. Jonathan, the son of Saul, defeated them at Michmash, and the Israelites were greatly elated with the victory and volunteered in great numbers, to drive the enemy away.

The Philistines then gathered themselves together for a great battle.

They marched a prodigious army into the country of Israel, and the Israelites became alarmed, and deserted Saul. They fled to caves and thickets, and rocks and high places, and pits, to hide themselves, so that there was but a small handful left with Saul. The whole country was in a panic, and Saul himself partook of the panic. He waited till the seventh day for Samuel, and as he did not come to offer sacrifices unto the Lord, he offered them himself. Just about the time he had made an end of offering his sacrifices, Samuel came, and Saul went out to meet him, to welcome him, in this time of distress and peril of the nation. The prophet asked him what he had done, and he told him, and why he had done it. Samuel charged him with having done foolishly, and assured him that the Lord would transfer the kingdom to another family. Their condition was certainly deplorable, for there was but six hundred soldiers left, but with them Samuel, Saul, and Jonathan, marched to Gibeah. Soon Jonathan, and his armor bearers had a glorious victory over an advanced garrison of the Philistines. Saul could see from the point he occupied, that the garrison was routed, and he desired to know who of his small army was gone.

The roll was called, and it was found that Jonathan, and his armor bearers, were absent. Saul at once called Ahiah, the priest, to consult the Lord and see whether he should attack the enemy.

While the priest was consulting, Saul beard a great noise, and finding that the army of the Philistines were killing one another, he pursued them.

About this time the deserters began to come out of their hiding places, and assist him in the pursuit of the enemy, killing them in the pursuit, as far as Ajalon. The rout would have been very fatal to the enemy, if Saul had not by a rash curse condemned the person to death who should stop the pursuit to take any refreshments. The Israelites grew faint in the pursuit and had they been strengthened with a little food, they might have gained a greater conquest. Jonathan, the son of Saul, did not know of the curse, and as he was following the enemy through a wood, he dipped the end of his staff in some honey, that dropped from a tree, and tasted a little of it.

In the evening as Saul's army gathered together, he consulted the Lord as to whether he should attack their enemy's camp at night, but the Lord gave him no answer, as a punishment for his rashness in fighting before the Lord had given him instructions, or advised him to commence the pursuit.

Saul thought there was some other one beside himself that had done wrong, and he rashly devoted the criminal to death, whoever he was. Lots were then cast, and Jonathan was taken. His offense was that of tasting honey as he passed through the wood; but his father said he should die, good as his excuse was for tasting it. And he would have executed his purpose, but the people said, Jonathan is our deliverer, and he shall not die, for he had not been guilty of crime. 1st Sam. xiv.

After this Saul kept a standing army, and he made Abner, the son of Ner, the captain of his host. Abner was Saul's uncle's son, and all the strong men, or valiant men in the nation, he took unto himself to serve in the army, and with his army he made war upon the Moabites, Edomites, Ammonites, and the Philistines.

In 1st Sam. xv., we have an account of his warring with the Amalekites, under an order from God to cut off the entire nation. With an army of two hundred and ten thousand he went against Amalek and ravaged his whole country, and cut off many of the people, and of their cattle; but he saved Agag, their king, and the best of their cattle alive, with some valuable movables. It is said: "But Saul and the people spared Agag, and the best of the sheep, and of the oxen, and of the fatlings, and of the lambs, and all that was good, and would not destroy them; but everything that was vile and refuse, that they destroyed utterly."

Saul came to South Carmel, "and set up a place," *i. e.*, a monument to mark his victory: then went down to Gilgal. Soon Samuel came to him and reproved him for not executing the divine order. He asked Saul what the bleating of the sheep and the lowing of the oxen meant, which he heard. He told him that these sheep and oxen were spoils he had taken in the war, with which to sacrifice unto the Lord.

The prophet charges him with doing a great wrong, and though Saul at first justified himself, yet he afterwards acknowledged his error and asked for pardon. He entreated Samuel to pray for him, but he seemingly refused, and turning from Saul was about to leave him, when the penitent king caught hold of his garment to detain him, and it was rent. Samuel then said to him, "So shall God rend the kingdom from thee and give it to a neighbor of thine that is better than thou." Saul then confessed his sin again, and entreated the prophet to honor him before the Elders of Israel, and turn in with him, that he might worship the Lord. He was fearful lest the people would look upon him with contempt, and rebel against him. The prophet complied with his request and joined him in public worship; after which he and the king of Israel parted, and never more met together in friendly counsel. Samuel never visited him again, and probably the only interviews they had after this was when Saul went to Ramah to arrest David, and when he came to him from the dead to warn him of his defeat and death at Gilboe.

The ability properly to govern Israel, was lost by Saul, and an evil spirit soon after this troubled him. David had been anointed by Samuel as Saul's successor. And as some of Saul's attendants advised him to procure a man skillful in music, to play before him during his fits of melancholy. David was procured, and was thus introduced to the court of Saul, and became his constant attendant. The music of David became effective, and Saul became strongly attached to him, and constituted him his armor bearer. When the Philistines pitched in Ephes-Dammim, and in the person of Goliath, the giant, defied the armies of the living God, Saul promised his eldest daughter to whoever should kill the giant, David performed the feat, and so won the prize. As David returned from the slaughter of the Philistines, the women of Israel came out to celebrate the victory by music and dancing. And they were heard by Saul to say, "Saul has slain his thousands, and David his tens of thousands." This made Saul jealous, and being greatly displeased, he sought opportunity to slay David. In his trouble of jealousy, one of his fits of melancholy came on him, and David played before him as at other times, and Saul having a javelin in his hand threw it at David, to kill him, but he escaped it. Saul then placed David in command of a thousand men, and sought occasion against him, but could find none. At length he promised David his elder daughter Merab, to wife, if he would be valiant for him, and fight the Lord's battles. He desired to prompt David to rush into danger, that he might be killed, and he did not really intend to give him Merab, for he gave her to another man: Adriel the Meholathite. Saul heard that his younger daughter was in love with David, and he said, I will give her to him that she may be a snare unto him. He told some of his attendants to tell David that he would give him Michal for one hundred foreskins of the Philistines. He thought, surely David will be killed before he has killed one hundred men, but in this he was mistaken, for David killed two hundred and brought the evidence to Saul, and the king gave him his daughter to wife. 1st Sam. xvii and xviii.

Saul was still intent on killing him, and made two ineffectual attempts. He threw a javelin at him, but missed his mark, and the instrument pierced the wall.

Saul then sent soldiers to his house to take him, but by the ingenuity of Michal he escaped. Still determined on taking David, when he heard that he was at Ramah he sent messengers, but they were thwarted. He then went in person to take him, but David escaped while Saul was divinely detained. 1st Sam. xix. Saul becomes very angry at Jonathan who plead before him for David, for he had given David permission to be absent at the feast of the new moon. That was the time Saul had certainly intended to kill him, and he was so enraged at Jonathan that he tried to kill him, for he cast a javelin at him. 1st Sam. xx.

Some time after this Saul bitterly complained that none of his servants had informed him of the accomplices of David. He upbraided his servants for infidelity towards him. 1st Sam. xxii: 7. Just at this time Doeg the Edomite stepped forward and informed Saul that he saw the son of Jesse at Nob, and that Ahimelech the priest gave him bread and the sword of Goliath, the Philistine. Saul was greatly enraged at the priest, and sent and brought him and all his family before him, and charged him with having conspired against him. Ahimelech asserted his innocence, but Saul condemned him and his fellow priests, with the inhabitants of the city. There were eighty-five priests slain that day—only one of the whole company escaping and that was Abiathar, who fled to David and informed him of the slaughter of the priests. It is quite likely he would have murdered the father and mother of David, but they went to their son who procured them a home in the country of Moab.

When Saul heard that David was in Keilah, a fortified city, he determined to go and seize him while there. David heard of it, and learning from the Lord that the men of Keilah would betray him he escaped. Saul learned that he was in the wilderness of Ziph, and he intended to go there and take him, probably depending on the Ziphites to betray him into his hands. Again David escaped and Saul heard of him in Maon, and went there to take him, but he was thwarted in his designs by being called into another part of his kingdom because of the Philistines invading it. 1st Sam. xxiii.

After Saul had returned from following the Philistines he heard that David was in the wilderness of Engedi, and he goes in search of him with three thousand men. Before he discovered David's camp he went into a cave to sleep. In that cave David and his men were hid; while Saul was asleep David arose and cut off the skirt of his robe, afterwards he showed it to Saul, and showed him how easily he might have killed him, but he would not. The conscience of the king smote him for having pursued an innocent person as he had David, and he returned to his home. 1st Sam. xxiv.

Saul gave Michal, David's wife, to Phalti, the son of Laish, and when he was informed, by the Zephites, of David's hiding place, again with thirty thousand men, he went in search of him. David sent out a small scouting party, and finds out where Saul is camped, and in company with Abishai, he went softly to the camp by night, and found them all asleep. He saw Saul sleeping within the trench, and his spear stuck in the ground by his bolster and a cruise of water, and Abner, the captain of his host, lay near him. He approached Saul, and took the spear and the cruise of water, and left the camp without waking them. In the morning, David called to Saul, and bade him send one of his servants to him, to return the trophies he had gathered from him during the night, and he chid Saul for his continued hostility to him. Saul humbled himself when he saw that David had again spared his life, and he promised he would no more persecute David. So he returned to his place, and David feeling that he could not depend on Saul's promises, sought refuge among the Philistines. 1st Samuel, xxvi.

The Philistines invaded the kingdom of Israel, with fresh vigor and earnestness. Saul was greatly troubled, and asked advice of the Lord, but he received no answer. At length he applied to the witch of Endor. After she became satisfied that the person who applied to her would not inform on her, for before this time all the witches and wizzards of the land that were known, had been put to death, she asked him who he wished to see from the spirit world, and he said the prophet Samuel, for he had died a little while before. After awhile the woman discovered that the person before her was Saul the king, in disguise, and she was afraid. But Samuel really appeared to the astonishment of the woman, and he demanded of Saul his reason for wishing an interview with him. He told him that he had made enquiry of the Lord, who had refused to give him any counsel or advice, either by dreams or vision, or by prophets. Samuel told him he need not expect to be comforted, for God had departed from him, and after intimating clearly to him that he should be slain in the coming battle, Samuel left him. He was probably alone with the spirit of the prophet, the woman having retired, but when she came in, she found him prostrate on the earth, without power to move or speak. She prepared some refreshments, and persuaded him to take them, and in the morning he returned to the camp, and took his position at the head of his forces to fight the battle they were preparing to fight. 1st Sam. xxviii.

The account of the Mt. Gilboa battle is given in 1st Sam. xxxi. It was a terrible fight, and the Israelites were routed, and very many of them fell down slain in the mount. As they fled the Philistines followed after them and overpowered them, and Saul and his sons, Jonathan, Abinadab and Melchishua, were slain. From the account given of the battle we may judge that Saul fought desperately. It is said he was hard pressed by the enemy, and begged his armor-bearer to kill him, that he might not fall into the hands of the uncircumcised Philistines; but his armor-bearer refused. Then Saul fell upon his own sword and died; and his armor-bearer, seeing the king was dead, fell also upon his sword and died. An Amalekite who was near by, seeing, it may be, some signs of life in Saul, thrust his sword through him, and taking possession of his crown and bracelets carried them to David, expecting, in all probabitity, a reward; but he was slain because he acknowledged to the murder of the king.

The day after the battle the Philistines found the bodies of Saul and his sons; and they cut off Saul's, head and stripped off his armor and sent it around amongst their people to satisfy them all of the victory they had obtained. The Philistines deposited Saul's armor in the house of their god, and fastened his body to the wall of Beth-shan. The men of Jabesh-gilead remembering with gratitude their deliverance, by the hand of Saul, from the Ammonites, sent their valiant men to recover the bodies, and having gained possession of them they buried them in a grove near their city, and mourned for seven days. Afterwards David removed their remains to the sepulcher of Kish.

Sometime during his reign Saul murdered many of the Gibeonites; and they demanded of David, after he was made king, reparation, in vengeance on the house of Saul. David gave them the two sons of Saul by Rizpah, and five of Merab's children, and the Gibeonites hung them as an atonement for Saul's murder of the people. [See Rizpah.]

Saul was at first a very humble young man, but he afterwards became proud, tyrannical and jealous. But the most inhuman and wicked act of his life was the murder of the innocent priests and people at Nob. Whatever his private character was, he was a bad king. He was a weak man; his conduct toward David proves this, as does his application to the witch of Endor. He was mortally wounded in the battle, and hence his last act need not be looked on as self-murder.

SAUL, 3—*Demanded, sepulcher, destroyer.*

Was a native of Tarsus, a city of Cilicia. He was miraculously converted, and called Paul, the great apostle to the Gentiles. [See Paul.]

SCEVA—[Se′vah,] *disposed, prepared.*

SCEVA was a Jew who resided at Ephesus. He is referred to in Acts, xix: 14–16, as being the chief of one of the orders, or classes of Jewish priests. He, with his seven sons, are noticed in the above reference. While Sceva was a chief priest, his sons made pretensions to exorcism, or casting devils out of men. They traveled about from place to place, on this business, but at Ephesus they undertook a case that they could not manage, and they finally adjured the devil by Jesus, whom Paul preached to come out of the person. The devil is represented as saying to them, "Jesus I know, and Paul I know; but who are ye?" The devil then used the possessed person as his instrument in handling the sons of Sceva so roughly, that they fled out of the house naked and wounded; or ran for their lives from the enraged man, possessed with the devil.

SEBA—[Se′ba,] *drunkard, that surrounds; according to the Syriac, old man.*

SEBA was the elder son of Cush, the son of Ham. There are four other sons of Cush mentioned in Gen. x: 7, viz: Havilah, Sabtah, Raamah and Sabtecha, and Raamah's two sons, Sheba and Dedan, are mentioned in the same verse.

SECUNDUS—[Se-kun′dus,] *the second.*

Was a friend of the apostle Paul, who is reported to have gone with the apostle from Corinth as far as Asia, on his way to Jerusalem. He was probably a devout christian, and fellow laborer. Acts, xx: 4.

SEDECIAS—[Sed-e-ci′as.]

Was the father of Maaseiah, and probably the same person, with the false prophet referred to in Jeremiah, xxix: 21-22.

SENAAH—[Se-na′ah.]

SENAAH is a person who is referred to in Ezra, ii: 35, among the Jews who returned from Babylon with the priests and Levites, and singers and porters. The family of Seenah numbered three thousand six hundred and thirty, and were very active in the accomplishment of the work, for which the Jews returned to Judah. This same family is referred to in Neh. iii: 3, as building the fishgate, and laying the beams thereof, and setting up the doors with the locks and bars.

SEGUB—[Se′gub,] *fortified, raised.*

Was the youngest son of Hiel, the Bethelite, who rebuilt Jericho, and realized the fulfillment of Joshua's prediction. He died just as his father finished the work of rebuilding the city. 1st Kings, xvi: 34.

SEIR—[Se′ir,] *hairy, demon, tempest, barley.*

SEIR is called the Horite, who inhabited the land of Lotan. The region of country where Esau lived for awhile, and where some of his children and grandchildren were born. The names of Seir's children are given in Gen. xxxvi: 21, viz; Lotan, Shobab, Zibeon and Anan, Dishon and Ezer, and Dishan, as also the name of his grandchildren. Gen. xxxvi: 22-30.

SEMACHIAH—[Sem-a-ki′-ah.]

SEMACHIAH was a descendant of Obed Edom, and one of the sacred porters. 1st Chron. xxvi: 7.

SENNACHERIB—[Sen-nak′-e-rib,] *bush of the destruction of the sword of drought.*

SENNACHERIB, was the king of Assyria. He invaded Judah, in the time of Hezekiah, in the fourteenth year of his reign. He besieged, and took, all the fenced cities. 2d Kings, xviii: 13. Hezekiah felt himself to be in extremity, and sent Senacharib word, that he would agree to any conditions of peace he would name. The Assyrian king accordingly subjected him to a tax of three hundred talents of silver, and thirty talents of gold. He paid it however, willingly, under the impression that Sennacherib would no longer war with him. He emptied his own house of silver, and the house of the Lord of gold, to meet this requisition. But in the stead of the Assyrian leaving him to enjoy himself in his subjection, he violated the agreement, and continued the war. He sent three of his generals to summons Hezekiah and the people of Jerusalem to a surrender; Tartan, Rabsaris and Rabshakeh halted near the city of Jerusalem in the fullers field, and made their demand. Hezekiah sent out three men to confer with them. But the generals of Sennacherib treated them with contempt, and offered them insult. Hezekiah's representatives asked them to say what they had to say in their own language, as they were competent to confer with them in Syrian language, but they refused and would talk to them loudly in the Hebrew language, in the hopes of creating dissatisfaction among the people. Sennacherib wrote Hezekiah a letter in which he boasted that he would compel him to a surrender, for he had it in his power to subdue Jerusalem as he had other cities. He then marched his army up to the walls of Jerusalem, and encamped in the valley of Tophet. The King of Judah was greatly distressed, and earnestly prayed to the Lord for help. The prophet Isaiah went to him in his distress, and assured him that his prayer was heard, and that the city of Jerusalem should be delivered; and that this haughty and defiant Assyrian, should be destroyed. The night before Sennacherib intended to take the city, the angel of the Lord went into his camp and passed through it as a destroyer, killing one hundred and eighty-five thousand of the Assyrian soldiery, and as it is thought the abominable and wicked general Rabshakeh among them. 2d Kings, xviii and xix; 2d Chronicles, xxxii and Isa. xxxvii, &c.

After this dreadful slaughter of Sennacherib's soldiers he returned home, and shortly after, two of his sons, Adramelech and Sharezer murdered him in the temple of his idol Nisroch. For an account of his death see Isa. xxxvii: 37, 38. And he was succeeded on the throne of Assyria by Ezar-haddon, his son.

SEORIM—[Se-o′-rim.]

Was one of the priests appointed by David when he divided them into twenty-four orders. His lot was the fourth. 1st Chron. xxiv: 8.

SERAIAH, 1—[Ser-a-i′-ah,] *prince of the Lord.*

SERAIAH was a high priest of the Jews. He was the son of Azariah and Jozedek, the father of Joshua. In Jer. li, we have an account of his capture by the captain of the guard at Jerusalem, and being taken a prisoner in company with Zephaniah, the second priest. The two were taken, with a eunuch that had charge of the men of war, and seven of the king's body guard, his scribe, and sixty of the people, by Nebuzaradan to Riblah, to the king of Babylon, and the king of Babylon cruelly murdered them.

SERAIAH, 2—*Prince of the Lord.*

SERAIAH was the son of Neriah, who was the son of Maaseiah, and this Neriah was the brother of Baruch. He was probably in a position of considerable importance in the kingdom, under Zedekiah. He may have been his steward, or probably he may have been the director of the presents that were borne from Zedekiah to Nebuchadnezzar a few years before Jerusalem was destroyed.

We have an account in Jer. li: 59–62, of the prophet Jeremiah committing to his hands a book, in which he had written of evils that should come upon Babylon; and the prophet Jeremiah gave him strict commandment when he came to Babylon, to read all the words of the book, and after he had read it, to declare that all the words of the book regarding Babylon should come to pass; "this place shall be cut off that none shall remain in it, neither man nor beast, but it shall be desolate forever." He was then ordered to fasten a stone to the book, and cast it into Babylon's great river, the Euphrates, and say: "Thus shall Babylon sink, and shall not rise from the evil that I will bring upon her; and they shall be weary."

SERED—[Se′-red.]

Was one of the sons of Zebulun, and is reckoned with Jacob's family in Egypt. Gen. xlvi: 14. And he was the head of the family of the Sardites. Num. xxvi: 26.

SERGIUS PAULUS, [Ser′-je-us, Pau′-lus,] *a net.*

SERGIUS PAULUS was the deputy governor of the island of Cyprus, at the time Paul and Barnabas were set apart by the church at Antioch to go unto the Gentiles. While these apostles were preaching the gospel in the synagogues of the Jews, in various parts of the island, they met with opposers and persecutors; yet the deputy himself was converted to the faith, and listened with great interest to the apostle preaching. At length Elymus a sorcerer sought to turn Sergius Paulus away from the faith and the apostle Paul rebuked him, and declared that he should be blind for a season, which came to pass. The deputy saw the miracle and was confirmed by it in the faith. Acts, xiii: 6–12.

SERUG.

SERUG was the son of Ragau or Reu, and the father of Nahor. Gen. xi: 22. We know but little concerning him, and it is doubtful whether there is foundation for the opinion that has been expressed, that Serug introduced idolatrous worship, or the worship of images of men who had been very useful in their life time.

SETH—*Put, who puts.*

SETH was the son of Adam. The account of his birth is in Gen. iv: 25: "And Adam knew his wife again, and she bare a son and called his name Seth; for God, said she, hath appointed me another seed instead of

Abel whom Cain slew." By this language we may understand that Eve, who named him, had it divinely revealed to her that this son should be in the line by which the Messiah was to come; and we find when the flood came and swept away the family of man from the earth, Noah and his family, who were descendants of Seth, continued to live and were preserved in the ark. Noah was the ninth from Seth and the tenth from Adam. So the genealogy of Christ, as given by Luke, iii, places Seth in the line, the first from Adam, and Shem the first from Noah.

Adam was one hundred and thirty years old when Seth was born, and it is said, in Gen. v: 3: "He begat a son in his own likeness, after his image." This language seems to allude to Gen. i: 26, when God said: "Let us make man in our own image." As Adam was a mortal, on account of the transgression of the law, imperfect and impure, Seth partook of his nature and qualities. In this respect he was like all the other children of Adam, though in the line of the coming Messiah.

Seth was the father of Enos, who was born unto him when he was one hundred and five years old; but he lived after the birth of Enos eight hundred and seven years, so that his age, at the time he died, was nine hundred and twelve years. Gen. v: 6-8. The posterity of Enos were, for a long time, true worshipers of the living God; but afterward, with the balance of the wonderfully increased family of man, they forsook God, for when God determined to deluge the world, the inhabitants had all strayed from him, except Noah's family, as we learn from Gen. vi.

SETHUR—[Se′-thur.]

SETHUR was of the tribe of Ashur, and was selected by Moses as one of the twelve spies, to search out and examine the nature and state of the land of Canaan. Numb. xiii: 13.

SHADRACH—[Sha′-drak,] *tender nipple, tender field.*

SHADRACH was one of the princes of Judah, taken with Meshech and Abednego and Daniel, into captivity to Babylon, when quite young. He, with his companions, was educated in the learning of the Chaldeans. His Jewish name was Hananiah, but the prince of the eunuchs called him Shadrach. Dan. i: 7. He, with his two companions, was on terms of intimacy with Daniel, and rendered him assistance by uniting with him in prayer for a revelation from God regarding the king's dream. Dan. ii: 17. After Daniel had interpreted the dream he was promoted in the kingdom to honor and great distinction, and his three friends were also promoted through the influence of Daniel, to a governorship, each of them. But afterwards their faith in God was severely tested, and their fidelity and faithfulness in their religion. They refused to obey the king by renouncing their religion and engaging in idolatry by worshiping the golden image that Nebuchadnezzar had set up. As a consequence of their refusal they were all three cast into the burning fiery furnace, heated seven times hotter than it was wont to be heated; but they were preserved and delivered, and honored by the king. Dan. iii. [See Abednego.]

SHAHARAIM—[Sha-ha-ra′-im.]

SHAHARAIM was a descendant of Benjamin, who lived in the country of Moab. He is referred to in the genealogy of Benjamin. 1st Chron. viii: 8. He either lived in Moab as an inhabitant or governed the country. It is said he begat children in the country of Moab. The names of his two wives are Hodesh and Hushim, and his posterity by them was very numerous. His children distinguished themselves by building and peopling several towns. Lydda and Ono are mentioned. And they drove the Philistines from Aijalon. The honorable persons of Shaharaim's posterity, who are mentioned, are said to have dwelt at Jerusalem. 1st Chron. viii: 28.

SHALLUM, 1—[Shal′-lum,] *perfect, peaceable.*

Was a son of Naphtali and Bilhah, and is referred to in the genealogy of Naphtali. 1st Chron. vii: 13. He is the same as is called Shillem in Num. xxvi: 49, who is said to be the father of the Shillemites. As there were forty-five thousand, four hundred Naphtalites, and only four families mentioned making up that number, we may reasonably suppose that Shallum's posterity was numerous.

SHALLUM, 2—*perfect, peaceable.*

SHALLUM was the son of Jabesh, and a king of Israel. We have an account of his conspiracy against, and murder of, Zachariah, and ascending the throne to reign in his stead, in 2d Kings, xv: 10. It is said he smote the king before the people, by which we may understand he killed him in a public assembly, and was probably approbated in his act by the people, who were tired of the reign of so wicked a king as Zachariah, though he had reigned but six months.

By the murder of Zachariah, the word of the Lord concerning Jehu was fulfilled. God promised him that his sons should sit on the throne of Israel to the fourth generation, and they did—Jehoahaz, Joash, Jeroboam, and Zachariah; thus his family was cut off. But the reign of Shallum was very short. He only reigned one month in Samaria, when Menahem, the son of Gadi, went up from Tirzah to Samaria and smote him. Who this Menahem was is not very certain, but possibly he was a general of King Zachariah, who determined to avenge the death of his master. After he had smitten Shallum he reigned in his stead.

SHALMANESER—[Shal-ma-ne′-zer,] *peace, tied, perfection and retribution.*

SHALMANESER, king of Assyria, is supposed to have been the son and successor of Tiglath-pileser. He is called Shalman by the prophet Hosea, and Enamassar in the book of Tobit. He appears and conquers Israel during the wicked reign of Hoshea in Samaria. Having conquered the kingdom and made it tributary, he made Hoshea his servant. Some time after he had made the king of Israel tributary to him, he found conspiracy in him. Hoshea had tried to shake off the Assyrian yoke by entering into a treaty with So, the king of Egypt, and he refused to send the annual tribute by Shalmaneser's messengers. This led the Assyrian to arrest Hoshea, and he bound him and cast him into prison. He then marched a powerful army into Samaria and besieged it for three years. He took the fenced cities and ravaged them—murdered their inhabitants in the most cruel and inhuman manner. Hosea. x: 14, says, "All thy fortresses shall be spoiled, as Shalman spoiled Beth-arbel in the day of battle; the mother was dashed to pieces upon her children." And the prophet Micah refers to the same destruction of Samaria in i: 5, 9.

After Shalmaneser had taken the kingdom of Israel and cruelly murdered many in the siege, and took her king and bound and imprisoned him. He carried away many of Israel into captivity in his own land, and placed them in different cities of the Assyrians and Medes. Shalmaneser then brought persons from different nations and placed them in the captured kingdom of Israel. He brought men from Babylon and Cutha, and from Ava and Hamath and Sepharvaim and placed them in the cities of Samaria. These people were very corrupt and wicked, and the Lord sent wild beasts among them, that devoured many of them. Shalmaneser then sent some of the priests that he had taken captive, back again to Samaria to teach the people how to worship God, and they incorporated the Israelite worship with the worship of their own gods. 2d Kings, xvii.

It is said that Shalmaneser after this commenced a war with the Tyrians, and besieged their capital, but died before he affected his object and was succeeded in the kingdom of Assyria by Sennacharib.

SHAMARIAH—[Sham-a-ri′-ah.]

SHAMARIAH was one of the sons of Rehoboam, born unto him of one of the wives he took in the family of David. 2d Chron. xi: 19.

SHAMGAR—[Sham′-gar,] *named a stranger, he is here a stranger, surprise of the stranger.*

SHAMGAR was the son of Anath, and a judge of Israel. He was the third judge of the people of Israel. Whether he was a man of any note before his judge-ship commenced, or before he took that position, we do not know. From the account given of him, which is Judges iii: 31, "And after him was Shamgar the son of

Anath, who slew of the Philistines six hundred men with an ox goad; and he also delivered Israel," we might suppose that he was a laboring man, engaged in cultivating his fields at the time that the Philistines were making inroads amongst them. He and his neighbors resisted them, and fought with them, and not having time to arm themselves with war weapons, they used their agricultural instruments, and Shamgar himself, with his ox goad, slew six hundred of them. The Philistine marauders were conquered, and terror-stricken, fled for their lives. Shamgar may have been rewarded by the people for his valor, by making him judge. Deborah, in her song, makes a reference to Shamgar, and the anarchy and confusion occasioned by the lawless Philistine banditti. Judges v and vi.

SHAMHUTH—[Sham′-huth,] *desolation, astonishment.*

The Izrahite, was the captain for the fifth month, when David instituted the monthly service of captains over twenty-four thousand men. 1st Chron. xxvii: 8.

SHAMIR—[Sha′-mir,] *prison, bush, less.*

SHAMIR was one of the ministers in the temple, under the order of service instituted in the time of David. 1st Chron. xxiv: 24.

SHAMMAH, 1—[Sham′-mah,] *loss, desolation, astonishment.*

SHAMMAH was the son of Agee, the Hararite. He was one of David's mighty men, the third in the order in which they are given. 2d Sam. xxiii: 11-17. It seems that a large marauding party of the Philistines, gathered in a field of the Gentiles, or as the parallel passage in 1st Chonicles, xi: 13, has it, a barley field, with a view of capturing, and carrying off into their land as captives, some Israelites among whom was Shammah. He is reported to have contended with this troop of Philistines, in the barley field, even after they had run the people away from the possession of it. He fought with them and killed a great number of them. The Lord through him wrought a great victory. He was accompanied by Eleazar, the son of Dodo, in this fight with the Philistines, and it is quite likely that they two, were of the three, that broke through the host of the Philistines, and brought David water from the well of Bethlehem. 1st Chron. xi: 18.

SHAMMAH, 2—*Loss, desolation, astonished.*

SHAMMAH was one of the thirty that David set over others, as an officer. He is called Shammah, the Horadite. 2d Samuel, xxiii: 25.

SHAMMAH, 3—*Loss, desolation, astonished.*

SHAMMAH was also one of the thirty, and is distinguished from the others by "the Hararite." It is true the first Shammah is called a Hararite, but he was of the three mighty men, more honorable than the thirty. 2d Sam. xxiii: 33.

SHAMMUA, 1—[Sham-mu′-ah] *that is heard, or obeyed.*

SHAMMUA was the son of Zaccur, of the tribe of Reuben, and one of the spies sent by Moses, to search out the land of Canaan. Num. xiii: 4.

SHAMMUA, 2—*That is heard, or obeyed.*

SHAMMUA was one of the sons of David, born unto him in Jerusalem. 1st Chron. xiv: 4.

SHAPHAN—[Sha′fan,] *a rabbit, wild rat, their lip.*

SHAPHAN was secretary of the temple in the time of king Josiah. 2d Kings, xxii: 8-9. We learn that he was the son of Azaliah, the son of Meshullam, and was appointed by the king, as scribe to the house of the Lord, when the breaches of the temple were being repaired. Josiah charged him to go to Hilkiah, the priest, and sum up the silver which is brought to the house of the Lord, gathered at the door of the temple by the keepers from the people. The money was to be delivered into the hands of those who were engaged in the repairs. It was to be used in purchasing material, and in compensating carpenters, masons and builders. Up to this time the money had not not been summed up, but paid out on orders presented.

While Hilkiah was engaged in the repairs, he found a book among the ruins, which proved to be a copy of the law of Moses, probably the original that was deposited in the ark. He gave it to Shaphan, and he read it. He then went to the king to make his report as to the money collected, and the disposition made of it. He then told the king of the book that Hilkiah had found, and read it in the hearing of Josiah, who was much affected by the reading of it. The king then sent it by the hand of Shaphan and several others, to Huldah, the prophetess. The deputation received her message, and carried it to Josiah. 2d Kings, xxii, and 2d Chron. xxiv.

SHAPHAT, 1—[Sha′-fat,] *a judge.*
SHAPHAT is referred to in Num. xiii: 5. He was the son of Hori, and of the tribe of Simeon. He was one of those who were sent by Moses to spy out the promised land; and among those who brought back an unfavorable report.

SHAPHAT, 2—*A judge.*
SHAPHAT was the father of the prophet Elisha. 1st Kings, xix: 16. We know but little about him, save that he lived at Abel-Meholah. He does not seem to object to his son entering upon the work and office of a prophet. He did not try to hinder him from obeying the divine call, but, after Elisha's feast to the people, parted with him affectionately and gave him to the Lord.

SHAPHAT, 3—*A judge.*
SHAPHAT, the son of Adlai, was placed by King David over that part of the herds that fed in the valleys. 1st Chron. xxvii: 29.

SHARAH—[Sha′-rah,]
Was the father of Ahiam, and is numbered with David's mighty men. 2d Sam. xxiii: 33.

SHAUL—[Sha′-ul,]
Was one of the sons of Simeon. He was the son of Simeon's Canaanitish wife, and numbered with the family of Jacob, who went down with him into Egypt to dwell. Genesis, xlvi: 10.

SHEALTIEL—[She-al′-ti-el,] *I have asked of God.*
Was the father of Zerubbabel. He was in the line of the Messiah, and as such is presented in Matthew i: 12, as also Luke iii: 27. He is called Salathial, the father of Zerubbabel.

SHEBA, 1—[She′-bah,] *compassing about, repose, old age.*
SHEBA was the son of Cush, called also Seba. He is referred to in Gen. x: 7, as the first-born of Cush. It is probable he gave the name of Sheba or Seba to the country in Arabia or Abyssinia that bears the name. In Psalms lxxii: 10, that country is referred to: "The kings of Sheba and Seba shall offer gifts," as also Isa. xliii: 3.

SHEBA, 2—*Compassing about, repose, old age.*
Was the grand-son of Cush, being the son of Raamah. Genesis x: 7. "And the sons of Raamah, Sheba and Dedan."

SHEBA, 3—*Compassing about, repose, old age.*
Was one of the sons of Joktan. Genesis x: 7.

SHEBA, 4—*Compassing about, repose, old age.*
The son of Jokshan, and the grandson of Abraham, by Keturah. It is supposed that from this person the Sabeans sprang, who robbed Job of his cattle, &c. See Gen. xxv: 3, and Job i: 15.

SHEBA, 5—*Compassing about, repose, old age.*
The son of Bichri, who decoyed the tribes of Israel into a revolt from David. Joab, David's general, followed him to Abel of Beth-maachah, and besieged the city. They cut off Sheba's head and threw it over the wall to him. 2d Sam. xx. [See Joab.]

SHEBNA—[Sheb′na,] *who rests himself, who is now captive.*
SHEBNA was the treasurer and secretary of king Hezekiah. He is referred to in 2d Kings, xviii; 18, as also in Isaiah, xxii: 15-20. He was sent with Eliakim and Joah, to Rabshekeh, the general of Sennacherib,

the king of Assyria, to hear the proposals to Hezekiah. From the account given of him in Isaiah, we may suppose that he was a proud and haughty officer, being careful to make a great show. He prepared himself a magnificent sepulcher, and it is quite likely built for himself costly and grand edifices. Isaiah is commissioned to prophesy against him, and declare that evil was before him. He should be carried away into captivity, loosing his estate and honor, as the treasurer and secretary of the king, and that he should not come to the sepulcher he had provided for himself. He was accordingly carried away by the Assyrian Sennacherib, or Esar-haddon, and died in dishonor and exile from his native land, and a captive of the conqueror of Israel.

SHEBUEL, 1—[Sheb′u-el.]

Was the son of Gershom, the son of Moses, and was ruler of the treasures, or constituted chief treasurer of the Levites. 1st Chron. xxvi: 24.

SHEBUEL, 2.

Was one of the sons of Heman, and when the lots were cast, and the singers were divided into twenty-four courses, the thirteenth came to him. 1st Chron. xxv: 4.

SHECHEM — [She′-kem,] *portion, the back, shoulders.*

Shechem was the son of Hamor the Hivite who was prince of the country of Shechem, or the country in which the city called Shechem, Sychem or Sychar was situated. It was here that Jacob bought a piece of ground and gave it to his son Joseph, Gen. xxxiii: 19, and in that parcel of ground Joseph's bones that were brought out of the land of Egypt were buried. Josh. xxiv: 32.

Shechem was the son of a prince, a Canaanite. While Jacob with his family tarried in the field he had bought of Hamor, for he spread his tents there, and erected an altar to his God, which he called El Elohe Israel, Shechem defiled Dinah, Jacob's daughter after which he tried to gain her affections and reconcile her to her disgrace. It is said he spake kindly unto her. This was an offence on the part of Shechem that the sons of Jacob would not look over. It seems that Shechem detained Dinah their sister as he made the effort to secure her as his lawful wife. For at the end of three days when Simeon and Levi went forth to slay Hamor and Shechem, they took her out of Shechem's house. Gen. xxxiv: 26.

In his anxiety to have Dinah for a wife Shechem said to his father, "Get me this damsel to wife," and Hamor the prince anxious to gratify his son, communed with Jacob, and afterwards when the sons come out of the field he communed with them on the subject, and in addition proposed to them that they should make marriages with his people, and his people with them, and that they should dwell in the land and trade with his people, and then fearing that his father would not succeed, Shechem spoke up and said unto Jacob and his sons, "Let me find grace in your sight, and what ye shall say unto me I will give." He agreed to give them anything they would ask so that they would grant his petition. They then proposed, (deceitfully) to Hamor and Shechem, that they would do as they desired, provided that all their males should submit to the rite of circumcision, and they refused on any other condition to grant them their request. They readily agreed to the conditions, and made them known to their people, who readily consented, and on the third day after the rite had been performed, the two sons of Jacob, Simeon and Levi, slew all the males of Shechem, coming upon them at a time when they were unable to defend themselves. Hamor and Shechem were both slain. Gen. xxxiv.

SHECANIAH—[Shek-a-ni′ah.]

Shecaniah was one of the priests appointed by David when he divided them into twenty-four orders. His lot was the tenth. 1st Chronicles, xxiv: 11.

SHEDEUR—[Shed′-e-ur,] *field, destroyer of fire.*

Shedeur was of the tribe of Reuben, and the father of Elizur, the prince who assisted Moses in numbering the tribes of Israel. Num. i: 5.

SHELAH—[She′-lah,] *that breaks, that undresses.*

Shelah was the younger son of Judah, by his Canaanite wife Shuah. He was quite young when his two brothers Er and Onan died, but his father pledged him to Tamar, his daughter-in-law, as a husband, as soon as he was grown. But the pledge was forgotten, and we judge, from the crime she committed with Judah, her father-in-law, to put him in memory of his promise, Shelah and Tamar were never married.

SHELEPH—[She′-lef,] *who draws out.*

Was the son of Joktan and the grandson of Eber, and is referred to in the posterity of Shem. Gen. x: 26.

SHELOMI—[She-lo′-mi.]

Was the father of Abihud, of the tribe of Asher, who as a prince assisted in dividing the land of Canaan. Num. xxxiv: 27.

SHELOMITH, 1—[Shel′-o-mith,] *my happiness, my recompense.*

Was of the tribe of Levi, and a descendant of Gershom through Shimei. He is noticed as the elder son of Shimei in the account we have of Solomon numbering the sons or descendants of Levi. 1 Chron. xxiii: 7-11.

SHELOMITH, 2—*My happiness, my recompense.*

Was of the family of Amram. He was the chief of the sons of Izhar. 1 Chron. xxiii: 18.

SHELOMITH, 3—*My happiness, my recompense.*

Was one of the sons of Rehoboam, born of Maachah, the daughter of Absalom. 2 Chron. xi: 20.

SHELOMITH, 4—*My happiness, my recompense.*

Was an Israelite woman whose father was an Egyptian. She was the daughter of Dibri, of the tribe of Dan. Lev. xxiv: 11. Her son was stoned to death for blaspheming the name of the Lord. The blasphemy he committed was under aggravating circumstances, viz: a quarrel with a man of Israel. But the circumstances under which he committed the sin did not justify it. Nor was he stoned to death because he was descended from an Egyptian, the father of Shelomith, for the law was, "Whosoever curseth his God shall bear his sin." The Israelite and the stranger, the native and the adopted, were under the same law.

SHELOMOTH—[Shel′-o-moth,] *my happiness, my recompense.*

Was one of the ministers in the temple under the order of service instituted in the time of David. 1st Chron. xxiv: 22.

SHELUMIEL—[She-lu′-mi-el,] *happiness, retribution of God.*

Was the son of Zurishhaddai, of the tribe of Simeon. He was the chief of that tribe, and associated with Moses and Aaron in managing the business of the nation at the time of their exodus from the land of Egypt. Num. i: 6. And when the tabernacle was fully set up he made an offering for his tribe. Num. vii: 36.

SHEM—*Name, renown, he that places.*

Shem was the second son of Noah, and is referred to first in Gen. v: 32. He, with Noah, his father, and his two brothers, Japheth and Ham, and the wives of each one of them—eight in all—were preserved in the ark when the destructive flood of water was upon the earth. After the ark had rested upon Mt. Ararat, and the waters had dried up, Shem, with his father and brothers, went forth from the ark. When Noah, ignorant, it may be, of the intoxicating qualities of wine, or the expressed juice of the grape, drank of it until he was drunk, and in a fit of drunkenness lay uncovered within his tent, and was treated so shamefully by Ham, it is said "Shem and Japheth took a garment and laid it upon both their shoulders, and went backward and covered the nakedness of their father." When Noah came out from under the influence of the wine, and knew what Ham had done, he pronounced a curse upon his descendants; and when he knew what part Shem and Japheth had acted, he pronounced blessings upon the descendants of both of them. Gen. ix.

The descendants of Shem, like the descendants of his brothers, were very numerous, and the territory of the earth peopled by his prosperity is referred to in Gen. x: 21, &c.

Although Japheth was the eldest son of Noah, yet Shem is always mentioned first. As proof that Japheth was the oldest, see Gen. x: 21, and 1st Chron. i: 5. In the former place it is said, "Japheth the elder," and in the latter the sons of Japheth are reckoned in their genealogy first. We suppose Shem is mentioned first because he was in the line of Messiah. See Matt. i, and Luke, iii. His chief excellency over his brothers, or his descendants over theirs, was this: that he was in the regular line from Noah of the coming "seed of the woman" that was to bruise the serpent's head. And to this probably Noah referred when he said, "Blessed be the Lord God of Shem, and Canaan shall be his servant. God shall enlarge Japheth, and he shall dwell in the tents of Shem." His family has been called, by way of eminence, the holy family, because the progenitors of the Messiah sprang from him.

SHEMAIAH, 1—[Shem-a-i′-ah,] *that obeys the Lord.*

SHEMAIAH was a prophet of the Lord, who, when Rehoboam raised a vast army in Judah, to subdue the ten tribes who had revolted under Jeroboam, spake to him against it. 2d Chron. xi: 4. He told Rehoboam that he should not go up, nor fight against his brethren, but the army should be disbanded and each man return to his house; and so Rehoboam was prevented from fighting with Jeroboam then. And when Rehoboam and his subjects forgot God, and forsook him, Shishak, the king of Egypt, took many of the fenced cities, and came up against Jerusalem. And the prophet, Shemaiah, came to Rehoboam, and the princes of Judah, and charged their sin upon them, and boldly declared that God had punished them in this way. The king and the princes believed him, and humbled themselves before God, when this prophet was ordered of the Lord to tell them, that as they had humbled themselves, he would not destroy them, but would grant them deliverance from Shishak, and he did, although the treasures of the house of Lord, and the treasures of the king's house were carried away. [See 2d Chron. xii.]

Shemaiah wrote the life and acts of Rehoboam.

SHEMAIAH, 2.—*That obeys the Lord.*

SHEMAIAH was one of the sons of Adonikam, a chief of those who went with Ezra from Babylon. Ezra, x: 21.

SHEMAIAH, 3.—*That obeys the Lord.*

SHEMAIAH was one of those who assisted Nehemiah in rebuilding the walls of Jerusalem. Nehemiah, iii: 29.

SHEMAIAH, 4.—*That obeys the Lord.*

SHEMAIAH was the father of Delaiah who, with several other princes, was sent in company with Macaiah, with a roll of threatening prophecies, or rather reported the roll to the king, and sent for Baruch to read them. Jeremiah, xxxvi.

SHEMAIAH, 5.—*That obeys the Lord.*

SHEMAIAH was the first-born son of Obed-Edom, and one of the sacred porters. 1st Chron. xxvi: 4.

SHEMEBER — [Shem-e′-ber,] *name of force, fame of the strong.*

SHEMEBER was the king of Zeboim, and was associated with the kings of Sodom and Gomorrah, Admah and Zoar, in a battle, in the vale of Siddim, with the confederate kings, Amraphel, Arioch, Chedorloamer and Tidal. These four kings conquered the kings of the cities of the plain. Genesis, xiv: 2–8.

SHEMIDA—[She-mi′-dah,] *name of knowledge, that puts knowledge, the science of the heavens.*

SHEMIDA was a descendant of the patriarch Joseph, and his name occurs in the summing up of the Manassites with the other Israelites in the plains of Moab. Num. xxvi: 32. He was the head of an extensive family called the Shemidaites. How many there were of his posterity in the time of Manasseh, as reckoned, which amounted to fifty-two thousand, seven hundred, we do not know.

SHEMUEL—[She′-mu-el.]
Was the son of Ammihud, of the tribe of Simeon, and one of the princes that assisted Joshua and Eleazar in dividing the land of Canaan among the tribes of Israel. Num. xxxiv: 20.

SHEPHATIAH, 1—[Shef-a-ti′-ah,] *The Lord that judges.*
SHEPHATIAH was one of the sons of David, born unto him in Hebron. There were six of them born there before he took up his residence in Jerusalem, viz: Amnon, Daniel or Chileab, Absalom, Adonijah, and Ithream. 1st Chron. iii: 1-3.

SHEPHATIAH, 2—*The Lord that judges.*
SHEPHATIAH, the son of Maachah, was the ruler of the tribe of Simeon. 1st Chron. xxvii: 16.

SHEPHO—[She′-fo,]
Was the son of Shobal and the grandson of Seir, the Horite. Gen. xxxvi: 23.

SHERAH—[She′-rah.]
SHERAH was the daughter of Beriah. She is referred to in 1st Chron. vii: 24, and must have been a person of some considerable importance. She built Beth-horen, the nether and upper; also Uzzeu-Sherah. The nether and upper Beth-horen were both in the tribe of Ephraim—one in the south and the other in the north of their inheritance. And Uzzeu-Sherah was, it is likely, a city of considerable size and importance in the same tribe.

SHESHBAZZAR—[Shesh-baz′zar,] *joy in tribulation, or of vintage.*
SHESHABAZZAR was probably the same person as Zerubbabel, the builder of the second temple. He is set forth in Ezra, i: 8, as a prince of Judah, in whose hands Cyrus placed the vessels of the house of the Lord, which Nebuchadnezzar had brought forth out of Jerusalem, and put in the house of his gods. And in the eleventh verse of the same chapter, it is said, "All the vessels of gold and silver were five thousand four hundred. All these did Sheshbazzar bring up with them of the captivity, that were brought up from Babylon unto Jerusalem." Sheshbazzar was probably his Chaldean name, while Zerubbabel was his Jewish name. Ez. v: 16. [See Zerubbabel.]

SHETHAR-BOZNAI—[She′thar-boz′na-i,] *that makes to rot and corrupt.*
SHETHAR-BOZNAI was engaged with Tatnai, who was governor of provinces belonging to the Persian empire, in enquiring as to the authority under which Zerubbabel and his companions acted in building the house of the Lord at Jerusalem. They acted very discreetly since they did not understand why these Jews were building the temple, they asked them, "Who hath commanded you to build this house, and to make up this wall?" They received a respectful answer, and then wrote to Darius, the Chaldean king, setting forth the facts clearly, with prudence and caution, and evidently without an exhibit of prejudice, and they closed their letter by asking the king how they should proceed in the matter. And they suggested to the king that search should be made for the decree of Cyrus, to which these Jews referred, if such a decree had been made, and they said, "Let the king send his pleasure to us concerning this matter." Ezra, v: 6-17.

Darius made search for the decree, and found it at Acmetha, in the province of the Medes, and we have a transcript of it recorded in Ez. vi: 3-5. Darius then confirms the decree, and sends the confirmation to Tatnai, and Shethar-boznai, and the result was, they encouraged the Jews to proceed with their work.

SHILLEM—[Shil′lem.]
Was the son of Naphtali, and is numbered with the family of Jacob, who went down into Egypt. Genesis, xlvi: 24.

SHIMEI, 1—[Shim′e-i,] *that hears, name of the heap, my reputation.*
SHIMEI was a brother of Laadan, and they were Gershonites, as we see in the reckoning of the sons of Levi, the descendants of Gershon, Kohath and Merari. 1st Chron. xxiii: 6-12. He had four sons, viz: Jahath, Zina, Jeush and Beriah. We gather

from the account given of Shimei, that his posterity was comparatively small, "he had not many sons." Being small, his family was united with that of Laadan, and the two were reckoned as one.

SHIMEI, 2—*That hears, name of the heap, my reputation.*

SHIMEI was a Benjamite, and a kinsman of Saul. He is brought to our notice as a hater of King David. When Absalom conspired against his father, and seduced the people from their allegiance to him, and was compelled to leave the city of Jerusalem to save his life, and fly to the wilderness. Though he was attended by his bodyguard, and many of his friends, yet this Benjamite met him and cursed him, and threw stones at the king, and accosted him in the most abusive and insulting language. He charged David with being a bloody man, and the murderer of the house of Saul. Abishai who was with David became so enraged that he asked the king to let him go at once and kill Shimei. But David would not allow it, for he reasoned with Abishai thus, "Behold, my son which came forth of my bowels, seeketh my life, how much more now may this Benjamite do it; let him alone, and let him curse, for the Lord hath bidden him," and so Shimei kept on cursing and throwing stones, and casting dust. 2d Sam. xvi.

After the rebellion headed by Absalom was crushed, the king returned again to Jerusalem, and on the way Shimei came to meet him, and knowing full well that he deserved death for his cruel treatment of David, he entreated for his life, acknowledging in the most humiliating manner his sin. Abishai who had desired to kill him when offering the insult to the king, and who was yet with David, asked if Shimei should not be put to death. He answered him that he should not, that no man should be put to death that day in Israel. It seems from the account given of his meeting David, that he was a powerful chieftain of the land, for he had a retinue of a thousand men, beside Ziba, the servant of the house of Saul, with his fifteen sons, and twenty servants. It was probably because of his authority and the retinue that he had with him, that he was so impudent to David when he was flying from Jerusalem. How humble he was, as he cast himself before the returning king, just as he stepped off the ferry boat on which he had crossed the Jordan. 2d Sam. xix. David pardoned him, but ever after that watched him and his conduct, and in his dying charge to Solomon said, "Hold him not guiltless, for thou art a wise man, and knowest what thou oughtest to do unto him; but his hoary head bring thou down to the grave with blood."

Solomon commanded Shimei to build a house in Jerusalem, and stay there, and not go forth from this city, for if he did he should die. He did not incarcerate him in a dungeon, though he probably deserved it; but Solomon made the city of Jerusalem his prison, and the penalty for escaping from Jerusalem, or going outside the walls, to pass over the brook Kidron, the king declared should be death. Shimei agreed to it, for he said; "The saying is good; as my Lord the King hath said so will thy servant do." All went on well with him for three years, when two of his servants ran away, and he heard of them in the country of Gath, and went after them to bring them back. Soon king Solomon learned that Shimei had been to the country of Achish and returned, and he sent and called him before him to account for his conduct in violating his obligation. It was indeed strange that he should so far forget the charge he was under from Solomon, as to rush into the very jaws of death, by following two fugitives; for had he reported to the king that two of his servants had gone, he would probably have had them returned. But he went himself after them. The king told him that for his offense he should die, and so he fell by the hand of Benaiah, the son of Jehoiada. 1st Kings ii.

SHIMEI, 3—*That hears, name of the heap, my reputation.*

He is called the Ramathite, and was placed by king David over the vineyards. 1st Chron. xxvii: 27.

SHIMEATH—[Shim′-e-ath,]

Was the father of Jozachar, one of the murderers of King Joash, at Millo. 2d Kings, xii: 21.

SHIMRON—[Shim′-ron,]

Was one of the sons of Issachar, and is numbered with the family of Jacob, who went down into Egypt to dwell. Gen. xlvi: 13.

SHINAB—[Shi′-nab.]

SHINAB was the king of Adnah, whose territory was invaded with that of the other four kings of the cities of the plain—Bera, king of Sodom; Birsha, king of Gomorrah; Shemeber, king of Zeboim; and the king of Zoar. The invaders were four kings, viz: Amraphel, king of Shinar; Arioch, king of Ellaser; Chedorlaomer, king of Elam; and Tidal, king of the nations. Gen. xiv: 1, &c.

SHIPHRAH—[Shif′-rah] *handsome, trumpet, that does good.*

SHIPHRAH was an Egyptian midwife who is spoken of in connection with Puah, another one of them, in Ex. i: 15. They were probably chief among this class of Egyptian women, which accounts for the king of Egypt giving the charge to them to kill all the male children of the Israelite women as soon as they were born: "If it be a son, then ye shall kill him; but if it be a daughter, then she shall live." They did not obey the command of the king fully, and the reason given is: "They feared God." Fearing God, they saved the men children alive. The God of the Israelites approved of the course of these women. "He dealt well with them, and made them houses."

SHIPHTAN—[Shif′-tan.]

Was the father of Kemuel, the prince of the tribe of Ephraim, who assisted in dividing the land. Numb. xxxiv: 24.

SHISHAK—[Shi′-shak,] *present of the bag, of the pot, of the thigh.*

SHISHAK was a king of Egypt, who is referred to in 1st Kings, xiv: 25, &c., as invading the land of Judea in the fifth year of Rehoboam. He came up against Jerusalem, and prevailed insomuch that he took away the treasures of the house of the Lord, and the treasures of the king's house. It is said he even took away all. He confiscated the shields of gold which Solomon had made, and Rehoboam made brazen shields in the stead of them, and committed them into the hands of those who formerly had possession of the golden shields, viz: the chief of the guard which kept the door of the king's house, and whenever the king went into the temple the guard carried the brazen shields before him, as he had formerly carried the golden shields.

We have a still more full account of Shishak coming against Rehoboam and Jerusalem in 2d Chron. xii: 2–9. There we learn that he commanded an army in that expedition, of twelve hundred chariots and six thousand horsemen, besides a very large number of the people who were not regular soldiery, but volunteers of the Lubim and Sukkiim, and Ethiopians.

SHITRAI—[Shit′-ra.]

SHITRAI, the Sharonite, was placed by King David over the herds that fed in Sharon. 1st Chron. xxvii: 29.

SHOBAB—[Sho′-bab,] *returned, turned back.*

Was one of the sons born unto David in Jerusalem. There were eleven of them. The following are their names: Shammuah, Nathan, Solomon, Ibhar, Elishama, Nepheg, and Japhia, Elishua, Eliada, and Eliphalet, as given in 2d Sam. v: 14–16.

SHOBACH—[Sho′-bak,] *your bonds, your nets, his captivity; according to the Syriac, a dove-house.*

SHOBACH was the general of the Syrians under Hadarezer. He is called the captain of the host. 2d Sam. x: 16. The Syrians had been hired by the Ammonites to make war upon David, and they did, but were defeated. Not being satisfied with their defeat, they determined to war upon David again, and Hadarezer gathered together a large army, and placed it in the charge of Shobach, his general. He had seven hundred chariots and forty thousand cavalry, or horsemen. But David's army conquered them again, and smote Shobach, their general, when the Syrians acknowledged themselves conquered and would no more help the Ammonites. 2d Sam. xvi: 19.

SHOBAL—[Sho′-bal.]

Was the eldest son of Seir, the Horite, who inhabited the land of Lotan. Gen. xxxvi: and in the 23d verse the following persons are named as his sons: Alvan, Manahath, Ebal, Shepho, and Onam.

SHOBI.

SHOBI was the son of Nahash, of Rabbah, of the children of Ammon. He, with several other friends of David, met him at Mahanaim with refreshments and provisions. "They brought beds, and basins, and earthen vessels, and wheat and barley, and flour and parched corn, and beans, and lentiles, and parched pulse, and honey, and butter, and sheep, and cheese of kine, for David, and for the people that were with him, to eat; for they said, For the people are hungry and weary and thirsty in the wilderness."

The father of Shobi is probably the one referred to in 2d Sam. x: 2, who showed kindness to David.

SHOHAM

Was one of the ministers in the temple under the order of service instituted in the time of David. 1st Chron. xxiv: 27.

SHOMER

Was the father of Jehozabad, one of the murderers of King Joash. 2d Kings, xii: 21.

SHUA—[Shu′-ah.]

SHUA was a woman of the tribe of Asher, noticed in the genealogy in 1st Chron. vii: 32. She was the daughter of Heber, and the sister of Japhlet, Shomer and Hotham.

SHUAH, 1—[Shu′-ah,] *pit, humiliation, meditation.*

SHUAH was one of the sons of Abraham by Keturah, and is referred to in Gen. xxv: 2, in company with his five brothers, Zimran, Jokshan, Medan, Midian and Ishbak.

SHUAH, 2—*Pit, humiliation, meditation.*

SHUAH was the daughter of a Canaanite. Gen. xxxviii: 2. She was a member of the family of Hirah, who lived in the city of Adullam. The Adullamite may have kept a house of entertainment which accounts for Judah being there, and possibly may account for Shuah being there also.

Judah is supposed to have been very young when he took this woman to wife and lived with her. She was one of another nation—yet Judah "took her" and she was the mother of Er and Onan, who were both wicked before the Lord and he slew them. She was also mother of Judah's son Shelah, and from Genesis, xxxviii: 5, we learn that about the time Shelah was grown, Shuah, Judah's wife, died.

SHUBAEL—[Shu′-ba-el.]

Was one of the ministers in the temple under the order of service instituted in the time of David. 1st Chron. xxiv: 20.

SHUHAM—[Shu′-ham.]

Was of the tribe of Dan, and the head of the family in that tribe called Shuhamites. Num. xxvi: 42.

SHUNI—[Shu′-ni.]

Was one of the sons of Gad, and is numbered with the family of Jacob, who went down into Egypt. Genesis, xlvi: 16. He was head of the family of Shunites.

SHUPHAM—[Shu′-fam.]

Was of the tribe of Benjamin, and the head of the family in that tribe called Shuphamites. Num. xxvi: 39.

SHUPPIM.

Was one of the sacred porters, and was associated with Hosah, another sacred porter, in keeping the westward gate. 1st Chron. xxvi: 16. He is supposed to have been captain of a thousand men.

SHUTHELAH—[Shu′-the-lah,] *plant, verdure, moist pot.*

Was one of the sons of Joseph, and of the tribe of Ephraim, and the head of the family of that tribe called Shuthalhites. Num. xxvi: 35.

SIBBECHAI—[Sib′-be-ka.]

SIBBECHAI, the Hushathite, slew at Gezer or Gob in the Philistine war, Sippai, that was of the children of the giants; and in the same war Elhanan slew Lahmi, the brother of Goliath, the Gittite; and Jonathan, David's brother, slew another giant who had twenty-four fingers and toes, and was of great stature. 1st Chron. xx: 4. Sibbechai was the captain of the eighth month when David instituted the monthly service of captains over twenty-four thousand men. 1st Chron. xxvii: 11.

SIDON—[Si´-don,] *hunting, fishing, venison.*

SIDON was the first-born son of Canaan, and the grandson of Ham, and is referred to in the posterity of Ham. Genesis, x: 15.

SILAS—[Si´-las,] *three, the third.*

SILAS was one among the primitive preachers of Christ's gospel, and was probably one of John's disciples, and it has been thought he was one of the two disciples, that John the Baptist sent to Jesus to ask him, "Art thou he that should come, or do we look for another?" Matt. xi: 3; but of this there is no certainty.

He was a companion of Paul, sent by the Antioch church, to the council at Jerusalem, and by that council he was sent, in company with Paul and Barnabas, and Judas, or Barsabas, to the various churches with the letters of the council. We learn from Acts, xv, and xvi, that he went with Paul after he and Barnabas separated, and became for a time that apostles constant companion. They went together through Syria, and Silicia, confirming the churches, and at Phillippi, the city of that part of Macedonia, they were both cast into prison, but they together rejoiced in their imprisonment, for at midnight they prayed and sang praises to God, and were not only miraculously delivered, but they witnessed the powerful conversion of the jailor.

When Paul was compelled to quit Thessalonica, Silas and Timothy went with him to Berea; but when it became necessary for the apostle to leave that place, Silas and Timothy remained behind, until the brethren that had conveyed Paul to Athens, returned with the commandment for them to come on; Acts, xvii, and xviii; and they left Macedonia and joined Paul again.

SILVANUS—[Syl-va´-nus,] *one who loves the woods.*

SILVANUS is supposed by some to be the same as Silas. In 2d Cor. i: 19, he is associated with Timothy, or Timotheus, as an associate preacher with Paul, and it is quite likely that the apostle refers to Silvanus in 2d Cor. viii: 18; "the brother whose praise is in all the churches." In both the epistles that Paul writes to the Thessalonians, he sends the salutations of Silvanus and Timothy. And it is thought he wrote, or transcribed the epistle to the Romans, calling himself "Tertius." Rom. xvi: 22. He also wrote, or transcribed, the first epistle of Peter. 1st Peter, v: 12; "By Silvanus, a faithful brother unto you, as I suppose, I have written." It is thought that Silvanus died after a faithful service of many years in the infant church, and that he probably suffered martyrdom, but of the manner of his death, or the precise time of it, we are not certain.

SIMEON, 1—[Sim´e-on,] *that hears or obeys,*

SIMEON was the second son of the patriarch Jacob. When he was yet a young man, he was associated with his brother Levi, in taking vengeance on the men of Shechem, for the injury that had been done to Dinah, their sister. The account of the stratagem and murder of Hamor, Shechem and the men of that place, is given in Genesis, xxxiv.

Simeon went down to Egypt with his brethren to buy corn. Joseph accused them all of being spies, and put them together in ward for three days, and at the expiration of that time, he liberated all of them, except Simeon, and sent them to their father with corn, under the command to bring their youngest brother, who was yet at home, down with them. "He took from them Simeon, and bound him before their eyes." It is thought that the reason Simeon was detained and bound by Joseph was, he was the one that bound Joseph, and put him into the pit. Simeon remained in Egypt till his brother came down the second time to buy corn, when he was brought out and again associated with them, and before he returned with them to their father, Joseph made himself known unto all. Genesis, xlii: 24.

When he went down with his father and brothers, and their families, into Egypt to reside, he had six sons. They were Jemuel, and Jamin, and

Ohad, and Jachin, and Zohar, and Shaul, and his descendants from five of these sons were very numerous. When they went out of the land of Egypt, there were fifty-nine thousand three hundred Simeonites that were able to bear arms, and they were under the command of Shelumiel, the son of Zuri-Shaddai. Gen. xlvi: 10; Exodus, vi: 15; Numbers, ii: 12.

We learn that the extensive families called Nemuelites, Jaminites, Jachinites, Zarhites and Shaulites, were Simeon's descendants. Num. xxvi: 12-13. Their spy to search out the promised land, was Shaphat, the son of Hori, and their representative to divide the land of Canaan, was Shemuel, the son of Ammihud. Numb. xiii: 5, and xxxiv: 20.

We have an account in Numbers, xxv, of the idolatry of the Israelites, at Shittim. They committed whoredom with the daughters of Moab, and sacrificed and bowed down to the gods of Moab. They joined themselves unto Baelpeor. As a tribe, they are implicated in the matter of Zimri and Cozbi, and a very large part of the twenty-four thousand that were cut off, were like Zimri of that tribe. This is pretty evident from the fact reported in Numbers, xxvi: 14, of the wonderful decrease of this tribe; there were but twenty-two thousand. And it may be that their very great wickedness for which they were thus punished, was the reason why Moses did not expressly bless them when he blessed the other tribes.

In Deut. xxxiii, we have an account of the prophetic declaration and blessings of Moses of the various tribes, but Simeon is left out. And we may see in the prophetic language of the dying Jacob, Genesis xlviii: 6, 7, an allusion to the descendants of Simeon, their sins and their punishment. "I will divide them in Jacob, and scatter them in Israel."

We have an account in Joshua xix: 1, 8, and in Jud. i: 1, 20, of the lot that was apportioned this tribe, or their inheritance within the inheritance of the tribe of Judah. The Simeonites and the children of Judah were associated together in attacking and conquering the Canaanites and Perizzites, and killing Adonibezek. The Simeonites never became noted as a tribe. They were not honored with any very distinguished or noted persons in their tribe, as the other tribes nearly all were, and their inheritance was very small. It is true that when David was made king of Israel, there were seven thousand one hundred of the Simeonites present and joining in the coronation ceremonies. 1st Chron. xii: 25.

They revolted as a tribe under Jeroboam with the other nine tribes, but many of them afterwards came back again and submitted to the King of Judah. In the time of Asa the strangers of Judah, Benjamin, Ephraim, Manasseh and Simeon, were gathered unto him. 2d Chron. xv: 9.

When Canaan was ravaged by the Assyrians, a body of the Simeonites retired southward and took possession of the country of the Amalekites. Their genealogy is given, and their taking possession of this. 1st Chron. iv: 24-43. We have an account of Josiah, during his reign and reformation, destroying idolatry in Judah, Manasseh, Ephraim, Simeon and Naphtali. 2d Chronicles, xxxiv: 6.

SIMEON, 2—*That hears or obeys.*

Simeon was an aged saint in Jerusalem, who was about the temple when christ was born. He had long waited for the coming Messiah, for God had told him by the spirit, that he should not die till he had seen the Savior. The character of this good man is presented briefly but clearly in Luke, ii: 25. "And behold there was a man in Jerusalem whose name was Simeon; and the same man was just, and devout, waiting for the consolation of Israel; and the Holy Ghost was upon him." It is further said that God, by the Holy Ghost assured him that he should not die before he had seen the Lord's Christ. Under the influence of the spirit, he went to the temple just at the time that Joseph and Mary presented the child Jesus there. As soon as his eyes, already dim with age, lighted upon the mother and her infant, his vision was strengthened, and his nature's failing fire was rekindled as he recognized in the person of that babe, the Savior of mankind. He sprang to the side of the mother and clasped her babe in his arms, "and blessed God, and said, Lord now lettest thou thy servant depart in peace, for mine eyes have seen thy salvation." He seemed now to be willing to die, nay more, he seemed desirous of immediate death, since he had seen the Savior of mankind, the light of the world, the glory of Israel.

Joseph and Mary listened with wonder and astonishment to this language of Simeon, as also to the declaration that this child "is set for the fall and rising again of many in Israel, and for a sign which shall be spoken against." There was something to them peculiarly strange in this language of the aged, just and devout Simeon. He evidently enjoyed, just at this time, the spirit of prophecy in a large degree; for he said to Mary, "Yea, a sword shall pierce through thine own soul also, that the thoughts of many hearts may be revealed." That prophecy was fulfilled when Mary, the mother of Jesus, looked on him as he hung in agony on the cross; and in deep sympathy with her sorrow-stricken soul, said, "Woman, behold thy son." Luke, ii: 26–35; John, xix: 26. It has been said that Simeon was the son of the Jewish Rabbi, Hillel, and the teacher of Gamaliel, who taught Saul of Tarsus.

SIMON, 1—[Si´-mon,] *that hears or obeys.*

SIMON was the son of Cleopas and Mary. He, with his brother James, the less, was the kinsman of our Lord. In Matt. xiii: 55, the entire family of Cleopas is referred to: "James, and Joses, and Simon, and Judas, and his sisters; are they not all with us?" See also, Mark vi: 3. Simon is said to have been the Bishop of the church at Jerusalem, after the death of his brother James, and that he was put to death by Trajan, after being terribly tortured for several days.

SIMON, 2—*That hears or obeys.*

SIMON, called Simon the Canaanite, or Simon Zelotes, was one of the twelve apostles. Matt. x: 4; Luke vi: 15. He was probably called the Canaanite because he was of Cana of Galilee, and it is thought he was called Zelotes because of his zeal, or furious bigotry against the right of the Romans to collect tax or tribute of the Galileans.

Where he spent his days, and performed his labor as an apostle, is not known. It is thought that he preached the Gospel in Egypt and other places, and was finally martyred with the apostle Jude.

SIMON, 3—*That hears or obeys.*

SIMON, surnamed Peter, was the brother of Andrew, and the first of the apostles chosen. He was probably the oldest man among the twelve, and heads the list of apostles. Matt. x: 2; Luke vi: 14. [See Peter.]

SIMON, 4—*That hears or obeys.*

SIMON, who is called the Pharisee, is referred to in Luke vii: 36, &c. He entertained the Savior in his house, and while Jesus sat at meat a woman came in that was a sinner, with a box of costly ointment, and anointed his feet. Simon knew the woman to be a sinner, and wondered that his distinguished guest did not repulse her. He thought within himself that Jesus did not know her character; but in this he was mistaken, for he not only knew what she was, but he knew the thoughts of Simon's heart. Addressing himself to Simon, Jesus said: "I have somewhat to say unto thee," and upon his expressing a willingness to hear him, Jesus reproved him for his thoughts, and commended this woman for her sacrifice, faith and love, and attentions to him. He gave Simon a very good reason for this woman's conduct, viz: much had been forgiven, and she loved much.

SIMON, 5—*That hears and obeys.*

SIMON, called Simon the leper, lived at Bethany, and entertained Jesus there. We have an account of him in Matt. xxvi: 6, &c., giving the hospitalities of his house to Jesus at the time that his body was anointed for his burial by a certain woman, supposed to be the Bethany Mary. The same circumstance is referred to in Mark, xiv: 3, &c.

SIMON, 6—*That hears or obeys.*

Was the father of Judas Iscariot. We know nothing further about him than this. He is mentioned in John vi: 71, and xii: 4.

SIMON, 7—*That hears or obeys.*

SIMON is called the Cyrenian, the father of Alexander and Rufus—two men who afterwards became noted christians. Three of the Evangelists give the account of this Simon carrying the cross for Jesus. Matt. xxvii: 32; Mark xv: 21; and Luke xxiii: 26. Whether he was a Jew or Gentile we do not know; nor do we know whether he sympathized with Jesus, and because of his sympathy was compelled to bear the cross. We only know that the Jews hailed him as he came near them, just as the sufferer had fallen the third time under the load, and they laid it upon him, or compelled him to carry one end of it. It is thought that this Simon afterwards became a preacher, and died a martyr.

SIMON, 8.—*That hears or obeys.*

SIMON was a tanner who lived by the sea-side, with whom Peter was lodging at the time he had the vision upon the house-top, which led him to go unto the Gentiles as a teacher. Peter went from Lydda to Joppa, at the call of the friends of Dorcas, whom he raised to life. After the miracle he tarried many days with Simon, a tanner. Cornelius was instructed to send to Joppa, to the house of Simon. His messengers went to the house, and were enquiring at the gate if Simon lived there, while Peter was thinking on the vision. The spirit bade him go down from the house-top, and receive their message and attend them, and he did so.

SIMON, 9—*That hears or obeys.*

SIMON was called Simon Magus. He was a noted sorcerer in the country of Samaria. He had acquired for himself a great name, and was looked upon as a very extraordinary person. But while the apostles preached Christ, and wrought miracles, and made many converts, Simon Magus professed to be converted to the christian faith, and was baptized. He looked on the apostles and their work with seeming admiration, and especially when he saw that by the laying on of hands the Holy Ghost was communicated to the people. He asked the apostles to give him power, that on whomsoever he laid hands they might receive it. He offered them money to give him that power. Peter rebuked him, saying: "Thy money perish with thee, because thou hast thought that the gift of God may be purchased with money," &c. The apostle then exhorted him to repent of his wickedness, for he was yet in the gall of bitterness, and in the bond of iniquity. Simon Magus then asked the apostle to pray for him—to intercede with God for him that the threatened evils might be averted. Acts viii: 5–24.

SIMRI

Was the chief of the sons of Hosah, and one of the sacred porters. 1st Chron. xxvi: 10.

SISERA — [Sis′-e-rah,] *that sees a horse or swallow.*

SISERA was a general under Jabin, king of Canaan. It was the Jabin with whom Barak, who commanded the army of Deborah, fought. He is introduced to our notice as the captain of Jabin's army; and we have an account of the battle he fought, and in which he was conquered, in Judg. iv.

The prophetess Deborah received a revelation from God to the effect that Israel should no longer be opposed by Jabin; and she called Barak and told him that the Lord would give their enemies into their hands,—that Sisera should be drawn out to the river Kishon, with his chariots and soldiery, to battle, and that the battle should go against him.

As soon as Sisera learned that Barak was preparing for battle he made ready his nine hundred iron chariots, and marshalling his entire army he went to battle. It was not long until the battle turned in favor of Israel, and the whole army of the Canaanites was utterly overthrown. The army was confounded, or thrown into confusion, so that Israel had little to do but to pass on, killing and pursuing; and the victory was so complete that not one of the vast army was left. Sisera himself fled away on foot, for he was compelled to abandon his chariot; and in his flight he turned into the tent of Jael, the wife of Heber, thinking, in all probability, that she would befriend him, and that in her tent he could be hid from his pursuers. He thought if Barak did pursue, he would not think of entering the apartment of the tent of Heber that Jael, his wife, occupied. But while he laid down in the tent to sleep, supposing himself to be quite secure, Jael went softly to him with a nail in one hand and a hammer in the other, and placing the point of the nail or spike on his temple, and holding it there a moment with one hand, with the other hand she wielded the hammer in driving it through his temples. He was lying there fast asleep and wearied exceedingly with the fatigues of the battle and his flight, and the piercing of his temples put him at once past all resistance, and he died. In a short time Barak, who was pursuing him, came up, and Jael showed him Sisera as he lay in her apartment of the tent pinned to the ground.

The mother of Sisera waited a long time for his return, but she waited in vain. She thought that he surely had been victorious, and was detaining to divide the spoil; but in this she was mistaken, for her son was dead, and Israel was exulting in victory. [See Barak.]

SITHRI. [or Zithri.]

SITHRI with his brother Mishael and Elzaphan, was a son of Uzziel, and a grandson of Kohath, of the the tribe of Levi. As Amram, the father of Moses, Aaron and Miriam was their father's brother, they sustained the relation of cousins to the illustrious trio who led Israel out of Egyptian bondage. Ex. vi: 22.

SO—*A measure for grain or dry matters.*

So was the king of Egypt. We have an account of a conspiracy in which Hoshea, the son of Elah, king of Israel joined himself with So, to shake off the Assyrian yoke, and free himself and his kingdom from the obligation to an annual tribute to Assyria. The consequence of this union of Hoshea and So, was the king of Assyria came up against Samaria and besieged it for three years, and finally took it and carried Israel captive to Assyria. 2d Kings, xvii: 4.

SOLOMON—[Sol′-o-m o n,] *peaceable, perfect, one who recompenses.*

SOLOMON was the son of David and Bathsheba, and the successor of his father to the throne of Israel. Though his name was Solomon, so named at his birth by his father, yet Nathan the prophet was sent by the Lord to the father and mother with another name, "Jedidiah," which signifies "beloved of the Lord." 2d Sam. xii: 25. This latter name was not designed to be the name by which he should be called, but to designate his character as the coming king of Israel, and the honor that God would confer upon him by making him the instrument of building the magnificent temple where God was to record his name, and dwell in the holy Shechinah. It is quite likely that Nathan gave David the information at this time that Solomon should succeed him, and that he should carry out his plan and design for building a temple to the Lord. This same prophet had told David before that the honor of building the Lord's house was to be reserved for his son, 2d Sam. vii: 5, and now he designated Solomon whom he calls Jedidiah, as that son.

Of the early part of Solomon's life we know but little. It is reasonable to suppose that he was educated with all the advantages and facilities of his time, and that his mind was well developed for his years when he attained early manhood. David knowing that Solomon was to build the temple, made great preparations during his lifetime for that important work, preparing materials and training his son up with great care. Adonijah the eldest son of David was about to usurp the throne before David died, which led him at once to place Solomon upon it. He ordered Nathan to have him anointed king, which was done with the greatest solemnity, after which his father directed him concerning the important work of his life, and reign, then gave him a solemn charge as to his conduct in all things—pronounced his blessing upon him and died. 1st Kings, ii: 1st Chron. xxii: 17.

Solomon was but eighteen years of age when he began to reign. He married an Ammonitess woman named Naamah two years before this, and and shortly after his reign began he married the daughter of Pharoah, king of Egypt, who either before or after their marriage became a proselyte to the Jewish religion—we judge this from the fact that we hear nothing of her idolatry, or of the religion of her country.

Young as Solomon was he felt the need of divine assistance for the performance of his duties as a sovereign. He earnestly desired success in his government, and sought after the Lord, and implored the divine favor. In company with his nobles and princes, he offered one thousand burnt offerings at Gibeon where the tabernacle of the Lord then was. And as a consequence of his earnest seeking and devotion, the very night after he had offered his sacrifice, the Lord appeared unto him and promised to give him whatever he would request. He immediately requested of the Lord to give him wisdom to qualify him for his important position of governing so great a people. The request that he thus made pleased the Lord—and it was met. He was not only granted wisdom, but honor and wealth such as no king before him had ever possessed, and no king after him should be equal to him.

When Solomen awoke from his vision he went to Jerusalem and offered up additional sacrifices before the ark of the Lord. He offered burnt-offerings, and peace-offerings, and made a feast to all his servants, as well as to his family. His wisdom was tested shortly after this, and developed by the judgment which he administered in the case of the two harlots who came to him with a dead and living child.

Solomon's kingdom was very extensive, and he divided it into cantons and appointed officers, giving them directions as to governing. The king's family was very extensive, and he had very many horses and chariots, and he himself exceeded all other men in wisdom and knowledge. He wrote many proverbs and songs, explained the nature of vegetables and animals of every kind then known. And it is said that the kings around him, who were tributary to him, or allies with him, would often send to him, or commune with him, to get the benefit of his wisdom.

The trade and commerce of Israel, under Solomon, was extensive. He traded in horses and fine linen with the Egyptians. He traded with Ophir for gold, and so with other countries where this precious metal was in abundance. We are informed that he made gold and silver as common in Jerusalem as the stones of the street, and he made cedar trees as plentiful as sycamores. He fitted out a fleet, that was managed by Tyrians, that made a trip to Ophir every three years, that brought back nearly two million pounds sterling. The number of songs that Solomon composed are given at one thousand and five, and the number of his proverbs at three thousand. See 2 Chron. i: 7–17; also 1 Kings, iv: 9–28, and x: 14–29.

When Hiram, the king of Tyre, heard that Solomon succeeded his father on the throne of Israel, he sent an embassy to congratulate him, and to open friendly communication with him. He received them and their embassage, and returned an answer, sending messengers to Hiram requesting him to render assistance in building a house unto the Lord. He let Hiram know that it was his desire to build a magnificent temple to the Lord, and his own people were not skillful in cutting timber and stone. The Israelites had not sawyers, carpenters, joiners nor builders equal to the Sidonians. Sidon was a part of the territory of Hiram, and its inhabitants were, many of them, skillful and expert workmen. Hiram entered at once into an engagement with Solomon to cut down cedars in Lebanon and bring them by sea in floats to Joppa, and so precise was the arrangement between these two kings regarding the timber to be furnished for the temple, that it was not only cut down and sawed, and hewed, and squared, but it was prepared fully, and finished to occupy its appropriate place in the magnificent building. The plan, and arrangement, and dimensions of the temple, and every piece of timber to be used in its construction was so perfectly understood by these two kings with Hiram the architect, that it was sent down the coast on rafts, and landed at the designated post, twenty-five miles from Jerusalem. At Joppa it was received by Solomon, and carried to the temple site and used in the construction of the building without any further use for ax or saw, because the timbers were ready to be put together. For the immense labor that Hiram performed, Solomon gave him, as a compensation, twenty thousand measures of wheat, twenty thousand measures of barley, twenty thousand baths of oil, and twenty thousand baths of wine. 2d Chronicles, ii: 10.

It was in the fourth year of Solomon's reign that the temple began to be built, and in seven years it was finished. Besides the large number of workmen who were servants of Hiram, king of Tyre, there were one hundred and fifty-three thousand, six hundred Canaanites employed, seventy thousand of whom were bearers of burdens, eighty thousand were diggers in the mountains and cutters of stone, and three thousand, three hundred were overseers of the work and workmen. They wrought in the work themselves, and had charge of the various pieces that were in the hands of the stonecutters and squarers; and besides these last-named overseers there was a reserve of three hundred to supply the places of such as fell sick or were disabled in any way. By the systematic arrangement entered into and prosecuted, all the materials, both of wood and stone, were prepared at a distance, so that there was nothing to do in building but to put them together. The sound of a hammer or iron tool was not heard in all the work of putting the material together; and Hiram, the architect, had charge of the foundry in the plain.

This massive structure was completed in seven years from the time it was begun, when it was publicly and devotionally dedicated to God. The account given us of the preparation for and dedication of the temple, is exceedingly interesting. Solomon united with the elders of Israel and all the people in the interesting and joyful ceremonies. The ark of the covenant was taken into it with the sacred things that were deposited therein; and with the ark he took the various utensils and ornaments and put them in their proper places, and the whole temple, as the services progressed, was filled with the cloud of the divine glory. So intense was the brightness that the priests were compelled for awhile to desist from their ministrations. "So the priests could not stand to minister because of the cloud, for the glory of the Lord had filled the house of the Lord." 1st Kings, viii: 11. Solomon then stood upon a scaffold, and turning his face to the temple prayed the dedication prayer, after which he turned toward the people and blessed them. God accepted his devotions, for fire came down from heaven and consumed the sacrifice on the altar, and again the temple was filled with divine glory; and the people were overawed, and reverently bowed with their faces and worshiped God.

Solomon made a sacrifice of twenty-two thousand oxen and one hundred and twenty thousand sheep; and as the altar of burnt offering was not large enough for this extensive sacrifice, the middle of the court was consecrated as an altar for sacrifice. After spending fourteen days in this dedication ceremony and sacrificing, Solomon dismissed the people, and they returned to their homes honoring God and blessing their king. See 1st Kings, vii, viii, ix; 2d Chron. iii–vii.

In addition to the temple, Solomon built a magnificent palace for himself and another for Pharaoh's daughter, his wife, and another still, called the House of the Forest of Lebanon, which was his royal residence part of the time. All these buildings were completed in twenty-two years, and Hiram, the king of Tyre, assisted him in building them. In order to reward him Solomon made him a present of twenty cities in the land of Galilee. But as these cities did not please Hiram he restored them to Solomon, who repaid him in some other way. Hiram called the cities "Cabul;" *i. e.*, "a remuneration with which I am displeased." He had lent King Solomon one hundred and twenty talents of gold, which was the occasion of Solomon's levy after the cities were not received, with which, in all probability, he raised the means and satisfied the claim.

Solomon took the city of Hamath-zobah and made its inhabitants tributary to him. He also built Tadmor in the wilderness, and he put in good condition for revenue the store cities in Hamath. He also built the upper and nether Bethhorons and Baalath, and Gezer. This last city was conquered by Pharaoh, king of Egypt, and given by him to his daughter, Solomon's wife.

Though Solomon did not require the Hebrews to labor in building his houses and repairing his cities, but required the Canaanites to perform the work, yet he taxed them to raise the money necessary to meet the expense; and these heavy taxes provoked them. Their taxes were the occasion of the complaint urged by the elders of Israel to Rehoboam, Solomon's successor: "Thy father made our yoke heavy, make thou it lighter." For it is said that his annual tax upon his own people was six hundred and sixty-six talents of gold, in addition to the presents from his allies and tributary kings, and the revenue of his commonwealth. His government was certainly a powerful and wealthy one.

But Solomon retained his wisdom for many years. It is said that the king of Tyre maintained a correspondence with him, and that their correspondence consisted, in part, of trying one another with hard questions. Whether this be so or not, we are assured in sacred history that the queen of Sheba heard of Solomon's fame, his wisdom, and his greatness, and came from her distant home to see him, and the development of his wisdom and greatness in the temple and the houses that he had built, and to puzzle him with difficult questions. She arrived at the capital of the kingdom, and looked with amazement upon the magnificent buildings, upon the court, and attendants, and table of the king of Israel. She saw the evidence of his greatness and wisdom, and fainted away with surprise. When she recovered from the shock she confessed freely that it far exceeded her expectations. "The half had not been told her." 1st Kings, ix, x; 2d Chron. viii, ix. She made valuable presents to King Solomon, such as none but the ruler of a wealthy kingdom could, and received valuable presents from him.

With all the grand and magnificent that has thus appeared in the person and character of Solomon, the latter part of his life was marked with bad and disgraceful conduct. He took to himself seven hundred wives and three hundred secondary wives, many of them were heathens and idolaters. The influence of these wives over him led him to forsake the Lord and his worship; for he plunged into the grossest idolatry and built heathen temples and erected heathen idols. Because of his wickedness, God was angry with him, and determined to rend his powerful kingdom in twain. When Solomon learned this, he became penitent for his sins, and many who read his life indulge the hope that he sought and found pardon, and that he finally died in the enjoyment of the divine favor. Whether this is so or not, it is quite likely that he wrote the book of Ecclesiastes after he had fallen, was reproved, and became repentant, and it is quite likely that he wrote a part of his Proverbs, especially those by which he warns his son to beware of the snares of wanton women. But if Solomon was forgiven, he was visited with temporal punishment, for Hadad, the Edomite, and Rezon, the Syrian, and Jeroboam the son of Nebat who afterwards led the ten tribes to revolt, gave him much trouble, and rendered him very uneasy. There are many things to admire in this king, and in the work he performed in the days of his strength. But his apostacy from God is to be regretted and deprecated.

Solomon reigned it is supposed about forty years, and as he was but eighteen years of age when he began, he was about fifty-eight when he died. Hence he died comparatively young for the time in which he lived. It is quite reasonable to suppose that his conduct brought on him a degree of premature infirmity. His history was written by the prophets Nathan, Abijah and Iddo.

He was buried in all probability in pomp and splendor, in the sepulcher of his father, in the city of David, and Rehoboam reigned in his stead. 1st Kings, xi.

SOSIPATER—[So-sip′a-ter,] *who defends or saves his father.*

Sosipater was probably the same person that is referred to in Acts, xx: 4, called "Sopater of Berea," who, with several others, accompanied Paul into Asia. He is referred to in Romans, xvi: 21, under the name Sosipater, in the salutations to the church, and in this place it is said he was a kinsman of the apostle Paul.

SOSTHENES—[Sos′the-nes,] *a strong and powerful savior.*

Sosthenes was the chief ruler of the synagogue at Corinth, and one of the first converts to christianity in that city. When Gallio refused to hear the accusations brought against Paul by the Jews, and drove them from the judgment seat, some heathen Greeks took Sosthenes, the chief ruler of the synagogue, and beat him before the judgment seat, or under the eye of Gallio; but he cared not for it, and took no notice of it. Acts, xviii: 12-17. This is probably the same person who was converted to christianity, and is called by Paul in 1st Cor. i: 1, Sosthenes, "our brother." If so, we may consider that he was an intimate friend and colaborer of Paul.

STEPHANAS—[Stef′a-nas] *a crown crowned.*

STEPHANAS was an early convert to the christian religion at Corinth. He was not only converted himself, but his family were all baptized. If there were adults, they believed with himself, and openly professed their faith. If there were infant children, they too were baptized. In 1st Cor. i: 16, Paul says, "I baptized also the household of Stephanus." This same person, in company with Fortunatus and Achaicus, visited the apostle Paul while at Ephesus, and were of great service to him. 1st Cor. xvi: 17-18: "They have refreshed my spirit." They were probably the bearers of a letter to Paul, and from him they were the bearers of this epistle to the Corinthians.

STEPHEN—[Ste′-fen.]

STEPHEN was one of the seven deacons selected to attend to some interests of the church, that were burdening the apostles, and somewhat hindering them in their work of faith and labor of love.

From the instructions given the disciples as to the selection of men to attend to these interests, we may gather that Stephen, with his companions, was in the estimation of his brethren a good man. Acts, vi: 3; "Look ye out seven men of honest report, full of the Holy Ghost and wisdom." Stephen and his companions were solemnly set apart by the imposition of the apostles' hands, and entered upon their important work.

It has been thought that he was one of our Savior's disciples, and that he was brought up like Saul of Tarsus, at the foot of Gamaliel, but of this we cannot tell. He was before his conversion, it is quite likely, a man of some note among the Hellinist Jews.

Being called to the work and office of a deacon, he was qualified for it. He was filled with the Holy Ghost, and preached the word as a deacon, with power, and in the demonstration of the spirit, and success crowned his efforts; "the word of God increased and the number of the disciples were multiplied." He not only preached successfully, but he wrought many and mighty miracles. "And Stephen full of faith and power, did great wonders and miracles among the people."

It was not long until certain Jews disputed with him, and not being able to compete with him in argument, or "resist the wisdom and spirit by which he spake, they suborned witnesses to swear falsely against him, declaring that he had blasphemed Moses and God. They soon succeeded in raising a mob and caught him and brought him to the council. They hurried him before the Jewish Sanhedrim and made a charge against him of speaking reproachfully against their honored temple and the law of Moses. They affirmed that Stephen had said that Jesus would abolish the law and destroy the temple. Stephen heard their accusation and stood up fearlessly, and undaunted, by these false charges. His countenance was lit up with a heavenly smile, as the Sanhedrim asked him, "Are those things so?"

Having an opportunity of speaking for himself, he told them what the dealings of God had been with the Jewish nation, and how wicked the nation had been, how they had incurred the divine displeasure, and felt God's judgments. He openly rebuked them for their murder of Jesus. He declared they had persecuted the prophets who had prophesied of the coming Savior, and now that he had come, they had put him to death. He said, boldly unto them, "Ye have been the betrayers and murderers of the holy and the just."

They heard this language of the good man condemning them, and "were cut to the heart, and gnashed upon him with their teeth." But still he was undaunted. He knew full well that the demonstration of feeling against him arose from murder in their hearts, and with early martyrdom in view, "he looked up steadfastly into Heaven, and saw the glory of God, and Jesus standing at the right hand of God," and in the hearing of the murderous multitude, he said: "Behold I see the Heavens opened, and the son of man standing on the right hand of God." They professed to be shocked with what he said, and to count it blasphemy, and, pretending to this, they stopped their ears, and ran upon him with one accord, and taking hold of him, they dragged him out of the city with great violence, and stoned him to death. The good man received all this abuse, and cruel treatment from his enemies, without a word of complaint or murmuring, and, indeed, with his last expiring breath, he offered up a fervent prayer to God, to forgive his murderers. He died praying for himself and for his enemies. His prayer for himself was, "Lord Jesus receive my spirit." In this prayer he involves the doctrine of the soul's immortality, and a conscious state of happiness for the good man immediately after death. But his prayer for his enemies is, as he kneels in their presence to receive the shower of stones, "Lord lay not this sin to their charge." How much like that prayer of the blessed Savior while hanging in agony on the cross. "Father forgive them, for they know not what they do."

After Stephen was thus murdered, his christian friends took charge of the body, and they carried to the burial, and made great lamentation over him. [See Acts, vi: 5–15.]

SUSANNAH—[Su-san′-nah,] *a lily, a rose, joy.*

This woman, we suppose, believed in Christ, as she is spoken of in connection with Mary Magdalene after her conversion, and with Joanna, the wife of Chuza, Herod's steward, as "ministering unto him of their substance." Like the other two women, she was, it is likely, a woman of position and property. Luke, viii: 3.

SUSI—[Su′-si,] *horse, swallow, moth.*

SUSI was of the tribe of Joseph. and the father of Gaddi, who was selected by Moses as one of the spies of the land of Canaan. Num. xiii: 11.

TAHAN—[Ta′-han.]

Was of the sons of Joseph in the tribe of Ephraim, and he was the head of the family of that tribe called Tahanites. Num. xxvi: 35.

TAHPENES—[Tah′-pe-nes,] *standard, flight.*

TAHPENES was the wife of Pharaoh, who gave his daughter to Solomon, the king of Israel, to wife, and possibly she was the mother of that beautiful woman. She was the sister of the wife of Hadad, the adversary of Solomon, who seems to have had the oversight and probably the education under her direction, of Genubath, the son of Hadad. 1st Kings xi: 20.

TALMAI, 1—[Tal′-ma,] *my furrow, heap of waters.*

TALMAI was the son of Anak, and of the race of the giants that were destroyed by the Israelites in Canaan. We have an account in Num. xiii, of the spies sent by Moses to search the promised land, and as they were proceeding on their journey they came to Hebron, where Ahiman, Shishai and Talmai, the children of Anak were, and we learn from Joshua xiv: 15, that the inheritance of Caleb took in the city of Hebron, and that he drove these three giants from his inheritance. See also, Joshua xv: 14.

TALMAI, 2—*My furrow, heap of waters.*

TALMAI was the king of Geshur, and the father of Maacah, whom David married; and this woman was the mother of Absalom. 2d Sam. iii: 3. When Absalom killed Amnon he fled to Talmai, the king of Geshur, his grand-father, and remained with him three years before he returned to his native land, and to David his father. 2d Sam. xiii: 37.

TAMAR, 1—[Ta-mar,] *a palm, palm tree.*

TAMAR was the wife of Er, the oldest son of Judah and Shuah his Canaanitish wife. Gen. xxxviii: 6. But because Er was wicked the Lord slew him, thus Tamar was left a widow. Judah then bade Onan marry his brother's widow. This was in accordance with a law that was afterwards well understood and practised upon, among the Israelites recorded in Deut. xxv: 5. "If brethren dwell together and one of them die, and have no child, the wife of the dead shall not marry without unto a stranger; her husband's brother shall (go in unto her and) take her to him to wife," etc. Onan was displeased at the requisition of the father, and was wicked, wherefore the Lord slew him also, and Tamar was again left a widow. Judah observant of this claim of a widow upon her brothers-in-law, bade Tamar wait until Shelah his youngest son was grown, and attained a proper age to marry, when he should be given her. She accordingly went to her father's house to tarry for a few years, until the marriage with Shelah could be consummated.

A few years passed away—the wife of Judah died, and Shelah attained a proper age for marriage, but had not been given unto Tamar. Judah went up with his friend Hirah the Adullamite, to the sheep shearers. Some one gave information to Tamar to the effect that her father-in-law was going to Timnath. She put off her widow's garments and decoyed him by acting the part of a prostitute. Judah was ensnared, and soon learned the fact, that his daughter-in-law had decoyed him, and the reason why she had done it, viz., that he had not fulfilled his promise, for though Shelah was grown, yet was he not given her as a husband. Tamar became the mother of twin sons for Judah, whose names were Pharez and Zarah. Pharez is honored by being in the line of genealogy from Judah to Christ. Matthew, i: 3.

**TAMAR**, 2—*A palm, palm tree.*

TAMAR was the daughter of David and Maacah, who was the daughter of the king of Geshur. She was consequently the sister of Absalom. She is introduced to our notice in 2d Samuel, xiii: 1. Absalom had a fair sister, whose name was Tamar. From this we may judge Tamar was a handsome woman. As, also, from the circumstance next narrated, viz: "Amnon, her half brother, loved her." But she fell a victim to the passions of Amnon, who acted under the wicked advice of Jonadab, her cousin. She plead with Amnon in the most tender and persuasive speech, but it was all of no avail. After she had been cruelly treated by Amnon, he drove her in anger from his presence; and feeling very keenly her disgrace and cruel treatment, she rent the garment that distinguished her as a king's daughter, and put ashes on her head, and went crying through the streets of the city. She met her brother Absalom, to whom she told the cause of her sorrow. Absalom pitied her, and felt keenly the disgrace of his sister, but he comforted her, and took her to his own house, where she remained desolate for several months.

Absalom treasured wrath in his heart against Amnon, and was not satisfied until he had avenged the wrong done his sister by killing him. What became of Tamar after Absalom fled and went to Geshur we know not, but we suppose Absalom remembered her; for after his return from his banishment, and his partial reconciliation to David, his father, amongst his children was a daughter whose name was Tamar, probably so named in memory of his injured sister, who may have died of a broken heart.

**TANHUMETH**—*Consolation, repentance.*

TANHUMETH, the Netophathite, was the father of Seraiah, one of the captains of the armies, who, hearing that Gedaliah was made governor by the king of Babylon, went to him to Mizpah. 2d Kings, xxv: 23.

**TAPHATH**—[Ta′-fath.]

Was a daughter of King Solomon, whom he gave to be the wife of the son of Aminadab, one of the twelve officers that were placed over the twelve districts to provide victuals for the king's household, monthly. 1st Kings, iv:11.

**TARSHISH** — [Tar′-shish,] *contemplation of the marble.*

Was one of the sons of Javan, the son of Japheth. There are four sons mentioned in Gen. x: 4, viz.: Elishah, Tarshish, Kittim and Dodanim. These four sons of Javan, with the three sons of Gomer, and the other five sons of Japheth—Magog, Madai, Tubal, Meshech and Tiras—are supposed to have settled in different parts of Asia and various kingdoms of Europe. In Gen.

x: 5, it is said, "By them were the isles of the Gentiles divided in their lands, every one after his tongue, with their families, in their nations."

TARTAK—*Chained, bound, shut up.*
Was an idol of the Avites, and is referred to with Nibhaz, another idol, in 2d Kings, xvii: 31. There is a difference of opinion among Jewish writers as to the form or figure of the idol Tartak. Some think it was made to represent the ass, while another important writer will have this idol to be the chariot of the sun, or the sun in his chariot.

TARTAN—[Tar′-tan,] *that searches, the gift of the turtle.*
TARTAN was one of the generals of Sennacherib, the king of Assyria. At the time that Sennacherib besieged Lachish he sent Tartan, Rabsaris, and Rabshakeh, with a part of his army, to demand of King Hezekiah and the inhabitants of Jerusalem a surrender. Rabshakeh was especially insolent to the messengers of Hezekiah. And when the destroying angel passed through the Assyrian camp and slew one hundred and eighty-five thousand of the soldiery, it is quite likely that two of the Assyrian generals were destroyed. See Isa. xxx, xxxiii, xxxvi, xxxvii. But it is likely that Tartan was not slain, for after this he is represented as leading the Assyrian hosts against Ashdod and taking it. Isaiah, xx: 1.

TATNAI—[Tat′-na-i,] *that gives.*
TATNAI was the governor of Samaria at the time that the returned Jews from Babylon were engaged in rebuilding the temple and the walls of their sacred city. He tried to hinder them in the work, as did his companions. We have an account of their efforts in Ezra, v: 3. He sent a letter to Darius informing him that they had tried ineffectually to stop them, and that these Jews that were engaged pretended that there was an edict of Cyrus appointing them to build it. And Tatnai suggested that search be made to ascertain whether there was such an edict. Darius accordingly made the search and found it, and then ratified it and ordered the Samaritans to give the Jews no further trouble, but allow them to go on with their work. Tatnai and his companions encouraged the Jews to proceed, and they did so, until it was finished. Ezra, vi: 13-16.

TEBAH—[Te′-bah,] *murder, a cook.*
He was the eldest son of Reumah, the concubine or secondary wife of Nahor. He is mentioned with three other sons of this woman, viz: Gaham, Thahash, and Maachah, in Gen. xxii: 24.

TEBALIAH—[Teb-a-li′-ah,]
Was one of the sons of Hosah, and he was one of the sacred porters. 1st Chron. xxvi: 11.

TEMA—[Te′-mah,] *admiration, perfection.*
TEMA was a son of Ishmael, hence a grandson of the patriarch Abraham. He is referred to in the generations of Ishmael. Gen. xxv: 15. He is supposed to have founded a city of the same name, referred to in Job, vi: 19; and the "troops of Tema," referred to there are supposed to be the descendants of the son of Ishmael.

TEMAN—[Te′man,] *south, Africa.*

TEMAN or TIMNAH, was the son of Eliphaz, and the grandson of Esau, and from him the Temanites, to whom Eliphaz, Job's friend belonged, descended. He is called in Gen. xxxvi: 42, a duke. Husham, another descendant of Esau, reigned in the land of Temani, when Jobab died. Gen. xxxvi: 34. There was an important city called Teman, that was built probably by this son of Eliphaz. It seems from Jeremiah, xlix: 20, that the inhabitants of Teman occupied nearly all the country of Edom, and the same fact seems to be set forth by the prophet, Amos, i: 11-12. The judgments of God were to be poured upon Edom, and the Lord says: "I will send a fire upon Teman which shall devour the palaces of Bozrah." The prophet Habakkuk makes a beautiful allusion to the country of Teman, and the symbols of the divine presence and glory, as they moved forward. "God came from Teman, and the holy one from Mt. Paran. Selah." Habakkuk, iii: 3.

TERAH—[Te′rah,] *to breathe, to scent, to blow.*

TERAH was the son of Nahor, and the father of Haran, Nahor and Abraham. His father was nine hundred and twenty years old when he was born. Genesis, xi: 24. And Terah was seventy years old when Haran was born unto him, for he was his oldest son, and Abram was the youngest of the three, not born, it is likely, until Terah was one hundred and thirty years old. Abram was seventy-five years old, when, with Lot, he departed from the land of Haran. His father, Terah, had just died at the age of two hundred and five, so that he must have been as old as we say, when Abram was born. Genesis, xii: 4. It is not certain that Terah and his family were idolaters at the time that God called Abram, if so he was likely converted about that time, for he, with Abram and Lot, left Ur, of the Chaldeans, to go to the land of Canaan, and at Haran, Terah died, when Abram and Lot went on. As Terah died and was buried at Haran, it is probable that his family remained there, except the two named, for we find the relationship afterwards in Padan-aram, in Mesopotamia. Nahor, one of the sons, built a city there. Isaac and Jacob both procured their wives from their relationship in this land. Genesis, xxv: 20, and xxviii: 6.

TERTIUS—[ Ter′shi-us,] *the third.*

TERTIUS was intimately associated with the apostle Paul, and may be, as some suppose, the same as Silas, who was his fellow laborer, and at one time, in Philipi, his fellow prisoner. He wrote the epistle to the Romans as Paul dictated it to him, or he transcribed the epistle that was sent to the church. Romans, xvi: 22, "I, Tertius, who wrote this epistle, salute you in the Lord."

TERTULLUS—[Ter-tul′lus,] *a liar, an impostor.*

TERTULLUS was a famous orator among the Jews, who was employed, or volunteered his services to prosecute Paul before Felix. We have an account of this matter in Acts xxiv: 1–10. Ananias, the high priest, with some Jewish Elders and Tertullus, went to Cesarea, whither Lysias had sent Paul. Arriving there, they informed the governor against Paul, and he was brought forth for trial. Tertullus then addressed the judge in a speech full of flattery and falsehood, after which the apostle was permitted to answer for himself; and we may judge that he satisfied Felix that he was not guilty of the crimes of which Tertullus charged him, for he commanded the centurion who had charge of Paul, to let him have liberty and allow his friends to minister unto him.

THADDEUS — [Thad′-de-us,] *that praises.*

THADDEUS, or LEBBEUS was the same person as Jude, the writer of the Epistle of Jude. In Matthew x : 3, Thaddeus is said to be his surname; "Lebbeus whose surname is Thaddeus." He was the kinsman or brother, as he is called, of Jesus. Luke vi: 16. He was the son of Cleopas. [See Judas.]

THEOPHILUS—[The-of′-fi-lus,] *a friend of God.*

THEOPHILUS was a noted christian, and an intimate acquaintance and friend of the evangelist, St. Luke. Some have thought that the name simply denotes any "friend or lover of God," as that is the import of the name. But in the manner in which it is used by St. Luke in directing his gospel, and also the Acts of the Apostles, we are certainly justified in believing it to be the proper name of a christian man. We may further suppose that he was a person of some note—a gifted and holy man. The first four verses of the 1st chapter of Luke's gospel is a preface written to Theophilus, commending to his attention and careful perusal the entire history that follows: the history of Jesus Christ, of whom he had heard, and in whom he believed. One grand object of Luke was to confirm this important person in the faith. Acts i: 1, makes a reference to the gospel written before to him. "The former treatise have I made, O Theophilus, of all that Jesus began to do and to teach."

THEUDAS—[Thu′-das,] *a false teacher.*

We have an account of this person in Acts, v: 36, or rather a reference made to him. "For before these days rose up Theudas boasting himself to be somebody; to whom a number of men, about four hundred, joined themselves: who were slain, and all, as many as obeyed him, were scattered and brought to nought." He set himself up as a noted person, trumpeted his greatness abroad. He was killed, and the four hundred men that joined him were either slain with him, or dispersed abroad.

THOMAS—[Tom′-mas,] *a twin.*

THOMAS, otherwise called Didymus, was one of our Savior's apostles, and is numbered with them in Matt. x: 3, and in other places where the list of names of the twelve is given. He had often been with Jesus to Bethany and enjoyed the hospitality of Lazarus and the two sisters, and appreciated their kindness. When Jesus heard that Lazarus was sick, after two days he said to his disciples, "Let us go into Judea again." His disciples were disposed to object because of the opposition and persecution that their master met with in Judea a little while before that. At length Jesus told them plainly, Lazarus was dead, and certified his intention to go to Bethany. No sooner had he done this than Thomas proposed to the other disciples that they all accompany him, thereby testifying their affection for the Bethany family, and if necessary die with their master, who would certainly endanger his life by returning to Judea. John, xi: 16. His affection for the bereaved sisters and his love for Christ must have been very strong.

In John, xiv: 5, we have an account of an interesting conversation between Jesus and Thomas. Jesus in order to comfort his disciples bade them be of good cheer, for "In my father's house are many mansions—I go to prepare a place for you—I will come again and receive you to myself," and he closed up this address by saying, "Whither I go ye know and the way ye know." Thomas professed ignorance and asked him whither he was going, and which way he would take, "Lord we know not whither thou goest, and how can we know the way?" Jesus then declared himself the way, the truth and the life—the grand medium of access to God the father.

After our Savior was risen from the dead, the same day he appeared to ten of the disciples and satisfied them that he was risen. They reported it to Thomas but he would not believe them. He did not say that they had not had an interview with their risen master, but he thought they were mistaken. They tried to convince him but all in vain—they told him that they had heard his well-known voice, saying, "Peace be unto you," nay more, they had seen his hands and his side. They had heard his words, and felt the blessed sensations produced by receiving the Holy Ghost; but Thomas said "except I shall see in his hands the print of the nails, and put my finger into the print of the nails, and thrust my hand into his side, I will not believe." In this state of mind he continued until the next Sabbath evening, when he assembled with the ten in their place of meeting. And while they were there Jesus appeared unto them. His appearance at this time seems to have been mainly to remove the doubts from the mind of Thomas, as to his resurrection from the dead.

He accosted them, as in the former case, with, "Peace be unto you," and, turning to Thomas, he said: "Reach hither thy finger and put it into the print of the nails, and reach hither thy hand and thrust it into my side, and be not faithless, but believing." This was the very evidence that the doubting disciple asked for; and he seemed to be quite overpowered with it, for he exclaimed: "My Lord and my God;" *i. e.*, It is enough. Now I know that Jesus has risen from the dead. The Savior rather reproved him for disbelieving so long by saying: "Blessed are they that have not seen, and yet have believed." John, xx: 24-29.

A short time after this Thomas, with others of the disciples, saw Jesus again. It was at the sea of Galilee. There were together seven of them, "Simon Peter, and Thomas called Didymus, and Nathaniel of Cana in Galilee, and the sons of Zebedee, and two others." John, xxi: 2. This was the third time that Jesus showed himself to his disciples after his resurrection; and, though Thomas was behind them all in that he had seen the Savior but once, and they had all seen him twice, yet now he is permitted to see him with only a part of them; and he is permitted to take bread and fish from his hands, and eat with them.

It is not certain where Thomas performed his apostolic labor. It is thought he preached at Jerusalem for many years, and then went to preach among the Parthians and Medes, and others, and that he finally suffered martyrdom in the East Indias, near to which, three or four centuries ago, Christians were found who called themselves by the name St. Thomas. It has been thought that this apostle preached in China.

TIBERIUS—[Ti-be′-ri-us,] *son of Tiber.*

Tiberius was a Roman emperor. He was adopted by Cesar-Augustus as his heir and successor. The mother of Tiberius married Cesar, which accounts, in part at least, for his being selected as heir to the emperor. In the beginning of his reign he behaved himself respectfully, and did honor to his position; but afterwards he became, it is said, peevish and fretful, cruel and oppressive.

About the sixth year of his reign, the Roman Senate ordered all the Jews to leave Rome, or submit to be made slaves. It is said that he made Pilate governor of Judea, in the thirteenth year of his reign. He took from the Jews the power of putting criminals to death; hence, when the Jews would put Jesus to death, they went to Pontius-Pilate to procure the sentence of death. It is said that he was prejudiced in favor of the Savior, and heard of his miracles with such great interest and admiration that he proposed to have Jesus numbered with the Roman deities, but was prevented by the Senate. He is also said to have favored Christians so much that he threatened with death any persons who molested them on account of their religion. See Luke, iii: 1.

TIBNI—[Tib′-ni,] *straw, understanding.*

We have an account of this person in 1st Kings, xvi, from which we learn that he was the son of Ginath. After the treason of Zimri, and the murder of Baasha, the king of Israel, by him, Omri turned against him, and with an army besieged Tirzah, where Zimri had stationed himself, and was reigning as king. The people, or soldiery in the camp, made Omri king, and he took the city. Zimri set the palace on fire, and died in the conflagration.

Part of the people then took up Tibni and determined to make him king instead of Omri. It is said the people of Israel were divided into two parts, half of the people following Tibni and the other half following Omri. It is probable that the former was the selection of the people for king, and the latter the selection of the army. The consequence of which was, Omri had the army and munitions of war with him, while Tibni had a raw, undisciplined host, that were almost without munitions of war. Yet they fought together, and Tibni was defeated and slain. It is said, 1st Kings, xvi: 22: "But the people that followed Omri prevailed against the people that followed Tibni, the son of Ginath; so Tibni died and Omri reigned."

TIDAL—[Ti′-dal,] *that breaks the yoke.*

Is called "king of the nations." Gen. xiv: 1. He was associated with Amraphel, Arioch and Chedor laomer, in a war with the kings of Sodom, Gomorrah, Admah, Zeboim, and Zoar. These four confederate kings were associated against the five Canaanite kings named above, and they prevailed against them. It is thought that the subjects of Tidal's kingdom were refugees from other kingdoms; hence, he is styled "king of the nations."

TIGLATH-PILESER—[Tig′-lath-Pile′-ser,] *that takes away captivity, miraculous.*

Tiglath-Pileser is sometimes called Tilgath-Pilneser. He was a king of Assyria, and probably the son of Pul, who prevailed against Israel during the reign of Menahem, and exacted of him a thousand talents of silver to confirm the kingdom unto him. Having received the exacted money of the king of Israel, Pul, the king of Assyria, left the land and went back into his own country. 2d Kings, xv: 19.

Tiglath-Pileser was the successor of his father, and received the kingdom at a time of prosperity and great power of the Assyrian empire. He was not satisfied, though, with the size and power of his empire, but sought to enlarge it. We have an account in 2d Kings, xv: 29, of his coming against Israel in the days of Pekah, their king, and taking several important cities, "Ijon and Abel-beth-maachah, and Janoah and Kedesh, and Hazor and Gilead, and Galilee, all the land of Naphtali, and carried them captive to Assyria." It seems that he was hired by Ahaz, the king of Judah, to fight against Pekah and Rezin, the king of Syria, who was associated with Pekah in efforts to take Jerusalem. Ahaz gave Tiglath-Pileser the silver and gold that was found in the house of the Lord and in the treasury of the king's house, sending it to him by a messenger. He took the money and met the wishes of Ahaz. He came into the country of Syria with his army, and engaged and conquered the king of Syria. "He took Damascus and carried the people of it captive to Kir, and slew Rezin." After his conquest Ahaz went to meet him at Damascus and acknowledge his obligation to him. 2d Kings, xvi.

It seems from Ist Chron. v: 26, that he and his father carried away into captivity the Reubenites and the Gadites, and the half tribe of Manasseh, and brought them unto Halah, and Habor, and Hara, and to the river Gozan. And we learn from 2d Chron. xxviii: 20, that though Ahaz hired him to help him against the king of Syria, and he did, and received a fair compensation for it; yet he was not fully satisfied, for he "distressed Ahaz and strengthened him not." We may judge that he ravaged a part of Judea.

Though Tiglath-Pileser slew Rezin, he did not help Ahaz either against the Philistines or against Pekah. He helped him a little, but distressed him much. He is supposed to have reigned about nineteen years, and was succeeded by Shalmaneser.

TIMNA—[Tim′-na.]

TIMNA was the concubine of Eliphaz, the son of Adah. Gen. xxxvi: 12. "And Timna was concubine to Eliphaz, Esau's son, and she bare to Eliphaz, Amalek." This Amalek was the father of the Amalekites, who became such bitter enemies to the Jews, and whom the Jews afterwards exterminated.

Timna was also the sister of Lotan, the Horite. Gen. xxxvi: 22. "And Lotan's sister was Timna."

TIMON—[Ti′-mon,] *honorable.*

Was one of the seven deacons of the early church. He was probably an Hellenist Jew. The name stands fifth in the list of deacons. Acts, vi: 1-6. We know nothing further of him.

TIMOTHY—[Tim-o′-thy.]

TIMOTHY or TIMOTHEUS, was a noted evangelist. From Acts, xvi: 1, we may gather that he was a native of Derbe or Lystra. His father was a Greek, but his mother was a Jewess. Whether his father was a convert to the christian religion or not, his mother Eunice, and his grandmother Lois were, and they together taught Timothy from a child the scriptures. They trained him up in the nurture and admonition of the Lord. 2d Tim. i: 5, &c. His pious training by these pious women, was the means that resulted in his early conversion. When Paul and Silas went to Derbe and Lystra, they found Timothy there a disciple. He became an intimate associate of Paul, his traveling companion and servant, and that apostle calls him his "beloved son." 1st Cor. iv: 17. Again he calls him his "own son in the faith," and his "faithful fellow worker." 1st Tim. i: 2. Timothy was ordained to the work and office of the ministry, by Paul. 2d Tim. i: 6. "Wherefore I put thee in remembrance that thou stir up the gift of God which is in thee, by the putting on of my hands." When Paul and Silas left Derbe and Lystra, Timothy accompanied them, and they made their way to Troas, where Paul had the vision that presented an open door to Macedonia, so that Timothy went with him to that country, and was at Philippi, Thessalonica, and Berea, and while the persecution was raging at Thessalonica, he and Silas suffered with Paul. At Berea, Silas and Timothy remained after the brethren had sent Paul away because the Thessalonians had stirred the Bereans up against him. Paul went to Athens, and tarried there until he was joined by Timothy and Silas. Acts. xvii: 16. Paul refers to this persecution, and the manner in which he and his companions had been exercised and preached the word of life. 1st Thess. ii: 2, also iii: 2, 3. In Acts, xviii: 5, we have an account of Silas and Timothy being with Paul at Corinth, and when the apostle wrote his epistles to the Thessalonians, which was done probably about this time, either from Athens or Corinth, Timothy and Silas or Silvanus, send their salutations to the church. See first verse of the first chapter of each of the epistles.

He continued to travel with Paul, and was obedient to him. By the appointment of the apostle, Timothy with other evangelists visited the churches of Ephesus, Macedonia and Corinth, for the purpose of establishing the christians in the faith. Acts xix: 22. "So he sent into Macedonia two of them that ministered unto him, Timotheus and Erastus." 1st Cor. iv: 17 and xvi: 10. He was left by Paul at Ephesus to guard the interests of the church when he went unto Macedonia, 1st Tim. i: 3, and while he was there he probably received their first Epistle in which Paul put him in mind of his charge, and gave him instructions as to proper conduct and gave him earnest exhortations to a faithful performance of his duty. After fulfilling his mission at Ephesus, he seems to have followed Paul into Macedonia, and was associated with him there, probably at Philippi, in labor.

About this time Paul wrote his 2d epistle to the Corinthians. The first verse of the first chapter, is a salutation of Timothy, joined with Paul, to the church. He attended Paul when he went to Corinth, and was with him when he wrote his epistle to the Romans and sent it by Phebe. Timothy with Lucius, Jason and Sosipater, sent their salutations to the church at Rome. After this, with others, he accompanied the apostle into Asia, Acts, xx: 4, and when Paul was at Rome, and wrote his 2d epistle to Timothy, in which he triumphs so gloriously in the prospect of death, he sent for him to come and see him as early as possible, and bring with him the cloak that he left at Troas, with Carpus and the books, and especially the parchments. 2d Timothy, iv: 9-13.

He did go to Paul and was with him awhile at Rome, during his imprisonment. He was with him when he wrote his epistles to the Philippians, and Colossians, as also the epistle to Philemon, for in the first verse of the first chapter, of each epistle, his salutations attend Paul's. He was not only with Paul, but for awhile he was a prisoner with him at Rome, and Paul refers to his imprisonment, or rather, to his being set at liberty. Heb. xiii: 23. "Know ye not that our brother Timothy is at liberty?" And Paul seems to have written, or sent, this epistle by Timothy. Thus, we observe, he was faithful to Paul, as long as Paul lived, and was especially dear to him.

What became of him after he left Paul, at Rome, we do not know, or where he spent the latter part of his life, or in what manner he died. As it is thought he was for many years the bishop of the church at Ephesus, he may have lived, and labored there, until he died.

TIRAS—[Ti′-ras.]

Tiras was one of the sons of Japheth. He is referred to in the generations of Noah as the seventh son of Japheth. Gen. x: 2. From Tiras, by a kind of general consent, it is reckoned the Thracians sprung. This people, we learn, were a very ignorant and idolatrous people, and exceedingly barbarous. They were divided into various tribes; and history informs us that the Greeks conquered them.

TIRHAKAH—[Tir-ha′-kah,] *inquirer, law made dull.*

Tirhakah was the king of Cush, in Arabia, or the Cush in Abysinia; and he is supposed to be referred to in Isaiah, xx: 4, &c., where the king of Assyria is represented as leading "the Egyptian prisoners, and the Ethiopian captives, young and old, naked and barefoot, even with their buttocks uncovered, to the shame of Egypt." But he is referred to by name in 2d Kings, xix: 9, as "Tirhakah, king of Ethiopia," who invaded

Sennacherib's kingdom at the time he was fighting against and trying to subdue Hezekiah and his kingdom. His object was to afford relief to Hezekiah or give him help against the Assyrians. But the Ethiopians and the Egyptians were taken prisoners, as we learn from the prophet Isaiah. The Jews were dispirited and terrified on account of it, but the Lord interfered and slew the hosts of Assyria. 2d Kings, xix: 35; Isa. xxxvii: 9–36.

TIRSHATHA—[Tir′-sha-tha,] *that overturns the foundation; in Syriac, that beholds time.*

TIRSHATHA was a name given to Zerrubbabel, the builder of the second temple, and also to Nehemiah, who rebuilt the walls of the sacred city. Ezra, ii: 63. "And the Tirshatha said unto them, that they should not eat of the most holy things till there stood up a priest with Urim and Thummim. See also Neh. x: 1, "And those that sealed were Nehemiah, the Tirshatha, &c." From both these quotations we may learn that the name was given both these persons, because of the work committed unto them, or the position they occupied as governors or overseers of the important work in which they were engaged. They were commissioners appointed by the Persian king to carry his orders to Jerusalem, and see that they were executed, hence they are both called the Tirshatha.

TIRZAH—[Tir′zah,] *benevolent, pleasant.*

TIRZAH was one of the five daughters of Zelophehad, who secured an additional law to the civil code of the Jews; a special enactment by which they were given an inheritance, and as heiresses, were not allowed to marry out of their own tribe, but were furnished with husbands from their father's brother's son. [See Hoglah.]

TITUS—[Ti′-tus,] *honorable.*

TITUS was an evangelist, eminent for his life and labors. He was a Gentile by birth, and though Timothy whose mother was a Jewess, and his father a Greek, was circumcised by Paul, yet Titus was never circumcised. Gal. ii: 3. "But neither Titus who was with me being a Greek was compelled to be circumcised." He became the attendant and assistant of the apostle Paul, and he honors him with the appellation of "partner and fellow-helper" in 2d Cor. viii: 23. He was a well-tried, and faithful helper of the apostle, one to whom he could confide the interests of the church. He therefore sent him to Corinth, giving him the strongest possible recommendations. The church received him cordially, and he labored acceptably and efficiently there, and returned to Macedonia to report his labors, and give Paul an account of the condition of the Corinthian church. The apostle was glad to receive Titus and especially comforted to hear the good report he made. 2d Cor. vii: 6. "Nevertheless God comforted us by the coming of Titus." Paul tells them how glad he was that they had been so kind. The church in Corinth had blessed Titus, and Titus had been a blessing to them. They had fully met his expectations and the expectations of Titus, for he had found them as a church, possessing all the excellencies that Paul had told him they possessed.

The apostle commended Titus for his faithful labors and earnest care for them, and desired his return to them. 2d Cor. viii: 6, 16. And it is quite likely that Titus and Luke were the bearers of Paul's 2d Epistle. We learn from Titus, i: 5, that Paul left him in Crete to settle the affairs of that church, and ordain elders in various cities, and as a guide for him in his important work, he set forth the qualifications for the ministry and gave him directions for life and doctrine. Paul wrote the epistle to Titus and sent it, claiming him as his "own son in the Gospel." Titus, i: 4. But the apostle sent after him to come and see him at Nicapolis, when he should send Tychicus and Artemus to supply his place awhile, and he bade him bring Zenas the lawyer, and Apollos with him. Titus, iii: 12, 13. In 2d Tim. iv: 10, we learn that Paul sent Titus to Dalmatia, and it is quite likely that he afterwards returned to Crete and labored there for several years. How long he labored, or where, after this, we do not know, or where he died.

TOB-ADONIJAH—[Tob′-ad-o-ny′-jah,] *my good God.*

He was one of the Levites sent by Jehoshaphat through the cities of Judah to teach the people the law of the Lord. 2d Chron. xvii: 8.

TOBIAH—[To-bi′-ah,] *the Lord is good.*

TOBIAH, the Ammonite, opposed the Jews very strenuously in their efforts to rebuild the temple and the walls of the city. He was associated with Sanballat, the Horonite. He is called in Neh. ii: 10, "the servant, the Ammonite." He seems to have been a joint governor with Sanballat, appointed by the Persian king. He mocked the Jews, and tried to prevent their completing the wall. We have a specimen of his mocking in Neh. iv: 3. "Now Tobiah, the Ammonite was by him, and he said: Even that which they build, if a fox go up, he shall even break down their stone wall." In Neh. vi: 1–12, we have an account of an effort that he made with Sanballat and Geshem to secure a conference with Nehemiah. Failing in this, they united in charging him with rebelling against the Persian king, and seeking to be made king himself. They then lay a snare, by hiring a false prophet, to put Nehemiah in fear, but they fail again. Tobiah then opens a secret correspondence with the nobles of Judah, and they in a treasonable manner carried on the correspondence. The Tirshatha discovers it and stops it. Neh. vi.

TOBIJAH—[To-bi′-jah.]

TOBIJAH was one of those of the captivity, who were with Zerubbabel after the second temple was built. There is an especial reference made to him in Zech. vi: 10–14. "Take of them of the captivity, even of Heldai, of Tobijah, and of Jedaiah, which are come from Babylon; and come thou the same day, and go into the house of Josiah, the son of Zephaniah." The prophet was ordered to take silver and gold, and make crowns and set them upon the head of the high priest, and upon the heads of Tobijah, Helem, Jedaiah and Hen. Thus was the glory of the Jewish priesthood hinted at, and the still greater glory of Christ and the christian dispensation.

TOGARMAH—[To-gar′-mah,] *which is all bone, strong.*

Was the son of Gomer and the grandson of Japheth. He is referred to in the genealogy of the sons of Noah. Gen. x: 3. There is difference of opinion as to who his descendants were; but it is quite likely that they are referred to in Ezek. xxvii: 14: "They of the house of Togarmah traded in thy fairs, with horses, and horsemen, and mules." If the allusion is to Togarmah, the son of Gomer, then his posterity traded with the Tyrians. From Ezek. xxxviii: 6, we learn that the posterity of Gomer and Togarmah will assist Gog and Magog against the Hebrews.

TOI—[To′-i,] *who wanders.*

TOI was the king of Hamath, in Syria. We have an account of him in 2d Sam. viii: 9–11. He was the friend of King David; and when David gained victories over Hadadezer, the king of Zobah, Toi sent congratulations to him. He did not send his salutations by some unimportant person, but he sent them by his own son Joram. The same is related in 1st Chron. xviii: 9, 10. It seems that the king of Zobah had warred with him and conquered him, and when he found that David had gained a victory over him he was exceedingly gratified, and not only congratulated him but made him rich presents. It is said "Joram brought with him vessels of silver, and vessels of gold, and vessels of brass," which David dedicated to the Lord, as he did the silver and gold that he took from various nations that he subdued.

TOLA, 1.—[To-′lah,] *worm, scarlet.*

TOLA was the eldest son of Issachar, one of the sons of Jacob. Gen. xlvi: 13. From Num. xxvi: 23, we learn he was the father of the Tolaites. The whole posterity of Issachar amounted to sixty-four thousand three hundred, and as there were but three other families named, the Punites, the Jashubites and Shimronites, it is likely the family of Tola was larger.

TOLA, 2.—*Worm, scarlet.*

TOLA was one of the judges of Israel. He was the tenth one that occupied this important position and succeeded Abimelech. Tola was the son of Puah, and the grandson of Dodo and he belonged to the tribe of Issachar. We have all that we can learn about him, in Judges, x: 1–2. It seems from the history of Israel as given in the book of Judges, that the various persons who served them in this capacity, were either before or after they became judges, deliverers of Israel. They avenged them of their adversaries. It is said in Judges, ii: 16: "The Lord raised up judges, which delivered them out of the hands of them that spoiled them."

It is quite likely that Tola performed signal deliverances for Israel, though they are not narrated. They had just passed through the strong and wicked reign of Abimelech. He restored peace and harmony in the land, and had prosperity during the twenty-three years of his reign, and when his successor, who was Jair, the Gileadite, came to be judge, the land was in peace and continued so the twenty-two years that he was judge.

The only thing further related of Tola, is, that he lived in Shamir, in Mount Ephraim, and that he died and was buried there.

TRYPHENA—[Tri-fe′-nah,] *delicate.*

TRYPHENA was one of two holy women mentioned in Rom. xvi: 12, saluted by the apostle: "Salute Tryphena and Tryphosa, who labor in the Lord." She was an assistant to the apostle in his great work. We may suppose she visited the sick, relieved the distressed, exhorted the feeble-minded, and strengthened the weak. She may have been, with the other holy women who are saluted as laborers in the Lord, a prophetess, and accustomed to pray and preach, for women did pray and prophesy, "having their heads covered."

TRYPHOSA—[Tri-fo′-sah,] *thrice shining.*

TRYPHOSA is associated with Tryphena as a co-laborer in the Lord with the apostle. Rom. xvi: 12. The two women occupied the same position in the church, and were abundant in labors.

TROPHIMUS—[Trof′i-mus,] *well educated.*

TROPHIMUS, with Tychicus, was a native of Asia, and with Sopater, Aristarchus and Secundus, and Gaius and Timothy, accompanied Paul when he would go into Macedonia. Acts, xx: 4. And when Paul went to Jerusalem to report his labors and successes to the apostles that were there, Trophimus was with him. Acts, xxi: 29. He seems to have been a traveling companion of Paul, for some time, and had been converted through his instrumentality. From 2d Timothy, iv: 20, we learn that he was taken sick while they were traveling together and the apostle left him awhile at Miletus.

TUBAL—[Tu′bal,] *the earth. confusion.*

TUBAL was the fifth son of Japheth. Gen. x: 2. We know but little, certainly, about him, for there is little said. He was, it is likely, the progenitor of a large tribe or tribes. And it is thought by some, that his descendants were associated with those of Meshech, his brother, as they seem to be reckoned together, for the phrase Meshech-Tubal is common in the scripture. See Ezekiel, xxxii: 26; xxxviii: 2–3; xxxix: 1. From these passages, we may suppose that the posterity of Tubal, with the posterity of his brother, are referred to and will act an important part against the people of God about the beginning of the millenium.

TUBAL-CAIN—[Tu′bal-ca′in,] *worldly possession, jealous of confusion.*

TUBAL-CAIN was the son of Lamech by his wife Zillah. Gen. iv: 22. He was the first worker in brass and iron. He was the first one to make cooking utensils and agricultural implements, that displayed any particular art. And he was the first one to make implements of war out of brass and iron.

It is thought that the Romans took their smith-god or vulcan from Tubal-cain. And it is thought to be quite reasonable—because of the import of the name, the occupation of the person, and the circumstances recorded regarding the Roman vulcan, viz: he had to wife Venus, which signifies beauty, and may answer to Naamah, the sister of Tubal-cain, which signifies beautiful.

TYCHICUS—[Tik′-i-kus,] *casual, happening.*

TYCHICUS was one of the primitive disciples, and, indeed, a noted evangelist, and companion of Paul. He, with several others, attended Paul when he went into Asia—Acts, xx: 4—and probably went with him to Jerusalem. Paul sent him to Ephesus with the epistle he wrote to the Ephesians. Eph. vi: 21: "But that ye also may know my affairs, and how I do, Tychicus, a beloved brother and faithful minister in the Lord, shall make known to you all things: whom I have sent unto you," &c. And when Paul wrote to Timothy the second Epistle, he informed him that he had sent Tychicus to Ephesus. 2d Tim. iv: 12. Paul also sent him to Colosse, and recommended him to the church as a faithful minister, and he sent the epistle to the church by him. Col. iv: 7. And he also sent him, in company with Artemus, to Crete, to fill the place of Titus while he should come to Nicopolis to see him. Some think that Paul appointed him as the successor of Titus to the church of Crete. Titus, iii: 12.

TYRANNUS—[Ty-ran′-nus,] *a prince, one that reigns.*

Is referred to in Acts, xix: 9, as a teacher at Ephesus, in whose school Paul preached. The apostle seems to have been permitted by Tyrannus to teach there daily for a long time; and the apostle's teaching was greatly blessed, for Jews and Greeks had an opportunity of hearing there the word of the Lord Jesus, and witnessing the astonishing miracles that God wrought by the hand of Paul.

UCAL—[Yew′-cal,] *power, prevalency.*

UCAL is a person referred to in Prov. xxx: 1. He is mentioned by the prophet Agur in connection with Ithiel, and the words of that prophet are addressed to them, "the prophecy the man spake unto Ithiel, even unto Ithiel and Ucal."

URI—[U′-ri,] *my light or fire.*

URI was the son of Hur and the father of the famous Bezaleel, who was appointed to construct the tabernacle, being "filled with the spirit of God, in wisdom and in understanding, and in knowledge, and in all manner of workmanship," etc. Ex. xxxi: 2. Uri was of the tribe of Judah and of the family of Pharez, who was in the line of the Messiah.

URIAH—[U-ri′-ah,] *the Lord is my light or fire.*

URIAH was a Hittite, and the husband of Bathsheba, who afterwards became David's wife, and the mother of Solomon, David's successor. He was one of the worthies of the king of Israel, an officer in his army, and was under Joab, when he fought with Ammon, and besieged the city of Rabbah. While the contest was going on between Joab and the enemies of Israel, David gave way to temptation, and committed the most wicked act of his life. And those sins against God were the occasion of the severest sorrow of his life. When he sent for Uriah to come to him from the army, his object was to screen the honor of Bathsheba and conceal his own crime. When he found he could not succeed, as he had hoped he would, he conceived murder in his heart, and wrote a letter to Joab, sending it by the hand of Uriah. That letter was virtually Uriah's death-warrant, and he bore it in his own hands to the commanding general: "Set ye Uriah in the front of the hottest battle, and retire ye from him that he may be smitten and die." Joab accordingly did so, assigning Uriah a place where he knew he would be in immediate danger, and it was not long until he was slain.

Joab thus sacrificed Uriah at the command of the king, but with him he sacrificed "some of the people of the servants of David." When the official report was made by Joab to David, and he was about to complain, they told him Uriah the Hittite, was dead also, and this pleased the king

When the news reached Bethsheba that her husband was slain, she mourned for him probably as was the custom, seven days, but David honored her by taking her as his wife. Uriah was certainly a brave, faithful, and an innocent, and incorruptible man. He refused while in the city to go home to his own house, and gave as his reason, "The ark of Israel and Judah abide in tents; and my lord Joab and the servants of my Lord, are encamped in the open fields, &c." He determined that he would sacrifice case and pleasure. "I will not indulge myself while all my fellow soldiers are enduring the hardships and fatigues of camp life, and the dangers of war; and even the ark of the Lord is exposed. 2d Sam. xi.

The murder of Uriah was charged upon David by Nathan the prophet. 2d Sam. xii: 9.

URIAS.

URIAS, or URIJAH was a true and faithful prophet, who warned the Jews of their approaching ruin, and affectionately admonished them to repent of their evil ways and turn to God. We have an account of him in Jer. xxvi: 20–23, from which we learn that he was the son of Shemaiah, of Kirjath-jearim. Jehoiakim was angry with him on account of his prophecies, and determined to put him to death. Urias heard of his purpose, and fled for his life into Egypt. The enraged king sent Elnathan and certain men into Egypt after him. They found him and brought him to Jehoiakim, who slew him with the sword, and cast his dead body into the graves of the common people—would not even allow him a prophet's burial.

URIJAH—[U-ri′-jah.]

URIJAH, or URIA. We have an account of this person in 2d Kings xvi: 10–16, from which we learn that he was an idolatrous priest, and in accordance with the wish of Ahaz, he made an idolatrous altar like the one that Ahaz saw at Damascus, when he went to meet the king of Assyria, and thanked him for his conquest of his enemies. In complying with the request of the king, Urijah committed sin against God, but especially did he commit sin in offering sacrifices on this altar instead of on the altar of his God.

UZ, 1—*Counsel; in Syriac, to fix.*

Uz was the elder son of Aram, one of the sons of Shem. There are three other sons mentioned in Gen. x: 23, viz., Hul, Gether, and Mash. The descendants of Uz are supposed to have peopled Syria, and were the founders of the city of Damascus. The descendants of Aram, the father of Uz were called Arameans, and afterward Syrians.

UZ, 2—*Counsel; in Syriac, to fix.*

Was the son of Dishan a Hosite, and is referred to in Gen. xxxvi: 28, with Aran his brother.

UZAL—[U′zal.]

UZAL was the 6th son of Joktan. He with his brothers it seems, from Gen. x: 30, had dwellings from "Mesha unto Sephar, a mount of the east."

UZZAH—[Uz′-zah,] *strength, a goat.*

UZZAH, with his brother Ahir, was the son of Abinadab, in whose house the ark of God was kept for a long time by the order of king David. We have an account in 2d Samuel, vi: of David going to Kirjath-jearim, with thirty thousand chosen men, to bring the ark up to Jerusalem. It had been in the house of Abinadab, and they took it out, and set it upon a new cart, and Uzzah and Ahio drove the cart. And when they came to a certain threshing-floor in the way, Uzzah put forth his hand to steady the ark, thereby violating a law that God gave to the Levites, by which they were forbidden, on pain of death, to touch it. For this offense of Uzzah, the Lord suddenly slew him. He fell down dead by the ark. It may be that he committed some other sin, but if he did we are not informed of it.

It is supposed that the garden in which king Amon was buried, was property that had belonged to this Uzzah during his life time. 2d Kings, xxi: 26.

UZZIAH—[Uz-zi′-ah,] *the strength of the Lord.*

UZZIAH was a king of Judah, called also Azariah. 2d Kings, xv. [See Azariah.]

UZZI—[Uz′-zi,] *my strength, my kid.*

UZZI was of the tribe of Levi, and in the line of the priests from Aaron to the captivity. 1st Chron. vi: 5.

UZZIEL, 1—[Uz-zi′-el,] *the strength of God.*

UZZIEL was one of the four sons of Kohath, and is referred to in the genealogy of the children of Levi. Ex. vi : 18. His three sons are referred to in verse twenty-two, Mishael, Elzaphan and Zithri. We learn from Lev. x : 4, that Uzziel was the uncle of Aaron, and his two sons Mishael and Elzaphan were commanded to carry Nadab and Abihu out of the sanctuary, where they had died for offering strange fire unto the Lord. Num. iii : 19; 1st Chron. vi : 2, 18.

UZZIEL, 2—*The strength of God.*

UZZIEL was the son of Bela. He with his brothers is reckoned a mighty man, or a man of valor. This Uzziel was of the tribe of Benjamin. See 1st Chron. vii : 7.

UZZIEL, 3—*The strength of God.*

UZZIEL was one of the sons of Heman, and is numbered among the officers of the temple, or rather among the singers and players of instrumental music. 1st Chron. xxv : 4, and the same person is referred to in 2d Chron. xxix : 14.

VAJEZATHA—[Va-jez′-a-thah.] The tenth son of Haman, the Jew's enemy. Est. ix : 9. He, with his brothers, at the request of Queen Esther, was hanged. They were all executed, and their bodies exposed as Haman's had been, that those who sought the destruction of the Jews might be filled with terror.

VASHNI—[Vash′-ni,] *the second.*

Was one of the sons of the prophet Samuel. 1st Chron. vi : 28. He is called Joel in verse 33, as also in 1st Sam. viii : 2. He was the first-born of Samuel, and an associate judge. [See Joel.]

VASHTI—[Vash′ti,] *that drinks, thread.*

VASHTI was the queen of Ahasuerus. We have an account of her in Esther, i : from which we learn that the king, her husband, in the third year of his reign, made a splendid feast to all his princes and nobles, during which he showed the riches and glories of his kingdom, and exalted himself among his people for one hundred and eighty days. Having made this feast to his princes, he followed it with a feast to all the people that were in the city of Shushan, his capital, and their feast lasted seven days, during which time he exhibited the grandeur and glory of his kingdom to the people, and permitted them to drink the royal wine, from the royal vessels, all of them who were disposed to drink. And those that were not disposed to drink were permitted to use their pleasure. And while Ahasuerus was thus making a feast to the men, Vashti made a feast to the women, for the men and women did not mix together in feasts in the east. About the close of the seven days feast that the king made to the men, and the feast that the queen made to the women, he gave an order to his seven chamberlains to bring Vashti before him with the crown royal upon her head, and show her beauty to the assembled multitude of men. This was to be the closing up of the king's great display. But Vashti thought it improper for her to be brought out thus and displayed. Her prudence and modesty was shocked at the idea of being exhibited before a crowd who had been engaged in revelry and bachanalian sports so long. She knew they were intoxicated with the display that had been made, and many of them were drunken, for they had drank freely of royal wine, day after day, and she refused to go at the king's command.

She showed a very large degree of courage in resisting the royal mandate, as well as commendable modesty. She must have known that she was running the risk of being deposed if not of losing her life. But she determined that she would rather give up the crown and her position as queen, than to be unchaste and immodest. The king must have had but little affection for her, for upon receiving her answer he turned to his wise men, as they were called, and asked what their advice was as to what he should do unto Vashti. One of them, answering for the rest, said, "Let there go a royal commandment from the king, and let it be written among the laws of the Persians and Medes, that Vashti come no more before the king Ahasuerus;

and let the king give her royal estate to another that is better than she." And Memucan, who gave this advice, gave as a reason for it, that Vashti had not only done wrong to the king but to all the princes and people throughout the province; for her deed was known or would be known to all the women, and they would despise their husbands and refuse to obey them, and give as a reason for it that the queen refused to obey the king. The king hearkened to his wise men and reduced Vashti to the position of a vassal, and after a time Esther was selected in her stead. Esther, ii: 17. [See Ahasuerus, Esther, &c.]

VOPHSI—[Vof'-si,] *fragment, diminution.*

He was of the tribe of Naphtali, and the father of Nahbi, who was selected by Moses as one of the spies of the land of Canaan. Num. xiii: 14.

ZAAVAN—[Za'-a-van.]
Was the son of Ezer, and the grand-son of Seir, the Horite. Gen. xxxvi: 27.

ZABAD, 1—Za'-bad,] *a dowry.*
A son of Nathan, born of the daughter of Sheshan. He occupies the position of a mighty man of David, and yet there is no record of great deeds performed by him. 1st Chron. xi: 41.

ZABAD, 2—*A dowry.*
Was an Ephraimite. 1st Chron. vii: 21.

ZABAD, 3—*A dowry.*
A son of Shimeath, an Ammonitess, one of the assassins of king Joash. 2d Chron. xxiv: 26.

ZABAD, 4—*A dowry.*
A man of Israel, of the sons of Zattu, who put away his strange wife at the command of Ezra. Ez. x: 27.

ZABAD, 5—*A dowry.*
One of the descendants of Hashum, who had married a foreign wife. Ez. x: 33.

ZABAD, 6—*A dowry.*
One of the sons of Nebo, whose name is mentioned under the same circumstances as the two preceding. Ezra x: 43.

ZABDI, 1—[Zab'-di,] *portion, dowry.*
Was the father of Carmi, and is referred to in Joshua vii: 1, &c., in the trespass of the Israelites in the matter of Achan, the son of Carmi. In 1st Chron. ii: 6, Zabdi is called Zimri. Judah had two sons by Tamar, viz: Pharez and Zerah, and Zabdi was the son of Zerah.

ZABDI, 2—*Portion, dowry.*
The Shiphmite, was placed by king David over the wine cellars. 1st Chron. xxvii: 27.

ZABUD—[Za'-bud.]
ZABUD was the son of Nathan and occupied the position, it is supposed, for King Solomon, of prime minister. It is said in 1st Kings, iv: 5, he "was principal officer and the king's friend."

ZACCUR, 1.
ZACCUR was of the tribe of Reuben, and the father of Shammua, who was selected as a spy from that tribe. Num. xiii: 3.

ZACCUR, 2.
ZACCUR was one of the sons of Asaph, and is numbered among the officers and singers that David separated for the sanctuary service. He, with his brothers, was probably a teacher of others. 1st Chron. xxv: 2, "which prophesied according to the order of the king."

ZACCHEUS—[Zak'-ke-us,] *pure, justified.*
ZACCHEUS was a chief publican who desired to see Christ, having heard of him as a noted man. Whether Zaccheus was a Jew or Gentile is not quite certain. We have our account of him in Luke, xix: 1–10, from which we learn that Jesus was passing from where he had been to Jerusalem, and in making the journey through Jericho this chief publican heard of him and was anxious to see him. He probably made unsuccessful efforts in the city on account of the crowd that gathered around Jesus—he being a man low of stature. He therefore passed on before the crowd and climbed up into a

sycamore tree by the roadside, where he could have a fair view of the distinguished stranger. To his astonishment, when Jesus reached a point in the way directly opposite the sycamore tree into which he had climbed, he stopped, and looking up, said, "Make haste and come down, for to-day I must abide at thy house." He had never spoken to Jesus, or had a sight of him before, and yet Jesus called him by name, and proposed thus to tax his hospitality by staying awhile at his house. Without any hesitancy he came down and took Jesus to his home. He was glad of the privilege of entertaining one so noted, and whom he was so anxious to become acquainted with. "He received him joyfully." The Jews murmured that he went with Zaccheus, "a man who was a sinner;" but in this was fulfilled his own declaration: "I came not to call the righteous but sinners to repentance."

The substance, even, of the conversation that Jesus had with Zaccheus is not given; but we may safely suppose that he talked with him about his spiritual and eternal interests. As a great Teacher he taught him spiritual lessons, for the publican became convinced of sin, and said to Jesus, "Behold, Lord, the half of my goods I give to the poor, and if I have taken anything from any man I restore him four-fold." I have not only a knowledge of sin, and a deep sense of guilt for my sins, but I am willing, so far as it is in my power, to make restitution for any injury I have done. Jesus then told Zaccheus, in substance, that his repentance and faith were genuine, and that he was accepted; and turning to his disciples, he said, "This day is salvation come to this house, forasmuch as he also is a son of Abraham."

ZACHARIAH—[Zak-a-ri′-ah,] *memory of the Lord.*

ZACHARIAH, or ZECHARIAH, was the son of the second Jeroboam, and succeeded his father to the throne of Israel. 2d Kings, xiv: 29. The reign of Zachariah was short; and it was a wicked reign, for it is said: "And he did that which was evil in the sight of the Lord, as his fathers had done. He departed not from the sins of Jeroboam, the son of Nebat, who made Israel to sin." Because of his wickedness he was, we may suppose, unpopular with the people, for it is said of Shallum, the son of Jabesh, that he smote Zachariah before the people. Many of them were engaged, it may be, in the conspiracy, and hence made no objection, but rather helped him to murder the king; and then they made Shallum king in the stead of Zachariah.

It is supposed that when Jeroboam died Zachariah was but an infant, and hence that several years elapsed from the death of the father until the son was crowned king. Some say it was twenty-three years, others (and the general opinion is) that it was only eleven years. But there was a prophecy made to Jehu that his sons should sit on the throne of Israel to the fourth generation. 2d Kings, x: 30. And this was fulfilled. Jehoahaz, Joash, Jeroboam, and Zachariah succeed Jehu. The same thing is referred to in Hosea, i: 4: "I will avenge the blood of Jezreel upon the house of Jehu." In the death of Zachariah by Shallum we see the prediction fulfilled, and the house of Jehu fails. Zachariah, the last of the family of Jehu, fell cruelly murdered among his people.

ZACHARIAS—[Zach-a-ri′-as.]

ZACHARIAS was a priest of the course of Abia and the father of John the Baptist. We may learn the entire scripture account of him from Luke, i. "He and his wife Elisabeth were both righteous before God, walking in all the commandments and ordinances of the Lord blameless." From this passage we are assured that they were eminently righteous. Elisabeth the wife of Zacharias had no children, and about fifteen months before our Savior was born, the angel of the Lord appeared unto Zacharias near the temple altar, while the priest was burning incense there. It was the angel Gabriel, and he assured the priest that his wife who had so long been barren, should have a son, and that his name should be called John, and further, that "the child should be great in the sight of the Lord, and should drink neither wine nor strong drink." He was informed that this child should be the messenger or forerunner of Messiah. Zacharias refused fully to credit the message of the angel, and for that refusal the angel told him he should be struck dumb, and remain so until the prediction regarding the birth of John should be fulfilled; and immediately he became dumb, and as he passed out of the temple he made signs to the people who were worshiping in the court, that he had seen a vision. When Zacharias had served his time at the altar, he went home and probably informed Elisabeth of the vision he had seen, and of the words of the angel. He continued to be without the power of speech until the child was born, and even then he was not restored, until a controversy was sprung between Elisabeth and her friends, as to the name of the child. She insisted that it should be named John. It is possible that Zacharias had in some way told her that the angel that appeared unto him, had said his name should be called John. The friends agreed with Elisabeth to submit the naming of the child to the father. They accordingly consulted him with signs, and he wrote that he should be called John. And immediately he recovered his speech, and broke out in rapturous strains of praise to God for the ground-work of faith that he now had for the speedy coming of Messiah; and as he looked upon the babe in its mothers arms, he prophesied that it should become a mighty teacher, and by his instructions should prepare the way of the Lord, by preparing the nation of the Jews to receive the Messiah.

ZADOK—[Za′dok,] *just, justified.*

ZADOK was the son of Ahitub. He was a priest and prophet, or seer. 2d Samuel, xv: 24–27. Zadok and Abiathar, who escaped from the city of the priests when Saul slaughtered them because that David had been befriended, were a sort of high priests in the time of David's reign. But Zadok seems to be the principal one, for David consulted him mostly. It may be, because he was a prophet as well as a priest.

When David fled from Jerusalem, on account of the rebellion of Absalom, Zadok had the ark borne as far as the brook Kidron, by the Levites. They evidently intended to take the ark on with David, but the king asked Zadok to carry the ark back again into the city. He was unwilling to have it exposed or borne away from Jerusalem. He accordingly, in company with Abiathar, carried the ark back again, and remained with them, that they might gather all the information regarding the rebellion that they could, and send it the king in the wilderness. He had a son whose name was Ahimaaz, and Abiathar had a son whose name was Jonathan; they also returned with them with a view of being couriers between Jerusalem and David's retreat. When Hushai, the Archite, David's particular friend, met him with his clothes rent, and earth upon his head, deeply affected by the sad calamity of the king, David, in his distress, appreciated the sympathy and kindness of Hushai, but he bade him return to Jerusalem, and defeat the counsel of Ahithophel, referring him to the fact that he would find Zadok and Abiathar, the priests there, in whom he might confide, for they would be ready to render him any assistance they could in favoring him, and the two sons of the priests would convey intelligence to him. 2d Sam. xvi: and xvii. When the battle was over, and Absalom was dead, Zadok and Abiathar spake unto the elders of Judah, that they should bring David back to Jerusalem at once, and they united in sending for David to return. 2d Sam. xix: 11–15. Zadok continued with David till the end of his reign, and when his successor was to be appointed David said, "Call me Zadok, the priest, and Nathan, the prophet, and Benaiah, the son of Jehoiada, and they came before the king." He then bade them prepare for the coronation ceremonies. "Cause Solomon, my son, to ride upon mine own mule, and bring him down to Gihon, and let Zadok the priest, and Nathan the prophet, anoint him king over Israel." They did as they were commanded, and Zadok poured the anointing oil upon the head of Solomon. 1st Kings, i. Thus we see, while Abiathar went with Adonijah, Zadok, after serving David through his reign, was honored by king Solomon. 1st Kings ii: 35—"put in the room of Abiathar," i. e., he came to be sole high priest after Abiathar's confinement, and was succeeded in the office by Ahimaaz, his son. 1st Chron. vi: 8.

And it would seem from 2d Chron. xxvii: 1, that there was another Zadok whose daughter Jerushah was the wife of king Uzziah, and the mother of Jotham.

It was probably the posterity of the Zadok who served in the priest's office during the reigns of David and Solomon, that is referred to in Ezekiel, xliv: 15: "But the priests, the Levites, the sons of Zadok, that kept the charge of my sanctuary when the children of Israel went astray from me, they shall come near to me to minister unto me; and they shall stand before me to offer unto me the fat of the blood, saith the Lord God. They shall enter into my sanctuary, and they shall come near to my table to minister unto me, and they shall keep my charge."

ZAHAM—[Za′-ham,] *crime, impurity.*

He was one of the sons of Rehoboam, born unto him of one of the wives he took in the family of David. 2d Chron. xi: 19.

ZALMON—[Zal′-mon,] *his shade, obscurity.*

He was an Ahohite, and one of David's mighty men. 2d Samuel, xxiii: 28.

ZALMUNNA—[Zal-mun′-nah,] *shadow, image.*

Zalmunna was a king of Midian, who, with Zebah, another king, was pursued by Gideon after the battle on the plains of Moab. Judg. viii: 4–12. Gideon, with his three hundred men, had passed over Jordan, "faint yet pursuing" the two Midianite kings, and he asked loaves of bread of the men of Succoth for his starving soldiery, and they refused it. He then told them after he returned he would punish them. He then asked bread of the men of Penuel, and they also refused. He threatened them with punishment also on his return, which threat he afterwards fulfilled to the letter.

Gideon overtook Zebah and Zalmunna with their host, and discomfitted them, bringing the two kings back with him, probably, as far as Succoth and Penuel. He questioned them as to some acts of violence they had committed at Tabor in murdering some of his relatives. At first the warrior bade Jether, his son, slay them, but he was a youth and afraid; therefore Gideon himself drew his sword and slew them both, and stripped their camels of the rich ornaments that were about their necks.

ZAPHNATH-PAANEAH—[Zaf′-nath-pa-a-ne′-ah,] *one that discovers hidden things; in the Egyptian tongue, a savior of the world.*

Was a name that Pharaoh, the king of Egypt, gave to Joseph after he had promoted him to be steward or superintendent of all his affairs, and placed upon him the badges of his new office. Gen. xli: 45.

ZEBADIAH, 1—Zeb-a-di′-ah,] *portion of the Lord.*

Was one of the sons of Shelamiah. He was one of the sacred porters. 1st Chron. xxvi: 2.

ZEBADIAH, 2—*Portion of the Lord.*

The son of Asahel, is reckoned in the course of his father when the monthly service was instituted. 1st Chronicles, xxvii: 7.

ZEBAH or ZIBA—[Ze′-bah,] *victim, immolation.*

Zebah was an associate with Zalmunna, as a king of Midian, who was pursued by Gideon, overtaken and discomfitted, and afterwards slain with the sword by the conqueror. Jud. viii: 10, 21. (See Salmunna.)

ZEBEDEE—[Zeb′-be-dee.]

Zebedee was father of the two apostles, James and John. Matt. iv: 21; and x: 2; Mark, i: 19, 20. The usual phrase in designating these two apostles is, "James, the son of Zebedee, and John his brother." He was a fisherman and was engaged with the sons in mending his nets when Jesus called them to be apostles.

ZEBUDAH—[Ze-bu′-dah.]

Zebudah was the daughter of Pedaiah of Rumah, and the mother of Jehoiakim. 2d Kings, xxiii: 36.

ZEBUL—[Ze′-bul,] *a habitation.*

Zebul was governor of the city of Shechem, appointed by Abimelech. When Gaal, the son of Ebed, conspired against Abimelech, Zebul heard of it, and his wrath was kindled and he immediately sent Abimelech word of the conspiracy, and of the fortifications that Gaal was preparing around the city, and he suggested to Abimelech to come up by night and lay in ambush until morning near the city, and then suddenly come upon Gaal and his forces. Early in the morning Gaal saw the approach of Abimelech and his men in the distance, and turning to Zebul, the governor, he said, "Behold there came down people from the top of the mountains." Zebul knew it was the approach of Abimelech, but he said to Gaal, "thou seest the shadow of the mountains as if they were men." But after a little while Gaal saw them coming down "by the middle of the land," and a large company coming by the plain. He now saw that it was Abimelech and his forces. Zebul referred him to what he had said about Abimelech, and told him to go out and fight with him, and he did, and only saved his life by flight. After this Zebul, the governor of the city, thrust him out, and would not let him remain in Shechem. Judges, ix: 28, 41.

ZEBULUN—[Zeb'-u-lun,] *dwelling, habitation.*

Zebulun was the sixth son of Jacob by his wife Leah, hence was one of the twelve patriarchs. His birth is announced in Gen. xxx: 20. When he was born his mother said: "God hath endowed me with a good dowry; now will my husband dwell with me, because I have borne him six sons; and she called his name Zebulun." In this language she alludes to the fact that Jacob dwelt mostly with Rachel. His position, as the sixth son of Leah, is given in Gen. xxxv: 23. The sons of Zebulun are referred to in Gen. xlvi: 14. They were Sered, Elon, and Jahleel; and from them sprung a numerous posterity. There were fifty-seven thousand four hundred warriors when they went out of the land of Egypt. Num. i: 30, 31. In Gen. xlix: 13, we have the dying father's prophetic benediction respecting the offspring of Zebulun: "Shall dwell at the haven of the sea; and he shall be for a haven of ships; and his border shall be unto Zidon." This prophetic declaration seems to be fulfilled in the inheritance that was given to Zebulun when the land of Canaan was divided. Joshua, xix: 10, &c.

When they went out of the land of Egypt the tribe of Zebulun was commanded by Eliab, the son of Elon; and the one that was sent as a spy to search the land of Canaan was Gaddiel, the son of Sodi, and their prince to divide the land was Elizaphan, the son of Panach. Num. xxvi: 23, 24; also xxxiv: 25. Their inheritance gave them a large amount of sea coast, and they carried on an extensive sea trade. They also had extensive fisheries, and were engaged in the manufacture of glass. It is said, in Deut. xxxiii: 19: "They shall call the people unto the mountain; there they shall offer sacrifices of righteousness; for they shall suck of the abundance of the seas, and of treasures hid in the sand." By this we may understand that they shall grow wealthy by their merchandise, and by their inventive genius they shall gather wealth, as well as notoriety, by manufacturing glass from the sand. It is understood that the tribe of Zebulun had revealed unto them the treasures of the sand by learning the method of manufacturing glass.

We learn from Judges, i: 30, that Zebulun did not drive out the Canaanites from at least two cities in their inheritance, Kitron and Nahalol, but they made the people dwelling in them tributaries to them.

When Deborah arose as a judge in Israel, Zebulun, with Naphtali, went up to the number of ten thousand men, and they were very active in routing the hosts of Jabin. Judges, iv: 10. And in the song of Deborah, Judges, v: 18, we have the following language: "Zebulun and Naphtali were a people that jeoparded their lives unto the death in the places of the field." And in Judges, vi: 35, we learn that they rallied to the help of Gideon against the Midianites and Amalekites; and the children of the East Gideon sent messages to them, as also to Manasseh, Asher and Naphtali, and they came up to meet him and assist him.

One of the judges of Israel, Elon, was a Zebulunite, as we learn from Judges, xii: 11, and he judged Israel fourteen years.

The tribe of Zebulun continued to be extensive for many years, for when David was coronated or crowned king of Israel, in Hebron, there were fifty thousand of the tribe that were true men—"they were not of double heart"—that brought large quantities of provisions to him, and united in turning the kingdom of Saul to him. 1st Chron. xii; 33. And they are mentioned in connection with Benjamin and Naphtali, by the Psalmist in the following language, Psalm, lxviii: 27, "There is little Benjamin with their rulers, the princes of Judah, and their counsel, the princes of Zebulun, and the princes of Naphtali."

When king Hezekiah invited all Israel to join him in holding a Passover to the Lord, he sent posts or messengers with his proclamation all over the country, from Dan to Beersheba, and though the messengers were generally mocked in Zebulun, as in other tribes, yet there were several who humbled themselves of the tribe of Zebulun, and came to Jerusalem, and entered heartily into Hezekiah's reformation. 2d Chron. xxx: 11.

The country inhabited by this tribe was blessed, and it is referred to by the prophet, Isaiah, ix: 1, 2, in his prophecy of Christ's birth, and the establishment of his kingdom. Their country was blessed with the instructions of the Great Teacher, and many of his miracles were performed there. Indeed, Capernaum, his "own city," was upon the sea coast in the borders of Zebulun and Naphtali, Matthew, iv: 12, and several of the disciples of Christ were gathered up by him from their original inheritance.

ZECHARIAH, 1—[Z e k´-a-r i-a h,] *memory of the Lord.*

Zechariah was the son of Jehoiada, the high priest of the Jews, and he is supposed to be the same person as Azariah. In 1st Chron. vi: 10, it is said, "Azariah executed the priest's office in the temple that Solomon built in Jerusalem." But whether Azariah was the same person or not, it is said in 2d Chron. xxiv: 20, Zechariah was the son of Jehoiada, the high priest, and that the spirit of God came upon him, and he stood above the people and charged their idolatry and wickedness upon them. He shunned not to charge the king's wickedness upon him; Joash became so enraged at the faithful prophet's warning that he ordered him to be stoned in the court of the house of the Lord. Zechariah's warning was in the following language: "Why transgress ye the commandment of the Lord that ye cannot prosper? because ye have forsaken the Lord, he hath also forsaken you." We must look upon Joash as a very contemptible and mean man to give an order thus to slay a prophet, and when we consider that Jehoiada, the father of Zechariah, had saved Joash from being murdered, and administered the government for him when he was too young to administer it for himself. (See Joash and Jehoiada.) But when Zechariah was dying he told them to rest assured that the Lord would avenge his death. 2d Chron. xxiv: 22. We may consider this person a true martyr to his religion, and to his profession as a prophet. See Matt. xxiii: 35. "That upon you may come all the righteous blood shed upon the earth, from the blood of righteous Abel, unto the blood of Zacharias, son of Barachias, whom ye slew between the temple and the altar." It is supposed that this Zechariah, the son of Jehoiada, is the one referred to by our Lord, and his cruel murder is brought to the remembrance of the Jews.

ZECHARIAH, 2—*Memory of the Lord.*

Zechariah was the son of Jebere-chiah or Barachiah. In 2d Chron. xxvi: 5, it is said of him "that he had understanding in the visions of God" by which we may understand that he could give the true interpretations of divine prophecies. He prophesied in the days of Uzziah and encouraged him to the practice of piety; and when he attempted to offer incense, it is quite likely that this Zechariah withstood him as did many others. He was one of the faithful witnesses referred to by name in Isa. viii: 2, that attested the prophet's writing concerning Maher-shalalhash-baz. "And I took unto me faithful witnesses to record, Uriah the priest, and Zachariah the son of Jebercheiah."

ZECHARIAH, 3 — *Memory of the Lord.*

ZECHARIAH or Zachariah was one of the twelve minor prophets. It seems that he returned from Babylon with Zerubbabel and while quite a young man began to prophecy. In Ezra, v: 1, we learn that Haggai and Zechariah the son of Iddo prophesied unto the Jews that were in Judea and Jerusalem. In his prophecies he exhorts the people to repentance and encourages them to build the temple. He had various visions which he made known to Zerubbabel and his builders, such as the vision of the four horns and four carpenters; the measuring of Jerusalem; the vision of Joshua, the high priest, with his associate priests; the type of the golden candlestick with the flying roll—and the vision of four chariots. He saw Heldai, Tobijah and Jedaiah, as well as Joshua crowned with crowns of silver and gold by which the glory of the New Testament church is set forth, Zech. iii, iv, v and vi. In the vii and viii he directs the Jews concerning the duty of fasting, and he presses upon them a variety of moral duties. They were to practice mercy and compassion, the one toward the other, and especially were to regard the wants of the widow and the fatherless, with the stranger and the poor, and be sure not to oppress them, etc. He predicts various wars—and the birth and sufferings in life of the Messiah. He predicts clearly the ruin of the Jewish Church, and the promulgation of the glorious truths of the gospel to the Gentiles, and he contemplates and predicts the glorious millennial era. He closes up his prophecies by declaring regarding the latter day that "there shall be upon the bells of the horses, holiness unto the Lord, and the pots in the Lord's house shall be like bowls before the altar." Zech. xiv: 20.

ZECHARIAH, 4 — *Memory of the Lord.*

Was one of the sons of Hosah, and one of the sacred porters. 1st Chron. xxvi: 11.

ZECHARIAH, 5 — *Memory of the Lord.*

Was the son of Shelamiah, and like his father, one of the sacred porters. He was the keeper of the northern gate. 1st Chron. xxvi: 14. He is also supposed to have been captain of a thousand men. 1st Chron. xxiii: 5.

ZEDEKIAH, 1—[Zed-e-ki′-ah,] *the Lord is my justice.*

ZEDEKIAH was the son of Josiah and the last of the Kings of Judah. His mother's name was Hamutal, the daughter of Jeremiah, of Libnah. He succeeded Jehoiachim as king, by the appointment of the King of Babylon, and the King of Babylon changed his name from Mattaniah to Zedekiah. 2d Kings xxiv: 17, &c. He began his reign when he was twenty-one years of age, and it continued eleven years. We are informed as to the character of Zedekiah as a king, "he did evil in the sight of the Lord, according to all that Jehoiakim had done." Though he had sworn to be tributary to the King of Babylon, who had appointed him king, he violated his obligations, and rebelled against him. Though he was faithfully warned from God by the prophet Jeremiah, and other prophets, he and his people refused to hear the warnings; and it is said in 2d Chron. xxxvi: 16, "They mocked the messengers of God, and despised his words, and misused his prophets, until the wrath of the Lord arose against his people, till there was no remedy." Both the king and his people, hardened their hearts, and indulged in gross idolatry, and other impieties. We have the fact set forth, as to the character of Zedekiah and the people of Judah, in Ezek. xvii: 13; there Zedekiah is said to have despised an oath that he took, and broke a covenant that he made, for which the Lord said he should not escape, but should die. We have an account in Jer. xxix, of a deputation sent to the King of Babylon by Zedekiah, probably with his first year's tribute; Elasah, the son of Shaphan, and Gemariah, the son of Hilkiah; and the prophet Jeremiah, sent letters to the captives in Babylon, by these messengers.

And in the fourth year of Zedekiah's

reign he went into Babylon in person in company with Seraiah; and Jeremiah sent prophecies by the hand of Seraiah into Babylon, and bade him read them, and then cast the roll with a stone fastened to it into the river Euphrates, that it might sink there; and then declared the sinking of the stone with the roll of prophecies against Babylon attached to it, emblematic of the destruction that should come upon Babylon, from which she should not recover. Jer. li: 59, &c.

It was in the ninth year of Zedekiah's reign, that he broke the solemn treaty with Nebuchadnezzar, and entered into a league with Pharaoh-hophrah, of Epypt, and other nations. He procured their assistance to throw off the yoke which was upon him and his people. As soon as Nebuchadnezzar, the King of Babylon, learned this he marched a large army into the country of Judea, and laid siege to Jerusalem. The captivity of Zedekiah was clearly foretold by the prophet Jeremiah. Jer. xxxiv: 1. And the prophet Ezekiel refers to the same thing. Ezek. xii: 8-21-26.

It seems that Zedekiah became alarmed when he found that the king of Babylon had laid siege to Jerusalem, and in his alarm he sent for the prophet Jeremiah to enquire of the Lord for him. As soon as the messenger that the king sent to the prophet reached him, they delivered their message to him, and the prophet promptly answered him, boldly setting forth the dreadful calamity that was coming upon Jerusalem, her people, and her king. Jer. xxi, xxvii, xxxix; 2d Kings, xxv. From these prophecies and declarations we learn that though Nebuchadnezzar raised the siege of Jerusalem in order to beat back the Egyptians,—thereby giving Jerusalem and its inhabitants a respite,—yet he returned, and a second time laid siege to the city until he conquered and took it. The prophet Jeremiah counseled the king Zedekiah to give up and submit himself to the mercy of the king of Babylon, for God had determined that Jerusalem should be taken. The king of Judah would not follow his counsels, cease his rebellion, and surrender himself up. The consequence of his refusal was, he brought upon himself greater misery and ignominy.

The city was finally taken. Zedekiah, with a number of his soldiery, fled in the night; but the Chaldeans pursued and overtook them near Jericho, or in the plains of Jericho. Jer. xxxix: 5. They then brought Zedekiah a prisoner to Nebuchadnezzar at Riblah, and the conquering king gave judgment against him. He then put Zedekiah's children to death, and the nobles and princes of Judah, before his eyes; after which Nebuchadnezzar put out Zedekiah's eyes, and had him bound with chains and carried to Babylon, where, after suffering for some time, he died, and was buried by his friends, or honorably interred, as the prophet had said he should be.

ZEDEKIAH, 2—*The Lord is my justice.*

Was a false prophet referred to in 1st Kings, xxii: 11-24. He was the son of Chenaanah, who persuaded Ahab to go up against Ramoth-gilead. Micaiah, a true prophet, declared Zedekiah a false prophet. At this he became angry and smote Micaiah on the cheek, and then insultingly said, "Which way went the spirit of the Lord to speak unto thee." The true prophet answered him by saying, "Behold, thou shalt see in that day, when thou shalt go into an inner chamber to hide thyself"—probably referring prophetically to some judgment of God that afterwards fell upon Zedekiah.

ZEDEKIAH, 3—*The Lord is my justice.*

Was the son of Maaseiah. Jer. xxix: 21, 22. It is said of him he prophesied a lie in the name of the Lord, and for it should be delivered into the hands of Nebuchadnezzar, and should be slain. We may suppose that he died the horrible death of "being roasted in the fire."

ZEEB—[Ze′-eb,] *wolf.*

Zeeb, with Oreb, is referred to in Judges, vii: 25. They were princes of Midian who fled before Gideon after the great battle in the plain of Moab. Under the command of Gideon, the Ephraimites watched at the fords of Jordan where the Midianites would be likely to cross on their way to their own country; and the children of Ephraim slew many of them, and found the two princes hid—one of them in a cavern of a rock and the other in the vat of a winepress, and they were both slain. Oreb was slain at the rock Oreb, and Zeeb "was slain at the winepress of Zeeb." The Ephraimites then brought their heads to Gideon on the other side of Jordan.

ZELEK—[Ze′-lek,] *the noise of him that laps.*

He was an Ammonite, and one of David's mighty men. 2d Samuel, xxiii: 37.

ZELOPHEHAD—[Ze-lo′-fe-had,] *The shade or tingling of fear.*

ZELOPHEHAD was the son of Hepher, and is referred to in Numbers, xxvii: 1, &c. He had no sons, but when he died left behind him five daughters. They were Mahlah, Noah, Hoglah, Milcah, and Tirzah. He was of the tribe of Manasseh, and died in the wilderness; but he did not die, as many of the Israelites did, for some particular sin committed. So his daughters say, when they make application to Moses for an inheritance in Canaan as heirs to their father, there being no son left. The Lord approved of their demand and Moses granted their request. So there was a special enactment provided to meet their case. They were required to marry such as were of the tribe of Manasseh, to which they belonged, so that the inheritance of their father should not be alienated from his tribe. See, also, Num. xxxvi, where we have the case of the daughters of Zelophehad presented by certain chiefs of the tribe of Joseph; and the matter was settled by Zelophehad's daughters marrying their cousins, or their "father's brothers' sons." Thus his inheritance was retained by his own children and continued in his own tribe.

ZELOTES—[Ze′lo-tes,] *jealous, full of zeal.*

Was the surname of one of the apostles, viz: Simon, the Canaanite. He is called Simon Zelotes. Luke, vi: 15. [See Simon, the Canaanite.]

ZENAS—[Ze′nas,] *living.*

ZENAS was a pious man who is referred to by Paul in his epistle to Titus, iii: 13. He is the only pious lawyer we read of in the scriptures. When the apostle was at Nicapolis, and Titus was about to make him a visit, he wrote, "Bring Zenas, the lawyer, and Apollos on their journey diligently;" from which we may judge that he was a noted christian, and an associate of the eloquent Appollos.

ZEPHANIAH—[Zef-a-ni′ah,] *the Lord is my secret, the mouth of the Lord.*

ZEPHANIAH was one of the minor prophets who lived and prophesied in the time of Josiah, the king of Judah. We learn from Zephaniah, i: 1. that he was the son of Cush, or Cushi, and the grandson of Gedaliah. He uttered a prophecy against Josiah, the king, because he allowed his children, when they grew up, to wear clothing like unto the princes of other nations, or robes of a foreign fashion. "They are clothed with strange apparel." In the first chapter of his prophecies, Zephaniah declares God's judgments against Judah. In the second, exhorts them to repentance, and in the third, utters sharp reproof against Jerusalem and its inhabitants.

ZEPHANIAH, 2—*The Lord is my secret, the mouth of the Lord.*

ZEPHANIAH was a deputy high priest under Seraiah, or a second priest. He is referred to in 2d Kings, xxv: 18. Here Nebuzar-adan, the captain of the guard, is represented as taking Zephaniah with Seraiah, and three door keepers, and a military officer, and five of the king's body-guard, and attendants, with the king's scribe, and sixty men of the people, and sending them to Riblah, where they were put to death by the king of Babylon. We have an account of Zephaniah in Jeremiah, xxi: 1, and xxxvii: 2. He is named as one of those by whom Zedekiah, the king, sent messages to the prophet Jeremiah, and requests for his prayers in behalf of him, and also of his kingdom. We learn from Jeremiah, xxix: 24–29, that Shemaiah sent letters unto Zephaniah, the son of Maasiah the priest, accusing Jeremiah of Anathoth, of being a madman, and deserving to be put in prison, and kept fast in stocks. Zephaniah read the letter in the ears of Jeremiah. Whether he was the Zephaniah who is referred to in Zechariah, vi: 10–14, as the father of Josiah, and the father of Hen, who were priests, we do not know. It is thought he lived too early to be the father of those priests.

ZEPHO—[Ze′-fo,] *that sees and observes.*

Was the son of Eliphaz, and the grandson of Esau. Gen. xxxvi: 11.

ZEPHON—[Ze′-fon.]

Or Ziphion, was a Gadite, and the head of the Zephonites, one of the powerful families of that tribe. Num. xxvi: 15. It seems from his position as given here, as well as the order of the children of Gad, as given in Gen. xlvi: 16, that he was the eldest son of his father.

ZERAH, 1—[Ze′-rah,] *east, brightness.*

Also called Zohar, was a son of Simeon. Gen. xlvi: 10. He was the fifth son, and we learn from Num. xxvi: 13, that he was the father of the Zarhites.

ZERAH, 2—*East, brightness.*

ZERAH was a powerful king of Ethiopia or Cush, who invaded Judah and was defeated by King Asa. The account of this invasion is given in 2d Chron. xiv: 9–15. Here we learn that Zerah had a host of fighting men, for they numbered one million, and besides he had three hundred chariots. The Lord interfered for Asa and smote the Ethiopians, so that they were conquered and fled before Judah, and the most of them were cut off. "Asa and the people pursued them unto Gerer, and the Ethiopians were overthrown that they could not recover themselves, for they were destroyed before the Lord and before his host; and they carried away much spoil."

ZERAH, 3—*East, brightness.*

Was of the tribe of Levi, and in the line of the priests from Aaron to the captivity. 1st Chron. vi: 21.

ZERAHIAH—[Zer-a-hi′-ah.]

Was of the tribe of Levi, and in the line of the priests from Aaron to the captivity. 1st Chron. vi: 6.

ZERESH — [Ze′-resh,] *misery, stranger.*

ZERESH was the wife of Haman, the enemy of the Jews. She is first introduced to our notice in Est. v: 10. Haman had attended a banquet of Esther in company with the king, and was overjoyed at the honor. But in addition to the first, he was invited to a second banquet on the morrow, and when he arrived at home that night he called together his friends and his wife Zeresh, to counsel with them as to what he should do to rid himself of Mordecai, the Jew, whom he could not bear to let live until the day of general slaughter. Zeresh, his wife, gave him counsel, and his friends joined her to the effect that a gallows be erected on which to hang Mordecai the next day. Haman adopted her counsel and made the gallows, but the next day passed away and the Jew was not executed; but in the stead the greatest honor had been conferred upon him. And Haman had been compelled to confer it in carrying out the king's wishes.

That day when the proud officer came home and reported what had taken place to his wife Zeresh, and all his friends, they seemed to join with Haman in his mourning, and they gave him an expression that indicated that they had dreadful forebodings of coming ill. "If Mordecai be of the seed of the Jews before whom thou hast begun to fall, thou shalt not prevail against him, but shall surely fall before him."

It was not long until the worst fears of Zeresh were realized, for the intelligence reached her before that day closed, that her husband was condemned to death, and that he was to be executed on the gallows that had been erected on which to hang the despised Jew. It was not long until the widow of Haman found that the ten sons were all slain. Thus she was left childless, as well as a widow. How long she survived this calamity, we do not know. It is probable that after it was found out that she counseled her husband to hang Mordecai, (if it was found out) that she too was slain by those who had put her husband and sons to death.

ZERI—[Ze′ri.]

Was also called Izri, and was one of the sons of Jeduthan, and when the lots were cast, and the singers were divided into twenty-four courses, the fourth lot came to him. 1st Chron. xxv: 3–11.

ZERUAH—[Ze-ru′ah,] *leprous, hornet.*

Was the mother of Jeroboam, the son of Nebat, who was employed at first by Solomon to superintend some of his improvements, and was afterwards the king of the revolted tribes. Zeruah was a widow woman. 1st Kings, xi: 26.

ZERUBBABEL—[Ze-rub′-ba-bel,] *banished, a stranger at Babylon, dispersion of confusion.*

ZERUBBABEL was the son of Salathiel and of the royal line of David. His position in the royal family is given clearly in the genealogy of Christ by Matthew, i: 12, where he is called Zorobabel. In Luke, iii: 27, he is called the son of Salathiel, as he is also in the former quotation, from which we may understand that Shealtiel and Salathiel are the same person.

Zerubbabel is mentioned in Ezra, ii: 2, as at the head, or in command of those who returned from Babylon. There were the children of the priests, the Levites, the singers, the porters, the servants of Solomon, and with them a great many who could not find their genealogy, or their family registers. In verses sixty-four and sixty-seven, we learn of the number of those who returned from Babylon; there were forty-two thousand three hundred and sixty, besides their servants, and the maids of whom there were seven thousand three hundred and twenty-seven. There were two hundred singing men, and singing women; and they had with them seven hundred and thirty-six horses, and two hundred and forty-five mules, four hundred and thirty-five camels, and six thousand seven hundred and twenty asses, besides a large amount of gold and silver and rich stuffs.

The Chaldean name of this person, was Sheshbazzar. Ezra, i: 8–11, and v: 14–16. Zerubbabel not only led this mighty host from Babylon to Judea, (having under his charge the valuables of the Chaldean king, sent by him, consisting of sacred vessels, gold, silver, &c.) But soon after he reached his native land, and saw again the cities of Israel, he built the altar of the God of Israel to offer burnt offerings on, according to the law of Moses. He instituted the Feast of Tabernacles, and then made his preparations to begin, as early as possible, the building of the temple, and in the second month of the second year, laid its foundations. The ceremonies of laying the foundations are recorded in Ezra, iii: 9–11. He had many obstructions laid in his way by the Samaritans, to prevent his rebuilding the temple, and he was compelled to cease from the work for a while. They stopped until the second year of the reign of Darius, king of Persia.

Zerubbabel then receives encouragement from two of God's servants, the prophets Haggai and Zechariah, and again proceeded with the building of the temple. Again they met with obstructions, and a letter was written to Darius, the king, which led him to have search made for the edict of Cyrus, under which Zerubbabel left Babylon, and entered upon this work. A transcript of the edict of Cyrus was found, and Darius confirmed it, and bade those who had opposed him to oppose him no more, but rather encourage him. Accordingly they did so. In comparatively a short time, the work was finished. The temple was dedicated, and the solemn Feasts of the Passover and of unleavened bread were kept, and the Jews rejoiced exceedingly. Ezra, iv, v and vi; Haggai, i and ii; Zech. iv: 6-10.

Zerubbabel had seven sons, whose names are given in 1st Chron. iii: 19–20, and a daughter whose name was Shelomith. The sons' names were Meshullam, Hananiah, Hashubah, Ohel, Berechiah, Hasadiah and Jushab-hesed. Two of these sons are called by other names in the genealogy of Joseph and Mary. Rhesa, from whom Mary was descended, and Abiud from whom Joseph came. Luke iii: 27, and Matthew, i: 13.

Zerubbabel was a very important personage, and performed a very important work in the building of the second temple, under the difficulties that surrounded him. There are some expressions in the book of the prophet Haggai, ii: 23, that seem to prefigure Christ: "In that day, saith the Lord of hosts, will I take thee, O Zerubbabel, my servant, the son of Shealtiel, saith the Lord, and will make thee as a signet; for I have chosen thee, saith the Lord of hosts." As he had all things necessary for re-building the temple at Jerusalem, he performed the work and completed it amid the rejoicing of the people. So Jesus builds the temple of his church amid the shoutings of the hosts of Heaven, and the redeemed on earth.

ZERUIAH—[Zer-u-i′-ah,] *pain, tribulation.*

ZERUIAH was the sister of king David, hence the daughter of Jesse. She was probably the eldest sister of David and his brothers, as she is mentioned first in 1st Chron. ii: 16. There we also learn she was the mother of Joab, the general of David's army, and of Abishai, who was such a valiant man and warrior; as also of Asahel, who was a noted runner, and was killed by Abner, the son of Ner, while pursuing him with murderous intent.

This woman is referred to in the same way that men are frequently referred to who are fathers of noted or illustrious persons. Almost as often as the name of the sons of this woman are given, she is referred to as their ancestress.

It may be that she was a woman of considerable note, more noted than her husband and the father of these sons, which was the reason why, especially Joab and Abishai, are so often called the sons of Zeruiah. David often complained of Joab, especially for his cruel and revengeful course. When Joab killed Abner, David said: "These sons of Zeruiah are too hard for me." 2d Sam. iii: 39.

ZETHAM—[Ze′-tham.]

Was the son of Laadan, a Gershonite Levite. 1st Chron. xxiii: 8.

ZETHAN—[Ze′-than,] *their olive.*

Was a Benjaminite of the sons of Bilhan. 1st Chron. vii: 10.

ZETHAR—[Ze′-thar,] *he that examines or beholds.*

One of the eunuchs or chamberlains of Ahasuerus. Est. i: 10.

ZIA—[Zi′-ah.]

One of the Gadites who dwelt in Bashan. 1st Chron. v: 13.

ZIBA—]Zi′-ba,] *army, fight, strength, stag.*

ZIBA was a servant of King Saul, whose treachery to his master, Mephibosheth, is related in 2d Sam. xvi. When the son of Saul desired to cast in his lot with the distressed David as he fled from Jerusalem, he bade his servant Ziba saddle an ass for him to ride upon, and he would follow David and suffer with him. Being lame, he was entirely dependent upon his servant. Ziba, instead of furnishing him the animal to ride upon, made ready and followed after David himself with a present and strong expressions of sympathy for the king; and he slandered his master, Saul's son, by saying that he was at Jerusalem and had turned against his benefactor, and anxiously looking for the restoration of his father's kingdom to him—a thing that Mephibosheth had not thought about. David hastily granted Ziba his master's property; but when afterwards he learned the facts in the case, he annulled the gift he had made to Ziba, placing him back again where he was before, viz.: He was to cultivate the land and give Mephibosheth one-half of the produce. Had he not been one of the servants of Saul in his life-time, David would probably have rewarded his treachery to his master with death. 2d Sam. xix: 24-30.

ZIBEON—[Zib′-e-on,] *iniquity that dwells, the seventh.*

Was the son of Seir, the Horite, whose posterity is referred to in Gen. xxxvi: 20.

ZIBIA.

A Benjaminite, probably one of the sons of Shaharaim, by his wife Hodesh. 1st Chron. viii: 9.

ZIBIAH—[Zib′-i-ah,] *deer, goat, honorable and fine.*

She was a native of Beer-sheba, and the mother of King Joash. 2d Kings, xii: 1, 2; 2d Chron. xxiv: 1.

ZICHRI, 1—[Zik′-ri,] *that remembers, a male.*

Was the son of Izhar the son of Kohath. Ex. vi: 21.

ZICHRI, 2, 3—*That remembers, a male.*

Were both Benjamites, the former of the sons of Shimhi, and the latter of the sons of Shashak. 1st Chron. viii: 19, 23.

ZICHRI, 4—*That remembers, a male.*

Was of the sons of Jeroham, also a Benjaminite. 1st Chron. viii: 27.

ZICHRI, 5—*That remembers, a male.*

Was a son of Eliezer, the son of Moses. 1st Chron. xxvi: 25.

ZICHRI, 6—*That remembers, a male.*

Was the father of Eliezer, a chief of the Reubenites in the time of David. 1st Chron. xxvii: 16.

ZICHRI, 7—*That remembers, a male.*

Was of the tribe of Judah, and the father of Amasiah. 2d Chronicles, xvii: 16.

ZICHRI, 8—*That remembers, a male.*

Was the father of Elishaphat, one of the conspirators with Jehoiada. 2d Chron. xxiii: 1.

ZICHRI, 9—*That remembers, a male.*

Was an Ephraimite hero in the invading army of Pekah, the son of Remaliah. 2d Chron. xxviii: 7.

ZICHRI, 10—*That remembers, a male.*

Was a priest of the family of Abijah, in the days of Jehoiakim, and is referred to in Neh. xii: 17.

ZIDKIJAH—[Zid-ki′-jah.]

Was a priest or family of priests who signed the covenant with Nehemiah. Neh. x: 1.

ZILLAH—[Zil′-lah,] *shadow, which is roasted, the tingling of the ear.*

ZILLAH was one of the wives of Lamech. She is referred to in connection with Adah the other, as being alarmed on account of the danger of the husband, who had slain a man in self-defense. Genesis, iv: 23. She was the mother of Tubal-Cain, the first artist, or worker in brass and iron. Gen. iv: 22. [See Adah.]

ZILPAH—[Zil′-pah,] *distillation, contempt of the mouth.*

ZILPAH was the handmaid of Leah, the wife of Jacob, given to her by Laban when she was married. Gen. xxix: 24. After Leah had borne Jacob four sons, and Rachel had set the example of giving her maid to her husband as a secondary wife, Leah gave Jacob Zilpah, her maid. Gen. xxx: 9. And Zilpah became the mother of two sons, Gad and Asher, who each became the head of powerful tribes. Gen. xxxv: 26.

ZIMRAN—[Zim′-ran,] *song, singer, vine.*

He was the oldest of Abraham's six sons by Keturah, and is referred to in Gen. xxv: 2. He is supposed to be the father of a numerous posterity.

ZIMRI, 1—[Zim′-ri,] *my field, my vine, my branch.*

ZIMRI was the son of Salu, a prince of the tribe of Simeon. He committed great wickedness in Israel, for which he was thrust through with an instrument of death by the zealous priest Phineas. His sin is recorded in Num. xxv: 6-14. It was that of going into the Midianitish camp and procuring a Midianitish princess for a wife and bringing her into the camp of Israel. This was contrary to the law governing the tribes of Israel as to marriage, and all the people were astonished at the act, and they wept at the door of the tabernacle of the congregation. But Phineas slew them both together.

ZIMRI, 2—*My field, my vine, my branch.*

ZIMRI was a general in the army of Elah, the king of Israel. He slew the king and placed himself upon the throne. He had charge, it seems, of one-half of the king's chariots, or commanded one-half of the cavalry of Elah's army. 1st Kings, xvi: 9, &c.

The king of Israel was indulging in drunkenness in the city of Tirzah, in the house of Arza, his steward. Zimri conspired against him, and came upon him while drunk, and smote him. He then killed all the family of Elah, that there might be none to claim the throne. He left not one of his relatives, and in this the prophecy, concerning the house of Baasha being destroyed, was fulfilled to the letter, as made by the prophet Jehu.

Zimri reigned seven days, when the army made Omri king, who at once besieged the city of Tirzah, where he dwelt in the palace of the king whom he had murdered. It was not long until Omri took the city; and when Zimri saw that it was taken, or was on the point of being taken, he set fire to the palace and burnt it down over his head, and so perished in the flames. Seeing he could not enjoy that palace with its riches and adornments, he determined that no one else should.

Zimri was a wicked man, and, coming to the throne as he did, he hardly deserves the name of king. In his short and wicked reign he walked in the way of Jeroboam and his sin.

ZINA OR ZIZAH—[Zi′-nah,]

Was one of the sons of Shimei who was the son of Gershom, of the tribe of Levi. 1st Chron. xxiii: 10. He is the same as Zizah, mentioned in the next verse, who was next to the chief of Shimei's sons.

ZIPHION OR ZEPHON—[Zif′-i-on.]

Was one of the sons of Gad and is numbered with his brothers among the grand children of Jacob who went down into Egypt to sojourn. The names of the others as given in Gen. xlvi: 16, are Haggi, Shuni, Ezbon, Eri, Arodi and Areli.

ZIPPOR—[Zip′-por,] *bird, crown; according to the Syriac, early in the morning.*

ZIPPOR was the father of Balak, who was the king of Moab at the time the Israelites pitched in the plains of Moab; and Balak hired Balaam to come and curse them. Zippor is not mentioned save as the father of Balak, as in Num. xxii: 2; iv: 10; Judges, xi: 25.

ZIPPORAH—[Zip-po′rah,] *beauty, trumpet.*

ZIPPORAH was the daughter of Jethro, the priest of Midian, and she was the wife of the celebrated Moses, the emancipator of Israel.

Moses probably saw Zipporah for the first time when he sat down by a well in Midian, after the fatigues of his flight from Egypt. The daughters of Jethro, seven in number, came to the well to draw water for their father's flocks. He assisted them, and the consequence was it did not take them as long as usual, which led their father to ask them on their return, why they "had come so soon to-day." They informed their father of the help that had been rendered them. Jethro asked them where the stranger was, for he should be entertained and fed for his kindness. Moses was called and gave Jethro an account of his eventful life, when a proposition was probably made to him to tarry with them. Moses agreed to it, and so became a shepherd.

Jethro gave him his daughter Zipporah to wife. This event fastened Moses to his family and interests, and he remained in Midian enjoying the society of this excellent family, and the affections of Zipporah, his wife, forty years. This woman became the mother of a son, and Moses called him Gershom, and immediately added, "I have been a stranger in a strange land." She also bore another son, Eliezer; and when Moses was commissioned to go to Egypt, he took his wife and sons and started with the wonderful rod of God in his hand. He had not, however, proceeded far, until his way was obstructed—"the Lord met him and sought to kill him." It seems that one of the sons of Zipporah had not been circumcised. Moses was probably reproved for neglecting this; and Zipporah, understanding the cause of the divine anger, and seeing that her child was in danger, hurriedly performed the rite and presented the proof of it to Moses.

It is thought, though the wife of Moses recognized the rite and performed the act she did, and so appeased the divine wrath, yet she was alarmed and returned to her father's house with her two sons, where she remained until she made the visit with her father and sons to Moses in the wilderness. When they went to see the husband and father, all Israel was encamped at the mount of God. Ex. xviii: 5: "And Jethro, Moses' father-in-law, came with his wife and his sons unto Moses into the wilderness, where they encamped at the mount of God." After tarrying awhile he returned home and left Zipporah and her sons with Moses; and yet we hear nothing more of her, and but little of her sons, Gershom and Eliezer. They and their families were incorporated with the Levites, and seemed to have the employment of taking care of the tabernacle and tent, performing some of the hardest service there. Num. iv: 24–28.

What became of Zipporah we do not know. She may have continued with Israel, or, when she saw her children settled, she may have returned to her father in the land of Midian.

ZIZA—]Zi′za,] *belonging to all; in Syriac, going back.*

Was one of the sons of Rehoboam, born of Maachah, the daughter of Absalom. 2d Chron. xi: 20.

ZOHAR—[Zo′har,] *white, shining, dryness.*

Was one of the sons of Simeon, and is numbered with the family of Jacob, who went with him down into Egypt. Gen. xlvi: 10.

ZOPHAI—[Zo′-fa.]

Was of the tribe of Levi, and in the line of priests from Aaron to the captivity. 1st Chron. vi: 26.

ZOPHAR—[Zo′-far,] *rising early, crown; in syriac, sparrow, goat.*

ZOPHAR was one of Job's three friends. He is called the Naamathite. This may be because he came from the town of Naama in the vicinity of Idumea. The first notice of him is in Job ii: 11. In company with Eliphaz and Bildad, he comes to Job to sympathize with him in his sorrows, "to mourn with and to comfort him." He formed an unfavorable opinion of Job, and twice spake against him. His first address to Job is chapter xi, and the second is chapter xx, &c. He, with the other two, were charged with having spoken wrong words against Job and against God, and the divine wrath was kindled against him; but he with his companions were pardoned in answer to Job's prayers. Job, xlii.

ZUAR—[Zu′-ar,] *small.*

Was of the tribe of Issachar, and the father of Nathaniel, the prince, who assisted Moses in numbering the tribes of Israel. Num. i: 8.

ZUPH—*That observes, roof.*

ZUPH was a Levite, and is referred to in 1st Chron. vi: 35, as one of the ancestors of the prophet Samuel. He is also referred to in 1st Sam. i: 1, in the account given of Elkanah, Samuel's father; and in 1st Sam. ix: 5, we have the country or city of Zuph referred to. It is likely that it was a country or city settled, or possessed by descendants of Zuph, and named in honor of him. Here the prophet Samuel lived, and was consulted by the son of Kish regarding the asses of his father, that he and his servant were hunting.

ZUR, 1—[Zur,] *stone, plan, form.*

ZUR was the father of Cozbi, and one of the five princes of Midian, who were slain by the Israelites, when Baalam fell. Num. xxv: 15; xxxi: 8.

ZUR, 2.—*Stone, plan, form.*

ZUR was the son of Jehiel, the founder of Gibeon. 1st Chronicles, viii: 30; ix: 36.

ZURIEL—[Zu′-ri-el,] *the rock, or strength of God.*

ZURIEL was the son of Abihail and a chief of the Merarite Levites, at the time of the exodus from Egypt. Numbers, iii: 35.

ZURISHADDAI—[Zu-ri-shad′-da-i,] *the Almighty is my rock, splendor, beauty.*

ZURISHADDAI is referred to in Num. i: 6, as the father of Shelumiel, of the tribe of Simeon. As Shelumiel was a prince of the tribe, it is likely that his father had occupied a prominent place in it.

# APPENDIX.

## EMBRACING THE BIOGRAPHY OF UNNAMED PERSONS.

*Abel—the Wise Woman of.*

Sheba raised an insurrection in the kingdom of Israel, and gained a party against David their king. Abishai and Joab follow him, and learning that he is in the city of Abel, they besiege it with a view of destroying it. About the time they had raised their embankment, and had their munitions of war ready for the attack, this wise woman of Abel, who was probably a governess in the city—demanded a conversation with Joab. She said, "Say, I pray you, unto Joab, come near hither, that I may speak with thee." 2d Sam. xx: 16. Joab came near and she plead with him to spare the city—urging that they were not enemies to David, neither did they sanction the insurrection of Sheba. Joab asked for a proof of the fact, that they had no sympathy with the insurrectionists—by putting Sheba to death and giving him evidence that he was executed, or else deliver his person to him. She told Joab that she would see to it, that Sheba was executed and his head should be thrown to him over the wall. She then went unto the people and in her wisdom spake to them. She showed them the propriety of their fulfilling this promise at once, that their city might be delivered. They accordingly executed Sheba and threw his head over the wall to Joab.

*Abimelech's Mother.*

This woman was a secondary wife of the famous Gideon, who delivered Israel from the Midianites and the children of the East. Gideon had many wives and many sons. Judg. viii: 30: "And Gideon had three-score and ten sons of his body begotten, for he had many wives."

This woman being a secondary wife, her son Abimelech could not inherit with the sons of Gideon's other wives. It is supposed this woman knew of the laws of inheritance, and yet she desired that it should be different in the case of her son, and hence designedly named him Abimelech, which signifies, "My father is king." She desired that her son should be raised to the government; and it is quite likely that she acted a prominent part in the revolution that was gotten up and prosecuted amongst the men of Shechem, which resulted in the death of all the sons of Gideon except Jotham, the youngest, who hid himself and so escaped the massacre.

*Abimelech's Murderer.*

The murderer of Abimelech was a woman. He had been a very wicked, aspiring, and bloody wretch. In order to assume the authority, he had slain, in one place, seventy half-brothers, and would have killed Jotham if he had not hid himself. He had not reigned three years until those who had selected him turned against him. He fought with the Shechemites and murdered them in large numbers; and hearing that a thousand of them had fled to the temple of Baal-Berith, he followed them there. He burned the temple and so destroyed them. He then went to Thebez, and attacked the tower in the midst of the city to which many had fled for safety. He gathered fuel and was about to set fire to it, so as to suffocate and destroy those who had fled to it, "when a certain woman cast a piece of millstone upon Abimelech's head, and all to brake his skull." She saw the oppressor and murderer from the top of the tower where she was, and hurling the piece of millstone down it struck him and fractured his skull. Whether she was recognized by Abimelech, and her intention understood before she threw it, we cannot tell; but he seems, after having received the fracture, to know who had done it, for he ordered the young man, his armor-bearer, "draw thy sword and slay me, that men say not of me a woman slew him." He felt that it would be a disgrace to be killed by a woman—and he feared that if he fell into the hands of his enemy thus wounded, they would put him to cruel torture. In compliance with his request his armor-bearer thrust him through, and he died. Thus we behold the judgment of God visited upon this wicked man and the cruel Shechemites. He fell by the hand of a woman, for if his armor-bearer had not thrust him through, he would have died from the fracture experienced by the stone hurled on him. Judges, ix: 53.

*Abraham's Trained Servants.*

There were three hundred and eighteen of them armed by Abraham to pursue after the confederate kings who had conquered the cities of the plain and taken Lot and his family prisoners. These trained servants of Abraham were joined with Aner, Eshcol and Mamre, with all the forces that they could muster, for they were confederate with Abraham. This company overtook the conquering kings and smote them, and recaptured the prisoners and spoils, and brought them back again.

His trained servants were all born in his own house. They were his family, and all of them had been under the salutary restraints of the pious patriarch, of whom God had said: "I know Abraham that he will command his household after him." Gen. xiv.

*Amalekite—he who Reported himself as Saul's Murderer.*

This Amalekite was a young man who, in his report to King David of the Gilboa battle, professed to have ended the sufferings of Saul while dying from his wounds on the battle-field; and he brought the crown which he had taken from the head of the fallen king, and the bracelet from his arm, and laid them before David as evidence that his report was true.

The report given of Saul's death in 1st Sam. xxxi: 3–5, says that he asked his armor-bearer to thrust him through with the sword, that he might not be abused and killed by the Philistines who would shortly pass over the field; but his armor-bearer would not, therefore Saul took his sword and fell upon it, and so killed himself. As evidence that he did kill himself, it is said, "when his armor-bearer saw that Saul was dead, he fell likewise upon his sword and died with him." And yet this young Amalekite says he slew him.

The strong probability is that this report of his to David was a base fabrication, gotten up under the impression that David would honor him; but in this he was mistaken. The future king of Israel charged the young Amalekite with killing the Lord's anointed, and took his own testimony as evidence of his guilt—or rather, executed him on his own confession. David called one of his young men and said, "Go near and fall upon him." The young man did so, and the Amalekite died. 2d Sam. i: 2–15.

*Angel who arrested Abraham on Mount Moriah.*

Abraham, in obedience to the divine command, had gone to Mount Moriah, in company with Isaac. The preparations for the sacrifice had been made, the altar was erected, the fire and wood prepared. And Isaac spoke unto Abraham, his father, and said, "My father;" and he said, "here am I, my son." And he said, "behold the fire and the wood; but where is the Lamb for a burnt offering?" And Abraham said, "my son, God will provide himself a Lamb for a burnt offering." Abraham then bound Isaac and laid him upon the altar, then stretched forth his hand, with the knife in it, to slay him.

The angel of the Lord called to him out of heaven, and bade him spare his son, approved him for his obedience, provided a ram in the stead of Isaac, and looked on while the good man offered it to God, in the stead of his son. The angel then called to him a second time, and confirmed, in the most solemn manner, the promise of blessings to himself and his family and to the nations of earth, in a Savior that should come of his family.

The angel that appeared here to Abraham, was the same person who was represented by the offering—the Lord Jehovah, the Jesus Christ of the New Testament. Genesis, xxii.

*Angel who appeared to Hagar.*

When Hagar fled from the face of her mistress into the wilderness, and sat by a fountain of water, the angel of the Lord found her, and bade her return and submit herself unto Sarai, giving her the promise of a son, and assured her that his posterity should be a mighty multitude. The angel gave her the name Ishmael, for her coming son, and gave as the reason, "Because the Lord has heard thy affliction." She looked upon the angel as the Lord Jehovah, for she called his name, "Thou God seest me." And she called the well, where he appeared unto her, "Beer-lahai-roi," the well of him which liveth and seeth me. Genesis, xvi: 1–14.

Fourteen years after this, Hagar was wandering about in search of water to save her life, and dying son Ishmael. In her extremity, the angel of the Lord, the same angel that talked with her and told her of Ishmael, called to her out of Heaven, and confirmed the covenant that had been made years before. He bade her lift up the dying boy, and assured her that he should be the head of a great nation. While she was in the act of lifting up her son in obedience to the command of the angel, her eyes were opened and she saw a fountain of water. "She went and filled the bottle with water, and gave the lad drink." Genesis, xxi.

*Angel who appeared to Gideon.*

When the Israelites were greatly alarmed because the Midianites and the Amalekites, and the children of the East, threatened them with destruction, they cried unto the Lord for deliverance. And the Lord heard them and sent a prophet unto them to reprove them and to instruct them. But God determined to deliver them out of the hands of their enemies, and an angel appeared to Gideon, the son of Joash, with a commission. This angel accosted Gideon with, "The Lord is with thee, thou mighty man of valor." He expressed fears as to his being able to deliver his people with so great an army against them; but his fears were allayed and all his objections removed by the miracles that were wrought before his eyes, and by the counsel given him by the angel. Gideon, desiring to express his regards for the angel, earnestly entreated him to tarry awhile until he made ready a present. He made ready a repast consisting of a kid, unleavened cakes, and broth, and brought it out to the angel. When he brought them he presented them to the angel, who bade him offer them as a sacrifice, and he took part in the offering. As Gideon took the flesh and the unleavened cakes and laid them on the rock, and poured out the broth, the angel put forth the end of his staff and touched the flesh and the unleavened cakes, and immediately there rose up fire out of the rock and consumed the sacrifice, when the angel departed from him.

Gideon seems to have been satisfied that he who appeared thus to him and did so wondrously, was a divine person. If it was not Jehovah himself it was his representative angel. He said, "Alas! O, Lord God! for because I have seen an angel of the Lord face to face." He feared that he would die, but his fears were allayed by a declaration from the Lord that he should not die.

From the importance of the work to which Gideon was here commissioned, and from the wonderful acts that were performed by the angel, we may suppose that this was the covenant angel —the Lord Jehovah of the Old Testament, who so frequently manifested himself in the office of an angel.—Judges, vi.

*Angel who appeared to Manoah's Wife.*

While the wife of Manoah was alone in the field, her attention was arrested by the appearance unto her of the angel of the Lord. Her own representation to her husband of the visitor was, "A man of God came unto me, and his countenance was like the countenance of an angel of God, very terrible." She was so awed by the appearance and presence of the angel, that she did not ask who he was, or whence he came.

The wife of Manoah had no children and the object of the angel's mission was to inform her that she should be a mother, and that her offspring should be a son; that he should be a prodigy of human strength, and the deliverer of Israel out of the hands of the Philistines. The angel instructed her as to her own habits until the child was born: "Drink not wine, nor strong drink, and eat not any unclean thing." He then instructed her as to the character of her child: that he should be a Nazarite unto God from his birth, and there should come no razor upon his head. She informed her husband of all that the angel had said, and he earnestly entreated the Lord that the angel might return unto him again, and repeat the instructions that had been given.

Accordingly the angel appeared to the woman again, as she sat in the field. She immediately ran and told her husband, who went out to see, and converse with the heavenly visitor. He gave to Manoah all the instructions he had previously given to his wife, regarding the child.

The instructions being finished, Manoah proposed to detain the angel while he prepared a repast. His visitant did not object to being detained, but objected to eating with him, and probably proposed to him to make an offering unto the Lord, and he would take a part in it. When Manoah asked after his name he refused to give it, but as the kid, with the meat offering, was provided and brought to the altar, which consisted of a stone imbedded in the earth in the field, "the angel of the Lord did wondrously, and Manoah and his wife looked on." He took an important part in the solemn sacrifice.

As the offering was placed there, the angel caused fire to come out from the rock and consume it, and as the flame ascended up to Heaven, and the astonished man and woman looked on the angel, he entered it, and amid its curlings ascended up into heaven. Jud. xiii: 3-10.

This angel was, in all probability, the same one that appeared to Moses at the burning bush; to Joshua, as a man of war; to Gideon, and touched the rock with the end of his staff, from which came out fire that consumed his sacrifice. It was the Lord Jehovah of the Old Testament; the Jesus Christ of the New Testament. And it may be that the name asked for by Manoah, and kept back by the angel, is referred to in his wondrous act. "And his name shall be called wonderful." Isaiah, ix: 6.

*Angel of the Lord Slaying One Hundred and Eighty-five Thousand Assyrians.*

Hezekiah, the king of Judah, was greatly troubled and distressed on account of the great army of Sennacherib, and the insulting taunts and threats that had been levelled at him. At length Isaiah predicts the destruction of Sennacherib's host. A very insulting letter was sent to the king of Judah to induce him to surrender—this letter was taken to the temple and spread before the Lord. It was the subject of Hezekiah's earnest prayer. That prayer was heard and answered, and the prophet Isaiah was sent to him to assure him that it was answered and that Jerusalem should be delivered and the Assyrians destroyed. That very night the angel of the Lord went out and smote, in the camp of the Assyrians, one hundred and eighty-five thousand soldiers—quietly and with the swiftness of lightning, the angel of death passed through the camp and touched this mighty host, and they died without creating enough disturbance to wake the sleepers around them, or attract the attention of the guard. "And in the morning when they arose early, behold they were all dead corpses." One tent after another was reported from, where a soldier was found dead, until when they came to number and lay their dead there were found to be one hundred and eighty-five thousand. 2d Kings, xix: 35.

*Angels—Three Entertained by Abraham.*

Abraham was dwelling in the plains of Mamre, and at mid-day he was sitting in the door of his tent, and lifting up his eyes he saw what seemed to be three men. They had the appearance of wearied travelers and his sympathies were roused for them. Rising from his seat he ran to them, and gave an earnest invitation to them to rest and be refreshed in his tent, before they pursued their journey farther. It may be, that they made as though they would go further, to test the strength of his feelings toward a wearied stranger which led him to insist that they should not go, but come in and enjoy his hospitality. They were persuaded to tarry in his tent, and he brought water to wash their feet, and at once, with the assistance of his wife, prepared a repast. Abraham gave directions as to the quantity of meal to be used in making cakes, viz., three measures—and he himself killed and dressed a calf. He then took the newly baked bread, the dressed calf and butter and milk, and set it before them; and they did eat while he stood under the oak of Mamre, near the tent, and engaged in an interesting conversation, during which we may suppose the Patriarch learned that they were angels; for one of them declared to him that Sarah, his wife, should have a son, though he was ninety-nine years of age, and his beloved Sarah was also very aged—yet they should be blessed with a son. He who made this promise to Abraham and Sarah, though in the form of a man, was the Lord Jehovah—the angel of the covenant. This intelligence filled the soul of the Patriarch with gladness, and he was loath to part with the strangers whom he had entertained as angels, "unawares." Accordingly as they rose to leave his tent, and journey toward Sodom, he determined to accompany them a part, at least, of the way. They had not proceeded far before the covenant angel determined to divulge to him the object of the mission in which they were engaged, viz., to destroy the cities of Sodom and Gomorrah.

As soon as Abraham learned this he became interested for the doomed cities. His kinsman Lot lived there and his family, and the cities had many inhabitants. He addressed the angel, whose true character he now understood, on behalf of the people devoted to destruction. He asked him if there were fifty righteous in the city, if he would not, for their sakes, spare them all; his petition was answered according to his desire. He then asked if there were but forty-five, then forty, then thirty, then twenty, and finally ten—this last petition was answered as he desired, and he left off to intercede for them, thinking surely there are ten that fear God; but in this he was mistaken. The covenant angel then left Abraham, and deputized his attendants to go on to Sodom where Lot dwelt and hasten his escape and the escape of his family before fire from Heaven consumed the city. They accordingly went and arrived at evening. Lot saw them as they entered the gate and rose up, for he was sitting in or near the gate, and met them with expressions of respect, and immediately urged them as strangers to tarry at his house for the night. In order to test his sincerity they made as though they would abide in the street all night, and not impose upon a private family. Lot pressed them earnestly, and they went in. He procured water and they washed their feet, after which he provided a repast and they partook of it.

These two angels had been observed by some of the men of Sodom as they entered the city, and in their wickedness they determined to do them violence that night; accordingly as night came on, a mob was raised that beset the house of Lot, and they demanded of him the men that were lodging with him. The good man tried to pacify them but failed. He even went out of the house and shut the door after him, and stood there for some time expostulating with them. They even threatened him with violence and rushed at his door to break it down. In this they failed, and the angels from within rescued Lot from their hands and power; they opened the door and pulled him in, and then smote the rebel crowd with blindness, partial if not entire, so that they could not find the door of the house.

The angels then entered into conversation with Lot regarding his family and relationship, and learned that his two daughters were espoused to husbands; and they directed him to gather them together and take them out of the city, for the object of their mission was to destroy it. Lot accordingly sought and obtained an interview with his sons-in-law, and urged them to accompany him out, but he seemed to them as one that mocked, and they would not go. As soon as the morning came the angels hastened Lot and his wife and two daughters out. They were somewhat slow; it may be the young women were loth to leave their betrothed behind them; but the angels took hold of the hand of Lot and his wife and his two daughters and brought them forth and set them without the city, and urged them to escape for their lives. They accompanied them to the outskirts of Sodom, then returned to destroy the city. They seemed to manifest the most intense anxiety for the welfare of Lot's family, urging them to flee to the mountains, and not look back or tarry in all the plain.

When Lot desired to go to Zoar, the angel permitted him to do so, in the stead of going to the mountain, and urged him to go quickly. When Lot and his family were thus saved (except his wife, who was disobedient and was punished), the angels returned from them and executed the divine decree by overthrowing the four cities of Sodom and Gomorrah, and Admah and Zeboim. Gen. xviii and xix.

*Babylon—the Queen of.*

When Belshazzar had been engaged a part of the night in his sacrilegious feast, and the hand-writing on the wall alarmed him, he had failed to find any among the wise men of Babylon, that could read the writing. The queen came into the banquet house, Daniel, v: 10, and reminded the king of Daniel, who possessed wisdom, and had been promoted to honor by the former king of Babylon. She entreats the king not to be discouraged by the failure of the wise men of Babylon, for Daniel had more than once rendered service to his grandfather, and would help him. Belshazzar credited what she said, and had Daniel called, who read the writing and gave him the interpretation thereof. The queen gives Daniel a very high character, "a man in whom is the spirit of the holy gods." She says further of him, "Light and understanding, and wisdom, like the wisdom of the gods, is found in him." She said further, that Nebuchadnezzar, his father, had made "him master of the magicians," and then she expresses her confidence in Daniel, by saying, "let him be called and he will show the interpretation." She had no doubt but the king, by applying to Daniel, would get the desired information. She was not mistaken, as the sequel proves.

*Bathsheba—the Child of.*

This child was illegitimate, Bathsheba being the wife of Uriah, an officer in David's army. The king of Israel sinned against God in this matter, for which God was angry with him, and by the prophet Nathan sorely reproved him. It was not long after Uriah was dead, and Bathsheba became David's wife, until the child was born; and while it was yet an infant it was struck with a disease of which it died in seven days.

Though David was very penitent for his sin, and earnestly implored the Lord for the life of the child, yet the child died, and the king of Israel comforted himself, after its departure, with the glorious doctrine of immortality—conscious, happy existence after death, and reunion of friends in Heaven: "I shall go to him, but he shall not return to me." 2d Samuel, xii: 12–23.

*Cain's Wife.*

It is unnecessary for us to conjecture or speculate, regarding this woman, as to who she was, and what natural relation she sustained to Cain, before they were husband and wife. She is introduced to our view as the mother of Enoch. Gen. iv: 17. "And Cain knew his wife, and she conceived and bare Enoch." She was, in all probability, associated with Cain in dedicating this son to God, that he might minister in the priest's office for their family—Cain, his father, being excluded from it, for the crime which he committed, in the murder of his brother.

While we may suppose that Cain heartily repented of his sin, and gave evidence to some extent of his repentance by dedicating Enoch to God, yet we may suppose that very much of the religious instruction that Enoch received in his early childhood and youth was imparted by his mother. She instructed him in the things of God, and impressed his mind and heart with the importance of the position he was to occupy and the important part he was to act in the family, viz., that of priest. And she looked with joy upon him as he developed his character and commenced his devotion to God, and the interest of the family as their priest, which devotion continued for more than three hundred years.

Knowing, as she did, that her husband was debarred the privilege of officiating as priest, she rejoiced that her son Enoch was accepted of God in his stead.

*Canaanitish Woman.*

She is brought to our view in Matt. xv : 22. St. Mark calls her, in vii : 26, a Syro-Phenician woman. The reason why she is called thus probably was, she lived in Phenecia, which at that time was looked upon as making a part of Syria, and was within the jurisdiction of the governor of Syria,

This woman, according to Christ's own declaration, was one of the most noted personages, for faith, that is brought to our view in the Gospels. According to one of the Evangelists, Jesus said to her, "O, woman, great is thy faith!"

This Canaanitish woman had heard of Christ's healing power—of wonderful cures he had performed—and she believed he had power to heal her daughter, who was "grievously vexed with a devil." Her address to Christ expressed the most intense feeling: "Have mercy on me, O Lord, thou son of David!" and then she opened the case to him. He whom she addressed heard her, and in his feeling heart there was sympathy for and to her. But he seemed not to regard her—to appearance paid no attention to her. His disciples were annoyed, and asked him to "send her away." He did not comply with their request, for he desired to let them see, what he was already acquainted with, viz.: that this woman had strong faith in him. It may be they were willing for the master to dismiss her after granting her request, as was his custom; and possibly they thought she had no claims upon him as she was a Canaanitish woman, and hence they desired him to send her away. Though he did not answer her, yet he did answer his disciples. His answer may have been intended as a partial rebuke to them; but as it was given in her hearing she seemed to be somewhat inspirited by it, for she approached nearer and worshiped him, and with all the earnestness of her soul, said, "Lord, help me." She felt that her case was important; and though she heard him say, "I am not sent but to the lost tribes of the house of Israel," she could not give it up. It was not on his part granting the request of his disciples—he did not openly spurn her, and she would not take what he had said as a refusal to help.

The Savior then noticed her, and addressing her for the first time, said, "It is not meet to take the children's bread and cast it to the dogs." This seemed to be virtually classing her with those of the heathens whom the Jews denominated dogs, while they rejoiced in the appellation of children. This did not discourage her; she acknowledged the justness of the classification, but she drew from it a strong argument in her own favor. She made a plea from it for help. She said, "Truth, Lord, but the dogs eat of the crumbs that fall from their master's table." She did not ask to be put on a level with the Jews; but in the abundance of miracle he was performing for the Jews, she begged that he would pity and help her, by curing her daughter.

The disciples had, probably, been looking on with astonishment while their master and this woman were in conference. They saw the force of her reasoning, and the expressed earnestness of her soul. I imagine they recognized her faith as she thus developed it.

*Captain of a Company of Syrians.*

The faithful prophet of God had reproved King Ahaziah for inquiring of Baalzebub, the God of Ekron, whether he should recover of his disease, as though there was no God in Israel to inquire of. And in addition to the reproof, Ahaziah was informed through his messengers that this man had said he should not come down from that bed on which he was gone up, but should surely die. The king of Israel became enraged at this and sent a captain with a company of fifty soldiers to take Elijah. The prophet sat upon the top of a hill and awaited the coming of the soldiers. The captain accosted him with, "Thou man of God, the king hath said come down." Elijah did not come but called fire down from heaven to consume the captain and his fifty soldiers. Ahaziah, undaunted by this circumstance, and determined to take him, sent another captain with a company of fifty—they also were consumed by fire from heaven. He then sent the third captain with his company. This officer, we may suppose, feared God and fully believed that the prophet was under the protection of the God of Israel. One hundred men and two commanding officers had been destroyed, and he feared lest he and his company should meet with a similar fate, and yet as an army officer he dare not fail to follow instructions. He accordingly approached the hill where Elijah was and plead with him for his life and the life of his men. He fell on his knees before the prophet and besought him, saying, "O, man of God, I pray thee let my life and the life of these fifty, thy servants, be precious in thy sight." As though he had said, I fear thy God who has manifested his power in thy protection, and in the destruction of more than a hundred men—now give up to me for the God who has thus protected thee will save thee from the wrath of the king, even in his very presence. Elijah then received direction from an angel of the Lord to go and appear before Ahaziah. He did so, and in the presence and hearing of the king repeated what he had declared to his messengers. The captain by addressing Elijah as he did saved his own life, and the life of the company he commanded. 2d Kings, i: 9, 15.

*Captain of the Lord's Host.*

Joshua had led the children of Israel across the Jordan, and was about to enter upon the conquest of the land of Canaan. Under the Divine direction, he circumcised the males of the children of Israel, for all their men of war who had been circumcised in Egypt had died in the wilderness, and none of those who were born after they left Egypt were circumcised.

After this Joshua had the Feast of the Passover observed and kept with solemn ceremony. The manna with which they had been fed in their wilderness state ceased to fall, and they began to eat of the produce of the land. Joshua, feeling that all things were in readiness for the work before him, having his army in readiness for battle—seems to have started out on a reconnoitering expedition toward Jericho, which was to be his first battle ground and conquest. He was probably alone as he neared the city, and may have been indulging fears that he could not take the strong city, or if he succeeded at all it would be with extreme difficulty. All at once a man stood over against him with a sword drawn in his hand. He looked at the warrior a moment, and then as a bold courageous general, drew near him and asked the significant question, "Art thou for us or for our adversaries." The answer came to him from the warrior, "Nay, but as captain of the Lord's host, am I now come." The leader of Israel was satisfied at once that he who stood before him was a divine personage and at once "fell on his face to the earth and did worship." He then asked for instructions from him who thus addressed him. "And the captain of the Lord's host said unto Joshua, Loose thy shoe from off thy foot; for the place whereon thou standest is holy, and Joshua did so."

It can hardly be supposed that this man of war was a created angel—else Joshua would not have worshiped him. Who, then, was it? It was the same person who appeared to Moses at the base of Horeb more than forty years before, and commissioned him to emancipate his down-trodden countrymen. Almost the same language is used to Joshua that had been used to Moses by the *I am* who spake to him from out the burning bush. It was the Jehovah of the Old Testament who appeared thus to Joshua as a man of war. Joshua, v: 13, 15.

*Children—Forty-two Killed by two Bears.*

Elisha was on his way to Bethel, and was recognized as the successor of the noted prophet Elijah, by those who committed offences here, and were punished with death. They who are called children here are supposed to have been young men. They had at least attained an age which marked them as accountable for their conduct. Some have supposed that they were students in a select school established on that road, and that the prophet was passing their school house, and being observed by them they called to mind the recent circumstance of Elijah's translation, and the mocking language which they used had reference to the upward flight of that holy man to heaven. "Go up, thou bald head; go up, thou bald head." If so, their sin was blasphemy, and their punishment, severe as it was, was not more than the crime deserved. The prophet recognized their great crime, and turning to them "cursed them in the name of the Lord." The voice of Elisha had but just fallen upon their ear in this fearful language when two she bears came out of the wood and attacked and destroyed forty-two of them.

It has been thought by some that instead of these young men being in attendance on a school, they had been engaged in the woods, out of which the bears came, in hunting, and these two she bears had been robbed of their whelps by them, and with the ferocity that belongs to a bear thus robbed they rushed upon and destroyed them. 2d Kings, ii: 23, 25.

*Damsel Possessed of Divination.*

We read of this damsel in the sixteenth chapter of the Acts of the Apostles. It seems after Lydia was converted, and invited the apostle to abide at her house, he left his former lodging, and went to her residence to tarry awhile; and while he was going, this maid, possessed of a spirit of divination, met him, and began to follow him with his companions, Luke, Silas and Timothy, and she cried as she followed them—"These men are the servants of the most high God, which show unto us the way of salvation." She did not thus follow them, and cry for an hour, or a day only; but she did this "for many days." Paul became wearied with the circumstance of her following and crying after them, and grieved lest Satan should use this to their hurt, by causing the people to imagine that they were in league with evil spirits; therefore, in the name of Jesus Christ, he commanded the evil spirit to come out of the damsel. The spirit obeyed, and came out of her. By her soothsaying she had brought her masters much gain. When they saw that she would no longer be of advantage to them in making money—that the hope of their gains was gone—they caught Paul and Silas, and in their rage, drew them into the market-place, with a view of accusing them. The multitude was excited against them, and they were beaten and imprisoned; but their imprisonment resulted in the conversion of the jailor.

As this damsel was delivered out of the hands of Satan by the power of Christ, it is quite likely she became a lover of Christ's cause, and lived and died a votary of it.

*Dead Man raised to Life by touching Elisha's Bones.*

The inhabitants of the land where Elisha's tomb was, were being invaded by bands of Moabites. One day, while they were engaged in burying a man, an alarm was given to the funeral train by the appearance of one of these marauding parties. They were just passing the sepulcher of Elisha, which was open, and through fear that they would be overtaken by the band, they threw the body into Elisha's grave, intending, it may be, after the danger was passed, to take it out and bury it where they had contemplated burying it. As soon as the form of the dead man, prepared for burial, touched the bones of the prophet, it was restored to life. This is the first and only miracle performed, where the bones of a dead man were the instrument. 2d Kings, xiii: 20, 21.

*Elect Lady.*

She was a Christian woman—a holy matron who, with becoming diligence had served the church. She was generally known, and as generally loved in the church. The apostle John, when very aged, wrote his epistles, the first to the Jewish Christians in general, and the second to the Elect Lady, while the third was written to Gaius.

From the epistle to this lady, we learn that John loved her, as the Christian religion requires love to one another, and that she was of good report among all the Christians. Her devotion to God and the interests of the infant church was known and admired. It would seem from the fourth verse of the epistle that she was the mother of a family and that her children were some of them "walking in the truth." If the apostle refers to her natural children, then we would judge some of them were converted, and were honoring God by living holy. If he is referring to her spiritual children, as a deaconess in the church, then we gather that some of them were adorning their profession. He exhorts them earnestly to love one another; gives various instructions for their spiritual benefit, and closes the epistle by expressing a purpose to pay her and her family a visit shortly. The Elect Lady was then an eminent, honorable Christian woman.

*Endor—Witch of.*

This was a woman that had escaped the slaughter that Saul had visited those with who professed to be in possession of familiar spirits, by which they could tell future events, and have communication with spirits. In 1st Sam. xxviii: 3, it is said, "And Saul had put away those that had familiar spirits, and the wizard, out of the land."

She lived at Endor, a city in the valley of Jezreel, not very far from where Saul and his army were encamped the night before the battle of Gilboa was fought. Saul saw the host of the Philistines, and was afraid. Their army was probably larger than his, and their preparations for war were superior, and their position in the contemplated battle had advantages which led him to fear. But the strongest grounds for his fears was so expressed in the sixth verse, when he enquired of the Lord. "The Lord answered him not neither by dreams, nor by Urim, nor by prophets." The Lord had departed from him, and was about to visit him with judgments. With his dreadful forebodings of coming ill, and no communications with God, he bade his servants seek him out "a woman that hath a familiar spirit, that I may go to her and enquire of her." His servants told him of the one who had lived at Endor. He disguised himself, and with two of his aids, who probably were also disguised, he went that night to see the woman, and inquire of her. He informed her as soon as he arrived for what intent he had come, and demanded of her, or through her, communication with a departed spirit. The woman made objection, and expressed her suspicions that they were laying a snare for her life. Saul assured her that was not the case, and pledged himself in the most solemn manner, to stand between her and all danger of that kind.

She then asked him what spirit she should bring up, and he said, "Bring me up Samuel." Soon Samuel appeared, but he was not brought up by the woman, but by the power of God. The Almighty, against whom Saul had sinned, saw fit to send the spirit of the prophet to the king, and Samuel once more communicated with him. When the real form of Samuel appeared to the eye of the woman, she was frightened, "and cried with a loud voice." The fact just then was communicated, in some way, to her, that the person who had applied to her, was the king himself, and she asked, "Why hast thou deceived me, for thou art Saul." As yet the king saw nothing, and asked the frightened woman to describe to him the appearance, and she did. Saul was satisfied that it was Samuel. The communication that Samuel made to him was solemn and affecting. "Moreover the Lord will also deliver Israel with thee into the hand of the Philistines; and to-morrow shalt thou and thy sons be with me; the Lord also shall deliver the hosts of Israel into the hand of the Philistines." What a solemn revelation to be made to a troubled king, by the spirit of him who had anointed him to be king, and been the prophet of Israel almost through his entire reign.

Saul was very deeply affected and fell with his whole length upon the ground in a swoon, where he remained for some time. As soon as he was recovered, she offered him such succour as his exhausted nature needed, and such as humanity would dictate to provide, and offer to one in the condition of Saul. But he refused to eat. His two servants that were with him joined in with the woman to persuade him to eat. And though his appetite and strength was gone, he yielded to their persuasions.

The woman had a fat calf, and she hastened to kill and dress it, and she baked unleavened bread, for there was not time to prepare leavened bread, and she brought it before Saul and his servants, and they did eat, after which they arose and went away to the camp.

It is thought by some, that this woman had power or control of spirits, and that she brought Samuel from the spirit world to the conversation with the King of Israel, if, indeed, Samuel appeared. The history undoubtedly warrants the conclusion, that Samuel did actually appear. But he was sent miraculously by the mercy of God, for the purpose of once more bringing the sins of Saul to remembrance; and warning him of his approaching death, "tomorrow thou and thy sons shall be with me." How solemn the revelation. The king was so fully advised thus of his approaching death, that he had an opportunity for making preparation, that he would not have had, if he had not thus been visited by Samuel. What an eventful night was that for Saul. He had just encamped with his soldiers, found out this woman, received the revelation from God, recovered from the swoon, ate his last meal, and by morning reached the camp, changed the clothes that disguised him, for his field armor, when the enemy were ready for fight, and at the head of the hosts he fell in battle. And what an eventful night for the "Witch of Endor." The men called on her and made known the object of their visit. Suspicions were roused and under them she trembled, lest they were trying to ensnare her and bring about her death. The fact was revealed to her that she was in the presence of the king, whom she feared. Unexpectedly to her Samuel actually appeared. The king swooned in her house, and afterward eat that which she had provided.

*Ezekiel's Wife.*

The only account we have of this woman is contained in Ezek. xxiv: 15–18, from which we may suppose she was much beloved by her husband, and that her death was a terrible calamity to him—a deep and dark dispensation of divine providence.

Ezekiel's wife died suddenly in the evening of a day that he had spoken unto the people in the morning, and had declared that God was about to destroy their city by the Chaldeans,—making his wife's death, which would be a sore trial to him, represent this sore calamity to them. As his wife, "the desire of his eyes," should be taken away with a stroke, so their city and sanctuary, which was the desire of their eyes, should be suddenly taken from them and destroyed.

There is something very peculiar in this account of the death of the prophet's wife. It is not to be supposed that she had committed sin for which she must die, or that the prophet had committed sin which must be punished by this terrible trial; but God, in his infinite wisdom, saw fit thus to afflict Ezekiel, in the sudden death of his companion, and then gave him directions as to how he was to be exercised under the affliction, in order to teach lessons to the people for practice.

God said, "Neither shalt thou mourn nor weep, neither shall thy tears run down. Forbear to cry, make no mourning for the dead, bind the tire of thy head upon thee, and put on thy shoes upon thy feet, and cover not thy lips, and eat not the bread of men."

Here we may suppose that the people, by the death of Ezekiel's wife, were to learn that no private affliction could equal this public calamity that, for their sins, was to be brought upon them. Ezekiel taught them that in this calamity they were to do as he had done—not complain of God for thus dealing with them; but they should not cover their lips, or eat the bread of men; their tires should be upon their heads, and their shoes upon their feet; they should not mourn nor weep, nor pine away for their iniquities, nor mourn one towards another.

*Hadad's Wife.*

We have the history of Hadad the Edomite in 1st Kings, xi: 14. This man became an adversary of King Solomon, but when he was in Egypt with Pharaoh, to whom he had fled when he was a little boy, he did not make known his intention to oppose the king of Israel. He saw that Pharaoh was at peace with Solomon and had given him his daughter to wife, and hence kept his opposition from the knowledge of the king of

Egypt. And Pharaoh gave him to wife the sister of his own wife. So that Hadad's wife was the sister of the queen. And this woman became for Hadad the mother of Genubath, who was raised up in Pharaoh's household.

*Harlot of Gaza.*

This woman, of whom we have an account in Judges, xvi: 1, was probably an inn-keeper, or the keeper of a house of entertainment in the city of Gaza. She may have been a very honorable woman, and the mistress of a reputable house of entertainment, and Samson stopped there for the night as a weary traveler. He was a man of note, and an avowed enemy of the Philistines, and they lay in wait for him to kill him in the morning. But he left the house of entertainment in the night and so escaped.

*Harlots Asking for Judgment.*

We have the account of them and their application to King Solomon for judgment in 1st Kings, iii: 16, 28. They both lived in one house, and each was delivered of a child about the same time. The one that came to the king to plead for her child says: The third day after her child was born, the other was delivered of a child, and she overlaid it. And after she found that her child was dead, then she arose and took my son and laid her dead child in my bosom in the stead. When she arose in the morning, or awaked from the sleep of the night—the dead child was laying by her; but when she came to look at it closely, behold it was not her son. She charged the woman with having done as above stated. She bitterly denied they came to Solomon for judgment; the case was such a one that it admitted of no formal proof, "there was no stranger with us in the house." They were alone at the time the transaction charged took place. The case, as thus presented to the king, was certainly a difficult one; but he saw that the tenderness and affection of the real mother might be tested, and so the fact be developed as to which of the two was the mother of the living child. After hearing the case he gave his decision, which was to appearance a very strange decision. "Divide the living child and give half to the one, and half to the other." Then the woman that came to the king for redress, said to him, "O, my Lord, give her the living child, and in no wise slay it." She said this because her bowels yearned over it as her own son. King Solomon marked her feeling. He saw how much rather she would give up her own son, than that he should be slain. The language in import was, "Spare the life of my son, even if I am not to be known as its real mother." But the other woman, not suspecting the aim of the wise king in this decision, said, addressing herself to the woman she had robbed: "Let it be neither mine, nor thine, but divide it." This expression condemned the woman and settled the matter, that she was not the mother of the child. Maternal affection had been fairly tested and developed. Solomon says, "Give her the living child, and in no wise slay it; she is the mother thereof." The suit was decided in favor of the complainant.

*Herodias—Daughter of.*

Her name is supposed to have been Salome, and she was, probably, the daughter of Philip, Herod's brother. It is supposed that Aristobulus, the brother of Herod and Philip, was the father of Herodias; hence, her daughter sustained the relation of niece to Herod, who was now her husband.

Herodias had become enraged at John the Baptist, because he had reproved her, and she meditated revenge. Herod, for her sake, had bound John and put him in prison. Matt. xiv: 3: "For Herod had laid hold on John and put him in prison, for Herodias's sake, his brother Philip's wife."

During the time that John was in prison, Herod's birthday came, and was observed, probably, with feasting; and in the midst of the pleasures of the day, the daughter of Herodias came into the apartment of the palace where Herod was, and danced. There was, in all probability, a large company of the king's admirers, who were invited guests to his birthday feast, present with him, when the young dancer entered and entertained them with her performance of dancing. Herod probably admired the beauty of her person, and listened to the expressions of admiration of the company; but he was pleased with her performance as a dancer, and joined with his guests in lauding the young woman. But he went further than mere laudations and admiration—under the excitement of the occasion he rashly promised, with an oath, that he would give her whatsoever she would ask.

How foolish was his proposition, and what a degree of weakness did it show! Mark, vi: 23: "Whatsoever thou shalt ask of me I will give it thee, unto the half of my kingdom." She went immediately to her mother to confer with her as to what she should ask. Her mother was not slow to give her an answer: "My daughter, ask the head of John the Baptist." Her vengeance was not yet fully wreaked; though John had been for her sake imprisoned, she desired his death. The daughter and dancer went in to Herod with haste, partaking of her mother's spirit of hatred to John, and said, "Give me here John the Baptist's head in a charger." What a request for a beautiful young lady to make to a king enamored with her beauty and skill in dancing! Behead John the Baptist, and bring me evidence of the fact that he is beheaded, by producing the head in a charger, that I can see it —that my mother may see it, and trace the lineaments on the distorted countenance of the man who dared to reprove her for choosing to become your wife! No wonder that the king was sorry, since her request was so cruel, that he made the promise; and sorry because he knew that John was an honorable and high-minded man, and correct in the reproof he administered. But Herod, for his oath's sake, sent an executioner and beheaded John, and they brought the head in a charger and gave it to her, and she gave it to her mother.

It is said that this young woman came to her death by falling or breaking through the ice on which she was walking, and that the ice closed, after her body had passed through, severing her head from her shoulders.

*Heth—Daughters of.*

They embittered the life of Rebekah, the wife of Isaac, as we learn from Genesis, xxvii: 46. "Rebekah said unto Isaac, I am weary of my life because of the daughters of Heth," &c. Rebekah had been brought from Mesopotamia by Abraham to be the wife of Isaac, and she greatly desired that Jacob who was her favorite, should go to Padan-aram and get a wife of his own relationship. She seems to be afraid that the daughters of Heth would so win upon Jacob's feelings, that he would do as Esau had done, marry among them. For Esau had married a Hittite woman. If she was not really afraid, she pretended to be, hence Isaac sent Jacob to his kindred to procure a wife.

*Isaac's Servants.*

We have an account of these servants when Isaac dwelt in Gerar. He had secured the respect of Abimelech, the king, and was permitted to dwell in the land, while the king gave a strict command to his people not to molest either Isaac or his wife. Thus protected and encouraged, he engaged in agricultural pursuits, and in taking care of his flocks and herds; and it is said of him: "He sowed in the land and received in the same year an hundred fold." His flocks and herds were very extensive, and his store of servants was large, insomuch that the people of the land envied him, and in all probability they were afraid of him.

The king of Gerar besought Isaac to go from him, giving, as his reason, "for thou art mightier than we." Accordingly he went and pitched in the valley; and he set his servants to digging wells of water or opening up the wells that Abraham digged when he was there, which the Philistines had filled up; and, in addition to reopening the wells of Abraham, "Isaac's servants digged in the valley and found there a well of springing water." When the herdmen of Gerar saw their success in procuring water, they claimed it and secured it; whereupon Isaac's servants digged another well; and that was taken from them, also. They then dug the well Rehoboth and were permitted to enjoy it.

The servants of Isaac, we suppose, like the servants of Abraham, were his own household, and were constantly governed by him. They performed for him the labor of tilling the ground, pasturing the flocks and herds, and such other work as Isaac's extensive estate and the care of his large household demanded. Genesis, xxvi.

*Jairus—Daughter of.*

Jairus was a ruler of the synagogue at Capernaum, it is supposed. He was not, like many of the rulers, an enemy of Christ's, as is evident from his conduct as narrated in connection with the resurrection of his daughter.

The daughter of Jairus was about twelve years of age when she was taken sick, and lay in a dying condition. Luke, viii: 42. "For he had one only daughter, about twelve years of age, and she lay dying." We suppose her father had used all the means within his reach—had had the skill of his family physician, but all to no avail. And believing in Christ's ability to heal her, he determined to apply to him, and he did, addressing him in the most touching manner. Mark v: 23. "My little daughter lieth at the point of death. I pray thee come and lay thy hand upon her, and she shall live." Jesus attended to his request and went to his house. The intelligence had reached them by a messenger, before they arrived at Capernaum, that his daughter was dead. But Jesus eased his strickened heart, by indicating that his daughter should be restored.

When they arrived, the friends of the family who had gathered in, and were mingling their sympathy with the bereaved family, were all put out of the apartment where the corpse was, and taking his three disciples, Peter, James and John, with the father and mother of the damsel, he entered the room. "And he took the damsel by the hand and saith unto her, *talitha-cumi;* which is, being interpreted, Damsel I say unto thee arise." She obeyed his command, and in a few moments the delighted parents rejoiced that she lived.

The daughter of Jairus is one of the few that were raised from the dead by Christ himself; and the case of her resurrection was a strong attestation of his Messiahship. How long she lived afterwards we know not, or what was her manner of life; but we may suppose, that with her parents, she became a firm believer in the truth of Christ's mission, and never forgot the scene that opened upon her vision when she first returned to consciousness.

*Jephthah's Daughter.*

Jephthah was the son of Gilead, but his mother was probably a Canaanite; and because he was the son of a woman of another nation—"a stranger woman"—his brothers would not allow him to inherit with them, and they "thrust out Jephthah." Judg. xi.: 2.

The Ammonites were greatly oppressing the Gileadites, and they desired deliverance. On making inquiry for a captain to head them, Jephthah was spoken of as a "mighty man of valor," and sent for to the land of Tob to come and fight for them against Ammon. They entered into a covenant with him, in which they promised if he would deliver them he should be their head. Jephthah sent an embassy to the enemy, and received an answer from them, to which he replied in a very spirited manner. His reply was not regarded by the enemy, and he prepared for battle.

Before Jephthah entered into battle with his enemy, he made a vow unto the Lord, Judg. xi: 30: "If thou shalt without fail deliver the children of Ammon into my hands, then it shall be that whatsoever cometh forth of the doors of my house to meet me when I return in peace, shall surely be the Lord's, and I will offer it for a burnt offering."

Jephthah obtained a great victory, and elated with it returned to Mizpah, where he lived. His daughter and his only child hearing of his victory and of his approach to the city, went out to meet him "with timbrels and with dances." This was not at all strange on her part, since it was an ancient custom for women to meet returning conquerors and honor them. Jephthah was greatly distressed when he saw his daughter coming to meet him, for the vow he had made before fighting the battle came to his mind; and addressing himself to the daughter he said, as he rent his clothes, "Alas, my daughter! thou hast brought me very low, and thou art one of them that trouble me; for I have opened my mouth unto the Lord, and I cannot go back." She seemed to understand the import of her father's language, and feel the sanctity of the obligation that was upon him. She saw how her father was brought down, and with the feelings of a dutiful daughter, she said: "My father, if thou hast opened thy mouth unto the Lord, do to me according to that which hath proceeded out of thy mouth."

What a picture is thus presented to our minds of piety and obedience! Though she was the daughter of a man now entitled to be the head of the Gileadites, yet she was willing to be sacrificed in the sense in which the promise of her father demanded it. But she gave the reason why she should thus suffer: "Forasmuch as the Lord hath taken vengeance for thee of thine enemies, even of the children of Ammon;" as though she had said, My father, if thou didst promise the Lord that whosoever first came forth from thy house to meet thee should be sacrificed, on condition of victory over thine enemies, be faithful to the Lord and fulfill thy vow. She asked but one request of her father, which request was granted. It was this: "Let me alone two months, that I may go up and down upon the mountains and bewail my virginity, I and my fellows." In this request it may be she simply asked the privilege of visiting her acquaintances and female companions for the space of two months, which she did, bewailing her virginity—sorrowing, as some think, that she could not be a mother in the line of the coming Christ, as many of every generation desired to be, and but one could be.

It is hardly likely that this vow of Jephthah, though it troubled him so much, demanded the death, by his hand, of the daughter. After two months had expired, she came to her father and yielded herself up as a sacrifice. Human sacrifices have always been an abomination to God. One of the reasons given why the Canaanites were driven out of their land was, they offered their sons and daughters in the fire to Moloch. It is not likely that he committed an act toward an innocent daughter that God had condemned in the people whom he fought and conquered. It may be that Jephthah offered a burnt offering to the Lord; but surely his daughter was not that burnt offering. In addition to the offering, he consecrated his daughter to God in perpetual virginity. In his devotion to God and his faithfulness to perform his vows, severe as was the stroke—she being his only child—he gave her to the Lord; and she knew no man, or continued a virgin all the days of her life. And the probability is, that, as long as she lived (and no longer than her life lasted) the daughters of Israel went yearly to lament the daughter of Jephthah, four days in the year. They went to see her and comfort her.

*Jeroboam—Wife of.*

She is brought to our view in 1st Kings, xiv, in connection with the account of the sickness and death of Abijah, the son of Jeroboam. The king sends his wife, disguised as the queen, to Shiloh to inquire of Ahijah, the prophet, what would be the result of the child's sickness. She, in accordance with the wish of her husband went, having all the solicitude of an anxious and alarmed mother, regarding the result of a dangerous sickness of her own son, for Abijah was her own son, and she had looked with fond affection upon him, and counted him the successor to the throne of Israel, of Jeroboam, his father. She took with her, presents from the king, and "feigned herself to be another woman." The prophet was aged and his eyes were dim, if, indeed, he was not quite blind. But it was revealed to him by the Lord, that the wife of Jeroboam was coming to him to inquire of him concerning her son. He detected her as she approached, and invited her to come in. He mildly reproved her for endeavoring to practice imposition, and immediately gave her the heavy tidings of God's anger towards Jeroboam, and his determination to cut off his house; and of the dishonor that should come upon many of his family. And as it regarded the child Abijah, his sickness the prophet declared unto her was unto death, and that she had seen her son alive for the last time; "when thy feet enter into the city, the child shall die." Hence, before Jeroboam's wife entered the royal palace and looked again upon the little sufferer, his mortal career was ended. She entered Tirzah, and as she came to the threshold of the door, the child died, and all Israel engaged in honoring him, for he was the only one of Jeroboam's family, or of this wife's children, that came to the grave in peace.

*Job's Wife.*

Job's wife is introduced to our notice in connection with the afflictions that he was called, for the trial of his faith, to pass through. She was the mother of the seven sons and three daughters of Job, and with him was deeply afflicted at the loss of property, servants and children. If, as we suppose, they were her sons and daughters, she must have felt exceedingly sorrowful when the intelligence was brought them that they were all dead. And while Job arose and "rent his mantle," and gave other evidences of his deep feeling, she was also giving vent to the sorrows of her heart in piercing cries and bitter wailings, though the sacred text does not show it. But it can hardly be said of her as it is said of Job: "In all this Job sinned not, nor charged God foolishly." The reason we think it cannot be, is, her conduct as narrated afterwards, when God tried the quality and quantity of Job's faith by allowing him to be afflicted with sore boils, "from the sole of his foot unto his crown," so that he became a very loathsome object, and needed the counsel and advice of a wise friend. He needed words of comfort poured into his ear and upon his lacerated and bleeding heart. Just then his wife ventured to counsel him, and, oh! what counsel for the wife of a good man to give him: "Dost thou still retain thine integrity? Curse God and die." Whatever the full meaning of this language is, it indicates a lack of faith in God on her part. While his heart in his afflictions was full of gratitude to God, her heart was filled with a contrary feeling. She seems to be almost, if not altogether, an infidel. The trials had come heavier on her than she could bear. Her children were all dead. Her husband's property was gone, and he afflicted with so loathsome a disease that his friends all shunned him. The prospect for her was that the name of her husband would soon perish, for they had no children to perpetuate it. Poverty stared them in the face, if her husband ever recovered of his disease. Her patience was gone. She gave vent to her fretful and murmuring feelings, and counseled Job to "curse God and die," or as some think, *bless God and die.* But how nobly did the sufferer reprove her: "Thou speakest as one of the foolish women speaketh. What? shall we receive good at the hands of God, and shall we not receive evil?" What philosophy was this. As though he had said to her: My knowledge of God, of religion, and of a future state, with our condition in this world, teaches me that we are not always to have prosperity, and plenty, and health. The God who gave me property and servants and children and health, or placed them in my charge, has a right to take them away when it shall please him. It may be that this same woman lived to see Job again in prosperity; saw his accusers confounded, and was the mother for him of the seven sons and three daughters that blessed the evening of his life.

*Lemuel—Mother of.*

It is not certainly known who King Lemuel was, possibly it was Solomon himself. If so Bathsheba, his mother, was the woman who is represented as uttering in the ears of her son, the proverbs recorded in Prov. xxxi. This queen mother expostulates with her son as to his future course of life. She pleads with him especially to avoid the two sins that so often go hand in hand, viz: drunkenness and lasciviousness. She counsels him to do good with his wealth, and use his power as a mighty king in administering justice with care, courage, and compassion. She then gives him a most glowing description of a virtuous woman, and the description is worth the study of all women. 10th and 30th verses inclusive.

*Lepers—the Four Famishing.*

Benhadad had besieged the city of Samaria and reduced its inhabitants and soldiery to the greatest necessity, for the head of an ass was sold for four-score pieces of silver, while the fourth part of a cab of dove's dung was sold for five pieces of silver. They were reduced to such necessity that they were dying of starvation, and women were eating their own children.

The king of Israel charged this dire necessity upon the prophet Elisha, and determined to destroy him. The messengers came to take him for death, and the king, determining to see his order executed, followed after them. While at the door of Elisha's house he heard his prophecy declaring that on the next day there should be great plenty in Samaria: "A measure of fine flour shall be sold for a shekel, and two measures of barley for a shekel in the gate of Samaria." One of the king's aids that attended him to the prophet's house, and that was anxious to see him executed, told the king that it was impossible for Elisha's declaration to be fulfilled: "If the Lord would make windows in heaven might this thing be?" Elisha then assured that man that he should see it with his eyes, but should not eat thereof; and in this matter the prophet's declaration was fulfilled to the letter, for the next day the people trod on him in the gate that he died, while they were rushing to the point to obtain the flour and barley that was selling according to the word of Elisha.

During the night, the Lord, by a miracle, had alarmed the Syrians, and they suddenly raised the siege of Samaria and fled, leaving their tents and horses, and all their equipments and stores.

There were four leprous men at the gate of the city in a starving condition, and, in their extremity, they determined to give themselves up to the Syrians; for, if they entered the city, they knew they would die, and they could but die by giving themselves up to the enemy; accordingly they arose and went toward the camp; but, to their astonishment, when they neared the camp, they found no guards. They came to the tents and entered, finding no occupants, and they saw no men throughout the entire encampment. They first, as starving men, satisfied themselves with food; then they gathered up silver and gold, and raiment, and went and hid it. So they pillaged several tents. They then determined to go back to the city and report that the Syrian army was gone, but all their tents and equipage were on the ground they had been occupying. They went and informed the guard, and soon the news spread through the city, and the king sent a small party out to ascertain the truth of the report. They followed the alarmed Syrians as far as the Jordan, and came back to report that they found it as the lepers had reported. Their enemy had fled from their encampment, leaving much behind them, and the way they had gone was strown with garments and vessels which had been cast away.

Thus these four lepers were instrumental in bringing relief, early that day, to the starving thousands of Samaria. 2d Kings, vi, vii.

*Levite's Secondary Wife.*

This Levite was of Mount Ephraim, and his concubine, or secondary wife, was of Bethlehem Judah. Judges, xix: 1. It is not certain from the presentation of this woman's case as given, that she was very disreputable, or that she was guilty of an act of conjugal infidelity. It may be that, as husband and wife, they did not agree, and mutually consented to separate, and the woman returned to her father's house. If she had been guilty of the improprieties and wickedness that some think she had, the Levite would not have gone after her to speak friendly to her, and bring her again to his house.

The father of the woman aimed to make up the difference between them, and probably succeeded after keeping the Levite at his house several days. He started with her and his attendants for his house in Mount Ephraim. As they were unable to reach home that day, they stopped for the night in Gibeah, of Benjamin. It was some time after they entered Gibeah, before they had an invitation for lodging. At length an aged man coming from his work, saw them as wayfarers in the streets, and approaching them, entered into conversation with them, from which conversation he learned who they were and whither they were going. The old man invited them to lodge with him—to come under his roof, and for the night enjoy his hospitality. The Levite agreed, and went into his house. But soon the house of the aged man was beset by wicked men, and they made cruel and wicked demands regarding the Levite and his party, and they could not be pacified by the aged man. At length the Levite, in order to save his own life and person, proved himself a graceless husband, by thrusting his wife out among the rabble, who with their cruelty and wickedness, occasioned her death. She died before the morning at the door of the house where the Levite, her husband, stayed.

The Levite, in the morning, cut the body of his deceased wife into twelve pieces, and sent a piece to each of the tribes of Israel, with an account of the barbarity and wickedness of the men of Gibeah, and also a request, we may suppose, that his wrongs be avenged.

There seems to have been a council called, and this Levite appeared before it, and represented his cause. The council consisted of the heads of eleven tribes. They unanimously resolved to avenge the wrong, and prepared for a war against Benjamin, on condition they did not give up the murderers of the Levite's wife. The Benjamites refused to do it, and the result was, the cities of Benjamin were all destroyed, and the Benjamites were destroyed as a tribe, except six hundred men who fled to the wilderness, who were afterwards provided with wives, and so were the means of saving the tribe from becoming utterly extinct.

*Lot's Wife.*

Her name is not given, but she was a favored woman in being the wife of so good a man as Lot. She may have been the wife of Lot at the time that the confederate kings conquered the country and took Lot and his family captives, and were hurrying away with them as captives taken in war, when Abraham, Lot's uncle, overtook them and smote them, "and recovered Lot and his goods, and the women also, and the people." But whether she was his wife then or not, she was when God determined to destroy the wicked cities of the plain and sent two angels to Sodom to inform Lot and hasten him out of the city with his family.

Whatever the character of Lot's wife was, whether, like her husband, she feared God in the midst of the wickedness around her, or partook of the spirit and wickedness of the Sodomites, she had a chance afforded her of escaping the punishment that was visited upon the city, for "the angels hastened Lot, saying, Arise, take thy wife and thy two daughters which are here, lest thou be consumed in the iniquity of the city." And so anxious were the angels for her salvation, and for the salvation of her husband and daughters, that they laid hold upon her hand. She seemed, for a time, to bid fair to escape, but, actuated by some motive, she disobeyed the injunction: Genesis, xix: 17: "Escape for thy life; look not behind thee; neither stay thou in all the plain; escape to the mountain, lest thou be consumed." She turned around in the flight and looked back to see, it may be, whether God was thus visiting the city with destruction. God had said, "look not back," but she said in action, I will look back. The judgment of God overtook her; terrible punishment was visited upon her: "She became a pillar of salt." The Almighty, who was raining fire and brimstone from Heaven upon the devoted cities, made her, for her disobedience, a public example of his vengeance; and her sin and her punishment have ever since been pointed to as a warning to others. Gen. xix: 26.

*Lot's Daughters.*

Their names are not given, but their number is—they were two. They had both of them entered upon marriage engagements, if the matter of their marriage was not already consummated as it probably was not, from what Lot says of them in Gen. xix: 8. The men to whom they were engaged in marriage or espoused, refused to believe the words of the angels regarding the coming destruction of the city, and hence they perished while the two young women escaped with their father to the mountain or rather to the little city of Zoar.

They had not dwelt in Zoar long until Lot feared to remain; his daughters joined him in all probability in fears, lest Zoar should be visited as the other cities had been visited, and yet they should be destroyed. Lot committed a great wrong when he entertained fears that Zoar would be destroyed, and when he proposed to his daughters that they should go to the mountains—the place where God at first commanded them to go. Had he remained the city would have been spared for his sake; and the stain that settles upon his character, on account of the shameful transaction recorded regarding him, would probably not have been there.

We are unable to excuse the daughters of Lot for their deception of their father—for the means on their part resorted to, to accomplish their purposes. And it is not to be wondered at that the descendants of their two sons, the names of which were Moab and Ben-ammi, were wicked. The Moabites who sprung from the first were gross idolators, and enemies to the chosen people of God —the children of Abraham. And the Ammonites who sprung from Ben-ammi, were in league with the Moabites — they were associated in idolatry and in their opposition to Israel. Gen. xix.

*Man of Benjamin, who went to Eli.*

This man belonged to the army of Israel, and only stayed with the routed army, after the battle, long enough to learn how many of the soldiers were slain, and that the ark of God was taken and Hophni and Phinehas were both dead. He was deeply afflicted over the defeat of Israel, and ran to Eli, as the bearer of sad news, but he came with his clothes rent and earth upon his head. These were the signs of sorrow and distress which he gave. By the former he signified that the Israelites were scattered and divided, and by the latter, he signified their deep humiliation.

When he came to Shiloh, Eli was sitting by the road side, waiting for intelligence and trembling for the result, and especially for the fate of the ark of God. Ere the Benjamite reached the point where Eli was, the whole city had learned through him the result of the engagement, and were engaged in lamentation and mourning. Eli had but time, on hearing their cries, to ask the cause, when the messenger arrived before him, and began to relate the casualties. He had hardly finished his message, when the aged priest fell backward before him, and broke his neck. 1st Samuel, iv: 12–18.

*Man of God and the Old Bethel Prophet.*

The names of these prophets are not given. Some have supposed that the name of the man of God who prophesied against Jeroboam's altar was Shemaiah, others have maintained that it was Joel, and still others that it was Iddo. But as the sacred historian has not given him a name it is useless to aim at securing one for him. He was a good man and a true prophet, commissioned by God to an important work, viz., that of prophesying against Jeroboam and his idolatrous altar. In the performance of his mission he went in accordance with the divine direction directly to the altar, and in the hearing of Jeroboam who stood by it declared the divine decree: "Behold a child shall be born unto the house of David, Josiah by name; and upon thee shall he offer the priests of the high places, that burn incense upon thee, and men's bones shall be burnt upon thee."

He then backed up his prophecy against the altar by a clear sign—Jeroboam saw the altar miraculously rent and the ashes poured out from the altar. He became enraged at the prophet and put forth his hand to take hold of him, thereby ordering those about him to arrest him—but as he did so his hand was withered—his whole arm became paralyzed, which affliction brought him to his senses and turning to the man of God he besought him to intercede with God in his behalf, that his hand might be restored to him again. The man of God did pray for him and God heard his prayer and restored the withered hand. Jeroboam felt greatly indebted to the prophet and proposed to him to go with him to his palace and rest and refresh himself, and receive at his hand a reward; but he told him he would not. The language of his refusal is as follows: "If thou wilt give me half thine house, I will not go in with thee, neither will I eat bread nor drink water in this place." The reason he gave for this bold refusal was, "For so it was charged me by the word of the Lord saying, Eat no bread nor drink water, nor turn again by the same way that thou camest." His mission being ended there the man of God turned to go to Judah by another way than the way he came.

It was not long after he left the rent altar, and the repentant king, until the sons of an old prophet that lived at Bethel, reported to their father all that the man of God had done that day. This old man is supposed to have been a backslidden prophet, one who had fallen from his steadfastness, and had been rejected by God. Though he may not have so far fallen, as to have become an idolater himself, yet his sons were probably idolaters, and had been engaged with Jeroboam at his worship. When the sons reported to their aged father the scenes of the day he became anxious to know more about the man of God, and he asked them which way he went; they told him, when he made ready and followed after him. He had not proceeded far till he overtook him. The man of God was sitting under the shade of an oak to rest himself; the old Bethel prophet accosted him with, "Art thou the man of God that camest from Judah?" He told him he was. He then gave him a cordial invitation to go back to his house and partake of a repast which he would provide. He told him that his orders were, not to stop to eat bread or drink water in that place, and that he who appointed him on the mission of prophesying against Jeroboam's idolatrous altar, had given him the orders. The old man then told him that he also was a prophet and that an angel spake unto him and bade him bring him back to his house, that he might eat bread and drink water, but the sacred historian says, "he lied unto him." The devil may have transformed himself into an angel of light, and spoken to the Bethel prophet to bring back this man of God, but he who had told him not to tarry certainly had not.

The man of God believed him and went back with him, and here was the sin for which he was punished. He ought not to have been satisfied with anything short of a direct communication from him who sent him on the errand. While engaged in eating, the word of the Lord came to him, either directly, or through this Bethel prophet, charging his sin upon him, and that he should be punished with death somewhere between Bethel and Judah. Immediately after the repast was finished, he left the house of the Bethel prophet, and began to journey toward his home. He had not proceeded far until he was met by a wild beast and slain. "A lion met him and slew him." Some travelers passing along, saw the dead body, and the lion standing by it, and they went and told the old prophet of Bethel, who immediately repaired to the place, and "he found his carcass cast in the way, and the ass and the lion standing by the carcass, the lion had not eaten the carcass, nor torn the ass." The Bethel prophet took possession of the body of the man of God, and took it back to Bethel for burial. He gave it possession of his own grave, and lamented over it saying, "Alas my brother." He then bade his sons bury him, when he died in the same sepulcher. He desired to have his bones laid beside the man of God. From this we may learn that he considered the prophet, who had thus come to his end, a great and good man, one by whom it would be an honor to lie in death. 1st Kings, xiii: 1–32.

The prophecy of this man of God was fulfilled regarding the altar of Bethel. More than three hundred years after this, when king Josiah, who was prophesied of by name, was carrying on his reform in the kingdom of Judah, in the destruction of idolatry, and of idolatrous temples. It is said he broke down the altar which Jeroboam built at Bethel, and utterly destroyed everything connected with it. While engaged in his destruction of idolatry at Bethel, Josiah had his attention directed to the sepulchers in the side of the mountain, and he ordered the bones taken out of the sepulchers and burnt on the altar, thereby polluting it. But he saw the sepulcher of the man of God, and the Bethel prophet, and knew it by an inscription upon a stone that closed it, or was near by it. He bade them let that sepulcher alone, or not move the bones. He had respect for the bones of one who had dared in the presence of the idolatrous Jeroboam to predict the overthrow of his altar, and of his system of idolatry. 2d Kings, xxiii: 15-18.

*Man of God who came to Eli.*

He was evidently a prophet of the Lord, and specially commissioned to prophesy the downfall of Eli's family, and the death of his two wicked sons, Hophni and Phinehas. He came to Eli and delivered his solemn charge, in which he referred him to God's goodness in selecting the tribe to which he belonged to honorable position among the tribes of Israel, and the family from which he was descended—that of Aaron—to be priests and ministers of holy things. He referred him to God's goodness to the Ithamar part of Aaron's family, in transferring the high-priesthood from Eleazar to them. And now he assured him that, because of the wickedness of his sons, this distinguished honor should be returned to the house of Eleazar.

God had promised that the high-priesthood should remain in the family of Aaron's younger son; and so it would, had they been faithful. Eli's sons had been very wicked, and he himself had been unfaithful, and now the prophet charges that unfaithfulness upon him, and gives it as the reason why the divine promise is annulled, and the divine decree reversed.

He still continues before Eli, and declares that even Shiloh shall be desecrated—a dreadful calamity shall fall upon Israel, in the capture of the ark and its sacred deposits, by their enemies; and that his two sons shall both be slain in one day, and his family shall entirely fail in the priesthood.

All this came to pass, for Abiathar was the last descendant of the house of Eli. 1st Sam. ii.

*Man of God who Encouraged the King to Attack the Syrians.*

Benhadad, the king of Syria, had thirty-two kings associated with him in besieging Samaria. His army was large and powerful, and he thought of nothing but success. He accordingly sent messengers with a very insulting message, to Ahab, the king of Israel; and insisted on pillaging the city of Samaria and bringing its king into the most abject servitude to him. Ahab, humiliated, proffered the insulting king of Syria all he asked; but the Elders of Israel checked him by saying, "Hearken not unto him, nor consent." Accordingly the king of Israel sent him word that he would not agree to the last part of the proposition he had made, viz.: that the Syrian soldiery should pass through the city and take whatever they pleased, after the wives and children, and silver and gold had been taken. Benhadad became enraged at this, and again vowed revenge, when the king of Israel, inspirited by the counsel of the Elders, sent him word that the battle was not over yet, and that it did not become a man who was preparing for a battle to boast as one who has fought and conquered. "Let not him that girdeth on his harness boast himself as he that putteth it off."

Just at this time, the man of God, who was a true prophet, approached Ahab and strengthened him for the coming contest. The prophet declared that this large army of the king of Syria should be conquered, and proceeded to give him instructions as to the manner of preparing for the battle. He was to take the young men, to the number of two hundred and thirty-two, and make the attack upon him in the pavilion, rush upon his tents ere he had time to prepare himself by throwing his army into line of battle, and then have his army of seven thousand Israelites to follow after him, and he did so. Benhadad, and the thirty-two kings that were helping him, were drinking themselves drunk in their tents. They rushed upon them and slew every one his man; Benhadad escaped on a horse with the horsemen. Thus the king of Israel followed the instructions of the prophet, and slew the Syrians with a great slaughter.

This same prophet then advised Ahab to increase his army and prepare himself for a second attack. He did so, and in the next battle slew one hundred thousand footmen. The Syrian army was followed as it retreated; and as it went into the city of Aphek, twenty-seven thousand more of them were killed by the falling of a wall, and Benhadad, and those that were left, surrendered to Ahab.

Who this prophet was, we cannot tell; some have thought it was Micaiah, the son of Imlah, and others that it was Elijah or Elisha; but of this we cannot be certain, as the name is not given. 1st Kings, xx: 13-30.

*Man that gathered sticks on the Sabbath.*

The brief history of this man is, that he was found by the children of Israel gathering sticks on the Sabbath day. And they that found him arrested and took him into the presence of Moses and Aaron for judgment, thereby bringing his case before all the congregation of Israel. Moses and Aaron knew that he had committed offence; but it was an offence that was not specified in their law of the Sabbath, hence they knew not what the penalty should be. They, therefore, put the man under guard until they might enquire of the Lord what should be done to him. "And the Lord said unto Moses, The man shall surely be put to death; all the congregation (of Israel) shall stone him with stones without the camp." Accordingly they brought him without the camp. and he was executed. If his act was not a plain and direct violation of the fourth commandment, still it was a violation of divine command, and of commands regarding the Sabbath. He seems to have been arrested as a Sabbath-breaker. Num. xv: 32-36.

We may judge, from the verses that immediately precede this reference, that his sin was presumptuousness, whereby he reproached the Lord. "He despised the word of the Lord, and brake his commandments;" and the penalty for that offence is said to be, "being cut off from among his people."

*Micah—the Mother of.*

This woman was of Mount Ephraim, and possibly, was a devoted servant of God. The transaction recorded of her is in Judges, xvii. She had collected together eleven hundred shekels of silver, which she "dedicated to the Lord." It was not her design to engage in idolatry, or to establish idolatrous worship in her house. At least there is no positive evidence that it was. She may have intended to make with it something to resemble some sacred thing in the tented temple.

Micah saw the money where his mother had concealed it, and took it. As soon as she missed it, she began to pour imprecations upon the head of the thief who had stolen it. Micah heard her language, and was afraid lest the curses should fall on him. He went to her and confessed that he had taken the money. He said, "The eleven hundred shekels of silver that were taken from thee, about which thou cursedest, and spakest of, also in mine ears, behold, the silver is with me, I took it." The mother of Micah was much gratified to learn that it was yet in the family. And when he restored it to her, she gave it back to him to use for the object for which she had intended it. The history indicates that he was not willing to appropriate the money to this object in person. It may be that he saw the impropriety in such a use of it that his mother did not.

But she took two hundred shekels and gave them to the founder, who made her an image, and it was placed in the house of Micah. So that we may judge that the son, if at first he was opposed to it, became reconciled, and argued with his mother that they should have a sanctuary at their house, a domestic temple; for, as it is stated, Micah made an ephod and teraphim, and consecrated one of his sons to serve in the priesthood, in his house of gods. It is likely that he aimed to imitate the sanctuary of God—in which was the ark, and the mercy-seat, and cherubim.

*Micah's Priest—the young Levite.*

This man Micah was an Ephraimite, and, in company with his mother, had erected a family temple and had in it an image which was with them an object of worship. He had also the paraphernalia of a priest in part—an ephod and a teraphim—and one of his sons was consecrated and served as a priest.

This young Levite was probably seeking employment, and coming to the house of Micah to lodge for the night, it may be, he was questioned as to the place from whence he hailed and whither he was going. He answered that he was a Levite, and was seeking a home and employment. Micah at once proposed to hire him to be a priest for him; and he agreed with him for ten shekels of silver a year, and a suit of clothing and his board. This young Levite served Micah for some time.

At length five Danites were passing that way and overheard him talking. It may be, he was performing service in the temple, and they knew it was not the dialect of the Ephraimites, and they asked him what he was doing there. He told them that he was hired by Micah as his priest. They asked him to serve them by asking God regarding the object of their mission, which was, to secure a home for themselves and a company of Danites who had sent them—whether they should prosper. He did ask for them, and, we judge, received a favorable answer, for he said to them: "Go in peace; before the Lord is your way, wherein you go." These Danites went on and selected the town of Laish, which was inhabited by a Zidonian colony that they thought could be easily conquered. They then returned to Zorah and Eshtaol and reported to the Danites who sent them out that this place could be secured. Then six hundred of them started out as warriors; and they took Mount Ephraim in their route, and, stopping at the house of Micah, one of the five men who were conducting them toward Laish, reported regarding Micah's temple and his Levite priest, and the whole company went toward the dwelling of the young Levite, and, stationing themselves near it, they sent the five men in, with instructions to take the graven image, and the ephod and teraphim, and carry it with them to their future home. The young Levite priest came out and expostulated with them against their action; but they would not hear, and, moreover, they compelled him to silence, but gave him an offer of employment with them; and they urged that it would be much better for him to become a priest for a large company, or for a tribe, than to remain as a priest for one man. He seems to have accorded to their wishes and rejoiced in the prospect of a more extended field of labor; and probably he had the offer of larger compensation. The young Levite then attended them, keeping in all probability, all the things that they had taken from Micah's temple, in his charge.

When they came to Laish and conquered it, they changed its name to Dan, calling it after the name of their tribe; and we may suppose that he who is called Jonathan, the son of Gershom, who, with his sons, were priests to the tribe of Dan until the days of the captivity of the land, was this same young Levite who had served Micah; if not, the Danites turned him off and took Jonathan in his place. Judges, xviii.

*Midianites—the two who encouraged Gideon.*

These two men belonged to the army of the Midianites. One of them had a remarkable dream in which he saw "a cake of barley bread tumbled into the host of Midian, and came into a tent, and smote it that it fell, and overturned it that it lay all along," and he related the dream to his fellow who at once interpreted it to mean that "the sword of Gideon, the son of Joash," should prevail against the Midianites, and they should all be delivered into his hand. These men were probably a part of the outside guard of the army, and Gideon had come in person, with his faithful servant, Phurah, to see how his enemy was situated, and to have his hands strengthened for the attack he was about to make. As soon as he heard the guards in conversation, he listened, and heard the dream related, and heard the interpretation given. He was immediately inspirited with courage and went back to his army and infused courage into them by saying: "Arise, for the Lord hath delivered into your hand the host of Midian."

Though the men of the Midianite army were not worshippers of the living God, yet the dream and the interpretation thereof, were both inspired of God, and accomplished the end for which God inspired them: to encourage Gideon to make the attack and to make it at once. Judges, vii: 9–15.

*Midianitish Merchantmen.*

They were a company of Ishmaelites, trading in spicery, and balm, and myrrh, with the Egyptians. As the cruel brothers of Joseph saw the caravan approaching, they agreed together to sell him to them, and let them take him down to Egypt and sell him as a slave. Accordingly, as the merchantmen approached they drew Joseph out of the pit and proposed to sell him. They agreed upon the price, which was twenty pieces of silver. It is supposed the price was twenty shekels, which would have been less than two dollars apiece for the ten brothers.

These merchantmen took him down into Egypt and sold him to Potiphar, the captain of the body-guard of Pharaoh. What the amount was for which they sold him we do not know, but it is quite probable that they sold him for much more than they gave. Gen. xxxvii.

*Moab—The King of.*

Jehoram, Jehoshaphat, and the king of Edom were engaged in war with Mesha the king of Moab. The Moabite army had been completely routed and his cities beaten down and his land ruined. He became greatly discouraged and wondered the cause of the success of his enemies against him. He became desperate in his feelings when he saw the probabilities of his being captured, and he determined if possible to make his escape. With seven hundred of his choicest soldiers he undertook to break through that part of the line of the army surrounding his city—formed by the Edomites, but he was repulsed and driven back. He then as a last resort took his eldest son and offered him as a burnt offering upon the wall. This was done we may suppose in the sight of the besieging army, and it came, as a desperate act of the king of Moab, to the knowledge of the surrounding nations, so that there was great indignation against Israel." They consequently raised the siege and departed from the city 2d Kings, iii: 26, 27.

*Naaman—the captive maid of.*

This captive maid was one that had been taken by a Syrian company from an Israelite family, during one of their expeditions in search of booty. 2d Kings v: 2. "And the Syrians had gone out by companies, and had brought away captive, out of the land of Israel, a little maid, and she waited on Naaman's wife." This little girl had been brought up by pious parents and had a knowledge of the true God, and had often heard her parents talk of the prophets of Israel, and particularly of the distinguished prophet Elisha.

Naaman, her master, was a leper, and she was led one day to say to her mistress, "would God my lord were with the prophet in Samaria, for he would recover him of his leprosy." As though she had said, I know of a prophet who could, and would cure my master of his disease, if he would only go to him.

Naaman was informed of what the little girl said, and he determined to make application. He did so, first to the king, and afterwards to Elisha, and was cured.

Thus we observe a little pious captive maid, made instrumental in curing her master of one of the most dreadful of all diseases, leprosy, and she was made an instrument, we may suppose in the conversion of this great man and his Syrian family. They were brought, we would suppose, all of them, to a knowledge of the truth and the true God.

*Nain—The Widow of.*

The record of this woman is in Luke, vii: 11–15. Her only son had died, and her numerous friends had gathered in to her desolate dwelling to console and comfort her in the bereavement. "Much people of the city was with her." From this circumstance we may judge she was a very reputable woman. She had endeared herself to her acquaintances by her many excellencies, and they came together to sympathize with her in the loss, and assist in burying the young man.

The bier-bearers and mourners, and her numerous friends, had just passed out of the gate of the city, going to the graveyard, as Jesus approached Nain. He knew the young man, and his relationship, as he knew all things. He looked upon the lone widow, now childless, "and had compassion on her;" and addressing himself to the woman, he said, "Weep not." An inquiry was raised in this stricken woman as to who it was that thus spoke; and her numerous friends wondered with her who this man was that said, Weep not. His voice and bearing indicated deep sympathy, but why did he give such a command? Could a woman, bereft as this widow was, refrain from weeping? Her son, an honorable young man, who she hoped would be her stay in the decline of life, was dead, and they were now about to bury him from her sight.

Leaving the side of the woman, who was following the bier, he stepped forward and touched it, thereby intimating to the bier-bearers that they should stop. They did so; and addressing himself to the dead young man, he said, "Young man, I say unto thee, arise!" He had no sooner uttered this command, than the dead man sat up and began to speak.

What a wonderful sight! A young man that was dead, being followed to his grave by a large concourse of friends of his widowed mother, — suddenly raised to life by the words of Jesus,—sitting up on the bier before their eyes, then still further satisfying them that he was alive by talking to them as they gathered around him!

It is worthy of remark that the sympathizing Jesus did not require this young man, brought up from the dominions of death, to follow him in his wanderings up and down in the world; but "he delivered him to his mother," —permitted him to go with her to her home, and as a dutiful son minister to her in her declining life. He had compassion on the widow, and restored her son to life and to her society.

*Noah's Wife and his Sons' Wives.*

The names of these four women are not given; but it is a remarkable fact that the souls preserved in the ark were eight—four of them being men and four of them women. Noah and his three sons, Shem, Ham, and Japheth, Noah's wife, and the wives of his three sons, were the source for re-peopling the earth; and may we not consider the polygamy of Lamach, Noah's father, rebuked by this circumstance?

God made known to Noah his intention to deluge the world, but bade him build an ark and take refuge with his wife his sons and their wives, in it, and he did.

This wife of Noah was probably the mother of the three sons, and was the eldest of the four women, which entitled her to the position of mistress of the family while in the ark.

True to the divine command, when all things were ready Noah's wife and her three daughters-in-law went with their husbands into the ark, where they remained until the waters were assuaged, when, by the divine command, the women went forth with their husbands from the ark under the divine promise that the world should not again be deluged, and under the command, "Be fruitful, and multiply and replenish the earth."

How long Noah's wife lived we do not know; but he himself lived after the flood three hundred and fifty years. They were an aged couple when the flood came, but the earth was peopled by the descendants of their three sons. The wives of Shem, Ham and Japheth lived, probably, to see their children and their children's children grow up around them. We must think of these women, as we think of their husbands, as being greatly honored of God, in linking the first great age of the family of man, with the ages that have succeeded each other since the flood. Gen. vii.

*Paul's Sister.*

Whether she was living when he was laboring and suffering in the cause of Christ, we do not know; but she was the mother of the young man who entered into the castle where Paul was bound, and informed him of the plot laid for his life. Paul asked the centurion to introduce the young man to the chief captain. He did so, and the plans of the council were thwarted. This young man was Paul's sister's son. Acts, xxiii: 16.

*Pharaoh's chief Butler and Baker.*

These two men were in the prison at the time Joseph was. They had offended the king of Egypt, and for their offense, they were imprisoned, while Potiphar, whose slave Joseph was, had been offended at him. The cause of the offense was a lie told by Potiphar's wife to blast the reputation of the faithful servant, because he would not accede to her wishes in sinning against God, as well as against his master. After these prisoners of Pharaoh had been awhile in prison, they each dreamed a dream during the same night, and in the morning were greatly troubled about the significance of their dreams. Joseph observed their state of mind, and enquired the cause. They answered him that they had each dreamed a dream, and desired an interpretation, but knew not who to apply to, for, said they, "there is no interpreter of it." Joseph then bade them tell him the dream, and intimated that he would give them the interpretation thereof. Accordingly they each related to him their dream, and he readily, under Divine direction, interpreted the dreams. In accordance with the interpretation of Joseph, the chief baker, in three days, was taken out of prison, condemned and hanged; and the chief butler, in three days, was taken out, and restored to his butlership.

From this we may judge the former was proved guilty of the crime, for which he was imprisoned, and the latter proved, by evidence elicited at the trial, innocent of the crime laid to his charge. Joseph, when he interpreted the chief butler's dream, charged him to remember him when he was restored to his butlership, and no doubt he promised to do so. And if he had been faithful to his promise and spoken of Joseph to the king, there would have been an investigation of the case, in all probability, and Joseph's prison life would have ended. But he forgot his promise to the sufferer, and bitterly reproached himself afterwards. Two years passed away, and all that time, the chief butler enjoyed the honors of his position as the cup-bearer of the king. But at length Pharaoh dreamed a dream which greatly troubled him, and he sought an interpretation of his dream, but all in vain. The Egyptian magician and wise man, could not interpret it. Just at this point, the chief butler remembered Joseph and his interpretation of his dream, three days before his head was lifted out of the prison. And he remembered his promise to Joseph, to speak of his case to the king; but two years had passed away, and he had failed—having never yet mentioned his case. He made an humble acknowledgment of his fault in forgetting Joseph, and then related the circumstance of his dream, and of Joseph's interpretation of it, and he showed the king that the interpretation had been fulfilled to the very letter. This presentation of Joseph's case to Pharaoh, led him to send hastily for Joseph, that he might come before him, and interpret his dream. Accordingly the prisoner was taken out of the dungeon; and arrayed in becoming attire, he appeared before Pharaoh, and met his wishes. After which, in the stead of being returned to his prison, he was promoted over all other officers in the land of Egypt, being second only to the king himself. Genesis, xli.

*Pharaoh's Daughter,*

Was led by Divine Providence, that memorable morning that Moses was taken from the water, to pass down the river-bank, and observe the ark in the flags by the brink, with the precious treasure in it. She exhibits the true feelings of a true woman, when she had compassion on the babe and said, "This is one of the Hebrews children."

And when the little Hebrew girl came up to her and said, "Shall I go and call thee a nurse of the Hebrew women, that she may nurse the child for thee?" she said to her, go. She had probably given expressions of strong feeling for the babe, and had made known a disposition to adopt the child, and raise it up in the court amid the wealth and pleasures of royalty.

Miriam went and called the child's mother, who was her own mother, and Pharaoh's daughter placed the babe in her charge, bidding her nurse it for her, and she would pay her wages. That mother would have gladly nursed the little one without compensation from the royal lady.

It is thought that Pharaoh's daughter did not acquiesce in the cruel edict of her father regarding the Hebrew male children; and that after she rescued Moses she succeeded in getting Pharaoh to abolish the law. Whether this is true or not, it is clear that the edict was not in force long after Moses was saved. Had it been in force many years it is not likely that their males would have amounted to the number of six hundred thousand effective men at the time of their departure from Egypt, as they did. Exodus, xii: 37. "Six hundred thousand on foot, that were men, besides children."

As soon as Moses attained a proper age to begin a course of education, the nurse gave him to Pharaoh's daughter, "and he became her son." His nurse, who was his own mother, we may suppose, felt keenly when he passed from her charge and became a member of the royal family, for her love was the love of a real mother. It may be that Pharaoh's daughter thought strange that the Hebrew nurse should have become so strongly attached to the child, as her feelings seemed to indicate, when she parted with him. And we almost wish that the royal lady had known the relation her adopted son sustained to the nurse. But that knowledge might have snapped a link, and so broken the chain of divine providences in the history of him who was to figure as the emancipator of a downtrodden race.

Pharaoh's daughter gave this Hebrew boy his name, and gives the reason why the name is settled upon him. "And she called his name Moses: and she said because I drew him out of the water. She had him placed under the care of competent educators for we are informed by Saint Stephen that "Moses was learned in all the wisdom of the Egyptians, and was mighty in words and in deeds."

We are not informed as to how long she lived: or as to how strong her attachments were for her adopted son, but we may suppose she looked with a degree of motherly pride upon him, as his mind was developed, and he attained position as a scholar. Ex. ii.

*Pharaoh's Daughter. — Wife of Solomon.*

It is said, in 1st Kings, iii: 1, "Solomon made affinity with Pharaoh, king of Egypt, and took Pharaoh's daughter and brought her unto the city of David, until he had made an end of building his own house, and the house of the Lord, and the wall of Jerusalem round about." It was not long after Solomon began his reign, that he entered into an alliance with the king of Egypt, probably with a view to strengthening his own kingdom, and in order to make the alliance permanent, he took Pharaoh's daughter to wife. It is quite doubtful whether he was justifiable in this marriage, since the law regarding marriage, was assuredly against it, she being heathen. Deut. vii: 3-4. "Neither shalt thou make marriage with them; thy daughter thou shalt not give unto his son, nor his daughter shalt thou take unto thy son; for they will turn away thy son from following me." Notwithstanding this law, and its violation in this case, there is no very plain and positive declaration, blaming him for this particular marriage. Though when the cause of Solomon's apostacy is given, it is said "he loved many strange women, together with the daughter of Pharaoh."

This woman, it is likely was, as is supposed, very handsome, and Solomon became strongly attached to her. He kept her in the city of David all the time he was building his house, and the house of the Lord. He bestowed honor upon her beyond what he bestowed on any other of his wives. He built what is called his own house, the house of the forests of Lebanon, and a house especially for Pharaoh's daughter. 1st Kings, vii: 8. And we learn from 1st Kings, ix: 24, that Solomon's wife, Pharaoh's daughter, came up out of the city of David unto the house which had been built for her. It seems to have been a separate house, and built specially for her, because she was a woman of another nation. In 2d Chron. viii: 8-11, it is said, "Solomon brought up the daughter of Pharaoh out of the city of David, unto the house he had built for her; for he said, My wife shall not dwell in the house of David, king of Israel, because the places are holy whereunto the ark of the Lord hath come."

And yet it is supposed, that this wife of Solomon, represents the church in the Canticles, or "Songs of Solomon." She is thought to be the spouse, and the ardent love of Solomon for her, was that which led to the sublime expressions that we have there, showing forth the glory of the church and the strong love of her head for her.

How long she lived we do not know, but we may suppose from the history of this king and his kingdom, that their union was pleasant, and possibly, politically advantageous.

*Phinehas— Wife of.*

Phinehas was the son of Eli, the priest. He fell in the battle with the Philistines, with his brother Hophni.

When the intelligence reached the venerable Eli, that the battle had gone against Israel, that his two sons were killed, and that the ark of God was taken, he was overcome with grief, and falling back from his seat, he broke his neck, or dislocated it by the fall and so died.

The wife of Phinehas heard the sorrowful tidings, and was deeply affected. And being near the time of delivery, the defeat of Israel, the death of her father-in-law, and of her husband, and the capture, on the part of the enemy, of the ark, was more than she could bear, and the pains of travail came upon her.

As she was about closing her eyes in death, they told her, "thou hast borne a son; but she answered not, neither did she regard it." 1st Sam. iv: 20. Before she died, she named the child, "Ichabod," signifying, "where is the glory." She gave the name, and then signified its import; "The glory is departed from Israel." Like Eli, her father-in-law, she felt for her people and for the cause of God, and mourned that the ark was taken. No wonder she said, "The glory is departed," for Israel's enemies had triumphed over them. The priests were slain, the chief magistrate was dead, and the ark with its sacred deposits, was in the hands of the uncircumcised.

*Philip—The Four Daughters of.*

It was Philip the Evangelist of whom we have an interesting account in Acts, viii: 5, 13. He was instrumental in the conversion of the Eunuch as is presented in Acts viii: 26-40, inclusive.

It seems that he lived at Cesarea; for when Paul and his friends left Miletus, touching at Patara, Tyre and Ptolemais, they arrived at Cesarea and entered into Philip's house, Acts, xxi: 8; "and we entered into the house of Philip the Evangelist, which was one of the seven and abode with him. And the same man had four daughters, virgins, which did prophecy." These four daughters of Philip had enjoyed from their infancy his counsels and advice—and they had been blessed with the exemplary life of their father who was fully devoted to God and his cause, and was a successful Evangelist. They were all unmarried and endowed with the spirit of prophecy. The miraculous gifts of the spirit were communicated to them. How extensively they labored we do not know, for we hear nothing more of them.

*Prophet—Widow of the.*

She is brought to our view in 2d Kings, iv: 1. Which one of the prophets she was the widow of it is not certainly known, but it is conjectured she was the widow of Obadiah. She was sorely oppressed by a merciless creditor and applies in her extremity to the prophet Elisha for counsel and advice. She comes to him to pour out the sorrows of her soul, and tell him her griefs. "The creditor is come to take unto him my two sons to be bondmen." This was more than she could endure, and she came as the wife of a prophet to him who had been acquainted with her husband and his faithful service before he died. Elisha felt for her and at once entered upon a plan of relief. He asked, "what hast thou in the house." She informed him that she was reduced to such extreme poverty that she had nothing "save a pot of oil." He then bade her go borrow empty vessels, as many as she conveniently could, and take them into her house and pour out the oil in her vessel into one and another of those she borrowed and set aside those that were full. She accordingly did as he had bidden her and all the vessels she had borrowed were filled. The prophet then bade her sell the oil and pay the debt, and live herself and her children of the rest.

*Putiel—Daughter of.*

Was the wife of Eleazar, the son and successor of Aaron to the office of the high priesthood. She was the mother of Phinehas, who performed a very daring and yet honorable act—for it was the occasion of turning away the divine wrath from Israel—God approved of it and pledged himself to prosper Phinehas and his posterity. The circumstance is related in Num. xxv: 6-8.

*Potiphar's Wife.*

Potiphar was Joseph's master. He had bought him of the Ishmaelites, who brought him down into Egypt. The wife of Potiphar then was his mistress, and while Joseph, "who was a goodly person and well favored," Gen. xxxix: 7, was performing faithfully the duties imposed upon him by his master, she laid a trap to ensnare him; but fortunately, the moral goodness of the young Israelite, with the favor of the God in whom he trusted, enabled him to shun the snare. He trusted in God, and the darts which were hurled at him fell harmless at his feet. It was not simply a snare set for once, to be removed by this woman if she was unsuccessful and never set again; but day after day his virtue was tried and proven, until the wife of Potiphar brought a false charge against him to her husband, and she presented what she was pleased to call the proof of the truth of her charge, "the garment that she had laid by until his lord came home."

Potiphar heard the charge, and saw the proof that she presented—was very angry at Joseph and cast him into prison, where he remained until he was called on to interpret the dream of Pharaoh, when he was promoted to great honor. His trust in the God of his fathers and his integrity were rewarded. Gen. xxxix.

*Queen of Sheba.*

We have an account of the visit of this royal lady to Solomon, and the effect that her visit had, in 1st Kings, x. She had heard of his fame and came from the far south country to see his wisdom and his wealth. She came with many hard questions if possible to puzzle him, to perplex him, and baffle his skill in answering questions. She beheld the temple and its worship, Solomon's own house, the house of the forests of Lebanon, and the house of his Egyptian wife. She beheld the magnificence and order of Solomon's court, of his table, and his attendants, and their apparel, and the ascent or steps by which he went up unto the house of the Lord, and she fainted. She was a woman of great taste, or she would not have come from a far country to see for herself the glory of Solomon and his kingdom. But when she saw it, like an artist viewing an exquisitely fine painting from the hand and brush of another, she was struck with astonishment and enraptured with its beauty and excellence. As soon as she recovered, she acknowledged to the king, that her expectations were more than met. "It was a true report that I heard in mine own land, of thine acts, and of thy wisdom." She acknowledged that before she left home she thought the reports exagerated, she did not believe the words. But now that she had come and seen for herself she was satisfied that the half was not told her. Her judgment is that his wisdom and glory, far exceed what she had heard. She gave a very natural expression of her feelings when she said, "Happy are thy men, happy are these thy servants which stand continually before thee, and hear thy wisdom," and she followed this expression with language, that would have done honor to the head or heart of an Israelite anywhere in the kingdom of Solomon. 1st Kings, x: 9. She made a present to King Solomon of a hundred and twenty talents of gold which was not less it is thought than four or five millions of dollars, besides spices of great value, and precious stones.

So great a king as Solomon, would not receive such a present without giving as great presents in turn. What it was that he presented her with, we do not know, but we are informed that he gave her all her desire, everything that she asked, Solomon gave unto her, and she returned to her own country, much gratified with her visit to the King of Israel.

*Reuel—the Seven Daughters of.*

They were young women at the time Moses went to the land of Midian, and were probably in charge of their father's flock. The future emancipator of Israel saw these seven daughters at the well where they were accustomed to water their father's flock. As he sat down by the well to rest and refresh himself, he saw them approach and fill the troughs with water that the flocks might drink. But there were shepherds near by who drove away Reuel's flock, and endeavored to get the advantage of the young women's labor by having their own flocks drink the water which was in the troughs. Moses saw their insolence, and immediately took the part of the young women and drove the shepherds away, or at least drove away their flocks, so that Reuel's daughters succeeded in watering theirs sooner than usual; and when they returned home, their father questioned them as to the cause of their early return home. They then related the incident that had transpired of the Egyptian helping them, and he sent them immediately after him to invite him into their house, and to eat bread with them.

Moses was accordingly invited by the daughters of Reuel, and became at once one of the family, and was married to Zipporah, who was, it is likely, Reuel's eldest daughter. Of the names of the other six daughters we are not informed. Ex. ii: 16–21.

*Rufus—the Mother of.*

Rufus was a chosen man in the Lord, or a choice man, and his mother was a noted Christian woman, who is saluted by the apostle in closing his Epistle to the Romans. Rom. xvi: 13: "Salute Rufus, chosen in the Lord, and his mother and mine." By this we judge that this good woman, who was the natural mother of Rufus, had been as a mother to Paul. He remembered her kindness and motherly affection, and in this epistle makes a record of it.

*Ruth—the Kinsman of.*

Boaz sat down in the gate of the city of Bethlehem, the morning after his intimacy with Ruth had ripened into thoughts of marriage, and the near kinsman of Elimelech passed along. He invited him to sit down near him, for he had a matter to present to him. Accordingly he sat down, "and he said unto him, Naomi, that has come again out of the country of Moab, selleth a parcel of land, which was our brother Elimelech's." I now propose to you, as the nearest kinsman, to buy the land and let the inhabitants and elders of Israel be witnesses to the purchase; but if you do not desire it, then I will buy it. He discovered that the right belonged to him, and, not knowing that there were any other conditions in it, he agreed to buy it. Boaz then informed him that there was a young widow, whose name was Ruth, that had an interest in the land, and he must take her as a wife with the purchase of the property. This he was unwilling to do; probably because he had a wife and did not desire another, and, as Boaz had none, he advised him to make the purchase. He said: "I can not redeem it for myself, lest I mar mine own inheritance. Redeem thou my right to thyself, for I can not redeem it." Accordingly Boaz complied with the requirements of the law, and, in the presence of the elders of Israel, married Ruth in purchasing the land. Ruth, iv.

*Samaria—Woman of, in extremity.*

This woman came to the king as we learn from 2d Kings, vi: 26, for help. One of the most terrible calamities that ever befel any city in a famine, had befallen Samaria. The woman in the hours of starvation had associated with another woman who had a son, who had in all probability like her son died but a little later of starvation. They had boiled and eaten her son, and her associate had pledged herself, the next day to boil and eat hers; but when the time arrived and hunger pressed them, and she demanded the fulfilment of the promise, the other woman refused, and she came with her complaint to the king, "Help my lord, O king!" The king asked her what was the complaint. She then told the horrible tale. The king was deeply distressed but could render her no relief.

*Samaria—Woman of, at Jacob's well.*

This woman lived in Sychar, a city of Samaria, near to Jacob's well. John, iv: 7. Jesus had left Judea to go into Galilee, because of the opposition and persecution he met with there. And as the road from Judea to Galilee passed through Samaria, it was a travel of two or three days; and when he reached Sychar, being fatigued with his travel, he stopped for awhile to rest. It was about noon, being the sixth hour. This may account for his fatigue, for his thirst, and also his hunger, for while he sat on Jacob's well the disciples were gone to the city to buy food.

While he was there alone, musing, this woman of Samaria came to draw water from the well. This was a common employment of females. As the woman came to the well, and was probably in the act of drawing the water, Jesus said to her: "Give me to drink," She was very much astonished that he should make this request of her as she saw he was a Jew and knew that the Jews and Samaritans had no dealings—and she ventured to express her astonishment to the stranger; "How is it that thou being a Jew, askest drink of me who am a woman of Samaria?" She could not understand why it was that this man could so far forget the prejudices of the Jews to the Samaritans as to ask a favor of her. The answer that Christ gave her was in keeping with his teaching to others. He turned the circumstance of her drawing water from the well—and his asking her for drink to spiritual use, just as he did the important circumstance of the priests' bringing water from the pool of Siloam to use in the temple service, on the last great day of the feast of Pentecost: "If any man thirst let him come unto me and drink." Jesus said to her, "If thou knewest the gift of God and who it is that saith to thee, give me to drink, thou wouldst have asked of him and he would have given thee living water." The Savior thus represents salvation. The Holy spirit in its saving influences on the heart, and as water quenches the thirst and invigorates the body—so he taught her that the grace of God communicated by the Holy spirit in salvation, quenches the thirst of the soul—and invigorates the spiritual man for the work of its high calling.

But the woman of Samaria did not understand the meaning of the Savior—she did not grasp the great spiritual truth that was being imparted—and she expressed her ignorance by saying, "Sir thou hast nothing to draw with, and the well is deep." She saw that he had no bucket and cord fastened to it with which to reach the water, and she said, "from whence then hast thou this living water?" She thought that he was assuming in this reason which she did not understand, something more than he should, hence she said, "Art thou greater than our father Jacob, which gave us this well, and drank thereof himself and his children, and his cattle? Jesus then teaches the spiritual lesson a little plainer as he says, "whosoever drinketh of this water shall thirst again; but whosoever shall drink of the water that I shall give him shall never thirst — it shall be in him, a well of water springing up into everlasting life." At this language the woman was astonished. There was something uncommon in the manner of the person who was teaching her and in the instruction itself. She expresses her ignorance by saying, "Sir give me this water that I thirst not, neither come hither to draw." She was ignorant yet of the Lord's meaning, but her curiosity was excited and she made this request.

Jesus then began to develop his character by letting her know that though he was a stranger to her she was not a stranger to him. He bade her go call her husband. The object he had in view evidently in making this demand was to lead her to consider her state, and to satisfy her that he knew her heart, and had been familiar with the actions of her life—she said, "I have no husband." He with whom she was talking said, "Thou hast well said I have no husband; for thou hast had five husbands, and he whom thou now hast is not thy husband." It is probable that the woman was engaged to be married but the matter was not yet consummated. The woman was very strongly impressed with these facts coming from one who was a stranger to her, and she concluded he was a prophet, and hence capable of deciding the question in dispute between the Jews and the Samaritans as to the proper place of worship. The Jews said Jerusalem was the place. The Samaritans say, "this mountain," probably meaning Mt. Gerizim, which was near to Sychar. Jesus thus continued his teaching, making spiritual worship the topic. "Woman believe me the hour cometh when ye shall neither in this mountain, nor yet at Jerusalem worship the father. But the hour cometh and now is, when the true worshipers shall worship the father in spirit and in truth." He declared to her the corruption of worship among the Samaritans — while the Jews continued to sacrifice only according to the law — and he declares to her that the Messiah is to come of the Jews. At this declaration of Christ she expressed her faith in the coming Messiah. When Jesus honored her by declaring most plainly that he was the Messiah; he had never spoken in such direct terms even to his disciples, concerning himself, before. The woman was so fully convinced that he was the Messiah that she left her water pot at the well and went into the city and reported it. If she did not boldly declare that he was the Christ, she told them that this person knew the secrets of hearts, for he had told her all things that ever she did. They knew that that was to be one of the characteristics of Christ, and she said, after making her report: "Is not this the Christ?"

This woman became, after this, a preacher of Christ. She spoke of him confidently to her friends and associates, and many of them, because of her words, believed on him. Those of the Samaritans who believed in Christ on her testimony, besought him that he would tarry with them, and he did, two days, and many others believed. "And they said unto the woman, Now we believe not because of thy saying, for we have heard him ourselves and know that this is indeed the Christ, the Savior of the world." John, iv: 42.

*Samson—the Mother of.*

The name of this celebrated woman is not known, but her son was the greatest prodigy of human strength ever born. Manoah, her husband, was a great and good man, and is supposed to have occupied a high position in the country, and to have had a strong hold upon the feelings of the people of Israel.

Samson's mother is said to have been celebrated for her beauty, moral excellence, and her great devotion in the service of God; and there are but few who have been honored more of God. She was visited by the angel of the Lord and informed that she should be the mother of a son, who should be a Nazarite unto God from his birth, and should commence the deliverance of Israel from the hand and power of the Philistines.

She was alone when the angel appeared to her; but though a timid woman and alone, she was by no means alarmed at the strangely glorious visitant. There the angel stood before her, and asked for her attention to the message he had brought: "Behold, now, thou shalt bear a son." She felt in her heart that this message was from God. No sooner was she left alone, than, with a joyful heart, she went in search of her husband and related to him the appearance and language of the angel.

Manoah listened with astonishment and expressed a desire for the reappearance of the angel. He said: "O, my Lord, let the man of God, which thou didst send, come again unto us and teach us what we shall do unto the child that shall be born unto us." This prayer was heard, for, while his wife was sitting in the field —probably where the angel appeared unto her before, and it may be she was earnestly asking for the re-appearance of the angel that her husband, who had loved her so long and so ardently, might be fully satisfied as to the truth of what she had communicated—the messenger re-appeared. As soon as she saw the angel, she ran hastily to where her husband was and informed him, and the two together came into his presence. Manoah, mustering all the courage he could command, addressed himself to the angel: "Art thou the man that spakest unto the woman? and he said, I am."

The mind of Manoah was clear, and he asked a repetition of the instruction given the woman regarding the child, intending to see that they were carried out. Accordingly the angel reiterated so far as was necessary, so that Manoah understood it. They then desired the angel to permit them to detain him awhile that they might give expressions of their regards in a repast, and that the angel might partake of their hospitality. He agreed to tarry awhile and observe their devotions while they offered a burnt offering to God. Here, in the history of this good woman, a sublime scene bursts upon our view. In company with her husband she prepared the offering, and they brought it into the presence of the angel and offered it unto God; "and the angel did wondrously." It may be that when the two placed their offering upon the rock, which served them as an altar, the angel bade them stand back while he performed the part in their devotions he determined to perform; and, when he approached their sacrifice, he touched it. As a consequence, the rock split, and, like the crater of a burning mountain, sent up a volume of flame. That flame enveloped the sacrifice and began to consume it. As the flame burned on, the angel of the Lord entered it, and, amid its curlings, ascended to Heaven whence he came. On beholding the wondrous departure of the angel, the two were struck with solemn awe; and, mingled with the reverence of Manoah, were fear and alarm lest he should die, having seen "an angel of the Lord." Addressing his wife, he said: "We shall surely die, because we have seen God."

Here again we observe excellencies in this good woman. She was as calm as a summer evening. In her heart she had a consciousness of divine approbation. Addressing her husband, she said: "If the Lord were pleased to kill us, he would not have received an offering at our hands. Fire would not have come from that rock and consumed our sacrifice; neither would the Lord have told us such things as he has revealed." As though she had said: How can we fear when God has manifested his love in answering our prayers and giving us the promise of a son, with instructions as to his training? Surely, she said: "If God had determined not to extend mercy to thee, he would not have dealt thus kindly." This was certainly most excellent reasoning, and no wonder if his fears were at once allayed.

Samson was born, and his mother followed faithfully the instructions of the angel regarding him. And in very early life, while yet at home with his mother, he was at times moved by the spirit of God, and his desires of delivering his country began to be developed. She lived to see him from his first unhappy marriage, for, in company with her husband, she procured Samson the woman as his wife; and how long after this she lived we know not.

*Samson—The First Wife of.*

She was a woman of Timnath, with whom Samson had fallen in love while at this frontier town of the Philistines. He went to his father and mother and told them of this woman, and of his having meditated marriage with her. And he said, Judges xiv: 2: "Get her for me to wife." His parents objected to it, they were devoted to God and law-abiding—and moreover from the birth of Samson they had looked anxiously upon him and they thought of the declarations of the angel who did "wondrously." They ventured to expostulate with him, "Is there never a woman among the daughters of thy brethren, or among all my people, that thou goest to take a wife of the tribe of the uncircumcised Philistines." Samson seemed to be somewhat impatient and dissatisfied at the counsel of his parents, for he said, "Get her for me, for she pleaseth me well." This seemed to be enough, they saw he was determined to marry the woman, and no longer tried to disuade him; had they known that Samson's choice was of the Lord they would have made no effort to stop him.

Not long after this Samson's father and mother went with him to Timnath; they had an interview with the woman concerning the matter of her marriage with their son. The espousals were made, and about a year after this Samson married her. On the day of the marriage he made a feast. In the midst of the ceremonies of the feast he put forth a riddle to his thirty companions, with a promise to give them thirty sheets, and thirty changes of garments if they would declare it—while they obligated themselves if they failed, to give him the same number. They had the seven days of the feast to expound the riddle; but the seventh day came and they were yet in the dark as to its meaning. They had gone to Samson's wife and asked her to confer with her husband and find it out, and they threatened if she did not do it they would burn her and her father's house with fire. She entreated Samson with tears to tell her the riddle, he made objections to telling her, but she continued to press him until he told her, and she went and told those who had made the threat, and so for the time being saved the life and property of her father's family. Just before the sun went down the seventh day, they came to Samson with the solution, and Samson saw at once that they had procured it from his wife. He charged them with taking a dishonorable course, and charged his wife with proving unfaithful to him. This seems to have been partly the occasion of his leaving his wife for a time—and it was the occasion of his slaying thirty men at Ashkelon, that he might meet the obligation of giving them thirty sheets and thirty changes of garments. It is doubtful whether Samson's wife was as blameable as many suppose. She was threatened with death and the destruction of her father's house if she did not make known to them the riddle. Is it to be wondered at, that she preferred to bring her husband under this obligation rather than endure the alternative.

And may we not suppose that Samson afterwards looked over this conduct, for he visited his wife with a present; but to his astonishment he found that his wife was given to another. His association with her was at an end—for she was the wife of another man. Samson felt he was wronged, and he avenged his wrongs by burning the corn of the Philistines. And they avenged this act of his by burning his wife and her father with fire, or it may be they did this cruel deed thinking it would please Samson whom they had begun to fear.

Samson's wife enjoyed his company but little for they were together but one week, and nearly all through that week she was in dread lest she should not find out the riddle. She was the wife of his companion only a short time when she was cruelly put to death.

*Shelomith—the Son of.*

This young man was of the tribe of Dan so far as his mother was concerned, but his father was an Egyptian. The young man seems to have been recognized among the Israelites, and allowed a home and reckoning with them, notwithstanding his father was of another nation.

For some cause or other he was engaged in strife with an Israelite, and, during the quarrel, the Egypto-Israelite "blasphemed the name of the Lord, and cursed." What his blasphemy and cursing consisted in we do not certainly know. It may be in the use of the name Jehovah, that the Jews held impious to pronounce, or it may be in the use of some name that designated an Egyptian deity or a false god. Whatever it consisted in it was a high crime, and they brought him immediately to Moses, who put him under guard until the Divine Will might be ascertained. Moses, therefore, applied to God for instructions to govern him in this case. The Lord bade Moses have him brought without the camp and let all the witnesses place their hands on his head, while the congregation stoned him to death. It was accordingly done, and all Israel was charged to look upon this case as a warning to others, for it was declared that whosoever cursed his God shall bear his sin, and he that blasphemeth the name of the Lord shall surely be put to death—the stranger who is incorporated with Israel, as well as he who is born in the Land. Leviticus, xxiv: 10–16.

*Simon's wife's mother.*

We know nothing more of this woman than is related in Matthew, viii: 15, and its parallel passages, Mark, i: 30, and Luke, iv: 38. It would seem that Peter was then a young married man, and this woman lived with him. She may have been a widow, and Peter's wife may have been her only daughter, with whom, after the marriage, she made her home. The Savior performed a noted miracle in healing her. He went into Simon's house, and this woman was laying sick with a fever. We suppose it was a very severe attack of a fever common to that climate, and to those times. Luke calls it a "great fever." By this, we may understand it was a severe case, in which all the means that had been used, had proved ineffectual.

Jesus cured her of the fever instantly. He approached her, "touched her hand, and the fever left her." The cure was not wrought slowly, and by a use of the means that were ordinarily brought to bear in such cases. It was not produced in the course of nature, or by means of medicine, but immediately upon Christ touching her hand, she was restored to health and strength, insomuch that she set herself at once to preparing a repast for them, and after she had prepared it, she served them while at meat: "Arose and ministered unto them."

*Shunamite woman.*
[See history of Elisha.]

*Sisera—the Mother of.*
We have no account of this woman, save in the song of Deborah and Barak. Judges v: 28–30. Her son was at the head of the army of Jabin, king of Canaan. And when he went to fight with Israel near Mt. Tabor, she was elated with the idea of his success. And when she saw him seated in his war chariot at the head of the nine hundred iron chariots of his king, she felt proud of him as her son. And we may judge from Deborah's description that she fully expected Sisera would soon return flushed with victory. But how was she mistaken. While she sat in her own room, or stood at the window of her apartment eagerly looking in the direction of the battle-field, and expecting all the time to see the war-chariot of Sisera and the victorious general approaching, victory had gone against her king and her son, and so complete had been the victory for Israel that there was not a Canaanitish chariot but had been taken in war, and there was not a single soldier of Sisera's vast army to bring the news to her of their defeat. Her son was probably the only one that escaped the slaughter of the battle-field, and he escaped to die by the hand of a woman, viz: Jael, the wife of Heber. Deborah represents Sisera's mother as looking out at the window, and crying through the lattice: "Why is his chariot so long in coming? Why tarry the wheels of his chariot?" Her attendants witnessed her anxiety and answered her. She received their answers and adds to them. She tries to satisfy herself in her anxiety by supposing that Sisera had had the victory, and was tarrying to divide and enjoy the spoils, and she fancied to herself that soon he would come decked and adorned as a great conqueror. This language of Deborah is a beautiful representation of the anxiety and impatience of the mother of Sisera at his delay; and it shows how exceedingly sanguine she was of his success. Soon we may suppose she heard of the defeat of Jabin's army; of the flight of Sisera, her son, the general, and of his cruel death in the tent, as he supposed, of a friend.

*Tekoah—the wise Woman of.*
Tekoah was a little city in the tribe of Judah, not many miles from Jerusalem. This wise woman lived there in widowhood. Joab, the general of David's army, selected her to be the bearer of a fictitious story to the king, the object of which was to induce David to send to Geshur for Absalom, his son, who had been there from the time he killed Amnon, his brother. Her story, as recorded in 2d Sam. xiv: 4–20, is a very ingenuous one. Whether Joab had anything to do with the formation of it, or not, we do not know. He probably had not. He knew her as a wise woman; he knew her as a widow, as a woman of sufficient years to give her application some weight with the king. Her wisdom was brought into exercise in framing her story so that the king could not divine her intention until she had concluded it.

She came to king David under the direction of Joab, feigning to be a mourner, clothed in habiliments suitable for a mourner, and, with undressed hair, she stood in the presence of the king to make her plea. Having secured the attention of David, she did the obeisance in his presence that was common in those days for any one approaching a ruling monarch with a request. But she followed her act of obeisance with the significant address made in much earnestness: "Help, O King!" Her appearance and this earnest appeal affected him, and he said: "What aileth thee?" As though he had said, I am ready to hear your request; make it at once. Seeing that the way was open, she related the fact of her widowhood: "My husband is dead." She then related a feigned story as to two sons, one of whom had slain the other—(or possibly it was a fact in her family history)—and that the whole family had risen against the one who had slain his brother, and assumed the position of avengers of blood; and they demanded of her that he be given up that he too may be slain. The consequence will be, she adds, if this son be slain the heir will be destroyed; my coal will be quenched, and my departed husband will have none left to perpetuate his name; my family will be extinct.

This was a very touching plea to King David, and his mind was made up at once to attend at least to her case. He said: "Go to thine house. I will give charge concerning thee." But the woman continued her plea: "My Lord, O King, the iniquity be on me and on my father's house, and the King and his throne be guiltless." As though she had said, If thou art afraid that the honor of thy throne will be tarnished or thine administration of justice questioned, if my son is not brought to punishment, I and my father's family will endure all the blame.

This had the effect to bring the king a little nearer to the point she desired, but yet he did not commit himself, and there was no solemn pledge or promise that proceedings should be stopped in the case of her son. She made one more plea, in all the earnestness of her soul, which was effectual. She referred David to the mercy of God, manifested when it was sought earnestly. She prayed him to show mercy promptly, lest it might be too late. The avengers of blood might do their work—then the case would be hopeless. My son is in imminent danger now, O king! render me help. David was so affected that he gave her the promise, under the solemnity of an oath, that her son's life should be preserved.

Having brought the king to this point, she made her plea plainly in behalf of Absalom. She showed, in a very forcible manner, how, if the king will deliver from death one of his subjects—a young man who had slain his brother—he was certainly to blame in not delivering his own son, who had committed a like act in slaying Amnon. She plead with the king to bring the young prince from his banishment his exile in Geshur. David felt the force of this reasoning, and he determined to send for Absalom. As soon as the woman had closed her application and acknowledged that the hand of Joab was in it, she left the king's presence and probably went to her home in Tekoah, while Joab received the order to send for Absalom and bring him home again.

*Woman diseased twelve years.*

We have an account of this woman, and her case and her cure, in Mark, v: 25–34. For twelve years she had suffered from this disease, which was of such a character that it excluded her from the temple and its services. She was not permitted to associate with her former friends, or mix in the congregation of Israel. She had been under the treatment of physicians. They had spent their skill, and failed to effect a cure, and she had reduced herself to poverty, "spent all she had." The disease was constantly growing worse, and she felt herself to be in extremity.

Having heard of Jesus, and of the miraculous cures he had performed, she greatly desired to see him, and make application for help in her case. And the day that Jairus found him and was conducting him to his house, she heard of him, and saw the crowd gathered about him. She came up to the company, and very earnestly desiring to present her case to him, she determined on an effort to get to him. But there were serious difficulties in the way. She was a lone woman—emaciated and feeble, and the crowd was great. How could she secure a position near enough to him to secure his attention, and even if she could do that, how could she represent her case to this great curer. Her faith in Christ's ability was strong, and moved by it she said, "If I may but touch his clothes, I shall be whole." It is not necessary that I represent the case to him. He will understand it if I can only get near enough to him to touch him. So saying, she began to press her way through the crowd, and succeeded, at last, in getting near enough to him to put forth her hand and touch him. No sooner had she done this than the disease was cured. She, who had "suffered many things of many physicians," and was not cured, was now made whole, instantly, by the great physician. What joy must have filled this woman's heart, as she realized she was healed of "that plague," and that the way was being opened for her to return to the temple, and, after an absence of twelve years, enjoy its privileges.

Jesus knowing that virtue had gone out of him, that a cure had been performed in the case of this woman—in order to bring out her acknowledgement, and commend her for her faith—said, "who touched me?" The disciples wondered that he should ask the question, since the multitude were pressing around him, but he told them he had performed a cure, and they had not witnessed it. The woman came forward and acknowledged the benefit she had realized, when Jesus said unto her, "Daughter, thy faith hath made thee whole; go in peace and be whole of thy plague."

*Woman who anointed Jesus' feet.*

Who this woman was we are not informed, but the record of her act is to be found in Luke, vii: 37–38. "And behold a woman in the city, which was a sinner, when she knew that Jesus sat at meat in the Pharisee's house, brought an alabaster-box of ointment, and stood at his feet behind him weeping, and began to wash his feet with tears, and did wipe them with the hairs of her head, and kissed his feet, and anointed them with the ointment." It is supposed by some, that this woman was Mary Magdalene; but of this, there is no proof. The strong probability is that she was a Gentile, who dwelt in Capernaum, or some other city, where Christ had been teaching, and that she was converted, and hearing that Christ was in the Pharisee's house, she came, and moved by pure love for Jesus, she approached him to perform the office of washing and anointing his feet. He was in the usual position of reclining at the table. She came behind him, and began to shower tears upon his feet, and she wiped them with her hair, and with affectionate tenderness, kissed them again and again. And having a box of precious ointment with her, she anointed his feet with it. She had procured the precious and costly ointment with her own means, and evidenced, in using it thus, her strong attachment for, and her love to Christ. She was highly commended by the Savior for this act, and Simon was mildly reproved for his want of courtesy in failing to procure water to wash his feet. He failed to treat the Savior as guests were usually treated. "I entered into thine house, thou gavest me no water for my feet; but she hath washed my feet with her tears, and wiped them with the hairs of her head. Thou didst not kiss me, but she hath not ceased to kiss my feet. My head with oil thou didst not anoint, but this woman hath anointed my feet with ointment." The Savior commends her for this strong expression of her love, and gives her strong and satisfactory assurances that her acts of love were appreciated and rewarded. She enjoyed a sense of divine favor, and as she closed her serving of Christ, she felt the joys of pardon and rejoiced.

*Woman afflicted eighteen years.*

The record of this case is in Luke, xiii: 11–13. She had had a spirit of infirmity for eighteen years, "and was bowed together, and could in no wise lift up herself." It was not a common case of infirmity, a nervous or spinal disease, but an infirmity produced by an evil spirit. That this is the case is evident from the sixteenth verse, "ought not this woman, being a daughter of Abraham, whom satan hath bound, lo! these eighteen years, &c."

This woman had come to the synagogue and was mingling with the worshipers, Jesus looked over the company that had gathered there, to whom as a teacher he was imparting instruction, and seeing this woman, he had compassion on her. He knew all the peculiarities of her case. He knew how long she had been afflicted, and how severe, and with how much difficulty she attended the synagogue service, and though she may not have thought of applying to him to be healed of her infirmity, yet he fixed his eye upon her, and "called her unto him." She accordingly came to him. It may be she came at his bidding to be taught, not thinking of having a cure performed. But as she waits to hear the instructions of Jesus, to her astonishment and joy, his voice falls upon her ear saying, "woman thou art loosed from thine infirmity." He accompanies this declaration with the significant act of laying his hands on her. She was healed immediately, "made strait and glorified God." *i. e.* She praised God in the presence of the congregation, for the signal and unexpected blessing that had been conferred upon her. Strange as it may seem, the ruler of the synagogue, objected to the praises of the woman, and to the miracle of healing, which had been done on the Sabbath day. He defended himself from the charge brought against him, and no doubt defended the woman for her praising.

*Zarephath— Widow of.*

This woman is brought to our notice in the history of the prophet Elijah, in 1st Kings, xvii. The prophet was preserved during the first months of the dearth and famine, by the brook Cherith. He was fed by ravens, who brought him "bread and flesh in the morning, and bread and flesh in the evening." But the brook was dried up, and Elijah was appointed to go to Zarephath in Zidon, and dwell during the remainder of the dearth with a woman who lived there. That woman was the Widow of Zarephath.

When the prophet arrived at the city, or as he was entering it, he met this poor widow. She was in search of a few sticks to make a fire, that, after she had prepared her last portion of food, she, with her son, might eat it, then give herself and her dear child up to starvation; for she knew not where to get that with which to prepare another meal. The prophet desired her to bring him a drink of water, and while she was going to get it, he called after her and asked that she would bring a piece of bread, also. The woman was quite willing to bring him water, but when he asked for bread she called to mind the fact that she had but enough meal and a sufficient quantity of oil to make one small cake; and she informed Elijah that she was just preparing to make a cake for herself and her son, that they might eat together their last meal. He told her to make a cake for him first, and then prepare for herself and her child; and then he gave her the declaration: "Thus saith the Lord God of Israel, The barrel of meal shall not waste, neither shall the cruse of oil fail." The woman believed the declaration of the prophet, obeyed his orders, and her house became his home. That woman and her son, and Elijah, lived for months on the last provisions she had, and the meal wasted not, nor did the cruse of oil fail.

About two years after this the widow's son died. She watched him through his sickness with fond affection, and when he died she approached the prophet with a sorrow-stricken air, and said, "What have I to do with thee, thou man of God? Art thou come unto me to call my sin to remembrance, and to slay my son?" Elijah felt keenly for the oppressed woman, and he took her son from her arms and carried him up into his own room and laid him on his own bed, and prayed for his life to be restored. His prayer was, "O Lord, my God, let this child's soul come into him again." His prayer was answered, and the child returned to life, and consciousness, and health; and he restored him to his mother.

We thus behold the power of God manifest in the resurrection of her son, and her own mind fully satisfied that Elijah was a true prophet, and that the word of the Lord by him was truth.

The history of this woman is attested to by Saint Luke, iv: 26: "But unto none of them was Elias sent save unto Sarepta, a city of Sidon, unto a woman that was a widow."

www.ingramcontent.com/pod-product-compliance
Lightning Source LLC
LaVergne TN
LVHW021316110826
845150LV00003B/583

* 9 7 8 1 4 2 5 5 5 7 5 2 2 *